AF569936

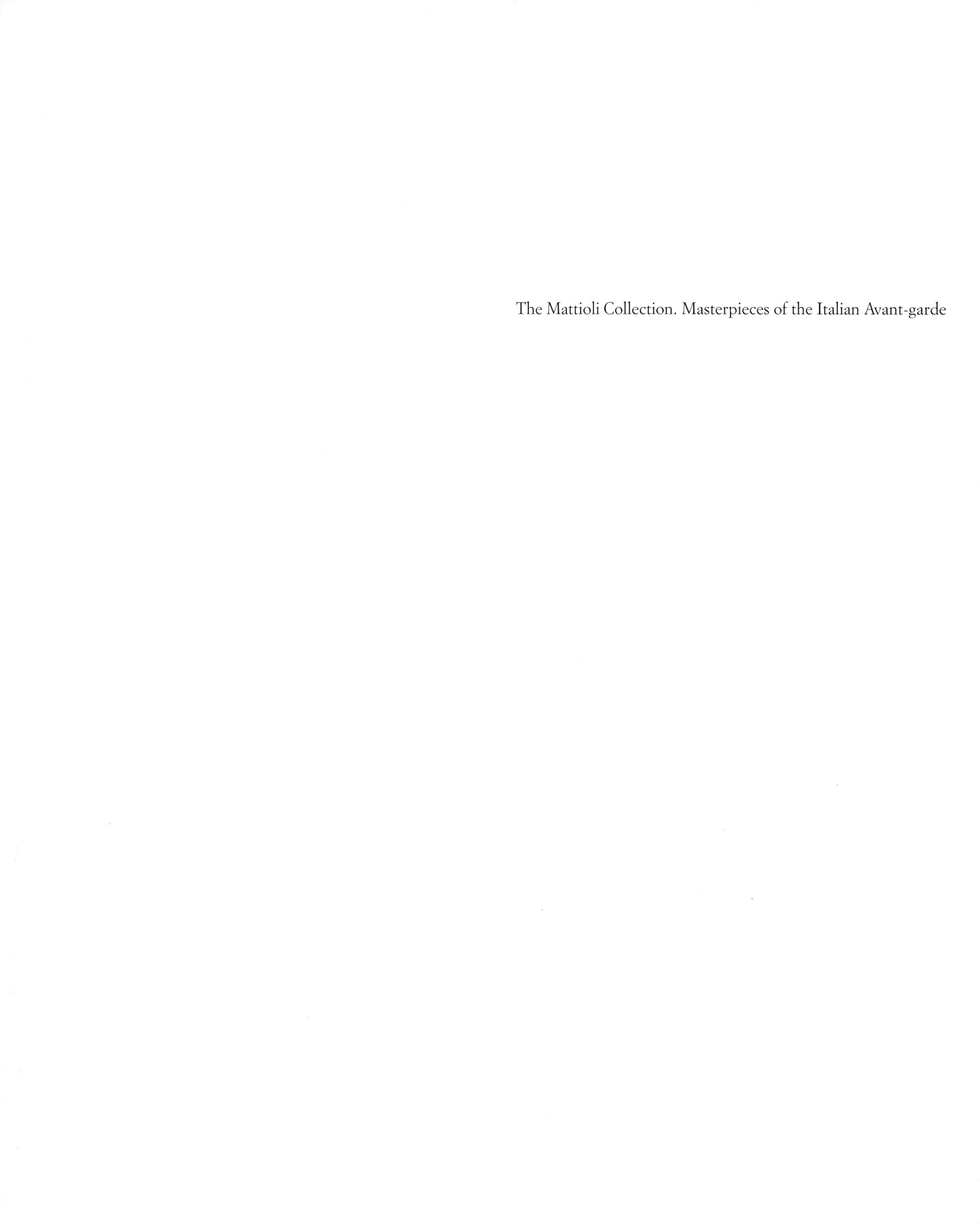

The Mattioli Collection. Masterpieces of the Italian Avant-garde

Peggy Guggenheim COLLECTION

The Mattioli Collection
Masterpieces of the Italian Avant-garde

Catalogue raisonné by Flavio Fergonzi

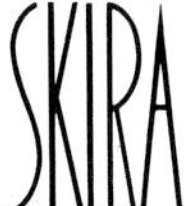

Cover
Umberto Boccioni
Dynamism of a Cyclist, 1913
(cat. no. 5)

Back cover
Gianni Mattioli
in his office, Milan,
late 1940s

Art Director
Marcello Francone

Editorial Coordination
Franco Ambrosio

Editing
Emma Cavazzini

Layout
Veronica Bellotti

Editorial supervision for English edition
Philip Rylands

Translations
Christopher Huw Evans
on behalf of Language
Consulting Congressi srl
Jennifer Franchina

Iconographical Research
Chiara Barbieri

First published in Italy in 2003
by Skira Editore S.p.A.
Palazzo Casati Stampa
via Torino 61
20123 Milano
Italy
www.skira.net

Printed and bound in Italy.
First edition
ISBN 88-8491-532-5

Distributed in North America and Latin America by Rizzoli International Publications, Inc. through St. Martin's Press, 175 Fifth Avenue, New York, NY 10010.
Distributed elsewhere in the world by Thames and Hudson Ltd., 181a High Holborn, London WC1V 7QX, United Kingdom.

Funding for this publication has been provided by:

a grant from the Kanbar Charitable Trust of the Jewish Community Endowment Fund, thanks to Maurice S. Kanbar in collaboration with the Murray and Isabella Rayburn Foundation; Regione del Veneto; Fondazione Cassa di Risparmio di Venezia; University of Trieste.

Contents

Preface

Since 1997 the Solomon R. Guggenheim Foundation has proudly placed on permanent exhibition twenty-six works from the collection of Gianni Mattioli at the Peggy Guggenheim Collection, Venice. When Mattioli's daughter, Laura Mattioli Rossi, entrusted these to our care, we promised to commission and publish a *catalogue raisonné* of those works. The present publication, by Flavio Fergonzi, fulfils this promise.

I would like to renew my thanks to Laura Mattioli Rossi for the trust she has shown in the Guggenheim Foundation by placing these masterpieces on show at the Peggy Guggenheim Collection. Her reasons for doing so go beyond mere considerations of opportunity or friendship. Her introductory essay to this catalogue is an important contribution, by a distinguished art historian in her own right, to our knowledge of Italian cultural history and to the history of twentieth-century art collecting. Numerous original documents are published here for the first time. Her history of her father's collection ends in 1953, the year when the collection was shown in Palazzo Strozzi, Florence (four years after Carlo Ludovico Ragghianti had hosted Peggy Guggenheim's collection there). But for Mattioli this was only the beginning. His programme was to spread the knowledge of the Italian avant-garde internationally. His own horizons had been immeasurably broadened in the immediate post-war period through his contacts with New York, with James Thrall Soby and James Johnson Sweeney. It is fascinating to read that when Mattioli visited Peggy Guggenheim's collection at the 1948 Venice Biennale his focus on the avant-garde became clearer, and that this had much to do with the shaping of his own collection — for example in the choices he made when a year later he was sifting through the Feroldi collection. His determination to make his collection (and hence modern Italian art) known internationally is evident from his readiness to privilege loans to exhibitions outside Italy (something his daughter has continued to do). From 1967 to 1972 his collection travelled to a dizzying number of cities: in America, Europe and Japan. This desire to set Italian art in an international context underlies Laura Rossi's choice of the Peggy Guggenheim Collection for the public display of her father's works — a museum where, thanks to the genius of a like-minded collector, works of Cubism, European Abstraction, Surrealism and American Abstract Expressionism, as well as of *pittura metafisica* and Futurism, offer a unique (in Italy) backdrop for Mattioli's paintings.

Given his ambitions for the promotion of Italian art, of which the formation of his collection was only one aspect, Mattioli would have been overjoyed by this catalogue, which is published both in English and Italian. It is a work of scholarship that amply fulfils the Guggenheim Foundation's mission, shared with all art museums, to study the works in its custody, while its English edition joins a bibliography on Italian early Modernism which is far too short. Despite Martin's 1968 book on Futurism, despite the presence in the United States of the now-dispersed Winston-Malbin Collection, and despite the early collecting of major works by the

Museum of Modern Art, Futurism remains relatively inaccessible to university curricula in the English-speaking world. The same is true of Metaphysical painting, and of the pure art of Giorgio Morandi — one of Italy's best-loved painters, who is virtually unknown to a non-specialist audience abroad.

The catalogue is by Flavio Fergonzi, to whom I would like to express my profound gratitude and admiration. With the discipline that is the hallmark of rigorous scholarship, Professor Fergonzi's quest for facts underpins every line of these catalogue entries. Speculation is left to others, who may base themselves on the truths that this catalogue documents. Yet there is nothing arid about these essays on Italian masterpieces. Paintings are set in the wider context of the history of their times: Sironi's interest in the fighter planes first used towards the end of the Great War, Balla's prophetic celebration of the planet Mercury only shortly before Einstein was to use its erratic perihelion as proof of his theory of relativity, Russolo's interest in Parisian Unanimist poetry, or Boccioni's cyclist as a document in the history of sport. There are images, almost amounting to narrative, that bring one close to the human moments when these works were created or collected. We can picture Balla in the winter of 1914, his daughter seated on his knee or at his feet, reading to her a child's illustrated book of astronomy before going to his studio to paint *Mercury Passing Before the Sun*; or Severini, at the end of June 1912, fresh off the train from Paris gleefully showing his friends in Milan reproductions of the latest Cubist works as well as his own white and blue dancers; or Morandi in the summer of 1914 painting the lush foliage of the Appenines near his country house at Grizzana, with Cézanne as his hero; or Peppino Ghiringhelli brow-beating the recalcitrant Pietro Feroldi into accepting Carrà's *The Engineer's Mistress*. Each entry is woven through with completely new information, of which the dating of Carrà's *Pursuit* to 1915 or the startling revelation of the presence of a bi-plane flying by moonlight in Sironi's *Composition with Propeller* are only two examples.

Flavio Fergonzi's methodology includes a critical history of each painting — the way each was received by exhibition reviewers and critics, thus reflecting changing tastes in art, which in turn determined the relative celebrity or obscurity of this or that work. Ideology or political ideas, such as Irredentism, Interventionism, Francophilia, nostalgia for the Italian Quattrocento, and the Return to Order permeate in one way or another not just the imagery of Carrà's paintings, but the way that critics viewed them. Morandi, who between the wars was secretive of his 1915 paintings influenced by Cubism, boasted of them in the post-war period when he could be seen as being precociously responsive to the French Cubist avant-garde. Professor Fergonzi offers us case studies in which art criticism and tastes in collecting become intelligible *tesserae* in the mosaic of social history, and this, at least in Anglo-Saxon art history, will set new standards for the *catalogue raisonné*.

I would like to thank others who have contributed to this catalogue: Lewis Kachur wrote the entry on Carrà's *Interventionist Demonstration*, while Gianluca Poldi and Nicola Ludwig have provided and analysed data offered by infrared reflectography of a number of the works. I would like also to thank Massimo Vitta Zelman, Stefano Piantini, Franco Ambrosio, Veronica Bellotti, Emma Cavazzini, Philip Rylands, Chiara Barbieri, Elena Cimenti, Jennifer Franchina and Christopher Huw Evans, all of whom have contributed to the production of the book in different and important ways.

As a contribution to the knowledge of modern Italian art, this catalogue matches precisely the mission of the Murray and Isabella Rayburn Foundation which, thanks to a grant from the Kanbar Charitable Trust of the Jewish Community Endowment Fund and thanks to the goodwill of Maurice S. Kanbar and Isabella del Frate Rayburn, helped to bring this project to fruition. Additional valuable support was provided by the Regione del Veneto, by the Fondazione Cassa di Risparmio di Venezia and the University of Trieste: my most sincere thanks go to them all.

Let us recall that Peggy Guggenheim's collection was from the beginning conceived as a museum of twentieth century art. Likewise, Gianni Mattioli, in the estimation of Ragghianti, made his collection "with the intention and spirit of an historian." We are proud to dedicate this catalogue to Gianni Mattioli in the centenary year of his birth.

Thomas Krens
Director
Solomon R. Guggenheim Foundation

Acknowledgments

In the years I have spent on this project I owe a debt of gratitude to many people, but two deserve particular mention. Laura Mattioli Rossi chose me to be the author of this catalogue. She has liberally given me the use of her father's archive and library, which she has maintained and kept up-to-date with exemplary care. She has helped me in every possible way, with her recollections, her advice and her encouragement. She has followed my research with passion and skill, discussing every hypothesis and conclusion, manifesting — with a candor for which I am especially appreciative — her doubts, her differences of opinion, or her approbation.

Philip Rylands coordinated the entire project and placed the resources of the Peggy Guggenheim Collection, Venice, at my disposal in the best way. However, his contribution did not end there. In the long process of revising the translations of the English edition of the catalogue, which he has edited, Philip checked every paragraph of the entries, verifying data, correcting minor imprecisions, urging me to enquire more deeply or to rethink my interpretations. It has been important for me to be able to count on his intelligence and his scrutiny. I want to add how much I have appreciated too the professionalism of the staff of the Peggy Guggenheim Collection, especially Chiara Barbieri, Liesbeth Bollen, Siro de Boni, Sandra Divari, Valentina Furlan, Gabriella Lewin, Jasper Sharp and Marco Trevisan.

During my researches for these twenty-six catalogue entries I have had the benefit of a continuous exchange of ideas with three youthful friends. With characteristic generosity Sileno Salvagnini supplied me with all kinds of information drawn from his wealth of knowledge of visual culture in Italy between the wars; I owe to Alessandro Del Puppo important notions regarding Balla, Boccioni and Carrà; Federica Rovati is writing her doctoral thesis on the late works of Boccioni, and our frequent discussions on matters of dating and chronology have been always precious. Questions from students have been stimulating when, in various lectures, I have talked of the content of parts of this catalogue: at the Scuola Normale Superiore of Pisa (on the invitation of Paola Barocchi), at the Schools for Specialization in Art History of the University of Siena (on the invitation of Enrico Crispolti), at the State University of Milan (on the invitation of Fernando Mazzocca), and at the University of Turin (on the invitation of Mimita Lamberti).

Others have contributed in positive ways to the completion of this publication. In Milan, where the largest part of my research has been conducted, I am grateful to Luisa Arrigoni and Matteo Ceriana of the Soprintendenza ai Beni Artistici e Storici, Maria Fratelli and Marina Pugliese of the Civiche raccolte d'arte, Antonello Negri, Giorgio Zanchetti and Paolo Rusconi of the Visual Arts Department of the State University, Pasquale Tucci and Gianluca Poldi of the Institute of General Applied Physics of the State University, Giacomo Agosti, Francesca Follia, Angela Occhipinti, Valter Rosa, Dario Trento and Francesca Valli of the Accademia di Belle Arti di Brera, Franco Ambrosio, Veronica Bellotti and Emma Cavazzini of the Studio Ambrosio; also Angelo Calmarini, Massimo Carrà, Luigi Cavallo, Anna Ceroni, Graziano Ghiringhelli, Claudia Gian Ferrari, Giovanna Ginex, Silvia Guastalla, Sergio Rebora, Giovanni Rossi, and Fabio Vittucci. In Turin: Alessandro Dorna. In Verona: Massimo Di Carlo and Laura Lorenzoni of the Galleria dello Scudo. In Venice: Nico Stringa of the Art History Department of the University of Ca' Foscari. In Trento: Gabriella Belli and Paola Pettenella of the Museo d'Arte Moderna e Contemporanea of Trento and Rovereto. In Udine: Barbara Cinelli of the Department of the History and Conservation of Cultural Goods of the Università degli Studi. In Trieste: Giuseppe Pavanello, Francesca Castellani, Enrica Cozzi, Alberto Craievich, Maurizio Lorber, Enrico Lucchese, all of the Department of History and Art History of the Università degli Studi; also Diana Arich de Finetti and Alessandro Sciarrone. In Bologna: Marilena Pasquali of the Museo Morandi. In Pisa: Donata Levi of the Department of the History of the Arts of the Università degli Studi. In Rome: Jennifer Franchina, who shouldered the task of translating the entries into English, Enrico Crispolti, the late Maurizio Fagiolo dell'Arco and Juan Casanovas of the Specola Vaticana. In Munich: Andrea Sironi. In Paris: Claire Laburthe and Cristina Maiocchi. In Madrid: Fernando De La Fuente Arranz of the Biblioteca Nacional de España. In New York Vivien Greene, Lewis Kachur (author of the entry for Carrà's *Interventionist Demonstration*) and Emily Braun, who made acute observations on the entry for Boccioni's *Materia*.

Several times, in Florence and Pisa, I had recourse to the counsels of Paola Barocchi, whose teaching has I hope left its mark on this catalogue.

I am also grateful to the directors and personnel of the following libraries and archives: in Milan, the Biblioteca Nazionale Braidense, the Biblioteca Civica Sormani, the art library of the Castello Sforzesco, the Biblioteca Trivulziana, the library and archives of the Accademia di Brera, the Biblioteca Feltrinelli, the library of the Department of Visual Arts and the library of the French Department of the State University, the library of the Civica Raccolta delle Stampe 'Achille Bertarelli', the library of the Museo del Risorgimento and the Civico archivio fotografico. In Turin: the library of the Galleria Civica d'Arte Moderna. In Venice: the Archivio Storico delle Arti Contemporanee. In Rovereto: the Archivio del 900 of the Museo d'Arte Moderna e Contemporanea of Trento and Rovereto. In Trieste: the Civica Biblioteca 'Attilio Hortis' and the library of the Department of History and History of Art of the State University. In Bologna: the Biblioteca dell'Archiginnasio. In Florence: the Biblioteca Nazionale Centrale, the Biblioteca Marucelliana and the Kunsthistorisches Institut. In Fiesole: the Fondazione Primo Conti. In Pisa the library of the Scuola Normale Superiore. In Rome: the archives of the Galleria Nazionale d'Arte Moderna. In Paris: the Bibliothèque Jacques Doucet.

A special thanks, finally, to my wife, who has been by my side throughout the various phases of my research and my writing.

This catalogue is dedicated to Mimita Lamberti, who taught me, in her lectures in Pisa, how paintings of the twentieth century should be studied.

Flavio Fergonzi

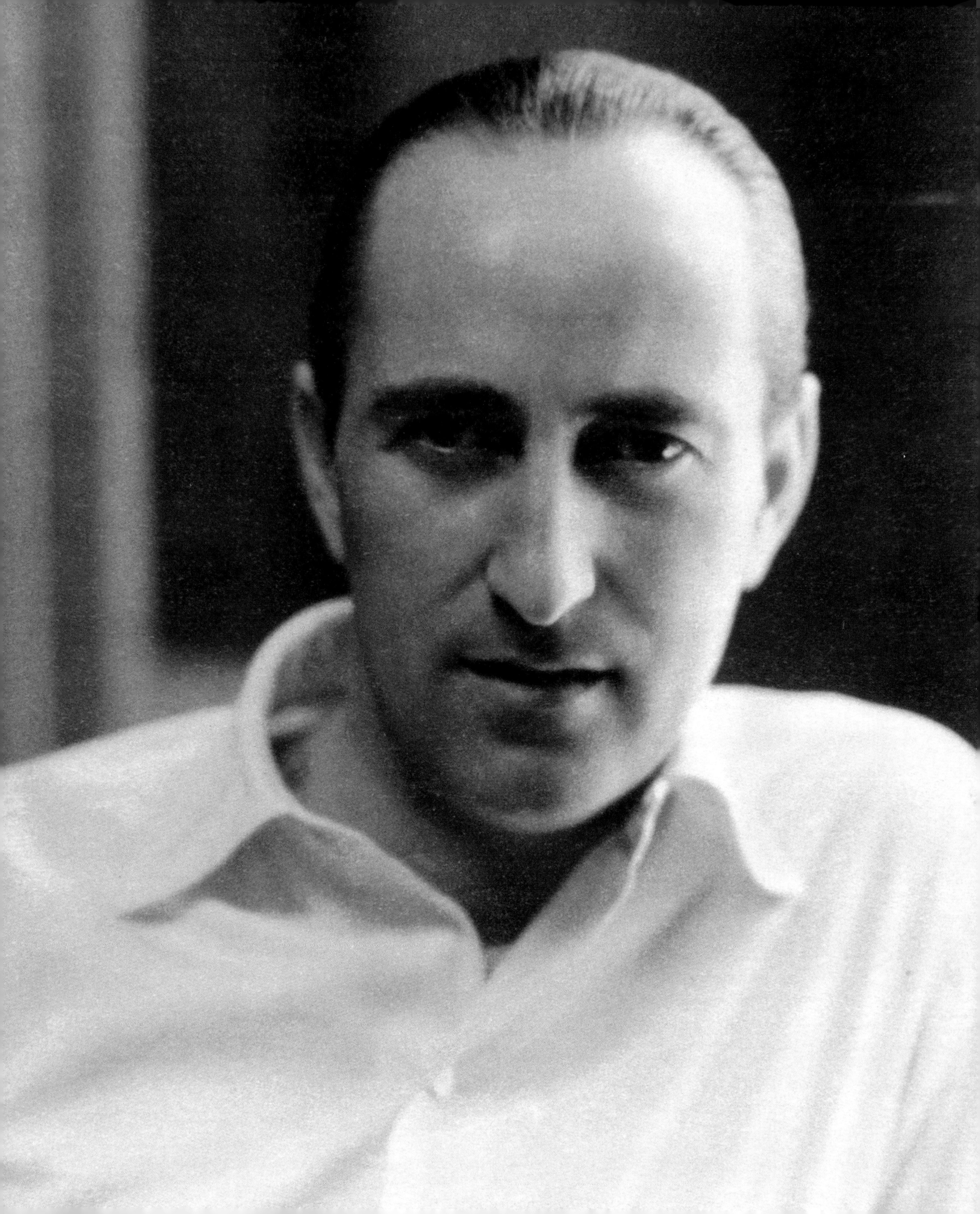

Laura Mattioli Rossi

The Collection of Gianni Mattioli from 1943 to 1953*

On a sheet of squared paper sent to my father Gianni Mattioli in September 1951, Pier Maria Bardi gave a brief but illuminating tribute to the collection that he had just seen: "Dear Signor Mattioli, your collection is something more than a collection of works of art; it constitutes, instead, one of the fundamental factors for peace in the world: the belief in art and in the history of humanity. Come and see us in Brazil where we are doing something similar. Yours, P.M. Bardi."[1]

The conscious decision to form a collection is a project of a very different kind from the casual acquisition of objects or works of art to decorate a home. Sometimes the desire to surround oneself with beautiful things is the first step toward the formation of a collection — a collection that may later take shape under the guidance of an increasingly refined taste and an ever more profound and specialized knowledge. In many cases a collector may be driven by an insatiable curiosity about the world that surrounds him (or her) and mixes *naturalia* and *artificialia*, or objects from different cultures, creating a unique setting in which to express his personality — to be shared only with an elite capable of appreciating the collection's qualities. Thus it was with the *Wunderkammern*, the pride of so many illustrious persons from the end of the Middle Ages to the beginning of the nineteenth century. Celebrated examples in the city of Milan were those of Canon Manfredo Settala (1600–80), whose collection, or what survives of it, is now in the Pinacoteca Ambrosiana, and — in more recent times — that of the critic Lamberto Vitali (1896–1992), who bequeathed his heterogeneous collection to several different civic institutions. In some cases it has been the vanity of an ancient family, or the desire to emulate the collections of those who can boast a nobility of much older date that constitutes the motivation for a commitment to art, while in others it is a sort of instinctive affinity binding the collector to an artist that forms the basis of patronage, as happened between the conductor Arturo Toscanini (1867–1957) and the painter Vittore Grubicy de Dragon (1851–1920).

Often, collections created for personal enjoyment and the private home take on such importance and size that they eventually find their way into museums, thus becoming accessible to the public. In such cases it is generally the owners themselves who take this decision, to assure these 'creatures' of theirs (and they themselves) a posthumous survival. In this way collectors have contributed to the creation or enrichment of innumerable museums all over the world and it is difficult to pick even a few names to exemplify a phenomenon so broad and general-

Fig. 1. *Gianni Mattioli, c. 1945*

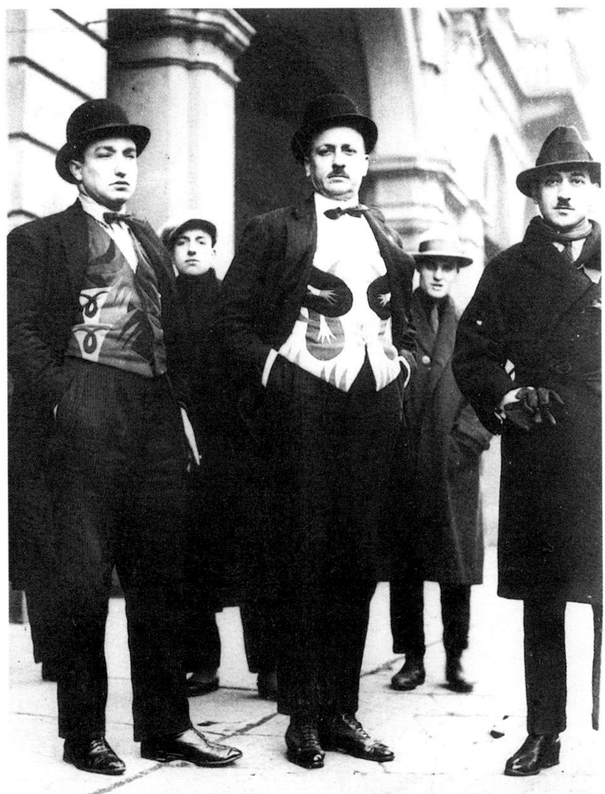

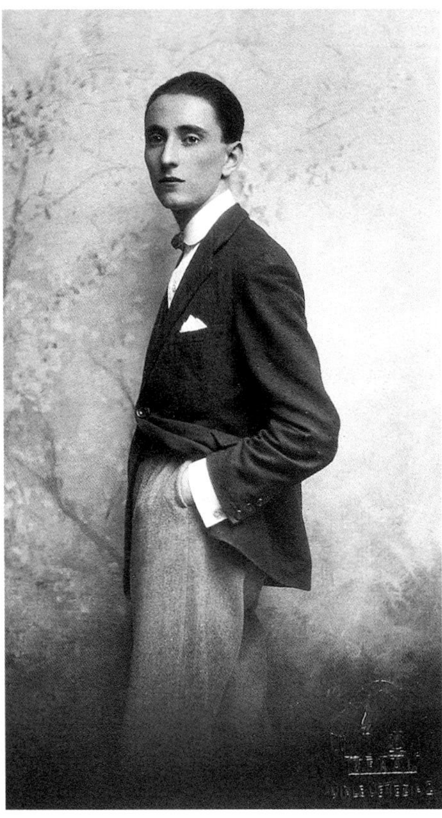

Fig. 2. *Depero, Marinetti and Cangiullo wearing Futurist vests, Turin, 1924*

Fig. 3. *Gianni Mattioli in the 1920s*

ized in space and time. For Milan, one could mention the donation of the Boschi Di Stefano Collection to the Civiche raccolte d'arte in 1973 and of the Emilio and Maria Jesi Collection to the Pinacoteca di Brera in 1981.

Gianni Mattioli is an exception to all this — as I trust will become clear from this account as well as from the documents in the appendix. From the beginning his purpose was to create a collection of modern and contemporary art that would be accessible to the public and that would reflect the importance and vitality of Italian art in the first half of the twentieth century at an international level. It was to foster the emergence of a civil consciousness that would help individuals — and consequently society — to become more fully aware of the dignity of the human condition: an affirmation of the positive aspects of humanity against its barbarities, against all the barbarities that he had experienced personally, from the hardships of his childhood and the hunger and poverty of his youth to the fascist dictatorship and the tragedies of the Spanish Civil War, World War II and the Holocaust.[2]

Even as an adolescent Gianni Mattioli cultivated a strong interest in contemporary art, as well as in literature and the theater: in 1918 he read enthusiastically Umberto Boccioni's *Pittura scultura futuriste*, and in 1921 he met Fortunato Depero at the time of Depero's one-man show at the Galleria Centrale d'Arte Moretti, in Palazzo Cova, Milan.[3] He then joined the Futurist group that was being reorganized in Milan under Filippo Tommaso Marinetti's leadership. In these years he came to know, among others, Anton Giulio Bragaglia, Francesco Cangiullo, Luigi Colombo called Fillia, Luigi Russolo and the architect Luciano Baldessari. He became a close friend of the poet and art critic Raffaele Carrieri (1905–84), who also frequented the circles of the avant-garde. On June 5, 1922 he wrote to his mother, who had moved to Angera after separating from her husband, of his great regret at being forced by his long working hours to turn down free tickets to Marinetti's play, which was to be performed at the Teatro Lirico that evening.[4] He would meet with the group of the Futurists whenever possible. In 1924 he traveled to Turin with them to see a performance at the Cinema Politeama by the Compagnia del Nuovo Teatro Futurista, which had made its debut on January 11 at the Teatro Trianon in Milan.[5] It was on that occasion, January 14, 1924, that a photograph was taken with Depero and Marinetti in the foreground wearing the Futurist vests that had been designed by Depero himself and worn on stage, along with Cangiullo on the right. Between the two main figures appears the head of my father, who told me that the picture was taken in Turin, in the vicinity of the Porta Nuova railroad station. The same year he was greatly impressed by Boccioni's one-man show at the Bottega di Poesia on Via Montenapoleone in Milan (March 10–21); he tried in vain to buy the works *en bloc* with the financial help of a friend.

Mattioli's ties to Marinetti had already loosened by the end of that year,[6] while relations with Depero and Fedele Azari grew closer. He collaborated with them on the publishing of the celebrated *libro imbullonato* (bolted book) titled *Depero Futurista*. Mattioli was never an adherent of second-wave Futurism, though he was friendly with artists such as Cesare Andreoni, Gherardo Dottori, Bruno Munari and Enrico Prampolini. Instead he played an important role in the acquisition of the collection of Boccioni's works formerly owned by Azari (who met an untimely death in 1930) by Ausonio Canavese — works which passed to the Civiche raccolte d'arte of Milan in 1934.[7]

It is revealing that at this time of his life Mattioli's mother expressed to him her hope, in a letter of 1935, that he would be able "without difficulty, to satisfy all your desires as an artist."[8]

A habitual visitor to exhibitions and galleries of modern art, his sympathy for the poetics of the avant-garde in the 1920s kept him aloof from the 'Novecento' movement. In the early 1930s his interests broadened and began to take in African art, Japanese painting and French art from Impressionism onward. He was especially keen on the work of Giorgio de Chirico, visiting his exhibitions at the Galleria Milano in Via Croce Rossa 6 (inaugurated April 27, 1931) and at the Galleria-Libreria il Milione in Via Brera 21 (May 7–22, 1938).[9] In the same year he seems also to have been in contact with Romeo Toninelli, and kept an issue of his magazine *Storia* containing reproductions of works by Gauguin.[10] It was probably in the second half of the 1930s that, thanks to a certain success he was attaining in his work,[11] he was able to afford paintings other than those of his friend Depero, such as de Chirico's *Gli Archeologi* (*The Archeologists*) of 1927 and Achille Funi's *Self-Portrait* of 1921.

In 1942 Mattioli visited, with interest and admiration, the exhibition of Pietro Feroldi's collection at the Pinacoteca di Brera (October–November). A lavishly illustrated volume was published to coincide with this, by the Edizioni del Milione, with an introduction by the writer Guido Piovene.[12] Evidence of his relations with the Pinacoteca di Brera in this period is provided by a copy of Fernanda Wittgens's book *Mentore* with a dedication from Ettore Modigliani, who gave it to him as a Christmas present in 1942.[13] This probably marked the beginning of the close friendship that bound Gianni Mattioli to Fernanda Wittgens up until her death in 1957. Although they were the same age, second cousins,[14] and shared a passion for art, they probably never met before the Feroldi exhibition at the Brera. I have been unable to trace any record of their contact prior to 1943, the year in which they began their clandestine activity together on behalf of Jews. I suspect that an article written by Fernanda on Boccioni in 1932 should be ascribed to the friendships that Wittgens had in the Jewish community rather than to a sympathy for Futurism stemming from an acquaintance with Mattioli.[15]

The first reference to Mattioli's desire to form "un museo di arte moderna" appears in a holograph will written by my mother Angela Maria Boneschi on July 17, 1943, at one of the most dramatic moments of World War II.[16] My mother, called Cici by her friends, was only twenty-four at the time and had married my father on October 24, 1940 in a wedding so eccentric and romantic that it attracted the attention of the newspapers:[17] it was held on board the ship *Victoria* of the Lloyd Triestino line, moored in Genoa harbor, with four sailors as witnesses and the bride's parents as the sole guests. The idea for this celebration was my father's, who in this unconventional way coped with a difficult situation without embarrassing his young fiancée. Not only was my father protestant, sixteen years older than his bride and the son of legally separated parents,[18] but from 1928 he had lived openly for several years with a married woman.[19]

Angela Maria's situation was little better: her father, Cav. Arturo Boneschi (Casteggio, 1878 – Milan, 1960), was a well-known entrepreneur in Milan, especially for his work as a film producer,[20] and after a series of economic ups and downs in Italy and India had established himself as a dealer in raw cotton, the same business as Gianni Mattioli's. Angela Maria's mother, Antonietta Marianna Colombari, called Maria (Intra, 1878 – Milan, 1957), was a worker in a local cotton mill when she met Arturo. After being together for a long period, they married on February 24, 1917 and lived for a while at Via Lauro 2 in Milan, where their daughter was born on March 29, 1919. Soon, mother and daughter began staying for the greater part of the year

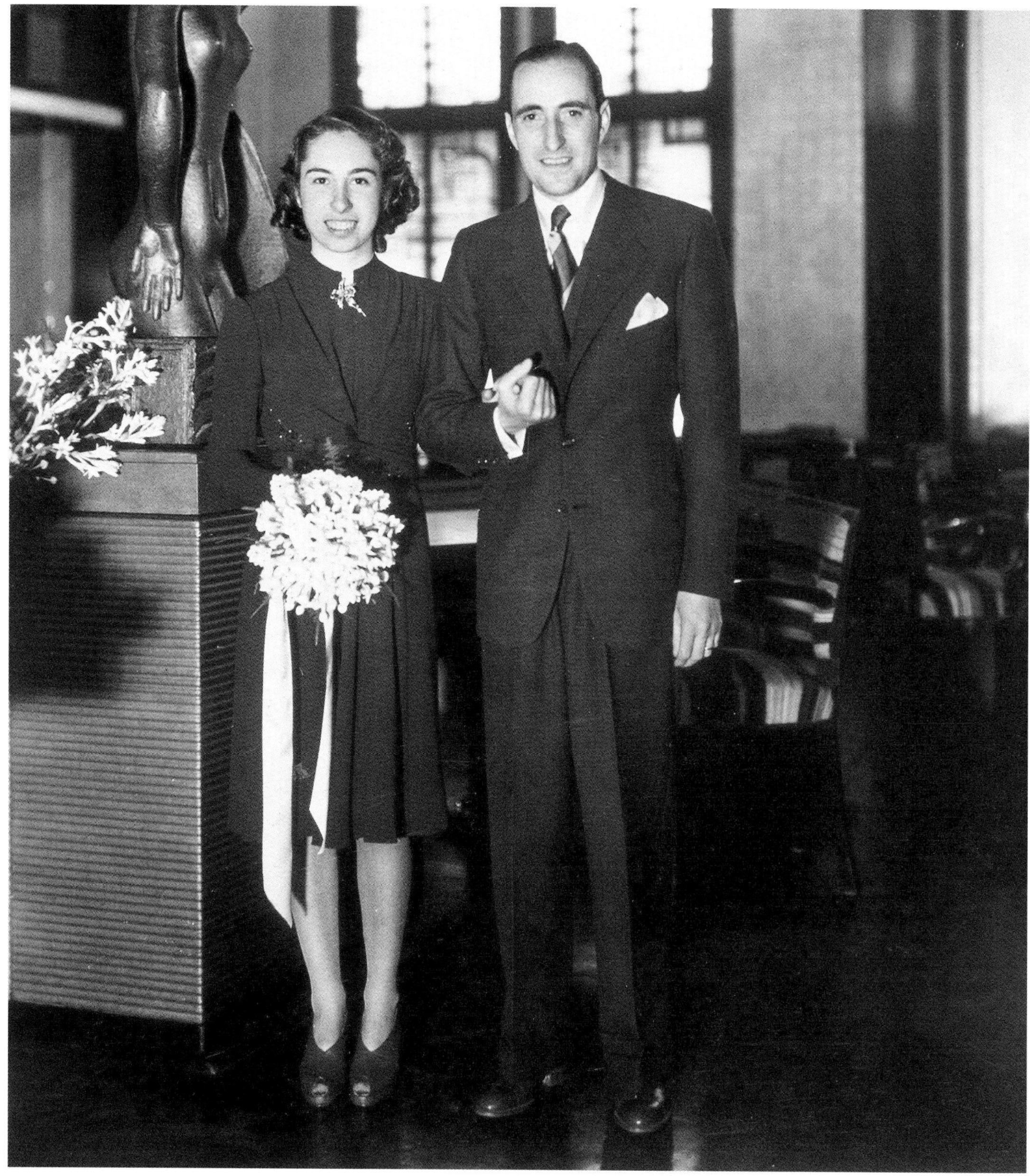

Fig. 4. *Gianni Mattioli and Angela Maria Boneschi after their marriage, October 24, 1940*

Fig. 5. *Gianni Mattioli and Angela Maria Boneschi in Meina, 1943*

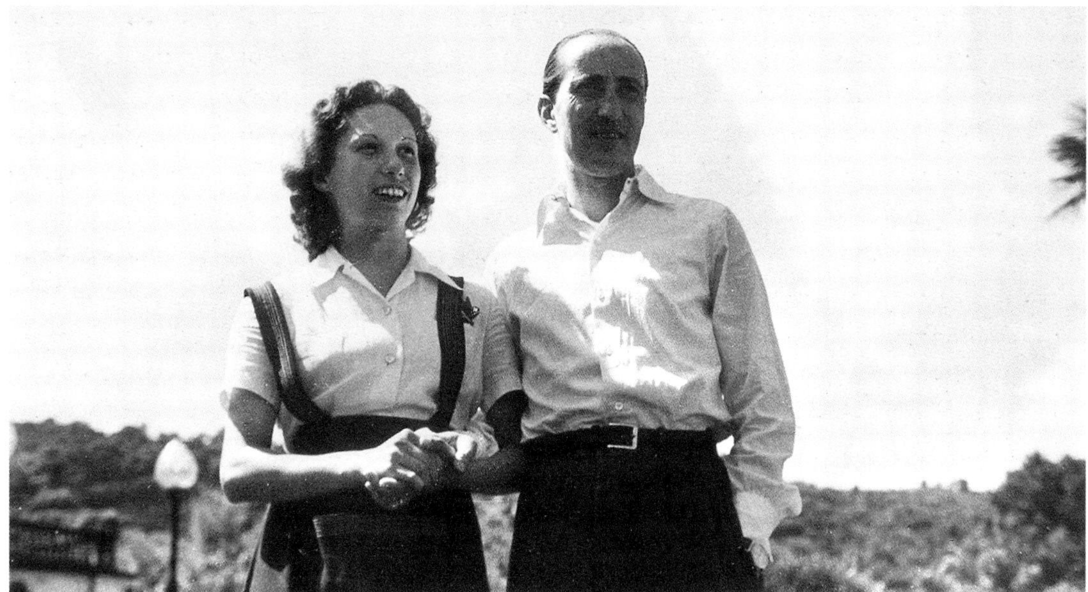

at an early nineteenth-century villa that Arturo bought for them at Meina, on Lago Maggiore.[21] Maria had no liking for city life and above all did not have the kind of education that would have allowed her to move comfortably in the upper middle-class circles to which her husband belonged. Thus Angela Maria attended elementary classes at a private school in Milan, the Istituto Salvoni, but then lived in isolation with her mother on Lago Maggiore.

Gianni Mattioli had met Arturo Boneschi in 1936 through his work.[22] His meeting with Boneschi's daughter took place early in 1938, on board the ship *Victoria* during the voyage to Egypt of the Italian delegation to the 18th International Cotton Congress, held in Cairo and Alexandria with the participation of King Farouk I, from January 26 to February 3. A postcard sent from Burgos in 1938 reveals that relations between the two cotton merchants were growing increasingly cordial. My parents became officially engaged in May 1940, and after their marriage moved in to the top floor of Via Manin 37.[23] But the first bombing raid on Milan, which took place the night of October 24–25, 1942, and a subsequent raid on February 14, 1943 induced them to renovate a farmhouse on the Boneschi estate at Meina and move there instead. For my father, the marriage signified not so much an improvement in his financial condition as the attainment of a higher social status.

During the war, Mattioli, declared unfit for military service because of his delicate constitution, traveled a great deal for work, maintaining contacts with the few textile mills still active. After his marriage he rented an office at Via Principe Amedeo 5 in Milan, spared by the subsequent bombing, where a *de facto* company for the trading of cotton was based from January 1941. On March 29, 1944 this became an unlimited partnership under the name 'Mattioli e Ghedini'.[24] Meanwhile in March 1943 Mattioli became joint owner with his father-in-law of a company trading in raw materials. In addition in 1942 he founded the 'Cantiere Navale Victoria' at Chioggia, which built three vessels and gave him the opportunity to pay frequent visits to Venice, as well as to Rome.

We know that Mattioli visited the Venice Biennale in 1942, as he had probably done on earlier occasions, and we know also that he saw the 'IV Quadriennale d'Arte Nazionale' at the Palazzo delle Esposizioni, Rome (May–July 1943), as testified by the presence of the catalogue in his library and above all by a letter of June 24, 1943 in which the committee responsible for the exhibition informed him that the sculptor Antonio Lucarda was willing to sell him the *Portrait of a Child* on show in room XI for 20,000 lire.[25] We do not know whether Mattioli actually bought the sculpture. In 1944–5 he took up charcoal drawing and more especially sculpture, under the guidance of the sculptor Gino Oliva. All that remains of this brief artistic activity are a few sheets with female nudes and a number of terracottas, including three heads of youths (which recall drawings by Giacomo Manzù from the 1930s and works by Arturo Martini from the second half of the 1920s),[26] as well as a female torso in marble, now lost.

1943 was a particularly difficult year for Mattioli. On March 7 Beatrice Bracciforti died at Angera and on April 7 Paolo Mattioli also died, in Milan. The loss of both his parents was followed by the bombing of Milan, from Saturday August 7 to Sunday August 15, in which much of the city burned and museums and monuments were destroyed. The *palazzo* of the Brera burned down, as did the Galleria del Milione with all its records, and the house at Via Manin 37 was heavily damaged.

Even on Lago Maggiore the situation was dramatic.[27] Many wealthy Jews had taken refuge on the Piedmontese shore of the lake in the hope that they would not be subjected to the same persecution in Italy as in the rest of Europe. Meina in particular housed many of these refugees, because of the ease with which they could come and go daily from Milan by train. From September 8, the *Leibstandarte Adolf Hitler* Armored Division occupied the Piedmontese side of the lake and immediately started hunting down Jews. On the night of September 13–14 the SS occupied 'Il Castagneto' at Baveno, a villa owned by Mario Luzzatto, a Jew who lived on Via Boscovich in Milan and a neighbor and friend of Arturo Boneschi, killing him and all his family. The SS arrived in Meina on September 15: they identified the Jews and shut them up in the Hotel Meina. The agony of the prisoners was played out in front of the whole town for a week, until September 22 and 23 when they were shot. For several days their bodies, bound with wire to large stones, continued to wash up on the shores of the lake, and the corpses of three children resurfaced right in front of Villa Boneschi. The German troops reached Arona around two in the afternoon on September 15. A few minutes before their arrival the Jarach family, close friends of the Boneschi, fled with a rowboat to the Lombardy shore. The SS occupied their house and scoured Arona, killing all the Jews. In the garden of Villa Jarach they found the abandoned automobile of a "signore da Milano" who had escaped on foot through the garden at the sight of the Germans, after persuading the Jarach to seek safety at the last moment. This mystery person was Gianni Mattioli. The SS, who took up permanent residence in the villa, decided to hold a party on Saturday September 18; the owner of the abandoned car turned up, bringing a German prostitute with him from Milan, and took advantage of the occupants' drunken state to make off with the automobile, a rare and precious asset in those days.

An undated note from Fernanda Wittgens, asking for an urgent appointment with Mattioli, and his carefully worded reply on September 16 testify to the involvement of both in the dramatic events of those days.[28] Fernanda supported the activity of the partisans of the 'Giustizia e libertà' formations, inspired by the 'Partito d'Azione', and was in direct contact with Ferruccio Parri, its leader. A relative of the Boneschi family with particularly close ties to Arturo and later a friend of Mattioli's, the lawyer Mario Boneschi was also active with Parri, and after the war became a member of the Constituent Assembly and a councilor in the Greppi administration of the municipality of Milan. After September 8 Wittgens worked to help as many Jews as possible to escape to Switzerland with the assistance of two groups: the first consisted of my father, who, thanks to his possession of an automobile and two passes (one obtained from the German command and one provided him by the partisans), transported the fugitives from Milan to his brother Ferdinando — called Nando — who had been evacuated to the home of the *podestà*, Cav. Alfredo Bellardi, at Galliate Lombardo (near Varese). My uncle, in agreement with

Fig. 6. *Gianni Mattioli,* Female Nude Seen from Behind, *drawing, December 1944*

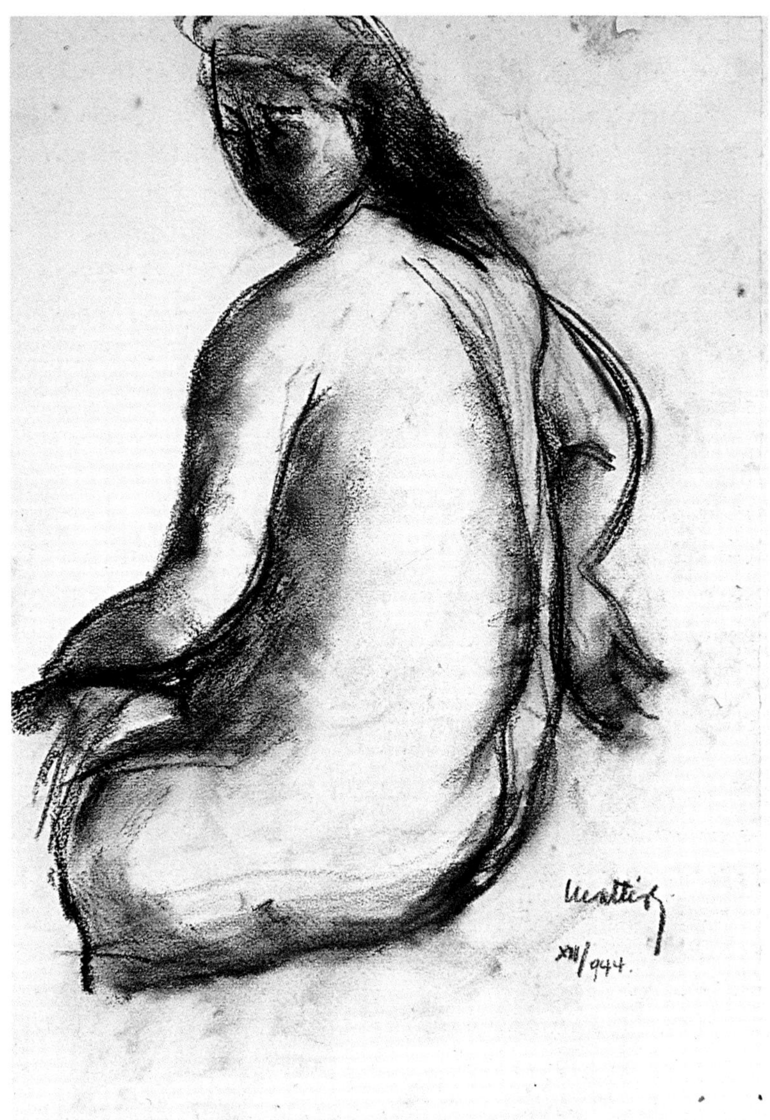

Bellardi, kept the Jews hidden until it was possible to smuggle them across the frontier into Switzerland by bribing the border guards. The best-known figure to go into exile by this route was Lamberto Vitali, who fled in November 1943, taking with him Amedeo Modigliani's painting *L'Enfant gras*, now in the Pinacoteca di Brera.[29] The second group was made up of four men and Adele Cappelli Vegni — doctor and longstanding antifascist, who sheltered escaping Jews at her house, the 'Villa San Vincenzo' at Torno on Lake Como — as well as the sisters Zina and Mariarosa Tresoldi, elementary schoolteachers who lived with Wittgens at Via Verga 15 in Milan.[30] This group succeeded in breaking Franco Momigliano out of the San Vittore prison. As a result of a tip-off several Jews were caught trying to cross the border at Como on the night of July 14, 1944, and all the members of the second group operating with Fernanda were arrested at dawn. On July 23, after preliminary interrogations in Como prison, all were handed over to the Special Tribunal for the Defense of the State in Milan. The men chose forced labor in Germany; the four women instead underwent trial, which was intended to set an example and was known as 'il processo delle Dame' (the trial of the Ladies). Fernanda wrote from prison to Gianni Mattioli, thanking him for the money offered to her family in those difficult months.[31] Wittgens was sentenced to four years' imprisonment, but served only seven months thanks to a false medical certificate that allowed her to be transferred to a clinic in the days of the fall of Nazi-Fascism.

A letter dated April 28, 1945 from Boneschi to the Mattiolis, who had come back to live in Milan,[32] testifies to the dramatic confusion of those days and their relief at knowing that all the partisans in the family, Fernanda, Mario Boneschi and Franco Mattioli, were safe.[33]

Wittgens described the impact that the experience of the war had made on her — feelings that were fully shared by my father, for these were the basis of their friendship and their collaboration — in clear and touching words in a letter sent to her friend Clara Valenti in Turin just before her death in 1957: "This letter passes on to you the torch of the 'sociality of art' that I have sought to light since coming out of San Vittore, having grasped the human problem in its fullness there. In other words that everywhere, even in prison, the 'human' can be saved from the 'bestial' and that art is perhaps one of the highest forms of defense of the 'human.' So, returning to Brera, I created the *living museum*."[34]

The second reference to the 'Mattioli collection' appears in a letter that Fortunato Depero sent to his friend Gianni from Serrada (Trento) on July 9–10, 1944, in which he wrote: "*Another idea*: Would you like to have *one* or *two* of your drawings appear in the collection that is being printed? That way you would begin to make known the existence of a *Mattioli Collection*: think about it!"[35] Depero was referring to the numbered edition of a portfolio of twenty-five drawings — on which he worked for much of 1944 — whose publication was made possible in the middle of October thanks to the financial assistance of my father. Thanks also to him, the book was put on sale in Milan in December, at the Hoepli bookshop on Corso del Littorio and at the Mondadori bookshop in Galleria Vittorio Emanuele II, and reviewed on March 4, 1945 by the *Corriere della Sera*.[36] In 1944 Mattioli took steps to ensure that the entry on Depero in the *Dizionario Comanducci* was made longer and better illustrated than originally planned.[37]

The correspondence between Depero and Mattioli, begun in 1922 and interrupted in 1936, was resumed sporadically after 1942. The artist had turned to his friend in July 1943 to obtain the money he needed to return to the United States, a move he had decided on for the "moral enhancement of my work and my name [...] and for a financial return, even modest, that here will never be possible with art, and that in N.Y. — given my previous experience, and the new means of approach to art — will not be difficult to attain."[38] In 1943 that journey was not possible because of the war, and at the end of the year the painter decided to live in Serrada with his wife Rosetta. Depero tried once more to make his fortune in America by going to New York in November 1947, again with Mattioli's financial help, but was obliged to return home in May 1949.

The renewal of relations between the two old friends gave my father the opportunity to acquire a series of works that had particularly fascinated him in his youth. In addition to the *Selvagetto* (*Little Savage*) of 1919 in wood, which the artist had given to him on the occasion of his one-man show at the Galleria Centrale d'Arte Moretti in 1921, Mattioli already possessed, in the house at Via Poerio 15,[39] the tapestries *Bambina e marinaio* (*Little Girl and Sailor*) of 1917 and *Due maschere tropicali* (*Two Tropical Masks*) of 1920, and the paintings *Diavoli di caucciù a scatto* (*Flip-Up Rubber Devils*) of 1919 and *Città meccanizzata dalle ombre* (*City Mechanized by Shadows*) of 1920, as well as two cushions probably identifiable with the *Ballerino in gomma* (*Rubber Dancer*) of 1920 and the *Diavolo nero* (*Black Devil*), this last previously owned by Fedele Azari. *Città meccanizzata dalle ombre* was a painting much admired by Carlo Belli. In 1919–20 it had inspired him to write a short story, which remained in manuscript form,[40] and in 1935 he cited it along with *La casa del mago* (*The Wizard's House*, also acquired by my father), the tapestry *Il corteo della Gran Bambola* (*The Procession of the Great Doll*) and *Villaggio sconosciuto* (*Unknown Village*) in his book *Kn*, published by Edizioni del Milione, describing this group of works as "the finest metaphysical pictures produced by this movement [...] spectacular visions of a magical naturalism superior to de Chirico himself."[41] In 1944 these works by Depero

Fig. 7. *Fortunato Depero,* Gianni and the Armadillo, *1946* *Private collection*

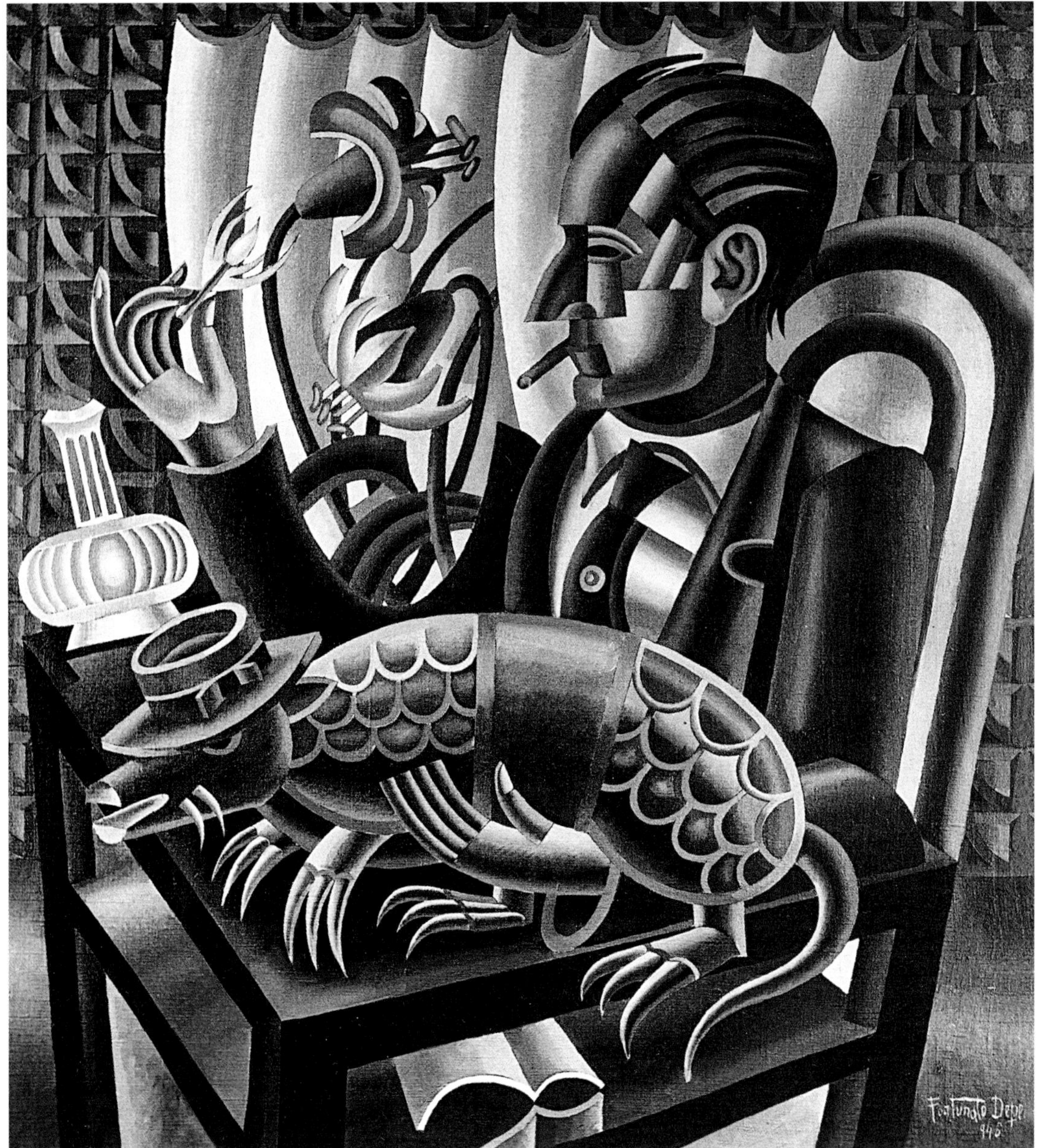

were joined by *Selvagetti* (*Little Savages*) of 1918 (whose original title was *I selvaggi rossi e neri* [*The Red and Black Savages*]), *Io e mia moglie* (*I and My Wife*) of 1919, *Natura morta accesa* (*Lit-up Still Life*) of 1936 and the charcoal drawings *Polenta a fuoco duro* (*Polenta on a High Flame*), *Il gallo* (*The Rooster*), and *Elasticità di gatti* (*Agility of Cats*), all sent from Serrada to Meina on May 27[42] and chosen by Mattioli on a visit to the Trentino in the first half of April.[43] Contacts with Raffaele Carrieri were also re-established on this occasion (Depero wished him to write an article[44]). Mattioli collected from him a group of drawings and "colored papers" (collage costume designs made for Diaghilev) from the second decade of the century that were still owned by the artist, which he then kept and bought little by little up until 1950.[45]

Differences soon emerged between Depero and the collector in the evaluation of the artist's work: Gianni preferred the early works and was looking for drawings from the years 1913–20, while Depero insisted on the importance of his more recent production. In order not to irritate him and to give him a hand financially, my father agreed to purchase a few recent drawings as well and helped him to sell a number of works.[46] In September 1945 Mattioli went to Rovereto, where he commissioned a portrait of himself and a design for a chandelier; he also offered him a one-man show at the Galleria del Camino in Milan the following year.[47]

1945 was in general a year of transition, which my parents once again spent in Milan. The end of the war brought a revival of business for manufacturing industries, especially in the fall, and therefore an increase in my father's commercial activity. With their return to the city it became possible for my parents to frequent old friends again, to make new ones, to go to the theater and read books, mostly by the American writers who were only published or obtainable in Italy after the fall of Fascism.[48] The house at Via Fratelli Gabba 9, into which the Mattiolis had moved in September 1945, was redecorated by the end of the year, in time to become a new meeting place.

1946 marked the start of a period of frenetic activity. Mattioli was in constant touch with Fernanda Wittgens, who was engaged in the work of rebuilding the city's museums and monuments, heavily damaged in the bombing, and with Ettore Modigliani, to whom my parents were particularly close during his son's fatal illness. They saw much of the brothers Aldo and Mario Boneschi and from 1947 onward, following the reconstruction of the theaters, they resumed their friendship with Arturo Toscanini, his daughter Wally and the actress Sara Ferrati.[49]

Mattioli strengthened his ties with the Milanese art galleries, and in particular with Gino Ghiringhelli — who for a short time transferred his gallery to Via Manzoni 26 — and his closest collaborators: Ambrogio Ceroni, bibliophile and old friend of Peppino Ghiringhelli, who during the unrest of 1945 left his post as secretary to the general manager of Ercole Marelli to work as a consultant in the field of contemporary art (he was to become famous for his fundamental monographs on Modigliani); Marco Valsecchi, who had been employed as an accountant in a timber firm before becoming a journalist and art critic; and Angelo Gritti, bachelor and wealthy property owner who had a great deal of free time and frequented these circles out of a passion for art. Gino, Ambrogio, Marco and Angelo formed with my father a group of close friends, with a propensity for intellectual talk but also for schoolboy pranks.

From March 9–31, 1946 a one-man show of Depero's paintings and drawings was held at Romeo Toninelli's gallery 'Il Camino,' on the corner of Via Sant'Andrea and Via Montenapoleone in Milan, with twenty-seven oils from the period 1944–6 and twenty-three drawings; the show included *Natura morta accesa* of 1936, that Mattioli had acquired a short time before. During his stay in Milan Depero came to know Gino Ghiringhelli, and corresponded frequently with my father throughout 1946.

Between April 10 and 18 Depero returned to Milan to meet John B. Salterini, his American friend who was visiting Italy and whom he wished to introduce to Mattioli in advance of the latter's imminent business trip to the United States.[50] That same year Salterini was to be Depero's go-between in his attempt to sell Boccioni's *Materia* (cat. no. 4) to the Museum of Modern Art in New York.

In a letter dated May 22, 1946, Depero told Mattioli that he had been informed in confidence that Boccioni's sister and her husband (Amelia and Guido Callegari), both ailing and suffering financial hardship, were "willing to sell some works of Boccioni's: either paintings — or drawings or etchings" and asked for permission to negotiate the purchase of works, even of minor ones.[51] Mattioli replied affirmatively by telegram,[52] and on June 11 Depero announced that he had bought a small view of the outskirts of Milan in oil from 1909[53] and four etchings.[54] He also proposed the purchase of a watercolor of the painter's mother, but it was deemed too expensive.[55] Receiving the payment with an accompanying letter on June 21,[56] Depero wrote back three days later: "There is one of Boccioni's major works in Verona — a painting of around 2 × 1.40 meters — *Materia*. Last year they were offered 100,000 for it — I have an idea for this work: to be precise I would like to propose it to the Museum of Modern Art in New York —

Fig. 8. *Gianni Mattioli in his office, Via Principe Amedeo 5, Milan, probably in the late 1940s*

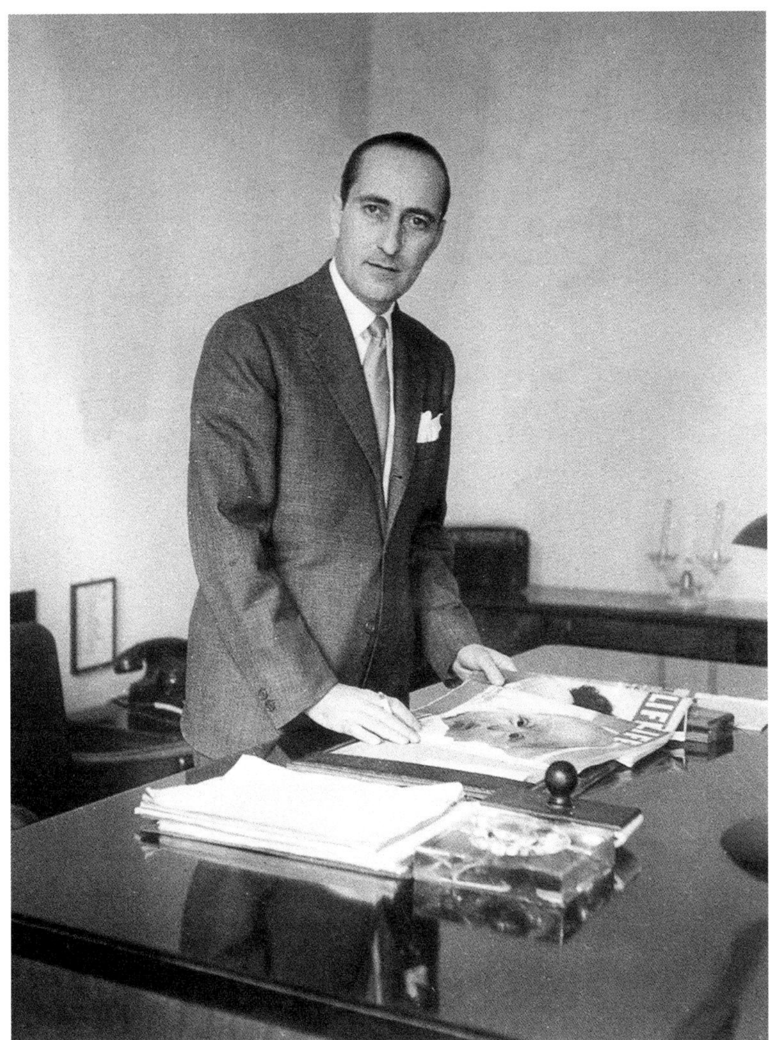

via Salterini. I would entrust you with the photographic and descriptive material *if you agree*, you could go yourself to Salterini. I think it might be a good deal and suggest (I don't know if this is right) that this time the profit be divided between *you-me* and *Boccioni's sister*. I believe that we could get a good price in N.Y."[57]

Mattioli, about to leave for the United States,[58] replied to Depero on July 4, 1946: "I will try talking about the large Boccioni picture in New York as you suggest. If I don't get anywhere over there I might think about the possibility of buying it myself if the price and conditions are not too onerous. So keep it 'on hold.' I hope to be back around the middle of August [...]."[59] My father had probably talked about the possibility of buying *Materia* with his group of friends at the Galleria del Milione and so Gino Ghiringhelli — taking advantage of Mattioli's absence from Italy — wrote to Depero on July 27, telling him that he was interested in acquiring works by Boccioni and in particular "a large and important painting whose exact subject I cannot recall right now."[60] Depero, chronically short of money and attracted by the prospect of a good deal, preferred to open negotiations with the Museum of Modern Art in New York through Salterini[61] and obtained from Amelia Callegari, owner of the work, official authorization to sell the painting in Italy or abroad.[62] He also wrote a report on *Materia* to send to America.[63] But at the end of 1946 James Johnson Sweeney, with whom Salterini had opened negotiations, resigned as director of the museum's Department of Painting and Sculpture (later to become director of the Solomon R. Guggenheim Museum). On December 30 the new director turned down the offer of the painting.[64] *Materia* remained the property of the artist's family until the beginning of 1948, when the gallery owner Romeo Toninelli went to Verona, where the Callegari were living, and bought around fifteen drawings and several paintings, including *Materia*, for the sum of 500,000 lire.[65]

On his trip to New York my father took with him a copy of Raffaele Carrieri's book *Giorgio De Chirico* (Milan, Garzanti 1942) which Peppino Ghiringhelli had asked him to give to James Thrall Soby, along with a letter of introduction, but he did not meet Soby personally on this occasion.[66]

Since March 1946 Mattioli had been friendly with the painter Arturo Tosi, whose studio was located above his office at Via Principe Amedeo 5. At the beginning of September Tosi gave one of his paintings to my father.[67] At the end of the year Mattioli sub-rented some rooms from him, in which to keep the works of art he now owned, evidently growing rapidly in number. He rented these rooms from December 31, 1946 to the end of June 1949.[68]

The year 1947 opened with a business trip to New York and Dallas from around January 20 to February 5. In spite of his heavy workload, Mattioli continued to pursue his passion for modern art and to frequent galleries and artists. He saw the exhibition 'Arte Astratta e Concreta,' held from January 11 to February 9 at Palazzo Reale in Milan, and showed one of his sculptures at the 'III Mostra Italiana di Arte Sacra per la Casa Cristiana' organized on the premises of the Angelicum in May–June.[69]

From a letter of July 4 from Gino Ghiringhelli, who had moved with his gallery and publishing house to Romeo Toninelli's address at Via Sant'Andrea 1, we learn that Mattioli bought a *Self-Portrait* by de Chirico that had previously belonged to Dr. Rodolfo Siviero, with the head of a woman in profile painted on the back. To make a greater profit from the sale, Ghiringhelli separated the two paintings, although this led Siviero to deplore the loss of paint from both works as a consequence of the intervention.[70]

Mattioli also maintained contact with Romeo Toninelli, president of the club known as the 'Circolo delle Arti - Le Grazie' at Via Sant'Andrea 1, who organized an exhibition of Flemish painting in the month of April, and on October 16 decided to merge with the 'Associazione Cultori e Amatori Arte Contemporanea,' headed by Marco Valsecchi. On December 2 the committee of the new arts club met for the first time to decide its program of activities: it was agreed that four exhibitions should be held, in the following order: Boccioni, curated by Raffaele Carrieri; Piccio, curated by Paolo D'Ancona and Roberto Pacchioni; Marussig, curated by Adriano Pallini and Gino Ghiringhelli; and Medardo Rosso, curated by Marco Valsecchi and Giovanni Scheiwiller. Lectures and concerts were scheduled, along with an exhibition possibly to be staged at the Galleria d'Arte Moderna on the nineteenth and twentieth centuries ('Ottocento e Novecento'),[71] in which all members of the association would be involved. A visit to the Reinhart Collection at Winterthur in Switzerland, with Giovanni Scheiwiller as guide, was also proposed.[72]

From a letter of January 23, 1948, we learn that Mattioli funded the staging of Piccio's exhibition on the premises of the Circolo delle Arti.[73] Boccioni's exhibition included the painting *Elasticità* of 1912, later in the Jucker Collection (now the property of the Comune of Milan).[74]

In 1948 Romeo Toninelli involved my father in the organization of the exhibition 'Twentieth-Century Italian Art,' to be mounted at the Museum of Modern Art in New York from June 28 to September 12, 1949. Toninelli was 'Executive Secretary for the Exhibition in Italy' and turned to the members of the Circolo delle Arti - Le Grazie for help in choosing and obtaining the works of art.[75] My father's name appears on the honorary committee at the beginning of the catalogue[76] along with those of some of the greatest Italian experts on modern art of those years, whom he certainly must have had the opportunity to meet. I have indirect information that in

Fig. 9. *Gianni Mattioli,* Head of the Infant St John, *terracotta, exhibited at the 'III Mostra Italiana di Arte Sacra per la Casa Cristiana' at the Angelicum, Milan, May–June 1947*

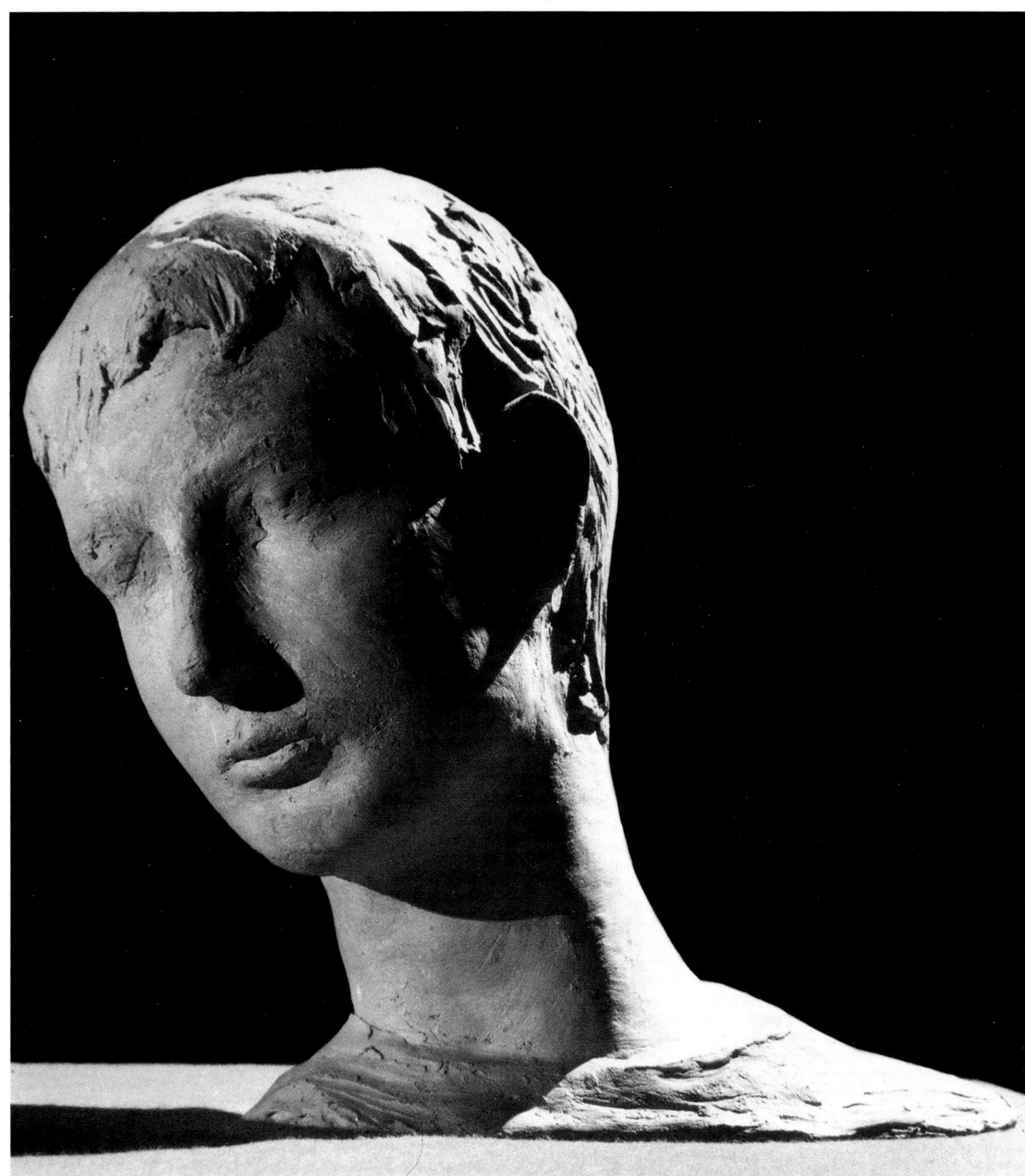

some letters exchanged between Soby and Barr now in the archives of MoMA mention is made of a visit to Medardo Rosso's studio at Barzio in the company of Gianni Mattioli and Fernanda Wittgens, although this took place after the exhibition, in October 1949. In any case my father was personally acquainted with the two curators of this important exhibition, which was one of the fundamental factors in making Italian modern art known to the wider world after the period of isolation imposed by the Fascist dictatorship, in a challenge to the acknowledged hegemony of French painting.

Mattioli's library testifies to the fact that he was a regular visitor to the museum on his business trips to America[77] and that in 1947 he had already bought W. R. Valentiner's book on the *Origins of Modern Sculpture* (New York 1946), in which the relationship between modern sculpture and pre-classical art is underlined, as well as the third edition of *Fantastic Art, Dada, Surrealism* published by the Museum of Modern Art, which emphasized the fantastical aspects of painting from the Renaissance to modern times, passing through Bosch and Goya, Chagall and Arp, and with reproductions of Giorgio de Chirico's *L'enigma dell'ora* (*The Enigma of the Hour*) and of *Le muse inquietanti* (*The Disquieting Muses*), both then in the Feroldi Collection.

Several works that were shortly to enter the Mattioli Collection were on show at the MoMA exhibition of 1949: Boccioni's *Materia* (cat. no. 4) then owned by Toninelli; Russolo's *Solidità della nebbia* (cat. no. 21) owned by Margherita Sarfatti; Carrà's paintings *Il cavaliere occidentale* (*The Western Rider*), belonging to Adriano Pallini, and *L'idolo ermafrodito* (*Hermaphroditic Idol*), owned by Carlo Frua De Angeli. My father appeared in the catalogue as owner by this time of paintings from the Feroldi Collection: Carrà's *L'amante dell'ingegnere* (cat. no. 10) and *Mattino sul mare* (*Morning over the Sea*), Morandi's *Natura morta con bottiglie e fruttiera* of 1916 (cat. no. 17) and Rosai's *Mio padre* (*My Father*).

In 1948, from April 20 to May 5, Mattioli was in New York on business and received the congratulations of the Associazione Cotoniera Italiana for his work on behalf of the industry.[78] In July he made contact with Tommaso Sillani, director of the Centro Italiano di Studi per la Riconciliazione Internazionale, and later with Ambassador Pompeo Aloisi[79] and J. D. Zellerbach, with whom he discussed the results of the Marshall Plan in Italy.[80] Over the following years he collaborated with this American program of aid for postwar construction in the sector regarding his own work as a merchant of raw cotton.

From March to May 1948 the 'Rassegna Nazionale di Arti Figurative' was held at the Galleria d'Arte Moderna in Rome, organized by the Quadriennale. On this occasion too a number of paintings were exhibited that were shortly to enter Mattioli's collection, including Russolo's *Solidità della nebbia* and Severini's *Ballerina blu* (cat. no. 22) in the Futurist section introduced by Benedetta Marinetti, as well as several works by Modigliani that were well known to my father, such as Lamberto Vitali's *L'Enfant gras* and the Milanese collector Adriano Pallini's *Portrait of Paul Guillaume* (now the property of the Comune of Milan, which bought it on Mattioli's recommendation).

The first Venice Biennale after the war, the XXIV, was held in 1948, and it is likely that my parents attended the inauguration. It was a particularly rich and ambitious event, which set out to present the theme of modern art in a prestigious and articulated manner. The large 'Mostra degli Impressionisti,' with almost a hundred works, was flanked by one-man shows of Chagall, Kokoschka and Picasso, organized with the help of the artists themselves, a retrospective on Klee, the exhibition of Peggy Guggenheim's collection, exhibitions dedicated to 'Tre pittori italiani dal 1910 al 1920' (including Metaphysical paintings by Carrà, de Chirico and Morandi) and the 'Fronte nuovo delle arti' movement (with works by Turcato, Santomaso, Corpora, Pizzinato, Guttuso, Vedova and Viani of 1947–8), retrospectives of Cesare Breveglieri, Arturo Martini, Gino Rossi and Scipione and monographic exhibitions of the work of Campigli, de Pisis, Maccari, and Mafai.[81]

My father was not listed among the lenders. There were works from the collections of Roberto Longhi, Lionello Venturi and Lamberto Vitali. The collections of Nino Barbantini, Pietro Feroldi, Carlo Frua, Emilio Jesi and Pietro Rollino are all mentioned and represented in the catalogue. Nevertheless a number of paintings were shown that Mattioli was soon to acquire, in addition to those belonging to Feroldi (whose collection he bought *en bloc* the following year): Carrà's *Il cavaliere occidentale* (then owned by Adriano Pallini) and *L'idolo ermafrodito* (Frua Collection), de Chirico's *Interno metafisco* (*Metaphysical Interior*, also Frua Collection) and Scipione's *La cortigiana romana* (*The Roman Courtesan*, then owned by Augusto Mascioli of Ivrea). Furthermore I know that my father later sought to buy, though in vain, Carrà's *Il gentiluomo ubriaco* (*The Drunken Gentleman*) from Frua and Carrà's *L'ovale delle apparizioni* (*The Oval of the Apparitions*) from Marcel Fleischmann in Zurich.

The Biennale certainly made a great impact on Mattioli. It gave him the opportunity to see some of Feroldi's paintings again and consider the possibility of buying them, since the Bres-

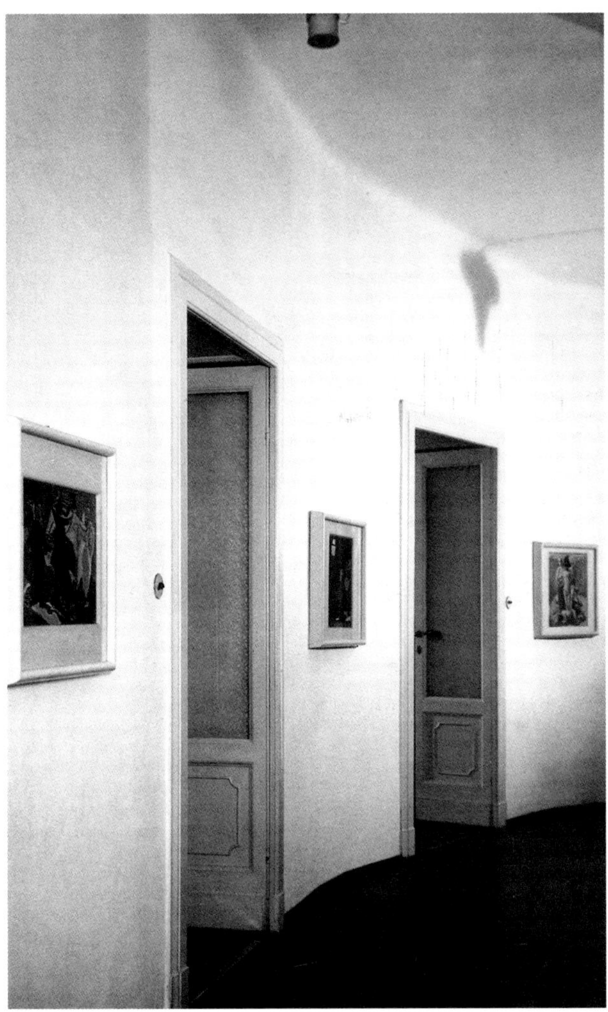

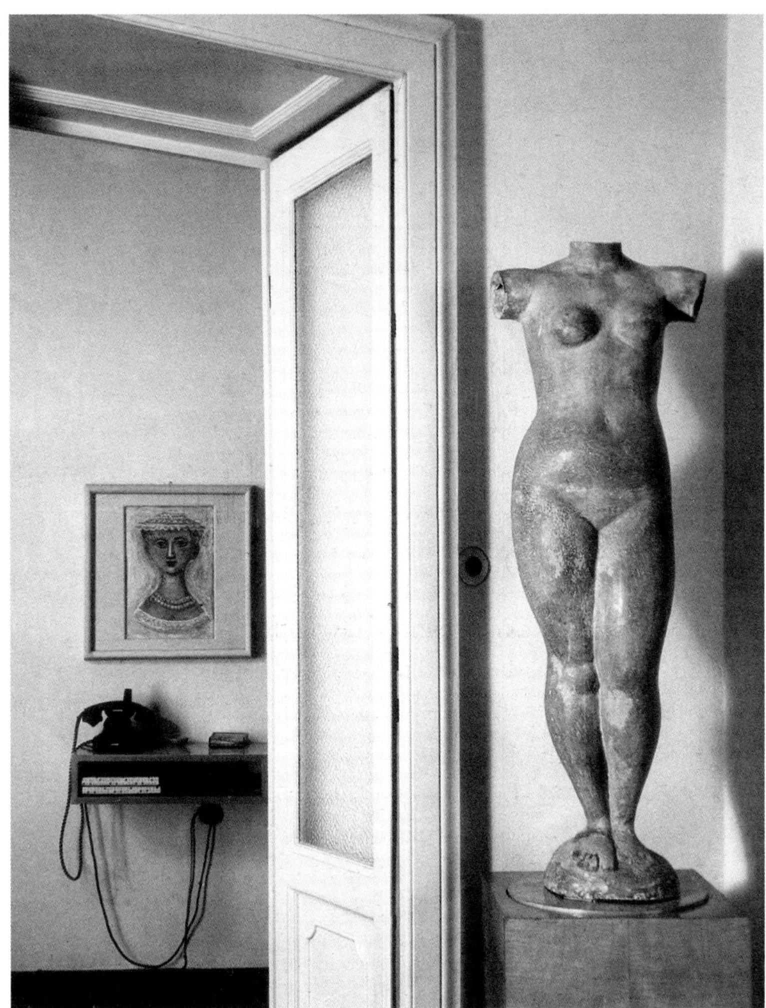

Figs. 10–11. *Mattioli's home, Via Gabba 9, Milan, probably September 1948: the entrance corridor and the telephone viewed from the living room*

cian collector had been trying to sell them since 1941[82] and for this had been in contact with the Galleria del Milione, which had always been his main point of reference.

Mattioli was struck not just by the Impressionists, whom he had been studying even during the years of the war, as is apparent from his library, but also by Peggy Guggenheim's collection, for its decidedly international character — something new for Italy — and for the freedom of expression displayed by the artists represented. Guggenheim's works probably made him think once more about the importance of the avant-garde movements in which he had believed in his youth, but whose historical importance and influence had not yet been recognized by Italian critics and collectors. The Biennale may also have induced my father to reflect on the need for a historical interpretation of all that had taken place in the first half of the twentieth century, based on key works of the leading artists, in order to shed light on the role played by Italian art in the international context, something that he probably thought was represented in too haphazard and qualitatively uneven a fashion in Venice.

From the end of 1948, at Mattioli's request, the Galleria del Milione sent regularly a statement of expenditure to the collector, who was now a frequent and valued customer.

The first of these notes is dated September 20, 1948 and lists the payment of 80,000 lire on March 26 for a still life with eggs by Casorati, of 30,000 lire on April 20 for an unidentified work by Mario Asnago, of the balance on July 20 for de Chirico's *Self-Portrait*, purchased from Siviero for 35,000 lire, of 45,000 lire for a picture of flowers by Soffici from 1929 (which had been sold by the Galleria del Milione to Siviero in June 1943), as well as the acquisition of a terracotta by Marino Marini for 400,000 lire on the same date, along with a landscape by de Pisis for 20,000 lire and a *Maternità* (*Motherhood*) in terracotta by Martini for 70,000 lire (which Mattioli was to donate to the Museum of Tel Aviv on June 1, 1950), and finally books for a total of 7,500 lire.[83]

A series of photographs of the house at Via Gabba 9, taken before the end of November of the same year,[84] sheds light on my father's taste at that moment, on the early appearance of his collection and on some of the acquisitions recorded in the statement from the Galleria del Milione.

The apartment had an entrance with a corridor that provided access to the other rooms. The decor was modern and some of the furniture, in the dining room and the bedroom for guests, had been designed by the architect Franco Albini. The pictures were all framed in the same simple way, with a strip of wood and an ivory-white matte, to give them the same dimensions and bring out their pictorial qualities. The whole house gave an impression of clarity and sobriety, with no frills but enlivened in its rigorous and essential lines by bunches of flowers and works of art. In the view of the corridor the paintings are seen at too steep an angle to be identifiable

Fig. 12. *Mattioli's home, Via Gabba 9, Milan, November 1948: the living room with* The Sacred Fish *by Giorgio de Chirico*

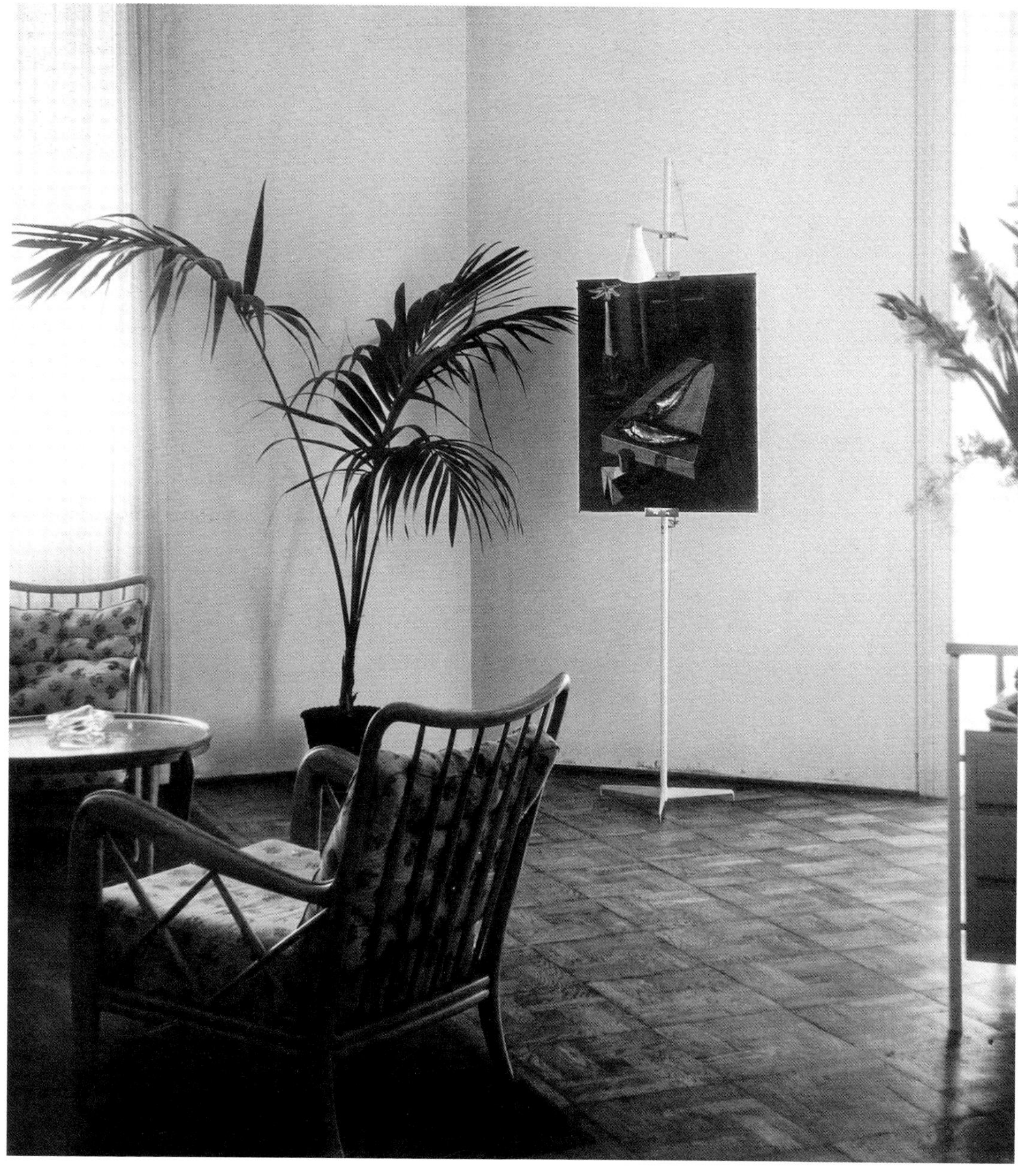

Fig. 13. *Mattioli's home, Via Gabba 9, Milan, probably September 1948: partial view of the living room, set up as a study*

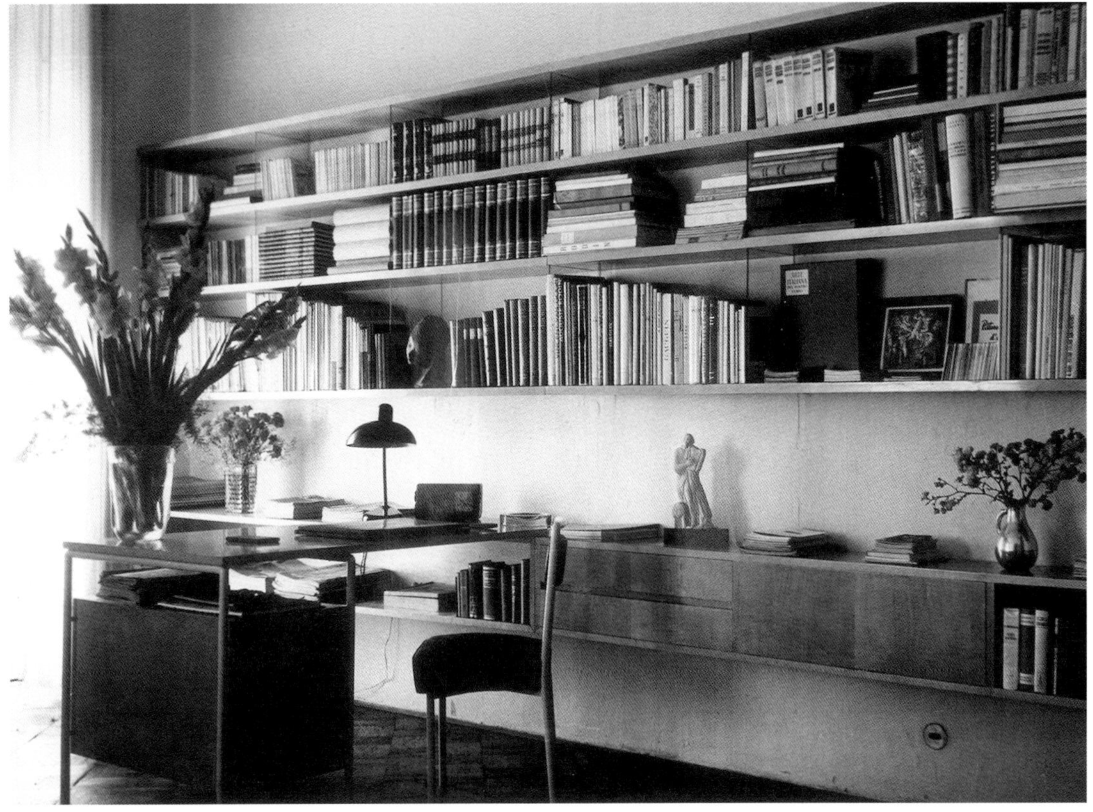

with certainty: it seems possible to recognize a still life by Severini and at the end *Nell'Arena* (*In the Arena*), a 1927 oil by de Chirico from his *Gladiatori* (*Gladiators*) series.[85] The telephone must have been located near the entrance, and above it hung a painting of the head of a woman wearing a hat by Massimo Campigli. The photograph was taken from the living room, where Marini's terracotta *Venus* of 1945, for which he paid the Ghiringhellis in September 1948, was located. The room looks simple and almost bare, but on an easel in one corner can be seen de Chirico's *I pesci sacri* (*The Sacred Fish*, now MoMA, New York), an emblematic work that Mattioli had on deposit from Carlo Frua at that time.[86]

My father told me that this famous and intelligent collector, perhaps the greatest of those years and a man with whom he had been friends since before the war, had lent him several works of which he was particularly fond — including Modigliani's portrait in profile of Lunia Czechowska — but that he had not always been able to acquire them.

One part of the living room was used as a study, with a desk made of wood and iron and a long bookshelf with many identifiable books on art as well as Arturo Martini's terracotta sculpture *Orfeo* (*Orpheus*) and Medardo Rosso's bronze *Bambino malato* (*Sick Child*).

The dining room had a round table in the center, on which was set Manzù's 1943 sculpture *Ragazza alla finestra* (*Girl at the Window*) — one of the Bergamasque artist's works closest to the style of Medardo Rosso — between a wall lined with a sideboard, closets, display cabinets and a grating from which to hang flower vases, and chairs set along the opposite side. From left to right above the chairs, one can identify Campigli's *Donna ingioiellata* (*Woman Decked with Jewels*) of 1942, formerly in the Giani Collection, de Chirico's first version of *Gli Archeologi* (painted in 1927), a *Still Life* by Morandi from 1946,[87] and Carrà's *Tramonto sul lago* (*Sunset on the Lake*) of 1922, previously owned by Rino Valdameri.

The bedroom would have looked bare if one whole wall had not been lined with two rows of pictures. Clockwise from the top left, one can recognize a *Natura morta con pere* (*Still Life with Pears*) by de Pisis, another still life by Tosi, a *Self-Portrait* of 1921 by Funi,[88] a still life by

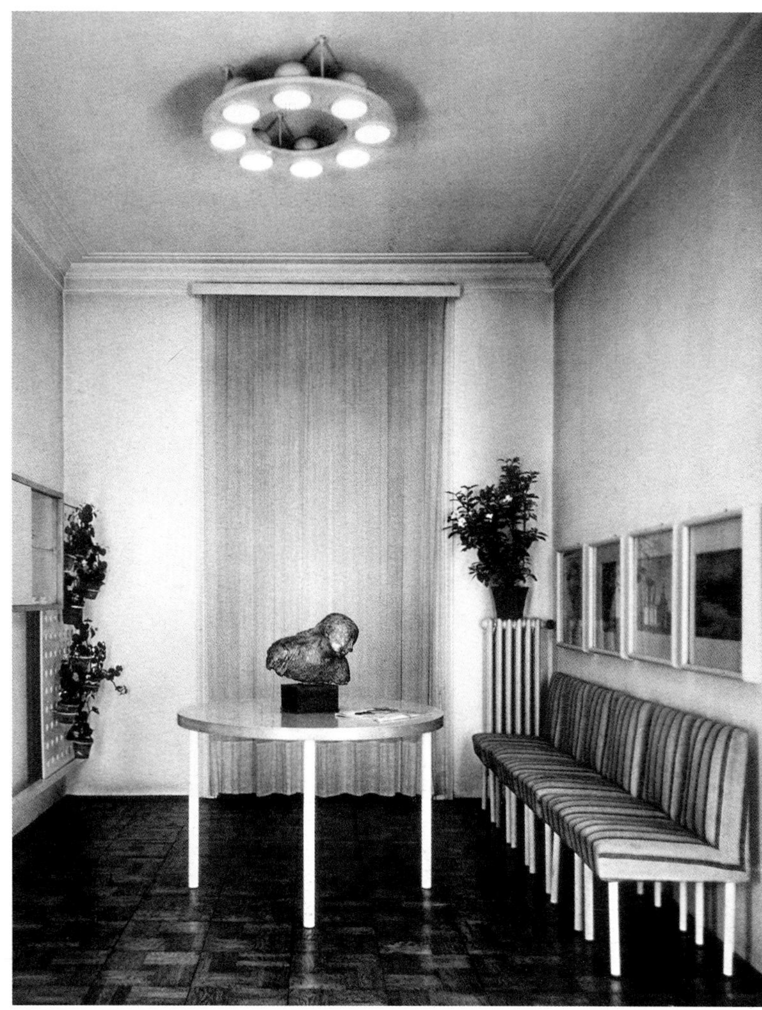

Fig. 14. *Mattioli's home, Via Gabba 9, Milan, probably September 1948: the dining room*

Severini that later entered the Mazzotta Collection,[89] Tomea's *Candele* (*Candles*) of 1942, Pompeo Borra's *Modella* (*Model*) of 1940,[90] a view of the island of San Giorgio in Venice by Guidi (probably painted at the request of Mattioli himself in 1946[91]), Sironi's *Donna seduta* (*Seated Woman*) of 1927 and Casorati's still life with eggs acquired from the Galleria del Milione in 1948.[92]

Above the sofa-bed in the guest-room hung a picture of horses by Giuseppe Cesetti, *Il vecchio porto a Viareggio* (*The Old Port at Viareggio*) of 1938 by Cesare Breveglieri[93] and a landscape by Umberto Lilloni from the period when he belonged to the Chiarismo movement.[94]

These images present us with a relatively traditional collection of modern art, with no foreign artists, no abstract works, no indications of his early friendship with the Futurists nor openings toward the avant-garde movements, and certainly nothing comparable to the collection that Peggy Guggenheim had mounted that same year in the gardens of the Venice Biennale: this reflected not just his as-yet narrower horizons, but also a smaller and more recent possibility of investment, compared to Guggenheim. The artists represented a cross-section of what the most scrupulous gallery owners and reputable critics (Giani, Piovene, Scheiwiller, Vergani) proposed to art lovers as established figures, in a cultural milieu that had not yet succeeded in distancing itself from the tradition of the nineteenth century. Moreover, there were none of the more politically committed painters, such as Guttuso or other members of the 'Corrente' group (my father regarded Guttuso as no more than a competent draftsman). The dispute, which was raging at that time, between supporters of a socially-engaged realism and defenders of artistic liberty in the name of formal abstraction, seems to have been wholly absent from the rooms of Via Fratelli Gabba. The outstanding artist appears to be de Chirico, represented by several works,

Fig. 15. *Mattioli's home, Via Gabba 9, Milan, probably September 1948: detail of the dining room*

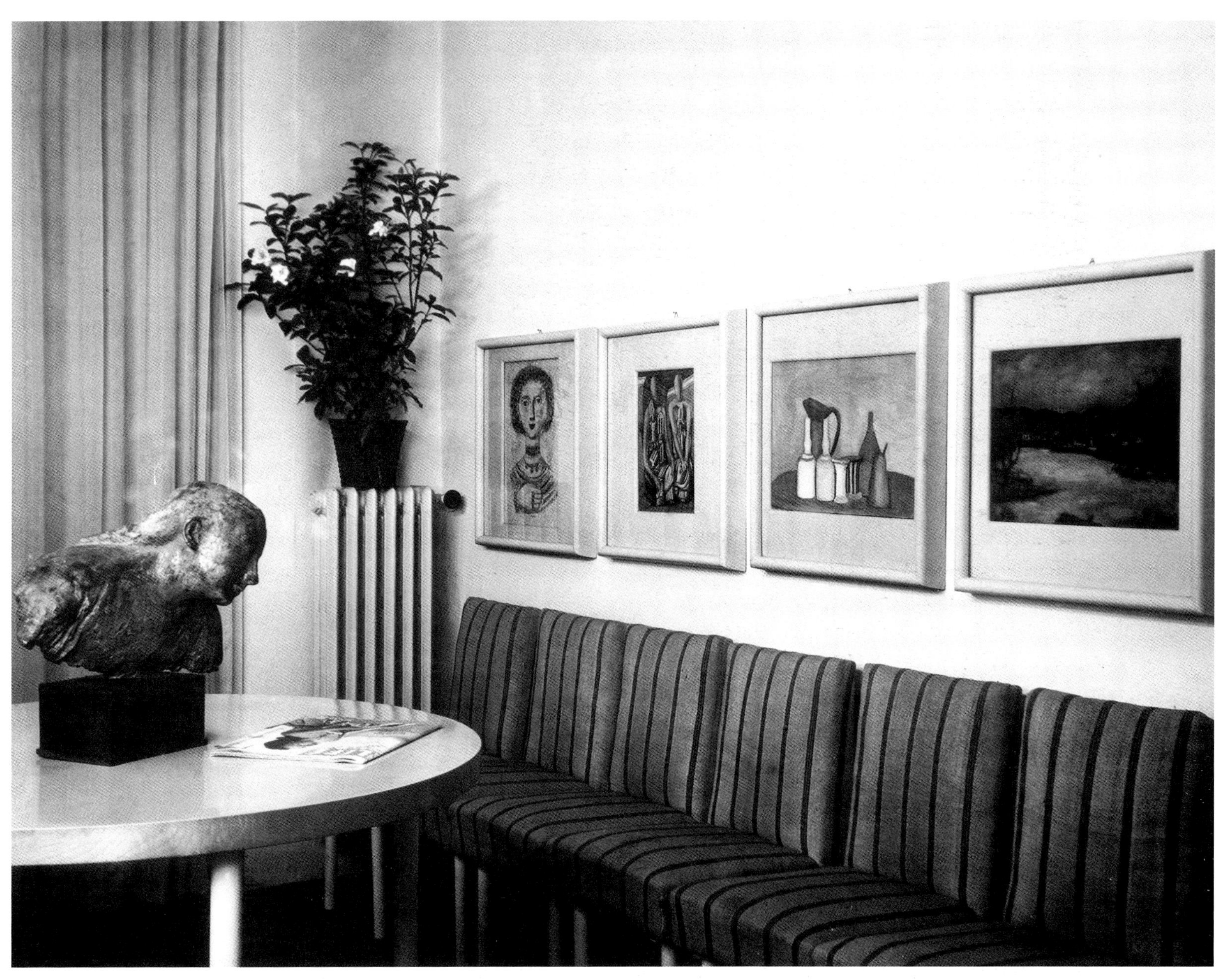

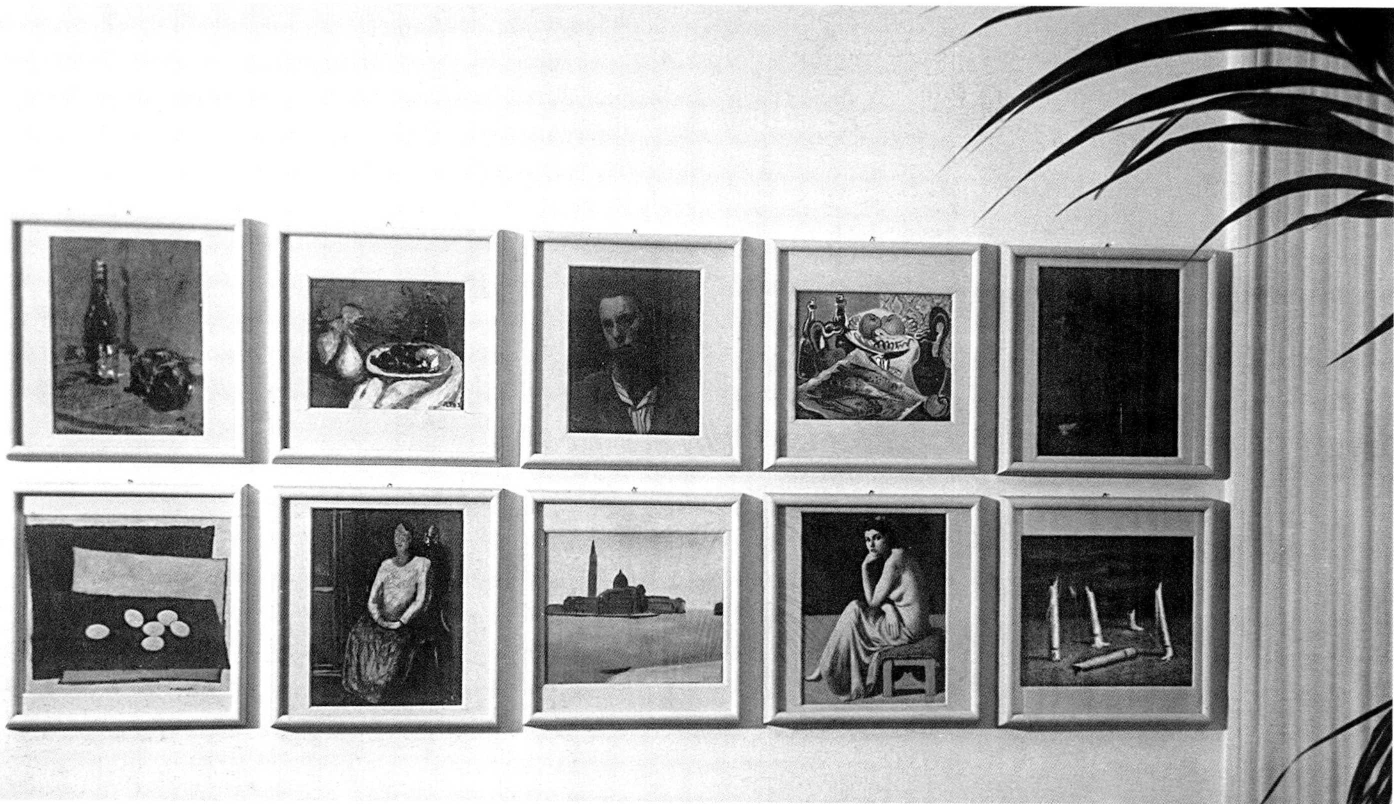

Fig. 16. *Mattioli's home, Via Gabba 9, Milan, probably September 1948: the wall opposite the bed*

all of high quality, that would later be sold by Mattioli on the grounds of the superiority of his Metaphysical period. Given this early date, on the other hand, the presence of sculptures by Medardo Rosso and Manzù is interesting. It is also remarkable to find Casorati's *Uova e carta gialla* (*Eggs and Yellow Paper*) in a Milanese collection, where parochial loyalties would normally have excluded a painter with such a high reputation in Turin. Apart from these considerations, what is striking is the high quality of all the works within the output of the individual authors, an indication of a sure and demanding eye, which aimed instinctively at a very rigorous selectivity. For sure, the paintings most remote from the taste of the day, such as Depero's early works and the early paintings by Boccioni, were kept elsewhere, in the small house renovated at Meina during the war and in the storerooms rented from Tosi. In reality, the apartment on Via Gabba demonstrated my father's difficulty in having a place of his own where he could nurture his own modernist tastes, without the risk of ostracism by Milanese society, cultured but still bound by aesthetic canons that had been shaped by its long isolation from the international scene.

In the fall of 1948 Mattioli acquired an apartment in a new building that was nearing completion at Via Manzoni 41/A. It was to become his definitive residence. The interior fitting and decoration, which should have been complete by the end of the year, prevented him from moving in until the following May. From the beginning the new house had a very different character from the previous one. It was a large and brightly-lit attic, facing onto the garden of Palazzo Borromeo, surrounded by a terrace with a splendid view of the cathedral and of the whole city: a place where he could entertain, therefore, and thus suited to his new position and to the circle of social contacts that came with it. To furnish this apartment my father bought for the first time antiques, Meissen statuettes and old masters: a painting attributed to Giorgione by Roberto Longhi, two still lifes from the school of Baschenis, pictures of the Flemish school and a portrait by Rosalba Carriera. The dining table was still circular, so that he could re-use his tablecloths, but it was now in Empire style, and the row of chairs was placed under a display cabi-

Figs. 17–18. *Mattioli's home, Via Gabba 9, Milan, probably September 1948: the main bedroom and the guest room*

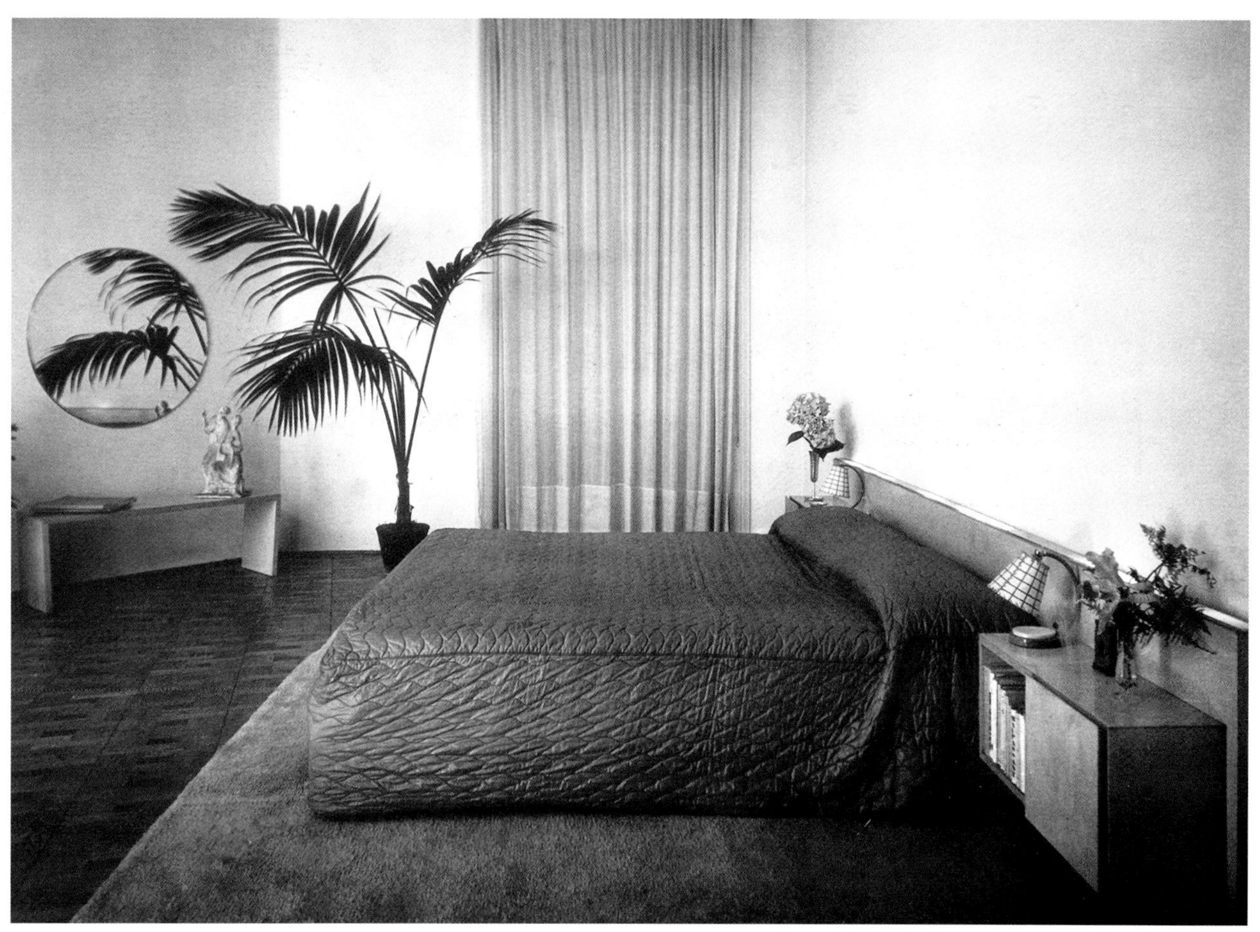

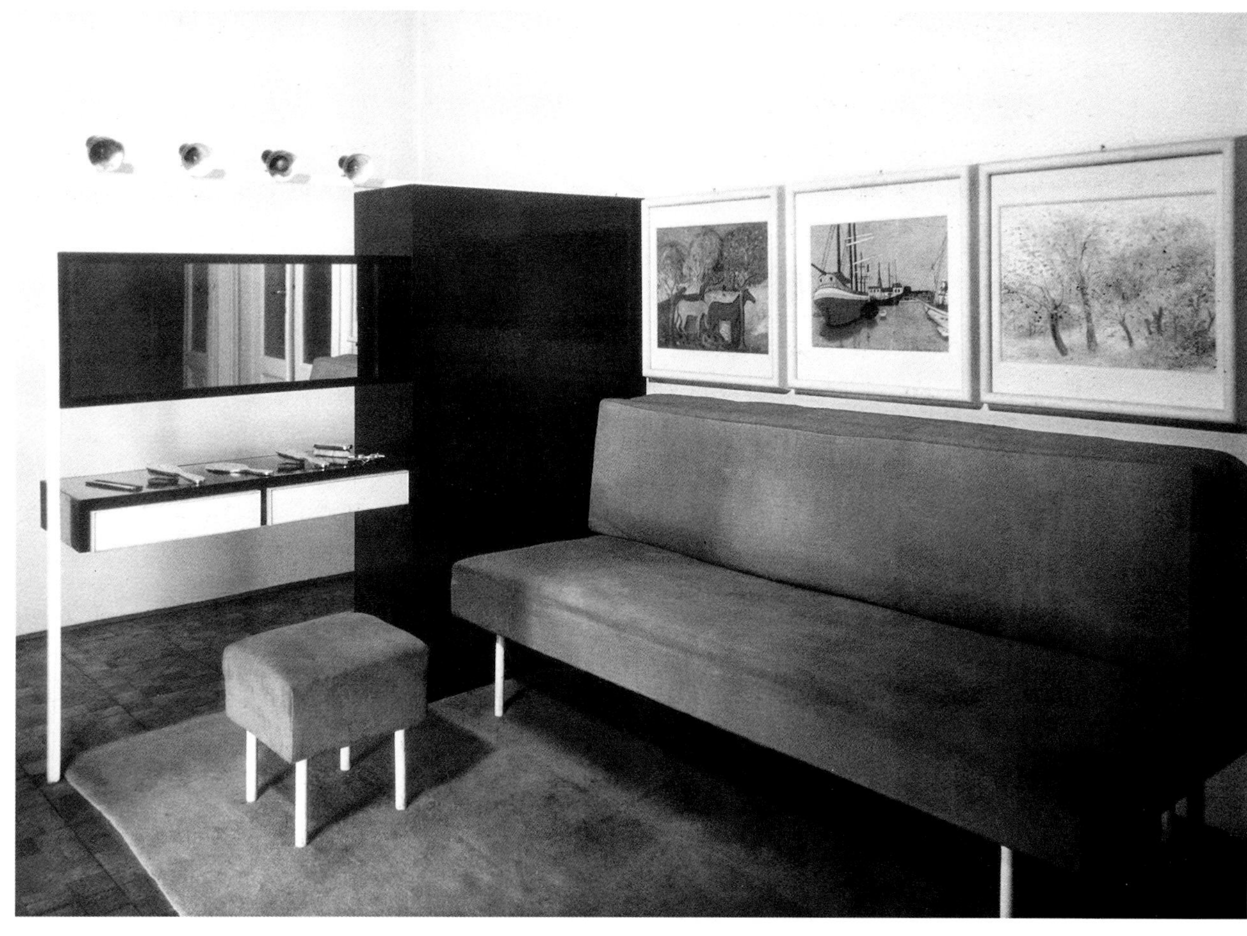

net containing a carriage in porcelain from Napoleon's wedding. A curious detail was provided by the drapes fitted with blue valances, identical to those that can still be seen today in the former home of Roberto Longhi.

Another feature, reflecting current taste for the 'fragment' (it was no coincidence that my father bought from Feroldi, and set on a gray ground by Morandi himself, a figure of a 1914 bather entitled *Frammento*[95]), was the wall above the double bed. It was no longer left conspicuously bare, as in Via Gabba 9, but was decorated with three icons, the one in the center representing the *Virgin and Child* and on each side icons with scenes from the lives of saints, cut into pieces so as to isolate one or more figures, scattered all over the available surface.

Obliged by his work continually to invite foreign businessmen and Italian industrialists with extremely old-fashioned tastes,[96] Mattioli adapted his home to their expectations and set up another place in which to install the contemporary art of which he was so fond.[97]

The year 1949 marked a turning point for Mattioli's collection, not just because of the move to the house on Via Manzoni and the renting of an apartment on the fourth floor of Via Senato 36 (to replace the rooms belonging to the painter Tosi at Via Principe Amedeo 5), but above all because of the new and ambitious dimension that it assumed with the acquisition of the Feroldi Collection.

The statement from the Galleria del Milione dated April 28, 1949[98] summarized the figures of the previous year and added the cost of the lining of Funi's *Self-Portrait*, the sale on March 30 of Sironi's small 1945 painting *Uomo e donna* (*Man and Woman*) for 28,000 lire, the rendering to the gallery of Tosi's *Natura morta con pere* for 32,000 lire, and the acquisition on April 28 of Medardo Rosso's bronze *Bambino malato* and Boccioni's *Landscape* of 1916[99] for 150,000 lire and of Marussig's *Alberi fioriti* (*Flowering Trees*) of 1917 for 120,000 lire.

On May 4, 1949, negotiations — which must have been arduous, to judge by the reductions achieved on the asking prices — were concluded on the purchase of eighty-seven pieces of the Feroldi Collection for a total of 26,000,000 lire. The seller undertook to complete the customs procedures relating to the paintings then on show at MoMA in New York and to have Mattioli's name appear as the new owner. The buyer guaranteed to "preserve the basic structure of the collection and to arrange it in the villa owned by the Boneschi family located in Meina (Lago Maggiore)."[100] Attached to the contract was a list of the works, from which at the last moment Feroldi removed de Chirico's *Notre Dame*: it comprised seventy-one paintings, nine drawings and eight sculptures.

In an impassioned letter Feroldi took leave of his collection, writing: "Above all I am gratified by the fact that the ensemble of the pictures transferred in this way not only will remain intact in their essential part, for which they have been recognized and appreciated by scholars (although neglected and ignored by my fellow citizens in Brescia), but will be merged with a group of other works of the same level and added to over the course of time so as to fill the current gap in Galleries of Modern Art in Italy."[101]

My father was fully conscious of the latter situation, as he had observed at first hand the efforts made daily by Wittgens for the restoration and enhancement of ancient works of art and for the reconstruction and reopening of the Milanese museums. The ties of friendship and cooperation that since 1947 had linked Fernanda to Paola Della Pergola, director of the Galleria Borghese in Rome, had further convinced her that the battle on behalf of the art of the twentieth century, so little and poorly understood by the public in general and by institutions in particular, should be conducted with private means by people with specific expertise and the ability to make rigorous choices. If Fernanda celebrated with her cousin the purchase of the Fe-

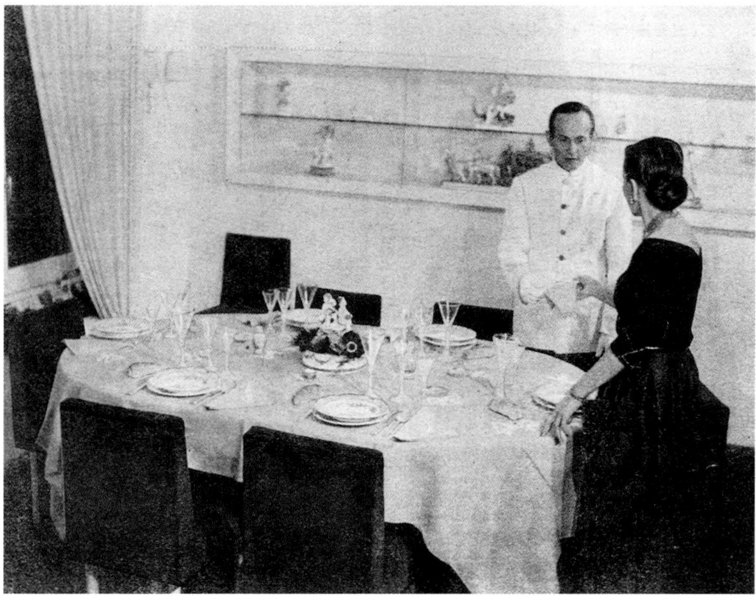

Fig. 19. *The dining room in Mattioli's home, Via Manzoni 41/A, Milan, 1950, published in* L'Illustrazione Italiana, *no. 1, January 1951, p. 83*

roldi works,[102] it was because he had acquired what was at the time the best-known collection in Italy, and one which appeared already complete in its own way, with the intention of utilizing only the pieces that he considered of greatest significance, to be placed alongside other works and thereby delineate a new history of modern Italian art. Notwithstanding the terms of the contract, Mattioli in reality already had in mind a new and different collection, based on criteria that he had always considered personal but that, after his visits to New York, now appeared international and universal. He was well aware of embarking on a road that constituted not just a cultural choice, but also a civil commitment and a political decision with regard to the dominant figurative culture of Italy at that time. His unorthodox position with respect to Cesare Brandi's idealism, Roberto Longhi's constant reference to French Impressionism, Lionello Venturi's political condemnation of Futurism, and the realism of socialist stamp proposed by the younger critics such as Raffaele De Grada, was the fruit of his early experiences and of his self-taught culture, but also the consequence of his more recent contacts with J. T. Soby and Alfred Barr, which had served to strengthen his intuitions and confirm his assessment of the importance of movements such as Futurism and Metaphysical painting.

A truly instinctive and temperamental collector, the lawyer Pietro Feroldi was a man of idealist culture, with a classicist education. He worked at the Banca Commerciale in Brescia and from the second half of the 1920s onward, with a considerable capital to invest, had begun to collect nineteenth-century Italian paintings. In 1930 he saw, probably at Carrà and Soffici's exhibition at P. M. Bardi's gallery in Milan, Carlo Carrà's painting *Mattino sul mare* of 1928, fell in love with it and started to build a collection of modern art.[103] In 1929 he met Carlo Belli, who lived in Brescia up until 1932 and who introduced him to the circles of the Galleria del Milione at the moment of its greatest vivacity. He was also in contact with Giuseppe Marchiori, Mario Broglio, Lionello Venturi and the principal collectors of Milan and Florence.

Feroldi's collection acquired considerable fame thanks to the exhibition devoted to it by the Galleria del Milione in 1933–4, entitled 'Mostra protesta del collezionista' and accompanied by issue no. 20 of the *Bollettino della Galleria del Milione*, which reproduced Lucio Fontana's *Testa di donna* (*Woman's Head*) in terracotta, a *Still Life* by Picasso (the first picture by the Spanish artist acquired in Italy), a small *Still Life* by Braque and Massimo Campigli's *Figure* (or *Donne con ombrello*) (*Figures* or *Women with Umbrella*) of 1932.[104] The exhibition was reviewed in 1934 in an article by Carlo Belli entitled 'Una collezione di provincia' in the magazine *Quadrante*.[105]

In addition to numerous loans to the most important exhibitions of modern Italian art, further official consecration of the collection came from the monograph published in 1942 (with a second edition in 1947) by the Edizioni del Milione, with an introduction by Guido Piovene, and the contemporaneous exhibition at the Pinacoteca di Brera. More information on the creation and character of the collection was published by Belli in 1962,[106] recounted to Mattioli in a letter of February 4, 1972,[107] and published by Sileno Salvagnini in his monograph *Il sistema delle arti in Italia 1919-1943*.[108]

From these writings, from the Feroldi–Belli correspondence (partly conserved in copies among my father's papers),[109] and from the list of the works in the collection at the time of the sale, it would seem to this writer that Feroldi's approach to figurative art developed on the basis of his earlier interest in nineteenth-century painting. His background led him to understand and appreciate chiefly the purely pictorial and tonal characteristics of painting, leaving him insensitive to other more conceptual or abstract aspects of art, often to the point of rousing the fury of his advisers Belli and the Ghiringhelli brothers.

An interesting example of this difference in understanding can be found in a letter sent by Gino Ghiringhelli to Feroldi on January 27, 1936, on the occasion of the latter's purchase of Carrà's *L'amante del'ingegnere* (cat. no. 10).[110] Feroldi, despite being extolled by his friends at the Galleria del Milione as the paladin of a new approach to collecting open to a historical vision of recent art, completely overlooked Futurism, had no desire to possess the abstract works that constituted the cutting edge of the early years of the Milanese gallery's activity, and appeared to accept Metaphysical painting only with reluctance. On this point, testimonies to the collector's personality are discordant but illuminating. Belli recalled in 1971: "When I managed to get *The Engineer's Mistress* and *The Disquieting Muses* into the collection, he hated me. Both pictures, brought to his house, were rejected and taken back twice, until I bullied him into accepting them with disgusting scenes."[111] But Feroldi had written to Marchiori in 1939: "Don't wonder at nor pity me: faced with the 'Disquieting Muses,' I fell to my knees and thought I am the madman who paid 50,000 lire for this painting. But I can tell you that it is, along with Modigliani, at the summit of all my values."[112] Other confidences made to Marchiori on March 29, 1939 reveal how Feroldi saw these works: "After the 'Muses' I acquired two more paintings from the Broglio Collection: 'Hector and Andromache' which is so to speak the matrix of all the others that followed. A splendor. Strong tones as in the Muses and an even tighter rhythm."[113] If the 'masticamenti faticosi' ('laborious mastication') of *L'amante dell'ingegnere* justified the collector's doubts at the moment of purchase (a painting long in gestation, and subject to numerous changes of mind), his judgment of the de Chiricos is expressed in terms of color and composition, in an evaluation based exclusively on pictorial merit.

Feroldi often showed independence of his advisers in his choices. If the majority of the Impressionist or French paintings that he continued to value highly and acquire outside the Milanese market did not stand up to the scrutiny of critics over time and prompted serious doubts over their authenticity, in some cases his eye prevailed over the arguments of the dealers (of whom he complained in a letter to Belli: "They have to stop insisting I buy a *piece* at every exhibition they hold"[114]). This was the case, above all, with Modigliani's *Nudo rosso* (*Red Nude*). In an undated letter to Belli, Feroldi wrote: "In the end Gino had to admit that the acquisition of the Modigliani was well done."[115]

The paintings about which he felt most strongly were Carrà's *Casine sul Sesia* (*Houses on the Sesia*), purchased together with *L'amante dell'ingegnere* and valued more highly,[116] Rosai's *Giocatori di Toppa* (*Toppa Players*) and *Mio padre*,[117] an old *Landscape* by Tosi painted at a time "when Tosi was straying between himself, Fontanesi and Segantini,"[118] as well as Morandis of

Fig. 20. *The apartment in Via Senato 36, Milan, in the early 1950s:* Girl on a Chair *by Giacomo Manzù and a drawing by Cézanne*

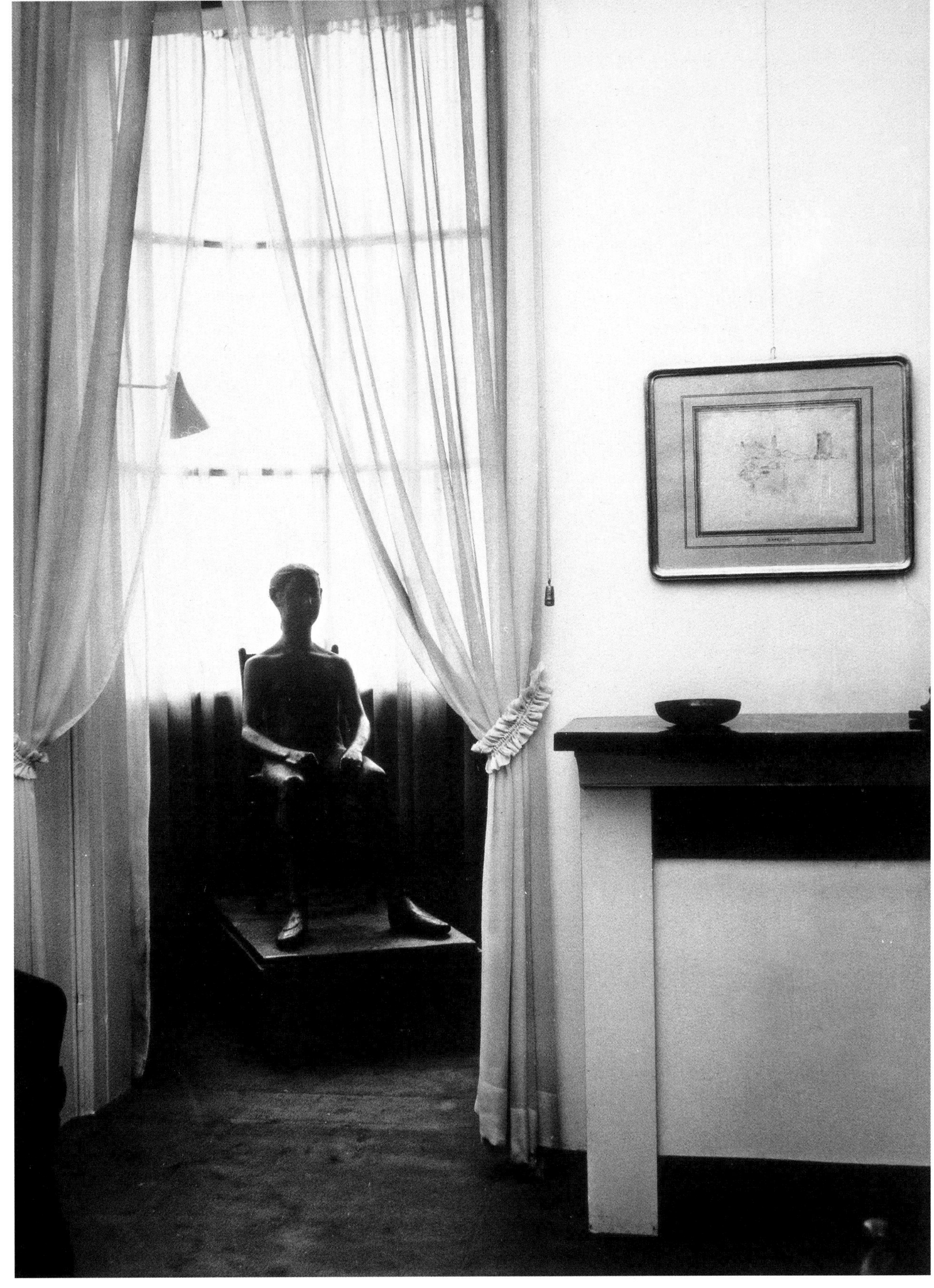

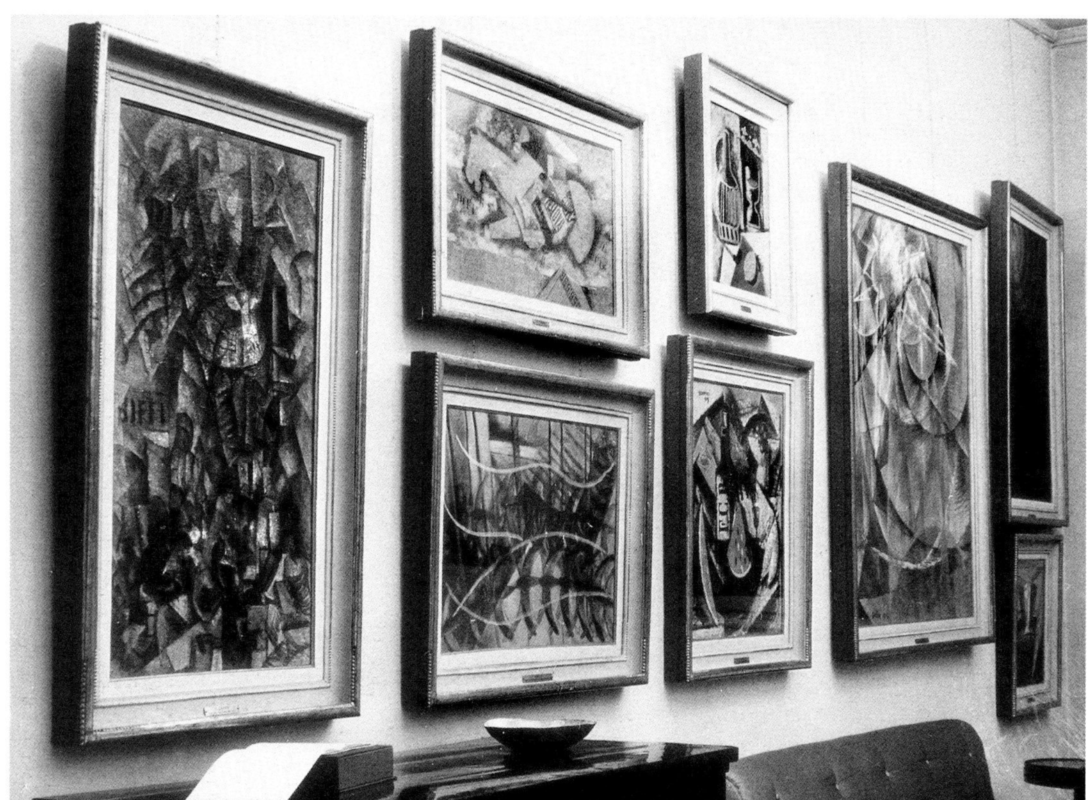

Fig. 21. *The apartment in Via Senato 36, Milan, in the early 1950s: the left wall of the first room, with Futurist works*

every period and Scipione. The last paintings he bought in 1941, to complete the collection in view of the imminent publication of the book, were by Rosai, Carrà, Morandi, de Pisis, Sironi, de Chirico and Guidi, along with a number of others considered of less significance — by Cesetti, Badoli, Marcucci, Birolli and De Rocchi.[119] These were unquestionably works that, in the international context, could be seen as representative of Italian visual culture. They were comparable in taste to that which marked the 'III Quadriennale romana' of 1939, but they had little in common with the avant-garde movements that had had important beginnings even in Italy.

My father's thinking was very different. His motive for buying the Feroldi Collection was primarily that of acquiring unique and seminal pieces of the Metaphysical period and from the years up to World War II. He wished to document the continuity and vitality of the role played in the history of Italian art by those movements at the beginning of the century, Futurism and Metaphysical painting, that he perceived as being the basis for the concept of 'modern art.'

Piovene declared that the Feroldi Collection was formed, instead, with the notion of defining Italian art in terms of its relation to French painting.[120] When the Brescian collector acquired many of the more significant works of the 1920s and 1930s, along with some particularly important earlier examples (consisting essentially of the three de Chiricos bought from Mario Broglio,[121] Modigliani's *Nudo rosso* and the Morandis), he was motivated by the belief that Impressionism lay at the base of modern painting: "The Italian painting of the period illustrated by the Feroldi Collection, during its development, appeared to be a painting of reconstruction."[122] But if, as Carlo Ludovico Ragghianti wrote in 1953, the Mattioli Collection was "put together with the intention and spirit of an *historian*,"[123] these words reflect my father's aim of outlining a history of Italian art intimately connected with the international scene and springing not out of Impressionism but out of the historic avant-garde movements, seen as the foundation of Modernism. From them germinated, in Italy as elsewhere in Europe, a new and intense production that lasted up until the end of the first half of the century: the history of fifty years of modern art, experienced by Mattioli at first hand and reconstructed through exemplary works chosen

Fig. 22. *The apartment in Via Senato 36, Milan, in the early 1950s: the right wall of the first room, with Futurist works*

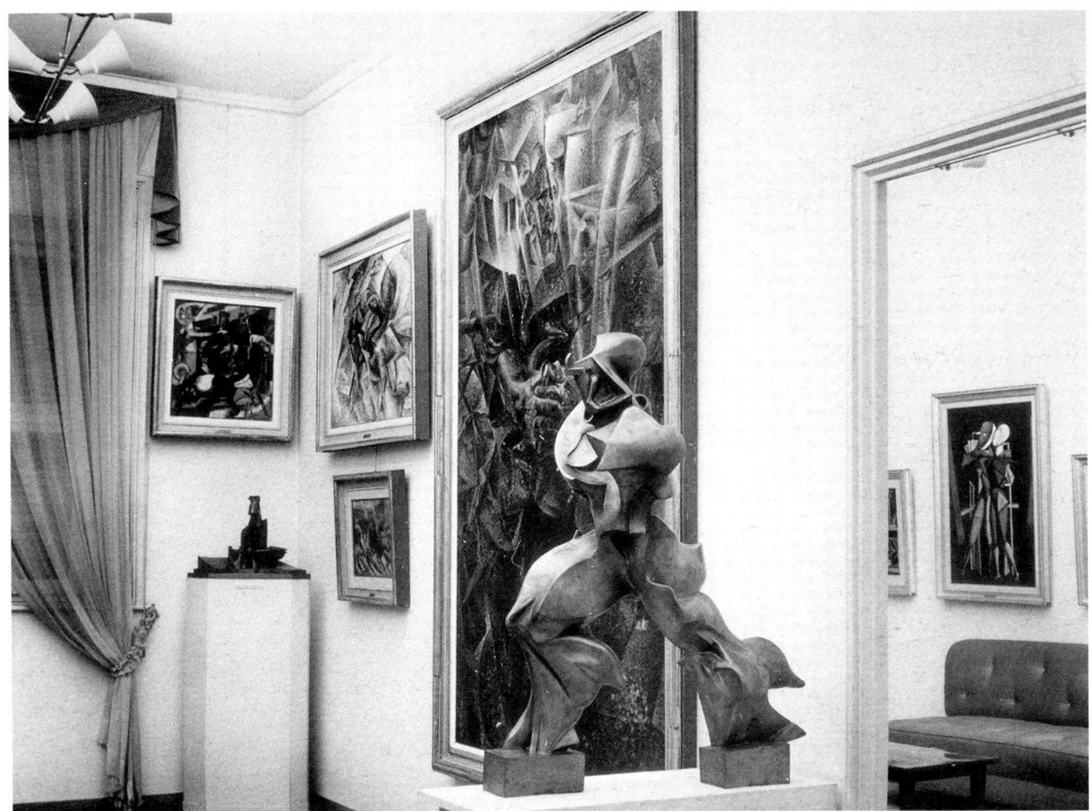

almost in reverse chronological order, starting from 1943–53 — the years in which he made the majority of his acquisitions — and working back to 1910, the year of the *Manifesto of the Futurist Painters*.

The 'essential part' of the Feroldi Collection that my father retained consisted of around forty works, while another thirty-five were sold off swiftly, by 1951 or shortly after, as the sum to be paid was very high for his means. He preferred to invest in the more important Futurist and Metaphysical paintings that he was able to track down on the market. The works he sold were: Carrà's *Crepuscolo* (*Twilight*), *Veliero* (*Sailboat*), *Capanni* (*Huts*), *Still Life* and *Assisi*; Cesetti's *Mandria* (*Herd*); de Chirico's *Self-Portrait*, *Uva* (*Grapes*) and *Cavallo* (*Horse*); de Pisis's *Canale* (*Canal*); Garbari's *La pigna* (*The Pine Cone*) and the drawing *Sibilla* (*Sybil*); Guidi's *Fanciulla* (*Girl*), *Bozzetto bagno* (*Bath Sketch*) and *Testina* (*Small Head*); Guttuso's *Fanciulla* (*Girl*); Longanesi's *Figura* (*Figure*); three landscapes by Morandi; Rosai's *Chiesa* (*Church*); Severini's *Still Life*; Soffici's *Paese* (*Village*) and *Nude*; Zandomeneghi's *Landscape* and *Donna in giardino* (*Woman in Garden*); Derain's *Testa* (*Head*); Picasso's *Still Life*; Renoir's *Landscape*; Utrillo's *Strada* (*Street*) and all the sculptures, including two important works by Marino Marini and Fontana's terracotta *Testa* (*Head*), which was reproduced on the cover of the *Bollettino della Galleria del Milione* in 1933. From this list it is easy to deduce the names of the artists who did not interest Mattioli: Cesetti, Garbari, Guidi, Guttuso, Longanesi and Zandomeneghi. Where de Chirico was concerned, he retained solely the Metaphysical paintings, excluding his later style of painting as a baroque regression, according to a critical interpretation that he shared with Lionello Venturi[124] and Roberto Longhi.[125]

His selection was strict and the axe fell, over a longer period, on practically all the French paintings and on the later Carràs and Rosais, the works identified as recent acquisitions in Feroldi's above-mentioned letter to Belli of December 1, 1941. Among the sales that might seem most surprising today were the three *Landscapes* by Morandi — two of which were probably painted in the war years at Grizzana — and the Picasso. An indirect explanation for these choices may be provided by some judgments expressed by Belli: "I insisted, for example, on the need to 'ditch' the mediocre Derain, the not very appealing Picasso, the lifeless drawing by Cézanne [...]"[126]; and again: "I didn't want the pressure of someone like Barbaroux convincing him to bring into the collection half-dozens of pictures by Tosi, Funi, Rosai, etc. The Ghiri[nghellis] were in despair because he let slip extraordinary opportunities, fixing perhaps on a Ferrazzi and spurning a Cubist Soffici (the splendid one of the watermelons),[127] or perhaps acquiring from who knows whom a run-of-the-mill Rosai for a sum that would have been enough to buy a Juan Gris! These were his failings. But then he escaped from us to Paris, Grenoble, Basel, and came back with a Utrillo, with Derain, with Matisse and Braque [...]."[128]

For the three Morandis the explanation was different: a very large number of pictures by the Bolognese master passed through my father's collection, including some interesting exchanges with other collections like that of Augusto Giovanardi. I believe that the motive for so many acquisitions and above all sales lies in the fact that the Galleria del Milione, the principal go-between for Milanese collectors after the war, represented Morandi, and so his paintings amounted to cash with the gallery in the case of onerous acquisitions or a need for liquidity. The Ghiringhellis themselves, as dealers, encouraged these continual movements of the works, from which they were sure of making a profit, as the artist's paintings were increasingly in demand.

The acquisition of the Feroldi Collection consolidated my father's social status, especially in cultural circles, and immediately bestowed on him the reputation of being one of the principal collectors of his time.

On June 19, 1949 he concluded the purchase of an important work by Modigliani from the son of the painter Italico Brass (cat. no. 12). Mattioli recalled the episode in these words: "[...] the work that gave me the most emotion, partly for the surprise of the encounter, is the *Portrait of Frank Haviland*, also by Modigliani, one of the very few 'fauve' paintings by this exceptional Artist. It was acquired, many years ago, by a painter, who kept it for himself, without telling anyone. When the owner died the painting came to light and in the summer of 1949, during the hottest months of the year, turned up in Milan. Once again fortune smiled on me, allowing me to come across it and obtain it."[129]

In the summer of 1949 my father began actively to search for the Futurist works that he had admired since his adolescence, even though critics like Venturi and friends like Wittgens discouraged him, arguing that it was just a youthful passion for a short-lived line of artistic research that had no solid value in the history of Italian art. In fact up until the exhibition of Italian art at MoMA in 1949 and the exhibitions of 1950 — of which I will have more to say — to which my father made a decisive contribution both as a lender as an adviser, the Futurist paintings of the second decade of the century were essentially ignored by the critical debate.[130]

Romeo Toninelli, who had bought works by Boccioni in Verona, wrote to Mattioli on June 8, 1949 — only a month after the acquisition of the Feroldi Collection — to tell him about the Italian exhibition at MoMA, but above all to offer him the painting *Materia* (cat. no. 4).[131] Despite an initial negative response,[132] my father bought the picture on December 21, 1949.[133]

In the winter of 1949 Gino Ghiringhelli, entrusted by Mattioli with the task of tracing important Futurist works, reported to him from Rome on the pictures he had seen in the homes of Benedetta Marinetti, Margherita Sarfatti and the Casella family:[134] they were *Elasticità* (*Elasticity*), *Dinamismo di un foot-baller*, *Antigrazioso* (*Antigraceful*) and a pre-Futurist *Self-Portrait* by Boccioni (of the same dimensions as another recently acquired by Mattioli), Carrà's *Portrait of Marinetti* and *Il pino sul mare* (*The Pine by the Sea*), Sironi's *Il ciclista* (*The Cyclist*), Funi's

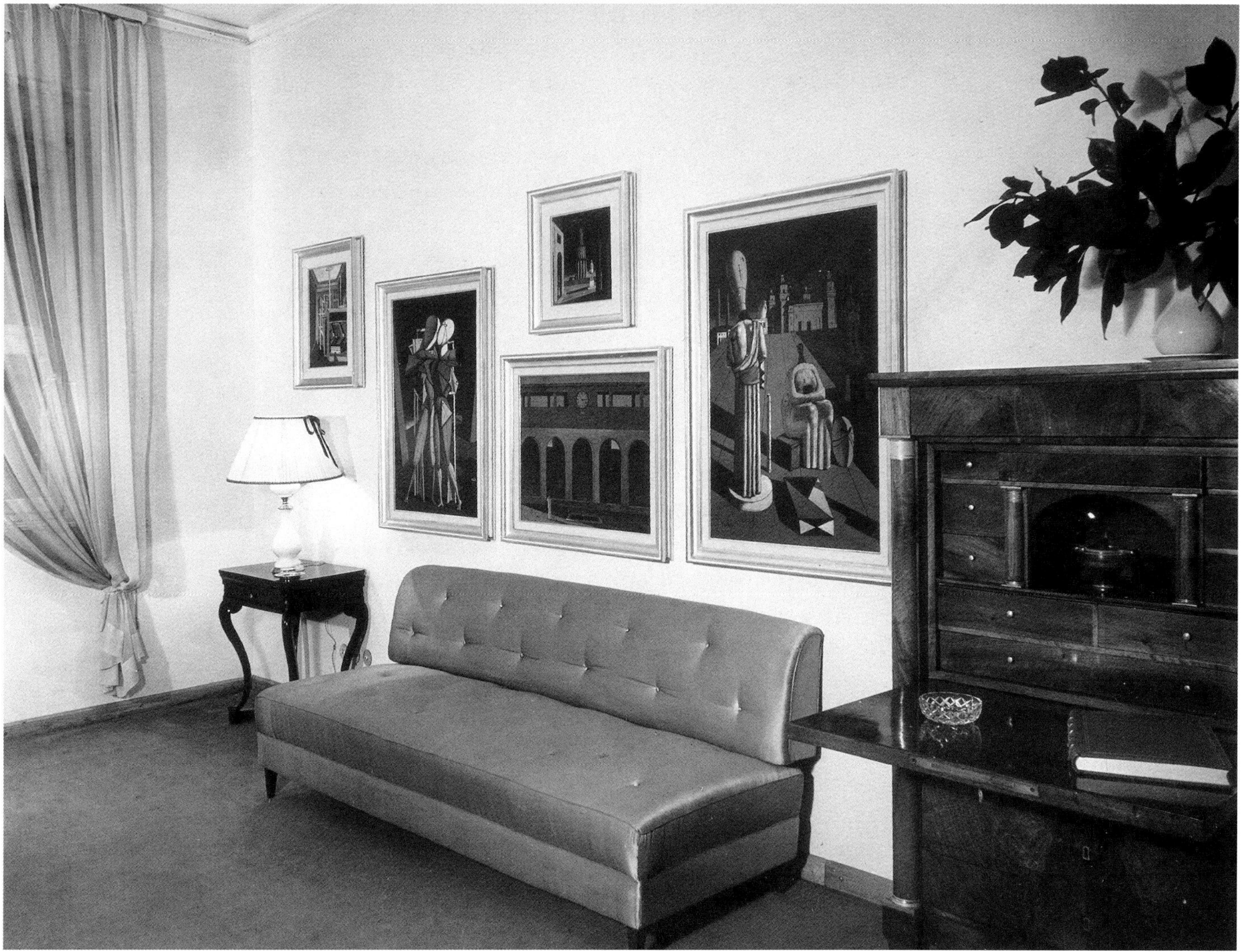

Fig. 23. *The apartment in Via Senato 36, Milan, in the early 1950s: wall with Metaphysical works*

Il motociclista (*The Motorcyclist*) and three works by Balla that were later acquired by Harry Winston.

Although my father was unable to buy any of these paintings, he made other important acquisitions in 1950. The account statements of the Galleria del Milione for that year are particularly complicated, in that they list the sales of works that had belonged to Feroldi, exchanges with other galleries, the cost of books, commissions and invoice stamp duty, as well as drawings or prints intended for friends or customers.[135] Numerous pieces entered the collection from the gallery. Among the most significant were five drawings by Boccioni with caricatures of Futurist friends, Campigli's *Donna velata con scialle* (*Woman Veiled with Shawls*, 1946), Carrà's collage *Inseguimento* (cat. no. 9), Klee's *Houses at Night* (1920), four drawings with horse and rider by Marino Marini, Arturo Martini's bronze *Portrait of Doctor Schwartz* (for which he paid the equivalent of around 500,000 lire, exchanging it for two pictures by Carrà and one by Morandi), two drawings by Modigliani, Morandi's *Fiori* (*Flowers*) of 1950 for 60,000 lire, two unspecified paintings by Gino Rossi, Sassu's *Cavalli* (*Horses*), Severini's *La chitarra* (*The Guitar*) of 1918, an unidentified Signac for 200,000 lire, three Sironis (an ink drawing depicting the *Bust of a Woman* of 1914, a Futurist tempera entitled *Composition*, 1916, and *La penitente* [*The Penitent*, 1945]: this later passed to the Giovanardi Collection) and a landscape by Vlaminck that turned out to be a fake. Again through Ghiringhelli, Mattioli acquired Russolo's 1912 painting *Solidi-*

tà della nebbia (cat. no. 21) from Margherita Sarfatti on May 8, 1950. Yet in spite of establishing friendly relations with Sarfatti, he was unable to persuade her to sell him *Antigrazioso*, the portrait of Margherita painted by Boccioni in 1912, of which she was particularly fond.[136]

Mattioli made donations to public institutions, including Sironi's *Composizione casa-figura* (*Composition with House-Figure*) to the Castello Sforzesco in Milan and four works (Morandi, *Still Life*, etching; Scipione, *Still Life*, oil; Arturo Martini, *Maternità* [*Motherhood*], terracotta; Sironi, *Uomo accanto a un fanale* [*Man Next to a Lamp*], oil) to the Bezalel National Museum in Jerusalem through professor Paolo D'Ancona, director of the Institute of Art History at the University of Milan. Finally, he gave Marinetti's volume *Umberto Boccioni* (Foligno 1927) to the library of the Museum of Modern Art in New York.

On January 30, 1950 my father wrote to his friend Depero to ask him for "a picture from your very early Futurist period that is in a fairly good state, if not perfect."[137] His reason for this was that he wished his friend to be represented at the exhibition of Italian art that was being organized in Paris, to make up for the great disappointment Depero felt at having been excluded from the American exhibition the previous year. He also took the opportunity to ask him who might have Futurist paintings by Balla and Russolo, which he had been unable to obtain from the artists' heirs. From an exchange of letters with Wittgens in April we learn of the proposal to buy Depero's large tapestry *Cavalcata fantastica* (*Fantastic Cavalcade*) from the collection of Umberto Notari: despite an initial refusal because the price was too high, the work entered Mattioli's collection.[138] In that same period Giampiero Giani sent my father the typescript for his monograph on Depero, which was published by the Edizioni della Conchiglia in February 1951.[139]

In addition to the Galleria del Milione and to his friend in Rovereto, my father turned to other sources to expand his collection further. He acquired Carrà's Futurist collage *Manifestazione Interventista (Festa patriottica)* (cat. no. 8) on June 19, 1950 from the Galleria Bolzani of Milan for 60,000 lire,[140] and Balla's *Mercurio transita davanti al sole* (cat. no. 2) from Mario Klaus on August 1 for 250,000 lire.[141] He also commenced an exchange of letters with Lionello Venturi, who had contacts in both the Parisian and the American market, in an attempt to procure works by foreign artists to set alongside his Italian paintings: these comparisons were to demonstrate not the derivation of modern Italian art from Impressionism, as Feroldi would have intended, but the parallels between the most advanced experimentation across the Alps and what was going on at the same time in Italy. His first request to Venturi, in April 1950, was for a painting by Cézanne, whom my father considered the common starting point for both the Cubism of Picasso and Braque and for Futurism, especially where Soffici, Morandi and even Boccioni were concerned. Venturi proposed six paintings to Mattioli, singling out as particularly interesting *Environs de Gardanne* of 1885–6 and *Marronnier et ferme du Jas de Bouffan* (*Chestnut Tree and Farmhouse at the Jas de Bouffan*) of 1885–7, for $55,000 and $50,000 respectively.[142] My father responded that he could not raise such sums at that time and put off the purchase. From Rome Venturi wrote to Mattioli again to ask him if he were still interested, as he recalled him being, in paintings by Rouault and Modigliani.[143] The answer was swift: Mattioli desired "a Rouault of fairly small dimensions, but very beautiful" and "the *Maria* that appears in the collection of Dr. Sabouraud in Paris in the last edition of Scheiwiller's little volumes."[144] In July Venturi managed to procure for Mattioli Cézanne's watercolor of *Rochers à Bibémus* (*Rocks at Bibémus*), of 1895–1900, which was acceptable to Mattioli both for the highly abstract character of its composition and for its much lower price than the previous paintings offered him, being a work on paper. For the Rouault Mattioli preferred to temporize until he could view a painting on which the artist was still working and for which Venturi had sent him the documentation.[145] However the search for a Rouault for the collection continued, spurred by Rouault's fame after the pres-

Fig. 24. *The apartment in Via Senato 36, Milan, in the early 1950s: works by Ottone Rosai and by Scipione on either side of a sculpture by Marino Marini* (Venus)

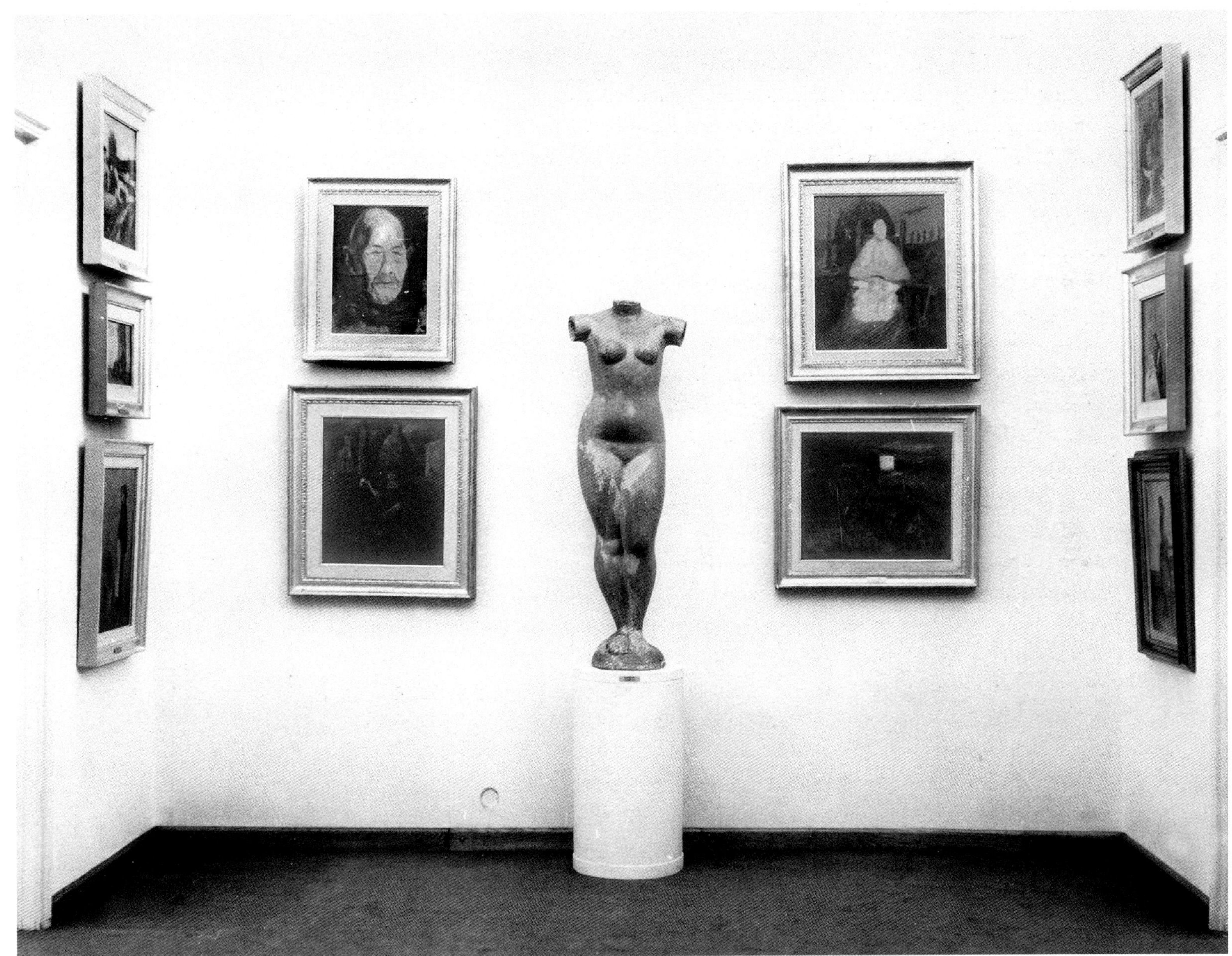

tigious exhibitions of 1945 and 1948[146] and Venturi's monograph of 1948.[147] On October 30 Venturi offered Mattioli five oils by Rouault, which — for financial reasons — my father preferred to pass up, acquiring only a small *Paysage biblique* (*Biblical Landscape*), obtained in Paris in exchange for an Utrillo. Through Lionello Venturi my father came into contact with Albert Skira and his publishing projects.[148]

Fig. 25. *The apartment in Via Senato 36, Milan, in the early 1950s: wall with works by Giorgio Morandi and, in the center of the room,* Horse *by Marino Marini*

The year 1950 was fundamental for creating an awareness of modern Italian art abroad, thanks to several exhibitions of great impact: in Brussels and Amsterdam curated by Lamberto Vitali, and in Paris and London under the patronage of the 'Amici di Brera,' an association of which my father was an active supporter and emeritus member.[149]

The first was held at the Palais des Beaux-Arts, Brussels, from January 28 to February 26.[150] It included the following works from the Mattioli Collection: three pictures by de Chirico, Scipione's *Studio per il Cardinal Decano* (*Study for Cardinal Dean*), Carrà's *L'amante dell'ingegnere* (cat. no. 10) and *Mattino sul mare* (*Morning over the Sea*) from the Feroldi Collection, the two Modiglianis, a still life by Morandi and Marini's portrait of the sculptor Fausto Melotti. Later, from March to May, the exhibition moved to Amsterdam.[151]

The exhibitions in Paris[152] and London[153] were promoted by the Italian government and were of particular importance both for the venues at which they were installed (the Musée National d'Art Moderne and the Tate Gallery) and for the fact that they represented an official acknowledgment of the value of a body of work that was practically unknown outside the country as a consequence of the long isolation imposed first by the Fascist dictatorship and then by the war. The works on show included about twenty Futurist paintings and four sculptures by Boccioni, a group of Metaphysical paintings by various artists, six pictures by Morandi, five by Sironi and nineteen works by Modigliani. The rigorous selection served to give a historical perspective to Italian artistic production and limited the field to those artists who could be recognized as "classics," as Paolo D'Ancona wrote in the introduction.[154] This was indeed a new reading of Italian art, and one that for the first time commenced with Futurism and not with the 'return to order' of the 1920s, continued with Metaphysical painting and placed the emphasis on a few artists, in line with the criteria that informed the Mattioli Collection and a few others that were destined to become famous, such as the Frua De Angeli, Jesi, Jucker and Pallini collections. My father took part in the Paris exhibition, attending the inauguration and lending sixteen works.

These exhibitions were accompanied in May by the publication of a special issue of the French magazine *Cahiers d'Art*, edited by Christian Zervos, devoted entirely to Italian art.[155] Mattioli actively contributed to its production up until November 1949, laying down the guidelines for the publication and offering hospitality to Zervos and Benedetta Marinetti for the meetings required to finalize the images and texts on Futurism. Serious misunderstandings emerged at the time of the distribution of the magazine and left my father and Fernanda Wittgens with feelings of rancor toward Zervos that they never overcame.[156] Yet *Cahiers d'Art* no. 1 of 1950 remains fundamental to an understanding of the transformation that the Mattioli Collection, not yet complete, had already brought about in the critical interpretation of the history of Italian art. In the preface Zervos pronounced negatively on the painting of Tiepolo and the whole of the nineteenth century in Italy, justifying the violently polemical positions taken by the Futurists at the beginning of the twentieth century. He praised the actions of Marinetti as founder of Futurism and immediately afterward cited the signatories of the first manifestos, Boccioni, Balla, Russolo, Carrà and Severini; the text continued with the Metaphysical painting of de Chirico and Carrà, a eulogy of the work of Modigliani (whose reputation was now firmly established

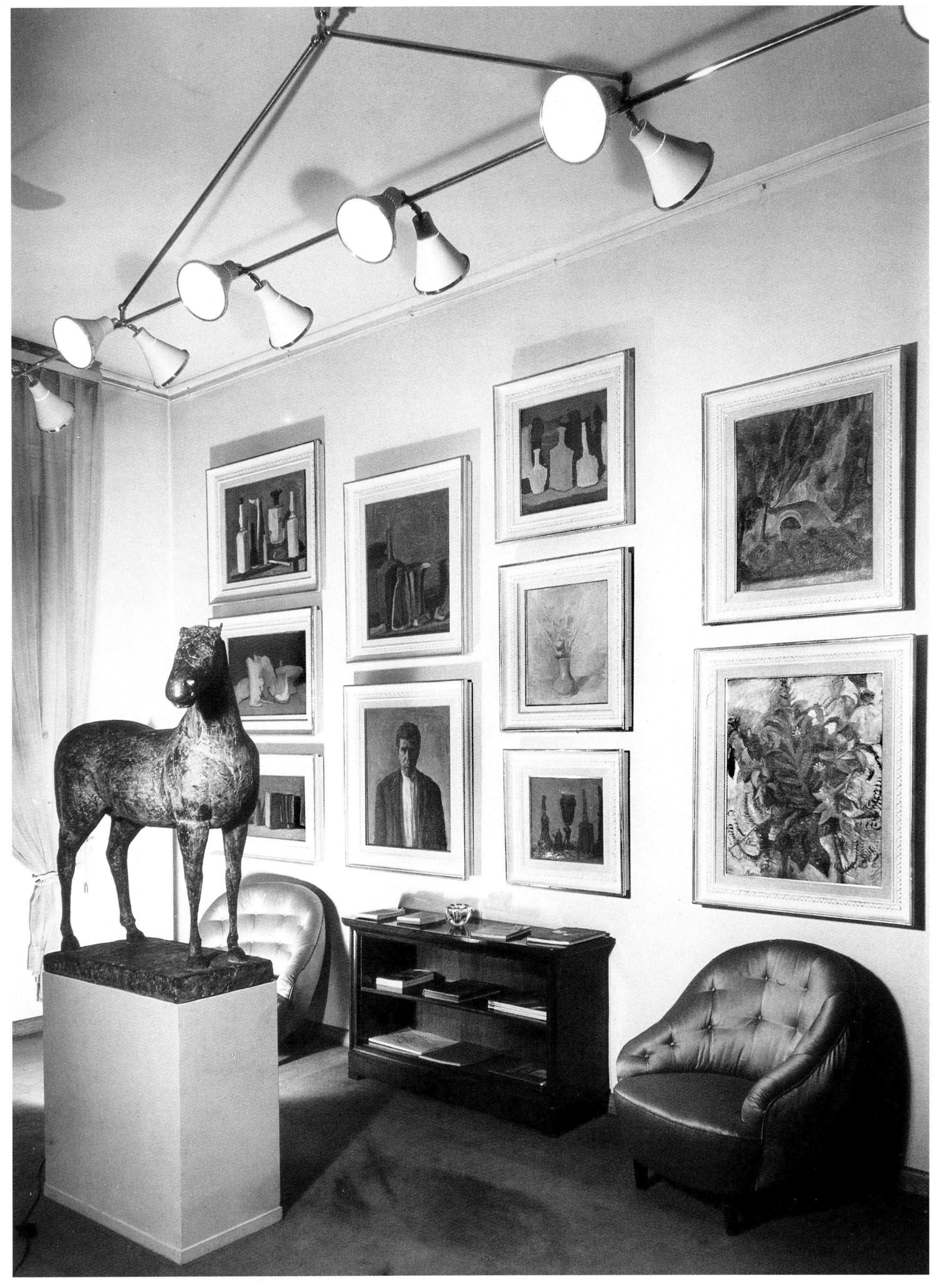

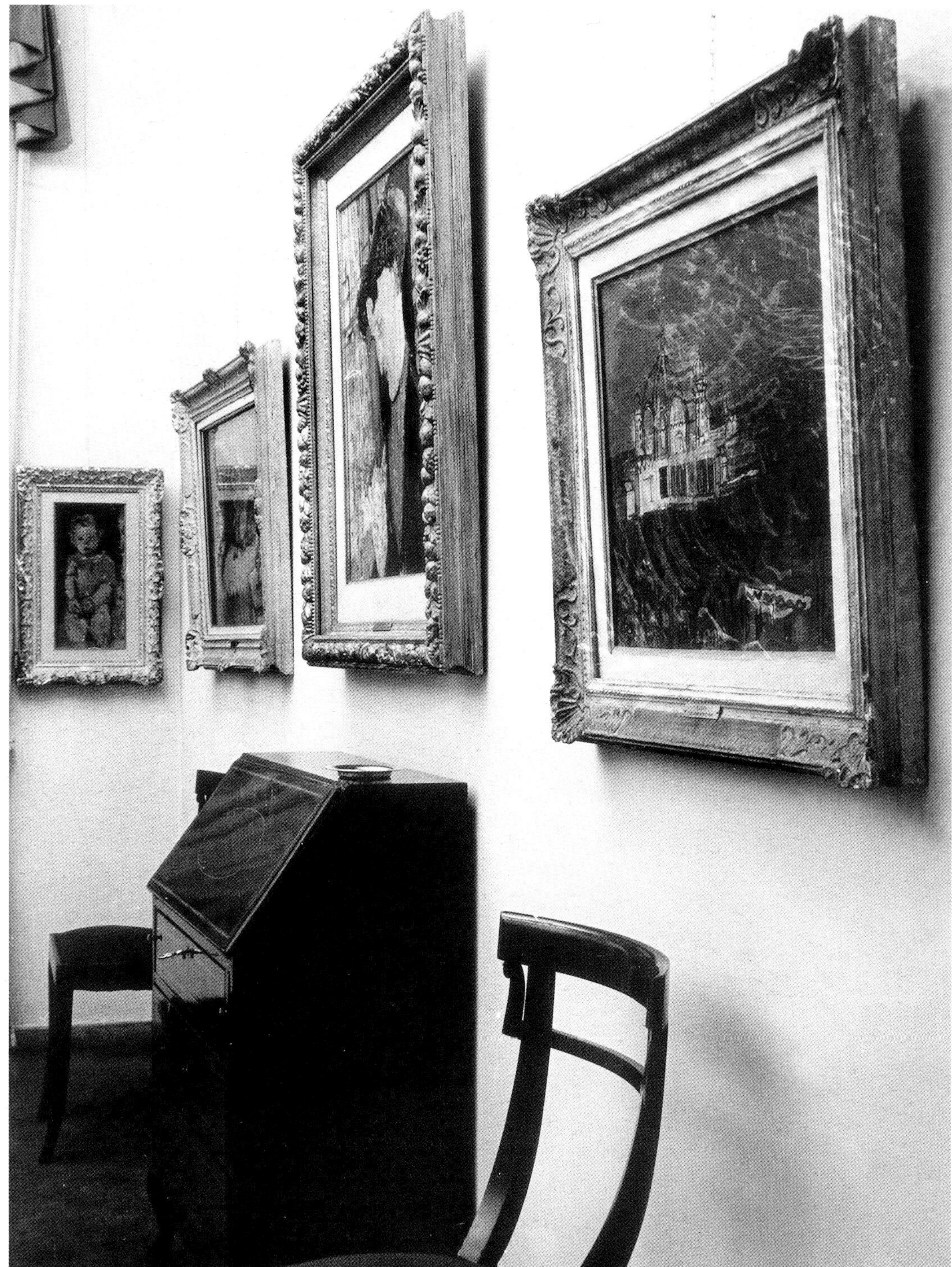

Fig. 26. *The apartment in Via Senato 36, Milan, in the early 1950s: works by the School of Paris, from the left,* Child *by Soutine,* Lovers *by Chagall,* Portrait of the Painter Frank Haviland *by Modigliani, and* The Casino in Nice *by Dufy*

among dealers and Jewish intellectuals) and with references to a number of artists who were also represented at the exhibitions in Paris and London.[157] The magazine opened with a review of Futurism compiled by Marinetti's widow: particularly long (around a hundred pages), it set out to present a historical profile of the movement up until 1950 and quoted several manifestos in their entirety.[158] The influence exercised by Mattioli's ideas on this unusual *incipit* to the history of Italian art and on the choice of the contents in general is clear from the fact that the paintings reproduced at the beginning of the majority of the chapters came from his collection.[159]

The last major exhibition of the year was 'Futurismo-Pittura Metafisica' at the Kunsthaus in Zurich,[160] the first to present modern Italian art exclusively through these two movements. In it were represented not just the signatories of the first manifestos, but also less some well-

Fig. 27. *The actress Sara Ferrati, the tenor Luigi Infantino and Gianni Mattioli in front of Balla's* Mercury Passing Before the Sun, *Via Senato 36, December 1954*

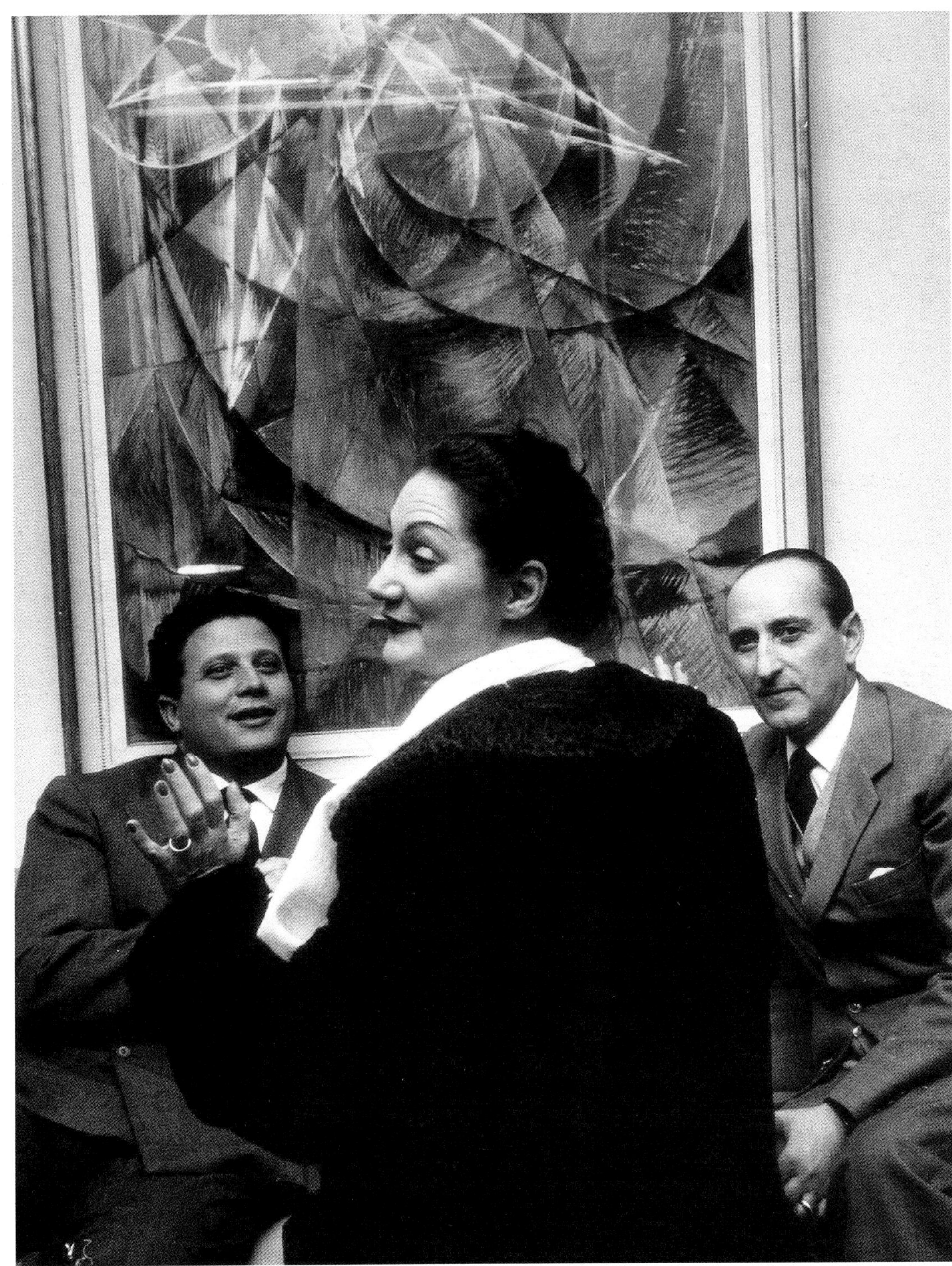

known artists such as Roberto Baldessari, Fortunato Depero, Enrico Prampolini, Ottone Rosai, Antonio Sant'Elia and others, while Metaphysical painting was illustrated by Carrà, Morandi and Sironi as well as de Chirico.

Mattioli lent fourteen works to the exhibition through the Soprintendenza alle Gallerie of Milan, which officially sponsored the project in the person of his cousin Fernanda Wittgens.

The XXV Venice Biennale of 1950 was organized by a committee on which the two most eminent critics of the moment, Roberto Longhi and Lionello Venturi, clashed fiercely. The outcome — which saw Longhi predominate with the monographic exhibition of Carrà's work from the 1920s onward, and the award of the Grand Prix for Italian painting to Carrà — must have looked a mixed bag to my father. Alongside the one-man show in memory of Giacomo Favretto, whom he detested, was a retrospective of Medardo Rosso, to which he lent two works: the model in plaster of *Bookmaker* and the *Portrait of Henri Rouart* in wax. His *Natura morta con chitarra* (*Still Life with Guitar*) was included in Severini's one-man show, although this interested him little: nor did other exhibitions awarded to Broglio, Magnelli and Semeghini. The exhibition of the five signatories of the early Futurist manifestos represented a notable opening towards this movement, still tainted by Fascism, with respect to the room it was given at the Rome Quadriennale of 1948, especially if one considers that it was flanked by retrospectives of the Fauves and the 'Four Masters of Cubism.' This was in fact the first official recognition of the historical role played by the Italian avant-garde in the international context. Mattioli lent Severini's *Ballerina blu* (cat. no. 22), and resolved to acquire Carrà's *La Galleria di Milano* (cat. no. 6) then owned by Magnelli. From the viewpoint of the historical confrontation of Cubists and Futurists the latter painting represented a key work and Mattioli was determined that it should be in his collection. But by then he was too well known on the market as a 'hunter' of works in the Futurist style and feared that his reputation might push the price too high. He contacted a succession of intermediaries, first Gino Ghiringhelli in Milan, then his friend Paolo Garretto and the publisher Gualtieri di San Lazzaro in Paris. The negotiations were long and difficult, and were concluded only in February 1951, for the sum of 750,000 French francs.[161]

At the Venice Biennale of 1950 my father certainly took pleasure in the works of Kandinsky and Le Douanier Rousseau, two of his favorite artists. Along with the painting and drawing by Rousseau that had passed from the Soffici and Feroldi collections into Mattioli's, there were two drawings by Rousseau belonging to Giorgio Morandi. 1950 saw the start of the friendship, based on mutual esteem, gifts of books and visits to exhibitions and places of art, which bound my father to Morandi for the rest of the artist's life.[162]

At the beginning of July 1950 Mattioli installed his collection in an apartment on the fourth floor of Via Senato 36, which he rented for this purpose. It was located in a modern building that faced onto the street, with three rooms illuminated by one window each, and onto an inner courtyard, adjoining the ex Palazzo del Popolo d'Italia, with one room originally used as a kitchen, another room and a bathroom, linked by a corridor. The corridor contained a collection of books; the kitchen had been closed to create a bow window that provided a worthy setting for *Bambina sulla sedia* (*Young Girl on a Chair*), a life-size bronze by Giacomo Manzù, and was fitted out as a cloakroom for visitors, while the internal room was turned into storage with shelves to hold paintings. In the other three rooms the works were constantly being rearranged, both to make room for new acquisitions and so as not to leave empty spaces during loans to exhibitions. The usual arrangement consisted of a drawing and a sculpture (*Il risveglio* [*The Awakening*] by Arturo Martini) in the entrance, while the first room was dedicated to Futurism, the second to Metaphysical painting and Italian works from the 1920s and 1930s, and the third to the School of Paris and foreign paintings. The pictures completely covered the walls, hung in two or three rows. The rooms maintained the appearance of a house and not a museum because of their small dimensions and because of the furniture — couches, armchairs, desks and tables, chest of drawers and bookcases — which provided surfaces on which to place things and comfortable seats for conversations and discussions. In addition to visits by appointment for scholars, collectors and friends, the collection was open to the public every Sunday morning up until the mid-60s, so that it frequently featured among the city's museums in the newspapers. There was no attendant to keep an eye on the apartment, but my father himself and some of his friends (such as Ceroni, Gritti and Valsecchi) took turns in the rooms, explaining the modern art to vis-

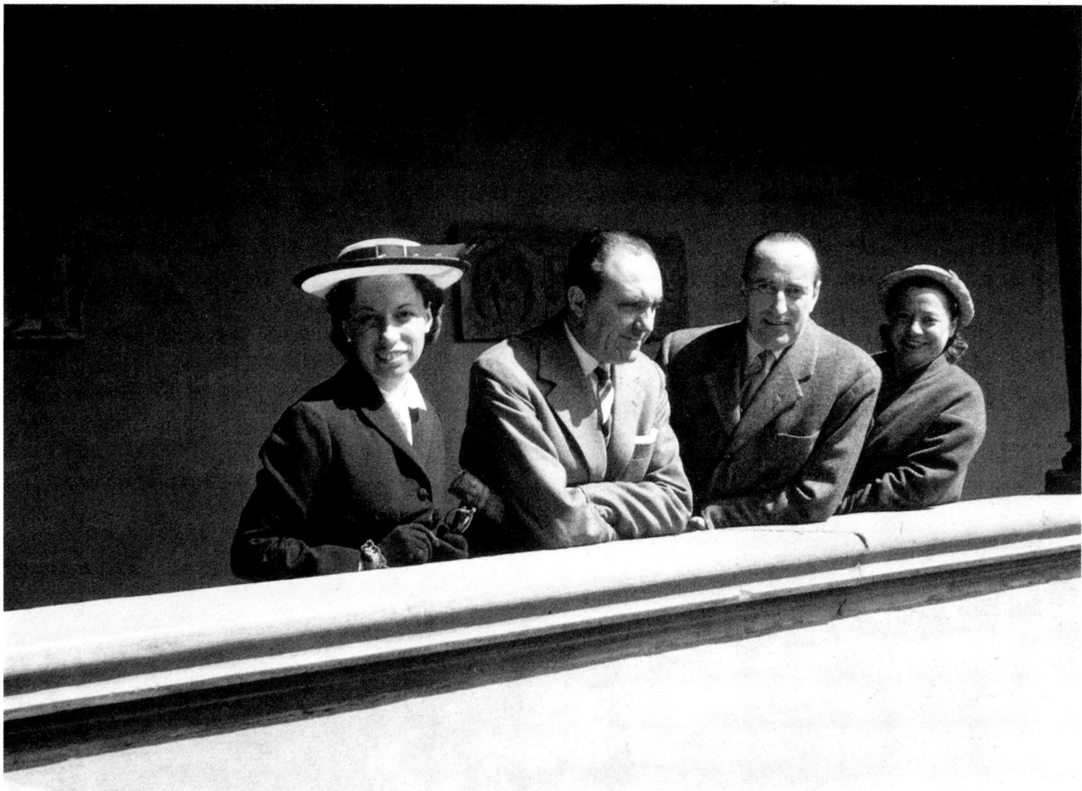

Fig. 28. *From left to right, Angela Maria Mattioli, Marco Valsecchi, Gianni Mattioli and Linuccia Ceroni in Florence, March 29, 1953*

itors.[163] The visitors' book records the names of the first guests: Paolo D'Ancona, with Fernanda Wittgens, Gian Alberto Dell'Acqua, and Angela Ottino della Chiesa.[164] Giacomo Manzù visited on July 8, 1950, the actress Sara Ferrati and her husband the tenor Luigi Infantino the next day, the critic Carlo Ludovico Ragghianti and Gino Ghiringhelli on July 11 and then the writer Giampiero Giani, Marino Marini, Lionello Venturi, Massimo Campigli and Margherita Sarfatti by the end of the year. Among visitors the following year were Professors Roberto Longhi and Annamaria Brizio, the painters Renato Birolli, Filippo de Pisis and Ottone Rosai, the collectors Riccardo and Magda Jucker and Augusto Giovanardi, the critics Fortunato Bellonzi, Maurizio Calvesi, Cesare Gnudi, and the poet Alfonso Gatto.

After the ceaseless activity of 1950, 1951 was for Mattioli a year in which to reflect on the choices he had made and to attend to the consolidation of the collection.

Now considered one of the most important collectors of his day, Mattioli saw the publication of his most extensive interview so far, "Come ho formato la mia collezione," in the January issue of the magazine *La Biennale di Venezia*.[165]

On February 15 he donated Campigli's painting *La scala* (*The Stairway*) of 1929 to the Civica Galleria d'Arte Moderna of Milan, for which he was an adviser on acquisitions.[166]

Mattioli's main concern in this period was to purchase paintings of particular historical and aesthetic significance, even at the cost of losing other works. Once again the correspondence with the Galleria del Milione and the statements it sent him provide precise information.

In January my father acquired one of Arturo Martini's most important sculptures from the *Valori Plastici* period, *Il centauro* (*The Centaur*), from the artist's companion[167] and Soffici's Futurist painting *Frutta e liquori* (cat. no. 26) from a Canadian collection.[168] In February he bought *La Galleria di Milano* (cat. no. 6), after the protracted negotiations referred to above, and on March 9 told Lionello Venturi about his recent acquisition of Carrà's *L'idolo ermafrodito* (from Carlo Frua De Angeli) in a letter. The letter also mentions the shipping to Italy of two Cubist paintings, one each by Picasso and Braque, purchased in the United States through the mediation of Venturi himself.[169] In June Morandi's *Natura morta con portaorologio* (cat. no. 16) of 1915 and de Chirico's *Interno metafisico con piccola officina* (*Metaphysical Interior with Small Factory*) of 1917 (this too formerly in Frua's collection) entered the collection from the Galleria del Milione. In September Marco Valsecchi brought three pictures to his notice (Morandi's *Rose* of 1917 [cat. no. 18], Modigliani's *Portrait of Paul Guillaume*, both from the Pallini Collection, and Sironi's *Paesaggio urbano* [*Urban Landscape*] of 1920–1 from the Sarfatti Collection),[170] of which Mattioli acquired only the Morandi. In November the Galleria del Milione charged him 2,500,000 lire for the purchase of Carrà's *Cavaliere Occidentale*. It was probably at the end of the year that he bought Marino Marini's bronze *Cavallo* (*Horse*) of 1939, praised by Wittgens in 1952 on the occasion of the solo exhibition given to the sculptor at the XXVI Venice Biennale.[171]

To pay for these acquisitions Mattioli sold a considerable number of works through the Ghiringhellis, including Carrà's *Capanni* (*Huts*) of 1927, de Chirico's *Self-Portrait*, Martini's bronze *San Marco e San Giusto* (*St Mark and St Just*), Picasso's *Still Life with Pipe*, Scipione's *Natura morta con piuma* (*Still Life with Feather*), an Utrillo and a Zandomeneghi (all from the Feroldi Collection), two landscapes by Morandi from 1936 and 1941, Boccioni's *Periferia* (*Suburbs*) and Marino Marini's *Portrait of the Artist's Wife* in wax and *Portrait of Melotti* in bronze.[172]

The loans Mattioli made to the '88 mostra Depero. Pittura e Arte applicata 1915-1951. Prima presentazione di pittura nucleare,' organized in the Sala Filarmonica of Rovereto in the summer — to which he lent fifteen paintings at the request of his old friend — also provided an opportunity to make a selection: Mattioli indicated to Depero himself six works to be sold.[173]

Depero's works had always constituted, for sentimental reasons, a separate *corpus* within the collection, motivated in part by a desire to help his old friend financially and to promote his image. Otherwise my father thought it expedient to represent the activity of each artist in the collection with few, particularly characteristic works. For him five paintings constituted the optimal number of works for each artist.

Two other aspects seem to characterize the handling of the collection in a new way from 1951 on: the interest in works on paper (considered an important form of expression complementary to that of oil painting or sculpture, but less expensive) and the desire to represent developments in contemporary art. This acquisition of works by artists emerging in the 1950s also reflected the need to keep expenditure within bounds.

Most of the works by new artists purchased in those years had been suggested by the Ghiringhellis and included, by way of example, Mario Asnago's *Sedia* (*Chair*), Bruno Cassinari's *Portrait of Mother Pons* of 1949, a painting by Santiago Cogorno, three by Mattia Moreni, Gino Romiti's *Gli oggetti* (*The Objects*) of 1950, four works by Atanasio Soldati and Sergio Vacchi's *Figura con toro* (*Figure with Bull*).[174] Over the following years my father acquired works by Afro, Giuseppe Ajmone, Renato Birolli, Gianni Dova, Gianfranco Fasce, Gino Meloni, Umberto Milani, Ennio Morlotti, Rufino Tamayo and Fritz Winter.[175]

As for works on paper, Mattioli acquired drawings by Carrà, Morandi and Rosai.[176] Such purchases continued the following year, chiefly with engravings and watercolors by Morandi.[177]

In 1952 Mattioli's links with the Galleria del Milione were particularly strong. The statements of account list Mattioli's principal acquisitions: André Derain's *Portrait of Léopold Zborowski* of 1920, which had previously belonged to Raffaele Carrieri;[178] *Natura morta con gli occhi* (*Still Life with Eyes*) of 1926 by de Pisis,[179] owned by Adriano Pallini; Carrà's *Paesaggio lacustre* (*Lakeside Landscape*) of 1922 from the Frua Collection and a still life by Morandi of 1931.[180] These

Fig. 29. *Angela Maria Mattioli in the entrance to Palazzo Venier dei Leoni, Venice, during a visit to Peggy Guggenheim's collection in Venice, July 1958*

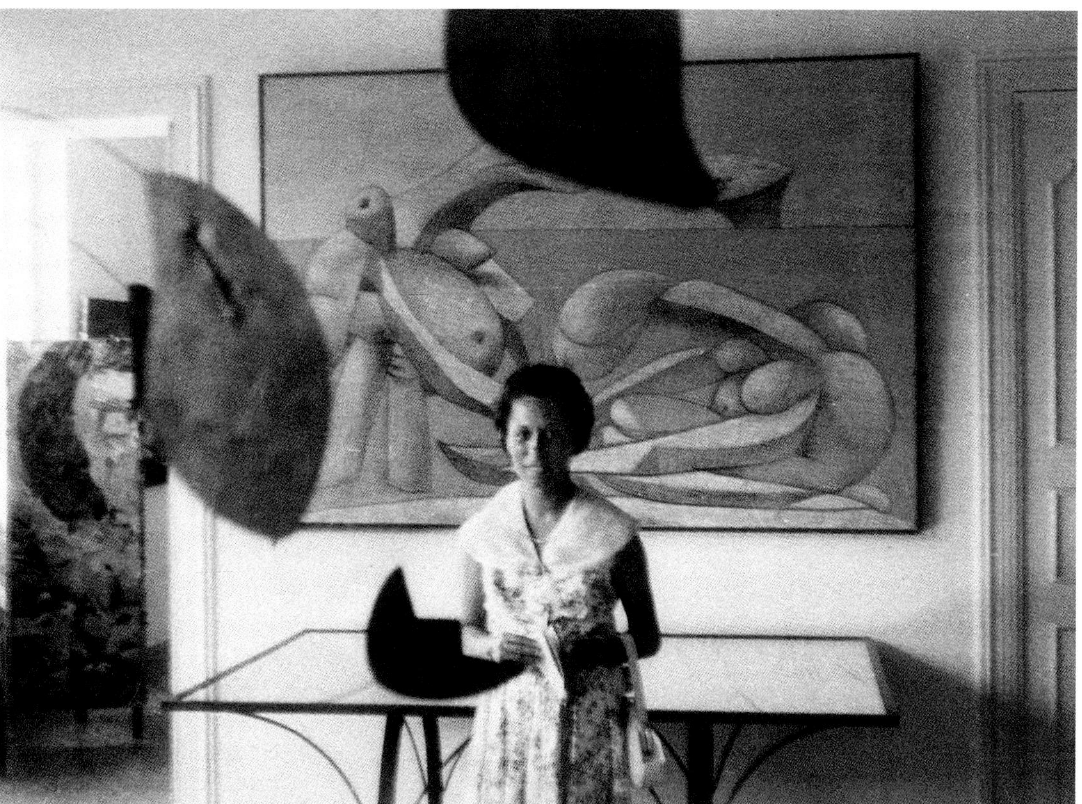

were followed shortly afterward by two temperas by Sironi and two 1952 oils by Morandi: one still life from the yellow cloth series and one of flowers.[181]

Although relations with the Ghiringhellis had grown increasingly amicable, the heavy mark-ups that the gallery applied on every purchase were a burden for my father in the face of the difficulties encountered in sales, which had been frequent in 1951. In February 1952 he set up a company with Gino Ghiringhelli, called 'G&G' (after the initials of the names Gino and Gianni), for the purchase and sale of works of art. In this way Mattioli reserved the right of preemption over the artists he considered most interesting and hoped to be able to acquire new works with a commission of 10% on the part of the gallery, while the Ghiringhelli reckoned on having greater financial liquidity at their disposal.

The company remained active until December 1954, when it was wound up, as my father had not benefited financially as he had hoped. In addition to the painters usually represented by the Ghiringhelli brothers, the company handled a large number of works by Sironi, who was still in difficulties over his Fascist past, and financed an exhibition by this artist and another by de Pisis in Copenhagen in 1953.

In November 1952 the Galleria del Milione opened its new premises at Via Bigli 2 in Milan. For the occasion, a special exhibition was mounted in the five rooms, to which my father contributed with the loan of around seventeen of the forty-nine works on show.[182] The event was celebrated with the first issue of the new series of bulletins published by the gallery. Two paintings in the Mattioli Collection, Morandi's *Natura morta con portaorologio* of 1915 (cat. no. 16) and Sironi's *Composition* of 1952, were reproduced. Gino wrote in the introduction: "art [should be] a total act of the human being in the fullness of his spiritual commitment against the continual decline of the time, and an intrepid call for truth, glimpsed and seized in an image, offered to society which will not be able to evade it for any reason." And again: "We have the certainty that just one of these works will suffice, will survive to indicate to what extreme limit of civilization this generation worked with desperate gentleness, offering a contribution to European culture that becomes clearer and more authoritative from day to day."[183] These were sentiments with which my father undoubtedly agreed.

The idea of the 'sociality of art' and the educational function of culture, definable as such only if addressed to a wide public and not just to a narrow circle of specialists, was something that Wittgens and Mattioli shared. To bring the general public into the Pinacoteca the Sovrintendente put a painting from the Brera on show in the windows of La Rinascente, the department store in Piazza del Duomo which was hugely popular in the early years of the economic miracle and of the emergence of a consumer society. In 1952 Mattioli began to collaborate systematically with magazines with a large circulation, getting journalist friends to write about works he owned. The first examples were the column 'Incontri con l'Arte Moderna' run by the young critic Guido Ballo in *Settimo Giorno*, in which articles on de Pisis, Morandi, Campigli, and Sironi appeared,[184] and Paolo Garretto's article in *Arbiter* entitled 'Garçonnière per sogni.'[185] Later, articles illustrated with works from the collection were to come out periodically in *Tempo*, *Gente*, *Epoca* and other non-specialist periodicals, making a decisive contribution not just to familiarizing the general public with modern art, but also to the fame of the individual paintings and of the collection as a whole.

The official consecration of the Mattioli Collection came in 1953 with the exhibition 'Arte moderna in una raccolta italiana,' held for one month from April 23 at Palazzo Strozzi in Florence and organized by Carlo Ludovico Ragghianti.

On January 7 Ragghianti approached my father on behalf of the 'La Strozzina' organization, telling him what a great thrill the visit of the previous year to the apartment on Via Senato had been for him and his students,[186] and asking him to allow the paintings in the collection to be shown first at Palazzo Strozzi in Florence and then in the Aula Magna of Pisa University. He added that it "represents the only collection of contemporary art in existence today that can be described as complete. An important experience in itself, but also, let me say, a so far unique example of a collection that already has the interest of the public and is made available to the public."[187] Mattioli at once reacted favorably to the offer, which evoked for him the exhibition of Peggy Guggenheim's collection at Palazzo Strozzi in 1949. The idea of staging the exhibition afterwards in Pisa was soon dropped. On January 21, 1953 On. Giorgio La Pira, mayor of Florence, thanked Mattioli for his willingness to lend the works he owned.[188] The exhibition proved a great success with the public and the critics: the catalogue, published by the Edizioni del Milione, was reprinted three times and the exhibition was given enthusiastic reviews by Guido Ballo, Alessandro Parronchi, Marco Valsecchi and Lionello Venturi.[189]

Ninety-five paintings (to which four more were added while it was being installed[190]), five sculptures and twenty-five drawings were exhibited. The show opened with the signatories of the early Futurist manifestos and with three early pictures by Soffici, continued with a substantial number of Metaphysical works of great importance and then moved on to the 1920s with paintings by Carrà, de Pisis, Funi, Rosai and Guidi. The 1930s and 1940s were represented by one picture by Rosai and others by Campigli, Scipione and Sironi. The room devoted to Morandi, with a total of eighteen works dating from 1913 to 1952, made a great impact.[191] A major draw for the public were the two paintings by Modigliani, in particular the celebrated *Nudo rosso*. The works by de Chirico included, in addition to the well-known Metaphysical masterpieces, *Gli Archeologi* of 1927 and *I biscotti di Ferrara* (*La Magie de la nuit*) (*The Biscuits of Ferrara* [*The Magic of the Night*]) dated 1916, although its presence in the collection is not documented elsewhere. The medium of sculpture was summarized by five emblematic examples, Medardo

Rosso's plaster model of the *Bookmaker*, Boccioni's *Sviluppo di una bottiglia nello spazio* (*Development of a Bottle in Space*) in bronze, an Arturo Martini of 1931, a Marino Marini of 1939 and a Manzù of 1949. The foreign paintings came in part from the Feroldi Collection, such as those by Matisse, Rousseau, Sisley, Soutine and Utrillo, but there were also the watercolor by Cézanne acquired through Lionello Venturi, three Cubist pictures, an important pastel by Chagall from 1923, the small Klee of 1920 and two Rouaults. The section devoted to graphic art presented several works that had formerly belonged to Feroldi, five drawings of high quality by Modigliani, two Futurist works by Carrà, three rare Morandis and works by Manzù and Marini from the 1940s. My father excluded from the exhibition Boccioni's *La Signora Massimino* and *Lo scultore Ripamonti*, choosing to open with Futurist works. He preferred instead to show these two portraits with an important group of Boccioni's works at the exhibition on art from Southern Italy entitled 'Mostra dell'Arte nella vita del Mezzogiorno d'Italia' that was staged in Rome from March to May 1953.[192]

In his introduction to the exhibition at Palazzo Strozzi, Ragghianti drew a profile of the collection. He complained of the difficulty the public faced in becoming acquainted with Italian art of the previous fifty years owing to the gaps and lack of organic unity that typified both public museums and temporary exhibitions. Given this situation, he asserted that Mattioli "has constructed what can quite rightly be called the first gallery of contemporary Italian art." He went on to say: "this collection has an original character, which distinguishes it sharply from any other, and forms its eminent value, apart from the artistic stature and representativeness of the individual works. Organized by a mature and cultivated mind, the collection does not represent the meeting point of episodic interests, or a reflection of particular impulses prompted by a long and assiduous involvement with modern painting. Artists, works, groupings, even the gaps that have still not been filled, make it immediately clear that the collection is governed by a vigilant principle, which prefers and discards, which weighs relationships and differences, which accompanies the desire to capture the most representative moment and work of an artistic personality (something that can often only be achieved with great patience and constant searching) with the subtle sense of finding and revealing the marks of a culture, the connections and articulations of a historical process that underlies the aesthetic characterizations."[193] His description of the Mattioli Collection as having been "put together with the intention and spirit of an *historian*"[194] was universally accepted henceforth.

The objects of this *catalogue raisonné* are the twenty-six works notified by the Italian Ministero della Pubblica Istruzione on September 4, 1973 on the basis of law 1089 of June 1, 1939, through the Soprintendente alle Gallerie Franco Russoli. The ministerial order laid down that the works subject to constraint on the basis of the aforementioned law constituted an indissoluble group, defining them "as a complex of exceptional artistic and historical interest for their very high aesthetic quality and as an irreplaceable testimony of crucial periods in the Italian painting of this century between 1910 and 1920, essentially those of Futurism and Metaphysical painting."[195]

I would like to express my gratitude to Philip Rylands for his determination to publish this catalogue raisonné, *and for having overseen with skill and dedication every phase of its production. I owe to him the proposal that I should write this essay. In addition he has most generously polished the English translation.*
The publication of this essay and of the entire volume would not have been possible without the hard work of the staff of the Peggy Guggenheim Collection, especially Chiara Barbieri, to whom I am most grateful.
A special thanks to Flavio Fergonzi for his constant advice, for his invaluable contributions to the content of my essay, and for his meticulous review of the text.
Much of the data published in Appendix I would have been incomprehensible had I not been able to consult the archives of the Galleria del Milione, which were opened to me in a spirit of friendship by Graziano Ghiringhelli.
Thank you to Linuccia and Anna Ceroni who contributed to this memoir with their personal recollections and who granted me access to the papers of the Archivio Ceroni; thank you to Massimo di Carlo for the identification of some of the works of art that appear in the photographs of my father's house in Via Gabba 9 in Milan; thank you to the Museo d'Arte Moderna e Contemporanea of Trento and Rovereto (MART) for permission to publish documents conserved in its archives; thank you to the Unione Femminile e Fondazione Elvira Badaracco, Milan, for access to documents pertaining to Fernanda Wittgens.
I am very grateful to Maria Benedetti, Enrico Stroppa and Barbara Geremia for their invaluable assistance in bringing order to the Archivio Mattioli.

* Titles of Italian works of art are left in Italian, except in cases in which the title is generic: *Portrait* (*Ritratto*), *Landscape* (*Paesaggio*), *Composition* (*Composizione*), and *Still Life* (*Natura morta*). Nor are translations given here for the twenty-six works that are in this catalogue. Translations are given in parentheses (or in the endnotes), at least for the first mention of the work. On rare occasions (Medardo Rosso's *Bookmaker* for example) the original title is in English.

[1] Archivio Mattioli, manuscript letter from P. M. Bardi to Gianni Mattioli, undated. According to the *Libro delle Firme dei Visitatori*, or *Visitors' Book* of Gianni Mattioli's collection at Via Senato 36, P. M. Bardi saw the collection on September 17, 1951. P. M. Bardi had inaugurated the first version of the Museo de Arte de São Paulo on October 4, 1947. On P. M. Bardi, Francesco Tentori's *P.M. Bardi*, Milan, Mazzotta 1990, remains fundamental. See the photograph at the beginning of *Appendix I, Documents*.

[2] Gianni Mattioli's parents, Paolo Mattioli (Milan, 1861–1943) and Beatrice Bracciforti (Milan, 1861 – Angera, 1943), separated in 1915: a sentence of the civil court of May 30, 1918 made the separation legal and assigned the blame to the husband, accused of concubinage and maltreatment. After running away from home in October 1919 to follow d'Annunzio to Fiume, Gianni Mattioli was obliged on his return to Milan at the end of 1920 to live with his father until 1922, contrary to what had been decided by the court, as his mother did not have enough money to support him. In 1923 he went to live in a rented room at Via Felice Casati 15, and maintained both himself and his mother on the wages of 300 lire a month he earned as a messenger. The hunger he endured up until around 1928 left a permanent mark on his health. In the spring of 1925 Mattioli went to London, where he worked at the Italian Embassy, officially as personal secretary to the Naval Attaché Ranieri Biscia, but in reality in charge of the coded messages of the Secret Services. As a consequence he became aware of many aspects of Mussolini's dictatorship and on his return to Italy kept away from politics. He was never a member of the Fascist Party and during the war did what he could to help victims of political persecution and Jews. In the years 1937–8 he went to Spain several times for reasons of work and was exposed to the atrocities of the civil war, of which he spoke with dismay until the last years of his life.

[3] The cloth tapestries made by Depero in 1920 for Umberto Notari, *Cavalcata fantastica* (*Fantastic Cavalcade*) and *Il corteo della Gran Bambola* (*The Procession of the Great Doll*) were also shown at this exhibition. Mattioli acquired the former on Notari's death in 1950. *Appendix I*, documents nos. 37 and 38. Mattioli also met Margherita Sarfatti and Umberto Notari himself at the exhibition.

[4] Archivio Mattioli, letter sent by Gianni Mattioli from Milan to Beatrice Bracciforti, June 5, 1922. *Il tamburo di fuoco* was performed at the Teatro Lirico in Milan on June 5, 1922, in the presence of the author, who came on stage to present the work to the audience. *Il Popolo d'Italia* published an unfavorable review of Marinetti's "tragedia africana" the following day.

[5] 'Burrascosa serata futurista al Trianon,' *Corriere della Sera*, Milan, January 12, 1924, p. 4; 'La serata futurista al Chiarella,' *La Gazzetta del Popolo*, Turin, January 15, 1924, p. 6. G. Lista (*La scène futuriste*, Paris, Editions du centre national de la recherche scientifique 1989, p. 411) stated that Depero's Futurist vests were first worn in public on the occasion of the tour by the Nuovo Teatro Futurista, which commenced in Milan.

[6] *Appendix I*, document no. 1: in a typewritten note the young Gianni Mattioli expressed his displeasure at the National Honors (*Onoranze Nazionali*) bestowed on Marinetti in Milan on November 23, 1924.

[7] L. Mattioli Rossi, 'C'era una volta,' in L. Mattioli Rossi (ed.), *Boccioni 1912 Materia*, catalogue of the exhibition at the Galleria dello Scudo, Verona, December 8, 1991 – February 16, 1992, Milan, Mazzotta 1991, p. 20.

[8] Archivio Mattioli, letter sent by Beatrice Bracciforti to Gianni Mattioli from Angera, November 28, 1935.

[9] Archivio Mattioli, invitations to the two exhibitions cited.

[10] Archivio Mattioli, *Storia, quindicinale illustrato di divulgazione*, year 1, no. 8, September 25, 1938.

[11] Up until the end of the 1930s my father worked for the firm Ettore Valesi, where he had been taken on in 1918, after interrupting his studies. He was promoted from the job of messenger to that of salesman, earning a higher salary. Free of family commitments, he also traveled abroad extensively: at the beginning of the decade to Turkey and then to Spain.

[12] *Le grandi raccolte d'arte contemporanea. La Raccolta Feroldi*, intro-

duced by Guido Piovene, Milan Edizioni del Milione 1942 (2nd ed. 1947). This was the first art book published in Italy to be illustrated exclusively with color plates. The choice of Guido Piovene, a reputable critic writing for the *Corriere della Sera*, as author of the introduction was taken as a personal affront by Carlo Belli, who had collaborated for many years with Gino Ghiringhelli on building up the collection and coping with the suspicious and recalcitrant attitudes of the Brescian collector (*Appendix I*, document no. 90).

[13] F. Wittgens, *Mentore. Guida allo studio dell'arte italiana*, Milan, Ulrico Hoepli Editore 1940.

[14] Fernanda Wittgens di Straytenau, belonging to an Austrian family that had settled in Milan during the reign of Maria Theresa, was born on April 3, 1903; my father was born on November 29 of the same year. Gianni Mattioli's maternal grandmother was Elisabetta, called Isabella Bellani, the sister of Rachele Bellani, Fernanda's paternal grandfather.

[15] Wittgens was a pupil of Paolo D'Ancona and collaborated with Ettore Modigliani. Lamberto Vitali invited her to write about Boccioni (F. Wittgens, 'Umberto Boccioni,' *Domus*, X, May 1932, pp. 264–8) on the occasion of the fiftieth anniversary of the artist's birth — a date celebrated with particular solemnity in Milan — and she wanted to illustrate the article with reproductions of many works owned by Vico Baer. All of these men of culture were Jewish. In 1935 Modigliani was dismissed from the Brera because of the racial laws. In 1941 Wittgens was appointed director of the Pinacoteca di Brera, and so it was she who promoted the exhibition of the Feroldi Collection along with Roberto Pacchioni and the Galleria del Milione, which at that time was located opposite the Pinacoteca, at Via Brera 21.

[16] *Appendix I*, document no. 4.

[17] 'Un originale matrimonio a bordo della "Victoria,"' *Il Secolo XIX*, October 25, 1940, p. 2; 'Un gesto gentile,' *Il Popolo Marinaro*, year XV, nos. 21–5, Rome, September 15 – October 28, 1940-XVIII, p. 8.

[18] Gianni Mattioli was born at Via Senato 8 in Milan on November 29, 1903, to Paolo, a teacher in the municipal schools, and Countess Beatrice Bracciforti. His parents had married on July 27, 1895. Giovanni, called Gianni, was the last born of three children, after Ferdinando (Milan, 1896 – Varese, 1983) and Isabella (born in January 1900 and dead only fifteen days later). Ferdinando Mattioli married Anna Bini and had a son, Franco Mattioli (Turin, 1917 – Milan, 1980), who became a lawyer. The banker Raffaele Mattioli, for whom Gianni Mattioli was often mistaken, was not a relative.

[19] The woman was named Franca De Eccher and had a little girl called Nora. Gianni Mattioli introduced her to his mother at the end of April 1928 and the two women became so close that Nora used to write often to Beatrice Bracciforti, calling her grandma. Even Fortunato Depero concluded his letters of this period with the phrase "salutami la tua Franca." The couple lived in her house, at Via Stradivari 7, from April 1933 to September 1935, and then at Via Poerio 15. Her name ceases to appear in Mattioli's papers from the end of 1936. In 1938, a few days before Christmas, Mattioli moved to Via Pinturicchio 29, still in Milan, where he lived until his marriage. In 1939 he took in his elderly and ailing mother.

[20] As a partner in Itala Film he participated in the making of the famous feature film *Cabiria* (1913–14), with screenplay by Giovanni Pastrone, inter titles by Gabriele d'Annunzio and music by Ildebrando Pizzetti. He also worked as a film producer in India.

[21] The title to the property was transferred on September 19, 1919.

[22] Archivio Mattioli, note from Arturo Boneschi to Gianni Mattioli, December 26, 1936. This was followed by two postcards sent to Arturo Boneschi by Gianni Mattioli from Burgos on June 21, 1937, and May 25, 1938.

[23] As a wedding present from a friend, my father received an autograph manuscript of André Gide, an author of whom he was especially fond.

[24] Gianni Mattioli was sole director of this company until his death in 1977.

[25] Archivio Mattioli, letter from the Ente Autonomo Esposizione Nazionale Quadriennale d'Arte di Roma to Gianni Mattioli, Rome, June 24, 1943-XXI.

[26] Gianni Mattioli took part in the 'III Mostra Italiana di Arte Sacra per la Casa Cristiana' mounted in May–June 1947 by the Franciscan friars of the Angelicum at Piazza Sant'Angelo 2 in Milan, showing the sculpture *Head of the Infant Saint John* (exhibition catalogue, p. 18), which was much appreciated by the critics. Indeed it was reproduced by the *Corriere Lombardo*, year II, no. 118, Sunday May 18, 1947, p. 3; it was given a positive mention by Costantino Baroni in his article 'Arte per la casa cristiana,' *Il Popolo*, year V, no. 118, Sunday May 18, 1947, p. 3; and it was mentioned by Franco Dacquati in his review 'La Mostra D'Arte Sacra all'Angelicum,' *Corriere degli Artisti*, year II, no. 8, Milan, May 20, 1947, p. 3. Well-known artists also took part in the exhibition, including Carlo Carrà, Giorgio de Chirico, Filippo de Pisis, Francesco De Rocchi, Trento Longaretti, Aligi Sassu, Fiorenzo Tomea, Orfeo Tamburi, Arturo Tosi, Arturo Martini and Francesco Messina.

[27] My parents, who witnessed these events, often spoke to me of what follows. The events were reconstructed in Marco Nozza's book, *Hotel Meina. La prima strage di ebrei in Italia*, Milan, Mondadori 1993.

[28] *Appendix I*, documents nos. 5 and 6.

[29] *Louise* or *The Fat Girl.* As a mark of his gratitude Vitali dedicated his monograph on Giorgio Morandi published by the Edizioni del Milione in 1964 to Gianni and Ferdinando Mattioli.

[30] On Fernanda Wittgens and her activity during the war see G. Ginex, 'Fernanda Wittgens e la socialità nell'arte (1903-1957),' *Risorgimento*, year XLI, no. 2, June 1989, pp. 161–9. Copies of some of the documents from Wittgens's archives are preserved at the Fondazione Elvira Badaracco in Milan.

[31] *Appendix I*, document no. 7.

[32] A letter from Gianni Mattioli to Fortunato Depero on March 22, 1945 (Archivio Mattioli) reveals that, since the house at Via Manin 37 was unfit for use after the bombing of 1943, Mattioli used a small apartment at Via Fatebenefratelli 5 for his brief stays in Milan. His 'Aprilia' car, which allowed him to move around faster and more safely than by train, was stolen on January 25.

As the journey to Lago Maggiore had become too long and dangerous following the bombing of the bridge over the Ticino, he decided to go back to live in the city permanently, and around the middle of March 1945 moved into Via Fratelli Gabba 5. At the beginning of September 1945 Mattioli was obliged to leave this apartment but found another at no. 9 on the same street. In a letter to Fortunato Depero dated September 3, 1945 (Archivio Mattioli), he told his friend that his new apartment was being renovated, and that Raffaele Carrieri had moved to Via Borgonuovo.

[33] *Appendix I*, document no. 8.

[34] Milan, Fondazione Elvira Badaracco, Fondo Fernanda Wittgens, cartella 1, busta 3, letter from Fernanda Wittgens to Clara Valenti, May 28, 1957. Fernanda Wittgens died of cancer at dawn on July 11, 1957.

[35] Archivio Mattioli, manuscript letter from Fortunato Depero to Gianni Mattioli, July 9–10, 1944.

[36] E. Radius, 'Disegni Depero,' *Corriere della Sera*, Milan, March 4, 1945.

[37] Entry for Depero in A. M. Comanducci, *Dizionario degli Artisti*, Bergamo, Ed. Arti Grafiche 1945.

[38] Archivio Museo d'Arte Moderna e Contemporanea of Trento and Rovereto, Fondo Fortunato Depero, no. 129, manuscript letter from Fortunato Depero to Gianni Mattioli, July 13, 1943.

[39] Archivio Mattioli, photographs of the interiors of Gianni Mattioli's home in the 1930s. A view of Milan taken from a window convinces me that this was the house at Via Poerio 15 and not at Via Stradivari 7 as I wrote in 1997 in 'Gianni Mattioli,' in *Capolavori della Collezione Gianni Mattioli*, Milan, Electa p. 13. Hence the photographs probably date from the winter of 1935.

[40] N. Boschiero, 'Carlo Belli: la vita,' in *Il mondo di Carlo Belli. Italia anni Trenta: la cultura artistica*, Milan, Electa 1991, p. 191.

[41] C. Belli, *Kn*, 2nd ed., Milan, Edizioni di Vanni Scheiwiller 1972, p. 136.

[42] Archivio Mattioli, manuscript letter sent by Fortunato Depero to Gianni Mattioli from Serrada, May 27, 1944.

[43] Archivio Mattioli, manuscript letter sent by Fortunato Depero to Gianni Mattioli from Serrada, April 14, 1944.

[44] Archivio Mattioli, copy of typewritten letter sent by Gianni Mattioli to Fortunato Depero from Milan, March 22, 1945, in which Mattioli informed his friend that Carrieri had not been able to write the promised article because the magazine *Domus* had ceased publication.

[45] Archivio Museo d'Arte Moderna e Contemporanea of Trento and Rovereto, Fondo Fortunato Depero no. 6963, typewritten letter sent by Gianni Mattioli to Fortunato Depero on October 14, 1944.

[46] Archivio Museo d'Arte Moderna e Contemporanea of Trento and Rovereto, Fondo Fortunato Depero no. 493, manuscript note of Fortunato Depero 'financial dealings with Gianni Mattioli' (from 1944 to February 13, 1950): the document tells us that Mattioli sold the tapestry *Costumi Atesini* (*Customs of the Adige Valley*) to the Ministero per le Corporazioni for 15,000 lire (also in Archivio Mattioli, letter from Gianni Mattioli to Fortunato Depero on October 14, 1944); *Landscape*, *Gondoliere* (*Gondoliers*), *Fiori* (*Flowers*) and a drawing in 1946 went to his business partner Rolando Ghedini for 78,000 lire; *Buffone* (*Buffoon*) to Sig. Castellani for 25,000 lire; *O la borsa o la vita* (*Your Money or Your Life*) of 1945 to the Milanese collector Adriano Pallini for 25,000 lire. In 1946 he bought for himself *Flora e Fauna magica* (*Magic Flora and Fauna*) of 1920 for 10,000 lire, *La casa del mago* (*The Wizard's House*) of 1919 for 10,000 lire, his own portrait *Gianni e l'armadillo* (*Gianni and the Armadillo*) and *Ballo di marionette* (*Dance of Marionettes*) for 60,000 lire and the *Uomo dai baffi* (*Moustachioed Man*) of 1945 for 25,000 lire on the occasion of the exhibition at the Galleria Il Camino.

[47] Archivio Mattioli, manuscript letter from Fortunato Depero to Gianni Mattioli, October 3, 1945: Depero told his friend that he was putting together photographs of the works to be shown at the exhibition in Milan, enclosed the design for the chandelier and asked him for photographs from which to paint the portrait, for which he had already begun the preparatory drawing. The portrait would be finished in January 1946.

[48] In these first few years after the war Mattioli tried to get hold of as many books on modern and contemporary art as possible. By way of illustration, I mention here the booklet *Henri Matisse,* published with an introduction by Jean Cassou to coincide with the exhibition 'Matisse-Picasso' at the Palais des Beaux-Arts in Brussels in May 1946. Another example is a note with which Fernanda, perhaps on the occasion of the 1948 Venice Biennale (where an important collection of Impressionist paintings was on show), accompanied the gift of a book on Manet that he wanted: "August 6 / Dear Gianni, / here is the only Manet / that I've found; I'm sorry that / it has few illustrations, but let's / hope that you like it anyway. / Kindest regards to Cicci [*sic*] and hope to see you soon in the new / atmosphere [...] but how much / cleaning still to be done, don't you think? / Affectionately / Fernanda", in Archivio Mattioli, manuscript letter from Fernanda Wittgens to Gianni Mattioli, undated.

[49] My father had a season ticket for second nights (turn B) at box no. 16 in the second row on the right at the Teatro alla Scala from 1947 to 1962 and was a member of the 'Amici del Teatro alla Scala' from 1947 until his death. He was also a life member of the 'Permanente' from 1948 and a member of the 'Amici di Brera' from its foundation.

[50] Archivio Mattioli, manuscript letter from Fortunato Depero to Gianni Mattioli, Rovereto, April 27, 1946.

[51] Archivio Mattioli, manuscript letter from Fortunato Depero to Gianni Mattioli, Rovereto, May 22, 1946, published in L. Mattioli Rossi (ed.), *Boccioni 1912 Materia* cit., 'Appendice 1,' no. 1, p. 231. See also *Appendix I*, document no. 10.

[52] Archivio Mattioli, telegram from Gianni Mattioli to Fortunato Depero on May 24, 1946: "Depero / Viale dei Colli 38 Rovereto / Received your express agreed leave you broad powers Boccioni acquisitions affectionately / Gianni."

[53] The painting can in all probability be identified with no. 414 in M. Calvesi, E. Coen, *Boccioni, l'opera completa*, Milan, Electa 1983.

[54] Two different versions exist of this manuscript letter from Fortunato Depero to Gianni Mattioli, June 11, 1946: one, certainly the draft that was not sent, in the Archivio Museo

d'Arte Moderna e Contemporanea of Trento and Rovereto, Fondo Fortunato Depero, no. 6984, and the other, shorter one in the Archivio Mattioli. *Appendix I*, document no. 11. The etchings were *La madre che cuce* (*The Mother Sewing*), *Signora con ventaglio* (*Lady with Fan*), *Signora seduta sul sofà* (*Lady Seated on the Sofa*), *Studio di vecchietta* (*Study of an Old Woman*), identifiable respectively with nos. 620, 285, 265 and perhaps 272 in M. Calvesi, E. Coen, *op. cit.*

[55] The work is identifiable with no. 935, *ibidem*.

[56] *Appendix I*, document no. 12.

[57] Archivio Mattioli, manuscript letter sent by Fortunato Depero to Gianni Mattioli from Rovereto, June 24, 1946. *Appendix I*, document no. 13. The letter was published with the incorrect date of May 24 in L. Mattioli Rossi (ed.), *Boccioni 1912 Materia* cit., 'Appendice 1,' no. 2, pp. 231–2.

[58] This was the first of a series of journeys made by my father to the United States for business reasons. Between the beginning of July and the beginning of September 1946 he went to New York, Dallas and New Orleans.

[59] Archivio Museo d'Arte Moderna e Contemporanea of Trento and Rovereto, Fondo Fortunato Depero, no. 6986, manuscript letter from Gianni Mattioli to Fortunato Depero, July 4, 1946, published in L. Mattioli Rossi (ed.), *Boccioni 1912 Materia* cit., 'Appendice 1,' no. 3, p. 232. *Appendix I*, document no. 14.

[60] Archivio Museo d'Arte Moderna e Contemporanea of Trento and Rovereto, Fondo Fortunato Depero, no. 7223/11, manuscript letter on notepaper headed 'Il Milione Galleria d'Arte-Edizioni' from Gino Ghiringhelli to Fortunato Depero, Milan, July 22, 1946; published in L. Mattioli Rossi (ed.), *Boccioni 1912 Materia* cit., 'Appendice 1,' no. 5, p. 232.

[61] Archivio Museo d'Arte Moderna e Contemporanea of Trento and Rovereto, Fondo Fortunato Depero, no. 5613, copy of a typewritten letter sent by John B. Salterini from New York to the Museum of Modern Art, New York, August 27, 1946 and no. 5614, copy of a letter sent by James J. Sweeney from New York to J. B. Salterini, September 5, 1946. Both letters are published in L. Mattioli Rossi (ed.), *Boccioni 1912 Materia* cit., 'Appendice 1,' nos. 6 and 7 respectively, p. 232. *Appendix I*, documents nos. 17 and 18.

[62] Archivio Museo d'Arte Moderna e Contemporanea of Trento and Rovereto, Fondo Fortunato Depero, letter sent by Fortunato Depero from Rovereto to Amelia Boccioni Callegari, October 11, 1946 (no. 5442) and by Amelia Boccioni Callegari from Verona to Fortunato Depero, October 14, 1946 (no. 5616), published in L. Mattioli Rossi (ed.), *Boccioni 1912 Materia* cit., 'Appendice 1,' nos. 8 and 9 respectively, pp. 232–3.

[63] Archivio Museo d'Arte Moderna e Contemporanea of Trento and Rovereto, Fondo Fortunato Depero, no. 5617: F. Depero, 'Relazione riguardante il quadro "Materia" di Umberto Boccioni,' Rovereto, October 1946, typewritten published in L. Mattioli Rossi (ed.), *Boccioni 1912 Materia* cit., 'Appendice 1,' no. 10, pp. 233–4.

[64] Archivio Museo d'Arte Moderna e Contemporanea of Trento and Rovereto, Fondo Fortunato Depero, typewritten letter sent by J. B. Salterini to Fortunato Depero from New York, December 6, 1946 (no. 3813 XXXV); copy of typescript letter sent by Dorothy C. Miller to J. B. Salterini from New York, December 30, 1946 (no. 5615); typewritten letter sent by J. B. Salterini to Fortunato Depero from New York, January 3, 1947 (no. 3813 XXXVII), published in L. Mattioli Rossi (ed.), *Boccioni 1912 Materia* cit., 'Appendice 1,' doc. nos. 11, 12 and 13 respectively.

[65] Thank you to Romeo Toninelli's son Luigi Filippo for this information.

[66] *Appendix I*, document no. 16.

[67] Archivio Mattioli, copy of typewritten letter from Gianni Mattioli to Arturo Tosi, Milan, September 14, 1946.

[68] Archivio Mattioli, records of quarterly payments.

[69] See note no. 26.

[70] Archivio Mattioli, typewritten letter on headed notepaper from Gino Ghiringhelli to Gianni Mattioli, Milan July 4, 1947, with enclosed copies of typescript letters sent by the lawyer Renzo Sabbadini to Gino Ghiringhelli from Florence on July 2, 1947, and by Gino Ghiringhelli to Renzo Sabbadini from Milan on July 3, 1947. The paintings in question correspond to nos. 5654 and 5655 in the registers of the Galleria del Milione. Mattioli later placed them on deposit at the gallery for re-sale.

[71] The title of the exhibition recalls that of Anna Maria Brizio's book *Ottocento Novecento*, whose first edition (Turin, UTET) had been published in 1939 and second edition in 1944, with a reprint in 1945.

[72] Archivio Mattioli, minutes of the Meeting of the Committee of the Circolo delle Arti held on December 2, 1947, at 9.30 p.m. in the assembly rooms. *Appendix I*, document no. 19.

[73] Archivio Mattioli, typewritten letter on notepaper headed 'Circolo delle Arti - Le Grazie' from the president Marco Valsecchi to Gianni Mattioli, Milan, January 23, 1948.

[74] The information is provided by Gino Ghiringhelli in his letter to Gianni Mattioli of December 22, 1949 (Archivio Mattioli).

[75] Archivio Mattioli, typewritten letter from Romeo Toninelli to Gianni Mattioli on notepaper headed 'Circolo delle Arti - Le Grazie,' Milan, June 25, 1948. *Appendix I*, document no. 20.

[76] *Twentieth-Century Italian Art*, by J.T. Soby and A. H. Barr, Jr., New York, ed. Museum of Modern Art 1949. The other members of the honorary committee were Giulio Carlo Argan, Palma Bucarelli, Carlo Cardazzo, Raffaele Carrieri, Pietro Feroldi, Riccardo Gualino, Riccardo Jucker, Roberto Longhi, Benedetta Marinetti, Franco Marmont, Adriano Pallini, Rodolfo Pallucchini, Camillo Poli, Pietro Rollino, Giovanni Scheiwiller, Cesare Tosi, Lionello Venturi and Mario F. Vespa.

[77] J. T. Soby, *Contemporary Painters*, New York, ed. Museum of Modern Art 1948; A. H. Barr, Jr., *Painting and Sculpture in the Museum of Modern Art*, New York, ed. Museum of Modern Art 1948.

[78] Archivio Mattioli, typewritten letter from the president of the Associazione Cotoniera Italiana to Gianni Mattioli, Milan, June 22, 1948.

[79] Archivio Mattioli, correspondence with the Centro Italiano di Studi per la Riconciliazione Internazionale, 1948.

[80] Archivio Mattioli, typewritten letter on notepaper headed 'United

States of America, Economic Cooperation Administration, Special Mission to Italy' from J. D. Zellerbach to Gianni Mattioli, December 16, 1948.

[81] *XXIV Biennale di Venezia. Catalogo.* Edizioni Serenissima, 1948. For further information on the exhibition see also: M. C. Bandera, *Il carteggio Longhi-Pallucchini, 1948-1956. Le prime Biennali del dopoguerra*, Milan, Charta 1999.

[82] Pietro Feroldi was worried about the fate of his collection, as he did not want it to be broken up but rather to continue to exist as a whole. His heirs were not interested in art, and so he wanted to find a home for it himself, but without depriving himself and his children of the financial value that it represented. Carlo Belli, ('Ritratto di Brescia 1929-1933,' *Il Bruttanome*, no. 2, 1962, pp. 160–1) recalled the discussions he had with Feroldi in this connection in 1941, during the preparation of the monograph on the collection published by the Edizioni del Milione. At first Feroldi intended to leave the collection to his children, but Belli tried to persuade him to make it available to the public. Originally they considered donating it to the Comune of Brescia, but Feroldi was not convinced, owing to the lack of interest in his collection in the city. Belli advised him to leave it to the Galleria Nazionale d'Arte Moderna in Rome, and the two of them went there to examine the possibility. On the eve of his definitive break with Belli, Feroldi wrote to him in laconic fashion: "The French to my children, the Italians to the State." But it seems that on the one hand the State remained numb to this opportunity and on the other the possibility of selling it to Mattioli, which emerged after the war thanks to the involvement of the Ghiringhelli brothers, who hoped to make a profit from the deal, induced Feroldi to cede his collection to my father on terms that he considered satisfactory: a substantial sum in cash and a guarantee that the basic core of the collection would be left intact.

[83] *Appendix I*, document no. 21.

[84] The *terminus ante quem* is provided by the presence of Tosi's *Natura morta con pere* (*Still Life with Pears*), deposited with the Galleria del Milione for sale on November 20, 1948, as emerges from its listing as no. 5285 in the gallery's inventory. Medardo Rosso's bronze, which is recorded as having been paid for on April 28, 1949 on the invoice of that date (Archivio Mattioli), was probably already on deposit at the gallery.

[85] C. Bruni Sakraischik, *Catalogo generale Giorgio de Chirico. Opere dal 1908 al 1930*, Milan, Electa 1974, vol. V, no. 322.

[86] On this subject see the fundamental essay by Paolo Fossati, 'Tema con variazioni, pesci,' in P. Fossati, *Storie di figure e di immagini*, Turin, Einaudi Saggi 794, 1995, pp. 236–69.

[87] Identifiable as no. 541 in L. Vitali, *Morandi. Catalogo generale*, Milan, Electa 1977.

[88] The painting is reproduced in black and white in O. Vergani, *Achille Funi*, Milan 1949, vol. 3 of the 'Galleria' series of monographs on modern Italian art edited by Orio Vergani.

[89] This is reproduced as no. 79 in G. Giani, *Gino Severini*, 'Pittori del Novecento' series, Milan, Edizioni della Conchiglia 1958.

[90] This is published as no. 39 in G. Scheiwiller, *Pompeo Borra*, Milan, Edizioni della Conchiglia October 19, 1941, vol. I in the series of monographs edited by Giampiero Giani.

[91] Archivio Mattioli, typewritten letter on notepaper headed 'La Piccola Galleria' to Gianni Mattioli, Venice, June 28, 1946, with an enclosed manuscript letter from Virgilio Guidi dated June 26, 1946.

[92] No. 5150 in the inventory of the Galleria del Milione, corresponding to the 1948 invoice sent to Mattioli, is identified as Casorati's picture *Uova e carta gialla* of 1940, oil on cardboard, 53 × 45 cm, on deposit from the artist, acquired by Mattioli. In G. Bertolino, F. Poli, *Catalogo generale delle opere di Felice Casorati. I dipinti (1904-1963)*, Turin, ed. Allemandi 1995, the same picture appears as no. 852 with the title *Uova*, oil on masonite, 31 × 40 cm, and dated to 1949.

[93] This is reproduced in G. Piovene, *Cesare Breveglieri*, Milan, Edizioni del Milione 1943, no. 26.

[94] My father possessed Emilio Radius's monograph *Umberto Lilloni*, Milan, S.A. Alfieri & Lacroix 1939.

[95] See cat. no. 14 for further details.

[96] In his notes my father jotted down a number of comments on his works of art that had amused him. Among them were: "You're a lucky man. You'll never have thieves in your house;" "Be careful, that Morandi is cheating you: you can't even tell whether the bottles he paints are full or empty." Archivio Mattioli, notes of Gianni Mattioli, undated.

[97] The dining room of the house on Via Manzoni was featured by Eva Garretto in 'Invito a pranzo,' *L'Illustrazione Italiana*, no. 1, January 1951, p. 83. The apartment on the fourth floor of Via Senato 36, where he kept his collection of modern art, was illustrated by Paolo Garretto in 'Garçonnière per sogni,' *Arbiter*, year XXV, 1952, no. 155, pp. 42–7.

[98] Archivio Mattioli, statement of account from the Galleria del Milione, April 28, 1949. *Appendix I*, document no. 22.

[99] This was no. 1136 in the gallery's registers, coming from the Jesi Collection in 1939, passing to Valdameri in 1942, then on deposit with Frua in 1948 and finally sold to Mattioli for 150,000 lire. The painting is no. 949 in M. Calvesi, E. Coen, *op. cit.*

[100] Archivio Mattioli, *Scrittura privata (bozza)*, draft of contract for Feroldi sale. *Appendix I*, document no. 23.

[101] Archivio Mattioli, typewritten letter on headed notepaper from Pietro Feroldi to Gianni Mattioli, Brescia, June 18, 1949. *Appendix I*, document no. 27. After his acquisition of the Brescian collection my father gave Wittgens Morandi's *Fragment* of 1914, which is visible behind the Superintendent in photographs taken in the winter of 1956–7. The painting was returned to Mattioli on Wittgens's death in 1957, much to the resentment of her family. See cat. no. 14 and fig. no. 14j.

[102] *Appendix I*, document no. 25.

[103] S. Salvagnini, *Il sistema delle arti in Italia, 1919-1943*, Bologna, Minerva Edizioni 2000, p. 226.

[104] *Bollettino della Galleria del Milione*, December 23, 1933–January 4, 1934, XII, no. 20.

[105] C. Belli, 'Una collezione di provincia,' *Quadrante*, no. 9, January 1934, pp. 2–11.

[106] C. Belli, 'Ritratto di Brescia 1929-1933,' cit.

[107] *Appendix I*, document no. 90. My father and Carlo Belli did not meet until the 1970s. In a handwritten letter sent from Rome on January

30, 1972 (Archivio Mattioli), Belli wrote to my father: "Dear Friend, / I must tell you first of all that I feel I have always known you, that I found you to be *precisely* the type that I imagined, and that I will never be able to understand how, having 'almost touched' for at least 40 years [if not half a century!], we never met."

[108] S. Salvagnini, *op. cit.*, pp. 316–27.

[109] Carlo Belli's entire archives are conserved at the Museo d'Arte Moderna e Contemporanea of Trento and Rovereto.

[110] Archivio Mattioli, manuscript and typewritten copy of Gino Ghiringhelli's letter to Pietro Feroldi of January 27, 1935 XIV. *Appendix I*, document no. 2.

[111] *Appendix I*, document no. 90.

[112] S. Salvagnini, *op. cit.*, p. 319.

[113] *Ibidem*, p. 320.

[114] Archivio Mattioli, copy of a letter from Pietro Feroldi to Carlo Belli, April 19, 1937.

[115] Archivio Mattioli, copy of a letter from Pietro Feroldi to Carlo Belli, undated.

[116] Archivio Mattioli, copy of a letter from Pietro Feroldi to Carlo Belli, January 20, 1936. On Carrà's paintings Feroldi wrote: "*The Houses on the Sesia*, verging on the transcendental, a real delight: I would like to keep the picture in front of my worktable. The *Mistress* in reality a bit intractable."

[117] Archivio Mattioli, copy of a letter from Pietro Feroldi to Carlo Belli, April 19, 1937: "Rosai's *My Father* is a gem in my collection." Copy of a letter from Pietro Feroldi to Carlo Belli, January 2, 1942: "I have bought Rosai's *Toppa Players* from Castelfranco (paying very dearly for it). Undoubtedly a great little picture [...]."

[118] Archivio Mattioli, copy of a letter sent by Pietro Feroldi to Carlo Belli, from Brescia, January 2, 1942.

[119] Archivio Mattioli, copy of a letter sent by Pietro Feroldi from Brescia to Carlo Belli, December 1, 1941. *Appendix I*, document no. 3.

[120] *Le grandi raccolte...* cit., p. VIII.

[121] The paintings by Giorgio de Chirico purchased by Feroldi from Mario Broglio for a total of 115,000 lire were *L'enigma dell'ora*, *Le muse inquietanti*, and *Ettore e Andromaca*, as can be deduced from Pietro Feroldi's letter to Carlo Belli on October 10, 1939 (Archivio Mattioli, copy).

[122] *Le grandi raccolte...* cit., p. VIII.

[123] C. L. Ragghianti, *Arte moderna in una raccolta italiana*, catalogue of the exhibition at Palazzo Strozzi, Florence, April–May 1953, Milan, Edizioni del Milione 1953, p. 7.

[124] L. Venturi, *Pittura contemporanea*, Milan, Ulrico Hoepli Editore undated [but 1947], pp. 39–40. Venturi considered the works of de Chirico between 1911 and 1917 to have inspired Surrealism. After 1920 "he remained a painter of great technical qualities, sometimes with a pleasant decorative feeling, but the years of his greatness, of his illuminations of the world, were over." This critical stance had great authority and, shared by my father and other important collectors, influenced the fortune and the complex story of the artist's later production.

[125] At the conclusion of a legal dispute begun on the occasion of the Venice Biennale of 1948, Longhi made a public attack on de Chirico's post-Metaphysical painting, publishing in the first issue of the magazine *Paragone*, which he had founded and edited, Antonio Fornari's article 'De Chirico e Rubens' (*Paragone Arte*, no. 1, January 1950, Florence, Sansoni, pp. 45–7).

[126] C. Belli, 'Ritratto di Brescia 1929-1933,' cit., p. 157.

[127] This painting, known by the title *Frutta e liquori* and dated 1915, entered the Mattioli Collection in 1951 after belonging to Carlo Frua (cat. no. 26).

[128] Archivio Mattioli, typewritten letter sent by Carlo Belli to Gianni Mattioli from Rome, February 4, 1971.

[129] G. Mattioli, 'Come ho formato la mia raccolta,' *La Biennale di Venezia*, year I, no. 3, January 1951, p. 26. *Appendix I*, document no. 67.

[130] Notable exceptions for that date were two Spanish publications: R. Benet, *Futurismo y Dada*, Barcelona, Ediciones Omega 1949; A. Cirici-Pellicer, *Surrealismo*, Barcelona, Ediciones Omega 1949.

[131] *Appendix I*, document no. 26.

[132] Archivio Mattioli, typewritten letter sent by Gianni Mattioli to Romeo Toninelli from Milan on July 1, 1949.

[133] Archivio Mattioli, manuscript statement by Romeo Toninelli, December 21, 1949. The correspondence relating to the purchase of *Materia* has been published in L. Mattioli Rossi (ed.), *Boccioni 1912 Materia* cit.

[134] *Appendix I*, documents nos. 29, 30, 31. These documents have been published in L. Mattioli Rossi (ed.), *Boccioni 1912 Materia* cit., 2nd enlarged edition on the occasion of the exhibition at the Fondazione Antonio Mazzotta, April 2–May 28, 1995, Milan 1995, 'Appendix I,' nos. 18, 19 and 20 respectively, pp. 235–7.

[135] *Appendix I*, documents nos. 32, 34, 36, 50, 59.

[136] *Appendix I*, document no. 72.

[137] *Appendix I*, document no. 33.

[138] *Appendix I*, documents nos. 37, 38.

[139] G. Giani, *Fortunato Depero Pittore*, Milan, Edizioni della Conchiglia 1951.

[140] *Appendix I*, documents nos. 44, 45 and cat. no. 8.

[141] *Appendix I*, document no. 54 and cat. no. 2.

[142] *Appendix I*, document no. 39.

[143] Archivio Mattioli, typewritten letter on notepaper headed 'Lionello Venturi, Corso Trieste 42, Roma,' from Lionello Venturi to Gianni Mattioli, Rome, June 21, 1950.

[144] Archivio Mattioli, typewritten letter from Gianni Mattioli to Lionello Venturi, Milan, June 23, 1950. My father is referring to G. Scheiwiller, *Amedeo Modigliani*, Arte Moderna Italiana no. 8, Milan, Ulrico Hoepli Editore 1950, pl. XIX, *Maria*, 1918, oil on canvas, 60 × 50 cm.

[145] *Appendix I*, document no. 51.

[146] J. T. Soby, C. O. Schulewind, *Georges Rouault*, New York, The Museum of Modern Art 1945. In 1948 a large exhibition was organized by the Kunsthaus Zürich.

[147] L. Venturi, *Georges Rouault*, Paris, Albert Skira 1948. L. Venturi and G. Salles were the curators of an exhibition of Rouault's work at the Musées des Beaux-Arts, Brussels (March 21–May 1, 1952) and at the Musée National d'Art Moderne, Paris (July 9–October 26, 1952). The Comune of Milan organized a Rouault exhibition at the Padiglione d'Arte Contemporanea in April–June 1954 which included two works from the collection of Gianni Mattioli: *Paysage biblique* (1939), and *Carmencita* (1948).

[148] Archivio Mattioli, typewritten letters between Gianni Mattioli and Albert Skira, dated May 19, 1950, May 25, 1950, May 27, 1950, November 28, 1950, December 5, 1950.

The series that Skira was publishing was called *Histoire de la peinture moderne*.
[149] *Appendix I*, document no. 43.
[150] 'Art italien contemporain,' Palais des Beaux-Arts, Brussels, January 28–February 26, 1950.
[151] 'Figuren uit de Italiaanse Kunst na 1910,' Stedelijk Museum, Amsterdam, March 3 – May 3, 1950.
[152] 'Exposition d'art moderne italien,' curated by P. D'Ancona, exhibition organized by the 'Amici di Brera,' Musée National d'Art Moderne, Paris, May–June 1950.
[153] 'Modern Italian Art,' exhibition organized by the Arts Council of Great Britain, Tate Gallery, London, June 25–July 31, 1950.
[154] Paolo D'Ancona, 'Preface,' in *Exposition d'art moderne italien*, Musée National d'Art Moderne, Paris 1950, no p. no.
[155] 'Un demi siècle d'art italien,' *Cahiers d'Art*, year 25, I, Paris 1950.
[156] *Appendix I*, documents nos. 46 and 49.
[157] C. Zervos, 'Vue d'ensemble sur l'Art italien moderne,' *Cahiers d'Art*, year 25, I, Paris 1950, pp. 3–8.
[158] Two reproductions show Boccioni's *Materia* (p. 35) and Carrà's *Portrait of Marinetti* (p. 77) prior to repainting by the two artists in 1913 and 1917–18 respectively. It is likely that *Cahiers d'Art* reproduced old photographs belonging to the Marinetti archive.
[159] These were de Chirico's *L'enigma dell'ora* in G. A. Dell'Acqua, 'La peinture "métaphysique,"' p. 121; Modigliani's *Nudo rosso* in U. Apollonio, 'Amedeo Modigliani,' p. 167; Carrà's *L'amante dell'ingegnere* in F. Arcangeli, 'La peinture italienne en 1920,' p. 193. It may be interesting to note the difference in the approach taken by Zervos's magazine and that of Umbro Apollonio's book *Pittura moderna italiana*, published by Neri Pozza in Venice in the same month of May 1950, which commences with the work of the painter Tosi.
[160] 'Futurismo-Pittura Metafisica,' Kunsthaus, Zurich, November–December 1950.
[161] *Appendix I*, documents nos. 55, 62, 63, 64, 65, 66, 70, 71.
[162] My father gave Morandi a copy of the issue of *Cahiers d'Art* on Italian art, and then chiefly volumes on Flemish painting, which the Bolognese artist studied with care. In 1951 he presented him with Signac's pencil drawing of a *Seated Figure of a Woman with Her Arms Folded*, bought through the Galleria del Milione on the French market, to which Morandi became very attached. The Bolognese painter visited my father's collection in Milan for the first time on April 30, 1951. For the correspondence between Mattioli and Morandi, see M. Pasquali, 'Morandi e il mondo dell'arte. 1950-1964,' in L. Mattioli Rossi (ed.), *Morandi ultimo. Nature Morte 1950-1964*, catalogue of the exhibition at the Galleria dello Scudo, Verona, December 14, 1997–February 28, 1998, and Venice, Peggy Guggenheim Collection, April–September 1998, Milan, Mazzotta 1997, pp. 213–28.
[163] Some coincidences should be pointed out. The Pinacoteca di Brera reopened to the public after repair of the damage inflicted by bombs during the war on June 9, 1950, thanks to the efforts of Fernanda Wittgens. She and Professor D'Ancona *de facto* inaugurated the exhibition of the Mattioli Collection at Via Senato 36 a month after that of the Brera, when Fernanda had recovered from a minor throat operation in June. As Superintendent, she initiated a revolutionary educational program at the museum in 1951, to which she also contributed personally.
[164] Dell'Acqua and Ottino della Chiesa were officials of the Soprintendenza alle Gallerie, and thus members of Wittgens's staff.
[165] *Appendix I*, document no. 67.
[166] *Appendix I*, document no. 69.
[167] *Appendix I*, document no. 68.
[168] *Ibidem*.
[169] *Appendix I*, document no. 73.
[170] *Appendix I*, document no. 78.
[171] *Appendix I*, document no. 85.
[172] *Appendix I*, documents nos. 74 and 79.
[173] *Appendix I*, documents nos. 75 and 77.
[174] *Appendix I*, documents nos. 68, 74 and 76.
[175] In 1949 the Galleria del Milione had mounted exhibitions by Cassinari, Morlotti and Birolli, in 1950 by Afro and in 1951 by Romiti, Vacchi, Ajmone, Chighine, Fasce, Carmassi and Milani; in the following years it held shows by Meloni, Cogorno, Dova, Tamayo and Winter. Carmassi's exhibition marked the launch of a series of small monographs devoted to new artists, edited by Marco Valsecchi. The painters chosen by Ghiringhelli and my father were almost always included in the Venice Biennales of those years: Carmassi, Milani and Tamayo at the XXV Biennale in 1950; Afro, Ajmone, Birolli, Cassinari, Dova, Meloni, Moreni, Morlotti and Romiti at the XXVI Biennale in 1952; Cogorno, Vacchi and Winter at the XXVIII Biennale in 1956.
[176] *Appendix I*, document no. 76.
[177] *Appendix I*, document no. 81.
[178] *Appendix I*, document no. 82.
[179] *Appendix I*, document no. 83.
[180] *Appendix I*, document no. 84.
[181] *Appendix I*, document no. 86.
[182] Not all the works can be identified from the information provided in the exhibition catalogue. They certainly included the following: Balla's *Mercurio transita davanti al sole* (cat. no. 2), Boccioni's *Forme uniche della continuità nello spazio*, Carrà's *La Galleria di Milano* (cat. no. 6), *L'idolo ermafrodito*, *L'amante dell'ingegnere* (cat. no. 10) and *Casine sul Sesia,* de Chirico's *Le Muse inquietanti* and *Ettore e Andromaca*, de Pisis's *Natura morta con gli occhi*, *Primavera a Parigi* and *Testa di vecchio*, Marini's *Giocoliere a cavallo* of 1949, Martini's *Ritratto del Prof. Schwartz,* Modigliani's *Nudo rosso*, Morandi's *Natura morta* of 1915 (cat. no. 16), Severini's *Ballerina blu* (cat. no. 22) and Sironi's *Composizione con cariatidi* of 1952.
[183] *Il Milione. Bollettino della Galleria del Milione*, new series no. 1, November 1952, Via Bigli 2, Milan, no p. nos.
[184] G. Ballo, 'La Venezia di De Pisis incominciò a Parigi,' *Settimo Giorno*, year V, no. 34, August 20, 1952, pp. 32–3; G. Ballo, 'Le bottiglie di Morandi non sanno di cantina,' *ibidem*, no. 37, September 10, 1952, pp. 32–3; G. Ballo, 'Le donne ad anfora di Massimo Campigli,' *ibidem*, no. 38, September 17, 1952, pp. 32–3; G. Ballo, 'Il poeta della periferia,' *ibidem*, no. 39, September 24, 1952, pp. 32–3.
[185] P. Garretto, 'Garçonnière per sogni,' *Arbiter*, year XXV, 1952, no. 155, January–February, pp. 42–7.
[186] The *Visitors' Book* has the entry 'Carlo L. Ragghianti e la scuola di Pisa' on April 29, 1952. Ragghianti held the chair in the History of Medieval and Modern Art at the Fac-

ulty of Letters and Philosophy of Pisa University and gave seminars at the Scuola Normale.

[187] Archivio Mattioli, typewritten letter from C. L. Ragghianti to Gianni Mattioli on notepaper headed 'La Strozzina. Mostre permanenti d'arte figurativa. Manifestazioni di cultura e di musica. Firenze Palazzo Strozzi,' January 7, 1952.

[188] Archivio Mattioli, typewritten letter on notepaper headed 'Il Sindaco di Firenze' from On. Giorgio La Pira to Gianni Mattioli, January 21, 1953.

[189] G. Ballo, 'Mezzo secolo di pittura europea a Palazzo Strozzi,' *Settimo Giorno*, year VI, no. 22, May 30, 1953, p. 32; A. Parronchi, 'La grande stagione dell'arte italiana moderna,' *La Nazione italiana*, year XCV, no. 100, Florence, April 26, 1953, p. 3; M. Valsecchi, 'Mezzo secolo a Firenze,' *Tempo*, year XV, no. 21, Milan, May 23,1953, p. 37; L. Venturi, 'Collezioni moderne,' *La Nuova Stampa*, year IX, no. 137, Turin, June 10, 1953, p. 3.

[190] These were two pictures by Tosi, one by de Pisis and *La Magie de la nuit* by de Chirico.

[191] In an article headed 'A Firenze, a Palazzo Strozzi' in the column 'Mostre d'arte' on p. 3 of *Il nuovo Corriere*, year IX, no. 100, April 26, 1953, the anonymous reviewer stated that the works on show were of "extraordinary interest, which will remain memorable not just for Florence: for example the large room dedicated in its entirety to Morandi, something that, for many years, it has not been possible to see publicly in Italy."

[192] *Mostra dell'arte nella vita del Mezzogiorno d'Italia*, catalogue of the exhibition, Palazzo delle Esposizioni, Rome, March–May 1953, Rome, De Luca Editore 1953, respectively no. 2 on p. 161 with the title *Donna alla finestra* (*Woman at a Window*) and no. 28 on p. 162.

[193] C. L. Ragghianti, *op. cit.*, pp. 6–7.

[194] *Ibidem*, p. 7. See also note 123 above.

[195] Decree of notification of the collection of Gianni and Angela Maria Mattioli issued by the Ministero della Pubblica Istruzione on September 4, 1973.

Caro Signor Mattioli,

la sua collezione è qualcosa di più di una raccolta di opere d'arte; per costituire, invece, uno dei fatti fondamentali per la pace nel mondo: il credere nell'arte e nella storia dell'umanità.

Vengo a trovarLa in Brasile come facciamo qualche di [illegible].

Suo P. M. Bardi

Appendix I - Documents

Compiled by
Laura Mattioli Rossi

This compilation of documents gathers texts, letters, contracts and accounts, in chronological order, that pertain both to Gianni Mattioli as a collector and to other cultural activities in which Gianni Mattioli was involved. The criteria for selection are twofold: documents that flesh out the profile of the collector himself, as delineated in my introductory essay, and documents relevant to the history of the works that are the subject of this catalogue raisonné. *With the exception of four letters that belong to the Fondo Depero del Museo d'Arte Moderna e Contemporanea of Trento and Rovereto (numbers 14, 15, 17, 18), all documents are preserved in the Archivio Mattioli. Two of the letters from the Ghiringhelli-Feroldi correspondence and the Belli-Feroldi correspondence (numbers 2 and 3) are photocopies given by Carlo Belli to Gianni Mattioli in February 1971. Mispellings have been corrected (excepting rare cases in which they have some historical significance); underlinings are indicated with italics, and, for uniformity's sake, the titles of works of art are given in italics if they appear in inverted commas in the original. Works of art mentioned in abbreviated form in the documents are, when possible, identified in square brackets. Graziano Ghiringhelli has provided essential assistance in identifying the works that passed through the Galleria del Milione: these were generally referred to in the accounts with the inventory number ('numero d'ingresso') with which they were recorded in the gallery registers. In this case, valuable information on provenance as it appears in the gallery registers has also been transcribed. The notes clarify briefly the people and circumstances that are mentioned fleetingly in the documents.*

Letter from Pier Maria Bardi to Gianni Mattioli, September 1951

1. Typescript by Gianni Mattioli (Archivio Mattioli)

[dated November 26, 1924 by the author in pencil on the *verso*]

Funerale del Futurismo

Domenica scorsa[1] solenni et ufficiali onoranze furono impiegate dalla decrepita civiltà per incatenare l'Aedo del futurismo. Si può compiacersi con la vecchia Eulalia per l'astuzia addimostrata ma non – certo – complimentare l'esaltatore del passo di corsa, del pugno e del salto per l'ingenuità con cui si è lasciato accalappiare e, forse, sottilmente schernire dal "defunto" che gli ha intessuto l'elogio.

Les Dieux s'en vont, D'annunzio [*sic*] reste.
La frustata marinettiana d'anteguerra si può oggi modificare così: les dieux s'en vont, l'homme reste.
Resta l'uomo con tutte le sue vanità che – purtroppo – neppure quindici anni di battaglie riescono ad annientare.
Ed ecco che un giorno l'invincibile ribelle, colui che aveva fuso il suo io nella violenta personalità pugilistica di Mafarka el Bar, si lascia ad un tratto docilmente legare dalla untuosità affettata di un ben composto comitato.
E sale tranquillo il palcoscenico di un teatro che tante volte aveva squassato coi suoi gridi incendiari, per ascoltare compunto quei noiosissimi discorsi ufficiali che fino a ieri eccitavano le sue più mordaci ironie.
Là, rigidamente vestito di nero – poiché in omaggio all'etichetta ha dimenticato nel cassetto colle idee che più amava anche i suoi esplosivi panciotti millecolorati – assiste sorridendo al funerale della sua magnifica anima incendiaria.
Che malinconia!

Mentre gli oratori parlavano, parlavano, parlavano mi tornavano nella mente con l'insistenza di un ritornello le parole del Commiato nel Notturno d'Annunziano.
"Ad una, ad una cadono tutte le aquile della battaglia ..."[2]
Ma che importa?

Anch'io sorriderò, o Marinetti dei miei primi sogni, pensando che oggi il futurismo è morto.
Ben morto.
E non lancerò più con te, dalla vetta del Gorisankar, vane sfide alle stelle.
Non mi curerò delle stelle del cielo.
Per il mio firmamento basteranno quelle – luminosissime – che costellano la mia anima.

Oggi come non mai, Mafarka el Bar canta nelle mie vene la più bella delle sue canzoni di guerra.

[1] The Futurist Congress and National Honors ('Onoranze Nazionali') for Marinetti took place in Milan on November 23, 1924.
[2] G. d'Annunzio, *Notturno*, Milan, Treves 1921, p. IX: the original text reads 'A una a una cadono le ultime aquile della battaglia'.

2. Copy of a typewritten letter, with manuscript additions, from Peppino Ghiringhelli to Pietro Feroldi, preceded by an accompanying manuscript letter from Peppino Ghiringelli to Carlo Belli (photostatic copy, Archivio Mattioli)

Caro Belli – come saprai Feroldi ha fatto la scorsa settimana una brutta telefonata, cui Gino[1] ha risposto un po' seccamente. 2 giorni dopo è venuto da noi, col muso, ma da buon amico, promettendo di non voler più discutere l'incidente e dichiarando di tenersi il quadro [C. Carrà, *L'amante dell'ingegnere* (*The Engineer's Mistress*)] (che Orombelli[2] gli avrebbe ripreso in cambio antichi più qualcosa in contanti). Poi, tornato a Brescia, ha trovato una mia lunga lettera che aveva tardato a giungergli. Subito mi scrisse un biglietto in cui affermava che se la lettera gli fosse giunta prima, avrebbe avuto molte cose da dilucidare. Con tale biglietto mi acclude copia di lettera scritta a te, in cui ritiene che io possa trovare spiegazioni che non aveva tempo di scrivermi. Mi sono messo subito stamani, appena ricevuto questo, a rispondergli questa lunga lettera di cui ti mando copia. Dimmi, ti pare cruda? Ma insomma con Feroldi non si può discutere. Non entra mai nel punto di vista dell'interlocutore, e infine si tratterebbe di dirgli che gli rimproveriamo non le sue critiche – che rappresentano interesse e intelligenza, benché esageri sui particolari, che devono essere libere e franche – ma il suo sistema di collezionista e il suo modo di discutere noi, le nostre argomentazioni e il nostro operato. Tu lo puoi fare meglio e lo sai fare meglio. Fallo tu. Come vedi io sono imbrogliato nel dirgli il mio parere: e già devo essere stato troppo duro. Egli deve imparare a distinguere il Feroldi che critica dal Feroldi che colleziona. Se colleziona Carrà non deve chiedere a Carrà quello che è di Giotto o quello che Carrà non ha saputo fare. È un peccato che non arrivi ad amare questo benedetto quadro: ma non si può fare a noi una colpa di avere forzato, sperando che arrivasse ad amarlo. E poi insisto che l'errore sta nella sua discussione. Il collezionista, e in genere il compratore di quadri, il committente, non ha diritto di chiedere all'artista quello che gli manca o sembra mancargli. Senza contare (inter nos) che questi scrupoli Feroldi se li fa solo sui pezzi importanti. Ciò che è giusto, ma se non dimenticasse che su gli altri pezzi non si sarebbe neppure sognato certi problemi, certe manchevolezze ecc. ecc. Scrivi francamente il tuo parere. Hai già avuto la poesia per un articolo sulla mostra Garbari? Ora ti spedisco il Bollettino. Ciao.

27 gennaio 1935 XIV [actually 1936]
Ma, caro Avvocato,
non abbiamo pensato di venderLe Giotto. Le abbiamo venduto un Carrà. Quando Lei mi avrà trovato un Carrà che non senta di suggerimenti (come del resto accade per qualsiasi artista che cerca, altrimenti non esisterebbero scuole né l'insegnamento degli antichi) e soprattutto un Carrà che sia una pittura "ordinata, netta, privilegio della concettuosità originaria e unigenia", pensando con tali parole a Giotto; e quando mi avrà trovato una metafisica *assolutamente* inedita in tutta la storia dell'arte: allora Le potrò dire che i Suoi ragionamenti non hanno perduto le proporzioni. Il procedimento creativo di Carrà esclude di per se stesso la possibilità di un Carrà senza artifici, senza sporchi, senza masticamenti faticosi. Tale è Carrà, e tale è tutta la grandezza morale di Carrà nella pittura italiana. 30 anni di cocciutaggine: questa la sua coerenza pittorica, e la coerenza tra gli elementi che va cercata in un suo quadro. Tipicamente noi abbiamo elogiato l'*Amante* per la sua collezione, pensando che Lei volesse *collezionare* Carrà in tutti i suoi meriti, e quindi anche in tutti i suoi difetti che stanno *implicitamente* (come sempre i veri meriti comportano i loro difetti).
Lei ci potrà ancora dire che questa è letteratura: ma a mio parere letteratura è ogni modo di esprimersi.
Per stare ai fatti, noi siamo stati molto più positivi (o almeno abbiamo creduto di esserlo). Vale a dire abbiamo insistito che, malgrado tutti i Suoi argomenti d'ordine *assoluto*, nella Sua collezione l'Amante dell'Ingegnere Le conveniva come il miglior Carrà disponibile, un Carrà assolutamente documentabile, e infine anche un Carrà per il quale Lei ha subito dimostrato un interesse spirituale ben vivo!
Davanti a questi *fatti*, pratici e per nulla letterari, abbiamo giudicato i Suoi scrupoli come una inquietudine di origine nobilissima, ma che per il buon equilibrio delle cose andava *vinta*. Del resto, è ovvio che abbiamo potuto vincere solamente perché c'era in Lei una convinzione.
Resta poi il fatto che a noi la metafisica non interessa che come *storia*. Ed è come storia che abbiamo *veduto* l'Amante nella Sua collezione. I Suoi esami scrupolosi e minuti del valore assoluto sono la natura stessa di un buon amatore collezionista. Ma è indipendentemente da essi che noi restiamo convinti dell'opportunità dell'ingresso del pezzo nella Sua collezione. Se non altro proprio per questo, che La fa tanto discutere. Perché *si collezionano* i punti cruciali dei problemi svolti nella storia dell'arte. Dunque avremmo anteposto considerazioni di *collezione* a considerazioni in senso *assoluto* (semmai – e non è neppur vero). Non considerazioni propagandistiche ad una disinteressata collaborazione con Lei in vantaggio della Sua raccolta.
Non comprendo bene a chi si riferisce nella lettera a Belli, ma mi par di capire che ritiene sbollita la valutazione del periodo metafisico di Carrà quale essa è uscita dal-

la mostra del dicembre. Permetta, la Sua intuizione non è autentica questa volta: è polemica. Non siamo stati noi a scoprire l'importanza di Carrà né dove Carrà è più importante, più "Carrà". È stata la critica da almeno 10 anni in qua: e poiché in Italia non esiste critica, è stata la critica straniera. In particolare la critica straniera che più ha conosciuto e studiato Carrà, la tedesca. Il compito del Milione anche questa volta è stato quello di aggiornare gli italiani e di porre in evidenza le buone ragioni del più vasto clima europeo. Le assicuro che i pareri che contano davvero a Milano avranno tratto da questa mostra, per sempre, la convinzione assoluta che il Carrà di primo piano è il Carrà metafisico e quanto del Carrà metafisico è continuato nelle maniere seguenti. E cioè le opere metafisiche hanno suggerito la ragione e l'origine della bellezza tipica del Carrà delle marine ecc. In questa proporzione anche il miglior pittoricismo delle ultime opere è stato nettamente condannato. Non parliamo del *Soldato a cavallo* [C. Carrà, *Soldier on Horseback*, 1934, exhibited in Carrà's solo show at the Galleria del Milione in December 1935] ecc.

Infine tutto questo non ha nulla a che vedere con le idee del Milione, cioè con l'arte astratta, ecc. Il nostro programma di Galleria è progr. di mercato. Sarebbe inutile che ci mettessimo a fare tutto il piacer nostro e le nostre convinzioni. Abbiamo invece sempre proceduto per gradi. L'anno scorso abbiamo sviluppato al massimo l'esposizione del pensiero e degli sviluppi astrattisti. Quest'anno era tempo, a parer nostro, di riprendere la discussione molto addietro: Carrà, Garbari, Marussig. Risaliremo fino a Semeghini, se ci sarà materialmente possibile. Tutto questo va inteso sempre nei riguardi della capacità di assimilazione della critica e del pubblico. Continuare nel programma dell'astratto fino a tutte le sue conseguenze, significherebbe in Italia restar presto in 10 persone a capirci. Una Galleria si propone una più larga sfera di comprensione, e noi crediamo nel controllo di una larga sfera, *anche per noi stessi*. Che resteremmo soli lo dimostrerebbe il solo fatto che Lei oggi p. es. ci rimprovera cose e modi che sono lontanissimi da noi: vale a dire che scrivendoci del metafisico rispetto al nostro atteggiamento per Carrà ha dimenticato la natura della questione, e le nostre particolari idee che con tale questione hanno nulla a che fare. Ha dimenticato p. es. il manifesto preposto al Bollettino 32 del 1934. Avremmo anche già spiegato sul Bollettino le ragioni contingenti, indipendenti dei nostri ultimi fini, del nostro programma di quest'anno, e dichiarato che le soluzioni contemporanee noi le vediamo sempre e più che mai nell'astratto e che l'anno venturo, se appena possibile, esporremo Mondrian e il maggior Kandinsky. Ma ci sembrava ridicolo aver l'aria di difenderci di una così intuitiva condotta pratica di Galleria: ripetere che abbiamo sempre distinto fra tendenze della Galleria e suo complesso programma informativo, di confronto, e di mercato. Ora, se anche l'avv. Feroldi può interpretare così, vediamo che tale dichiarazione è dovuta, e la faremo.

Caro avvocato, se io ho potuto accennare alle influenze *momentanee sull'umore* da parte dell'ambiente bresciano e milanese, pensavo evidentemente non agli esami critici da Lei fatti: cioè al suo tormento, che non lascia in pace né Lei né noi (e che non bisogna dimenticare che ci fa, per se stesso e nei suoi limiti, un piacere enorme); ma pensavo ai Suoi scatti che portavano le conseguenze dei Suoi esami nel campo pratico della collezione, della storia, del prezzo, e del valore relativo, sul quale solamente discutiamo il nostro operato. Pensavo alla Sua telefonata, in cui mi parve trattarsi addirittura della *dignità* dell'opera e delle sue buone ragioni relative alla Raccolta Feroldi, e della nobiltà delle nostre intenzioni nel consigliarLa.

Ora queste cose, dopo la Sua visita, sono evidentemente cadute. Ma resta questa scia di confusione che Lei continua a fare tra le sue cose.

Così pure non intendevo dire che Lei fosse contravvenuto alla cordialità dei nostri rapporti, nel senso esteso della parola. Le ho appunto scritto a lungo del *qualche cosa in più* che esiste fra noi e la Sua Raccolta.

Stringendo crudamente le cose (e dopo tutto questo spero che vorrà collocare le mie affermazioni su di un piano polemico superiore a quanto delle persone sappiamo reciprocamente) ci dobbiamo chiedere se infine Lei non esagera le proporzioni di ogni cosa. Abbiamo sempre premesso che Lei non deve badare solo alla Collezione. Ma non fino al punto di ascoltarsi tutti i dubbi, altrimenti, obbedendo a una convinzione assoluta, Lei getterebbe un giorno anche il Matisse. Tant'è vero che Lei ha composto una Raccolta, e una Raccolta è appunto una miniera di dubbi e di confronti e cioè, con un temperamento come il Suo, di tormento perenne. Ci dica un poco infine se potevamo protestare meno davanti alla conclusione definitiva che si deve trarre dal Suo tono, pel quale il Carrà diventa uno degli affari peggiori da Lei fatti.

Come vede, la discussione va fatta come la facciamo noi. *Da una parte* tutti i Suoi appunti, dall'altra la relatività di tutte le cose umane e il nostro entusiasmo perl'opera, la grandezza, la metafisica di Carrà e la difficoltà di trattare questo garbuglio nei limiti esatti di ogni elemento. Con tutti i pareri contrari che possiamo avere, resta il fatto della nostra convinzione di averla fatta passare sopra tutti i dubbi, incoraggiandoLa ad ascoltare la voce più importante dentro di Lei: quella che Le proviene [illegible line]

[1] Gino Ghiringhelli was director and co-owner of the Galleria del Milione and brother of the writer.
[2] The writer's *lapsus* for Alessandro Mazzucotelli, owner of the painting; Count Alfonso Orombelli was a collector in the same period.

3. Letter from Pietro Feroldi to Carlo Belli (photostatic copy, Archivio Mattioli)

Brescia, 1° dicembre 1941 XX

Caro Belli,

ho ricevuto il tuo espresso. Non ho mai visto la lunga lettera che tu hai scritto a Peppino né me ne fu mai parlato. Tanto più mi meraviglia in quanto parecchie volte ho fatto cadere il discorso sopra il tuo prolungato silenzio. Una sola volta Peppino mi disse che tu avevi scritto delle molte occupazioni che hai, ma del libro, dei particolari ai quali accenni assolutamente nulla. Al punto

che non potendo più pensare a disegni da intercalare nel testo, abbiamo deciso di far seguire alle tavole a colori quattro o cinque grandi tavole coi migliori disegni della mia raccolta cioè Modigliani, Rousseau (perché ho anche un bellissimo disegno "nudo femminile" di Rousseau sempre proveniente da Soffici) Scipione, Marini e Picasso.
All'elenco già ci pensavo ma certo che i miei dati non bastano nel senso ch'io vorrei, non come si fa nei cataloghi delle vendite, ma come in quelli "ragionati" francesi, accennare all'inquadramento dell'opera nell'antologia dell'autore.
Di scultura non facciamo nulla: però ho suggerito a Gino la riproduzione della prima pagina interna e sotto il frontespizio del *Nudo* di Marini, che tu non hai mai visto.
Ritengo poi necessario che di ritorno da S. Remo e passando da Milano faccia una punta qui preferibilmente insieme con Gino. Infatti è necessario che tu conosca anche le cose che ho introdotto nella raccolta quasi con lo scopo precipuo di colmare le lacune e di rendere più interessante il volume con qualche motivo *pittorico* a togliere quella che potrebbe apparire austerità eccessiva della parte centrale.
I nuovi acquisti sono questi: Rosai, *Chiesa di Poggio al Caiano* 1920; pure di Rosai, *Interno di Caffè* 1941; Carrà, *Crepuscolo* 1922; *Assisi* 1940; sempre di Carrà, *Cascine* 1941; Morandi, *Natura morta* 1941; pure di Morandi, *Paesaggio dell'Appennino* 1940; altro *Paesaggio* 1941; De Pisis, *Ritratto* 1924; *Natura morta al mare* 1927; Sironi, *Composizione* 1919; De Chirico, *Autoritratto* 1919; *Natura morta* 1921; Guidi, *Figura* 1921.
Non ti parlo dei minori che entreranno nell'elenco generale ma non nelle tavole: Cesetti, Badodi, Marcucci, Birolli, De Rocchi.
Come tu vedi ci saranno non meno di dodici tavole di cui non conosci gli originali.
Valdameri[1] era stato preso dalla smania di voler arrivare primo. Questo non l'avrei permesso, e neanche gli sarebbe stato possibile. Poi è entrato nella combinazione di fare la mostra alla galleria Roma[2], mostra che, per insufficienza di spazio si limiterà a tre autori: Carrà, De Chirico e Morandi. D'altra parte la collezione Valdameri a ben guardare è tutta in quei tre.
Del lavoro ne resta molto, ma io spero di arrivare per l'aprile.
Da tutto l'insieme puoi capire che questa mia fatica e quella ancora che devo compiere mi porteranno *dissanguato* al traguardo.
Spero dunque di rivederti presto qui.
Tuo Feroldi

[1] Rino Valdameri, Milanese lawyer, president of the Accademia di Brera and an important collector.
[2] 'LI-LII Mostra della Galleria di Roma con opere della collezione dell'avv. Valdameri,' Rome, Galleria di Roma, January 27–February 10 and February 14–28, 1942.

4. Manuscript will of Angela Maria Boneschi in Mattioli (Archivio Mattioli)

Meina 17 luglio 1943
La sottoscritta Angela Maria Boneschi in Mattioli in possesso di tutte le sue facoltà mentali dichiara che in caso di morte desidera che tutto quanto è di sua proprietà, e precisamente: la parte della casa di Via Stendhal intestata a lei, i suoi gioielli, le pellicce, gli abiti i libri ed anche tutte le altre sue piccole cose diventino di proprietà di suo marito Gianni Mattioli. A Mamma e Papà lascia la libertà di scelta tra le cose che erano di Sua proprietà prima di sposarsi perché le abbiano per suo ricordo.
Sarebbe un suo vivo e grande desiderio che la villa di Meina venisse lasciata dai suoi genitori il giorno della loro morte a Suo marito Gianni, perché possa effettuare il comune progetto di trasformarla in un museo d'arte moderna, e poi perché a Meina io ho *nonostante tutto* [crossed out in the manuscript] voluto un gran bene e perché lì Gianni mi potrà sempre ritrovare!
Vogliatevi sempre tutti tanto bene, che i vostri cuori siano sempre vicini e uniti, ed il mio cuore sarà sempre vicino a voi.
Mamma e papà, vi raccomando Gianni, vogliategli bene come a me stessa, perché lo merita, è sempre tanto buono con me, mi ha voluto bene, bene tanto tanto e per me è stato tutta la mia vita.
Angela Maria Boneschi in Mattioli

5. Manuscript letter from Fernanda Wittgens to Gianni Mattioli (Archivio Mattioli)

[1943]
Caro Gianni,
avrei molto piacere di vederti oggi; non dico a colazione perché sono arrivata da un viaggio interminabile e sono impresentabile. Ma p.e. verso le 14 potrei essere al tuo ufficio.
A Brera ci sono soldati tedeschi ma si entra liberamente.
Aspetto un tuo appuntamento
Fernanda[1]

[1] Fernanda Wittgens, cousin of Gianni Mattioli and Soprintendente alle Belle Arti (later alle Gallerie) della Lombardia.

6. Copy of a typewritten letter from Gianni Mattioli to Fernanda Wittgens (Archivio Mattioli)

Meina, 16 settembre 1943
Cara Fernanda,
Mi è stato recapitato oggi qui a Meina il tuo gentile biglietto. Io credo di poter essere a Milano verso i primi della settimana prossima e farò in modo di avvisarti tempestivamente del mio arrivo; se tu però avessi qualche cosa di urgente da comunicarmi, puoi mandare un biglietto a mio suocero (Signor Arturo Boneschi – Via Boscovich, 18 – Milano) il quale fa la spola giornalmente fra Meina e Milano.
Se invece tu ritenessi di fare una scappata a Meina, tanto io quanto la Cici[1] saremmo felicissimi di riceverti, anche se i momenti non ci permettono l'esposizione di festoni e bandiere.
Assieme alla Cici ti mando i più affettuosi saluti.

[1] Angela Maria Mattioli née Boneschi.

7. Manuscript letter from Fernanda Wittgens to Gianni Mattioli (Archivio Mattioli)

giovedì 19 [October 1944; the letter was sent from the prison of San Vittore, Milan]
Carissimo Gianni,
avrai saputo dall'Angela di una mia lettera a te che ha avuto per strada un incidente per un'errata consegna a mia cognata. Non so se l'hai ricevuta o no. Ad ogni modo ti riconfermo quello che era il suo contenuto: cioè che io sento una gratitudine infinita per ciò che fai per me e per i miei in quest'ora.
Prima il conto con Barbieri; poi l'avvocato ora addirittura i pacchi ... che dirti caro cugino? Quello che già ti avevo scritto; mentre per il mio orgoglio avrei veramente sofferto di ricevere da chiunque altro, da te non ho proprio pena perché so con quanta spontaneità anzi con quanta gioia tu dai e come la Cicci sia d'accordo con te in ogni tua opera buona.
Il bello è che per eccesso di delicatezza tu capovolgi la situazione e parli da debitore! Altro che Boltraffio [G. A. Boltraffio, *Ritratto di donna* (*Portrait of a Woman*), oil on panel, 49 x 37 cm; the painting had recently been acquired by Gianni Mattioli at the suggestion of Wittgens herself] dovrei io renderti!
Ma so che questo linguaggio del dare e avere ti dispiace. E allora ti dirò solo grazie e basta; ma in quel grazie è, oltre alla gratitudine, un affetto veramente fraterno. Pensa che nella serenità assoluta del mio pensiero rimasta inalterata in questi tre mesi l'unica nube era la responsabilità materiale verso i miei; e tu col tuo aiuto hai fatto il miracolo di cancellare anche questa pena. Ora posso attendere serena gli avvenimenti qualunque siano.
Qui non si sta male: leggo, studio e guardo il panorama umano offerto da tante diverse donne politiche e no (queste ultime a volte molto divertenti: facciamo veramente spesso delle risate anche qui!).
Peccato non ci si possa vedere. Ci vorrebbero raccomandazioni in questura e prefettura perché qualcuno ha colloqui tutte le settimane e persino (quelli di villa Triste) tutti i giorni; ed è certo una pressione esercitata dalla questura e dalla prefettura sul direttore di qui. Ma non conviene impazzir tanto per una cosa che col tempo si otterrà.
Intanto grazie ancora affettuose e un abbraccio a te e Cicci
Fernanda

8. Typewritten letter, with manuscript additions, from Arturo Boneschi to Gianni and Angela Mattioli (Archivio Mattioli)

[on 'Arturo Boneschi / Export – Import / Milan - Turin – Bombay' letterhead]

Meina, 28 Aprile 1945
Carissimi Cici e Gianni,
La carissima vostra di ieri ci ha sollevati dall'ansia che avevamo in questi giorni e ci ha fatto tanto piacere. Non era assolutamente possibile avere vostre care nuove e nemmeno notizie precise di Milano e degli avvenimenti. Senza telefono e senza radio perché rotti i fili della forza eravamo qui esitanti e per nulla tranquilli.
Possiamo finalmente ora assicurarvi che stiamo bene e che finalmente ci troviamo un po' tranquilli perché anche noi quì [*sic*] abbiamo passati giorni di grande agitazione. Infatti mentre in un primo tempo sembrava tutto passato giunse notizia che la colonna tedesca dell'Ossola si ritirava e marciava su Arona. Verso le diciassette circa cominciarono cannoneggiamenti e sparatorie; più tardi si fermava la colonna a Meina ed in gran parte davanti a noi. In complesso siamo stati ancora fortunati, sembra per il parco ed il lago che rappresentavano per loro una incognita quindi si sono recati a dormire in paese da diversi privati ecc. di modo che oltre alle noie spaventi ecc. hanno avuto anche danni materiali di qualche entità. Ma non era ancora finita ed al mattino trovammo spalancati i cancelli; da una rapida constatazione però nulla di manomesso. Più tardi sparatorie tra partigiani e tedeschi e fascisti. Vennero altri tedeschi che saliti sul tetto con mitraglie ecc. sparavano alla più bella ma infine fatte le somme, grande spavento, ma nulla di male.
Finalmente alla sera partita la colonna abbiamo potuto riposare e rasserenarci. Pazienza, rimaneva però sempre la nostra preoccupazione per voi a Milano che come detto, ignoravamo assolutamente tutto. Ad ogni modo ora è passata e speriamo bene.
Ieri abbiamo avuta la corrente e quindi le prime notizie della radio.
Sento con rincrescimento che lo zio Carlo è stato ammalato e che ora però va meglio e vi preghiamo di telefonare a nostro nome dando nostre notizie e porgendo i nostri più cari saluti a tutti.
Ci fa molto piacere di avere buone nuove della Sig. Fernanda, di Franco[1] e dell'avvocato Mario[2].
Vi preghiamo di inviare alla Fast[3] la qui unita lettera e speriamo che si possa combinare in modo da poter intervenire per l'Assemblea ad ogni modo se ciò non fosse possibile, sarà bene che Gianni si accordi coll'Avv. Mario e Rag. Saladino in modo di fare loro nel miglior modo. Accludo lettera che avevo scritto in precedenza e che può ancora servire per quanto da fare.
Speriamo avrete ricevuto i tre panini da Michele[4] ed ad ogni buon conto ve ne mandiamo altri tre anche un po' di verdura che speriamo vi servirà in questi momenti.
Siamo ansiosi di abbracciarvi ad ogni modo attendete che tutto sia calmo prima di muovervi. Vi mandiamo tanti e tanti baci affettuosi
papà e mamma

Grazie di tutte le notizie forniteci e dei giornali. Vedete di darci vs. notizie. Il telefono non va ancora appena possibile telefoneremo. Tanti baci in parti uguali con supplementi in ogni modo.
Il bestiame tutto bene compresi i 5 tacchinetti che sono birichini divertentissimi

[1] Franco Mattioli, partisan of CLNAI, nephew of Gianni Mattioli.
[2] Mario Boneschi, partisan of CLNAI and member of the Partito d'Azione.
[3] A commercial company of which Arturo Boneschi was the owner.
[4] Michele Perego, Gianni Mattioli's chauffeur.

9. Manuscript letter from Fortunato Depero to Gianni Mattioli (Archivio Mattioli)

Rovereto 9 dicembre 1945
Carissimo Gianni,
Ho qui il tuo ultimo espresso e sono in attesa di tue notizie (che tardano ad arrivare) dal tuo ritorno da Roma. Mi dicevi che partivi il 24 *scorso* e saresti rimasto assente circa una settimana. Quindi immagino che ora sarai di nuovo a Milano e non avrai in vista per il momento altre partenze. Pregoti di comunicarmelo. Io non mi muovo fino a che non ho la certezza di trovarti tranquillo costì. Mi avevi promesso una lettera con il tuo espresso e quindi l'attendo. Intanto io lavoro tutti i giorni inchiodato con saldi ma spuntati pennelli allo sgabello ed al cavalletto.

Flora e fauna magica è *arrotolato* in attesa di partire con me.

Gianni e l'armadillo [F. Depero, *Gianni e l'armadillo* (*Ritratto di Gianni Mattioli con un armadillo*) (*Gianni and the Armadillo* (*Portrait of Gianni Mattioli with an Armadillo*), oil on canvas, 1945-6] è interamente disegnato e riportato sulla tela pronta. In questi giorni attacco con i colori. Rosetta[1] è entusiasta per averti pienamente colpito. Nella posa e nella espressione il tuo tipo l'ho felicemente imbroccato e l'armadillo che reggi in braccio ti aggiunge un delicato senso di bontà. Con l'altra mano porgi un fiammifero acceso, che sembra un bocciolo di fiore.
E fiori stanno sul fondo, fra il tuo profilo e la mano, come sorretti dall'arco del braccio. Il gesto ti dà un'aria galante di cavaliere (quale sei) anche se le tue sottili labbra chiuse ed il naso affilato ti diano una espressione di uomo fermo e deciso diretto alle sue mete. Vi lavorerò con amore e diligenza augurandomi buon esito. Ma quando ti sarò più vicino – avrò modo di ritrarti variamente.

Ho fatto ricopiare a mano tutto il nuovo manoscritto del progettato libro sulle mie ideologie – da mio nipote – ed a giorni sarà pronto – l'originale resterà in mia mano mentre la copia posso lasciarla in visione al probabile editore – Lo esamineremo assieme – sicuro di poter trascorrere molte ore felici vicino a te.
Intanto pazienza. Avevo pensato ad un primo titolo "STILE D'ACCIAIO" che sarebbe molto efficace – ma per varie ragioni sono incerto e ne avrei pensato un secondo "CHIAREZZA e STILE".

Lotto con i mozziconi dei pennelli ogni mia ricerca è vana

Ho aggiunto alcuni nuovi capitoli e precisamente "STATICA" "Ritorno" "Estetica della Macchina" ed "Onore al Cubismo".
Quest'ultimo e di attualità ed è una onesta difesa ed elogio a Picasso ed il suo movimento trascurato dai pseudo-futuristi.

Salute ottima e volontà di lavoro accanita nel modo più inguaribile. Rosetta mi prega di volerla particolarmente ricordare alla tua Cici. Le domanda se ha ricevuto la sua lettera. È afflitta perché in questi giorni si è bruciato il motore dell'acqua e quindi dobbiamo prenderla fuori casa e si è fatto molto freddo. Tutti i giorni c'è sempre qualche cosa di nuovo e qualche seccante sorpresa. Ed ora buona notte – anche domenica ho lavorato tutto il giorno.
ti abbraccio sempre tuo
F. Depero
Il dramma dei pennelli mi rende idrofobo e malinconico!

[1] Rosetta Amadori, wife of Fortunato Depero.

10. Manuscript letter from Fortunato Depero to Gianni Mattioli (Archivio Mattioli)

Rovereto, 22 maggio 1946
Carissimo Gianni,
Nel timore di una tua tempestiva partenza ti ho fatto telefonare dall'Ufficio di un mio amico (anche perché abito lontano e sarebbe stato un disagio il dover attendere molte ore per il contatto con Milano). Ti ringrazio di quanto hai risposto ed ora ti invio la presente per chiarificarti la faccenda.
Ho ricevuto da Abano lettera da una nostra conoscente e nello stesso tempo amica della sorella di Boccioni, con la quale *(in forma riservata)* mi comunica che la Signora Boccioni e suo marito sono ammalati ed in serie condizioni finanziarie. Questa nostra conoscente ieri di ritorno da Abano è venuta a trovarci ed a spiegarmi a voce quanto mi aveva brevemente scritto, precisandomi che i coniugi Boccioni sarebbero disposti a cedere qualche opera di Boccioni: o dipinto – o disegno o acquaforte. Dato che tu mi avevi autorizzato di trattare personalmente per qualche acquisto, *ho subito detto che sarei disposto io ad acquistare qualche cosa purché di modeste dimensioni e di relativa spesa*. Perciò desidererei sapere da te se sei ancora della stessa idea e quale somma a tale scopo intenderesti disporre.
Attualmente i coniugi Boccioni si trovano a Coredo e le opere si trovano parte a Coredo e parte a Verona. Mi dovrei recare quindi a Coredo per prendere visione ed acquistare in forma amichevole ciò che meglio mi sembra opportuno e per tuo conto.
Se invece desideri avere notizie informative sulle dimensioni – con fotografie – la faccenda si complica. I Signori Boccioni comprenderanno che si tratta di terze persone – faranno altri prezzi e probabilmente – scarseggeranno di foto e magari saranno titubanti sulle trattative. Comunque – appena avrò tue precise notizie mi recherò a Coredo e ti scriverò. L'acquisto, magari per ora modesto, credo potrebbe essere immediato se (come eravamo d'accordo) effettuato per mio conto e nel modo nel quale mi sono espresso con l'amica della Signora Boccioni. Naturalmente se non ci fossero opere degnamente figurative (se pur modeste) declinerei l'acquisto – come pure nel caso la richiesta fosse elevata. A scanso di equivoci ti assicuro che curerò scrupolosamente il tuo interesse *artistico* ed *economico*, nel senso più disinteressato – e solo per l'amicizia che ci lega.
L'acquisto dovrebbe essere trattato anche con partico-

lare tattica ed è per questo che si sono rivolti a me.
Affettuosi a te e Cici da me e Rosetta
Tuo F. Depero
N.B.: Ho già ordinato i 50 metri di cornici.

11. Manuscript letter from Fortunato Depero to Gianni Mattioli (Archivio Mattioli)

Rovereto [11] giugno 1946
Caro Gianni, grazie dei saluti avuti a 1/2 Macconi. Ti informo che sono stato a Coredo dal signor Callegari[1] marito della sorella di Boccioni[2]. Di Boccioni non hanno molte cose da scegliere. A Verona ce ne sono altre sette da vedere. Andrò in questi giorni.
Per il momento ho preso un piccolo dipinto ad olio – di modesta pretesa – di buona conservazione – firmato – del 30.IX.1909. È un paesaggio – dipinto su tavoletta di legno (30 × 35) tecnica divisionista – rappresenta una prospettiva di via periferica milanese. È luminoso. L'ho pagato 10,000. Mi sembravano molte – ma dato che mi hanno regalate inoltre quattro acqueforti – ho accettato.
Le acqueforti rappresentano:
1. la madre che cuce.
2. signora col ventaglio.
3. signora seduta sul sofà.
4. studio di vecchietta.

Vedrò se a Verona riuscirò a trovare qualche bel disegno.

Li farò mettere tutti sotto vetro ed incorniciati.

I 50 metri delle cornici sono pronti – costano 30 lire al metro – dimmi se te li devo spedire subito o se attendi che ti spedisca tutto assieme. Potresti anche prendere tutto con te, quando verrai a trovarmi. Fai come meglio credi – sono a tutta tua disposizione.
Anche per il rimborso di queste spese farai globalmente con tuo comodo.
Sto studiando giornalmente il francese. Semplici ed utili esercizi riguardanti le mie idee artistiche. Ottimo materiale per mie eventuali conferenze all'estero, o scritti propagandistici.
Non ho ricevuto ancora notizie da Sartoris[3]. Proseguo diligentemente con i dipinti.
Scrivimi del tuo viaggio in America. Lo sai che le tue notizie sono sempre ansiosamente attese.
Ti abbraccio tuo
Depero

Ti allego una fotografia di un bell'acquarello che sarebbe acquistabile. *La madre* cm 52 × 63 cm. Chiedono 50,000 – ma potrei averlo per 40 – tenterò 35. È uno degli ultimi lavori fatti prima di morire. La ragione del prezzo è questa: Hanno ancora disponibili poche opere e poi ci si trova di fronte ad uno scomparso.
Scrivimi pur sinceramente il tuo pensiero. Non posso spendere forti cifre senza la tua approvazione

Tante affettuosità alla tua Cici da me e Rosetta. Dimmi quando potremo avervi a Rovereto? Salutami caramente Ghedini[4]

[1] Guido Callegari.
[2] Amelia Boccioni Callegari.
[3] Alberto Sartoris, architect and theorist of functionalist architecture.
[4] Rolando Ghedini, business partner of Gianni Mattioli.

12. Copy of a typwritten letter from Gianni Mattioli to Fortunato Depero (Archivio Mattioli)

Espresso
Milano, 21 Giugno 1946
Carissimo Depero,
Ho ricevuto la tua cara lettera con l'unita fotografia dell'acquarello di Boccioni e ti ringrazio sentitamente.
Circa il mio viaggio in America è successa una cosa strana: io che sono un individuo senza troppa importanza ho avuto subito il benestare americano, viceversa il Signor Crespi[1], che è un pezzo grosso e insieme al quale devo fare il viaggio, non avrà il suo visto che il 28 Giugno nel pomeriggio.
Siccome bisogna inoltre avere i visti di transito francesi e svizzeri, presumo che la mia partenza per New York non potrà avvenire che verso il 5/10 del prossimo Luglio. Comunque ti comunicherò tempestivamente la data definitiva della mia partenza.
Ti ringrazio dell'acquisto della piccola tavoletta di Boccioni. Ti sarei molto grato se a mezzo di Saetta tu potessi farmela avere con cortese sollecitudine perché vorrei farla montare prima della mia partenza. Le quattro acqueforti, se tu mi permetti, desidererei le tenessi tu, in compenso anche della fatica fatta.
Circa l'acquerello de *La madre* benché veda dalla fotografia che è veramente bello, mi sembra enormemente caro perché, sulla base di 35/40.000 lire vendevano a Milano un bel ritratto di signora ad olio, e tu sai che gli acquerelli hanno un valore di mercato notevolmente inferiore. Bisognerebbe quindi che il prezzo venisse sensibilmente ridotto per poter pensare di acquistarlo.
Sono contento che siano pronti anche i 50 metri delle cornici e ti sarei molto grato se, assieme al dipinto di Boccioni, tu potessi farmeli avere al più presto, sempre a mezzo Saetta. Ti accludo perciò assegno circolare di £. 25.000 (£. 10.000 Boccioni + 15.000 cornici) e ti ringrazio per il tuo affettuoso interessamento.
Cici sta sempre bene e ti ricorda con me affettuosamente. Salutami caramente Rosetta, scrivimi presto e gradisci un caro abbraccio.
Tuo affez.mo [G. Mattioli]
alleg/ 1 assegno

[1] Guido Crespi, textile manufacturer.

13. Manuscript letter from Fortunato Depero to Gianni Mattioli (Archivio Mattioli)

Rovereto, 24 giugno 1946
Mio caro Gianni,
stamane ho ricevuto il tuo ultimo espresso in data 21 c.m. contenente l'assegno di 25 mila. Domani o dopodomani partirà il collo a mezzo Saetta, composto di:
1-) dipinto Boccioni
2-3-4-5-) quattro acqueforti di Boccioni
6-) una tempera di E. Prampolini.

Tutti e sei sono incorniciati e sotto vetro.
Un fascio di listelli di cornice in faggio evaporato. Ti osservo che circa 13 metri sui 50 sono stati usati per i sei lavori sopra elencati.
Sta bene per le 10.000 – date alla Signora Boccioni-Callegari – delle quali ti allego la relativa ricevuta.
Per le altre 15 mila hai fatto un calcolo troppo generoso – anche calcolando le spese avute sia di viaggio che di vetri e per le acqueforti e tempera che desidero inviarti, oltre alle cornici. Ti ringrazio per ora di tutto cuore e per quanto ti sono ancora debitore ne parleremo al nostro prossimo incontro.
Stop.
Per l'acquerello di Boccioni hai ragione – se credi – scrivimi a quanto di massimo si può offrire – se ti interessa – che scriverò lettera a Coredo.
Stop.
A Verona non sono ancora stato – andrò in questi giorni. Ci sarebbe a Verona uno dei maggiori lavori di Boccioni – un dipinto di metri 2 × 1.40 circa – *Materia*. Lo scorso anno hanno offerto 100.000 – su questa opera avrei un'idea: precisamente desidererei proporla per il Museo d'Arte Moderna di New-York a 1/2 Salterini[1]. Affiderei a te il materiale fotografico e descrittivo e *se sei d'accordo*, ti potresti recare a N.Y. di persona da Salterini. Credo che si potrebbe fare un buon affare e ti suggerirei (non so se sbaglio) questa volta di suddividere il soprapprezzo fra *te – me – e sorella di Boccioni*. Credo che a N.Y. si potrebbe spuntare una buona cifra. Comunicami pur sinceramente il tuo netto pensiero. Tieni questa notizia riservata – ed interessati quali sarebbero eventualmente le formalità – le difficoltà ecc. ... Intanto io potrei scrivere a Salterini informandolo del tuo arrivo e di questo mio progetto. Per ora mi attengo ad un tuo sincero giudizio e consiglio.
Per oggi ti abbraccio – assieme a Rosetta – con molte affettuosità alla tua Cici –
Non dimenticarmi al Signor Boneschi – a Ghedini ed altri amici –
Lavoro con molta soddisfazione –
tuo Fortunato Depero
All'ultimo momento vengo a sapere che oggi è S. Giovanni
Un miliardo di auguri

[1] John B. Salterini, friend of Depero and resident of New York.

14. Manuscript letter from Gianni Mattioli to Fortunato Depero (Archivio Museo d'Arte Moderna e Contemporanea of Trento and Rovereto. Fondo Fortunato Depero no. 6986)

Milano, 4 luglio 1946
Caro Depero,
due righe in fretta prima della mia partenza che è fissata per domani da Genova sul "Vulcania".
Ho ricevuto il quadro e le acqueforti di Boccioni in perfetto stato, assieme alle cornici, e ti ringrazio di vero cuore.
Per il grande quadro di Boccioni vedrò di parlarne a New York, come tu dici. Se non riuscissi a combinare laggiù potrei forse studiare la possibilità di acquistarlo io stesso se a prezzo e condizioni non troppo onerose. Vedi quindi di tenerlo "in sospeso".
Spero di essere di ritorno verso metà Agosto e ti avviserò immediatamente non appena rientrato a Milano.
Tante cose affettuose alla tua Rosetta, ed a te un fortissimo caro abbraccio.
tuo Gianni

15. Manuscript letter from Gino Ghiringhelli to Fortunato Depero (Archivio Museo d'Arte Moderna e Contemporanea of Trento and Rovereto. Fondo Fortunato Depero no. 7223/11)

[on 'Il Milione Galleria d'Arte' letterhead]

Caro De Pero [*sic*],
l'amico Mattioli mi parlò tempo fa di alcuni Boccioni che tu gli avevi proposti.
Tra questi mi ricordo di un grande dipinto importante che ora non mi sovviene a memoria il soggetto esatto.
A me interessa aver opere di Boccioni. Mi potresti dare esatte informazioni al fine di poterle trattare per l'acquisto?
Scusami se mi rivolgo a te ma la cosa mi interessa vivamente e ti sarei gratissimo se mi aiuti in questa ricerca.
Grato di tutto e con la viva preghiera di venirci a trovare presto a Milano ti saluto cordialmente.
Ma dammi notizie del tuo lavoro.
Tuo Gino Ghiringhelli
22/7/46

16. Typewritten letter from James T. Soby to Peppino Ghiringhelli, with an accompanying manuscript letter from Peppino Ghiringhelli to Gianni Mattioli (Archivio Mattioli)

[on 'Il Milione. Edizioni d'arte e di cultura' letterhead]

31 agosto 1946
Preg.mo Signor Mattioli,
tornando a ringraziarLa del cordiale interessamento a tutte le nostre questioni, mi pregio inviarLe copia di una lettera di Mr Soby[1], tradotta, ricevuta ora, la quale vi scrisse in seguito del di Lei interessamento a N.Y.
Con i più deferenti saluti
Peppino Ghiringhelli

21 agosto 1946
Caro Sig. Ghiringhelli
Il libro di Carrieri su De Chirico[2] mi è pervenuto, e la ringrazio molto per l'invio. Spero che al ricevimento della presente il Sig. Lanza sia già venuto alla vostra Galleria per il saldo del mio dare. Mi è pervenuta in questi giorni una sua lettera nella quale mi significa che era in partenza per Milano e quindi vi avrebbe visitati. Alla sua partenza dall'America gli detti del danaro e gentilmente mi promise che avrebbe sistemato la mia pendenza con voi.
Ho ricevuto una lettera molto utile dal Sig. Lamberto Vitali, con molte precise informazioni che mi abbisognavano. Mi ha citato due libri (o piuttosto un libro ed

una rivista) che se potete farmele avere vi sarei molto grato. Sono: Cesare Brandi, *Morandi*, ediz. Le Monnier, Firenze 1942; Marco Valsecchi, *Una pagina per De Chirico*, Lettere ed Arti, Venezia Vol. 2° n° 4, 1946. Mi potete pure inviare Giuseppe Raimondi, *Anni di Bologna*, che mi avete annunciato nella vostra ultima lettera. Vi ringrazio.
Ho avuto due colloqui con Monroe Wheeler[3] circa la distribuzione in Italia tramite vostra Galleria delle pubblicazioni del Museum of Art. Poiché lo rivedrò fra una settimana circa, ritornerò sull'argomento. Spero di intrattenervi presto al riguardo.
Vi assicuro che sarò felice di incontrare il Sig. Mattioli. Vado sovente a New York (sono solo 100 miglia da qui) e spero di incontrarlo. Spero di esserne informato direttamente o tramite il Museo d'Arte Moderna dove sempre sanno dove trovarmi. Spero di avere il piacere di intrattenermi con lui e sarò felice di aiutarlo in tutti i modi per la ricerca delle persone che desidera conoscere a New York.
Sono felice di apprendere che avete trovato il mio libro, *Il primo De Chirico*, di vostro interesse, e spero che la seconda edizione sia più completa e documentata. Avevo l'intenzione di venire in Italia prima dell'apparizione della prima edizione, ma poi scoppiò la guerra. Spero tuttavia di venire in Italia la prossima primavera per un lungo soggiorno. Nel contempo voi mi siete stati di grande aiuto e di questo ve ne sono molto grato.
Coi migliori saluti
James T. Soby
29 Mountain Spring Rd.
Farmington, Conn.
U.S.A.

[1] Trustee from 1942 of the Museum of Modern Art, New York, department head for painting and sculpture from 1943 to 1945 and later curator and organizer of important exhibitions.
[2] R. Carrieri, *Giorgio De Chirico*, Monografie d'Arte di 'Stile', Milan, Garzanti 1942.
[3] Director of temporary exhibitions at the Museum of Modern Art, New York, from 1935 to 1965.

17. Copy of typewritten letter from John B. Salterini to the Museum of Modern Art, New York (Archivio Museo d'Arte Moderna e Contemporanea of Trento and Rovereto. Fondo Fortunato Depero no. 5613)

New York, 27 agosto 1946
Gentili signori,
un artista italiano, di nome F. Depero, appartenente al movimento che all'inizio del secolo veniva chiamato futurista, scrive di possedere una delle opere più tipiche di Umberto Boccioni, intitolata *Materia*. È un grande dipinto a olio, di circa 2 × 2,40 metri, perfettamente conservato. Umberto Boccioni è stato uno dei massimi esponenti di quel movimento futurista italiano da cui sono emersi molti artisti di fama internazionale, fra cui appunto Fortunato Depero di Rovereto, in provincia di Trento. Secondo la sua descrizione, l'opera di Boccioni oggetto della proposta è una delle più tipiche e significative della sua tecnica. Depero o il proprietario del dipinto desidererebbero vederlo esposto in un'istituzione del prestigio del Museum of Modern Art di New York. Per quanto riguarda il prezzo, so che chiederebbero più di 3000 dollari. Non sono tuttavia al corrente dei dettagli e, dato che non sono un mercante d'arte, vi comunico questa informazione come membro amichevole della vostra istituzione; in passato ho già sottoposto alla vostra attenzione le opere dei disegnatori sudamericani che successivamente sono state esposte, poco prima della guerra, nel vostro Museo.
Se siete interessati, potete contare sul mio interessamento puramente amichevole, con il chiaro intendimento che, per questa trattativa, non esigerò né accetterò alcun compenso in denaro.
Con i più distinti saluti
John B. Salterini

18. Copy of typewritten letter from James J. Sweeney to John B. Salterini (Archivio Museo d'Arte Moderna e Contemporanea di Trento e Rovereto. Fondo Fortunato Depero no. 5614)

New York, 5 settembre 1946
Egregio Signor Salterini,
La sua lettera in merito al quadro *Materia* di Umberto Boccioni, attualmente in possesso di F. Depero, mi ha vivamente interessato.
Avrei molto piacere di vederne una fotografia. Va senz'altro che non è possibile giudicare la qualità di una creazione artistica da una fotografia, però mi darebbe una idea generale del suo posto nei lavori dell'artista.
Se possibile Vi pregherei di chiedere al Sig. Depero di comunicarVi altri dati e dettagli a sua disposizione – la data, la provenienza, ecc.
Le ne sarò veramente grato. E le sono anche grato di avere pensato di scriverci in merito a questo quadro.
Distinti saluti
James Johnson Sweeney

19. Minutes of the meeting of the committee of the Circolo delle Arti held on December 2, 1947 at 9.30 p.m. in the members' rooms (Archivio Mattioli)

Presenti i Sigg: Romeo Toninelli, Presidente, Attilio Scaglia, Livio Ghiringhelli, Prof. Costantino Baroni, Prof. Guglielmo Pacchioni, Prof. Paolo D'Ancona, Raffaele Carrieri, Architetto Ing. Giovanni Muzio, Adriano Pallini, Dottor Alberto Rossi, membri, unitamente ai Sigg. Marco Valsecchi, Prof. Dell'Acqua, Giovanni Scheiwiller, in rappresentanza questi ultimi dell'Associazione cultori e amatori arte contemporanea.
Assenti giustificati: Avv. Amilcare Lanza (rappresentato da Toninelli), Comm. Edmondo Gorini, Ing. Luigi Paleari, Dott. Gianni Mattioli (che ha delegato a rappresentarlo il Prof. Gino Ghiringhelli).
Assenti senza giustificazione: i Sigg. Pietro Feroldi e il Prof. Ignazio Batti.
Il Presidente datane lettura, pone in discussione l'ordine del giorno, e vengono prese all'unanimità le seguenti deliberazioni:

a)- *Situazione Finanziaria.*
Il Presidente fa presente la critica situazione finanziaria del Circolo, comportante al 30 novembre un deficit di L. 237.873,70 come da distinta allegata e fa appello ai Membri azionisti e collezionisti per una spontanea elargizione [che] abbia a consentire di coprire immediatamente – in parte – il predetto deficit, nonché permettere di acquistare un primo quantitativo di combustibile necessario per il riscaldamento delle sale sociali.
Il presidente si prenota per L. 50.000; mentre gli altri membri e precisamente i Sigg. Scaglia, Lanza, Peppino Ghiringhelli, Livio Ghiringhelli, Adriano Pallini e Alberto Rossi, sottoscrivono cadauno la somma di L. 25.000; in totale vengono così raccolte L. 200.000.
Il Presidente si riserva di interpellare gli assenti, Ing. Paleari, Gianni Mattioli, sperando che gli stessi abbiano ad imitare il generoso gesto degli altri membri.
Il Presidente ringrazia vivamente gli offerenti, assicurando che si cercherà di contenere il più possibile le spese di esercizio dei Circolo tentando inoltre di aumentare la quota sociale da L. 7.000 a L.10.000 nonché di ottenere nuove iscrizioni.
Si passa poi a discutere il punto b) relativo alla fusione del Circolo con l'Associazione cultori e amatori arte contemporanea e dà comunicazione di una lettera del Sig. Marco Valsecchi in data 3 ottobre 1947, che dà il gradimento a detta fusione.
Gli intervenuti prendono nota con vivo compiacimento della cosa ed accettano la proposta del Presidente di nominare un Vice Presidente /Segretario Generale nella persona del Sig. Marco Valsecchi che accetta; al più presto verrà data forma legale a tale decisione, modificando convenientemente lo statuto del Circolo che viene fissata per il 20 dicembre e alla formazione del calendario per le prime quattro mostre interne che restano stabilite come segue:
I° mostra: Boccioni, pitture, sculture e disegni prefuturisti e futuristi, ordinata da Raffaele Carrieri, dal 20 dicembre al 15 gennaio.
2° mostra: Piccio, pitture selezionate, ordinata dai Professori D'Ancona e Pacchioni dal 20 gennaio al 15 febbraio.
3° mostra: Marussig, pitture selezionate, ordinata da Adriano Pallini e dal Prof. Gino Ghiringhelli dal 20 febbraio al 15 marzo.
4° mostra: Medardo Rosso, sculture, ordinata da Valsecchi e da Scheiwiller dal 20 marzo al 15 aprile.
Vengono inoltre determinate delle manifestazioni culturali intermedie, come segue: (data approssimativa):
22 dicembre: Carrà e Sironi parleranno di Boccioni.
10 gennaio: concerto per clavicembalo tenuto dal maestro Malipiero.
25 gennaio: Francesco Flora parlerà di Ugo Foscolo e delle sue lettere d'amore inedite.
10 febbraio: una manifestazione solista di canto con elemento da stabilirsi.
Viene inoltre progettata una *Mostra Esterna* per settembre da tenersi possibilmente nelle sale della rappresentanza della Galleria d'Arte Moderna in Milano con il tema: *Ottocento/Novecento*, ordinata dall'intero gruppo studiosi del Circolo, e con la collaborazione di altri competenti i cui nominativi verranno determinati successivamente.
Inoltre il Sig. Marco Valsecchi propone una attività editoriale del Circolo sotto forma di cartelle litografiche a tiratura ridotta, da porsi in vendita ai soci, e al riguardo verrà sottoposto al Comitato un progetto concreto studiato dallo stesso Presidente.
Viene anche progettata una visita alla raccolta Reinhart di Winterthur (Svizzera) e viene dato incarico al Sig. Giovanni Scheiwiller che accetta di prendere contatto con il suddetto Collezionista.
Il Presidente ringrazia tutti gli intervenuti per il loro intervento tanto importante per la riuscita della istituzione e toglie la seduta alle ore 23.

Romeo Toninelli, Presidente
Attilio Scaglia
Livio Ghiringhelli
Prof. Costantino Baroni
Dott. Alberto Rossi
Marco Valsecchi
Giovanni Scheiwiller
Prof. Guglielmo Pacchioni
Prof. Paolo D'Ancona
Raffaele Carrieri
Arch. Ing. Giovanni Muzio
Adriano Pallini
Prof. Dell'Acqua

20. Typewritten letter from Romeo Toninelli to Gianni Mattioli (Archivio Mattioli)

[on 'Circolo delle Arti – Le Grazie Via S. Andrea, 1 – Milano' letterhead]

Milano, 25 Giugno 1948
RT/st

Egregio Signor
Gianni Mattioli
Via Principe Amedeo 5
Milano

Egregio Signore,
di ritorno da New York mi affretto a informarLa che il Comitato del Museum of Modern Art – presieduto da Nelson A. Rockfeller – ha approvato, su proposta di James Thrall Soby, l'esposizione d'Arte Contemporanea Italiana in Stati Uniti fissandola per la primavera 1949. Sono in attesa di maggiori dettagli scritti che Le comunicherò non appena mi saranno giunti.
Con l'occasione l'informo che sto concludendo con la Libreria Nazionale di New York un'esposizione del Libro Italiano d'Arte da tenersi il prossimo inverno e sarà mia premura tenerLa informato degli sviluppi di questa seconda iniziativa.
Cordialmente La saluto
Romeo Toninelli[1]

[1] Dealer and owner of the Galleria Il Camino in Via Montenapoleone in Milan; he was the Italian agent of James Thrall Soby and Alfred H. Barr, Jr., for organizing the exhibition 'Twentieth-Century Italian Art' held at the Museum of Modern Art, New York, from April to September 1949.

21. Account from the Galleria del Milione to Gianni Mattioli (Archivio Mattioli)

Milano 20 settembre 1948
Preg. Sig. Gianni Mattioli
Via Fr. Gabba
Milano

Ci pregiamo inviarle come da Lei richiesto situazione contabile ad oggi.
1948
marzo
26 - vs/ acquisto Casorati N. 5150 [F. Casorati, *Uova e carta gialla* (*Egg and Yellow Paper*), 1940, oil on cardboard, 53 × 45 cm, deposit of the artist] L. 80.000
27 - vs/ saldo Casorati L. 80.000
aprile
2 - bolli fatt. Casorati L. 1.400
20 - vs/ acquisto Asnago N. 4062 [*sic*, but actually N. 5167, M. Asnago, *Bambino* (*Child*), oil on canvas, 43 × 30 cm], L. 30.000
maggio
15 - cornice al Sironi N. 4062 L. 5.000
15 - vetro al Sironi L. 250
giugno
30 - libri nel mese di marzo L. 3.000
luglio
7 - vs/ versamento L. 100.000
20 - liquidato pendenza Siviero per De Chirico a Siviero per foderatura L. 25.000
20 - dato Soffici 3315 [A. Soffici, *Fiori* (*Flowers*), 1929, oil on cardboard, 50.5 × 66 cm] L. 45.000
20 - al mediatore Silva L. 10.000 = 80.000
20 - vs/ acquisto terracotta Marino [M. Marini, *Venere* (*Venus*), 1945, terracotta, h. 113 cm] L. 400.000
20 - vs/acquisto De Pisis N. 4970 [F. de Pisis, *Landscape*, oil on canvas, 54 × 65 cm, provenance from Milani] L. 20.000
20 - vs/acquisto terracotta Martini 4586/1 [A. Martini, *Orfeo* (*Orpheus*), terracotta, 30 cm in height, provenance from the artist] -17 [A. Martini, *Maternità* (*Motherhood*), terracotta, 36 cm in height, provenance from the artist] L.70.000
20 - bolli fattura N. 2 Martini L. 850
22 - vs/ versamento L. 200.000
30 - libri nel mese di luglio L. 4.500
agosto
28 - vs/ versamento L. 100.000
settembre
14 - vs/ versamento L. 100.000
sommano L. 695.000 = L. 580.000
vs/ dare a saldo L. 115.000

22. Account from the Galleria del Milione to Gianni Mattioli (Archivio Mattioli)

Milano 28 aprile 1949
Preg. Sig. Gianni Mattioli
situazione alla data odierna;

1948
marzo
30 - libri a credito nel mese L. 3.000
luglio
1 - liquidazione Siviero per De Chirico
1 - mediazione a Silva L. 10.000
1- rimborso a Siviero per foderatura L. 25.000
1 - A Siviero ns/ Soffici L. 45.00
========== L. 80.000
7 - Vs/ versamento in conto L. 100.000 così ripartite
- ai 2 Forni saldo conto L. 36.650
- al Milione in conto L. 63.350 = 63.350
22 - Vs/ versamento in conto L. 200.000,-
così ripartite;
- ai 2 Forni saldo conto L. 90.000
- al Milione in conto L. 110.000
========== L. 110.000
31 - libri nel mese L. 4.500
agosto
28 - Vs/ acquisto terracotta Martini L. 400.000
settembre
14 - Vs/ versamento in conto L. 100.000
30 - libri nel mese L. 5.975
ottobre
1 - prestito alla Galleria L. 1.200.000
30 - zinco dipinto da Sironi L. 24.000
30 - libri nel mese L. 6.100
novembre
1 - prestito alla Galleria L. 100.000
18 - prestito alla Galleria L. 300.000
25 - venduto De Chirico N. 5289 [G. de Chirico, *Gladiatori nel circo* (*Gladiators in the Ring*), oil on canvas, 38 × 46 cm] L. 120.000,-
25 - bolli fattura vendita De Chirico L. 2.000
30 - libri nel mese L. 4.000
dicembre
30 - libri del mese L. 22.000
1949
gennaio
15 - pagato doppia foderatura e restauro suo autoritratto Funi L. 3.500
febbraio
29 - restituito libro Orlando Furioso L. 3.200
a riportare L. 555.075 = L. 2.096.550

1949 riporto L. 555.075 = L. 2.096.550

marzo
30 - venduto Sironi N. 3661 [M. Sironi, *Uomo e donna* (*Man and Woman*), 1945, media unknown, on cardboard] L. 28.000
30 - bolli fatt. vendita Sironi 360
30 - libri nel mese 300
aprile
2 - venduto Tosi N. 5285 [A.Tosi, *Natura morta con pera* (*Still Life with Pear*), oil on canvas, 40 × 32 cm] L. 32.000

sommano L. 555.735,- 2.156.550
ns: dare a saldo L. 1.600.815

1949 riporto a nuovo L. 1.600.815

aprile

28 - vs/ acquisto Medardo Rosso – [*Bambino malato* (*Sick Child*)] (bronzo) L. 330.815

28 - vs/ acquisto Boccioni - Paesaggio N. 1136 [U. Boccioni, *Landscape*, 1916, oil on canvas, 55 × 33 cm, from Emilio Jesi (1939), later Rino Valdameri (1942) and Carlo Frua De Angeli (1949)] L 150.000

28 - vs/ acquisto Marussig - Alberi N. 1473 [P. Marussig, *Alberi fioriti* (*Trees in Bloom*), 1917, oil on canvas, 55 × 70 cm, from Rossi] L. 120.000

sommano L. 600.815 = L. 1.600.815
ns: dare a saldo L. 1.000.000

23. Draft of a simple contract ('scrittura privata') between Pietro Feroldi and Gianni Mattioli (Archivio Mattioli)

I sottoscritti
Feroldi Avv. fu residente a Brescia
e
Mattioli Giovanni detto Gianni fu Paolo residente a Milano
Stipulano e convengono
1) l'Avv. Feroldi vede e vende con la presente al Sig. Mattioli, che accetta, n. 87 pezzi, come da elenco controfirmato dalle parti ed allegato alla presente, i quali costituiscono la "Collezione Feroldi" nell'attuale sua consistenza, opere tutte che il venditore dichiara di sua esclusiva proprietà e possesso, libere da pesi, oneri o diritti di terzi.
2) Il prezzo della presente vendita è fissato dalle parti in lire ventiseimilioni da versarsi dal compratore al venditore o rispettivi avanti causa come appresso:
seimilioni alla firma di questo atto
diecimilioni alla fatturazione dei primi 15 pezzi
cinquemilioni entro il 31 dicembre 1949
cinquemilioni entro il 30 marzo 1950.
3) La proprietà della Collezione si trasferisce ad ogni effetto al momento della firma della presente, mentre l'acquirente si riserva di procedere al ritiro delle opere ripartitamente ed a proprio insindacabile giudizio; nel frattempo il venditore viene costituito custode della Collezione nel suo complesso ed in ogni singola opera, e si obbliga alla diligenza necessaria ed opportuna data la particolare natura degli oggetti affidati alle sue cure.
4) Le formalità in corso relativamente all'esposizione a New York di parte delle opere della Collezione saranno condotte a termine dal venditore il quale provvederà peraltro ad impartire tempestive e tassative istruzioni all'ente organizzatore della mostra perché i pezzi vi figurino esposti al nome del Sig. Mattioli ed allo stesso siano esclusivamente indirizzate tutte le relative comunicazioni.
5) Il venditore si obbliga a costituire l'acquirente beneficiario di tutte le polizze di assicurazione della Collezione sia in Italia che all'estero fin dal momento della firma del presente atto.
6) L'acquirente provvederà di conservare la ossatura essenziale della raccolta e di organizzarla convenientemente nella villa di proprietà Boneschi sita in Meina (Lago Maggiore).
7) Le parti si riservano di predisporre e perfezionare di comune intesa le opportune scritture definitive del presente accordo e si obbligano sin d'ora reciprocamente ad adempiere l'una verso l'altra quelle formalità che fossero comunque ritenute necessarie al miglior perfezionamento dello stesso. In particolare il venditore si impegna a provvedere a sue cure *e spese* [crossed out nel testo] alla fatturazione secondo gli accordi che verranno presi in capo all'acquirente delle opere compravendute al prezzo unitario che il compratore gli indicherà, e ciò man mano saranno ritirate; per le opere da esporre a New York la fattura verrà compilata prima della loro spedizione da Brescia.
8) La stesura degli atti di cui al precedente articolo è affidata ai Signori Avvocati .... Feroldi di ... Franco Mattioli i quali fungeranno anche per quanto possa occorrere, da arbitri amichevoli compositori, senza obbligo di formalità di sorta, designando ove necessario quale terzo l'Avv. Vermondo Brugnatelli.
9) Il venditore dà tutte le più ampie garanzie d'uso mentre l'acquirente dichiara di sottoporsi agli oneri ed obblighi imposti dalle autorità tutorie del patrimonio artistico nazionale.
10) La firma della presente vale anche quale quietanza per il primo versamento di cui al precedente paragrafo 3),
Letto approvato e sottoscritto in Milano in duplice esemplare il .... maggio 1949 alle ore ...
Avv. Pietro Feroldi

Elenco opere Raccolta Feroldi[1]

DE CHIRICO
1 - Le muse inquietanti = Tav. 10
2 - Ettore e Andromaca = Tav. 11
3 - Enigma dell'ora = Tav. 8
4 - La grande torre = Tav. 9
5 - Autoritratto = Tav. 12
6 - Don Chisciotte
7 - Uva = Tav. 13
8 - Notre Dame [crossed out]
CARRÀ
9 - Amante ingegnere = Tav. 1
10 - Tramonto a Belgirate = Tav. 2
11 - Casine sul Sesia = Tav. 3
12 - Mattino al mare = Tav. 4
13 - Capanni
14 - Velieri = Tav. 5
15 - Assisi
16 - Natura morta
MORANDI
17 - Paesaggio = Tav. 18
18 - Frammento bagnanti
19 - Natura morta = Tav. 19
20 - Fiori = Tav. 20
21 - Conchiglie = Tav. 21
22 - Natura morta = Tav. 22
23 - Natura morta = Tav. 23
24 - Bottiglia bianca
25 - Paesaggio bolognese
26 - Paesaggio sottobosco = Tav. 24
27 - Paesaggio con casine = Tav. 25
28 - Piccola natura morta

29 - Fiori
30 - Paesaggio con brolo
31 - Natura morta = Tav. 26
32 - Natura morta blu
33 - Acquarello
SCIPIONE
34 - Bozzetto Cardinale = Tav. 30
35 - Studio pel Cardinale = Tav. 31
36 - Natura morta
DE PISIS
37 - Boulevard Sebastopol
38 - Ritratto di vecchio = Tav. 7
39 - Natura morta [crossed out] Venezia
CAMPIGLI
40 - Donne con l'ombrello = Tav. 6
SIRONI
41 - Il cavallo bianco = Tav. 32
GUIDI
42 - Fanciulla tedesca = Tav. 15
43 - Testina
44 - Bozzetto per il bagno = Tav. 6 (fasc. Guidi)
TOSI
45 - Sensore
46 - Natura morta = Tav. 36
ROSAI
47 - Mio padre = Tav. 27
48 - Giocatore di toppa = Tav. 29
49 - Chiesa a Poggiocaiano = Tav. 28
50 - Natura morta
SOFFICI
51 - Nudo = Tav. 34
52 - Paesaggio
GARBARI
53 - La Pigna
LONGANESI
54 - Donna romana
CASSINARI
55 - Testa di donna
GUTTUSO
56 - Donna alla finestra
SEVERINI
57 - Natura morta
ZANDOMENEGHI
58 - Donna in giardino = Tav. 37
59 - Paesaggio
DERAIN
60 - Testa di ragazza = Tav. 41
MATISSE
61 - Donna seduta = Tav. 40
UTRILLO
62 - Lapis à Gill [*sic* for Le Lapin Agile] = Tav. 38
63 - Paris à banlieu = Tav. 39
ROUSSEAU
64 - Natura morta = Tav. 43
SISLEY
65 - Le Loing = Tav. 44
BRAQUE
66 - Natura morta = Testata pag. I°
PICASSO
67 - Natura morta = Tav. 42
SOUTINE
68 - Bambino
RENOIR
69 - Paesaggio a Cagne
MODIGLIANI
70 - Nudo rosa = Tav. 17
FUNI
71 - Natura morta = Tav. 14

Disegni:
ROUSSEAU
72 - Nudino = pag. XVIII°
CEZANNE
73 - Estaque = pag. IX°
MODIGLIANI
74 - Testa = pag. XV
PICASSO
75 - Maternità = pag. XXI°
GARBARI
76 - Sibilla = pag. VII°
LEGER
77 - Tre figure
SCIPIONE
78 - Nudo di donna
DE CHIRICO
79 - Cavalletto = pag. XI°
MARINO
80 - Nudo = pag. XXII°

Sculture:
MARINI
81 - Nudo grande, bronzo
82 - Ritratto di Melotti
MARTINI
83 - Mia figlia
84 - Bozzetto
85 - San Marco
MESSINA
86 - Ritratto
ROMANELLI
97 - Ritratto
FONTANA
88 - Testa donna, terracotta
===========
[manuscript] cancellato il n. otto (restano 87 pezzi)
Avv. Feroldi

[1] The plate numbers ('Tav.') refer to *Le grandi raccolte d'arte contemporanea. La Raccolta Feroldi*, presented by Guido Piovene, Milan, Edizioni del Milione 1942.

24. Typewritten list giving the estimated price and the sale price of the works from the Feroldi collection (Archivio Mattioli)

Raccolta Feroldi

N.	Riferimento	Artista	Titolo	£[1]	£[2]
1		Carrà	Amante ingegnere	1.000	680
2	1078	" "	Crepuscolo	300	190
3	5436	" "	Casine sul Sesia	300	190
4		" "	Mattino al mare	350	215
5	5437	" "	Veliero	340	200
6	5434	" "	Capanni	200	120
7	5455	" "	Natura morta	150	85
8	5435	" "	Assisi	150	85
9	5456	Campigli	Figure	180	100
10	5464	Cesetti	Mandria	25	15
11	1087	De Chirico	Enigma dell'ora	900	600
12	923	" "	La grande torre	600	380
13		" "	Muse inquietanti	4.000	2.550
14	1082	" "	Ettore Andromaca	2.000	1.275
15	1606	" "	Autoritratto	600	380
16	1607	" "	Uva	300	190
17	1043	" "	Cavallo	150	90
18	5454	" "	Cavalletto	20	12
19	5457	De Pisis	Vecchio	150	90
20	5458	" "	Parigi	100	60
21	5429	" "	Canale	65	35
22	5463	Funi	Natura morta	120	70
23	3993	Garbari	La pigna	100	60
24	5481	" "	Disegno La Sibilla	20	10
25	1650	Guidi	Fanciulla	100	60
26	2760	" "	Bozzetto bagno	100	60
27	5426	" "	Testina	45	25

N.	Riferimento	Artista	Titolo	£[1]	£[2]
28	5462	Guttuso	Fanciulla	35	20
29	5429	Longanesi	Figura	10 12.410	6
30	5483	Marino	Disegno	20	12
31		Modigliani	Nudo	8.000	5.100
32	5480	“ ”	Disegno	80	50
33	5442	Morandi	Frammento bagnante	300	190
34	5448	“ ”	Paessaggio 1914	400	250
35		“ ”	Bottiglie e fruttiera	750	490
36	5439	“ ”	Fiori	300	190
37	5446	“ ”	Nat. morta (conchiglie)	300	190
38	5438	“ ”	Natura morta scura	300	190
39	5443	“ ”	Natura morta caraffa	300	190
40	5444	“ ”	Paesaggio 1941	300	190
41	5445	“ ”	Paesaggio 1941	300	190
42	5449	“ ”	Natura morta	300	190
43	5447	“ ”	Paesaggio 1936	300	190
44	5451	“ ”	Natura morta 1941	300	190
45	5441	“ ”	Fiori campestri	250	150
46	5450	“ ”	Paesaggio	300	190
47	5440	“ ”	Acquarello	80	50
48	5452	“ ”	Natura morta	300	190
49	5453	“ ”	Natura morta	300	190
50		Rosai	Padre	200	120
51		“ ”	I giocatori di toppa	160	100
52	5431	“ ”	Chiesa	120	70
53	5461	“ ”	Fruttiera	90	50
54	5427	Scipione	Natura morta	250	150
55	5428	“ ”	Studio Cardinale	450	320
56		“ ”	Cardinale	500	340

N.	Riferimento	Artista	Titolo	£[1]	£[2]
57	5482	Scipione	Disegno	23	12
58	5489	Severini	Natura morta	45	26
59	5459	Sironi	Cavallo	180 27.908	100 17.713
60	5432	Soffici	Paese	50	30
61	5433	“”	Nudo	100	60
62	2226	Tosi	Sensore	70	40
63	5460	“”	Natura morta	120	75
64	5466	Zandomenghi	Donna giardino	290	180
65	5467	“”	Paesaggio	220	125
66	5476	Braque	Natura morta	270	160
67	5478	Cézanne	Disegno	220	75
68	5465	Derain	Testa	500	300
69	5477	Léger	Disegno	630	17
70	5472	Matisse	Figura	1.500	960
71	5473	Picasso	Natura morta	900	600
72	5479	“”	Maternità (disegno)	100	60
73	5474	Renoir	Paese	350	220
74	5471	Rousseau	Natura morta	3.650	2.370
75	5468	Sisley	Paesaggio	1.500	960
76	5475	Soutine	Bambino	550	320
77	5469	Utrillo	Strada	1.000	640
78	5470	“”	Lapin	900	600
79	1502	Rousseau	Disegno	900	600
			SCULTURE		
80		Marino	Nudo grande-bronzo	500	320
81		“”	Ritratto di Melotti	200	120
82		Martini	Mia figlia-terracotta	180	100
83		“”	Bozzetto-bronzo (Vittoria)	180	100
84		“”	San Marco-bronzo	200	120

N.	Riferimento	Artista	Titolo	£[1]	£[2]
85		Messina	Ritratto-bronzo	100	55
86		Romanelli	Ritratto-bronzo	100	55
87		Fontana	Tesa donna-terracotta	100 41.808	55 26.500

[1] Estimated price; [2] Sale price

25. Manuscript letter from Fernanda Wittgens to Angela Maria and Gianni Mattioli (Archivio Mattioli)

[on 'Pinacoteca di Brera – Milano' letterhead]

5 maggio 1949
Carissimi,
almeno un fiore vi dica quello che Fernanda esuberante nelle cose piccole ma taciturna nelle grandi non riesce a dirvi: la commozione per il gesto di Gianni e della sua Cicci di salvare all'Italia i documenti della civiltà artistica moderna. Il nastrino è tricolore perché il gesto è, prima ancora che di passione artistica, di italianità.
Vi abbraccio con affetto e *gratitudine*
Fernanda

A Cicci e Gianni Mattioli, via Manzoni 41a

26. Typewritten letter from Romeo Toninelli to Gianni Mattioli (Archivio Mattioli)

[on 'Palazzo Serbelloni-Milano' letterhead]

Milano, 8 Giugno 1949
RT/st

Egregio Signor
Dr. Gianni Mattioli
Via Manzoni 41 a
Milano

Caro Mattioli,
Le mando la distinta delle opere rappresentate nell'Esposizione in modo che Lei possa subito vederne l'importanza, in attesa di ricevere il catalogo che mi farò premura di farLe pervenire ai primi di luglio.
Circa la *Materia* sarei naturalmente lieto che andasse a far parte della Sua Fondazione, italiana, piuttosto di un'altra istituzione straniera, anche perché si tratta dell'opera più importante di Boccioni.
Il quadro misura 150×230 ed è stato esposto in tutte le capitali d'Europa e già una volta in America; pubblicato, come Lei sa, per la prima volta nel libro sul futurismo di Boccioni; poi sull'*Histoire de l'Art Contemporaine* [*sic*] di Christian Zervos – edizione Cahier d'Art, Paris – tav. 357 nel 1938, sul giornale "Comœdia" di Parigi il 21 giugno 1913 e sulla rivista inglese "The Sketch" il 29 aprile 1914, documenti dei quali io possiedo la copia originale. Dell'opera, come Le è noto, non esiste nessuna variazione o altre repliche.
Lei conosce l'offerta che ho avuto ($ 6500,-) e che io ritengo inadeguata; andrebbe benissimo invece nel caso nostro, pronto anche, se crede, a trattare la somma visto lo scopo culturale della Sua Fondazione.
È superfluo raccomandarLe la massima segretezza soprattutto per quanto si riferisce al valore che, nel caso ci accordassimo, metà dovrebbe essere versato in America e metà in lire a Milano con Suo comodo.
Attendo Sue notizie a New York per la fine del mese con preghiera di indirizzare presso Mr. Wheeler - c/o Museum of Modern Art - II West - 53rd Street - N.Y.
Con molti cordiali saluti.
Toninelli

Boccioni – futurista: 2 sculture – 10 pitture – 16 disegni o gouache
De Chirico – metafisica e romantico: 10 opere più disegni
Modigliani ; 2/3 sculture - 10 opere - 6 disegni
Carrà - futurista, metafisico e marine : 9 opere più disegni
Morandi - dal metafisico fino al 1949 : 13 opere - 5 acqueforti
Campigli : 6 opere
Sironi - futurista, metafisico fino al 1949 : 6 opere
Scipione : 4 opere
De Pisis : 4 opere
Manzù: 5 bronzi grandi e piccoli - 6 disegni
Marino Marini : 8 bronzi grandi e piccoli - 15 disegni
Martini Arturo : 4 bronzi e terracotte
Rosai - futurista : 6 opere
Casorati : 4 opere
Mafai : 4 opere
Balla - futurista : 4 opere - 6 disegni o gouache
Fazzini : 4 bronzi - 4 disegni
Tosi : 3 opere
Guidi : 2 opere
Borra : 2 opere
Fontana - ceramiche : 3 opere
Soffici - futurista : 2 opere
Donghi : 2 opere
Severini - futurista : 9 opere

Oltre una rappresentanza di giovani come Guttuso 6, Afro 2, Cassinari 3, Santomaso 2, Cagli 1 tempera e 1 disegno e alcuni altri.

27. Typewritten letter from Pietro Feroldi to Gianni Mattioli (Archivio Mattioli)

[on 'Avv. Pietro Feroldi – Brescia' letterhead]

18 giugno 1949
Egr. Sig. Gianni Mattioli
Milano

A conclusione dei nostri colloqui che si sono svolti in un ambiente di sincera cordialità, Le preciso le mie decisioni che hanno già incontrato il Suo consenso.
Lei ha conosciuto le cause che mi vi hanno portato. Non mi era più possibile custodire tutta la mia raccolta negli angusti locali, nei quali ho dovuto trasferirmi per volontà della Banca proprietaria, dai maggiori e ben illuminati che godevo in precedenza. Inoltre (e la circostanza assumeva gravità eccezionale), ho dovuto adattarmi a un ingresso comune e promiscuo con altri inquilini dello stesso piano dove il mio studio non risulta difeso che da una portina a vetri.
Tuttavia non senza titubanza per la sua gravità, ho accolto la di Lei gentile proposta di trasferire parte della mia raccolta a Milano, per ora, in locali messi a disposizione da Lei, mantenendole sempre il carattere di aperte al pubblico.
Soprattutto mi ha lusingato il fatto che il complesso dei quadri così trasferiti, non solo rimanga intatto nella parte sostanziale, per cui essi sono stati riconosciuti ed apprezzati nel campo degli studiosi (anche se negletti e trascurati in Brescia dai concittadini), ma venga fuso con un gruppo di altre opere del medesimo livello e sempre arricchite in prosieguo di tempo così da colmare l'attuale lacuna di Gallerie d'Arte Moderna in Italia.
Un impulso così alto doveva agire sul mio animo con forza determinante a quella decisione che, Ella vorrà comprendermi, rappresenta per sempre per me il dolore di un distacco.
Prendo atto con animo grato delle cortesi profferte che Ella mi fa di considerarmi sempre persona di casa nelle sale che ospiteranno la raccolta.
Voglia, egregio amico, darmi il benestare della presente lettera il cui contenuto porterò a conoscenza della Sovrintendenza delle Arti.
La saluto con deferenza e viva cordialità
Pietro Feroldi

28. Tyewritten statement by Avv. Alessandro Brass, followed by a manuscript statement signed by Boniface Allasia (Archivio Mattioli)

Venezia, 19.6.1949
Dichiarazione
Dichiaro che il quadro dipinto ad olio su cartone, della misura 59,5 × 72,5, raffigurante *Portrait de Frank Haviland* eseguito da Amedeo Modigliani circa nel 1915 e da me affidato per la vendita alla Signora R. Boniface Allasia (Milano, Viale dei Mille 27), proviene dalla collezione del defunto mio Padre il pittore Italico Brass dal quale lo ho ereditato essendo io il suo unico erede. *Detto quadro è quindi di mia esclusiva, libera ed assoluta proprietà.* = Detto dipinto fu esposto nel 1931 presso la Galleria Marcel Bernheim di Parigi ad una Mostra postuma delle opere di Amedeo Modigliani ivi tenuta nel Giugno 1931 ed è quello che figura nell'elenco del catalogo di detta Mostra. Detto quadro è l'originale della riproduzione a pag. II del volume "Modigliani" di Arthur Pfannstiel, pubblicato a Parigi nel 1929 dall'editore Marcel Seheur.
In fede
Alessandro Brass

Dietro pagamento il quadro sopra citato è stato da me ceduto al Signor Gianni Mattioli.
In fede
Boniface Allasia
il 19.9.49

29. Manuscript letter from Gino Ghiringhelli to Gianni Mattioli (Archivio Mattioli)

[on 'Galleria d'Arte Il Camino mostre periodiche d'arte – Il Milione opere d'arte – Milano Via S. Andrea n. 1' letterhead]

Roma 17 dicembre 1949

Caro Gianni,
eccoti la relazione di queste mie due giornate piene a Roma. Marinetti: ebbi l'appuntamento per il caffè dopo la colazione a casa sua ieri pomeriggio. I dipinti della mostra di New York[1] non li ha ancora ricevuti. Vidi però il Boccioni *Giocatore di calcio* (*Foot Baller*) e ne ho avuto una grande impressione tanto che non mi so spiegare come non è stato scelto dagli americani. Di gran lunga superiore a *Materia*, di poco più piccolo (circa 160 in quadro); è il dipinto più vicino ai cubisti perché il soggetto è completamente dominato da un perfetto sincronismo plastico, più acceso di essi nel colore sul tema azzurro.
L'autoritratto sempre di Boccioni pre-futurista, bello ma non superiore assolutamente al tuo recentemente acquistato del quale ha le stesse misure.
Di Carrà il ritratto di Marinetti, già Contessa Casati, che non mi piacque molto.
Tre Balla discreti.
La conversazione è stata subito impostata su un suo netto rifiuto a vendere malgrado le mie precise offerte di pagamento per contanti. Ella non può vendere così subito perché le opere sono per testamento di proprietà delle bambine, e poi perché Ella pensa suo dovere per la memoria di Marinetti cederli a una fondazione che dovrebbe riunire tutte le opere futuriste pittoriche e letterarie. Quindi cedere tutto il blocco con tutta la storia critico letteraria custodita in 5 casse e comprendente ben 5 manoscritti inediti di Marinetti.
Poi mi disse che altri da Milano le hanno chiesto da oltre un anno il Boccioni *Elasticità* ma che Ella non lo ha ceduto pur sentendosi impegnata moralmente, e a un certo punto tirò fuori il tuo nome. Vidi il pericolo di creare una gara e per smontarla e dimostrarle che poi chi comprende la grandezza di Boccioni e del futurismo sono pur sempre poche persone ho scoperto le carte di-

cendole che io comperavo per il mio cliente Mattioli, e la fretta era motivata per essere in vendita ora a Milano il dipinto *Materia* con una richiesta in partenza su uno, e che io prevedo di poter avere a un massimo di 800 e la nostra incertezza tra i due pezzi per essendo *Materia* più noto e più archetipo. Reagì prontamente a questa mia esposizione con giudizi di riserva per questo dipinto esponendosi forse fin troppo.
Ma la sua decisione era stata troppo esplicita sull'apertura della conversazione e io capivo che non avrei condotto nulla in porto.
Ella forse verrà a Milano il 22 e si farà viva da te. Io l'ho lasciata facendole intravedere che io personalmente mi interessavo alla pubblicazione degli ultimi manoscritti inediti di Marinetti, specialmente di uno dal titolo "Milano città futurista" e che poi avrei cercato di agire a Milano per la formazione di una fondazione sul Movimento futurista.
Né mi era possibile ottenere di più sul momento. Ho lasciato invece l'incarico al dott. Monotti che mi aveva fissato l'appuntamento e che mi aveva accompagnato di proseguire in questi giorni la penetrazione adducendo il motivo che per legare la Edizione del Milione alla pubblicazione del manoscritto e per trovare alleati alla fondazione è opportuno cedere un pezzo e allargare così l'interesse e gli impegni sul futurismo. Monotti, che è il mio agente fidato e provato a Roma, agirà in questo senso in questi giorni e l'ho lanciato che faccia un'offerta a 600 in pronti contanti, a salire fino a 700.
Se Benedetta[2] venisse veramente a Milano in questi giorni regolati.
Mi scordavo di dirti che prima di lasciarla mi sono fatto promettere che in ogni caso si ritenga impegnata prima di cedere un pezzo a chiunque farmi un telegramma con diritto di prelazione. Ella ha pienamente accettato.
Poi sono stato dalla Sarfatti. Anch'essa non vende però mi ha fatto accompagnare per vedere tutti i pezzi.
Interessante: Boccioni *L'antigrazioso* futurista della forza e del tipo *Bevitore* di Jucker. Dimensioni 80 × 80 circa. Molto bello nel tono grigi e rossi, importante e significativo. Per: Sironi: *Ciclista* olio su cartone 70 × 80 circa con carte collate. Importante.
Funi: il *Motociclista* = tempera su cartone 120 × 80 ottimo pezzo futurista.
Con il conte Gaetani, genero della Sarfatti[3] ho avuto due lunghi colloqui nei quali nel ripetermi che la Contessa non aveva intenzione di vendere voleva indagare sulla cifra che io avevo intenzione di spendere. Gli ho precisato che un Sironi può raggiungere un massimo da 200 a 300 e che un Boccioni sui 500. Fu dopo queste mie precisazioni che si decise a portarmi a vedere le opere. Vidi anche 2 Severini di scarso valore.
Concludendo:
lasciare lavorare Monotti con Benedetta e al mio ritorno a Roma dare l'assalto decisivo sui 700 per *Elasticità*.
Fallendo questo, agire sulla Sarfatti per l'*Antigrazioso* sulle 500-600. Però io vorrei sentire il tuo parere e scrivimi a: G.G. presso Krugell=Minori (Salerno).
io tengo il tesoro affidatomi intatto su di me. Io parto domani per Napoli.
In attesa ti saluto caramente
tuo Gino Ghiringhelli

[1] 'Twentieth-Century Italian Art,' New York, The Museum of Modern Art, April-September 1949.
[2] Benedetta Cappa Marinetti, widow of Filippo Tommaso Marinetti.
[3] Livio Gaetani, husband of Fiammetta Sarfatti, daughter of Margherita.

30. Copy of Typewritten letter from Gianni Mattioli to Gino Ghiringhelli (Archivio Mattioli)

Espresso

Milano, 20 dicembre 1949
Caro Gino,
ho ricevuto oggi la tua gradita lettera di sabato e mi affretto a risponderti.
Ti ringrazio per le esaurienti notizie datemi circa i contatti romani. Ecco in breve righe il mio parere, visto che tu lo richiedi e non vuoi approfittare della carta bianca da me datati:
Marinetti: Sono quasi vent'anni che non rivedo il *Footballer* di Boccioni e potrei anche sbagliarmi. Ricordo però che si trattava di un grande quadro quadrato e per il mio gusto di allora non lo avrei messo in primissima fila. Però può darsi che mi sbagli e rivedendolo mi ricreda. Comunque, sia per il soggetto che per le dimensioni, non ne riterrei opportuno l'acquisto. Punterei invece su *L'Elasticità* e sulla cifra da te detta sono senz'altro d'accordo.
Mi potrebbe anche interessare, se ad un prezzo conveniente, uno dei tre Balla che tu definisci discreti.
Sarfatti: *L'anti-grazioso* di Boccioni è il quadro di cui ti avevo parlato e se ben ricordi, ti avevo detto che a me piace in un modo straordinario. Riterrei opportuno acquistarlo se sulla base da te indicata. Idem per Sironi e Funi.
Ad ogni modo, come dettoti, hai carta bianca; cerca di fare per il meglio. L'ideale sarebbe se tu potessi, lasciando eventualmente anche una caparra, avere l'impegno dei singoli pezzi e definire di comune accordo al tuo ritorno a Milano.
Perdona i fastidi che ti do, dimentica i quadri e passa un bel Natale col sole, mare e cielo e senza collezionisti!
Coi più vivi auguri anche da parte di mia moglie, gradisci i miei più affettuosi saluti.

31. Manuscript letter from Gino Ghiringhelli to Gianni Mattioli (Archivio Mattioli)

[on 'Il Milione Galleria d'Arte Moderna' letterhead]

Atrani, 22 dicembre 1949

Caro Gianni,
spero avrai avuta la mia lettera da Roma che ti dava relazione esatta di quanto avevo visto e ti proponevo il Boccioni.
Da Roma non ho avuto in questi giorni altre notizie, ma le aspetto.
Non so quindi se la Sig.ra Benedetta è venuta il giorno 22 (cioè oggi) a Milano, come mi disse lo sperava, e nel qual caso cercherà di te e ti sarà possibile concludere il discorso iniziato da me e forse così convincerla ad entrare nel concetto della cessione.

Sia perché in fondo l'offerta di denaro liquido la lusinga più di quanto non lo voglia confessare, sia perché il dipinto nella tua raccolta sarebbe pur sempre vivo e utile ai fini della storicità del futurismo per la pubblicazione in colori che ne faremo con una diffusione che nessun museo pubblico è in grado di fare. E poi in definitiva ci invoglierà ad appoggiare le pubblicazioni che costituiranno la base per una documentazione storico bibliografica del movimento futurista dal '10 al '40, delle grandi pubblicazioni il Museo ne sarà il depositario degli originali.

Nel caso che Benedetta non intenda retrocedere dal suo proposito di non cedere, noi abbiamo sempre la possibilità di un accordo con la Sarfatti per l'*Antigrazioso* e il Sironi *Ciclista* che sono due dipinti di alto interesse, e pei quali si potrebbe sentire con un'offerta complessiva di 700.

Come ti ho scritto il Boccioni della Marinetti *Elasticità del cavallo* non l'ho ora rivisto perché non ancora riconsegnato dalla mostra di New York, però lo ricordo assai assai bene per averlo esposto al Circolo delle Grazie due anni fa, cosicché lo posso a memoria confrontare con l'*Antigrazioso* e ritenere che se il primo è più aderente agli enunciati del dinamismo futurista, il secondo, più vicino ai cubisti, è pittoricamente e plasticamente più realizzato, sostenuto su valori grigi contrastati e con pochi elementi in rosso. Cosicché si può dire che entrambi hanno un'importanza fondamentale nella produzione di Boccioni, né io saprei in definitiva a quale dei due dare la precedenza nella scelta.

A Roma, e questo non te lo scrissi, mi sono anche interessato a fondo per la raccolta Casella e presto spero sapere qualcosa in merito, soprattutto per il Carrà *Pino sul mare*, e di questo tieni molta segretezza.

Con me conservo naturalmente intatta la busta che mi hai consegnato.

Non appena avessi notizie da Roma ti risponderò. Intanto gradirei avere un tuo scritto con il tuo pensiero.

Non devi però ritenere che se non ho voluto concludere subito, né mi era possibile senza un'intesa con te, possa continuare un fatto che pregiudichi dei vantaggi. Vi ho riflettuto e sono anche convinto che un rialzo dei futuristi dovrà certamente avvenire, non sarà così istantaneo. Il futurismo assumerà sempre maggiore importanza più entrerà nella storia, ma il suo valore commerciale sarà sicuramente di lenta affermazione, pur essendo sicuro.

Approvo senz'altro il tuo interesse per questo movimento e rivedendo nei giorni scorsi a Roma questi pezzi, mi sono maggiormente convinto di questa verità.

In attesa di leggerti, per l'indirizzo rivolgiti a Ceroni[1] che ha la situazione aggiornata dei miei spostamenti, ti auguro buone feste e ti prego di trasmettere i miei omaggi alla tua Gentil Signora.

Qui vado completando alcuni gravi lacune che avevo per non avere visto mai gli originali dell'arte che si trovano in questa superba regione Salernitana.

Con care cordialità

Credimi tuo aff.

Gino Ghiringhelli

[1] Ambrogio Ceroni, employee of Galleria del Milione and author of important studies on Amedeo Modigliani.

32. Account of the Galleria del Milione to Gianni Mattioli (Archivio Mattioli)

Milano 12 gennaio 1950
Preg. Sig. Gianni Mattioli

Situazione alla data di oggi;
1949
maggio
10 - pagato dogana arrivo cornici dipinti da Brescia L. 2.861
10 - mancia facchini e colazione allo chaffeur a Brescia L. 3.000
giugno
1 - vernice pei dipinti avuti da Brescia L. 670
11 - venduto Rosai N. 5431 [O. Rosai, *Chiesa di Poggio a Caiano* (*Church in Poggio a Caiano*), 192[?], oil on canvas, 30 cm wide, ex Feroldi] L. 70.000
30 - pagato telaio suo De Pisis L. 535,-
luglio
10 - vs/ acquisto Campigli N. 4023 [M. Campigli, *Composizione di figure* (*Figure Composition*), 1942, charcoal, 29.5 × 46 cm, on deposit] L. 11.000,-
10 - vs/ acquisto Sironi N. 3683/1 [M. Sironi, *La mia amica Margherita* (*My Friend Margherita*), lithographic pencil, 26 × 17 cm, on deposit from the artist] L. 4.500,-
25 - supporto legno maschera Marini L. 1.600
26 - zinchi rame Modigliani e Carrà L. 41.500
settembre
10 - zinchi rame per De Chirico (*Muse*) L. 22.000
10 - cassa imballaggio per Modigliani inviato a Venezia L. 3.500
14 - pagato per foto Modigliani L. 1.200
novembre
5 - pagato base statua Marino L. 7.435
5 - pagato per foto Scipione L. 1.200
15 - venduto Soffici N. 5432 [A.Soffici, *Paese* (*Village*), oil on canvas, 34 × 41 cm, ex Feroldi] L. 30.000,-
15 - libri nel mese di aprile dalle Edizioni L. 30.150
30 - pagato foto ritratto Modigliani L. 1.200
30 - telegramma alla Colomba L. 230
30 - catalogo mostra Bruxelles L. 2.500
dicembre
15 - venduto Martini *Mia figlia* L. 100.000
15 - venduto Guidi N. 1650 [V. Guidi, *Ragazza tedesca* (*German Girl*), 1931, 45 × 51 cm, ex Feroldi] L. 60.000
15 - ns/ teca tipo grande con 6 vetri L. 16.000
15 - vs/ acquisto Albers N. 523 [J. Albers, *Züsammen* (*Together*), 1933, woodcut, 23 × 22 cm; *Gegenüber* (*Opposite*), 1933, woodcut, 45 × 25 cm] e 525 e bolli fattura L. 20.300
20 - cornicette, vetri, cornici e passe-partout disegni Marini e Carrà L. 3.000

sommano L. 174.831 = 260.000,-
vs/ avere a saldo L. 85.619

33. Copy of typewritten letter from Gianni Mattioli to Fortunato Depero (Archivio Mattioli)

Espresso
Milano, 30 Gennaio 1950
Via Principe Amedeo, 5

Caro Depero,
Ho ricevuto la tua cara lettera del 28 corrente. Mi interesserebbe di conoscere *al più presto* se tu hai un quadro della tua primissima epoca futurista, che sia in stato abbastanza buono, anche se non perfetto.
In caso affermativo, vedi di farmelo avere con la maggiore velocità, perché tenterei di metterlo nel gruppo futurista che pare si faccia a Parigi.
Mi interesserebbe inoltre di sapere chi può avere dipinti futuristi di Balla e di Russolo; Balla non ha più alcuna opera – solo un disegno che mi ha mandato poco fa – e la Famiglia Russolo non ha più assolutamente nulla. Tu non conosci e ricordi nomi di raccoglitori od amici che possano avere loro opere? Anche per questo siimi preciso con la tua consueta velocità.
Tanti cari saluti a Rosetta anche da parte di mia moglie e tu gradisci un affettuoso abbraccio

34. Account from the Galleria del Milione to Gianni Mattioli (Archivio Mattioli)

Milano 6 febbraio 1950

Preg. Sig. Gianni Mattioli
situazione contabile ad oggi;
- Vs/ avere come da situazione precedente 85.619
- Vs/ acquisto Guidi N. 2189 [V. Guidi, *Paesaggio con uomini e dirigibile* (*Lanscape with Men and Dirigible*), oil on panel, 72 × 58 cm, from the father of the artist] 60.000
- bolli fattura vendita Guidi 980
- versate a Johnson per vs/ conto 34.000
- Vs/ acquisto libri dalle Edizioni di ottobre 6.830
- Vs/ acquisto libri dalle Edizioni di novembre 27.300
- vs/ acquisto dipinto Severini N.8 100.000 [G. Severini, *La guitare* (*The Guitar*), 1918, oil on canvas, 80 × 65 cm]
- pagato per N. 5 montature disegni Boccioni 2.500,-
- versate 1° acconto a Rosmini[1] 100.000,-
- rimborsato versamento a Rosmini 100.000,-
- 2° versamento a Rosmini 50.000,-
- ns/ provvigione per vendita Morandi da Lei effettuata 20.000,-
- pagato per vetro al vs/ Modigliani 1.350
- vs/ acquisto Campigli N. 5652 [M. Campigli, *Donna velata con scialle* (*Woman Veiled with Shawls*), 1946, oil on canvas, 48 × 82 cm, from Balzarotti] 220.000
- bolli fattura acquisto Campigli 1.850
- pagato fattura N. 68 Cromografiche per cliché suo Modigliani 57.900,-

sommano 682.710 185.619
ns/ avere a saldo L. 497.091

11.2.1950 = versate £. 500.000 = [manuscript]

[1] Egle Rosmini, ex companion of Arturo Martini.

35. Typewritten letter from Giovanni Ponti to Gianni Mattioli (Archivio Mattioli)

[on 'Ente Autonomo La Biennale di Venezia' letterhead]

Venezia, 12 marzo 1950

Egregio Signore,
La ringrazio vivamente per la concessione delle opere di Sua Proprietà per la XXV Biennale.
Mi spiace soltanto che Lei abbia già impegnato *Materia* di Boccioni, dipinto che mi sembrava indispensabile per una mostra sul futurismo.
Segnalo ai sottocommissari della Mostra di Medardo Rosso le due opere in Suo possesso e non mancherò di tenerLa informata sulle loro decisioni.
Con rinnovati ringraziamenti, voglia gradire i nostri migliori saluti.

Il Commissario Straordinario
On. Prof. Giovanni Ponti[1]

[1] Commissioner extraordinary of the Ente Autonomo 'La Biennale di Venezia' and president of the exhibition.

36. Account from the Galleria del Milione to Gianni Mattioli (Archivio Mattioli)

Milano 30 marzo 1950
Preg. Sig. Gianni Mattioli
Principe Amedeo 5

Situazione alla data d'oggi;
1950
gennaio
31 - ns/ avere come da situazione prec. L. 497.091
febbraio
10 - vs/ versamento L. 500.000
10 - vs/ acquisto N. 5 disegni Boccioni L. 66.000
10 - bolli fatt. acquisto Boccioni L. 900
10 - vs/ acquisto 2 dip. Gino Rossi L. 100.000
10 - da noi venduto De Chirico N. 1043 di vs/ proprietà [G. de Chirico, *Cavallino* (*Foal*), oil on canvas, 33 × 22 cm, ex Feroldi] L. 90.000
10 - bolli fatt. 377/378 vendita De Chirico L. 1.900
15 - versate a Egle Rosmini per vs/ conto L. 60.000
15- N. 2 telefonate a Venezia per vs/ dip. Modigliani L. 470
23 - venduto Campigli N. 5653 vs/ propr. [M. Campigli, *Testa di fanciulla* (*Head of a Young Girl*), 1945, oil on canvas, 33 × 47 cm] L. 90.000
27 - vs/ acquisto Funi N. 3046/ [A. Funi, *Nudo* (*Nude*), 1928, oil on canvas, 58 × 64 cm] L. 2.000
27 - vs/ acquisto Sironi N. 3682/4 [M. Sironi, *Palcoscenico* (*Stage*), tempera, 23 × 24 cm] L. 2.500
27 - vs/ acquisto Marussig N. 1683/18 [P. Marussig, *Chiesa di campagna* (*Rustic Church*), 1935, pencil, 16 × 12 cm] L. 1.000
27 - vs/ acquisto Paulucci [*sic*] N. 1583/9 [E. Paulucci, group of six drawings] L. 1.000,-

27 - vs/ acquisto Guidi N. 3274/1 [V. Guidi, *Nudo seduto* (*Seated Nude*), 1944, pen, 18 × 24 cm, deposit of the artist] L. 2.000
27 - vs/ acquisto Miori N.3426/2 [L. Miori, *Bosco con casolare* (*Wood with Hut*), 1944, ink, 24 × 17 cm] 1.500
marzo
8 - pag/ clichè zinco per Modigliani L. 28.500
8 - pag/ clichè zinco per Chagall L. 27.500
8 - pag/ clichè zinco per grande Breveglieri L. 63.500
20 - vs/ acquisto Signac L. 200.000
22 - vs/ versamento L. 200.000
22 - bolli fatt. 384-385 Signac L. 980
22 - al restauratore per la divisione n. 2 Rossi, doppia foderatura e restauro L. 10.000
22 - al restauratore per doppia foderatura e restauro al Morandi (*Fiori*) L. 7.000
22 - versate a Egle Rosmini per vs/ conto L. 40.000

sommano L. 880.000 = L. 1.113.841
ns/ avere a saldo L. 233.841 = L. 1.900 [manuscript]
L. 1.111.941 [manuscript]
L. 880.000
L. 231.941 [manuscript]

5/4/1950 versate a saldo L. 231.941 [manuscript]

37. Manuscript letter from Fernanda Wittgens to Gianni Mattioli (Archivio Mattioli)

[on 'Sovrintendenza alle Gallerie – Milano' letterhead]

21 sera [pencil addition: 20.04.50]
Caro Gianni
ho trovato finalmente la lettera per l'arazzo [F. Depero, *Cavalcata Fantastica* (*Fantastical Cavalcade*), 1920, tapestry in lenci cloth, 273 × 376 cm, property of Umberto Notari] e te la mando. Vorrei però che tu non facessi sacrifici. Mi pare un po' caro, perché per tutti gli altri arazzi chiede £ 500.000 e per questo solo la cifra di tutto è … un po' molto.
Grazie ancora per tutte le tue affettuosità, in questi 40 giorni di passione per l'apertura di Brera mi vedrai spesso molto giù: sai che quando si è alla fine la responsabilità schiaccia. Ma ho anche tanta serenità e so che finirà bene.
Ti abbraccio fraternamente
Fernanda

38. Copy of typewritten letter from Gianni Mattioli to Fernanda Wittgens (Archivio Mattioli)

Milano, 21 Aprile 1950
Cara Fernanda,
Ti ritorno la lettera di Notari[1]. Data la particolare mia amicizia con Depero, egli mi pratica dei prezzi sempre molto bassi.
Mi sembra che la cifra richiesta per l'arazzo della *Cavalcata* sia così elevata, da non presentare l'opportunità di una seria controfferta.
Penserei dunque, se tu sei d'accordo, di dare passata alla cosa.
Grazie ancora di tutto e tanti, tanti cari saluti

[1] Umberto Notari, publisher, collector, patron of Fortunato Depero, friend of the Futurists and financial supporter of the 'Novecento Italiano' group.

39. Typewritten letter from Lionello Venturi to Gianni Mattioli (Archivio Mattioli)

[on 'Lionello Venturi. Corso Trieste 42, Roma' letterhead]

24 Aprile 1950

Sig. Gianni Mattioli
Via Manzoni 41 A
Milano

Caro Sig. Mattioli,
Subito tornato a Roma da Milano dove la cortesia Sua e della Signora mi procurarono un soggiorno molto piacevole, volli assaggiare le possibilità del mercato internazionale relativo a Cézanne. Le risposte non si sono fatte attendere ed eccone il risultato. Lei ha, immagino, il mio libro su Cézanne[1] e quindi cito il numero del mio catalogo:

No. 373 Dollari 35,000 [*Portrait de Chocquet* (*Portrait of Chocquet*), 1879-1882, 46 × 38 cm]
" 436 " 55,000 [*Environs de Gardanne* (*Environs of Gardanne*), 1885-1886, 60 × 73 cm]
" 445 " 24,000 [*Le Clos normand* (*The Normandy Field*), 1885-1886, 50 × 65 cm]
" 451 " 40,000 [*Maison dans la campagne aixoise* (*House in the Aix Countryside*), 1885-1887, 79 × 85 cm]
" 464 " 50,000 [*Marroniers et ferme du Jas de Bouffan* (*Chestnut Trees and Farm of the Jas de Bouffan*), 1885-1887]
" 792 " 24,000 [*Arbres et rochers* (*Trees and Rocks*), 1900-1906, 61 × 50 cm]

Poiché il Cézanne che Lei comprasse sarebbe il solo esposto al pubblico in tutta Italia, mi pare che dovrebbe essere tale da dare da solo il carattere tipico del maestro. E perciò escluderei sia il n° 373 che per quanto bellissimo è un po' speciale, sia i numeri 445, 451 e 792 che anche se meravigliosi non sono punti di arrivo dell'attività di Cézanne e per una ragione o per l'altra non darebbero al giovane pittore italiano il senso pieno e completo di quello che è stato Cézanne.
Resterebbero in gara i numeri 436 e 464, ambedue bellissimi e perfetti e famosi.
Il 464 è anche uno dei pochi quadri di Cézanne che sia stato firmato da lui, cioè è stato da lui considerato come finito e perfetto, e tale da dargli soddisfazione. Aggiunga che il quadro si trova a Parigi, e quindi Lei può vederlo facilmente. Possiamo combinare di farvi un salto per vederlo. D'altra parte il 436 che si trova a New York, è un poco più grande e costa 5mila dollari di più. Forse per il 464 posso ottenerLe una piccola riduzione, per il 436 nessuna riduzione. Comunque sono due tali capolavori che preferirei di non fare io stesso la scelta.

Con il più devoto ossequio alla Signora, La saluto cordialmente
Lionello Venturi

[1] L. Venturi, *Cézanne. Son art, son œuvre*, Paris, Rosenberg 1936.

40. Copy of typewritten letter from Gianni Mattioli to Lionello Venturi (Archivio Mattioli)

Milano, 27 Aprile 1950
Via Manzoni N. 41/A

Gentile Professore,
Ho ricevuto la Sua gradita lettera del 24 corrente e Le sono molto grato per quanto in essa mi comunica.
Le indicazioni circa le disponibilità e le quotazioni di Cézanne, sono per me particolarmente interessanti, ma – come dettoLe – per quest'anno almeno non penso di avere possibilità di procedere all'acquisto di pezzi di tale importanza per la mia raccolta.
Nel momento in cui il mio desiderio avrà – come ardentemente spero – la possibilità di concretarsi, mi permetterò di disturbarLa e di chiedere il Suo cortese appoggio.
Con tutta probabilità, io sarò a Parigi l'8 maggio e mi fermerò sino all'11, in modo da poter assistere all'inaugurazione della Mostra d'Arte Moderna Italiana. Se in quest'occasione Lei pure si trovasse a Parigi, sarei veramente felice di passare qualche ora in Sua compagnia e potremmo vedere assieme il Cézanne 464, a titolo informativo.
Conto di farLe avere presto il secondo gruppo di fotografie promessoLe e la piantina dell'appartamento di Via Senato.
Per ora ho incominciato ad appendere i quadri tenendo conto dei Suoi preziosi suggerimenti, ma non sarà possibile ottenere una sistemazione organica finché non mi saranno ritornate le opere attualmente ad Amsterdam, Parigi e Venezia.
Desidero porgerLe ancora un grazie per tutta la bontà e l'interessamento da Lei dimostratimi. Voglia gradire i miei più devoti saluti.
Suo dev.mo
[G. Mattioli]

41. Manuscript letter from Fernanda Wittgens to Gianni Mattioli (Archivio Mattioli)

[on 'Pinacoteca di Brera – Milano' letterhead]
9 mattina [later addition: 'maggio 1950']

Caro Gianni,
tutto bene. D'Ancona[1] sedotto da te (sei un genio!) parte domani. Stamattina mi ha telefonato Dell'Acqua[2] che era indispensabile perché sarebbe nato uno scandalo. Egli è ospite del governo francese. Confermata la cerimonia semplice ma solennissima perché celebrata dagli Esteri e Istruzione francese.
Evviva! Ci copriremo di gloria noi Amici di Brera! Tutto questo significa che i nostri quadri sono piaciuti.
Dell'Acqua e Ghiringhelli sono felici.
Ghiringhelli ti fa dire che è all'Hotel du Rhône
Rue Rousseau
tel. Gutenberg 59-00
Buon viaggio. Felice che tu ci rappresenti così simpaticamente a Parigi ti abbraccio
Fernanda

La mia cipria è
N'aimez que moi (!!!)
colore Ivoire nacré, da Caron
Rue de la Paix 10.
Non rivelare questi segreti del Sovrintendente

[1] Paolo D'Ancona, founder and first holder of the chair of History of Art at the Università Statale of Milan from 1923 to 1938, barred from teaching following the anti-Jewish racial laws and reinstated as director of the Institute from 1945 to 1955.
[2] Gian Alberto Dell'Acqua, official of the Sovrintendenza alle Gallerie della Lombardia.

42. Manuscript letter from Fernanda Wittgens to Gianni Mattioli (Archivio Mattioli)

[on 'R. (*sic*) Sovrintendenza alle Gallerie – Milano' letterhead]

25 maggio [19]50
Caro Gianni,
ti mando la risposta di Pallucchini[1] che può servirti per lo Duca[2].
Ho detto a Cicci per la visita della Della Pergola[3] alla tua collezione. Quando vuoi: io sono occupata solo dalle 15 alle 16 domani in tribunale ma posso in tutte le altre ore. Sarò molto contenta di fare quattro chiacchere carine.
Ciao
Fernanda

Se sei troppo occupato con i tuoi clienti posso condurre io la Della Pergola e poi andiamo magari a salutare la Cicci

[1] Rodolfo Pallucchini, Secretary of the Venice Biennale.
[2] Giuseppe lo Duca, writer.
[3] Paola Della Pergola, director of the Galleria Borghese and personal friend of Fernanda Wittgens.

43. Typewritten letter from the vice-presidents of the Associazione Amici di Brera to Gianni Mattioli (Archivio Mattioli)

[on 'Associazione Amici di Brera e dei Musei Milanesi – Milano' letterhead]

31 maggio 1950
Gentile signor Mattioli,
mentre La ringraziamo vivamente per il generosissimo contributo apportato alla realizzazione della Mostra del Novecento Italiano attualmente allestita nel Musée National d'Art Moderne di Parigi, ci è gradito comunicarLe che la Mostra stessa ha avuto un solenne riconoscimento ufficiale con l'intervento all'inaugurazione di S.E. Jox, di S.E. Quaroni Ambasciatore d'Italia a Parigi, di alte personalità dell'amministrazione francese delle Belle Arti, dei rappresentanti del corpo diplomatico e della stampa.

Dalle prime segnalazioni a noi pervenute si delinea fin d'ora il successo della nostra iniziativa che indubbiamente costituirà un importante apporto alla conoscenza dei più alti valori dell'arte italiana nel quadro dell'arte europea contemporanea.
Abbiamo il piacere di annunciarLe che nella seduta di Consiglio del 29 maggio, la S.V. è stata nominata all'unanimità socio benemerito degli "Amici di Brera"; quale socio e collaboratore della Mostra Le offriamo un esemplare dello speciale volume di Cahiers d'Art che Christian Zervos ha voluto pubblicare in occasione della nostra manifestazione, e che Le verrà spedito direttamente da Parigi.
Anche a nome del Consiglio Le porgiamo il nostro saluto riconoscente,
i Vicepresidenti
[illegible signatures]

44. Typewritten letter from Bruno Bolzani to Gianni Mattioli (Archivio Mattioli)

[on 'B. Bolzani Galleria d'Arte – Milano' letterhead]

Milano 17.6.1950
Egr. Sig. Mattioli Gianni
Milano
Via Manzoni 41 A
Non so se il Dott. Paolo Stramezzi le ha già parlato di un magnifico quadro di Carrà futurista di mia proprietà [C. Carrà, *Manifestazione interventista* (*Festa patriottica*) (*Interventionist Demonstration* [*Patriotic Holiday*]), 1914]. Ad ogni modo, dietro suggerimento dello stesso, mi permetto prima di cederlo ad altri, di sottoporlo alla Sua attenzione sapendolo un raccoglitore di queste opere.
Lieto di una sua visita, gradisca i miei distinti saluti.
B. Bolzani

45. Copy of typewritten letter from Gianni Mattioli to Bruno Bolzani (Archivio Mattioli)

Milano, 19 giugno 1950
Spett.
Galleria Bolzani
Milano
Corso Matteotti, 20
Raccomandata
Ho il piacere di accompagnarVi assegno di £ire 60.000.- a saldo del quadro futurista papier collé di Carrà [C. Carrà, *Manifestazione interventista* (*Festa patriottica*) (*Interventionist Demonstration* [*Patriotic Holiday*]), 1914], oggi da Voi vendutomi.
Vogliate gradire i miei più distinti saluti.

46. Copy of typewritten letter, with manuscript corrections, from Fernanda Wittgens to Benedetta Cappa Marinetti (Archivio Mattioli)

San Remigio di Pallanza, 21.6.50

Cara Benedetta,

la tua lettera mi raggiunge quassù mentre sono convalescente di una piccola operazione alla gola fatta subito dopo l'inaugurazione di Brera. Di qui proseguirò per l'alta montagna e sarò a Milano solo a metà luglio. Gli "Amici di Brera" prima che io partissi mi hanno detto che tutto è regolare, e difatti le opere d'arte da Parigi sono andate regolarmente a Londra. Infatti la Mostra di Londra non era un'ipotesi ma una certezza, *fissata insieme a quella di Parigi dal novembre*; e difatti i quadri tuoi sono stati assicurati per Parigi-Londra. Non comprendo come possa esserti nato il dubbio per Londra. Ad ogni modo ho mandato una lettera agli "Amici di Brera" che ti scriveranno.
Per Zervos[1] risponderò una specie di lettera-testamento così sarà tutto chiaro.
Io ho cercato, d'accordo con gli amici di Zervos, di aiutarlo; ma lui ha reso impossibile l'aiuto. Rifacciamo una volta per sempre la storia.
1° - Progetto del Cahier d'Art: novembre 1949.
Preoccupata della vendita di un'opera sull'arte italiana, faccio incontrare Zervos col distributore di libri francesi in Italia Caputo. Zervos stabilisce con Caputo che, per vendere, ci vuole un libro che costi sui 2700 frs. Caputo si impegna a prenderne molte copie anche 500 se Zervos gli dà la priorità di 15 giorni sulla vendita.
2° - *Maggio 1950*. Zervos scrive a Frua[2] che ha fatto un Cahier d'Art grandioso e chiede se sottoscrizioni degli "Amici di Brera", Frua sente la situazione (gli "Amici di Brera" sono in costituzione e non hanno capitali) e risponde che gli "Amici" non possono e che lui e Mattioli sono impegnati con la Mostra. Zervos dunque sa *prima che deve agire con i librai e cercare diffusione*. Invece non perfeziona l'accordo con Caputo. Scrive a me che Caputo non si fa vivo. Protesto, e Caputo dice che è Zervos che tace. Allora scrivo a Zervos e lui dice che Caputo è un fallito e gli deve del denaro. E allora perché l'ha messo di mezzo? Morale: esce il Cahier d'Art. L'Italia è zeppa di pellegrini, si potrebbero far vetrine di Cahier d'Art, lanciarlo ecc. Zervos non manda copie. Facciamo fare recensioni, ma il libro non c'è. Parlo con gli editori perché lo comprino e lo smercino. Nessuno vuole farlo. Ma Einaudi (che si assume di finanziare il libro di Zervos sulla Sardegna) consiglia di appoggiarsi a Ghiringhelli che è pronto a lanciare il libro.
Zervos *per dispetto* risponde che si guasterebbe con Hachette, che non può fare sconti a particolari ecc. Gli contesto che oggi ancora Caputo ha il libro col 50% di sconto. *Su questo punto Zervos non risponde*. Nel frattempo viene fuori il racconto romanzato dell'impegno di Gianni per 1000 copie! Conosco Gianni: se dice una cosa la fa pagandola all'ultimo sangue. E in un anno conosco Zervos: la realtà è per lui un gioco che varia secondo le sfumature della sua immaginazione. Sicché, cara Benedetta, credo a Gianni. Ti dirò di più. Non gli avevo detto nulla della lettera di Zervos con quel racconto; ma Zervos ha riscritto a me e ha scritto a Frua. E Gianni e Ghiringhelli insieme sono dipinti male anche per l'acquisto di un Braque. Ho *dovuto* dare a Gianni la lettera di Zervos. Non avrei mai voluto farlo, ma Gianni ha diritto di difendersi.
Conclusione: non ci sono copie in Italia. Gli "Amici di Brera" ne hanno comprate alcune direttamente, ma sic-

come le pagano £ 11.700 mentre da Caputo costano £ 8.000 nessuno sarà così stupido da ordinare direttamente. Io ho fatto una Conferenza-Stampa e, in occasione della Mostra di Londra, usciranno altre recensioni. Se Zervos mandava duecento copie in deposito a Ghiringhelli lo si sarebbe aiutato a venderle. *Così Zervos ha fatto fallire ogni aiuto.* Restano le cento copie che S.E. Andreotti ha promesso di comperare per propaganda. Ha voluto la richiesta ufficiale degli "Amici di Brera" che è stata mandata appoggiata da un amico di Gianni il dott. Bodrero e siamo in attesa dello sviluppo della pratica. *Abbiamo coscienza di aver fatto il massimo nella situazione reale.* Ti dirò di più: ho capito ora che abbiamo pagato cara la collaborazione di Zervos al lancio dell'Arte Italiana a Parigi. Io sono stoffa di soldato, e gioco sempre forte; quindi a me, per quanto sia stata attaccata direttamente in modo poco simpatico per una donna, non fa male. Non sono stata ferita. Ma agli *"Amici di Brera"* è dispiaciuto trovarsi colpiti dalle antipatie di Zervos che si sono riversate su di loro, poveri capri espiatori. Su queste antipatie che Zervos ha, io ho molto meditato. Tutti quelli che creano sono odiati: una parte dunque è fatale. Ma la quantità di odio per cui Zervos veramente è un isolato, questa dipende non dal suo potere creativo ma da quell'altro potere, negativo e distruttivo che, purtroppo, si incrocia in lui. Io l'ho sperimentato in questi mesi; e ho giurato a me stessa che, come amico, individualmente, per il suo grande ingegno continuerò a considerarlo e a tenere i legami. Ma non lo porterò in una iniziativa collettiva e sociale perché lui stesso, per il primo, distrugge le basi di ogni collaborazione. Se avesse preso accordi preventivi e precisi per il Cahier d'Art, se avesse chiesto *prima* l'impegno invece di dichiarare che gli bastava l'aiuto datogli da Gianni col mese di soggiorno in Italia e da me per le fotografie, se non sbandava fuori dei limiti col Cahier a 4.500 frs. non si verificavano tutte queste recriminazioni. Se da *lui stesso non partivano tante chiacchiere*, non si sarebbe aperto l'immondezzaio dell'articolo di Guido di San Lazzaro[3] su "Omnibus".
Ecco dunque tutta la verità. Non ti avrei parlato mai così, se le lettere di Zervos non creassero un angoscioso dramma a cui tu fai coro con la tua lettera. Basta di essere messi in stato di accusa quando si ha la coscienza pulita e si è agito con perfetta lealtà e coerenza. La nostra coscienza individuale e di *italiani* è *pulitissima* e respingiamo ogni chiara o larvata accusa di indifferenza o, peggio, di aver mancato alla generosità. Sono gli altri che hanno creduto che la generosità fosse debolezza, e ora sono stritolati dalla ribellione. Bisogna non suscitare mai nei generosi il senso di essere stati giocati.
Scrivo a te così perché tu sei donna che vedi gli estremi: a nessun altro potrei parlare così.
E bisogna che ti dica anche che *non risponderò ad una tua risposta*. Troppo grande è lo sforzo già di scriverti di queste cose in questi giorni in cui mi concedo finalmente – avendola pagata con un'operazione leggera ma pericolosa – una tregua spirituale. Mi sono rifiutata a Milano di entrare nel gioco di martirizzamenti che Zervos ama. Sono rimasta sempre armoniosa e serena anche vicina a questo curioso gigante del bene e del male, dell'intelligenza e della povertà ... ma lasciamo le definizioni. Non mi lascio torturare nemmeno a distanza. Faccio tutto il possibile; campagna di stampa, Andreotti per le cento copie, coccolamento di Einaudi perché collabori e assuma impegni ecc. Ma nessuna azione su Gianni, nessuna pressione su creature di alto livello spirituale che devono essere libere di agire secondo la loro coscienza. E nessun rimorso mio perché ho la coscienza pulita. Ecco il mio testamento che è un suggello definitivo sulla questione Zervos. Scusami ma ora sono proprio stanca. A metà luglio sarò di nuovo sulla breccia.
Con saluti amichevoli

[1] Christian Zervos, director of the magazine *Cahiers d'Art*.
[2] Carlo Frua De Angeli, textile manufacturer and Milanese collector.
[3] *Lapsus* for Gualtieri di San Lazzaro, art critic residing in Paris and editor of the review *Spazio*.

47. Typewritten letter from Mordechai Narkiss to Gianni Mattioli (Archivio Mattioli)

[on 'The Executive Of The Zionist Organization - The Bezalel National Museum – Jerusalem' letterhead]

3 - VII - 1950
Illmo
Signor Gianni Mattioli
Via Manzoni 41
Milano

Egregio Signor Mattioli,
Ci è stata particolare gioia ed onore di apprendere dalla Signora Cohen-d'Ancona del generoso dono datoci al nostro museo:
Giorgio Morandi, *Natura morta*, acquaforte.
Scipione, *Natura morta*, dipinto a olio.
Arturo Martini, *Maternità*, terracotta.
Mario Sironi, *Uomo accanto al fanale*, dipinto a olio.
Siamo entusiasti del Suo amichevole aiuto per il nostro lavoro d'educazione artistica, propagando così l'arte italiana moderna nel nostro giovane stato. Vorremmo che apprenda che apprezziamo moltissimo il Suo atteggiamento nobile verso di noi.
Naturalmente, non sarà dimenticato di rimarcare il nome del generoso donatore.
Ringraziandola sinceramente di nuovo siamo
colla più profonda stima
M. Narkiss[1]
Direttore

[1] Mordechai Narkiss, founder of the National Museum of Jerusalem.

48. Typewritten letter from Mario Fabiani to Gianni Mattioli (Archivio Mattioli)

[on 'Citta' di Firenze - Mostra di Pittura Contemporanea Italiana in Germania' letterhead]

Firenze, 6 luglio 1950
Illustre Signore,
la Città di Firenze ha assunto la realizzazione di una Mostra di Pittura Contemporanea Italiana in Germania, or-

ganizzata dallo Studio Italiano di Storia dell'Arte di Firenze.
La Mostra, che consisterà di circa 250 opere d'arte, avrà luogo fra l'ottobre 1950 e il maggio 1951 nella Galleria della 'Amerika-Haus' di Monaco di Baviera, e nei Musei di Hamburg, Mannheim e Colonia.
La Mostra è posta sotto il patronato di S.E. Carlo Sforza Ministro degli Affari Esteri, e del dr. Ehard, Presidente del Consiglio dei Ministri della Baviera.
Il Comitato d'Onore della Mostra in Germania è formato dal Presidente del Consiglio dei Ministri della Baviera, dal Ministro della Pubblica Istruzione S.E. Hundhammer, dal Segretario di Stato Sattler, dai Sindaci delle Città di Hamburg, Mannheim, Monaco e Colonia, dal Direttore della Sezione Culturale della 'Amerika-Haus', etc.
Il Comitato Esecutivo Germanico è composto dai sigg. dr Hanfstaengl, Direttore Generale delle Belle Art della Baviera; dr Degenhart, direttore dei Musei di Monaco; dr Ludvig Grote, organizzatore delle Mostre internazionali della Città di Monaco; Mr Stefan Munsing, Direttore della 'Amerika-Haus'; dr Werner Haftmann. Il Comitato italiano è quello segnato in calce.
L'attuale Mostra costituisce la prima grande manifestazione di cultura artistica italiana in Germania, nel quadro della ripresa dei rapporti e degli scambi culturali tra i due Paesi.
La invito a far parte del Comitato Generale di detta Mostra, e sono certo che Ella vorrà onorarci con la Sua ambita adesione, che La prego di volermi cortesemente confermare, indirizzando al Sindaco di Firenze, presso Studio Italiano di Storia dell'Arte, Palazzo Strozzi, Firenze.
Mi abbia frattanto a nome della Città, nonché del Comitato Esecutivo della Mostra, coi più cordiali ringraziamenti e saluti

Il Sindaco di Firenze
Mario Fabiani

49. Copy of a letter from Gianni Mattioli to Christian Zervos (Archivio Mattioli)

Milano, 14 luglio 1950

Egregio Signore [Zervos, manuscript],
ho ricevuto la sua del 30 giugno.
Il fatto che la sig.ra Marinetti abbia ascoltato la nostra comunicazione telefonica non cambia per nulla la situazione; infatti mi sono incontrato con la Signora al suo passaggio di Milano, e le ho dato ogni informazione sulla pratica che il Dr. Bodrero, dietro raccomandazione di Fernanda e mia, stava svolgendo alla Presidenza del Consiglio a Roma a favore del "Cahier d'Art", né Ella mi ha parlato d'altro. D'altra parte anche Fernanda ha parlato nello stesso giorno e lungamente con la Sig.ra Marinetti, senza che le facesse cenno di alcun ipotetico mio impegno.
Fernanda ha tenuto, come tiene, tutti i contatti anche perché in questi ultimi tempi io sono stato molto occupato (lavoro ogni giorno sino alle otto e mezza di sera) ed in più sono stato molto preso per seguire mia moglie nei primi giorni di vita della nostra bambina.
Tutto questo però non sposta la questione di una virgola.
Lei ha capito ben poco di me se può pensare che io faccia la distinzione fra un impegno morale e un impegno materiale: per il mio modo di sentire, sono esattamente la stessa cosa.
Ma mentre io avevo unicamente promesso di fare quanto mi era possibile per il buon esito del "Cahier d'Art", come ho fatto e sto facendo tuttora, Lei ha scritto non a me è vero ma a Fernanda e a Frua:
1° che io avevo preso l'impegno di fare acquistare 1600 esemplari del "Cahier" ridotti (bontà sua) a 1000 e di anticipare subito l'importo a Lei.
2° che io avevo dato l'incarico al Sig. Ghiringhelli di acquistare tramite suo un Braque ritirando tre giorni dopo la mia parola.
Queste due asserzioni sono assolutamente false ed offensive per me.
La vera ricchezza non ci viene data solo dai mezzi materiali ma dalle cose buone che la vita ci può offrire. Mi sento anch'io – ma non so se Lei potrà comprenderlo – un poco più povero dei bei tempi dell'Albergo Manin per aver perduto una illusione.
Non ho nessun gusto per la polemica e questa poi è anche per me particolarmente dolorosa. Le sarò grato se vorrà fare, come io farò, punto con la presente.

50. Account from the Galleria del Milione to Gianni Mattioli (Archivio Mattioli)

Milano 18 luglio 1950

Preg. Sig. Gianni Mattioli
Situazione ad oggi;
1950
marzo
30 - suo debito come da situazione precedente L. 233.841
30 - suo versamento a saldo L. 231.941
30 - bonifico su detto conto L. 1.900
aprile
1 - monografia Bordoni ecc. ecc. L. 3.500
6 - zinco rame De Chirico - *Ettore e Andromaca* L. 24.500,-
10 - suo acquisto Cogorno N. 5737 [S. Cogorno, *Testa di donna* (*Head of a Woman*), oil on canvas, 38 × 73 cm, deposit of the artist], L. 40.000
maggio
8 - ns/ provvigione acquisto Russolo [L. Russolo, *Solidità della nebbia* (*Solidity of Fog*), 1912, oil on canvas, from Margherita Sarfatti] versata L. 30.000
8 - suo prestito per Campigli della Galleria Arte Moderna L. 385.000
9 - da noi venduto suo Sironi N. 4042 [M. Sironi, *Mare con monti* (*Sea with Mountains*), 1946, tempera on paper, 30.5 × 23.5 cm, deposit of the artist] (L. 16.000) L. 14.400
9 - parte bolli fattura vendita L. 250
15 - ns/ versamento a Rosmini vs/ debito saldo L. 40.000
20 - pagato basamenti bronzi L. 25.000
20 - pagato zinco grande Morandi *Fiori* L. 71.000
25 - ns/ teca completa di vetri L. 15.000

giugno

1 - prestateci L. 1.000.000

1 - acquisto e pagato Sironi N. 5725/1 [M. Sironi, *Composizione casa-figura* (*Composition with House-Figure*), tempera, 60 × 30 cm, acquired from the artist] per Castello Sforzesco L. 30.000

1 - pagatoci ns/ provvigione per opere regalate a D'Ancona L. 25.000

15 - prestateci per raccolta Poli L. 1.000.000

16 - suo acquisto disegni Marino 5626/1-2-3-4 [M. Marini, *Giocoliere a cavallo* (*Juggler on Horseback*), 29 × 38 cm; *Giocoliere acrobata su cavallo* (*Acrobatic Juggler on Horseback*) 29 × 38 cm; *Uomo a cavallo* (*Man on Horseback*), 29 × 38 cm; *Cavaliere sdraiato su cavallo* (*Rider Lying on a Horse*), 29 × 38 cm] L. 64.000

16 - suo acquisto Soffici N. 3607/1 L. 15.000 [A. Soffici, *Landscape*, 1938, pencil on paper, 22 × 25.5 cm]

16 - suo acquisto Sironi N. 3765/2 L. 10.000 [M. Sironi, *Tre figure e un bambino* (*Three Figures and a Child*), pencil and charcoal, 22 × 32 cm]

16 - suo acquisto Martini N. 5633/7 [A. Martini, *Figura* (*Figure*), pen, 27 × 44 cm, deposit of Egle Rosmini] L. 30.000

16 - suo acquisto Marussig N. 1683/3 [P. Marussig, *Uomo sulla sedia* (*Seated Man*), 1916, pencil, 35 × 26 cm] L. 6.000

16 - suo acquisto De Pisis N. 3249/2 [F. de Pisis, *Nudo di giovane seduto* (*Seated Nude Youth*), 1944, sepia and watercolor, 23.5 × 32 cm, deposit of the artist] L. 5.500

20 - ns/ versamento a Cairola[1] (oltre al Guidi N. 5650 [V. Guidi, *Venezia, S. Giorgio* (*Venice, San Giorgio*), oil on canvas, 49 × 39 cm] - Morandi N. 4049 [G. Morandi, *Bottiglie bianche e boccale* (*White Bottles and Jug*), 1946, oil on canvas, 52.5 × 33 cm, acquired from the artist] - Carrà N. 5455 [C. Carrà, *Still Life*, 1942, oil on cardboard, 50 × 40, ex Feroldi] L. 40.000

20 - pagato per selezione cartolina Modigliani L. 6.500

20 - pagato per sdoganamento suoi Cahiers d'Art L. 1.000

20 - pagato per suo acquisto Sironi N. 4000 [M. Sironi, *Tempera periodo futurista* (*Tempera Futurist Period*) tempera, 61 × 73.5 cm, on deposit from Signora Sironi, returned 1.10.1946] (prezzo acq. Poli) L. 75.000

20 - pagato per suo acquisto Sironi N. 4385 [M. Sironi, *Manichino* (*Mannequin*), tempera, 68 × 49 cm] (prezzo acq. Poli) L. 45.000

20 - pagato per suo acquisto Sironi N. 5776 [M. Sironi, *La penitente* (*The Penitent*), oil on canvas, 60 × 50 cm] (prezzo acq. Poli) L. 65.000

20 - pagato per suo acquisto Sironi N. 5782 [M. Sironi, *Composizione con cavaliere* (*Composition with Rider*), oil on panel, 28 × 20 cm] (prezzo acq. Poli) L. 30.000

20 - pagato per suo acquisto Sironi N. 5778 [M. Sironi, *Alleluia*, oil on canvas, 40 × 50 cm] a Gritti (prezzo acq. Poli) L. 45.000

976.091,- 2.718.241,- [manuscript]

1950 riporto 976.091,- 2.718.241,-

giugno

30 - quota bolli acquisto Sironi fatt. 424/425 L. 2.160

30 - ns/ provvigione 10% sugli acquisti dei 5 Sironi della raccolta Poli ceduti a prezzo d'acquisto (L. 260.000) L. 26.000

30 - pagate N. 2 basi in legno sculture 8.200,-

30 - ns/ provvigione acquisto Sironi di Gaetani[2] 10.000,-

30 - ns/ provvigione suo acquisto *Dr. Schwarz* di Martini [A. Martini, *Ritratto del dott. Schwarz* (*Portrait of Dr Schwarz*), 1931, bronze, h. 40 cm] con cambio fatto con Cairola - valutato L. 450.000- L.45.000

luglio

6 - suo prestito L. 800.000

6 - suo acquisto dipinto Klee [P. Klee, *Case di notte* (*Houses at Night*), 1920, oil on panel, 17 × 28 cm] L. 200.000

6 - ns/ provvigione 10% su acquisto Klee L. 20.000

6 - sua rimessa in Svizzera per Klee L. 148.222

6 - pagato retino per zinco Chagall L. 600

12 - N. 4 Cahiers d'Art a L. 7.500 L. 30.000

12 - pagato a Bacci per 5 foto caricature disegni Boccioni L.2.500

12 - pagato a Bacci per 2 foto dipinto Rossi - 2 Morandi (per America) e 1 Signac L. 3.200

12 - libri forniti in giugno dalle Edizioni (4.500 + 8.960 + 1.260 + 420) L. 15.140

15 - suo acquisto Morandi *Fiori* N. 5746 [G. Morandi, *Vaso di fiori* (*Vase of Flowers*), 1950, oil on canvas, 26 × 34 cm, acquired from the artist] L. 60.000

15 - parte bolli fatt. 436/437 per acq. Morandi L. 1.000

sommano L. 1.399.981 L. 3.666.46

nostro dare Galleria a saldo L.2.266.572

[1] Stefano Cairola, owner till 1948 of the Galleria della Spiga in Milan, then of Galleria Cairola.

[2] Livio Gaetani, son-in-law of Margherita Sarfatti.

51. Copy of typewritten letter from Gianni Mattioli to Lionello Venturi (Archivio Mattioli)

Milano, 20 Luglio 1950

Gentilissimo Professore,

Faccio seguito alla nostra conversazione telefonica e desidero ancora una volta ringraziarLa di vero cuore per la cortesia che Lei sempre mi dimostra.

Come dettoLe per il Rouault sono del parere di attendere il dipinto ad olio in preparazione che spero riesca bello come il suo! Le confermo invece l'acquisto dell'acquerello di Cézanne rappresentante le rocce di Bibémus [P. Cézanne, *Rochers à Bibémus* (*Rocks at Bibemus*), 1895-1900, watercolor on paper, 47 × 31 cm] al prezzo da Lei indicatomi; mi voglia dire come debbo procedere per il pagamento ed io mi affretterò ad effettuarlo secondo le Sue indicazioni. Quando l'opera Le sarà pervenuta concorderemo insieme per il ritiro.

La ringrazio ancora tanto tanto sia per il Suo interessamento che per il Suo valido ed intelligente appoggio.

Mi auguro di avere presto il piacere di rivederla e frattanto La prego di gradire i miei più devoti saluti.

Suo

[G. Mattioli]

P.S. Accluso alla presente Le ritorno le due fotografie dei Rouault.

52. Manuscript letter from Mario Klaus to Gianni Mattioli (Archivio Mattioli)

Roma 31 luglio 1950
Egregio Signor Mattioli,
ho trattato per il Mercurio che passa davanti al Sole [G. Balla, *Mercurio passa davanti al sole* (*Mercury Passing Before the Sun*), 1914, tempera on paper, 120 × 100 cm].
Bellissimo di colore e di disegno; contrariamente a quanto scritto sul Cahiers d'art, la misura è 100 × 130 firmato in basso a sinistra Balla 1914 (!). Probabilmente lo hanno fotografato in parte per comodità di pubblicazione.
Come Le dissi è una tempera su carta, ma così fresco di colore da essere molto più gradevole di un olio. Posso fornirglielo a £ 270.000 (duecentosettantamila) *franco* Milano.
Potrei venire su verso la fine settimana.
Grato di un'immediata risposta, La saluto distintamente
Mario Klaus

53. Manuscript letter from Gino Ghiringhelli to Gianni Mattioli (Archivio Mattioli)

Caro Gianni,
Sono arrivato oggi, dopo aver lasciato i coniugi Ceroni a Napoli in luna di miele.
Qui mi attendeva un espresso che ti compiego perché ne vedi il testo
Che ne pensi? Evidentemente Magnelli[1] da Parigi vuole palleggiare tra l'offerta avuta da Garretto[2] e Venezia
Vista la cosa sotto questo punto di vista come comportarci? È importante che Gian Ferrari sia con noi.
Io proporrei di trasmettergli la stessa che Garretto ha fatto a Parigi.
Telegrafami il tuo pensiero e cioè quello che debbo rispondere per telegramma a Venezia. Il mio indirizzo anche telegrafico è: Ghiringhelli - Posta Atrani
Resto in attesa.
Qui è una delizia il paesaggio, però fa caldo assai e questa notte a Napoli né io né i Ceroni abbiamo potuto dormire.
La Sig.ª Zanchi è commossa per il vostro regalo e vi ringrazierà quando ... si sarà rimessa dallo stupore.
Scusami la fretta. Ma lo zelo di Gian Ferrari[3] esige urgenza.
Con cari e cari saluti
credimi tuo aff.mo
Gino Ghiringhelli
31.7.1950

[1] Alberto Magnelli, nephew of Alessandro Magnelli, former owner of C. Carrà's *La Galleria di Milano* (*The Galleria in Milan*), 1912.
[2] Paolo Garretto, draftsman, friend of Gianni Mattioli.
[3] Ettore Gian Ferrari, head of the sales office of the Venice Biennale (where *La Galleria di Milano* was in the meantime exhibited) and owner of the Milanese Galleria Gian Ferrari.

54. Copy of a letter from Gianni Mattioli to Mario Klaus (Archivio Mattioli)

Raccomandata - Espresso
Milano, 1 Agosto 1950
Via Manzoni N° 41/A -
Egregio Signor Klaus,
Faccio seguito alla nostra telefonata e Le accompagno assegno di £. 250.000.- per il Balla di cui Lei mi ha parlato con Sua del 31 Luglio u.s.
L'attendo sabato a Milano e Le porgo i miei migliori saluti.
dev.mo
[G. Mattioli]

55. Manuscript letter from Gino Ghiringhelli to Gianni Mattioli (Archivio Mattioli)

[on 'Il Milione Galleria d'Arte Moderna' letterhead]

Atrani, 8.8.50
Caro Gianni,
ebbi il tuo telegramma e l'espresso e ti ringrazio. A Venezia telegrafai l'offerta valida per un milione. Tenendo presente che per la vendita alla Biennale è dovuto il 15%, Magnelli avrebbe un netto di 850 quindi non superiore alla offerta di Garretto.
Da Venezia Gian Ferrari accusandomi ricevuta al mio telegramma mi scrive di aver trasmessa l'offerta con la sua "opera di persuasione affinché la somma venga accettata". Teme però "che la risposta non sia quale noi l'attendiamo, dato che l'opera era stata assicurata per 2 e mezzo" e conclude "comunque stiamo a vedere".
Gli ho risposto che le cifre di assicurazione hanno sempre un valore cautelativo specie quando non si paga il tasso; che il Futurismo, visto anche le recenti recensioni di Londra, non gode poi grande favore di critica in sede estetica, salvo di una certa importanza nel campo di una discussa priorità nell'avanguardia europea; che in ogni modo il mio sforzo è di fermare il "*pezzo*" a Milano, perché entri in una raccolta che sarà quasi pubblica ed è proprio per questa ragione che confido nella sua efficace collaborazione confermandogli però il promesso riconoscimento personale. L'ho ringraziato delle sue premure concludendo che restiamo in attesa della risposta di Magnelli e vedremo se ci saranno altre offerte e se supereranno la nostra. Credo che Gian Ferrari ci aiuterà sinceramente.
Ed ora dovrei dirti di queste mie giornate d'ozio. Ti scrivo davanti alla finestra a balcone della mia stanza, nuda e bianca, che sta a picco sul mare e spazia sulla distesa di colore possente. I monti della costa amalfitana fanno da maestosa quinta, già in ombra, al fondale lontano e tutta scintillante di rosa e azzurri chiarissimi quale appare la sottile striscia della piana di Pesto a ridosso dei monti del Cilento. Dalle rocce sottostanti il sciacquio dell'onda, il pigolio di uccelli dall'agrumeto e lo stridere di una cicala: qui ha veramente stanza il riposo e lo spirito si ricrea.
Vedi un po' se ci sto bene ... tanto da lasciarmi tentare da una pretesa letteraria! Purtroppo penso che già un terzo del mio soggiorno è trascorso, ma ... ma penso an-

che agli amici cari rimasti costassù e, non ti nascondo, con una certa malinconia (di quali complicazioni è mai fatto il nostro spirito?!).
Penso spesso a te con profonda dolcezza, al tuo rifugio che hai saputo crearti ai margini della pianura milanese, prodigiosamente (è il vocabolo esatto) intimo, raccolto che fa tanto bene all'anima. E ne ho conforto perché se hai dimostrato più assiduità di me nello sfidare l'intera canicola in sede a Milano, alla sera ti puoi ricreare lo spirito in tale quiete fra la tua famiglia e meritatamente. Così mi è caro pensarti e augurarti bene e pace.
Con la Signora Zanchi, mia buona e fedele entusiasta compagna fra questa superba natura, parliamo sovente di te con viva simpatia ed ella mi prega di presentare alla Signora e a te i suoi vivi omaggi.
Da parte mia una ... fiera protesta al tuo invito di tenermi lontano per questo riposo dai collezionisti, tra i quali crederti e includerti, e un caldo e affettuoso saluto a tutta la tua famiglia e a te da chi crede di asserti amico affezionatissimo.
Gino Ghiringhelli

56. Copy of a typewritten letter from Gianni Mattioli to Lionello Venturi (Archivio Mattioli)

Milano, 26 Settembre 1950
Via Principe Amedeo N. 5-

Egregio Professore,
Innanzitutto un grazie di cuore per la Sua gentile accoglienza e per la cortesia dimostratami. Unito alla presente Le ritorno l'opuscolo prestatomi, con i miei più vivi ringraziamenti.
Un mio conoscente di Parigi mi ha offerto un Cézanne che dalla fotografia – che mi permetto unirLe – non mi sembra il migliore ottenibile. Il prezzo però – che non conosco ancora esattamente – pare sia particolarmente basso e quindi "abbordabile" anche da me.
Non so se il quadro sia autentico, nonostante le dichiarazioni che lo accompagnano e di cui Le accludo pure copia. Se lo fosse, potrei eventualmente trattarlo riservandomi di cederlo quando mi sarà possibile acquistarne uno più bello. Lei lo conosce ? Mi vuol dire la Sua opinione ?
Grazie anche per questa nuova cortesia e gradisca i miei più cordiali saluti.
dev.mo
[G. Mattioli]

57. Typewritten letter from Lionello Venturi to Gianni Mattioli (Archivio Mattioli)

[on 'Lionello Venturi. Corso Trieste 42, Roma' letterhead]

Roma 28 settembre 1950

Sig. Gianni Mattioli
Via Principe Amedeo 5
Milano

Caro Sig. Mattioli,
Sono io che Le sono grato della sua visita a Roma e della Sua cortesia.
Purtroppo il Cézanne è falso. Ne ho veduti parecchi di simili. Il figlio di Cézanne era un piccolo industriale che dopo il fallimento ha vissuto dando certificati per opere false di suo padre. Pace all'anima sua.
Mille cordiali saluti dal Suo

Lionello Venturi

58. Typewritten letter from Caio Mario Cattabeni to Gianni Mattioli (Archivio Mattioli)

[on 'Comune di Milano - Ripartizione Educazione' letterhead]

Protocollo n. 123967 al 2259/50

Milano 6 ottobre 1950

Ill.mo Dott. Gianni Mattioli
via Manzoni, 41-a
Milano

Oggetto: Commissione Consultiva per la Galleria d'Arte Moderna

La Commissione Consultiva di Studio nominata da questo Assessorato con incarico di coadiuvare l'Amministrazione nel riallestimento della Civica Galleria d'Arte Moderna, ha espresso il voto di potere in una più larga formazione farsi interprete delle varie correnti critiche che militano in tale campo specifico.
Pertanto su assenso della Giunta Municipale mi onoro di invitarLa a far parte di detta Commissione la quale per il corrente anno risulta composta oltre che da Lei dai Signori: Comm. Frua De Angeli, Raffaele Calzini, Prof.ssa Fernanda Wittgens, Lamberto Vitali, prof. Costantino Baroni, prof. Paolo D'Ancona, dott. Paolo Stramezzi, dott. Marco Valsecchi, prof.ssa Stella Matalon.
Con la fiducia che Ella voglia accogliere l'invito, e con tutta stima,

L'Assessore
(prof. Caio Mario Cattabeni)

59. Account from the Galleria del Milione to Gianni Mattioli (Archivio Mattioli)

Milano 28 ottobre 1950

Preg. Sig. Gianni Mattioli
Milano

Situazione contabile alla data d'oggi;

1950
luglio
18- ns/ avere come da situazione precedente L. 2.266.572
23 - costo zinco Sironi (*Bevitore*) L. 23.500

agosto
1- telefonate urgenti alla Biennale L. 580
1 - pagato base in legno per M. Rosso L. 7.500
1 - pagate N.2 teche in fleches L. 27.500
1 - Vs/ acquisto dipinto Wlaming [*sic*] N. 5812 [M. Vlaminck, *Strada di paese* (*Villlage Street*), oil on canvas, acquired from Di Maio] L. 110.000 in sospeso – [manuscript]
1 - parte bolli fatt. 442 acquisto Wlaming [*sic*] L. 1.000
settembre
7 - Vs/ acquisto Dufy N. 4897/3 [R. Dufy, neither signed nor dated, Barbanti deposit] L. 8.000
25 - N. 1 Cahier d'Art spedito a Morandi L. 8.250
22 - pagato a Meloni dipinto *Cavallo* L. 27.500
ottobre
2 - Ns/ provvigione su acquisto N. 2 disegni Modigliani L. 10.000
3 - venduto Carrà N. 1078 [C. Carrà, *Crepuscolo* (*Twilight*), 1922, oil on canvas, 50 × 35 cm: property of Il Milione by exchange Valdameri with Morandi of the Quadriennale as well as Morandi 1079; December 1939: Simonetti by exchange for Marussig no. 1022; June 1949: Mattioli deposit] di vs/ proprietà L. 190.000
3 - venduto De Chirico N. 1607 [G. de Chirico, *Uva* (*Grapes*), 1924–5, tempera on cardboard, 27 × 35 cm, ex Feroldi] di vs/ proprietà L. 190.000
3 - versate ad Egle Rosmini in conto Martini L. 130.000
3 - ns/ provvigione su acquisti Baer[1] L. 40.000
4 - pagato a Borra per dipinto *Cavallo* L. 33.000
4 - pagato a Usellini L. 22.000
4 - Vs/ versamento a Usellini L. 20.000
8 - Vs/ acquisto del Carrà N. 5836 (*Inseguimento* - papier collè) L. 200.000
10 - pagato a Sassu per dipinto *Cavalli* L. 27.500
10 – pagato dipinto *Cavalli* di Sironi L. 25.000
12 - sua cessione dipinto Garbari N. 3993 [T. Garbari, *La pigna* (*The Pine Cone*), 1924, oil on cardboard, 38 × 45 cm, ex Feroldi] a L. 100.000 valutato L. 60.000 ° L.40.000
12 - sua cessione dip. Soffici N. 5433 [A. Soffici, *Studio di nudo* (*Study of a Nude)*, oil on canvas, 34 × 41 cm, ex Feroldi] a L. 80 mila - valutato L. 60mila ° L. 20.000
20 - pagato per N. 20 tavolette in legno L. 10.000
20 - pagato per applicazione a tavoletta del dip. Cavalli di Sironi L. 2.000
20 - pagato foderatura Balla grande L. 7.500
20 - pagato foderatura Balla piccolo L. 4.500
a riportare L. 785.330 = L. 2.866.572
° Incassati direttamente da Sig. Mattioli [manuscript]

1950 riporto L. 785.330 L. 2.866.572
ottobre
24 - Vs/ acquisto Sironi 5842 (tem. futurista) [M. Sironi, *Busto di donna* (*Bust of a Woman*), 1914, ink on paper, 13.5 × 19 cm, acquired from Mimì Sironi] L. 25.000
24 - Vs/ acquisto Sironi 5843 (tem. futurista) [M. Sironi, *Composition*, 1916, tempera, 20 × 27 cm, acquired from Mimì Sironi] L. 25.000
24 - Vs/ acquisto Morandi 5830/1 (acquaforte) [G. Morandi, *Still Life*, 1915, etching, artist's proof, exchanged for another Morandi] L. 10.000
L. 845.330 = L. 2.886.572
Vs/ avere a saldo L. 2.021.242
N.B. - Nella rimanenza a Vs/ credito è compreso il prestito da Voi fatto di L. 385.000 per l'acquisto del Campigli al Museo del Castello.

[1] Vico Baer, resident of New York, friend and collector of Boccioni's work.

60. Typewritten letter from Lionello Venturi to Gianni Mattioli (Archivio Mattioli)

[on 'The Ambassador, Park Avenue, 51st to 52nd Streets, New York 22, N.Y' letterhead]

30 ottobre 1950

Sig. Gianni Mattioli
Via Principe Amedeo 5
Milano

Caro Sig. Mattioli,

Dopo quindici giorni di visite alle gallerie, ecco quello che ho trovato e che può interessarLa:

ROUAULT

presso Paul Rosenberg:
1. *Pitre* (attribuito al 1927, credo sia più tardo 1930-1936)
molto bello di forma, colori vivaci. 26 1/4 × 19 1/4 inches, cioè grande per un Rouault.
Dollari 6500.00

2. *Tête de Pierrot*, 1936, stupendo di colore, profondo, un gran pezzo. 24 1/2 × 18 3/4 inches. Sempre grande per un Rouault.
Dollari 5800.00

presso Knoedler:
3. *Face à face*, 9 1/2 × 13 1/2 inches. Bello, ma piccolo.
Dollari 4000.00

4. *La plume blanche*, c. 1937. Stupendo. 24 1/4 × 29 1/2 inches.
Dollari 10000.00

presso Theodore Schemp:
5. *Ballet russe*, 29 1/2 × 21 inches. Brillante ed elegante.
Dollari 4.000.00

Credo che di questi quadri di Rouault, quello che più rivela il potere creativo dell'artista (eccettuata la *Plume Blanche* che costa troppo) è la *Tête de Pierrot*, di Rosenberg.
Considerati i prezzi raggiunti da Rouault (mi sono sentito domandare 15 e 18.000 dollari) non mi pare che 5800 dollari siano un prezzo eccessivo.

Circa i Degas, che pure ho cercato, preferisco scrivere a Lei quando abbia trovato meglio. Finora per una ra-

gione o per l'altra, nulla che io possa consigliarLe di acquistare.
Ho veduto una serie di quadri moderni, nei musei e presso i privati, da sbalordire, ma la lira costa troppo poco rispetto al dollaro.

Mille cordiali saluti a Lei e alla Signora,

Lionello Venturi

61. Copy of a typewritten letter from Gianni Mattioli to Lionello Venturi (Archivio Mattioli)

Milano, 10 Novembre 1950
- Via Manzoni n° 41/A -

Egregio Professore,

Ho avuto la Sua gentile lettera del 30 ottobre u.s. con le fotografie dei Rouault che Le ritorno unite alla presente.

Benché sia pienamente d'accordo con Lei sull'indubbia qualità dei pezzi mandatimi in visione e non sia rimasto insensibile al fascino della *Tête de Pierrot*, trovo che i prezzi richiesti oggi in America per queste pitture sono per me troppo elevati.

Lei stessa mi aveva indicato come valore per un pezzo simile al dipinto molto bello di Sua proprietà, la base di 3.000- dollari, e miei amici di Parigi mi hanno anche recentemente confermato che un'opera sicura ed abbastanza importante si può ottenere a circa 1.000.000 di Franchi Francesi. Le quotazioni da Lei segnalatemi, sono il doppio della base sulla quale io contavo di rimanere. Di conseguenza, preferisco per il momento dare passata alla cosa ed attendere il pezzo che eventualmente Lei potrà avere da Rouault stesso, ad un prezzo più equo.
Nel frattempo, da alcuni miei conoscenti ho potuto avere un *Paesaggio biblico* [G. Rouault, *Paysage biblique* (*Biblical Landscape*), 1939, oil on panel, 25 × 34 cm] che dalla fotografia mi sembra molto bello, benché un po' piccolo (misura 25 × 35). Detto Paesaggio per me è permutabile alla pari con l'Utrillo del 1925, che, come Lei forse ricorderà, non era molto di mio gusto e che lei stessa non considerava un pezzo da conservare nella collezione.
Il valore del mio Utrillo è oggi di £. 1.000.000 circa che vuol dire avere il pezzo francese per 500.000 Franchi.
Le sono comunque grato per il disturbo che si è presa per me e se vorrà tenermi informato della data del Suo arrivo in Italia, mi farò premura di venirla a salutare a Roma.
Le auguro di vero cuore che il Suo soggiorno americano sia felice e le porti tutte quelle soddisfazioni che Lei può desiderare e merita.
Mia moglie Le ricambia il Suo gentile ricordo ed io La prego di gradire i miei più cordiali saluti.
dev.mo
[G. Mattioli]

Prof. Lionello Venturi
The Ambassador
New York - (USA)

62. Manuscript letter from Gualtieri di San Lazzaro to Paolo Garretto (Archivio Mattioli)

[on 'Spazio-Rassegna delle arti -Redaction Parisienne-M.G.di San Lazzaro' letterhead]

13 novembre [1950]
Caro Garretto,
ho avuto la tua lettera. Sono finalmente riuscito ad aver la fotografia del Rouault, la quale però non dà che una pallida idea della drammatica intensità dell'originale. Te la mando, ma non credo affatto alla possibilità di simili affari per corrispondenza. Il quadro è già stato venduto a un americano che ha versato un anticipo di 600mila franchi (su 1.100.000 fr.) ma sembra che quest'americano non riesca a pagare il resto, è già in ritardo. Il proprietario del quadro si è comunque riservato di restituire l'anticipo e di riprendere la propria libertà d'azione, se l'altro entro 15 giorni non si faccia vivo.
A proposito del quadro di Carrà [C. Carrà, *La Galleria di Milano* (*The Galleria in Milan*), 1912], spero di poter dire a Mattioli qualcosa di nuovo, fra qualche giorno. Gli scriverò direttamente, come mi hai chiesto.
Ho terminato un libro che potrebbe avere un certo successo di vendita, una specie di romanzo. Che ne pensi di Garzanti? È capace di lanciare un libro? Non vorrei che facesse la fine degli altri due, sebbene l'ultimo si sia un po' venduto.
Affettuosamente, tuo
San Lazzaro

63. Copy of a typewritten letter from Gianni Mattioli to Gualtieri di San Lazzaro (Archivio Mattioli)

Milano, 20 Novembre 1950
Egregio Signor
Gualtieri di San Lazzaro
Parigi

L'amico Garretto mi ha informato dell'esito delle démarches fatte a Parigi per il quadro *La Galleria di Milano* di Carrà.
Poiché non ero al corrente che della cosa poteva occuparsi Lei, avevo informato dell'interesse che portavo all'opera diversi Amici e quindi ritengo che alcune, se non tutte, le richieste pervenute per il dipinto in parola siano originate dalla mia domanda.
Attraverso la Signora Garretto, io avevo fatto una offerta direttamente a Magnelli di £ 1.000.000.-, e qualora il proprietario fosse disposto a cedere l'opera su questa base, Lei potrà in qualsiasi momento farmi invio del dipinto e mi troverà pronto a versare immediatamente detta cifra più, se permette, £ire 200.000.- di mediazione per Lei, perché non trovo giusto che abbia a disturbarsi senza alcun compenso.
Non so se mi sarà possibile venire preso a Parigi; mi auguro comunque di aver modo di rivederLa e frattanto Le porgo i miei migliori saluti.
dev.mo
[G. Mattioli]

64. Typewritten letter from Gualtieri di San Lazzaro to Paolo Garretto (Archivio Mattioli)

[on 'Spazio-Rassegna delle arti -Redaction Parisienne-M.G. di San Lazzaro' letterhead]

27 novembre [1950]
Caro Garretto,
scusami, anche presso Mattioli, se rispondo con qualche giorno di ritardo. Il possessore del quadro di Rouault è ancora in viaggio e solo fra due o tre giorni saprò se consente a farlo fotografare. Quanto alla *Galleria* di Carrà, per quanto grande sia il mio desiderio di guadagnare le due cento mila lire promessemi dal tuo generoso amico, non posso dirti ancora nulla di preciso. Magnelli ha avuto delle offerte più cospicue (un milione e mezzo) che non si è ancora risolto di accettare. Come faccio ad offrirgli un milione? Per quanto possa volermi bene, non potrà certo per farmi guadagnare 200 mila lire, perderne, lui, cinquecento. Comunque domani sera viene a cena da me, e cercherò di sapere qualcosa. Scusami presso Mattioli di non rispondergli direttamente, ma non ho il suo indirizzo. Sarebbe bene ch'egli scoraggiasse, con molto tatto, altri intermediari, non per permettere a me di fare l'affare, ma nel proprio interesse, se vuole veramente avere il quadro. Bisognerebbe poi sapere chi ha avuto l'imprudenza di offrire un milione e mezzo. Se non è lo stesso Mattioli, bisognerebbe sorvegliare le mosse dell'avversario.
Salutami tanto tua moglie, e credimi
tuo affmo
San Lazzaro

65. Typewritten letter from Gualtieri di San Lazzaro to Gianni Mattioli (Archivio Mattioli)

30, Rue Jacob, Paris 6
4 dicembre
Egregio dottor Mattioli,
mi scusi se non Le ho risposto prima, ma non mi è stato facile in questi ultimi tempi vedere Magnelli, e esplorarne le intenzioni.
Come avevo già detto a Garretto, sono state fatte a Magnelli per la *Galleria* di Carrà varie offerte, sia dall'Italia che dall'estero. Egli non ha accettato nemmeno le due offerte più alte pervenutegli, una dall'Italia e l'altra dall'estero, di un milione e mezzo di lire. Perciò non ho creduto trasmettergli la Sua, di appena un milione. Se potessi offrirgli anch'io un milione e mezzo di lire (per lui) sono però quasi certo di riuscire a convincerlo, sebbene il fratello, cui il quadro appartiene, gli abbia fissato la cifra di due milioni.
La ringrazio di quanto Ella gentilmente mi propone per la mia mediazione. Sarei lieto di poter concludere quest'affare per Lei, ma non posso evidentemente sperare di decidere, sia pure un caro amico come Magnelli, ad accettare, per farmi piacere, un'offerta molto inferiore ad altre già fattegli e non accettate.
Mi creda, in attesa di una Sua risposta, e con i più cordiali saluti
Suo dev.mo
G. di San Lazzaro

66. Copy of a typewritten letter from Paolo Garretto to Gualtieri di San Lazzaro (Archivio Mattioli)

Milano 7 Dicembre 1950
Via Santo Spirito 24
Carissimo San Lazzaro,
ho visto Mattioli e gli ho detto quanto mi hai chiesto di dirgli in merito al quadro di Carrà ed a quello di Rouault. Gli ho anche consegnato la lettera a lui diretta. Il suo indirizzo è il seguente e ti prego di prenderne nota:
Sig. Gianni Mattioli / Via Principe Amedeo 5 / Milano
Egli mi ha poi telefonato per avvertirmi che mi mandava una nota (sempre sul Carrà) e mi pregava di scriverti in via confidenziale per informarti di quanto contenuto in detta nota. Io ti mando la nota direttamente e, come vedi, le cose stanno come ti dissi a Parigi per telefono: tutte le offerte fanno capo a Mattioli che è l'unico interessato al quadro. L'offerta di Brera è un'offerta fatta da una galleria e la galleria prima offre e poi cerca i soldi.
In ogni modo io credo che lui sarebbe anche disposto a pagare più di un milione, se ciò fosse proprio indispensabile. Vedi tu cosa puoi fare e fagli una proposta concreta, direttamente, magari, poiché ora conosce la situazione da quando gli ho mostrato le tue lettere e deve poter prendere una decisione in merito. La mia impressione personale è che (conoscendo il tipo) si sia messo in testa di avere QUEL quadro perché fa pendant ad uno di Boccioni che è su una parete della sua galleria: per un po' che ne trovi uno della stessa grandezza e futurista addio interesse in quel Carrà. Tanto più che già ha comperato una tela futurista di Carrà ma più piccola. Sai come son questi collezionisti! Dunque bisognerebbe battere il ferro ora che è ancora caldo.
Da quando cerca il Rouault tutti i vari Ghiringhelli gli cercano e trovano Rouault, e perciò finirà col trovare quel che cerca.
Caro San Lazzaro ti saluto molto ed anche mia moglie ti manda i suoi saluti

67. Gianni Mattioli, 'Come ho formato la mia raccolta,' La Biennale di Venezia, I, 3, January 1951, pp. 25-6

[Illustrations: photo-portrait of Gianni Mattioli; Amedeo Modigliani, *Ritratto del pittore Frank Haviland* (*Portrait of the Painter Frank Haviland*); Umberto Boccioni, *Landscape*, 1916; Giorgio Morandi, *Self-Portrait*, 1930]

Prima dei quadri cominciai a raccogliere ritagli di giornale, molti e molti anni fa, da ragazzo. Mi piacevano i dipinti moderni (erano gli anni del futurismo e della metafisica) e li occhieggiavo nelle esposizioni o nelle vetrine, a quell'epoca rare, delle gallerie milanesi. Ma, naturalmente, non avevo allora i soldi per acquistarli, e così, munito di forbici, ritagliavo tutti gli articoli sull'arte moderna che apparivano sui giornali del tempo.

Ritagli e ritagli da riempirne degli album, che tuttora conservo. Se debbo essere sincero, vorrei trascorrere ancora oggi quelle ore di quieto lavoro e d'appassionata lettura, ma purtroppo non ne ho più il tempo.

Un giorno quella mia collezione si arricchì, insperatamente, di una bella tavola a colori, riproducente un dipinto del Blaue Reiter. Ricordo di averla vista in un negozio di macchine da scrivere tedesche, che stava in via Brera; serviva da réclame. Era da poco finita la guerra del 1918. La guardai con desiderio per qualche giorno e finalmente mi decisi ad entrare per chiedere di acquistarla. Osservarono un po' sorpresi quel ragazzino (dovevo avere ancora i calzoni corti) e dopo breve consultazione me la regalarono.

Fra i primi acquisti, ricordo invece – di lì a pochi anni – uno alla Bottega di Poesia, che allora si apriva in via Monte Napoleone, diretta da Emanuele Castelbarco: due disegni di Boccioni, due piccoli fogli che portai gelosamente a casa.

Di ritaglio in ritaglio, di disegno in disegno, passano gli anni e comincio a portare a casa anche qualche dipinto, che amavo cambiare di posto, sull'una o l'altra parete, col piacere di vivere accanto ad essi in una continua sorpresa. Avevo il *Tramonto sul lago* del 1922 di Carlo Carrà, gli *Archeologhi* [*sic*] di De Chirico del 1927, la *Donna ingioiellata* di Campigli, una *Natura morta* di Giorgio Morandi, de Pisis, Funi, Guidi, Sironi, Tosi ed un gruppo di futuristi oltre a sculture di Martini, Manzù e Marini. Più che seguire un criterio di scuola o dedicarmi ad un solo autore, ho sempre preferito compiere una specie di antologia, che andavo man mano selezionando, fra le opere degli artisti della mia generazione, o con essa viventi. E sono sempre stato grato – e lo sono tuttora – a tutti gli artisti per le emozioni che mi hanno donato con le loro opere.

La nuova guerra mi costrinse, purtroppo, a sfollare tutto, e sentii fortemente quella separazione. Ebbi davvero il senso della pace, quando riportai quelle opere nuovamente a Milano.

Debbo ammettere che la fortuna mi fu favorevole in più di una occasione e tanto più lo fu il giorno che mi concesse, qualche anno fa, di imbattermi con un bel gruppo di opere che, pur non possedendole, avevo imparato ad amare da tempo. Tra gli altri dipinti c'era il *Nudo rosa* di Amedeo Modigliani, le *Muse inquietanti* e l'*Ettore e Andromaca* di Giorgio de Chirico, l'*Amante dell'ingegnere* di Carlo Carrà, alcune *Nature morte* di Morandi. Attraverso un raro caso di umana comprensione e di reciproca simpatia, nacque così questo apporto di notevole importanza per la mia collezione, la quale poteva ormai contare su un gruppo di opere che spaziava dal Futurismo alla Metafisica, al miglior Novecento, a Scipione incluso.

Dovessi dire qual è l'opera che tuttora preferisco, per quanto mi riesca difficile scegliere, direi il *Nudo rosa* di Modigliani, per l'estrema sua purezza. Ma l'opera che mi ha dato più emozioni, anche per la sorpresa dell'incontro, è il *Ritratto di Frank Haviland*, pure di Modigliani, uno dei pochissimi dipinti "fauve" di questo eccezionale Artista. Esso venne acquistato, molti anni fa, da un pittore, che lo tenne presso di sé, all'insaputa quasi di tutti. Venuto a mancare il possessore il dipinto tornò alla luce nell'estate del 1949, durante i mesi del maggior caldo, comparve a Milano. Anche questa volta la fortuna fu con me benigna, se fece in modo che io lo potessi incontrare e prendere.

Il mio proposito ora sarebbe di selezionare sempre più la raccolta di opere italiane e, integrando anche il nucleo delle opere straniere, dar vita ad una piccola galleria privata – ma alla quale chiunque abbia interesse per l'arte possa accedere – ora siano rappresentati i principali movimenti che si sono svolti in Europa, dall'Impressionismo in avanti, e faccia testimonianza dell'arte nata nel tempo in cui fui chiamato a vivere.

68. Account from the Galleria del Milione to Gianni Mattioli (Archivio Mattioli)

Milano 7 febbraio 1951

Sig. Gianni Mattioli
Situazione alla data di oggi;

1950
ottobre
30 - riportasi Vs/ avere come da situazione precedente L. 2.021.242
novembre
6 - pagate a Bacci per 4 foto suoi bronzi di Marini L. 5.100
6 - spese di viaggio Dr. Ceroni a Bellinzona ed Ascona L. 3.950
7 - N. 2 telefonate Uff. vendita Biennale L. 1.120
7 - telefonata a Vallecchi (Firenze) L. 280
11 - zinco Modigliani (cartolina) L. 20.000
20 - pagato Campigli per dipinto *Cavallo* L. 38.500
21 - a noi accreditate come da vs/ ordine per provvigione vendita Utrillo L. 100.000
21 - venduto dip. Zandomeneghi N. 5467 (già coll. Feroldi) [F. Zandomeneghi, *Landscape*, oil on panel, 30 × 43 cm, ex Feroldi] L. 125.000
22 - pagato Miori per dipinto *Cavallo* L. 22.000
25 - venduto dipinto Carrà N. 5434 (già coll. Feroldi) [C. Carrà, *Capanni* (*Huts*), 1927, oil on panel, 41 × 33 cm, ex Feroldi] L. 120.000
27 - Vs/ prestito alla Galleria L. 150.000
30 - spese viaggio a Torino per ritiro dip. Soffici rientrato dall'America L. 3.800 [A. Soffici, *Frutta e liquori* (*Fruit and Liqueurs*), 1915, from the Israel collection, Montreal]
30 - Vs/ prestito alla Galleria L. 350.000
dicembre
30 - pagate al corniciaio Tauro per listelli L. 2.800
30 - spese telegrafiche Bloch (Parigi) per disegno Seurat L. 1.782

1951
gennaio
10 - suo acquisto terracotta *Centauro* [A. Martini, *Centauro* (*Centaur*), 1921, terracotta, h. 27 cm] da Egle Martini a L. 200.000. Dedotto L. 130.000 versate il 30/10/950 L. 70.000
12 - pagato restauro Carrà futurista L. 2.500
12- pagato per stiratura, ritoccatura, intelaiatura a N. 2 dip. Depero L. 11.000
12- pagato per nuovo telaio e foderatura Soffici rientrato America L. 4.000

a riportare L. 286. 832 = L. 2.766.242

1951
riporto L. 286. 832,- 2.766.242,-
gennaio
12 - rimborsate a Egle Rosmini spesa imballo Martini *La dormiente* 7.000
13 - in conto restituzione parte prestiti, ns/ versamento L. 1.000.000
14 - pagate alla tipografia Esperia note N. 607 e 628 cartoncini auguri Natale e buste L. 13.100
17 - Vs/ acquisto dipinto Cassinari [B. Cassinari, *Ritratto di madre Pons* (*Portrait of Mother Pons*), 1949, oil on canvas, 90 × 70 cm] L. 60.000
17 - telegramma a Bloch per disegno Seurat L. 785
30 - Vs/ acquisto olio Soldati N. 5877 [A. Soldati, *Segreti* (*Secrets*), panel, 35 × 30 cm] L. 30.000
30 - Vs/ acquisto olio Soldati N. 5886 [A. Soldati, *Architettura* (*Architecture*), 1950, oil on panel, 29 × 53 cm] L. 35.000
30 - Vs/ acquisto N. 2 tempere Soldati 5888/5889 [A. Soldati, *2 Compositions*, 1950, oil and tempera on paper, from the artist] L. 25.000
30 - pagate a Mari per N.15 spagliacci cartone per vs/ disegni L. 8.000
30 - spese Gino per viaggio a Firenze per Rosai e Vallecchi L. 12.000
febbraio
6 - Vs/ acquisto vaso grande Gambone 90.000,-
6 - Vs/ acquisto vaso piccolo Gambone 25.000,-
6 - Vs/ acquisto olio Usellini N. 4975 [G. Usellini, *Regata d'amore* (*Love Regatta*), tempera on canvas, 140 × 60 cm, from the artist] 80.000
1.672.717,- 2.766.242,-
Vs/ avere a saldo 1.093.525,- ==========

N.B. Nel ns/ Dare in L. 1.093.525 vi sono comprese e L. 385.000 prestate alla Galleria Civica per l'acquisto di Campigli.

Presso il Sig. Mattioli rimangono in sospeso le sottonotate opere di ns/ proprietà:
- M. Rosso - *Conversazione in giardino* - cera.
- Campigli - *Le amazzoni* - dipinto olio
- Marussig - *Vaso e mandolino* olio
- Severini - *Paysanne romaine* olio
- Martini - disegni acquarellati N. 5689-5633 [the only identifiable work is A. Martini, *Nudo accovacciato* (*Crouching Nude*), 1940, pencil, 33 × 30.5 cm, from Egle Rosmini]

69. Copy of a typewritten letter from Gianni Mattioli to Costantino Baroni (Archivio Mattioli)

Milano, 15 Febbraio 1951
Via Manzoni 41/A-
Egregio Prof. Baroni[1],
Se la cosa può essere utile alla Civica Galleria d'Arte Moderna di Milano, Le comunico che vorrei fare dono del dipinto di Massimo Campigli *La scala* firmato 1929, dipinto che Lei conosce e per il quale ebbe a dimostrare particolare interesse.
In attesa di un Suo cenno, La saluto cordialmente.
Dev.mo
Gianni Mattioli

[1] Costantino Baroni, director of the Civici Musei of Milan.

70. Typewritten letter from Gualtieri di San Lazzaro to Gianni Mattioli (Archivio Mattioli)

30, Rue Jacob-Paris 6
Lunedì 26 febbraio [1951]
Tel. Danton 82.10

Egregio dottor Mattioli,
solo oggi, dopo tre mesi di trattative, spesso penose, posso finalmente dirLe quanto segue a proposito del quadro di Carrà.
I Magnelli, che come Lei sa, non avevano accettato l'offerta di un milione e mezzo di lire (offerta sia pure praticamente inesistente, come Lei mi fece scrivere da Garretto) non avendo nessuna intenzione di vendere il quadro, cedendo finalmente alle mie insistenze, acconsentono a venderLe *La Galleria* di Carrà, esposta all'ultima Biennale e alla mostra di Zurigo, per *settecentocinquantamila franchi* netti, pagabili a Parigi, nelle mani di Alberto Magnelli. Il quadro si trova in Italia, e Lei potrà, appena effettuato il versamento, ritirarlo o farselo spedire a Milano.
Questo prezzo, è superiore a quanto Lei aveva offerto, ma come già Le scrissi, sulla sua offerta non era possibile arrivare a trattative.
Decida Lei, e mi faccia avere una risposta con cortese sollecitudine. Quanto alle duecento mila lire per me, evidentemente mi rendo conto che la sua promessa era basata su un'altra cifra. Dai Magnelli, che ritengono di avermi fatto un grande favore, fissando il prezzo di 750 mila franchi, non avrò nulla, ma Lei non si preoccupi di me. Non Le mancheranno altre occasioni per farmi guadagnare qualcosa. In ogni caso non vorrei che il premio promessomi fosse un ostacolo alla conclusione dell'affare, perché non sono stato mosso da un desiderio di lucro, sia pure legittimo.
Con i più cordiali saluti, mi creda
Suo aff.mo
Gualtieri di San Lazzaro

71. Copy of a typewritten letter from Gianni Mattioli to Gualtieri di San Lazzaro (Archivio Mattioli)

Milano, 28 Febbraio 1951
Egregio Signor M.G. di San Lazzaro,
Ho ricevuto la Sua gradita lettera del 26 corrente e Le

do senz'altro il benestare per *La Galleria* di Carrà al prezzo indicatomi. Entro qualche giorno dal ricevimento della presente, prego Lei od il Signor Magnelli di passare dal Signor M. Charpentier – 10, Rue Commines – Parigi – Telefono: Turbigo 68.00 (suocero di Garretto), il quale provvederà a regolare la cosa.
In realtà il prezzo del dipinto è un po' elevato, ma desidero confermarLe l'acquisto anche per non prolungare ancora le Sue fatiche in ulteriori trattative.
Desidero però che Lei mi permetta di corrisponderLe il premio di £it. 200.000.- per tutto il disturbo avuto e La prego di volermi dire se preferisce il controvalore a Parigi, oppure se debbo versare le Lire in Italia a persona che Lei mi indicherà.
Ho appreso dall'Amico Paolo [Garretto] che le condizioni di salute di Sua moglie sono sempre poco buone e Le faccio di vero cuore tanti tanti auguri.
Ancora un grazie per il Suo gentile interessamento e nella speranza di aver presto il piacere di vederLa, voglia gradire i miei migliori saluti.
dev.mo
[G. Mattioli]

72. Manuscript letter from Margherita Sarfatti to Gianni Mattioli (Archivio Mattioli)

4 marzo 1950 [actually 1951], Roma
Egregio e caro amico, mi perdoni, la prego, se ho tardato tanto a risponderle. Lo scambio di lettere con il mio figliuolo a Parigi è stato piuttosto laborioso, io insistevo per qualche proposta, nel senso che lei sa, lui si dichiara incapace di trovare qualcosa d'interessante per una somma con cui, egli mi scrive, "non si può far tremare W. Str., non sarebbe gentile!" Perciò, io che mi sarei rassegnata al dispiacere di vendere una tela a me carissima se vi fossi stata incoraggiata per ragioni di contingenza pratica, torno ora alle ragioni del sentimento. Ho molto esitato perché proprio mi dispiace di darle un dispiacere, ma il dispiacere di vendere è grande per me. Lei ama i quadri da lei raccolti, dunque deve comprendermi. Per me poi ogni tela, e soprattutto l'*Antigrazioso*, è legata ad una quantità di ricordi preziosi, all'affetto e alla premura di mio marito, al mio entusiasmo per le nuove tendenze che pugnacemente difesi quando da tutti avversate! E anche alla balda figura di Boccioni, con tutto il suo complesso di gravi difetti, snob, arrivista, vanitoso ecc. ecc., ma ciò malgrado o forse anche per il suo egotismo ed egoismo (giacché gli esseri umani attirano anche per le loro cattive qualità!) malgrado ciò, dico, *charmeur*. Una personalità forte, di cui io a Milano fui la primissima ad accorgermi, assai prima ch'egli avesse neppure incontrato Marinetti: e che aiutai a mettere in luce e in valore.
Caro amico, vuole ella dimostrarmi che non mi serba rancore per la piccola delusione che mi vedo obbligata a darle? Allora mi mandi una cartolina per dirmelo, oppure mi faccia una telefonata, perché so che ella non ama perdere tempo a scrivere! Il che non toglie che il suo articoletto nitido e preciso sul periodico *La Biennale*[1] sia scritto benissimo. Gli ho dato un'occhiata da amici ma spero che lei si ricordi di prestarmelo. Lo restituirò!
Adesso le chiedo anche di darmi, se può, un'informazione. La Galleria Internazionale di via Gesù 13 è una casa buona e seria? mi hanno scritto che vorrebbero comperare due miei Mancini, e questa pittura dell'Ottocento, per quanto sia bella, e i due Mancini miei sono stupendi, mi interessa meno e sarei disposta a trattare con questa galleria, se è seria. E si ricordi lei per favore 1) di chiedere all'amico Ghiringhelli per l'acquisto di un Morandi, che vorrei comperare; 2) di non mancare alla promessa visita, ma stavolta non più tanto fuggevole né meteorica, e completata dall'altra metà.
E me la saluti affettuosamente, con un bacino alla piccolina.
Le posso assicurare che se fossi stata disposta a separarmi dal mio caro *Antigrazioso*, lo avrei venduto e lo venderei sempre a lei piuttosto che a qualsiasi altri, per l'amicizia e la simpatia, e perché lei ama l'arte di amore caldo e disinteressato quanto il mio. E mi voglia bene lo stesso.
affma Margherita Sarfatti

[1] G. Mattioli, 'Come ho formato la mia raccolta,' *La Biennale di Venezia*, I, 3, January 1951

73. Copy of a typewritten letter from Gianni Mattioli to Lionello Venturi (Archivio Mattioli)

Milano, 9 Marzo 1951
Egregio Professore,
ricevo oggi la gradita Sua del 7 corrente con i ritagli di giornale e La ringrazio.
Il Picasso [P. Picasso, *Homme à la mandoline* (*Man with Mandolin*), 1911] ed il Braque [G. Braque, *Still Life*, 1911] non sono ancora arrivati dall'America. Il vapore sul quale sono stati imbarcati è atteso a Genova verso il 15 corrente mese; sarà mia premura scriverLe nuovamente non appena mi perverranno.
Non credo mi sia possibile venire a Parigi durante il Suo soggiorno; ad ogni modo tengo presente il Suo indirizzo. Chissà che non mi capiti un'occasione propizia!
Circa il Chagall ed il Rouault, pur ringraziandoLa sentitamente per il Suo costante gentilissimo interessamento, penserei ad acquistarli solo se si tratta di una vera occasione (che forse è un po' difficile).
In questi ultimi tempi, oltre ai due quadri che Lei sà, ho acquistato *La Galleria di Milano* di Carrà e l'altro metafisico che mi interessava pure di Carrà cioè *L'idolo ermafrodito*: il mio Ministero delle Finanze gradirebbe quindi una temporanea battuta di arresto.
Ad ogni modo se Lei troverà qualche cosa di particolarmente interessante e me lo segnalerà inviandomi le fotografie, gliene sarò sempre grato.
Mi ricordi ai Suoi Cari tutti e coi migliori auguri per il Suo viaggio a Parigi, voglia gradire i miei cordiali devoti saluti.
dev.mo
[G. Mattioli]

74. Account from the Galleria del Milione to Gianni Mattioli (Archivio Mattioli)

2 maggio 1951

Sig. Gianni Mattioli
Situazione ad oggi;

1951
febbraio
6 Vs/ avere come da situazione precedente L. 1.093.525
"16 addebito zinco in rame dipinto Klee L. 25.000
marzo
6 storno suo versamento alla Galleria Arte Moderna per Campigli L. 385.000
10 pagato a Rossi per restauro N.1 Balla L. 3.000
10 pagato a Rossi per foderatura e ritocco a N. 1 Depero 131 × 90 L. 7.000
10 venduto dipinto Morandi N. 5444 [G. Morandi, *Landscape*, 1941] L. 190.000
10 venduto dipinto Morandi N. 5447 [G. Morandi, *Landscape*, 1936] L. 190.000
17 rimborsate a Ceroni spese viaggio a Firenze per vs/ conto L. 16.000
22 vs/ acquisto Morandi N. 5934 [G. Morandi, *Still Life*, 1936, watercolor on paper, 32 × 23 cm, from Scheiwiller] L. 25.000
22 vs/ acquisto Carrà N. 5935 [C. Carrà, *Figura uomo con bicchiere* (*Male Figure with Glass*), 1924, pencil, 22 × 32 cm, from Scheiwiller] L. 35.000,
22 vs/ acquisto Rosai N. 5936 [O. Rosai, *Uomini che giocano* (*Men Playing*), pencil, 18 × 13 cm, from Scheiwiller] L. 15.000
22 vs/ acquisto Romiti N. 5951 [G. Romiti, *Gli oggetti* (*The Objects*), 1950, oil on canvas, 70 × 50 cm, deposit of the artist] L. 30.000 [ex Scheiwiller - manuscript]
31 pagato a Della Rotta per restauro Chagall e Rosalba L. 8.500
31 Vs/ acquisto Moreni N. 5892 [M. Moreni, *Barche e reti* (*Boats and Nets*), 1950, oil on canvas, 70 × 60 cm, deposit of the artist] L. 50.000
31 Vs/ acquisto Moreni N. 5893 [M. Moreni, *Composizione in rosso* (*Composition in Red*), 1950, oil on canvas, 100 × 80 cm, deposit of the artist] L. 40.000
31 Vs/ acquisto Moreni N. 5894 [M. Moreni, *Reti*, (*Nets*) 1950, oil on canvas, 70 × 60 cm, deposit of the artist] L. 40.000
aprile
12 pagato a Della Rotta per restauro Signac L. 5.000
13 pagato a Rossi per restauro Soffici L. 5.000
13 pagato a Rossi Scipione *La cortigiana* L. 7.500
pagato a Rossi per restauro Scipione *Cavallino* L. 7.500
21 venduto Boccioni *Paesaggio* [*Periferia* - manuscript] L. 290.000, L. 261.000
21 parte bolli fatt. 575/576 vendita Boccioni L. 990
30 libri delle Edizioni
nel luglio 950 L. 1.345
agosto 1950 L. 280
gennaio 1951 L. 9.450
febbraio 1951 L. 5.700
febbraio 1951 L. 1.225
marzo 1951 L. 5.600
L. 729.090 = 1.734.525

riporto L. 729.090 = L. 1.734.525,-

vs: avere a saldo L.1.005. 435

N.B. opere di ns/ proprietà ancora in sospeso ed in vs/ possesso:

- M. Rosso - conversazione in giardino
- Campigli - *Le amazzoni*
- Marussig - N. 5304 [P. Marussig, *Vaso e mandolino* (*Vase and Mandolin*), 1925, oil on canvas, 46 × 40 cm, deposit of Frua De Angeli]
- Severini - N. 7 [G. Severini, *Paysage romain* (*Roman Landscape*), 1918, oil on canvas, 65 × 81 cm, from Rosenberg, 1937]

tappeto rosso

75. Copy of a typewritten letter from Gianni Mattioli to Fortunato Depero (Archivio Mattioli)

Milano, 8 Giugno 1951
Caro Depero,

Ho ricevuto la tua del 5 Giugno. Anch'io sto poco bene e sono molto stanco e pieno di preoccupazioni per l'ufficio.

Ti ho spedito, come da tuo desiderio, un altro rotolo di 30 fogli di cellophane identico al campione e spero che vadano bene.

Ho parlato con Giani[1] il quale ti spedirà o manderà a me quello che può trovare di pagine sciolte e illustrazioni del libro. Credo però che abbia poco perché un mese fa circa, ha traslocato il suo stabilimento e non so cosa avrà portato nel nuovo degli scarti.

Ti allego distinta delle tue opere in mio possesso e ti prego di ritornarmi una copia segnandomi con una crocetta quelle che desideri ti vengano spedite per la Mostra. Nel frattempo, se ci fossero dei titoli inesatti o delle date sbagliate, vedi di correggermeli in modo che possa mettere a posto la rubrichetta della mia raccolta.

Ricordami affettuosamente a Rosetta (alla quale so che Cici ha scritto direttamente) con un grazie da parte mia per i bellissimi fiori. A te molti pensieri affettuosi.

DIPINTI

- SELVAGGETTI - TEATRO PLASTICO
olio su tavola - 1918 -

- IO E MIA MOGLIE
olio su tela - 1919 -

- DIAVOLI DI CAUCCIÙ
olio su tela - 1919 -

- FLORA E FAUNA MAGICA
olio su tela - 1920 -

- CICLISTA VELOCE
olio su tela - 1922 -

- TRENO PARTORITO DAL SOLE
olio su tela - 1924 -

- IL BEVITORE (1ª Edizione dell'Uomo dai Baffi)
olio su tela - 1925 -

- ARATURA
olio su tela - 1926 -

- NATURA MORTA ACCESA
olio su tavola - 1936 -

- L'UOMO DAI BAFFI
olio su tavola - 1944 -

- GLI AUTOMI
olio su tela - 1945 -

- GIANNI E L'ARMADILLO
olio su tela - 1946 -

- RICAMATRICE
olio su tela - 1922 -

- CITTÀ MECCANIZZATA DALLE OMBRE

- LA CASA DEL MAGO
olio su tela - 1923-

DISEGNI

RITRATTO DI GILBERT CLAVEL
- acquarello - 1916 -

PITTURA ASTRATTA
- disegno acquarellato - 1915 -

DISEGNO ASTRATTO
- disegno acquarellato -

IL GALLO
- disegno a carbone - 1932 -

ELASTICITÀ DI GATTI
- disegno a carbone - 1932 -

POLENTA A FUOCO DURO
- disegno a carbone - 1943 -

NITRITO IN VELOCITÀ
- disegno a tempera - 1922 -

FIGURE (Riprodotto su "Valori Plastici")
- disegno a matita -

ARAZZI

CAVALCATA FANTASTICA - 1920 -

DUE MASCHERE -

PROPRIETÀ GHEDINI

- VASO DI FIORI
olio su tavola - 1944 -

- COLEOTTERO VENEZIANO
olio su tavola - 1944 -

- PROSPETTIVA ALPESTRE
olio su tavola - 1944 -

PAESAGGIO ALPINO
- disegno a carbone - 1945

[1] Giampiero Giani, man of letters and Milanese publisher, author of the small book *Fortunato Depero Pittore*, Milan, Edizioni della Conchiglia 1951, to which this letter refers.

76. Account from the Galleria del Milione to Gianni Mattioli (Archivio Mattioli)

Milano 30 giugno 1951
Preg. Sig. Gianni Mattioli
situazione alla data d'oggi;

1951
aprile
30 - Vs/ avere come da situazione precedente L. 1.005. 435
maggio
5 - N.1 zinco in nero di vs/ dipinto riprodotto nel catalogo Tosi L. 3.300
10 - pagato foto dipinto Carrà *Galleria* L. 1.600
22 - spese viaggio Ceroni a Torino L. 8.000
30 - suo acquisto dip. Asnago N. 6013 [M. Asnago, *Sedia* (*Chair*), oil on canvas, 60 × 70 cm, deposit of the artist] L. 60.000
giugno
4 - versate dal Sig. Mattioli L. 100.000
4 - spese di viaggio Sig. Gino e Ceroni a Bologna per ritiro dipinto Morandi [G. Morandi, *Natura morta con portaorologio* (*Still Life with Clock Case*), 1915] L. 15.000
4 - pagato al restauratore Rossi per dipinto Scipione *Cardinale* L. 30.000
12 - pagato foto Emmer N. 10 copie Carrà L. 2.500
12 - suo acquisto dipinto Cogorno *Cavallino* L. 20.000
22 - suo acquisto Sironi N.6061 [M. Sironi, *Contrabbandieri* (*Smugglers*), 1951, oil on cardboard, 50 × 40 cm, acquired from the artist] L. 105.000
22 - suo acquisto Vacchi N. 6067 [S. Vacchi, *Figura con toro* (*Figure with Bull*), 1950, oil on canvas, 90 × 115 cm, deposit of the artist] L. 45.000
25 - ns/ provvigione per *Piccola Officina* [G. de Chirico, *Interno metafisico con piccola officina* (*Metaphysical Interior with Small Factory*), 1917, oil on canvas, 46 × 36 cm] accordataci dal Sig. Mattioli L. 315.035
25 - versate dal Sig. Mattioli L. 500.000

sommano L. 605.435 = 1.605.435
riporto conto a nuovo L. 1.000.000

77. Copy of a typewritten letter from Gianni Mattioli to Fortunato Depero (Archivio Mattioli)

Milano, 5 Luglio 1951
Caro Depero,
Ho ricevuto la tua del 1° corrente e sono lieto che le tue tempere ti siano arrivate regolarmente. Ho definito oggi gli accordi con Monti & Gemelli (che sono gli speditori abituali di Brera ed i migliori che ci siano a Milano) per l'invio del gruppo delle tue opere, che partirà senz'altro ai primi della prossima settimana.
Le opere che ti invierò sono le seguenti:
- *Io e mia moglie*
- *Diavoli di caucciù*
- *Flora e fauna magica*
- *Ciclista veloce*
- *Treno partorito dal sole*
- *Il bevitore* (*1ª edizione dell'Uomo dai baffi*)
- *Aratura*
- *Natura morta accesa*
- *L'uomo dai baffi*
- *Gli automi*
- *Ricamatrice*
- *La casa del mago*
- *Ritratto di Gilbert Clavel*
- *Vaso di fiori*
- *Coleottero Veneziano*
Come vedrai, ho aggiunto alla lista di quelle da te segnate, *L'Aratura* e *La casa del mago*, perché reintelaiate e ripulite mi sembra che siano venute molto bene e che valga la pena di esporle.
Poiché sono del parere che ciò che maggiormente valorizza le opere di un artista è che esse siano divise fra diversi proprietari e raccoglitori, esaminando il gruppo dei vari dipinti in mio possesso, sono venuto nella determinazione che potrei cederne qualcuno se durante la Mostra ci fosse interesse da parte di qualche Ente o privato per opere tue di date non recenti. I pezzi che eventualmente cederei sono i seguenti:
- *Gli automi*
- *La casa del mago*
- *Il bevitore* (*1ª edizione dell'uomo dai baffi*)
- *Ciclista veloce*
- *Aratura*
- *Ricamatrice*
Per il prezzo naturalmente ti lascio la più ampia libertà.
Cici e Laura stanno bene e sono andate per un periodo di tempo sopra Stresa in montagna. Io conto di raggiungerle domani e di rimanere con loro fino a lunedì, riposandomi un poco.
Ancora molti auguri, saluti affettuosi a Rosetta ed a te un abbraccio
tuo
[G. Mattioli]

Depero
Tenere

Selvaggetti
Io e mia moglie
Diavoli di caucciù
Flora e fauna magica
Treno partorito dal sole
Natura morta accesa
L'uomo dai baffi
Gianni e l'armadillo
Città meccanizzata dalle ombre
-
Ritratto di Clavel (acquarello)
-
Nitrito in velocità
Figure
Il gallo
Elasticità di gatti
-
Cavalcata fantastica
Due maschere

Cedere

Ciclista veloce
Il bevitore
Aratura
Gli automi
Ricamatrice
Casa del mago

78. Typewritten letter from Marco Valsecchi to Gianni Mattioli (Archivio Mattioli)

Milano, 19 Settembre 1951
Caro signor Mattioli,
da qualche giorno la fortuna mi concede di rintracciare vecchie pubblicazioni; e stamane, su una bancarella, ho trovato un fascicolo che le allego. Come vede, è un numero speciale apparso nel 1933, in occasione delle onoranze a Boccioni, nella Villa Reale di Milano. Mi permetta di offrirglielo per la sua biblioteca; e le sarà tanto più caro se considera l'invio autografo di Depero, che appare sul frontespizio.
I miei viaggi (finalmente finiti) e le sue partenze serali ci hanno impedito i simpatici incontri nella galleria di via Senato. Quando li riprenderemo? lei sa il piacere che essi sempre mi procurano.
Mi rammento del suo desiderio di affinare via via la scelta dei suoi dipinti; e mi rallegro alla notizia che finalmente la *Natura morta* 1915 di Morandi, dopo lo strappo, le è stata consegnata. Non la molli più, consideri che è tra i più rari e bei pezzi di Morandi. Da parte mia spero di dedicarle un saggio, che mi conceda di studiare lo sviluppo morandiano dal 1911 al 1920; sto già raccogliendo il materiale necessario.
Se volesse effettuare altri acquisti parimenti preziosi (e al caso procedere a eventuali cambi), penso a un gruppo di dipinti che non dovrebbe lasciarsi sfuggire, qualora l'occasione li mettesse sulla sua strada. Sono dipinti che io considero fondamentali, sia storicamente che esteticamente; e cioè:
1) *Rose* - 1917 - di Morandi (periodo metafisico) ora proprietà Pallini
2) *Paesaggio urbano* - 1920/1 - di Sironi, ora propr. Sarfatti

3) *Paul Guillaume* - 1916 - di Modigliani, ora propr. Pallini (avrebbe così, con gli altri due, i tre più bei dipinti di Modigliani ora in Italia, oltre a completare la sua collezione di tutti i modi di Modigliani; penso anche alla rarità di questi dipinti e alla caccia internazionale, specie dopo la mostra americana)
Questi i primi tre: naturalmente ci sarebbero altri cambi e acquisti da fare: un bel Rosai, per esempio, un Rosai futurista da reggere il confronto con quello di Soffici già in suo possesso, un Campigli del periodo 1918-24; e non mancherò di segnalarglieli man mano che mi verranno a conoscenza. E finisco con l'augurarle la buona fortuna per *Via Toscanella*!
Mi ricordi, la prego, alla sua gentile signora e gradisca i miei più cordiali saluti. Il suo
Marco Valsecchi

79. Account from the Galleria del Milione to Gianni Mattioli (Archivio Mattioli)

Milano 20 ottobre 1951

Egr. Sig. Gianni Mattioli
Via Principe Amedeo N.5
Città

Colla presente Vi segnaliamo di aver venduto in questi giorni le sotto specificate opere di vs/ proprietà ai prezzi stabiliti nell'elenco in Vs/ mani, e vi abbiamo accreditato di L. 2.736.000 sul Vs/ conto.

N. 6156 - Balla *Ottimismo* L.120.000
N. 1606 - De Chirico *Autoritratto* L. 700.000,-
N. 4048 - Marino *Ritratto moglie* (cera) L. 80.000
N. 6161 - Marino *Ritratto Melotti* (bronzo) L. 200.000
N. 5620 - Martini *Lo zio* (bronzo) L. 170.000
N. 5621 - Martini, *Scoccombrina* (terracotta) L. 200.000
N. 6162 - Martini *S. Marco e S. Giusto* (bronzo) L. 250.000
N; 4373 - Marussig *Donna sul divano* L. 120.000,-
N. 5473 - Picasso *Natura morta pipa* L. 1.000.000,-
N. 5702 - Rossi G. *Paesaggio* [*Burano* - manuscript] L. 80.000
N. 6157 - Scipione *Natura morta piuma* L. 300.000
N. 6159 - Tosi *Tunnel a Levanto* L. 200.000

sommano L. 3.420.000,-
dedurre ns/ provvigione 20% L.684.000
importo vs/ avere L. 2.736.000

Colla massima stima

80. Account from the Galleria del Milione to Gianni Mattioli (Archivio Mattioli)

Milano 3 novembre 1951

Sig. Gianni Mattioli
Milano

Situazione alla data d'oggi;

1951
giugno
27 - Suo avere come da situazione precedente L. 1.000.000 [L. 1.005.435 - manuscript]
luglio
21 - pagato all'Esperia per cartoncini L. 5.900
settembre
10 - spese viaggio a Rovereto L. 7.000
15 - pagato trasporto dipinto Morandi *Nudi* a Bologna L. 2.500
24 - ns/ provvigione per raccolta Feroldi L. 1.000.000
24 - suo versamento eventuale acquisto dipinto Morandi di Jucker [(5196) - manuscript] L. 100.000
ottobre
29 - suo acquisto dip. Morandi N. 5196 [G. Morandi, *Fiori* (*Vaso con rose*) (*Flowers* [*Vase with Roses*]), 1917, oil on canvas, 50 × 58 cm: 31.5.1948: deposit Frua; 7.11.49 Pallini lire 495.000; 5.10.51 our purchase from Pallini lire 400.000; 9.10.1951 Mattioli lire 600.000] L. 600.000
29 - per vendita sue opere come da distinta già trasmessa L. 2.736.000
29 - pagato a Rossi per foderatura e stiratura N. 2 grandi Depero L. 42.000
29 - venduto tempera Sironi N. 4360 [M. Sironi, *Composition*, tempera on paper, 41 × 34 cm, deposit from Zanchi] L. 16.000
29 - pagato zinco de Pisis per pouchette L. 21.000
30 - venduto suo Guidi N. 5426 [V. Guidi, *Piccolo ritratto* (*Small Portrait*), 1934, oil on cardboard, 27 × 34 cm] a L. 33.000 (26.400)
30 - suo acquisto dip. Carrà N. 6133 [C. Carrà, *Il cavaliere occidentale* (*The Western Rider*), 1917, oil on canvas, 67 × 52 cm, bought from Pallini 1.500.000] L. 2.500.000

sommano L. 4.178.400 = L. 3.878.400
ns/ avere a saldo L. 300.000,-

7.11.51
a saldo ass. N. 081527
Cred. Italiano =L. 300.000= [manuscript]

81. Account from the Galleria del Milione to Gianni Mattioli

1 febbraio 1952
Preg. Sig. Gianni Mattioli
Situazione contabile alla data d'oggi;

1951
ottobre
30 Vs/ dare come da situazione in tale data L. 300.000
novembre
8 - Vs/ versamento a saldo L. 300.000
10 - Vs/ acquisto Martini *Figliuol Prodigo* [1933, bronze sculpture, h. 36 cm] L. 200.000
14 - venduto Cesetti N. 5464 [G. Cesetti, *Maremma*, oil on panel, 59 × 38 cm, ex Feroldi] a L. 40.000 (32.000)
dicembre
1 - Vs/ acquisto Morandi N. 5953 [G. Morandi, *Cac-*

*tus**- watercolor drawing, 1918, 11 × 19.5 cm, from Pallini] L. 60.000
14 - per libro *Piero della Francesca* L. 10.000
14 - suo acquisto acqueforti Morandi N. 4101/10 [G. Morandi, *Landscape*, etching, 26 × 19 cm] a N. 6096/2 [G. Morandi, *Montagne* (*Mountains*), 1929, etching, 17 × 13.5 cm] montate L. 40.000
29 - pagato per 3 copie foto bronzo Marino L. 600
29 - pagato per 3 foto a suoi dipinti Morandi L. 4.200
31 - per zinco Morandi metafisico (a suo tempo strappato) L. 66.500,-
31 - suo acquisto Rosai N. 6234 [O. Rosai, *Viale dei colli* (*Street of the Hills*), 1950, 65 × 50 cm, oil on canvas; manuscript: deposit of the artist] L. 80.000

1952
gennaio
15 - suo acquisto Klein L. 20.000
25 - pagato per foderatura Soutine L. 6.500
30 - suo acquisto 1 Pollaiolo e 1 Bernini L. 500
L. 788.300 = L. 332.000
ns/ avere a saldo L. 456.300,-

2/2/52 Frs.400 × 158 = fatti accreditare da Winterthur a Henri Kaeser - Lausanne L. 63.200
L. 393.100 [manuscript]

* Acquistato un Morandi e consegnato al Sig. Pallini in cambio del disegno acquarellato *Il cactus* 1918 [manuscript]

5/2/51 - Ass. N. 090732 - Cred.Italiano = L 393.100- [manuscript]

82. Letter from Gino Ghiringhelli to Adriana Cristina with an account from the Galleria del Milione to Gianni Mattioli (Archivio Mattioli)

Gent.ma Sig.na Cristina[1],
le allego la distinta di tutte le opere di proprietà Sig. Mattioli in deposito presso di noi coi prezzi di stima.
Tutte queste opere passano ora in carico come d'accordo alla G. & G.[2]
I prezzi di stima sono stati fatti unitamente al Sig. Mattioli.
Per il momento, non vi sono altre variazioni alla G. & G.
Coi più cordiali saluti
Gino Ghiringhelli

Le allego una nota che è fuori dalla contabilità G. & G. e che prego di passare al Sig. Mattioli

Milano 13 marzo 1952

Sig. Gianni Mattioli
Milano

situazione alla data d'oggi;

1952
gennaio
31 - Vs/ dare come da situazione precedente L. 456.300
febbraio
1 - Vs/ rimessa a saldo L. 456.300
20 - pagato per N. 3 foto a vs/ dipinti Sironi L. 4.200
22 - pagato per vs/ acquisto Derain N. 6319 [A. Derain, *Portrait of M. Zborowsky*, oil on canvas, 37 × 44 cm, from Raffaele Carrieri] L. 600.000 (600.000)
marzo
5 - Pagato al fotografo Emmer per N. 22 selezione a colori dipinti vs/ collezione L. 154.000
13 - Vs/ acquisto dipinto Rosina Viva N. 6346 [R. Viva, *Fiori sul mare* (*Flowers by the Sea*), 1951, oil on canvas, 40 × 50 cm] L. 70.000
L. 1.284.500 = L. 1.056.300
Ns/ avere a saldo 228.200

15/3/52- Pagato Ass. N. 3260718 -B.ca Popolare- [manuscript]

[1] Adriana Cristina, Gianni Mattioli's secretary.
[2] Company founded in 1952 by Gianni Mattioli and Gino Ghiringhelli for trading in art.

83. Account from the Galleria del Milione to Gianni Mattioli (Archivio Mattioli)

Milano 31 marzo 1952

Sig. Gianni Mattioli

Situazione alla data d'oggi;

1952
marzo
1 - Vs/ dare come da situazione precedente L. 228.200
20 - Vs/ rimessa a saldo L. 228.200
25 - Vs/ acquisto De Pisis N. 6256 [F. de Pisis, *Gli occhi* (*The Eyes*), oil on cardbaord, 72 × 56.5 cm, from Pallini] L. 350.000
27 - Vs/ acquisto Meloni N. 6367 [G. Meloni, *Controluce* (*Contre-jour*), 1951, oil on canvas, 60 × 80 cm, deposit of the artist] L. 90.000

sommano L. 668.200 = L. 228.200
vs/ dare a saldo situazione odierna L. 440.000
L. 668.200 = L. 668.200

1/4/52- Ass. N. 3260722 -B.ca Popolare- L 440.000 [manuscript]

84. Account from the Galleria del Milione to Gianni Mattioli

Milano 20 luglio 1952
Sig. Gianni Mattioli
Situazione conto personale

consegnato 1 pouchette Meloni L. 400
consegnato 1 libro Soffici L. 1.800 (1.800)
pagato per restauro pastello Rosalba [Carriera] L. 9.500
pagato per restauro De Chirico *Magia Notte* L. 5.000

pagato per restauro Sironi *Bevitore* L. 8.500
pagato per restauro Carrà *Paesaggio* L. 6.120
pagato per foto Wlaming [*sic*] con 4 copie L. 2.200
pagato per foto Carrà *Manifestaz. futurista* con 10 copie L. 3.400
pagato per foto Chagall con 2 copie L. 1.800
pagato zinco a 5 colori suo dipinto Romiti nella pouchette L. 28.400
Ns/ provvigione 10% su dipinto Carrà N. 3378 [C. Carrà, *Paesaggio lacustre* (*Lakeside Landscape*), 1922, oil on canvas, 50 × 34 cm, from Frua De Angeli] già in sociale e dal sig. Mattioli prelevato L. 26.000
idem su Morandi N. 6437 [G. Morandi, *Still Life*, 1931, oil on canvas, 50 × 63 cm, from Mascioli] L. 60.000
spesa spedizione foto sue opere al Museum of Modern Art L. 2.450
pagato 2 zinchi formato grande per suoi dipinti Sironi da pubblicarsi sulla monografia L. 102.600

Importo dare sig. Mattioli L. 257.770

Riepilogo

- Importo avere Sig. Mattioli per Soc. G. & G. L. 486.250
- a dedurre conto personale Sig. Mattioli L. 257.770°

ns/ versamento a saldo in data odierna L. 228.480

° per questo importo versato assegno sul c/c Belinzaghi c/ GG [manuscript]

85. Manuscript letter from Fernanda Wittgens to Gianni Mattioli (Archivio Mattioli)

[on 'Sovrintendenza alle Gallerie / Milano' letterhead]

14 agosto [1952]
Caro Gianni,
ti penso finalmente "statico", e mando a te Cici e Laura un caro augurio e un saluto pieno di affetto.
Dalla mamma notizie buone, sempre, naturalmente, transitorie e alterne. Ma la vita là è tranquilla.
Ho visto la Biennale: è piuttosto deprimente, ed è bene vederla a settembre perché il caldo è feroce.
Sicché rinuncio per ora all'idea gioiosa di una tua corsa qui. Ci torneremo a settembre. L'acquisto del cavallo di Marino[1] è stata veramente un'ispirazione. È l'unica cosa grande della Biennale e non v'è paragone con le altre stesse opere sue.
Sicché la nostra galleria sarà un trionfo.
Per il resto questo gran Bazar che è l'Excelsior mi diverte abbastanza nella sua anormalità di gente e di vita.
L'esperienza cinematografica è molto interessante e te ne riferirò al ritorno. Certo le basi della civiltà moderna sono cambiate con il cinematografo e bisogna tenerne conto.
Il 22 sarò a Milano e spero di rivederti e di fare una corsa all'Alpino. Un caro abbraccio Fernanda

[1] M. Marini, *Cavallo* (*Horse*), 1939, bronze.
[2] In the Marino Marini gallery at the XVI Venice Biennale, curated by Marco Valsecchi.

86. Account from the Galleria del Milione to Gianni Mattioli (Archivio Mattioli)

Milano 31 dicembre 1952

Sig. Gianni Mattioli
Milano

Situazione alla data d'oggi;

1952
settembre
18 - pagato per foto ai vs/ dipinti Sironi e Morandi L. 5.400
25 - cliché formato cartolina Rosai *Il padre* L. 21.000
25 - cliché formato cartolina Soutine *Bambino* L. 20.500
dicembre
13 - Vs/ acquisto tempera Sironi N. 6523 [M. Sironi, *Composizione chiara* (*Light Composition*), 1952, tempera on paper, 31 × 43.5 cm, from the artist] composizione con cornice e vetro L. 85.000
16 - N. 2 acqueforti Chagall (per Valsecchi) L. 20.000,-
16 - Vs/ acquisto dipinto Morandi *Fiori* N. 5731 [G. Morandi, *Vaso fiori con fondo chiaro* (*Vase of Flowers with Light Background*), oil on canvas, 30.5 × 35 cm, from the artist] con cornice e vetro L. 200.000
18 - N. 2 zinchi formato grande dei suoi dipinti di Boccioni L. 90.000
20 - Vs/ acquisto tempera Sironi *Composizione* N. 6559 [M. Sironi, *Composition*, 1952, tempera on paper, 34 × 49.5 cm, from the artist] con cornice e vetro L. 85.000
23 - N. 1 acquaforte Chagall (per Carrieri) L. 10.000
23 - Vs/ acquisto dipinto Morandi *Natura morta* N. 6438 [G. Morandi, *Natura morta con cestino e panno giallo* (*Still Life with Small Bowl and Yellow Cloth*), 1952, oil on canvas, 40 × 40 cm, from the artist] con cornice L. 200.000
23 - Vs/ acquisto dipinto Morandi *Natura morta* N. 5891 [G. Morandi, *Natura morta, bottiglie* (*Still Life, Bottles*), 1950, oil on canvas, 45 × 35 cm, from the artist] con cornice L. 200.000
29 - pagato per N.10 zinchi formato cartolina per vs/ dipinti (×) L. 223.000
29 - N.3 riviste "Art Plastique - Biennale" L. 3.000
29 - pagato fotocolor dipinto Campigli per riproduzione su rivista "Settimo Giorno" L.12.500
Importano L. 1.175.400

(×) - Renoir *Gabrielle* - Gauguin *Giovane tahitiana* - Rousseau *Natura morta* - Picasso *Uomo mandolino* - Gris *Bottiglia bordeaux* - Braque *Duo per flauto* - Derain *Ritratto* - Matisse *Donna* - Utrillo - Rouault

87. Account from the Galleria del Milione to Gianni Mattioli (Archivio Mattioli)

Milano 28 aprile 1953
Sig. Gianni Mattioli

Situazione contabile ad oggi;

1953
febbraio
10 - suo acquisto Marino N. 6650 [M. Marini, *Cavallo* (*Horse*) 1953, tempera and oil on cardboard, 35 × 50 cm, from the artist] e bolli fatt. L. 111.000
12 - nota Olgiati 31/1/53 per zinchi Dufy, Carrà e Rosai L. 79.000
12 - pagato a Marconi per spagliaccio in tela a suo De Chirico 2.500
15 - libri a Ragghianti per mostra Strozzina (N. 1 Feroldi, 10 cartoline e 2 pouchette) L. 4.000
15 - suo acquisto Sironi N. 6667 [M. Sironi, *Composizione con cavallo* (*Composition with Horse*), 1953, oil on paper, 100 × 80 cm, from the artist] (ora spedito in America) L. 350.000
marzo
2 - a Valsecchi: acquaforte Morandi N. 6677/1 [G. Morandi, *Landscape*, 1932, etching on Japon paper 1/10] L. 20.000
2 - a Valsecchi: acquaforte Morandi N. 6680/1 [G. Morandi, etching on Fabriano paper] 15.000,-
3 - pagato fatt. N. 16 Clari per foto ai Morandi con copie L. 1.800
3 - pagato fatt. N. 29 Clari per N. 21 foto varie a suoi dipinti L. 35.000
aprile
11 - suo acquisto dip. Ajmone N. 6653 [G. Ajmone, *Natura morta dalle arance* (*Still Life with Oranges*), 1953, oil on canvas, 60 × 50 cm, from the artist] L. 50.000
11 - libro Marini lusso copia N.7 L. 15.000
18 - pagato a Marconi per N. 3 cornici oro fino a suoi dipinti L. 40.000
20 - pagato a Marconi per cornice Marino L. 6.500
20 - pagato per 50 ritagli "Eco stampa" L. 4.300
20 - ns/ versamento per suo acquisto De Pisis *Parigi* [F. de Pisis, *Primavera a Parigi* (*Springtime in Paris*), 1928, oil on canvas, 55 × 45 cm] L. 300.000
21 - suo rimborso acquisto De Pisis L. 300.000
25 - suo acquisto acq. Morandi N. 6677/7 japon [G. Morandi, *Landscape*, 1932, etching on Japon paper, 7/10] L. 20.000
25 - suo acquisto Morandi N. 6680/7 [G. Morandi, etching on Fabriano paper, 1/65] L. 15.000
25 - suo acquisto Morandi a Forti; acquaf. Morandi N. 6677/43 L. 15.000
25 - suo acquisto Morandi N. 6680/43 [G. Morandi, etching] L. 15.000,-
25 - suo acquisto Morandi a Righi N. 6678/50 [G. Morandi, etching] L. 15.000,-
25 - suo acquisto Morandi N. 6680/50 [G. Morandi, etching] L. 15.000
a riportare L. 1.129.100 = L. 300.000

1953 a riportare L. 1.129.100 = L. 300.000,-
aprile
25 - suo acquisto libro De Chirico L. 1.800
da noi venduto 1 catalogo mostra Strozzina L. 400

L. 1.130.900 = L. 300.400
ns/ avere a saldo L. 830.500

88. Account from the Galleria del Milione to Gianni Mattioli (Archivio Mattioli)

Milano 2 giugno 1953

Sig. Mattioli

1953 situazione contabile al 30 maggio 1953:
maggio
5 - spesa spedizione cataloghi a Firenze L. 1.950
5 - acquisto 60 buste grandi per spedizione cataloghi L. 1.500
5 - acquisto libro Cristofanetti L. 600
8 - suo acquisto dipinti Ajmone N. 6729 [G. Ajmone, *Still Life*, 1953, oil on canvas, 65 × 55 cm, from the artist] e 6730 [G. Ajmone, *Natura morta in blu* (*Blue Still Life*), 1953, oil on canvas, 73 × 60 cm, from the artist] L. 120.000
8 - spesa montatura suo disegno Carrà L. 700
9 - spedizione cataloghi a Firenze L. 1.250
9 - spedizione N. 55 cataloghi pacco raccomandato L. 3.300
10 - spedizione cataloghi a Firenze L. 2.000
15 - importo N. 2 note per zinchi catalogo Firenze L. 147.000
25 - suo acquisto N. 3 dipinti Cristofanetti N. 6764 [F. Cristofanetti, *Bateaux* (*Boats*), 1949, oil on canvas, 92 × 74 cm, from the artist], N. 6765 [F. Cristofanetti, *Paysage* (*Parigi*) (*Landscape* [*Paris*]), 1949-50, oil on canvas, 65 × 50 cm, from the artist] e 6768 L. 250.000
25 - suo acquisto dipinto Cristofanetti regalato alla Galleria d'Arte Moderna di Milano N. 6763 [F. Cristofanetti, *Bateaux (USA)* (*Boats [USA]*), 1941, oil on canvas, 81 × 100 cm, from the artist] L. 60.000
25 - N. 3 cartoline Morandi L. 100
25 - pagato per N. 3 invii cataloghi a Firenze L. 6.900
sommano L. 583.300

a dedurre;
resa dipinto Ajmone N. 6653 [G. Ajmone, *Natura morta dalle arance* (*Still Life with Oranges*), 1953, oil on canvas, 60 × 50 cm] acquistato da noi e pagato in precedenza L. 50.000
ns/ avere a saldo L. 535.300

[15/6 Regolato con assegno Cred. Comm.le - manuscript]

89. Account from the Galleria del Milione to Gianni Mattioli (Archivio Mattioli)

Milano 30 settembre 1953

Preg. Sig. Mattioli

1953 situazione conti alla data odierna:
giugno
6 Spese per catalogo Strozzina;
6 - pagato zinco copertina 9.200
6 - al legatore per cataloghi 1526 a L. 20 [each] L. 30.520

6 - al legatore per cataloghi 1540 a L. 20 [each] L. 30.800
6 - all'Esperia per cataloghi 1500 a L. 235 [each] L. 352.500
25 - Versatoci dalla Strozzina per N. 1266 cataloghi venduti a L. 240 cadauno L. 308.840
25 - Rimborso alla Strozzina per foto eseguite L. 15.000
25 - spesa benestare Bancario spedizione Braque a Zurigo L. 1.650
luglio
18 - pagato zinchi Ajmone e Marino L. 58.800
20 - Per N. 12 telefonate a Firenze e N. 1 Zurigo L. 14.470
27 - Pagato cornicetta acquarello Tosi L. 2.000
28 - N. 1 libro La Tour L. 600
settembre
5 - Rimborso a Ceroni per telefonate a Firenze L. 2.980
18 - Suo acquisto Carrà N. 2869 [C. Carrà, *Marina a Moneglia* (*Seascape at Moneglia*), 1921, oil on canvas, 38 × 43 cm] L. 750.000
L. 1.268.520 = L. 308.840

ns/ avere a saldo L. 959.680 [corrected by hand L. 964.680]

Riepilogo

Ns/ avere come da situazione L. 959.680 [corrected by hand L. 964.680]
A dedurre avere situazione G. & G. L. 662.380

ns/ avere a pareggio L. 297.300 = 959.680 [corrected by hand L. 302.300]

90. Typewritten letter from Carlo Belli to Gianni Mattioli (Archivio Mattioli)

Roma, 4 febbraio 1971
Caro Mattioli,
mi scusi del ritardo con il quale rispondo alla Sua del 21 gennaio, e anche per il tempo che dovrà perdere nel leggere (se Le interesserà), una lettera che già da queste prime righe minaccia una esagerata dilatazione. Ma occorre un preambolo.
L'avvocato Pietro Feroldi, che conobbi nel 1929 quando, come giornalista fui mandato a Brescia (e dove rimasi fino al 1932 per trasferirmi poi a Roma), era persona di rara intelligenza, amante specialmente della pittura e della musica, lettore di classici e di moderni, perennemente agitato da uno spirito nobile e avvampante. A codeste virtù aggiungeva un carattere a dir poco antipatico: violento nei giudizi come negli atteggiamenti, capace d'impennate irrimediabili contro cose e contro persone, demoniacamente frettoloso e trinciante in ogni commercio con i suoi simili, e capace di villanie incredibili. Tutto ciò è (o almeno era ai miei tempi), molto "bresciano".
Lo trovai che collezionava croste locali, salvo un Piccio e, mi pare, un Ranzoni. Ciò contrastava non poco con lo spirito particolarmente aperto che possedeva. Mi fu facile portarlo ad apprezzare i valori della cultura allora attuale: il mio seme cadeva su un terreno fertilissimo e assai preparato a riceverlo, e oggi sono sicuro ch'egli avrebbe percorso la strada, che poi ha percorso, anche se non vi fosse stato il nostro incontro. Ma forse con titubanze e cadute anche maggiori di quelle che continuamente ebbe. Capì la importanza di certi fenomeni, come la metafisica e l'astratto, ma ne rimase ostinatamente sordo. Quando riuscii a ficcargli nella raccolta l'*Amante dell'ingegnere* e *Le muse inquietanti*, mi odiò. L'uno e l'altro quadro, portatigli in casa, furono respinti e ripresi per due volte, finché non gliegli imposi di prepotenza con scenate disgustose. Le lettere che gli scrissi per quei due quadri (e per il *Gentiluomo ubriaco* che non volle assolutamente)! I telegrammi, le telefonate, i colloqui! Si accendeva di entusiasmo per questi miei interventi, ma dopo un po', eccolo preso da nuovi dubbi e da vere disperazioni. La metafisica lo turbava. L'astratto non lo poteva sopportare. Non riuscii che a portargli un Fontana (ma figurativo) e un Soldati più metafisico che astratto. In fondo, egli amava la pittura 900, quella che piaceva alla Sarfatti, ma capiva e come, i francesi. Aveva un concetto sicuro dei valori *propriamente pittorici*, e li sapeva cogliere anche in certi quadretti dell'ultimo Ottocento di gusto pessimo. Superava questa componente negativa *per amore vero* della pittura. Intelligenza acuta e cultura soda (sapeva di greco e latino), lo ponevano in condizione di esprimere giudizi lampanti sia sulla pittura che sulla scultura, non meno che sulla musica di cui era ghiotto, oltre che buon intendente avendo studiato il violino da giovane.
Una medesima comunanza d'interessi (provengo anch'io dalla musica), suggellò per oltre dodici anni la nostra amicizia, finita, ahimè, tempestosamente. "Tu sei stato la fiamma della mia raccolta", mi scriveva spesso; "Senza di te sarebbe mancato lo stile ..." eccetera. Erano dichiarazioni di amore che seguivano sempre (oppure precedevano) aspre polemiche e tensioni fino al limite della rottura. Non poteva tollerare di avere torto (e spesso lo aveva): inveiva allora contro me e rovesciava contumelie sopra i Ghiringhelli che gli erano sinceramente amici, anche se facevano il loro mestiere di mercanti. Io non volevo che sotto la pressione di Barbaroux si lasciasse convincere a portare nella raccolta mezze dozzine di Tosi, di Funi, di Rosai ecc. I Ghiri[nghelli] si disperavano perché si lasciava scappare occasioni straordinarie, puntando magari su un Ferrazzi e sdegnando un Soffici cubista (quello splendido delle angurie), o magari acquistando da chissà chi il solito Rosai per una somma che gli sarebbe bastata a comperare un Juan Gris! Queste erano le sue cadute, ma poi ci scappava a Parigi, a Grenoble, a Basilea e ritornava con Utrillo, con Derain, con Matisse e con Braque...
Insomma la nostra amicizia fu sempre difficilissima e se i Ghiri[nghelli] ogni tanto potevano mandarlo al diavolo poiché di clienti ne avevano sempre; per me, non mercante, mosso da esclusivi interessi culturali, ciò non era possibile. Non so quante volte ricucii gli strappi violenti ch'egli operava nel tessuto della nostra amicizia, e so io quanto costarono codesti rammendi al mio orgoglio giovanile. Posso aver sbagliato anch'io, s'intende; ma se mi avesse ascoltato qualche volta, oggi Lei, caro Mattioli,

avrebbe potuto avere i più bei Kandinsky, e Klee e Gris che allora si affacciavano assai timidamente al mercato. E non le dico dei Fontana, dei Melotti, dei Soldati e dei Licini, che sempre mi scartò con ostinazione.
Comunque, lavorai per dodici anni a comporgli una collezione *corretta*, convincendolo a scartare, a scartare, a scartare e ad acquistare con estrema oculatezza. Qualche volta riuscii, qualche altra no. Ma dell'amore che posi in codesto lavoro sarebbero testimonianza centinaia e centinaia di lettere, di espressi, di telegrammi, di telefonate, di colloqui, se la maggior parte di questo materiale non fosse andato perduto durante la guerra. A Brescia, nel 1929-32, io lavoravo di notte, lui di giorno quando io dormivo. Ci vedevamo alla domenica e durante la settimana ci scrivevamo lettere e bigliettini. Quando venni a Roma, e poi in giro per il mondo, la nostra corrispondenza non cessò: anche due lettere al giorno non gli bastava. Sempre si lamentava dei miei "lunghi silenzi" e andava in furia se gli ricordavo mie lettere rimaste senza risposta. Veniva spesso a Roma, ma sempre come un fulmine tra un treno e l'altro, imprecando contro la città e contro di me che osavo viverci. Verso il 1938 lo convinsi a pubblicare la sua raccolta in un bel volume. Ci vollero tre anni per convincerlo! Ma intanto aderì a preparare le tavole a colori, lavoro che andò avanti per altri lunghi anni tra entusiasmi, depressioni e risollevamenti degni di miglior causa. Per tre anni ci scrivemmo sempre sullo stesso tema: le tavole, la mia prefazione, la bibliografia. Che pazienza! Venne finalmente il giorno fatale: nella primavera del 1942 gli mandai il manoscritto di prefazione giacché le tavole erano pronte. Prima, poiché volevo essere ben sicuro, lo avevo fatto leggere ai Ghiri[nghelli], a Licini, a Melotti, a Bardi, a Bontempelli e a Emilio Cecchi, i quali lo avevano trovato (mi scusi, sa) eccellente. Può figurarsi quale fu la mia sorpresa quando me lo vidi ritornare indietro con correzioni e soppressioni di interi periodi, operate da Feroldi. Non andava. Aderii per puro spirito di tolleranza ad alcune correzioni ad altre no. Mi scrisse che la mia prefazione non valeva niente e che io non ero in grado di presentare la sua collezione. Pensai a uno scherzo, ma il tradimento mi apparve chiaro quando, recatomi a Milano, seppi che da mesi, *prima ancora che io mi mettessi a scrivere quella prefazione*, egli aveva segretamente commissionato la stessa a Guido Piovene! Allora, Piovene scriveva sul "Corriere della Sera" con firma prestigiosa e pubblicitaria, mentre io ero il deprecato autore di *Kn* di cui dovevo vergognarmi, secondo la critica ufficiale di allora. Questa fu la ragione segreta del tradimento e ... la ricompensa di un'amicizia totale e disinteressata. Non lo potei perdonare mai. Verso il 1950 mi mandò messaggi e ramoscelli d'ulivo. Li respinsi. Mi mandò anche a dire che non solo si era pentito, ma che era anche rimasto tremendamente deluso della prefazione del Piovene. Non me ne importò nulla. La ferita che mi aveva inferto non poteva più chiudersi. Non volli più vederlo. Seppi poi della sua morte.
Ecco la storia. Sfrondandola del fatto personale e considerandola soltanto sulla base dei pochi documenti rimasti (le 200 lettere che Le invio a parte), essa testimonia sì un amore straordinario per l'arte coltivato con pari vigore dal Feroldi e da me, e ne sono sicuro che la chiara intelligenza e l'acume critico di cui egli era dotato, uniti, a qualche mio modesto consiglio, abbiano giovato non poco a creare chiarificazioni a certi orientamenti nell'opinione degli Intellettuali di allora, voglio dire alla formazione di una cultura lontana da equivoci e da banalità, frequenti, allora, non meno che oggi.
Mi scusi, caro Mattioli, ma questo preambolo, anche se lungo e personale, dovevo farlo a Lei, erede di un bene che tanta fatica costò anche a me! [...]

Carlo Belli

Appendix II - Gianni Mattioli, Writings and Bibliography

Compiled by
Barbara Geremia

Gianni Mattioli - Published Writings

1919
'Uno strano cibo siamese,' *Il Giornale Illustrato dei Viaggi*, XXXV, no. 34, August 24, 1919, p. 12.
1921
'Ignoto militi,' *Il Crepuscolo*, November 10, 1921, p. 1.
'Per studiare,' *Il Crepuscolo*, November 25, 1921, p. 3.
1922
'Dedicato alle persone per bene,' *Il Crepuscolo*, January 5, 1922, p. 1.
1924
'I Beritt' ('Rassegna Filodrammatica' section), *L'Ambrosiano*, September 23, 1924, p. 4.
'Corale Verdi' ('Rassegna Filodrammatica' section), *L'Ambrosiano*, September 30, 1924, p. 4.
'Circolo Volta' ('Rassegna Filodrammatica' section), *L'Ambrosiano*, October 21, 1924, p. 3.
'Arte moderna' ('Rassegna Filodrammatica' section), *L'Ambrosiano*, October 28, 1924, p. 3.
'Resistenza' ('Rassegna Filodrammatica' section), *L'Ambrosiano*, October 28, 1924, p. 3.
'Arte moderna' ('Rassegna Filodrammatica' section), *L'Ambrosiano*, November 7, 1924, p. 3.
'Salone solari' ('Rassegna Filodrammatica' section), *L'Ambrosiano*, November 18, 1924, p. 3.
'Arte e diletto' ('Rassegna Filodrammatica' section), *L'Ambrosiano*, November 25, 1924, p. 3.
'Salone Solari' ('Rassegna Filodrammatica' section), *L'Ambrosiano*, December 2, 1924, p. 3.
'Compagnia amici dell'arte' ('Rassegna Filodrammatica' section), *L'Ambrosiano*, December 16, 1924, p. 3.
'Monviso' ('Rassegna Filodrammatica' section), *L'Ambrosiano*, December 16, 1924, p. 3.
1925
'Arte moderna' ('Rassegna Filodrammatica' section), *L'Ambrosiano*, January 20, 1925, p. 3.
'Poliziano' ('Rassegna Filodrammatica' section), *L'Ambrosiano*, January 23, 1925, p. 3.
'Arte e diletto' ('Rassegna Filodrammatica' section), *L'Ambrosiano*, January 29, 1925, p. 3.
'Arte e diletto' ('Rassegna Filodrammatica' section), *L'Ambrosiano*, March 4, 1925, p. 3.
1951
'Come ho formato la mia raccolta,' *La Biennale di Venezia*, I, no. 3, January 1951, pp. 25–6.
1957
'La parola agli artisti,' *Il Popolo di Milano*, April 14, 1957, p. 3.
1958
'Cultura e televisione,' *Le Arti,*' VII, no. 11, February 1958, p. 6.
1961
'Somigliava a Ninchi...,' *Il Giornale Letterario*, XIV, no. 7/8, July/August 1961, p. 4.
'Sironi,' *Il Giornale Letterario*, XIV, no. 9, September 1961, p. 4.

Gianni Mattioli Bibliography

1947
C. Baroni, 'Arte per la Casa Cristiana,' *Il Popolo*, May 18, 1947.
Corriere Lombardo, May 18, 1947 (reproduction of *San Giovannino* by Gianni Mattioli).
F. Dacquati, 'La mostra d'arte sacra,' *Corriere degli Artisti*, II, no. 8, May 20, 1947, pp. 3–4.
1949
M. Valsecchi, 'Pochi quadri nella nebbia,' *Oggi*, no. 41, November 17, 1949, p. 38.
1950
C. B., 'Milanesi alla Biennale,' *Il Popolo*, February 24, 1950.
1951
Galdino, 'Fondazione Feroldi-Mattioli incantato regno dell'arte,' *Il Lunedì del Giornale di Brescia*, December 24, 1951.
1952
P. Garretto, 'Garçonniere per sogni,' *Arbiter*, XXV, no. 155, January–February 1952, pp. 42–7.
L. A., 'Collezioni private d'arte contemporanea,' *Milano Cultura*, I, no. 9 – II series –, November 21, 1953, p. 9.
1953
L. Venturi, 'Collezioni Moderne,' *La Stampa*, June 10, 1953.
C. L. Ragghianti, 'Arte italiana moderna,' *SeleArte*, I, no. 6, May/June 1953, pp. 43–52.
C. L. Ragghianti, 'Arte moderna in una raccolta italiana,' in catalogue of the exhibition (Palazzo Strozzi, Florence, April–May), Milan, Edizioni del Milione 1953.
1955
C. Ravioli, 'Ingresso libero per tutti la domenica mattina,' *La Notte*, October 26–7, 1955.
1956
R. Pallucchini, 'Il problema delle gallerie d'arte moderna in Italia,' lecture held on October 20, 1954 at the Gal-

leria d'Arte Moderna a Milano. Congress of the Associazione Nazionale dei Direttori e Funzionari dei Musei Locali, Milan, 1956, p. 13.
'Rivelata una galleria dalla Campagna dei musei,' *Corriere Lombardo*, October 16–17, 1956.
G. Grando, 'Visita ad una raccolta d'arte moderna,' *Atti del Collegio Regionale degli Architetti*, no. 12, December 1956, pp. 9–10.
1957
'Gallerie' section, *Corriere Lombardo*, December 5–6, 1957.
1958
F. Russoli, 'Una collezione esemplare,' *Settimo Giorno*, XI, no. 12, March 20, 1958, pp. 42–7.
'Sono aperte per voi' section, *Avanti!*, April 5, 1958.
'Ragghianti critica la cultura come moda,' *Messaggero Veneto*, May 3, 1958.
'Taccuino – Pinacoteche e Musei' section, *Avanti!*, May 7, 1958.
'Arte moderna in via Senato,' *Il Giorno*, May 25, 1958.
O. Vergani, 'È o non è Milano una "grande città"?,' *Corriere della Sera*, June 15, 1958.
1959
R. Borghello, 'Sintesi d'arte moderna in una galleria milanese,' *Messaggero Veneto*, January 17, 1959.
'La pinacoteca in famiglia,' supplement of *Il Giorno*, May 24, 1959.
'La pittura intesa come amore,' *Termal*, I, no. 86, June 1959, pp. 27–8.
Capolavori d'arte moderna nelle raccolte private. Mostra inaugurale della Civica Galleria d'Arte Moderna, Torino, catalogue ed. by M. Valsecchi (Civica Galleria d'Arte Moderna, Turin, October 31–December 8), Milan, Edizioni dl Milione 1959.
1960
Aremond, 'Una raccolta privata d'arte moderna è aperta al pubblico,' *Famiglia Meneghina. Rassegna di vita milanese*, XXXIV, no. 3, May–June 1960, pp. 18–19.
1961
F. Arcangeli, *Maestri del disegno contemporaneo in una raccolta privata di arte moderna a Milano*, Milan, Vanni Scheiwiller Edizioni 1961, pp. 5–12.
1962
F. Dentice, 'I manovratori,' *L'Espresso*, VIII, no. 11, March 4, 1962, pp. 16–17.
Letter from M. Polacco, Milan, 'Collezionisti,' in the section 'Lettere al Direttore' [L. Russo], *L'Espresso*, VIII, no. 9, March 18, 1962, p. 2.
1963
L. Bortolon, 'Come acquistare quadri d'autore senza spendere cifre favolose,' *Grazia*, no. 1183, October 20, 1963, pp. 54–61.
1966
'Un fatto de Il Giorno,' *Pagine e schermi*, II, no. 2, February 1966, pp. 10–11.
'A quale collezione puntava la gang?,' *Il Giorno*, February 27, 1966.
1967
M. Valsecchi, 'C'è da scegliere anche oggi' ('Parliamo d'Arte di Marco Valsecchi'), *Il Giorno*, January 20, 1967.
M. Valsecchi, 'Vent'anni d'arte cancellano i segni dell'alluvione,' *Tempo*, XXIX, no. 12, March 21, 1967, pp. 72–7.
F. Dentice, 'Pittori in cassaforte,' *L'Espresso*, May 28, 1967, pp. 22–3.
G. Ballo, 'L'investitore esteta,' *Successo*, IX, no. 10 – new series –, October 1967, pp. 106–13.
Masters of Modern Italian Art from the Collection of Gianni Mattioli, catalogue of the exhibition curated by F. Russoli (The Phillips Collection, Washington, DC, November 30, 1967 –January 14, 1968; Dallas Museum of Fine Arts, Dallas, February 1–March 3, 1968; The San Francisco Museum of Arts, March 16–April 21, 1968; the Detroit Institute of Arts, Detroit, June 19–July 21, 1968; The William Rockhill Nelson Gallery of Arts, Kansas City, October 6 –November 17, 1968; The Museum of Fine Arts, Boston, January 23–February 23, 1969; Olivetti, New York, March 5– April 5, 1969; Palais des Beaux-Arts, Brussels, September 9–October 12, 1969; Louisiana Museet, Copenhagen, November 8–December 14, 1969; Hamburger Kunsthalle, Hamburg, February 19–March 30, 1969; Museo Español de Arte Contemporaneo, Madrid, November–December 1970; Palacio de la Virreina, Barcelona, December 1970–January 1971; Museo de Arte Contemporaneo, Seville, January–February 1971; The National Museum of Modern Art, Kyoto, April 15–May 21, 1972; The National Museum of Modern Art, Tokyo, May 31–July 9, 1972), Washington, DC, H. K. Press 1967.
1967–8
Miro Damaro (F. Passoni), 'La cultura dell'arte – le scienze dell'uomo,' *Auto Chic!*, IV, no. 14, December 1967/February 1968, pp. 28–9.
1968
G. Mascherpa, 'Ogni sette giorni si può visitare la sua casa,' *Gente*, January 3, 1968, p. 75.
D. Buzzati, 'Milano per miopia fiscale rischia di perdere un tesoro,' *Corriere della Sera*, February 11, 1968.
'Un'intensa attività prevista nel programma della giunta di Aniasi,' *Parliamoci*, VII, no. 46, February 1968, pp. 6–7.
C. Gian Ferrari, 'Come Milano incoraggia il collezionismo,' *La Loggia dei Mercanti. Bollettino del sindacato nazionale mercanti d'arte moderna*, II, no. 1–2, March 1968, pp. 9–10 (reproductions of works in the collection in the whole publication).
Mar. Peno., 'L'arte e il Fisco,' *Avanti!*, November 17, 1968.
1970
P. Waldberg, 'Paragonabile a Mattioli,' *Corriere della Sera*, March 8, 1970.
'Raccolte di carattere particolare' section, *Tutta Milano*, June 1970, p. 46.
'Raccolte di carattere particolare' section, *Tutta Milano*, July 1970, p. 46.
L. Vincenti, 'Giriamo nelle case vendendo a rate migliaia di capolavori,' *Oggi*, XXVI, no. 44, 1970, pp. 3-11.
1971
M. Valsecchi, 'Come una festa il nostro '900' ('Parliamo d'Arte di Marco Valsecchi'), *Il Giorno*, February 27, 1971.
1972
V. Scheiwiller, *Milano '52-'72, Milano 70/70*, catalogue of the exhibition (Museo Poldi Pezzoli, Milan), Milan, Edizioni Edi Stampa 1972, p. 122.
F. Passoni, 'I 'Depero' di Mattioli,' *Pictogramma*, bulletin no. 2, October 1972.
'Uno scultore per Stravinsky,' *Il Giorno*, December 9, 1972.
1976
M. Valsecchi, introduction to *Arte moderna a Milano*, Cassa di Risparmio delle Provincie Lombarde, Milan, 1976, pp. 7–13.
1989
I benemeriti di Milano (ed. P. Migliorini), Comune di Milano – Edizioni Il Mondo Positivo, Milan 1989, p. 57.
1990
G. A. Dell'Acqua, 'Morandi e i collezionisti lombardi,' in *Morandi e Milano*, exhibition catalogue (Palazzo Reale, Milan, November 22, 1990–January 6, 1991), Milan, Electa 1990, p. 34.
1991
L. Mattioli Rossi, 'C'era una volta,' in *Boccioni 1912 Materia*, catalogue of the exhibition curated by L. Mattioli Rossi (Verona, Galleria dello Scudo), Milan, Edizioni Mazzotta 1991, pp. 17–26 (II edition 1995).

1993
R. Bossaglia, 'I segreti dei super collezionisti,' *Corriere della Sera*, January 10, 1993.
Letter from R. Bossaglia, 'Non Raffaele Mattioli ma Gianni Mattioli,' 'Lettere e idee' section, *Corriere della Sera*, January 12, 1993.
1997
L. Mattioli Rossi, 'Gianni Mattioli,' in L. Mattioli Rossi, E. Braun, *Capolavori della Collezione Gianni Mattioli*, Milan, Electa 1997, pp. 9–20.
P. Rizzi, 'Arriva il Museo del Futurismo,' *Il Gazzettino*, August 20, 1997.
E. Tantucci, 'I tesori del futurismo,' *Il Mattino di Padova*, August 23, 1997.
A. Masoero, 'I Futuristi avevano un amico,' *Panorama*, August 28, 1997, pp. 94–5.
G. Borgese, 'Collezioni. Addio Milano Crudele,' *Corriere della Sera*, August 31, 1997.
C. Bertelli, 'Almeno Boccioni resterà accanto a Léger e Braque,' *Corriere della Sera*, August 31, 1997.
'Diventa americana ma resta in Italia,' *Il Giornale dell'Arte*, September 1997, p. 98.
'Ventisei capolavori della Collezione Gianni Mattioli nelle "barchesse" della galleria Guggenheim,' *Il Giornale di Vicenza*, September 3, 1997.
F. Fracchini, 'Da Boccioni a Morandi risplende l'arte del Novecento,' *Il Quotidiano*, September 6, 1997.
F. C., 'Guggenheim/Tutti Futuristi amici di Gianni Mattioli,' *Avvenire*, 7 September 1997.
A. Vattese, 'La Materia del Novecento,' *Il Sole 24 Ore*, September 7, 1997.
N.O. Covero, 'Capolavori dell'avanguardia,' *L'Indipendente*, September 9, 1997.
P. Marino, 'Colpo grosso in laguna il tesoro del '900,' *La Gazzetta del Mezzogiorno*, September 12, 1997.
R. Franke, 'Exil im eigenen Land,' *Berliner Morgenpost*, September 15, 1997.
M. Brusini, 'Maestri del Novecento in ... collezione,' *Il Secolo d'Italia*, September 20, 1997.
L. Gigliotti, 'Il fattorino autodidatta con il gusto dell'arte,' *La Voce Repubblicana*, October 1–2, 1997.
F. Tedeschi, 'Magie di un grande collezionista,' *La Provincia di Como*, October 10, 1997.
G. Vonmetz Schiano, 'Ma questi Futuristi li abbiamo solo noi,' *Alto Adige*, October 12, 1997.
F. Lorenzi, 'Alla Guggenheim i Feroldi perduti da Brescia,' *Il Giornale di Brescia*, October 13, 1997.
D. Polaczek, 'Der bestrafte Sammler,' *Frankfurter Allgemeine*, October 28, 1997.
A. Sciacca, 'Milano dorme, Venezia ringrazia,' *L'Eco di Bergamo*, October 31, 1997.
M. G. Messina, 'Milano cede i suoi gioielli d'arte. Ricompare a Venezia la "Collezione Mattioli",' *L'Unità*, December 27, 1997.
1998
D. Coia, entry for 'Mattioli, Gianni,' in *Dictionary of Art*, ed. J. Turner, New York, Grove 1996.
'Double Vision,' *Orient Express Magazine*, XV, no. 1, 1998, pp. 26–30.
E. Pontiggia, 'La Raccolta Mattioli,' *Ars*, II, no. 4, April 1998, pp. 84–91.
2000
A. C. Quintavalle, entry for Collezioni d'arte,' in *Enciclopedia Italiana*, appendix 2000, vol. I, Rome, Istituto della Enciclopedia Italiana, founded by Giovanni Treccani 2000, pp. 383–94.
P. Rylands, 'Peggy Guggenheim e la sua fondazione a Venezia,' *Il Notiziario della Banca Popolare di Sondrio*, no. 82, April 2000, pp. 160–3.
2001
K. Beber, entry for 'Mattioli, Gianni' in *Dizionario del Futurismo*, ed. E. Godoli, Florence, Vallecchi 2001, pp. 717–18.
2002
L. Mattioli Rossi, entry for 'Fortunato Depero,' in *Mecenati e pittori*, catalogue of the exhibition curated by L. Mattioli Rossi (Villa Menafoglio Litta Panza, Biumo Superiore [Varese], April 20–July 14), Milan, Skira 2002, p. 34.

Reviews on line

1997
B. Malipiero, 'At the Fondazione Guggenheim in Venice: 'Capolavori della Collezione Gianni Mattioli,' 'Events' section, *Dolce Vita*, 1997 (www.dolcevita.it).
G. Grossato, 'Venezia – Peggy Guggenheim Collection,' 'Appuntamenti d'Arte' section, *Nautilus. Immagini e Cultura*, II, October 1997 (www.inews.it).
2000
M. M. Friel, 'Picasso in leasing,' 'Economia' section, *Nautilus. Immagini e Cultura*, V, December 2000 (www.inews.it).

Catalogue

Flavio Fergonzi

Explanatory Notes to the Catalogue

Each of the entries in this catalogue has three sections:
a. technical data, consisting of, in order: artist's name and biographical data (for the first entry only), title, date, medium, dimensions, inscriptions and provenance;
b. a discussion of the principal issues, such as dating, style, content and meaning, that contribute to our full understanding of the work;
c. exhibition and bibliographical listings, in chronological order.
The criteria for each of these sections are as follows.

a. Technical Data

a.1. Artist's Name and Biographical Data
All of the works have been extensively documented and constitute key works in their respective artist's *oeuvres*. Their autograph status has never been questioned in the literature, nor is it discussed in this catalogue. Since monographs exist on each of the artists, biographical data has been limited to the date and place of birth and death. Biographical data relevant to the entry is included in section *b.*

a.2. Title
The title is given first in English, followed by the Italian title. The titles are those enshrined in the history of the Mattioli Collection: those adopted for the handbook published at the time that the collection was placed on deposit at the Peggy Guggenheim Collection in Venice (Mattioli Rossi, Braun 1997) and which were in turn codified in the collection's exhibition history (*Florence* 1953[a]; *Washington, DC* 1967-*Tokyo* 1972).
One or more variant titles are given, in parentheses, if: 1) the Mattioli title does not correspond to the title given by the artist (this is the case with cat. no. 8, the collage named by Carlo Carrà *Patriotic Holiday-Freeword Painting* but which entered the Mattioli Collection as *Interventionist Demonstration*); 2) the work was given a different title when it was published for the first time, or first listed in an exhibition catalogue, or in a contemporary or near-contemporary document (for example cat. no. 25 was given the title *Still Life* by its author, Ardengo Soffici, in 1918 [*Rome* 1918[a]] and *Lemon, Pipe etc.* in 1920 [*Florence* 1920], before the artist himself renamed the work *Small Trophy* [Papini 1933]); 3) the work was known by a different title prior to its purchase by Mattioli (the titles of cat. nos. 17 and 18, Morandi's *Still Life* and *Flowers* respectively, were substituted over a period of time by titles that the collector himself preferred: *Bottles and Fruit Bowl* and *Roses*).
Section *c.* (the exhibition and bibliographical appendices) enables the reader to track significant variations, if any, in the title even after Mattioli's purchase of the work: the variant title is given in parentheses at the end of the listing.

a.3. Date
This is the date of the execution of the work as deduced from section *b.* The given date may differ from that which is inscribed on the work by the artist. In the event that an artist reworked a painting after a documented lapse of time, the date of the reworking is specified (e.g. '1912, reworked 1913' in the case of cat. no. 4, *Materia* by Umberto Boccioni). A more precise dating within the year is when possible discussed in section *b.* In the appendices in section *c.* (exhibitions and bibliography) dates are noted when they differ from the date given in this catalogue.

a.4. Medium and Support
This refers to the medium and support of the work in its present state. Conservation is discussed in this section only when this involved transferring the work from its original support to another (e.g. the tempera on paper glued to canvas in the case of Giacomo Balla's temperas, cat. nos. 1 and 2), but not otherwise (e.g. the replacement of the canvas support after the detachment of the paint surface in cat. no. 16 by Giorgio Morandi; relining of canvases, or other types of conservation treatment). In such cases, conservation is discussed, and when possible dated, in section *b.*

a.5. Dimensions
These are in centimeters for paintings and collages and in millimeters for drawings. Height precedes width.

a.6. Inscriptions
Inscriptions in the artist's hand, whether on the *recto* or *verso*, stretcher or support, are noted here. Section *b.* discusses inscriptions that are no longer legible but which are referred to in the earlier critical literature (e.g. the date 1912 written on the back of cat. no. 19, *Dynamism Bar San Marco* by Ottone Rosai, which can no longer be read owing to lining with a new canvas). Section *b.* also mentions other documentation on the *verso* (writing, stamps, labels) when this is relevant for chronology, provenance or exhibition history. When identifying the position of these inscriptions, and indeed when there is any mention of left or right, this refers to the viewpoint of the spectator, unless otherwise stated.

a.7. Provenance
This records, chronologically, documented changes in ownership of the work. Question marks indicate when the date on which the work changed hands is uncertain, or if the name of the owner is in doubt. When a sale has been brokered by a third party (private person or gallery), the phrase 'with the mediation of...' appears. Section *b.* provides documentary references and discusses any issues raised by provenance.

b. The Text

This part of the entry deals in detail with all the issues raised by the work: its date, its iconography, its relationship to preparatory studies or other works of art, its ideological or programmatic relationship to contemporary cultural and artistic discourse; its visual sources; its technical and stylistic peculiarities; its critical fortune and its place in the history of collecting. Some of these issues are already lodged in the critical debate about the work to date; others are raised here for the first time. Given the definition of this book as a *catalogue raisonné*, the emphasis is placed on matters of chronology and iconography, analysis of preparatory works, identification of visual sources, and the reconstruction of the work's provenance.
The date of the work has been arrived at by cross-comparing the date either given on the support by the artist himself or customarily assigned to the work in the literature, with other references that may serve as reliable *terminus post quem* or *ante quem*: letters, archives, catalogues, publications or contemporary photographs. As far as possible all newspaper clippings used in the collages have been tracked down, and these naturally serve as *terminus post quem*. In support of such references, and in place of them when they are lacking, other considerations have also been taken into account (technique, style, or content) that serve to place the work in relation to other works by the same artist or by other artists. In some of the more complex cases (cat. nos. 4, 9, 17, 25 for example), this has led to a rather broad review of the artist's entire production in the period under examination.
The iconography of the work, when this is not self-evident (such as in cat. nos. 1, 4, 8, and 9), is discussed in terms of its title, of the repertoire of the artist's interests and awarenesses, and in general of the historical and cultural context in which the work was produced.
Preparatory studies, directly related works and later derivations are consistently included with the purpose of reconstructing the development of the artist's motif. When possible these have been included in the comparative illustrations.
As for matters of style, and in general of the formal framework and intellectual intentions of the work, interpretive or descriptive declarations by the artist himself (in manifestos, statements, letters and any other texts) have been privileged. Possible coeval visual references have been tracked down, and these are always supported by evidence of how the artist could have known them (first hand experience, photographs, publications or letters).
Special attention is given to provenance and to the work's critical fortune, whether visual or literary, before its entry to the Mattioli Collection. This has the benefit of helping to place the collector's choices in the appropriate cultural perspective. Certain of the twenty-six works (such as for example *The Engineer's Mistress* by Carlo Carrà, cat. no. 10) were already famous at the time they were bought by Mattioli; others, including almost all of the Futurist works, entered the canon of Italian twentieth-century art only after they entered Mattioli's celebrated collection. Changes in the works ownership are established both from standard sources (such as sale contracts, exhibition catalogues, labels glued to the back of the work), and occasionally recourse from the typewritten files of the Mattioli archives (identified as 'Archivio Mattioli, file for the work'), in which the information is derived directly from the collector.
The entries do not provide answers to all the questions that are raised. In certain areas of particular controversy (for example, the chronology of *Materia* within Umberto Boccioni's production in 1912 and its priority or succession to other related works), the author has declined to adopt a position, marshalling what is known for certain, and drawing subordinate conclusions that may favor resolution of the larger problem in the future. In others (for example, the explanation of how the title of Giacomo Balla's *Paths of Movement + Dynamic Sequences* relates to the visual evidence, or the possible links between Balla's *Mercury Passing Before the Sun* and Albert Einstein's studies of relativity, or the visual sources for Giorgio Morandi's *Bottles and Fruit Bowl*), the author's hypotheses are put forward even while other, alternative solutions are acknowledged.
The comparative illustrations are intended to aid the reader's understanding of the relevant passages in the entry. Generally these document the preparatory studies, other related works, the visual sources, and key moments in the history of the work.

c. The Appendices

c.1. Exhibitions

This lists in chronological order and in abbreviated form (place and date), the exhibitions in which the work has been shown, followed by the relative catalogue number. The page number is included only when necessary for the identification of the work. In exhibition catalogues without numeration, only the page number is specified. Full details of the exhibitions cited are in the chronological list of exhibitions at the end.

If the work was exhibited with a title differing from that given at the beginning of the entry, this is added in parentheses. A question mark signifies uncertainty whether the work displayed is securely identifiable with the subject of the entry.

The list of exhibitions is a census in the strict sense of the loan of the work to exhibitions, such as can be deduced from catalogues, from the Mattioli archives, and from the critical literature surrounding the exhibitions themselves. Thus exhibitions are also included in the following cases: 1) when the catalogue omits mention of a work that was nevertheless on exhibition; 2) when no catalogue was printed; 3) when the author has been unable to find a copy of the catalogue. Such cases are identified as follows: 'not in catalogue', 'no catalogue printed', 'catalogue not traced'. When appropriate they are followed by a note explaining the presumed or certain presence of the work in the exhibition.

When instead a work is listed in the catalogue of an exhibition to which it was not in fact loaned, the exhibition is not listed, and its catalogue listed instead in the bibliography.

Only the earliest reproduction of the work in chronological terms is listed among both exhibitions and the bibliography.

In order to distinguish references to exhibitions from the abbreviated bibliographical references, exhibitions are given in italics if they occur in footnotes. They are instead in normal font in Appendix *c.1.*

c.2. Bibliography

This lists, in chronological order and abbreviated form (author, year, page number), the critical literature relevant to the work. In the case of daily, weekly or twice-monthly periodicals, the precise publication date is given, without the page number. Publications are included only when they specifically refer to the subject of the entry. Publications of indirect relevance to the entry are quoted and listed in detail in section b: this is particularly relevant where preparatory studies for major works are discussed (such as those for *Paths of Movement + Dynamic Sequences* by Giacomo Balla, cat. no. 1, or *The City Rises* by Umberto Boccioni, cat. no. 3), involving the vast literature linked to the final version which is obviously pertinent to the interpretation of the Mattioli paintings.

Letters or other archival documents are listed under the dates they were written, rather than when they may have been published.

Generally bibliographical items are included according to the following criteria. The complete traceable bibliography is given up to the time when Mattioli acquired the work. After this date, when owing to the fame of the collection and because Mattioli himself campaigned for the works to be reproduced as often and as widely as possible the bibliography grows exponentially, a more selective approach is adopted: publications are now listed because they contribute new ideas, approaches or facts to the literature; other items are included because they are perceived as relevant to the work's critical fortune, given their historical importance, the renown of the author, or the breadth of circulation.

Notes on the translation

Philip Rylands

The original language of this catalogue is Italian (excepting cat. no. 8). Given the importance of titles in reconstructing dates, exhibition history and provenance, all titles are recorded in the original language for the use of scholars, primarily in the footnotes but also in the text itself, in the captions to the figures that illustrate the entries, and most obviously directly after the English title(s) of the work at the beginning of each entry.

The word 'scomposizione' occurs frequently in stylistic analysis as well as in the titles of Futurist and Cubist works of art. The English word 'fragmentation' has been preferred to 'decomposition', with its suggestion of decay, or the relatively rare and awkward 'discomposition'.

Translations of quotations are as literal as possible, retaining even peculiarities of punctuation. This is in order to preserve the original, often singular and dated diction, whether colloquial in letters or poetic in passages of art criticism.

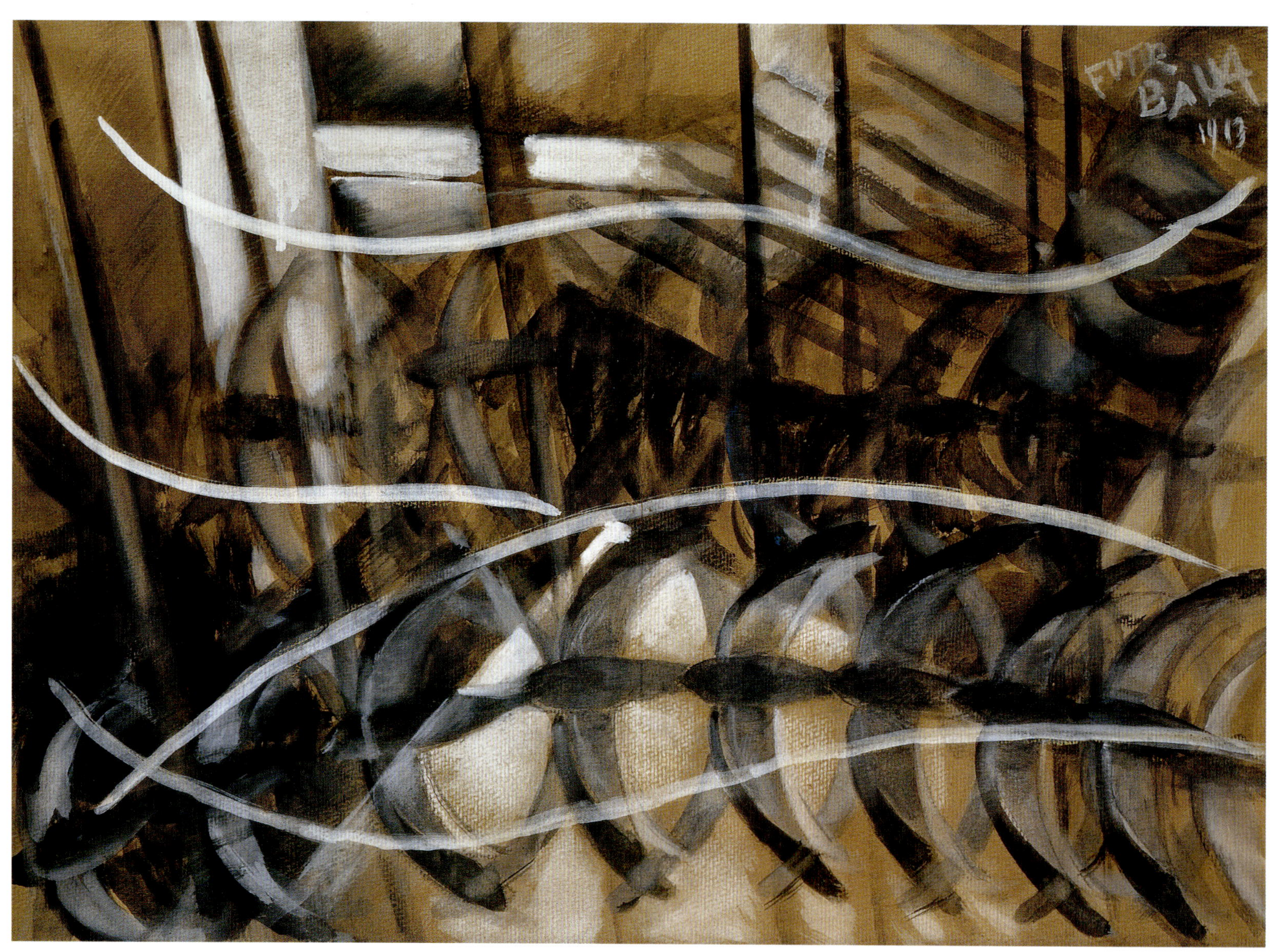
FUTR
BALLA
1913

1

Giacomo Balla (Turin, 1871 – Rome, 1958)

Paths of Movement + Dynamic Sequences (Swifts in Flight; Swifts in Flight–Study)

Linee andamentali + successioni dinamiche (Rondoni in volo; Rondoni in volo-studio), 1913

Tempera on paper laid on canvas
49 × 68 cm

Inscription: *recto*, signed upper right: 'FUTUR / BALLA / 1913'

Provenance: property of the artist; 1950: Gianni Mattioli

Exhibitions: Zurich 1950?, no. 7 (*Schwalbenflug. Studie II*, 1913); Florence 1953[a], no. 5 (*Rondoni in volo,* 1913); New York 1954, no. 6 (*Swifts: Paths of Movement + Dynamic Sequences*); Turin 1957, no page nor catalogue number (*Linee andamentali*, 1913); Rome 1959, no. 55 *(Linee andamentali+successioni dinamiche*, 1913); Winterthur 1959, no. 1; Munich 1959–60, no. 1; Venice 1960, p. 13, no. 7; Turin–Milan 1961, no. 30; Cologne 1962, no. z/6, fig. 144; Turin 1963, no. 84; Washington, DC 1967–Tokyo 1972, no. 26 (Washington, DC–Hamburg), no. 25 (Madrid–Seville), no. 26 (Kyoto–Tokyo); Rome 1971–2, no. 33; Newcastle upon Tyne 1972–London 1973, no. 3; Paris 1973, no. 7; Milan 1973–4, no. 231; Düsseldorf 1974, no. 16; Venice 1986, p. 97; Saint-Paul de Vence 1992, no. 22; Barcelona 1996, no. 10

Bibliography: Garretto 1952, p. 43 (illus.); Ragghianti 1953, p. 9; Haftmann 1955, p. 122, no. 252; Ballo 1956, p. 16; Drudi Gambillo, Fiori 1958–62, vol. I, p. 400 (*Rondoni in volo*), vol. II, pp. 90, 157, no. 97 (*Volo di rondini*); Marchiori 1960, no. 25; Carrieri 1961, no. 80; Crispolti 1963, p. 16; Crispolti, Drudi Gambillo 1963, p. 66 (*Linee andamentali+successioni dinamiche*); Ballo 1964[b], vol. I, p. 91; Barricelli 1966, p. 35; Calvesi 1967, pp. 130, 142–3,

Although Giacomo Balla signed both manifestos of Futurist painting in 1910, his work had little in common with that of other Futurist artists, in Milan, until early 1913. While Umberto Boccioni and Carlo Carrà were striving for a plastic dynamism based on the dislocated spaces and interpenetrating objects of the language of Cubism, Balla in 1912 was concerned with the analysis of movement. He broke it down into sequences of distinct images (the positions of a violinist's hand, the oscillations of a moving leash, the succession of a girl's steps) and focused on linear rhythms. His studies for *Swifts: Paths of Movement + Dynamic Sequences*, initiated in the spring of 1913, marked the beginning of Balla's interest in new formal devices: intersecting planes and a synthetic pattern (the wavy line) to represent the passage of a moving body.

Balla dedicated a series of six tempera and oil studies[1] as well as various preparatory drawings in pencil and charcoal (some with touches of red) to the subject of swifts in flight which he observed from his studio overlooking the park of the Villa Borghese. The culmination of this cycle is unanimously considered to be the oil on canvas now in the Museum of Modern Art in New York (96.8 × 120 cm, fig. 1d), the only work both documented in a contemporary photograph[2] and with a verifiable early exhibition history.[3] Of the entire series, the tempera on paper laid on canvas in the Mattioli Collection is the closest to the painting in New York. The birds are placed along the same curving trajectories that intersect the broken lines of the gutters around the balcony and the straight lines of the French-door frames; the light is comparably subdued, with brownish tones probably implying dusk, when swifts fly through the sky with their piercing cries; a series of prominent wavy white lines (the 'paths of movement' in the title), whose meaning is controversial, traverse the foreground.

Balla's daughter Elica, in a memoir written late in life that opens with recollections of her father, remembered that he was fascinated by swifts in flight even in his pre-Futurist period ("What joy those swifts in flight gave the artist who would later make a painting and then the endless series of analytical studies of their flight for his 1913 Futurist study *Swallows* [*sic*] *in Flight + Paths of Movement*"[4]). Confirmation of this can be found in a letter Balla wrote to his family from Düsseldorf, datable to July 1912: "The only thing I can compare to my past existence are the swifts, exactly like those in Rome."[5] However, apart from his fondness for even the most commonplace animal and vegetable life, to which those who knew Balla testified, there are other possible reasons for his choice of the motif of flying swifts.

The first of these were the studies of birds in flight by the physiologist Etienne-Jules Marey, in his famous photographs taken in rapid succession. Giovanni Lista and Marta Braun have reconstructed the occasions on which Balla may have encountered the work of Marey and his photographic plates. These were exhibited in 1898 at the first 'Congresso Fotografico Nazionale' in Turin, the artist's birthplace, and two years later in the 'metrophotography' and 'chronophotography' galleries of the 1900 'Exposition Universelle' in Paris, which Balla visited. Again, Marey's chronophotography books were discussed at the 'Congresso Internazionale di Fisiologia' in Turin in 1902, held at the same time as the 'Esposizione Internazionale di Arti Decorative'. Furthermore, closer to the time when Balla was working on the swifts series of which the Mattioli tempera is a part, an important *corpus* of prints was presented at the 'Esposizione Fotografica Internazionale' held in Rome in 1911.[6] There can be no doubt that Balla studied certain of these chronophotographs: that of a seagull flying upwards (1886, fig. 1h) may have prompted the rapid and rhythmical beating of the wings of the swifts.[7] However, Balla's sources in this case were not only photographic. Marey's most widely circulated scientific texts (*La Méthode graphique dans les sciences expérimentales*, 1878; *Le Vol des oiseaux*, 1890) were illustrated with drawings based on his chronophotographs and these were probably available to Balla while observing the swifts flying over the Villa Borghese gardens. The side views of the various angles of the flapping of the birds' wings may have influenced his early drawings in the series;[8] the tabulated plate with outlines of flight projected on three different registers

notes 99–100, p. 437; Fagiolo dell'Arco 1968, p. 17; Apollonio 1970, pl. VII (*Study of Ongoing Lines [Swallows]*, 1913); Sani 1971, pp. 160–1; Velani 1971, pp. 115, 121, 125, 129; Lista 1982, no. 356, p. 211 and 509–10 (*Linee andamentali + successioni dinamiche - Volo di rondini*); Roche-Pézard 1983, p. 383; Balla 1984, p. 167; Boess 1988, pp. 115–16; Antolini 1991, p. 464; Crispolti 1992, pp. 467–8; Braun 1992, p. 306; Marziali 1996, pp. 142–3; Rylands 1997, p. 50; Fagiolo dell'Arco 1998[a], p. 24

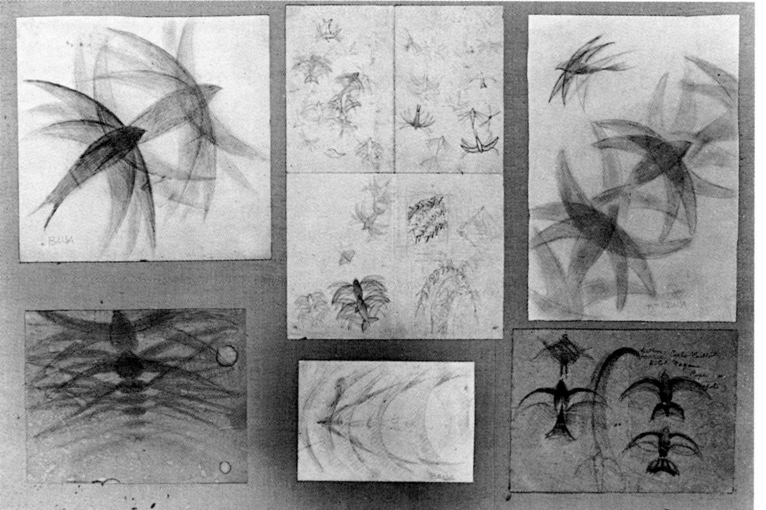

Fig. 1a. *Giacomo Balla,* Six Studies of Swifts in Flight, *pencil on paper, 1913. Rome, Galleria Nazionale d'Arte Moderna*

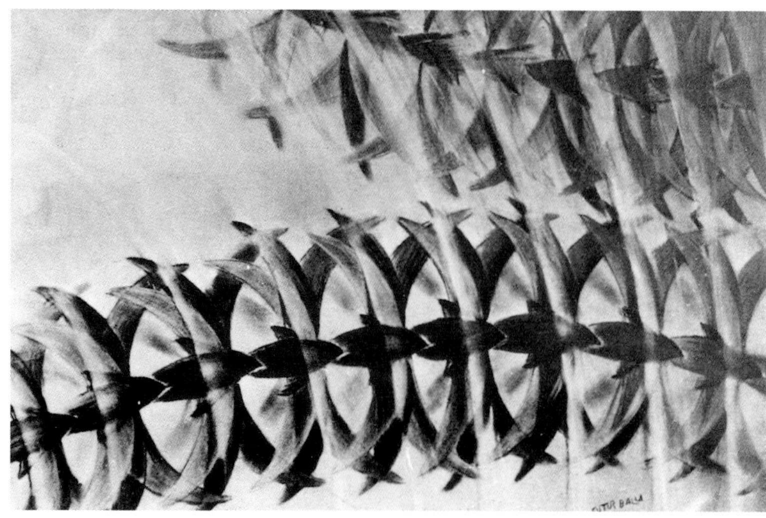

Fig. 1b. *Giacomo Balla,* Volo di rondoni (Flight of Swifts*), charcoal and pastel on paper, 1913. Paris, private collection*

Fig. 1c. *Giacomo Balla, Study for* Linee andamentali + successioni dinamiche, *pencil and charcoal on paper, 1913. Private collection*

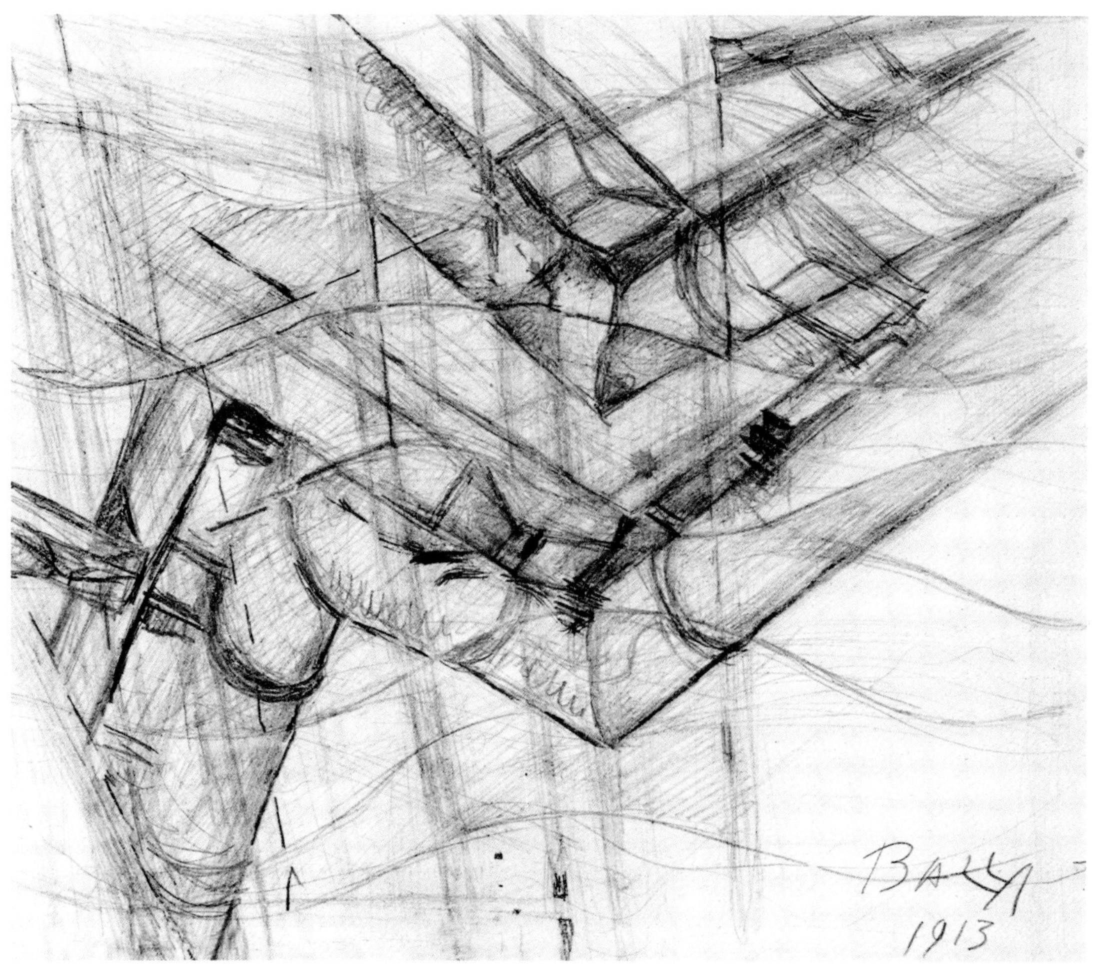

(fig. 1i)[9] may have suggested the 'paths of movement' which were maintained even in the final versions of the image;[10] finally, the linear depiction of their flapping wings when soaring into the wind (fig. 1k)[11] may explain the brusque and apparently incomprehensible addition of a second line in the upper left of the Mattioli tempera.

Maurizio Fagiolo dell'Arco has pointed to a second possible source: the scientific studies of Leonardo da Vinci, an artist particularly dear to Balla.[12] The artist even took Leonardo, together with books by Dante, Foscolo and Leopardi, as reading matter on his trip to Düsseldorf in 1912.[13] In 1892 Leonardo's *Codice sul volo degli uccelli* (*Codex on the Flight of Birds*) entered the Biblioteca Reale in Turin, where Balla could have seen it given that he lived there until 1895. It was published in 1893 in a fine edition by Teodoro Sabachnikoff and Giovanni Piumati. In the sheets describing the behavior of birds in relation to different types of flight and differing wind conditions, Leonardo made sketches of birds in repetitive sequences of movement, in which the direction of the wind is indicated by dense parallel pen strokes. The clear reproductions on the right-hand pages of the Sabachnikoff-Piumati edition of the codex served to isolate single drawings on the white ground (fig. 1l) and to place them in relation to Leonardo's text on the facing pages.[14] Balla's attention would have been drawn to the analysis of the movement of birds through sequential repetition, and may have been the inspiration for the layout of his early drawings.

Another relevant factor is that in 1913, in order to represent speed, Balla retrieved graphic devices invented earlier for different subjects. In one of his pencil studies for the luminous radiance of *The Street Lamp*,[15] the arrows of multicolored light (an acute wedge, crossed by an arc-like motif through its center) resemble the stylized swifts in the early drawings of the series.

Finally it is worth mentioning a couplet in a poem by Corrado Govoni, 'La città morta', published in *Lacerba* in March 1913, in which the flight of a swift is compared to "an arrow / poisoned in springtime."[16] This testifies to the circulation of the semantic constellation swift/arrow/speed in Futurist circles during the months when Balla was beginning his studies for *Swifts: Paths of Movement + Dynamic Sequences*.

The sequential arrangement of the studies for the final painting constitutes the first real difficulty when studying the series; the matter is further complicated by the fact that it cannot be excluded *a priori* that Balla executed some components of the series after completion of the painting now in the Museum of Modern Art in New York.

Balla began by studying the subject of flying swifts in pencil on small sheets (some of which were later assembled on a single support [fig. 1a];[17] others remained separate[18]) or on larger separate sheets.[19] They range from profile views to views from above and frontally from below and were probably made with the aid of chronophotography, since in some cases Balla captured the moment of flight, invisible to the naked eye, when the tip of the wing turns toward the bird's head. Sometimes the focus is limited to the mechanics of the flapping wing (the bird is seen in only two forward-moving positions, but each consists of five different angles of beating wings), while in others the focus is on the broad trajectory, covering an entire arc (with a sequence of evidently less analytical positions). The silhouette of the bird seen from above, with three overlapping positions of the flapping wings,[20] is studied with strong decorative simplification in a tempera on paper;[21] then, in an oil on canvas,[22] the motif is set against a background of broad wedges of divided colors. The technique in this background is similar to that in *Girl Running on a Balcony*,[23] a painting executed not later than February 1913. In a large charcoal and pastel study (fig. 1b),[24] the motif of the bird seen from above with three different positions

Fig. 1d. *Giacomo Balla,* Rondoni: Linee andamentali + successioni dinamiche *(*Swifts: Paths of Movement + Dynamic Sequences*), oil on canvas, 1913. New York, The Museum of Modern Art, purchase*

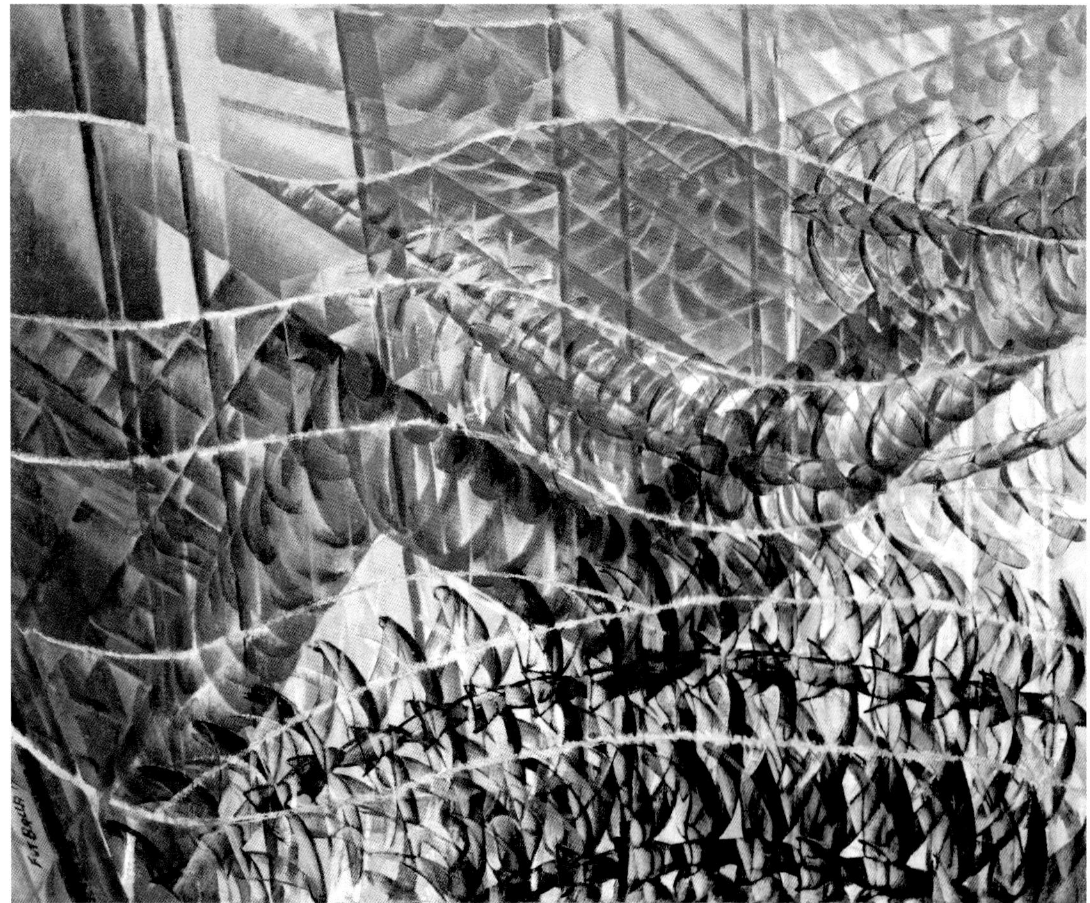

Fig. 1e. *Detail of fig. 1d*

Fig. 1f. *Detail of cat. no. 1*

Fig. 1g. *Giacomo Balla,* Linee andamentali + successioni dinamiche (Paths of Movement + Dynamic Sequences)*, tempera on paper, 1913. Private collection*

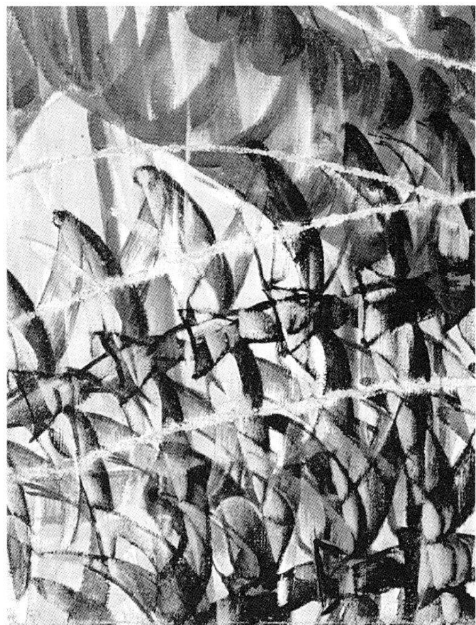

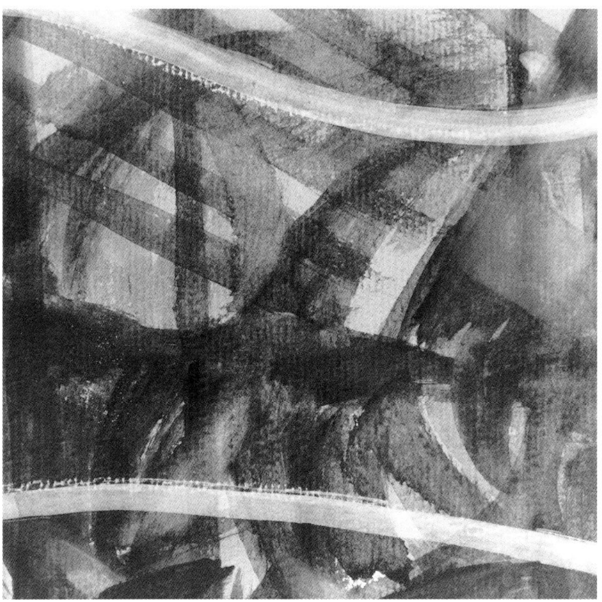

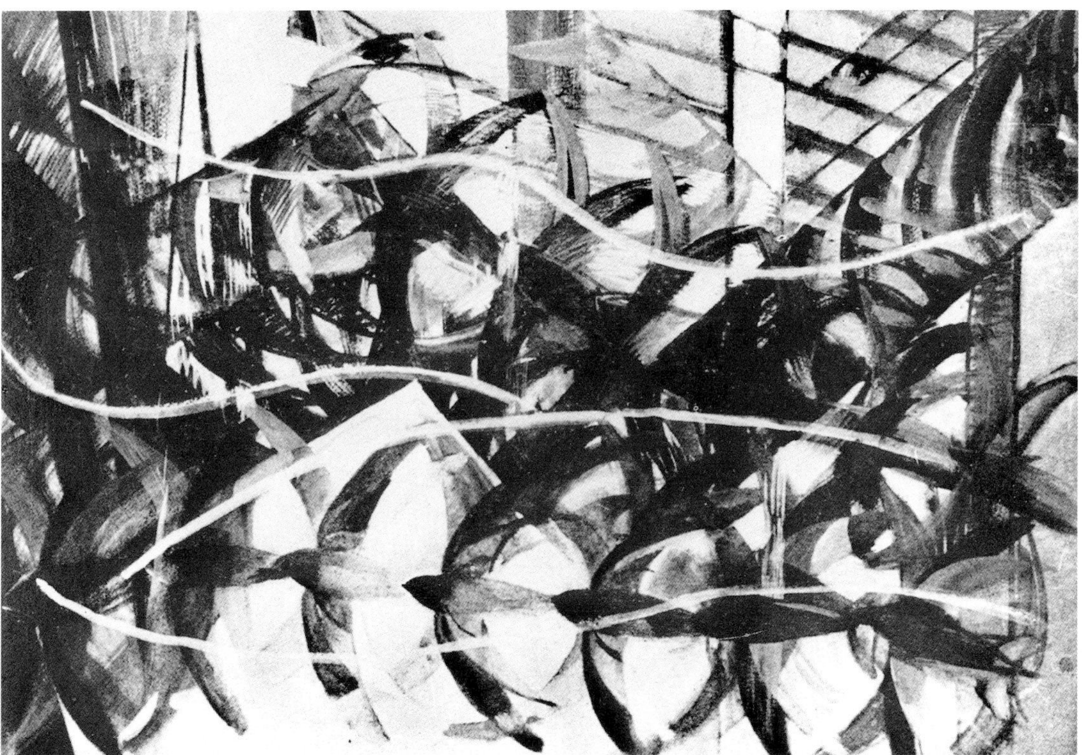

of its beating wings (and a fourth lightly sketched) is multiplied to create an arc running from left to right along the lower part of the drawing, while a swift repeats the movement in the opposite direction in the upper part.

At a certain point Balla began to study the surroundings of his motif, and this precipitated a decisive shift away from the somewhat decorative, two-dimensional studies hitherto. In a small sketch in a private collection, a careful description of volumes in perspectival space, he drew the eaves with their wooden supports as well as the gutter, viewed from below: the detail of the gutter is repeated higher on the sheet (fig. 1c).[25] The lighter vertical lines seem to represent the French-door frames through which the gutter was seen from inside the studio. Swifts as such are absent from the drawing but instead a series of wavy lines (integral to the drawing and not later additions) traverse the sheet from left to right. In another, possibly later drawing (since exactly the same subject is drawn in a more precise hand), three swifts in tight formation flying from left to right have been added, as if seen from inside the room against the background of the sky.[26]

It is not easy to position these two drawings and the Mattioli tempera in a chronological sequence culminating in the finished painting in the Museum of Modern Art (fig. 1d). The Mattioli study seems indebted to the first drawing in only a limited way (fig. 1c: broadly, in the viewpoint from below and the uprights of the doorframe which scan the composition in the vertical sense). In other respects it is closer to solutions developed in the Museum of Modern Art painting (the reduction from two gutters to one; the passage of the swifts in the foreground; the extension of the doorframes to the right). But it also differs both from the final painting and from the other drawing: the wavy lines are four instead of the seven in both the drawing and the New York painting. Thus the Mattioli tempera may represent Balla's first attempt to overlay the passage of the birds, analyzed in paint, onto his drawings of the eaves (which would explain why the right-left direction, previously found in the above-mentioned oil painting catalogued by Lista as no. 355, is maintained). Compared to others in the series, the Mattioli painting is singular for its luminosity (the clear light that strikes the frames and reverberates in repeated effects of transparency) and its color scheme (an overall brown monochrome accented by liquid dark marks and by the white of the lit areas). This is obtained by extremely simple means: the black marks representing the swifts and the white washes are executed on unprimed paper. The light is more metallic, the chromatic range richer (with yellow, green and blue passages) and the composition more contrived in the Museum of Modern Art painting.[27]

It seems clear that, with the Mattioli tempera, Balla was trying for the first time to combine two hitherto separate cycles of studies (that of the bird's flight and that of the gutter) into a coherent chiaroscuro whole. The white 'paths of movement' lines may not have been painted at the same time as the rest of the painting. They appear to have been brushed over an already dry surface, together with the signature (in 1913 the artist was not yet signing his works 'Futur Balla'[28]) but not the date, which seems to have been added at yet another moment, in a smaller hand and with thicker paint. The close vicinity of the date of the Mattioli tempera on paper to that of the Museum of Modern Art canvas is proved by a detail in the execution of both works. Balla originally drew the 'paths of movement' lines in yellow pastel on the Mattioli tempera, and this still shows through in certain places on the right side; only later did he cover them with fluid white strokes in tempera (fig. 1f). The 'paths of movement' in the New York painting are also yellow, and are obtained not by adding but by subtracting color, by scraping the surface to reveal the priming (fig. 1e). Balla may have been experimenting with yellow lines in the Mattioli tempera, to assess the effect they would have in an oil painting, and then overpainted them with white to restore the chromatic harmony of the whole.

The other two tempera studies in this series do not seem to complicate the sequence that is being proposed here. The first, a tempera on paper like the Mattioli painting but of slightly larger dimensions (50×76 cm: fig. 1g),[29] is similar in its right-to-left direction of the swifts' flight and in the comparable four wavy white lines; but it is closer to the Museum of Modern Art painting in its depiction of the last piece of the gutter on the left. The second, even larger tempera (58×84 cm),[30] is painted in a more abbreviated and generalized style and with a different palette (brick red with blue touches). It portrays the passage of a single swift (low down, moving from left to right) and lacks the 'paths of movement' lines omnipresent in the studies where swifts and gutters are combined. This seems to be a simplified re-visitation of the composition previously achieved in the Museum of Modern Art painting.

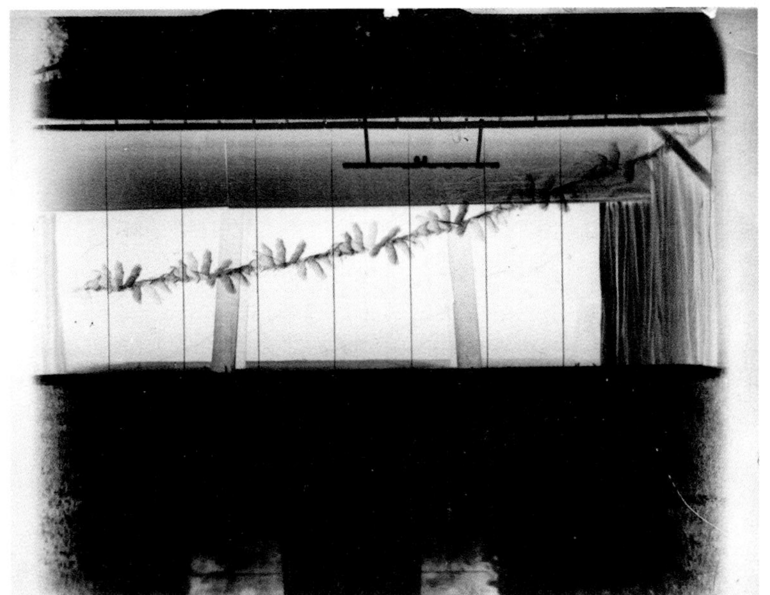

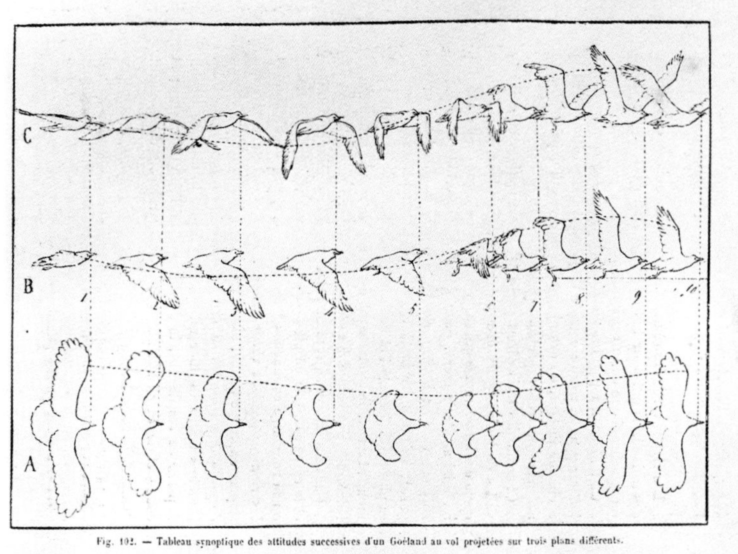

Fig. 1h. *Etienne-Jules Marey,* Flight of a Seagull, *chronophotograph, 1886. Paris, Collège de France*

Fig. 1i. Tableau synoptyque des attitudes successives d'un Goéland au vol projetées sur trois plans différents, *in E.-J. Marey,* Le Vol des oiseaux, *1890*

The second important problem posed by the Mattioli tempera is the meaning of the work *vis-à-vis* its title. In particular, there are differences in opinion about the meaning of the first of the two syntagmas of the title (*Paths of Movement*), which is generally agreed to refer to the wavy horizontal white lines which surface from the time the balcony setting first appears (with, as we have seen, one exception — Lista's catalogue no. 354). It has been read as a synthetic representation of the artist's repeated walking to and fro (in his studio or on the balcony) while observing the flying swifts.[31] Alternatively it may stand for a synthesis of the trajectories of the birds' flight paths[32] superimposed on the dynamic sequence of the beating of their wings.

There is no decisive argument in favor of either interpretation. When one of the paintings in the series (most probably that of the Museum of Modern Art) was exhibited at the Doré Galleries in London late in April 1914, it appeared with the English title *Walking Lines – Dynamic Successions*:[33] even with due caution for the circumstances (translation of titles into foreign languages in early Futurist exhibitions was most often the responsibility of the gallery owner; who explained the meanings of the titles to him is unclear), this translation would unequivocally remove any doubt in favor of the former interpretation (later English translations of the first syntagma of the title were more neutral and denotative: *Progressive Lines* or *Paths of Movement*[34]). Balla legitimated this explanation many years later when replying to a questionnaire from the Museum of Modern Art in 1952[35] and, orally, on other occasions.[36] However, this makes certain characteristics shared by the principal works of the series hard to explain: the strokes are overly varied and extend too far (they cross the gutter in one drawing) to represent the passage of the artist along the narrow balcony. Furthermore the multiplication of the points of view turns the artist into the fixed observer of a scene also comprised of his own movement. Prior to this, when Balla used undulating horizontal lines to express movement, he did so to suggest the passage of a body perfectly visible in the painting itself. This can be seen in a study for *Leash in Motion*[37] and in a study for *Girl Running on a Balcony*[38] (fig. 1n), in which a continuous wavy line follows the hem of the girl's dress through the various sequences of its positions. An interpretation of the 'paths of movement' as a synthesis of the motion of the birds' wings (the most circumstantiated explanation for this is Giovanni Lista's reference to the line called 'the stereoscopic trajectory of movement' by Marey[39]) also has its problems: the lines, even in the Mattioli tempera, do not always refer explicitly to the passing swifts, but animate the foreground of the painting independently. Moreover in Marey, who is un-

levier est placé horizontalement sur une planchette à laquelle on imprime des oscillations verticales. Dans ces conditions de mouvements continuellement variés imprimés à l'appareil, la masse qui charge le levier présente continuellement une résistance par son inertie; quand le tambour s'élève, la masse abaisse la mem-

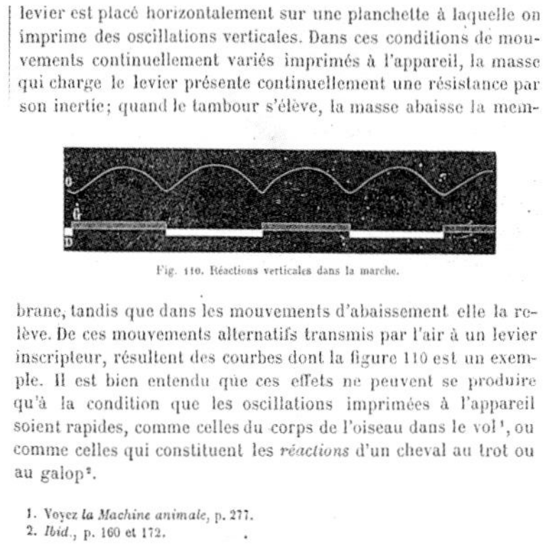

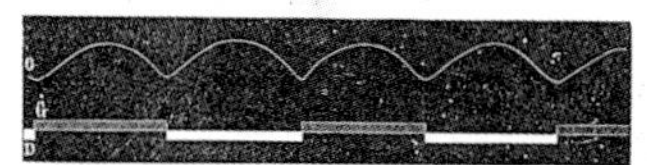

Fig. 110. Réactions verticales dans la marche.

brane, tandis que dans les mouvements d'abaissement elle la relève. De ces mouvements alternatifs transmis par l'air à un levier inscripteur, résultent des courbes dont la figure 110 est un exemple. Il est bien entendu que ces effets ne peuvent se produire qu'à la condition que les oscillations imprimées à l'appareil soient rapides, comme celles du corps de l'oiseau dans le vol[1], ou comme celles qui constituent les *réactions* d'un cheval au trot ou au galop[2].

1. Voyez *la Machine animale*, p. 277.
2. *Ibid.*, p. 160 et 172.

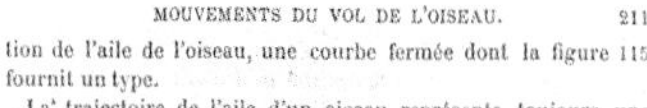

MOUVEMENTS DU VOL DE L'OISEAU. 211

tion de l'aile de l'oiseau, une courbe fermée dont la figure 115 fournit un type.

La trajectoire de l'aile d'un oiseau représente toujours une

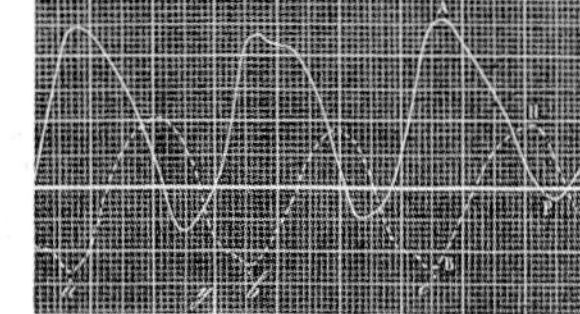

Fig. 114. Courbes des deux ordres de mouvement de l'aile d'un pigeon. AP, ligne pleine, mouvements dans le sens antéro-postérieur. HB, ligne ponctuée, mouvements de haut en bas.

sorte d'ellipse dont les deux axes sont fort inégaux. Le grand axe est incliné en bas et en avant par rapport à la direction

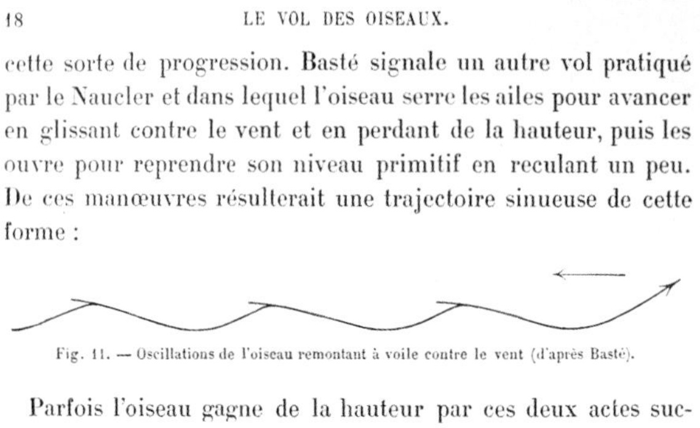

18 LE VOL DES OISEAUX.

cette sorte de progression. Basté signale un autre vol pratiqué par le Naucler et dans lequel l'oiseau serre les ailes pour avancer en glissant contre le vent et en perdant de la hauteur, puis les ouvre pour reprendre son niveau primitif en reculant un peu. De ces manœuvres résulterait une trajectoire sinueuse de cette forme :

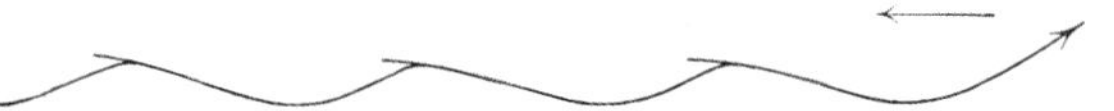

Fig. 11. — Oscillations de l'oiseau remontant à voile contre le vent (d'après Basté).

Parfois l'oiseau gagne de la hauteur par ces deux actes suc-

Fig. 1j. *Pattern of oscillations of the movement of a man and the flight of a pigeon, in E.-J. Marey,* La Méthode graphique dans les sciences expérimentales, *1878*

Fig. 1k. Oscillations de l'oiseau remontant à voile contre le vent, *in E.-J. Marey,* Le Vol des oiseaux, *1890*

doubtedly the key source for the whole cycle of studies, the undulating line used by Balla for the 'paths of movement' always referred to the trajectory of a moving human being: the trajectory of the flight of birds, whether their beating wings are represented in a forwards-backwards motion or in an up-down direction, makes a different pattern, with more acute angled peaks (fig. 1j).[40]

The only certainties are that Balla worked on studies with swifts painted against a neutral background without undulating lines and that at a certain point he studied a setting of eaves and doorframes and introduced these wavy lines. Planning a painting focused on the passage of swifts seen from his studio, he may initially have intended to represent the birds' trajectories as simple synthetic lines (as in the drawing catalogued by Lista as no. 360: fig. 1c); later he must have realized that inserting the swifts, studied separately with analytic methods focused on the beating of their wings, made the superimposition of the synthetic lines over the sequences of objects in flight too mechanical. At this point he would have separated the swifts' trajectories from the oscillations of the line (a process easily discernible in Lista 358), and maintained this division through the rest of the cycle. As his work progressed, the meaning of these lines may have changed with respect to his initial intentions, or at least to their justification. Aided by the theories and examples of the photodynamics of Anton Giulio Bragaglia (who in a photograph titled *Man Walking* had obtained the white lines of movement of a man passing, made almost invisible by the length of the exposure: fig. 1m), Balla perhaps only then introduced the motif of the artist walking in his studio: he may have suggested it to Boccioni for the French translation of the caption (*Lignes d'allure* [*Paths of Walking*]) when the painting was illustrated in *Pittura scultura futuriste*;[41] he may then have been so explicit on the point afterwards as to cancel any possible doubt for the translation in London, and thereafter continued to adopt the same interpretation of the motif.

Many factors complicate the chronology of Balla's paintings between February 1913 and the first half of the following year: the unusual volume of his production over this period;[42] his working simultaneously on various cycles;[43] the difficulty in identifying with certainty the paintings sent to exhibitions; and the habit of inscribing dates on paintings at some time after their execution.[44] Despite this, dating the studies for *Swifts: Paths of Movement + Dynamic Sequences* does not seem particularly problematic. If by the end of September 1913 all the painters in the Futurist group, excepting Soffici, had delivered the photographs for publication in Boccioni's book,[45] the Museum of Modern Art version was already finished and photographed by this date (it appeared as the first of the sequence of five reproductions of paintings by Balla). The same *terminus ante quem* applies therefore to the Mattioli tempera. This confirms the chronology posited by Elica Balla,[46] based on the recollections of her father, according to which the painting is the fourth and last of the analytic studies of movement, exe-

Fig. 11. *Leonardo da Vinci, Two studies of the flight of birds, in* I Manoscritti di Leonardo da Vinci. Codice sul volo degli uccelli e varie altre materie, *1898*

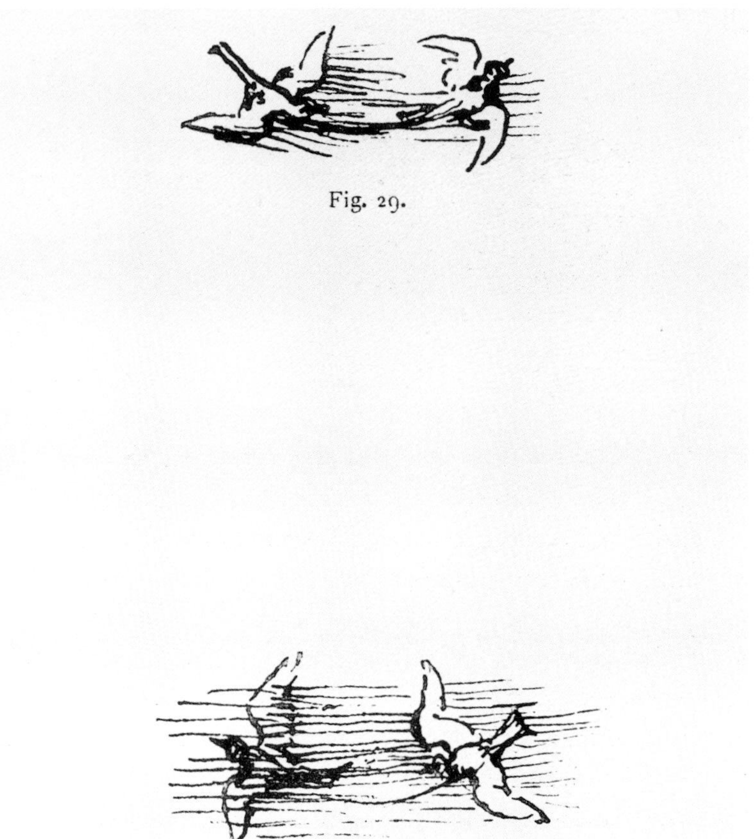

cuted after the February 1913 show in Rome where the first three (*Leash in Motion*, *The Rhythm of the Violinist*, *Girl Running on a Balcony*) had been exhibited.[47] According to Elica Balla, *Swifts: Paths of Movement + Dynamic Sequences* was painted in 'May–June 1913' and the theoretical corollaries derived from it were developed in the months immediately following ("during the summer Balla was immersed in a study of the 'paths of movement' or impalpable movement, as he called these sources of research on movement"[48]). It is difficult to include it in the "four paintings of movement (still realistic) but incredibly advanced and very strange compared to a year ago"[49] which Boccioni told Severini he had seen two days before Christmas 1912 in Balla's studio in Rome, and only three of which had been exhibited, together with the older *The Street Light,* at the Costanzi show in Rome.[50] The swifts series would have bridged the period of his representation of movement by repetition (as in *Leash in Motion* and *Girl Running on a Balcony*) and that of the interpenetration of objects and their geometric stylization, which began with his studies of speeding automobiles (one of which Balla had already begun in April 1913[51] while another, with the title *Plasticity Lights × Speed*, was documented by its exhibition and catalogue illustration in the November 1913 'Lacerba' show[52]).

It seems that none of the series of swifts in flight seen from the studio balcony was sent to the 'Lacerba' show. There is no proof that the work in the catalogue called *Luminous Sequences × Displacements* was a study for the oil painting at the Museum of Modern Art, as has been suggested,[53] nor even that it was the painting itself.[54] Excluding *Plasticity Lights × Speed*, that was illustrated in the catalogue, we know little about the three remaining paintings which Balla sent to Florence. They were certainly studies on paper (the artist referred to them in a letter as "drawings" or "studies"); Balla himself wrote their titles on the backs of the sheets;[55] and their geometrical and schematic quality was remembered with irritation by Soffici four decades

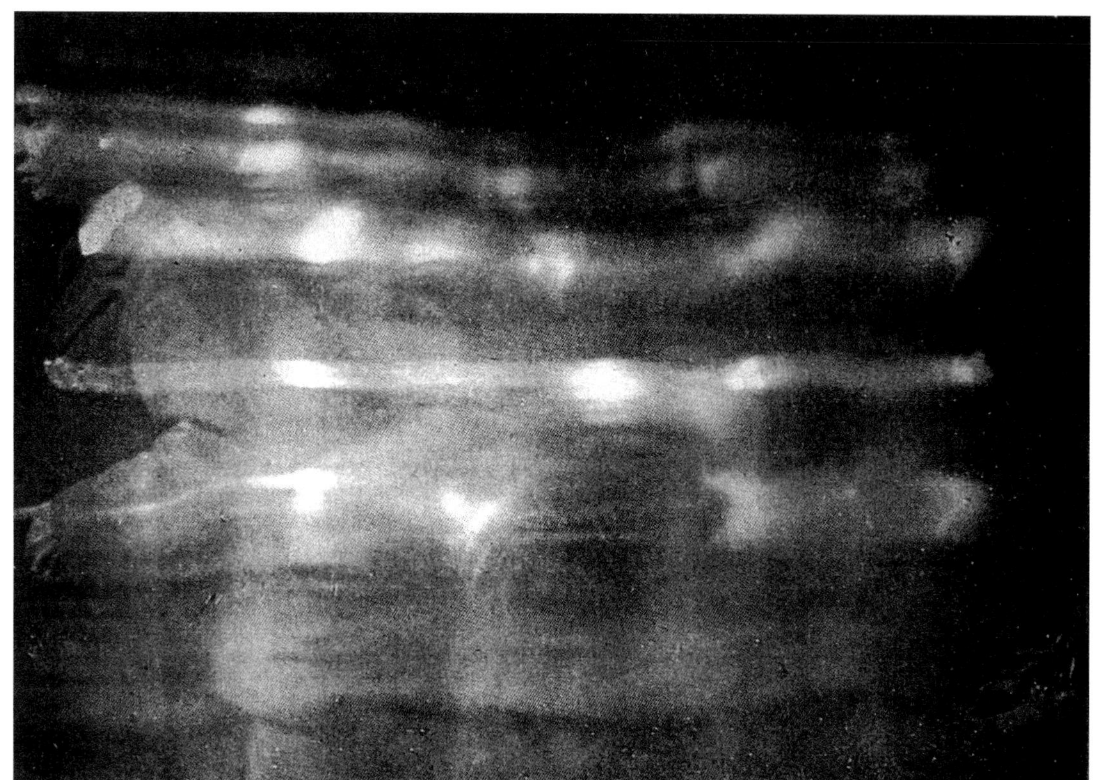

Fig. 1m. *Anton Giulio Bragaglia,* L'uomo che cammina (Man Walking), *photograph, 1912. Rome, Raccolta A. Vigliani Bragaglia, Centro Studi Anton Giulio Bragaglia*

later ("skeleton-like planes, curves, geometric angles, all tinted rather than painted, and only echoed, one might say, by many parallel lines at various distances"[56]). *Luminous Sequences × Displacements* was sent from Florence to the Galleria Sprovieri exhibition in Rome in February–March 1914, together with *Swifts: Paths of Movement + Dynamic Sequences*, now in New York, and it seems improbable that Balla would have exhibited in the same room a painting and one of its studies under such different titles. The title *Paths of Movement + Dynamic Sequences* also appears in a sequence of three other titles (*Abstract Speed, Plasticity Lights × Speed, Layers of Atmosphere*) on sheet no. 12 in one of Balla's notebooks published in 1974 by Maurizio Fagiolo dell'Arco.[57] References to the Sprovieri show on the neighboring page 17 and, above all, the exact similarity between this list and the first four illustrations of Balla's works in Boccioni's book, with a simple inversion of the third (*Abstract Speed*) and fourth (*Plasticity Lights × Speed*) titles, do not justify speculations about pre- or post-dating any of them.

Even stylistic considerations confirm the mid-1913 date. The basic scheme is an evolution of *Girl Running on a Balcony* (whose horizontal passage is superimposed on the vertical segments of the railing), completed by February 1913. Low down in a sheet close to the abovementioned drawing for this painting, with the continuous line along the hem of the dress,[58] appear the same eaves subsequently studied in greater detail in the drawings for *Paths of Movement + Dynamic Sequences.*[59] Finally, the structural complexity of the Museum of Modern Art painting, with its systematic use of broken lines and interpenetrating planes, relates directly to *Plasticity Lights × Speed*, exhibited in November 1913 at the 'Lacerba' show.

Painted between the spring and summer of 1913, the *Paths of Movement + Dynamic Sequences* series is linked to two fundamental factors in the development of 1913 Futurist poetics: Boccioni's articles in *Lacerba* and Anton Giulio Bragaglia's experiments with photography. Balla had been friendly with the latter since late in 1912 (Balla posing in front of his *Leash in Motion* is the subject of one 'photodynamic'[60]). Bragaglia's images were exhibited in March 1913 at the Galleria Romagna in Rome[61] and published late in June 1913 in sixteen plates of the second edition of *Fotodinamismo futurista*, as well as in various periodicals. The text of Bragaglia's booklet was fundamental to Balla's imagery in the late spring of 1913. Its terminology, which was completely extraneous to official Futurist theorizing, was almost literally echoed by Balla in the title of his painting: "*andature* di ritmi"[62] becomes "linee *andamentali*," "statica *successiva*" or "momenti *successivi*"[63] become "*successioni* dinamiche." Some of Bragaglia's theories recur, with a certain precision, in the painting's formal ideology. Trajectories of movement are independent of the reality of the objects depicted ("the lines representing movement are continuous and do not represent the reality of the phenomenon at all"[64]); the trajectory of movement has the capacity to suggest its "intermovemental states" to the eye;[65] the rhythm of one movement is "sufficient for an entire painting and possesses the force to compose an immense harmonious poem."[66] Bragaglia's conception of the representation of movement was stigmatized by the Futurists in a note appearing in October 1913 in *Lacerba* as being incompatible with plastic dynamism.[67] By this time it had become Balla's most feasible way of countering Boccioni's "unique form," the "synthesis of the states of motion of an object"[68] which deforms the object into a spiral: thanks to Bragaglia's example, Balla was able to give new meaning to the dynamic trajectory of movement polemically belittled by Boccioni to the role of "passage of one state of repose to another state of repose".[69] The various versions of *Paths of Movement + Dynamic Sequences* correspond therefore to Balla's quest for an alternative to Boccioni's dynamism, by attempting, relative to his works of 1912, more complex solutions for spatial construction and the multiplication of perceptions.

The Museum of Modern Art painting was one of the few that Balla presented again after World War I. With the title duly stripped of its Futurist connotations (*Swallows in Flight*), it was exhibited in the large solo section dedicated to Balla (consisting of ninety-three works) at the 1928 'Amatori e Cultori' exhibition in Rome.[70] In 1936, together with *Leash in Motion*, it represented Balla's Futurism and his "technique of kinetic simultaneity"[71] in the seminal 'Cubism and Abstract Art' exhibition at the Museum of Modern Art, New York.[72] The title of the work was linked to Balla's name in Agostino Mario Comanducci's popular art dictionary in the

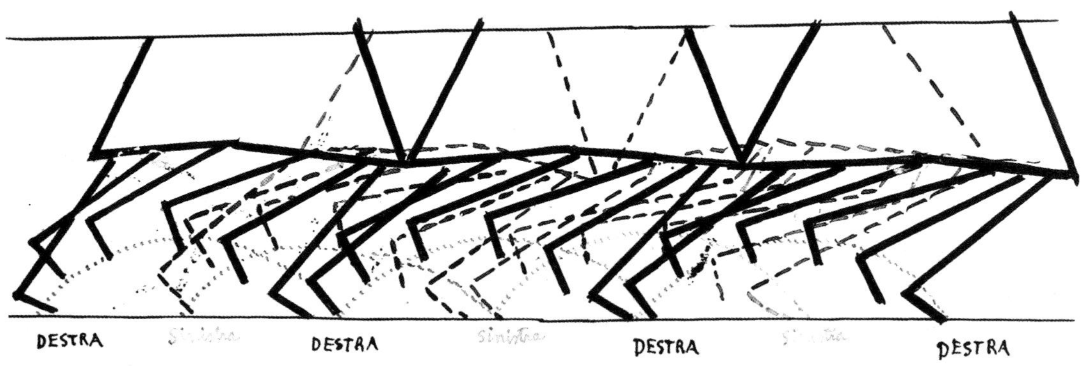

Fig. 1n. *Giacomo Balla, Study for* Bambina × balcone (Girl Running on a Balcony), *ink on paper, 1912. Milan, Civiche raccolte d'arte, Grassi Collection*

mid-1930s[73] and in an important book by Vincenzo Costantini on contemporary painting.[74] The same painting was also the starting point for the 'Balla Renaissance' during the second post-war era: called *Flight of Swallows Gutter Sky*, it was exhibited at the 'V Rassegna Nazionale di Arti Figurative' in 1948,[75] acquired by Alfred Barr for the Museum of Modern Art in New York[76] and shown again that year in the 'Twentieth-Century Italian Art' exhibition, by then as property of the Museum.[77]

Meanwhile Balla had set the preparatory tempera aside (folded in half, the fold being clearly visible, running from top to bottom) where it lay, forgotten for many years. It was acquired from the artist by Gianni Mattioli in 1950.[78] There is a possibility that it can be identified with the second of the works called *Schwalbenflug Studie I* and *II*, exhibited in 'Futurismo-Pittura Metafisica' in Zurich, November–December 1950.[79] A manuscript list (October 1950) of the works sent to Zurich includes a 'Balla Futurista 1913', valued at 200,000 lire, which would be compatible with the Mattioli study for *Paths of Movement + Dynamic Sequences*.[80] Instead the frequently published assertion (including recent studies[81]) that it was exhibited at the VI Quadriennale in Rome in 1951–2 is surely mistaken, and the *Swifts in Flight (study)* with which it is confused can be identified instead, thanks to a catalogue illustration, with the version catalogued by Lista as no. 359.[82] Thus the first certain public showing of the Mattioli work, with the title *Swifts in Flight*, was in Florence in 1953, at the Palazzo Strozzi exhibition of Mattioli's collection (where it was listed in the catalogue as a tempera on paper, without mention of its lining with canvas[83]): Carlo Ludovico Ragghianti's preface limited it, along with Balla's other paintings and the Russolo, to a "non-constructive but decorative and almost melodious declination of Futurism."[84] The painting had been published for the first time in the Milanese magazine *Arbiter* the previous year, hanging on a wall of Gianni Mattioli's home in Via Senato 36, next to another Balla painting (cat. no. 2) and to *Solidity of Fog* by Luigi Russolo (cat. no. 21).[85]

[1] Lista 1982, no. 351, 354–7, 359.
[2] Boccioni 1914, unnumbered plate (the first of five dedicated to Balla). The book was published in March 1914 but the date of the final compilation of the photographs, excepting the Soffici reproductions, is known from a letter whose date, early October 1913, can be established by its contents, from Umberto Boccioni to Ardengo Soffici in Drudi Gambillo, Fiori 1958–62, vol. I, p. 296.
[3] *Rome* 1914[a], p. 26, no. 11; *London* 1914, no. 43; *San Francisco* 1915–16, no. 1136.
[4] Balla 1984, p. 167.
[5] Undated letter (known to be of July 1912) from Giacomo Balla to his family, in Fagiolo dell'Arco 1968, p. 29.
[6] Lista 1984, p. 22; Braun 1992, pp. 293–6.
[7] Braun 1992, nos. 166, 308.
[8] Marey 1890, p. 13.
[9] *Ibidem*, p. 173, fig. 102.
[10] As maintained by Lista 1979, pp. 158–9 and Lista 1982, pp. 42–54.
[11] Marey 1890, p. 18.
[12] Fagiolo dell'Arco 1968, p. 17; Fagiolo dell'Arco 1998[a], pp. 23–4.
[13] Letter from Balla in Düsseldorf to his family, dated December 5, 1912, in Balla 1986, p. 170.
[14] Sabachnikoff, Piumati 1893, p. 77, figs. 29–30; p. 79, fig. 31; p. 89, figs. 45–50.
[15] New York, The Museum of Modern Art, Christopher Tietze Fund: Lista 1982, no. 202.
[16] Govoni, March 15, 1913.
[17] Lista 1982, no. 350.
[18] Lista 1984, no. 1075; *Rome* 1989, p. 185, no. B/2.
[19] Lista 1982, no. 353.
[20] Using the technique of overlaying photographic negatives according to Dortch Dorazio 1970, unnumbered page.
[21] New York, private collection: Lista 1982, no. 351.
[22] Private collection: *ibidem*, no. 355.
[23] Milan, Civiche raccolte d'arte, Grassi Collection: Caramel, Pirovano 1973, no. 343; Lista 1982, no. 290.
[24] Paris, private collection: *ibidem*, no. 352.
[25] *Ibidem*, no. 360.
[26] Rome, private collection: *ibidem*, no. 358; according to Dortch Dorazio 1970, no. 90, "a preliminary study".
[27] Dortch Dorazio 1970, no. 95.
[28] As seems to be proven by the reproduction of *Penetrazioni dinamiche d'automobile* (*Dynamic Penetrations of an Automobile*), in Boccioni 1914, unnumbered page.
[29] New York, private collection: Lista 1982, no. 359; for a discussion of the work see Dortch Dorazio 1970, no. 93.
[30] New York, private collection: Lista 1982, no. 354; for a color reproduction see Calvesi 1967, p. 131.
[31] Calvesi 1967, p. 142, based upon a suggestion by Virginia Dortch Dorazio, whose source was the artist himself; Fagiolo dell'Arco 1968, p. 17; Dortch Dorazio 1970, no. 93; Sani 1971, p. 160; Braun 1992, p. 306; Fagiolo dell'Arco 1998[a], p. 24; Del Puppo 2001, p. 104. Close to this interpretation is that of Roche-Pézard 1983, p. 383, who seems to read the wavy white lines as reflections on the windowpane caused by

2

Giacomo Balla

Mercury Passing Before the Sun (*Mercury Passing Before the Sun Seen Through a Telescope*)

Mercurio transita davanti al sole (*Mercurio passa davanti al sole*; *Mercurio passa davanti al sole visto nel cannocchiale*), 1914

Tempera on paper lined with canvas
120 × 100 cm

Inscriptions: *recto*, signed lower left: 'BALLA 1914'; *verso*: signed upper right: 'BALLA 1914 / RIPRODOTTO / SUL / CAHIERS / D'ART' (fig. 2a)

Provenance: property of the artist; July 1950: Gianni Mattioli, with the mediation of Mario Klaus

Exhibitions: Zurich 1950, no. 9 (*Merkur von der Sonne vorbeiziehend*); Rome 1951–2?, p. 39, no. 6 (*Mercurio passa davanti al sole visto nel cannocchiale*); Venice 1952, ex catalogue (a label glued to the stretcher testifies to the painting's presence in the exhibition); Milan 1952, II Gallery, unnumbered (*Mercurio passa davanti al sole*); Florence 1953[a], no. 6 (*Mercurio passa davanti al sole visto da un cannocchiale*, 1914); São Paulo 1953–4, p. 5, no. 3; New York 1954, no. 7 (*Mercury Passing Before the Sun*); Kassel 1955, no. 17; Turin 1957, unnumbered; Rome 1959, no. 60 (the caption to plate 1 erroneously refers to no. 49); Winterthur 1959, no. 6; Munich 1959–60, no. 4; Milan 1960 [no. 3]; Venice 1960, p. 13, no. 8; Paris 1960–1, no. 6; New York 1961–Los Angeles 1962, no. 16; Vienna 1962, no. 66; Turin 1963, no. 108 (*Mercurio transita davanti al Sole, visto col cannocchiale*, 1914); Milan 1966[a], no. 2; Washington, DC 1967–Tokyo 1972, no. 28 (Washington, DC–Hamburg), no. 27 (Madrid–Seville), no. 28 (Kyoto–Tokyo); Rome 1971–2, no. 40; Rome 1973, p. 197, unnumbered; Paris 1973, no. 8; Milan 1973–4, no. 232; Düsseldorf 1974, no. 23; Venice 1986, p.198; Düsseldorf 1987, no. 0.1; London

This painting was first published in 1950, with the title *Mercure passant devant le Soleil.*[1] In 1963, Enrico Crispolti and Maria Drudi Gambillo related it for the first time to a specific astronomical event, the partial eclipse of the sun by Mercury on November 7, 1914.[2] They did so (in the catalogue of the Giacomo Balla retrospective exhibition at the Galleria Civica d'Arte Moderna e Contemporanea in Turin) by matching the artist's date on the painting (and on another of the same series, also exhibited in the 1963 Turin show[3]) with a passage from the widely-read *Almanacco Bemporad 1914*, quoted in full in the catalogue. Published at the beginning of each year, the 1914 almanac announced the coming event the following November, and described its characteristics (frequency, duration, and how it would it appear).[4] This assured that anticipation of the event spread wider than merely professional circles.

Balla's painting poses a preliminary problem: the difficulty of reconciling the 1914 date and the November 7 eclipse with the fact that the event had not yet acquired the considerable importance it was to have for the history of twentieth-century science. The age-old problem of the irregularity of Mercury's perihelion was explained by Albert Einstein only in 1915.[5] Observations made during the planet's next passage across the sun, on May 27, 1924, constituted one of the fundamental experimental verifications of the theory of general relativity. It is surprising therefore that Balla should have dedicated so ambitious a cosmological painting to such a modest eclipse prior to the moment, some years on, when the same event would become proof of a theory of immense philosophical implications (a new ontological status of energy, the definition of curved and finite space, the gravitational dilation of time). In 1914 only a narrow circle of specialists in Italy were aware of Einstein's research, nor had any of Einstein's published writings yet treated the subject of Mercury's orbit.[6]

Furthermore there is no verifiable history of the Mattioli tempera, nor of the several painted or drawn studies related to it, prior to 1950. These two considerations (the later fame of the eclipse and the lack of historical documentation of the series) are nevertheless insufficient to justify a suspicion that the Mattioli *Mercury* was painted after 1914. Strong stylistic analogies bind it (and other works in the series) to Balla's works dateable with certainty between the end of 1914 and early 1915. On the back of the version of *Mercury Passing Before the Sun* that formerly belonged to Harry L. Winston[7] (the only version traceable with certainty to an historic Futurist collection between the wars, that of Filippo Tommaso Marinetti), there is a sketch which Marianne Martin correctly related to the cycle of *Interventionist Demonstrations* of 1915.[8] Indeed, the works stylistically closest to the Mattioli painting can be found precisely in this *Interventionist Demonstrations* series. In the tempera *Waving*[9] (fig. 2c) Balla used the same palette (blue triangles against a ground of various orange tones) and inserted strong black curvilinear accents over the compositional structure of intersecting diagonals. The round contours in the Mattioli painting show the same black shading with repeated fine linear brushstrokes as the collage *Crowd + Landscape*.[10] Balla soon abandoned this type of painting in favor of flatter shapes and novel experiments with tonal shading. The stylistic congruence of the Mattioli tempera with works by Balla securely dateable to 1914–15 leaves little room for postdating its execution. We need instead to reconstruct the motives that prompted Balla to represent, at the end of 1914, this particular astronomical event of November 7.

The passage of Mercury across the sun on November 7, 1914 lasted a little over four hours and took place in Italy in full daylight, from 10:58 a.m. to 3:08 p.m. Observation in Rome was facilitated by weather conditions of fair visibility (*La Tribuna* the following day reported a variable sky, clearing toward midday thanks to wind) so that even amateur astronomers with modest equipment would have been able to see it. Balla was an astronomy buff (in a strongly Symbolist painting of 1910 he had depicted *The Constellation of Orion*[11]) and owned a simple telescope without a viewfinder, formerly preserved in the artist's home-museum (though it is not known whether it was already in his possession in 1914). This was catalogued in early twentieth-century publications as a 'Type 1' instrument (the least powerful, with a lens up to 57 mm, a maximum focus length of 85 cm and a 35× enlargement eyepiece) with which the stars could be seen magnified up to 8×, as well as the phases of Venus.[12]

The passage of Mercury in front of the sun in November 1914 was an event that astronomy amateurs could hardly have overlooked. It followed by just a few months a more spectacular event, the total eclipse of the sun on August 21, which awakened a general interest for observing the sky. It was also announced (though a day too soon) in the best known and most popular astronomy manual then available in Italy, that of Camille Flammarion.[13] Its importance was stressed in the most widely-distributed Italian astronomy atlas, by Giovanni Naccari ("the passage of Mercury will perhaps enable us to learn more about the atmosphere surrounding the planet; to measure more exactly that small globe's diameter; to explain more completely the problem of the irregularities it encounters along its orbit").[14] Reports of the event reached well beyond specifically professional circles. In addition to the *Almanacco Bemporad 1914* mentioned above, the two major Roman dailies *Il Messaggero* and *La Tribuna* highlighted the news item on November 6. Another possible source for Balla was the recently published *Libro del cielo* by the polygraph Adolfo Padovan: this small volume in the 'Biblioteca dei Ragazzi' series of the Istituto Editoriale Italiano, with embellished margins by Duilio Cambellotti (a long-standing friend of Balla), narrated the discovery of the celestial mysteries by some children under the guidance of an elderly amateur astronomer, just as Balla would have talked to his daughters (as remembered by Elica Balla[15]). In the story, Mercury is a mysterious planet, hard to observe, which only recently had "stopped mocking us with its elusiveness, as astronomers are now able to find it with stronger telescopes, even by day in full sunlight, and are getting ready to catch it by surprise the next time it passes in front of the solar disc, on November 6 of this year of 1914."[16] The same booklet illustrated the corona observed during the 1860 eclipse of the sun with a picture with three colors (fig. 2h) ranging from an intense blue to a vivid orange-red, not unlike those used by Balla in his painting. Balla's evident passion for astronomy, his recollection of a recent spectacular eclipse of the sun, a certain insistence in the popular press about the event, and perhaps an echo of the scientific debate on the irregularity of the planet's perihelion: all these motives seem, after all, more than enough to cause Balla to ob-

1989, no. 13; Madrid 1990–1, p. 224; Saint-Paul de Vence 1992, no. 23; Barcelona 1996, no. 15; Venice 2000, p. 267

Bibliography: Zervos 1950, p. 66, detail illus. (*Mercure passant devant le soleil*, 1914); Garretto 1952, p. 43, illus. whole; Ragghianti 1953, p. 9; Haftmann 1955, no. 75; Castelfranco, Valsecchi 1956, p. 73; Drudi Gambillo, Fiori 1958–62, vol. I, p. 400, vol. II, pp. 97 and 158, no. 136 (*Mercurio che passa davanti al sole visto col cannocchiale*); Calvesi 1959, p. 32; Recupero 1959, pp. 61–2; Haftmann 1960, vol. II, p. 150; Marchiori 1960, no. 26; Taylor 1961, pp. 64–5 and 141–2; Carrieri 1961, p. 109 and no. 86; Brizio 1962, pp. 498 and 502; Bellonzi 1963, p. 58; Crispolti 1963, p. 20; Crispolti, Drudi Gambillo 1963, pp. 72–4; Vallier 1963, pp. 164 and 272; Ballo 1964b, p. 91; Pierre 1966, pp. 30, 34, 41, 126, 132, 151; Barricelli 1966, p. 47; Calvesi 1966, pp. 88–9; Calvesi 1967, pp. 137 and 152; Fagiolo dell'Arco 1967, p. 15; Crispolti 1967, pp. 322–3; Muller, Elgar 1967, p. 95; Martin 1968, p. 200 and pl. 215; Fagiolo dell'Arco 1968, p. 26; Hamilton 1970, p. 222; Dortch Dorazio 1970, no. 133; Sani 1971, p. 164; Velani 1971, pp. 115–17, 125, 129; Hofmann 1971, pp. 42, 131 and fig. 113; Bowness 1972, p. 134; Fagiolo dell'Arco 1974, p. 9; Tisdall, Bozzolla 1977, p. 192; Spate 1979, p. 42; Lista 1979, p. 41; Calvesi 1980, pp. 192–3; Crispolti 1980b, p. 120; Lista 1982, p. 82; no. 398, p. 224; pp. 511–12; Roche-Pézard 1983, p. 386, no. 25; Balla 1984, pp. 346–50; Messina, Nigro Covre 1986, pp. 302–3 and no. 127; Coen 1986, p. 46; Schmidt 1987, pp. 36–7; Poggianella 1995, p. 462; Marziali 1996, pp. 144–5; Fagiolo dell'Arco 1997, pp. 19–23; Rylands 1997, p. 52; Matitti 1998, p. 41; Lista 2000, p. 93; Naubert, Riser 2000, pp. 122–3; Benzi 2001, p. 24; Fonti 2001a, p. 27; Lista 2001, p. 127

Fig. 2a. Verso *of cat. no. 2*

Fig. 2b. *Detail of cat. no. 2, in* Cahiers d'Art*, 1950*

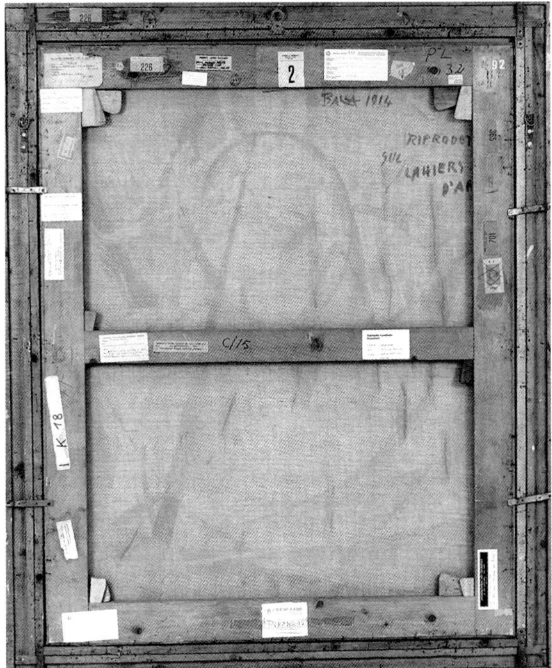

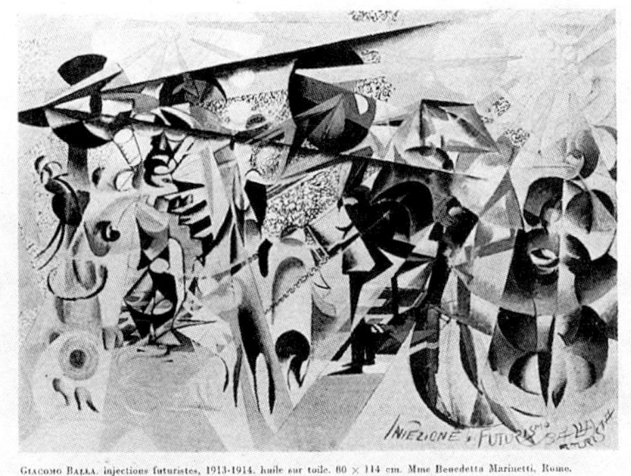

Giacomo Balla, injections futuristes, 1913-1914, huile sur toile. 80 × 114 cm. Mme Benedetta Marinetti, Rome.

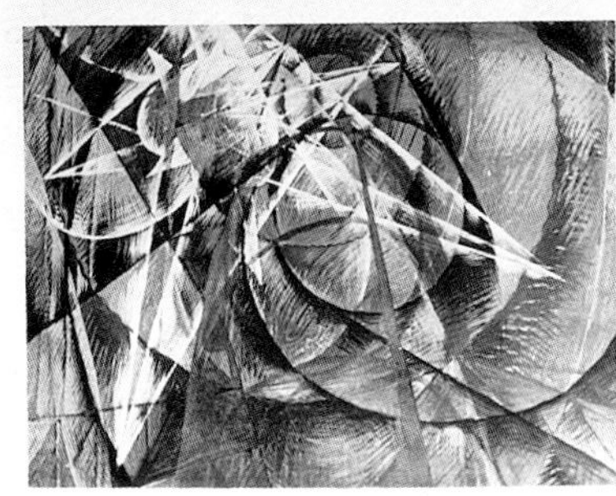

Giacomo Balla, mercure passant devant le soleil, 1914, huile sur carton. [illegible]

serve the November 7, 1914 passage of Mercury and to derive from it an ambitious series of pictorial studies.

In the Mattioli painting, Mercury is the tiny dark ball at the peak of the narrow, compact cone of green shadow which projects from the base of the Mattioli painting. The sun can be identified as the highest and smallest of the orange circles, outlined in red and made ragged by solar eruptions. The path and proportions of the eclipse are painted realistically. Mercury cuts across the sun on a chord far to the south, corresponding to its real trajectory during the November eclipse (the moment portrayed is well advanced, coinciding with the last phase of the event[17]). Mercury in its November orbit is at the perihelion, its minimum distance from the sun, and therefore the disproportion (1:10 1/2) between the two masses as seen from the Earth is at its maximum. Even the palette, based on orange sienna, is not unrealistic given the conditions of observation of the phenomenon. For studying the passage of Mercury across the sun, the astronomy manual of Guglielmo Meyer recommended attaching a smoked glass to the telescope to attenuate the sun's rays: in this way Mercury would stand out as "a perfectly black disk"[18] against the orange ball of the sun. In a more detailed report of the event in Italy, by the Brera Astronomical Observatory, "Mercury appeared as a brownish spot perfectly visible".[19]

The painting, however, represents more than merely Mercury's passage seen through a telescope. Information which Balla gave his daughter Elica at a later date (she was born on October 30, 1914, only a week before the event) included the dynamics of his observation and better explains the image's complex structure. Balla had set out to compose a painting with

> "lines that give the sensation of the movement of the observer, at the telescope, who looks outside and inside it. These lines interpenetrate with the instrument and the sun. The white sun, which harms the naked eye outside the telescope, contrasts with the orange color of the flaming globe seen through the black glass. Forms and colors constitute a new pictorial complex since the subject was strongly felt by the artist and the telescope magnifies — it is no more the poor small instrument but is the eye more powerful than man's that captures in its visual circle the tiny planet as it passes before the yellow disk of the sun."[20]

The lines following this passage are flawed by errors and contradictions: the eclipse is dated June 1914, perhaps confusing it with the total eclipse of the sun on August 21 of that year, which was certainly a more spectacular event with a greater impact; furthermore the chronology of the pictorial studies is interwoven with the turbulent political events of the summer, which determined the dates of Balla's final visit to the Löwenstein family in Düsseldorf. Nonetheless this recollection is fundamental to an understanding of the presence of two distinct but simultaneous views in the painting: one through the telescope filtered by the smoked glass (in which the sun appears red and the rest is generally brownish in tone) and the other of the sky as seen by the naked eye outside the telescope (where the sun, in the upper left, appears extremely white and radiant, and where Balla was able to insert slices of the cobalt blue sky). The latter point of view thus allowed him to depict the telescope as a green tube thrusting towards the sun.

Aside from the fact of direct observation of the phenomenon, two other components of the painting should be mentioned. The first, noted by Maurizio Fagiolo dell'Arco,[21] is Balla's awareness of the deformations, ambiguities and multiplications to which views of the sky were subjected by the superimposition of atmospheric strata. This had been the theme of two earlier paintings, *Layers of Atmosphere*[22] (fig. 2d) and *Celestial Orbits*.[23] The frame of vision enclosed by the telescope is depicted by a black line which multiplies and approximates to a spiral motif: it is similar to that used in the *Dynamism of an Automobile* paintings, and Balla used it again for the inside of the telescope in the Mattioli tempera.[24] The second component is his use of astronomical sources other than the passage of Mercury across the sun in 1914. Giovanni Lista noted the impact of Jules Jannsen's celebrated photographs of Venus eclipsing the sun in 1874,[25] but Balla may have relied on sources of a different kind from the stark simplic-

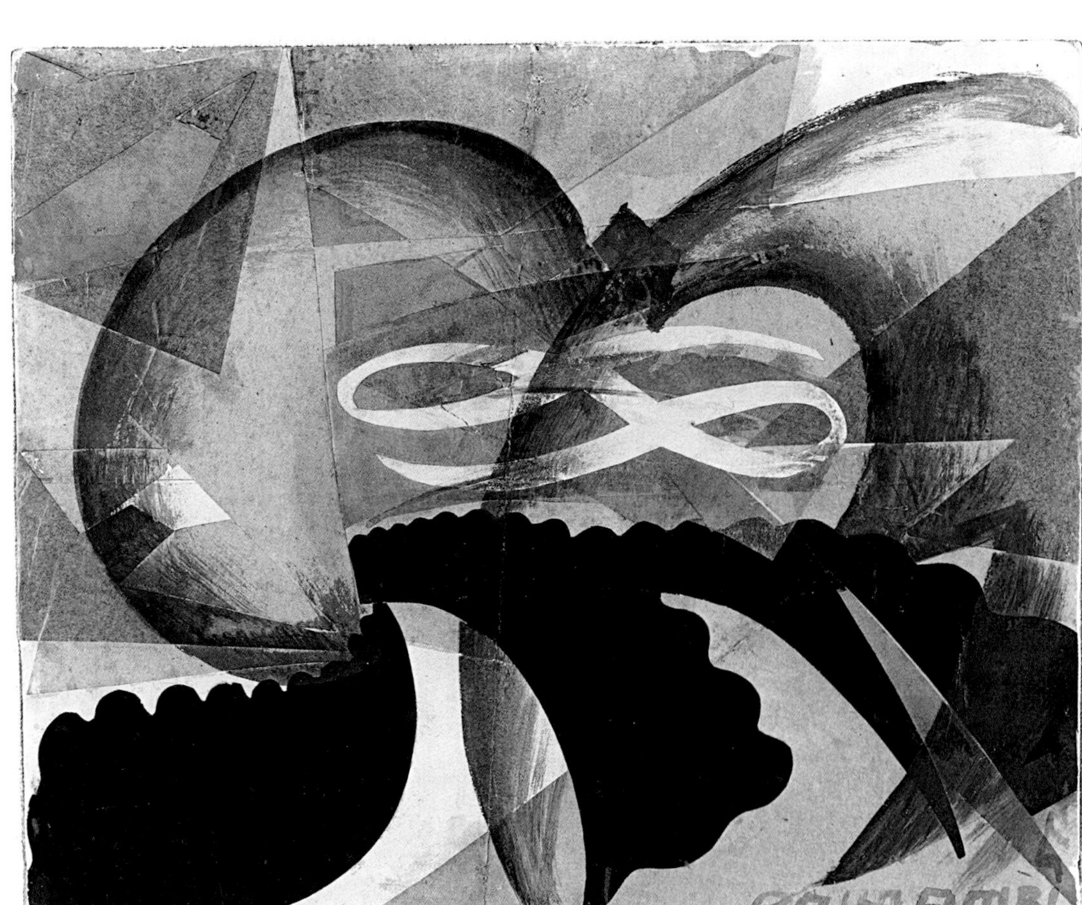

Fig. 2c. *Giacomo Balla,* Sventolamento (Waving*), tempera and collage on paper, 1915. Milan, Civiche raccolte d'arte, Jucker Collection*

Fig. 2d. *Giacomo Balla,* Spessori d'atmosfera *(Layers of Atmosphere), 1913, in U. Boccioni,* Pittura scultura futuriste, *1914*

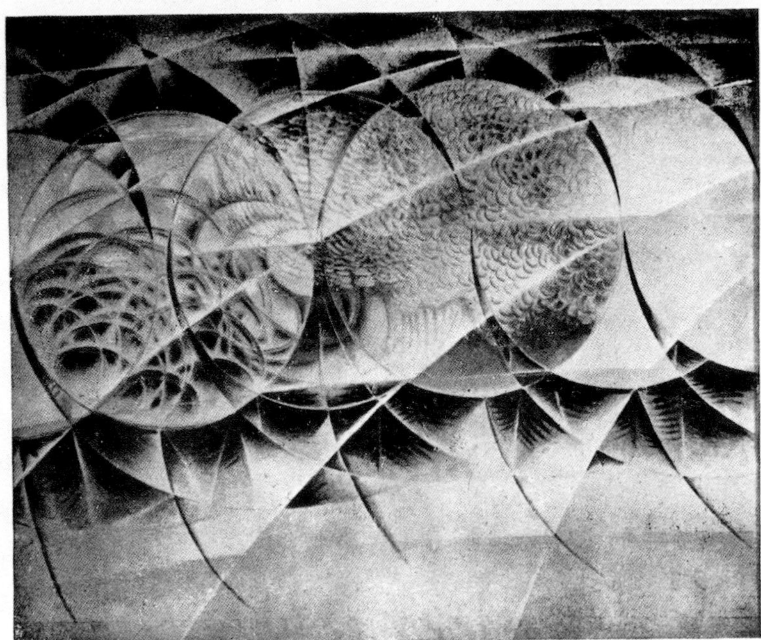

BALLA. – **Spessori d'atmosfera (1913) Epaisseurs d'atmosphère**

ity of Jannsen's images. In a small German astronomy manual, published by Ferdinand Möbius in 1906 and surely accessible to Balla on his trips to Düsseldorf in 1912–14, the diagram of Venus' passage between the sun and the earth is represented with a drawing[26] (fig. 2i) which is similar to the schema Balla used in his Mercury series: the sweeping arc on the left describing the trajectory of Venus is a constant compositional element in the early studies of the series; the circular pattern of the orbits intersected by the triangles of merging lines resembles the motif of the curved lines traversed by the luminous white points of the sun's rays in the Mattioli tempera.

In a recent study, in advance of the as yet-unpublished *catalogue raisonné* of Balla's paintings, Maurizio Fagiolo dell'Arco analyzed five drawings, eight temperas and one oil which he related to Balla's cycle on the November 1914 eclipse.[27] Excluding the first (in which the present writer is unable to identify either the profiles of the sun and the planets or the outline of the telescope, elements shared by all studies in the series) and the last (which seems to belong to a later period on stylistic grounds), the twelve remaining works can be subdivided into three distinct groups.

The first group includes the studies in which the sun is not explicitly portrayed as a white source of light to the left of the telescope, but merely radiates some areas with white highlights.[28] Instead Balla privileged the relation of the sun disk to another, larger circle closer to the viewfinder, the consequence in some way of multiple images of the star inside the telescope cone. The surface is subdivided into zones produced by the intersection of curved lines (the sun multiplying its own disk, the telescope eyepiece) and straight lines (among which the axis of the telescope is a point of reference). In some studies the small dark circle of Mercury is already situated in the same place allocated to it in the final version.[29] In the largest and most developed study of the series[30] (fig. 2e) the circle of the sun is surrounded by a dark halo, perhaps the circumference of the telescope lens, which will become one of the most characteristic features of the subsequent series.

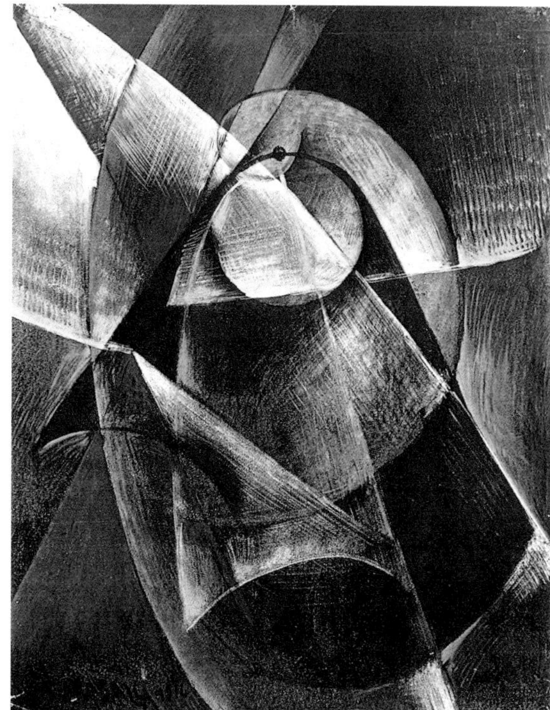

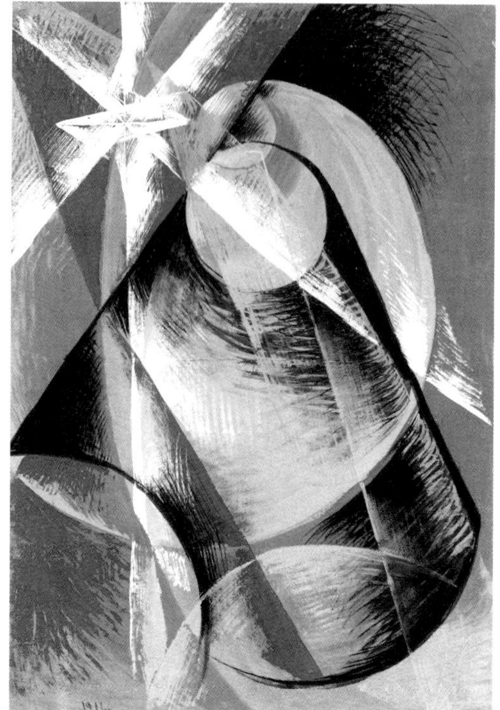

Fig. 2e. *Giacomo Balla,* Mercurio transita davanti al sole *(*Mercury Passing Before the Sun*), tempera on paper, 1914, in* Omaggio a Giacomo Balla, *Rome, Fondazione Origine, 1951*

Fig. 2f. *Giacomo Balla,* Mercurio transita davanti al sole *(*Mercury Passing Before the Sun*), tempera on paper, 1914. Vienna, Museum Moderner Kunst Stiftung Ludwig*

In a second, more compact group of three works the white prismatic dazzle of the sun seen with the naked eye partially overlaps the round orange sun seen through the telescope, traversing it with a bright diagonal.[31] Despite the similarity of drawing, the pictorial *ductus* in these three works is very different: the oil in the Musée National d'Art Moderne in Paris, painted on unusual corrugated paper, repeats, though with a duller execution, with flatter fields of color and more dissonant colors (acid green and electric blue), all the chromatic and chiaroscuro devices in the Vienna painting (fig. 2f), the largest of the series and the only one executed on two sheets joined together, painted in a very liquid tempera that made possible the rapid feathery brushstrokes. As Elica Balla recalled when describing the genesis of the painting, its double point of view allowed the artist to suggest the silhouette of the telescope seen from above.

The works in the third group have the common denominator of a variation of the sun placed on the upper left.[32] It is depicted as a white ball, bristling with peaks, and becomes the most important component of the composition, with its rays thrusting almost to the middle and to the right margin of the rectangular pictorial field (fig. 2g). With a single exception,[33] the silhouetted dot of Mercury is present in the whole group. Balla made the telescope more specific, as its shaft moved to an axial position, and accentuated the multiplication and reciprocal interrelation of the celestial bodies which makes the Mattioli painting one of the freest and most successful of Futurist paintings. Critics have stressed its "glistening, smoldering display of cosmic pyrotechnics"[34] and the posture of the painter, whose "eye seems to lose itself in the vast space and complex order of an evolving universe."[35]

The reading of certain passages in Marinetti's manifesto *Distruzione della sintassi* (*Destruction of Grammar*) was surely one of the incentives for Balla to translate his passion for observing the sky into Futurist imagery. In the second section, headed 'Dopo il verso libero le parole in libertà' ('After Free Verse Words-in-Freedom') published in November 1913 in *Lacerba*, men of letters and artists were invited to seek ways of representing "the spectacles and dramas of the infinitely large" and "the speeds of the stars."[36] The direct depiction of the multiplication of the solar disk and the character of abstract spectacle of cosmic light in the Mercury series has provoked scholars to look for more precise textual sources. Maurizio Calvesi noted analo-

Fig. 2g. *Giacomo Balla,* Mercurio transita davanti al sole (Mercury Passing Before the Sun*), tempera on paper, 1914. Private collection*

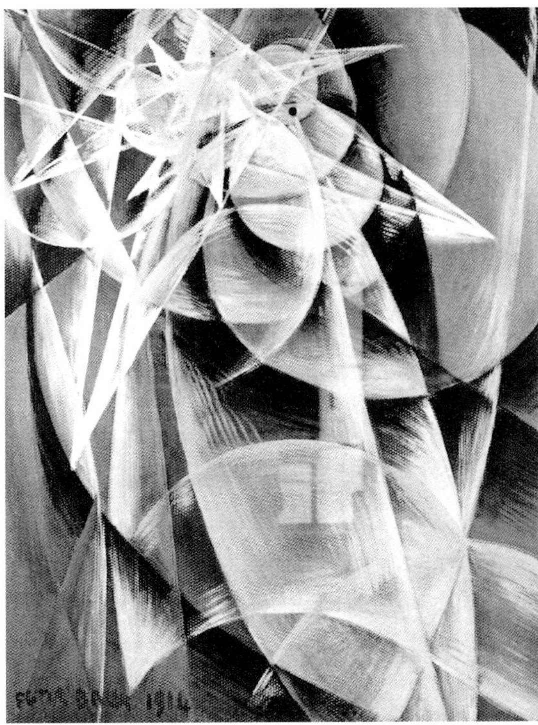

gies with an essay text by Anton Giulio Bragaglia (inventor of Futurist photodynamics and in contact with Balla from at least 1912), 'L'innamorato del sole', published early in 1912 in the Roman periodical *Patria.*[37] In a sort of "allegorical-autobiographical tale" the protagonist Gianni Rachi discovers the fascination of the luminous Volta arc lamp which creates "a disk just as splendid as the shining golden sun" with "the dazzling, sparkling red clarity of molten copper." The luminous disk acts on the eye in ways not dissimilar to that depicted by Balla, in expanding movements alternating with sudden rotations, contractions and multiplications:

> "the disk still seemed to rotate and expand further, then immediately shrinking and then, all of a sudden, becoming very tiny like a far-away sun lost in the immense desert and darkness of an unknown world, then to plunge forward again, resplendent and breathless. It shrank again, and expanded, and rotated and rotated flashing, and advanced with sudden breadth and multiplied into innumerable suns in a wonderful, stupendous way".[38]

Giovanni Lista has emphasized the importance of the re-publication in October 1914, in the Roman theosophical review *Ultra*, of excerpts from Ardengo Soffici's declaration of Bergsonian poetics titled 'Raggio', first published in the July 1914 issue of *Lacerba.*[39] *Ultra* would have been familiar to Balla since one of his friends, Antonio Ballatore of Turin, a general in the army and member of the Italian theosophical society, was on the staff.[40] Soffici described the contiguity between the perceiver and that which is perceived as "a globe of light that shoots its rays in all directions according to the force which it has, onto the things of this world, beyond the moon, the sun and the stars, through the cosmic night."[41] Despite hypotheses advanced on various occasions, the esoteric reference to a "'coniunctio mercurialis' performed by the triangle, the symbolic form of penetration,"[42] and "veiled references to the alchemical process"[43] have not yet been convincingly demonstrated.

Research over the last two decades has tended to relate the Mattioli version of *Mercury Passing Before the Sun* to contemporary Parisian avant-garde experiments:[44] in particular to Robert Delaunay's 1913 series of *Formes circulaires*, in which a sun or a moon is represented by a radiation of multicolored haloes (and especially in the case of two paintings called *Soleil. Lune. Simultaneité 1* and *2* [*Sun, Moon. Simultaneity*], in which two heavenly bodies appear simultaneously in the same painting). Beyond a general formal resemblance (limited to the mutual presence of one or more circles reverberating in space, while triangular modules are absent from Delaunay's work), no verifiable direct link can be found. Balla's awareness of Delaunay's cosmic subjects is certain, given that thirteen works (with titles such as *Sun, Moon, Simultaneous Sun Moon, Simultaneous Contrast Movement of Color Depth, Prism Sun*) are listed in the catalogue of the 'Erster Deutscher Herbstsalon' at the Der Sturm gallery in Berlin on September 20, 1913,[45] to which Balla also sent two paintings, and given the polemics between Delaunay and the Futurists following the exhibition of *Solar Disks, Simultaneous Form: To the Great Constructor Blériot* at the 1914 Salon des Indépendents in Paris.[46] That Balla ever saw Delaunay's paintings first-hand can probably be ruled out. He may have had second hand knowledge through black-and-white illustrations in *Montjoie!*, edited by Ricciotto Canudo (limited in this case to *Solar Disks*),[47] since the issue dedicated to the 1914 Salon des Indépendents was sent to Gino Severini convalescing in Anzio[48] and Severini could have shown this to Balla, with whom he was in contact during the months of his obligatory sojourn in Lazio.[49]

Balla was surely aware of the pictorial interest in cosmological themes which began to be felt in the Italian Futurist milieu in the fall of 1913 or spring of 1914. He shaped his treatment of such themes in the light of the formal motifs dear to him: the doubling of moments of seeing (an eye looking alternately down the telescope and directly at the sun); the dynamic multiplying of images depicted in clear, spiral designs; the theme of astronomical observation through a telescope. In this writer's view, the most interesting reference point for defining the basic graphic scheme of the most advanced studies in the series (the Mattioli version, the tempera in Vienna, the study formerly in the Winston-Malbin Collection) was his encounter with Gino Severini. In Anzio during the winter of 1913–14, Severini was painting abstract compositions in which the dense triangularity of the basic image has curved elements laid over it.

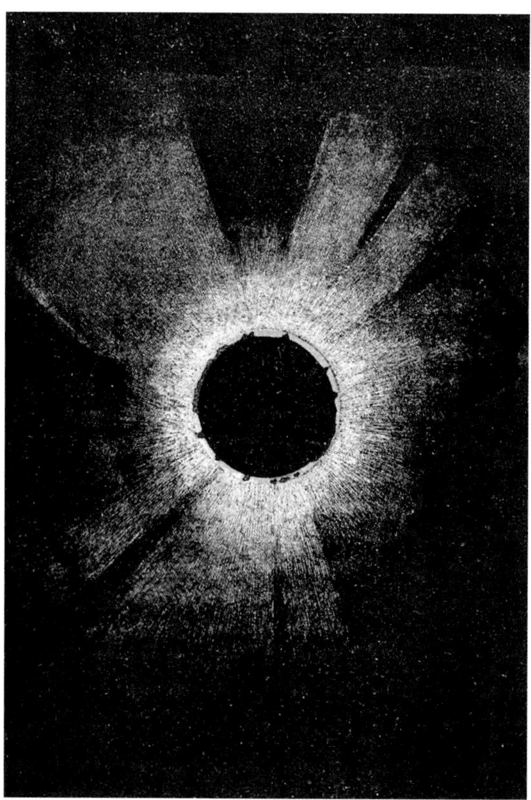

Fig. 2h. *The solar corona during the total eclipse of 1860, in A. Padovan,* Il libro del cielo, *1914*

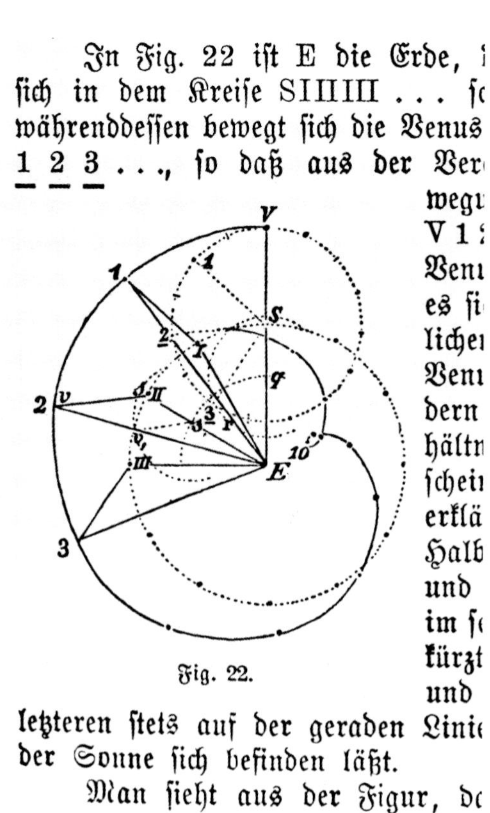

In Fig. 22 ist E die Erde,
sich in dem Kreise SIIIIII . . . s
währenddessen bewegt sich die Venus
1 2 3 . . ., so daß aus der Ver
wegu
V 1
Venu
es si
liche
Venu
dern
hältn
schei
erklä
Halb
und
im s
kürzt
und
letzteren stets auf der geraden Lini
der Sonne sich befinden läßt.
Man sieht aus der Figur, da

Fig. 2i. *Diagram of the passage of the planet Venus before the Sun, in A. F. Möbius,* Astronomie, *1906*

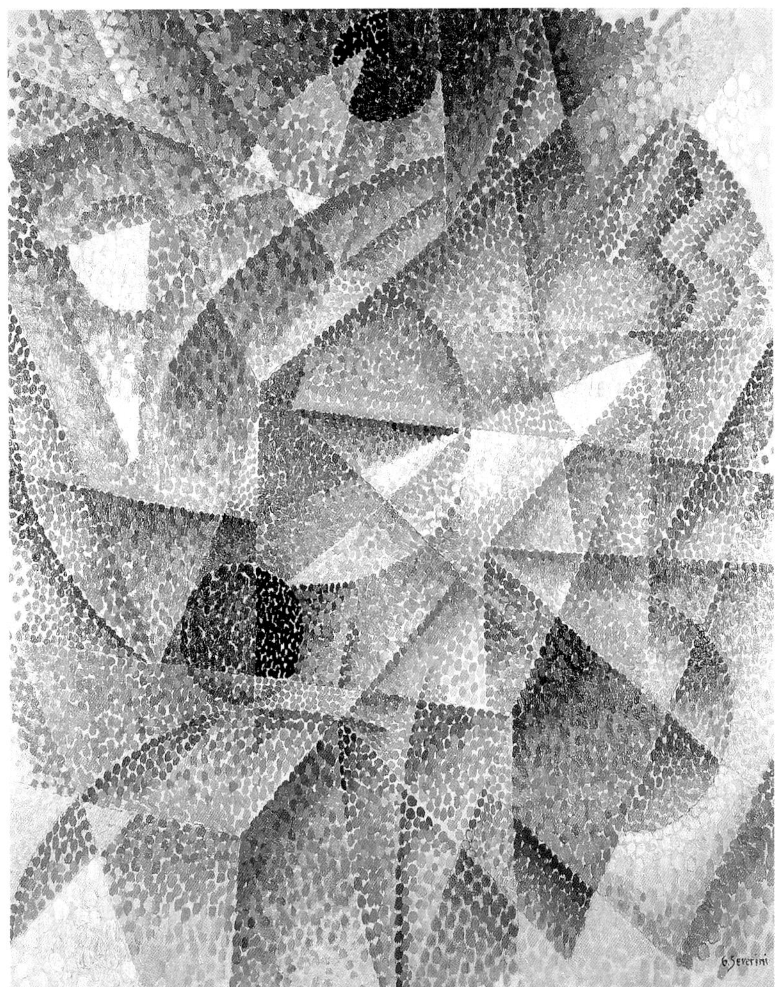

Fig. 2j. *Gino Severini,* Espansione sferica della luce *(*Spherical Expansion of Light*), oil on canvas, 1913–14. Utica (New York), Munson-Williams-Proctor Institute Museum of Art*

In *Spherical Expansion of Light*[50] (fig. 2j) multiple acute angles in constant tension spring from a central circle. Balla's dense hatching in the final paintings of *Mercury Passing Before the Sun* turned Severini's static *pointillé* into a new, tense, dynamic texture.

The subsequent history of the twelve studies in the *Mercury* series is unusual even given the general ill fortune of Balla's Futurist paintings until the after the second World War. Though it is possible that one work from the series was shown at the 'Fu Balla e Futurista' exhibition in December 1915 at the Sala d'Arte Angelelli in Rome (the catalogue does not list the works),[51] and although Marinetti owned a tempera in the series which remained in his widow's collection until 1954 when Harry Lewis Winston acquired it,[52] the silence (critics, exhibitions, documents) which surrounded the entire series for thirty-five years is surprising.[53] Furthermore this was in spite of detailed reports of visits paid to the artist's studio[54] and retrospective exhibits or surveys of the heroic Futurist era. It was only in 1950 that a modest photograph of the upper part of the Mattioli painting was published (and captioned with a mistaken technique and without the owner's name) in a special issue of *Cahiers d'Art* on Italian art of the first half of the twentieth century, edited by Christian Zervos[55] (fig. 2b).

In November 1950, a few months after the *Cahiers d'Art* publication, one of the series was exhibited at the 'Futurismo-Pittura Metafisica' show in Zurich, with the title *Mercur von der Sonne vorbeiziehend* and the generic indication 'private collection'.[56] This was the large tempera acquired in July by Gianni Mattioli for the sum of 250,000 lire.[57] Mattioli seems to have sent another of the same series, smaller and omitted from the catalogue, to the Zurich show.[58] Only after the sale to Mattioli was the paper laid on canvas, which still today is its support. An accounting note from the Galleria del Milione to Gianni Mattioli dated October 20, 1950 records a cost of 7,500 lire for the laying of the 'Balla grande' on canvas and of 4,500 lire for the 'Balla piccolo.'[59] Between July and October 1950 Balla signed the canvas lining (through which the darker marks of the tempera, the shape of the telescope and the spirals around the sun are visible), with the date, noting the fact that the work had been illustrated in *Cahiers d'Art* a few months earlier (fig. 2a).

Thus the Mattioli work was the first painting of the series to be published and to have an exhibition history at a time when Balla, according to a statement in 1951, was beginning to "pull out the old Futurist canvases [set] aside twenty years earlier," surprised by their historical reevaluation.[60] The second work to re-emerge is the one that was exhibited at the 'Omaggio a Giacomo Balla' in April 1951,[61] discovered, as Piero Dorazio recalls, by himself and by the painter Edgardo Mannucci in an overhead storage space in the kitchen of the Balla home.[62] The third was exhibited at the 1951–2 Rome Quadriennale;[63] this was probably the tempera which later passed to the Museum Moderner Kunst Stiftung Ludwig in Vienna.[64] The fourth is the version once owned by Benedetta Marinetti, acquired by Harry Winston in 1954 and exhibited for the first time in Ann Arbor (Michigan) in 1955, at a show of his collection.[65]

[1] Zervos 1950, p. 67.
[2] Crispolti, Drudi Gambillo 1963, p. 72, no. 108.
[3] Vienna, Museum Moderner Kunst Stiftung Ludwig: Fagiolo dell'Arco 1997, no. 12 (but fig. 13).
[4] *Almanacco* 1914, p. 18.
[5] Mercury's perihelion, as proved by observations made by Jean-Joseph Leverrier in 1859, shifts slightly according to a precession which contradicts Newton's universal law of gravitation by 42" of the arc per century (Roseveare 1982, pp. 3–37). The definitive explanation of this anomaly was announced by Albert Einstein in a corollary to the theory of general relativity published in an issue of *Sitzungsberichte* of the Berlin Academy of Sciences, in the fall of 1915 (Einstein 1915, pp. 831–9). The publisher did not distribute the journal in Italy because of the restricted circulation of scientific publications in enemy territory during the war.
[6] Beginning in 1919, and especially in 1921, the year he was awarded the Nobel Prize for Physics, Einstein became a legendary figure whose theories were widely circulated and discussed in the most popular periodicals, even in Italy (Maiocchi 1985, pp. 49–70). In the years prior to 1914, the electronic foundations of the theory of relativity, published by Einstein in 1905 and known as "restricted relativity," were of little interest in Italy and confined to a few university professors (Tullio Levi-Civita, Roberto Marcolengo, Giovanni Giorgi, Max Abraham). In particular, the matter of the irregularity of Mercury's orbit was never associated in Italy with Einstein's studies: in 1912, when the possible gravitational implications of the theory of restricted relativity were discussed in *Il Nuovo Cimento* by Max Abraham, from 1909 professor of rational mechanics at the Politecnico in Milan and a fierce rival of Einstein's, Abraham was able to argue the definitive decline of the theory of relativity (Abraham 1912, pp. 480–1). The first, fundamental application of the theory to the gravitational field, published by Einstein in 1913 together with the mathematician Marcel Grossmann, had left the matter of Mercury's orbit still unresolved (Einstein, Grossmann 1913, pp. 3–22), while a specific study of the question, undertaken by Einstein and Michele Besso ('The Einstein-Besso Manuscript on the Motion of Mercury's Perihelion,' in Einstein 1995, pp. 344–473), remained unpublished and made no impression of any kind either in specialist or amateur circles.
[7] Fagiolo dell'Arco 1997, no. 8.
[8] *Dimostrazioni interventiste*: Martin 1973, p. 56.
[9] Milan, Civiche raccolte d'arte, Jucker Collection: *Milan* 1992–3 [no. 2].
[10] *Folla + paesaggio*, formerly New York, Barnett-Malbin Collection: *New York* 1973, no. 20.
[11] *La costellazione di Orione*, Rome, private collection: *Venice* 2000, p. 266.
[12] Flammarion 1904, p. 700; the artist's telescope was illustrated for the first time in Dortch Dorazio 1970, no. 132.
[13] Flammarion 1913, p. 420.
[14] Naccari 1911, p. 40.
[15] Balla 1984, p. 11.
[16] Padovan 1914, p. 83; the erroneous date was derived from Flammarion 1913, p. 420.
[17] Abetti 1915, p. 26.
[18] Meyer 1900, p. 122.
[19] Celoria 1914, p. 809.
[20] Balla 1984, pp. 346–8.
[21] Fagiolo dell'Arco 1997, p. 19.
[22] Whereabouts unknown: Lista 1982, no. 310. The painting was illustrated in *Pittura scultura futuriste* by Umberto Boccioni (Boccioni 1914, unnumbered plates, second Balla illustration) and was exhibited at the Galleria Sprovieri in February of that year (*Rome* 1914[a], p. 26, no. 10, with the title *Spessori d'aria + dinamismo d'elica*).
[23] *Orbite celesti*, private collection: Lista 1982, no. 309, speculatively dated to 1913.
[24] As correctly interpreted by Crispolti 1967, p. 181.
[25] Lista 1979, p. 41.
[26] Möbius 1906, p. 82.
[27] Fagiolo dell'Arco 1997, pp. 19–23.
[28] *Ibidem*, nos. 2, 3, 5, 6, 9.
[29] *Ibidem*, nos. 3, 5, 6.
[30] Formerly New York, Slifka Collection: *ibidem*, no. 9; an old repro-

duction (*Rome* 1951, no. 2) makes it possible to locate the small circle of Mercury, no longer visible owing to the poor condition of the work.

[31] In ascending order of size: the oil in Paris, Centre National d'Art Contemporain Georges Pompidou; a tempera in a private collection; the large 18 × 99 cm, now in Vienna, Museum Moderner Kunst Stiftung Ludwig (*ibidem,* nos. 10, 11, 12).

[32] A drawing (385 × 290 mm) from a private collection; a tempera on paper laid on canvas (45 × 34 cm); the tempera (65 × 50 cm) formerly in the Marinetti and then in the Winston-Malbin Collections; the Mattioli tempera (*ibidem*, nos. 4, 7, 8, 13).

[33] *Ibidem*, no. 7.

[34] Martin 1968, p. 200.

[35] Taylor 1961, p. 64.

[36] Marinetti, November 15, 1913.

[37] Calvesi 1980, pp. 191–2.

[38] Bragaglia, February 29, 1912.

[39] Lista 1979, p. 41.

[40] Matitti 1998, p. 40.

[41] Soffici, July 1, 1914.

[42] Calvesi 1966, pp. 88–9; later Fagiolo dell'Arco 1967, p. 15.

[43] Matitti 1998, p. 41.

[44] Spate 1979, p. 42; Messina, Nigro Covre 1986, pp. 302–3; Naubert, Riser 2000, pp. 122–3.

[45] *Soleil, Lune, Soleil Lune Simultané, Contraste Simultané Mouvement de couleur, Prisme soleil*: *Berlin* 1913, p. 15, nos. 78–98.

[46] *Disques solaires, simultané forme: au grand constructeur Blériot*: *Paris* 1914, no. 877; Breunig 1960, pp. 586–9.

[47] *Disques solaires*. Salmon, March 18, 1914; on Delaunay's critical success between 1913 and 1914, Rousseau 1999, pp. 247–64.

[48] Letter from Gino Severini to Carlo Carrà, dated March 9, 1914 ("tell me what you think of the sharpshooting by Delaunay and his wife") in Carrà, Severini 1983, p. 285; letter from Gino Severini to Guillaume Apollinaire, dated March 30, 1914 in Apollinaire 1992, p. 167.

[49] As proven by a note of greetings written together to Apollinaire, dated December 3, 1913 in Apollinaire 1992, p. 167.

[50] Utica (New York), Munson-Williams-Proctor Institute Museum of Art: Fonti 1988, no. 199; *New Haven* 1995–6, no. 14, illus. p. 87. The painting was exhibited in *Rome* 1914[a], p. 27, no. 4 or 5 with the title *Spherical Expansion of Light (centripetal)*; Fonti 2001[a], p. 27, is the most recent to write on this relation.

[51] *Rome* 1915, unnumbered pages.

[52] Martin 1973, no. 17.

[53] The presence of a work in the series in *Rome* 1918[b], claimed by Recupero 1959, p. 62, is pure invention.

[54] For instance, Venna, January 15, 1918; Santamaria, August 15, 1920.

[55] Zervos 1950, p. 67.

[56] *Zurich* 1950, no. 9.

[57] Archivio Mattioli, letter from Mario Klaus to Gianni Mattioli, dated July 31, 1950, with the sale offer of the tempera for 270,000 lire (*Appendix I*, document no. 54); letter from Gianni Mattioli to Mario Klaus, dated August 1, 1950, closing the sale for 250,000 lire (*Appendix I*, document no. 52).

[58] Archivio Mattioli, receipt signed by the Soprintendente alle Gallerie Fernanda Wittgens and dated October 27, 1950, with a list of the paintings in the Gianni Mattioli Collection sent to the 'Futurismo-Pittura Metafisica' show in Zurich: this includes a *Mercury Passing Before the Sun no. 1* valued at 500,000 lire and a *Mercury Passing Before the Sun no. 2,* valued at 250,000 lire. The latter work can be identified with a pastel on paper (65 × 50 cm) inventoried with the number 5899 in the register of purchases and sales of the Galleria del Milione and sold by Gianni Mattioli to Cesare Tosi in May 1952 (information courtesy of Graziano Ghiringhelli). This pastel was not included in Fagiolo dell'Arco 1997 but was exhibited in *Rome* 1989, no. B/14.

[59] Archivio Mattioli, accounting note from the Galleria del Milione to Gianni Mattioli, dated October 28, 1950 (*Appendix I*, document no. 59).

[60] Statement by Giacomo Balla in 1951, in Velani 1971, p. 116.

[61] Formerly New York, Slifka Collection: Fagiolo dell'Arco 1977, no. 9, in its present state of conservation.

[62] Interview with Piero Dorazio in Pirani 1989, pp. 51–2.

[63] *Rome* 1951–2, p. 39, no. 6.

[64] Fagiolo dell'Arco 1997, no. 12; this identification is suggested in Crispolti, Drudi Gambillo 1963, p. 73.

[65] Fagiolo dell'Arco 1997, no. 8; *Ann Arbor* 1955, p. 9, no. 6.

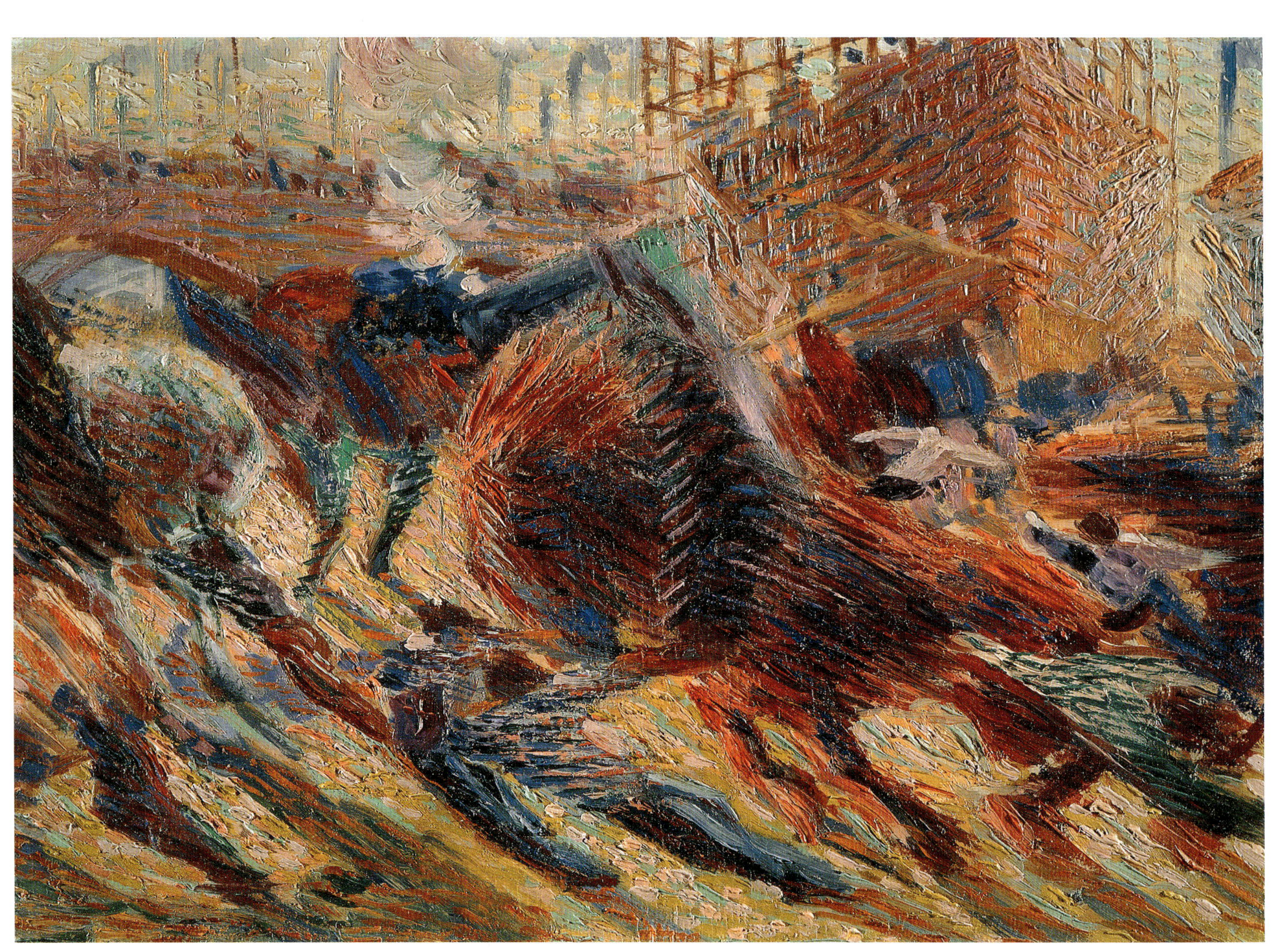

3

Umberto Boccioni (Reggio Calabria, 1882 – Sorte, Verona, 1916)

Study for *The City Rises* (Study for *Labor*)

Studio per *La città che sale* (Studio per *Il lavoro*; Studio per *La città sale*; Studio per *La città che sorge*), 1910

Oil on cardboard
33 × 47 cm

Provenance: property of the artist; ?: private collection, Lombardy; ?; Rolando Ghedini, Arona (Novara); before June 1952: Gianni Mattioli

Exhibitions: Milan 1916–17?, no. 147 or 153 or 189 (*Studio per il Quadro 'La città sale'*) or 213 (*Studio-Idea per il quadro 'La città sale'*); Venice 1952, p. 396, no. 53 (*Bozzetto per la 'Città che sorge'*); Florence 1953[a], no. 1 (*La città che sale*, bozzetto); New York 1954, no. 11; Amsterdam 1958, no. 56; Rome 1959, no. 78; Winterthur 1959, no. 15; Munich 1959–60, no. 9; Venice 1960, p. 14, no. 26; New York 1961–Los Angeles 1962, no. 29; Venice 1966, p. 7, no. 32; Washington, DC 1967–Tokyo 1972, no. 2; Turin 1969, no. 330; Milan 1970, no. 139; Paris 1973, no. 12; Milan 1974, no. 96; Düsseldorf 1974, no. 41; Venice 1986, p. 118; Paris 1994–Tokyo 1996, p. 78 (Paris–Barcelona), no. 54 (Tokyo); Rome 2000–1[a], no. 97

Bibliography: Argan, Calvesi 1953, pp. 17 and 34 (illus.); Ragghianti 1953, p. 8; Calvesi 1958[a], p. 155; Drudi Gambillo, Fiori 1958–62, vol. I, p. 412, vol. II, pp. 212 and 264, no. 218; Marchiori 1960, no. 2; Taylor 1961, pp. 35–6, no. 28, p. 142; Carrieri 1961, p. 31; De Grada 1962, pp. 83, 173, 180, pl. 61; Bellonzi 1963, pp. 60, 66–8; Ballo 1964[a], pp. 223–4, pl. 129; Ballo 1964[b], pp. 64–6; Perocco 1965, pp. 102, 104; Ballo 1966, pp. 66–7; Calvesi 1967, pp. 53, 68–72; Fiori 1968, no. 2439; Martin 1968, pp. 85–7; Bruno 1969, no. 119i, pl. XIX; Marinetti 1969, p. 101, fig. 16; Birolli 1970, pp. 139–40; Calvesi 1973, notes 20–1;

Given his flair for theoretical synthesis, his idealism and his gift for tactics, Umberto Boccioni assumed the leadership of his fellow Futurist painters in Milan early on. He it was who drafted most of the two Futurist painting manifestos, of February and April 1910. He was the first to exhibit his work under the label of Futurism (in a one-man show at Ca' Pesaro, Venice, July 1910), and was the first to speak publicly about the principles of the new painting (at a lecture in Rome, May 29, 1911). In 1910 Boccioni found himself addressing the difficult task of transferring Divisionist technique and Symbolist subjects (which for him represented the apex of pictorial modernity) to the new ideological context of Marinetti's Futurism. The Mattioli oil study is a significant testimony of this phase of Boccioni's experimentation. It is also one of the key surviving preparatory studies (the third largest after a drawing formerly in the collection of Vico Baer,[1] fig. 3b, and the tempera in the Jesi Collection,[2] fig. 3j), for *Labor*, one of the founding works of Futurist painting. Measuring nearly three meters in width, this was exhibited in April 1911 at the 'Mostra d'Arte Libera' in the Padiglione Ricordi in Milan. It now belongs to the Museum of Modern Art, New York, and bears the title *The City Rises*[3] (fig. 3a).

In its large definitive version *Labor* marked a clear watershed in Boccioni's career. It was his first important work directly focused on Futurist poetics, both in its theme, echoing Marinetti in 1909 ("We shall sing of the great crowds in the excitement of labor"[4]), and in its application of pictorial principles sanctioned by the April 11, 1910 *Technical Manifesto of Futurist Painting* ("moving objects constantly multiply themselves, they are deformed and succeed each other like vibrations in the space they move through"[5]). *Labor* also provoked the first violent schism among Boccioni's critics. It was mocked (at the exhibition "couples help one another to avoid laughing"[6]), and severely criticized even by Nino Barbantini, a critic who had been sympathetic to Boccioni in the preceding months (Barbantini scolded him for a concept "executed with uncertainty in an inadequate form" and for his lack of "clarity and of organic cohesion"[7]). However, it was also the object of unexpected praise from various quarters, ranging from the Socialist-leaning daily *Il Secolo* ("a highly personal vision of art" achieved by representing modern life made of "the convulsive strain of draft horses," of "trams passing along a distant horizon and laborers toiling or immersed in a blue cloud of dust"[8]), to the conservative news-sheet *La Perseveranza* ("the orgy of color takes nothing away from the reality, but rather, adds a frisson of life"[9]). The fact that Boccioni exhibited the painting again in the February 1912 Futurist group show at the Galerie Bernheim-jeune in Paris[10] indicates that he considered it the first product of a new era, capable of holding its own *vis-à-vis* the Parisian audience and critics. The change of title for the occasion (*La Ville monte* supercedes *Labor*, which was preceded in turn by a series of intermediate titles inspired by humanitarian socialist sympathies, such as *Men* and *Giants and Pygmies*) marked a decisive turn toward Marinetti, whether one attributes the responsibility for this to Marinetti himself and to "certain images of Promethean symbolism in his poetry",[11] or to Boccioni, seeking to "make [the theme of labor] explode in an optimistic expectation of its outcomes" and to reduce it to a "purely physical [value], that is, to the parameters of energy and of movement".[12]

The catalogue of the large posthumous retrospective of Boccioni's work at the Galleria Centrale d'Arte, Palazzo Cova, Milan, (December 28, 1916 – January 14, 1917) lists, next to the final version of *The City Rises*,[13] four *bozzetti* (identified as 'Study for' or 'Idea for' the painting)[14] and a 'drawing for the large painting.'[15] The latter can confidently be identified with the only surviving drawing which is large in scale and extensively detailed[16] (fig. 3b); the four *bozzetti* match the four extant color studies: aside from the Mattioli study (the only oil version, whose exhibition history thus began precociously in 1916) these are: a small tempera on paper, 140×200 mm[17] (fig. 3h), a tempera on board, 17.5×30.5 cm, formerly in the Borgese Collection[18] (fig. 3i), and the above-mentioned tempera on cardboard in the Jesi Collection, 37×60 cm[19] (fig. 3j).

The 1916–17 catalogue is silent about the ownership of the works on view. This makes it difficult, henceforth, to identify the collectors of these four color studies and their presentation in later exhibitions. The version of *The City Rises* in the collection of Vico Baer listed in the Boccioni exhibition at the Galleria Bottega di Poesia in Milan in 1924[20] is the same that later passed to the Jesi Collection[21] (fig. 3j). It is not possible to identify Boccioni's nineteen 'drawings in tempera' shown at the 'III Biennale romana' in 1925, nor does more precise information emerge from contemporary newspaper articles covering the event. The selection of works for the 1933 Boccioni retrospective at the Castello Sforzesco in Milan (for which there was no catalogue) included the large final painting (fig. 3a, then in the Busoni Collection) as well as the large drawing, the small tempera on paper and the tempera that later went to the Jesi Collection,[22] all three then in Baer's collection (figs. 3b, 3h, 3j). In 1949, the study for *The City Rises* owned by the art dealer Romeo Toninelli shown at the New York Museum of Modern Art's 'Twentieth-Century Italian Art' exhibition can be identified, because of its size, with the tempera formerly in the Borgese Collection[23] (fig. 3i). The unique oil study for *The City Rises* reappeared for the first time at the 1952 Venice Biennale, in an international Divisionism exhibition, by this time the property of Gianni Mattioli.[24]

What little we know about the Mattioli oil from 1916 to 1952 we owe to Laura Mattioli Rossi's oral recollection. Rolando Ghedini, Gianni Mattioli's business partner, gave him the sketch. Ghedini's brother, an antique dealer in Arona, had bought it from an unidentified private collection in Lombardy consisting mainly of nineteenth-century drawings. Its entry into the Mattioli Collection immediately made it the most widely exhibited and reproduced of the four surviving studies. In 1953 Carlo Ludovico Ragghianti described it as "much more synthetic and fiery than the painting".[25]

An industrial city, probably inspired by Milan,[26] is sketched in the background of the oil study. Large horses in the foreground arch their backs under the strain of dragging their heavy loads, urged on by laborers apparently overwhelmed by an irrepressible force, emphasized by the long brushstrokes that follow the direction of their efforts. The Mattioli study is the outcome of a lengthy drafting process which can be recreated rather precisely thanks to the numerous surviving drawings and studies.

Poggialini Tominetti 1979, pp. 79–80; Birollli 1983, pp. 63–71; Calvesi, Coen 1983, no. 683; Roche-Pézard 1983, p. 477; Salaris 1985, p. 40; Coen 1986, pp. 28–30; Calvesi 1994, pp. 22–5; Lista 1994, p. 77; Schneede 1994, pp, 60, 63, fig. 42; Agnese 1996, pp. 206–8; Rylands 1997, p. 54; Spinazzè 2000, pp. 256–7 (illus., in reverse)

Fig. 3a. *Umberto Boccioni,* La città che sale (Il lavoro) *(*The City Rises [Labor]*), oil on canvas, 1910–11. New York, The Museum of Modern Art, Mrs Simon Guggenheim Fund*

Fig. 3b. *Umberto Boccioni, Drawing for* La città che sale*, pencil and chalk on paper, 1910–11. New York, The Museum of Modern Art, Mrs Simon Guggenheim Fund*

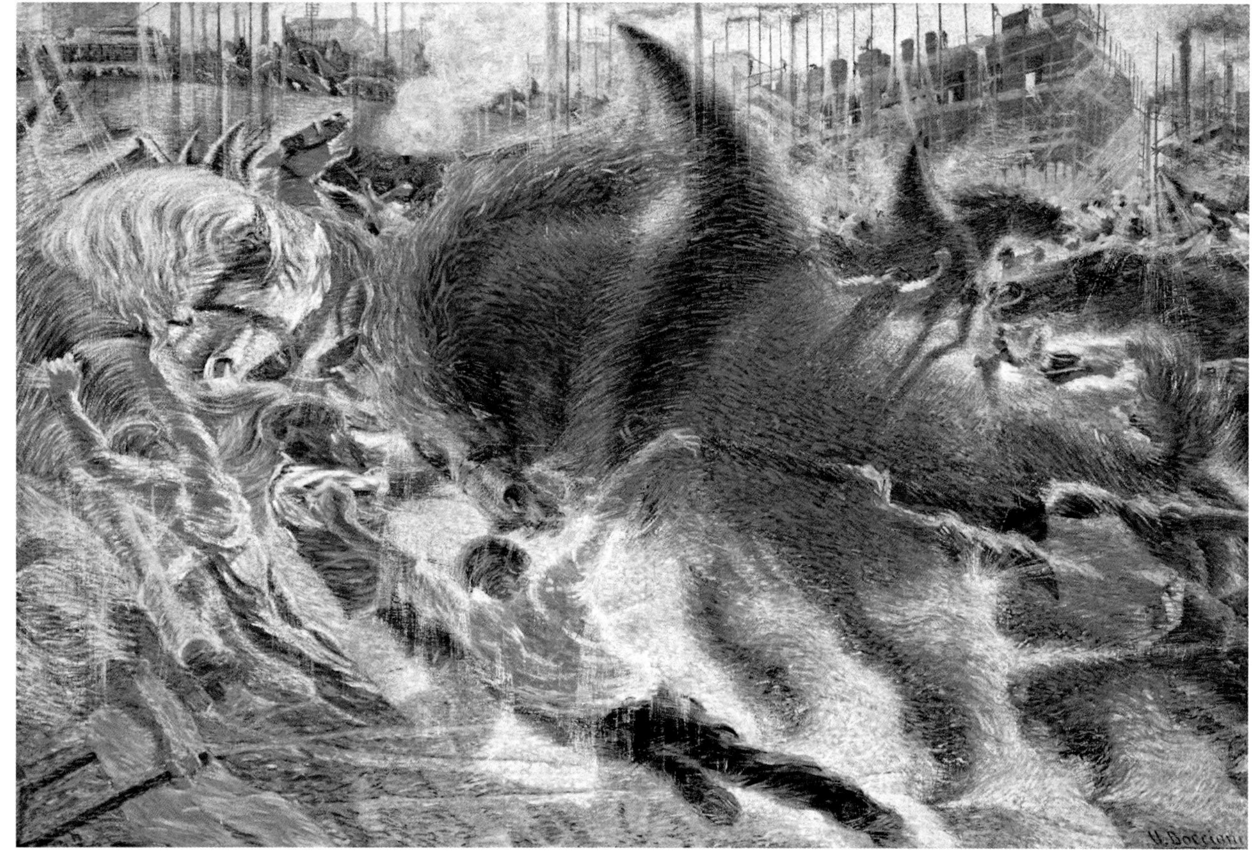

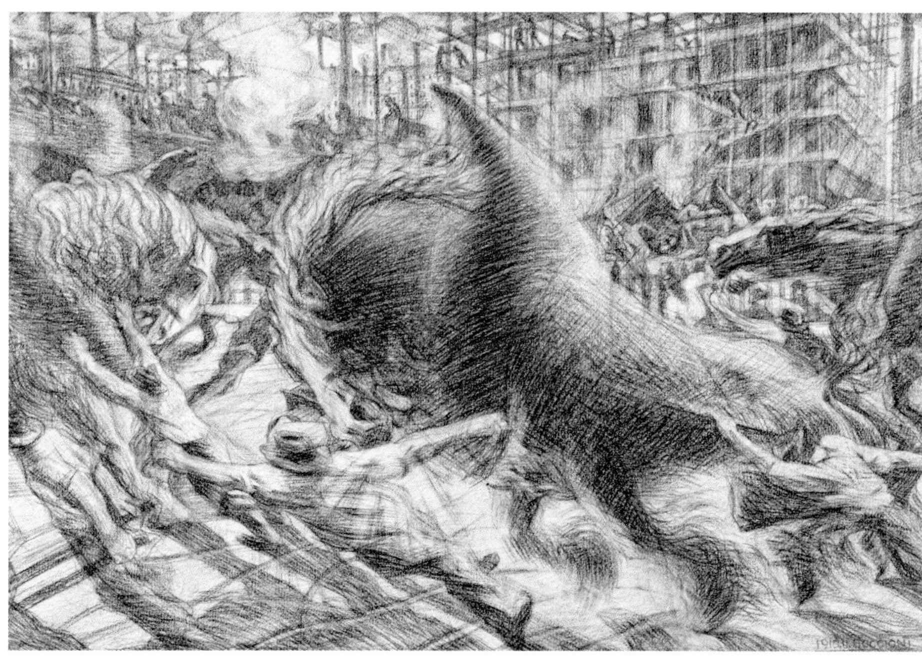

A photograph taken during Boccioni's first visit to Paris in April–August 1906 captures the artist in the act of making a pencil study of a horse harnessed in a large collar.[27] Drawings by Boccioni of the same subject, with the focus on the large collar harness, become more numerous around 1910.[28] At a certain point Boccioni began to sketch in the background and to yoke the horses to a loaded wagon.[29] Beginning with two India ink drawings, on the *recto* and *verso* of a single sheet,[30] the horses grow in number, in a setting in which people start to appear: the motif of the man on the left who adds his own efforts to the struggle of a horse pulling a huge weight, which was the subject of separate studies by Boccioni, gradually increases in importance.[31] In one of these drawings (fig. 3c) — which was crucial in terms of the development of the motif — the right and left horses face each other, the outlines of the horses begin to multiply (two, led by men walking in front, are clearly visible in the middle distance in the center of the sheet; three others are summarily sketched further back), and finally Boccioni roughs in an urban setting.[32] At this point the essential composition of *Labor* has materialized, and in a subsequent drawing we see the horse to the left posturing strenuously, its legs stiffened and its weight balanced by the counter-thrust of the workman — a motif that Boccioni retained through to the final version of the painting.[33]

The core motif, that of a man assisting a gigantic toiling horse, descends from figurative sources symbolizing Work in the opening years of the century. Carlo Ludovico Ragghianti[34] pointed to a large sculptural relief by Gustave Debrie entitled *Le Coup de collier* (*The Thrust of the Draft Horse*) as Boccioni's source for the final version of *The City Rises*. This was exhibited at the Paris Salon in 1904[35] and reproduced the same year in *L'Art Décoratif*[36] (fig. 3k), a Parisian magazine consulted by many Italian artists in this period. For the motif of the horse arched with its muscles swollen by extreme effort (which is the sole subject of some preparatory studies[37]), Boccioni may have had recourse to more easily comprehensible models such as a bronze with the same title as Debrie's relief by the Belgian sculptor Joseph Kemmerich (fig. 3l, shown at the 'Exposition Triennale des Beaux-Arts' in Ghent in 1906 and acquired by the museum of Brussels[38]). Again, in July 1910, contemporary with Boccioni's studies for *Labor*, *L'Art Décoratif* published a powerfully muscular *Cheval* in bronze, its front legs stationary, by De Mounard.[39]

We can locate the effective turning point of Boccioni's studies for *Labor* in this phase. The composition seemed to acquire a new meaning as the artist abandoned his focus on single episodes and seemed to strive for more generalized symbolic content. In three letters written after he had begun the painting (one of them after it had been completed), he declared his intention to create a work of art radically different in character from anything that had preceded it: "a great synthesis of labor, light and movement" painted "without a model" in which the artist's skills were subordinated "to the ultimate cause of emotion".[40] By his own admission, Boccioni sought to express "that sense of fatal destiny in the crowds at work"[41] by conjuring "a complete mental vision [...] infinitely superior to any more or less subjective reproduction of real life".[42] In a hitherto unpublished drawing[43] (fig. 3d), a rapid pencil sketch, workers accompanying the surging thrust of draft animals are depicted on the same flattened diagonal that we see in the final version of the painting. The same drawing includes a large building with a steeply sloped roof in the middle of the background. This may be explained as an evolution of the gigantic pyramid bearing down in three earlier drawings, probably studies for an unexecuted painting in which gentlemen in top hats from Boccioni's *The Police Raid* seem to be observing the draft horses in *Labor*.[44]

This group of studies, with the horses all heading to the left, have their summation in a drawing formerly in the Winston-Malbin Collection which includes several components of the final painting[45] (fig. 3e): the laborer with a wheelbarrow and another holding back the draft horse on

Fig. 3c. *Umberto Boccioni,* Cavalli e figure *(*Horses and Figures*), ink on paper, 1910. Private collection*

Fig. 3d. *Umberto Boccioni, Drawing for* La città che sale*, pencil on paper, 1910. Trieste, private collection*

Fig. 3e. *Umberto Boccioni, Drawing for* La città che sale*, pencil on paper, 1910. Private collection*

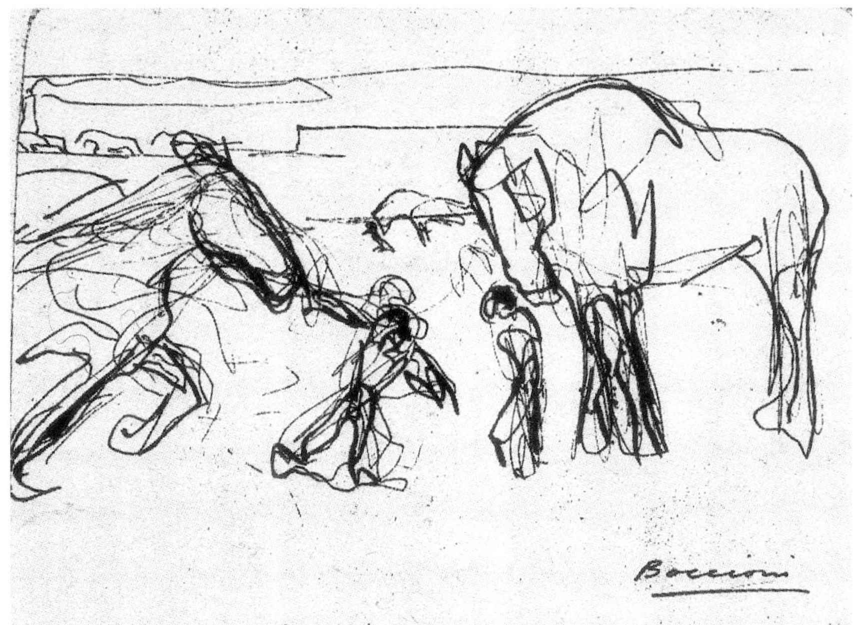

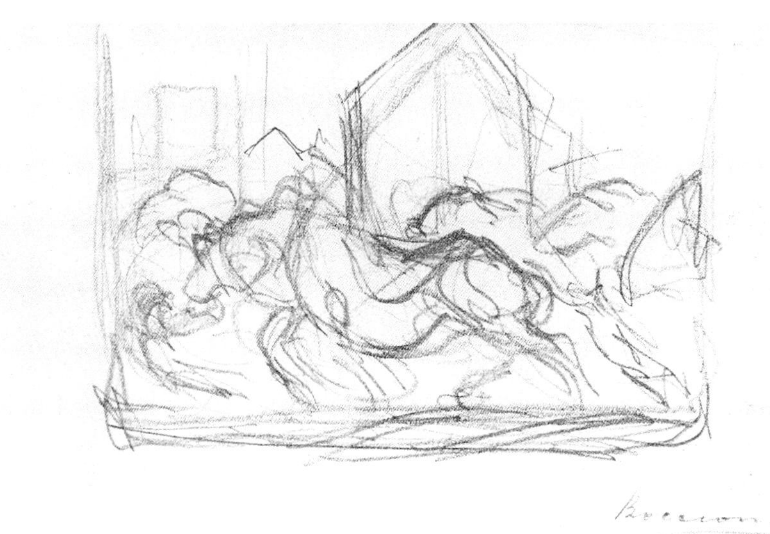

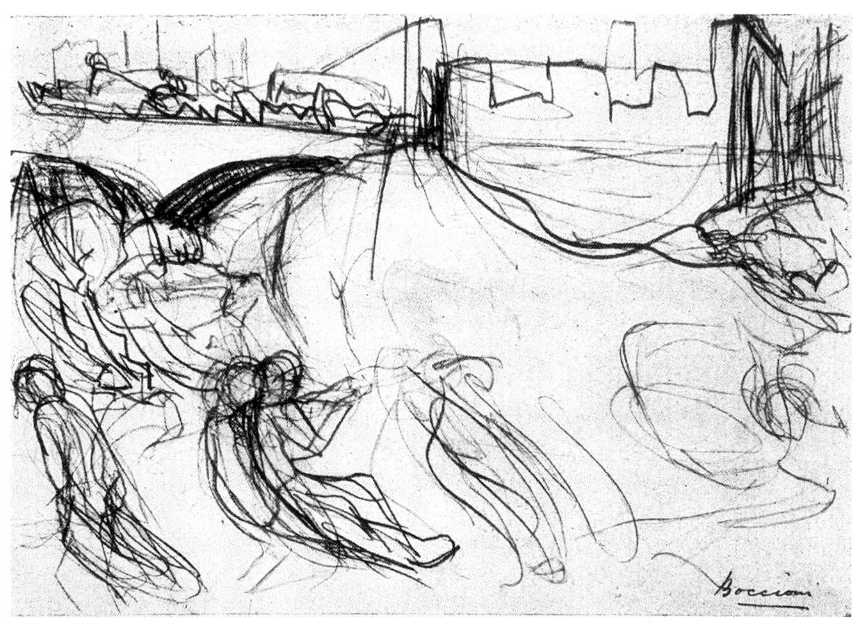

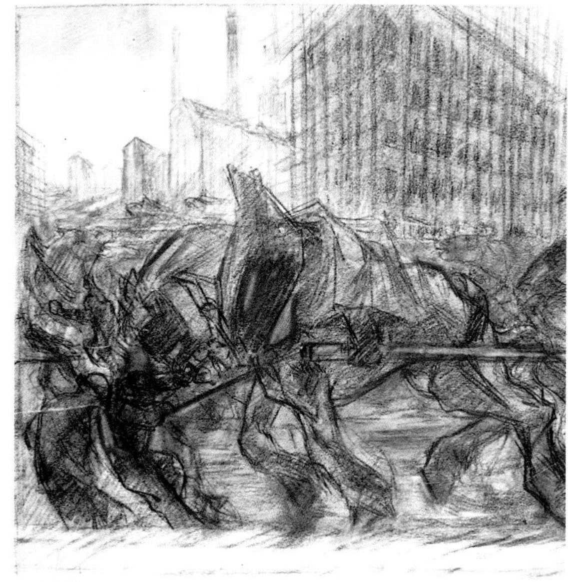

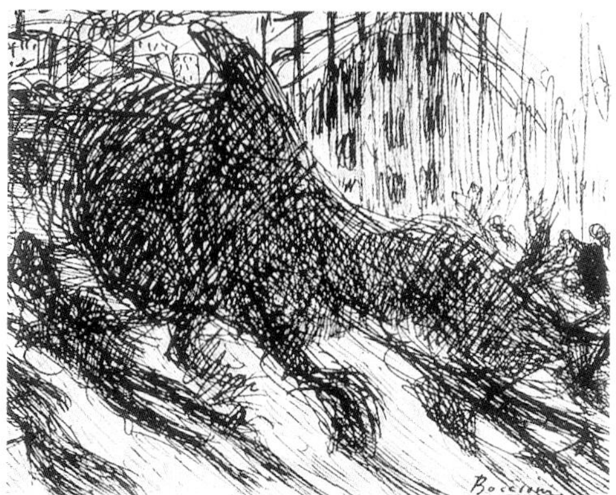

Fig. 3f. *Umberto Boccioni,* Giganti e pigmei (Giants and Pygmies)*, pencil on paper, 1910, detail. Turin, Galleria Civica d'Arte Moderna e Contemporanea*

Fig. 3g. *Umberto Boccioni, Drawing for* La città che sale, *ink on paper, 1910. Private collection*

the left, the two men hauling the large central horse, and the horse's head that intrudes on the right margin. Having found his motif, Boccioni cropped it (eliminating many of the details on the left) and attempted to insert it, with the title *Day*, in the center of an ambitious triptych that he was planning and which he was calling *Giants and Pygmies.*[46] The triptych did not progress beyond a detailed drawing[47] (fig. 3f), though the aborted project was not in vain: by narrowing the field of vision for this mooted central panel, the horse in the foreground comes to dominate the entire scene. In a pen sketch with a backlit effect (fig. 3g), Boccioni represented the horse as an enormous winged Pegasus with its head and neck on a larger scale than the rest of the body.[48] This may be the moment at which, as first observed by Maurizio Calvesi, Boccioni turned to two separate sources in the work of Gaetano Previati.[49] He admired Previati more than any other contemporary Italian painter and would inevitably have visited the Previati retrospective, with two hundred paintings, that opened in January 1910 at the Palazzo della Permanente, Milan. This show included two triptychs, *Il giorno* (*The Day*) and *L' Eroica* (*Heroic*)[50] (fig. 3m), in which in the central sections horses like Boccioni's have heads arched over as they gallop, constructed with the same long filament-like brushstrokes.[51] Exhibited in the same room as *L'Eroica* was *Galere pisane* (*Pisan Galleys*),[52] whose sails may have suggested the strange wedge-shaped silhouette and luminous structure of the enormous pointed collars with which the horses in *Labor* are harnessed.

The above-mentioned drawing (fig. 3g), with the horse portrayed against the light, is the closest of the group to the Mattioli study and constitutes the bridge to the remaining studies: the large (572 × 851 mm) pencil drawing formerly owned by Vico Baer[53] (fig. 3b) and the four color studies whose problematic chronology is discussed here for the first time. Thus the group consists of six works: the former Baer drawing (fig. 3b), the four studies (the Mattioli oil, Calvesi-Coen no. 681 [fig. 3h], the Estorick tempera [fig. 3i], the Jesi tempera [fig. 3j]), and the final painting (fig. 3a). These vary in four principal ways:

1. *The relative scale of the large red foreground horse in the field of vision.* In the Mattioli study the point of view is more distant; the tip of the blue yoke is located roughly three-quarters of the way up the composition. In the Baer drawing the horse is brought closer to the spectator as if by a photographic zoom, making the yoke stand out against the scaffolding in the background. The yoke is closer to the upper edge in the Estorick study and actually touches it in the tempera study (fig. 3h; private collection, henceforth Calvesi, Coen no. 681), in the Jesi study and in the large final painting.

Fig. 3h. *Umberto Boccioni, Bozzetto for* La città che sale (Gli uomini)*, pencil and tempera on paper, 1910. Milan, private collection*

Fig. 3i. *Umberto Boccioni, Bozzetto for* La città che sale*, tempera on board, 1910. London, Estorick Collection*

Fig. 3j. *Umberto Boccioni, Bozzetto for* La città che sale*, tempera on cardboard, 1910. Milan, Pinacoteca di Brera, Jesi Collection*

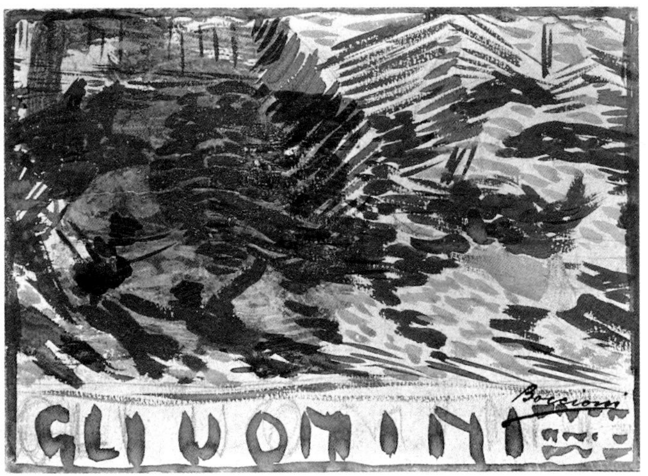

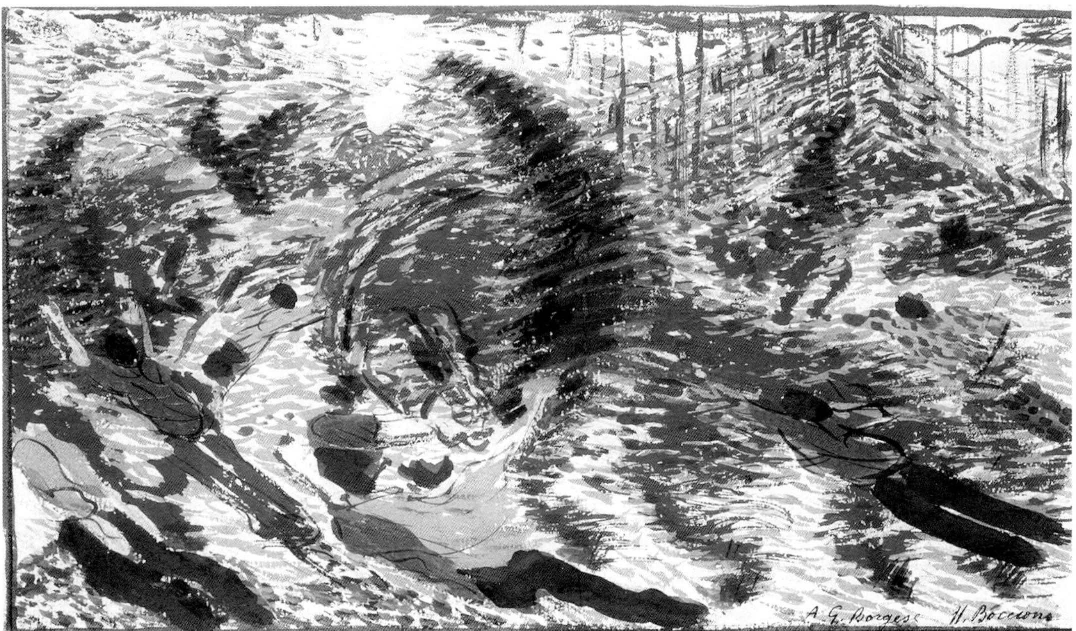

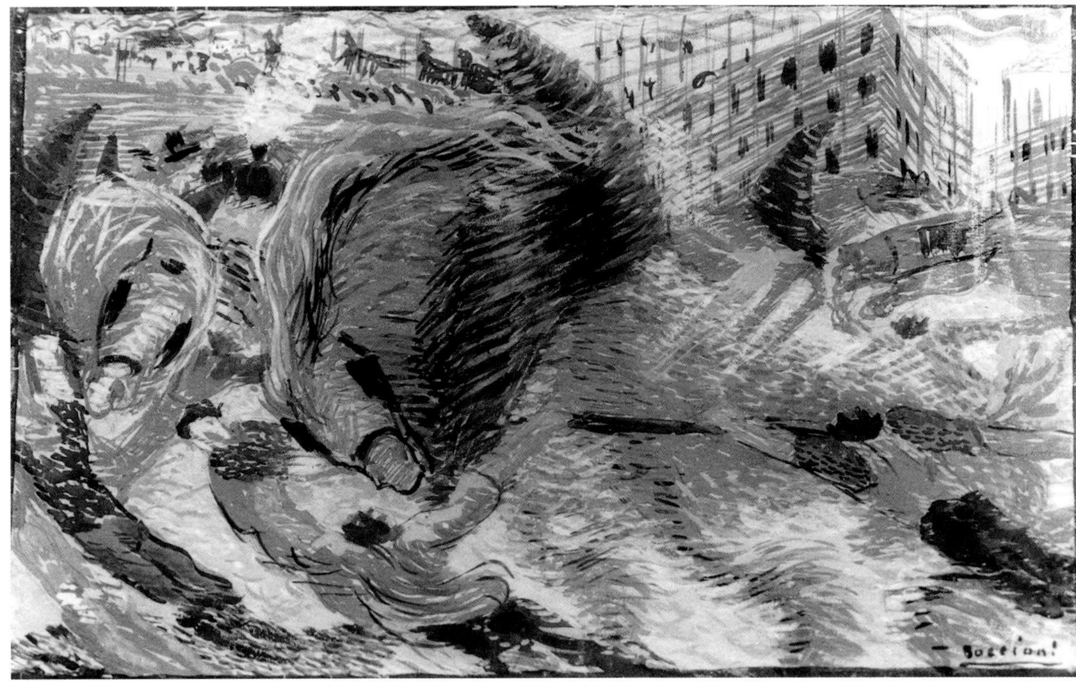

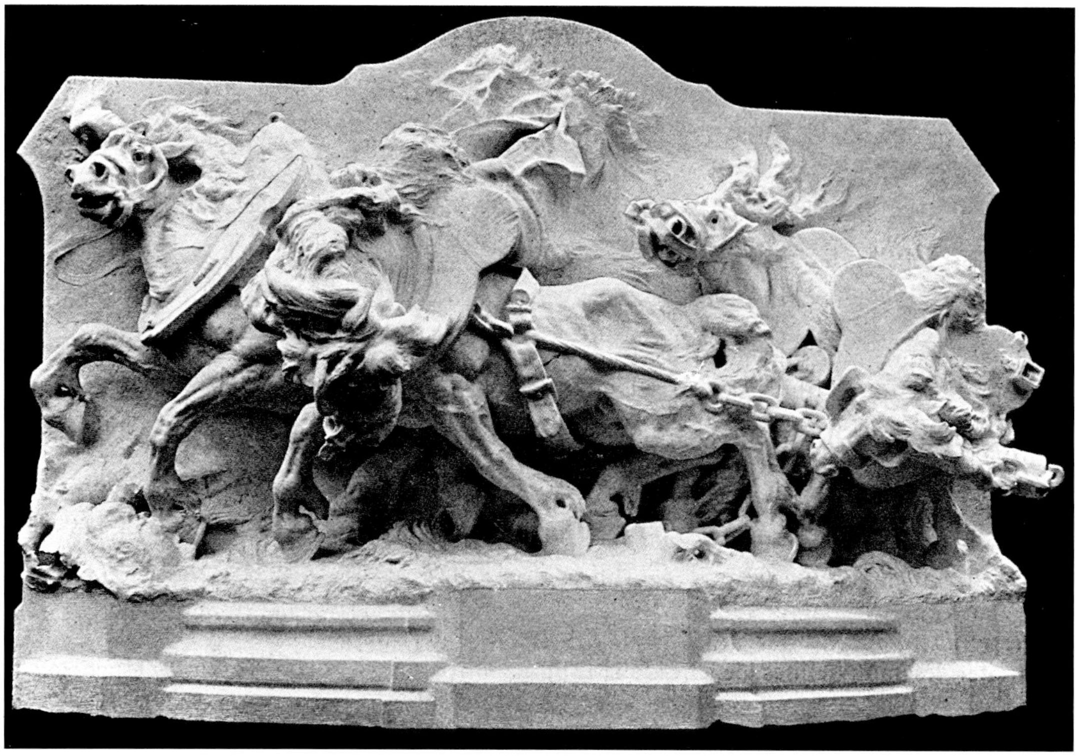

Fig. 3k. *Gustave Debrie,* Le Coup de collier (The Thrust of the Draft Horse), *in* L'Art Décoratif, *1904*

2. *The distance between the heads of the two principal horses facing one another (colored red and white in the final painting) and the figures in the gap between them.* In the Mattioli study there is considerable space between the two horses, and two small laborers are inserted between the heads. The horses are closer in the Baer drawing and only one small man leading a horse is visible between them. Similarly, in the trio consisting of the Estorick study, the Jesi study and the final painting, a single man is visible, though closer to the foreground, leaning to the right and wearing a green shirt. Many of the details in the much abbreviated tempera study Calvesi, Coen no. 681 are indecipherable.

3. *The pose and position of one of the two workmen leading the large red horse (the one farther to the left, the only one that turns its head to the viewer in the final painting).* Illegible in the tempera study Calvesi, Coen no. 681, this figure merely flanks his co-worker in the Mattioli study, but moves behind the latter and is almost concealed by him in the Baer drawing and is noticeably higher and farther off, behind the large horse's muzzle, in the Estorick and Jesi studies as well as in the final painting.

4. *The background detail behind the back of the central horse.* A tilted cart unloads building materials in the Baer drawing while in the other studies and in the final painting a horse moves from left to right with the usual pointed yoke.

On the basis of these observations, it is clear that the Mattioli study is not the final preparatory study for the painting, as is usually claimed,[54] since the compositions of the Estorick and Jesi studies are closer to that of the New York painting. Evaluating how the Baer drawing (fig. 3b) relates to the Mattioli study is more complicated. Guido Ballo and Maurizio Calvesi considered it the last phase of development prior to the final painting,[55] while for Ester Coen it is *d'après* the latter:[56] indeed, its chiaroscuro precisely replicates the chromatic effects of the painting, and the substitution of the draft horse with the barrow in the lower left corner can be understood as a later variant of the large, final canvas. Even so, chronological placement of this drawing is ambiguous: certain details (the electric tram silhouetted behind the wall on the upper right or details of the scaffolding around the house on the upper left) can only be found in the final painting, while others seem to belong to a phase preceding even the Jesi and Estorick studies.

The Mattioli study, then, represents the first pictorial synthesis of the scene once all its components had been defined: it is the first color study, with a generally cooler and more strident palette than the other studies and the final painting. The alteration in the spatial treatment of the composition between the Mattioli study and the later Jesi and Estorick studies in effect revolutionized the meaning of the painting, transforming it from an urban scene with horses and laborers into a painting with strong Symbolist connotations, in which a red horse in the foreground fills the scene and monopolizes attention. Boccioni, as recounted in a letter of 1910–11, was aware that the painting underwent change as it was being transferred to the final canvas ("I multiplied the inspiration and the painting has become more populous more violent than before. The crowd has grown"[57]). This transformation entailed understandable problems for a painter unaccustomed to working on such a large surface,[58] and the last studies may have been executed for the purpose of coping with the development of the large painting even after it had been begun. Barbantini, who saw the huge canvas of *Labor* in June 1911 after examining the preparatory works in Boccioni's studio, was perhaps alluding to a certain confusion in Boccioni's process, and to a premature and over precipitous transfer to full scale when he suggested "that the work may have been insufficiently prepared, and perhaps should have been worked out in advance in greater depth and over a longer period of time".[59]

Even if Boccioni had not set to work on the large canvas with all the extant studies already executed (as Zeno Birolli speculates[60]), the matter really only concerns the last two (Estorick and Jesi). The *terminus ante quem* of the Mattioli study is therefore a letter from Boccioni to Barbantini in which the painter maintained that he would "begin a 2 × 3 meter painting on Wednesday." Though undated, the letter can be placed in August 1910 thanks to a reference to the summer exhibition at Ca' Pesaro, Venice, that was inaugurated on July 16, 1910, in the context of which Barbantini had organized Boccioni's first one-man show. For this exhibition Boccioni had chosen to exhibit his *Periferie* (*Suburbs*) series, which was the immediate precedent for the rich palette of "convulsive chromatic fragmentation"[61] in the Mattioli study. Thus the chronology confirms Boccioni's execution of the Mattioli study for *Labor* soon after the drafting of the *Technical Manifesto of Futurist Painting,* and supports its status as his first programmatic attempt to apply pictorially the principles it declaimed.

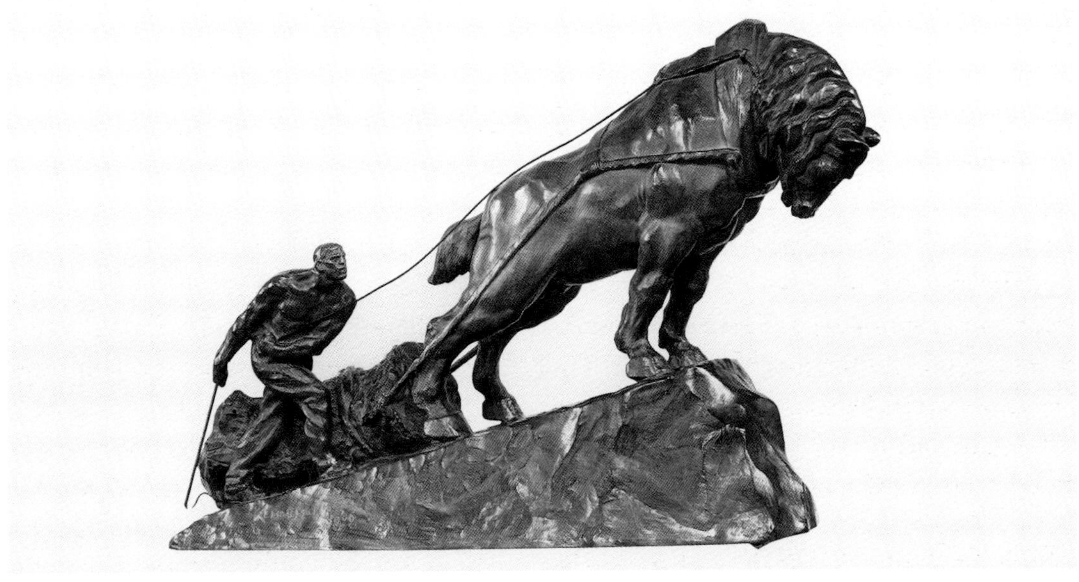

Fig. 31. *Joseph Kemmerich,* Le Coup de collier (The Thrust of the Draft Horse)*, bronze, 1906. Brussels, Musées Royaux des Beaux-Arts de Belgique*

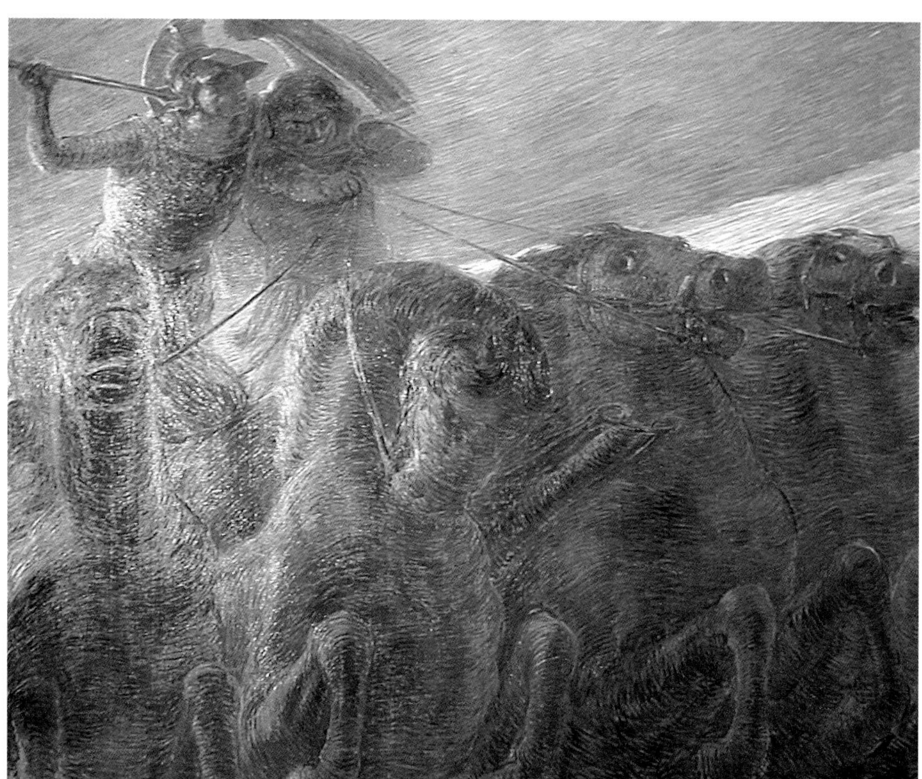

Fig. 3m. *Gaetano Previati,* L'Eroica (Heroic)*, central panel of the triptych, oil on canvas, 1907. Rome, Headquarters of the Associazione Mutilati e Invalidi di Guerra*

[1] New York, The Museum of Modern Art: Calvesi, Coen 1983, no. 684.
[2] Milan, Pinacoteca di Brera, Jesi Collection: *ibidem,* no. 682.
[3] *Ibidem*, no. 675.
[4] Marinetti, February 20, 1909. The translation is from the catalogue of the exhibition *Newcastle upon Tyne* 1972–*London* 1973, p. 25.
[5] Boccioni *et al.*, April 11, 1910. The translation is from the catalogue of the exhibition *Newcastle upon Tyne* 1972–*London* 1973, p. 29.
[6] *Uomo di Pietra*, May 6, 1911.
[7] Barbantini, May 19, 1911.
[8] Signed c.c. May 2, 1911.
[9] Signed d.b. May 1–2, 1911.
[10] *Paris* 1912[a], p. 24, no. 6.
[11] Lista 1980, p. 43.
[12] Calvesi 1976, pp. 259–60.
[13] *Milan* 1916–17, no. 70.
[14] *Ibidem*, nos. 147, 153, 189, 213.
[15] *Ibidem*, no. 308.
[16] This is the previously mentioned Calvesi, Coen 1983, no. 684.
[17] Private collection: *ibidem*, no. 681.
[18] London, Estorick Collection: *ibidem*, no. 680, with an autograph dedication by Umberto Boccioni to Giuseppe Antonio Borgese.
[19] *Ibidem*, no. 682.
[20] *Milan* 1924, p. 34, no. 33, in the 'Paintings' section.
[21] Identification made possible by autograph notes by Maria Jesi on the back of a photograph of the work (Sovrintendenza al Patrimonio Storico, Artistico e Demoetnoantropologico, Milan, fototeca).
[22] Rovati 2001, pp. 304–8, respectively no. 145 (*La Ville monte*, oil, 200 × 300 cm, Busoni, Berlin), no. 42 (*La Ville qui monte*, drawing, 870 × 590 mm, Vico Baer), no. 38 (*La Ville qui monte*, tempera, 21 × 14 cm, Vico Baer), and no. 121 (*La Ville qui monte*, tempera, 60 × 35 cm, Vico Baer).
[23] *New York* 1949, p. 126.
[24] *Venice* 1952, p. 396, no. 53.
[25] Ragghianti 1953, p. 8.
[26] The comparison in Capano, Negri 1992–5, p. 258, between the house under construction in the background (particularly as detailed in Calvesi, Coen 1983, no. 672, just prior to the Mattioli oil study) and the thermoelectric plant in Piazza Trento in Milan seems convincing to this writer. A theory has recently been advanced that the final painting may be set in Rome, during construction of buildings for the 1911 'Esposizione Internazionale' (Calvesi 1994, pp. 23–5; Spinazzè 2000, pp. 256–7) on the basis of the presence of the tram crossing the Flaminio bridge, but this was inaugurated later, in May 1911.
[27] Verona, Archivio Pollini; the photograph is published in Ballo 1964[a], p. 35, no. 17.
[28] Calvesi, Coen 1983, nos. 538, 540, 544–5.
[29] *Ibidem*, no. 558.
[30] These are the *recto* and *verso* (Calvesi, Coen 1983, nos. 667–8) of the sheet formerly in the Harry Winston Collection (Taylor, Martin 1973, no. 158). See fig. 3c.
[31] Calvesi, Coen 1983, no. 669.
[32] *Ibidem*, no. 667.
[33] *Ibidem*, no. 677.
[34] Ragghianti 1965, pp. 16 and 23.
[35] *Paris* 1904, no. 2829.
[36] Rambosson 1904, p. 33.
[37] Calvesi, Coen 1983, no. 665.
[38] Brussels, Musées Royaux de Beaux-Arts de Belgique, inv. 3850: Van Lennep, undated, p. 245.
[39] Roches 1910, p. 19.
[40] Letter from Umberto Boccioni to Nino Barbantini, undated (but September 1910), in Boccioni 1971, p. 343.
[41] Letter from Umberto Boccioni to a lady, undated (but 1911), in Drudi Gambillo, Fiori 1958–62, vol. I, p. 233.
[42] Letter from Umberto Boccioni to Nino Barbantini, undated (but May 1911), in Boccioni 1971, p. 345.
[43] Formerly in the Gino De Finetti Collection, now in a private collection in Trieste: the drawing was probably acquired by De Finetti at the Umberto Boccioni retrospec-

tive in 1924 at the Galleria Pesaro, Milan.

[44] *La retata*: Calvesi, Coen 1983, nos. 661 and 663–4.

[45] *Ibidem*, no. 676; Taylor, Martin 1973, no. 192.

[46] Calvesi, Coen 1983, no. 673.

[47] Turin, Galleria Civica d'Arte Moderna e Contemporanea: *ibidem*, no. 672.

[48] Private collection: *ibidem*, no. 679. A wide range of references for this *Pegasus*, from Caravaggio to Redon, was postulated by Martin 1968, pp. 86–7.

[49] Calvesi 1958, p. 155.

[50] *Milan* 1910, nos. 29 and 82.

[51] On the meaning of this reference, see also Ginex 1999, pp. 72–3.

[52] *Milan* 1910, no. 78.

[53] New York, The Museum of Modern Art: Calvesi, Coen 1983, no. 684.

[54] Birolli 1970, no. 137; *Venice* 1986, p. 118; Rylands 1997, p. 54; Spinazzè 2000, pp. 256–7. Taylor (1961, p. 142), to the contrary, dates the Jesi study after the Mattioli study.

[55] Ballo 1964[a], p. 224; Calvesi 1973, no. 21.

[56] Coen 1988[b], p. 99.

[57] Letter from Umberto Boccioni to a lady, undated (but 1911), in Drudi Gambillo, Fiori 1958–62, vol. I, p. 233.

[58] As it was impossible for Boccioni to execute the large painting in his studio in Via Adige 23, he temporarily obtained a larger one on the Società Umanitaria premises: Agnese 1966, pp. 206–7.

[59] Barbantini, May 19, 1911.

[60] Birolli 1983, p. 63.

[61] Poggialini Tominetti 1979, p. 79.

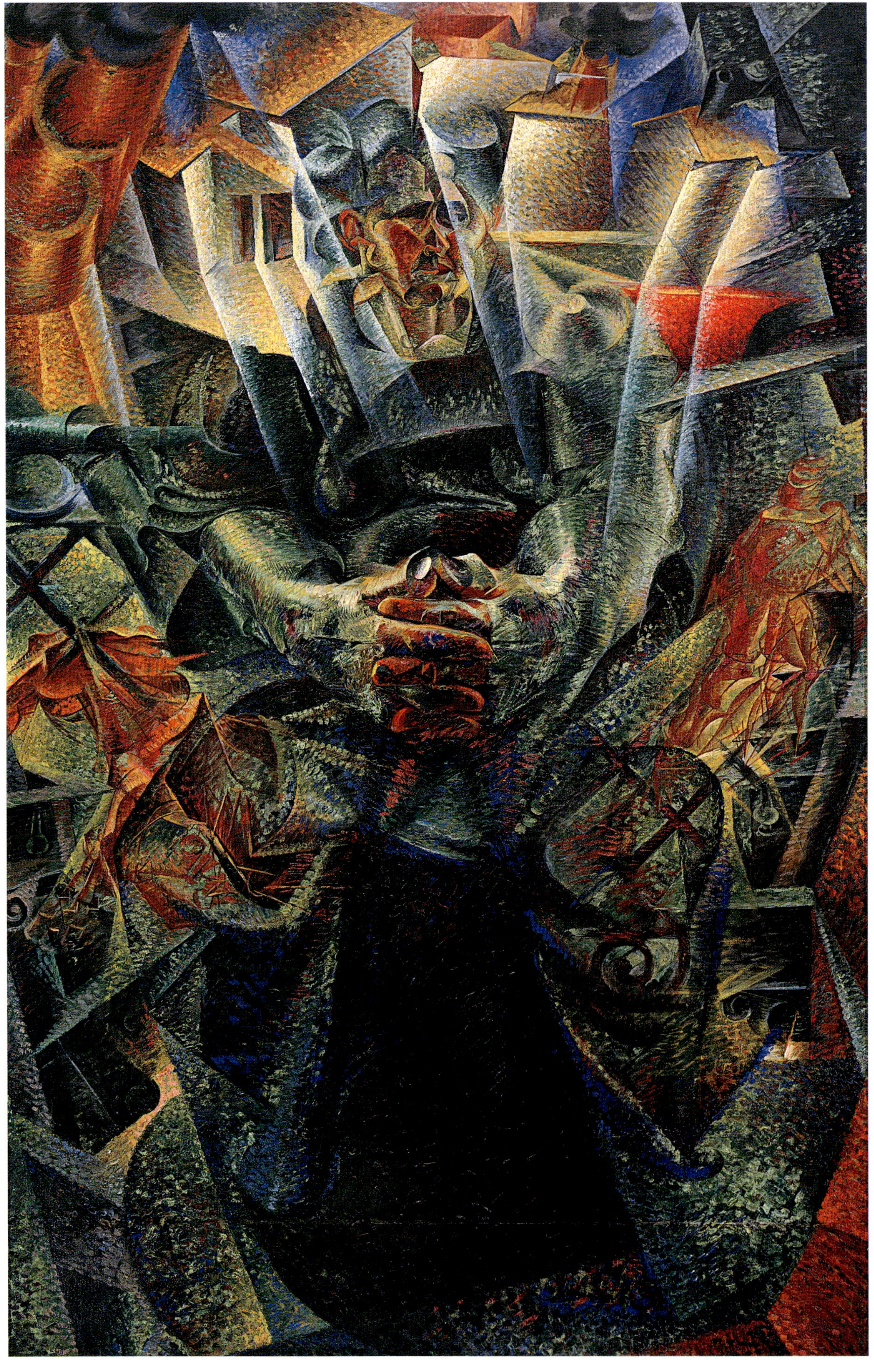

4

Umberto Boccioni

Materia, 1912, reworked 1913

Oil on canvas
226 × 150 cm

Inscription: *verso*, signed on the canvas: 'U. Boccioni' (fig. 4a)

Provenance: property of the artist; 1916: Cecilia Forlani, Milan; 1927: Amelia Callegari Boccioni, Verona; 1949: Romeo Toninelli, Milan; December 1949: Gianni Mattioli, with the mediation of Vittorio Barbaroux

Exhibitions: Rome 1913, p. 21, no. 21 (*Materia*); Rotterdam 1913, p. 19, no. 1; London 1914, p. 25, no. 4; San Francisco 1915–16, no. 1142; Milan 1916–17, p. 48, no. 49; Geneva 1920–1, p. 17, no. 26; Paris 1921 (the catalogue has not been traced by the author, though *Materia*'s presence in the exhibition is documented by a label on the reverse of the painting); Milan 1924, no. 24; Rome 1925, p. 47, no. 1, pl. 87 (repr. upside down); Milan 1933, no. 101 (the catalogue not traced by the author, though *Materia*'s presence in the show and its catalogue number are documented by a label on the back of the painting); New York 1949, no. 39, fig. 10, p. 126; Paris 1950, no. 11; Zurich 1950, no. 26; Florence 1953[a], no. 2; São Paulo 1953–4, p. 7, no. 10; Kassel 1955, no. 65; Rome 1959, no. 77; Winterthur 1959, no. 25, pl. 8; Munich 1959–60, no. 18, pl. 6; Venice 1960, p. 15, no. 86; Washington, DC 1967–Tokyo 1972, no. 3; Paris 1973, no. 25; Milan 1973–4, no. 162; Düsseldorf 1974, no. 56; Venice 1986, p. 129; London 1989, no. 25; Madrid 1990–1, p. 227; Verona 1991–2, no. 25; Saint-Paul de Vence 1992, no. 25; Milan 1995, no. 25; Milan, 1995–6, no. 31; Barcelona 2000–1, no. I.1

Bibliography: Cecchi, March 23,

Materia was Boccioni's most important and ambitious painting of 1912 and, after *The City Rises* (1910–11), his second largest canvas to date (subsequently Boccioni painted only one other canvas on a comparable scale, the slightly larger *Dynamism of a Soccer Player*, 1913–14). Boccioni himself was aware of its status as the single most important painting of that crucial year of work following the first Futurist exhibition in Paris in February 1912: *Materia* opened the sections dedicated to Boccioni's paintings in exhibitions during the first half of 1913 (Rome, February–March; Rotterdam, May–June), bumping into second place the *States of Mind,* the triptych that had opened all the group shows of 1912 and which for Boccioni, more than any other paintings, embodied the anti-Cubist posture he aggressively declared in the catalogue.[1] In this sense, *Materia*'s subsequent exhibition history is significant. Absent from the smaller group shows of 1913 (the Florentine 'Lacerba' show in November, where it was substituted by *Horizontal Construction* [fig. 4h][2] and the two Rome and Naples shows at the Galleria Sprovieri at which Boccioni exhibited only works of 1913), *Materia* was included instead in the two major international Futurist exhibits in 1914–15: in London at the Doré Galleries in April–May 1914 and in San Francisco at the 'Panama-Pacific International Exposition' in 1915. Two years after its execution, Boccioni evidently still considered this painting, together with *Elasticity*, among the few works capable of holding its own with the work of the subsequent two years, marked by a more explicit dynamism and a more developed plastic and chromatic abstraction.

Materia depicts the artist's mother, Cecilia Forlani, seated in front of a narrow balcony (its wrought iron railing is clearly visible) affording a view over an industrial urban panorama. Nearby houses and roofs, rendered in a fractured style of the Cubist formal language of 1909–10, are flanked by red factory chimneys billowing smoke. Leonardo Capano and Antonello Negri have identified the balcony itself, that still exists on Via Adige 23 in Milan, the address of Boccioni's studio-apartment from 1909 to February 1913[3] (fig. 4b). The railing, the same as is depicted in paintings from 1909 (*Sister on the Balcony*) to 1911 (*The Street Enters the House*, fig. 4k) is painted with surprising realism while, to left and right moldings and scroll brackets can also be related to actual details of balconies on the two neighboring buildings. The townscape visible through the French window of the Boccioni apartment was dominated by two imposing industrial buildings, the Besozzi-Marzoli mill (of which one of the coupled windows appears next to the mother's head), and the municipal thermoelectric plant, whose three tall chimney stacks are painted to the left exactly as seen from the balcony, in the adjacent Piazza Trento. Period photographs show crowds of men and horses yoked to carts in front of the two factories. This is the explanation for the two bright red figures, a horse trotting toward the left and a man walking to the right, which seem to merge with the foreground according to principles of simultaneity of perception ("At times, on the cheek of the person with whom we are talking [...] we see the horse that passes in the distance"[4]), already codified in the April 1910 *Technical Manifesto of Futurist Painting*.

The critical history of the studies for *Materia*, culminating in 1991 with the catalogue of a show dedicated solely to this large painting (henceforth Verona 1991–2), have isolated three key issues. The first is its chronological position in the complicated repertoire of Boccioni's production in 1912, particularly in relation to a smaller canvas called *Horizontal Construction*[5] (fig. 4h), to a large drawing of the same subject (fig. 4g, in turn called *Materia* or *Horizontal Construction*: Calvesi, Coen no. 754[6]) and to Boccioni's first efforts as a sculptor: his plaster *Head + House + Light* (fig. 4j) destroyed in 1917, was considered even by the earliest commentators as "a plastic translation of the painting *Materia*."[7] The second issue concerns the more strictly stylistic aspects of the painting, particularly Boccioni's relation to the Cubist archetype which changed radically with respect to his works of the preceding year. The third is that of the painting's iconography and ideology, with its important psychological (the complex relationship between the artist and his mother, whose presence looms over the image like a gigantic totem), scientific and philosophical components. In this context the relation of the painting's title, subject matter and visual ideology to the writings of Henri Bergson (especially *Matière et Memoire*, 1896), which lay at the heart of Italian cultural debate at the time and which were first pointed out by Maurizio Calvesi,[8] is fundamental. *Matière et Memoire* was one of Marinetti's favorite texts and was certainly known to Boccioni, who quoted and discussed excerpts in his article 'Fondamento plastico della pittura e scultura futuriste' in *Lacerba*, March 15, 1913.

a. The Chronological Question

Materia is one of the "six works of painting" that Boccioni proudly announced in a letter to Vico Baer in February 1913 that he had produced in the space of a frenetic year:[9] writing (the manifesto of sculpture and the book he would call *Pittura scultura futuriste*), trips abroad and

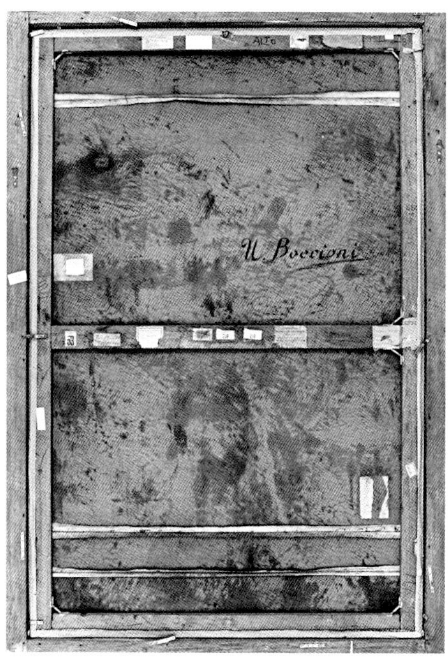

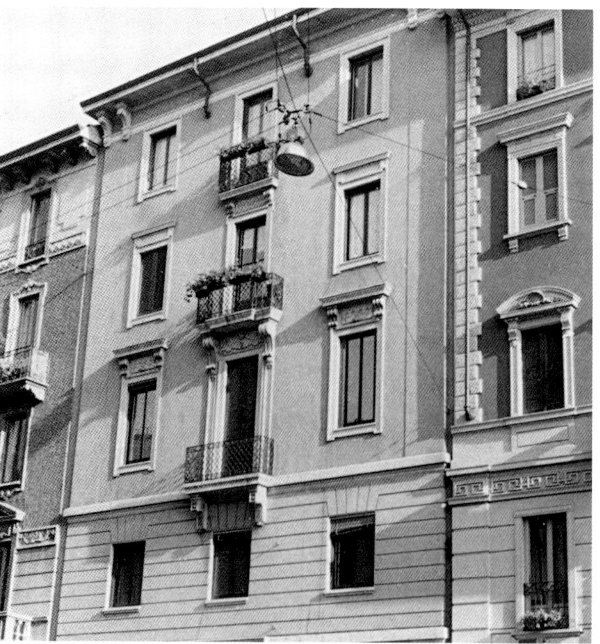

1913 (*Materia*); Longhi, April 10, 1913; Pascazio 1913, p. 36: Warnod, June 21, 1913 (illus. in its first state); Letter from Mario Sironi to Umberto Boccioni, undated (but autumn–winter 1913), in Agnese 1996, p. 321; Cajumi, December 10–11, 1913; Cantù 1913, p. 138; Boccioni 1914, pl. 7 (illus. in the definitive version); Longhi 1914, p. 17; *Sketch*, April 29, 1914; Sarfatti, September 24, 1916; Marinetti 1919, between pp. 28 and 29; Lancelotti 1926, p. 54 (illus. upside down); Marinetti 1930, in *Enciclopedia* 1929–37, vol. VII, p. 236; Buzzi 1933, p. 17; Depero 1933, p. 40; Severini 1933 (illus. at end of text); Carrà, June 22, 1933; Nicodemi, July 16, 1933; Costantini 1933, p. 128; Barr 1949, p. 12 and p. 126, no. 10; Carrieri 1950, p. 49, pl. 55; Sironi Zervos 1950, p. 13; Zervos 1950, p. 35 (illus. in its first state); Valsecchi 1952, pl. 1; Argan, Calvesi 1953, p. 34 and 44; D'Ancona 1953, pl. 3; Calvesi 1958[a], p. 168; Drudi Gambillo, Fiori 1958–62, vol. I, p. 412, vol. II, pp. 222 and 268, no. 275; Maltese 1960, pp. 430–1, fig. 155; Carrieri 1961, pl. 19; Taylor 1961, pp. 85 and 93; De Grada 1962, p. 175, pl. 73; Bellonzi 1963, pp. 62 and 68; Ballo 1964[a], no. 463, pp. 321–2; Ballo 1964[b], pp. 75 and 78; Calvesi 1967, pp. 59 and 63; Martin 1968, pp. 151–3 and fig. 113; Bruno 1969, no. 148a and pl. XXXVIII; Apollonio 1970, between pp. 32 and 33; Rye 1972, p. 58; Kozloff 1973, pp. 178, 194; Pampaloni, Verdone 1977, p. 80; Tisdall, Bozzola 1977, pp. 76–7; d'Harnoncourt 1980, pp. 23–4; Ballo 1982, pp. 50–1; Birolli 1983, pp. 20, 150 and fig. 21; Calvesi, Coen 1983, no. 752; Roche-Pézard 1983, pp. 363–5, no. 70, p. 483; Coen 1988, no. 60, pp. 138–9; Verzotti 1989, p. 120, no. 119; Antolini 1991, pp. 467–8; Anzani, Pirovano 1992, vol. I, pp. 116, 120–1; Capano 1991, pp. 146–216; Capano, Negri 1991, pp. 253–5; Dalai Emiliani 1991, pp. 65–82; Marinelli 1991, pp. 142–4; Mattioli Rossi 1991[a], pp. 17–26; Mattioli Rossi 1991[b], pp. 231–52; Negri 1991, pp. 27–42; Putrella 1991, pp. 83–114; Rosci 1991, pp. 43–64; Sandroni 1991, pp. 221–3; Di Genova 1993, pp. 191–2; Schneede 1994, pp. 105–13, fig. XXI; Frontisi 1994, pp. 9–22; Capano, Negri 1995, pp. 258–9; Dalrymple Henderson 1995, pp. 26–8; Lamberti 1995, pp. 227 and 295; Rossi 1995, p. 222; Agnese 1996, pp. 281–3, 291; Poggi 1997, pp. 31–7; Rylands 1997, pp. 56–9; Spate 1997, pp. 128–31, figs. 4. 10–11; De Milia 1998, pp. 26, 35, 46; Antliff 2000, pp. 730–1; Calvesi 2000, pp. 18–19; Del Puppo 2000[a], pp. 77, 126, 141, 145, 156, 167; Siligato 2000, p. 26; Lista 2001, pp. 106–7

Fig. 4a. Verso *of cat. no. 4*

Fig. 4b. *The house on Via Adige, Milan, where Boccioni painted* Materia

Fig. 4c. *Umberto Boccioni in his studio at the Bastioni di Porta Romana, Milan, in front of* Materia *before its final retouching, August–September 1913*

Fig. 4d. *Umberto Boccioni,* Materia, *before retouching, in August–September 1913, in* Comœdia, *June 21, 1913*

the weaving of a network of alliances had conspired to restrict his time and drain his energy from painting and from his first efforts at sculpture. The six new paintings were most probably all exhibited in the foyer of the Teatro Costanzi in Rome, with the titles *Materia*, *Elasticity*, *Fragmentation of Figures at a Table* (fig. 4l), *Horizontal Construction* (fig. 4h), *Antigraceful*, and *Abstract Dimensions* (fig. 4i).[10] With their pronounced stylistic oscillations they place serious obstacles in the way of a convincing reconstruction of their temporal sequence.

Among Boccioni's surviving works of 1912, two paintings (*Horizontal Construction* [fig. 4h] and *Abstract Dimensions* [fig. 4i]), two sculptures (*Head + House + Light* [fig. 4j] and *Antigraceful*), and a series of drawings[11] are close to *Materia* stylistically and thematically. The trio formed by the two paintings *Materia*/*Horizontal Construction* and the sculpture *Head + House + Light* has been the object of lengthy discussion. For Marianne Martin the two paintings were more or less contemporaneous: *Horizontal Construction*'s "expression of 'pure art' in terms of calculated mathematical values" did not contradict Boccioni's attempt to paint in *Materia* a strongly iconographical work, a "majestic *madre*, or even a modern worker's *maestà*." She had no doubt, instead, about the derivation of *Head + House + Light* from *Horizontal Construction*.[12] Guido Ballo situated *Horizontal Construction* (with the title *Horizontal Volumes*) before *Materia* and related the sculpture *Head + House + Light* to the latter.[13] In the 1983 general catalogue of Boccioni's work, Maurizio Calvesi and Ester Coen did not focus on the issue, but published the Munich painting ahead of the Mattioli painting,[14] a sequence repeated by Ester Coen in her catalogue of the 1988 Boccioni exhibition in New York.[15] This created two couples constituted by *Materia* and *Head + House + Light* on the one hand, and *Horizontal Construction* and *Antigraceful*, in the sculptural version, on the other: for Calvesi *Head + House + Light* was executed "at the end of 1912 with its painted twin, *Materia*"[16] and Coen considered *Antigraceful* "an almost literal translation of the painting [*Horizontal Construction*]."[17] In the catalogue of the 1991–2 Verona exhibition, Marco Rosci reversed the sequence, judging *Horizontal Construction* a "markedly Cubist rereading of *Materia*," and situated it even after the first sculptures, "a later phase which further retrieved and formalized in paint the plastic and polymateric discourse of *Head + House + Light*."[18] However, in the same catalogue Leonardo Capano ordered the group differently in his entry for a drawing close to *Head + House + Light*: the sculpture was placed at the end of the sequence, after *Horizontal Construction*.[19] More re-

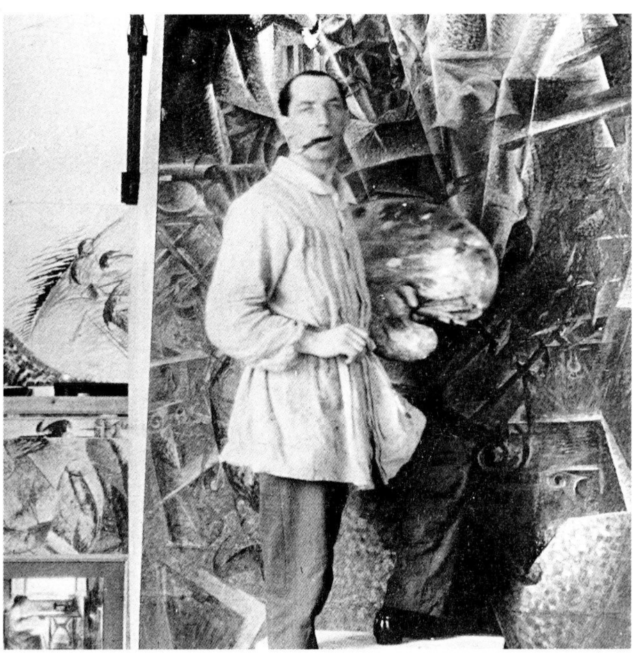

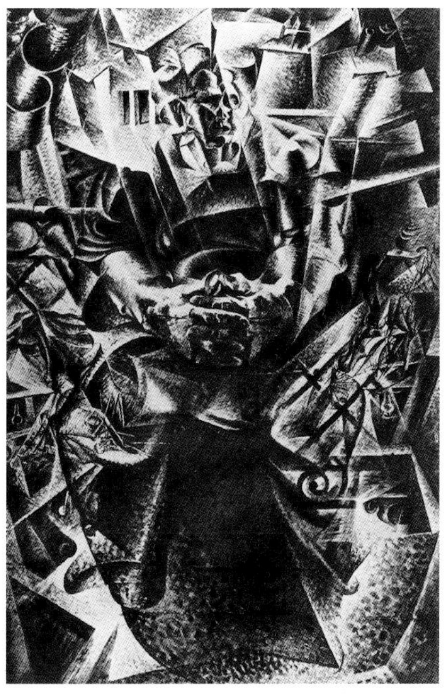

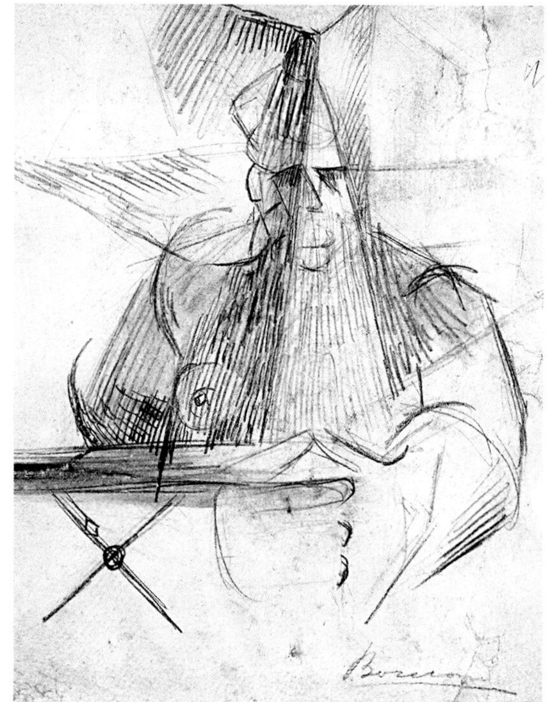

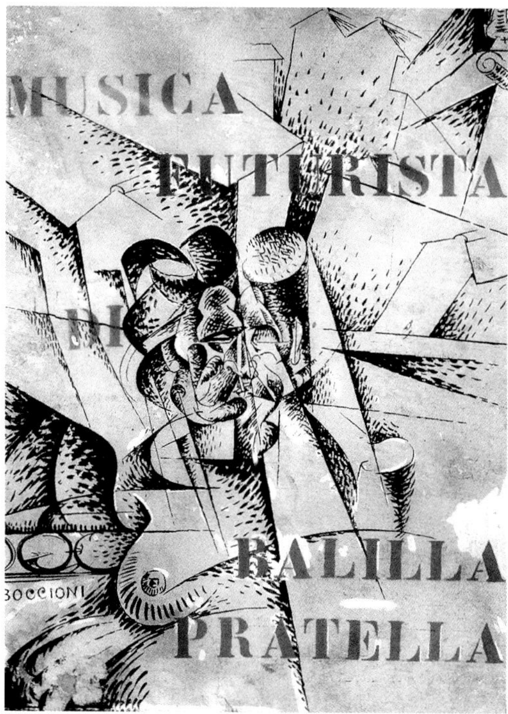

Fig. 4e. *Umberto Boccioni, Study for* Materia, *pencil on paper, 1912. Milan, Fondazione Antonio Mazzotta*

Fig. 4f. *Umberto Boccioni, Study for the cover of the book* Musica Futurista *by Balilla Pratella, tempera and ink on paper, 1912. Ravenna, Raccolta Pratella*

cent studies have either reconfirmed the general descent of *Head + House + Light* from *Materia*[20] or else have accepted the sequence which postdates *Horizontal Construction* with respect to *Materia*[21] in accordance with the conclusions drawn in the Verona exhibition. Uwe Schneede, in a monograph on Boccioni published in 1994, considered *Horizontal Construction* pendant to and contemporary with *Materia* and executed simultaneously.[22] We owe this confusion to the fact that no contemporary evidence (writings by Boccioni, letters or any other documentation) provides any clue about how and when *Materia* was painted. Its *terminus ante quem* remains February 21, 1913 (not February 11 as indicated in Verona 1991–2[23]), the date of the inauguration of the show in the foyer of the Teatro Costanzi, Rome.

The present writer has not formulated definitive conclusions regarding the exact date of *Materia* or its position in the sequence of works to which it is related. What follows is simply a catalogue of the data (chronological, documentary, material) pertinent to this vexed question, as well as some possible inferences.

1. Of the six new works exhibited by Boccioni in Rome on February 21, 1913, the identities of three are certain: *Materia, Elasticity* and *Fragmentation of Figures at a Table* (fig. 4l). Two others are good probabilities. Emilio Cecchi wrote briefly on *Horizontal Construction* in his review of the Rome show[24] and the painting we know today by that title (fig. 4h) was illustrated for the first time in 1916 by Margherita Sarfatti, as *Horizontal Constructions*.[25] *Antigraceful* was illustrated and dated 1912 in *Pittura scultura futuriste* (1914) and by the time of the Rotterdam exhibition in May 1913 was already owned by Sarfatti. The identity of *Abstract Dimensions* with the painting in the Civiche raccolte d'arte of Milan is more complicated (fig. 4i). The latter appears, hanging in Boccioni's studio, in a photograph of uncertain date.[26] There was no painting with this title in the December 1916 Boccioni retrospective, while the painting now in Milan was shown at the 1920 Geneva exhibition as *Study for a Head*.[27] At the time the Canavese Collection was left to the City of Milan in 1934, the painting was inventoried as *Study of a Head-The Mother*; it was not until 1953, in the monograph by Giulio Carlo Argan and Maurizio Calvesi, that it acquired the title *Abstract Dimensions (Portrait of the Mother)*.[28] It may be noted that if *Horizontal Construction* was the painting now in Munich and if *Abstract Dimensions* was the

Fig. 4g. *Umberto Boccioni, Study for* Costruzione orizzontale, *pencil and pen on paper, 1912. Milan, Civico gabinetto dei disegni*

painting now in the Civiche raccolte d'arte, Milan, then Boccioni exhibited in Rome three works with the same subject (portraits of his mother) in a zoom-like sequence (from the full length of *Materia* to only the head in *Abstract Dimensions*) with three very different titles.

2. Boccioni placed his paintings for the Costanzi exhibition catalogue in the following order: *Elasticity* first, then *Fragmentation of Figures at a Table*, *Horizontal Construction* and *Antigraceful*. (*Materia*, as noted above, was omitted from this sequence as it was the opening work of the room and placed even before the 1911 *States of Mind*.) The variant sequence of the illustrations in *Pittura scultura futuriste* (1914) does not contradict this order: *Horizontal Construction* has been dropped and *Materia* inserted at the end of the series, after *Antigraceful*; the first pairing of *Elasticity-Fragmentation of Figures at a Table* still stands, however, before the second pairing (*Horizontal Construction-Antigraceful* in the Rome catalogue and *Antigraceful-Materia* in the 1914 book). It is not clear what value to attribute to these two series. However, in his 1914 book, Boccioni seemed intent on putting his works (and those by the other five artists similarly illustrated) in a rough chronological order.

3. Boccioni's travels in 1912 can be reconstructed with reasonable certainty thanks to his published letters. He was in Paris in February for the Futurist group show at Bernheim-jeune; he then accompanied the paintings to London, returning to Paris towards the middle of March in time to visit the Salon des Indépendants.[29] He was in Berlin for the installation of the Der Sturm show at some point during the first and second ten days of April.[30] After passing through Milan,[31] he returned to Berlin before May 20 to conclude the sale of his paintings to the banker Borchardt and to oversee their shipment to Brussels.[32] From June he resided in Milan for the summer[33] and part of the fall until November, when he returned to Paris as Severini's guest to visit the Salon d'Automne.[34] He was in Milan again from November until the inauguration of the Costanzi show, paying a short visit to Rome before Christmas.[35] In effect, he spent only two periods of time working in a continuous manner in his Milan studio during 1912: from June

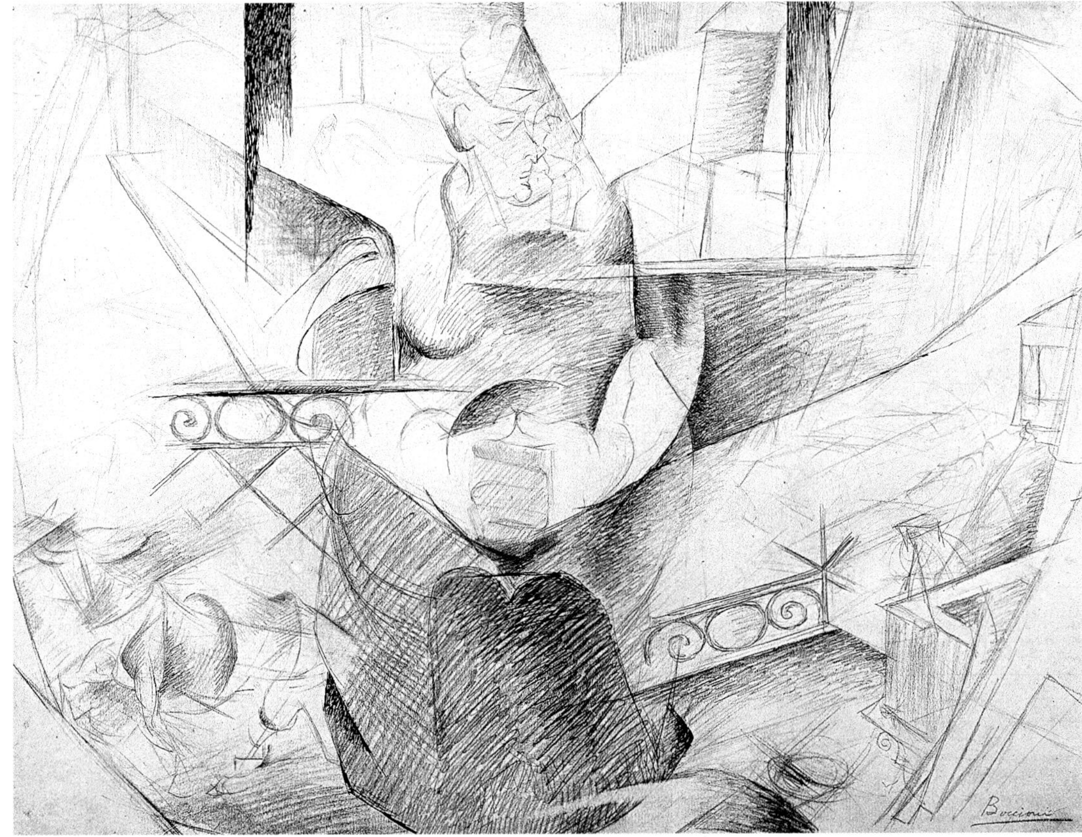

to October, fresh from the stimuli of his spring travels abroad, and from November to January 1913, after his important first-hand experience of Cubist paintings at the Salon d'Automne.

4. The *Technical Manifesto of Futurist Sculpture* was conceived in Paris in March 1912,[36] dated April 11, 1912 and published at the end of September 1912. We can, however, be sure that it had been written by July. Marinetti sent it as a "primizia" (meaning a pre-publication viewing) to Aldo Palazzeschi in an undated letter together with the recently published *I poeti futuristi*, of which the first reviews appeared in the press in July 1912.[37] The dating of the sculptures has only one firm point: the well-known letter in which Boccioni told Severini of his difficulties with sculpting ("Then I am struggling with sculpture: I work, work, work and know not what I render"). This letter has been correctly situated by Calvesi in the second half of November 1912, based on the chronological information it contained.[38]

5. A drawing of Boccioni's mother on the balcony, very similar to the upper part of *Materia*, can be dated with certainty (fig. 4f): it served as the cover illustration of Balilla Pratella's *Musica futurista* (a book published in the early months of 1913, despite the 1912 date) and was sent by Marinetti in a parcel to Pratella on November 26, 1912.[39] Therefore Boccioni's invention of his mother's fractured and subdivided face in the Mattioli painting had been made before this date.

6. The support of *Materia* is not a single piece of canvas. Boccioni took an almost square canvas (162 × 150 cm), to which he then added two strips of the same width to the top and

Fig. 4h. *Umberto Boccioni,* Costruzione orizzontale (Horizontal Construction)*, oil on canvas, 1912. Munich, Bayerische Staatsgemäldesammlungen, Pinakothek der Moderne*

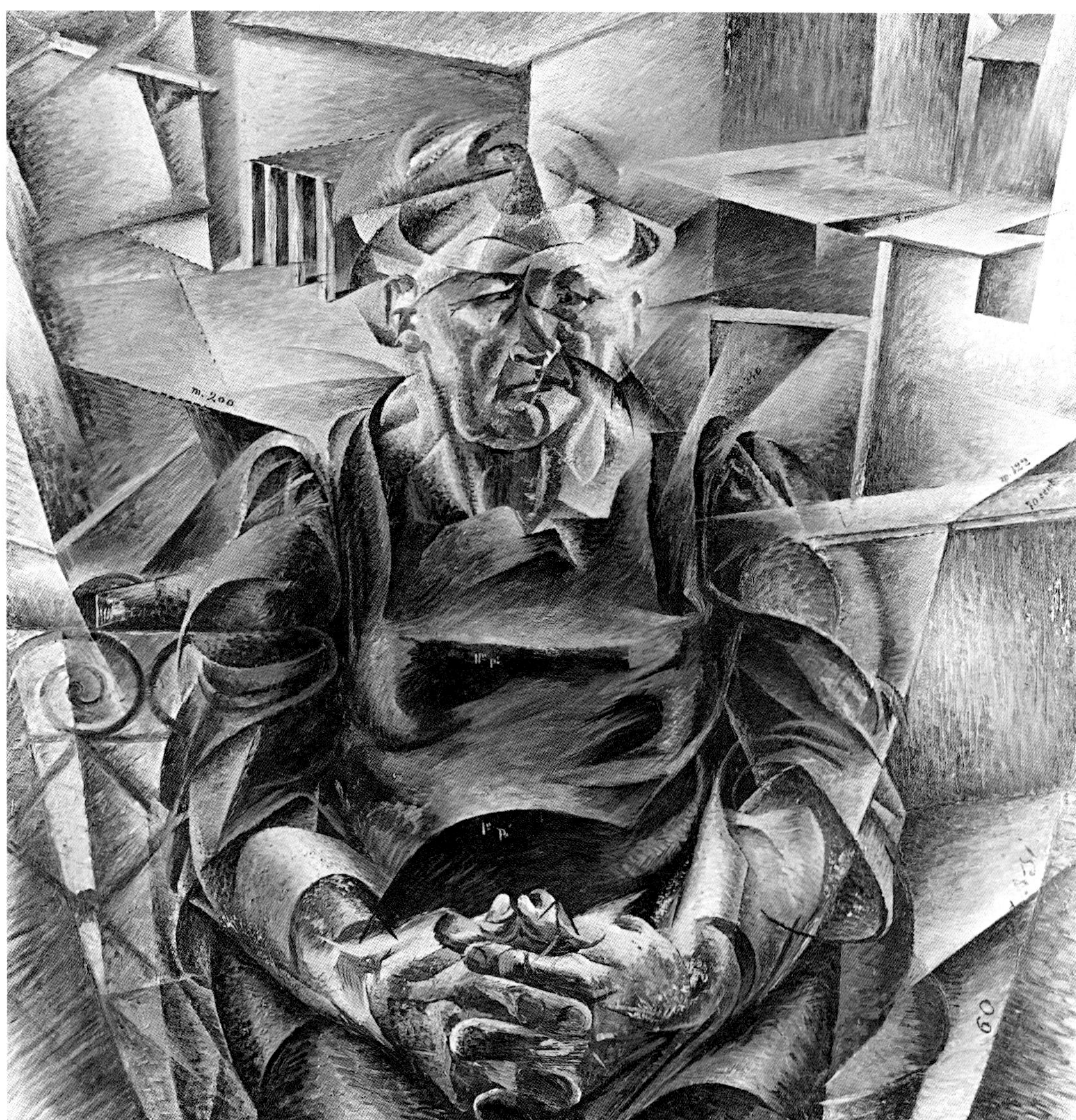

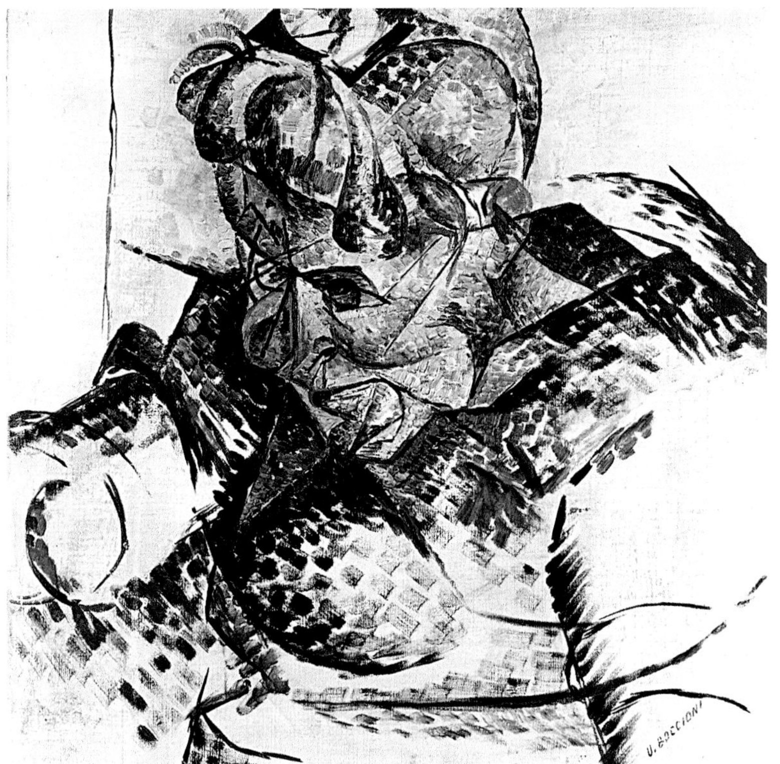

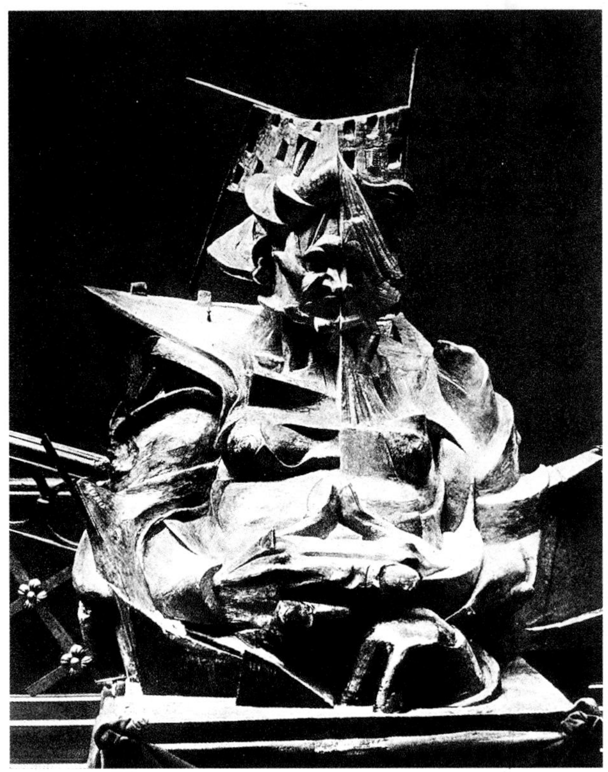

Fig. 4i. *Umberto Boccioni,* Dimensioni astratte *(*Abstract Dimensions*), oil on canvas, 1912. Milan, Civiche raccolte d'arte*

Fig. 4j. *Umberto Boccioni,* Testa + casa + luce *(*Head + House + Light*), plaster and iron, 1912. Destroyed*

bottom, measuring respectively 15 cm and 26 cm in height, subsequently adding another strip 23 cm high, its seam stitched in the opposite direction, to the bottom (fig. 4a).[40] The process seems to have been typical of Boccioni's work on large paintings, as it is also apparent in *Dynamism of a Soccer Player* at the New York Museum of Modern Art. As the upper addition occurs along the mother's forehead, it is impossible to suppose that this strip of canvas could have been sewn on after the composition had been planned in terms of a nearly square format. The back of *Horizontal Construction* in Munich reveals unequivocally that it has neither been cut nor its format diminished.

7. Boccioni reworked *Materia* after its first exhibition in the Teatro Costanzi foyer. Leonardo Capano noticed a difference between the first published photograph of *Materia*,[41] illustrating an article by André Warnod in the Parisian weekly *Comœdia* on June 21, 1913 (fig. 4d), and subsequent photographs, the first of which was inserted by the artist into *Pittura scultura futuriste*.[42] The variations are significant though not decisive. In the lower left of the painting, the mother's skirt was originally separated by a firmer outline and the adjacent area, now dominated by a semicircular motif was, instead, occupied by the conspicuous jutting corner of a balcony.[43] In Marco Rosci's opinion, the *Comœdia* photograph could not record an earlier stage of the painting predating the Rome exhibition. The first state (probably shortly before Boccioni began his retouches) is visible in a series of three photographs [44] (fig. 4c) which portray the artist in his new studio-apartment at the Bastioni di Porta Romana 35, rented in February 1913, before his departure for Rome,[45] but to which he actually moved only in March (the new address was communicated to Gino Severini in a letter datable around March 30, 1913).[46] However, the retouching could not have been executed, as has been suggested,[47] in the interval between the Rome show, prolonged at the Colonna pavilion, and the inauguration of the exhibition in Rotterdam (March 18, 1913) because the paintings were packed for shipment in Rome and sent directly to Holland without passing through Milan.[48] Boccioni must have retouched the painting the following August, after the paintings had returned from Rotterdam, as demonstrated by the three photographs that show the incomplete *Dynamism of a Cyclist*, an oil on canvas finished in the fall of

1913 (see cat. no. 5). Thus Boccioni's *pentimenti* to the lower half of the painting, obliterating elements which separated the skirt too distinctly from its setting and which therefore interfered with the reciprocal interpenetration of figure and environment, can be dated well into 1913.

8. A comparison of pictorial techniques, as visible to the naked eye, of *Materia* and *Horizontal Construction*, reveals the following difference: the brushwork in *Materia* is denser and choppier while that in *Horizontal Construction* is more liquid and rapid, with parallel strokes. However, certain parts of *Horizontal Construction* (the dress covering the mother's forearms, her hands, neck and head) are painted in a manner similar to that of *Materia* — small touches of thick paint with strong highlights. We are looking at an evident reworking of the paint surface over a first layer handled quite differently: it is not possible however to say whether this took place before Boccioni began work on *Materia* (as we see it today) or after the larger painting was finished, with the intention, at least in part, of harmonizing the technique of the two paintings (between January and early February Boccioni wrote to Severini that he was retouching the paintings for the Rome show[49]).

9. Strictly, Calvesi, Coen drawing no. 754 (fig. 4g) is exclusively related to neither *Materia* nor *Horizontal Construction* (fig. 4h). It is close to *Materia* in its full-length view of the mother and its inclusion of the horse on the lower left, in some literal details (in the view of the city that frames the mother's head, the façade of the house with a sloped roof on the right recurs only in *Materia*) and in some of its key spatial relations (the mother's elbow to the left is situated at exactly the same height as in *Materia*, while in *Horizontal Construction* it is lower, at half the height of the railing). Other details of the drawing (the characteristic rays of light in the form of a downward-spreading cone which sub-divide the mother's face; the serpentine line of the neck of the dress leading down to her breast) are closer to *Horizontal Construction*. There is no reason why the drawing could not be a preparatory study from which Boccioni derived elements by turn for one or other painting, or, again, a graphic reworking of one previously-executed oil in anticipation of the next.

10. In a comparison between *Head + House + Light* (fig. 4j) and the two paintings, the closer relationship is clearly between the sculpture and *Horizontal Construction*. The principal mo-

Fig. 4k. *Umberto Boccioni,* La strada entra nella casa (The Street Enters the House), *oil on canvas, 1911. Hanover, Sprengel Museum Hannover*

Fig. 4l. *Umberto Boccioni,* Scomposizione di figure a tavola (Fragmentation of Figures at a Table), *oil on canvas, 1912. Whereabouts unknown*

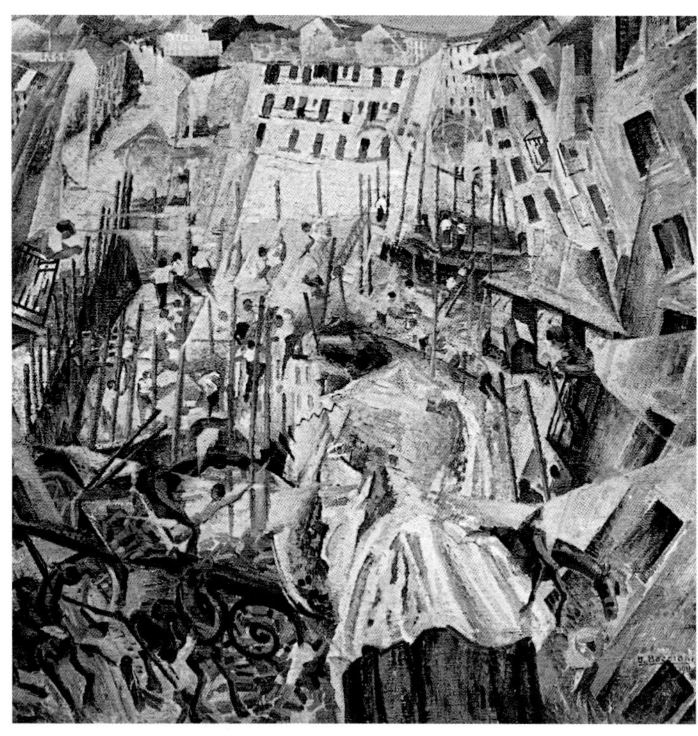

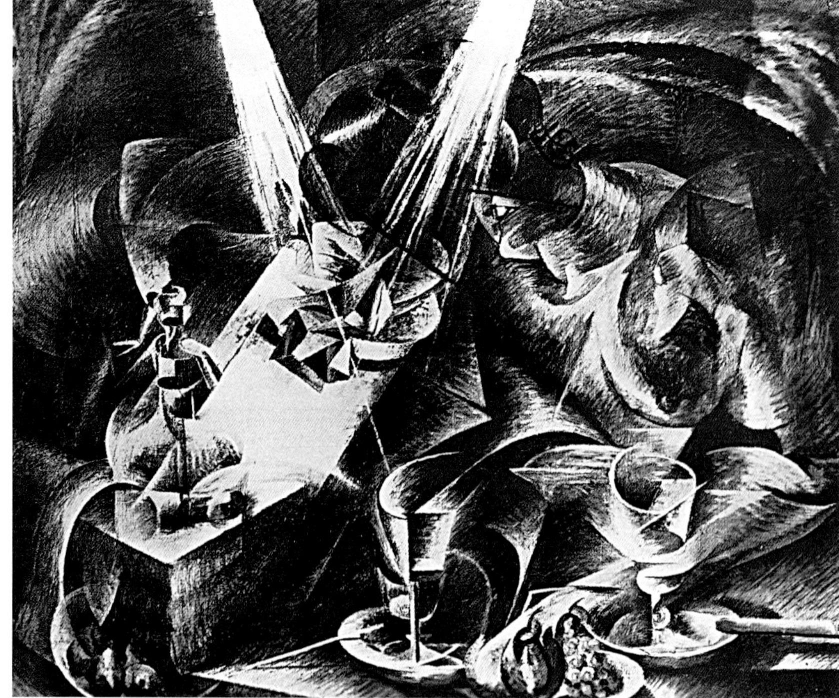

Fig. 4m. *Marcel Duchamp,* Nu descendant un escalier n. 2 (Nude Descending a Staircase, no. 2)*, oil on canvas, 1912. Philadelphia, The Philadelphia Museum of Art, The Louise and Walter Arensberg Collection, 1950*

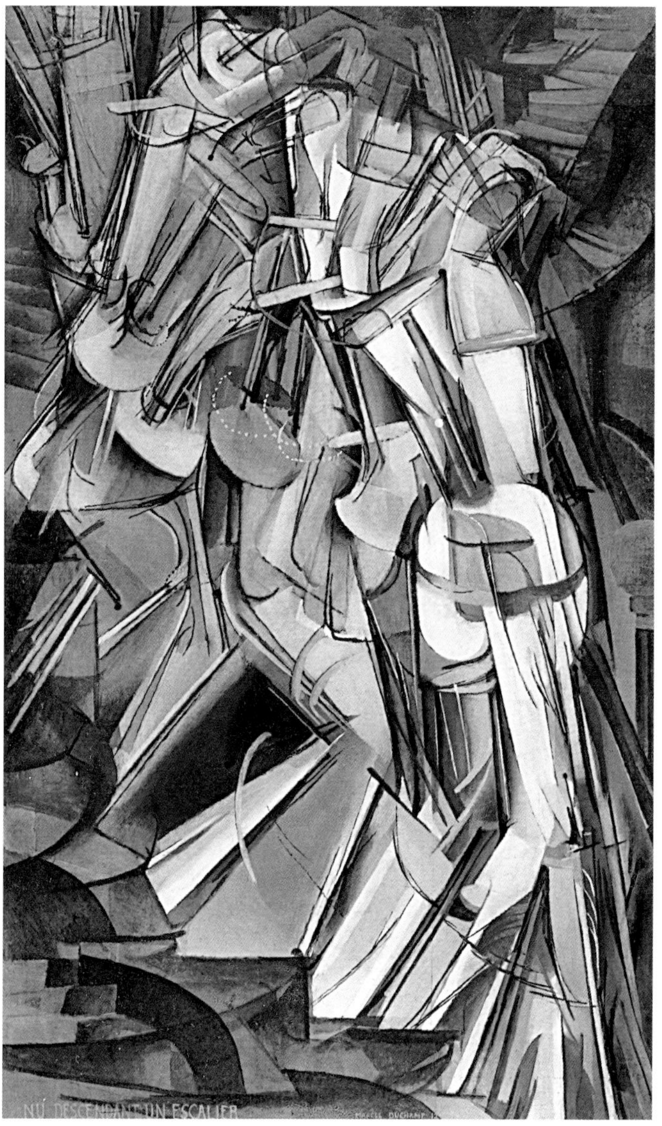

tif of light (in the sculpture, in all the drawings related to it[50] and, partially, in *Horizontal Construction*) is the cone-shaped beam originating from the crown of the head and running vertically to the center of the face: this axis is absent from *Materia*, where the rays of light are parallel, generated by two different points in the background landscape. The inclined plane over the mother's breast in *Head + House + Light* is identical to that in *Horizontal Construction*, while it tips in the opposite sense in *Materia*. The strange overturned plate-like form on the mother's shoulder in *Materia* is absent from both *Head + House + Light* and *Horizontal Construction*. Moreover, the hairdo of concentric spirals in the sculpture is closer to that of *Horizontal Construction* than to the bubble-like forms in *Materia*. Both *Head + House + Light* and *Horizontal Construction* contain inscriptions ("muro", the house's street number "45", and another illegible word on the shoulder of the sculpture, as well as more precise indications of space, such as "I° piano" and "II° piano", or distances expressed in meters and centimeters in the painting) which are absent in *Materia*. Thus a group consisting of *Horizontal Construction,* the sculpture *Head + House + Light* and its respective drawings can be identified as distinct from *Materia*.[51]

Possible conclusions are few at this point.

1. Some parts of *Horizontal Construction* resemble in technique the *States of Mind* (second version) of 1911. The two lower corners of the painting, to left and right, show the same thread like strokes with two alternating colors as the beating rain in *Those Who Go* (in 1912

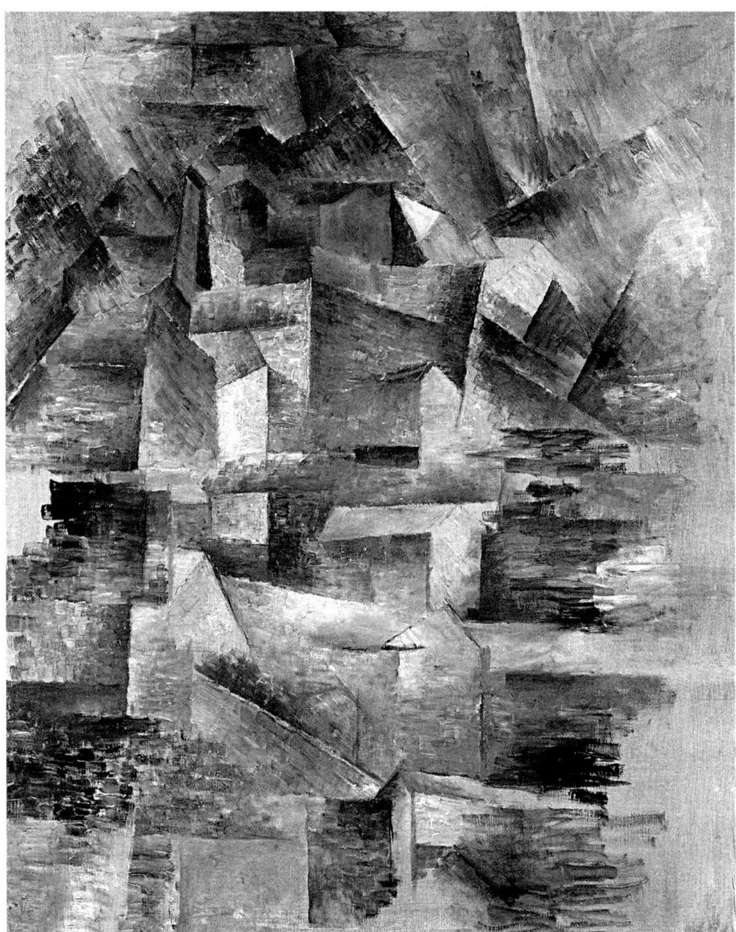

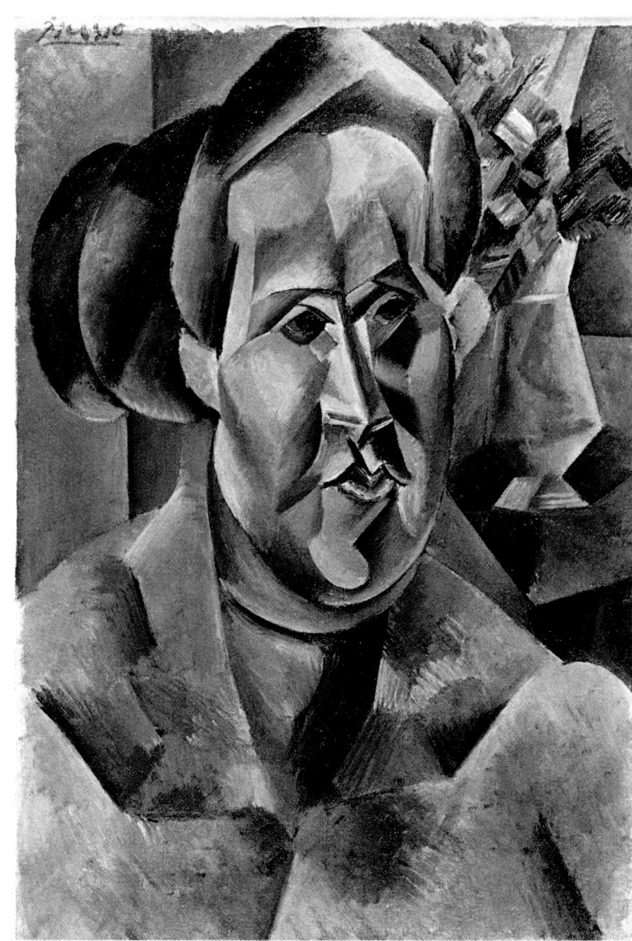

Fig. 4n. *Georges Braque,* Les Usines du Rio Tinto à L'Estaque (The Rio Tinto Factories at L'Estaque*), oil on canvas, 1910. Paris, Centre National d'Art Contemporain Georges Pompidou, Gift of André Lefèvre*

Fig. 4o. *Pablo Picasso,* Portrait de Fernande, *oil on canvas, 1909. Düsseldorf, Kunstsammlung Nordrhein-Westfalen*

the same technique can be found in only certain passages of *Fragmentation of Figures at a Table*, as far as one can tell from the black and white photograph of the now lost painting, fig. 4l). This observation does not conclusively pre-date *Horizontal Construction* with respect to *Materia.* Boccioni could conceivably, however unlikely, have painted *Materia* first and *Horizontal Construction* after, returning then to stipple the entire paint surface of *Materia* and the face and hands only of *Horizontal Construction* with the thicker brushwork.

2. In November Boccioni was at work on sculpture and he executed drawings of his mother's head, one of which was sent via Marinetti to Balilla Pratella. This drawing, in the modeling of the face, the form of the hairdo and the angle at which the rays of light fall, is closer to *Materia* than to either *Horizontal Construction* or *Head + House + Light*. It has all the characteristics of a *d'après* and it is therefore probable that, by that date, *Materia* had been partially executed or at least planned in detail. It is worth noting that the large dimensions and the complexity of the Mattioli painting presuppose a relatively long period of time, two months or more, for its execution.

3. The only work that can feasibly be related to *Elasticity* is *Fragmentation of Figures at a Table* (fig. 4l), by reason of their shared insistence on sine curves in their draftsmanship. The two paintings are side by side in the Teatro Costanzi show catalogue and in *Pittura scultura futuriste* and placed before *Horizontal Construction* (in the former) or before *Materia* (in the latter). In other words, Boccioni insisted on placing first, in a sequence in an exhibition and then in a series of photographic illustrations, a period of graphic elegance exemplified by *Elasticity*, and then a period marked by the layered drafting, the complicated (and even disjointed) compositional handling of *Materia* and *Antigraceful*. It is worth noting that Boccioni's return to painting in 1913 (with thick impastos of color and the choppy broken brushwork of the two versions of *Dynamism of a Human Body*[52]), makes more sense as an evolution of *Materia* than of *Elasticity*.

Fig. 4p. *Detail of cat. no. 4*

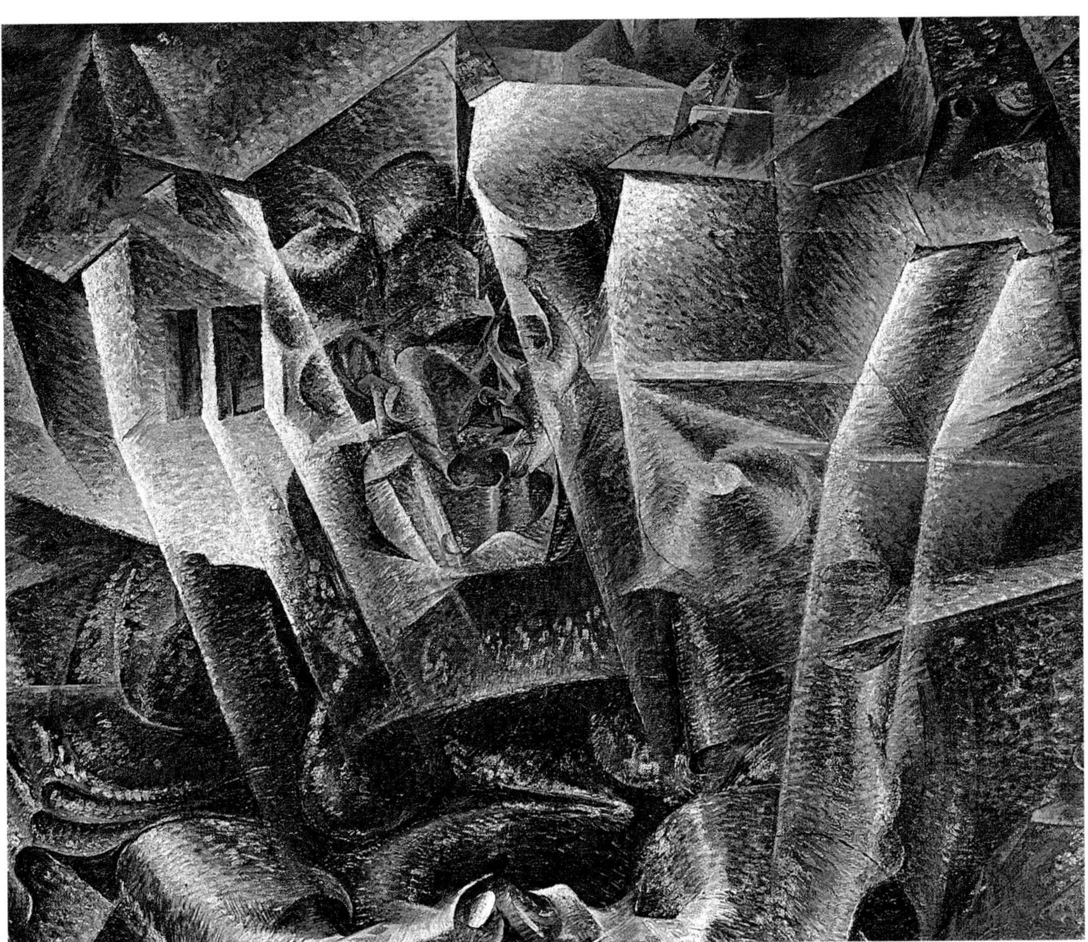

4. At the end of 1912 Boccioni was already executing the first series of sculptures that would be exhibited the following June in Paris; but he decided to exhibit only paintings at the February 1913 Teatro Costanzi show.

For a series of reasons *Horizontal Construction* may be considered a pictorial attempt to anticipate certain effects of his experiments in sculpture (its proximity to *Head + House + Light*, the presence on the painting of inscriptions underscoring the spatial location of the figure, the clarity of volumetric construction). In this respect its relationship to *Materia* is less important in terms of which was painted first than for its revelation of the different pictorial visual ideology that drove them: using the same subject matter, Boccioni focused on the relation between figure and setting, but placed the emphasis in *Materia* on the dynamics of the forces released by this relation, while in *Horizontal Construction* he explored the system of spatial relations.

Though there is no surviving testimony by Boccioni of his execution of *Materia,* two excerpts from his theoretical writings seem directly related to the formal themes of the painting and usefully situate it chronologically in the second half of 1912. The first of these, in *Pittura scultura futuriste*, 1914 (the first draft of which, as Boccioni stated in a letter, was finished by the end of December 1912[53]), concerns the relation between object and environment, the indivisible unity of a thing and the space surrounding it:

> "So then, we conceive the object as a nucleus (centripetal construction) from which the forces come (lines-forms-force) that define it in its environment (centrifugal construction) and determine its essential nature. We thereby create a new concept of the object: the object-environment, conceived as a new *indivisible unit.*"[54]

The second excerpt, from a text published in March 1913 in *Lacerba*, touches on the idea of atmosphere as a solid system of relationships between things: Boccioni was working on the sculptures for his exhibition in Paris in June (or else was pondering them, in the event that they were already finished), and recalled the "materiality which is alive between one object and another" in the painting he had recently completed:

> "... when I say that for sculpture it is necessary to model the atmosphere, I mean that I suppress, that is to say I leave aside the sentimental and traditional value of atmosphere [...] but consider this atmosphere a materiality which is alive between one object and another, which varies its plastic quality and, instead of glossing over it like a breath, since culture has taught me that the atmosphere is gaseous, impalpable, etc., etc., I feel it, I seek and grasp it, I accentuate it, in the variations by which it is imprinted by light, by shadows and the currents of the forces of bodies. Therefore I create the atmosphere!"[55]

b. The Formal Aspects and Their Relationship to Sources

The subject of a woman at a window or balcony was central to Boccioni's painting at least since his *Portrait of Signora Massimino* of 1908: its value for him lay in its capacity to bring the outside world into the perceptual realm of the person portrayed. In 1911 it recurs in one of Boccioni's first fully achieved Futurist paintings, *The Street Enters the House* (fig. 4k), exhibited with the title *On the Balcony* at the Famiglia Artistica in Milan in December of the same year.[56] Boccioni's mother is depicted with her back to us. To represent the series of buildings around her, which open onto the building site populated by laborers, Boccioni reworked one of the first Cubist images he had seen, a photographic reproduction of *La Tour Eiffel* by Robert Delaunay (in the version sent to the 1911 Salon des Indépendents and destroyed in Berlin in 1945[57]): by rendering the crowd of workers in duplicated poses and with flattened forms, Boccioni was attempting to express the Futurist idea of the multiplication of figures in certain conditions of perception, an attempt he had already made (though without any awareness of Cubism) in *Mourning* and *Labor*.

The motif of *Materia* is substantially the same as that of *The Street Enters the House*, though the mother has been turned through 180° to face the viewer (and the painter). The compositional structure has become more complex. Convex elements (the clasped hands, the curve of the arms) are combined with concave elements (the curved plane running from the mother's bust to her knees, the circle of buildings which form a crown around her head); centrifugal forces (the diagonals and rays emanating from the joined hands) conflict with other, centripetal forces (the enveloping townscape). Antonello Negri[58] has indicated how Boccioni, influenced by Cézanne's letters, theorized the interaction of these forces in a passage in *Pittura scultura futuriste*: to Boccioni "the sphere creates horizontal dilations and suggests expansive possibilities."[59] Both photographic (contemporary experiments with the wide-angle lens[60]) and pictorial sources (Parmigianino's *Self-Portrait in the Mirror* in the Kunsthistorisches Museum, Vienna[61]) have been cited to explain the optical distortion which results in the prominence of the gigantic hands in the foreground.

In 'Les Exposants au public,' the preface to the catalogue of the first Futurist exhibition in Paris signed by all five exhibitors, Boccioni, the author, explicitly addressed the situation portrayed in *The Street Enters the House* and reiterated in *Materia*:

> "In painting a person on a balcony, seen from inside the room, we do not limit the scene to what the square frame of the window renders visible; but we try to render the sum total of

Fig. 4q. *Albert Gleizes,* Portrait de Jacques Nayral, *oil on canvas, 1910–11. London, Tate*

Fig. 4r. *Albert Gleizes, Drawing for* L'Homme au balcon *(*Man at the Balcony*), in A. Gleizes, J. Metzinger,* Du "cubisme", *1912*

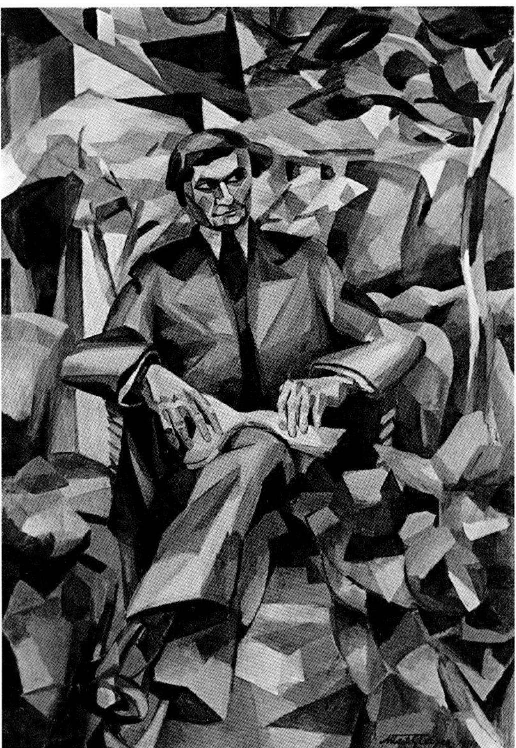

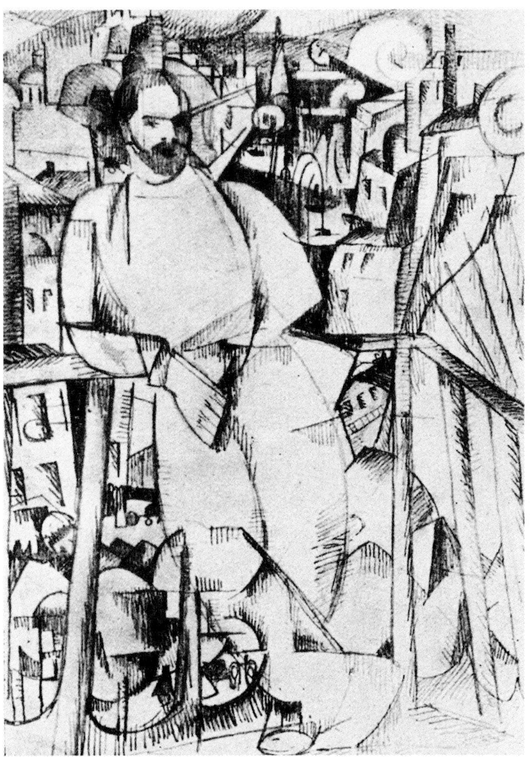

> visual sensations which the person on the balcony has experienced; the sun-soaked throng in the street, the double row of houses which stretch to right and left, the beflowered balconies, etc. This implies the simultaneousness of the ambient, and, therefore, the dislocation and dismemberment of objects, the scattering and fusion of details, freed from accepted logic and independent from one another."[62]

Marco Rosci has stressed the extent to which *Materia* is a complete "conceptual and spatial overthrow" of this passage.[63] In representing the scene (a woman at a balcony and a townscape behind), Boccioni withdrew his attention from the analytical fragmentation of perceptions, the eruption of the outdoors into the interior, such as he described to his Parisian public in 1912; instead he emphasized the solidity and structural convexity of the figure that imposes itself on the spectator. Marisa Dalai Emiliani discovered a significant variation of the passage cited above when it was translated into Italian and printed in the catalogue of the 1913 Costanzi exhibition:[64] in the translation (or in the correction of the proofs, to which Boccioni personally attended[65]) the "ensemble de sensations *visuelles* qu'a éprouvées *la personne* au balcon" was changed to "the complex of *plastic* sensations experienced by *the painter* on the balcony."[66] This variant, a hint of which was present already in the caption for the painting in the Sackville Gallery catalogue, London, March 1912,[67] testifies to Boccioni's development in 1912 and resolves an important contradiction: the painter traditionally extracts himself from the painted scene, observing it at one remove, in front of him, while at the same time registering the plastic sensations which emanate from the picture's center — the sitter in a portrait for example. According to Dalai Emiliani, "the antinomy between the observer and the person observed, or better yet, the person observed observing, that is, between the subject and the object, is overcome for the first time thanks to the effective negation of a fixed *point of view*, of a *distance* of fixed perspective construction, of the use of the pictorial surface itself as the sole *plane of projection*."[68]

As always with Boccioni, the quest for his sources, especially where the international avant-garde of painting is concerned, is a matter of distinguishing different levels. They may be precise evocations (the man on the right, for example, obviously refers to Marcel Duchamp's *Nude Descending a Staircase no. 2*, submitted for exhibition at the Indépendents in March 1912, fig. 4m);[69] or they may be models of which the artist was aware and which he transcribed in a different pictorial language; or thirdly, simple formal appropriations for the purpose of bringing the painting up to date in a modernist sense.

The buildings in the background betray a clear awareness (which had considerably matured with respect to his paintings in the fall-winter of 1911–12) of the techniques of fragmenting volumes seen in Cubist works of 1909–10. One might usefully compare them to the neatly faceted solids in *The Rio Tinto Factories at L'Estaque* by Georges Braque (fig. 4n)[70] or *The Oil Mill* by Pablo Picasso.[71] With complementary colors and with the play of the force-lines, Boccioni overturned the principles of monochromy and frozen immobility in his Cubist sources, but preserved the governing centripetal force which draws the objects strongly toward the vertical axis. The interlocking of the various volumes in Braque's and Picasso's paintings is reinforced by the use of chiaroscuro, an effect which is artificially heightened in the black-and-white reproductions that Boccioni was certainly examining. Such chiaroscuro is invigorated in *Materia* by the harsh lighting (of such force that the corners of the buildings are connected to the woman's hands with beams of pale blue light) and by a systematic application of contrasting complementary colors (orange-azure, red-green), which emerge with special force in the generally dark tonality of the entire canvas.

The mother's face, constructed by intersecting curved lines, reveals a precise debt to the faces of Picasso's female portraits of 1909, such as *Portrait of Fernande* (fig. 4o),[72] *Head of Woman*,[73] or *Woman with Pears*[74] which Boccioni could have seen in Paris in 1912 (and perhaps in Berlin, at the home of a collector). The two-part division of the plane of the forehead, the compression of the nose which is reduced to a flat triangle, the prominence of the cheekbones, and the modeling of the twice-dimpled chin, are all analogous. Yet Boccioni's use of arcs and spirals to describe the features of the face is extended to the rest of the painting, which thereby acquires an original dynamic tension.

However, more pertinent comparisons for *Materia* are with paintings of seated or standing figures which directly confront the viewer, meaning not so much Paul Cézanne's *Madame Cézanne in a Red Armchair* mentioned above[75] as the Cubist paintings that were at the center of contemporary debate. Boccioni surely cast a polemical eye over the large, faceted *Portrait of Jacques Nayral* by Albert Gleizes[76] (fig. 4q, exhibited at the 1911 Salon d'Automne which was the occasion of Boccioni's first direct encounter with Cubist painting) in which the sitter, his large hands in the foreground, is posed in a way similar to the mother in *Materia*. A more direct relation, which has already been pointed out,[77] is with Gleizes' *Man at the Balcony*[78] (fig. 4r) in which the life-size figure stands in stark relief against a balcony railing in a solidly static representation that would have been an easy target from Boccioni's anti-Cubist standpoint. Boccioni would have been more challenged by Picasso's contemporary paintings of the same subject. He surely found the 1910 *Portrait of Daniel-Henri Kahnweiler*[79] (fig. 4s) hostile and incomprehensible, despite elements in common with *Materia* such as the joined hands and a comparable imposing frontality. Picasso's earlier paintings, less tough than the more recent ones dominated by obsessive faceting, adapted more easily to Boccioni's play of references. Among the seated women of 1909, a *Woman Seated in an Armchair* (fig. 4t, spring 1909),[80] painted with a dark palette of greens and ochers and with prominent silvery lights on the face and breast, could be seen at Kahnweiler's gallery. Boccioni may have noted the woman's pose (the curve of the arms is closed by the joined hands) and other compositional devices such as the diagonal in the upper left which closes the background and frames the subject. But above all he may

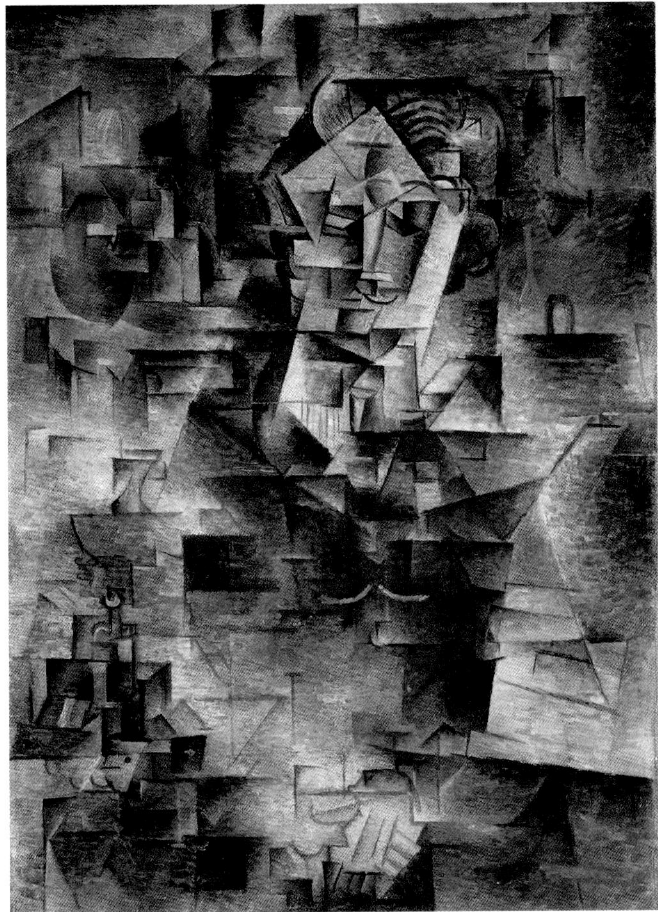

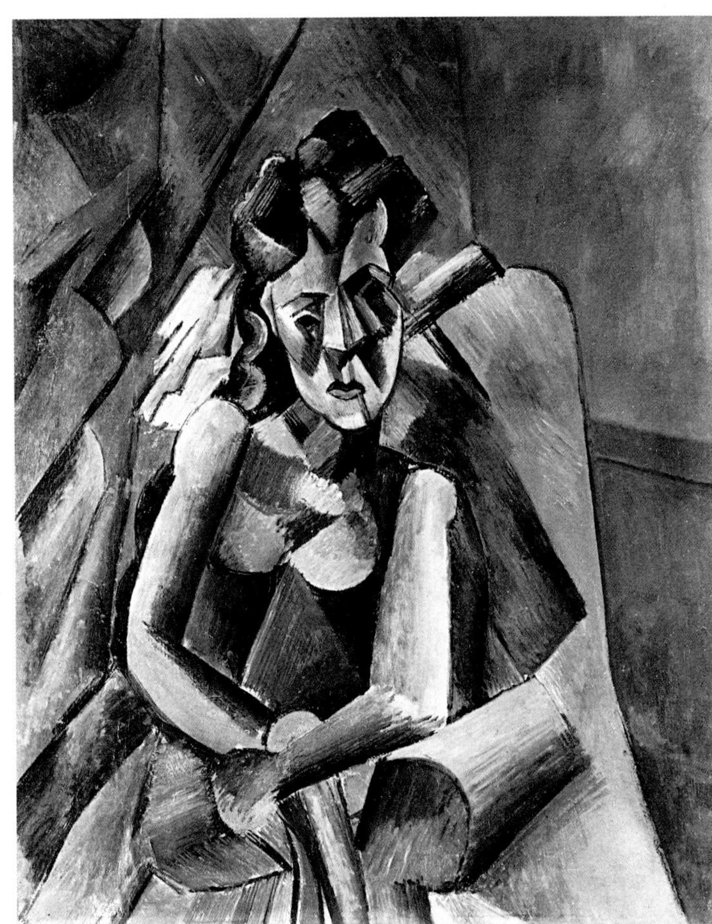

Fig. 4s. *Pablo Picasso,* Portrait de Daniel-Henri Kahnweiler, *oil on canvas, 1910. Chicago, The Art Institute of Chicago, Gift of Mrs Gilbert W. Chapman in memory of Charles B. Goodspeed*

Fig. 4t. *Pablo Picasso,* Femme assise dans un fauteuil (Woman Seated in an Armchair*), oil on canvas, 1909. Berlin, Staatliche Museen zu Berlin - Preussischer Kulturbesitz Nationalgalerie*

have appropriated certain details of the face: the hair is depicted in terms of clustered globular forms, the lips are silhouetted and outlined in black in a similar way, and the forehead is grafted onto the hair by the intersection of two curved lines.

More strictly contemporary Cubist compositions presented other, perhaps more meaningful stimuli. One of the rooms of the 1912 Salon d'Automne, visited by Boccioni during his Parisian trip in November 1912, was dominated by the large *Woman in Blue* by Fernand Léger[81] (fig. 4u). As explained above, *Materia* would have been nearing completion in the artist's studio in Milan at this time. Nevertheless his encounter with Léger's painting, of similar dimensions (it measures 193 × 130 cm), of the same subject (a large seated figure located on the vertical axis, cut off in the same way above the head and beneath the feet, framed by a landscape in a surrounding oval) and with a surprisingly similar construction (the arms join together in a curve with the hands conspicuously placed at the geometrical center of the canvas, the point at which the two expanses of the bust and the skirt separate), certainly had a decisive impact on Boccioni. He drew from it specific details (the geometric motif of the chimney stacks in the upper left corner of *Materia* seems too close to the corresponding motif in *Woman in Blue* to be a coincidence) but above all he found here a strong incentive to challenge the almost abstract juxtapositions of Léger's zones of flattened, contoured color with a truculently dynamic language, rich in chiaroscuro effects, of intersecting planes grafted into alternating reliefs and counterreliefs, hollows and mounds.

c. The Title and Meaning of the Painting

Calling the painting *Materia* was a brilliant invention Boccioni's, or of whomever may have suggested it to him. An abstract term, ennobled by centuries-old philosophical and scientific tradition, was chosen as the title of a painting with an ordinary and recognizable subject (a person at a balcony), but with a monumental format and a revolutionary formal ideology. In Boccioni's Futurist works it interrupted the long sequence of straightforward thematic titles (*The Laugh*, *The Police Raid*), or titles savoring of Symbolism (*Those Who Go*, *The City Rises*, *Modern Idol*) or titles of explicit logical provocation (*The Street Enters the House*), or of ostentatious technical jargon (*Simultaneous Visions*, *Abstract Dimensions*). *Materia* takes us into a conceptually more ambitious terrain.

In 1912 'materia' was a word with much-discussed and manifold meanings. The Larousse *Grand Dictionnaire Universel*, the well-known encyclopedic compendium of late nineteenth-century erudition, traced it "to the Sanskrit *matram*, measure and matter, from the same root *ma*, to make by hand, to construct, to measure."[82] In the same years the derivation of the term from the Latin *mater* was still current and continued to be so in Italy even up to 1937, in for example Ottorino Pianigiani's etymological dictionary ("others identify this word directly with the Latin, *mater*, mother, which goes back to the same root [*matram*] and explains: prime substance from which others are formed"[83]). The three terms 'materia' (matter) 'madre' (mother) and 'mano' (hand) in this family of words derived from the same etymon are densely interwoven in Boccioni's painting. In a psychoanalytic reading of *Materia*, Fausto Petrella noted that the etymology of words can, on the unconscious level, activate metaphorical thought and images which favor the emergence of hidden connections that the use of language obscures.[84] The artist's mother, with whom he had an extremely close relationship that was recorded by his contemporaries ("he loved his mother more than anything else in the world"[85]) and who was his favorite model from the middle of the second decade onwards, would have prompted this chain of associations and given life to the painting. The anti-idealizing process which Boccioni applied to his mother was conducted on two fronts: he first deformed her physical appearance, underscoring her enormous, graceless hands in the foreground, and then emptied her of any symbolic pre-eminence by emphasizing her relation to surrounding 'matter.' Recent studies of *Materia* have drawn attention to Boccioni's ambivalent posture denoting violence/castration implicit in his portrayal of his mother,[86] or to Boccioni's explicit adoption of Marinetti's concept of a passive female body awaiting permeation by an active male force.[87]

Furthermore 'materia' was a fashionable word in these years: Italian current affairs periodicals gave wide-coverage to the theory of the electromagnetic basis of matter formulated by Wilhelm Ostwald, 1909 Nobel Prize Winner, whose principal work was translated into French in 1912.[88] Some recent studies have stressed the connection between Boccioni's painting and this field of science: the materialization of the light rays binding the mother to the ambient has been compared to Faraday and Maxwell's theory of electromagnetic waves,[89] while the atmosphere wrapped around the figure has been described as being traversed by molecular oscillations of matter-energy.[90] But the clearest source for Boccioni's use of the term 'materia' was its occurrence in Bergson's philosophy: according to Bergson, "matter" meant "the sum total of images" perceived by a person, and the syntagma "perception of matter" represented the same complex of images "placed in relation to the possible action of a certain, determinate image, my body."[91] Boccioni's first hand knowledge of Bergson's writings most probably dates to 1912, the time of his conception of and early studies for *Materia*. Prior to this date 'matter', with philosophical implications of any kind, appears nowhere in the artist's essays and letters (the "terror of matter that suffocates me", which Boccioni wrote in his diary in 1908, merely recorded his fear of failing to find an adequate technique for converting idea into image[92]). In a letter to Carrà from Berlin, datable to mid-April 1912, Boccioni used the word in a Bergsonian sense for the first time, as a complex of images perceived and coordinated by the ego:

Fig. 4u. *Fernand Léger,* Femme en bleu *(Woman in Blue), oil on canvas, 1912. Basel, Öffentliche Kunstsammlung Basel, Kunstmuseum, Gift of Raoul LaRoche*

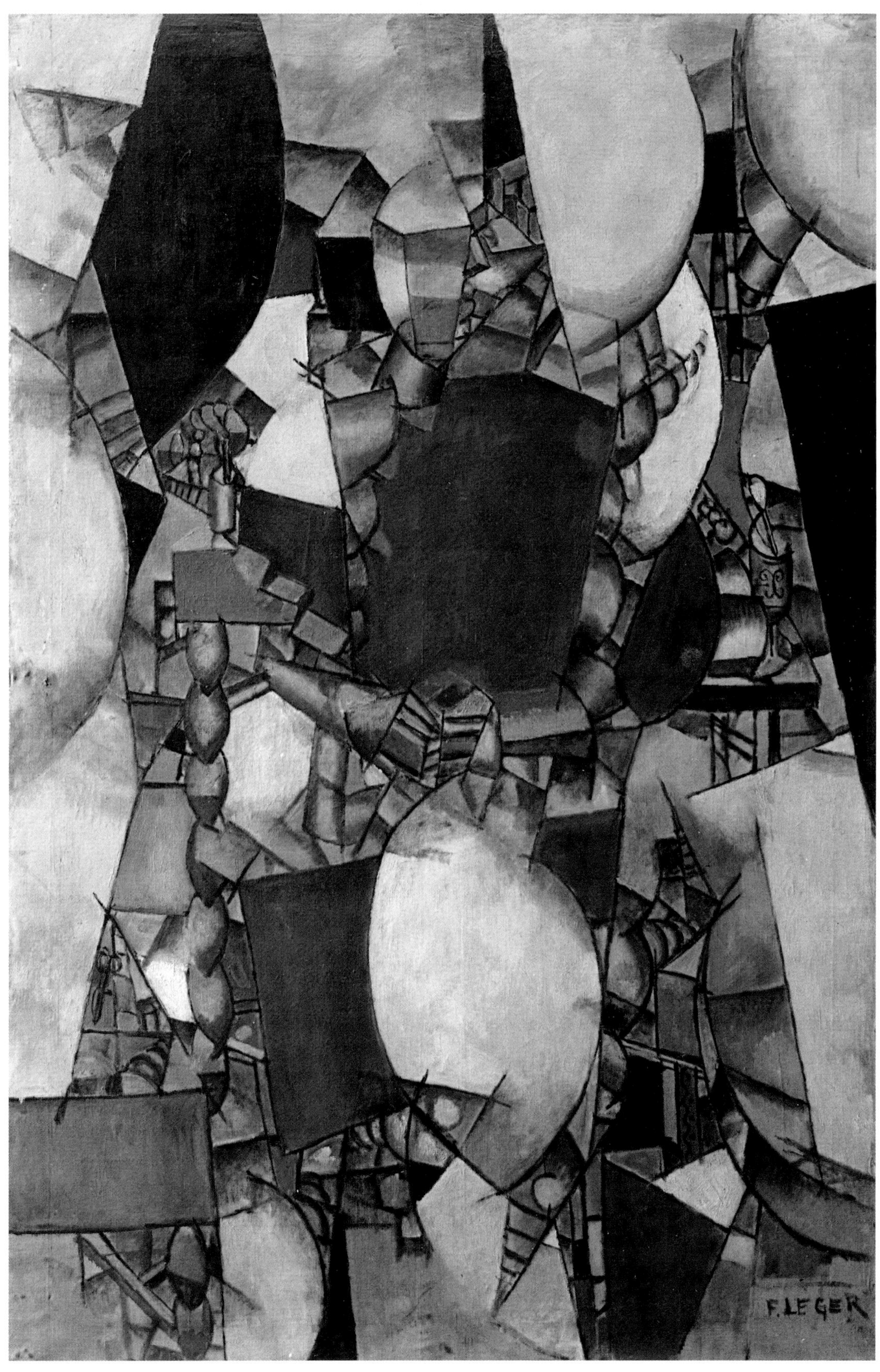

"the greatest truth lies outside the pictorial (as I understood it until yesterday): *I am not interested for the moment in anything but matter expressed according to me myself* … et tout le reste est littérature."[93]

Toward the end of the first decade of the century, Bergson had come to monopolize even in Italy a large segment of philosophical debate, and between 1911 and 1912, following his lecture tour in Italy and England,[94] Bergson's fame was at a peak. The theories of a man who could justifiably be referred to as "the philosopher in fashion"[95] had already invaded the arena of artistic debate. In 1910 Soffici had employed the Bergsonian theory of the perception of objects "in the relationship they have with our needs" to explain the perspectival deformations of the new Cubist painting.[96] Meanwhile resistance to a philosophy that was perceived as too pervasive was beginning to grow among the writers of *La Voce*: there was, according to Prezzolini, a new "hunger for order and discipline" founded on the necessity, so well expressed in the paintings of Cézanne, to "give solidity, firmness, cubicity to the forms of things."[97]

During his travels abroad, in the spring of 1912, Boccioni surely encountered a climate particularly receptive to Bergsonian discourse adapted to artistic matters: concepts of duration, memory and intuition, drawn for the most part not from original texts but from abridgements (of which contemporary magazines were full) had been abundantly utilized for interpreting the new Cubist painting in important articles (of which Boccioni was certainly aware even if indirectly) by Tancrède de Visan, Jean Metzinger, Roger Allard and Albert Gleizes.[98] Within the year, references to Bergson, especially in the context of investigations of the concept of simultaneity, became routine among Futurist painters. Even an artist with as little propensity for theoretical speculation as Gino Severini stated in the introduction to his one-man show at the Marlborough Gallery in London in April 1913 that "to perceive — says Bergson — is, after all, nothing more than an opportunity to remember."[99]

On his return to Milan in the summer of 1912, Boccioni was evidently keen to clarify and test against Bergson's original texts the ideas he had gathered during the spring. The precise congruity of many of the notions expressed by Boccioni in *Pittura scultura futuriste* (such as the identification of the subject who perceives with the object perceived, the distinction between absolute and relative motion, the theory of muscular sensation) with Bergson's writings has been demonstrated in a study by Brian Petrie.[100] The political implications of Bergson's theories of space-time as understood by Boccioni have been the object of a recent study by Mark Antliff.[101] However no one has yet inquired how Boccioni accessed the French philosopher's works. In an undated note published by Zeno Birolli in 1971 (the *terminus ante quem* is March 1913, when a part of the note was used in Boccioni's first article in *Lacerba*[102]), Boccioni transcribed a passage from *Matière et Mémoire* on the condition of matter (its indivisibility, thus contradicting standard definitions in popular dictionaries of the time[103]), with the purpose of refuting accusations that Futurist painting was cinematographic:

"All division of matter into independent bodies with absolutely determined contours is an artificial division."[104]

This note, which includes quotations as well as a reading list, allows us to reconstruct the facts of Boccioni as a reader of Bergson, which took place for the most part in the libraries of Milan: the number he transcribed (with a slight error: 7.4.D.41 in place of F.4.D.41) next to his note of Giovanni Papini's translation from Bergson, *La filosofia dell'intuizione*, corresponds to the call number of the Biblioteca Nazionale Braidense. The notes he took from the first, 1896 edition of *Matière et Mémoire* (also available at the Braidense) show us the degree of superficiality with which Boccioni glanced through the philosophical text. As one would in a hasty reading, he copied almost exclusively the brief phrases in italics that stressed key concepts (on pages III, 4, 6, 74, 163, 213, 215, 218 — where he found the passage cited above on the indivisibility of matter — 225 and 252, the opening lines of the author's *résumé*). Unsystematic though his reading of the book may have been, Boccioni found there concepts and images he would pour almost literally into *Materia*: the origin of representation from the body's "center of action;"[105] the continuous action of centripetal and centrifugal forces that bind the person who perceives to the object of perception (p. 6), the image of the body which occupies the center of the perceptive world and with its movement changes the images perceived (p. 10), the perceptive centers of the body which connect to objects with actual rays (p. 27), the living body as a center and departure point from which is reflected, on the surrounding objects, the action that these objects exercise on it (p. 47), the impossibility of delineating a separation between a body and the objects it perceives (pp. 48–9).

Recent studies of *Materia* have largely overlooked Maurizio Calvesi's important insight on Marinetti's role as mediator of Boccioni's introduction to Bergson and his concept of matter.[106] In Marinetti's *Technical Manifesto of Futurist Literature*, published with the date May 11, 1912 as an introduction to *I poeti futuristi*,[107] the term 'matter', in the strictly Bergsonian sense of a network of perceived images, was obsessively repeated nine times, and Marinetti was obliged to defend himself (in his August 11, 1912 *Risposta alle obiezioni*[108]) from accusations of having appropriated Bergson too blatantly. Boccioni, who was constantly in the company of Marinetti in Milan in the summer of 1912, must have been particularly responsive to all the contexts in which Marinetti engaged the term 'materia' ("lyrical obsession of *matter*" to balance against human psychology; matter which is to be withdrawn from the contemplation of an ego "distracted, cold, too self-absorbed, full of prejudices, of wisdom and human obsessions;" "*matter*, which possesses an estimable continuity in its impulse towards greater fervor, greater movement," whose essence must be penetrated and "the deaf hostility which separates it from us" destroyed).

d. The History and Critical Fortune of the Painting

When it was shown in Rome in 1913, *Materia* failed to receive critical attention in proportion to its large ambition and to the strategic position it had been assigned as the first painting in the catalogue. The choice not to reproduce it in reviews was perhaps owing to the difficulty of rendering the image legibly in black and white in newspapers and magazines; by contrast, the alluring subject, the clear fragmentation of the forms and the shrill palette of *Elasticity* made it the most admired and reproduced painting of the show.

While polemical reviews of the Teatro Costanzi exhibit ignored *Materia*, more benevolent critics appreciated isolated aspects of the painting, or even single passages. Roberto Longhi was struck by its capacity to generate movement by the use of concentric waves:

> "By studying the superficial planes of Cubism, in order not to chill matter but to release its power, [Boccioni] came to conceive it as a superimposition of planes that fall away, that emerge from the husk as if surrounding a compact central nucleus: and it is the rotating movement given this kernel that causes the outer form to roll up, like Saturn freeing itself of its rings. All this becomes clear when observing how the metal of the railing in *Materia* rises up, assimilated: each small undulation is followed to its farthest limit, launched into the most violent orbit; the little projection of the first joint of the thumb is sufficient to make it rise up in a barrier of flesh."[109]

Emilio Cecchi preferred the upper portion, with its orderly decorative scoring:

> "... in one part of *Materia* [...] not only does [Boccioni] obtain a solid connection of the planes of light, of force-lines, of cubic solids, etc. but, with the play of refractions [...] produces chords now slow, now vibrato, modulations of colors abstract and precious; and perhaps he lacks only a more noble material and greater art of transparencies and polishes for the effect to be surer and more profound. But at least the Persian carpet, the purely decorative surface are achieved by him always."[110]

Arnaldo Cantù instead focused his attention on the gravitation of masses toward the center of the painting, the mother's large hands:

> "The painting *Materia* represents a solemn figure with powerful hands entwined on her lap, almost as if seen through a subaqueous light, closed in a sober and well-defined rigidity of planes, constructed with a sort of inverse perspective whose masses, whose planes and whose volumes moving from the base of the painting could be said to gravitate with their acute angles and with their tangent rays toward the center of the depiction."[111]

Little critical attention was given *Materia* in reviews of the 1913 show in Rotterdam (though the photograph of the first version of the painting, before its completion, began to circulate and was published in *Comœdia* in June as "a painting which contains the same research" as the sculpture *Head + House + Light*[112]). The same was true of the 1914 show in London (where it was confused with *Dynamism of a Soccer Player* but published in its definitively retouched version[113]) and of the San Francisco exhibition in 1915–16. Still unsold at the time of Boccioni's death, *Materia* was exhibited at the December 1916–January 1917 retrospective exhibition at Palazzo Cova, Milan, together with three studies, most likely drawings:[114] here too the lack of interest in *Materia* is surprising, to the point that it was omitted from the twenty-two works illustrated in the catalogue and was illustrated only once in the torrent of articles in the press when Boccioni died and when the large commemorative exhibition was held in Milan.[115] *Materia* was evidently a painting insufficiently dynamic for wartime rhetoric that sought in Boccioni "divine joy"[116] or the "virile bliss of conquest",[117] but was also too Cubist-oriented when, in the celebrations after his death, Boccioni came to be perceived as a "classic [...] temperament" who dreamed of leading speed "into the realm of synthesis and order."[118]

It is to Marinetti that we owe the subsequent exhibition history of the painting. Its presence in the numerous exhibitions to which it was sent testifies both to Marinetti's desire to keep alive the memory of the heroic years of Futurism and his attempt to make an important sale that would help Boccioni's impoverished mother. *Materia* was exhibited at the 1920–1 Boccioni retrospective curated by Enrico Prampolini at the 'Exposition Internationale d'Art Moderne' in Geneva, and again in 1924 in another retrospective at the 'Bottega di Poesia' gallery in Milan (where it failed to sell at the auction held on March 19 and 21, but where it was admired for the first time by the young Gianni Mattioli[119]); and again at the 'III Biennale romana' the following year (*Materia* was published upside down in the catalogue; for reviewers of the show, dominated by discussions of the new classicism, Boccioni's art was a very remote problem). When Boccioni's mother died in 1927 the painting passed to the artist's sister Amelia, who had married Guido Callegari in 1910. *Materia* remained in their house in Verona until June 1933; it was then loaned to the large retrospective show in the Sala del Consiglio Segreto of the Castello Sforzesco (Milan), an exhibition without a catalogue that was intended by its organizers to tie historical Futurism to the art of its weaker followers of the 1930s. Though *Materia* was frequently mentioned in reviews of the event and sometimes illustrated (only in texts by exponents of Futurism itself, such as Paolo Buzzi and Fortunato Depero), it was overwhelmed by the much-admired figurative paintings, whether pre- or post-Futurist, and by those belonging to Marinetti (the three *States of Mind* and *Dynamism of a Soccer Player*) which drew to themselves all illustrations and critical comment. In the most widely distributed art magazine in Italy, *Emporium*, Vincenzo Costantini noted that the luminist tendency in *Materia* derived from the tradition of the Lombard school of painting, but could not resist the canonical comparison with *Elasticity*, in which "the fundamental problem of Boccioni's theory is addressed in greater depth."[120]

The painting's re-emergence during the second postwar era and its purchase by Gianni Mattioli can be reconstructed thanks to a series of documents preserved in the Fondo Depero of the archives of the museum of Rovereto and in the Archivio Mattioli, all published in the catalogue of the monographic exhibition on *Materia* held in Verona in 1991–2[121] and re-published here in *Appendix I*, document nos. 13, 15, 17, 18, 26 and 29. On May 22, 1946, Fortunato Depero told Gianni Mattioli that the Callegari–Boccioni couple intended to sell a series of works, including *Materia* for which an offer had been made the previous year of 100,000 lire. Depero's plan was to buy the painting and then re-sell it to the Museum of Modern Art, New York, sharing the profit between himself and the Boccioni family (which would have received 250,000 lire of the $3,000 total sale price). This was frustrated by James Johnson Sweeney's resignation as director of the museum. When, two and a half years later, *Materia* was among the paintings by Boccioni in the 'Twentieth-Century Italian Art' exhibition at the Museum of Modern Art, it was listed as the property of Romeo Toninelli, an art dealer who had evidently inserted himself in the negotiations between the Boccioni–Callegari family and Depero. In December *Materia* was sold by Toninelli, through Vittorio Barbaroux, to the 'Fondazione Gianni Mattioli.' The collector chose it ahead of *Elasticity* and *Dynamism of a Soccer Player*, which were for sale by Marinetti's widow at the same time, despite its higher price (Gino Ghiringhelli spoke in a letter of an asking price of a million lire and a probable settlement for around 800,000 lire for *Materia*, against 600–700,000 lire for the two Marinetti paintings) and despite the reservations of Ghiringhelli who, fuelled by a firm anti-Cubist prejudice, preferred *Dynamism of a Soccer Player* to *Materia*, because of its "subject completely dominated by a perfect plastic synchronism."[122]

[1] *Rome* 1913, p. 21, nos. 1–4; *Rotterdam* 1913, p. 19, no. 1–4. Rosci 1991, p. 45, stresses the significance of *Materia*'s preeminent position in the catalogues of the two exhibitions.
[2] *Florence* 1913–14, p. 21, no. 3, with the title *Dimensioni orizzontali*.
[3] Capano, Negri 1991, pp. 253–5; Capano, Negri 1995, pp. 258–9.
[4] Boccioni *et al.*, April 11, 1910.
[5] Munich, Bayerische Staatsgemäldesammlungen, Pinakothek der Moderne: Calvesi, Coen 1983, no. 751.
[6] Milan, Civico gabinetto dei disegni: *ibidem*, no. 754 called *Studio per Costruzione orizzontale*; in *Verona* 1991–2, no. 24, with the title *Studio per 'Materia'*.
[7] Cajumi, December 10–11, 1913; Longhi (1914, p. 17) was of the same opinion.
[8] Calvesi 1967, pp. 209–17.
[9] Letter from Umberto Boccioni to Vico Baer, dated February 19, 1913, in Boccioni 1971, p. 366.
[10] *Materia, Elasticità, Scomposizione di figure a tavola, Costruzione orizzontale, Antigrazioso, Dimensioni astratte*; *Rome* 1913, nos. 1, 5, 6, 7, 8, 9.
[11] Corresponding to Calvesi, Coen 1983, cat. nos. 754–61.
[12] Martin 1968, pp. 152 and 165.
[13] Ballo 1964[a], p. 321; the sequence is accepted by Bruno 1969, nos. 147–9 and repeated in Ballo 1982, p. 51.
[14] Calvesi, Coen 1983, nos. 751–2.
[15] Coen 1988[b], nos. 59–60.
[16] Calvesi 1983[b], p. 110.
[17] Coen 1988[b], p. 212.
[18] Rosci 1991, pp. 49 and 55.
[19] Capano 1991, p. 210: the relative entry was that for *Studio per "Testa + casa + luce"*, Milan, Civico gabinetto dei disegni, Calvesi, Coen 1983, no. 761.
[20] Spate 1997, p. 131; but not Calvesi 2000, pp. 18–19, who considers the sculpture earlier than *Materia*.
[21] Poggi 1997, p. 33; Velani 1999, p. 54.
[22] Schneede 1994, pp. 113–14.
[23] *Verona* 1991–2, p. 225.
[24] Cecchi, March 23, 1913.
[25] Sarfatti, September 24, 1916.
[26] The photo is reproduced in *Verona* 1991–2, p. 214.
[27] *Studio per una testa. Geneva* 1920–1, no. 27; an identification with the painting now known as *Dimensioni astratte* is possible thanks to the exhibition label still glued to the back, with the title *Studio di testa (la madre)*.
[28] Argan, Calvesi 1953, p. 30.
[29] Letter from Umberto Boccioni to Vico Baer from Paris, dated March 15, 1912, in Boccioni 1971, p. 349.
[30] Letter from Umberto Boccioni to Nino Barbantini from Berlin, dated April 13, 1912, in *ibidem*, pp. 351–2.
[31] Letter from Umberto Boccioni to Herwarth Walden from Milan, dated May 8, 1912, *ibidem*, p. 354.
[32] Letter from Umberto Boccioni to his family from Berlin, undated (but prior to May 20, 1912), in Lorenzoni 1995, p. 270.
[33] Maurizio Calvesi's postdating (Calvesi 1983[a], pp. 108–9) of the letters from Boccioni to Carrà and Severini, usually dated June–July 1912 (Boccioni 1971, pp. 357–9), definitively excluded the possibility of Boccioni's trip to Paris in June 1912.
[34] Letter from Umberto Boccioni to Vico Baer from Paris, dated November 9, 1912, *ibidem*, pp. 362–3.
[35] Letter from Umberto Boccioni to Gino Severini, dated January 11 (actually dated January 1) 1913, *ibidem*, pp. 363–4.
[36] Letter from Umberto Boccioni to Vico Baer from Paris, dated March 15, 1912, *ibidem*, p. 349.
[37] Letter from Filippo Tommaso Marinetti to Aldo Palazzeschi, undated (but July 1912), in Marinetti, Palazzeschi 1978, pp. 79–80; the first review was Calza, July 21, 1912.
[38] Undated letter from Umberto Boccioni to Gino Severini in Boccioni 1971, p. 359: the traditional dating of August 1912, formerly proposed by Drudi Gambillo, Fiori 1958–62, vol. I, p. 249 on the basis of a recollection by Gino Severini (Severini 1946, p. 167) and accepted by Pacini 1970, pp. 12–14, was corrected by Calvesi 1983[a], p. 108.
[39] Letter from Filippo Tommaso Marinetti to Balilla Pratella, dated November 26, 1912, in Lugaresi 1969, p. 38. References to Ojetti in the preceding letter, dated November 8, 1912, confirm the dating of Balla's visit to Milan, as well as the one following, in January, 1913.
[40] Rossi 1995, p. 222.
[41] Warnod, June 21, 1913.
[42] Boccioni 1914, unnumbered plate.
[43] Capano 1991, pp. 200–2.
[44] Drudi Gambillo, Fiori 1958–62, vol. I, facing p. 160; Ballo 1964[a], p. 17, fig. 1; Rosci 1991, p. 46.
[45] Letter from Umberto Boccioni to Vico Baer, dated February 19, 1913, in Boccioni 1971, p. 366.
[46] Letter from Umberto Boccioni to Gino Severini, undated (but approx. March 31, 1913), *ibidem* 1971, p. 367.
[47] Rosci 1991, p. 47.
[48] As can be deduced from a letter from Filippo Tommaso Marinetti to Giovanni Papini dated April 11 (1913), according to which the paintings would be packed and sent to Rotterdam on the 15th: Fiesole, Fondazione Primo Conti, Archivio Papini. My thanks to Federica Rovati for bringing the letter to my attention.
[49] Letter from Umberto Boccioni to Gino Severini, dated January 11, 1913, in Boccioni 1971, pp. 364–5.
[50] In chronological order beginning with Calvesi, Coen 1983, no. 760.
[51] *Ibidem*, nos. 759–60; no. 761 has the look of a *d'après* of the sculpture.
[52] Both Milan, Civiche raccolte d'arte: Calvesi, Coen 1983, nos. 859 and 883.
[53] Letter from Umberto Boccioni to Gino Severini, dated January 11, 1913, in Boccioni 1971, pp. 364–5: "My book was finished by December 1".
[54] Boccioni 1914, p. 110.
[55] Boccioni, March 15, 1913.
[56] *Milan* 1911; the painting can be identified thanks to the description in Sarfatti, December 12, 1911.
[57] Spate 1979, fig. 127; for the reproduced photograph which Boccioni used as a medium, see Allard 1911, p. 60 and Calvesi 1958[a], pl. 58a.
[58] Negri 1991, pp. 38–9.
[59] Boccioni 1914, p. 184; the Cézanne source, a letter to Emile Bernard dated July 25, 1904 (see Doran 1995, pp. 47–8), was probably encountered by Boccioni in the 1912 book version rather than in its original publication in the October 1907 issue of *Mercure de France* (as stated in Fratelli 2000, p. 18).
[60] Lista 1979, pp. 18–21.
[61] Dalai Emiliani 1991, p. 79.
[62] The English translation is that of Apollonio 1973, p. 47. Boccioni *et al.* 1912, pp. 5–6.
[63] Rosci 1991, p. 50.
[64] Dalai Emiliani 1991, p. 77.
[65] Letter to Vico Baer, dated February 19, 1913, in Boccioni 1971, p. 366.
[66] *Rome* 1913, p. 8, the present writer's italics.
[67] *London* 1912, p. 21: "He also reproduces what he would see by looking out on every side from the balcony."
[68] Dalai Emilani 1991, p. 77.
[69] Philadelphia, The Philadelphia Mu-

seum of Art: despite the fact that it appeared in the catalogue, the painting was rejected by the exhibition committee (Lebel 1959, pp. 8–11). For its relation to Boccioni's painting see Rylands 1997, p. 59, which reverses Calvesi's position on the subject: Calvesi 1959, pp. 26–7.

[70] Paris, Musée National d'Art Moderne: Worms de Romilly, Laude 1982, no. 68.

[71] *Le Moulin de huile*, France, private collection: Daix, Rosselet 1979, no. 277, formerly Kahnweiler and reproduced in des Prureaux, December 7, 1911.

[72] Düsseldorf, Kunstsammlung Nordrhein-Westfalen: Daix, Rosselet 1979, no. 288.

[73] *Tête de femme*, Rio de Janeiro, Museu de Arte Moderna: *ibidem,* no. 291.

[74] *Femme aux poires*, New York, The Museum of Modern Art: *ibidem*, no. 290 (formerly Berlin, Flechtheim).

[75] *Madame Cézanne dans un fauteil rouge*, Boston, Museum of Fine Arts: Rewald 1996, no. 324. The reference is made by Capano 1991, pp. 203 and 205; the painting was formerly in Italy in the collection of Egisto Fabbri, Florence, and its reproduction was circulated by Ardengo Soffici: Soffici 1908, p. 323 and Rodriguez 1994, p. 23.

[76] London, Tate: the painting was also reproduced in October 1912 in *Du "cubisme*:" Gleizes, Metzinger 1912, unnumbered plate.

[77] D'Harnoncourt 1980, pp. 23–4.

[78] Philadelphia, The Philadelphia Museum of Art: the painting was exhibited at the 1912 Salon d'Automne and the reproduction of one of its preparatory drawings (or more likely a *d'aprés*) was published in Gleizes, Metzinger 1912, unnumbered plate.

[79] Chicago, The Art Institute: Daix, Rosselet 1979, no. 368; its appearance in *Camera Work* in 1912, in an issue for sale at the 'Libreria della Voce', testifies to its diffusion among the Italian Futurists; for a comparison between the two works see Dalai Emiliani 1991, pp. 73 and 76.

[80] New York, private collection: Daix, Rosselet 1979, no. 269, where it was published that the painting had belonged to Kahnweiler, archive no. 163.

[81] Basel, Öfflentliche Kunstsammlung Basel, Kunstmuseum: Green 1976, p. 47; Cooper, Tinterow 1983, p. 208. The painting was exhibited in *Paris* 1912[b], p. 150, no. 1005.

[82] Larousse 1873, vol. X, p. 1337.

[83] Pianigiani 1937–8, *ad vocem.*

[84] Petrella 1991, p. 95.

[85] Carrà 1916, p. 23.

[86] Spate 1997, pp. 128–31.

[87] Poggi 1997, pp. 31–7.

[88] Ostwald 1912, pp. 243–63.

[89] Dalrymple Henderson 1995, p.28.

[90] Lista 1995, p. 443.

[91] Bergson 1896, p. 7.

[92] Boccioni 1971, p. 304.

[93] Letter from Umberto Boccioni to Carlo Carrà, undated, after April 12, 1912, *ibidem*, p. 353.

[94] Antliff 1993, p. 4.

[95] Chiappelli, May 7, 1911.

[96] Soffici, September 22, 1910.

[97] Prezzolini, February 15, 1912.

[98] Messina, Nigro Covre 1986, pp. 59–90.

[99] Severini 1913, p. 3.

[100] Petrie 1974, pp. 140–7.

[101] Antliff 2000, pp. 720–33.

[102] Boccioni, March 15, 1913.

[103] Rigutini, Fanfani 1875, p. 945; Tommaseo, Bellini 1861–79, vol. IV, p. 147.

[104] Boccioni 1971, p. 442.

[105] Bergson 1896, p. 4.

[106] Calvesi 1967, pp. 209–17.

[107] Marinetti 1983, pp. 46–54. The book was published at least a month later, given that the reviews came out in July: Calza, July 21, 1912.

[108] Marinetti 1983, p. 55; the matter is discussed in De Maria 1983, pp. LXIX–LXXX.

[109] Longhi, April 10, 1913.

[110] Cecchi, March 23, 1913.

[111] Cantù 1913, p. 138.

[112] Warnod, June 21, 1913.

[113] *Sketch*, April 29, 1913.

[114] *Milan* 1916–17, p. 48, no. 49; p. 56, nos. 276–8.

[115] Sarfatti, September 24, 1916.

[116] Marinetti 1916, p. 10.

[117] Simoni 1916; the Futurist painting hung in the place of honor toward the back was, significantly, *Dynamism of a Soccer Player*, formerly the property of Marinetti, as seen in a photograph published in *Secolo Illustrato*, January 15, 1917.

[118] Sarfatti 1917, p. 48.

[119] Mattioli 1951, p. 25; Mattioli Rossi 1991[a], p. 19.

[120] Costantini 1933, p. 128.

[121] *Verona* 1991–2, pp. 231–7.

[122] Letter from Gino Ghiringhelli to Gianni Mattioli, dated December 17, 1949, Archivio Mattioli (*Appendix I*, document no. 29).

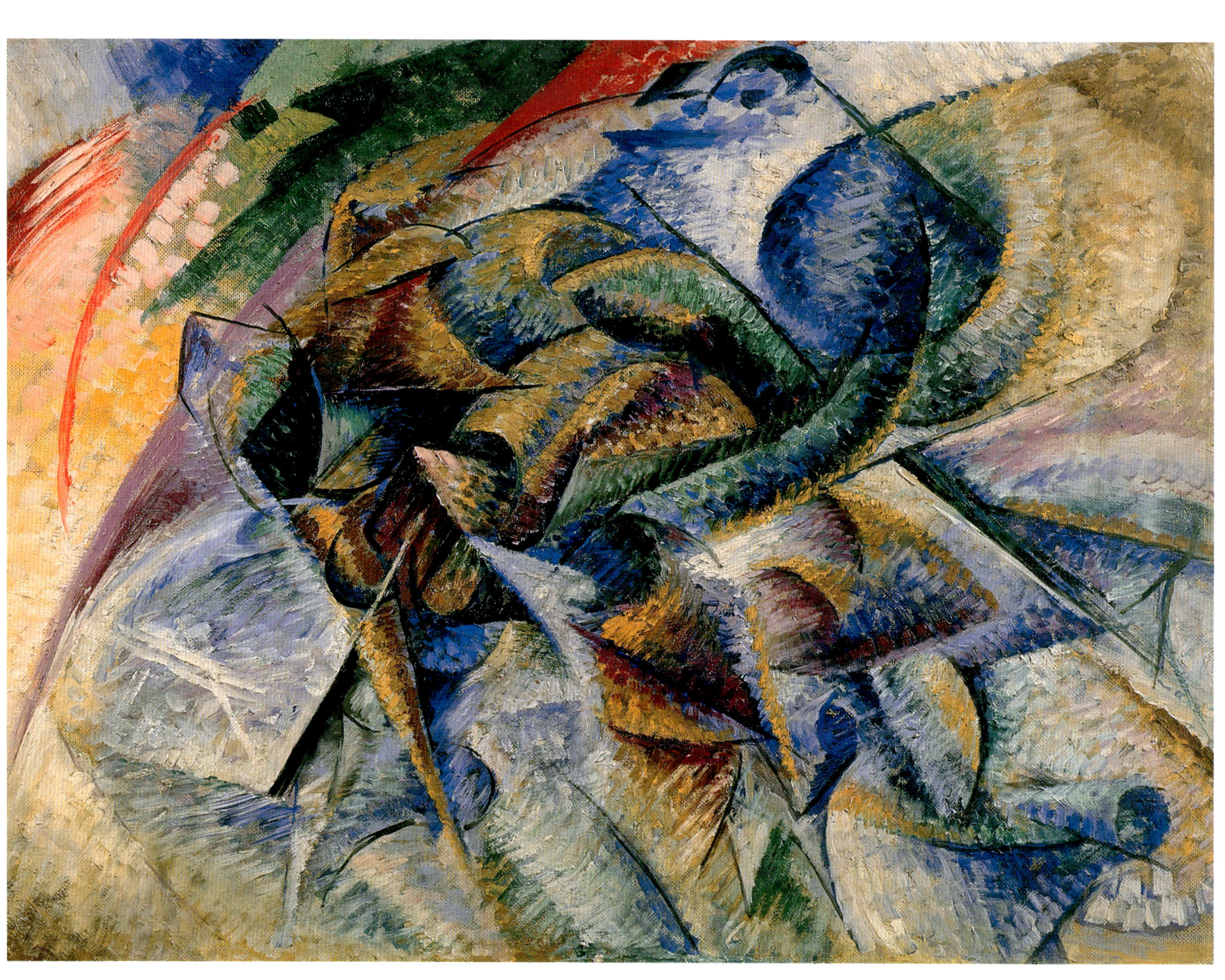

5

Umberto Boccioni

Dynamism of a Cyclist

Dinamismo di un ciclista, 1913

Oil on canvas
70 × 95 cm

Inscription: *verso*, signed on the canvas: 'U. Boccioni' (fig. 5a)

Provenance: property of the artist; ?: Vittoria Colonna di Sermoneta, Rome; after 1953: Signora Chittaro, Rome; June 1955: Gianni Mattioli, with the mediation of the Galleria del Milione

Exhibitions: Florence 1913–14, p. 21, no. 2 (*Dinamismo di un ciclista*); London 1914, p. 25, no. 2 (illus. p. 23); Rome 1914[a], p. 23, no. 2; San Francisco 1915–16, no. 1140; Milan 1916–17, p. 48, no. 47; Rome, 1955–6, p. 54, no. 2; Munich 1957, p. 50, no. 22; Rome 1959, no. 89; Winterthur 1959, no. 29; Munich 1959–60, no. 22; Venice 1960, p. 16, no. 48, fig. 8; New York 1961–Los Angeles 1962, no. 55; Cologne 1962, no. g/13; Hamburg 1963–Frankfurt 1964, no. 27; Milan 1966[a], no. 1; Venice 1966, p. 12, no. 89; Washington, DC 1967–Tokyo 1972, no. 9; Newcastle upon Tyne 1972–London 1973, no. 112; Paris 1973, no. 31; Milan 1973–4, no. 171; Düsseldorf 1974, no. 75; Venice 1986, p. 134; London 1989, no. 24; Saint-Paul de Vence 1992, no. 28; Frankfurt 1995, no. 355; Barcelona 1996, no. 56; New York 2001, no catalogue; Tokyo 2001, p. 37

Bibliography: Boccioni 1914, unnumbered plate (illus. with the title *Dinamismo di un ciclista*); Soffici 1914, unnumbered plate; Barr 1949, p. 13; *Twenty-Century* 1949, p. 126; Carrieri 1950, pp. 59, 61, pl. 69; Valsecchi 1950, unnumbered plate (*Dinamismo di un ciclista*, 1912–14); Zervos 1950, p. 41 (*Dynamisme d'un cicliste*,

Dynamism of a Cyclist is exemplary of Boccioni's artistic concerns in the second half of 1913. Following a period in which he had dedicated himself to sculpture, he turned his attention to the nude figure in action, stressing its muscular tensions, its trajectory through space, and its relation to its environment. He conceived the body in movement as a 'unique form' incorporating the dynamic synthesis of its passage from one point in space to another. Boccioni's paintings, generally characterized at this time by a renewed chromatic intensity, were the pictorial application of ideas he published in a series of essays in the Florentine bi-monthly *Lacerba*, beginning March 1913.

The depiction in the second decade of the twentieth century of a racing cyclist, straining his body and doubled over his vehicle, added the new dimension of competitive sport, a modern entertainment *par excellence*, to the still novel image of the bicycle as represented at the turn of the century. The apotheoses of cycle races were the great Franco-Belgian classics and, as of 1909, the Giro d'Italia. Reports, leg-by-leg, of Italian cycle races perceived as mighty contests between champions appeared in the most widely read sports newspaper *La Gazzetta dello Sport* and compensated in Italy for the lack of a literary tradition (such as existed instead in France) in which the heroics and velocity of cyclists were celebrated in works ranging from the popular novel (*Le Recordman* by Rémy Saint-Maurice, 1898) to epics of irony (*Le Surmâle* by Alfred Jarry, 1902[1]).

Boccioni probably drew his inspiration for this painting by attending an actual cycle race. The first preparatory studies for the painting[2] incorporate details that relate them to period photographs (the front wheels of other cyclists are clearly visible behind the rear wheel of the main subject, who is pulling away in a break or a sprint: figs. 5c–5d). In May 1913 the keenly anticipated sprint finish of the fifth Giro d'Italia (won by Carlo Oriani,[3] protagonist of a spectacular comeback from behind) was cheered by a crowd of 100,000 in the Trotter stadium in Milan, and it is easy to imagine Boccioni, already a frequent visitor for the purpose of his studies of horses, among them.[4] *Lo Sport Illustrato*, a successful new Milanese sports bi-monthly founded in April 1913, diligently reported the cycling season in articles copiously illustrated with snapshots that held the reader's attention year-round, nurturing the modern myth of the cyclist with tales of his endeavors and trials (fig. 5b). The number 15, painted by Boccioni in this final version only, on the cyclist's tabard, signals a realistic detail from modern life precisely when, at the conclusion of a long series of drawings, Boccioni's formal abstraction peaked.

The cycle race represented, in Futurist ideology, a typical circumstance in which man could attain the desired de-humanization through fusion with a machine. Marinetti made no secret of his preference for automobiles and airplanes (in the founding manifesto of Futurism in 1909 the driver of the automobile was vexed by "two cyclists" wavering "like two arguments" over a "stupid dilemma"),[5] but the bicycle was for him an example "of the great Futurist aesthetic,"[6] or one of the symbols of modern life characterized by "an acceleration of life [...], a physical, intellectual and emotional balancing act on the tightrope of speed."[7] In 1913, none of the original signatories of the 1910 manifesto had yet painted a cyclist in action, but the subject had already incited their fantasy. It is interesting to discover, in the text of a lecture on Futurist painting delivered by Boccioni in Rome at the Circolo degli Artisti on May 29, 1911, a passage (attributed to an "example by Carrà" referring perhaps to a text read during a *soirée*) which seems to anticipate by two years precise details of the Mattioli painting (the forward projection of the cyclist's head which almost touches the front wheel or the corresponding inclination of his body behind which, because of the exertion, is almost parallel to the ground):

> "Citing an example of another Futurist painter, my dear and great friend Carlo Carrà, I shall tell you that in painting for example a man speeding along on a bicycle we shall try to reproduce the instinct for speed that determines the action, not the visible physical forward motion of the cyclist. It doesn't matter to us that the cyclist's head might touch the edge of the wheel or his body stretch out behind losing itself in vibrations to infinity with an obvious deception of sight, since it is the sensation of the race, not the cyclist that we wish to depict."[8]

In his manifesto *L'immaginazione senza fili e le parole in libertà* (*Imagination without Strings and Words-in-Freedom*) of May 11, 1913 Marinetti affirmed the centrality of competitive sport in Futurist sympathies ("Passion, art and idealism of Sport. Concept and love of the 'record'").[9] This appeal to sports and sporting records from the pen of the leader of the movement came to have a special meaning for Boccioni in the late spring of 1913. He was concerned with reaffirming the ideological superiority and chronological precedence of the Italian Futurists over the French Cubists,[10] especially following a clear shift towards the return of the subject and of color in certain paintings in the Salon des Indépendants, which were hailed with approval by the most influential critics from Apollinaire to Warnod.[11]

1913); Argan, Calvesi 1953, p. 30; Purchase note, dated June 28, 1955 (Archivio Mattioli); Account note from the Galleria del Milione, dated December 17, 1955 (Archivio Mattioli); Castelfranco, Valsecchi 1956, p. 72, pl. 4; Drudi Gambillo, Fiori 1958–62, vol. I, p. 412, vol. II, pp. 238 and 272, no. 362; Francastel 1959, p. 2; Crispolti 1960, vol. IV, pp. 169–70; Marchiori 1960, no. 8; Carrieri 1961, pl. 20; Taylor 1961, pp. 96–8, illus. p. 96; De Grada 1962, p. 178, fig. 91; Ballo 1964[a], no. 558 and pp. 325–6, 330, 503, 510, illus. pl. I, p. 10; Mathey 1967, p. 185; Martin 1968, pp. 160–1, fig. 132; Bruno 1969, no. 170; Apollonio 1970, pp. 148–9, no. 72; Kozloff 1973, pp. 203–4, fig. 88; Calvesi 1976, p. 245; Tisdall, Bozzolla 1977, p. 82, fig. 81; Birolli 1983, p. 20; Calvesi, Coen 1983, no. 884; Roche-Pézard 1983, p. 169, no. 87, p. 480, fig. 45; Coen 1988, no. 73a, pp. 166–8; Verzotti 1989, no. 129, p. 130; Gombrich 1990, p. 18, no. 10; Di Genova 1993, pp. 219–21; Schneede 1994, pp. 169–74, fig. XXVII; Lemaire 1995, p. 55; Marziali 1996, p. 163; Rylands 1997, p. 60; Spate 1997, p. 134 (illus.); Del Puppo 2000[a], pp. 156–7; Lista 2001, p. 122

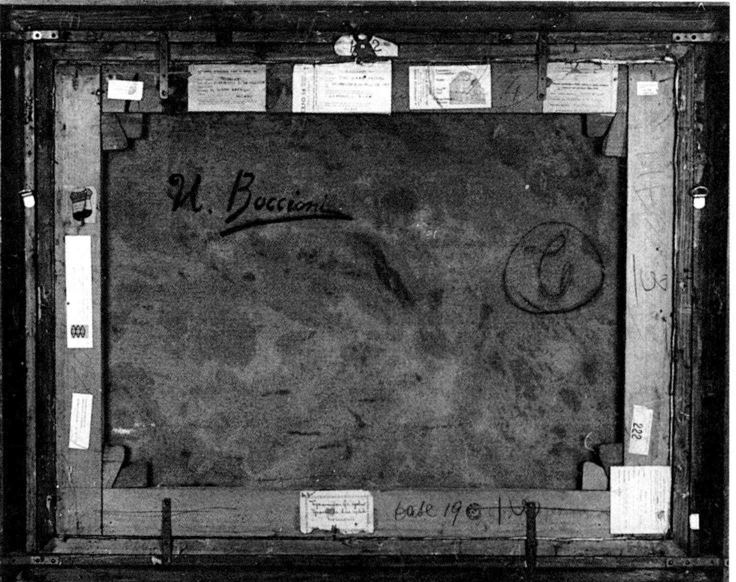

Fig. 5a. Verso *of cat. no. 5*

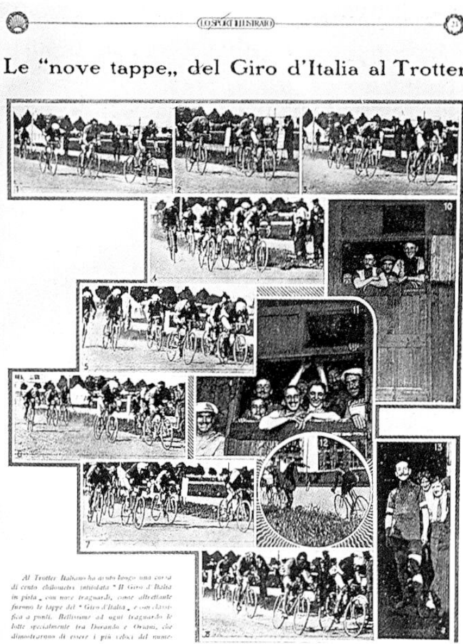
Le "nove tappe,, del Giro d'Italia al Trotter

Fig. 5b. *The laps of the Giro d'Italia at the Trotter, Milan, in* Lo Sport Illustrato, *June 15, 1913*

It is likely that the most direct source for the painting was not French. Boccioni almost certainly knew a canvas by Lyonel Feininger, *Cyclists*, exhibited in 1912 at the XXIV Berlin Secession and illustrated that year in an issue of the Parisian review *Les Tendences Nouvelles*[12] (fig. 5l). It represented a group of racing cyclists, their bodies doubled over under the strain of the race, and certain elements (the cut-off of the foreground cyclist, with wheels partly outside the visual field) found their way into the Mattioli painting. But the real impetus for *Dynamism of a Cyclist* came to Boccioni from Paris. He must have been surprised and vexed by the enthusiasm elicited by paintings with sporting themes at the Indépendents (*The Soccer Players* by Albert Gleizes,[13] *The Cardiff Team, Thirteenth Representation* by Robert Delaunay,[14] classified by Apollinaire as "the most modern canvas of the Salon"[15]), reproductions of which he at once asked Severini to procure.[16] It is also possible that Boccioni was aware of Jean Metzinger's *At the Cycle-Race Track*[17] (fig. 5k), either directly or through a photographic reproduction, even if it was not exhibited in 1912: this painting represents the last dash in the Paris-Roubaix race in 1912, with a geometric synthesis that fixes the cyclist's movements in an artificially frozen posture. Marinetti's manifesto, published when the most heated polemics were already over, may have been an important stimulus for finding an alternative to the tidy calibration of Cubist paintings on the subject of sports (and to the orderly composition of triangular shapes in Feininger's *Cyclists*). It also constituted the ideological basis for the violent dynamism and the vivid colors of both Boccioni's paintings of athletes in action, painted within ten months of each other, *Dynamism of a Cyclist* and the larger and slightly later *Dynamism of a Soccer Player* (which immediately entered Marinetti's own collection).[18]

There is some uncertainty about the early exhibition history of the Mattioli *Cyclist*. According to the entry in the Boccioni *catalogue raisonné*, it was exhibited at the 'Lacerba' Futurist show which opened in Florence in November 1913.[19] The identity of no. 2 in the catalogue (*Dinamismo di un ciclista*) with the Mattioli painting could be questioned on the basis of a passage in a review of the show in the December issue of *Quartiere Latino*, in which the writer, Ugo Tommei, recalled a drawing titled "*Dynamic of a Cyclist* in pen, published in *Lacerba*, excellent study of movement."[20] The context does not make it clear whether the drawing illustrated in the October 15, 1913 issue of *Lacerba* (to which Tommei referred: fig. 5d)[21] was exhibited in place of the painting at the Via Cavour show, or else was only mentioned for argument's sake, for its more comprehensible dynamic qualities. Another review of the Floren-

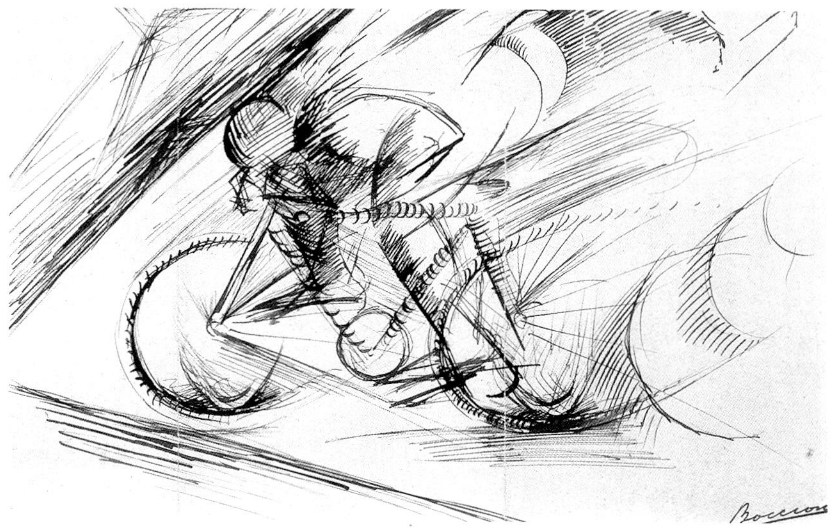

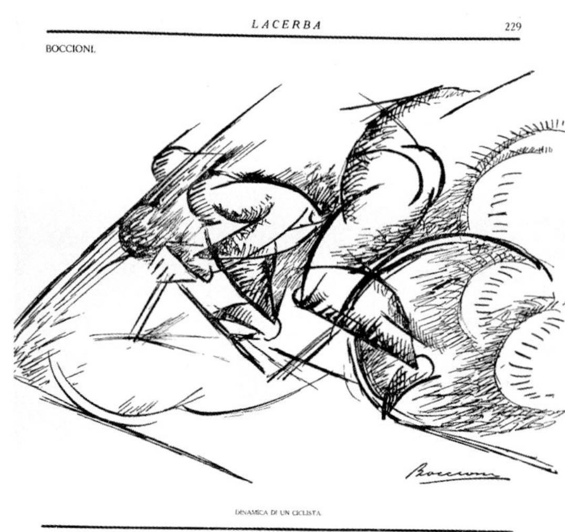
LACERBA 229

BOCCIONI.

DINAMICA DI UN CICLISTA

Fig. 5c. *Umberto Boccioni, Study for* Dinamismo di un ciclista, *pen on paper, 1913. London, Estorick Collection*

Fig. 5d. *Umberto Boccioni,* Dinamica di un ciclista *(*Dynamic of a Cyclist*),* *in* Lacerba, *October 15, 1913*

tine show, by Luigi Fallacara in the periodical *Humanitas* (Bari), seems instead to refer to the Mattioli painting: Fallacara associated *Dynamism of a Cyclist* with a *Ballerina* by Severini, with the large *Dance of the Pederasts* by Soffici and with the *Speeding Automobile* by Russolo in a series of "orgies of color,"[22] an observation which would exclude the pen drawing. Other considerations favor the argument that the painting rather than the drawing was exhibited in Florence. The drawing, already conspicuously illustrated a month and a half earlier in the periodical of the Florentine Futurists, would have been an unlikely choice for Boccioni to exhibit it again in the 'Lacerba' show.

The same duo of titles, *Nude* and *Dynamism of a Cyclist*, introduced the section of Boccioni's paintings at three exhibitions, in Florence, in Rome (Galleria Sprovieri, from February 11, 1914) and in London (Doré Galleries, from April 13, 1914), spanning the period from December 1913 to June 1914.[23] There can be no question that the Mattioli *Dynamism of a Cyclist* was exhibited in London, as it was illustrated in the catalogue[24] and a label from the show is still glued to the stretcher. Thus the decision to exhibit drawings of cyclists beside the oil painting would have been limited to the Sprovieri show in Rome.[25]

The most certain chronological fact in the painting's execution is the above-mentioned publication of a drawing similar to the final resolution of the canvas in the October 15, 1913 issue of *Lacerba* (fig. 5d). The drawing was in Soffici's hands by September 28[26] and the title *Dynamism of a Cyclist*, communicated in a letter from Boccioni to Soffici on October 1, 1913,[27] was significantly corrected by the latter for publication in the periodical into the less Marinetti-influenced title, *Dynamic of a Cyclist*. The painting was surely executed in September. The partly-painted canvas (the road on the left is only sketched in paint over an outline of the scene) is visible in three photographs taken in Boccioni's studio at the Bastioni di Porta Romana 35[28] (fig. 5h). These photographs represent a valuable *terminus post quem*: Boccioni posed next to *Materia* (cat. no. 4) in late August, before retouching it after its return to Milan from its showing in Rotterdam.[29] It is likely that the oil version of *Dynamism of a Cyclist* was painted soon after the drawing was made, which was, as we have seen, certainly before the end of September.

Dynamism of a Cyclist is logically situated in the stylistic sequence of Boccioni's 1913 works after the ten sculptures exhibited at his June show at the Galerie La Boëtie, Paris. The reduction of the cyclist's muscles into tapering spiral shapes grafted one onto another with glittering effects of light ("The lights succeed again in cleaving the central body in movement as if they sought to dismantle it in its race with itself. It is infinitely dispersed in the atmosphere"[30]) recalls the way Boccioni constructed figures in his sculpture. Moreover, the violent intrusion

Fig. 5e. *Umberto Boccioni, Study for* Dinamismo di un ciclista, *pen, watercolor and India ink on paper, 1913. New Haven (Connecticut), Yale University Art Gallery, Gift of Collection Société Anonyme*

Fig. 5f. *Umberto Boccioni, Study for* Dinamismo di un ciclista, *pen and brush and ink on paper, 1913. Milan, Civico gabinetto dei disegni*

Fig. 5g. *Umberto Boccioni, Study for* Dinamismo di un ciclista, *watercolor on paper, 1913. Milan, Civico gabinetto dei disegni*

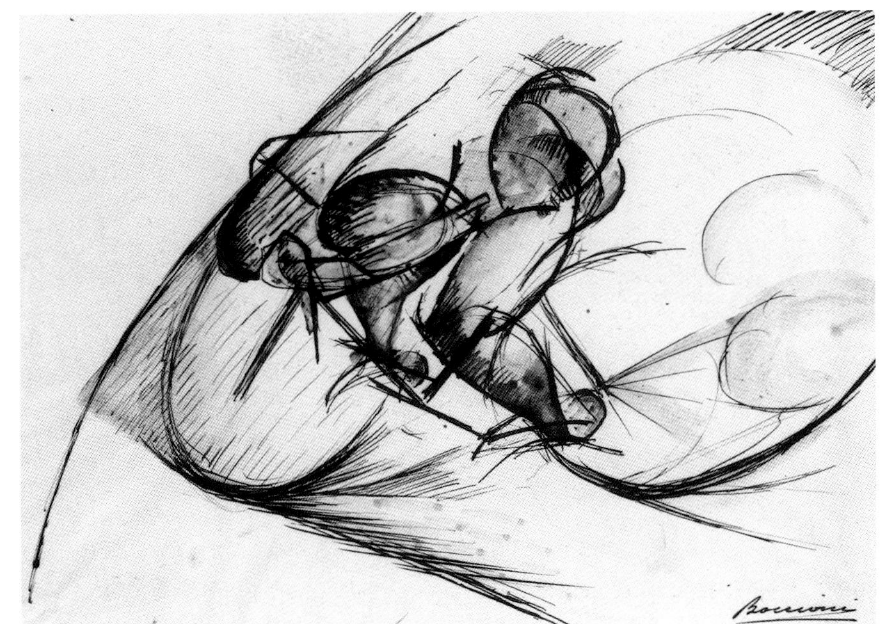

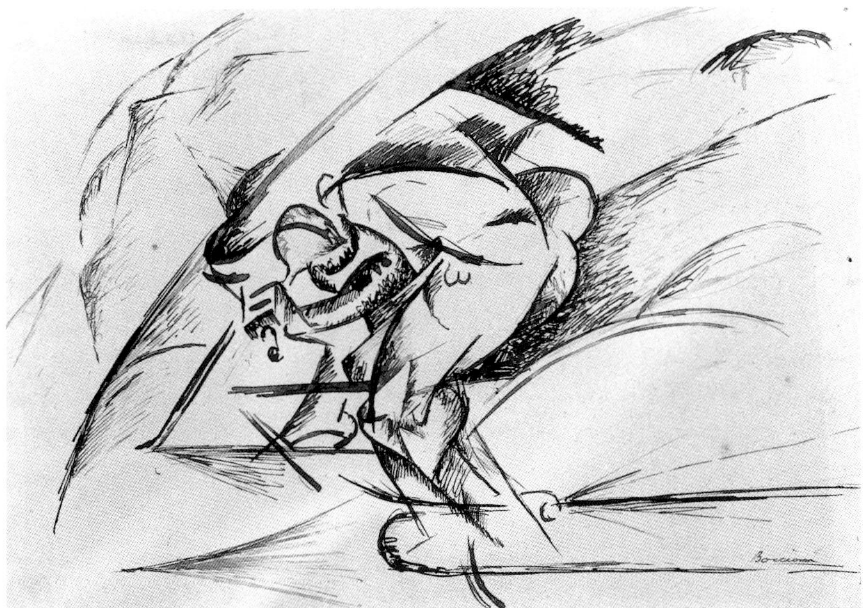

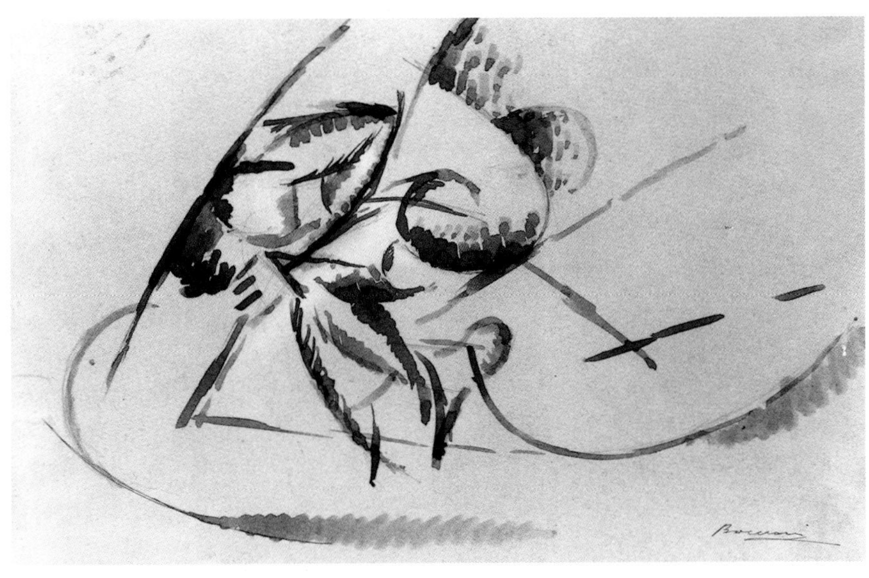

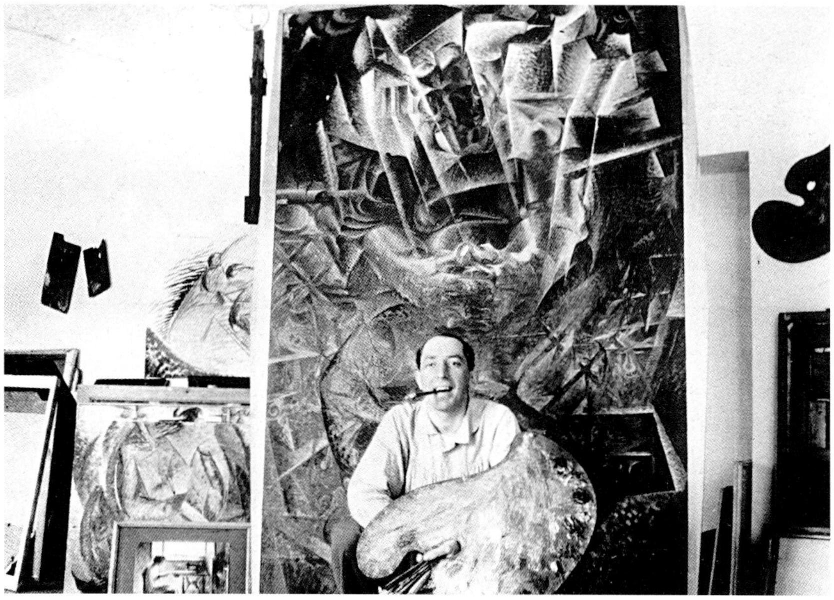

Fig. 5h. *Umberto Boccioni in his studio at the Bastioni di Porta Romana, August–September 1913: left,* Dinamismo di un ciclista *during execution*

into the arabesque of arcs and sine curves of straight lines that intersect in acute angles is a process inherited from those of Boccioni's watercolor drawings which were closest to his sculptures and which had by this time already traveled with his series of plasters to the show in Paris[31] (fig. 5i). Other more incidental considerations support the dating in the second half of 1913. Boccioni the sculptor, who returned from Paris in July convinced of the stagnation of Cubism, which "seemed to be going nowhere,"[32] had taken up painting again, experimenting with a particular livid and high-keyed palette. Confirmation of this comes from contemporary writings and, indirectly, from letters between Carrà and Soffici. During the summer Boccioni had been discussing the matter of a new, fiery color scheme with Carrà (who, in a manifesto published in *Lacerba* on September 1, called for "reds that shout, greens that scream, yellows that can never be explosive enough"[33]). He also discussed the subject in letters to Soffici. The latter, after receiving the texts for the summer issues of *Lacerba*, described the two Milanese artists as "tormented [...] because of aesthetic and, above all, pictorial matters" and warned them about "the ardor of their colors:" in his view, what was needed was a chiaroscuro that would fit the Italian tradition of tonal painting, with the capacity to give back "solidity and consistency to the visible world."[34] Statements by Boccioni such as that in favor of "the use of colors with pure tones applied simultaneously and for contrasts, for affinities and for gradations" to obtain a "dynamism of color that was hitherto made static by the continuity of chiaroscuro" (published in *Lacerba* in August[35]) left Soffici puzzled but throw light on the substance of Boccioni's theory of color in the second half of 1913 and the choices he made for the Mattioli *Dynamism of a Cyclist.* The yellow ground painted directly onto the priming of the canvas enhances the brilliant colors with an unprecedented degree of luminosity (red, green, purple, yellow, blue) both in the local color and in the broad patches of broken color. As Marianne Martin has observed "no external light to speak of exists apart from that generated and reflected by the pigments themselves."[36]

The term that most frequently recurs in the titles of Boccioni's paintings in the catalogue of the 'Lacerba' show was 'complementarism,' evidence of the renewed importance that color held for him in the second half of 1913. His painting of a cyclist was the only one to include the fateful word 'dynamism' (also used by Carrà for a sporting subject, *Dynamism of a Boxer*). The matter of dynamism dominated obsessively the declarations, manifestos, articles and letters of the Futurist painters in 1913. The word had a different meaning according to who was

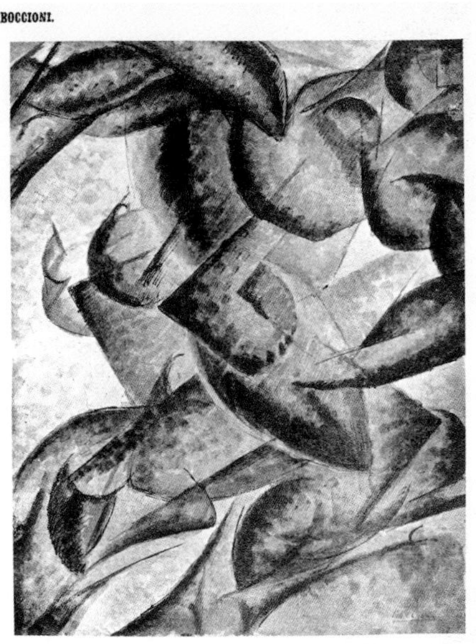

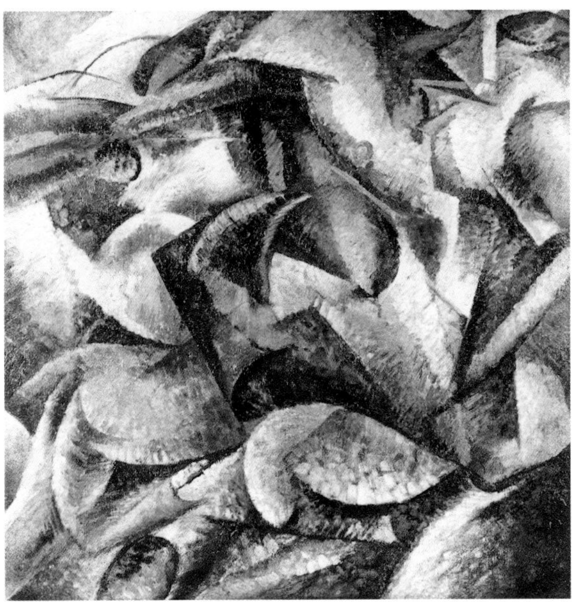

Fig. 5i. *Umberto Boccioni,* Dinamismo muscolare *(*Voglio sintetizzare le forme uniche della continuità nello spazio*) (*Muscular Dynamism *[*I Want to Synthesize the Unique Forms of Continuity in Space*]), in* Lacerba, *March 15, 1914*

Fig. 5j. *Umberto Boccioni,* Dinamismo di un corpo umano *(*Dynamism of a Human Body*), oil on canvas, 1913. Milan, Civiche raccolte d'arte*

using it: "continuance" united to "displacement, which is necessarily included in it" according to Severini;[37] a plastic expression of the "currents" of the "centers of the forces" of a body, which determine its "weight, size and gravity" according to Carrà;[38] the possibility of modifying the rhythm of an object by making "the planes and volumes of the surrounding objects" enter it, according to Soffici.[39] For Boccioni in 1913, the concept of 'dynamism' was clarified above all through his practice of sculpture.

His point of departure, stated emphatically in the introduction to his first sculpture show, openly derived from the theories of Bergson:

> "To show a body in movement I try not to show its trajectory, that is, its passage from one state of repose to another state of repose, but force myself to secure the unique form which expresses its *continuity in space*."[40]

In work of the previous months focused on the plaster sculptures representing human bodies in movement,[41] Boccioni had succeeded in putting behind him the notion of dynamism as a cinematographic sequence of acts:

> "We do not subdivide visual images, we look for a sign, or better, a unique form to substitute the new concept of continuity for the old concept of division."[42]

When, in the summer, he began painting again and initiated the series of studies that would lead to *Dynamism of a Cyclist*, the adjective 'lyrical' (as a synonym of 'pure formal value'), which Soffici and Longhi were already fond of using, became associated with the concept of 'dynamism':

> "It is not, then, only the observation of the object in movement that creates dynamism. It is not only the trajectory from point A to point B of any object that moves us. Dynamism is the lyrical concept of bodies interpreted by a form which synthesizes the infinite manifestation of their relativity between absolute and relative motion."[43]

A passage in *Pittura scultura futuriste* (written by Boccioni for the most part in 1912, revised and finished by the fall of 1913, and published in 1914) defines the concept of 'dynamic form,'

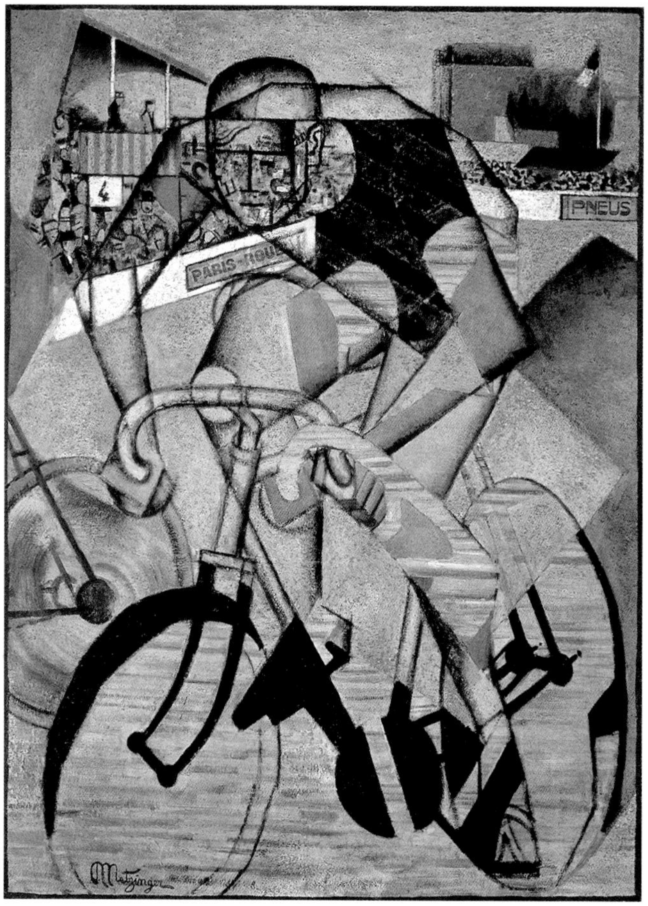

Fig. 5k. *Jean Metzinger,* Au Vélodrome (At the Cycle-Race Track)*, oil and collage on canvas, 1912. Venice, Peggy Guggenheim Collection (The Solomon R. Guggenheim Foundation)*

with its capacity to blend the object and its environment, and this may be taken as a revealing commentary on the Mattioli painting:

> "The dynamic form, for its changeable and evolving essence, is a sort of invisible nimbus between an object and an action, between relative motion and absolute motion, between the visible and the invisible, between the object and its own indivisible setting. It is a kind of analogical synthesis dwelling on the borders between the real object and its plastic-ideal power and can only be grasped by flashes of intuition."[44]

Preparatory work on the painting is documented by approximately ten surviving drawings which illustrate its coherent evolution on two separate fronts.[45] The first consisted of a progressive liberation from the initial motif, taken from real life: in a drawing in the Estorick Collection the frame of the bicycle is clearly defined and the cyclist is portrayed in a still realistic pose[46] (fig. 5c). By the end of this phase, in which Boccioni was striving to achieve a synthesis of the motif (a watercolor in the Civico gabinetto dei disegni at the Castello Sforzesco, Milan,[47] fig. 5g), he had almost entirely eliminated the bicycle (its wheels survive) and isolated the athlete's posture, represented summarily by the tangle of muscles which he would maintain in the finished painting. The second line of progression was the systematic substitution of the straight lines characteristic of the early drawings with more flexible lines: the two dominant force-lines that come together in a peak (as they still do in the drawing published in October 1913 in *Lacerba*,[48] fig. 5d) transform into two curves that frame the cyclist's movement with a more elastic silhouette (in this sense, the progression is highly evident if one places Calvesi, Coen catalogue numbers 890, 891, 892, 888 in sequence). In the last two drawings (figs. 5e–5f) one can observe the beginning of the process

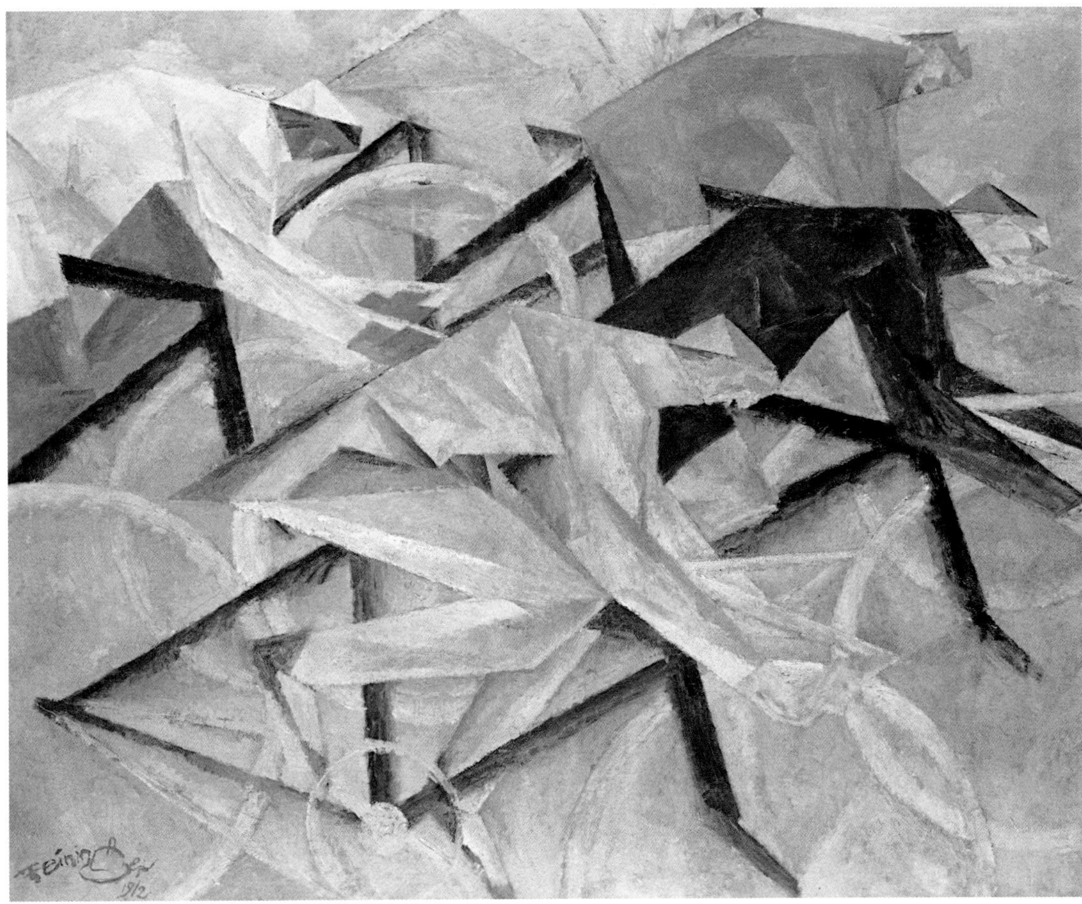

Fig. 5l. *Lyonel Feininger,* Radfahrer (Cyclists), *oil on canvas, 1912. Washington, DC, National Gallery of Art, Collection of Mr and Mrs Paul Mellon*

of relating object to atmosphere (which Boccioni so often theorized): the curving lines spread to the horizon and connect with the spirals of the athlete's muscles. Added to this is a decisive zoom on the cyclist's body: in one of the last of the drawings[49] (fig. 5f) and in the Mattioli painting, the lower portion of the wheel is outside the painting's frame of view. In the previously-mentioned manifesto *L'immaginazione senza fili e le parole in libertà* (May 1913), Marinetti had recommended the use of the straight line both to assure a more effective mechanistic quality in the representation of speed and a dehumanization of the content of the work of art ("Nausea of the curved line, of the spiral and of the tourniquet. Love of the straight and of the tunnel"[50]). The initial choice of an acute angle as a synthetic formula for suggesting rapid motion to the left may have come from Marinetti's notions but it can also be related to studies of a speeding automobile on which Giacomo Balla was working in Rome between the spring and fall of 1913: in these Balla systematically used a triangular shaped wedge. The subsequent transformation of straight lines into curved lines, and the change in their function (from a peak circumscribing the cyclist in order to synthesize his movement, to the emanation of the cyclist's movement which spreads outwards) was the outcome of the process of exploring spiral forms in sculpture.

The traditional Symbolist curved horizon, the use of pure, luminous colors with a strongly lyrical purpose (especially in the upper left portion of the painting, as in *Dynamism of a Human Body* in the Civiche raccolte d'arte, Milan,[51] fig. 5j), the black outlines around a figure at first glance almost indistinguishable — all these features recall contemporary or slightly earlier works by Wassily Kandinsky.[52] Boccioni certainly knew the illustrations to the Russian painter's *Über das Geistige in der Kunst*, which he discussed in a passage in *Pittura scultura futuriste*.[53] He may have seen *Impression V* of 1911 (Paris, Centre National d'Art Contemporain Georges Pompidou,[54] fig. 5m), which shares with *Dynamism of a Cyclist* its general handling

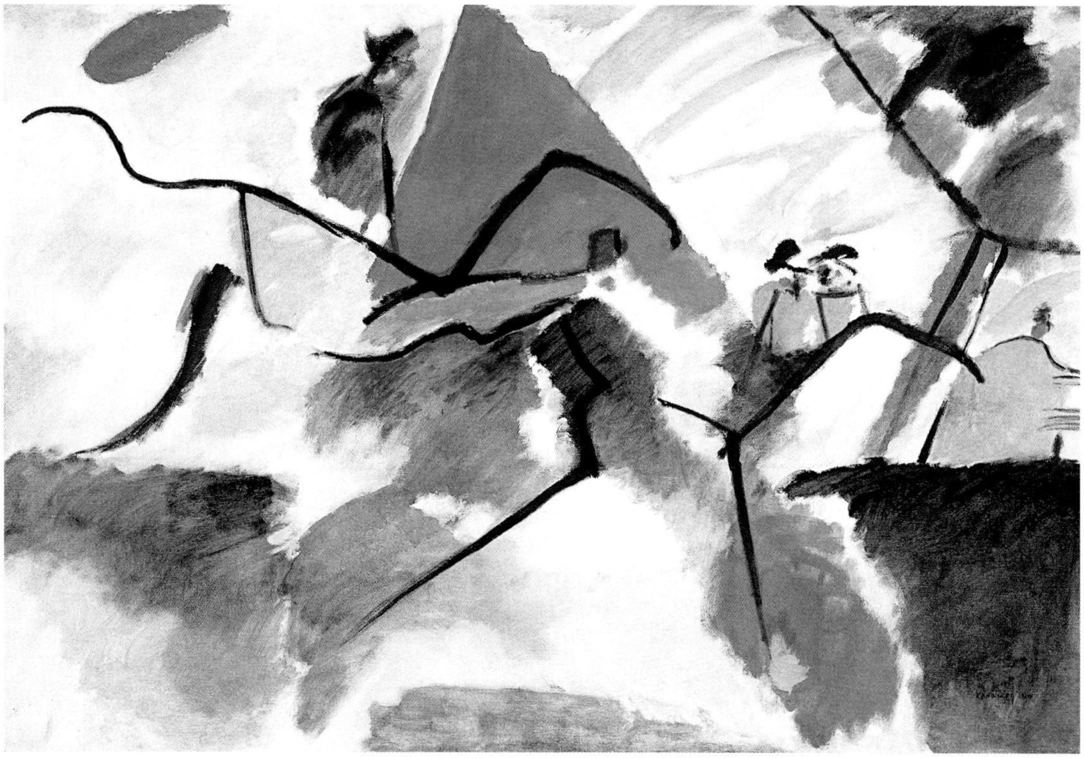

Fig. 5m. *Wassily Kandinsky,* Impression V, *oil on canvas, 1911. Paris, Centre National d'Art Contemporain Georges Pompidou*

and reliance on black outlines. He had probably also seen the reproductions in a Kandinsky album published in 1913 by 'Der Sturm' (in which he could have studied the curved sky in the 1913 *Landschaft mit roten Flecken I*[55]). Again, Boccioni could have viewed works by Kandinsky as early as 1912 in Paris or Berlin: whether at Walden's gallery during his Berlin sojourn in April 1912 (he wrote of a "musical composition" in a letter to Carrà[56]) or at the 1912 Salon des Indépendants (several *Improvisations* were reported in the widely-read review by Guillaume Apollinaire[57]), which was open at the time of one of Boccioni's trips to Paris in the spring of that year.[58]

Dynamism of a Cyclist was the last and most advanced work by Boccioni to be illustrated in the two official contemporary texts on Futurist art, *Pittura scultura futuriste* by Boccioni and *Cubismo e futurismo* by Ardengo Soffici. Boccioni considered it one of the key moments in his artistic career. Thus it was included in the highly selective exhibition at the Doré Galleries in London in April 1914[59] together with the later and more ambitious *Dynamism of a Soccer Player*, with the two works that best represented his production in 1912 (*Materia* and *Elasticity*), as well as with an unidentifiable *Nudo (complementarismo dinamico di forma e colore)* (*Nude [Dynamic Complementarism of Form and Color]*) and a series of ten drawings documenting his sculptural activity. In the following year, the same selection of works but without the drawings, now considered a sort of canon of Boccioni's Futurism, was presented at the 'Panama-Pacific International Exposition' in San Francisco. After appearing as number 47 in the 1916–17 retrospective at the Galleria Centrale d'Arte at Palazzo Cova, its history becomes difficult to follow and there is no definite trace of it until 1953, when, in the catalogue of works edited by Maurizio Calvesi, in an appendix to Argan's monograph on Boccioni, it was listed in Rome in the collection of the Duchess of Sermoneta.[60] Vittoria Colonna, amateur painter, student of Adolfo Venturi's art history courses at the University of Rome and wife of don Leone Caetani, Duke of Sermoneta, hosted Boccioni in her villa in Pallanza in July 1916, a few days before his death.[61] Boccioni may have given the painting to the Duchess or she may have purchased it at a later date, perhaps at the time of the Boccioni retrospective in April 1922 at the Casa d'Arte Bragaglia, where, however, neither the catalogue of the show nor contemporary press reviews make it possible to reconstruct the checklist of works exhibited.[62] A statement of accounts and a note preserved in the Mattioli Archive allow us to fix the date of purchase by Gianni Mattioli (June 28, 1955), the amount paid (3,100,000 lire, plus a 10% commission for the Galleria del Milione as mediator), and the name of the seller, a certain Signora Chittaro.[63]

[1] Bergman 1962, pp. 14–15.
[2] Calvesi, Coen 1983, nos. 887 and 890–1.
[3] Longoni, May 23, 1913.
[4] Marinetti 1969, pp. 61 and 86.
[5] Marinetti, February 20, 1909.
[6] Marinetti *et al.*, April 27, 1910.
[7] Marinetti, June 15, 1913.
[8] Boccioni 1972, p. 26.
[9] Marinetti, June 15, 1913.
[10] Boccioni, April 1, 1913.
[11] Apollinaire, March 18, 1913; Warnod, March 18, 1913.
[12] Washington, DC, The National Gallery of Art: Hess 1961, pp. 58 and 327.
[13] *Les Joueurs de football*, Washington, DC, The National Gallery of Art.
[14] *L'Equipe de Cardiff, troisième représentation*, Paris, Musée d'Art Moderne de la Ville de Paris.
[15] Apollinaire, March 18, 1913.
[16] Letter from Umberto Boccioni to Gino Severini, dated March 13, 1913, in Boccioni 1971, p. 367.
[17] *Au Vélodrome*, Venice, Peggy Guggenheim Collection (The Solomon R. Guggenheim Foundation): the dating of this painting to 1912 has been convincingly demonstrated by Schmid, Weddingen 1998, pp. 229–58.
[18] *Dinamismo di un footballer*, New York, The Museum of Modern Art: Calvesi, Coen 1983, no. 895. Its earliest certain public appearance was in *London* 1914, no. 5. According to Martin (1968, p. 160), the two paintings were contemporary.
[19] *Ibidem,* p. 489, no. 884.
[20] Tommei, December 24, 1913.
[21] Calvesi, Coen 1983, no. 890.
[22] *Danza dei pederasti* and *Automobile in corsa*; Fallacara 1913, p. 370.
[23] *Florence* 1913–14, p. 21, nos. 1–2; *Rome* 1914[a], p. 23, nos. 1–2; *London* 1914, p. 25, nos. 1–2.
[24] *London* 1914, p. 23.
[25] *Rome* 1914[a], p. 23, no. 11 (*Penetrazione angolare [Bicicletta]*) and no. 18 (*Ambiente emotivo di una bicicletta*).
[26] Postcard from Ardengo Soffici to Carlo Carrà, dated September 28, 1913, in Carrà, Soffici 1983, p. 39.
[27] Letter from Umberto Boccioni to Ardengo Soffici, dated October 1, 1913, in Boccioni 1971, p. 373.
[28] Ballo 1964[a], p. 17, fig. 1; Rosci 1991, p. 46.
[29] Rosci (1991, p. 47) demonstrated that *Materia* could not have been in Boccioni's studio at the Bastioni di Porta Romana 35, where he carried out the last retouches, prior to March 1913, therefore after the painting had left for the Costanzi show. A letter from Filippo Tommaso Marinetti to Giovanni Papini, dated April 11 [1913] (Fiesole, Fondazione Primo Conti, Archivio Papini) specifies that the paintings were sent directly from Rome to Rotterdam, a fact that excludes work on the painting by Boccioni in his studio between the two shows. The Futurist paintings were sent back from Rotterdam to Milan around August 20, as is proved by Carrà's sighting of Soffici's painting *Scomposizione dei piani di un lume* hanging on the wall of Marinetti's living room, as recounted by Carrà in a letter to Soffici dated August 23 (Carrà, Soffici 1983, p. 33).
[30] Birolli 1983, p. 20.
[31] Calvesi, Coen 1983, nos. 860, 867–70.
[32] Undated letter from Umberto Boccioni to Vico Baer (but early in July 1913), in Boccioni 1971, p. 370.
[33] Carrà, September 1, 1913
[34] Letter from Ardengo Soffici to Carlo Carrà, dated July 27, 1913, in Carrà, Soffici 1983, p. 30.
[35] Boccioni, August 15, 1913.
[36] Martin 1968, p. 160.
[37] Severini 1913, p. 6.
[38] Carrà, March 15, 1913
[39] Soffici, April 15, 1913.
[40] Boccioni 1913, p. 5.
[41] *Espansione spiralica di muscoli in movimento*; *Sintesi del dinamismo umano*; *Forme uniche della continuità nello spazio*; *Muscoli in velocità*. Calvesi, Coen 1983, nos. 854–7.
[42] Boccioni, March 15, 1913.
[43] Boccioni, August 15, 1913.
[44] Boccioni 1914, p. 199.
[45] Calvesi, Coen 1983, nos. 885–94.
[46] *Ibidem*, no. 887.
[47] *Ibidem*, no. 893.
[48] *Ibidem*, no. 890.
[49] *Ibidem*, no. 888.
[50] Marinetti, June 15, 1913
[51] Calvesi, Coen 1983, no. 859.
[52] This affinity was proposed for the first time in Martin 1968, p. 160.
[53] Boccioni 1914, pp. 292–5.
[54] Paris, Centre National d'Art Contemporain Georges Pompidou: Kandinsky 1912, between pp. 98 and 99; Roethel, Benjamin 1982, no. 397.
[55] Essen, Museum Folkwang: Roethel, Benjamin 1982, no. 459; *Kandinsky* 1913, p. 12.
[56] Undated letter from Umberto Boccioni to Carlo Carrà (but after April 12, 1912), in Drudi Gambillo, Fiori 1958–62, vol. I, p. 239.
[57] Apollinaire, March 25, 1912.
[58] A letter dated March 15, 1912 was sent to Vico Baer by Boccioni from Paris: Boccioni 1971, pp. 349–51.
[59] Instead it was not in the show in Naples at the Galleria Sprovieri held at the same time, as hesitantly maintained by Calvesi, Coen 1983, no. 884: *Penetrazione angolare – bicicletta* and *Ambiente emotivo di una bicicletta* (*Rome* 1914[a], p. 23, nos. 11 and 18; *Naples* 1914, p. 25, nos. 15 and 22) are, therefore, preparatory studies.
[60] Argan, Calvesi 1953, p. 30; thus 'Duchess of Permolata,' published in *New York* 1949, p. 126, needs to be corrected.
[61] Agnese 1996, pp. 367–74.
[62] *Rome* 1992, unnumbered pages; Verdone, Pagnotta Guidetti, Bidetti 1992, pp. 380–1.
[63] Archivio Mattioli, accounting note of the Galleria del Milione, dated December 17, 1955: on June 28, 1955, the price of the *Cyclist* was debited at 3,100,000 lire plus 310,000 lire for the gallery's commission; Archivio Mattioli, account dated June 28, 1955 with the annotation by the Galleria del Milione "Suo acquisto Boccioni dalla Chittaro".

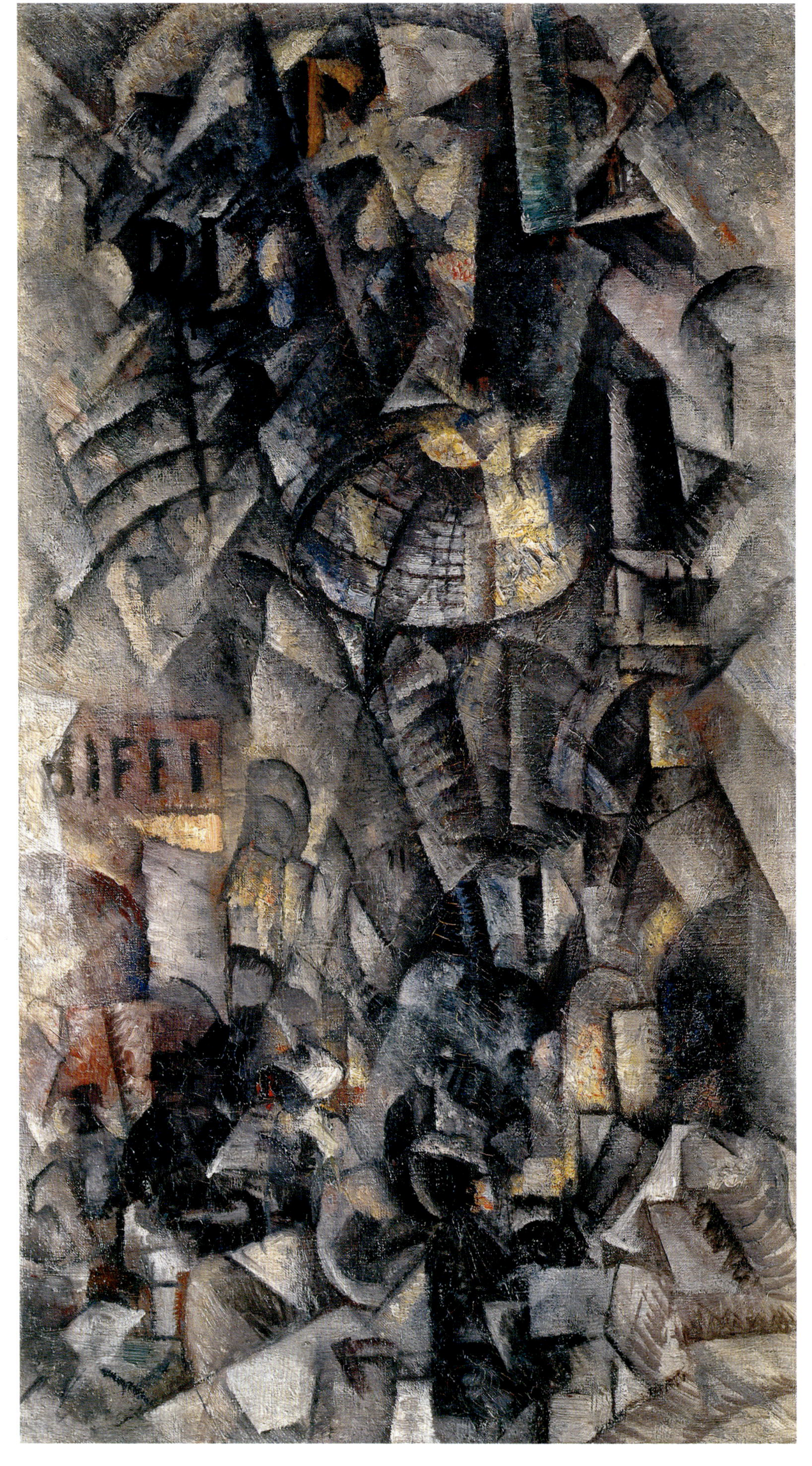

6–7

Carlo Carrà (Quargnento, Alessandria, 1881 – Milan, 1966)

The Galleria in Milan (*Galleria of Milan*)
Study for *The Galleria in Milan*, 1912

La Galleria di Milano (*Galleria di Milano*)
Studio per *La Galleria di Milano*, 1912

Cat. no. 6
Oil on canvas
91 × 51.5 cm

Provenance: property of the artist; March 1914: Alessandro Magnelli, Florence; 1950: Alberto Magnelli, Paris; February 1951: Gianni Mattioli, with the mediation of Gualtieri di San Lazzaro

Cat. no. 7
Pencil and charcoal on paper
370 × 210 mm

Inscription: *recto*, signed lower left: 'Carrà 1912'

Provenance: property of the artist; ?: Galleria del Milione, Milan; before 1953: Gianni Mattioli

Exhibitions cat. no. 6: Rome 1913, p. 23, no. 2 (*Galleria di Milano*); Rotterdam 1913, p. 20, no. 2 (*La Galleria in Milano*); Florence 1913–14, p. 223, no. 14 (*Galleria di Milano*); Rome 1937, p. 14, without cat. no.; Milan 1942[a], no. 26; Milan 1942[b], catalogue not printed; Venice 1950, p. 61, no. 25; Zurich 1950, no. 42; Milan 1952, unnumbered; Florence 1953[a], no. 10; São Paulo 1953–4, p. 8, no. 19; New York 1954, no. 21; Kassel 1955, no. 103; Rome 1955–6, p. 55, no. 10; Amsterdam 1958, no. 62; Rome 1959, no. 112; Winterthur 1959, no. 50; Munich 1959–60, no. 45; Venice 1960, p. 17, no. 66; Paris 1960–1, no. 71; New York–Los Angeles 1962, no. 76; Milan 1962[c], no. 5; Cologne 1962, no. g/29; Hamburg 1963–Frankfurt 1964, no. 31; Washington, DC 1967–Tokyo 1972, no. 13 (Washington, DC– New York), no. 12 (Brussels–Hamburg), no. 11 (Madrid–Seville), no. 13 (Kyoto–

Carrà painted *The Galleria in Milan* in 1912 after his brief trip to Paris in February of that year, a visit which put him in direct contact with the art movements of the international avant-garde. Taking as his starting point a formal structure close to that of the Cubist paintings he had seen first-hand in artists' studios and at Daniel-Henri Kahnweiler's gallery, Carrà created here a characteristic Futurist work on the subject of night life in Milan. The compact construction of the image, the rich and refined palette and, not least, Carrà's challenge to Cubism on its own terrain of the fragmentation and analysis of form immediately gave this painting the status of an outstanding example of Italian Futurist painting.

In 1912 the Galleria Vittorio Emanuele II, inaugurated with lavish ceremony in 1867, was a civic monument almost fifty years old, bound to an era of by-then obsolete post-unification values. Yet it still represented for the Futurists the venue *par excellence* symbolizing modern Milan. Strategically located between two symbols of the city, the Duomo and La Scala, it was a third pole, consecrated to commerce and fashionable society, and a thriving witness to the energy generated by city life. Its fame in this respect endured even after the turn of the century. Foreign guidebooks described it as the "most beautiful emporium in Europe,"[1] where "sparkling cafés with red couches and gold-leaf mirrors alternate in colorful abundance with shops of dazzling luxury," to be admired especially "in the evening, when everything becomes resplendent and ablaze with the light of the electric lamps."[2]

Marinetti loved the Galleria (he called it "a high glass hemisphere [...] a pleasing example of an imperious aesthetic of machinery"[3]); but above all he sensed the symbolic and propagandistic value of the Futurists' presence under its vaults. It was habitually frequented by painters and poets who strolled there (Gino Severini recalled his 1912 debut, clothed in shabby but consciously elegant dress),[4] who argued in Savini's café-restaurant where Marinetti had open credit,[5] or who sought inspiration for modern themes (Boccioni, as remembered by Marinetti, used his "sharp eyes" for studying situations and moods of the kind that appear fleetingly in Carrà's *Galleria*, such as the "perspiring intrepid waiters balancing silver sweet-dishes with ice-cream"[6]). From the summer of 1914 the Galleria was designated an ideal venue for staging interventionist demonstrations certain to attract the instant attention of public opinion and the press.

Carrà's frequenting the Galleria coincided with his conversion to the ranks of the Futurists and with the albeit modest improvement in his social status that this entailed. Before 1910, in place of the luxurious café-restaurants of the Galleria, Carrà patronized the smoky taverns near the Porta Tenaglia, crowded with anarchists and socialists, and after 1906 the student cafés near the Brera between Corso Garibaldi and Via dei Fiori Chiari.[7] As a habitué of Savini, Carrà included the Galleria in a series of paintings beginning in 1909 that represented modern Milan: Piazza Beccaria and its night lighting, Piazza della Scala with its opera-goers exiting among workers shoveling snow, Piazza del Duomo etched by its trams, the train station with its metal roof and its inmates of suffering humanity.[8]

Nevertheless, to paint the Galleria was an unusual choice in terms of recent and traditional Milanese art. In a city where the most important Italian school of perspective, the Accademia delle Belle Arti of the Brera, was operative, the Galleria was inexplicably neglected by local painters, perhaps because it was too difficult to represent, with its impenetrable light shed by the vaulted glass roof.

There are no paintings of the Galleria between 1872 (when Angelo Morbelli, coldly insensitive to its characteristic luminous aquarium-like atmosphere, painted a view of the dome and transepts,[9] fig. 6c) and 1910, when Umberto Boccioni, in *Riot in the Galleria* (fig. 6d), portrayed a night-time commotion outside the door of Savini, viewed from an angle not dissimilar to that of Morbelli's painting.[10] Boccioni's picture, executed in an up-to-date French *pointilliste* style, was exhibited in Milan twice between 1910 and 1911,[11] and was certainly known to Carrà. While Boccioni skirted the problem of the glass vault by adopting a high viewpoint, thereby crushing to the pavement the whirling vortexes of night-lifers and prostitutes, Carrà structured his composition on the provocatively direct relation of two distinct and remote planes. In the foreground is a café scene, occupying the lower part of the painting, with two groups of elegantly-dressed clients seated at tables[12] while an out-sized waiter holding a tray erupts from the right. In the second plane is the glass vault, whose luminous fragmentation, multiplied by the nocturnal lighting, impresses its scansion of chiaroscuro across the entire canvas.

In Boccioni's *Riot in the Galleria*, set late at night, no tables impede the concourses of the Galleria. Yet it was standard practice, at lunch and dinner times, for both the Biffi Restaurant (open on one side of the octagon) and Savini (facing the shortest arm of the Galleria, towards Via Ugo Foscolo) to put out tables, and not just a single row hugging the wall, such as one sees in period photographs (fig. 6a).[13]

A cartoon depicting the inside of the Galleria from the same position as Carrà's painting, published in September 1911 in the humorous weekly *L'Uomo di Pietra* (fig. 6b), shows the extent to which the prepared tables invaded the octagon, hampering pedestrian traffic. This was the cause of bitter complaint, as indicated by the acidic couplet captioning the cartoon: "L'è giust che quand i sciori hinn dree a disnà / El pubblich l'abbia minga de passà!" ("It is right that when the gentlefolk come to dine / The public has difficulty passing by!"). Carrà's *The Galleria in Milan*, with customers at the tables, the Biffi sign (written in the right sense, and thus seen from outside the restaurant), and the easily visible architectonic structures of the vault, has its own spatial logic, with implications of neither an indoors/outdoors simultaneity nor a synthesis of different moments of perception. If, in the portrayal of rich clients at the tables, there is still a hint of social polemic (comprehensible for an artist of declared Socialist leanings like Carrà), then it is no accident that the scene is set not at Marinetti's Savini, but in front of Biffi, a locale scorned by the Futurists for its traditionally more bourgeois clientele and stately atmosphere and sometimes chosen by them as the setting for their violent brawls.

The Galleria in Milan marks an important stage in Carrà's Futurist development. The artist himself, in his autobiographical memoir published in 1943, attributed to it a primary role:

Tokyo); Prato 1971, no. XI; Rome 1972, p. 115, no. 5; Paris 1973, no. 43; Milan 1973–4, no. 133b; Venice 1986, p. 139; Paris 1994–Tokyo 1996, pp. 77–8; Rome 1994–5, pp. 206–7; Milan 1995–6, p. 159; Barcelona 1996, no. 65; Hanover 2001, no. 148

Bibliography cat. no. 6: Soffici 1913, unnumbered plate (*La Galleria di Milano*); Cecchi, March 23, 1913; Letter from Giovanni Papini to Carlo Carrà, dated March 24, 1913, in Papini, Carrà, p. 342; Letter from Carlo Carrà to Giovanni Papini, dated March 7, 1913, in Carrà, Papini 2001, p. 15; Letter from Giovanni Papini to Carlo Carrà, dated March 24, 1913, in Carrà, Papini 2001, p. 16; Longhi, April 10, 1913; Pascazio 1913, p. 96; Tarchiani, December 7, 1913; Tommei, December 24, 1913; Cantù 1913, p. 138; Boccioni 1914, unnumbered plate (*Galleria di Milano*); Soffici 1914, unnumbered plate; Letters from Carlo Carrà to Giuseppe Sprovieri, dated March 29, 1914, and April 3, 1914, in Drudi Gambillo, Fiori 1958–62, vol. I, pp. 322–3 and 327; Letters from Carlo Carrà to Alberto Magnelli, dated April 23 and 30, 1914, in Abadie 1989, pp. 175–6; Franchi 1918[a], p. 47; Cecchi, May 21, 1925; Soffici 1926, p. 7; Soffici 1928, pl. 2; Lega, January 15, 1927; Bardi 1930, pl. 2; Costantini 1934, p. 198; Belli 1935, p. 129; Nicodemi 1935, p. 130; Longhi 1937, p. 9, pl. II; Anceschi, January 1, 1939; Costantini 1940, pp. 204–5; Répaci 1942, p. 575; Testori 1942, p. 6; Carrà 1943, p. 189; Pacchioni 1945, p. 46 and pl. 4; Soby 1949, p. 12; Apollonio 1950, p. 60; Carrieri 1950, pp. 50 and 62, pl. 56; Zervos 1950, p. 83; Letter from Gualtieri di San Lazzaro to Paolo Garretto, dated November 13 [1950] (Archivio Mattioli); Copy of letter from Gianni Mattioli to Gualtieri di San Lazzaro, dated November 20, 1950 (Archivio Mattioli); Letter from Gualtieri di San Lazzaro to Gianni Mattioli, dated December 4 [1950] (Archivio Mattioli); Letter from Gualtieri di San Lazzaro to Paolo Garretto, dated December 4, 1950 (Archivio Mattioli); Letter from Paolo Garretto to Gualtieri di San Lazzaro, dated December 7, 1950 (Archivio Mattioli); Letter from Gualtieri di San Lazzaro to Gianni Mattioli, dated February 26 [1951] (Archivio Mattioli); Copy of a letter from Gianni Mattioli to Gualtieri di San Lazzaro, dated February 28, 1951 (Archivio Mattioli); Ragghianti 1953, no. 9; Haftmann 1955, no. 71; Castelfranco, Valsecchi 1956, p. 30, pl. 12; Ballo 1956, no. 18; Valsecchi 1956, p. 197; Drudi Gambillo, Fiori 1958–62, vol. I, pp. 322–3, 327, 428, vol. II, pp. 294, 280, no. 16; Pacchioni 1959, pl. 11; Giedion Welcker 1959, unnumbered page; Maltese 1960, p. 295; Marchiori 1960, pp. 55–7; Haftmann 1960, vol. II, pp. 150, 159; Carrieri 1961, p. 45, pl. 58; Taylor 1961, pp. 75–9; Rosenblum 1962, p. 182; Valsecchi 1962[a], pp. 5, 12, pl. III; Bellonzi 1963, p. 88; Carli, Dell'Acqua 1964, vol. III, p. 440, fig. 523; Ballo 1964[b], p. 80; Calvesi 1967, p. 89; Mascherpa 1967, pp. 113–14, 117; Carrà 1967–8, vol. I, no. 5/12, p. 221; Martin 1968, pp. 151–2, fig. 112; Bigongiari 1970, pp. 7–8; Carrà 1970, no. 33, pl. IX; Rye 1972, pp. 51, 54; Ballo 1973[b], p. 15; Kozloff 1973, p. 170, pl. 70; Fagone 1978, p. XX; Tisdall, Bozzolla 1977, pp. 59–60; Roche-Pézard 1983, pp. 197–8, 347–8, 390–2, fig. 53; Bagatti, Vanghetti, Porto 1984, pp. 62–3; Messina, Nigro Covre 1986, pp. 316–17; Coen 1986, pp. 34 and 37; Fugazza 1988, p. 396; Schulz-Hoffmann 1988, p. 125, no. 13; Antolini 1991, p. 469; Di Genova 1993, pp. 198–9; Guzzi 1994[b], pp. 206–7; Lamberti 1995, pp. 268–9; Lemaire 1995, pp. 47, 53; Marziali 1996, pp. 170–1; Rylands 1997, p. 64; Del Puppo 2000[a], pp. 156, 169

Exhibitions cat. no. 7: Florence 1953[a], no. 104 (*La Galleria di Milano*, 1912); New York 1961–Los Angeles 1962, no. 75; Milan 1967, no. 20; Washington, DC 1967–Tokyo 1972, no. 11 (Washington, DC–Hamburg), no. 12 (Madrid–Seville), no. 11 (Kyoto–Tokyo); Düsseldorf 1974, no. 103; Venice 1986, p. 624; Paris 1994–Tokyo 1996, p. 78

Bibliography cat. no. 7: Ballo 1956, p. 14 (illus., *Studio in bianco e nero per "La Galleria"*); Drudi Gambillo, Fiori 1958–62, vol. I, p. 428, vol. II, p. 280, no. 13, p. 294; Arcangeli 1961, fig. XIX; Calvesi 1967, p. 40; Carrà 1970, no. 33; Carrà, Russoli 1977, no. 57; Carrà 1996, pp. 48–9; Rylands 1997, p. 63

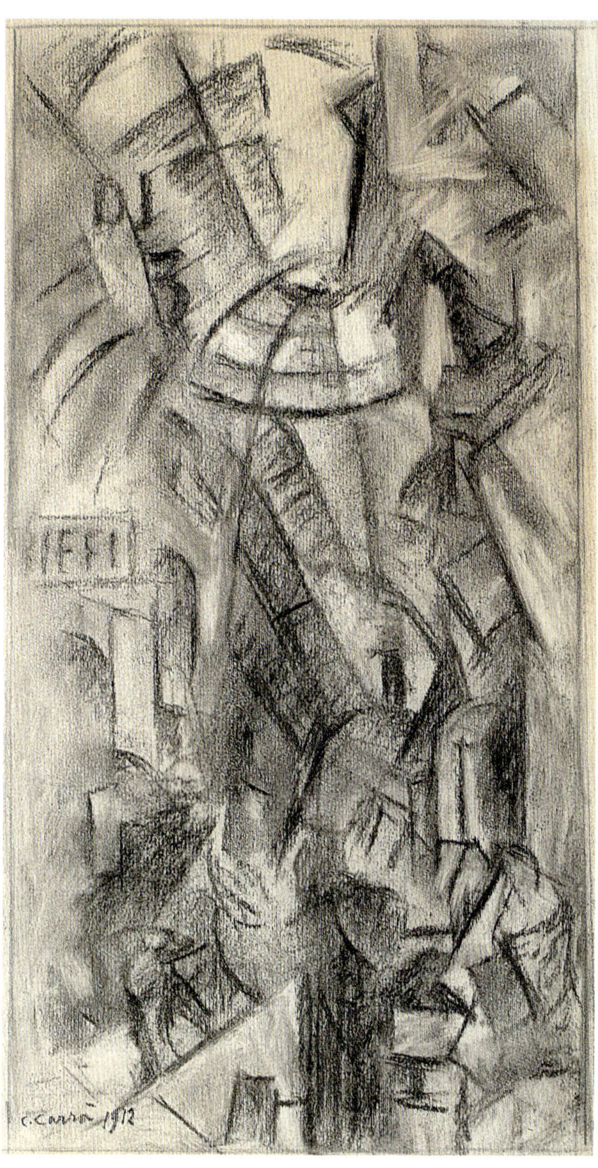

Cat. no. 7

> "I consider this painting of mine a culminating point of my artistic activity in that period. I remember that while painting it, I was so fascinated by the subject and by the guiding concepts that were leading me, that for a period I could paint nothing else."[14]

Carrà's retrospective opinion of the work was surely influenced by the judgement of Roberto Longhi, Italy's most authoritative art critic, who in 1937, a quarter of a century after the painting had been completed, recognized it as a masterpiece in a sort of canon of Futurist painting, together with that of *Rhythms of Objects*:[15]

> "... that *Galleria in Milan*, cavern of quivering stalagmites, which compared to Boccioni's passionate distortions, to Soffici's delectable cartoons during his brief Futurist 'scherzo', to Severini's childish and patient cutouts, [is] and [will remain one of the] most beautiful examples of the 'movement'; it ages [...] in fact excellently, even compared to the more famous examples of its cousin Cubism; whether they be the macabre caricatures of Picasso the dynamiter, or the most musical remnants of the upholsterer Braque."[16]

Carrà, in the early 1940s, was especially aware of the centrality of the painting in current debate about the by-then distant years of early Futurism. In the two principal books of theory on modern painting written in Italy at that time, *Cubismo e oltre* by Ardengo Soffici (1913) and *Pittura scultura futuriste (Dinamismo plastico)* by Umberto Boccioni (1914), the inclusion of an illustration of *The Galleria in Milan* implied a tribute to an Italian painting that consciously measured itself against the language of Cubism and at the same time safeguarded the elements of color, simultaneity and modern subject matter so central to the Futurist credo. International critics later stressed this singular balance between Cubism and Futurism: for a painting "clearly aimed at creating a sense of a noisy ambiance," where "the spectator can enter the picture, and the composition closes around him,"[17] Carrà chose the stylistic solution of "an animated, excellent cubism, quite thoroughly enlisting the French formal vocabulary in the service of Futurist simultaneity."[18]

The Galleria in Milan was painted at some time between February 1912 (it was not among Carrà's paintings at the first Futurist painting exhibition, at the Galerie Bernheim-jeune, Paris) and February 1913 (the date of its first exhibition, in the Futurist show in the foyer of the Teatro Costanzi in Rome[19]). Despite Marianne Martin's hypothesis (without explanation) that Carrà's first idea for the painting predated his February 1912 trip to Paris,[20] and Maurizio Calvesi's dating "certainly well into 1912,"[21] there is no secure evidence for somehow compressing this twelve-month span. Next to strongly narrative works (*Leaving the Theater*, *The Funeral of the Anarchist Galli*[22]) and paintings of a harsh disorderly expressionism, the February 1912 Paris exhibition showed one quite different painting, *Woman and Absinthe*,[23] which already demonstrated Carrà's conscious adherence to Braque's and Picasso's Cubist manner, evidently seen during his brief visit to Paris in October 1911. Carrà, together with Marinetti, Boccioni and Russolo, returned to Paris in February 1912 for the inauguration of the Futurist exhibition (though on March 22 he was already back in Milan, probably without having been present at the inauguration of the Salon des Indépendants on March 19) and this accentuated the pro-Cubist tendency in his work. He visited Daniel-Henri Kahnweiler's gallery where Braque and Picasso's works painted at Céret in the summer of 1911 were visible, and their influence was in some respects conveyed to *The Galleria in Milan*. Its composition, structured around the vertical axis, which draws to it the dense agglomeration of forms, the crowded texture of broken or curved lines etched in black, the vibrant lights and

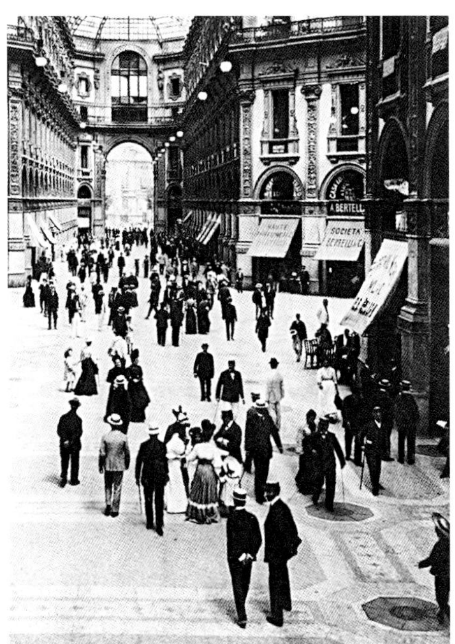

Fig. 6a. *The Galleria of Milan in 1905. Milan, Civiche raccolte fotografiche, Castello Sforzesco*

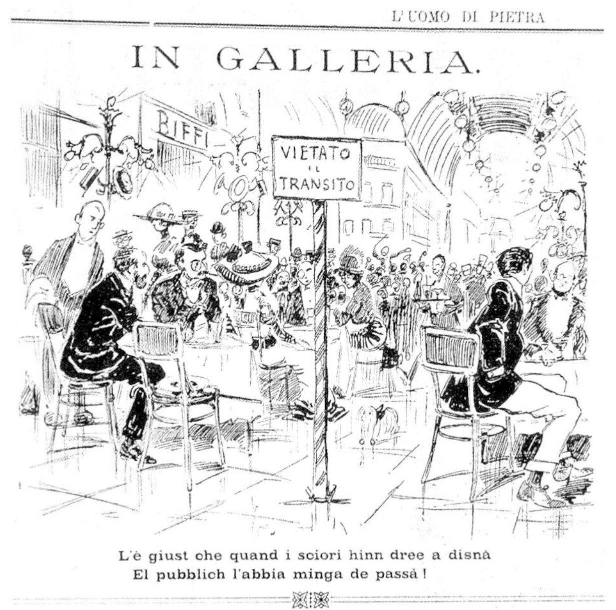

Fig. 6b. *Anonymous,* In Galleria, *in* L'Uomo di Pietra, *September 23, 1911*

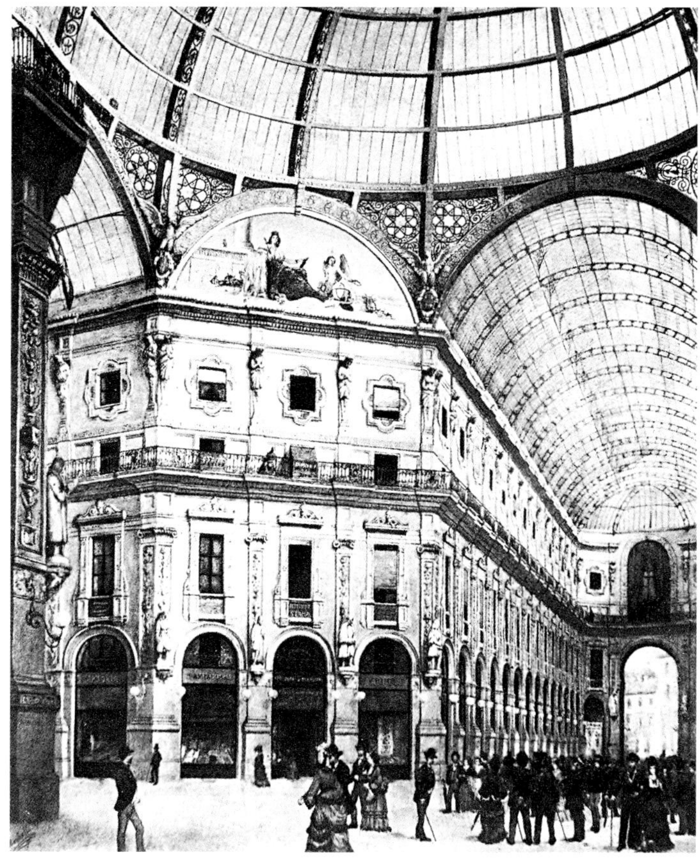

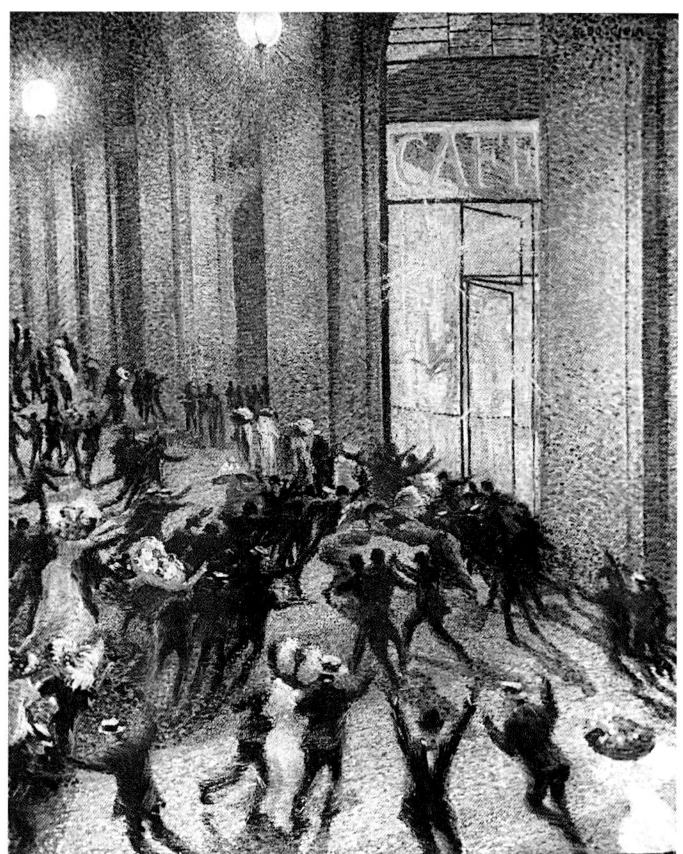

Fig. 6c. *Angelo Morbelli,* La Galleria di Milano *(*The Galleria in Milan*), oil on canvas, 1872. Milan, private collection*

Fig. 6d. *Umberto Boccioni,* Rissa in Galleria *(*Riot in the Galleria*), oil on canvas, 1910. Milan, Pinacoteca di Brera, Jesi Collection*

darks that generate the faceted surface, seems to respond to paintings by Picasso such as *The Accordionist*[24] (fig. 6e; this is comparable for the way space is materialized as well as in the snail-shell form to the right of the BIFFI sign), or *Man with a Pipe*[25] (in which the lettering may explain the insertion, in Carrà's painting, of DI and the number 3 on the Galleria vault), or paintings by Braque such as *Man with Mandolin*[26] (for the intensity of the highlights and the strong centripetal tension along the vertical axis).

However, *The Galleria in Milan* cannot be explained exclusively by Carrà's trip to Paris in February 1912; it was also the outcome of further exposure to Parisian art in the months that followed. During the summer, Boccioni asked Gino Severini to gather as much information as he could about the latest Cubist production[27] and Severini, passing through Milan, obliged with a series of reproductions keenly anticipated by the Savini Futurist group.[28] Together with the photographs, he showed them and discussed his recently completed *Blue Dancer*, now in the Mattioli Collection (cat. no. 22), in which clients of the dance hall in the background resemble the café customers in the foreground of *The Galleria in Milan* (figs. 6f–6g); moreover, Severini's analysis of broken forms, especially in the two upper corners, is similar to that adopted by Carrà. In the fall, Italian controversy over Cubism began to heat up. The first important theoretical treatment of the new art was published in October: *Du "cubisme"* by Albert Gleizes and Jean Metzinger, a copy of which was bought by Carrà and is still today in the artist's archives. The critical debate, launched the previous year by Ardengo Soffici's (unillustrated) article on Picasso and Braque,[29] now entered its most animated phase, with contributions from Henri des Prureaux, Ugo Ojetti and, once more, Soffici.[30]

The Cubist paintings Carrà saw after his return from Paris had little in common with the extreme spatial and conceptual *tabula rasa* of Picasso's or Braque's most recent art. *Du "cubisme"* more abundantly illustrated the popular Salon Cubists (Jean Metzinger, Albert Gleizes,

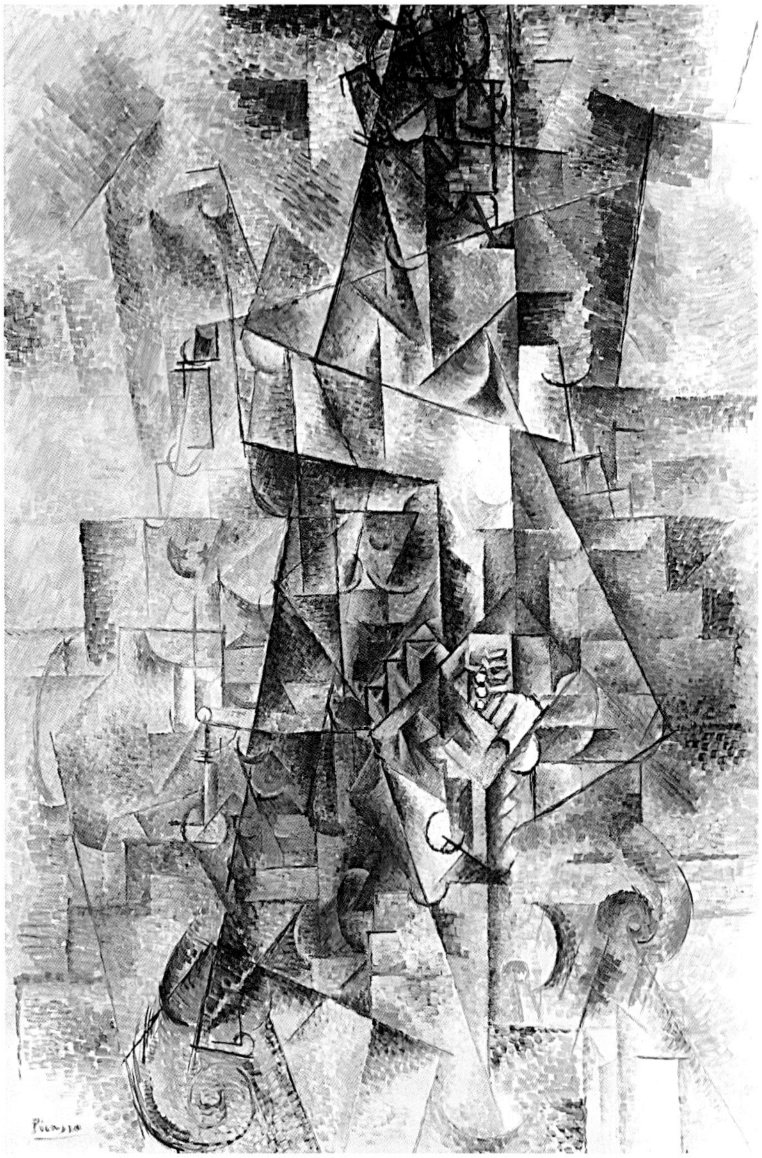

Fig. 6e. *Pablo Picasso,* L'Accordéoniste (The Accordionist)*, oil on canvas, 1911. New York, Solomon R. Guggenheim Museum, Gift of Solomon R. Guggenheim, 1937*

Fernand Léger). The names of Delaunay and Léger began to circulate,[31] while the novelties that most attracted Severini's attention at the 1912 Salon d'Automne were paintings by Metzinger, Léger and Gleizes.[32] As in the work of the latter artists, the single spatial units created by the fragmentation of form in *The Galleria in Milan* tend to recompose themselves, recompacting and generating new volumes. This phenomenon was most evident in the paintings of Fernand Léger, with their mosaics of strongly lit and shaded *tesserae*: *The Smokers*,[33] painted between 1911 and 1912, could have been seen by Carrà in February 1912 at the gallery of Kahnweiler, to whom it belonged[34] (the treatment of the upper right corner seems particularly close to *The Galleria in Milan*, fig. 6h); *The Wedding*,[35] with its numerous fragmented figures hemmed in by the setting, was exhibited at the Indépendants the same year;[36] a *Landscape* and *Houses and Smoke* (fig. 6i), with their studied alternation of curved and broken lines, were both illustrated in *Du "cubisme"* (in the same book a 1910 *Nude* by Metzinger [fig. 6j] provided an accessible and succinct example of spatial analysis).[37] Moreover, Carrà's waiter in the foreground to the right (his face, which perhaps drew too much attention to itself, is concealed with a patch of blue-black paint) is reminiscent of the tubular surfaces painted with parallel stripes in *Nudes in a Landscape*,[38] a work already exhibited and widely discussed at the 1911 Indépendants. In all of these paintings we find recognizable figures bound to their

Fig. 6f. *Detail of cat. no. 6*

Fig. 6g. *Gino Severini,* Ballerina blu (Blue Dancer), *oil on canvas, 1912, detail. Mattioli Collection, on deposit at the Peggy Guggenheim Collection, Venice*

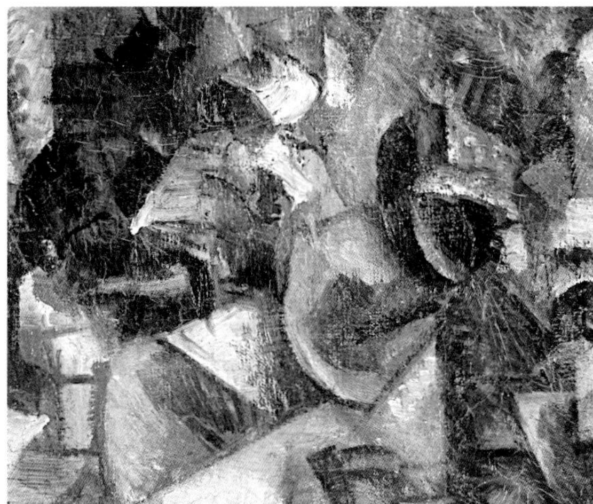

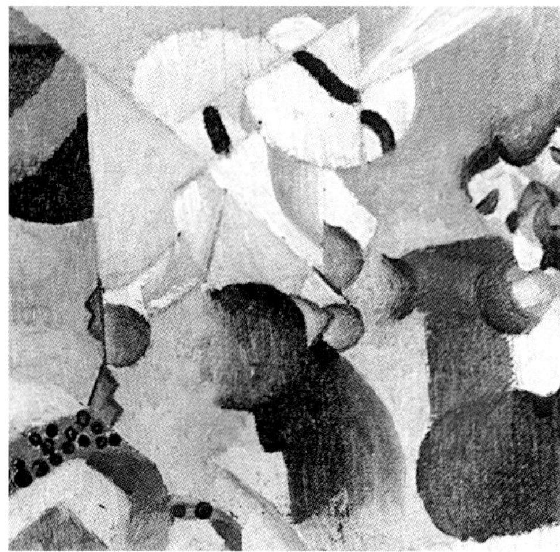

ambient with a Cubist technique of *passage* and fragmented planes of a kind that Carrà could readily adapt to his own work. If one of his goals was the "pursuit of solidity," as he confided a year later to Ardengo Soffici,[39] these images were of more use to him than those by Picasso or Braque. The more synthetic tendencies of Cubist technique and composition were better suited to Carrà's interest in color.

In *The Galleria in Milan*, on top of the over-all blue-gray tonality, he added black contour lines and then, in bold relief, the lights that impart the nocturnal atmosphere of the café, with a technique still residually divisionist (alternating stippling and impasto) and with a series of heavily-worked tonal passages in the tradition of late nineteenth-century Lombard painting: these colors ranged from yellow and pink to bright red and violet in obedience to the notion of synesthetic perception which Carrà formalized the following year in *La pittura dei suoni, rumori, colori* ("in restaurants and cafés [the sounds, noise and smells are predominantly] silver, yellow and violet").[40]

This duplication of language (an experiment with delicate, nuanced color grafted onto a Cubist grid) was what attracted the interest of Italian critics when the painting was shown together with other works by Carrà in the foyer of the Teatro Costanzi, Rome (February–March 1913, the first Futurist show to be held in Italy), and when it was shown again in late November at the 'Lacerba' exhibition in Florence. In Emilio Cecchi's view, Carrà had "the qualities of a colorist mellow, fiery and succulent, without loss of other qualities, diaphanous, glassy," though he was also "approximate, obscure" in his somewhat unthinking acceptance of Cubist theory, "in his fragmentations and reconstructions of planes and volumes."[41] This way of looking at the painting was essentially shared by all. For a group of painters known for the violence of their colors, it came as a pleasant surprise to encounter color modulations "graduated in precise tones" giving "a musical sensation, like that of a gently sustained note which then fades away"[42] and that successfully evoked "entirely the sense of oppression felt by the painter [when faced with] the architectonic muteness of the arches and [with the] depth of the cupola"[43] Arnaldo Cantù was captivated by the "shadows and lights cast by the artificial lighting on the glass panes of a livid whiteness streaked as if permeated by thin blue shivers."[44] Nicola Pascazio, writing in the periodical *Humanitas*, coined the term "Cubist Impressionism" for the painting.[45]

Roberto Longhi's reading of the painting was notable for its visual acuity. In tune with the international visual-aesthetic debate, he combined ideas sympathetic to Boccioni's anti-Cubist polemics and his awareness of the hostility of the periodical for which he was writing (*La Voce*) to Ugo Ojetti, powerful art critic of the *Corriere della Sera* and arbiter and of an official and retardataire taste, with an explanation of the painting's complex tonalities. For Longhi the richness of Carrà's tones served to dissolve visible matter:

> "Carrà is traveling the same route [of overcoming Soffici's Cubism]. Of rather Cubist tendencies is in fact *The Galleria in Milan*, a most solid painting, one might even say perspectivally structured, in which the consuming intensity of the chiaroscuro, which reduces its originally warm and luminous colors to a few particles wrapped in shadow, as if under ashes, the void expanded by the light of the overturned chasm of the dome (Ojetti passes beneath it every day, but notices nothing), and above all the peeling away of the matter in sharp acute angles lend the composition an essential constructive nature."[46]

The painting was shown in only some of the Futurist exhibitions of 1913. For example, it was exhibited in Rotterdam in May but not in the smaller selection at the 'Herbstsalon' in Berlin (where Carrà, having been invited to show only three works, sent more recent paintings).[47] It appeared again at the 'Lacerba' show, Florence, in the winter of 1913–14 but not at the Galleria Sprovieri in Rome the following February.[48] In March 1914, while Carrà was in Paris and Sprovieri was composing a list of works to exhibit at the Futurist show in Naples in May–June, *The Galleria in Milan* was sold to a Florentine collector, Alessandro Magnelli, a wealthy textile merchant and former collector of the Macchiaoli, who had admired the painting some months earlier at the 'Lacerba' show. The mediator for the sale was the collector's nephew, the young painter Alberto Magnelli, who had been in Paris with Carrà in March. Carrà proudly announced to Sprovieri on March 29 that the painting had been bought by a "young gentleman, [...] a fervent admirer of Futurism, [who] bought a Picasso painting of the latest period and a sculpture by Archipenko *Caroussel Pierot* [*sic*] which was on exhibition at the Indépendants."[49] The canvas was shipped from Rome to Florence towards mid-April[50] and its sale price was paid to the artist within the month. In his 1943 autobiography Carrà recorded both the price (750 French francs, much less therefore than the 1500 Dutch florins, equal to 3120 French francs, which had been the asking price the previous year in the catalogue of the Rotterdam exhibition[51]) and the detail that the first installment had enabled him to extend his stay in Paris in the spring of 1914.[52]

The fact that *The Galleria in Milan* had entered a private collection in Florence meant that it was not shown over the next decade in exhibitions that defined the canon of Carrà's painting: the one-man show at the Galleria Paolo Chini (December 1917–January 1918), with paintings exclusively from Milanese collections, and the gallery dedicated to Carrà at the 1925 Rome Biennale. However, awareness of the painting was maintained by Florentine writers as well as by scholars and friends who visited the Magnelli Collection. In a nearly thirty-year period (from 1914 to 1942, coinciding with the critical eclipse of historical Futurism) it was exhibited only once, at the Galleria di Roma in 1937.[53] Yet its critical history gave it special status in the history of the Italian avant-garde, endowing it with the capacity, despite its Futurist appearance, of anticipating the core motifs of Carrà's post-1920 art. A hint of this manifested itself at the height of the Metaphysical period (Raffaello Franchi in *La Raccolta* in 1918 noted its ability to convey "the intense pleasure of a harmony for its own sake, the ultimate, classic [pleasure] that many people show they understand"[54]). But its critical status established itself later, in the 1920s. Emilio Cecchi, for example, who in 1925 was pulling together the threads of nineteenth-century Tuscan painting in the quest for a tenuous link to the early twentieth century, perceived in *The Galleria in Milan* clear signs of Carrà's shift towards an art of landscape rich in lush natural tones:

Fig. 6h. *Fernand Léger,* Les Fumeurs (The Smokers)*, oil on canvas, 1911–12. New York, Solomon R. Guggenheim Museum*

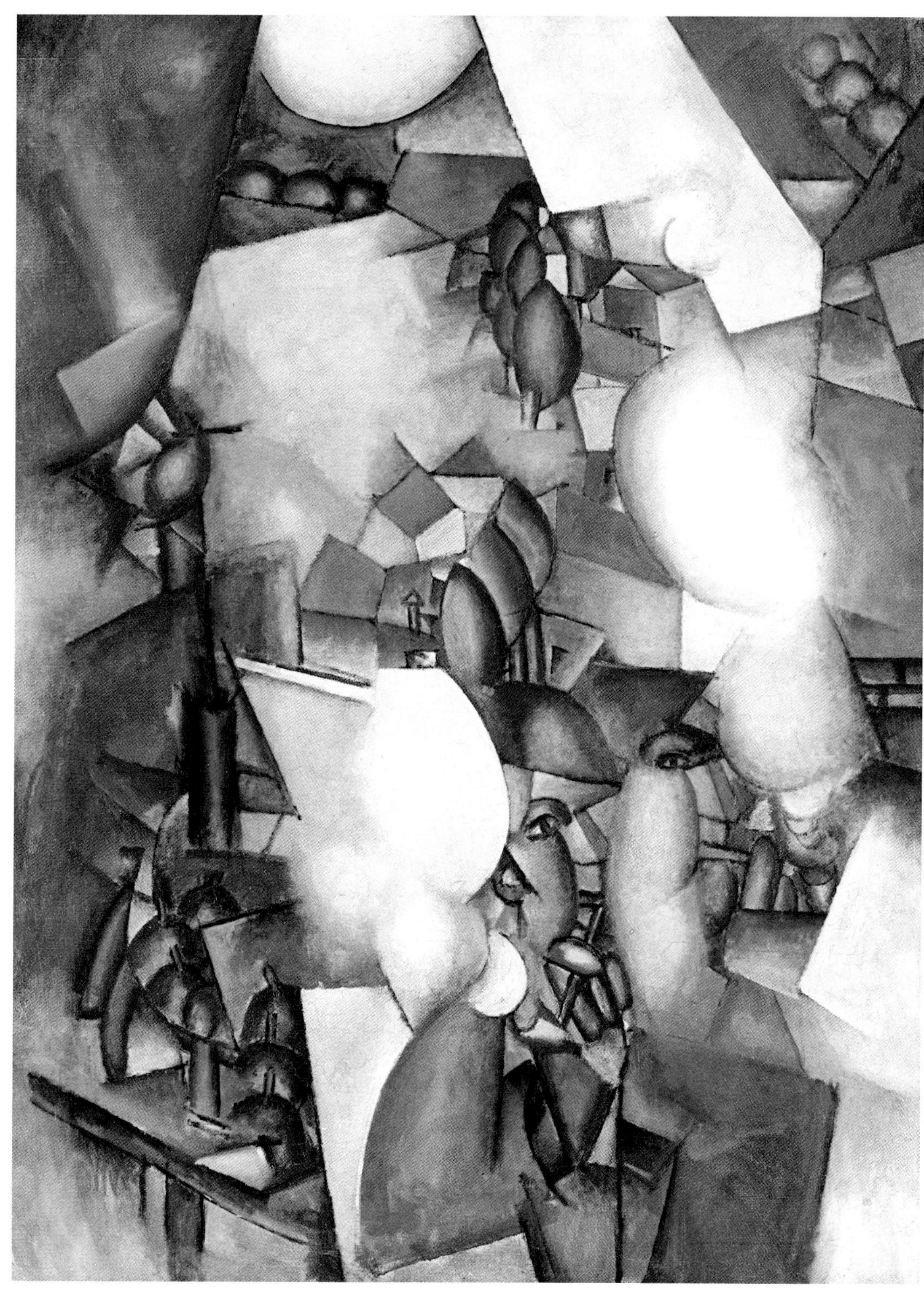

> "Taking the most healthy part, that could approximately be called *cubist*, of the first and best Futurism, he picked up and left; and that was final. Meanwhile, his palette was already the same as it is today; it suffices to recall *The Galleria*, with its quiet range of blues, ash-colors and green, to understand generically in terms of their color what are the landscapes painted in Valsesia and on the lakes."[55]

At the de Chirico–Carrà–Merello show in 1926 at the Galleria Pesaro in Milan, the work, though not on exhibit, was mentioned in the catalogue's introduction by Ardengo Soffici, now a convinced supporter of a burdensome nationalistic *rappel à l'ordre*, as a landscape fundamental to the history of painting of the second decade of the century. In Carrà, the Futurist,

> "... the vigor of the stroke, the dramatic play of chiaroscuro, the grandiosity of arabesque; or the solidity of the impastos, the refinement of the color relations, the mysterious richness of the spatial architecture, all reach a truly high degree. To a very high degree, unsurpassed by any of us, in this kind of pictorial expression, attains a *Galleria in Milan*, a masterly piece, a plastic symphony of browns, reds, turquoises and silvery whites, which is still the positive paragon of how Futurism could be of service to an artist of depth, who could never be content, as his colleagues were, with astonishing the public with superficial masquerades, but who stood his ground and strove, even by those revolutionary means, to reach the *pictorial* essence, the basis and hidden foundation of our true tradition."[56]

A year later another Tuscan painter, Achille Lega, a confirmed ultra-nationalist with ideological convictions diametrically opposed to those that engendered *The Galleria in Milan*, wrote of it in *Selvaggio* as "the most important of Futurist paintings":

> "... it shall remain the definitive work of this period, with an essential constructive sense, novel in its color scheme of whites, of browns, of reds and of deep blues: a painting which shall survive and with the passing of time be ever more important."[57]

In the years that followed, *The Galleria in Milan* was to be perceived equally as an anticipation of the new classical realism ("the breaking up of the component parts of the image is disposed in such a way as to give nonetheless the sense of perspective of a view seen in depth and where the cerebral intuition of forms materializes in logical sequences"[58]) and, in an environment of fierce hostility to the Novecento movement, as a free impression of light effects, with "rays from Gothic stained glass observed by the whirling eyes of a tightrope walker plunged into a void"[59] as its subject.

By the time *The Galleria in Milan* was shown in Carrà's solo exhibition at the 1950 Venice Biennale, it belonged to the collection of Alberto Magnelli in Paris.[60] Negotiations for Gianni Mattioli's purchase of the painting, conducted by Ettore Gian Ferrari and Paolo Garretto, began even while the Biennale was still open. The sale was concluded only in March of the following year, thanks to the intervention of Gualtieri di San Lazzaro, a Florentine art dealer living in Paris since the 1930s who was particularly active in promoting Italian avant-garde art internationally in the second postwar era. The agreed price was 750,000 French francs (circa 1,376,000 lire),[61] which Mattioli felt was "in reality somewhat steep"[62] but which he paid, given the painting's historical importance and the fact that he was competing with the Pinacoteca di Brera.[63]

Fig. 6i. *Fernand Léger,* Maisons et fumées (Houses and Smoke)*, in A. Gleizes and J. Metzinger,* Du "cubisme"*, 1912*

Fig. 6j. *Jean Metzinger,* Nu (Nude)*, in A. Gleizes and J. Metzinger,* Du "cubisme"*, 1912*

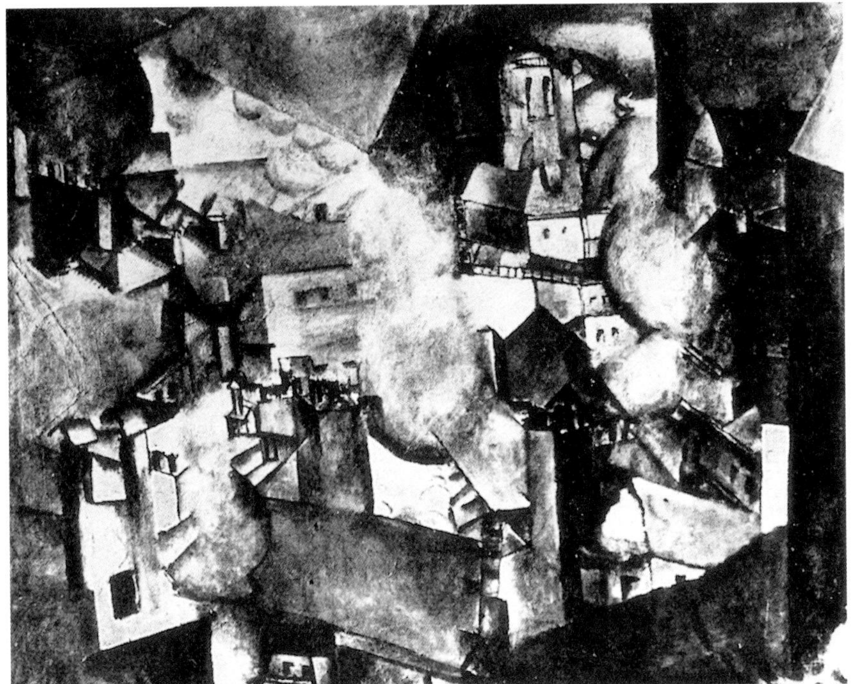

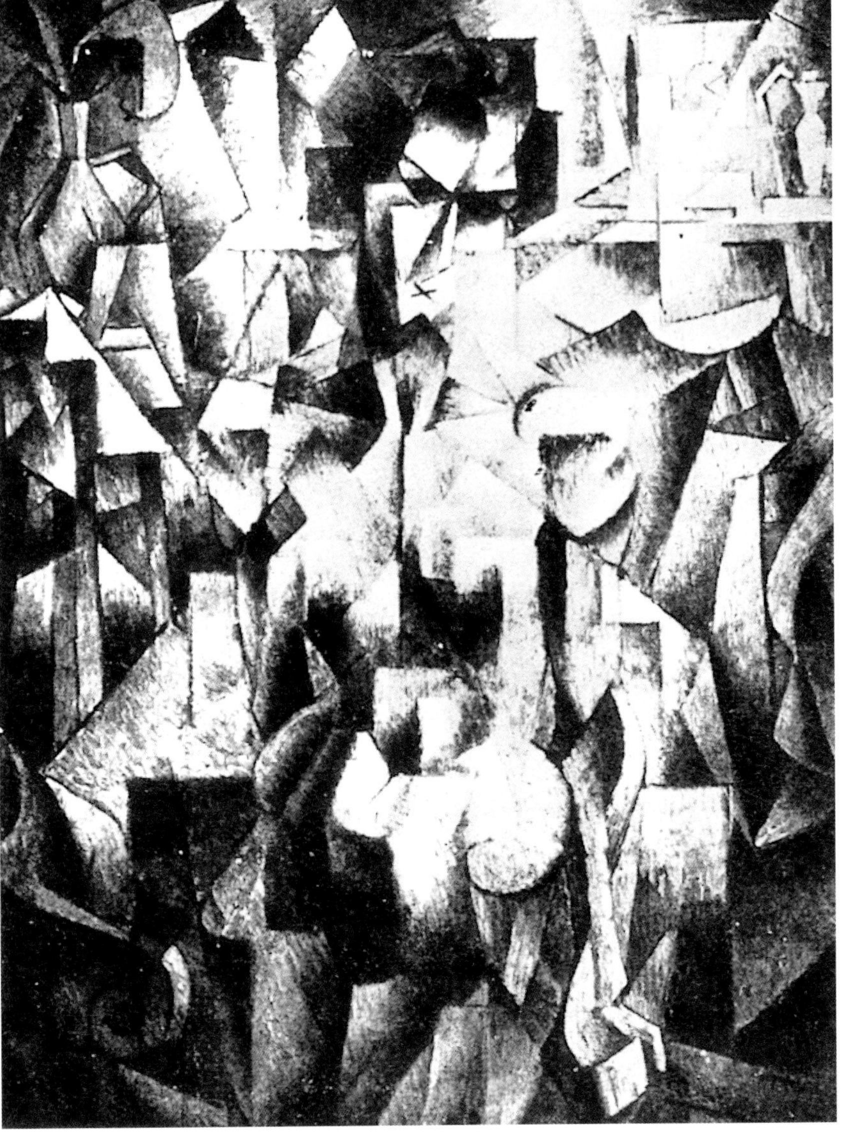

The Mattioli Collection includes a preparatory drawing for *The Galleria in Milan* (cat. no. 7), acquired prior to 1953[64] from the Galleria del Milione.[65] This and a second, more schematic drawing[66] are the only surviving studies for *The Galleria in Milan*. (A drawing published as *The Milan Galleria* in the catalogue of the 1949 exhibition of Italian art in New York[67] and dated 1913 should according to this writer be excluded, even as an autonomous development out of the painting, and should be read in the horizontal sense.[68])

The sequence of the two drawings and their relationship to the oil painting represent still unresolved problems. Philip Rylands has observed how "both drawings confirm that Carrà's composition and many of the forms were already decided prior to beginning work on the canvas" and that "a greater complexity of forms across the whole of the finished painting was a natural consequence of working on more than double the scale when he took up his oil paints."[69] Certainly, compared to the painting, there are fewer details down the left and right sides in the Mattioli drawing (especially in the lower left, which evolved in a quite different way in the oil). This may result from Carrà's formal progression, which began with models such as Braque and Picasso's paintings of 1911: the frame in the drawing does not truncate forms that would otherwise appear to continue beyond, but rather the marks thin out to the point of disappearing before reaching the limits of the image. Moreover, the drawing sketches in a looser way some important passages that shape the light (such as the scythe-shaped forms that enliven the roof in the upper center of the painting) and many of the black edging lines (the motif like a snail shell to the right of the BIFFI sign is missing, which in the painting is developed from a window in the drawing). Compared to the painting the drawing gives a more legible architectonic impression of the whole (a complex spatial system generated by the crossing of the four nave-like spaces under the central cupola whose rational structure is, in the painting, convulsed by the fragmenting effect of light). In the lower part of the drawing, however, the café scene is relatively confused. The table on the left, set back from the foreground, where two clients sit, is barely sketched; the positioning of the two figures seated at the foreground table is unclear; the odd waiter who enters from the right corner is less distinct, even if one can make out the head which was to be obliterated in the painting. The execution of the canvas had therefore the effect both of multiplying the quantity of visual information and of rendering it less legible by the techniques of fracturing and sub-dividing the forms by light.

The nature of the drawing in the Carrà Collection is quite different, with a more cryptic *facture* and sketchy chiaroscuro. It appears to be a derivation of the Mattioli drawing, and provides no additional information about the evolution of the painting, nor does it present us with variants later discarded during execution. It transcribes the first drawing but in a more summary manner: in the lower part the rich chiaroscuro texture of the Mattioli drawing is ignored and the spatial tension between the foreground and the far distance, that is one of the painting's strengths, is missing. The principal difference between this and the Mattioli painting and drawing consists in the suppression of the café people in the foreground scene, thus distorting the meaning of the image. It was quite probably an independent exercise, based on the Mattioli drawing but without any direct relation to the sequence of studies for the painting.

[1] *Venedig, Mailand* 1899, p. 171.
[2] Holtzmann 1899, p. 137.
[3] Marinetti 1969, pp. 11–12.
[4] Severini 1946, p. 158.
[5] Zuccoli, May 11, 1913.
[6] Marinetti 1969, p. 107.
[7] Carrà 1943, pp. 67, 79, 90–1, 108.
[8] Carrà 1967–8, vol. I, nos. 2/11, 4/09, 3/09, 1/11: *Milan* 1987, no. 10.
[9] Private collection: Gambi, Gozzoli 1982, no. 111/g.
[10] Milan, Pinacoteca di Brera, Jesi Collection; Calvesi, Coen 1983, no. 657.
[11] Coen 1988, pp. 93–4.
[12] Immediately identified as such by early reviewers (Civ., February 22, 1913); therefore not merely "passers-by" (Guzzi 1994[b], p. 206).
[13] Beltrami 1906, p. 95; Titta Rosa 1970, fig. 12; Zanchi, Bottelli undated, p. 39.
[14] Carrà 1943, p. 189.
[15] *Ritmi di oggetti*, Milan, Pinacoteca di Brera, Jesi Collection; Carrà 1967–8, vol. I, no. 7/11.
[16] Longhi 1937, in Longhi 1984, p. 42.
[17] Taylor 1961, p. 75.
[18] Kozloff 1973, p. 170.
[19] *Rome* 1913, p. 23, no. 3.
[20] Martin 1968, p. 151.
[21] Calvesi 1967, pp. 89–90.
[22] *Uscita da teatro*, *I funerali dell'anarchico Galli*: respectively London, Estorick Collection (Carrà 1967–8, vol. I, no. 4/09) and New York, The Museum of Modern Art (*ibidem*, vol. I, no. 8/11).
[23] *La donna e l'assenzio*: private collection (*ibidem*, vol. I, no. 4/11).
[24] Ex Paul Guillaume Collection, now New York, Solomon R. Guggenheim Museum: Daix, Rosselet 1979, no. 424.
[25] *L'Homme à la pipe*, Fort Worth, Kimbell Art Foundation: Daix, Rosselet 1979, no. 422.
[26] *Homme à la mandoline*, formerly owned by Kahnweiler, now New York, The Museum of Modern Art: Worms de Romilly, Laude 1982, no. 99.
[27] Undated letter from Umberto Boccioni to Gino Severini (but June–July 1912) in Drudi Gambillo, Fiori 1958–62, vol. I, p. 246.
[28] Severini 1946, p. 157.
[29] Soffici, August 24, 1911.
[30] Des Prureaux, October 31, 1912; Ojetti, November 8, 1912; Soffici, November 21, 1912.
[31] Ojetti, November 8, 1912; Soffici, November 21, 1912.
[32] Letter from Gino Severini to Umberto Boccioni, dated October 29, 1912, in Lorenzoni 1995, p. 271.
[33] New York, Solomon R. Guggenheim Museum: Green 1976, p. 37.
[34] Cooper, Tinterow 1983, p. 206.
[35] *La Noce*: Paris, Musée National d'Art Moderne de la Ville de Paris; Green 1976, p. 42.
[36] Spate 1979, p. 245; Messina, Nigro Covre 1986, p. 308; Carrà missed seeing the show but could easily have obtained a reproduction of the painting.
[37] Gleizes, Metzinger 1912, unnumbered plates.
[38] *Nus dans un paysage*, Otterlo, Rijksmuseum Kröller-Müller; Green 1976, p. 21.
[39] Letter from Carlo Carrà to Ardengo Soffici, dated July 14, 1913, in Carrà, Soffici 1983, p. 25.
[40] Carrà, September 1, 1913.
[41] Cecchi, March 23, 1913.
[42] Tarchiani, December 7, 1913.
[43] Tommei, December 24, 1913, p. 7.
[44] Cantù 1913, p. 138.
[45] Pascazio 1913, p. 96.
[46] Longhi, April 10, 1913.
[47] *Berlin* 1913, p. 14, nos. 72–4.
[48] Despite the fact that, as we know from two letters from Carrà to the dealer Giuseppe Sprovieri (dated March 29, 1914 and April 3, 1914), the painting was in Rome at Sprovieri's gallery at the time the show opened: Drudi Gambillo, Fiori 1958–62, vol. I, pp. 322–3 and 327.
[49] Letter from Carlo Carrà to Giuseppe Sprovieri, dated March 29, 1914, *ibidem*, vol. I, pp. 322–3.
[50] Letter from Carlo Carrà (from Milan) to Alberto Magnelli, Paris, dated April 23, 1914, in Abadie 1989, p. 175.
[51] Roche-Pézard 1983, p. 197.
[52] Carrà 1943, p. 189.
[53] *Rome* 1937, p. 14; contrary to a statement by Guzzi (1994[b], p. 206), the reproduction in Bardi 1930, pl. 2, does not testify to its presence in a contemporary show at the Galleria Bardi, where only works from after 1922 were shown (Milan, Archivio Storico Civico, Biblioteca Trivulziana, Fondo Bardi, Cartella 9, carta 3196: *Distinta dei quadri esposti da Bardi*; with thanks to Paolo Rusconi for this reference).
[54] Franchi 1918[a], p. 47.
[55] Cecchi, May 21, 1925.
[56] Soffici 1926, p. 7.
[57] Lega, January 15, 1927, p. 3.
[58] Nicodemi 1935, p. 130.
[59] Répaci 1942, p. 575.
[60] *Venice* 1950, p. 61, no. 25.
[61] Archivio Mattioli, letter from Gualtieri di San Lazzaro to Gianni Mattioli, dated February 26, 1951 (*Appendix I*, document no. 70).
[62] *Ibidem*, copy of the letter from Gianni Mattioli to Gualtieri di San Lazzaro, dated February 28, 1951 (*Appendix I*, document no. 71).
[63] *Ibidem*, letter from Paolo Garretto to Gualtieri di San Lazzaro, dated December 7, 1950 (*Appendix I*, document no. 66).
[64] *Florence* 1953, no. 104.
[65] Archivio Mattioli, in the relevant file for the work.
[66] Carrà Collection: Carrà, Russoli 1977, no. 58.
[67] *New York* 1949, p. 127.
[68] As printed, correctly, in Carrà, Russoli 1977, no. 68.
[69] Rylands 1997, p. 62.

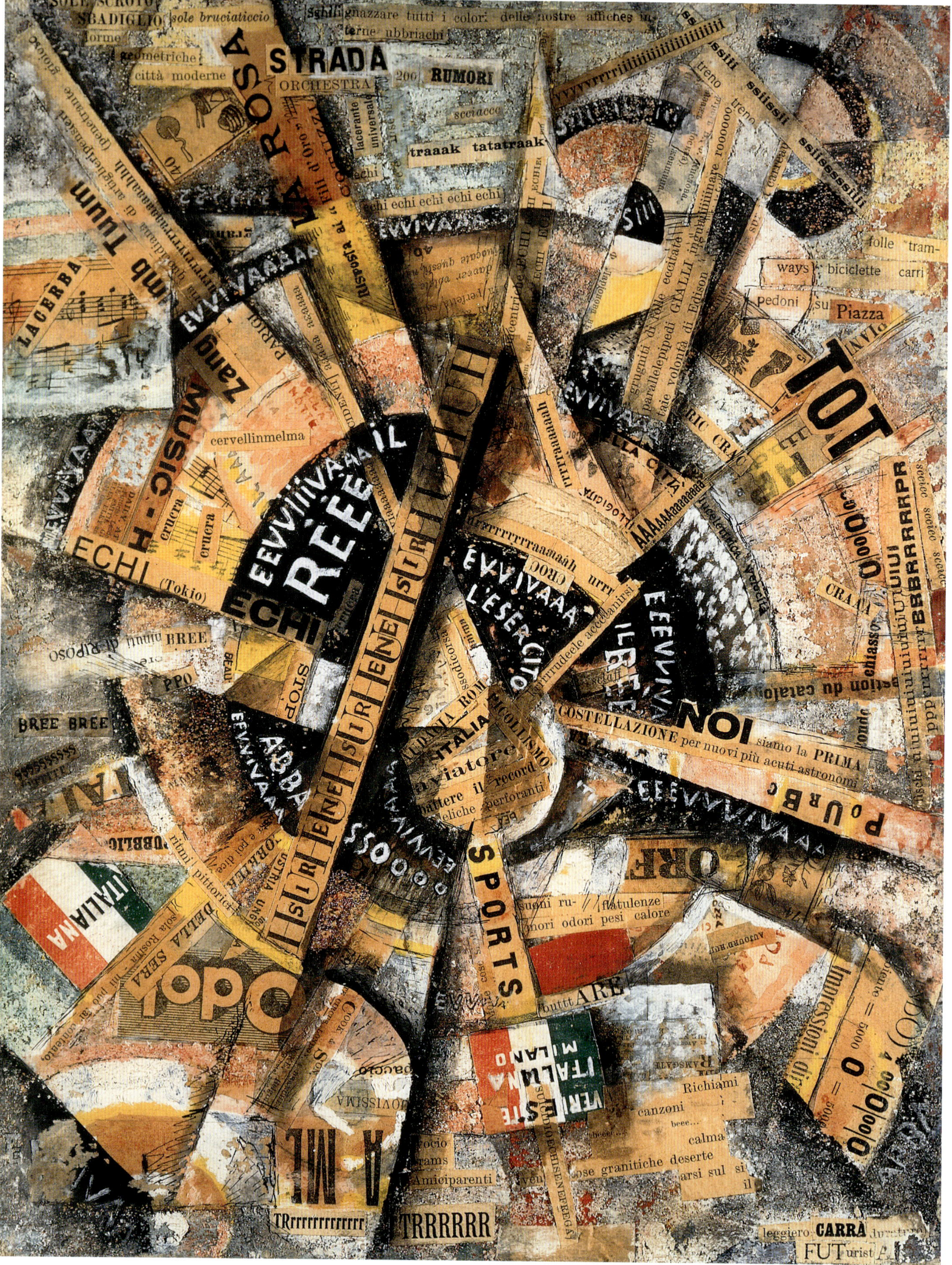
SBADIGLIO
sole bruciaticcio
Sghignazzare tutti i colori delle nostre affiches
città moderne
LA ROSA
STRADA
ORCHESTRA
RUMORI
traaak tatatraak
echi echi echi echi
LACERBA
folle tram-
ways biciclette carri
pedoni su Piazza
TOT
MUSIC-H
cervellinmelma
ECHI
(Tokio)
EVVIVAAA
L'ESERCITO
BREE BREE
COSTELLAZIONE per nuovi più acuti astronomi
NOI
siamo la PRIMA
battere il record
SPORTS
suoni ru- flatulenze
mori odori pesi calore
ITALIANA
ITALIANA
MILANO
Richiami
canzoni
calma
cose granitiche deserte
TRrrrrrrrrrrrr
TRRRRRR
CARRA
FUTurist

8

Carlo Carrà

Interventionist Demonstration (*Pictorial-poem*; *The Patriotic Holiday*; *Patriotic Holiday-Pictorial Poem*; FREEWORD PAINTING-*Patriotic Holiday*; *Patriotic Holiday-Freeword Painting*)

Manifestazione Interventista (*Poema-pittorico*; *La festa patriottica*; *Festa patriottica-poema pittorico*; DIPINTO PAROLIBERO-*Festa patriottica*; *Festa patriottica-dipinto parolibero*; *Dimostrazione interventista*), 1914

Tempera, pen, mica powder, paper glued on cardboard
38.5 × 30 cm

Inscription: *recto,* signed lower right, with printed papers: 'leggiero CARRÀ duraturo FUTuristA'

Provenance: property of the artist; ?: Galleria Bolzani, Milan; June 1950: Gianni Mattioli

Exhibitions: Milan 1917–18 (*Festa patriottica-dipinto parolibero*); Zurich 1950, no. 43 (*Dimostrazione interventista*, 1913); Florence 1953[a], no. 8 (*Manifestazione interventista*, 1913); New York 1954, no. 22 (*Manifestation for Intervention*, 1914); Rome 1959, no. 109 (*Manifestazione interventista*, 1914); Winterthur 1959, no. 52 (*Manifestazione interventista*, 1914); Munich 1959–60, no. 47 (*Manifestazione interventista*, 1914); Venice 1960, p. 17, no. 68 (*Manifestazione interventista*, 1914); New York 1961–Los Angeles 1962, no. 81 (*'Free-word' painting-Patriotic Celebration*, 1914); Milan 1962, no. 8 (*Manifestazione interventista*, 1914); Washington, DC 1967– Tokyo 1972, no. 20 (*'Free word' Painting-Patriotic Celebration*, 1914); Brussels–Berlin 1971, no. 15 (*Manifestazione interventista*, 1914); Milan 1972, no. 13 (*Manifestazione interventista*, 1914); Paris 1973, no. 45 (*Manifestation interventionniste ou Peinture-mots en liberté*, 1914); Milan 1973–4, no. 133c (*Manifestazione interventista*, 1914); Düsseldorf 1974, no. 106 (*Manifestazione interventista*, 1914); Berlin 1977, no. 3/401 (*Manifestazione interventista*, 1914); Frankfurt 1977–78, no. 3/401, (*Manifestazione interventista*; *Dipinto parolibero-Festa patriottica* 1914); Venice 1986, p. 163 (*Manifestazione interventista*, 1914); Paris

Carlo Carrà's *Interventionist Demonstration* (henceforth *Festa patriottica*, given the history of its title) is a landmark of his career, and one of the signature works of Futurism, both of art and of writing. It is a mixed media collage-painting, composed entirely of patches of color and words, primarily cut and pasted from printed sources, which create "a boisterous Futurist synaesthesia of sights, smells and sounds."[1] As such, "with *Festa patriottica* the Futurist effort to synthesize the resources of poetry and the visual arts reached its apogee."[2] In this "plastic abstraction of civic tumult," form and content support multiple levels of meaning and interpretation.[3] On one level it is an emblem of Futurist *parole in libertà* (free wordism), that when closely read proves to be a painted manifesto as well. It proclaims the primacy of Futurist experimentalism, and suggests echoes of Futurist influence spreading world-wide.

As a painted textual appropriation, Carrà's collage should be contextualized in terms of writing as much as art. It is one of the prime examples of Filippo Tommaso Marinetti's definition of *parole in libertà*. Indeed the title of one of Marinetti's own early *parole in libertà*, *Zang Tumb Tuum* (of March 1914), is cited along an axis towards the upper left corner of *Festa patriottica*. (Marinetti's onomatopoeic title imitates the sound and echo of cannon fire in the Balkan fighting.) Carrà was inventive in the language he applied to this mixed media work. Thus he referred to it first in correspondence as a "poema pittorico" ("pictorial poem") and subsequently as *Dipinto parolibero* when first published in the Futurist periodical *Lacerba*.[4] Another letter, from Marinetti to Soffici, co-signed by Carrà, shows that the *Lacerba* title and capitalization were carefully specified.[5] It indicates as well the presence of Marinetti around its naming, in seeking invented terms to define its hybrid status.

Festa patriottica is closely related to Carrà's own and others' *parole in libertà*, most of which appeared in *Lacerba*. Seven articles from this magazine's pages account for almost every printed source selected and pasted into the collage. Indeed the artist was literally dependent on *Lacerba*'s layout as the source for the most typographically complex and experimental words and sounds in the work. The latter include the extended 'rrrraaahhhh's at the center, "vocio grugniti di folle eccitate" ("grunting clamor of excited crowds") from his own manifesto *1900-1913. Bilancio* (fig. 8a), as well as 'TRrrrrrrrr' at the lower center, and 'traaak tatatraak' at the upper center, both car noises from Marinetti's *Correzioni di bozze + desideri in velocita*.[6] Carrà also clipped from Marinetti, *Dunes* (fig. 8b), Boccioni, *Man + Valley + Mountain*, Gus-

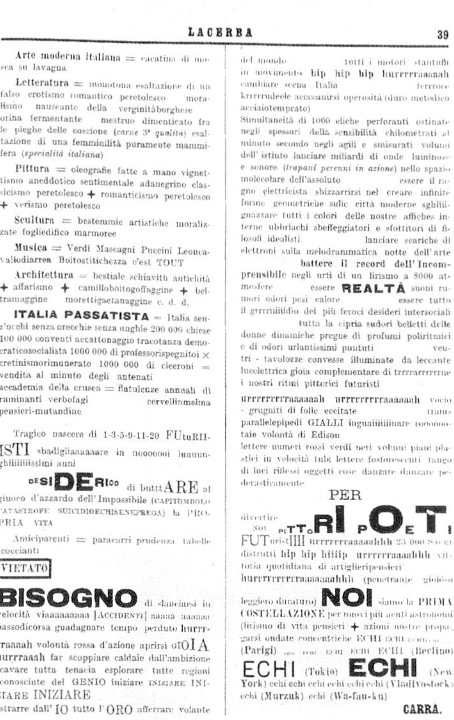

LACERBA 39

Arte moderna italiana = cacatina di mosca su lavagna

Letteratura = monotona esaltazione di un falso erotismo romantico peretolesco moralismo nauseante della verginitàborghese orina fermentante mestruo dimenticato fra le pieghe delle coscione (*carne 3ª qualità*) esaltazione di una femminilità puramente mammifera (*specialità italiana*)

Pittura = oleografie fatte a mano vignettismo aneddotico sentimentale adanegrino classicismo peretolesco + romanticismo peretolesco + verismo peretolesco

Scultura = bestemmie artistiche moralizzate fogliedifico marmoree

Musica = Verdi Mascagni Puccini Leoncavallodiarrea Boitostitichezza c'est TOUT

Architettura = bestiale schiavitù antichità + affarismo + camilloboitogoffaggine + beltramaggine morettigaetanaggine c. d. d.

ITALIA PASSATISTA = Italia senz'occhi senza orecchie senza unghie 200 000 chiese 100 000 conventi accattonaggio tracotanza democraticosocialista 1000 000 di professorispegnitoi × cretinismorimunerato 1000 000 di ciceroni = vendita al minuto degli antenati
accademia della crusca = flatulenze annuali di ruminanti verbofagi cervellinmelma pensieri-mutandine

Tragico nascere di 1-3-5-9-11-20 FUtuRIIISTI sbadigliaaaaaare in nooooooi luuuunghiiiiiiiissimi anni

DESIDERIco di buttARE al giuoco d'azzardo dell'Impossibile (CAPITOMBOLO CATASTROFE SUICIDIOECHISENEFREGA) la PROPRIA VITA

Amiciparenti = paracarri prudenza tabelle scoccianti

VIETATO

BISOGNO di slanciarsi in velocità viaaaaaaaaa |ACCIDENTI| aaaaa aaaaaa passodicorsa guadagnare tempo perduto hurrrraaaah volontà rossa d'azione aprirsi GIOIA hurrraaah far scoppiare caldaie dall'ambizione scavare tutta tenacia esplorare tutte regioni sconosciute del GENIO iniziare INIZIARE INIZIARE INIZIARE
estrarre dall'IO tutto l'ORO afferrare volante del mondo tutti i motori stantuffi in movimento **hip hip hip hurrrrraaaaah** cambiare scena Italia ferroce krrrrudeele acceccanirsi operosità (duro metodico acciaiotemprato)
Simultaneità di 1000 eliche perforanti ostinate negli spessori della sensibilità chilometrati al minuto secondo negli agili e smisurati volumi dell'istinto lanciare miliardi di onde luminose e sonore (*trapani perenni in azione*) nello spazio molecolare dell'assoluto essere il ragno elettricista sbizzarrirsi nel creare infinite forme geometriche sulle città moderne sghiiiignazzare tutti i colori delle nostre affiches interne ubbriachi sbeffeggiatori e sfottitori di filosofi idealisti lanciare scariche di elettroni sulla melodrammatica notte dell'arte **battere il record dell'Incomprensibile** negli urti di un lirismo a 8000 atmosfere essere **REALTÀ** suoni rumori odori pesi calore essere tutto il grrriiiiidio dei più feroci desideri intersociali tutta la cipria sudori belletti delle donne dinamiche pregne di profumi poliritmici e di odori urlantissimi puntuti ventri - tavolozze convesse illuminate da leccante lucelettrica gioia complementare di trrrarrrrrne i nostri ritmi pittorici futuristi

urrrrrrrraaaaaah urrrrrrrrraaaaaah vocio - grugniti di folle eccitate trams parallelepipedi GIALLI inguaiiiiiinare rooooootaie volontà di Edison
lettere numeri rossi verdi neri volumi piani plastici in velocità tubi lettere fosforescenti tango di luci riflessi oggetti cose danzare danzare pederasticamente

PER divertire noi PITTORI POETI FUTuristIIII urrrrrrraaaaahhh 23 000 Sacri distrutti hip hip hiiiip urrrrraaaahhh vittoria quotidiana di artiglieripensieri
hurrrrrrrrraaaaaaahhh (penetrante gioiosa leggiero duraturo) **NOI** siamo la PRIMA COSTELLAZIONE per nuovi più acuti astronomi (lirismo di vita pensieri + azioni nostre propagarsi ondate concentriche ECHI ECHI echi echi (Parigi) echi echi ECHI ECHI ECHI (Berlino) ECHI (Tokio) **ECHI** (New York) echi echi echi echi echi echi (Vladivostock) echi (Murzuk) echi (Wa-fan-ku)

CARRA.

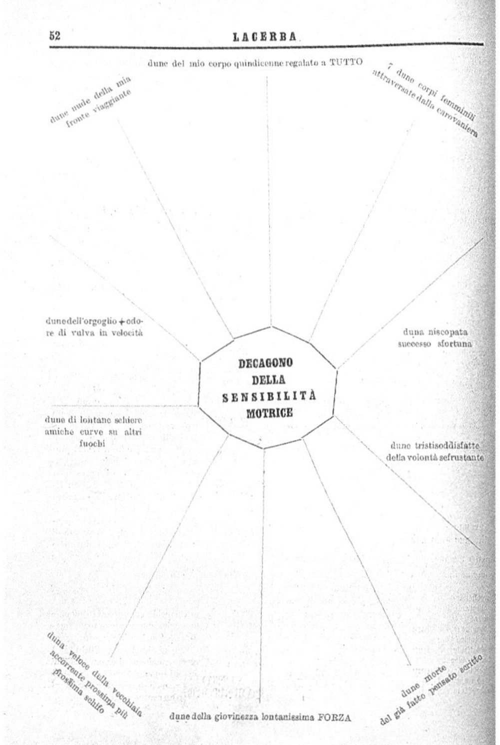

52 LACERBA

dune del mio corpo quindicenne regalato a TUTTO

dune nude della mia fronte viaggiante

7 dune corpi femminili attraversate dalla carovaniera

dunedell'orgoglio + odore di vulva in velocità

duna niscopata successo sfortuna

DECAGONO DELLA SENSIBILITÀ MOTRICE

dune di lontane schiere amiche curve su altri fuochi

dune tristisoddisfatte della volontà sefrustante

duna veloce della vecchiaia accorrente prossima più prossima schifo

dune della giovinezza lontanissima FORZA

dune morte del già fatto pensato scritto

tave Five, *Sports*, Soffici, *Stroll*, and Cangiullo, *Evenings in Honor of Yvonne*.[7] Together they offer a cross-section of the themes and authors of experimental *parole in libertà* which became prevalent in the dynamically redesigned *Lacerba* of 1914. Carrà's own involvement is underscored by the nineteen different writings and manifestos he contributed to *Lacerba* from 1913–14. Somewhat surprisingly, this was the most of any Milanese Futurist, one more than even Marinetti himself.[8] They speak to Carrà's commitment to *parole in libertà* as an independent pursuit at this moment.

Thus it is telling that as a composition *Festa patriottica* is closest not to other Carrà collages, but rather to two examples of his *parole in libertà* likewise from 1914: *Report of a Milanese Nightwalker* (fig. 8c) and *Thirteen Introspections* (*Tredici introspezioni*). Both have strongly centered designs, concentric circles crossed with radiating linear spokes. Both evoke the urban center, the signs, posters and sounds of the multinational city. *Report* is based on a late night stroll through Milan's Galleria, and includes a running total of other people encountered, from fifteen prostitutes to one Englishman. Like *Festa patriottica* it includes bits of sheet music, place names, snatches of foreign words, numerals and the like.[9] And in both, multifarious themes are united as perceptions of the central author.

These two *parole in libertà*, along with *Festa patriottica*, were influenced by an early image poem by Guillaume Apollinaire entitled 'Lettre-Océan,' published in *Les Soirées de Paris* of June 15, 1914 (fig. 8d) and hailed in *Lacerba* the following month. Alan Windsor has convincingly argued that Carrà would have been aware of Apollinaire's new experiment in calligrammes, itself inflected by Marinetti's theory and practice of *parole in libertà*.[10] 'Lettre-Océan' contains two relevant images: one of twelve radiating linear spokes, the other of concentric circles, both suggesting signals emanating from the telegraph station atop the Eiffel Tower. In certain specific sounds, notably the wailing 'Hou Hou Hou' of the siren, 'Lettre-Océan' specifically anticipates *Festa patriottica*. In the latter Carrà modified a printed 'UHUHUH' sound by cutting off the first U, and then intermittently hand-lettering the word *sirene* to specify the sonic source. And as we will see, Carrà also adopted the metaphor of

1990–1, p. 183 (*Manifestazione interventista*, 1914); Vienna 1993–Frankfurt 1994, no. 8 (*Manifestazione interventista*, 1914); Barcelona 1996, no. 72 (*Manifestazione interventista*, 1914)

Bibliography: Letter from Carlo Carrà to Ardengo Soffici, dated June 23, 1914, in Carrà, Soffici 1983, pp. 58–9 (*Poema-pittorico*); Letter from Carlo Carrà to Ardengo Soffici, dated July 4, 1914, *ibidem*, p. 60 (*La festa patriottica*); Letter from Carlo Carrà to Ardengo Soffici, dated July 11, 1914, *ibidem*, p. 60 (*Poema pittorico*); Letter from Carlo Carrà to Gino Severini, dated July 11, 1914, in Drudi Gambillo, Fiori 1958–62, vol. I, p. 341 (*Festa patriottica-poema pittorico*); Letter from Filippo Tommaso Marinetti to Gino Severini, dated July 15 (1914), in Pacini 1970, p. 26; Letter from Gino Severini to Carlo Carrà, dated July 19, 1914, in Carrà, Severini 1983, p. 295; Letter from Filippo Tommaso Marinetti to Ardengo Soffici, dated July 21 (1914), in Drudi Gambillo, Fiori 1958–62, vol. I, pp. 341–2 (*DIPINTO PAROLIBERO [Festa patriottica]*); Letter from Gino Severini to Carlo Carrà, dated July 22, 1914, in Carrà, Severini 1983, p. 296; *Lacerba*, August 1, 1914, illus. (*DIPINTO PAROLIBERO [Festa patriottica]*); Letter from Bruno Bolzani to Gianni Mattioli, dated June 17, 1950 (Archivio Mattioli); Letter from Gianni Mattioli to Bruno Balzani, dated June 19, 1950 (typewritten copy, Archivio Mattioli); Ragghianti 1953, p. 9 (*Manifestazione interventista*); Drudi Gambillo, Fiori 1958–62, vol. I, pp. 341–2, vol. II, p. 289, no. 43 (*Manifestazione interventista*); Pacchioni 1959 (*Manifestazione interventista*, 1915); Carrieri 1961, p. 150, pl. 62 (*Manifestazione interventiva*); Seitz 1961, p. 27; Taylor 1961, pp. 109–11; Rosenblum 1962, p. 187 and note 131; Pierre 1966, pp. 32 and 158; Calvesi 1967, p. 164; Martin 1968, pp. 193–4, fig. 195 (*Dipinto parolibero-Festa patriottica*); Carrà 1967–8, vol. I, no. 8/14 (*Festa Patriottica*); Apollonio 1970, no. 94; Carrà 1970, no. 52 (*Manifestazione interventista [Festa Patriottica]*); Pacini 1970, p. 26; Rye 1972, pp. 90–1; Kozloff 1973, pp. 207–13; Lista 1973, p. 320; Windsor 1977, pp. 144–52; Bohn 1979, pp. 246–71; Argan 1977, p. 200, fig. 36; Tisdall, Bozzolla 1977, pp. 176 and 187; Carrà, Soffici 1983, pp. 58–60; Roche-Pézard 1983, pp. 441–4; Bohn 1986, pp. 9–14, 24–8; Perloff 1986, pp. 54, 61–4, 77, fig. 2.7; Poggi 1992, pp. 25, 223–5; Lista 1993, pp. 54–5; Stoss 1993, p. 16; Bohn 1994, pp. 670–81; Fossati 1995, pp. 53–4; Marziali 1996, pp. 172–3; Orban 1997, pp. 52, 81–2; Rylands 1997, p. 66; Humphreys 1999, pp. 66–7; Del Puppo 2000ᵃ, pp. 164–5; Shell 2000, pp. xxii, xxiii, 62–119, 399; Poggi 2002, pp. 731–4, 748, fig. 11 (*Patriotic Festival*)

sound waves or signals radiating from a central beacon. Equally suggestive are Apollinaire's phrases 'Viva le Roy' and 'Evviva il Papa,' which closely anticipate the 'Eevviiivaaa il Rèèè,' 'Evvivaaa l'Esercito' shouts that Carrà painted around the center of his work.[11]

The collage's format reinforces these connections to literature. It is not on canvas but rather a paper-based support, and its size (38.5 × 30 cm) is only slightly larger than a typical book page. It was first published in the pages of *Lacerba*, in the context of other *parole in libertà*, before it was exhibited in an art gallery. Interestingly, it is signed not by hand, but rather by the printed papers 'leggiero CARRÀ duraturo FUTuristA' ('lighthearted Carrà durable Futurist') pasted at the lower right.

The work also bears comparison to a word-drawing by Gino Severini called *Danza Serpentina*, published in *Lacerba* of July 1, 1914 (fig. 8e). This immediately elicited a letter from Carrà, who was struck by the similarity to his own recently-completed *Festa patriottica.*[12] Severini's 'graphic poem' also drew positive comment from Apollinaire and Marinetti.[13] It included strong centered vectors and a jumble of complex word-associations.

There are hints of Carrà's 1913 manifesto *La pittura dei suoni, rumori e odori* (*The Painting of Sounds, Noises and Smells*) in Severini's enumerated bright colors ('rosso, viola, verde, verdissimo' ['red, violet, green, very green']) and the words 'luce calore odore' ('light heat smell'). There are also, for Severini, unusually bellicose allusions to a 'Palla Mauser' and to the sound of gun fire.

Carrà's collage was first exhibited in Milan under the title *Festa patriottica (dipinto parolibero)* in 1917. One should also note that Carrà did not find it appropriate to include it in *Guerrapittura* of 1915. This anthology of writings and drawings included twelve 'disegni guerreschi' ('war drawings') among them the collage *Pursuit* (cat. no. 9). Despite this clear

Fig. 8a. *Carlo Carrà,* 1900–13. Bilancio, *in* Lacerba, *February 1, 1914*

Fig. 8b. *Filippo Tommaso Marinetti,* Dune (Dunes), *in* Lacerba, *February 15, 1914*

Fig. 8c. *Carlo Carrà,* Rapporto di un nottambulo milanese (Report of a Milanese Nightwalker), *ink and collage on paper, 1914. Milan, private collection*

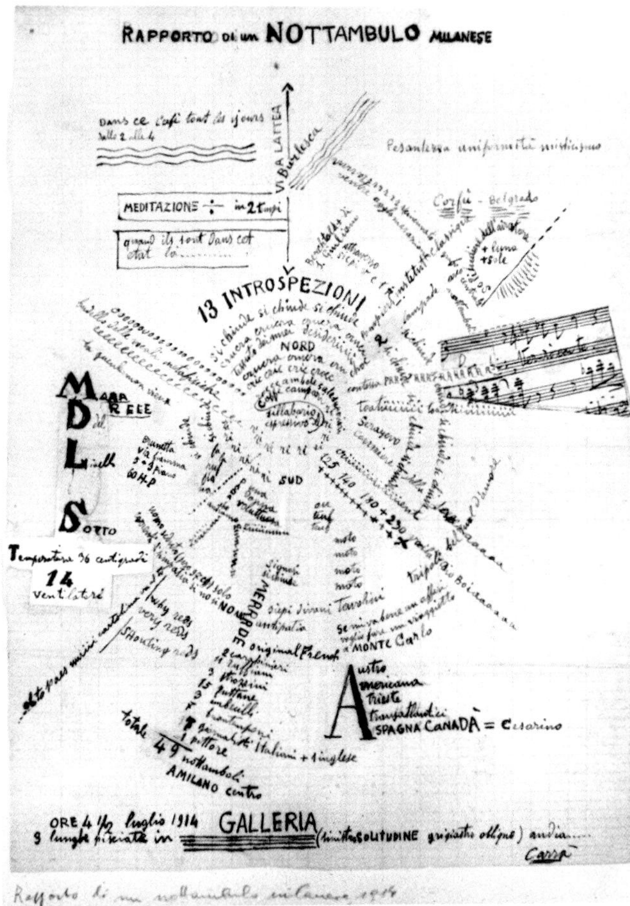

documentation, *Festa patriottica* has since World War II been more frequently entitled *Manifestazione interventista*.[14] The contrasting titles reflect the significant split between what can be surmised of the context and intention when the collage was made, versus the context of its early public reception. Many historians and critics have not taken the trouble to consider exactly when in 1914 the collage was created, and have incorrectly assumed that it was a belligerent statement made after the outbreak of war. In fact it was made shortly before hostilities were declared, and thus before a call for intervention would have been relevant.

This is the view Willard Bohn has detailed repeatedly, most recently proposing that the collage was largely made in the last two weeks of June 1914. He suggests it may refer to a national (and nationalist) holiday, the 'Festa dello Statuto' of early June, which celebrated Italian unification, as the initial stimulus for what Carrà referred to as his 'tumulto cittadino' ('civic tumult'). This view is shared by Fanette Roche-Pézard.[15] She notes that the work is patriotic, and Irredentist, without being specifically Interventionist. More recently Oliver Shell has elaborated on this view, connecting the work to rioting that broke out in the 'Settimana Rossa' ('Red Week') following a shooting in Ancona during the 'Festa dello Statuto' of June 7, 1914.[16]

Thus the collage includes at the lower right an Irredentist banner referencing Trieste, then controlled by Austro-Hungary (whose name appears at the lower left, next to the siren sound) and long a sore point with the Italians. Some of the more suggestive phrases like '[vitto]ria quotidiana di artiglieripensieri' ('daily victory of the artillerythoughts') at the upper left also lend a militaristic mood. When published in *Lacerba* on August 1, 1914, *Festa patriottica* coincided with Germany's first declaration of war, against Russia, followed two days later by France. Marinetti immediately began to advocate intervention in the Futurist circle. He successfully sought to "transform *Lacerba* into a political newspaper with the sole aim of

Fig. 8d. *Guillaume Apollinaire,* Lettre-Océan, *in* Les Soirées de Paris, *June 15, 1914*

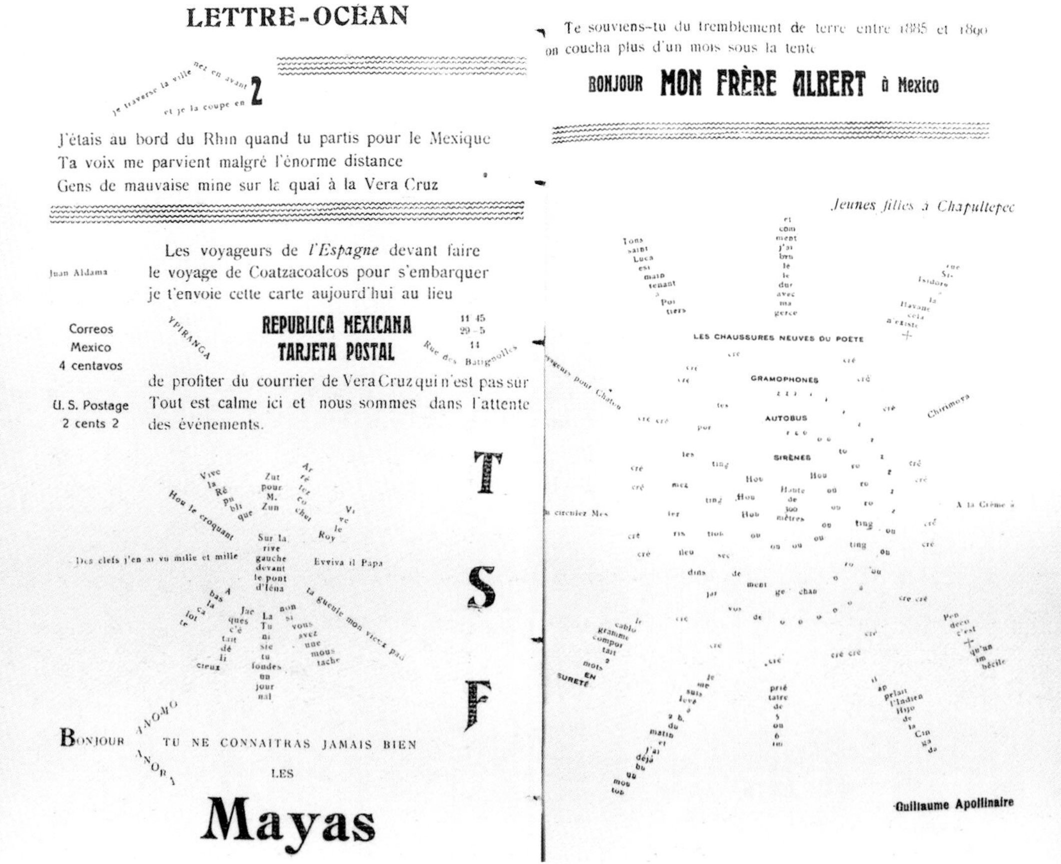

Fig. 8e. *Gino Severini,* Danza serpentina *(Serpentine Dance), in* Lacerba, *July 1, 1914*

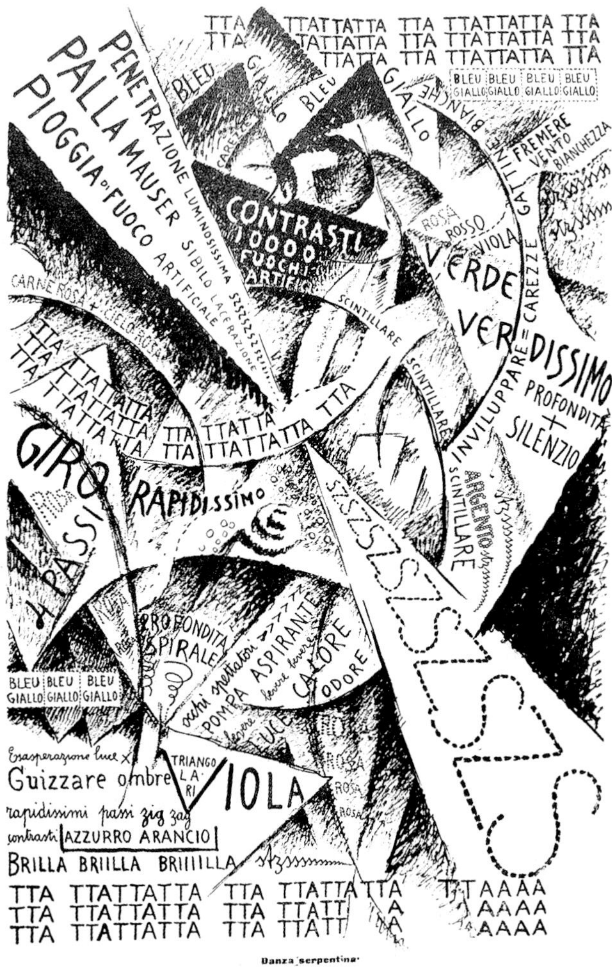

preparing the Italian climate for the war with Austria."[17] As received, *Festa patriottica* soon became an unintentional poster for Italian intervention. Indeed it seemingly anticipated the Futurist protests at the Teatro Dal Verme, September 18–19, 1914, with their cries of 'viva l'esercito' ('long live the army'). There Marinetti waved an Italian flag, while an Austrian one was torn up. As a result, the word 'TOT' prominent at the upper right of *Festa patriottica* has been misunderstood as a German word: an implicit cry for 'death' to the German-speaking Austrians. In fact, as Bohn has demonstrated, it is the commercial name of an anti-heartburn pill manufactured in Milan.[18] The same word appears, more clearly postered to the side of a building, in Carrà's drawing *Down the Street* (*Per la strada*, 1913). As such, it is a contemporary commercial design, like the Odol toothpaste or mouthwash logo that is placed diagonally across from it (fig. 8f). These examples suggest the role played by advertising and mass media as part of his 'tumulto cittadino.' To Shell the "swirling fantasy of urban commodity culture" including these health products implies a broader social hygiene, "a paradigm of political consensus and nationalist unity."[19]

The center of the collage highlights the words 'aviatore / battere il record' ('aviator / beat the record'). At this time the pioneers of flight captured the public imagination, including that of the Cubists Braque and Picasso (with their allusions to the Wright brothers) as well as, somewhat later, Mario Sironi. Throughout these years adventurous pilots competed in meets for the highest altitude, as well as the longest time in the air, creating records which were successively broken. Bohn suggests that there may have been flights in connection with the 'Fe-

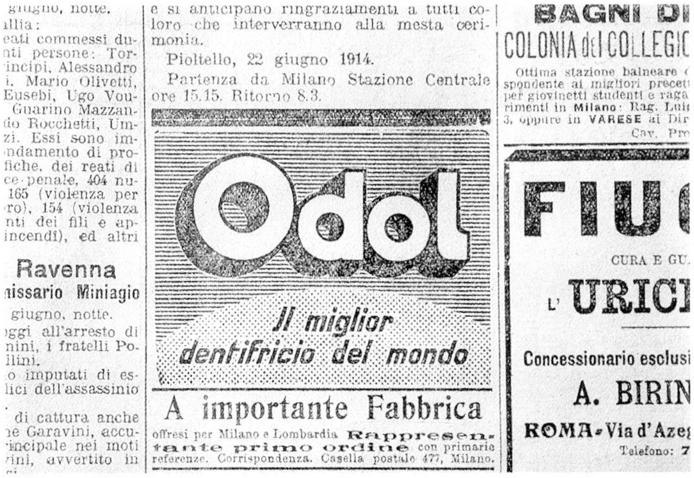

Fig. 8f. *Advertisement for Odol toothpaste, in* Corriere della Sera, *June 22, 1914*

sta dello Statuto,' thus generating a 'pilot's eye' overhead view for the collage. In this reading the flattened pictorial field is analogized to a map of Carrà's city of Milan, with a central square (Piazza del Duomo) and radiating tram lines. (Carrà had painted a 1909 Divisionist view of the Piazza del Duomo choked with yellow trams and crowds.) Longtime owner Gianni Mattioli believed to the contrary that it was a view in this square looking upwards, as leaflets flutter to the ground.[20]

On April 1, 1914 Mario Betuda had published 'Looping the Loop' in *Lacerba*, a *parole in libertà* evoking a stunt pilot's spirals in flight. But there are more telling associations to aviators. Another is that the collage evokes a head-on view of an airplane propeller, with the radiating spokes suggesting its whirling spin. This gains credence with comparison to a very large and well-known aviation painting of early 1914: Robert Delaunay's *Tribute to Blériot* (fig. 8g). At its lower left is a partly abstracted image of an airplane seen head-on, its upright propeller stilled. Yet its circular motion is suggested with the swirling colored disks he often painted. Delaunay's monumental canvas was his major submission to the spring 1914 Salon des Indépendants, where it garnered the favorable response of Apollinaire, among others. The French poet wrote of its "labyrinths of swirling futurism,"[21] terms that the visiting Carrà and Soffici would have noted. They had journeyed to Paris at just this moment, with this Indépendants exhibition a focal point of their itinerary. As a theme of contemporary life and technology — Louis Blériot was lionized in 1909 as the first to fly the English Channel — it was already of a Futurist-type.

Indeed, Carrà this same year produced a *parole in libertà* in direct homage to Blériot, shaped like his monoplane, with a propeller in front (fig. 8h). Its word-shapes include references to 'Looping' and 'spirale,' thus rhyming with the concentric spins of *Festa patriottica*, as well as Betuda's example. The words 'Parigi' and extended 'ecco's also recur, strongly suggesting that one reading of the 'aviator's record' at the center of *Festa patriottica* is as an allusion to Blériot's historic flight across the Channel.

On another level the 'aviators' are the Futurists themselves, pioneers of new horizons. This is underlined in Carrà's extensive pasting of phrases from his manifesto 'Bilancio,' initially published as a summary of the development and achievement of Futurism (fig. 8i). This is the source for 'aviatore/ battere il record' which in the manifesto is clearly analogized to Futurist art. The same is true of the prominent phrase 'NOI siamo la PRIMA COSTELLAZIONE per nuovi più acuti astronomi' ('WE are the FIRST CONSTELLATION for new sharper astronomers'; figs. 8i–8j), extending as a strong spoke from the center to the right, where 'Noi' is the Futurist group. The reference to COSTELLAZIONE recalls the resounding metaphor closing the Founding Manifesto: "Ritti sulla cima del mondo noi scagliamo, una volta ancora la nostra sfida alle stelle!..." ("Erect on the summit of the world, once again we hurl defiance to the stars...") while it also anticipates the *Ricostruzione futurista dell'Universo* (*Futurist Reconstruction of the Universe*). This universe centers on a Futurist 'sole bruciaticcio' ('burning sun,' upper left of *Festa patriottica*), radiating its influence over the artistic planets in its orbit.

As the manifesto 'Bilancio' itemizes, Futurism's impact spread worldwide, as far afield as Russia (where Marinetti had recently lectured), New York and Tokyo. The smaller and larger 'echi' repeated in the clippings suggest lesser or greater degrees of Futurist influence, with various cities including Paris named. At the same time the typography conveys loudness or volume. Thus the concentric circle design is a metaphor not only of many sounds echoing across the city, melded with the aviator's whirling propeller, but also the worldwide resonance of the Futurist style. On this level it is not only the *aviatore* but also the Futurists ('NOI') who embodied the central words 'ITALIA AUDACIA ROMPICOLLISMO' ('Italy Audacity Foolhardiness'). Carrà's collage is thus a proud manifesto, proclaiming Italian Futurism as the new sun, and the Futurist artists as the audacious astronomers of a new artistic Universe.

As a word-image collage, its immediate impact was on the pasted papers of Dada artworks and typographic design. Some works of Berlin Dada even share the collage manifesto

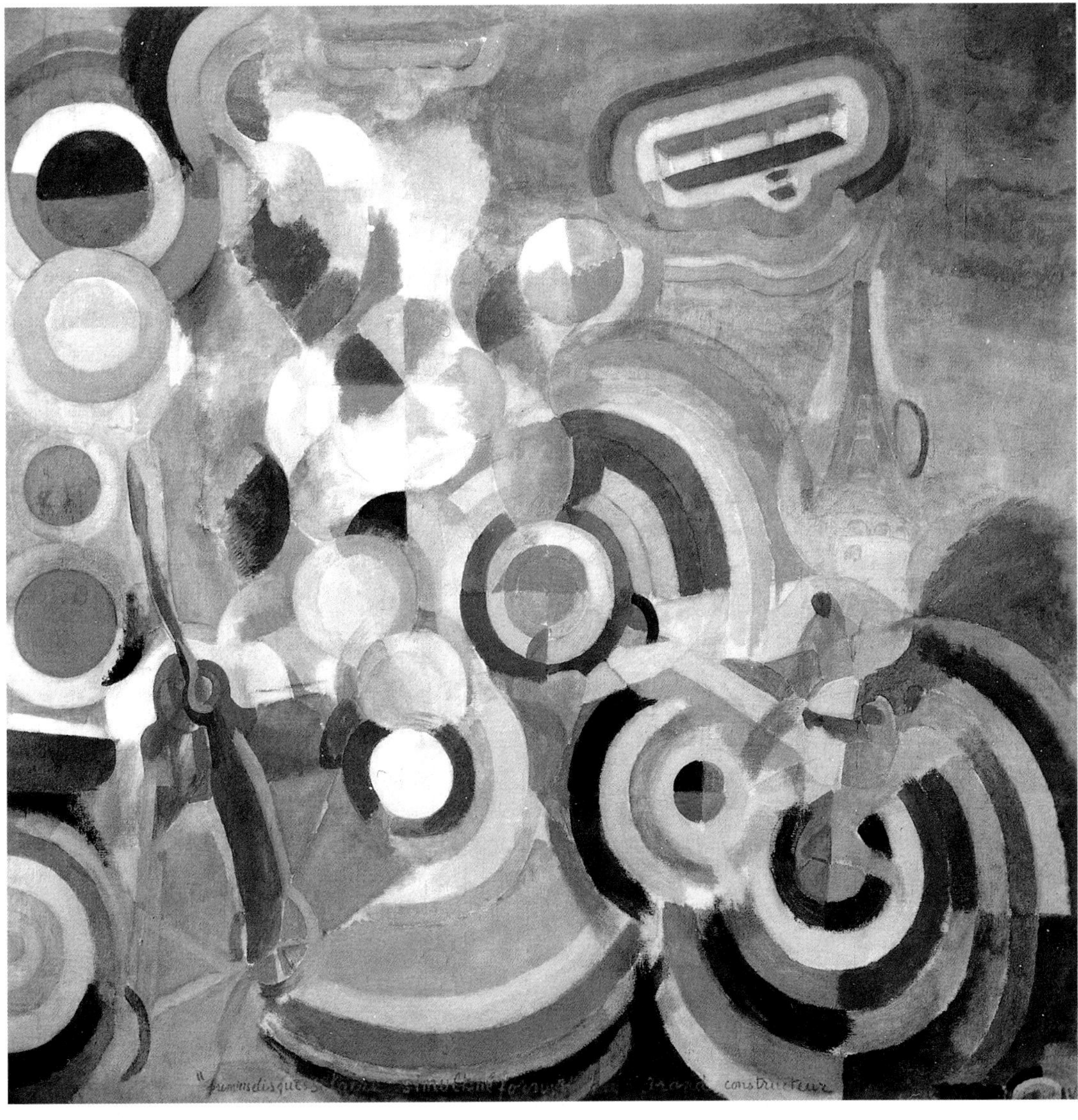

Fig. 8g. *Robert Delaunay,* Hommage á Blériot *(*Tribute to Blériot*), oil on canvas, 1914. Basel, Öffentliche Kunstsammlung Basel, Kunstmuseum*

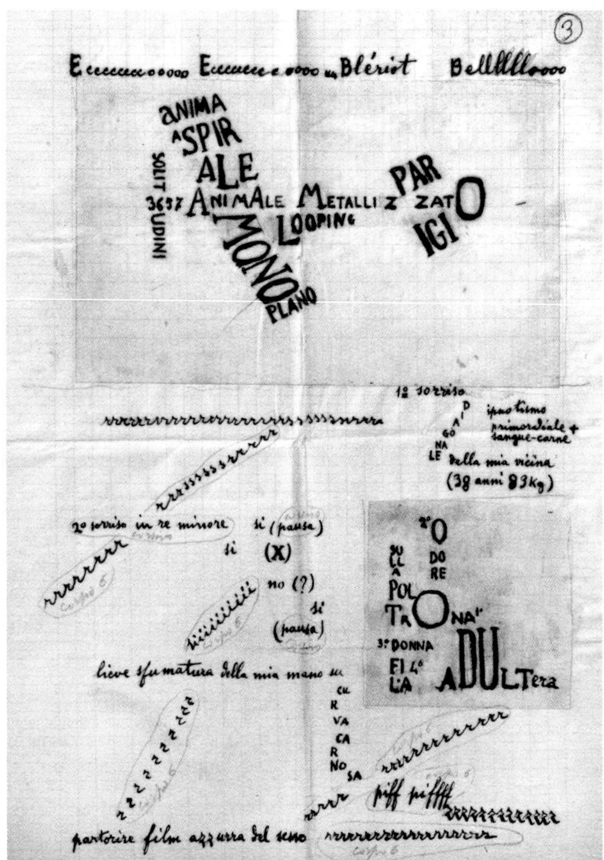

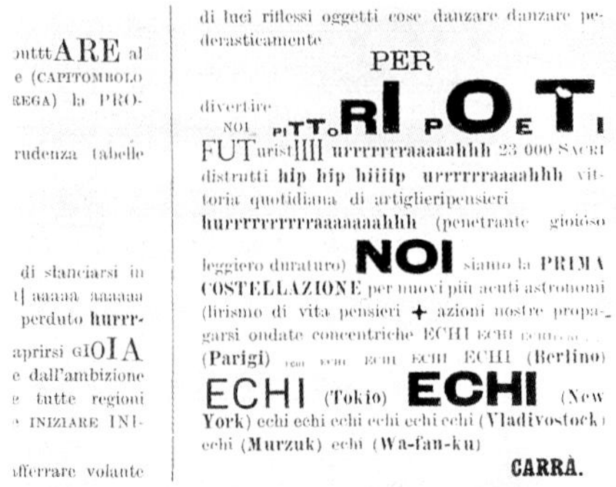

Fig. 8h. *Carlo Carrà,* Ritmi grafici con aeroplano (parole in libertà) (Graphic Rhythms with Airplane [Words in Liberty]), *ink and pencil on paper. Milan, private collection*

ntttARE al
e (CAPITOMBOLO
REGA) la PRO-
rudenza tabelle
di slanciarsi in
t| aaaaa aaaaaa
perduto **hurrr-**
aprirsi GIOIA
e dall'ambizione
e tutte regioni
INIZIARE INI-
afferrare volante

di luci riflessi oggetti cose danzare danzare pederasticamente
PER
divertire
NOI **PITTORI POETI**
FUTuristIIII **urrrrrraaaahhh** 23 000 SACRI distrutti **hip hip hiiiip urrrrrraaaahhh** vittoria quotidiana di artiglieripensieri **hurrrrrrrrraaaaaahhh** (penetrante gioioso leggiero duraturo) **NOI** siamo la **PRIMA COSTELLAZIONE** per nuovi più acuti astronomi (lirismo di vita pensieri + azioni nostre propagarsi ondate concentriche ECHI ECHI echi... (**Parigi**) echi echi ECHI ECHI ECHI (**Berlino**) ECHI (**Tokio**) **ECHI** (**New York**) echi echi echi echi echi echi (**Vladivostock**) echi (**Murzuk**) echi (**Wa-fan-ku**)

CARRÀ.

Fig. 8i. *Detail of fig. 8a*

element, such as Raoul Hausmann's *Dada Siegt* (1920). Its 'Dada worldwide' message, here in part ironic, recalls Carrà's vision of Futurism's global impact.

The studies of Bohn, Windsor and others listed in the bibliography suggest the considerable fascination with *Festa patriottica* among Anglo-American scholars. This stems from its notable exhibition history once it became part of the Mattioli Collection. It was part of an important Futurism show at the prominent Sidney Janis Gallery in 1954, also a showcase for New York School artists. The work was chosen for color illustration in the accompanying catalogue. This was notably followed by inclusion in the Museum of Modern Art's 'Futurism' exhibition of 1961, again with a color plate. This landmark show toured the United States. Both these venues assured that it was widely seen by New York artists, even as it was becoming one of the iconic works of Futurism for scholars.

Subsequently, with the more recent rise of 'word as image' as an ongoing area of exploration in art since around 1960, parallel to the development of concrete poetry, *Festa patriottica* has gained a second life as its most significant forebear in the early modernist generation. One might speculate about its impact on 'word artists' at this moment. For instance, Alan Kaprow's *Words* installation of 1962 brings the word-as-image into three-dimensional space[22] (fig. 8k). Kaprow even utilized record players to emit literally the kinds of words and sounds that Carrà conveys typographically. There are innumerable other examples in this generation, which was less concerned with the specific politics of such works than with their innovative use of typography. A recent exhibit, 'Poetry plastique', mapped how this mode continues in the present, with even a suggestive early drawing by Robert Smithson containing repeated "echoes."[23] Looking back on the whole century, the echoes of influence that *Festa patriottica* proclaimed have been unexpectedly fulfilled.

Lewis Kachur

Fig 8j. *Detail of cat. no. 8*

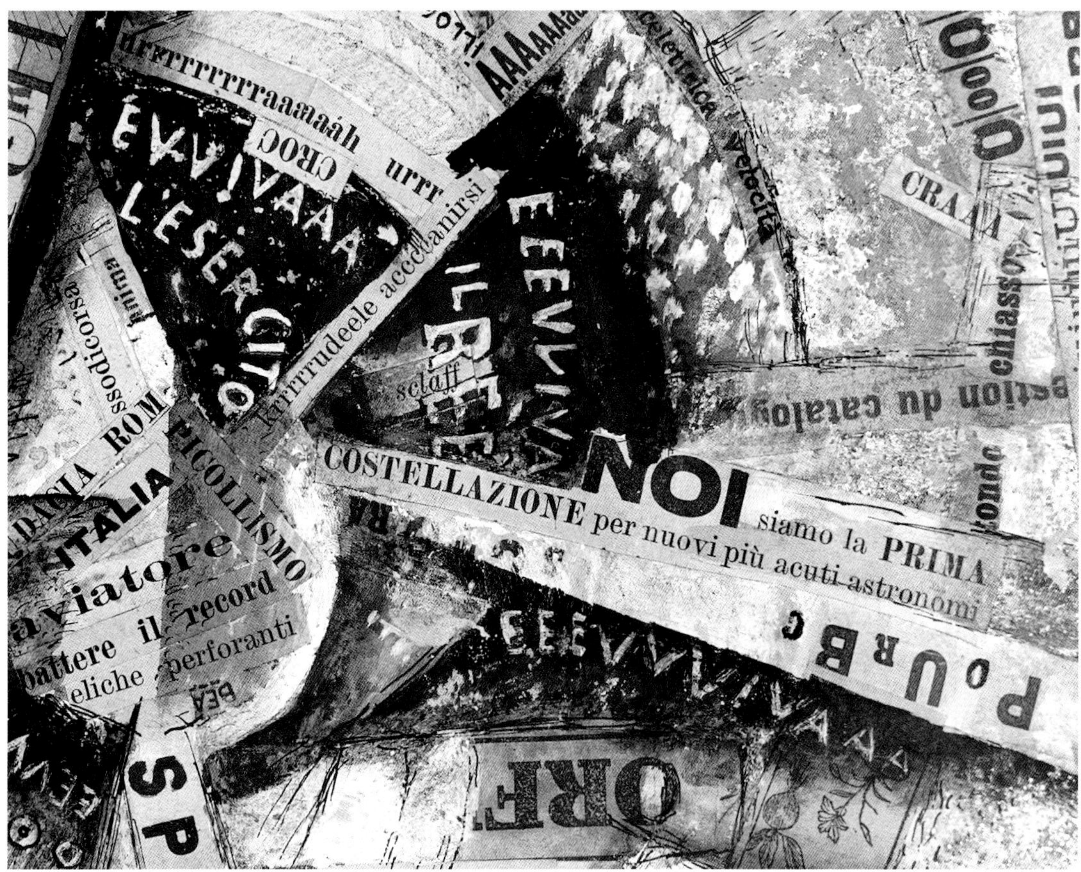

For an extended period the provenance of this collage is a mystery. In the catalogue of the one-man show held at the Galleria Paolo Chini between December 1917 and January 1918 the lack of any indication of ownership (which was specified in the cases of works in the collections of Penazzo, Notari and Marinetti) would seem to indicate that *Festa Patriottica* had not in the meantime found a buyer. The few reviews of the exhibition are silent on this collage,[24] or refer to it with severe disapproval ("things from an ethnographic exhibition, of a savagery full of melancholy mystery"[25]). Reactions elicited by the exhibition in numerous letters between various artists and critics[26] focused on the characteristics of volumetric austerity in Carrà's works of 1916–17, ignoring the entire selection of his Futurist paintings, collages and drawings in the show. Henceforth, as with all the most radical Futurist images, *Festa patriottica* disappeared from circulation: no critical mentions, reproductions, nor loans to exhibitions of any kind until after World War II. It is not known whether the collage remained in Carrà's possession all these years, or whether it had passed into a private collection. Gianni Mattioli bought it from the Galleria Bolzani, which had opened in the 1930s in Via Matteotti in the center of Milan and which dealt mainly in late nineteenth-century painting and Lombard Chiarismo.[27] Two documents in the Mattioli archives enable us to date the purchase: in a letter of June 1950 the gallery owner Bruno Bolzani wrote to Mattioli at Paolo Stramezzi's suggestion, offering "a magnificent picture by Carrà *Futurista* that I own;"[28] two days later a letter from Mattioli states that he had purchased the "futurist *papier collé* picture" for the sum of 60,000 lire,[29] a very low price and a clear indication of the lack of interest in Italy at that time for Futurist collages. A few months later, in November, *Festa patriottica* was exhibited in 'Futurismo-Pittura Metafisica' in Zurich, with the title *Dimostrazione interventista*:[30] in the thirty-five years since its execution, its publication in *Lacerba* in 1914 with its original title had evidently been forgotten and its precise historical meaning lost. The first significant

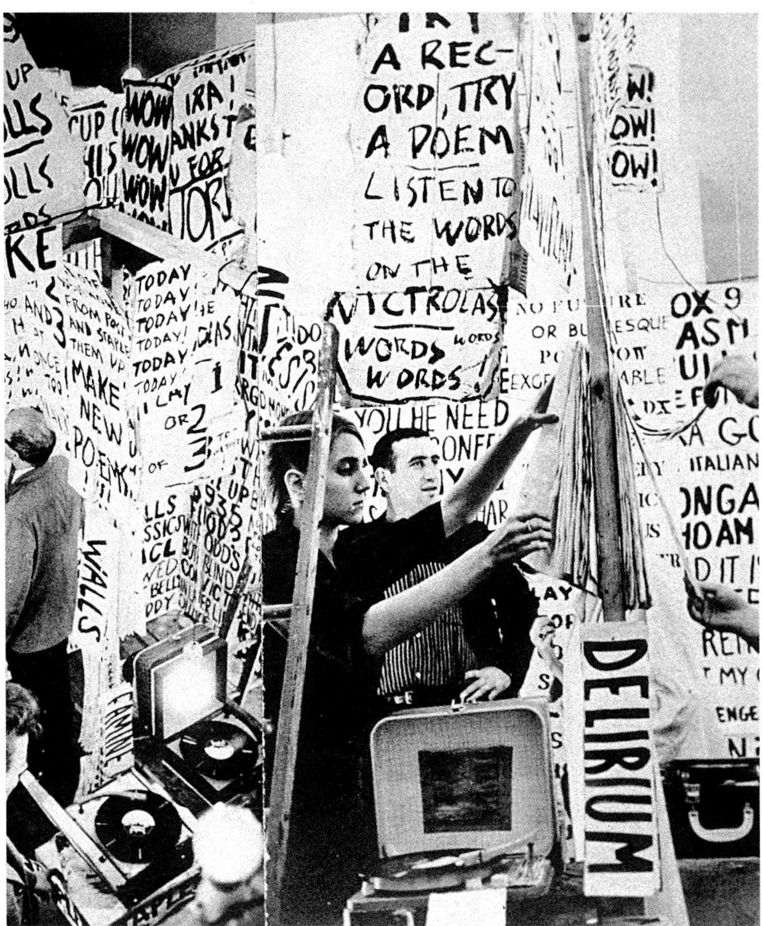

Fig. 8k. *Allan Kaprow,* Words, *installation, Smolin Gallery, New York, 1962*

critical mention of the work comes three years later, when Carlo Ludovico Ragghianti ranked it, now firmly titled *Manifestazione interventista*, among the masterpieces of the Italian avant-garde: a "powerful gyroscope that reveals all its structural energy, and, even, its monumentality," giving it the status of the most accomplished product of Futurist poetics, superior to contemporary works by Boccioni for its capacity "to mobilize [...] dynamically, in three dimensions, with a kind of billowing delirium, the entire image."[31]
Flavio Fergonzi

1 Rylands, 1997, p. 66.
2 Poggi, 1992, p. 225.
3 Letter of Carlo Carrà to Gino Severini, dated July 11, 1914, in Drudi Gambillo, Fiori 1958–62, vol. I, p. 341.
4 Letter from Carlo Carrà to Ardengo Soffici, dated June 23, 1914, in Carrà, Soffici 1983, p. 59; the first reproduction was in *Lacerba*, August 1, 1914; see Windsor 1977, 148–9.
5 Letter from Filippo Tommaso Marinetti to Ardengo Soffici, dated July 21, 1914, in Cavallo 1986, p. 231.
6 'Proof Corrections + Desires in Speed.' The two texts were published in *Lacerba,* February 1, 1914, p. 39, and December 1, 1913, respectively. See Bohn 1982, p. 126 and note 7, and Bohn 1986, p. 25 and note 46.
7 *Dune*, *Uomo + vallata + montagna*, *Sports*, *Stroll*, *Serate in onore di Yvonne*. Boccioni and Five are from the same issue as Carrà's own manifesto (February 1), as is the musical staff at the upper left, which is from a composition by Pratella. 'Dune' and Soffici are from the next issue, February 15, 1914, while Cangiullo's is by far the latest, June 15, 1914, and thus provides one *terminus post quem* for the completion of the collage.
8 Tisdall, Bozzolla, 1978, p. 169. See their useful chapter 9 on *Lacerba.*
9 It is analyzed in detail in Bohn, 1986, pp. 30–6.
10 Windsor 1977, pp. 149–50. Since this article, Carrà's June 23, 1914 letter to Soffici has been published, which confirms that he saw and liked Apollinaire's calligramme (Carrà, Soffici 1983, pp. 58–9).
11 Windsor 1977*,* pp. 149–50.
12 Letter from Carrà to Severini, dated July 11, 1914, in Drudi Gambillo, Fiori 1958–62, vol. I, p. 341. He goes on to say "2 giorni fa l'ho portato dal fotografo" ("two days ago I took it to the photographer").
13 Severini 1946, p. 156.
14 *Zurich* 1950, no. 43, with the Italian title *Manifestazione interventista*. Carrà 1967–8, vol. I, p. 824, no. 8/14 as *Manifestazione Interventista*.
15 Bohn 1982, pp. 126–8, and Roche-Pézard 1983, pp. 440–1.

[16] Shell 1998, pp. 81–3.
[17] Letter from Filippo Tommaso Marinetti to Balilla Pratella, in Tisdall, Bozzolla 1978, p. 174.
[18] Bohn 1994, p. 674. The word is cut from Ardengo Soffici's 'Passeggiata' published in *Lacerba*, February 15, 1914. Its diverse dual implications may have both appealed to Carrà.
[19] Shell, 1998, p. xxii.
[20] Mattioli's views came out of "his background in the milieu of Marinetti" (letter from Philip Rylands, February 21, 2001); see also Rylands 1997, p. 66. This author's view is that this and Bohn's interpretations go astray in seeking meaning in traditional representation.
[21] *L'Intransigeant*, March 3, 1914, in Apollinaire 1960, p. 434.
[22] Among many others, see Kachur 1992.
[23] Sanders, Bernstein 2001. The Smithson drawing is entitled *Echoes* (1962). Another word-drawing recalling Carrà's example is Jackson Mac Low, *A Vocabulary* (1963), p. 31.
[24] Bevilacqua, January 13, 1918.
[25] Fanciulli, January 10, 1918.
[26] Letter from Alberto Savinio to Carlo Carrà, dated February 18, 1918, in *Venice* 1979, pp. 122–3.
[27] Negri undated, pp. 17–18.
[28] Letter from Bruno Bolzani to Gianni Mattioli, dated June 17, 1950: Archivio Mattioli, *Appendix I*, document no. 44.
[29] Letter from Gianni Mattioli to the Galleria Bolzani, dated June 19, 1950: Archivio Mattioli, *Appendix I*, document no. 45.
[30] *Zurich* 1950, no. 43: the title was in Italian and the work was dated 1913.
[31] Ragghianti 1953, p. 9.

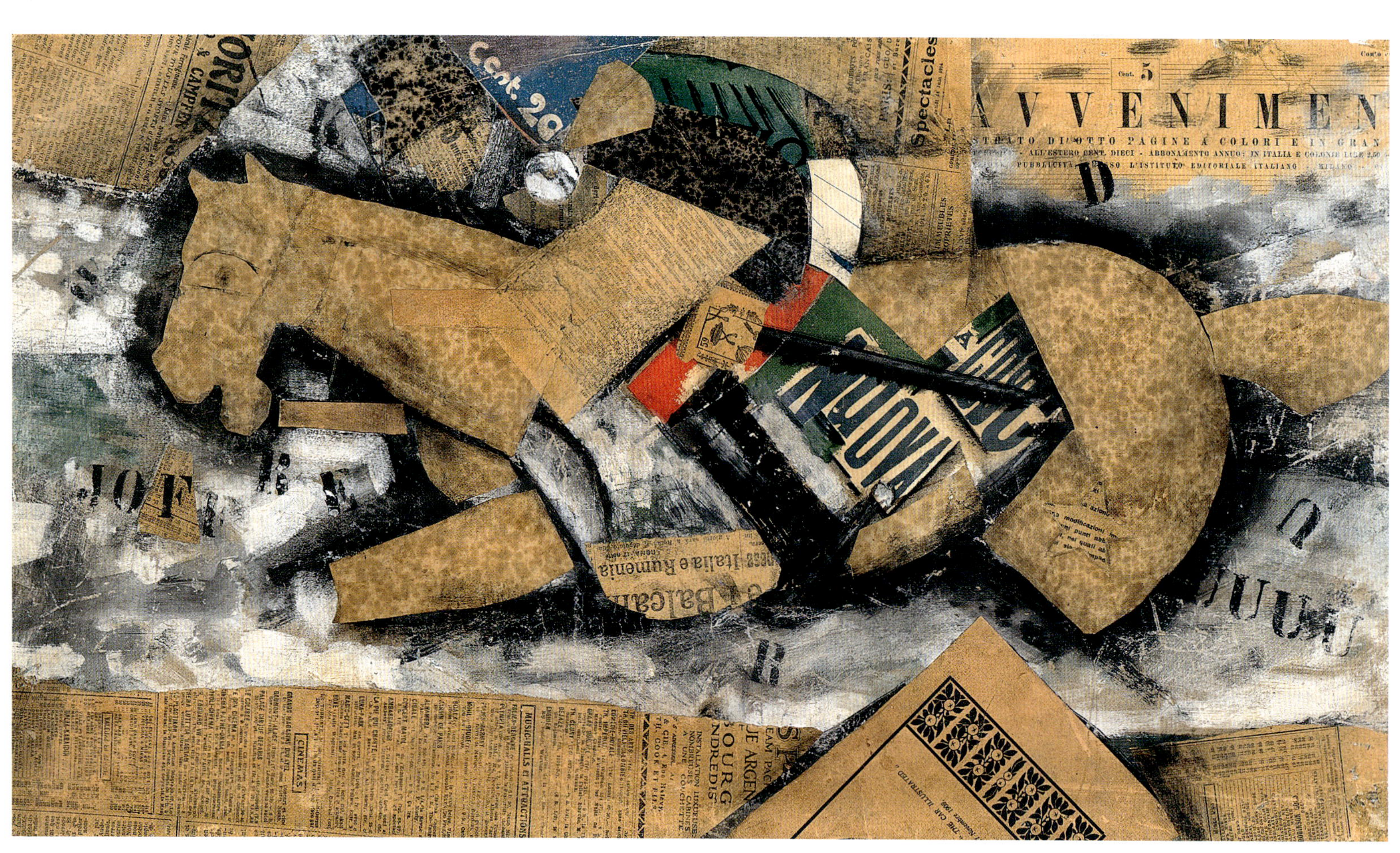

9

Carlo Carrà

Pursuit (*Horse and Rider*)

Inseguimento (*Cavallo e cavaliere*), 1915

Tempera, charcoal and collage on cardboard
39 × 68 cm

Provenance: 1915: Umberto Notari, Milano; ?: Galleria del Milione, Milan; October 1950: Gianni Mattioli

Exhibitions: Florence 1953*, no. 12 (*Cavallo e cavaliere*, 1915); São Paulo 1953–54, p. 8, no. 20 (*Cavallo e cavaliere*, 1915); New York 1954, no. 23; Lausanne 1955, no. 15 (*La Poursuite*, 1915); Rome 1959, no. 107 (*Inseguimento*); Winterthur 1959, no. 53; Munich 1959–60, no. 48; Venice 1960, p. 17, no. 67 (*Inseguimento*, 1914); New York 1961–Los Angeles 1962, no. 82 (1914); Milan 1962, no. 7 (1914); Washington, DC 1967–Tokyo 1972, no. 16 (Washington, DC–Hamburg), no. 15 (Madrid Seville), no. 16 (Kyoto–Tokyo); Prato 1971, no. XIVa (1914); Rome 1972, p. 115, no. 7 (1914); Paris 1973, no. 46 (1914); Milan 1973–4, no. 133d (1914); Düsseldorf 1974, no. 107 (1914); Venice 1986, p. 161 (1914); Madrid 1990–1, p. 232 (1914); Vienna 1993–Frankfurt 1994, no. 50 (1914); Berlin 1994, no. II, 35 (1914); London 1994, p. 63 (1914); Venice 1996, no. 14 (1914)

Bibliography: Carrà 1915, p. 31 (illus., *Inseguimento*); Letter from Ardengo Soffici to Carlo Carrà, dated April 28, 1915, in Carrà, Soffici 1983, pp. 80–1; Letter from Giovanni Papini to Carlo Carrà, dated August 22, 1915, in Papini, Carrà 1986, p. 357; Conti 1919, p. 28; Raimondi 1942, p. 7; Account from the Galleria del Milione, dated October 28, 1950 (Archivio Mattioli); Carrieri 1950, pp. 81–2 (*Collaggio da Guerra Pit-*

The year 1915 saw Carrà progressively loosening his ties to the Milanese Futurists, and to Boccioni in particular. Aside from any personal resentments accumulated over the years, Carrà felt increasingly remote from Boccioni's credo of dynamism, the fragmentation of forms and simultaneity. In its place, with the complicity of Ardengo Soffici as theorist, he was arduously in search of a more concrete figuration combining modernity, popular tradition and a lyrical feeling for objects. *Pursuit*, still Futurist in its subject, in certain technical choices (the application of cuttings from newspapers) and in its intended use (for reproduction in a book published by Edizioni Futuriste di Poesia), represents nevertheless a decisive step in Carrà's move away from Futurism towards a new interest in primitive forms cleanly contoured in space.

Pursuit is difficult to place in the *corpus* of paintings depicting World War I. It portrays a rider on horseback galloping after an enemy (the wartime theme is confirmed by its publication in 1915 as a plate in Carrà's *Guerrapittura*[1]) but, as has been pointed out, his clothing "looks more like [that] of a jockey than a warrior" and his cylindrical hat is especially incongruous in its large scale.[2] The topical echoes of war in the texts surrounding the horse and rider (the name of Marshal Joffre, victor of the Battle of the Marne in September 1914, is stenciled under the horse's muzzle; the Balkan predicament is alluded to in a scrap of newspaper prominently placed by the soldier's boot) cohabit with clippings of an entirely different sort (classified ads, music and sports events and an automobile advertisement), arousing in the viewer a sort of Dadaist disorientation.[3] The horse and rider resemble marionettes, and the mood, suspended between dream and reckless adventure, has little in common with the codes of triumphant propaganda commonly used by the Futurists in their representations of war. As Richard Cork has written, "the entire conception of the picture belongs to the nursery rather than the battlefield."[4]

Despite the fact that in recent years *Pursuit* has consistently, with a single exception,[5] been assigned to the year 1914 (the words 'Jeudi, 11 juin 1914' which can be read on a fragment of newspaper in the upper center of the picture refer to the entertainment events that day in Paris), it can confidently be post-dated to 1915. January 3, 1915 was the inaugural date of publication of the Milanese illustrated weekly, *Gli Avvenimenti*, whose masthead can be seen in the upper right corner. The newspaper fragment cut in a rough semicircle that stands for the horse's chest, with its reference to the Balkan war and to Italy and Rumania's shared tempo-

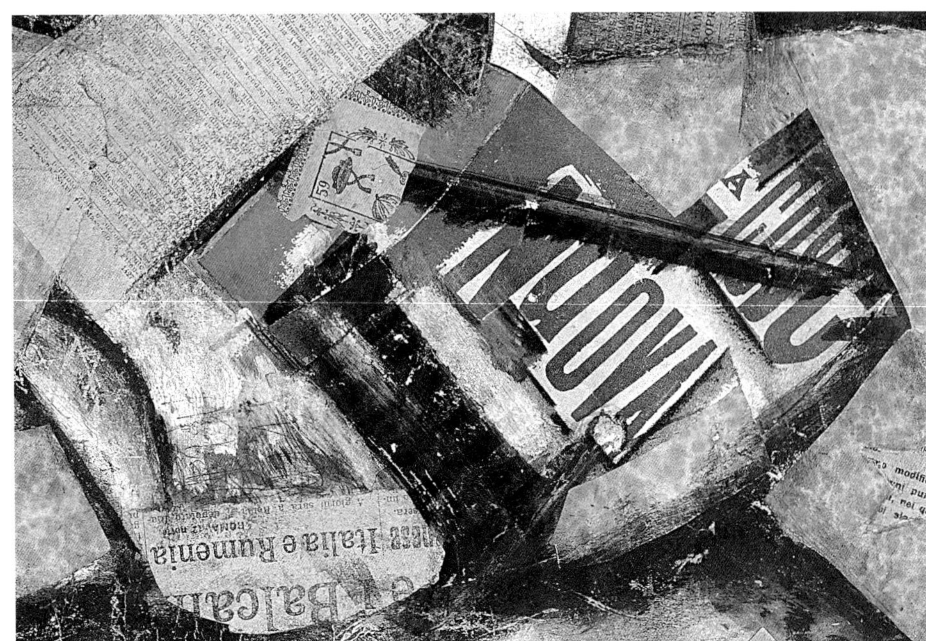

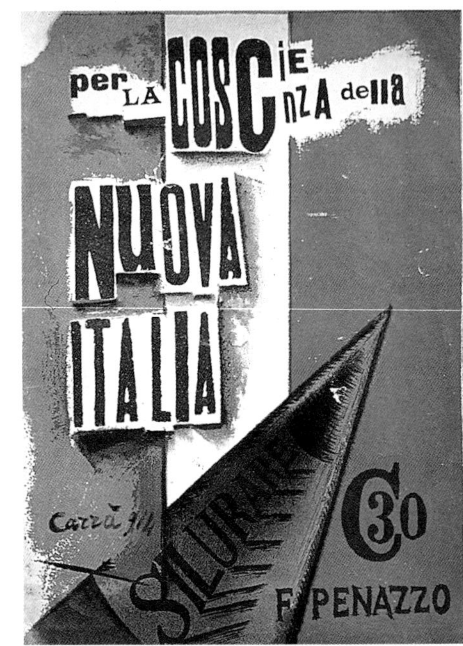

rizing policy (the place, date and time, "Roma, 12 notte" are legible), is cut from page 4 of the January 13, 1915 edition of *Il Popolo d'Italia* (fig. 9c). Finally, the column of classified ads wedged between the galloping rider's torso and leg was cut from page 5 of the *Corriere della Sera* of February 9, 1915. The work was certainly finished by the end of March 1915 (when Carrà announced in a letter to Soffici the imminent publication of the book *Guerrapittura*[6]), though an earlier *terminus ante quem* may be February 20, when Carrà signed and dated the essay *Non sono uno specialista* NO! which served as an introduction to the book's texts, words-in-freedom plates and illustrations. The use of an eight-month-old newspaper clipping may be explained by the fact that Carrà, intending to represent a cavalry officer who was French, could not lay hands on anything more recent: most probably Soffici left him this French daily (that of June 11, 1914) when, following his return from Paris towards the middle of June 1914, they met soon after in Milan for the consignment of a plate for *Lacerba*.[7]

Post-dating *Pursuit* to the beginning of 1915 relocates it to a specific phase of his production which can best be defined in the context of all Carrà's collages of 1914–15. A preliminary, more conventionally Futurist phase, characterized by "research which, judged superficially might seem simple 'trompe l'œil', whereas in reality it is a more direct expression of reality,"[8] coincided with the shipment of two works to the May–June 1914 Futurist show at Giuseppe Sprovieri's gallery:[9] *Dynamic Construction on a Horizontal Axis* and *Dynamic Construction on an Oblique Axis* (fig. 9e, including the announcement of Russolo's Futurist 'intonarumori' concert on April 21, 1914).[10] This was followed soon after by a phase marked by references to popular culture and by "forms of colored cardboard in relief,"[11] of which *Still Life with Syphon* (fig. 9f, with a legible clipping from the April 28, 1914 issue of the sports daily *La Gazzetta dello Sport*)[12] was published in *Lacerba* on July 1. Carrà's 'pictorial poem' the Mattioli *Patriotic Holiday* (cat. no. 8), published in *Lacerba* on August 1, was made between June and July.[13] It was taken for photographing on July 11, together with three other pictures: probably *Suburban Café* (a fragment of the May 15, 1914 issue of *Lacerba* provides its *terminus post quem*), possibly *Flask and Glass* (dated by Carrà 'maggio 1914' in ink) and *Chandelier*.[14] A six-month hiatus followed (during which the multimedia *Noises of a Night Café* may be dated,[15] fig. 9g) until we come to the drawings and collages that were to illustrate *Guerrapittura*, including *Pursuit*. The only extant testimonies to his return to collage in 1915 are

tura, 1914–15); Ballo 1956, pp. 18 and 24 (*Cavallo e cavaliere*); Pacchioni 1959, no. 12 (*Inseguimento*, 1915), Drudi Gambillo, Fiori 1958–62, vol. I, p. 428 (*Cavallo e cavaliere*), vol. II, pp. 288 and 295, no. 40 (*Inseguimento*); Marchiori 1960, p. 63 (*Inseguimento*, 1914); Carrieri 1961, p. 157, fig. 63 (*Inseguimento*, 1915); Taylor 1961, pp. 110–12; Ballo 1964b, vol. I, pp. 80 and 100 (*Cavallo e cavaliere*, 1915); Carrà, Waldberg, Rathke 1968, p. 27 (*Inseguimento*, 1914); Martin 1968, pp. 199–200, fig. 212 (1914); Carrà 1967–8, vol. I, no. 9/14, p. 261 (1914); Apollonio 1970, no. 95 (1914); Carrà 1970, no. 53 (1914); Rye 1972, pp. 92–3; Russoli 1977, p. 12; Argan 1977, p. 200, no. 114b (1914); Tisdall, Bozzola 1977, pp. 186–7; Roche-Pézard 1983, pp. 445–6, no. 126, fig. 58 (1915); Poggi 1992, pp. 238–241, fig. 139 (late 1914); Di Genova 1993, pp. 295–6 (1914); Cork 1994, pp. 63–4 (1914); Lemaire 1995, p. 55 (1914); Licht 1996, p. 181 (1914); Rylands 1997, p. 68 (1914); Shell 2000, pp. 159–63

Fig. 9a. *Detail of cat. no. 9*

Fig. 9b. *Carlo Carrà, cover of F. Penazzo,* Per la coscienza della Nuova Italia, *Milan 1914*

Fig. 9c. Il Popolo d'Italia, *January 13, 1915*

Fig. 9d. *Flyer with predictions of the* Pianeta della fortuna. *Milan, Civica raccolta delle stampe Achille Bertarelli*

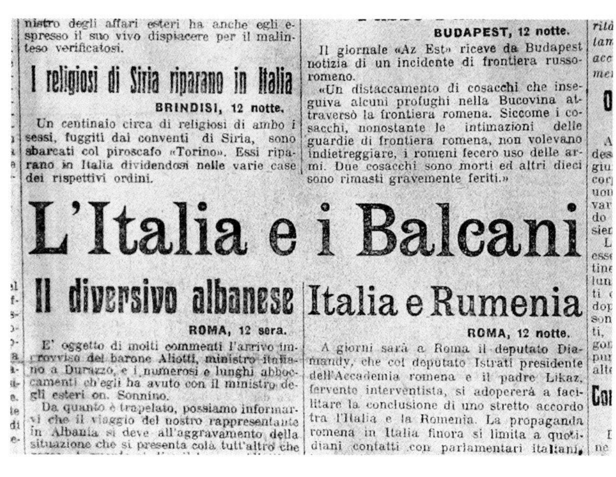

nistro degli affari esteri ha anche egli espresso il suo vivo dispiacere per il malinteso verificatosi.

I religiosi di Siria riparano in Italia

BRINDISI, 12 notte.

Un centinaio circa di religiosi di ambo i sessi, fuggiti dai conventi di Siria, sono sbarcati col piroscafo «Torino». Essi riparano in Italia dividendosi nelle varie case dei rispettivi ordini.

BUDAPEST, 12 notte.

Il giornale «Az Est» riceve da Budapest notizia di un incidente di frontiera russo-romeno.

«Un distaccamento di cosacchi che inseguiva alcuni profughi nella Bucovina attraversò la frontiera romena. Siccome i cosacchi, nonostante le intimazioni delle guardie di frontiera romena, non volevano indietreggiare, i romeni fecero uso delle armi. Due cosacchi sono morti ed altri dieci sono rimasti gravemente feriti.»

L'Italia e i Balcani

Il diversivo albanese

ROMA, 12 sera.

E' oggetto di molti commenti l'arrivo improvviso del barone Aliotti, ministro italiano a Durazzo, e i numerosi e lunghi abboccamenti ch'egli ha avuto con il ministro degli esteri on. Sonnino.

Da quanto è trapelato, possiamo informarvi che il viaggio del nostro rappresentante in Albania si deve all'aggravamento della situazione che si presenta colà tutt'altro che

Italia e Rumenia

ROMA, 12 notte.

A giorni sarà a Roma il deputato Diamandy, che col deputato Istrati presidente dell'Accademia romena e il padre Likaz, fervente interventista, si adopererà a facilitare la conclusione di uno stretto accordo tra l'Italia e la Romenia. La propaganda romena in Italia finora si limita a quotidiani contatti con parlamentari italiani,

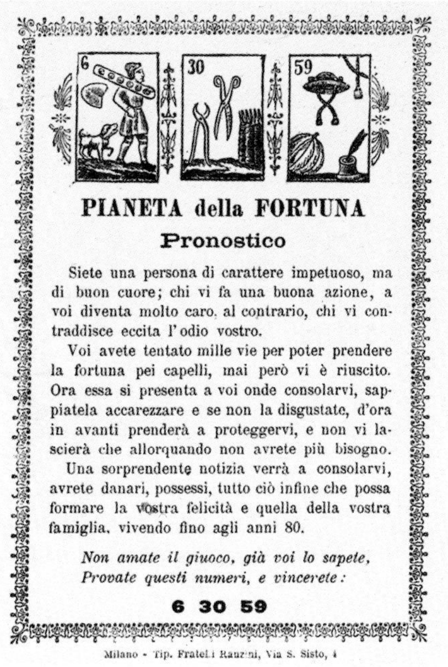

6 30 59

PIANETA della FORTUNA

Pronostico

Siete una persona di carattere impetuoso, ma di buon cuore; chi vi fa una buona azione, a voi diventa molto caro. al contrario, chi vi contraddisce eccita l'odio vostro.

Voi avete tentato mille vie per poter prendere la fortuna pei capelli, mai però vi è riuscito. Ora essa si presenta a voi onde consolarvi, sappiatela accarezzare e se non la disgustate, d'ora in avanti prenderà a proteggervi, e non vi lascierà che allorquando non avrete più bisogno.

Una sorprendente notizia verrà a consolarvi, avrete danari, possessi, tutto ciò infine che possa formare la vostra felicità e quella della vostra famiglia, vivendo fino agli anni 80.

Non amate il giuoco, già voi lo sapete,
Provate questi numeri, e vincerete:

6 30 59

Milano - Tip. Fratelli Rauz[illegible]i, Via S. Sisto, 4

the later *Composition*[16] (with newspaper clippings from July of the same year), *The Flask* (dated 1915) and *Negro Acrobat*.[17]

Thus *Pursuit* may be detached from the group of collages executed in the late spring of 1914. It can be situated halfway between that date and Carrà's experiments that led to his return to volumetric figuration in late 1915 and which marked his definitive rejection of Futurism. The horse in particular, isolated in space by the black tempera nimbus that surrounds it, has little in common with works of 1914 and seems a direct antecedent of those "concrete forms [...] placed in space" that Carrà announced to Soffici in December 1915.[18] These led the painter toward a primitivism influenced by Giotto and the Douanier Rousseau.

Two issues are key to understanding Carrà's work in the second half of 1914. The first was the psychological reaction, shared by all the Futurists, to the outbreak of war in August on the Franco-German front. Suddenly, in his letters to Soffici, anguished soul-searching about his work ceases and is replaced by impassioned interventionist and pro-French declarations. Only in November did Carrà begin to work again with fresh enthusiasm, buoyed by his awareness that in time of war "true art will find a new momentum to discover ways hitherto unknown": he defined this new production as "plastic syntheses which, observed in periods of inertia, seem to me folly."[19] Secondly Carrà, after completion of the Mattioli *Patriotic Holiday* (cat. no. 8), seemed to enter a period of crisis: his attempt at a work of literature-painting, composed of legible words like a musical score,[20] marked the most advanced point of his experimentation but also, for the first time, rocked the foundations of his craft as a painter.

In the last months of 1914, Marinetti played the card of interventionism with increasing conviction, inviting Futurist artists to focus on topical themes of war: there existed, as he explained to Severini, an opportunity to publish "a great and very important periodical, on the war, three-quarters filled with illustrations of drawings and paintings."[21] The periodical in question was most probably *Gli Avvenimenti*, published by Umberto Notari,[22] owner of the Istituto Editoriale Italiano, who subsequently decided instead to use photographs, thus disappointing the Futurists' expectations. Writers and artists in Marinetti's circle found themselves, especially after the disagreements with the Florentine editors of *Lacerba*, in possession of works they did not know what to do with. Marinetti actively addressed the matter on various fronts, the first of which (through Sibilla Aleramo) was to approach *La Grande Illustrazione*, a sump-

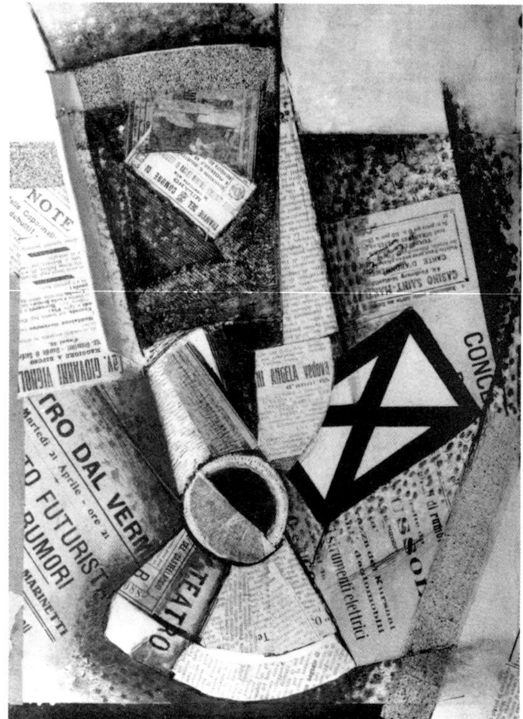

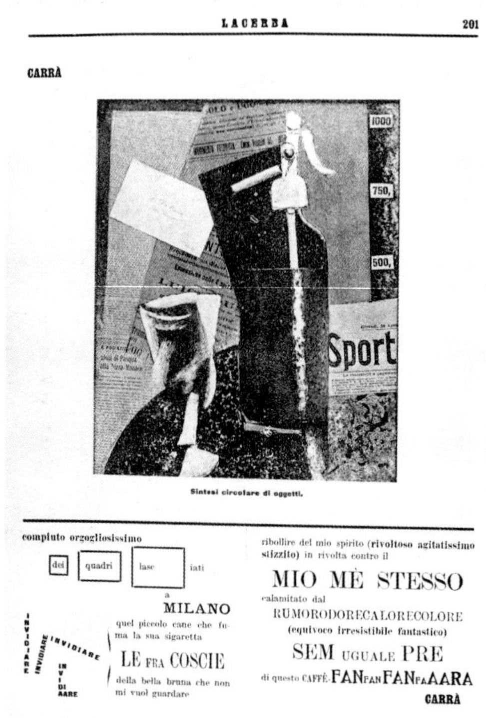

LACERBA 201

CARRÀ

Sintesi circolare di oggetti.

compiuto orgogliosissimo

dei quadri lasc iati

a

MILANO

quel piccolo cane che fuma la sua sigaretta

LE FRA COSCIE

della bella bruna che non mi vuol guardare

INVIDIARE INVIDIARE INVIDIARE INVIDIAARE

ribollire del mio spirito (rivoltoso agitatissimo stizzito) in rivolta contro il

MIO MÈ STESSO

calamitato dal

RUMORODORECALORECOLORE

(equivoco irresistibile fantastico)

SEM UGUALE PRE

di questo CAFFÈ-FANFANFANFAAARA

CARRÀ

Fig. 9e. *Carlo Carrà,* Costruzione dinamica su asse obliquo *(*Dynamic Construction on an Oblique Axis*), tempera and collage on board, 1914. Private collection*

Fig. 9f. *Carlo Carrà,* Sintesi circolare di oggetti *(*Natura morta con sifone*) (*Circular Synthesis of Objects *[*Still Life with Syphon*]), 1914, in* Lacerba*, July 1, 1914*

tuous monthly published in Pescara. In addition to works by the Belgian Futurist Marc Demarle, a tempera and collage by Umberto Boccioni, *Charge of the Lancers*[23] (fig. 9l), was published in the January 1915 issue and a drawing by Gino Severini, *Sketch for a Picture*[24] (fig. 9m, with three galloping cossacks of the Russian army armed with lances, whose bearskins are transformed into top hats not unlike the one in Carrà's *Pursuit*), appeared in February. One might speculate that Carrà's *Pursuit* was among those works on the theme of war solicited by Marinetti and then rejected by Notari for *Gli Avvenimenti*: the title of Notari's periodical is clearly visible in the background of Carrà's collage and Notari himself was to be its first owner. The two works by Boccioni and Severini illustrated in *La Grande Illustrazione* are related to Carrà's collage. This can be explained as a direct (and polemical) reply to Boccioni's tempera which showed, as has been stressed,[25] a war image in accordance with Futurist orthodoxy. A squadron of lancers leaps from a backdrop of news reports and confronts the viewer, enveloping him in the action. More complex, and subtle, is the relation of *Pursuit* to Severini's *Sketch for a Picture*, published in February on the exact date of the last of Carrà's newspaper clippings, and to another contemporary drawing by Severini, *Amazons*,[26] which portrays two women on horseback. It is evident that both artists, at the same time, were setting out to simplify the forms of a horseman, and to neutralize dynamic movement within a finite, closed profile.

Carrà's collage represents the last product of a period dedicated essentially to works on paper and which is documented by the illustrations to *Guerrapittura*. The eleven 'war drawings' (*disegni guerreschi*) accompanying the reproduction of *Pursuit* (ten precede it and one, *Conclusion*, significantly inscribed with the words 'Bomboni su Vienna' ['bonbons over Vienna'], follows it) re-present the entire stylistic range of Carrà's work from the preceding two years: from the canonical Futurist fragmentation of form (*Wartime Sky* [*Cielo di guerra*]) to the words-in-freedom plate (*Naval War in the Adriatic* [*Guerra navale nell'Adriatico*]) and his apparent attention to popular imagery (*War Prisoners* [*Prigionieri di guerra*] which seems to replicate the language of anti-German cartoons in the *Almanacco della guerra 1915* published

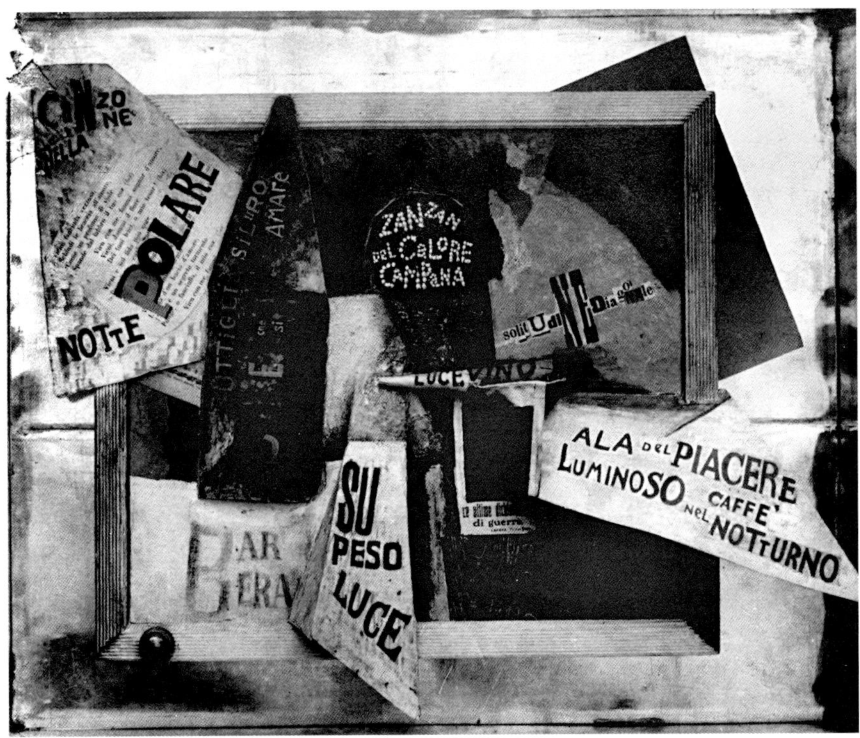

Fig. 9g. *Carlo Carrà,* I rumori del caffè notturno *(*The Noises of the Night Café*), multimedia collage, 1914. Whereabouts unknown*

by *Lacerba* in December 1914). The main components of several drawings are pasted clippings from the headlines of the incessant war bulletins: the Futurists themselves admitted that these obsessed their imaginations in the months prior to Italy's entry into the war. Carrà privileged one newspaper in particular, *Il Popolo d'Italia,* whose editor-in-chief was Benito Mussolini: only recently launched (the inaugural issue was dated November 15, 1914), this was the voice of those revolutionary splinter groups that had recently left the Socialist Party, who supported the entry of Italy in the war and who sought to emphasize the nature of war as a grandiose and fascinating spectacle on the chessboard of the world. Two drawings, *Wartime Sky* and *Prisoners of War*, used passages from the same page of the December 19, 1914 issue of *Il Popolo d'Italia*, highlighting bulletins of the French counter-offensive on the Belgian front and the German retreat from the Russian cavalry on the Polish front; fragments in *Hulan + Belgian Landscape* (fig. 9i) were cut from the January 8, 1915 edition (a summary of press on the Italian occupation of Valona; the presidency of the Fascio Interventista in Milan assigned to a grandson of Garibaldi); as we have seen, the most visible collage in the center of *Pursuit* derives from the January 13, 1915 issue of *Il Popolo d'Italia.*

Two plates from *Guerrapittura* in particular should be considered in direct relation to *Pursuit*. The first is *Hulan + Belgian Landscape*,[27] in which a galloping French lancer anticipates the posture (and a certain playful, mechanical character in the action) of the rider in the Mattioli collage. It must have been executed earlier (there are clippings from January 8 whereas the clippings in *Pursuit* are as late as February 9): speed disintegrates the forms in a still-Futurist manner and Carrà strengthened the force-lines of movement with pencil. A second plate in *Guerrapittura*, called *Penetrating Angle of Joffre over the Marne against 2 Germanic Cubes* (fig. 9h; the title is preceded by the following note: "La notte del 20 Gennaio 1915 sognai questo quadro" ["The night of January 20, 1915 I dreamed this painting"]),[28] is related to *Pursuit* by its reference to the victorious Battle of the Marne fought between September 5 and 12, 1914, and to its victor, General César-Joseph-Jacques Joffre. Linda Landis and Christine Poggi have explained the drawing as directly connected to the waging of the battle on the Franco-Ger-

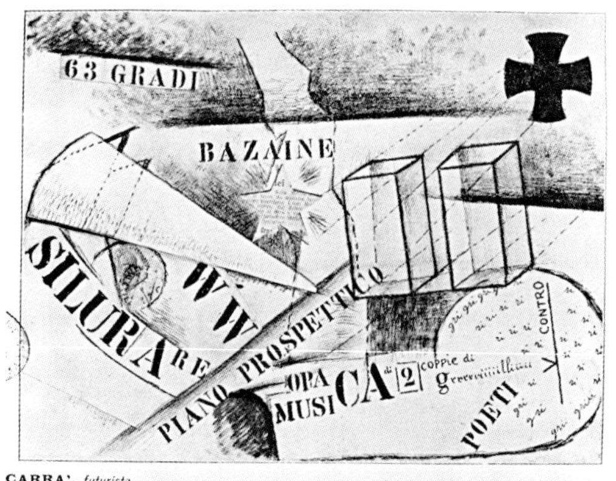

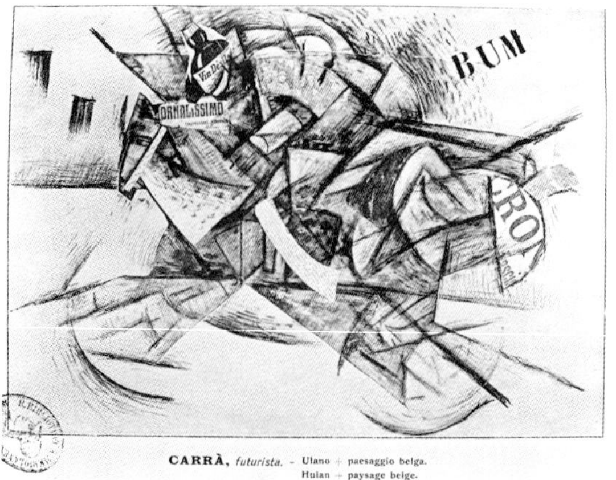

Fig. 9h. *Carlo Carrà,* Angolo penetrante di Joffre sopra Marna contro 2 cubi germanici *(*Penetrating Angle of Joffre over the Marne against 2 Germanic Cubes*), 1915, in* Guerrapittura*, 1915*

Fig. 9i. *Carlo Carrà,* Ulano + paesaggio belga *(*Hulan + Belgian Landscape*), 1915, in* Guerrapittura*, 1915*

man front (a somewhat remote event by January 1915):[29] it offers a summary representation of the battlefield traversed by the river, troops in formation and airplanes engaged in the encounter (a German Fokker and Albatros B II and a French Morane). The composition is dominated by the clash between the weight and inertia of the elements on the right and the lightness, the dynamism of those on the left: the "music of two pairs of crickets" launched against the line of the German army.

The notion of agility triumphing over ponderous immobility was linked to the Futurist interpretation of war: on the final page of the book Carrà inserted the *tavola parolibera* 'Sintesi futurista della guerra' ('Futurist Synthesis of the War', conceived in the wake of the interventionist demonstrations in September, 1914) in which the war was 'synthesized' as a Futurist wedge weighing on the anti-Alliance countries (France was endowed with "speed, elegance, spontaneity, explosiveness, self-possession" ("*velocità, eleganza, spontaneità, esplosività, disinvoltura*") pitched against Austro-Germanic nostalgia. In *Pursuit*, the odd little square of collage pasted conspicuously on the rider's red trousers may be read in this sense (fig. 9a). It was cut from a page of the *Pianeta della fortuna* (*Planet of Fortune*) series, printed at the beginning of the century by the Milanese typographer Ranzini, with a prediction of three winning numbers for the game of Lotto[30] (fig. 9d): the numbers included 59, the one Carrà selected, flanked by drawings of four objects (a cardinal's hat and cord, an inkwell and a squash: symbols traditionally associated with this number in the Lotto game). It is unlikely that this can be explained merely by Carrà's passion (frequently professed in his writings and letters at the time) for anachronistic ephemera of popular culture. Both the context of the Lotto game of chance and the profile of the player attached to the three numbers ("you are a person of impetuous character, but with a good heart [...] you have tried many ways to seize fortune by the hair, from now on she will protect you and will not leave you") refer to an irrational faith in chance, fickle and unpredictable, which decides the course of events. Between mid January and early February 1915, when the war on the Belgian front was languishing in extenuating trench warfare following the January 7–14 German victory at Soissons, hope for a swift resolution (with fortune's assistance) led by the hero of the Marne must have filled the dreams and thoughts of Carrà (and of Marinetti too, given that on February 11, 1915 he published a words-in-freedom pamphlet titled *Mountains + Valleys + Streets × Joffre* [*Montagne + Vallate + Strade × Joffre*] centered on Joffre's visit to the front after the triumph of the Marne[31]). This hope may have transmitted itself to the optimistic vision of *Pursuit*.

Pursuit marks a development beyond the other drawings/collages reproduced in *Guerrapittura* (all of early 1915 despite the date 1914 penciled on some by Carrà after their publication[32]), and not simply because of its technical complexity. The soldier-jockey who non-

Fig. 9j. *Carlo Carrà,* Fantino a cavallo (Jockey on Horseback*), pencil on paper, 1914, in G. Raimondi,* Disegni di Carlo Carrà*, 1942*

Fig. 9k. *Carlo Carrà,* Cavallo e cavaliere (Horse and Rider*), temper and ink on lined paper, 1912. Milan, Civiche raccolte d'arte, Jucker Collection*

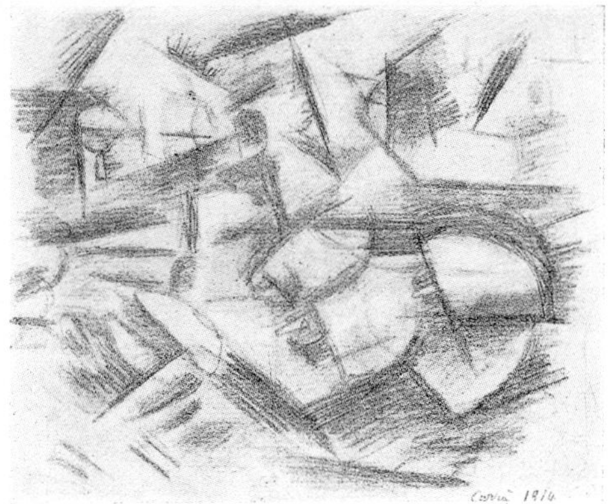

FANTINO A CAVALLO - 1914.

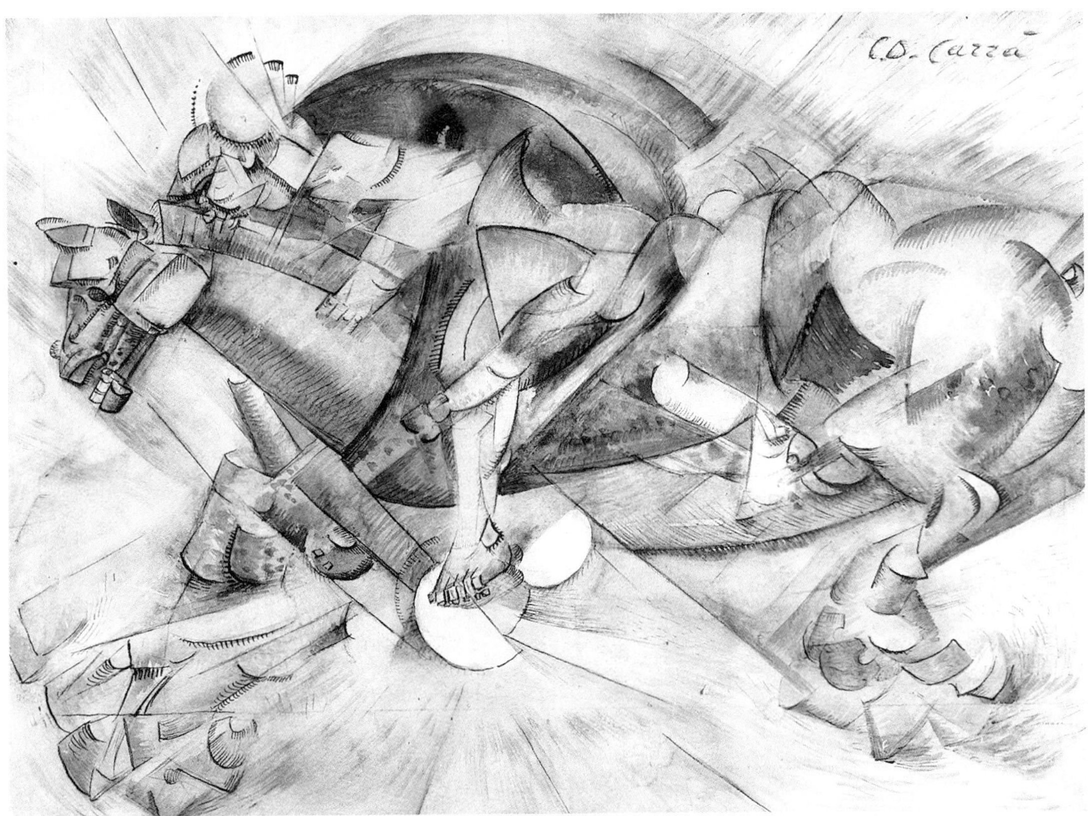

chalantly traverses the battlefield scattering words of wartime news together with sports reports and classified advertising represented, for Carrà, a new conquest. The agility and dynamism he associated with Frenchness went hand-in-hand with, for the first time, a subtle aloofness from the event portrayed. On the one hand, the contamination of current political events with facetiousness can be related to the ideology of Marinetti, as expressed in the manifesto *Il teatro di varietà* of 1913 (in which, in one example, the tragic Balkan situation was dismissed in a rapid, ironical sketch);[33] on the other hand, Carrà's reduction of the horse to a toy may be explicable by his interest in popular or folk art, as theorized in a text of spring 1914: folk art is postulated as the only possible source for the "new aesthetic values that respond to the great needs of our spirit, desirous at all costs of creating a primordial-modern."[34]

Examination of the process with which the collage was made, by looking at the superimposition of layers, tends to confirm Carrà's intention to create a plastically structured image. Carrà prepared the cardboard support with a thin white priming and then sketched the scene in tempera. Traces are still visible in the horse's outline. He hinted at a naturalistic back-

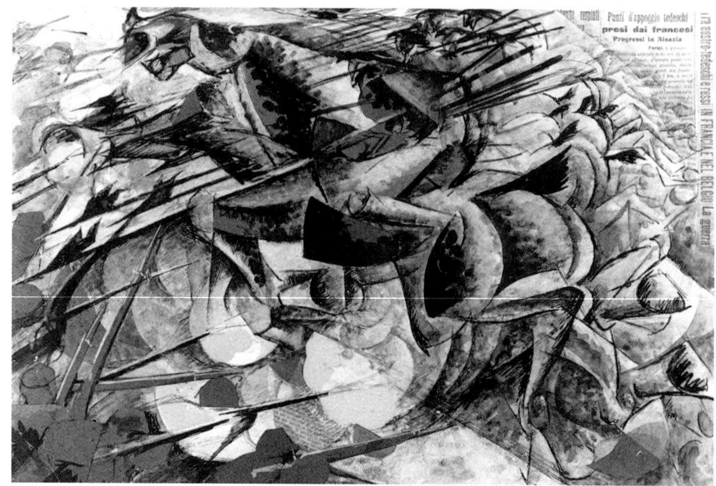

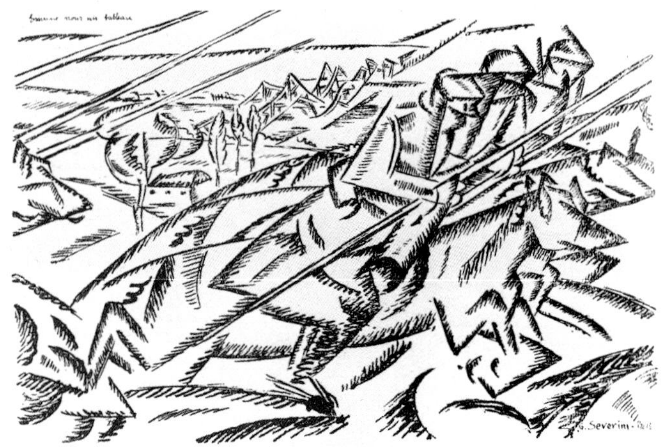

Fig. 9l. *Umberto Boccioni,* Carica di lancieri *(*Charge of Lancers*), tempera and collage on board, 1915. Milan, Civiche raccolte d'arte, Jucker Collection*

Fig. 9m. *Gino Severini,* Esquisse pour un tableau *(*Sketch for a Picture*), in* La Grande Illustrazione*, February 1915*

ground with a coat of green paint (green emerges in front of the horse's muzzle and especially along the edge of the triangular form on the bottom). At this point the artist began to work on the outer edges of the image with collage in the following sequence: the clipping from the sports page of the French newspaper in the upper left; the fragment of *Gli Avvenimenti* in the upper right; the long strip from the French newspaper along the base. He then added, with the brush, touches of whitish or gray tempera, to lend movement to the neutral background and to muddy the papers hitherto used (this is the only such intervention in Carrà's collages of 1914–15, while it was common practice with Boccioni and Soffici). He then shaped the horse from pieces of pale yellow, lightly marbled paper (this is not foxing, since it appears thus in the 1915 plate in *Guerrapittura*). The unnatural, toy-like appearance of the horse was obtained by simply placing the papers next to each other (head and neck, front leg, back end of the belly, large hindquarters, tail) without actually joining them. Next came the rider. The three-color polychromy and the lettering on the rear flank of the horse are cut from the cover, designed by Carrà himself in 1914, of an interventionist pamphlet by Francesco Penazzo, *Per la coscienza della Nuova Italia* (fig. 9b); he also used a piece of stiff, mottled black paper (similar to that used a few months later for a detail in *Composition* in the Pushkin Museum, Moscow[35]) for the torso and abdomen and for the cylindrical helmet. In only two points along the rider's contour did Carrà later add papers that define his body in negative: the French newspaper clipping of Parisian entertainments of June 11, 1914 forms the curve of the galloping rider's back and overlays the January fragment from *Gli Avvenimenti*; the central clipping with the classified ads from the February 9, 1915 issue of *Corriere della Sera* is the wedge that determines the angle of the rider's leg and torso and fractionally overlaps the square from *Pianeta della fortuna*. These inserts generate a visual alternation of solids and voids that evokes still the process of plastic fragmentation. The last addition, the cutting from *Il Popolo d'Italia* of January 13, 1915 which represents the horse's breast, has the value of sealing the image with a strong constructive sense. In the final stages he softened the horse's silhouette with black washes and added, again in black, the boot and the lance. He also painted in black the letters forming the name 'JOFFRE' and the onomatopoeic 'UUUU' sequence of letters on the right. This process confirms his preference for closed, finite forms in a general intent to enhance clear cut silhouettes.

The subject of horse and rider invites comparison with earlier works of the same subject by Umberto Boccioni (beginning with *Elasticity* of 1912[36]); indeed, the horse made of assembled parts, with the air of a toy that could be taken apart, brings to mind Boccioni's mixed-media *Dynamism of a Speeding Horse + Houses* (fig. 9n), although the question of which was made

Fig. 9n. *Umberto Boccioni,* Dinamismo di un cavallo in corsa + case (Dynamism of a Speeding Horse + Houses), *multimedia sculpture, 1915. Venice, Peggy Guggenheim Collection (The Solomon R. Guggenheim Foundation)*

first remains open.[37] But the horse and rider theme had been a favorite of Carrà's from the beginning of the century. In his 1908 *Horsemen of the Apocalypse*[38] the skeleton on horseback wrapped in a red flag at the center of the picture was derived from a painting legendary to Milanese artists with Socialist sympathies, *The Horrors of War* by Gaetano Previati, which was painted for the Padiglione della Pace at the 1894 'Esposizioni Riunite' in Milan[39] and published as an illustration in Manzoni's *Promessi Sposi* (Hoepli) in 1900.[40] The *Horsemen of the Apocalypse* can be considered the prototype of an intermediate work by Carrà of great importance for *Pursuit*: *Horse and Rider* in the Jucker Collection at the Civiche raccolte d'arte, Milan (fig. 9k).[41] Here Carrà used the characteristic techniques of plastic dynamism to represent the galloping horse seen from the side, with its rider urging it on. The horse, however, betrays an embryonic shift towards the plastic synthesis of its constituent parts (the unity of the neck and head for example) which Carrà would maintain through *Pursuit* and beyond: the metaphysical toy that is *The Western Rider*[42] of 1917 (fig. 9o), set in a landscape with perspective gleaned from Paolo Uccello's frescoes in Santa Maria Novella, Florence, is an evident reiteration of *Pursuit* both in its figurative arrangement and its subject[43] — the western spirit of France, two years on, launched against the hated Germany.

There exists a drawing which can justly be considered the preparatory study for *Pursuit*, though it is not included in the major catalogue of Carrà drawings. In *Jockey on Horseback*, dated (perhaps *post facto*) 1914 and published in 1942 by Giuseppe Raimondi[44] (fig. 9j), the invention of *Pursuit* was almost perfected both in its horse-rider group and in the landscape

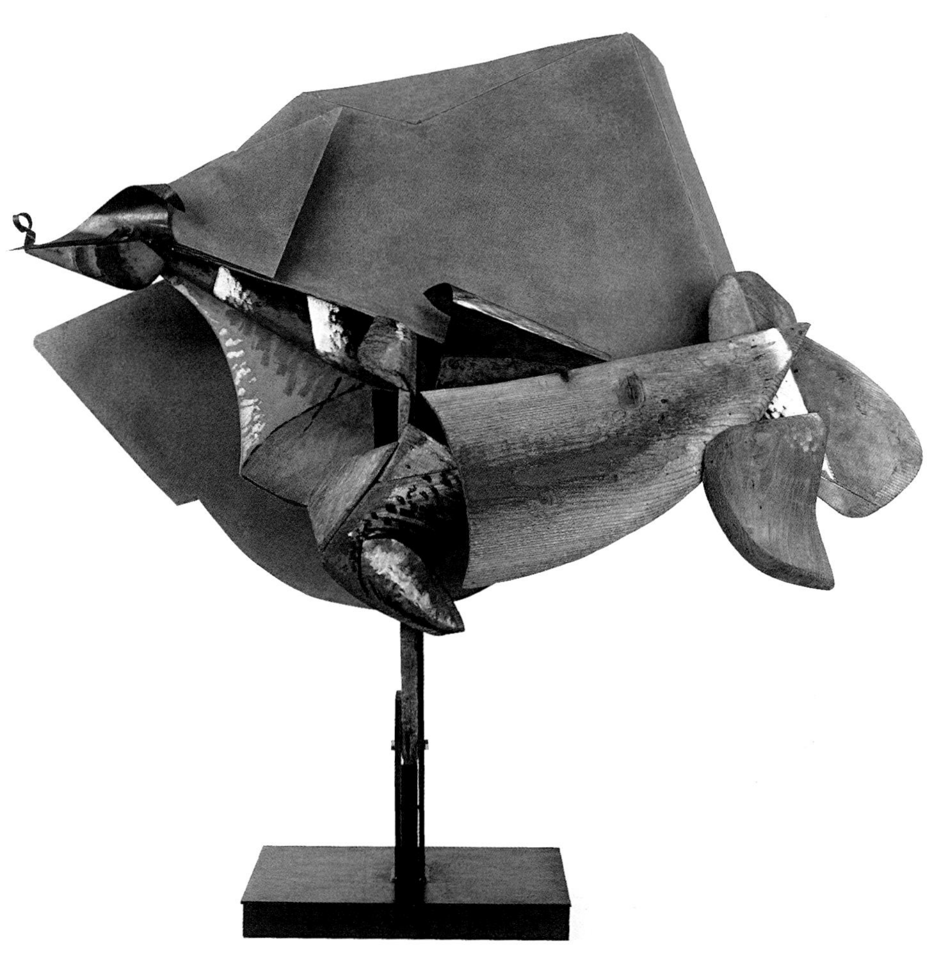

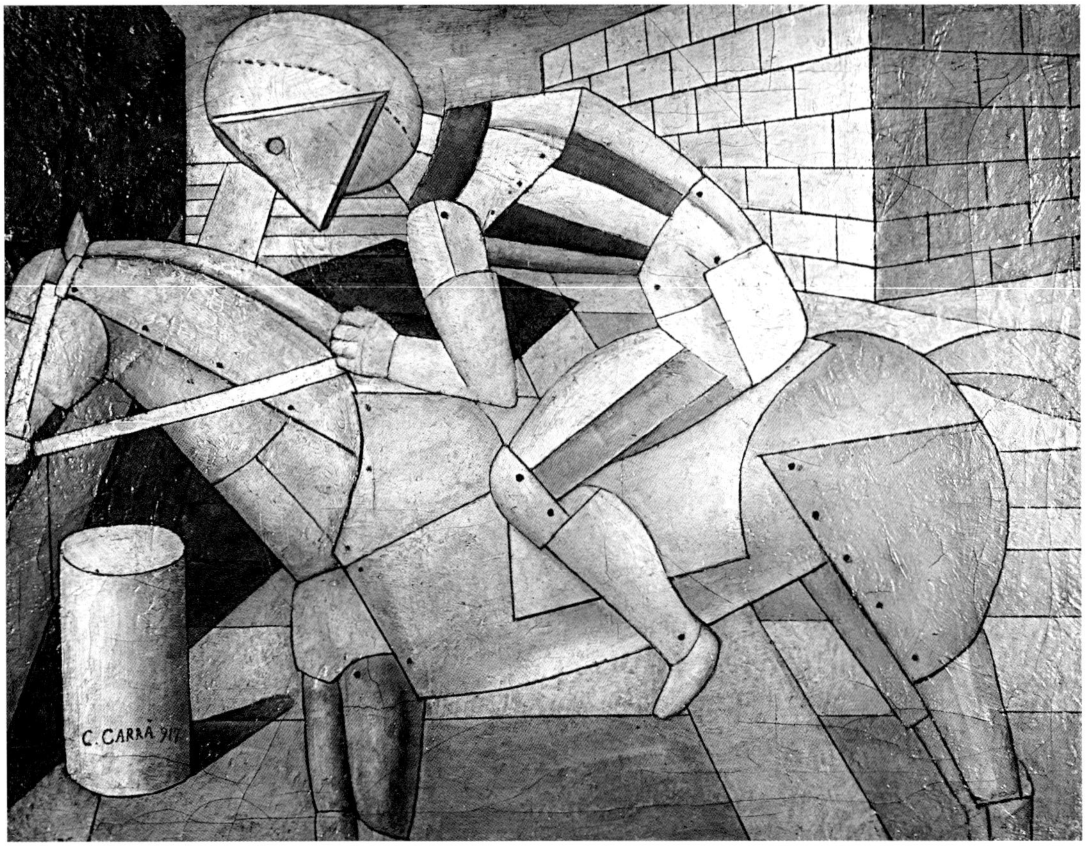

Fig. 9o. *Carlo Carrà,* Il cavaliere occidentale (The Western Rider), *oil on canvas, 1917. Private collection*

background. In the collage for *Guerrapittura* Carrà translated the drawing's many triangulations into a less busy composition, stressing the continuity of the outlines of the horse and simplifying the chiaroscuro pattern. This change testifies very clearly to Carrà's formal development in the crucial months of his decision to go beyond Futurist plastic dynamism.

Though the theme occurred in Carrà's pre-Futurist work, and was later developed in a tempera and a drawing of his Futurist period, he was surely aware of similar works being produced by the international avant-garde in those crucial years of 1912–14 that would have confirmed the vitality of his invention. In June 1914 the periodical *La Plume* illustrated an article by Jean Christophe with *War* (1894, fig. 9p) by Henri Rousseau,[45] an artist of whom Carrà was especially fond following his visit to Paris in March–April of that year:[46] had Carrà seen the reproduction, he would certainly have remarked the horse centered in the composition leaping triumphantly and with impassive indifference over the ground strewn with corpses. Even closer to Carrà's collage, and already recognized as a derivation of Rousseau's prototype,[47] is a 1911 painting by Wassily Kandinsky, *Lyrical* (fig. 9q),[48] with a rich exhibition history between 1911 and 1914 and which was reproduced in 1912 in the 'Blaue Reiter' almanack[49] as well as the album dedicated to Kandinsky by 'Der Sturm' in 1913.[50] Carrà may have appropriated some of its details, such as the background with two curtain-like forms which frame the horse and rider toward the top; or the waving line of the ground which begins to rise toward the right; or certain details of the rider such as the lance held horizontally behind the body to accentuate the visual effect of swiftly galloping.

Pursuit, which was already the property of Umberto Notari at the time of the publication of *Guerrapittura*, was omitted from Carrà's one-man show in December 1917–January 1918 at the Galleria Paolo Chini (where Notari had lent his later *The Romantics* and where, in the drawing section, several of the drawings for *Guerrapittura* were shown[51]). However, its reproduction in the 1915 book did not pass unobserved. *Pursuit* was admired especially in

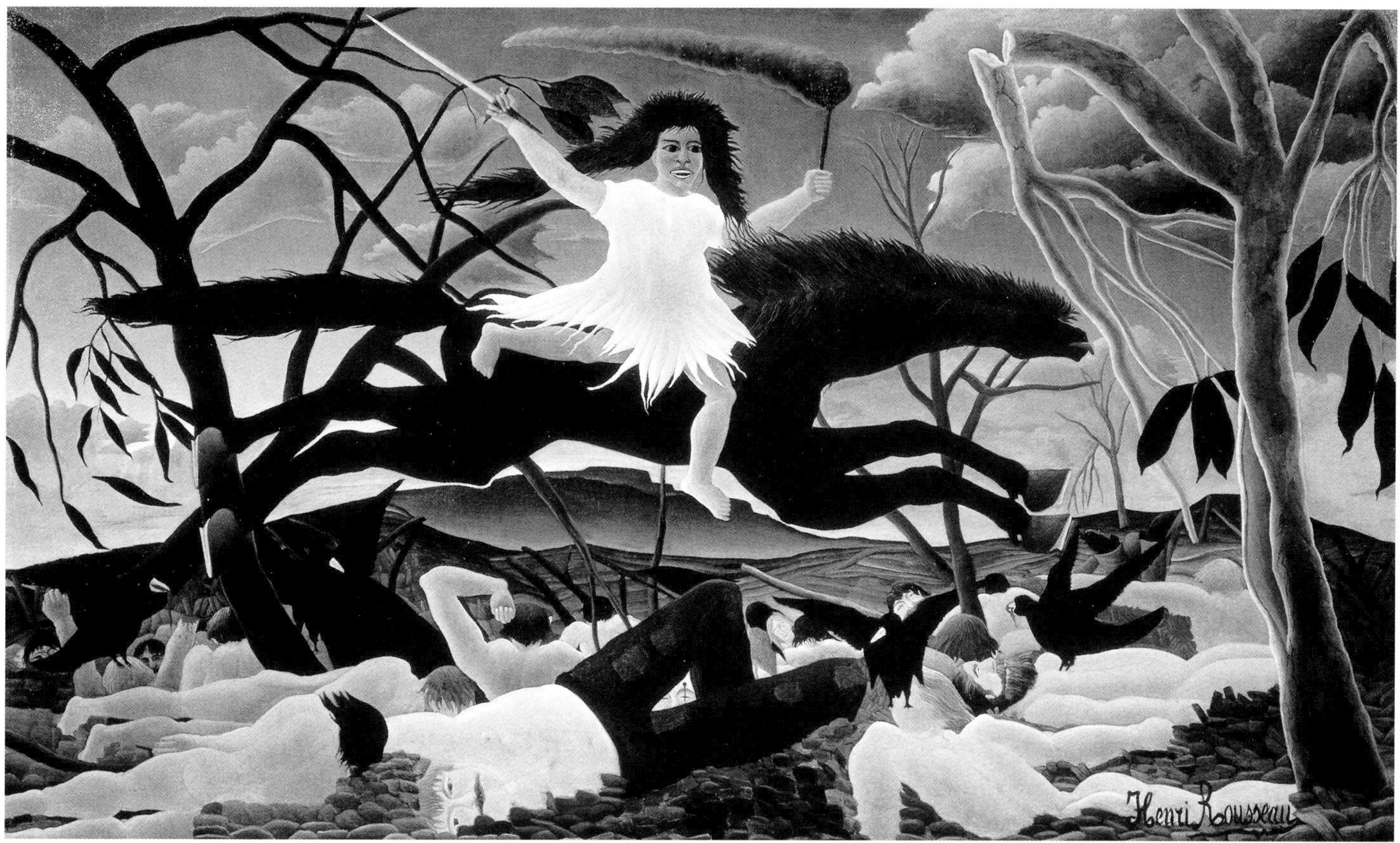

Fig. 9p. *Henri Rousseau,* La Guerre (War)*, oil on canvas, 1894. Paris, Musée d'Orsay*

Florence where it was hailed as a positive development by those who considered excessive Marinetti's influence on the drawings preceding it: Soffici praised it in a letter to Carrà for its "sobriety" and the "plastic qualities, *pictorial* and of sincerity",[52] while Papini considered it "the most beautiful and the most plastic" in the book.[53] After the war, when conversion to classicism was in the air, the Florentine Futurists looked back wistfully at its formal qualities: Primo Conti remembered "the panel shining and grainy of *Pursuit*" as "the last gift Carrà could make for us, as a farewell. As this gift is beautiful, we accept it without rancor."[54] Notari kept the work in his collection for more than thirty years but, in line with the general critical disregard of Futurist collages in the following two decades, he neither exhibited nor allowed it to be published. *Pursuit* only re-emerged, with the title *Horse and Rider* (*Cavallo e cavaliere*), at the 1953 exhibition of the Mattioli Collection in Palazzo Strozzi, Florence. Gianni Mattioli had acquired it in October 1950 from the Galleria del Milione for the sum of 200,000 lire.[55]

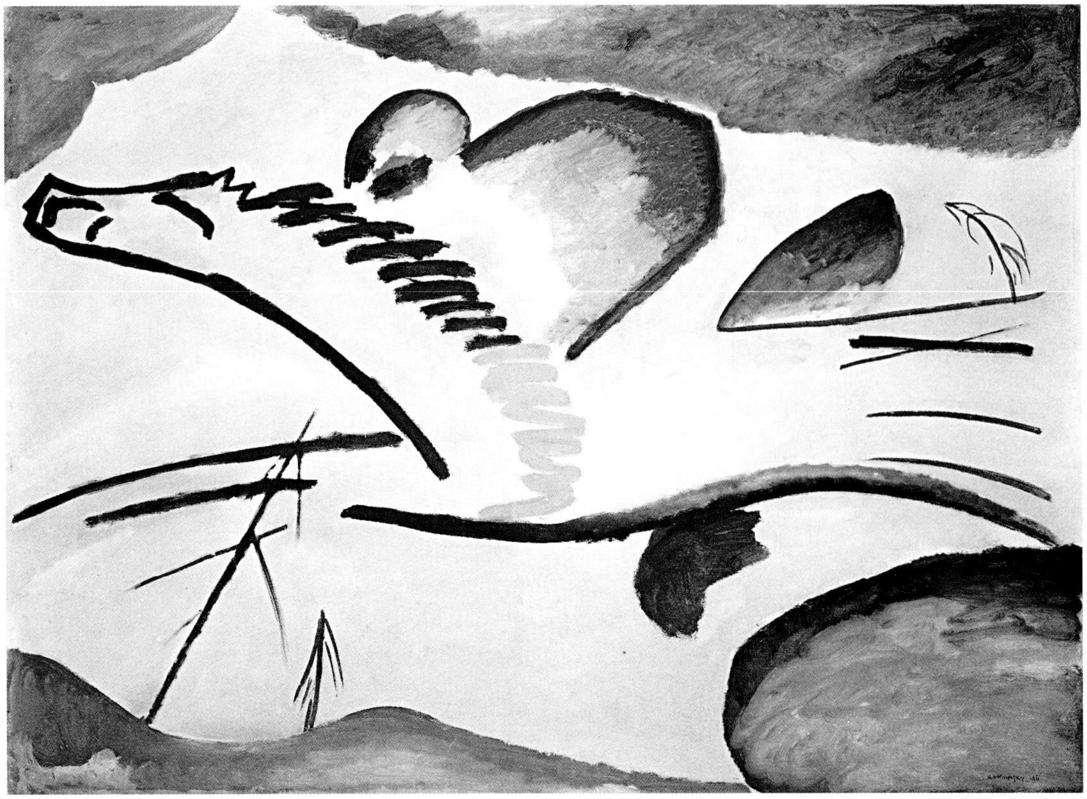

Fig. 9q. *Wassily Kandinsky,* Lyrisches (Lyrical)*, oil on canvas, 1911. Rotterdam, Museum Boijmans Van Beuningen*

[1] Carrà 1915, p. 31.
[2] Martin 1968, pp. 199–200. Certain details of the rider (the black boots, the red trousers, the lance) resemble those of the uniform of the light cavalry, 5th Regiment, of the French army (Funcken 1970, vol. II, p. 25); when in battle dress these soldiers wore a cylindrical hat or helmet with a short visor. But the unusual height, color and shape of the rider's hat in *Pursuit* suggest to the present writer a civilian hat, a stove-pipe or top hat, which could make sense in the context of a strategy elsewhere in this collage of contaminating military with society iconography.
[3] Martin 1968, pp. 198–9; Poggi (1992, p. 238) has pointed out that the mix of French and English (the inclusion of *The Car Illustrated*) in the collage may allude directly to Carrà's hopes of an alliance between Italy and the two countries in a war against the Empires.
[4] Cork 1994, p. 64.
[5] Roche-Pézard 1983, p. 445.
[6] Letter from Carlo Carrà to Ardengo Soffici, dated March 25, 1915 in Carrà, Soffici 1983, p. 80; thus Roche-Pézard (1983, p. 445) was mistaken in moving the date to the summer of 1915.
[7] As documented by a postcard from Ardengo Soffici to Carlo Carrà, dated June 26, 1914, in Carrà, Soffici 1983, p. 59.
[8] Letter from Carlo Carrà to Ardengo Soffici, dated April 30, 1914, *ibidem*, p. 52.
[9] *Naples* 1914, p. 26, nos. 3–4.
[10] *Costruzione dinamica su asse orizzontale* and *Costruzione dinamica su asse obliquo*, both New York, private collections: respectively Carrà 1967–8, vol. I, no. 1/14 and, probably, no. 7/14.
[11] Undated letter from Carlo Carrà to Ardengo Soffici (but May 1, 1914), in Carrà, Soffici 1983, p. 53.
[12] *Natura morta con sifone*, private collection: Carrà 1967–8, vol. I, no. 3/14.
[13] Gianni Mattioli Collection, on deposit at the Peggy Guggenheim Collection, Venice (see cat. no. 8): *ibidem*, vol. I, no. 8/14; for dates see the letters from Carlo Carrà to Ardengo Soffici, dated June 23 and July 4, 1914, in Carrà, Soffici 1983, pp. 58–60.
[14] *Caffè di sobborgo*, *Fiasco e bicchiere*, and *Candeliere*, all in private collections: respectively Carrà 1967–8, vol. I, nos. 4/14, 6/14, 5/14.
[15] *I rumori del caffè notturno*, whereabouts unknown: *ibidem,* vol. I, no. 2/14; Poggi (1992, p. 193) dates the work to the final months of 1914 thanks to an unidentified newspaper clipping with the "latest declarations of war," which broke out in August.
[16] *Composizione*, Moscow, Pushkin Museum: Carrà 1967–8, vol. I, no. 2/15.
[17] *Il fiasco*: *ibidem*, vol. I, no. 4/15; *Acrobata negra*: *ibidem,* vol. I, no. 1/13 (whereabouts unknown); in the artist's general catalogue the latter work is inexplicably dated 1913 despite the perfectly legible fragment of an issue of the fortieth year of the *Corriere della Sera*, founded in 1876.
[18] Letter from Carlo Carrà to Ardengo Soffici, dated December 27, 1915, in Carrà, Soffici 1983, pp. 93–4.
[19] Letter from Carlo Carrà to Ardengo Soffici, dated November 21, 1914, *ibidem*, p. 69; for a recollection of the Futurists' creative block after the outbreak of war, see Soffici 1955, p. 427.
[20] Fossati 1995, pp. 49–58.
[21] Letter from Filippo Tommaso Marinetti to Gino Severini, dated November 20, 1914, in Drudi Gam-

billo, Fiori 1958–62, vol. I, pp. 349–50.
[22] As deduced from a letter from Umberto Notari to Francesco Cangiullo, dated February 4, 1915, *ibidem*, vol, I, pp. 351–2.
[23] *Carica di lancieri*, Milan, Civiche raccolte d'arte, Jucker Collection: Calvesi, Coen 1983, no. 925; the motif was inspired by a clipping from the January 5, 1915 edition of *Corriere della Sera*.
[24] *Esquisse pour un tableau*, whereabouts unknown: Fonti 1988, no. 224. The drawing illustrated *Les Cosaques,* a prose-poem by Paul Fort.
[25] Coen 1989, p. 190; Poggi 1992, p. 240.
[26] Fonti 1988, no. 226a.
[27] *Ulano + paesaggio belga*: Carrà 1915, p. 19; Carrà, Russoli 1997, no. 179 (whereabouts unknown).
[28] *Angolo penetrante di Joffre sopra Marna contro 2 cubi germanici*: Carrà 1915, p. 29; Carrà, Russoli 1977, no. 142 (private collection).
[29] Landis 1983, pp. 64–5; Poggi 1992, pp. 240–1.
[30] A copy exists in the Civica raccolta delle stampe Achille Bertarelli, Milan, call number SPP.m.18-7; my thanks to Federica Rovati for calling this to my attention.
[31] Caruso, Martini 1974, p. 41.
[32] Carrà, Russoli 1977, nos. 136, 140, 141, 142.
[33] "And now let us take a peek at the Balkans: King Nicholas, Enver-bey, Daneff, Venizelos, punches in the tummy and slaps between Serbs and Bulgars, a tirade and its all over:" Marinetti, October 1, 1913.
[34] Carrà, June 1, 1914.
[35] Carrà 1967–8, vol. I, no. 2/15.
[36] Milan, Civiche raccolte d'arte, Jucker Collection: Calvesi, Coen 1983, no. 799.
[37] *Dinamismo di un cavallo in corsa + case*, Venice, Peggy Guggenheim Collection (The Solomon R. Guggenheim Foundation): Calvesi, Coen 1983, no. 903. The standard dating of 1914–15 (Rudenstine 1985, p. 99), later accepted by Angelucci, Rylands (1992, pp. 134–5), or narrowed to 1914 by Coen (1996[a], p. 61), has been moved to March–April 1915 by Enrico Crispolti on the basis of a report in a Futurist review, *La Balza* of April 27, 1915: according to this Boccioni had completed "in these days a large plastic Futurist assemblage (sculpture) titled *Dynamism of a Speeding Horse + Houses*:" Crispolti 1988, p. 200, note 21.
[38] *Cavalieri dell'Apocalisse*, Chicago, The Art Institute, Mr And Mrs Harold X. Weinstein Collection: Carrà 1967–8, vol. I, no. 2/08.
[39] *Gli orrori della guerra*: Fiori 1968, no. II, p. 606, fig. 839.
[40] Manzoni 1900, p. 483.
[41] The Jucker tempera on paper has been dated by some (Taylor 1961, p. 75; Martin 1968, pp. 152–5) to 1912, thus making possible its identification with the mysterious *Speed Dismantles the Horse*, exhibited in February 1913 at the Teatro Costanzi show in Rome (*Rome* 1913, p. 23, no. 7) and summarily described by critics on that occasion (Mastrigli, February 23–4, 1913) but mistakenly considered by others (Carrà 1967–8, vol. I, n. 1/14) a later 1914 evolution of the 1912 prototype. The *terminus ante quem* is its reproduction in Nebbia 1913, p. 437.
[42] *Il cavaliere occidentale*, private collection: Carrà 1967–8, vol. I, no. 6/17.
[43] As already perceived by Raimondi 1942, p. 7.
[44] *Ibidem* 1942, pl. VI; a later version seems to be the drawing in Carrà, Russoli 1977, no. 106.
[45] This information comes from Hoog 1984, p. 128.
[46] Monferini 1996, pp. 63–4.
[47] Lindsay, Vergo 1982, vol. I, p. 28.
[48] *Lyrisches*, Rotterdam, Museum Boijmans Van Beuningen: Roethel, Benjamin 1982, no. 377.
[49] Marc 1912, p. 9.
[50] *Kandinsky* 1913, p. 58.
[51] *Milan* 1917–18, nos. 8, 31, 36–7, 43.
[52] Letter from Ardengo Soffici to Carlo Carrà, dated April 28, 1915, in Carrà, Soffici 1983, pp. 80–1.
[53] Letter from Giovanni Papini to Carlo Carrà, dated August 22, 1915, in Papini, Carrà 1986, p. 357.
[54] Conti 1919, p. 28.
[55] Archivio Mattioli, account of the Galleria del Milione, dated October 28, 1950: the purchase of the "papier collé *Inseguimento*" is dated October 8, 1950, with the stock entry number 5836 (*Appendix I*, document no. 59). In a subsequent statement, dated February 7, 1951 (*Appendix I*, document no. 68), Mattioli was noted as owing lire 2,500 for the restoration of a "Carrà futurista" which can be identified with *Pursuit*.

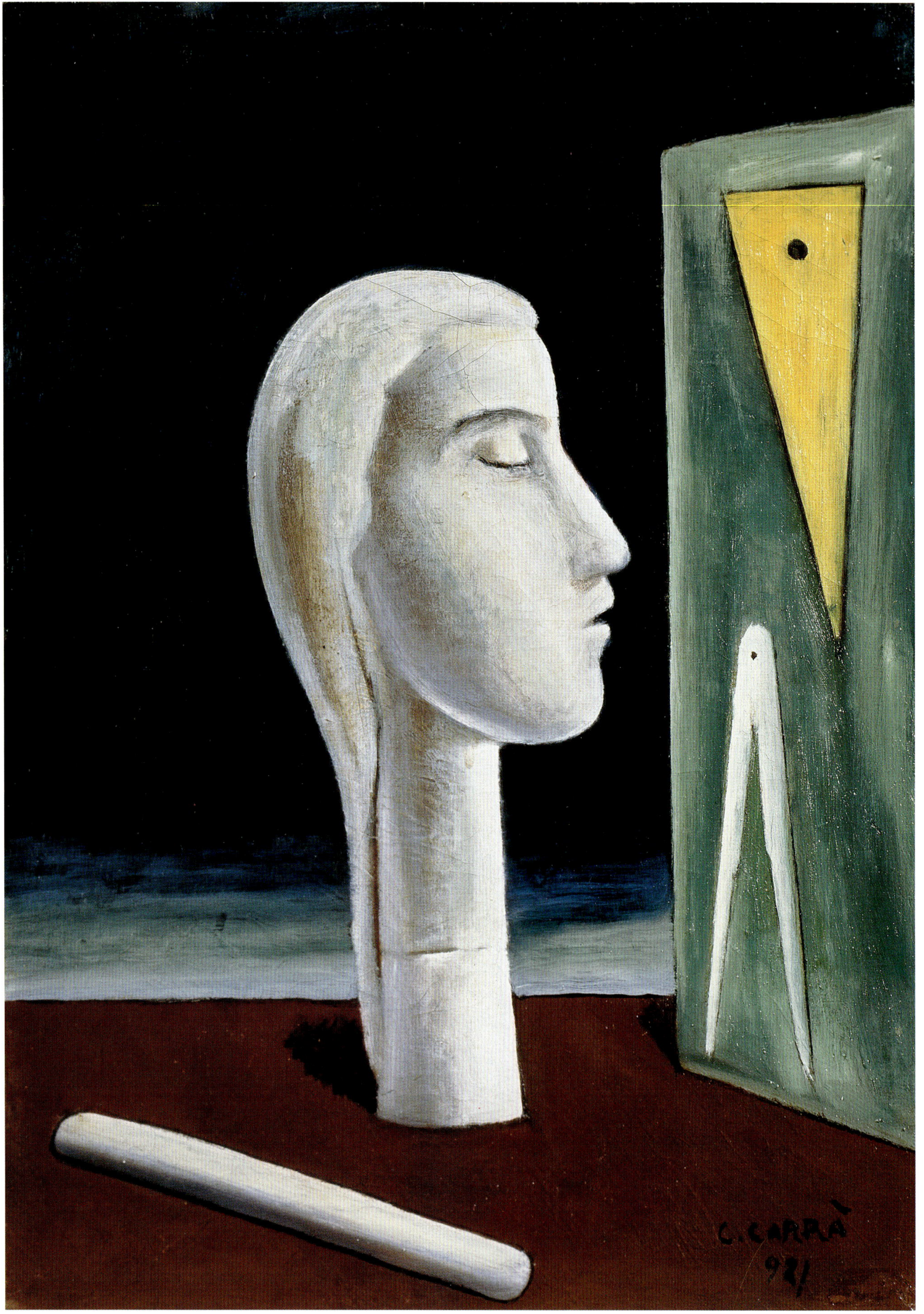
C. CARRÀ
921

10

Carlo Carrà

The Engineer's Mistress (*The Engineer's Wife*; *The Engineer's Woman*)

L'amante dell'ingegnere (*La moglie dell'ingegnere*; *Donna dell'ingegnere*), 1921

Oil on canvas
55 × 40 cm

Inscription: *recto*, signed lower right: 'C. Carrà 921'

Provenance: property of the artist; August 1923: Mario Broglio, Rome; October 1924: property of the artist, Milan; 1926: Alessandro Mazzucotelli, Bergamo; January 1936: Pietro Feroldi, Brescia, with the mediation of the Galleria del Milione; May 1949: Gianni Mattioli

Exhibitions: Alessandria 1921, catalogue not traced (its presence, with the title *Donna dell'Ingegnere*, is documented in the June 18, 1921 edition of *La Stampa*); Milan 1922, catalogue not traced (its presence is documented by the photograph in *Primato* 1922, p. 45); Turin 1923, no. 333 (*L'amante dell'ingegnere*); Rome 1925, p. 33, no. 24 (illus. pl. 20); Milan 1926, p. 43, no. 10 (*L'amante dell'ingegnere*, 1921); Milan 1935, no. 47; Rome 1937, p.14, unnumbered; San Francisco 1939, p. 22, no. 5; Zurich 1940, not in catalogue (the painting's presence in the exhibition is documented by a label on the *verso*); Milan 1942a, no. 18; Milan 1942[b], catalogue not printed; Venice 1948, p. 29, no. 12; Milan 1948, catalogue not traced (its presence attested by information in the Archivio Mattioli, file for the work); Cairo 1949, no. 64; New York 1949, p. 128 and pl. 41; Amsterdam 1950 catalogue not traced (its presence attested by information in the Archivio Mattioli, file for the work); Brussels 1950, no. 13; London 1950, no. 29; Paris 1950, no. 26; Zurich 1950, no. 123; Milan 1952, unnumbered; Florence 1953[a], no. 15; Ostend 1953, cata-

The Engineer's Mistress is a pivotal work in Carrà's career. Usually considered the last episode in the chapter of Carrà's Metaphysical painting, which began in 1917, it synthesizes the expressive character of Carrà's *metafisica* and some of its postulates: the gap between the picture's straightforward title and its stubbornly indecipherable subject; its iconography, with objects typical of the paraphernalia dear to Giorgio de Chirico, such as the fragment of the statue and the drawing instruments; and its ambiguous perspective. At the same time, given the particular quality of the light and the handling of paint, *The Engineer's Mistress* seems to open the way to the mellow tones of Carrà the landscape painter of the 1920s. It should be noted however that the latter characteristic, which has strongly conditioned the painting's critical reception, was mitigated when it was cleaned in 1988 by Giovanni Rossi: following the removal of a layer of brown varnish that dulled the colors, the picture surface regained its enameled hues and the precision of its light effects.

On the first occasion that Carrà was given the opportunity to exhibit his art in a coherent way, he himself acknowledged *The Engineer's Mistress*'s status as a painting bridging two distinct phases of his production. In the 1925 III Biennale of Rome (where Carrà was given a gallery to himself) it was the only one among many Metaphysical works illustrated in the catalogue with a Valsesia landscape opposite, *Sunset on the Mountains*,[1] in what amounted to a dialogue. In a show at the Galleria Pesaro, Milan in 1926, *The Engineer's Mistress* came after the solidly Metaphysical *Solitude* and before no fewer than twenty-four landscapes.[2] In the series of plates in a little book on Carrà published by Hoepli in 1928 it was inserted between the oppressive box-like space of *The Builder's Son* and the open air, the new–found neo-Giottesque perspective, of *Pine Tree by the Sea*.[3]

The work has been among the most fortunate of all Italian paintings of the first half of the century: its presence in renowned collections (Mazzucotelli, Feroldi, Mattioli); its promotion by means of a systematic campaign in the press as well as picture postcards circulated by Italy's most important modern art gallery, the Galleria del Milione; its captivating iconography — all this has made it an important point of reference in the Italian critical debate on figurative art. During the 1920s and 1930s, it represented the case for an Italian way of *metafisica*, as an art of plastic construction (*costruzione plastica*) and an alternative to the literary complexities and international eclecticism of de Chirico. In the second postwar era, the painting was co-opted as an icon of the popular theories of Existentialism: Carlo Ludovico Ragghianti writing in 1953 considered it a "now popular [image] and, in its candid search for a world [conjured] from the chaos of fragments and uncertainties, very often set up as a virtual symbol of modern life."[4] It was no accident that Gianni Mattioli chose to reproduce this work on the flyer that advertised the opening of his collection to the public in his apartment in Via Senato, Milan in the early 1950s (fig. 10b).

The Engineer's Mistress is signed and dated 1921 on the front of the canvas, but whether or not the signature and date were applied at the time of execution is uncertain. In a black-and-white photograph widely circulated in the 1920s[5] and in another photograph made for the catalogue of the 'Terza Biennale Romana' in 1925 (in which the number 34 in the lower left refers to the room in which the paintings were hung and to the catalogue number), the signature and date are not visible against the dark background. As late as 1930 the painting was still being illustrated and captioned with the date 1917.[6] But despite this (Carrà may have signed and dated the canvas at a later time, in his broader and more sloping hand of the late 1920s or early 1930s), and contrary to the complex vicissitudes of postdating and retouching of others of Carrà's paintings of that period, there are no plausible stylistic or documentary motives for questioning the date 1921. In some passages the handling of paint resembles that of *Pine Tree by the Sea*, which certainly dates from 1921 (such as, for example, the loaded brushstrokes of the dawn light along the horizon, absent from Carrà's metaphysical work up to 1920). Furthermore, the painting's first exhibition, as demonstrated here, was in June 1921, immediately, surely, after its execution.

In this sense the date 1920 inscribed by Carrà on two works related to *The Engineer's Mistress* is not an issue. The first can be read on a smaller (24 × 19 cm) version of the Mattioli painting formerly in the Estorick Collection and now in a private collection in New York[7] (fig. 10c). This belongs to a series of replicas, or better 'revisitations,' of important works of 1919–22 that Carrà executed between the late 1930s and early 1940s, with the characteristic feathery brushwork of that period.[8] The second instance of the 1920 date occurs on the base of a large drawing of *The Engineer's Mistress* with all the characteristics of a *d'après*.[9] It can be grouped with other drawings which share several features (the same dimensions, squaring and technique) and which reiterate, each with a comparably summary handling and each generously pre-dated, important Metaphysical paintings such as *The Drunken Gentleman*, *My Son*, *Penelope*, *Solitude*, and *The Daughter of the West*.[10] The *d'après* status of at least one of these drawings, the reworking of *Solitude*,[11] is uncontestable: contrary to the 1917 date inscribed on it, it shows the painting precisely as it was after Carrà's modifications carried out after 1921,[12] thus rendering an earlier dating impossible.

Of the other works on paper connected to *The Engineer's Mistress*, all of which relate to an advanced state of Carrà's invention, the most interesting would seem to be a pencil drawing dated 1921 in ink (and therefore possibly a later addition)[13] (fig. 10d): the small differences *vis-à-vis* the final version of the painting (the nut still joining the two arms of the compasses which will eventually shrink to a dot; the profile of the statue-figure which has a lower forehead and a longer nose) tend to indicate Carrà's desire to reduce further the already meager naturalism of the drawing. Infrared reflectography of the oil painting (fig. 10e) reveals that the artist was exploring some details in the drawing at a time when the final canvas was already begun: Carrà had first painted the round nut of the compasses like that in the drawing, but in a different position, at the height of the nose; furthermore the set square, contrary to its appearance both in the drawing and in the final version of the painting, was originally horizontal and was mounted on a broader support which extended to the left, passing behind the profile of the head (fig. 10e).

Though *The Engineer's Mistress* was executed in 1921, it was most probably conceived earlier. Evidence for this occurs in a passage of Filippo de Pisis' critique of Carrà's solo show at the Galleria Paolo Chini in Milan (December 1917–January 1918) published early in 1918 in *La*

logue not traced (its presence attested by information in the Archivio Mattioli, file for the work); Kassel 1955, no. 108; Turin 1959, p. 41, no. 7; Milan 1962[c], no. 24; Milan 1966[a], no. 8; Florence 1967[a], no. 842; Washington, DC 1967–Tokyo 1972, no. 19 (Washington, DC–Hamburg), no. 18 (Madrid–Seville), no. 19 (Kyoto–Tokyo); Prato 1971, no. XXVI; Berlin 1977, no. 3/627; Frankfurt 1977–8, no. 3/627; Venice 1989, p. 385; Madrid 1990–1, p. 269; Rome 1994–5, p. 236

Bibliography: De Pisis, February 12, 1918? (*La moglie dell'ingegnere*); *Stampa*, June 18, 1921 (*Donna dell'ingegnere*); *Primato* 1922, p. 45, illus. (*L'amante dell'ingegnere*), Zanzi, May 10, 1923; Thovez, May 20, 1923; Gobetti, July 11, 1923; Letter from Carlo Carrà to Mario Broglio, dated October 15, 1924 (Milan, private archive); Sarfatti 1925[a], pp. 41 and 43, Lancellotti 1926, p. 34; Soffici 1926, pp. 11 and 14; Soffici 1928, unnumbered plate; Bardi 1930, no. 5 (*L'amante dell'ingegnere*, 1917); Sarfatti 1930, pl. 11; Scheiwiller 1930, p. 32; Bartolini, January 11, 1931; Cremona, June 15, 1932; Vitali, April 21, 1934; Solmi, December 6, 1935; Letter from Gino Ghiringhelli to Carlo Belli, dated January 12, 1936, in Boschiero 1991, p. 233; Letter from Pietro Feroldi to Carlo Belli, dated January 20, 1936 (photostatic copy, Archivio Mattioli); Letter from Peppino Ghiringhelli to Pietro Feroldi, dated January 27, 1936 (photostatic copy, Archivio Mattioli); *Milione* 1936, no. 45, unnumbered page; Costantini 1936, p. 44; Letter from Gino Ghiringhelli to Carlo Belli, dated May 18, 1936 (photostatic copy, Archivio Mattioli); Ragghianti 1936, pp. 252–3; Longhi 1937, pl. 10; *Pittori* 1938, vol. II, pl. 1002; Anceschi, January 1, 1939; Arcangeli 1942, p. 9; Testori 1942, p. 6; Torriano 1942, unnumbered page; Giolli 1942, p. 260; Briganti, July 15, 1942; Piovene 1942, p. XII; Carlo Belli, unpublished typescript introduction to the Raccolta Feroldi catalogue, before May 1942 (Rovereto, MART, Archivio del 900, Fondo Belli); Carrà 1943, p. 240; Pacchioni 1945, p. 47 and pl.14; Arcangeli 1948, p. 28; Mango 1949, p. 25; Soby 1949, p. 23; Carrieri 1950, p. 143; Mattioli 1951, p. 25; Ragghianti 1953, p. 10; Haftmann 1955, p. 187; Castelfranco, Valsecchi 1956, p. 32; Valsecchi 1958, pp. 46 and 71; Pacchioni 1959, pl. 31; Maltese 1960, p. 329; Marchiori 1960, no. 19; Valsecchi 1962[a], pp. 7 and 24; Ballo 1964[b], vol. I, p. 193; Calvesi, November 15, 1964; Calvesi 1966, p. 155;

Carrà 1967–8, no. 7/21, pp. 20, 30, 35, 131, 171, 237, 249, 254, 268, 291–3, 351; Carrà, Waldberg, Rathke 1968, fig. 34; Argan 1970, pp. 592–3; Carrà 1970, pl. XXVIII, no. 91, p. 92; De Micheli 1971, pp. 17–18; Calvesi 1981, pp. 63–4; Calvesi 1982, p. 124; Fossati 1988, p. 47; Fugazza 1988, p. 395; Appella 1991, pp. 13–30; Boschiero 1991, p. 216; Cinelli 1991, pp. 212–13; Calvesi 1992, p. 16; Anzani, Pirovano 1992, pp. 138 and 143; Monferini 1994, pp. 83 and 87; Guzzi 1994[b], p. 236; Hergott 1994, p. 107; Rylands 1997, p. 70; Salvagnini 2000, pp. 318 and 32

Gazzetta Ferrarese. At the prompting of Giorgio de Chirico, whom Carrà had excluded from a show they had planned together,[14] de Pisis wrote a text focused not on the works exhibited in the show but in a more general way on the theoretical basis of Ferrarese *metafisica*, well-known to him since he was regularly in the company of de Chirico and Carrà in Ferrara during 1917.[15] The list of Carrà's most recent works in de Pisis's article ("his best paintings and [those] carried out in a period of intense work"[16]) holds some surprises: together with works already executed and certainly exhibited in Milan (*Solitude, Metaphysical Muse*), de Pisis mentioned works no longer identifiable either because they were destroyed or subjected to a title change, or perhaps because they were only in the planning stage (*The School Teacher, The Little Fish*), as well as one called *The Engineer's Wife*, which can feasibly be considered an anticipation by four years of the Mattioli painting. It is not possible to deduce from de Pisis's text whether the picture called *The Engineer's Wife* had in fact already been painted or whether it was merely an idea for development that Carrà mentioned when his young reporter friend visited him in his studio in Milan in January 1918.[17] The only certain fact in this context is that the details of the underdrawing visible with infrared reflectography are directly on the preparation of the canvas, thus excluding that Carrà painted the version we know today as *The Engineer's Mistress* over a previous version.

Carrà's title is not easy to explain; nor is the search for too-literal correspondences necessarily productive. In a letter to Mario Broglio in 1919 in which he communicated the captions for three illustrations of paintings for publication in an issue of *Valori Plastici*, Carrà stated that his titles were "simple indications."[18] Maurizio Calvesi has proposed separate iconographical interpretations on two occasions. In 1982 he read the stone bust herm as a *virgo methaphisica*, with its closed eyes "as if dazzled by the unveiled epiphany of the set square" (an attribute referred by Calvesi to the metaphysics of Giovan Battista Vico) and of the compasses.[19] But in an earlier interpretation, of 1964, he had suggested that the source was a *pièce* by Filippo Tommaso Marinetti called (when first published in 1909) *Les Poupées électriques*.[20] The engineer in the play, a certain John Wilson, falls under the spell of mechanical robots that he himself had invented, and finds in them the true flame of passion, "a prodigious stimulant for the heart, like alcohol for my love."[21] Marinetti's play was performed in Turin in 1911; then, after radical rewriting, it reappeared on tour in 1913 with the title *Elettricità (sintesi futurista)*. Carrà attended a performance in Bologna in January 1914, as we know from a letter to Ardengo Soffici.[22] In the edition published in 1920, by then called *Elettricità sessuale*, the engineer-protagonist Riccardo Marinetti asserted the need for keeping the physical presence of his beloved at a distance in order for his love to be kept alive ("One must [...] then create artificially the mystery, around the body of the beloved ... forget flesh previously explored ... distance yourself from it even forget it so that it will one day become obsessive, so that it becomes unfamiliar and new!").[23] According to Calvesi's second interpretation the engineer, represented by the tools of his trade (set square and compasses), is flanked on the picture's surface, in a dialogue of love, by the object of his desire transformed into a cold *simulacrum*.

The backdating of the initial idea for the painting to the end of 1917 diminishes the otherwise insurmountable difficulty of relating a text by Marinetti of the first decade to a painting by Carrà of 1921, by which time Carrà both in his ideological convictions and because of personal resentments had drifted away from the Futurist leader. Yet, given the work's content as it was painted in 1921, it is hard to justify the casual substitution of the mechanical puppet with a sculpted head: the latter was, around 1920, an object of crucial importance in Carrà's return to plastic values and to museum tradition. Even if Marinetti's *pièce* was not after all the direct iconographical basis for the painting, it may nevertheless have been one of the agents that inserted and consolidated the figure of the engineer in Carrà's pictorial imagination. In turn of the century Italy the

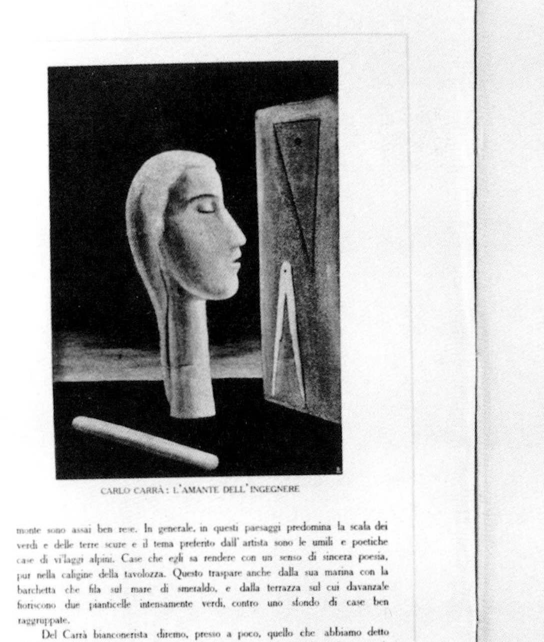

CARLO CARRÀ: L'AMANTE DELL'INGEGNERE

monte sono assai ben rese. In generale, in questi paesaggi predomina la scala dei verdi e delle terre scure e il tema preferito dall'artista sono le umili e poetiche case di villaggi alpini. Case che egli sa rendere con un senso di sincera poesia, pur nella caligine della tavolozza. Questo traspare anche dalla sua marina con la barchetta che fila sul mare di smeraldo, e dalla terrazza sul cui davanzale fioriscono due pianticelle intensamente verdi, contro uno sfondo di case ben raggruppate.

Del Carrà bianconerista diremo, presso a poco, quello che abbiamo detto del Carrà pittore, tavolozza a parte naturalmente.. I suoi disegni vogliono esprimere un sentimento e cercano di accentuarlo con deformazioni di figure e di cose. Credo che si possa, che si debba raggiungere lo stesso risultato senza bisogna di

34

CARLO CARRÀ: IL FIGLIO DEL COSTRUTTORE

questo. E lo prova lo stesso Carrà in alcuni suoi disegni che, per essere moderni, non rinunziano alla logica della forma. Vediamo, così, il gruppo di minuscole casette bene composte; la vivace, rapida marina, tanto delicata di segno; una testa fortemente segnata, profonda di sentimento; uno studio di nudo che rende bene il dinamismo della figura; una donna stilizzata, sì, forse troppo nelle gambe interminabili, ma dal cui volto traspare una rassegnata sofferenza; una barchetta a vela, infine, che è una delle cose sue migliori. Quando, dunque, il Carrà vuole, dimostra di sapere dipingere e disegnare senza trucchi da primitivo e, tuttavia, senza mettersi sulle vie già battute. Questo ci fa sperare che egli trovi la sua strada e che la trovi non sacrificando la propria personalità.

L'americano Maurice Sterne si dice che sia molto conosciuto in Italia. Confesso la mia ignoranza, ma, prima di oggi, ne ignoravo la esistenza. Non vi saprei, quindi, informare nè dove nacque, nè quando, nè con chi ha studiato, nè

35

Fig. 10a. *Cat. no. 10 flanked by* Il figlio del costruttore (The Builder's Son) *in A. Lancellotti,* La Terza Biennale Romana, *1926*

engineer was a protagonist *par excellence* of modern society (the *Programma politico futurista* signed by Marinetti, Boccioni, Carrà and Russolo in 1913 looked forward to an Italy founded on a class of "very many engineers" as well as chemists, mechanics and businessmen[24]) but was at the same time a player in the bourgeois milieu remote from Carrà's circle of contacts. The role of the engineer therefore seems ambiguous, suspended between a heritage of Positivist shibboleths ("Balla and Boccioni," according to a letter from Soffici to Carrà in 1915, "will only ever do metaphysics as mechanical engineers"[25]) and tomorrow's man of action. Giorgio de Chirico's father Evaristo had been an engineer, and hints of his profession appear in many of de Chirico's Metaphysical paintings: the small *The Nostalgia of the Engineer* (1916 or 1917) was exhibited with the Massine Collection in the foyer of the Teatro Costanzi in Rome on April 9, 1917.[26] This was the first of de Chirico's paintings to gain recognition in Italy. It contains a jumble of squares and complicated engineers' instruments as well as something resembling a blackboard, on which a loaf of bread is painted, drawn with the same hesitant perspective as the panel on the right in *The Engineer's Mistress.*

In 1921 Carrà decisively shifted his position and gave to the term 'engineer' the meaning of expert in construction, in the sense of a practice fundamental to any painter. He had celebrated the constructive rationality of the Italian pictorial traditional in a famous essay of 1916, *Paolo Uccello costruttore*, in which the fifteenth-century artist, a passionate student of mathematics and perspective, was identified as the key figure in the re-conquest of volumes in modern painting. At a time when Carrà was turning his back on de Chirico, his desire to neutralize literary complexity with a quest for pure sculptural values is easily comprehensible. As early as 1917 he countered the drafting squares hanging in de Chirico's paintings of 1916–17 with the more rational and neo-primitive *Still Life with a Set Square* (exhibited at the Galleria Paolo Chini in the winter of 1917–18).[27] In 1921 therefore, in response to a painting by de Chirico such as *Hermetic Melancholy* of 1919[28] (in which there is a plaster bust, a box with similar spatial ambiguity and a baton that regulates the perspective scale, fig. 10i), it is natural to imagine Carrà painting an allegory

Fig. 10b. *The Mattioli Collection flyer, with a reproduction of cat. no. 10*

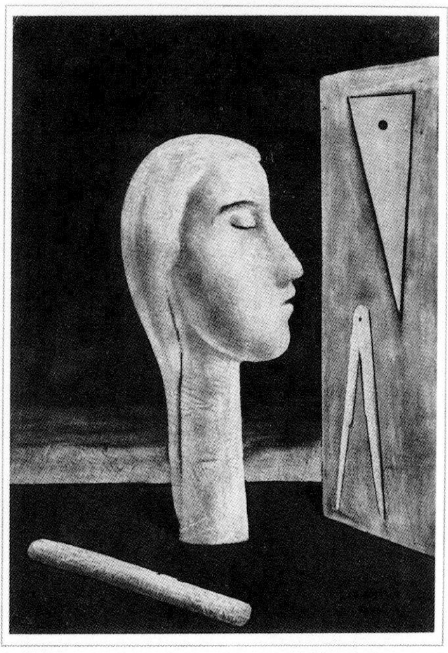

Raccolta privata d'Arte Moderna

with a metaphysical aura such as *The Engineer's Mistress*, which conjugates a similar repertoire of objects: the artist's self-portrait as an engineer-builder, metaphorically represented by a set square and compasses, in amorous juxtaposition (as told to the present writer by Carrà's son Massimo, who was given this explanation by his father[29]) with the petrified herm of Ines Minoja, the woman he had recently married and who, in 1921, was expecting their first child. The woman in the painting became the symbol of Carrà's fascination for the art of the past and combines influences that amount to a compendium of Carrà's enthusiasms at that moment: in the preparatory drawing (fig. 10d) she resembles cameo profiles of ancient Indian miniatures that were collected and published in a small book by Valori Plastici around 1920;[30] she evokes fifteenth-century models such as Piero's *Battista Sforza* in the double portrait of the Duke and Duchess of Montefeltro at the Uffizi[31] (fig. 10f); the Madonna in one of the paintings that had been crucial to Carrà in his training, Piero's *Brera Altarpiece* in the Pinacoteca di Brera, Milan (fig. 10g), has her eyes closed in concentrated prayer, her features rounded-off and psychologically inert (thus purely plastic, according to the interpretation of the period). In the same years Piero's *Brera Altarpiece* attracted the attention of painters sensitive to the poetry of space, as demonstrated a few months later when Felice Casorati reworked it in his *Silvana Cenni* (1922).

In this context, of Carrà distancing himself from de Chirico, a crucial work from a slightly earlier period of Carrà's production, *The Drunken Gentleman* of 1916–17[32], becomes relevant: here a foreground male herm is placed in the company of elementary forms in plaster (a bottle, a polychrome baton, a cylinder) while a small panel emerges in the background. From the retrospective viewpoint of 1921, *The Drunken Gentleman* could be seen as a precursor: it was Carrà's first attempt (and the first by his generation of Italian artists) to give back to volumes their solidity, to locate them in an illusionistic spatial box, and to allegorize with them the artist's condition (his head as herm, surrounded by the instruments of his craft). It is significant that in 1921, the same year as the execution of *The Engineer's Mistress*, Carrà offered *The Drunken Gentleman* (fig. 10h) for re-publication in an issue of *Valori Plastici* (year III, no. 1).

Some of the mystery of this expressionless head, with its eyes closed, may be dispelled by a reading of Carrà's contemporary essay 'Misticità e ironia nella pittura contemporanea', published in the summer 1920 issue of *Valori Plastici*. Beginning with a quotation (which this writer has been unable to identify), the artist noted that "the word *mystical* is usually derived from a Greek word meaning to close, as if to indicate he who closes his lips to keep secret that which cannot be revealed; but the same Platonists have it derive instead from the act of closing the eyes, so that one can see more, internally."[33] In the July 1920 issue of *La Ronda*, Giorgio de Chirico had claimed the need, in order to bring about the classical rebirth of modern painting, for a new mysticism (which would perpetuate a linear historical development that ran from Greece through the Renaissance to Germany, from Polygnotus to Max Klinger, and to which the writer proudly felt himself bound[34]). Carrà was fiercely critical of de Chirico's position. His was "a purely aesthetic faith [which] expresses itself in a form sufficient to itself."[35] The stone herm loved by the painter-engineer may therefore represent the only object of adoration permitted to a modern mystic: painting, with its profound and mysterious laws.

Though painted in 1921, *The Engineer's Mistress* was not among the works that belonged contractually to the dealer Mario Broglio (which were to be published in *Valori Plastici* and exhibited in the German tour of 'Valori Plastici' in 1921 and at the Primaverile Fiorentina in 1922). It remained instead in the hands of Carrà who, in an open challenge to Broglio's timorous efforts to sell his work, planned its early exhibitions (reconstructed here for the first time). In June 1921 *The Engineer's Mistress* was exhibited, together with *The Mill of St Anne*[36] and a large number of drawings, at the 'Esposizione Provinciale d'Arte' of Alessandria, the first non-partisan art exhibition in which Carrà had participated for a decade and an evident tribute to the city of his birth. This writer has not traced the catalogue, but an anonymous review in *La Stampa* mentioned a *Donna dell'ingegnere* (*Engineer's Woman*) among the two "newest canvases" by Carrà.[37] Seven months later, in January 1922, the painting was sent to the show 'Pittori contemporanei italiani' with which Enrico Somaré inaugurated his 'Bottega di Poesia' gallery. Here too, the failure to trace the catalogue is compensated for by contemporary publications: the work was illustrated in the February 1922 issue of *Il Primato Artistico Italiano*, of which Somaré was the militant art critic.[38] Relations between Carrà and Somaré opened in 1920 with a bitter critical duel,[39] and the debate continued at arm's length, though in a more conciliatory tone, in periodicals the following year: it comes as no surprise therefore that when Somaré inaugurated his new gallery with a group show of artists ranging from the Divisionists to the 'Return to Order', Carrà chose to send a painting predicated on a tonal and romantic *metafisica*.

Unsold in Milan, the painting was shown again the following year in Turin at the 'Esposizione Nazionale di Belle Arti' at the Parco del Valentino,[40] where Felice Casorati had been commissioned by the presidency of the organizing body to install a room of new Italian tendencies. *The Engineer's Mistress* was shown together with *The Builder's Son* (in its first appearance after a radical repainting of the 1918 version) in a room dominated by de Chirico at his most Boecklinian and by five paintings by Casorati at his most Mantegnesque. Carrà was critically embattled:[41] he who "took on the chin — like a boxer down on his luck — every day thousands of insults and abuse from visitors" exhibited "some so-called paintings that confirm among the profane the opinion that there persists in him a madness painful and tragic, a secret reasoning insanity." This was written by Emilio Zanzi, a Catholic critic open to modernism but who declared himself at a loss to understand what the paintings meant:

> "... however hard I tried, however hard some of my friends who are quite expert in philosophical hermeneutics tried [...], none of us, together, managed to solve the charades, the re-

Fig. 10c. *Carlo Carrà,* L'amante dell'ingegnere (The Engineer's Mistress), *oil on canvas, c. 1940, in M. Drudi Gambillo, T. Fiori,* Archivi del Futurismo

Fig. 10d. *Carlo Carrà,* L'amante dell'ingegnere (The Engineer's Mistress), *pencil on paper, 1921. Rome, Galleria Anna d'Ascanio*

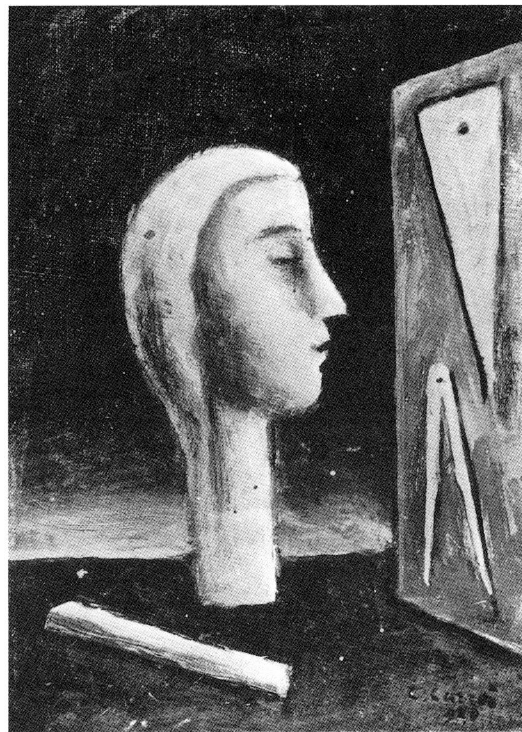

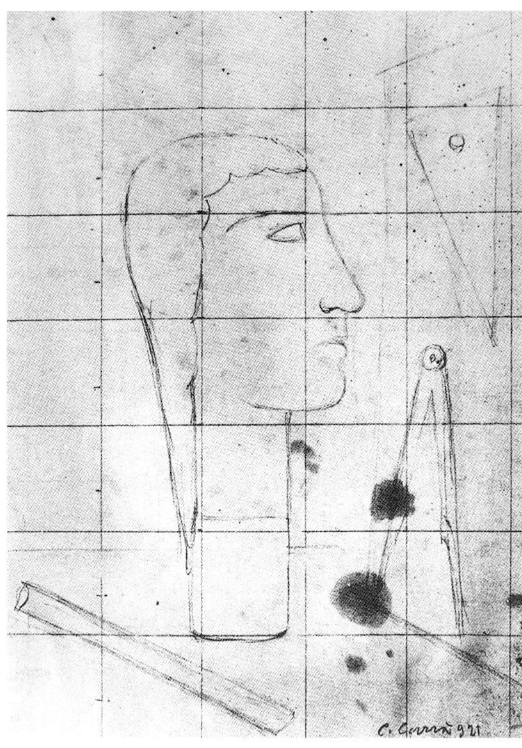

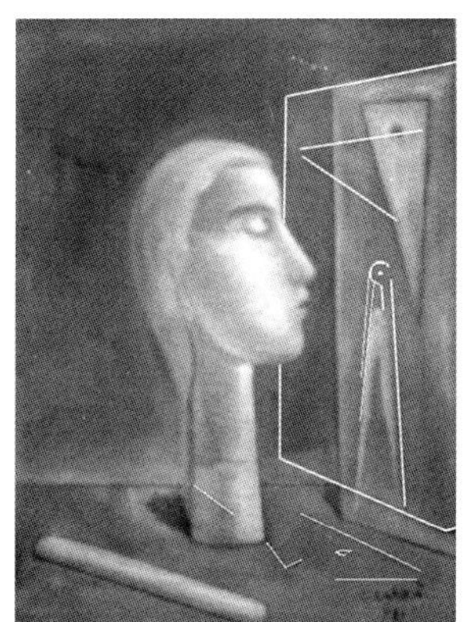

Fig. 10e. *Infrared reflectography image of cat. no. 10*

buses, the puzzles of these style-less, ultra-barbaric, ultra-childish paintings, with no hint that might reveal at least the draftsman, the caricaturist, the brazen imp or the naive poet."[42]

The painting's presence in Turin provoked a great deal more incomprehension (Carrà was, by turn, defined a "grotesque" artist,[43] author of "comical puppets"[44] or, at worst, accused of "mischievous, teasing apparitions"[45]), but younger visitors found his work especially intriguing. Together with *The Builder's Son*, *The Engineer's Mistress* indelibly impressed the memory of the eighteen-year-old Turinese painter Italo Cremona, who described the two paintings impeccably from memory in an article published in 1932 in *Il Selvaggio*:

"... two little canvases shining and poor, painted with devilish modesty, discharged in simple frames and appearing as if by chance in the grand show in Turin between de Chirico and Casorati, still grate in my memory: colors never seen before or even imagined, so new that perhaps, to feel again their wonder, I should open again one of those fragile boxes of hardened watercolor paints brought to me by the Holy Child at Christmas. An absurd pink, an enchanted grass green, the red of a king's robes, the black of the Devil and a white that was unnecessary [...] To soil them... to use them... was the end of the joy. These are memories of ten years ago and to recall them whole is a struggle because of the too many thoughts that pile up to weaken my clear vision of them, to the point of obscuring them entirely.

"Let this retrospective comparison with a child's paint box suffice.

"Now, though reminding myself of them each in turn (having also seen them later in photographs), it is hard for me to picture them distinctly and there is no way to separate the hole in the set square in the 'Mistress' from the grid of racquet strings in the other, the pavement of that one from the long neck of the engineer's companion. What is certain is that, with such works, Carrà began to exist for my adolescent self, with a hundred other paintings now almost all sunk to the bottom while he is still afloat."[46]

In a letter from Carrà to Broglio of August 1923 we learn that the two paintings were shipped to Rome after the closing of the Turin show, on the basis of a new contract between the artist and the dealer.[47] But Broglio's failure to meet the terms of the contract prompted Carrà, in October 1924, to demand their return, mentioning specifically *The Engineer's Mistress*.[48] The painting was once again in the artist's possession when it was exhibited in what was to be the first occasion that Carrà was given a room of his own in a major group show in the 1920s, the 'Terza Biennale Romana'.

Its special relationship with *The Builder's Son* (and the crucial role of both paintings in Carrà's stylistic development) was rendered explicit not only by their presence in the gallery but also by the way they were illustrated in the catalogue[49] (fig. 10a). This exhibition was an important turning point in the painting's history: Italian critics saw in it the moment in which Carrà put behind him the cold intellectualism of Metaphysical painting. According to Margherita Sarfatti, *The Engineer's Mistress* was the decisive painting that released Carrà from "the enclosure, the rarefaction, the artifice of Metaphysical painting, toward the light and the joy of the atmosphere."[50]

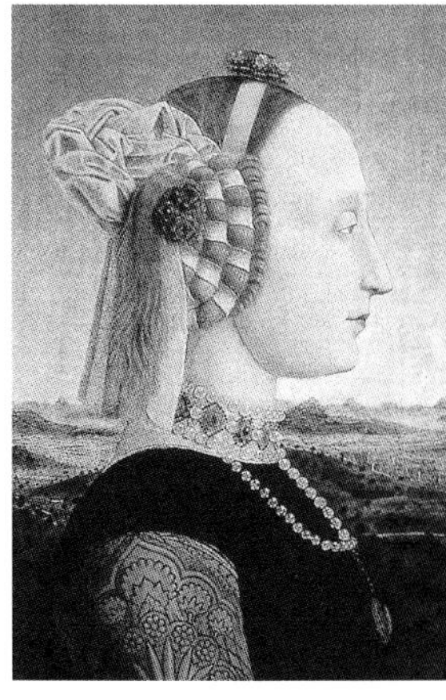

Fig. 10f. *Piero della Francesca,* Portrait of Battista Sforza, *tempera on panel, c. 1465. Florence, Galleria degli Uffizi*

In February the following year, the work, still with no indication of ownership, appeared in a group show at the Galleria Pesaro, Milan, together with paintings by Giorgio de Chirico and Rubaldo Merello. It was the only one among Carrà's Metaphysical paintings to be illustrated in the catalogue, and it underlined, together with three landscapes, his shift by this time toward a naturalistic language.[51] Its purchase (for the modest sum of 1000 lire) by Alessandro Mazzucotelli, which is usually said to have taken place in 1925,[52] should be moved back to somewhere between 1926 and 1928. It was published in the latter year in Hoepli's monograph on Carrà in the *Arte Italiana Moderna* series, with a preface by Ardengo Soffici and a caption naming its new owner.[53] Thus *The Engineer's Mistress* entered the collection of a rising figure in the Milan art world, a master of artistic wrought-iron from Bergamo and owner of a successful craft industry soon to become secretary of the Lombard Federation of Fascist Artists and later, in the 1929 elections, a deputy in Parliament.

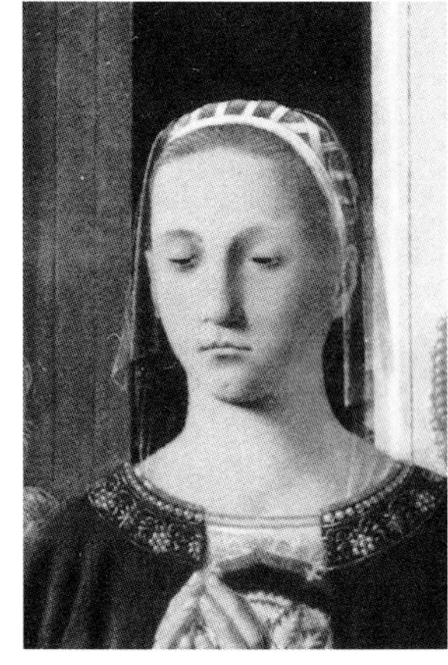

Fig. 10g. *Piero della Francesca,* The Brera Altarpiece *(detail), tempera on panel, 1472–4. Milan, Pinacoteca di Brera*

He was a long-standing friend of Carrà's (he had been one of the organizers of the 'Esposizione Libera' in the Ricordi Pavilion in 1911) and an important early Futurist painting (*Piazza del Duomo a Milano*) is recorded as being in his collection into the 1930s.[54]

The Engineer's Mistress remained in the Mazzucotelli Collection for less than a decade. It was not included in the Carrà–Soffici show at the Galleria Bardi in 1930[55] but was presented instead at a show of Carrà's paintings at the Galleria del Milione in November–December 1935.[56] The gallery's newsletter boasted that this was "the first exhibition of Carrà with the intention of placing the development of an artist so fundamental to contemporary Italian painting in a historical context."[57] *The Engineer's Mistress* was a key work in the gallery's attempt to affirm the artist's continuity despite the changes in his style:

> "Italianness and tradition, which we can recognize today in *The Engineer's Mistress* of 1921 or in the mannequins exhibited next to the recent works, now seem to us an obvious and natural feature of his production as a whole [...] Behold the Italianness, so marked as to declare itself distinctly as an 'exportable' value, unmistakable in the broader arena of modern Europe of the time."[58]

Placed on the Milan market as a Modernist masterpiece, the painting was well received by contemporary critics who awoke at last to the strong links connecting Carrà's Metaphysical period to the works that followed: "the profound and almost antique pictorial and formal sense of *The Engineer's Mistress* does not negate but rather to the contrary continues the gifts, always pictorial, that we find again in *Pescatori* [*Fishermen*]."[59]

Fig. 10h. *Carlo Carrà,* Il gentiluomo briaco *(*The Drunken Gentleman*), 1916–17, in* Valori Plastici, *1921*

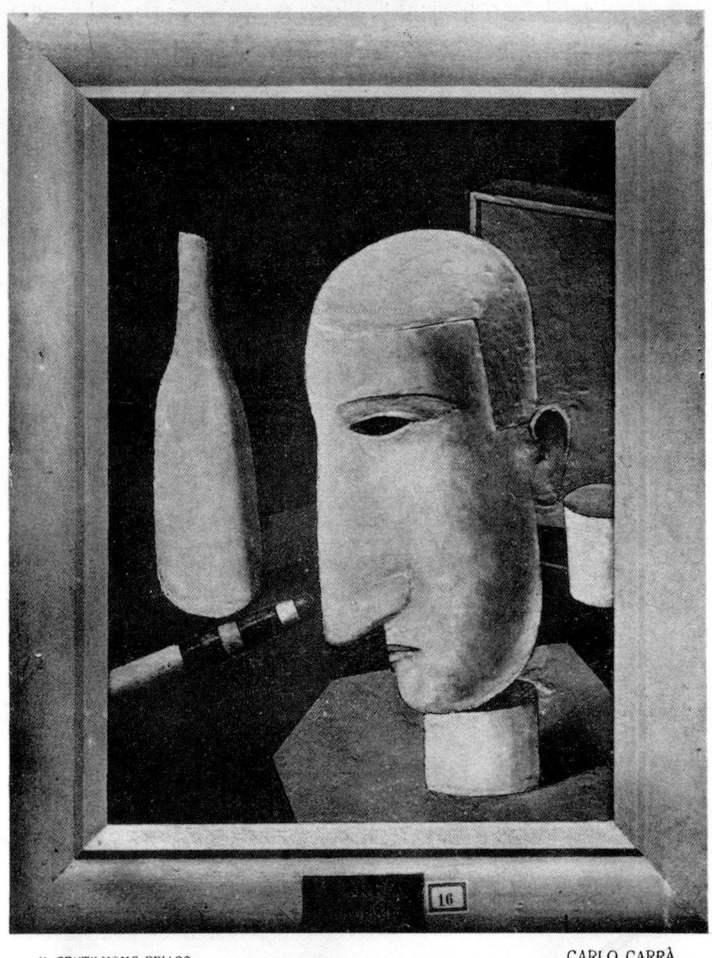

IL GENTILUOMO BRIACO
Proprietà Piccoli

CARLO CARRÀ

Fotoinc. S. Michele - Roma

The attention which il Milione lavished on *The Engineer's Mistress* had a specifically commercial intent. The following January, Gino Ghiringhelli, the gallery director, attempted a sale for 12,000 lire (as told by Ghiringhelli to Carlo Belli in a postcard of January 12, 1936[60]) to Pietro Feroldi, a lawyer and il Milione's most valued client, who already possessed three seascapes and a landscape by Carrà.[61]

The sale met with unexpected obstacles and Belli, looking back on the incident in a letter, recalled the collector's distrust of Metaphysical painting:

> "[Feroldi] understood the importance of certain phenomena such as *metafisica* and abstraction, but was stubbornly blind to them. He despised me when I managed to insert *The Engineer's Mistress* and *The Disquieting Muses* into his collection. Both paintings, when brought to him at home, were rejected and sent back twice, until I forced them upon him with terrible rows."[62]

This episode is an example of the difficulties experienced by the new generation of collectors, habituated to recent tonal and neo-Expressionist trends, when faced by the tougher intellectual content of paintings of more than fifteen years earlier. Even Feroldi, in a letter to Belli in January 1936, admitted this:

"You may know from Ghiri[nghelli] that the Mistress and the Sesia (small houses on) came into the collection, (almost) closing its door [...] 'The Houses on the Sesia' is moving to the point of being almost transcendental; a true joy. I would like to hang the painting in front of my desk. The Mistress is actually a bit testy. Metaphysical, but one hundred percent Carrà with his black hair and his snappy voice. I admire this serious, mysterious, deep painting, but feel unable to desire it. And how expensive it is! Nevertheless we'll see, over time!"[63]

A selling price of 11,000 lire was agreed[64] but the matter was not yet over. Seven days later, in a letter to Pietro Feroldi from Peppino Ghiringhelli, Gino's brother (of which a copy was sent to Carlo Belli by the exasperated Ghiringhelli himself), one can read between the lines in some detail the collector's bewilderment about the painting he had now bought. The Galleria del Milione, as emerges from a note accompanying the letter, was willing to retrieve the painting, "which Orombelli (certainly a lapsus for Mazzucotelli) would take back in exchange for some old masters plus some cash":

"But, dear Lawyer, we have not thought of selling you a Giotto. We have sold you a Carrà. When you find me a Carrà with no hint of influences [...] and above all a Carrà in a style that is 'orderly, clear, sole outcome of an original conceptuality true only to itself,' thinking with these words of Giotto; and when you have found me a metaphysical [Carrà] *absolutely* new in the entire history of art, then I will be able to tell you that your arguments are not unreasonable. Carrà's creative process excludes in itself the possibility of a Carrà that is artless, unsullied, free of laborious reworkings. Such is Carrà, and such is the whole moral stature of Carrà in Italian painting. Thirty years of stubborn pride: that is his pictorial integrity, and the integrity of the parts that should be sought in his painting. As always we recommended *The Mistress* for your collection, thinking that you wished to collect Carrà with all his merits, and therefore with all his defects as well (true merit will ever have its share of defects). We [...] insisted that, despite all your arguments of an *absolute* kind, that *The Engineer's Mistress* was suitable for you as the best Carrà available, a totally documented Carrà, and in the end a Carrà for which you immediately showed a very lively spiritual interest! [...]
"The fact remains that we are only interested in *metafisica* as *history*. And it is as history that we *saw The Mistress* in your collection. Your careful and detailed analysis of the absolute value are part of the very nature of a good collector *amateur*. But it is independently of this [analysis] that we are still convinced of how appropriate it is that this piece should enter your collection. If for no other reason than the fact that it causes you to argue so. Because key moments of the problems addressed in the history of art should be collected [...]
"It seems to me that you think Carrà's Metaphysical period has fallen in value since its presentation in the show in December. Forgive me, your intuition misses the mark this time: it is polemical. It was not we who discovered Carrà's importance nor where Carrà is more important, more 'Carrà.' It has been the critics over at least the past 10 years [...] I assure you that the opinions which count in Milan will be forever and absolutely convinced by this show that the outstanding Carrà is Carrà the Metaphysical painter, together with that part of Carrà the Metaphysical painter which endures in his subsequent styles. In other words, the Metaphysical works have suggested the logic and origin of the beauty typical of Carrà in his seascapes, etc."[65]

The entry of Carrà's painting into the Feroldi Collection and its price were long discussed by the Milanese. A letter from the same Ghiringhelli to Belli a few months after the purchase men-

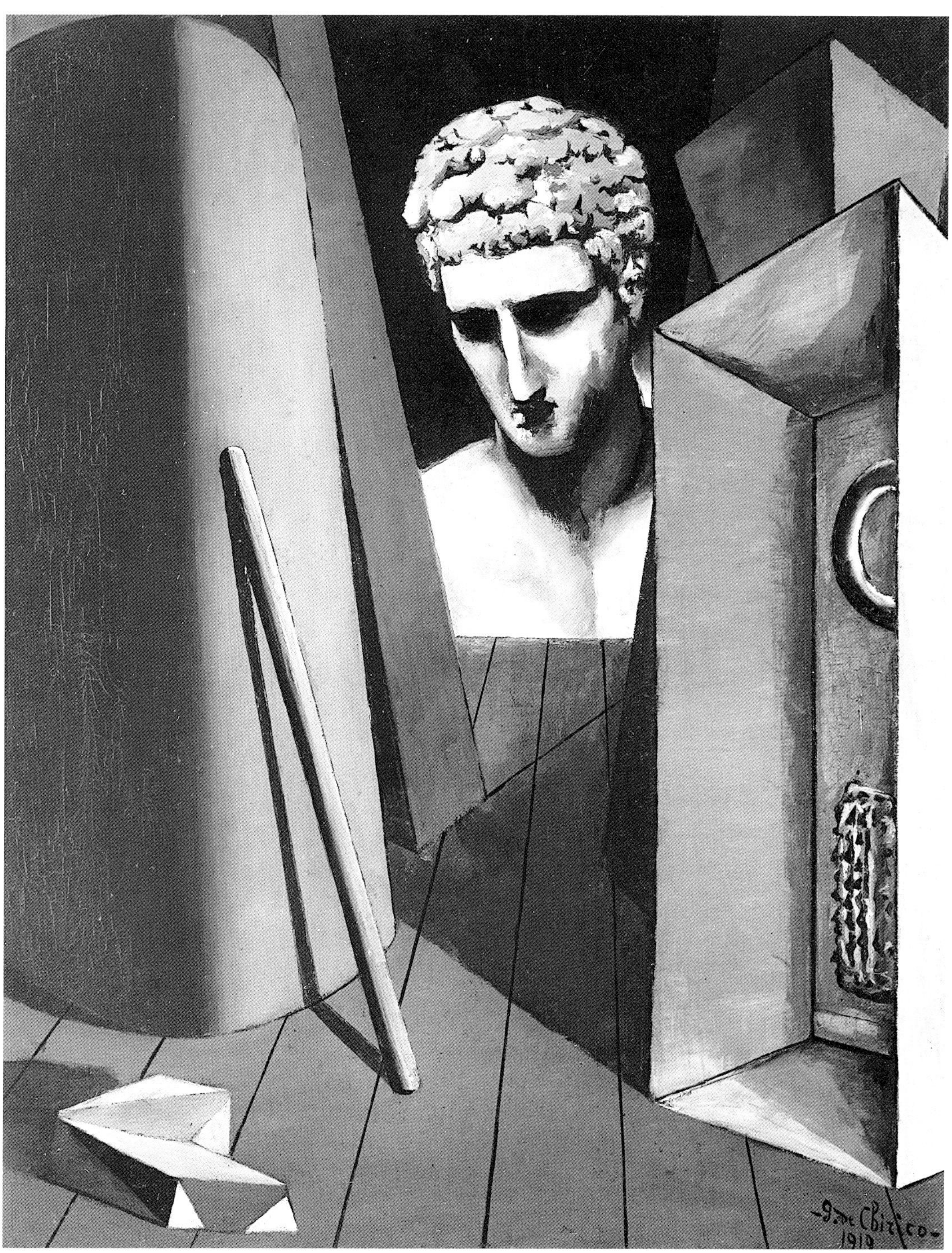

Fig. 10i. *Giorgio de Chirico,* Malinconia hermetica *(Hermetic Melancholy), oil on canvas, 1919. Paris, Musée d'Art Moderne de la Ville de Paris*

tions the opinions of an abstract painter (Mauro Reggiani), two painters of the Chiarismo movement (Umberto Lilloni and Giuseppe Cesetti) and a collector and prominent art critic (Lamberto Vitali):

> "I have to start by saying that a new chapter of the story came up recently, dreamed up by Lilloni (and maybe Cesetti) on a visit to Brescia, according to which Reggiani had said during an argument at the Brera that *The Engineer's Mistress* was not a good painting. Rubbish, of course. Reggiani, defending Carrà in an argument with Lilloni, who was demolishing him [...], stated the same thing which had given rise to the misunderstanding in Lamberto Vitali's judgement, that is to say, that the true Carrà was that of the mannequins rather than 'The Mis-

> tress' [...] All things told, more doubts and hearing provincial gossip about *The Mistress*. Don't tell me I didn't have the requisite style in my polemic with Feroldi."[66]

Feroldi loaned the painting, by this time perceived as a sort of moral exemplar for younger painters ("Poverty, but also harsh lucidity, need for transparency and coherence; no immediacy or concession or sensuality"[67]), to the 'Omaggio ai 16 artisti italiani' at the Galleria di Roma in June 1937.[68] It was then selected (by Roberto Longhi[69]) for Carrà's section in the Golden Gate Exhibition in San Francisco in 1939. In 1942 it was exhibited twice, each time in Milan: in the spring it was the centerpiece of a room at the large Carrà show in the otherwise empty galleries of the Pinacoteca di Brera,[70] and a few months later it was shown again in the same rooms when the Feroldi Collection was put on display.[71] In this way interpretations of the painting multiplied. Generally this meant an emphasis on its difference from de Chirico (compared to de Chirico's paintings, "*The Engineer's Mistress* [...] is less rich in overt allusions to the fantastic. Its world is poor, dull, chaste, and in this lies its poetry, and its freedom from any illustrative tendency"[72]), as well as an appreciation of the embryo of tonal painting that could be traced there: "its geometric rigor already yields to subtle modulations and tonal transitions, with a sense of distance like the presage of aerial perspective;"[73] "the blue of the background — no longer a frozen void, but already sky — extends through the dense shadows of an evening, an early evening still hesitant in its virgin breadth!"[74]. A fine and little-known reading of the work by Francesco Arcangeli, based on the aura of luminous nightmare that permeates the scene, is a good example of the fascination this painting exercised on the new generation of critics:

> "The severed head, the stick, the compasses and the set square take on a glow, dense and devoid of feeling, they slowly trickle between those hard edges transformed by the igniting and by the fading of light and of shadow into dimly tender settings, in predestined wombs. The head is absorbed in impassioned sleep and the eye of the artist loves and wounds it in equal measure. The braid of hair on the point of fusing, in the amorous half-light, with the curve of the neck, meets the long scar of shadow that painfully pushes apart their embrace; while on the dangling neck impasted in an ivory white the tiny wound etches itself yet catches the light along its lip. By the enchanted light of a melancholy hour the black and white of the volumes are instilled with the sky's night blue and the table's desolate brown. All as if a firm intelligence hindered in its movements had entered the solitary and sweetly threatening flow of a nightmare."[75]

In 1949 Alfred Barr and James Thrall Soby chose *The Engineer's Mistress* to close the Metaphysical section of the 'Twentieth-Century Italian Art' exhibition at the Museum of Modern Art in New York.[76] In May of the same year the work was bought by Gianni Mattioli for the sum of 680,000 lire (although estimated at one million), the fourth most important painting in the Feroldi Collection.[77]

[1] *Tramonto sui monti*, private collection: catalogued by Carrà 1967–8 as no. 15/24; *Rome* 1925, pls. 20–1.
[2] *Solitudine*, Zurich, private collection: catalogued by Carrà 1967–8 as no. 3/17; *Milan* 1926, p. 43, no. 10.
[3] *Il figlio del costruttore* and *Il pino sul mare*, both paintings in private collections: catalogued by Carrà 1967–8 as nos. 5/21 and 1/21 respectively; Soffici 1928, unnumbered plates.
[4] Ragghianti 1953, p. 10.
[5] Beginning with *Primato* 1922, p. 45.
[6] Bardi 1930, pl. 5.
[7] Now New York, private collection: Drudi Gambillo, Fiori 1958–62, vol. II, p. 292, no. 53.
[8] Carrà 1967–8, no. 36/40, with the title *Studio da 'L'amante dell'ingegnere'* and dated 1940; this study is still inexplicably dated 1920 in Noble 1997, pp. 22–4 and p. 33, note 50.
[9] Carrà, Russoli 1977, no. 393, 420 × 335 mm.
[10] *Il gentiluomo briaco*, *Mio figlio*, *Penelope*, *Solitudine*, *La figlia dell'Ovest*: *ibidem*, nos. 226, 239, 280, 290, 321.
[11] *Ibidem*, no. 280.
[12] Evidence for the appearance of the first version of *Solitudine* is the illustration in *Milan* 1917–18, no. 26. In 1921 the painting illustrated in *Valori Plastici* (III, no. 1, between pp. 8 and 9) was still in its first state, when it was more literally indebted to de Chirico's Metaphysical paintings. For a comparison of the two versions see Guzzi 1994[a], p. 131.
[13] Carrà, Russoli 1977, no. 400.
[14] Baldacci 1997, pp. 378–80.
[15] Filippo de Pisis visited the exhibition on January 6, 1918: Zanotto 1996, pp. 95–6.
[16] De Pisis, February 12, 1918.
[17] Letter from Filippo de Pisis to Mario Zucchini, dated January 15, 1918, in Zanotti 1996, p. 95.
[18] Letter from Carlo Carrà to Mario Broglio, dated May 19, 1919, in Morelli 1988, p. 334.
[19] Calvesi 1982, p. 124.
[20] Calvesi, November 15, 1964.
[21] Marinetti 1909, pp. 134 and 132.
[22] Letter from Carlo Carrà to Ardengo Soffici, dated January 22, 1914, in Carrà, Soffici 1983, p. 46.
[23] Marinetti 1920, p. 35.
[24] Marinetti *et al.*, October 15, 1913.
[25] Letter from Ardengo Soffici to Carlo Carrà, dated April 28, 1915, in Carrà, Soffici 1983, p. 81.
[26] *La nostalgie de l'ingénieur*, now in Norfolk (Virginia), The Chrysler Museum: for a reconstruction of the exhibition history of this painting, see Baldacci 1997, pp. 324 and 430.
[27] *Natura morta con la squadra*, Milan, Civiche raccolte d'arte, Jucker Collection: Carrà 1967–8, no. 36/40.
[28] *Malinconia hermetica*, Paris, Musée d'Art Moderne de la Ville de Paris: catalogued in Baldacci 1997, no. 146; this was reproduced in the third plate of *de Chirico* 1919.
[29] Verbal communication from Massimo Carrà to the author, October 8, 1998.
[30] Tavolato, Kheiri, undated, pls. 34–6.
[31] Cinelli 1991, pp. 212–13.
[32] *The Drunken Gentleman* was painted before Carrà met de Chirico. Carrà (1916[b] pp. 270–1) refers to the "gentiluomo briaco" as "my recent picture" ("mio recente quadro"). The details of the panel in the background and above all the polychrome baton in the foreground suggest that Carrà reworked (updated) the painting, with de Chirico's art in mind, prior to the painting's exhibition and publication in the catalogue of *Milan* 1917–18, no. 16.
[33] Carrà 1920[b], p. 70.
[34] De Chirico 1920, pp. 506–11.
[35] Carrà 1920[b], p. 71.
[36] *Il mulino di S. Anna*, private collection: Carrà 1967–8, no. 4/21.
[37] *Stampa*, June 18, 1921.
[38] *Primato* 1922, p. 45; Rusconi (1998, p. 87) failed to locate the catalogue when researching specifically the 'Bottega di Poesia'.
[39] Somaré 1920, p. 33; Carrà 1920[a], pp. 67–8.
[40] *Turin* 1923, no. 333.
[41] A reconstruction of the critical debate can be found in Rovati 2000, pp. 287–8.
[42] Zanzi, May 10, 1923.
[43] Quadrone, April 14, 1923.
[44] Thovez, May 20, 1923.
[45] Gobetti, July 11, 1923.
[46] Cremona, June 15, 1932.
[47] "Let me know if my paintings from Turin have reached Rome." Milan, private archive, letter from Carlo Carrà to Mario Broglio, dated August 7, 1923. In June Carrà had received an advance from Broglio, accepting monthly payments of three subsequent installments: *ibidem*, letter from Carlo Carrà to Mario Broglio, dated June 26, 1923.
[48] "I also beseech you *immediately* to send back the paintings of mine still in your possession, including *The Engineer's Mistress*:" Milan, private archive, letter from Carlo Carrà to Mario Broglio, dated October 15, 1924.
[49] Lancellotti 1926, pp. 34–5.
[50] Sarfatti, March 27, 1925.
[51] *Milan* 1926, p. 11.
[52] Carrà 1970, no. 91.
[53] Soffici 1928, unnumbered plate.
[54] Longhi 1937, p. 19.
[55] This information in Guzzi 1994[b], p. 236, is based on the illustration of the painting in Bardi 1930, pl. 5, and confirmed by the list of works actually exhibited: for this document see note 53 of cat. nos. 6–7.
[56] *Milan* 1935, no. 47.
[57] *Milione* 1936, no. 45, unnumbered page.
[58] *Ibidem*.
[59] Costantini 1936, p. 44.
[60] Boschiero 1991, p. 233.
[61] *Milione* 1933, no. 20, unnumbered page.
[62] Translator's note: "sordo" literally means deaf; "blind" is the sense however: letter from Carlo Belli to Gianni Mattioli, dated February 4, 1971, Archivio Mattioli (*Appendix I*, document no. 90).
[63] Letter from Pietro Feroldi to Carlo Belli, dated January 20, 1936, Archivio Mattioli, photostatic copy.
[64] Letter from Gino Ghiringhelli to Carlo Belli, dated January 20, 1936, cited in Rosazza Ferraris 1998, p. 169.
[65] Archivio Mattioli, photostatic copy of the letter from Peppino Ghiringhelli to Pietro Feroldi, dated January 27, 1935 (the inscribed date, January 27, 1935 XIV, should be 1936 since the letter refers to Carrà's exhibition the preceding December), with an accompanying note from Peppino Ghiringhelli to Carlo Belli.
[66] Archivio Mattioli, letter from Peppino Ghiringhelli to Carlo Belli, dated May 18, 1936, photostatic copy.
[67] Ragghianti 1936, p. 253.
[68] *Rome* 1937, p. 14, unnumbered catalogue.
[69] Brandi 1990, p. 146.
[70] *Milan* 1942[a], p. 6, no. 18.
[71] Piovene 1942, pl. 1.
[72] *Ibidem*, p. XII.
[73] Torriano 1942, unnumbered page.
[74] Testori 1942, p. 6.
[75] Arcangeli 1942, p. 9.
[76] Soby 1949, pl. 41.
[77] Archivio Mattioli, typewritten list of works in the Feroldi Collection: *Appendix I*, document no. 24.

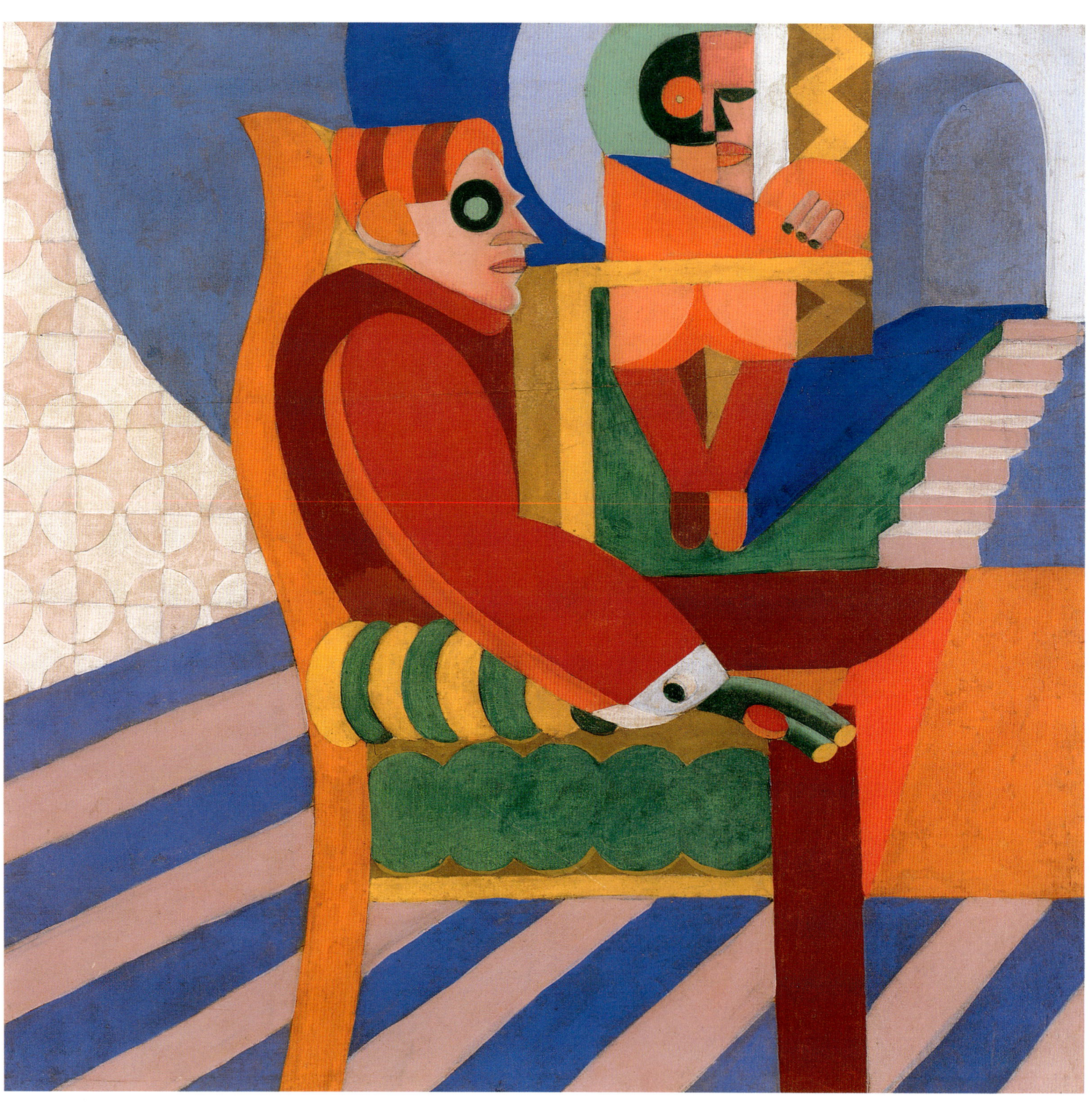

11

Fortunato Depero (Fondo, Trento, 1892 – Rovereto, Trento, 1960)

Portrait of Gilbert Clavel (Double Portrait; Portrait of the Writer Clavel; Portrait of Clavel)

Ritratto di Gilbert Clavel (Doppio ritratto; Ritratto dello scrittore Clavel; Ritratto di Clavel), 1917

Oil on canvas
70 × 75 cm

Provenance: 1917: Gilbert Clavel, Capri; 1927? René Clavel, Basel?; before 1962: Gianni Mattioli

Exhibitions: Capri 1917, no. 26 (*Doppio ritratto*, 'quadro a olio'); Viareggio 1918? (catalogue not traced); Florence 1918, no. 119? (*Ritratto dello scrittore Clavel*); Milan–Genoa–Florence 1919, no. 50 (*Ritratto di Clavel*, property of Clavel); Milan 1962[a], no. 12 (*Ritratto di Clavel*, 1917, illus.); Milan 1962[b], no. 6; Washington, DC 1967–Tokyo 1972, no. 36 (Washington, DC–Hamburg), no. 35 (Madrid–Seville), no. 36 (Kyoto–Tokyo); Bassano del Grappa 1970, no. 128; Milan 1971, no. 2; Bonn–Kassel 1973, no. 32; Trento 1973, no. 34; Milan 1973–4, no. 273; Venice 1986, p. 182; Rovereto 1988–Milan 1989, no. 7

Bibliography: Letter from Gilbert Clavel to Fortunato Depero, dated August 22, 1918 (Rovereto, MART, Archivio del 900, Fondo Depero, ms. no. 1357); Giani 1951, p. 18; Ballo 1962, p. 2; Passamani 1970[a], p. XXVI; Passamani 1970[b], pp. 37–8; Passamani 1981, pp. 102–5, 292–3, no. 382; Scudiero 1987, p. 60, pl. 12; Fagiolo dell'Arco 1988, pp. 71–2, 78, 88–9; Belli 1994, pp. 18–19; Rylands 1997, p. 72

Admitted to the Futurist movement at age twenty-three in 1915, Fortunato Depero was one the most experimental and versatile artists of the Italian avant-garde. As early as the time of the manifesto *Ricostruzione futurista dell'Universo*, March 11, 1915), written with Giacomo Balla,[1] Depero envisioned a total fusion of the arts and a transcending of the traditional distinctions separating painting and sculpture. Between 1915 and 1917, his production included large words-in-freedom panels, three-dimensional constructions, dynamic architecture, sets and costumes for the theater, early experiments in Futurist-inspired applied arts, as well as abstract paintings in the style of Balla. By 1917 Depero had developed a completely new style which blended vestiges of the Secessionist style from his training, archaisms inspired by ancient figurative civilizations, echoes from the nascent Metaphysical movement and the fantasy of the man-automaton. The portrait in the Mattioli Collection is one of the first and most important examples of this new period in Depero's art.

The subject, Gilbert Clavel (Basel, Switzerland 1883–1927), is a hazy figure about whom no serious study has yet been written. Born into a wealthy family of textile manufacturers originally from Lyon, he studied the Humanities and Natural Sciences[2] and, like many young people of his generation, was interested in the esoteric and occult, which he combined with his studies of ancient civilizations, especially Egyptology. This led him in 1911 to make a long journey to Luxor, Thebes and Aswan.[3] Born a hunchback and tormented by various illnesses, he lived in Italy from 1906 on, to convalesce from an attack of tuberculosis. In 1910, in Positano, he restored and then moved into the Torre del Formillo.[4] However, the greater part of his time was spent in Capri, where he occupied the villa 'La Saida' on the high Anacapri plateau. He mixed with the resident international community of Capri (Jacques d'Adelswart Fersen, Robert de Tournel and Axel Munthe among others), and was conspicuous for his eccentric clothing, his exhibitionist, anti-conformist behavior, dandyism and frequent abuse of alcohol and drugs.[5] Toward the end of 1916, thanks in part to his command of the Russian language, he and Italo Tavolato came into contact with the company of the Ballets Russes when it was stationed in the Naples area; in this way they met Diaghilev, Massine, Bakst and Stravinsky.[6] In the summer of 1917 we find Clavel exchanging letters with Pablo Picasso and Jean Cocteau.[7] The first of his very rare texts translated into Italian by Italo Tavolato dates from 1918: a short story in the Metaphysical vein, *Un istituto per suicidi*, illustrated by Fortunato Depero for the Roman publisher Lux, and three articles for the review *Valori Plastici* (a brief essay on Picasso, another

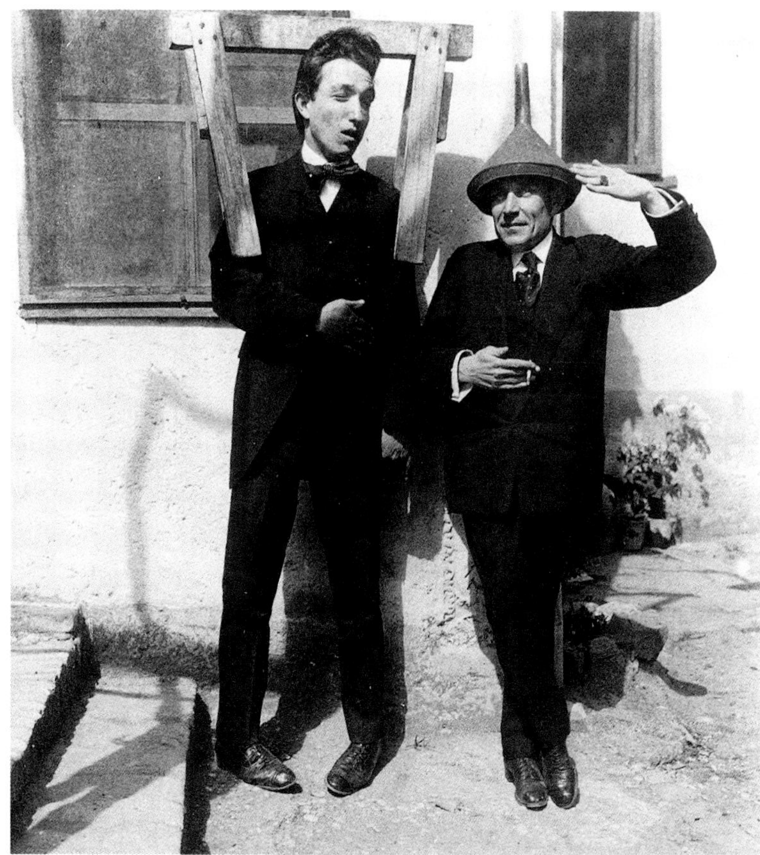

Fig. 11a. *Fortunato Depero and Gilbert Clavel in Capri in 1917. Rovereto, Museo Fortunato Depero*

on the 'teatro plastico', and a study on an Egyptian subject which was to be printed separately as a book by Valori Plastici publications in 1920[8]). In 1918, Clavel began to invest his energies and financial resources in the production of Depero's *Balli plastici*. But at about this time he fell victim to the German stock market crash which considerably depleted his income.[9] His health progressively deteriorated during the 1920s. He returned to Basel in 1927 and within the year committed suicide. His few published texts were collected and reissued in a book in German by his sister in 1930.

The encounter in 1917 between the 25-year-old Depero and the 34-year-old Clavel was described by the former in a 1940 autobiographical text. Between the end of 1916 and the beginning of 1917 Depero was designing, in his Viale Giulio Cesare studio in Rome, the sets and costumes for *Le Chant du Rossignol*, a Ballets Russes production set to music by Igor Stravinsky to be staged in Paris late in the spring and for which, probably in April, Diaghilev was to cancel the contract. Through Michail Semenov, a music critic and Diaghilev's secretary, Clavel visited Depero's studio and recognized in the exotic artifice of the ballet sets a visual equivalent to the strangeness of the narrative scenes in *Un istituto per suicidi*:

> "Michele Semenoff brought a friend to my studio one day: a small man, hunchback with a rectilinear nose, like a triangle, with gold teeth and little feminine shoes, with a crystalline, nasal laugh. A man of nerves and will, highly cultured. A professor of Egyptian history, researcher and observer with the sensibility of an artist, writer, a lover of the people, of verse and metaphysics [...] He had lived for a long time in Aswan, Capri and Positano [...]. Composer of lyrics, he was also a pleasure-seeker and a sufferer. His name is Gilbert Clavel. He enters my studio and is startled. He finds himself unexpectedly in the world of his dreams. He tells me that he is writing a short novel which takes place on an island covered with un-

Fig. 11b. *Fortunato Depero,* Uomo e tavolo - Clavel *(*Man and Table – Clavel*), pencil on paper, 1917. Rovereto, Museo Fortunato Depero*

Fig. 11c. *Fortunato Depero,* Il poeta e scrittore svizzero Gilbert Clavel *(*The Swiss Poet and Writer Gilbert Clavel*), pen and India ink on paper, 1917, in B. Passamani,* Fortunato Depero*, 1981*

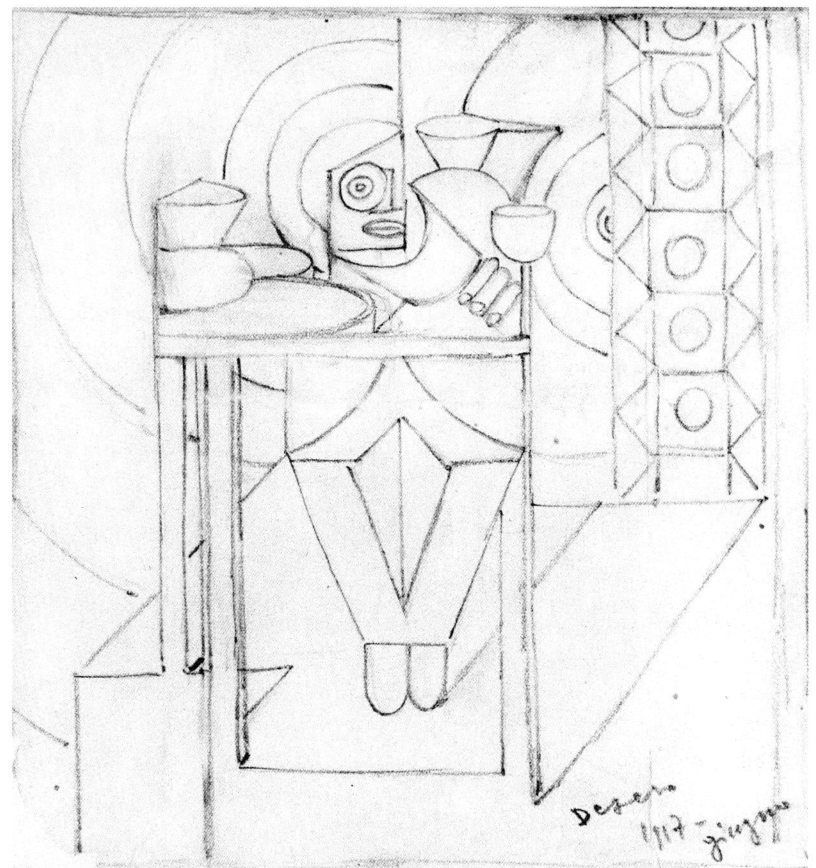

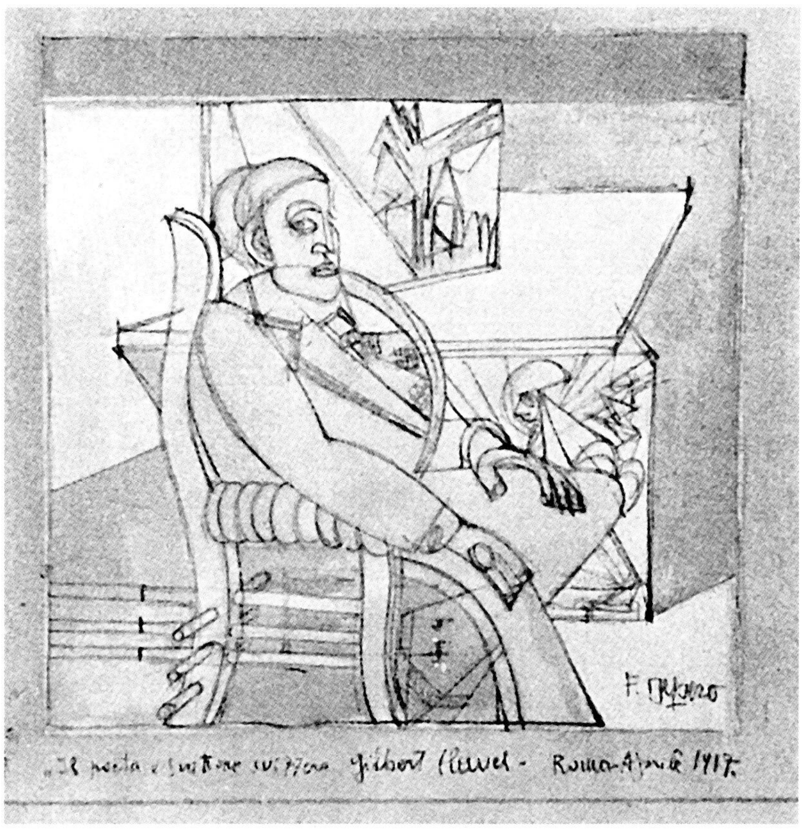

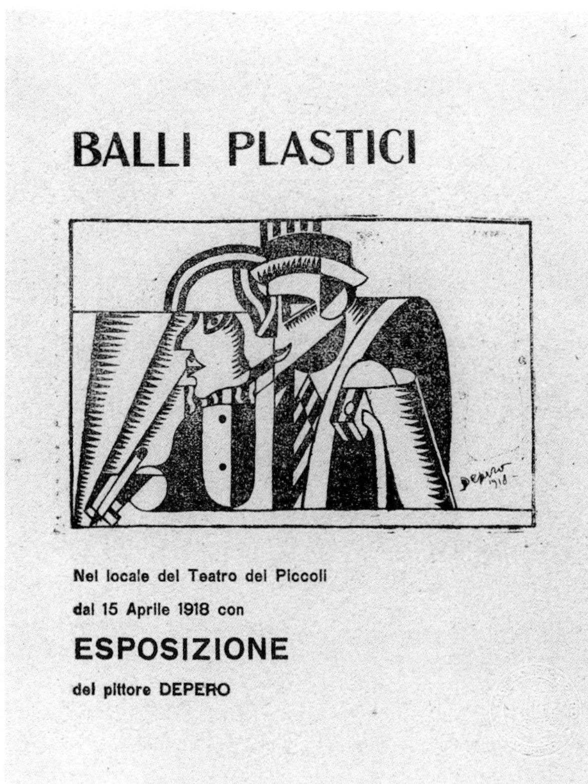

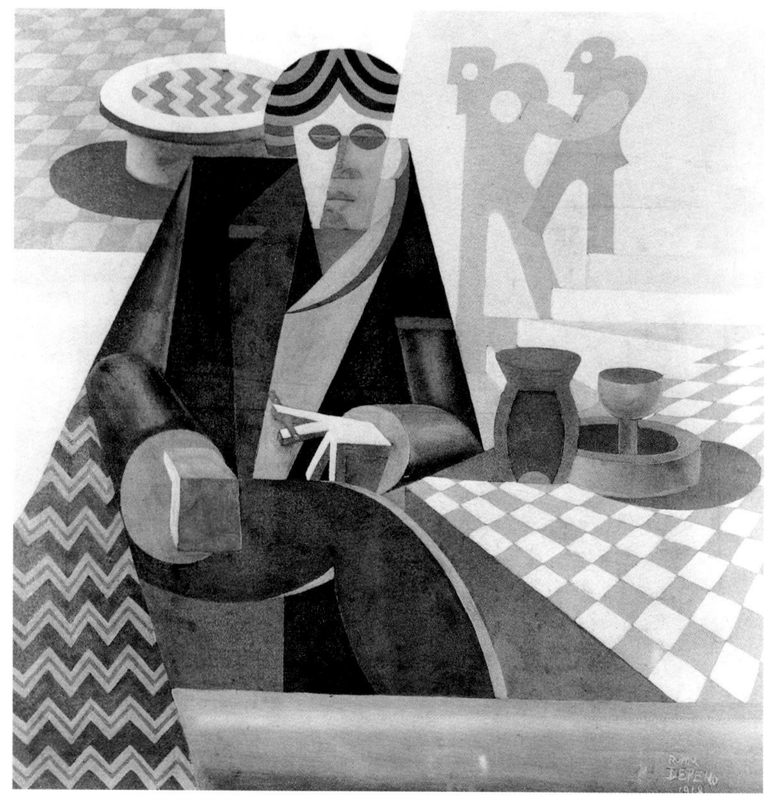

Fig. 11d. *Fortunato Depero, cover for the catalogue of* Balli plastici (Plastic Dances)*, April 1918*

Fig. 11e. *Fortunato Depero,* Ritratto di Gilbert Clavel (Figura seduta al caffè) (Portrait of Gilbert Clavel [Figure Seated at the Café])*, oil on canvas, 1918. Milan, Civiche raccolte d'arte*

real vegetation of crystal in enchanting, iridescent colors, of a mechanistic style, on which one lives a life of illusions. As soon as he sees the model for the plastic sets I have created for the *Ballets Russes*, he is struck and becomes pensive. It is the flower-decked island of his dream that he finds constructed and within his grasp. That is how we meet and become friends. After a few days our mutual understanding becomes fraternal and profound, and he invites me to Capri as his guest."[10]

Depero spent June to September 1917 on the island in a house rented by Clavel. The summer was enlivened not just by the usual resident community, but also by writers who had formerly been part of the *Lacerba* circle (Italo Tavolato, Theodor Daubler), by aristocratic ladies with Modernist tastes (Marchesa Casati Stampa, the Princess of Bassiano) and by intellectual women (Clotilde Marghieri, Sibilla Aleramo)[11] as well as by a brief visit from Marinetti. Depero's work of this period is documented by a one-man show in a room at the Café Morgano in Capri (September 8–16): in addition to oil paintings, watercolors and drawings inspired by Capri, Depero exhibited costume designs for *Le Chant du Rossignol*, figurines for *Il giardino zoologico* by Francesco Cangiullo, six charcoal illustrations for Clavel's book, two studies which were a prelude to the *Balli plastici* project, and three carpets made of Spanish cloth.[12]

It is very probable that the Mattioli painting was number 26 in the catalogue-invitation of the show, with the title '*Doppio ritratto* (quadro a olio)' ('*Doube Portrait* [oil painting]'). Among no fewer than nine portraits of Clavel on exhibition, this was the only oil. Of all Depero's surviving or known portraits of the Swiss poet dateable to 1917, this is the only one in which the sitter appears twice. Given its size and importance, it would have been natural for it to open the 17-painting section of works belonging to Clavel, and that its title should have been the only one printed in uppercase lettering in the catalogue. A useful clue as to its date is provided by a drawing (*Man and Table – Clavel*[13]: fig. 11b), dated 'June 1917' by the artist, which is a study for the small frontal figure of Clavel in the upper right and which differs in only a few details from the oil. More interesting and complex is the relation of the painting to a second drawing (a detailed pen study with India ink washes) which Depero inscribed on the cardboard support 'Il poeta e scrittore svizzero Gilbert Clavel'[14] (fig. 11c) together with the place and date, 'Roma, Aprile 1917'. This is evidently the first study for the Mattioli painting: Clavel is seen in near profile (with a slight turn of the head towards the viewer), posed in the same way in the same armchair. Depero's inscription (dated a month before his sojourn in Capri) and the setting (the maquette of the set for *Le Chant du Rossignol* is visible on the table behind[15]) situate the drawing in Depero's Viale Giulio Cesare studio in Rome.[16] Thus the Mattioli painting was executed from a sketch made some months earlier. In Capri Depero added the figure in the background, based as we have seen on a separate study dated June 1917, and then trimmed certain details to give priority to the broad areas of flat color. With respect to the Rome drawing he removed the references to his own works in the studio as well as the too-insistent perspective effect of the chair legs; he also fused Clavel's right leg with that of the chair and relinquished important details such as the left hand resting on his thigh and the left foot, with its little pointed feminine shoe. As for the later drawing with the small frontal Clavel, he suppressed the right table leg, the drinking glass and the two pitchers on the table. He abandoned the primitive trapezoidal profile of the head, assimilating it into the scheme of concentric circles dominating the background. Finally, he simplified the decorative Greek pattern which served as a backdrop on the right.

In 1917 Depero seems to have been especially intrigued by the notion of the double portrait. In a portrait of Filippo Tommaso Marinetti[17] (fig. 11f), which required particular care because of its subject and size, and which was surely executed during Marinetti's stay in Capri in July 1917, he replicated the bust of the founder of Futurism in the lower left corner, multiplying his presence and implying a holiday mood, without intellectual pretensions.

There can be no doubt that the double Clavel portrait in the Mattioli Collection is set instead in the Anacapri villa owned by the writer. The room corresponds to recollections by contemporaries of the house "immaculate and bare, except for the fairy-tale carpets [...] radiant like Persian miniatures"[18] with its ceramic tiles, visible on the left, characteristic of Capri,[19] whose two-color design lend rhythm to the surface of the wall behind. Clavel is seated in the foreground in an armchair with striped fabric and dressed in a blazing red suit. (The latter imprinted itself on visitors' memories[20] and was painted again by Depero in another large portrait of Clavel bought by the Marchesa Casati when she visited the artist's studio in Capri[21] and which remained in her collection at least until 1951.[22]) In the frontal portrait in the background Clavel is seated at the table which eye-witnesses remember covered in pitchers and glasses brimming with refined iced drinks that Depero had depicted in his drawing but then suppressed in the painting. Clavel's ungainly body is in no way idealized: his hump, his head sunk in his shoulders and his short legs are almost caricatured. This was not casual. Depero was transforming Clavel's deformity into an important, independent object of creative investigation (his hunched back became the subject of many paintings and drawings in 1917–18) and in this way helped his friend to change his attitude to his own body by ridiculing one of the principal causes of his anguish.[23] First-hand witnesses tell how Depero himself often stuffed under his jacket "a cushion to make a hump like Clavel's for symmetry"[24] and in 1918 he portrayed himself in a drawing in his friend's company as a hunchback (fig. 11d).[25] Clavel's reaction, upon receipt in November 1917 of a drawing by Depero, in which he is portrayed with his deformity in evidence, was completely focused on the fantastic transfiguration of his body. "Your last [letter] with a very beautiful drawing, the white-shadow hump has become a new human creation, not deformed but of a superior life. And the legs are colossal bridges and gates, houses, buildings, beneath the human vibration."[26]

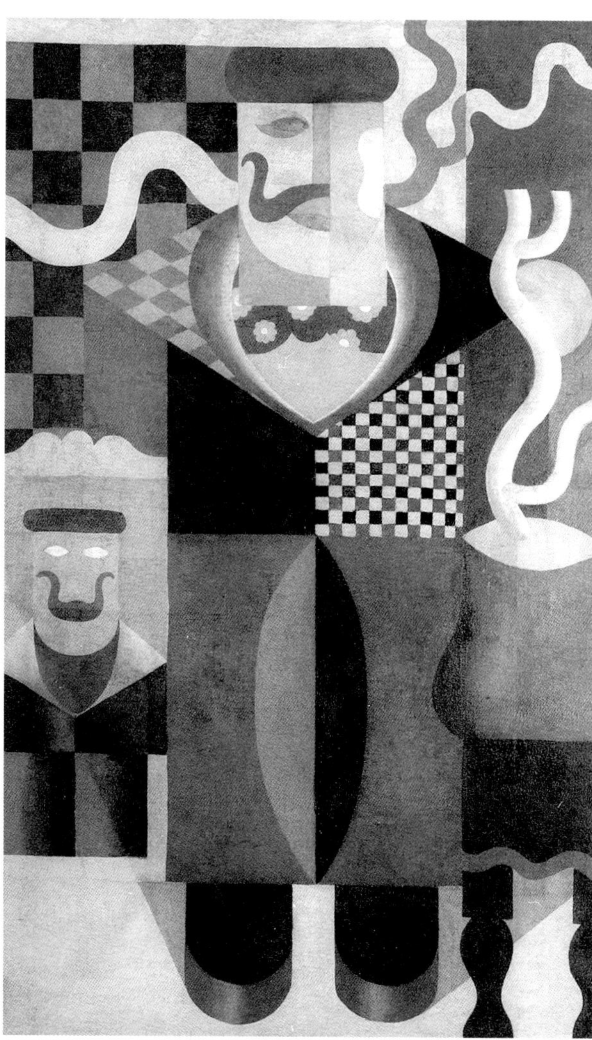

Fig. 11f. *Fortunato Depero,* Doppio ritratto di Filippo Tommaso Marinetti *(*Double Portrait of Filippo Tommaso Marinetti*), oil on canvas, 1917. Rovereto, Museo Fortunato Depero*

The painting's stylistic key lies in the inflexion of that Egyptian art which was the principal interest of the portrait's subject. It is probable that Clavel discussed Egyptian art with Depero while looking through photographs collected in the Capri house and that the painter, fascinated, drew from them characteristic poses and a specific pictorial language as a sort of intellectual tribute to his friend. The impassive profile in the foreground portrait, the way the subject is sitting, the armchair reduced to a cubic box on a perfect axis, the arm elegantly relaxed with the long, tubular and jointless fingers (fig. 11h), all recall the typology of the seated figure in Egyptian art. Some famous comparable examples are the fresco with Nefertari playing chess in the tomb in the Valley of the Queens in Thebes (fig. 11i) and the relief representing the superintendent Maiy in the funeral chapel of the vizir Ramosé in tomb number 55 in Thebes (fig. 11j; this may also be a source for the three diagonal fingers unattached to the hand of the small, frontal Clavel).[27] Clavel's eye, depicted as two concentric circles, is reminiscent of the Egyptian code for the eyes of animals, like that of the golden head of a vulture strategically placed on the cover of the widely-used manual of Egyptian art by Hedwig Fechheimer.[28] Another Egyptian feature is the decision to combine figures of different sizes in a single representation and apparently in the same plane. Moreover in the most important photographic compendium of Egyptian sculpture then available, the author von Bissing occasionally combined frontal and profile images of certain works in the same plate (fig. 11g).[29] The small Clavel perched frontally at the table (fig. 11k), closed in an angular geometric scheme, with his large stylized feet hanging vertically, is reminiscent of basalt statuary of the XII dynasty (such as the super-

Fig. 11g. *Front and profile view of Amenemes III, in* Denkmäler Ägyptischer Skulptur, *1914*

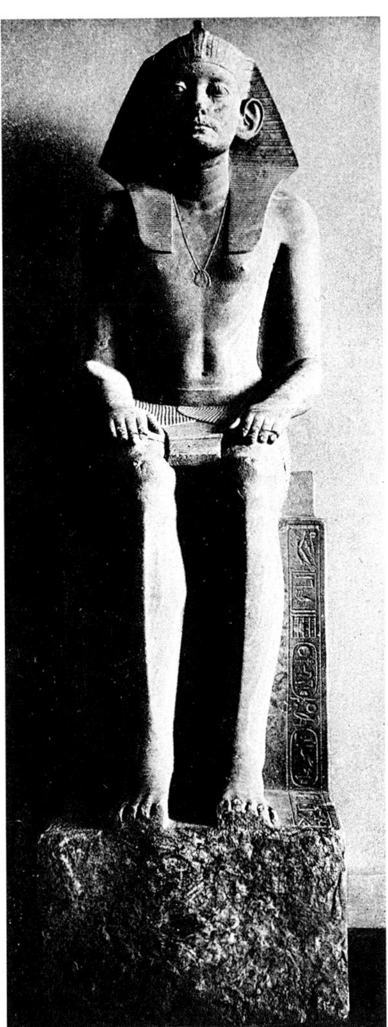

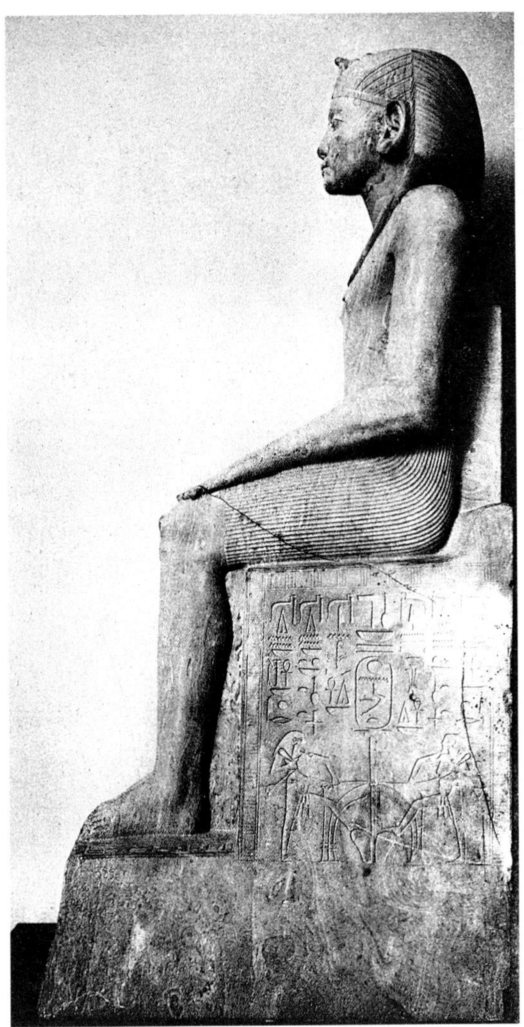

intendent Khertihotep in orange stoneware in the Egyptian Museum in Berlin, fig. 11l) or small statuettes from the XX–XXI centuries B.C. already well-known from the plates of late nineteenth-century picture books of Egyptian art[30] (fig. 11m). Some details (the particular form of the mouth, the Greek zig-zag in the background) echo the hieroglyphs that typically surround pictorial and sculptural portrayals. On one occasion this appropriation of Egyptian forms attracted the attention of a perceptive reviewer of Depero's work. The young painter-writer Filippo de Pisis, faced by Depero's works in a group show, 'La Pittura d'avanguardia' at the Kursaal in Viareggio in August 1918 (where the Mattioli portrait may have been exhibited), offered for comparison "the scenes of certain Egyptian monuments, awesome, spectral, expressive precisely in their elegance and skeletal simplicity and in their ineffable rhythm."[31]

The Mattioli *Portrait of Gilbert Clavel* represents a high point of two-dimensional stylization and compositional rigor in Depero's *oeuvre* that was never to be surpassed. Within the grid of the underdrawing, still visible here and there, Depero carefully laid in areas of even color with fluid paint, often in strident contrasts of complementary colors (the pink and sky blue of the carpet; the green and yellow of the armrest of the chair; the emerald of the chair cover and the scarlet of his jacket). Chiaroscuro is abolished (excepting the shadow implying the tubular shape of Clavel's two green fingers in the foreground) and any sense of spatial depth has been eliminated by juxtaposing areas of "pure color hues"[32] which, with equal luminosity, cling to the paint surface as in marquetry. The composition is based on obsessively repeated motifs (the concentric circles of the eye continue on the wall behind; the strips of alternating colors

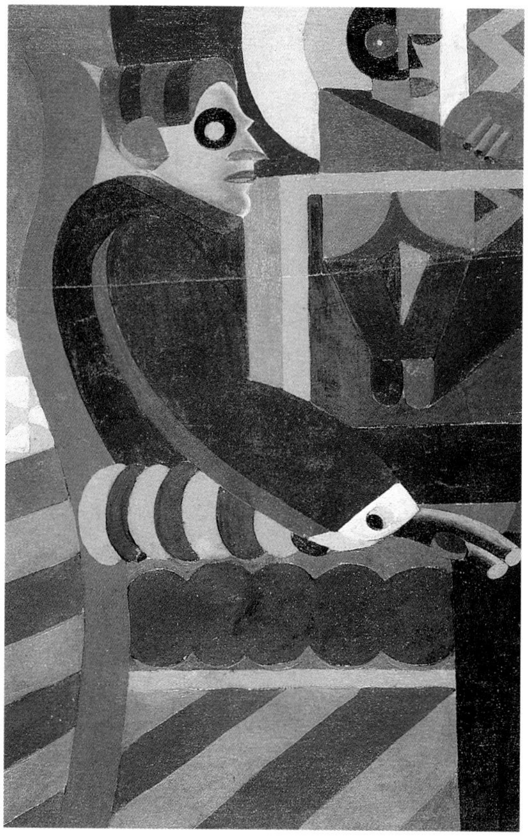

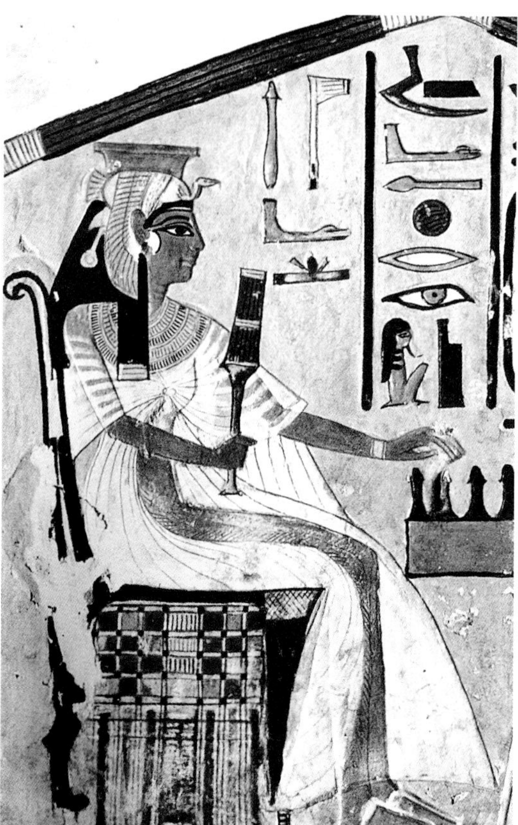

Fig. 11h. *Detail of cat. no. 11*

Fig. 11i. Queen Nefertari Playing Chess, *fresco, XIII century B.C. Thebes, Tomb of Nefertari*

lend rhythm to the carpet in the foreground, then to the seat of the armchair and to the stairway in the background) and on the insertion of a strong diagonal component (the stripes on the carpet, the profile of the stairs) in an orthogonal system, exactly as in other works painted in Capri at this time (the watercolors *Sailor* or *Woman in a Window*, nos. 9 and 13 in the Café Morgano show of September 1917). This formal system was the outcome of the months spent in contact with Clavel. Depero left definitively behind him the dynamic tensions of the paintings exhibited at his one-man show in Rome in May 1916, as well as the sharp angles and distinct chiaroscuros of his costume designs for *Le Chant du Rossignol*. A drawing published in *Sic* of May 1917, dedicated to Clavel but executed in April in Rome as indicated by an inscription in Depero's hand, highlights the new stylistic departure from May onwards.[33] Yet this phase of Depero's work, exemplified by the Mattioli *Portrait of Gilbert Clavel*, was shortlived. In works executed slightly later (the eight full-page illustrations for *Un istituto per suicidi*, already complete when Depero left for Rome, or charcoal drawings exhibited with the title *Architetture sintetiche* at the September show in Capri), figures and objects assume a metallic density — they are clearly modeled with lights and darks, and cast shadows that emphasize their corporeal presence. This was the direction in which Depero was moving in late 1917-early 1918. In a later *Portrait of Gilbert Clavel* (dated 'Roma 1918,'[34] fig. 11e) the ashtray and glass on the table have a precise volumetric quality, the lapel of the jacket seems cut from a thick layer of cardboard and the arms are painted with the requisite chiaroscuro for the simulation of a tubular form.

In a memoir of 1940 Depero recalled the extent to which the atmosphere of the Capri summer had contributed to the luminous patchwork of the Mattioli painting. He was surrounded by "an iridescent palette," with the "rainbow scenery of the hypnotizing Neapolitan gulf" nearby, where "the blue of the sky is inlaid on the floors," and where reality appeared "translucent," enlivened by the splendor of the ceramics "with various yellow and light blue patterns."[35] The

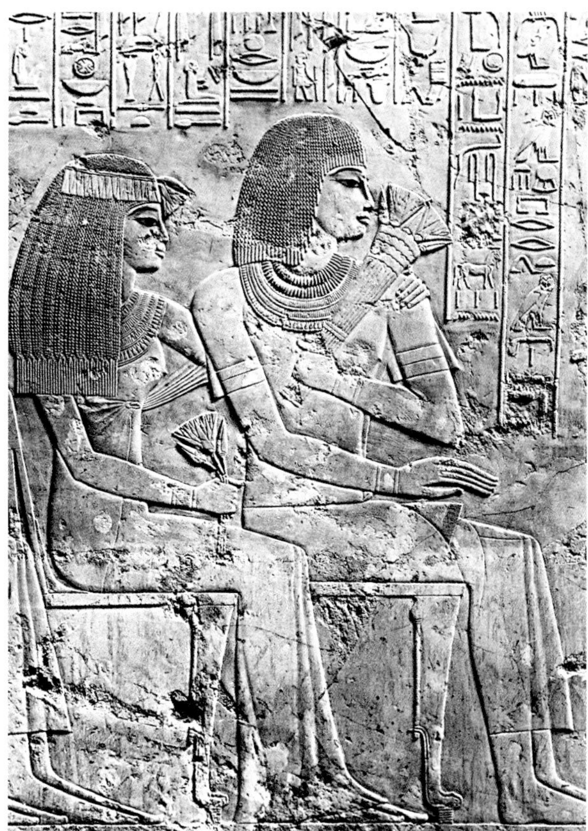

Fig. 11j. The Superintendent Maiy and His Bride, *bas-relief. Thebes, tomb no. 55, funeral chapel of the vizir Ramosé*

new turn of events in the 1917 summer became a departure point for that radical evolution of pictorial linguistics which Depero recounted in a famous 1919 declaration:

> "I geometrified, compacted and crystallized the lights, metallicized the shadows, brought to any solid matter that could possibly be resolved by mechanical construction the whole range of emotions and plastic sensations. Everything in my most recent works is constructed with rhythm, ultra-evident logic of relations and contrasts of colors and forms, so as to shape a unique and strong whole. As a reaction to the Impressionist style, I invented a flat, simple, geometric, mechanical style: primal and clear form; complementary color done in flat and curved planes in a geometric sense; a return to a severe perspective of the body implicit but unseen; a highly rigorous plastic consideration of values; rhythmic and architectonic relations of minimal, invisible details [...] I am not satisfied with a color range nor with plastic relations between things, but struggle always to find the line which fuses and supports the most disparate elements of an architectonic unit."[36]

Following the Capri show in September 1917, the history of the painting cannot be reconstructed with certainty. Portraits of Clavel appear in almost all exhibitions of Depero's work between 1918 and 1922,[37] but they were never illustrated and reviewers always passed them by (with one exception, which was not however the Mattioli painting[38]), giving their attention instead to the novelties (figurines, toys, cushions, tapestries) that Depero periodically introduced. The only certain piece of information appears in the catalogue of the March 1919 'Grande Esposizione Nazionale Futurista', Milan, in which it was noted that one of two portraits of Clavel on exhibit was the property of the writer (given the importance of the show, this could plausibly have been the Mattioli painting). In the dozens of letters from Clavel to Depero between 1917 and 1920 preserved in the Fondo Depero in Rovereto, it is unclear which works in Clavel's collec-

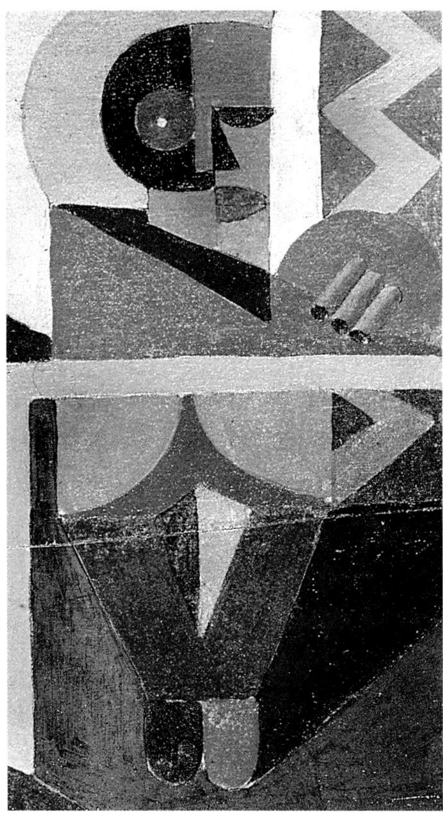

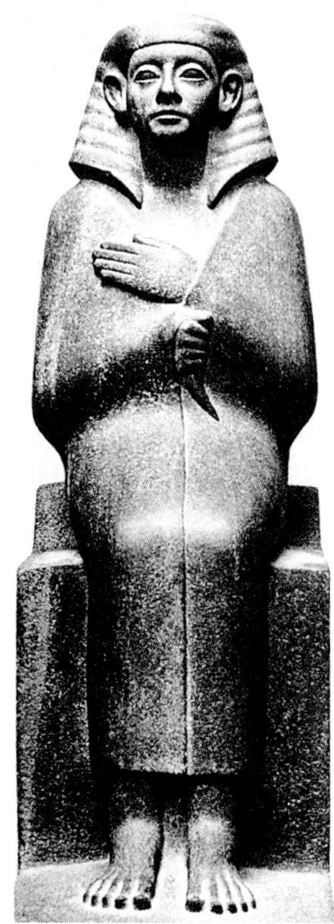

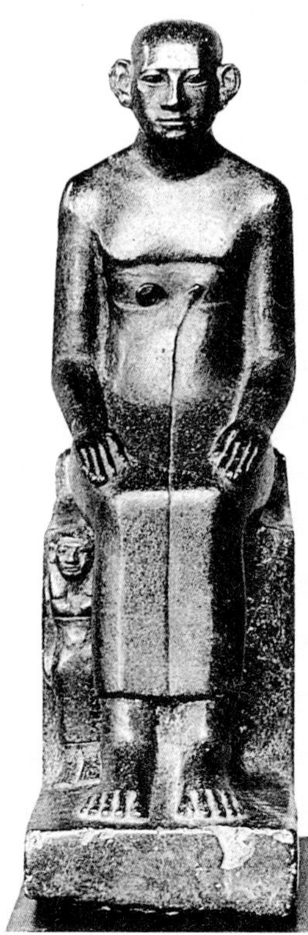

Fig. 11k. *Detail of cat. no. 11*

Fig. 11l. The Superintendent Khertihotep, *XII Dynasty, in* Aegyptische und Vorderasiatische Alterthümer aus den Koeniglichen Museen zu Berlin, *1895*

Fig. 11m. *Statuette with a Portrait of a Dignitary, c. 2,200 B.C., in* Aegyptische und Vorderasiatische Alterthümer aus den Koeniglichen Museen zu Berlin, *1895*

tion remained in Capri after 1917 and which were returned to Depero to enable him to exhibit them (from two letters of October–November 1917 we learn that Clavel shipped works by Depero from Capri to Rome, but with no further details).[39] The only reference to the painting in the correspondence occurs in a letter of August 1918 in which Clavel tells Depero of the effect of drugs given him by a Neapolitan doctor for an operation on his jaw, but his shaky Italian makes it unclear whether or not he was referring to a painting actually in his house at that time:

> "They gave me so much cocaine that I became half mad for ten days — one night I felt myself separated completely in two — which means that I encountered myself in an empty room but in front of myself. I see this thing in a large painting by you that could be called 'the duplication.'"[40]

Forgotten for three decades, the painting seems to have re-emerged in 1951, according to information provided by Giampiero Giani, in Basel in the collection of René Clavel, Gilbert's brother.[41] At some point between the end of the 1950s and the beginning of the 1960s it was acquired by Gianni Mattioli, a friend of the artist over several decades.[42] Its first exhibition in a historic show was in 1962 when the catalogue indicated its ownership as the Mattioli Collection in Milan.[43]

[1] Balla, Depero, March 11, 1915.
[2] 'Sprovieri' 1983, p. 144.
[3] Clavel 1920, pp. 25–32; Bondi 1979, pp. 9–10; Passamani 1981, p. 291.
[4] Fermani, Lambiase 1983, p. 154.
[5] Peyrefitte 1959, p. 247; Fermani, Lambiase 1983, pp. 149–71; Bragaglia 1988, p. 26; Bignardi 1996, pp. 184–5.
[6] Belloli 1979, pp. 327–32; Fagiolo dell'Arco 1988, pp. 71–3.
[7] Letter from Enrico Prampolini to Bino Sanminiatelli, dated August 12, 1917, in Drudi Gambillo, Fiori 1958–62, vol. II, p. 55.
[8] Clavel 1918, pp. 11–13; Clavel 1919, pp. 10–14; Clavel 1920, pp. 25–32.
[9] Rovereto, MART, Archivio del 900, Fondo Depero, letters dated October 30, 1917 (ms. no. 3136), October 5, 1918 (ms. no. 1358), January 21, 1919 (ms. no. 3150), and February 15, 1919, partially published in *Capri* 1988, p. 53.
[10] *Depero* 1940, p. 203.
[11] Fermani, Lambiase 1983, pp. 62–3.
[12] *Capri* 1917, unnumbered page; Passamani 1981, pp. 292–3.
[13] *Uomo e tavolo - Clavel*, Rovereto, Museo Fortunato Depero: *Bassano del Grappa* 1970, no. 125a.
[14] Trento, private collection: *Bassano del Grappa* 1970, no. 125b.
[15] A shipment from Rome to Capri of material to exhibit at the September show at the Sala Morgano is documented (letter from Gilbert Clavel to Fortunato Depero, dated July 17, 1917 in Rovereto, MART, Archivio del 900, Fondo Depero, ms. no. 3136) but the catalogue of the show makes no mention of the set design maquette for *Le Chant du Rossignol*.
[16] Passamani 1970[b], p. 37. Later, dated 'Capri 1917', this is therefore the sketch with Clavel at his work table published in Belloli 1979, p. 327 (where its ownership is given as the collection of Giovanni Acquaviva, Milan).
[17] Rovereto, Museo Fortunato Depero: *Paris* 1996, no. 13.
[18] Margheri 1982, p. 333.
[19] *Depero* 1940, p. 204.
[20] Bragaglia 1988, p. 26.
[21] *Depero* 1940, p. 402.
[22] Giani 1951, p. 18.
[23] Biondi 1969, p. 16.
[24] Bragaglia 1970, p. LXII.
[25] Illustrated on the cover of the 'Balli Plastici' show catalogue in Rome in the foyer of the Teatro dei Piccoli in April 1918, in *Rovereto* 1988–*Milan* 1989, p. 29.
[26] Letter from Gilbert Clavel to Fortunato Depero, dated November 5, 1917, in Rovereto, MART, Archivio del 900, Fondo Depero, ms. no. 1341.
[27] A relevant account of Clavel's visit to the Theban tombs with the frescoes of Nefertari is in Clavel 1920, pp. 25–7.
[28] Fechheimer 1914, cover.
[29] Von Bissing 1914, pl. 24 (Amenemes III of the central kingdoms at the Cairo Museum) and pl. 45 (Amenofi IV of the XVIII dynasty).
[30] *Koenigliche* 1895, with inventory numbers 10115 and 8430.
[31] The extract of the lecture is anthologized in *Trento* 1921, p. 7.
[32] Giani 1951, p. 4.
[33] In Fagiolo dell'Arco 1988, p. 25.
[34] Milan, Civiche raccolte d'arte: Caramel, Pirovano 1973, no. 120.
[35] *Depero* 1940, pp. 204–8.
[36] Depero 1919, p. 9.
[37] *Florence* 1918, no. 119 (*Ritratto dello scrittore Clavel*); *Milan–Genoa–Florence* 1919, no. 50 (*Ritratto di Clavel* property of Clavel) and no. 51 (*Ritratto di Clavel*); *Milan* 1921, no. 94 (*Clavel-Ritratto 1918*).
[38] Aniante, January 27, 1919.
[39] Letters from Gilbert Clavel to Fortunato Depero, dated October 25 and November 15, 1917, in Rovereto, MART, Archivio del 900, Fondo Depero, mss. nos. 1340 and 3132.
[40] Letter from Gilbert Clavel to Fortunato Depero, dated August 22, 1918, in Rovereto, MART, Archivio del 900, Fondo Depero, ms. no. 1357.
[41] Giani 1951, p. 18.
[42] Archivio Mattioli, file for the work.
[43] *Milan* 1962[a], no. 12 (listed as Milan, private collection).

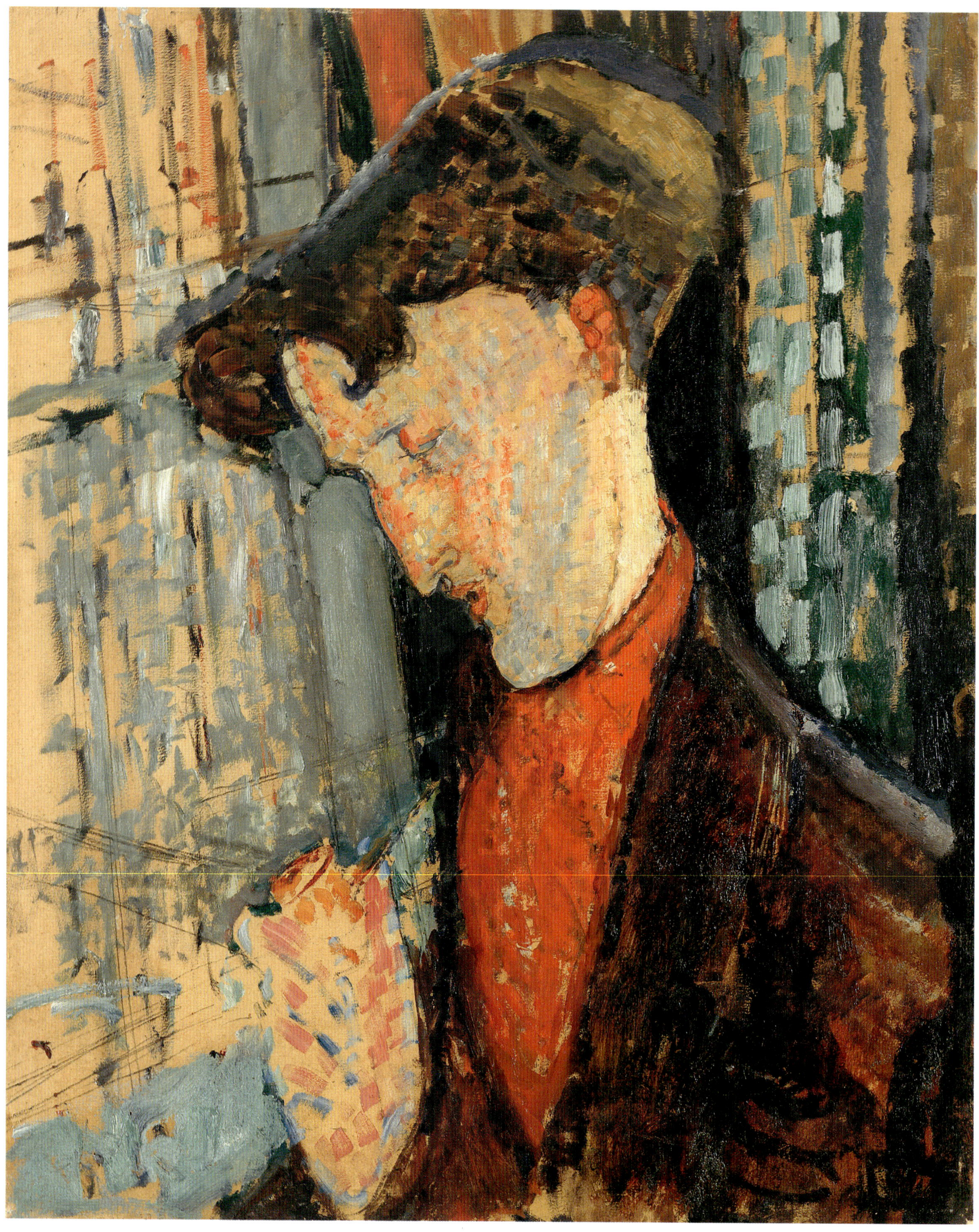

12

Amedeo Modigliani (Leghorn, 1884 – Paris, 1920)

Portrait of the Painter Frank Haviland

Ritratto del pittore Frank Haviland, 1914

Oil on board
73 × 60 cm

Provenance: before 1929: Adolphe Basler, Paris; before 1929: C. Zamaron, Paris; before 1929: S. Reinke, Überlingen, Germany; before 1931: Galerie Marcel Bernheim, Paris; ?: Italico Brass, Venice; 1943: Alessandro Brass, Venice; September 1949: Gianni Mattioli, with the mediation of R. Boniface Allasia and the Galleria Annunciata

Exhibitions: Paris 1931, catalogue not traced (the presence of the work in the exhibition is documented by a statement by Alessandro Brass, dated June 19, 1949: Archivio Mattioli, *Appendix I*, document no. 28); Brussels 1950, no. 61 (*Portrait de M. Havilland* [*sic*], 1914); Amsterdam 1950, catalogue not traced (the presence of the work in the exhibition is documented in the Archivio Mattioli, file for the work); Paris 1950, no. 43; London 1950, no. 59; Cleveland–New York 1951, p.16; Florence 1953[a], no. 20; Bern 1955, p. 6, no. 5; Milan 1958, no. 8; Turin 1959, p. 42, no. 23; Frankfurt 1963, no. 6; Milan 1966[a], no. 3, Florence 1967[a], no. 438; Washington, DC 1967–Tokyo 1972, no. 70 (Washington, DC–Hamburg), no. 68 (Madrid–Seville), no. 70 (Kyoto–Tokyo); Paris 1975–6, no. 46; Martigny 1990, no. 28

Bibliography: Pfannstiel 1929, p. 7 and facing p.11 (*Portrait de Frank Haviland*, 1915); Statement by Alessandro Brass, dated June 19, 1949 (Archivio Mattioli, file for the work); Scheiwiller 1950, pl. II (*Ritratto di Frank Haviland*, 1914, illus.); Mattioli 1951, pp. 25–6; Ragghianti 1953, p. 11;

The sitter, who poses in profile with his pipe in his hand and his eyes half-closed engrossed in thought, is the painter Frank Haviland (1886–1971), a figure in Parisian art circles in the second and third decades of the century and a friend of numerous avant-garde artists. Born and educated in France but of American origin (he was a descendant of David Haviland, who moved to France from the United States in the mid-nineteenth century and founded an important porcelain factory in Limoges), Frank Haviland first studied music and then came into contact with Picasso in 1910 and turned to painting. He signed his pictures, which were in an ingenuously 'Cubified' realist style, 'Frank Burty', from the surname of his mother's father, the critic and writer Philippe Burty.[1] Haviland was distinctive in Picasso's circle for his refined elegance (Fernande Olivier remembered him as "tall, fair, very distinguished, very young […], solicitous and reserved"[2]) and for his wealth. Between 1910 and 1915 he helped many artist friends financially, and was particularly close to the Spanish sculptor Manolo (Manuel Martínez Hugué) with whom he went several times to Céret in the company of Picasso, Braque and Gris. Haviland was also painted by Juan Gris in a portrait of 1913,[3] for which there is an important preparatory drawing (fig. 12c):[4] the cigarette, the fall of his long hair, his shoe string tie and top hat characterize a type of elegance both dandyish and formal. Haviland's habitual kindness and unselfishness must have fascinated Modigliani, who was himself known for his aristocratic manners: he sometimes went to paint in Haviland's studio on rue Schoelcher in Montparnasse[5] and was probably helped by him in moments of financial difficulty.

Two versions of the painting exist: in addition to the Mattioli painting, there is another with an identical support though slightly smaller (62.2 × 49.4 cm, Los Angeles County Museum of Art, fig. 12e).[6] This was formerly owned by Haviland but was sold at auction at the Hôtel Drouot on October 20, 1926.[7] Furthermore a study of the artist's face similar to that in the two painted portraits exists in a drawing acquired by the Musée d'Art Moderne de la Ville de Paris in 1980 from Haviland's heirs (fig. 12d).[8]

The comparison between cat. no. 12 and the painting in Los Angeles raises the obvious question, though it has not been previously addressed, of which of them was painted first. Relative to the Mattioli painting, the Los Angeles version gives us more information about the setting (the backs of stretched canvases stacked in the studio and a penciled-in drinking glass on the table lower left) and about the sitter's clothes (the scarf, red in the Mattioli painting, becomes an elegant fabric bordered with a black strip and decorated with little red cross-shaped motifs evidently reminiscent of Cézanne); finally, Modigliani accentuated the strange profile of the head, now longer and more stylized. The degree of finish in the two paintings is similar (in the Mattioli version the brown velvet jacket is more finished; in the Los Angeles version the hand holding the pipe is defined in greater detail) and Modigliani chose, in both versions, to exploit the expressive potential of lack of finish: for example the paint condenses into colored planes around the head to give prominence to its clear outline.

However certain signals argue in favor of giving precedence to the Mattioli painting. Only here is there retouching to the contour of the cranium: in the upper part a pale blue line and a dark blue shape merging with the background accentuate the deformation of the back of the head to the same degree as in the Los Angeles painting which, however, lacks any comparable *pentimenti* (below the paint surface one can make out a simple line drawing faithfully followed by the brush). In addition there are clues that suggest a passage from a more realistic image to a more stylized one. Haviland's right eye in the Mattioli painting is just visible whereas it has vanished completely in the pure profile of the Los Angeles painting. The less elongated shape of the head in the Mattioli painting more closely resembles that of Haviland himself, as seen in photographs taken at his wedding in Céret in 1914 (fig. 12a) or in Paris in the same year (fig 12b).

The drawing does not apparently contribute to a resolution of the question. The curve of the nape of the neck is less pronounced (as in the Mattioli painting before the blue retouches), the right eye of the subject is visible and the tuft of hair on his forehead is closer to that of the Mattioli version than to that in Los Angeles. Other features, particularly the attenuation of the face and the exaggerated tapering of the outline of the neck, move the drawing closer

Descargues 1954, no. 13; Pfannstiel 1956, p. 66, no. 34 (1914–15); Castelfranco, Valsecchi 1956, p. 63; Ceroni 1958, pp. 55–6, no. 34; Modigliani 1958, p. 81; Russoli 1958, pl. 3; Bellonzi 1963, pp. 133, 136; Werner 1967, pp. 78–9; Crispolti 1968, pp. 14, 21; Ponente 1969, pp. 15, 30, pl. 10; Ceroni 1970, p. 90, no. 44 and pl. VII; Lanthemann 1970, no. 47; Warnod 1975, p. 104; Mann 1980, pp. 94–5; Lassaigne 1981, p. 17 and no. 44; Castieau-Barrielle 1987, p. 108; Rose 1990, p. 113; Marchesseau 1990, p. 214; Parisot 1991, no. 6/1914; Schmalenbach 1991, p. 37; Patani 1991, p. 77, no. 49; Durieu 1995, pp. 68–9; Kruszynsky 1996, pp. 32–3; Rylands 1997, p. 7

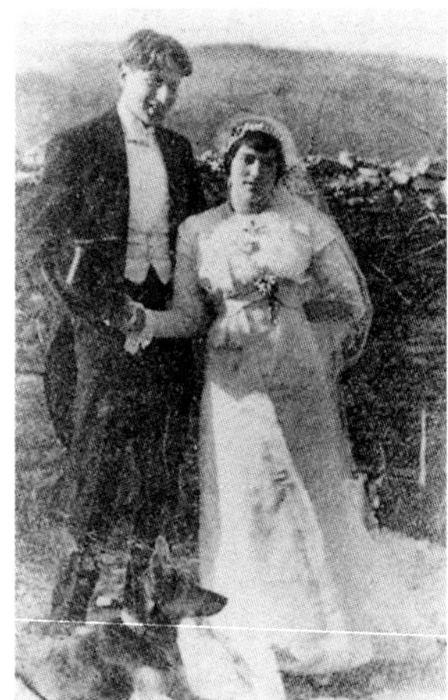

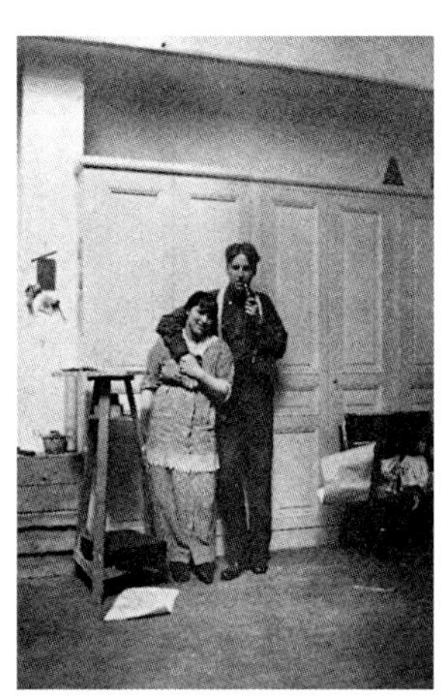

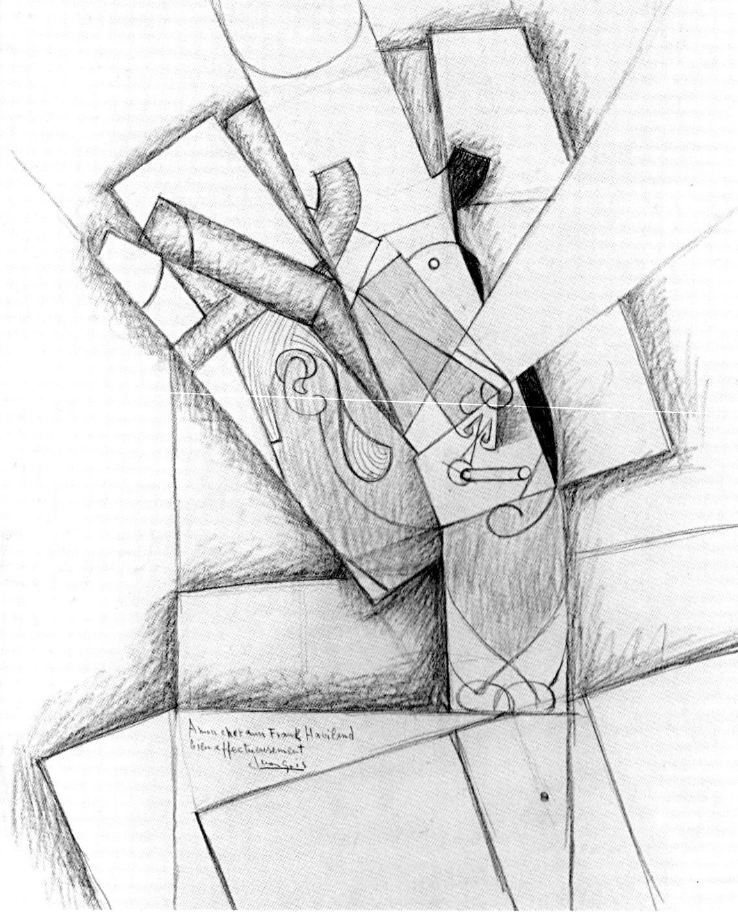

Fig. 12a. *Frank and Joséphine Haviland photographed in Céret on their wedding day, January 8, 1914. Paris, Fonds Pageard*

Fig. 12b. *Frank and Joséphine Haviland photographed by Pablo Picasso, 1914. Paris, Archives Picasso, Musée Picasso*

Fig. 12c. *Juan Gris,* Le Fumeur (Portrait de Frank Haviland) (The Smoker [Portrait of Frank Haviland]), *pencil and charcoal on paper, 1913. New York, The Metropolitan Museum of Art, Jacques and Natasha Gelman Collection, 1998*

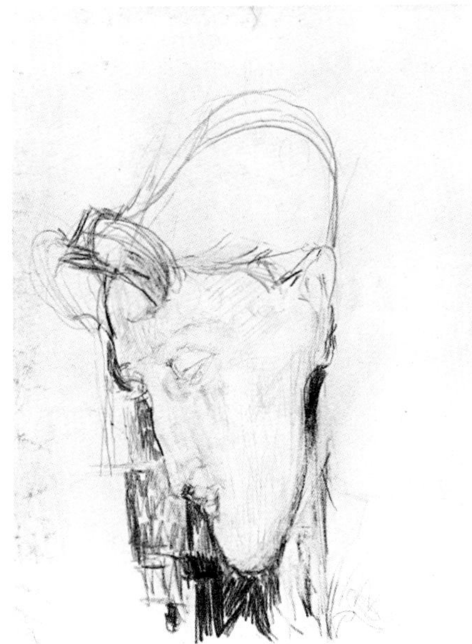

Fig. 12d. *Amedeo Modigliani,* Ritratto di Frank Haviland (Portrait of Frank Haviland), *pencil on paper, 1914. Paris, Musée d'Art Moderne de la Ville de Paris*

Fig. 12e. *Amedeo Modigliani,* Ritratto di Frank Haviland (Portrait of Frank Haviland), *oil on board, 1914. Los Angeles, Los Angeles County Museum of Art, Mr and Mrs William Preston Harrison Collection*

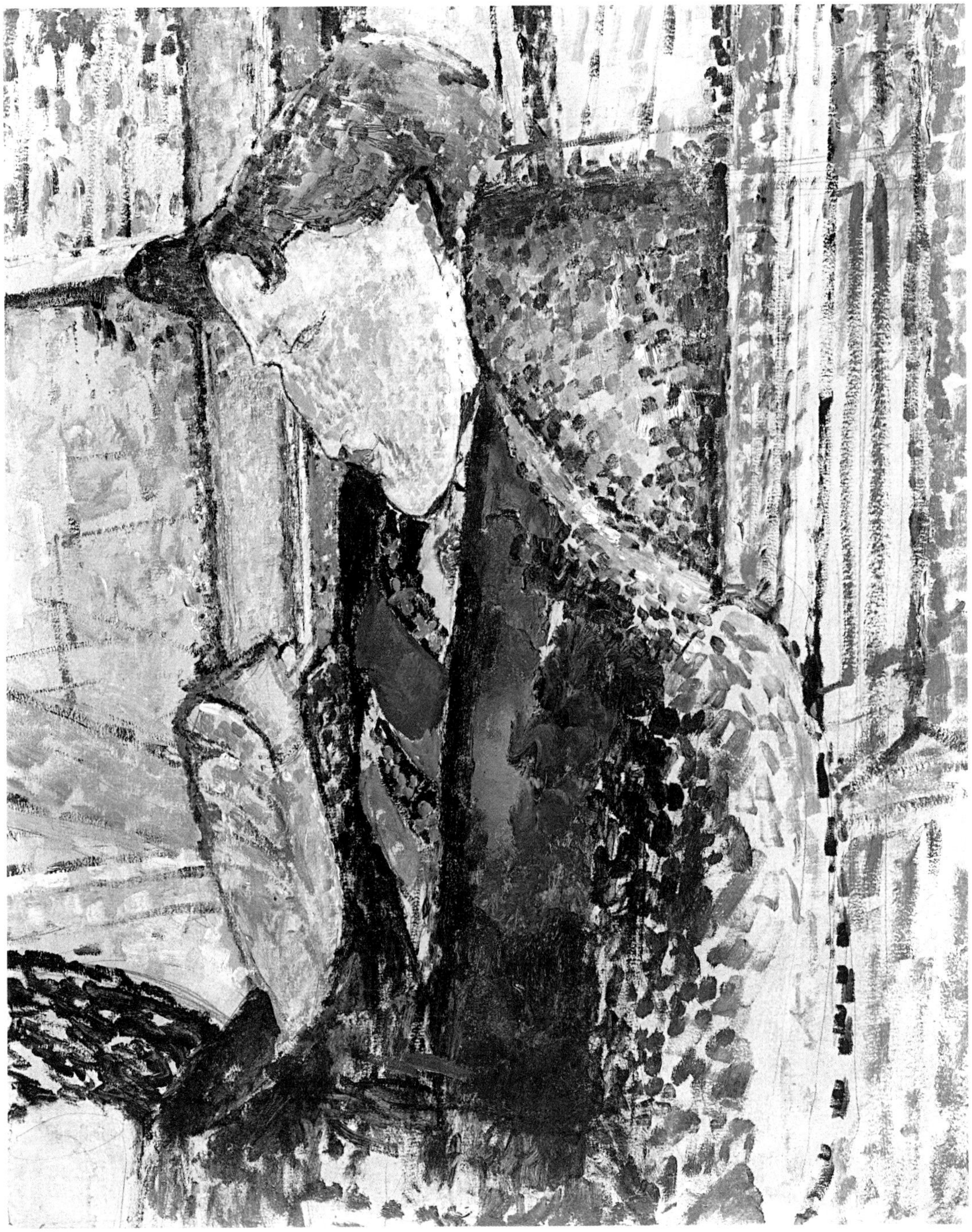

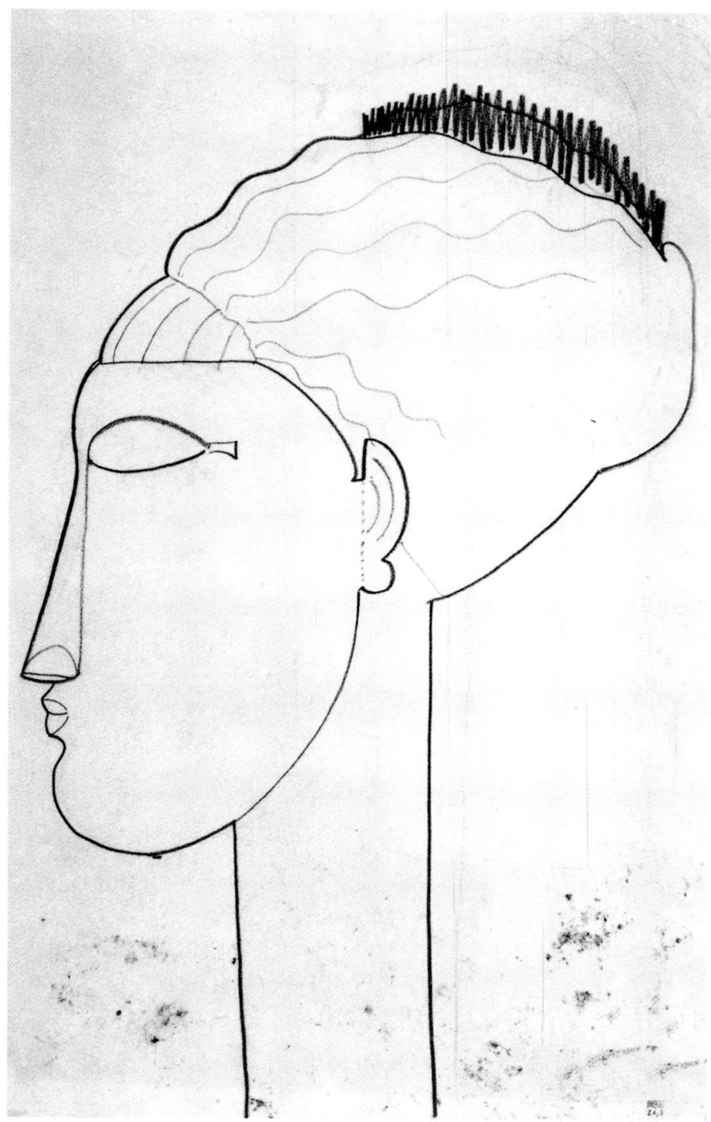

Fig. 12f. *Amedeo Modigliani,* Cariatide in profilo (Caryatid in Profile)*, pencil on paper, 1912. Paris, Noël Alexandre Collection*

to the Los Angeles painting. It is possible therefore to suppose that Modigliani first portrayed Haviland in the Mattioli painting and then later, separately, developed certain stylistic characteristics (the attenuation of the profile, the reddening of the cheek, the bell-shaped form of the hair, the elongation of the body) in the subsequent version.

Published for the first time in the fundamental 1929 catalogue by Arthur Pfannstiel with the date 1915 (while cautioning that it "may be prior to that date"[9]), the painting is now unanimously dated 1914.[10] After his return from Leghorn, now known to have taken place in April–June 1913,[11] Modigliani gave up sculpture (to which he had dedicated himself since 1911) and began a series of painted portraits in a style which he was swiftly to abandon: the relation of the figure to space is left uncertain; the broken and choppy brushstrokes generate a vibrant luminous effect; the sitter's faces and physical attributes are distorted to the point of caricature (the puffy and exotic features of Diego Rivera [fig. 12h] for example, or the long neck of Beatrice Hastings). Despite some decidedly pictorial aspects (the bright colors reminiscent of the Fauves, the attempt to represent an indoor atmosphere with thickly impasted touches of the brush), the portrait of Frank Haviland is still strongly indebted to the months that Modigliani had spent working on sculpture. The choice of the pure profile which, after the 1909 *The Cello Player*[12] (with the sole exception of the portrait of *Lola de Valence*[13]) was to recur only in 1918, derives from his studies for the caryatids and for the sculpted heads of 1912–13.

Fig. 12g. *Amedeo Modigliani,* Cariatide (Caryatid)*, pencil, pen and watercolor on paper, 1913. Chicago, The Art Institute, Gift of Amy McCormick*

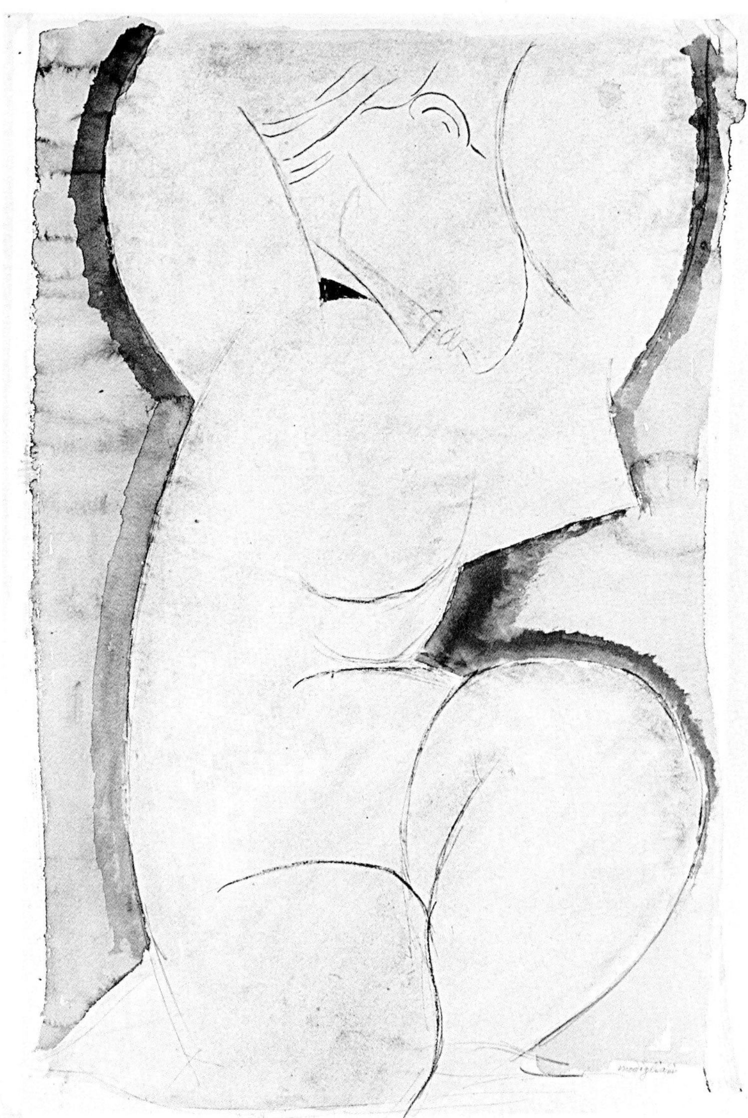

The hair bunched up at the back of the head in a compact mass is seen in profile heads in drawings collected by Paul Alexandre[14] (fig. 12f). Some of the features that characterize this portrait, such as the elegant and melancholy inclination of the face, the high positioning of the ear and the silhouette of the lips and chin, closely resemble the watercolor studies of caryatids[15] (see for example fig. 12g). The portrait of Frank Haviland represents therefore an important link in the *corpus* of Modigliani's paintings: he appropriated a repertory of stylizations from his long experience of making studies on paper for sculpture, and at the same time initiated a tendency to linear elegance reminiscent of Tuscan painting in the fourteenth and fifteenth century.

The early history of the painting is intricate and difficult to reconstruct with precision, for lack of reliable evidence about the market for Modigliani's works in the 1920s. In 1929, when the first catalogue of his paintings was published, Arthur Pfannstiel located it in Germany, in the Reinke Collection in Überlingen, but mentioned its earlier presence in two Parisian collections: from that of Adolphe Basler (prolific writer of books illustrated with French modern art, and author in 1931 of a monograph on Modigliani) it passed to that of a certain C. Zamaron, about whom little is known and who lent two of the three paintings in his collection to the 1926 Modigliani retrospective at the 'Salon des Artistes Indépendants.'[16] Shortly thereafter the painting reappeared on the market. It was acquired by Marcel Bernheim and was exhibited in

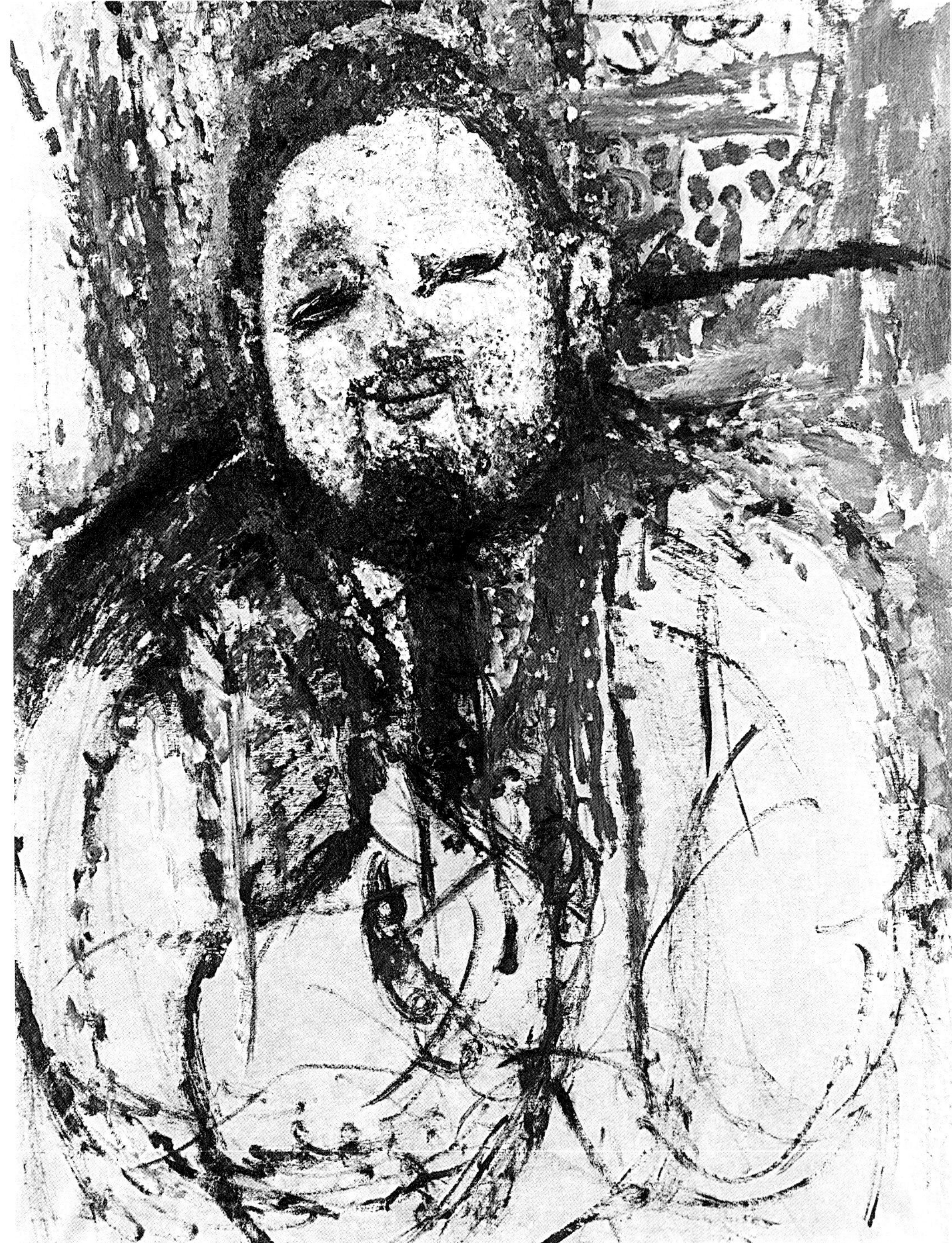

Fig. 12h. *Amedeo Modigliani,* Ritratto di Diego Rivera (Portrait of Diego Rivera*), oil on canvas, 1914. São Paulo, Museu de arte de São Paulo Assis Chateaubriand*

the 'Rétrospective Modigliani' in June 1931 in his gallery.[17] Information is scarce from this point on. Gianni Mattioli purchased the portrait in September 1949 from the heirs of Italico Brass (1870–1943),[18] a Venetian painter with an important collection of sixteenth- and seventeenth-century art[19] (in which however there is no evidence of other twentieth-century masterpieces) which was broken up and sold after his death. In a brief text of 1951 in which Gianni Mattioli recounted the criteria which were driving his collecting, he spoke of the *Portrait of Frank Haviland* as the "work that gave me the most emotion" both for its rarity ("one of the very few 'fauve' paintings by this exceptional artist") and for the "surprise of the encounter" (a painting which had been "acquired, many years ago, by a painter, who kept it for himself, without telling anyone").[20] He also stated that the painting had "appeared in Milan, in the summer of

1949": the heirs of Italico Brass entrusted the sale of the painting to Signora Boniface Allasia,[21] though the Galleria Annunciata, Milan, seems also to have become involved in the transaction, since a label with the accession number 1121 is glued to the stretcher. In January 1950, the painting, by this time part of the Mattioli Collection, was included in the contemporary Italian art exhibition organized by the Venice Biennale which traveled to Brussels, Amsterdam, Paris and London.

[1] Loize 1966, pp. 27–32; Rewald 1989, pp. 119–21.
[2] Olivier 1933, p. 138.
[3] *Le Fumeur*, Madrid, Thyssen-Bornemisza Collection.
[4] New York, The Metropolitan Museum of Art, Jacques and Natasha Gelman Collection: *New York* 1989[a], pp. 119–21.
[5] Castieau-Barrielle 1987, p. 108.
[6] Los Angeles County Museum of Art, Mr and Mrs William Preston Harrison Collection: Patani 1991, no. 48.
[7] Pfannstiel 1929, p. 7.
[8] Paris, Musée d'Art Moderne de la Ville de Paris, inv. AMD 80.871: *Paris* 1981, no. 140; Patani 1994, no. 28. The most recent general catologue of Modigliani's drawings identified a drawing of a *Head* summarily outlined in pencil with strokes of gouache and watercolor now in the Kunsthaus Zürich as a *Portrait of Frank Burty Haviland*, dating it 1911–12 (Patani 1992, no. 123). The date was later shifted to 1914 (Decroocq 1999, p. 186). However it is hard to see a resemblance to the painter here. His face seen frontally is elongated, like a bell, as in the two oil portraits; the lips are similarly small and feminine; but it does not have Haviland's characteristic aristocratic aquiline nose, which Modigliani was keen to stress in the two oil portraits. The style of drawing would seem to suggest a later date than that proposed by Patani. Neither at its first known exhibition (*Bern* 1955, p. 11, no. 49), nor at the Modigliani exhibition in Paris in 1981 (where it was reproduced in the catalogue as *Tête de femme*: *Paris* 1981, no. 157) was this drawing related to Haviland.
[9] Pfannstiel 1929, p. 7.
[10] Ceroni 1958, pp. 45–6, no. 34; Lanthemann 1970; Parisot 1991, no. 6/1914; Patani 1991, p. 77, no. 49.
[11] Alexandre 1993, pp. 102–9.
[12] *Il suonatore del violoncello*, Geneva, Galerie Krugier: Patani 1991, no. 32.
[13] New York, The Metropolitan Museum of Art: *ibidem*, no. 54.
[14] Alexandre 1993, nos. 189–209; p. 183, no. 9.
[15] For instance, the watercolor with *Caryatid*, 1913–14, Chicago, The Art Institute, Gift of Amy McCormick donation: *Paris* 1981, no. 127.
[16] *Paris* 1926, nos. 3105–6; both paintings were called *Figures*; the chronological sequence of the thirteen paintings in this exhibition, with the two Zamaron paintings towards the end, and in any case after works from 1916, would seem to rule out the presence of the Haviland portrait.
[17] *Paris* 1931, catalogue not traced.
[18] Archivio Mattioli, statement of provenance and authenticity of the painting signed by Alessandro Brass, son of Italico Brass, dated June 19, 1949; statement by *idem* of the sale of the painting to Gianni Mattioli, dated September 19, 1949 (*Appendix I*, document no. 28).
[19] Ivanoff 1941, pp. 71–80; Malni Pascoletti 1991, pp. 43–52.
[20] Mattioli 1951, p. 26.
[21] Archivio Mattioli, statement of Brass, dated June 19, 1949: the painting had been "affidato per la vendita alla Signora R. Boniface Allasia (Milano, Viale dei Mille 27)" (*Appendix I*, document no. 28).

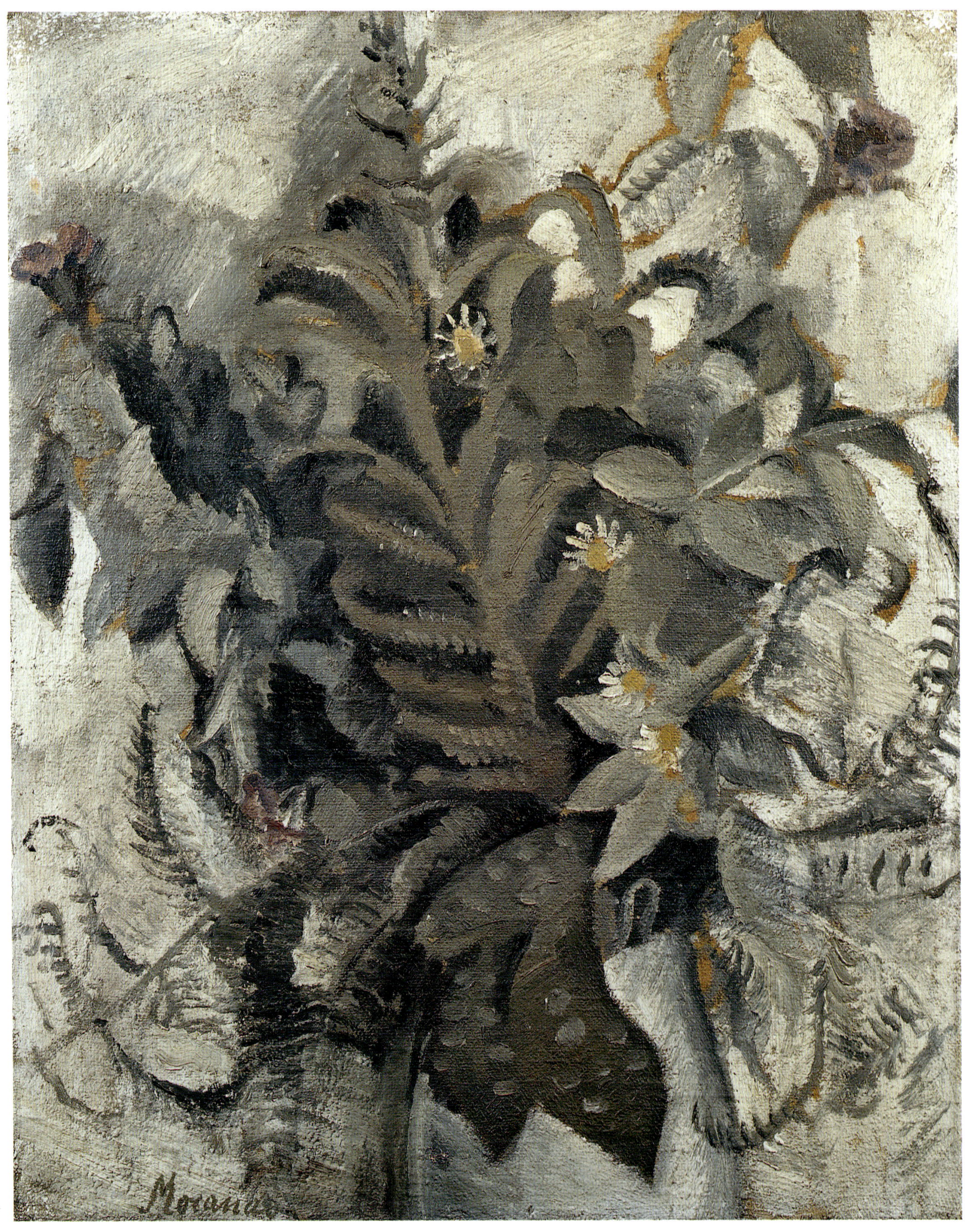
Morandi

13

Giorgio Morandi (Bologna, 1890–1964)

Flowers

Fiori, 1913

Oil on canvas
68 × 55 cm

Inscription: *recto*, signed lower left: 'Morandi'

Provenance: property of the artist; March 1950: Gianni Mattioli, with the mediation of the Galleria del Milione

Exhibitions: London 1950, no. 70 (*Flowers*); Zurich 1950, no. 152; Florence 1953[a], no. 22; Turin 1959, no. 25; Paris 1960–1, no. 509; Bern 1965, no. 4; Venice 1966, p. 27, no. 3; Bologna 1966, no. 4; Washington, DC 1967–Tokyo 1972, no. 71 (Washington, DC–Hamburg), no. 69 (Madrid–Seville), no. 71 (Kyoto–Tokyo); Milan 1971, no. 3; Rome 1973, no. 4

Bibliography: Statement of account of the Galleria del Milione, dated March 30, 1950 (*Fiori*; Archivio Mattioli); Raimondi 1951, p. 20 and fig. 8 (*Fiori*, 1913); Garretto 1952, p. 43; Bardi 1957, fig. 1; Ragghianti 1953, p. 14; Vitali 1964, fig. 6; Arcangeli 1964, pp. 35–6; Raimondi, November 24, 1966; Giuffré 1970, p. 12 and pl. 2; Del Monte 1973, p. 31; Solmi 1978, p. 17, fig. 10; Solmi 1985[a], p. 27; Cavallo 1989, p. 7; Pasini 1989, pp. 25–6; Rylands 1997, p. 76

In the history of Italian twentieth-century painting, the youthful work of Giorgio Morandi is usually interpreted as a case of anomalous but superlative apprenticeship that is hard to explain in the cultural context in which he grew up. Trained in the artistically provincial city of Bologna in the early years of the century, Morandi was impervious to the lingering modes of international realism and symbolism still dominant in Italy. Instead he painstakingly assimilated the pictorial languages of Cubism and Futurism, though without ever actively participating in either of those avant-gardes. With the help of a few carefully chosen critical and visual aids, he purposefully turned toward French painting in the line of descent from Cézanne, painting pictures with a solid constructive sense in a narrow but highly modulated palette.

Lamberto Vitali's general catalogue of Morandi's paintings inventories only thirty-four works prior to the Metaphysical period in 1918[1] (a small number of juvenilia, for the most part owned by the Museo Morandi in Bologna, can now be added to these[2]). In fact the artist destroyed the majority of his early works, both because he was dissatisfied with their quality and in order to eliminate paintings that were too obviously exercises in the manner of other artists — masters that he studied intensely but then repudiated because they were extraneous to Cézanne or Rousseau, the only influences he was willing to acknowledge. (On a visit to Morandi's studio in June 1918, Emilio Cecchi wrote to his wife of "certain heads" in which the artist was "more lyrical, but also more broken and patchy with borrowed elements: from Greco, Derain."[3])

The few paintings that survived were released by Morandi into the public domain in three distinct phases. Some were bought by Mario Broglio[4] and in part published in the periodical *Valori Plastici* in an issue (year II, no. 3) appearing between the end of 1921 and the beginning of 1922. Others emerged on the art market and in collections (mainly Milanese) during the 1930s in ways still requiring documentation[5] (two exceptions are the purchases by Pietro Feroldi in this catalogue, nos. 14 and 15). The critical date for this is 1939, when the first six paintings in Morandi's solo section at the 'III Quadriennale romana' and the first ten plates in the book by Arnaldo Beccaria published a few months later made available to a wider public early works known previously only to a small circle of amateurs. The majority of the paintings of 1910–17 reappeared on the market or were published in exhibition catalogues, books and periodicals after the end of World War II. Morandi was singled out by the more informed critics (Roberto Longhi, Cesare Brandi, Carlo Ludovico Ragghianti) as the only Italian artist ca-

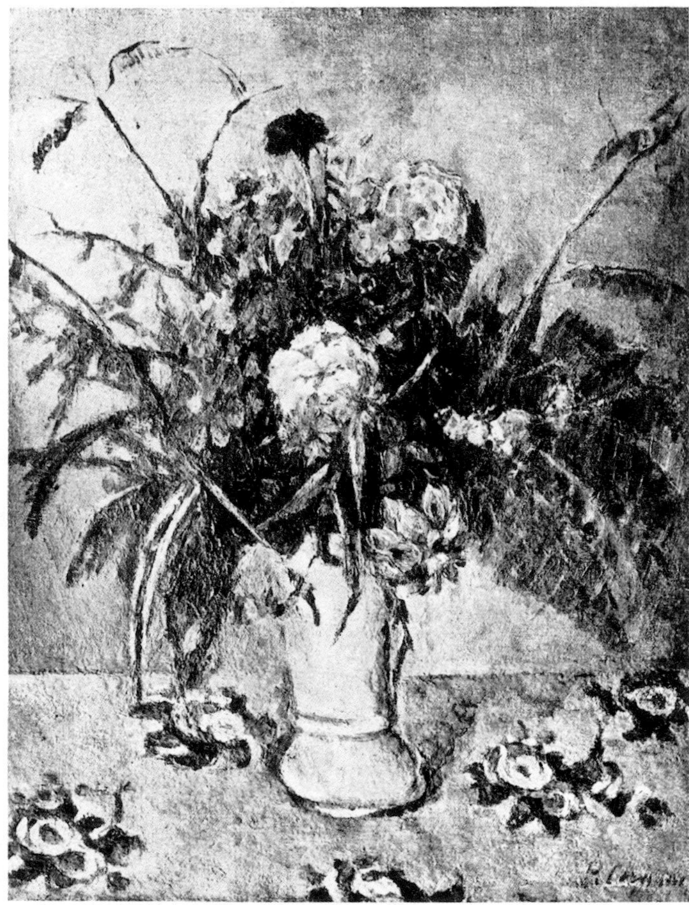

Fig. 13a. *Paul Cézanne,* Le Vase des fleurs sur un tapis fleuri *(*Vase of Flowers on a Flowered Carpet*), in V. Pica,* Gl'Impressionisti Francesi*, 1908*

pable of holding his own against the most acclaimed international contemporary painters. Furthermore the awarding of a first prize at the 1948 Venice Biennale placed him in the limelight in a period of frenetic collecting activity. Pictures that Morandi had kept to himself, or shown in his home to the few visitors that came, or which had long since passed to a small group of friends, mostly men of letters (Giuseppe Raimondi, Mino Maccari, Leo Longanesi) progressively, during the 1950s, acquired prominence in the history of twentieth-century Italian art.

This vase of flowers falls in the third group. Gianni Mattioli bought it from the artist through the Galleria del Milione before March 1950,[6] and promptly loaned it to the 'Modern Italian Art' show organized by the 'Amici di Brera' and by the Italian Institute at the Tate Gallery in London in June–July of the same year.[7] The painting has no certain exhibition history prior to this. Severo Pozzati told Carlo Ludovico Ragghianti that he remembered it among the Morandis exhibited in a show of five young Bolognese artists in a room in the Hotel Baglioni in Bologna.[8] But the lack of a catalogue and the vagueness with which the event was reported in the local press frustrate any possibility for verifying this.[9]

A year after Mattioli's purchase, *Flowers* was reproduced for the first time among the illustrations for an essay by Giuseppe Raimondi dedicated to the parallel development of Carrà and Morandi in the 1910s. The close reading of Morandi's work by this Bolognese writer, a friend of the artist since 1916, included references to Modernist painting (Matisse and Derain) of which the young Morandi in 1913 could hardly have been aware, but which served to place him in an international context:

Fig. 13b. *Henri Rousseau,* Still Life *(*White Vase with Pansies and Other Flowers*), in W. Uhde,* Henri Rousseau, *1911*

Fig. 13c. *Odilon Redon,* Fleurs dans un vase *(*Flowers in a Vase*), in* L'Art Décoratif, *1913*

> "A painting of intense beauty, dated 1913, has re-emerged from time. It is of some 'Flowers' in which, in the dense inlay of colors sustained by the armature of stems, by the veins of the leaves, the undeniable lesson of Cézanne filters in a lucidity of intellect and in an 'impassioned' poetry of the level of contemporary or slightly earlier compositions by Matisse. In a form, therefore, and a spirit already removed from the observation and from the rigor, more narrowly conforming to Cézanne, of Derain, so to speak. The petals already become thicker, in these flowers, with their pulp of suffering, the leaves are spotted with a red-brown of ancient elegy, which rings out in the two famous compositions of 'Flowers' of '18."[10]

Henceforth *Flowers* was a fixture of the early Morandi canon as an episode of exceptional vitality of touch and color. Later interpretations acknowledged such qualities as "the outpouring of an overflowing vitality of color, of brushstroke and of plastic-spatial passages,"[11] "a pressure immediate, dense, potent [...] of the natural image,"[12] "a shadow of devilish vitality,"[13] "a surplus of energy" which generates a dense "material pulp."[14]

The essay by Raimondi quoted above stated that *Flowers* was 'dated 1913,' thus raising an unresolved question: today the painting has no trace of an autograph date, and nor was one visible in the photograph published in 1951 in *Paragone*. It may be that Raimondi made a mistake, or simply intended to say something else, such as "that Morandi recalled painting it in 1913"; then again it cannot be excluded that the work was dated on the back of the coarse original canvas, which was strengthened by relining immediately after its purchase.[15] The dating of Morandi's youthful works relies, in the absence of autograph dates on the canvases, on the artist's own recollections, which were even from early times prone to imprecision.[16] The suspicion that *Flowers* may after all belong to 1914 arises from its strongly Cézannesque quality, above all in the character of the brushstrokes. This would be more readily explicable if Morandi had had the opportunity for the first time to see originals by Cézanne (in the spring of 1914 at the exhibition of thirteen watercolors loaned by Bernheim-jeune to the 'II Esposizione del-

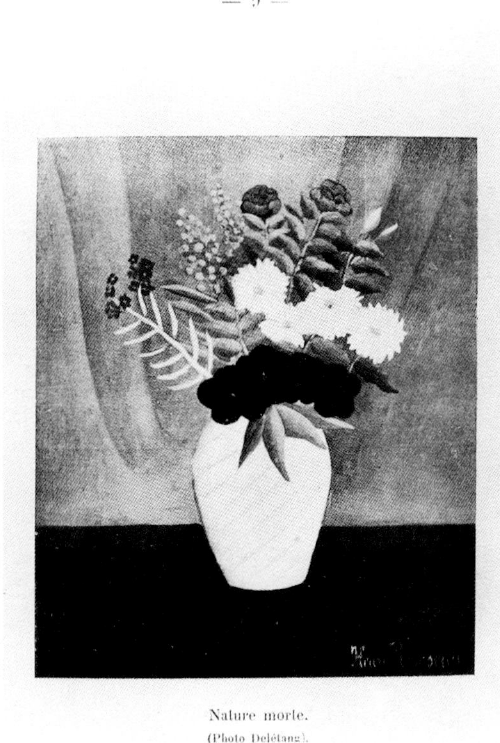

— 9 —

Nature morte.

(Photo Delétang).

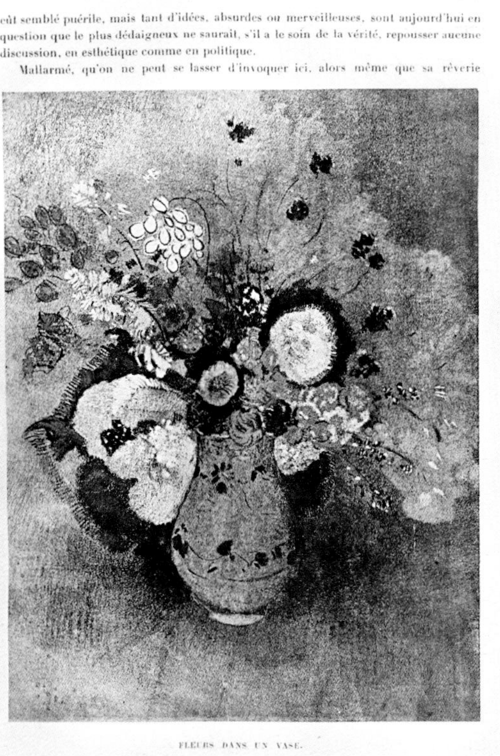

L'ART DÉCORATIF 17

eût semblé puérile, mais tant d'idées, absurdes ou merveilleuses, sont aujourd'hui en question que le plus dédaigneux ne saurait, s'il a le soin de la vérité, repousser aucune discussion, en esthétique comme en politique.

Mallarmé, qu'on ne peut se lasser d'invoquer ici, alors même que sa rêverie

FLEURS DANS UN VASE.

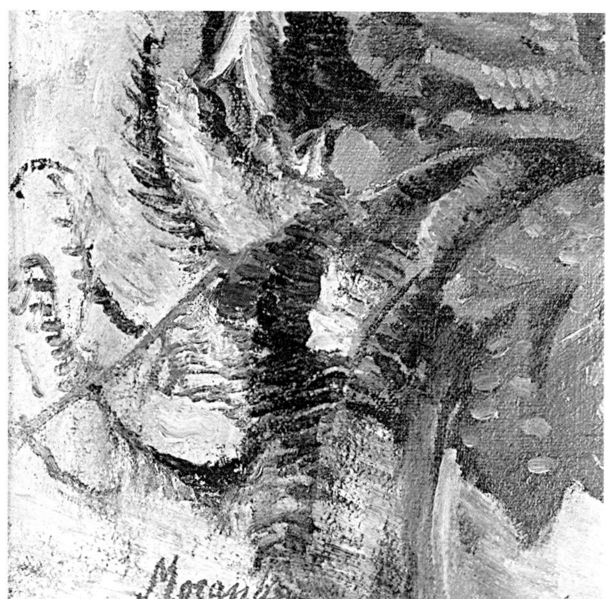

Fig. 13d. *Detail of cat. no. 13*

la Secessione romana'[17]) or after the publication of sixteen Cézannes in a little book published late in 1914 by Libreria della Voce.[18] Another small volume from the same series, printed the same year, offers a further admissible precedent in a plate illustrating *Flowers* by Henri Rousseau (fig. 17h).[19]

But a closer look at the circulation of sources makes it possible to explain Morandi's awareness of these Modernist exemplars prior to 1914. The principal source of the painting, as has been noted,[20] is a *Vase of Flowers* by Cézanne[21] reproduced in 1908 from a block provided by Durand-Ruel, in a book by Vittorio Pica on the French Impressionists[22] (fig. 13a), which we know that Morandi owned and avidly consulted ("Morandi himself recalled the impression made on him by Vittorio Pica's book when [...] he was able to meditate on the lesson that those plates, even though lacking the support of color, offered him; and above all he mentions the few reproductions of paintings by Cézanne"[23]). From this black and white, clearly legible image, Morandi derived the explosion in all directions of the structured mass of flowers and leaves, in which the ferns silhouetted against the neutral background are literal quotations. The bright touches on the leaves of the Mattioli painting can be explained as Morandi's attempt to replicate the rhythm of Cézanne's lights and darks conveyed by his laden brushstrokes. As for Rousseau, Vitali recalled that, even before the plates of the Libreria della Voce volume, reproductions in a more extensive monograph by Wilhelm Uhde of 1911 entered Morandi's visual repertoire, "which Morandi could have seen in the bookshops of his hometown."[24] In *White Vase with Pansies and Other Flowers* of 1910, illustrated by Uhde[25] (fig. 13b), we see the same formula of the convex vase standing out against the background, the same motif of spiky leaves which spread to mask the rim of the vase, and the same insistent outlining of the flowers. Further justification for the 1913 date comes from the only usefully comparable painting in Morandi's *oeuvre*. In a summer *Landscape* in a private collection[26] (fig. 13e), undated but certainly painted a year earlier than the summer of 1914 (when Morandi revealed a more confidently Cézannesque style in two of his famous landscapes[27]) the construction of the foliage standing out against the sky in the upper left corner is painted in a way similar to that of the ferns in Mattioli *Flowers* (fig. 13d).

The forceful thrusting of this spray of foliage and flowers toward the viewer, which makes *Flowers* unique among the numerous Italian paintings of this genre in the 1910s, may derive from another source: the illustrations in the periodical *L'Art Décoratif*, which was widely cir-

Fig. 13e. *Giorgio Morandi,* Landscape, *oil on canvas, 1913. Private collection*

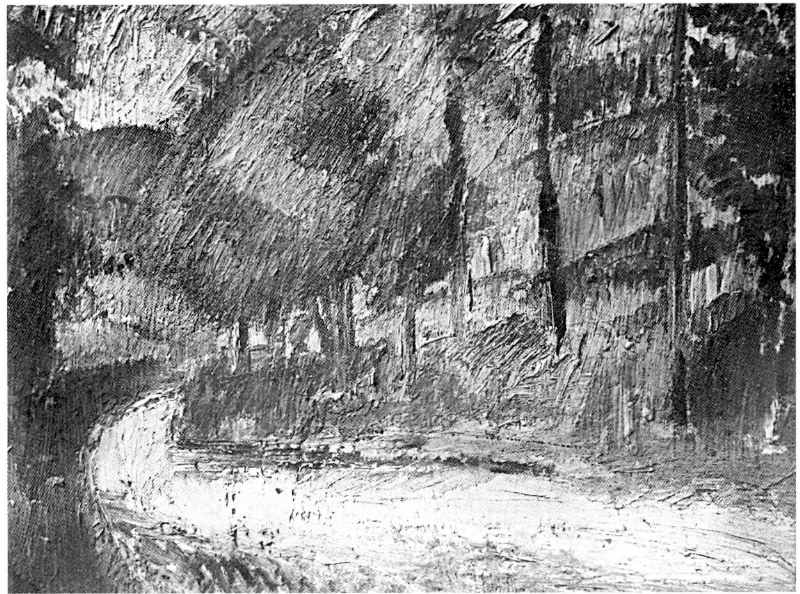

culated in Italy and of which Morandi is known to have owned the June 1912 issue with an article on Seurat.[28] Paintings of flowers in vases by Odilon Redon were published in an article by André Salmon in January 1913[29] (fig. 13c), and share with Morandi's painting the tangled explosion of flora erupting from the modest vase and the boldly silhouetted profiles of the flowers against the neutral ground. Redon probably served to mediate, for Morandi, between the radiant palette of the three, unfortunately no longer identifiable, still lifes of flowers by Auguste Renoir that Morandi admired at the IX Venice Biennale in 1910,[30] and the primitive stasis of Henri Rousseau's still life, intuited in the writings of Ardengo Soffici and seen, around 1913, in the photographs in Uhde's book.

[1] Vitali 1977, nos. 1–34.
[2] Pasquali 1996, no. 1–6.
[3] Cecchi 1990, p. 28.
[4] Vitali 1977, nos. 8, 25 and 30 (identifiable thanks to the December 26, 1919 contract between Morandi and Broglio, nos. 6–8 in Vitali 1983, Appendix, unnumbered pages), and no. 29; Beccaria 1939, pl. X (identifiable from the photograph in the *Valori Plastici* archive, in Rivosecchi 1988, p. 142).
[5] A preliminary survey can be found in Garberi 1990, pp. 20–33.
[6] Mattioli Rossi 1997, p. 16.
[7] *London* 1950, no. 70.
[8] Ragghianti 1969, p. 61.
[9] Forti, March 22, 1914; Mazzuccato, March 22, 1914; Sani, March 23, 1914.
[10] Raimondi 1951, p. 20.
[11] Ragghianti 1953, p. 14.
[12] Arcangeli 1964, p. 36.
[13] Solmi 1985[a], p. 27.
[14] Pasini 1989, p. 25–6.
[15] Archivio Mattioli, statement of accounts between the Galleria del Milione and Gianni Mattioli, dated March 30, 1950; on March 22, 1950, 7,000 lire was debited for the "relining and restoration of Morandi [flowers]". *Appendix I*, document no. 36.
[16] An extreme case is the mistaken dating to 1917, in the engravings catalogued in Vitali 1957, nos. 50 and 51, of two paintings certainly of 1916 (Vitali 1977, nos. 26 and 28).
[17] Arcangeli 1964, p. 60.
[18] *Cézanne* 1914.
[19] Merion (Pennsylvania), Barnes Foundation: *Rousseau* 1914, no. 5; Vallier 1969, no. 239.
[20] Rylands 1997, p. 76.
[21] *Le Vase des fleurs sur un tapis fleuri*, Paris, private collection: Venturi 1936, no. 181; Rewald 1996, no. 316.
[22] Pica 1908, p. 199.
[23] Vitali 1964, p. 12.
[24] *Ibidem*, p. 13.
[25] Uhde 1911, pl. 9; Vallier 1969, no. 257b.
[26] Vitali 1977, no. 8.
[27] Mattioli Collection, no. 15 in the present catalogue: Vitali 1977, no. 16, dated 1914; Milan, private collection: *ibidem*, no. 17.
[28] Arcangeli 1964, p. 25.
[29] Salmon 1913, pp. 6, 17.
[30] *Venice* 1910, pp. 40–1, nos. 14, 21, 22.

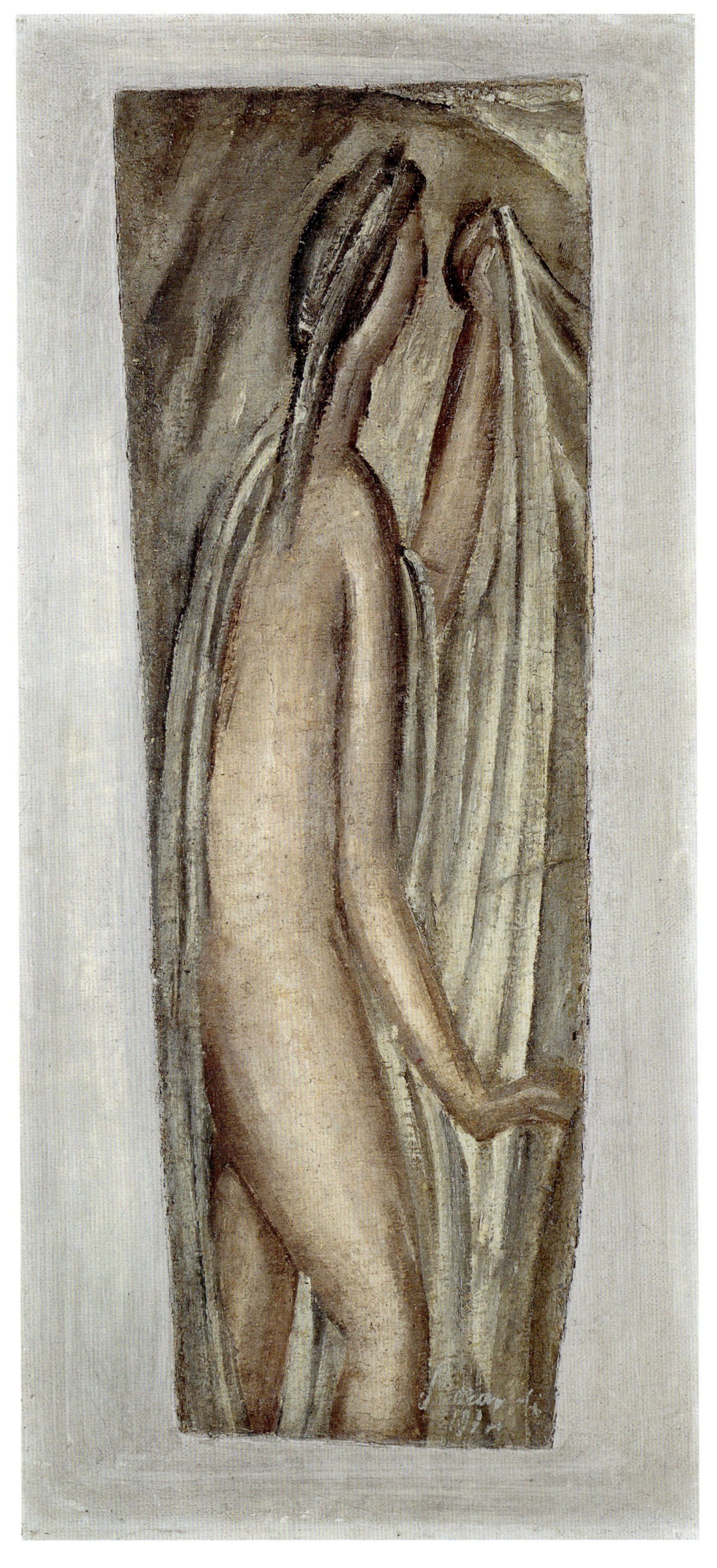

14

Giorgio Morandi

Fragment (Fragment of Bathing Women)

Frammento (Frammento di bagno di donne), 1914

Oil on canvas laid on canvas
66 × 30 cm

Inscription: *recto*, signed lower right: 'Morandi 1914'

Provenance: property of the artist; before January 1937: Galleria del Milione, Milan; January 1937: Pietro Feroldi, Brescia; May 1949: Gianni Mattioli

Exhibitions: Milan 1937, without cat. no., illus. prior to the painting of the borders of the canvas; Milan 1942[b], catalogue not printed; Turin 1959, p. 42, no. 26; Bern 1965, no. 9; Florence 1967[a], no. 1190; Washington, DC 1967–Tokyo 1972, no. 72 (Washington, DC–Hamburg), no. 70 (Madrid–Seville), no. 72 (Kyoto–Tokyo); Rome 1973, no. 11; Paris 1987, no. 3; Madrid 1990–1, p. 252

Bibliography: *Milione* no. 50, 1937, unnumbered page; Letter from Pietro Feroldi to Carlo Belli, dated January 6, 1937 (photostatic copy, Archivio Mattioli); *Milione* 1937, no. 51, unnumbered page; Moretti, January 28, 1937; Costantini 1937, p. 164; Della Porta, October 1, 1938; Letter from Cesare Brandi to Giorgio Morandi, dated December 25, 1938, in Brandi 1990, p. 155; Brandi 1939, p. 245 (*Frammento di un bagno di donne*); Raimondi 1951, pp. 22–3 and pl. 10, illus. after the painting of the margins of the canvas; Giani 1958, no. 51; Arcangeli 1964, pp. 64–5, fig. 6 (*Bagnante*); Vitali 1964, p. 18 (*Bagnante*, 1915) and no. 15 (*Nudo*, 1915); Ragghianti 1969, p. 59 and fig. 55; Del Monte 1973, pp. 37–8; Vitali 1977, no. 15 (*Nudo femminile*); Solmi 1978, pp. 25–6, fig. 17; Solmi 1985[a], p. 35; Pasini 1989, p. 28 (*Nudo*);

This 'fragment', and to an even greater extent the *Landscape* which follows it in this catalogue, are works in which Morandi explicitly measured himself against the painting of Paul Cézanne. Italian figurative artists discovered Cézanne very late: from 1908 he was central to Ardengo Soffici's aesthetics and criticism, but it was only in 1914 that Boccioni and Carrà began to understand the revolutionary significance of his work when, in a retrograde move, each felt the need to return to the sources of modern painting. Morandi, whose knowledge of Cézanne's paintings was virtually limited to black-and-white photographic reproductions, perceived in them at once a perfect lens through which to view his own pictorial world. From the *Baigneuses* he derived the slow tempo of his compositions, the tendency to solidify form and to immobilize bodies through a process of archaic synthesis; in the *Landscapes* he was enthralled by the challenge of representing the structure of things by using a compact grid of brushstrokes which crystallized the luminous vibrations of the *plein air*.

Morandi's studies of the female nude are limited to only three extant paintings: besides *Fragment*, of 1914, in which a bather is draped in a white cloth, the artist saved only two other, more complex compositions from destruction, one larger[1] (fig. 14b) and one smaller[2] (fig. 14c). The only other known instance is the watercolor with a *Nude* dated April 6, 1918[3] (fig. 14d) which was also the first to be made known when it was acquired by Mario Broglio the following year and illustrated in the penultimate issue of *Valori Plastici* (year III, no. 3, published end of 1921/early 1922). The two paintings of nudes from 1915 seem, for stylistic reasons, to constitute a series distinct from the Mattioli painting. The more schematic drawing of the bodies and the freer chiaroscuro pattern relate them to the series of small *Bathers* painted in 1908 by André Derain;[4] however, this series (as opposed to Derain's larger paintings of bathers), since it entered the art market only later and was nowhere reproduced photographically, was certainly unknown to Morandi in the 1910s.

Already called *Fragment* when exhibited for the first time in 1937,[5] and described as a "fragment of a destroyed *Women Bathers*" in a list of Morandi's youthful works compiled by Cesare Brandi in 1939 on the basis of information from the artist,[6] this painting has from the beginning manifested its fragmentary status — like a precious relic salvaged from the destruction of most of Morandi's production down to 1916. Morandi cut the bather from a composition which had included other figures, executed on a canvas of an unusually ambitious size. Part of a leg or arm belonging to another figure is visible on the lower right, where the canvas

Pasquali 1990, p. 20 (*Nudo*); Castagnoli 1990, p. 34 (*Nudo*); Rylands 1997, p. 78; Messina 1998, pp. 21–2; Salvagnini 2000, fig. 74

is more narrowly cropped. Down the right side visible traces of black, perhaps charcoal, delimit that part of the canvas to be cut away. The cutting thereby obtained, painted on the coarse canvas typical of Morandi's early work, has been glued onto a larger canvas of finer weave and stretched on a new stretcher. Today the supporting canvas is covered by a layer of gray tempera, giving the overall impression, as noted by Philip Rylands, of a detached fresco.[7] However, this addition of gray paint came after the laying of the cropped canvas on its new support. In a photograph published in January 1937 in the Galleria del Milione *Bollettino* (fig. 14a), the weave of the bare canvas is visible (even though the image crops most of the margins).[8] Only later, perhaps after Gianni Mattioli's purchase of the painting in 1949, was this outer portion of the canvas painted gray. It was published in its new state by Giuseppe Raimondi in *Paragone* in July 1951, and it is probable that Morandi himself effected the change.

The subject, though unusual in Morandi's *oeuvre*, need not surprise us. It was difficult for a young painter between late 1913 and the following spring, returning from a crucial visual *tour de force* in Florence and Rome, to escape the appeal of the nude in painting, previously stigmatized as anti-modern in Futurist manifestos but which had become, in a period of only a few months, a cogently topical subject in the critical discourse of Italian art. At the Florentine 'Lacerba' exhibition in November 1913–January 1914, which Morandi certainly saw, a *Nude* opened the section dedicated to Boccioni, and four nudes were included in that of Carrà.[9] At the subsequent selling exhibition organized in the same rooms by the art dealer Gonnelli, Ardengo Soffici exhibited three oils and three drawings of this subject,[10] and at the 1914 'II Secessione romana' the group of Matisse drawings loaned by Bernheim-jeune were mainly studies of the nude.[11]

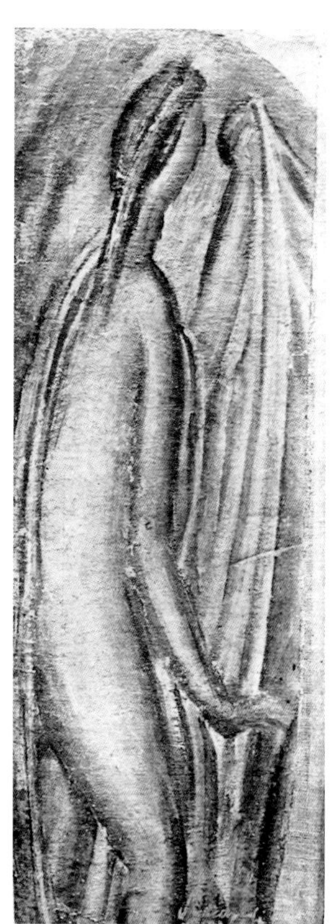

Fig. 14a. *Cat. no. 14 before the painting over of the margins of the unprimed canvas, in* Il Milione, *1937*

But Morandi's principal visual resource late in 1914 — after a summer of experimenting with still lifes in a manner influenced by Cubism, of painting landscapes that paid tribute explicitly to Cézanne, and of studying Giotto in Padua and Vitale da Bologna in the Mezzaratta frescoes — were perforce the rare illustrations in contemporary art publishing. Lamberto Vitali has stressed that the origin of the series of nudes should be traced "according to what the author himself declares,"[12] to the *Five Bathers* by Paul Cézanne[13] (fig. 14e) which belonged at that time to the Florentine collector Egisto Fabbri and which was reproduced, with the title *Composition*, in the small volume on Cézanne published by La Voce in 1914:[14] the pose and the gestures of the figure standing on the left, which closes the calibrated arabesque of bodies in Cézanne's painting, are reworked by a Morandi in search of models of pre-classical severity. *Five Bathers* was published again in the *Almanacco della Voce 1915* (which appeared late in 1914) as an advertisement for the periodical's activities as an art publisher; in the same *Almanacco*, the woman on the right in a woodcut by Ardengo Soffici called *Lo specchio* (*The Mirror*), previously illustrated in the December 5, 1912 issue of *La Voce* (fig. 14f), may have impressed Morandi by the primitive simplicity of her anatomy. As Franco Russoli has noted,[15] the principal source for Soffici's woodcut was a drawing of nudes by Picasso of 1909 (fig. 14g) which entered Soffici's collection in 1910.[16] Morandi in turn could have known this drawing from its reproduction in the November 1912 issue of *La Voce*.[17] Finally, the relation between the Mattioli *Fragment* and the large Derain nudes in his Gothicizing period was for Lamberti Vitali "a small critical enigma,"[18] since he was unable to discover how Morandi, in Italy, could have seen them. Furthermore the influence of Derain was strenuously denied by the artist himself ("to whom it was a blunder to hint at, for example, derivations from Derain"[19]). This contact now has a documentary basis thanks to Maria Grazia Messina[20] who discovered a reproduction in a 1913 issue of *Emporium*[21] of one of the crucial versions of the *Bathers* (now in the Národní Galerie, Prague,[22] fig. 14h).

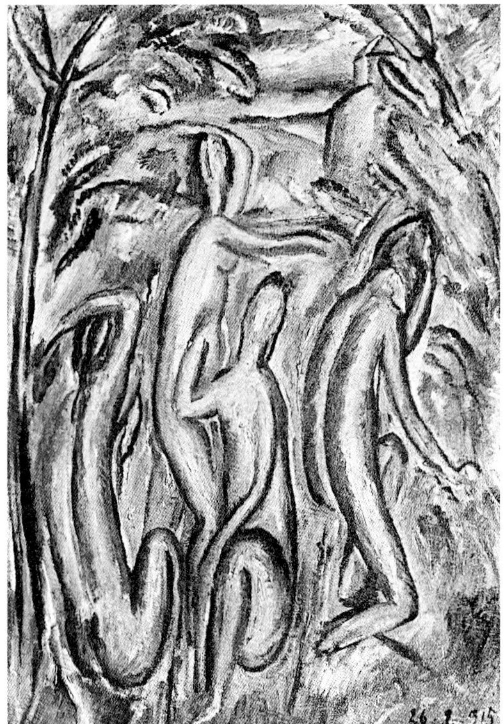

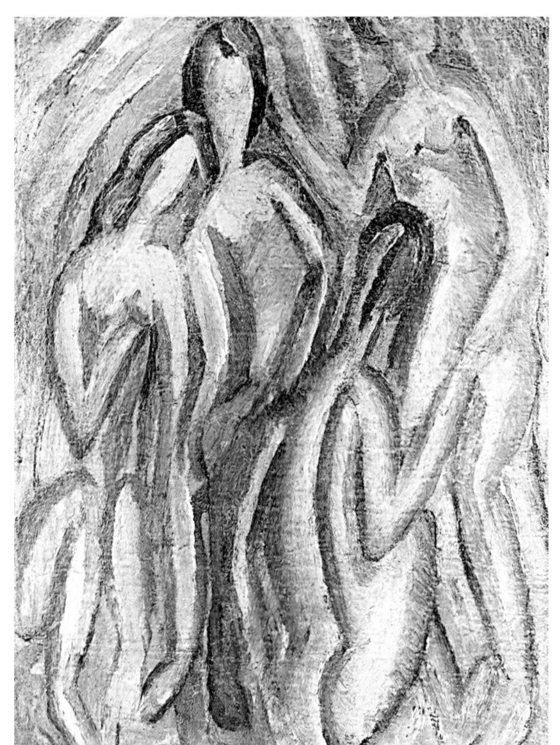

Fig. 14b. *Giorgio Morandi,* Bagnanti (Bathers)*, oil on canvas, 1915. Private collection*

Fig. 14c. *Giorgio Morandi,* Bagnanti (Bathers)*, oil on canvas, 1915. Rome, Galleria Nazionale d'Arte Moderna*

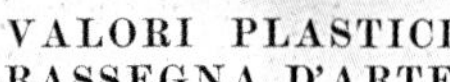

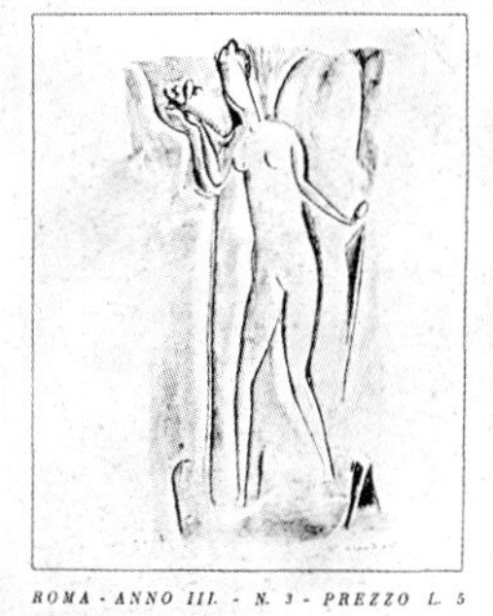

Fig. 14d. *Giorgio Morandi,* Nude, *watercolor, 1918, in* Valori Plastici*, 1921, year III, no. 3, end of 1921–beginning of 1922*

Morandi's nudes (before they dropped from sight for two decades) received some attention in the earliest critical literature. They may plausibly be identified with the "studi di stile" ("studies of style") to which Riccardo Bacchelli alluded in 1918, considering them "the least successful and most troubled by reminiscences," but also "the genre that offers the most pretexts and play for the imagination," but with too many "lapses into sensuality."[23] More interesting that year was an explicit reference to the nudes in a text by Raffaello Franchi, who speculated that they were studied from sculptural models made by Morandi himself: "the group of human figures" would have derived from "clay models, marked by perspective features with areas of color, closed and perfect within the confines of their own volume."[24] This hypothesis, repudiated by Lamberto Vitali probably at Morandi's own insistence,[25] has recently been revived on the discovery of terracottas fashioned by the artist in his youth.[26]

The Mattioli painting, whether in its original state with several nudes or as the fragment with a single figure we know today, remained in Morandi's studio until it was acquired in the first days of 1937 by the Galleria del Milione. In a letter dated January 6, 1937 the lawyer Pietro Feroldi wrote to tell Carlo Belli of having seen "the *Fragment* by Morandi which I bought right away" in the rooms of the gallery the previous day.[27] The painting was exhibited a few weeks later at an important exhibition called '20 firme in una mostra collettiva' in which the Galleria del Milione set out, after seven years of exhibiting, to review the principle developments and trends in Italian art in the 1930s. Morandi, who had been in contact with Gino Ghiringhelli since 1934,[28] but whose name only now appeared for the first time in one of the gallery's catalogues, was in the company of artists adored by Milanese collectors (de Chirico, Carrà, Severini) and of others making new reputations as Modernists in Milan in the 1930s (Fontana, Licini, Melotti). The pre-eminence given *Fragment* by its full-page reproduction in the gallery bulletin and by Ghiringhelli's insistence on comparing it to the work of Giorgio de Chirico,[29] an artist certainly more widely discussed and popular than Morandi, promoted it to the status of a key work in the history of Italian art of the second decade of the century.

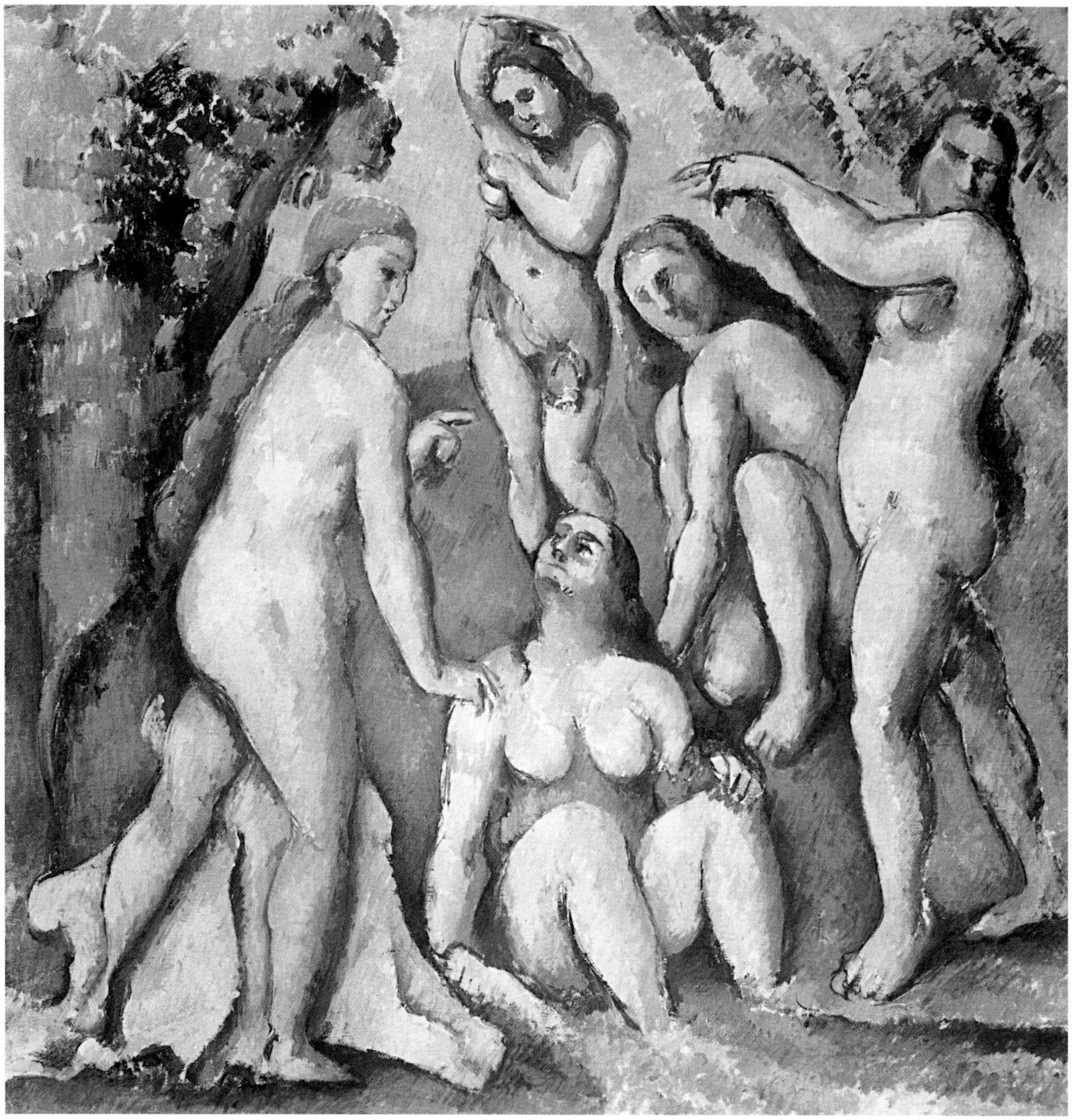

Fig. 14e. *Paul Cézanne,* Cinq baigneuses (Five Bathers)*, oil on canvas, 1885–7. Basel, Öffentliche Kunstsammlung Basel, Kunstmuseum*

However, it was difficult for Italian critics reviewing the show to agree on its quality: many ignored it or considered it an anachronistic 'Cubist' survival.[30] Only Vincenzo Costantini, attentive chronicler of the Milanese art world, was able to appreciate a painting he described as "exquisite, exceptionally refined in color and spiritual, stylistically elongated in, I would say, an ascending sense."[31] Perhaps because of these difficulties *Fragment* was excluded from the second edition of the show, in which several works were substituted, in Genoa at the Galleria Genova.[32] But the novelty of a young Morandi, contrary to his fame as a delicate painter of intimate themes, who was capable of tackling the painting of a figure boldly subjected to a deforming force, made an impression and provoked discussion. The following year a reproduction of *Fragment* was centrally placed in a photomontage of contemporary paintings and sculptures (with works by Carlo Carrà, Arturo Martini, Marino Marini, Lucio Fontana and Corrado Cagli) labelled *Le opere di certi modernisti è chiaro che denigrano la razza* (*The Works of Certain Modernists Clearly Denigrate the Race*)[33] (fig. 14i) with which *Perseo*, the militant Fascist art review published in Varese, enacted a chapter of its anti-modern polemic in the critical transitional period between the publication of the *Manifesto della razza* (July 14) and the issuing of the racial laws (November 10). Surprisingly, in late 1938, Cesare Brandi's curiosity about the work was aroused when reviewing material for his fundamental essay 'Cammino di Morandi': a photograph of the work shown to him by Morandi provoked him to inquire into the matter of the influence of Cézanne and

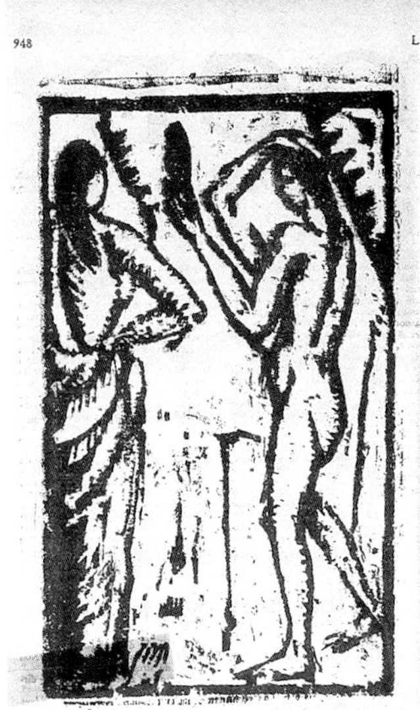

948 LA VOCE

Non mi hai detto ieri che te
zire quando hai saputo della
per l'estero?
— Oh sì! ti amo, ma com
altrimenti...
— Ah, ah, ah... Si amano
Perchè dunque ad un tratte
Perchè sei convulsa e tremanc
Perchè bevi tanto? Forse p
distruggere in te l'effetto delle
Oh! non tormentarmi più!..
molto triste e affranto. — Sa
d'essere amato da te... Ti an
Poi con improvvisa energia
amo! ti amo! ti amo!...
Ma non potè dire altro; l
spense in un sospiro come l'
frange sulla spiaggia. Una
pausa seguì. Poi le sussurrò
— Hai tu capito finalmente
all'anima mia il terribile mis
cato di nasconderlo... Ma qu
stata da me... Per me non se
Ella lo guardò sgomenta; g
bocca le si contrassero, tort
goscia interna; i loro sguard
rono e si fissarono lungamen
— Questo è terribile — r
e una strana paura l'invase,
lei respirasse un alito infuoca
— Sì, è terribile — ripetè
sciamente.
Di nuovo regnò un lungo
provvisamente ella balzò in p
imperiosa:
— Vattene a casa!... Va!..
Egli ne fu stupefatto, non c
la sua voce umile e suppliche
— No, Agai! Io non posso
da te.
— Ma cosa desideri dunq
ella a denti stretti.
— Nulla... nulla... Cosa po
da te.. soggiunse poi sorride
mente. — Fino a ieri esistev
che cosa che mi faceva paura
Temevo l'incesto... e mi pre
disperazione quando rividi e
avevo festeggiato le mie orgie
però ella ha cessato d'esse
Oggi, in lei vedo solo la do
più d'ogni cosa al mondo...
sangue del mio sangue, parte
e, forse per questo, ti amo
arrestò. — Hai paura di q
Agai?
— Io non ho nessuna pa
ridendo con disprezzo.
— Ma... ma...
Egli la guardava atterrito e
come se la sua vita dipendess
rola di lei che lo avvolge
sguardo penetrante e freddo,

A. SOFFICI. - *Lo specchio.*

— Come hai fatto presto a diventare padrona di te! Eppure poco fa tremavi di emozione, ancora adesso tremano convulse

il suo viso si animò, soffriva e gli occhi ardevano d'un martirio infinito, terribile.
— Parla!... va oltre!... seguita!... —

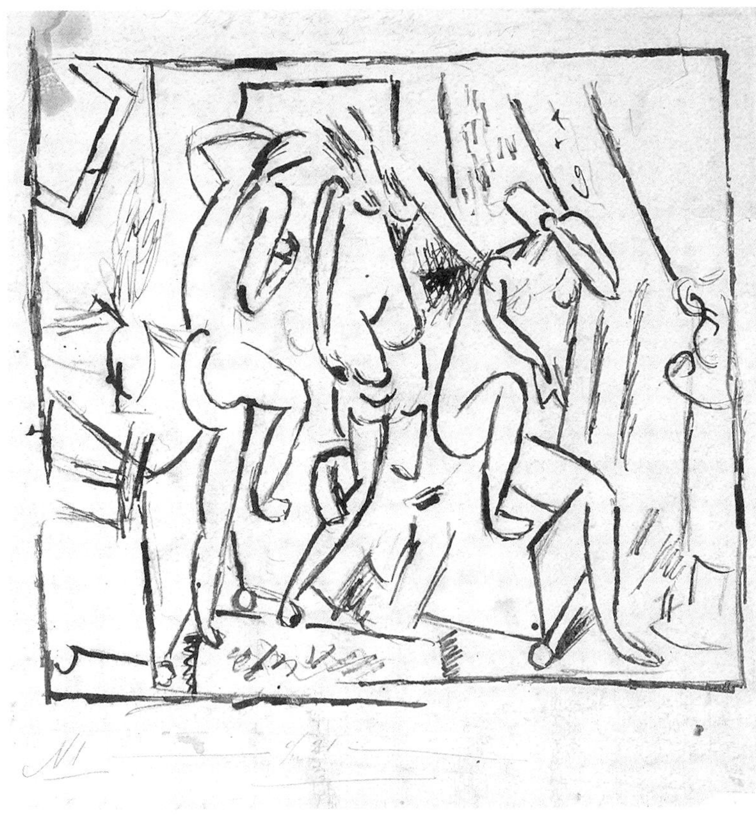

Fig. 14f. *Ardengo Soffici,* Lo specchio (The Mirror)*,* *in* La Voce*, December 5, 1912*

Fig. 14g. *Pablo Picasso,* Donne al bagno (Women Bathing)*, ink on paper, 1909. Milan, private collection*

Fig. 14h. *André Derain,* Female Group (Bathers)*,* *in* Emporium*, 1913*

ANDRÉ DER AIN: GRUPPO FEMMINILE.

mediocre cultore d'arte, noi vorremmo che altra osservazione si facesse, oggi, che la difesa della razza è diventata crociata nazionale.

E per restare in argomento ci piace riportare, oltre le illustrazioni,

na del Cardellino) il disegno del volto, l'atteggiamento degli occhi e soprattutto l'espressione sono tipicamente quelli delle donne nostre.

« Si passi a Leonardo, al Correggio e più avanti al Tiziano. Mutano

cento all'ottocento, anche se non tutta sublime.

Per sei secoli gli artisti italiani hanno nobilitata ed elevata la stirpe nei suoi caratteri etnico-biologici raffigurandola nei lineamenti caratteri-

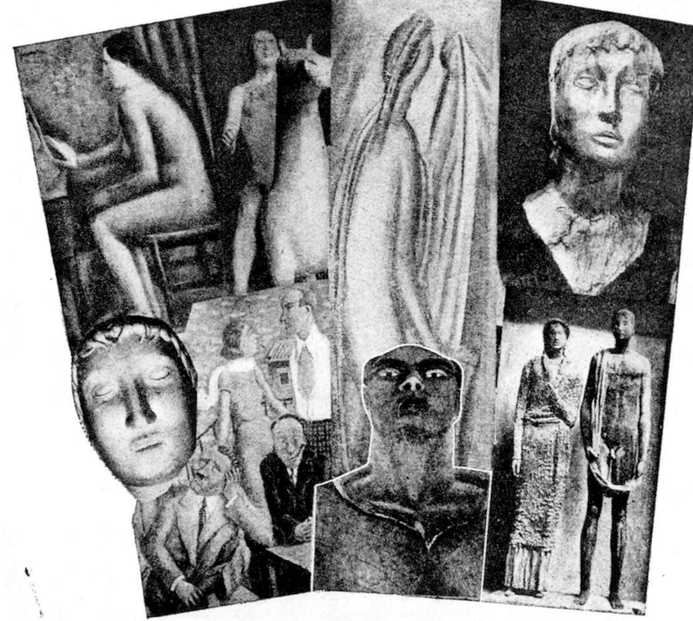

LE OPERE DI CERTI MODERNISTI È CHIARO CHE DENIGRANO LA RAZZA

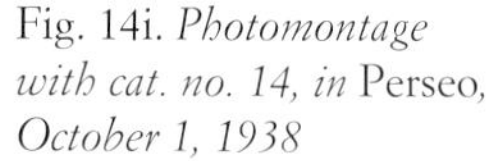

Fig. 14i. *Photomontage with cat. no. 14, in* Perseo, *October 1, 1938*

Modigliani on the young artist.[34] While Morandi allowed the reference to Cézanne, his reaction to that of Modigliani was entirely different. Although Morandi's reply is missing, the artist's annoyance can be felt between the lines of a susbequent cautious letter written by Brandi:

> "If I mentioned the name of Modigliani, it was because, in those youthful things of which you had the photographs (especially the figure of the isolated woman with some branches in the background), your figurative interpretation developed from Cézanne some linear motifs that brought to mind similar solutions by Modigliani. Besides, there are no traces of him in other works."[35]

Fragment entered Mattioli's collection with the sale of the Feroldi Collection in May 1949. The price was 190,000 lire, against an estimate of 300,000 lire, a standard valuation for Morandi which was ascribed to thirteen of the sixteen paintings in the collection.[36] It passed immediately to Fernanda Wittgens, then Soprintendente alle Gallerie in Lombardy, in recognition of her part in the sale of the Feroldi Collection (a photograph shows the scholar at work with the painting hanging behind her,[37] fig. 14j) but it was returned in 1957, upon her death, to Via Senato 36, Milan, where the Mattioli Collection was then installed. The difficulty of assimilating it with the more widely-diffused notion of Morandi's style lies behind the rarity with which it was either exhibited or reviewed in the 1950s (an exception is Raimondi's reading of the work in 1951, in which he admired the "depth of space contained and developed in a sense of verticality, so to speak, almost 'gothic'"[38]). The large color reproduction that Morandi himself requested in the book edited by Lamberto Vitali in 1964 and the attention dedicated to it by Francesco Arcangeli in his 1964 monograph ("an archaism, one might say, general, not deriving from any specific source beyond a broad reference to Cézanne. It has a primitive significance seeking universality in its purity and essentiality'")[39] have led from the 1960s onward to ever-increasing interest in the work.[40]

Fig. 14j. *Fernanda Wittgens in her office, with cat. no. 14 behind her*

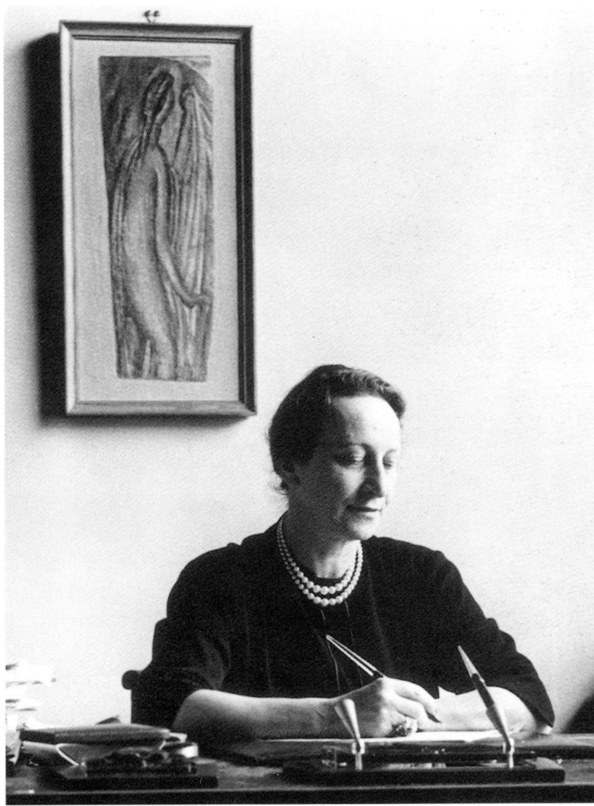

[1] Private collection: Vitali 1977, no 21, dated '26.2.1915'.
[2] Rome, Galleria Nazionale d'Arte Moderna: *ibidem*, no. 22, dated '1915'.
[3] Private collection: Pasquali 1991, no. 1918/3.
[4] *Baigneuses*. Paris, Musée d'Art Moderne de la Ville de Paris: Kellermann, 1992, no. 396; Paris, Musée Picasso: *Paris* 1994–5, no. 69.
[5] *Milan* 1937, no. 27.
[6] Brandi 1939, p. 245.
[7] Rylands 1997, p. 78; the gray tempera ground was particularly favored by the purist taste of Milan during the early 1950s (Mattioli Rossi 1999, pp. 90–1).
[8] *Milione* 1937, no. 50, second cover page.
[9] *Florence* 1913–14, p. 21, no. 1; p. 22, nos. 8, 9, 10, 12.
[10] Cavallo 1986, p. 208.
[11] *Rome* 1914[b], pp. 39–41.
[12] Vitali 1964, p. 18.
[13] *Cinq baigneuses*, Basel, Öfflentliche Kunstsammlung Basel, Kunstmuseum: Rewald 1996, no. 554.
[14] *Cézanne* 1914, no. 8; Venturi 1936, no. 542; Rewald 1996, no. 554.
[15] Russoli 1976, p. 46.
[16] Milan, private collection: Cavallo 1999, p. 14.
[17] Soffici, November 21, 1912.
[18] Vitali 1964, p. 18; also Pasquali 1990, p. 20.
[19] Russoli 1976, p. 46.
[20] Messina 1998, p.22.
[21] Nebbia 1913, p. 427.
[22] Kellermann 1992, no. 394.
[23] Bacchelli, March 29, 1918.
[24] Franchi 1918[b], p. 118.
[25] Vitali 1964, p. 18.
[26] Solmi 1985[a], pp. 33–4.
[27] Letter from Pietro Feroldi to Carlo Belli, dated January 6, 1937, in Archivio Mattioli, photostatic copy. Feroldi liked Morandi's nudes and in 1938 he also bought the watercolor formerly belonging to Broglio: according to the collector, it had "a few points of contact with the fragment I bought from Gino Ghiringhelli: this one intact and complete, a standing figure, hieratic stride with fruit in the hands [*sic*] and palms on the side. Yellow-red tonality and violet chiaroscuro in the background. I think it is a perfect thing": letter from Pietro Feroldi to Carlo Belli, dated October 10, 1938, Archivio Mattioli, photostatic copy.
[28] Pasquali 1989, p. 21.
[29] *Milione* 1937, no. 51, unnumbered page.
[30] Moretti, January 28, 1937.
[31] Costantini 1937, p. 164.
[32] A detailed review of the works in Riva, April 20, 1937, must substitute for the impossibility of finding the catalogue.
[33] Della Porta, October 1, 1938.
[34] Letter from Cesare Brandi to Giorgio Morandi, dated December 18, 1938, in Brandi 1990, p. 151.
[35] Letter from Cesare Brandi to Giorgio Morandi, dated December 25, 1938, *ibidem*, p. 155.
[36] Archivio Mattioli, *Elenco raccolta Feroldi* (*Appendix I*, document no. 24).
[37] Mattioli Rossi 1997, p. 17.
[38] Raimondi 1951, p. 22.
[39] Arcangeli 1964, p. 65.
[40] Solmi 1978, pp. 25–6; Pasini 1989, p. 28; Messina 1998, pp. 21–2.

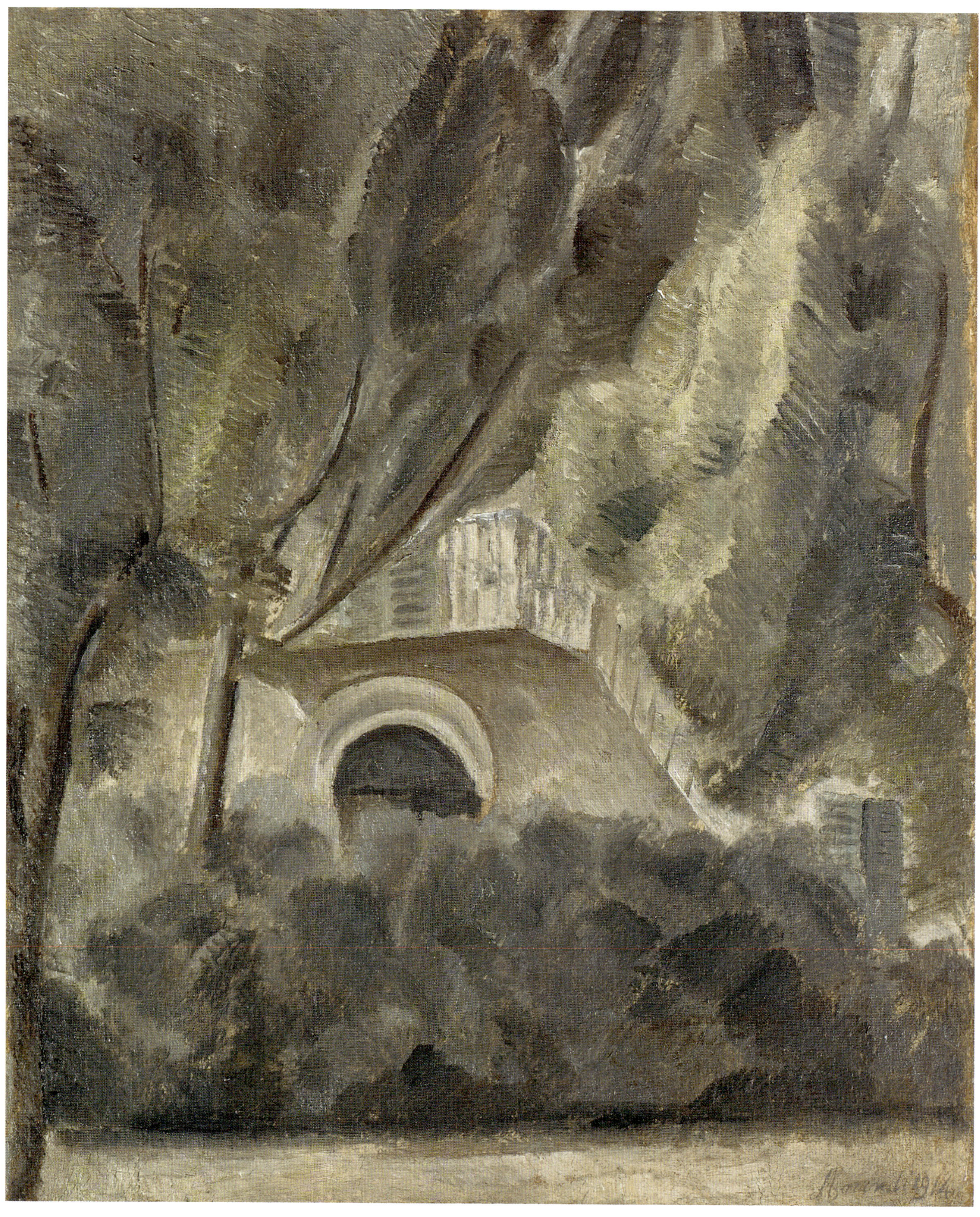

15

Giorgio Morandi

Landscape

Paesaggio, 1914

Oil on canvas
58 × 48 cm

Inscription: *recto*, signed lower right: 'Morandi 1914'

Provenance: property of the artist; June 1938: Pietro Feroldi, Brescia; May 1949: Gianni Mattioli

Exhibitions: San Francisco 1939, p. 22, no. 19; Florence 1953[a], no. 23; Turin 1959, p. 42, no. 27; Bern 1965, no. 6; Florence 1967[a], no. 1189, illus.; Washington, DC 1967–Tokyo 1972, no. 73 (Washington, DC– Hamburg), no. 71 (Madrid–Seville), no. 73 (Kyoto–Tokyo); Milan 1971, no. 6, illus. p. 34; Rome 1973, no. 7; Paris 1987, no. 4

Bibliography: *Pittori* 1938, pl. 1008, illus.; Letter from Pietro Feroldi to Ottone Rosai, dated June 21, 1938, in Corti 1994, p. 118; Letter from Carlo Belli to Pietro Feroldi, dated June 29, 1938, in Boschiero 1991, pp. 216–17; Brandi 1939, p. 245; unpublished typescript by Carlo Belli presenting the Feroldi Collection, before May 1942 (Rovereto, MART, Archivio del 900, Fondo Belli, p. 9); Piovene 1942, pl. 17; Gnudi 1946, fig. 1; Garretto 1952, p. 43; Ballo 1960, p. 24; Marchiori 1960, pl. 40; Arcangeli 1964, p. 63, fig. 5; Vitali 1964, pl. 10; Siblik 1965, pl. 3; Raimondi, November 24, 1966; Monti 1967, p. 96, fig. 215; Giuffré 1970, p. 12; Del Monte 1973, p. 34; Vitali 1977, no. 16; Solmi 1978, p. 11; Riccòmini 1985, pp. 16–17; Solmi 1987, p. 15; Pasini 1989, pp. 28–9; Dell'Acqua 1990, p. 37; Castagnoli 1990, p. 32; Garberi 1990, p. 25; Pasquali 1996, p. 430; Rylands 1997, p. 80

In his catalogue of Morandi's paintings Lamberto Vitali speculated that *Landscape* was among the paintings in the first ever exhibition to which Morandi submitted work, a brief event in March 1914 in the Hotel Baglioni in Bologna,[1] and this supposition has been accepted.[2] However the identification of the paintings Morandi sent to this show is problematic: no catalogue was printed and the only landscape that was included, according to a review by Ascanio Forti ("a strange landscape in which the tones scale down from an intense green to an ashen white, with just a small touch of red"[3]), does not apparently correspond to the Mattioli painting. No confirmation of Vitali's hypothesis can be found either in the scant information provided by Morandi (who insisted that he had destroyed many of the paintings exhibited in Bologna[4]) or in the fragmentary recollections of another of the five exhibitors, Severo Pozzati, as told to Carlo Ludovico Ragghianti (in which no mention was made of this painting[5]). In particular, the date 1914 inscribed on *Landscape* (the date appears to be brushed into still wet paint at the time of execution) and its inclusion in the Baglioni exhibition are in evident contradiction. The scene is a detail of the hills around Grizzana: in Emilia Romagna the lush vegetation that screens and frames the house (allowing us only to glimpse the door, a railing and two windows) grows only during the late spring or summer, and certainly not before the end of March. It is hardly likely therefore, in the case of an artist always faithful to the reality of his motifs, that Morandi would have painted *Landscape* between January and March 1914, in time for the Bologna show.

Landscape was surely painted during the summer of 1914, after Morandi's first experience of original paintings by Cézanne — the watercolors sent by Bernheim-jeune to the 'II Secessione romana' which opened in March. Even if the dense texture of Morandi's oils in this picture is very different from the rarefied translucent patterns of Cézanne's watercolors, they offered Morandi the chance to study characteristics of Cézanne's technique that were difficult to intuit from the photographs that had been his only source till then: the parallel strokes of the brush in the wall of vegetation visible in *Tree Among Rocks*[6] or the suffused chiaroscuro pattern of plants framing the house in *House and Trees*,[7] both of them watercolors exhibited at the Secession.

However, the quest for Morandi's sources in photographic reproductions of the period (better suited to the protracted lengths of time Morandi required to internalize these images) gives as usual the best results. In the case of Cézanne, one may add to publications already several years old — the article by Ardengo Soffici of 1908, Vittorio Pica's monograph on French Im-

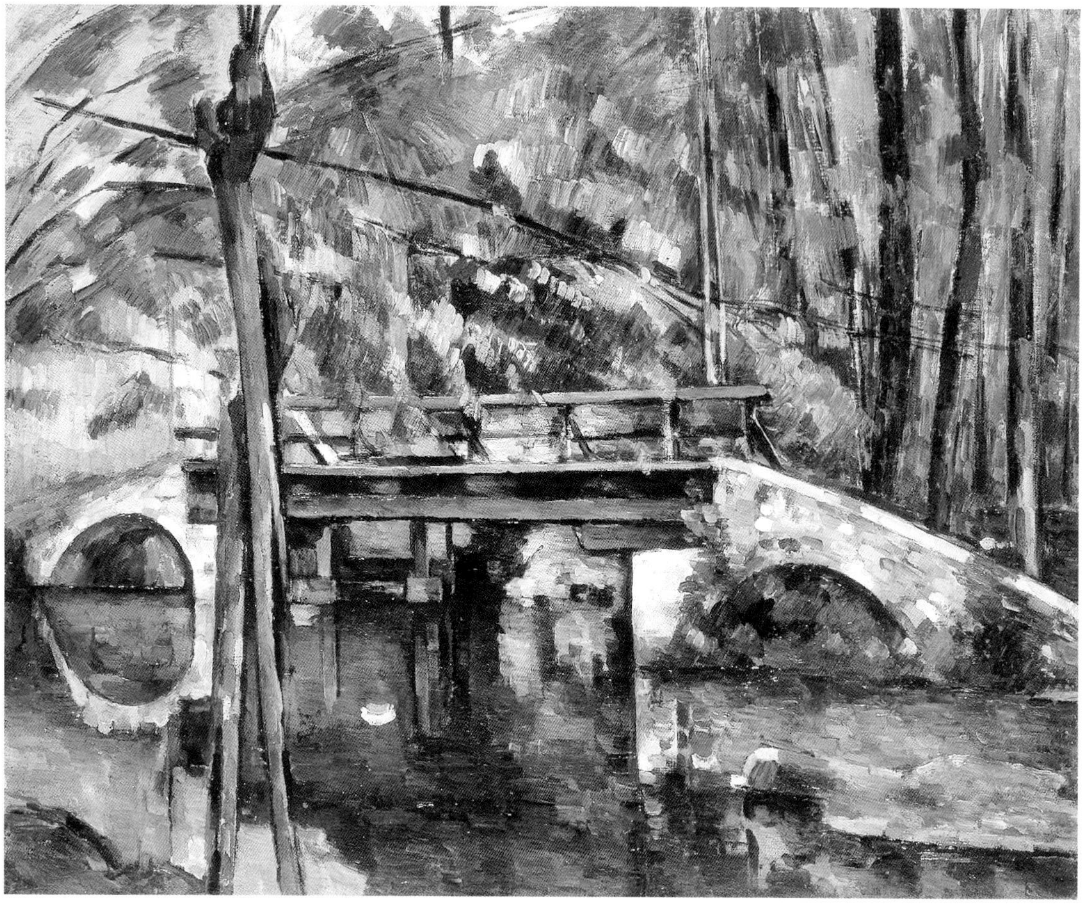

Fig. 15a. *Paul Cézanne,* Le Pont de Maincy (The Bridge of Maincy), *oil on canvas, 1879–80. Paris, Musée d'Orsay*

pressionism of the same year, and the article by Elie Faure in 1911 in *L'Art Décoratif* (in which Morandi could usefully have examined the construction of the tree's leafy branches in dense parallel strokes of *The Harvest,*[8] the motif of trees screening the house in *A Corner of the Woods,*[9] and the relationship between houses and foliage in *Landscape*[10]) — a considerable number of reproductions that appeared in the course of 1914. These were illustrations for the luxurious monograph published by Bernheim-jeune and for the small volume in the *Artisti moderni* series published by Libreria della Voce, and finally those of the large illustrated edition of Ambroise Vollard's book. The most credible Cézannesque source for the Mattioli *Landscape* appeared in the first of the three, which was available to Morandi because it was on sale at the Libreria della Voce and was immediately acquired by the Biblioteca Marucelliana in Florence, where Morandi occasionally would go. A plate reproducing *The Bridge of Maincy* [11] (fig. 15a) was surely long contemplated by Morandi, for its compositional scheme and above all the chiaroscuro pattern of its landscape. Working before the motif in Grizzana, Morandi was able to adapt the diagonal of the access ramp of Cézanne's bridge on the right to the stairs leading to the upper floor of the house; the bridge fenced in by the parapet has become the shaded balcony railing; finally he shifted the mysterious dark, semicircle void of the bridge arch to the center and transformed it into the lunette of the door, similarly framed with light.[12] Thus Morandi found for himself, in the countryside of Grizzana, a motif matching Cézanne's invention of a light, glowing central form almost overwhelmed by encroaching foliage.

As was characteristic of Morandi in 1913–14, the predominantly Cézannesque style is annexed to elements drawn from other prominent contemporary artists: the trees on the left, constructed in cryptic, oval-shaped modules were common in landscapes by Henri Matisse (which he may have seen in the now unidentifiable landscapes by Matisse that were exhibited by ro-

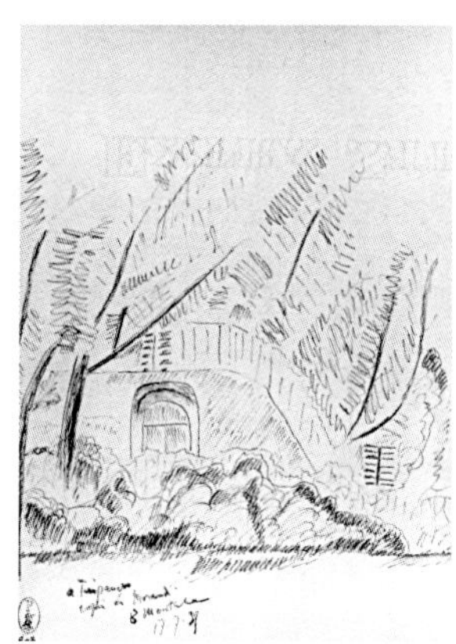

Fig. 15b. *Eugenio Montale,* Paesaggio con alberi e casa *(*Landscape with Trees and House*), copy of cat. no. 15, ink on paper, 1939. Pisa, Università degli Studi, Gabinetto Disegni e Stampe, Timpanaro Collection*

tation at the 1914 'Secessione romana' show[13]) and in the work of Derain (in addition to the reproduction of *Window on the Park* in the 1913 *Rassegna Contemporanea,*[14] there was that of *The Pines* in the much-discussed *Cubistes, futuristes, passéistes* by Gustave Coquiot in 1914,[15] and of the *Provence Landscape* published in February of the same year in *Les Soirées de Paris*[16]).

Landscape survived Morandi's drastic destruction of many works from his early years and reappeared twenty-five years later when (parallel to the sending of the 1914 Jesi *Landscape* to the 'III Quadriennale romana' in 1939[17]) it was chosen to represent the landscape genre in Morandi's early work at the 'Golden Gate Exhibition' in San Francisco in 1939[18] (its identification is certain since the sticker from the show is still glued to the stretcher). It already belonged to Pietro Feroldi by this time. The date of its purchase is revealed in a letter of June 1938 from Feroldi to Ottone Rosai who, sometime earlier, had helped to put the collector directly in touch with Morandi:

> "I have been on the Thursday of Corpus Domini at Morandi's, before whom I felt that I should kneel. I acquired (thanks to your benevolence) several things, among which a 1914 landscape, the sublimest poem I've ever seen."[19]

The painting immediately qualified as a masterpiece among Morandi's landscapes (Carlo Belli, in his introduction [later rejected] to the catalogue of the Feroldi Collection, perceived "a *levitas* of the Giottesque touch"[20]). It was selected by the Galleria del Milione for illustration in the third series of color reproductions of modern masterpieces placed on sale in November, 1938.[21] Evidence of its appreciation by the best intellectual milieu of the time (when the fashion for Morandi peaked, at the time that the room dedicated to his work was on view at the 1939 Rome Quadriennale) is a copy made with pen and ink by Eugenio Montale[22] (fig. 15b). Montale could have seen the painting in January 1939 when, as testified by a stamp on the stretcher, the painting was stored at the Florence Soprintendenza before being shipped to San Francisco, or alternatively he could have copied it from the plate published by the Galleria del Milione. Together with the Feroldi Collection, *Landscape* was sold to Gianni Mattioli in 1949 for 250,000 lire (as against its estimate of 400,000 lire[23]), the second highest price among Morandis in the collection.

[1] Vitali 1977, no. 16.
[2] Pasquali 1996, p. 430.
[3] Forti, March 22, 1914.
[4] Arcangeli 1964, p. 61.
[5] Ragghianti 1969, p. 61.
[6] *Profil de rocher près des grottes au-dessus de Château Noir*, New York, private collection: *Rome* 1914[b], room 8, no. 16; Rewald 1983, no. 436.
[7] *Paysage de Provence*, Germany, private collection: *Rome* 1914[b], room 8, no. 39; Rewald 1983, no. 390. For an identification of the watercolors in Rome, see Fergonzi 1993, pp. 25–6.
[8] *La Moisson*, Japan, private collection: Soffici 1908, p. 328; Venturi 1936, no. 249; Rewald 1996, no. 301.
[9] *La Côte des bœufs, Pontoise,* private collection, on loan to the Museum of Art, St Petersburg (Florida): Pica 1908, p. 199; Venturi 1936, no. 173; Rewald 1996, no. 312.
[10] *Bords de la Marne II*, private collection: Faure 1911, p. 120; Venturi 1936, no. 629; Rewald 1996, no. 624.
[11] *Le Pont de Maincy*, Paris, Musée d'Orsay: Bernheim-jeune 1914, pl. XXXVII, with the title *Le Pont*: Venturi 1936, no. 396; Rewald 1996, no. 436.
[12] This is not "the eye of stone opened on the hill" as suggested by Solmi 1987, p. 11.
[13] Fergonzi 1993, p. 22, note 38.
[14] *Fenêtre sur le parc*, New York, The Museum of Modern Art, Abby Aldrich Rockefeller Fund; del Re 1913, between pp. 136 and 137; Kellermann 1992, no. 321.
[15] *Les Pins*, Coquiot 1914, between pp. 16 and 17.
[16] *Paysage de Provence*, St Petersburg, The Hermitage: Kellerman 1992, no. 241.
[17] *Paesaggio*, Milan, Pinacoteca di Brera, Jesi Collection: Vitali 1977, no. 8.
[18] *San Francisco* 1939, no. 19.
[19] Letter from Pietro Feroldi to Ottone Rosai, dated June 21, 1938, in Corti 1994, p. 118.
[20] Rovereto, MART, Archivio del 900, Fondo Belli (unpublished typescript), before May 1942, p. 9.
[21] *Milione* 1938, no. 59. The series of postcards is illustrated in Boschiero 1991, p. 217.
[22] Severini 1959, no. 803; the sheet was then dedicated and given to Sebastiano Timpanaro on July 17, 1939.
[23] Archivio Mattioli, *Elenco raccolta Feroldi* (*Appendix I*, document no. 24).

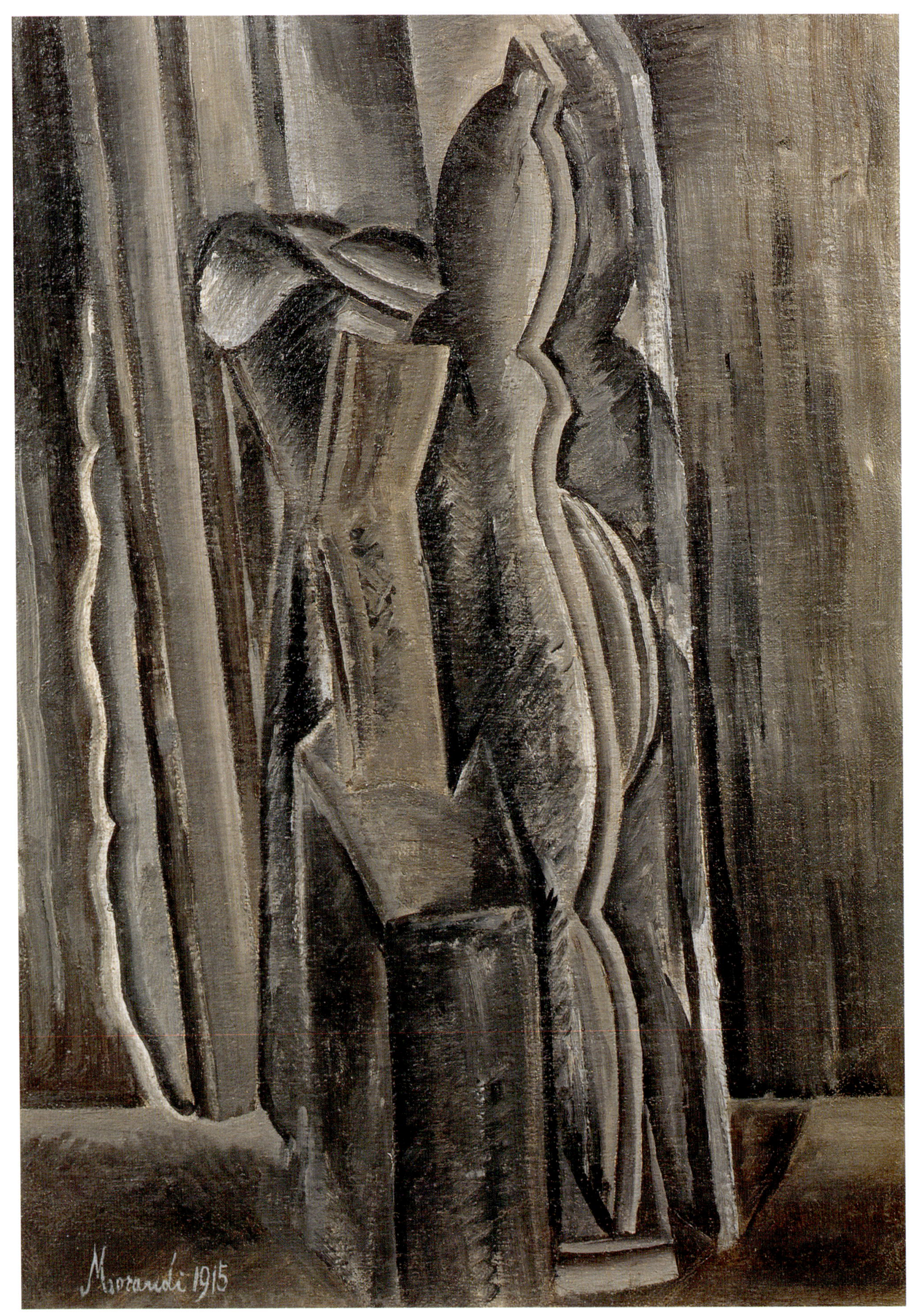
Morandi 1915

16

Giorgio Morandi

Still Life with Clockcase (Still Life)

Natura morta con portaorologio (Natura Morta), 1915

Oil on canvas
74.5 × 53 cm

Inscription: *recto*, signed lower left: 'Morandi 1915'

Provenance: property of the artist; June 1951: Gianni Mattioli, with the mediation of the Galleria del Milione

Exhibitions: Milan 1952, unnumbered page, illus. (*Natura morta*); Florence 1953[a], no. 24, pl. 5 (*Natura morta con l'orologio*); Turin 1959, no. 28, p. 42, pl. 13 (*Natura morta*); Milan 1964, unnumbered (*Natura morta*); Bern 1965, no. 11; Venice 1966, p. 27, no. 6 (*Natura morta con l'orologio*); Bologna 1966, no. 8; Washington, DC 1967–Tokyo 1972, no. 74 (Washington, DC–Hamburg), no. 72 (Madrid–Seville), no. 74 (Kyoto–Tokyo); Milan 1971, no. 7; Rome 1973, no. 10; Bologna 1975, no. 2; Paris 1987, no. 6; Venice 1989, p. 364; Kamakura 1989–Kyoto 1990, no. 4; Madrid 1990–1, p. 253

Bibliography: *Milione* 1952 no. 1, unnumbered page, illus. (*Natura morta*); Valsecchi, May 23, 1953; Castelfranco, Valsecchi 1956, p. 57; Drudi Gambillo, Fiori 1958–62, vol. II, pp. 422, 435, no. 2 (*Natura morta*); Marchiori 1960, no. 41 (*Natura morta con l'orologio*); Bellonzi 1963, pp. 99, 106; Arcangeli 1964, pp. 67–8, fig. 10 (*Natura morta*); Valsecchi 1964, pp. 4, 8–9, pl. 1; Vitali 1964, pp. 17–18, pl. 14 (*Natura morta*); Siblik 1965, pl. 5; Mathey 1967, p. 187; Ragghianti 1969, p. 46, fig. 54; Apollonio 1970, no. 109; Giuffré 1970, pp. 14–15; Del Monte 1973, p. 37; Vitali 1977, no. 23 (*Natura morta*); Abramowicz 1990, p. XLV; Castagnoli 1990, pp. 32, 34; Rylands 1997, p. 82

We know of no still lifes by Morandi between the *Still Life* with glass objects of 1912 (dated on the back of the canvas)[1] and 1914–15, when Morandi painted a group of three still lifes, similar in subject matter and in style, catalogued by Vitali as numbers 13, 18 and 23. The first of the group, belonging to the Giovanardi Collection and on deposit at the Museo di Arte Moderna e Contemporanea of Trento and Rovereto (fig. 16a), is dated July 14, 1914 on the back[2] (now hidden by a lining canvas). The second, today in the Centre National d'Art Contemporain in Paris (fig. 16b), is an evident development of the first and is dated 1914 on the canvas. The last of the group, the Mattioli painting, is dated 1915. The *verso* of the canvas was used for a study for *Bathers,* dated February 26, 1915[3] (fig. 14b). As noted by Francesco Arcangeli,[4] Morandi recalled that the study for *Bathers* was made after the execution of the Mattioli *Still Life*, thus compressing the date of the latter into the first two months of 1915. The date of *Still Life with Silver Platter*[5] (fig. 16e) (1914) is less secure: it was dated 1914 when it was first published, in 1932,[6] but it is perhaps closer to the Mattioli painting, with which it shares the emphatically illuminated ridges that define the contours of the objects. Despite this hiatus of almost a year and a half in the catalogue of surviving works, Morandi's production of still lifes in 1913 and the first half of 1914 was not significantly interrupted, since of four paintings he sent to the 'Esposizione Libera Futurista Internazionale' at the Galleria Sprovieri, Rome, in April–May 1913,[7] three were still lifes. One of these belonged to the series of "vetrerie in penombra" (glassware in shadow)[8] already shown at the group show held slightly earlier at the Hotel Baglioni,[9] but the two others testify to a lost phase Morandi's work, certainly prior to the spring of 1914.

Morandi's paintings of still life, nurtured from his earliest years as "a zone free of misunderstandings caused by content"[10] and in continuous dialogue with the rare examples of the international avant-garde that were available in photographic reproduction in Italy in those years (illustrations of Cubist works published in *Lacerba*, the *Dodici opere di Picasso* in the *Maestri moderni* series edited by La Voce, the illustrations in *Cubismo e futurismo* by Soffici, the plates in *Du "cubisme"* by Gleizes and Metzinger), must be understood in an intellectual environment which was overtly Modernist. Henri des Prureaux, a painter and collector active between Florence and Paris and a brilliant propagandist of Cubism, wrote of the still life in an article in *La Voce* in 1911 as the modern genre *par excellence*: "our dictionary, and also our treatise on harmony and our grammar"; it opened the door to "an abstract painting, almost occult [...], child of the spirit of analysis and individualism."[11] In 1912, Ardengo Soffici interpreted the still life's line of descent

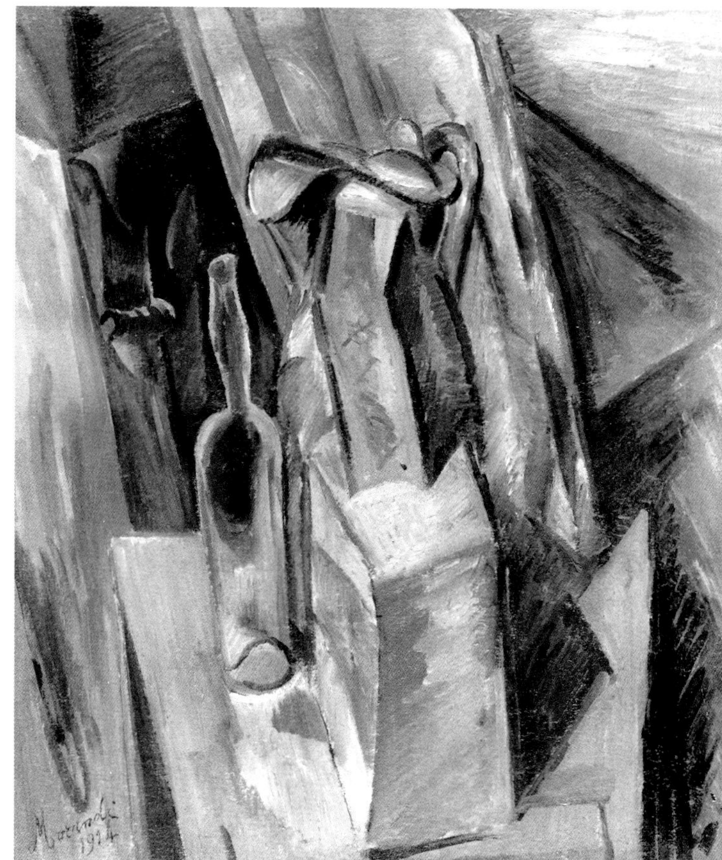

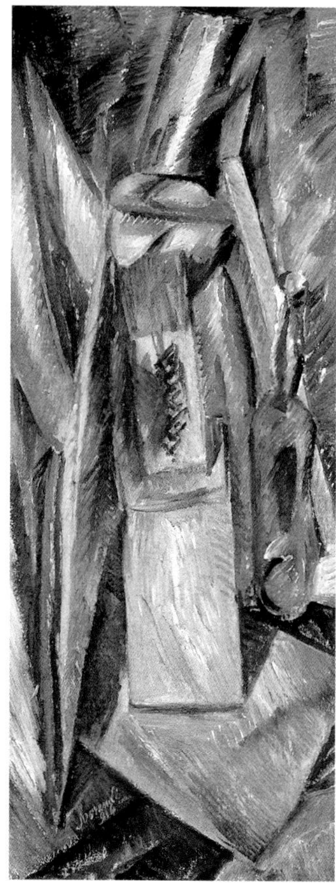

Fig. 16a. *Giorgio Morandi,* Still Life, *oil on canvas, 1914. Trento, Museo di Arte Moderna e Contemporanea of Trento and Rovereto, Giovanardi Collection (deposit)*

Fig. 16b. *Giorgio Morandi,* Still Life, *oil on canvas, 1914. Paris, Centre National d'Art Contemporain Georges Pompidou*

from Chardin to Cézanne in a wholly conceptual way, with Cubism clearly in mind: for these artists the still life made it possible to "condense the spiritual universe in a simple, visible form."[12]

Comparison with the three still lifes which preceded the Mattioli painting and with one surviving drawing enables us to identify most of the objects that are represented. The central section of the painting consists of a grouping of a solid with a rectangular base (perhaps a tea box[13] or a tin can for saving leftover paint), a small book placed upon it and, behind, a pitcher or a metal watering-can also visible in the Giovanardi still life (fig. 16a). The luminous wavy line on the left belongs to the edge of a tray, easily recognizable and viewed from the same angle in the contemporary drawing (fig. 16c).[14] To the right of the book and the box, the strange flat object with an eccentric profile placed on a stand is a mantel clock whose front is visible in *Still Life with Silver Platter* (fig. 16e), where one can also glimpse the round case of its face. As in the Giovanardi painting, a reflecting object, perhaps a diptych mirror, closes the composition behind (in the Mattioli painting it parallels the contour of the clock), while other spatial divisions are added to the left, a motif prefigured in the still life in the Musée National d'Art Moderne (fig. 16b).

Apart from these painted still lifes, the Mattioli painting is also closely related to the first work that Morandi allowed to appear in print in Italy, an etching of a still life[15] published by Giuseppe Raimondi in the second issue of *La Raccolta* (Bologna, April 15, 1918; fig. 16d). The relationship between the print (undated on the plate but usually assigned to 1915) and the Mattioli painting is not clear. Morandi's etchings usually replicated in reverse a composition previously executed as a drawing or painting. More rarely the etching comes first, in which case it would be in the same sense as the subsequent painting. Here however, the etching reverses most of the elements in the painting (the edge of the tray, the pitcher, the box and the book), but the back of the clock is oriented in the same direction as in the painting. Some elements have disappeared (the open diptych mirror on the right), others are inserted from earlier paintings (the cylindrical bottle with its strange swollen neck from the Giovanardi and Paris still lifes, figs. 16a, 16b), and others, structured (like the above-mentioned drawing [fig. 16c] but reversed) by what seem to be the vertical divisions of a place for storing crockery[16] are quite new, such as the non-descript vegetables on the right (thistle or celery?).

Given the etching's more developed spatial arrangement (all the objects in a still life for the first time lined up against the background, thus absorbing the abrupt spatial projection of the central objects in the Giovanardi painting still apparent in the Mattioli painting) and its abstracting tendency (Giuseppe Raimondi memorably wrote of the "dogmatic severity of Monsieur de Saci, in Pascal" and that "something afflicted and scholastic" from *Inni Sacri* by Alessandro Manzoni[17]) it can best be dated at the conclusion of this sequence of studies, directly after the Mattioli painting. As such, Morandi considered it his first solid achievement worthy of publication. But this was not his attitude to the Mattioli *Still Life*, the back of whose canvas he used for another painting: it was consigned to the limbo of endeavors withheld from public view, destined exclusively for his private use.

It is clear that Morandi, in this series of three still lifes with the pitcher, box and book, was conjugating elements of Cubist grammar. For example, the Giovanardi still life seems indebted, for the dislocation of its planes, to Picasso's *The Oil Mill*[18] (fig. 16f), published in 1911 in *La Voce*[19] and again, in 1914, as an illustration of the Picasso volume in the series *Maestri Moderni*;[20] for the fragmentation of the objects, Morandi seems to have looked at a still life by Georges Braque, *Violin, Glass and Knife* (1910)[21] (fig. 16g), which was reproduced by Soffici in *Cubismo e futurismo*.[22] But the tightening up and flattening of space in the Mattioli still life and the different handling of paint (in place of the broad and generalized brushstrokes in the 1914 paintings, a more regimented texture of parallel strokes and a darker palette) makes it necessary to look for other models, above all André Derain, an artist rarely reproduced in Italian art publications of the period and a model stubbornly denied by Morandi in later years.[23] The painting which constituted the essential reference for *Still Life with Clockcase* seems to this writer Derain's *Still Life on a Table* formerly in the Shchukin Collection[24] (fig. 16h). Morandi could have examined this in a reproduction from a block belonging to Kahnweiler in *Du "cubisme,"*[25] which was sold in the Libreria La Voce and which was often to be found in artists' studios of the time. The pitcher on

Fig. 16c. *Giorgio Morandi,* Still Life, *charcoal, 1915, in G. Ramous,* Giorgio Morandi. I disegni, *1949*

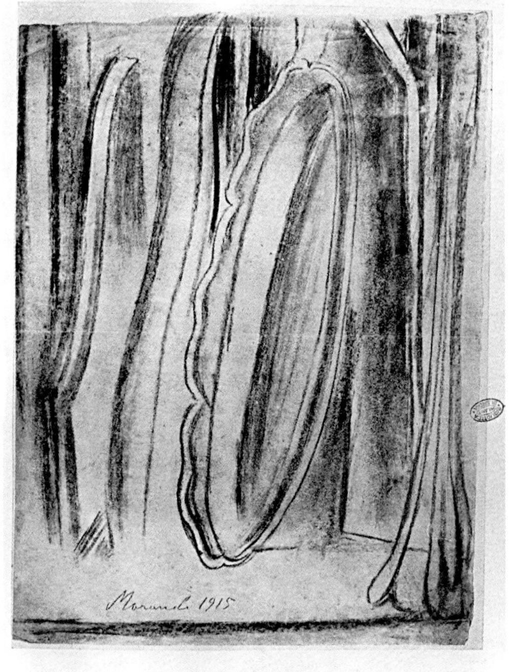

Fig. 16d. *Giorgio Morandi,* Still Life, *etching, 1915, in* La Raccolta, *1918*

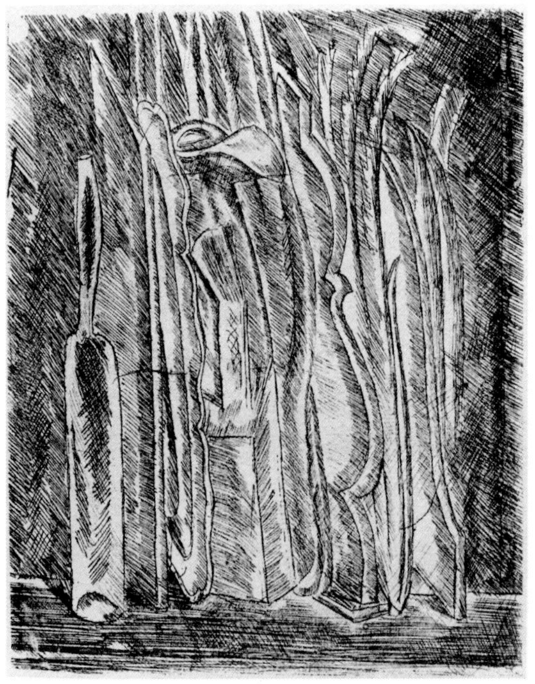

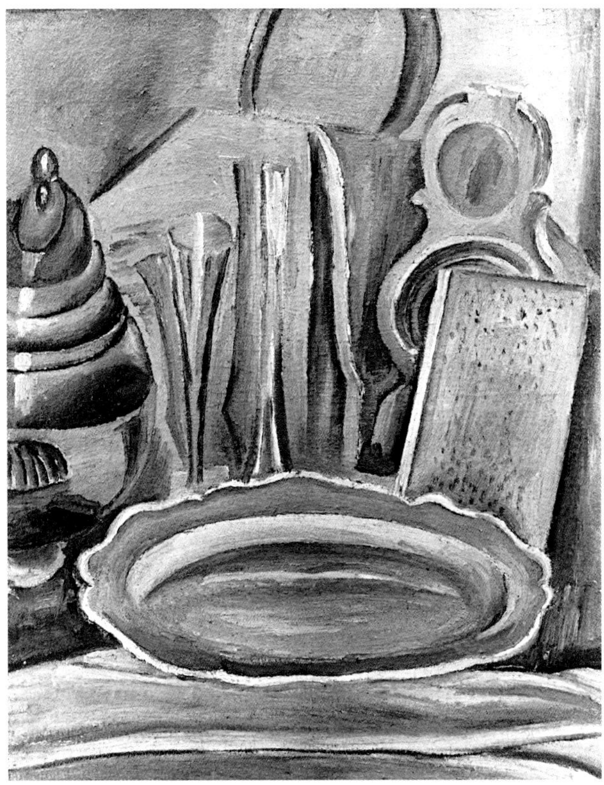

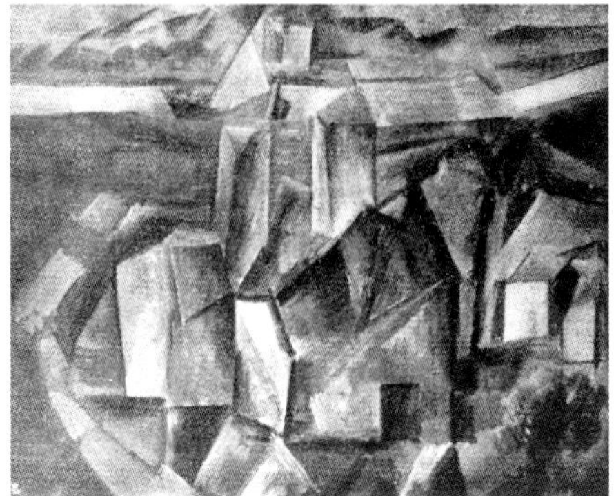

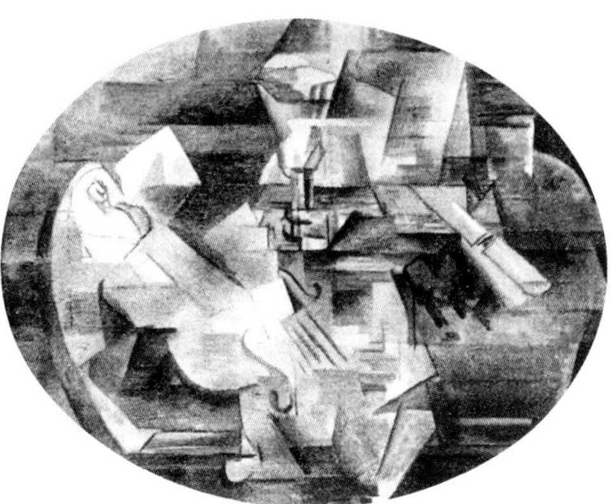

Fig. 16e. *Giorgio Morandi,* Natura morta con il piatto d'argento *(*Still Life with Silver Platter*), oil on canvas, 1914. Rome, Galleria Nazionale d'Arte Moderna*

Fig. 16f. *Pablo Picasso,* Le Moulin à huile *(*The Oil Mill*), in* La Voce*, December 7, 1911*

Fig. 16g. *Georges Braque,* Nature morte avec violon, verre et couteau *(*Still Life with Violin, Glass and Knife*), 1910, in A. Soffici,* Cubismo e futurismo*, 1914*

the table, standing in profile, the solemn graduated grouping of objects, the chiaroscuro rhythm in which the somber tones are interrupted by strong highlights, the background scanned by a dense sequence of verticals — these elements were studied by Morandi and provoked him into compacting within a single coherent motif the spatial caprices of the two earlier still lifes of 1914.

The distinctly Cubist-inspired style of the series with the pitcher, box and book contributed to its rapid fall from favor in the cultural climate of the 'return to order.' In the first monographic essay dedicated to Morandi by an Italian critic, Riccardo Bacchelli stigmatized his friend's attachment to "that mediocre Metaphysic which goes by the name of Cubism," while at the same time acknowledging "that Morandi had mainly appropriated from it a criterion of purity, that is, of essentiality."[26] In 1939, the engraver Luigi Bartolini, divided from Morandi by a proud sense of rivalry, drew attention not without perfidy to sources of Morandi's work which he thought would discredit the artist's growing fame with the more nationalistic public ("he comes from Cézanne. He also comes from Cubism. I have seen, in his studio, certain of his efforts, old and avant-gardist"[27]) and at the same time indicated the accessibility of such paintings in Morandi's home-studio in Via Fondazza.

Morandi kept the series hidden for over three decades, but it had a natural rise of fortune in the second postwar era, when adherence to the historic avant-garde became a mark of prestige for an Italian painter. The Mattioli painting was the first of the three to be published. Detached in 1951 from the *verso* of *Nudes* (which would then enter the Rollino Collection) at the request of Gino Ghiringhelli and with the artist's consent,[28] *Still Life with a Clockcase* was relined and sold by the same Ghiringhelli, director of the Galleria del Milione, to Gianni Mattioli.[29] In a letter to the collector in September 1951, the young critic Marco Valsecchi expressed his enthusiasm for the acquisition ("Don't let go of it; think of it as one of the rarest and most beautiful works by Morandi"[30]). It was exhibited the following year at the inaugural show on the new premises of the Galleria del Milione in Via Bigli, Milan, and prominently illustrated in the catalogue: in the context of an anthology of Italian works intended to celebrate "the polemics of the distant years

Fig. 16h. *André Derain,* Nature morte sur une table (Still Life on a Table), *oil on canvas, 1912. St Petersburg, Hermitage*

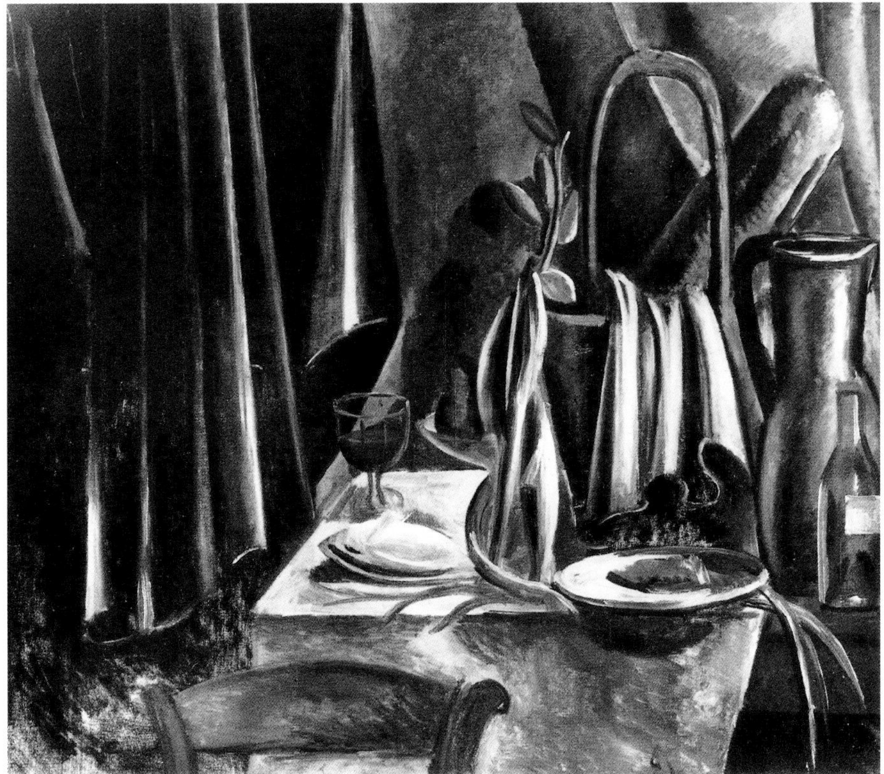

in Via Brera" Morandi's still life was perceived as an important turning point (even though in effect it was absent from view during the 1930s). Its Cubist style served perfectly as a weapon in the battle against the new realism fought by the Galleria del Milione in these years: in the exhibition's introductory text, Morandi's experimental visual language was interpreted not as a posture of formalist isolation but as "adherence in more subtle ways to the fate of humanity".[31]

[1] *Natura morta*, Milan, private collection: Vitali 1977, no. 4.
[2] Arcangeli 1964, p. 63 and Fergonzi 1998, p. 48.
[3] Vitali 1977, no. 21; the two painted surfaces were detached from their support only in 1951 (*Bologna* 1997, unnumbered page).
[4] Arcangeli 1964, p. 67.
[5] *Natura morta con il piatto d'argento*, Rome, Galleria Nazionale d'Arte Moderna: Vitali 1977, no. 19.
[6] Soffici 1932, plate.
[7] *Rome* 1914[c], p. 21, nos. 1–3.
[8] Forti, March 22, 1914.
[9] According to Morandi's recollection, published in Ragghianti 1969, p. 61.
[10] Lamberti 1997, p. 27.
[11] Des Prureaux, June 11, 1911.
[12] Soffici, July 11, 1912.
[13] Rylands 1997, p. 82.
[14] Private collection: Pasquali, Tavoni 1994, no. 1915,3.
[15] Vitali 1957, no. 3.
[16] According to Raimondi 1941, p. 164.
[17] Raimondi 1948, p. 150.
[18] France, private collection: Daix, Rosselet 1979, no. 277.
[19] Des Prureaux, December 7, 1911.
[20] *Picasso* 1914, pl. 8.
[21] Prague, Národní Galerie: Worms de Romilly, Laude 1982, no. 65.
[22] Soffici 1914, unnumbered plate.
[23] Russoli 1976, p. 46.
[24] *Nature morte sur une table*, St Petersburg, The Hermitage: Kellermann 1992, no. 286.
[25] Gleizes, Metzinger 1912, unnumbered plate.
[26] Bacchelli, March 29, 1918.
[27] Bartolini, February 12, 1939, p. 175.
[28] *Bologna* 1997, unnumbered page.
[29] Mattioli Rossi 1997, p. 16; a *terminus ante quem* for Mattioli's purchase of the work is provided by a debit from Mattioli's account of 15,000 lire on June 4, 1951 for "travel expenses Sig. Gino [Ghiringhelli] and [Ambrogio] Ceroni to collect Morandi painting": Archivio Mattioli, account of the Galleria del Milione dated June 30, 1951 (*Appendix I*, document no. 76). The detached verso of the canvas, with the composition of *Nudes* was sent back to Morandi in Bologna on September 15 following (*ibidem*, accounts of the Galleria del Milione, dated November 3, 1951: *Appendix I*, document no. 80).
[30] Archivio Mattioli, letter from Marco Valsecchi to Gianni Mattioli, dated September 19, 1951 (*Appendix I*, document no. 78).
[31] *Milione* 1952, unnumbered page.

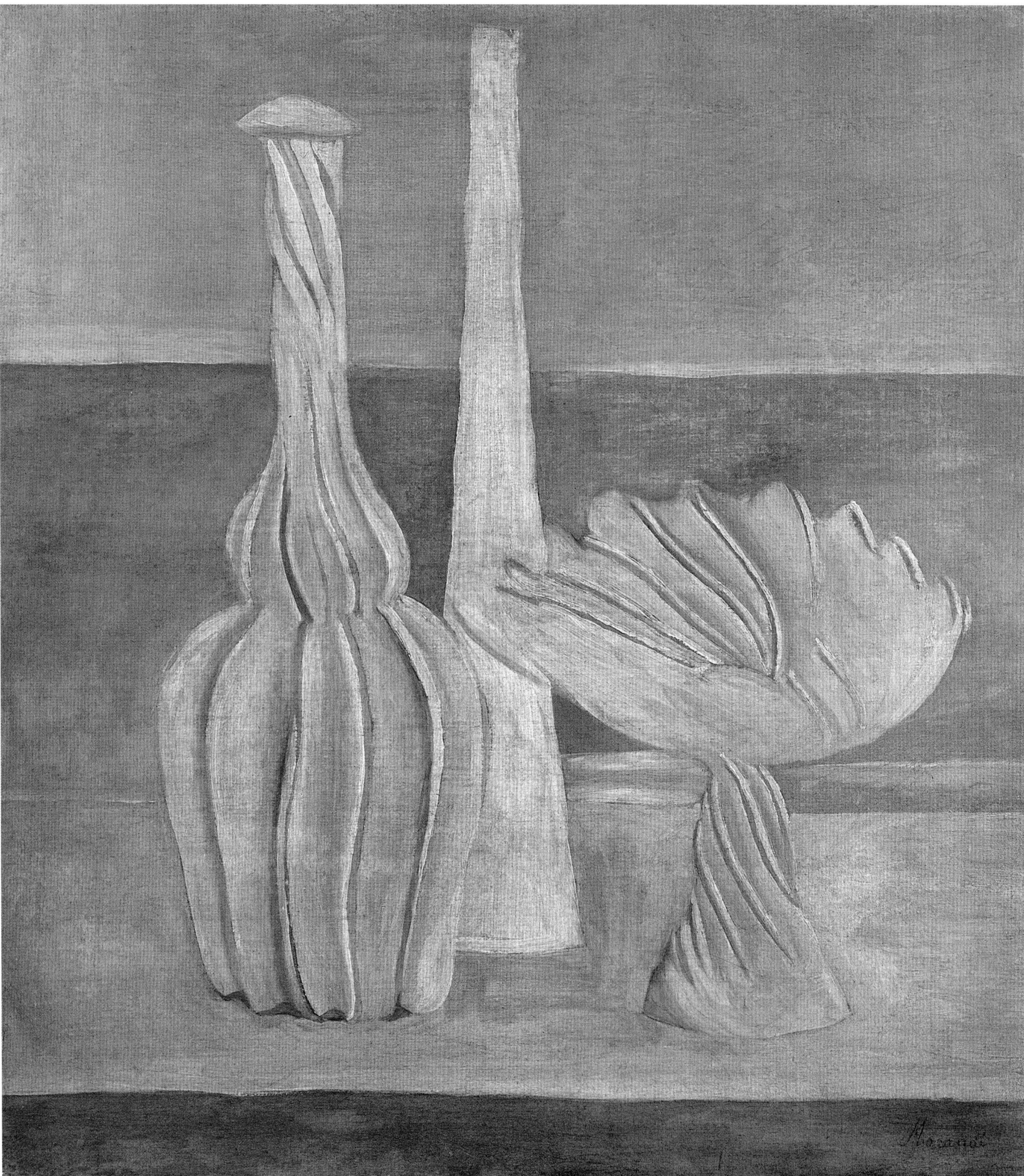
Morandi

17

Giorgio Morandi

Bottles and Fruit Bowl (Still Life)

Bottiglie e fruttiera (Natura Morta), 1916

Oil on canvas
60 × 54 cm

Inscriptions: *recto*, signed on lower right: 'Morandi' (fig. 17a); *verso*, signed upper center of the lining canvas: 'Morandi 1916' (fig. 17b)

Provenance: property of the artist; before October 1939: Pietro Feroldi, Brescia; May 1949: Gianni Mattioli

Exhibitions: Venice 1948, p. 30, no. 29 (*Natura morta*); New York 1949, pl. 58 and p. 132 (*Still Life with Bottles and Fruit Dish*); Zurich 1950, no. 155 (*Stilleben*); Florence 1953[a], no. 25, fig. 6 (*Bottiglie e fruttiera*); Rome 1955–6, p. 58, no. 64; Winterthur 1956, no. 4; Turin 1959, no. 29, p. 42; Naples 1964–Rotterdam 1965, no. 336 (Naples), no. 191 (Zurich–Rotterdam); Bern 1965, no. 13; Milan 1966[a] (no. 4); Venice 1966, p. 27, no. 10 (*Bottiglie e fruttiera*); Bologna 1966, no. 10; Florence 1967, no. 1191; Washington, DC 1967–Tokyo 1972, no. 75 (Washington, DC–Hamburg), no. 73 (Madrid–Seville), no. 75 (Kyoto–Tokyo); Milan 1971, no. 9, illus. p. 58; Rome 1973, no. 12; Bologna 1975, no. 3; Paris 1987, no. 8; Venice 1989, p. 367; Kamamura 1989–Kyoto 1990, no. 6; Madrid 1990–1, p. 255

Bibliography: Letter from Cesare Brandi to Giorgio Morandi, dated December 18, 1938, in Brandi 1990, p. 151; Beccaria 1939, pl. VII (*Natura morta*); Letter from Pietro Feroldi to Carlo Belli, dated July 1, 1941 (photostatic copy, Archivio Mattioli); Unpublished typescript by Carlo Belli, introducing the Feroldi Collection, before May 1942 (Rovereto, MART, Archivio del 900, Fondo Belli, p.

This still life with three objects (from left to right, a fluted oil bottle, a long bottle of "maraschino di Zara"[1] and a fruit bowl with spiral decorations) is one of Morandi's most celebrated masterpieces. It entered the public domain for the first time in 1939 in a small book on Morandi by Arnaldo Beccaria.[2] The caption of its illustration gave the date 1916 and its ownership as the Feroldi Collection. Today the painting is signed on the lower right of the canvas (fig. 17a) in an unusually rounded hand, and, more surprisingly, in pencil, a medium which Morandi did not customarily use on oil paintings; the signature, followed by the year 1916, is repeated in pencil on the lining canvas (fig. 17b), in a more pointed hand more closely resembling Morandi's signature as we know it. The signature on the front can be read in the photograph (fig. 17c) when the painting was published for the first time in 1939.[3] The signature and date in pencil on the *verso* of the canvas were inevitably added after the painting's execution and after its relining. The 1939 photograph shows us a canvas with some conservation problems, with lifting and abrasions which are absent in the color photograph published in 1942 in the catalogue of the Feroldi Collection.[4] The latter photograph was probably taken after a restoration that may have included the relining: Morandi spoke of the painting as "very damaged and restored" in a letter of May 1948, when he was attempting to block its exhibition in the XXIV Venice Biennale.[5]

The painting's subject had been known for more than a decade before its publication, thanks to an etching of the same motif in reverse[6] (fig. 17c), with a signature and date (1917) that contradict the 1916 date invariably given the painting from the time of its first publication in 1939. Morandi exhibited this etching at the 1928 Venice Biennale with the title *Natura morta*:[7] the date when the plate was etched (1928) is confirmed in a letter sent by the artist to Carlo Alberto Petrucci, director of the Calcografia Nazionale in Rome, together with the correction of the date of the painting from which the engraving had been made ("keep in mind that the 1917 date is erroneous. The painting is of 1916."[8]). The sending of this etching to the first Biennale to which Morandi had been invited (in the print rather than the painting section) is significant for the history of the painting itself. Morandi, more than a decade after its execution, evidently considered the latter a solid achievement and the undue emphasis placed on the date ("added by covering the cross-hatching with priming varnish before the etching," according to Giuseppe Trassari Filippetto's technical explanation[9]) was evidently intended to draw the attention of Biennale visitors to a work of ten years earlier, by a painter still disregarded by the majority. The engraving was executed from the painting and not from a preparatory drawing. It imitates details specific to the handling of the paint, such as the thickness of the brushstrokes of the tall central bottle or the slight addition of white light along the 'horizon' directly above the fruit bowl.

The date on the etching, all the odder because Morandi was not prone to historicizing his work (though it shares this feature with a plate of the same year which replicated, with the date 1917, a painting of *Flowers* generally agreed to be of 1916[10]), requires explanation. One hypothesis may be as follows. In 1928, the two paintings were still in Morandi's studio, but neither of them was dated: Morandi was not aided, in attributing to them their correct dates, by the painting closest to the Mattioli *Still Life*, a composition with the same three objects in reverse and a fourth bottle on the left[11] (fig. 17f: henceforth Vitali 29), which was in the 'Valori Plastici' exhibitions in 1921 in Germany,[12] which remained the property of Mario Broglio beyond 1928,[13] and which is clearly dated June 23, 1916. Only when Morandi had obtained the photograph of Vitali 29 (which we know he procured from Rome in February–March 1929[14]) or when he saw the painting itself at the 1939 Quadriennale,[15] would he have been reminded of the correct year of execution of the Mattioli painting. It is true that Morandi's memory might have been jogged by the date July 2, 1916 visible on a painting similar in technique and palette, with two bottles, a pitcher, a box and a coffee-pot[16] (fig. 17g, henceforth Vitali 27) which, as Carlo Ludovico Ragghianti recalled, was "nailed for years high above the door of Morandi's studio,"[17] but he seems not to have taken advantage of this.

The matter of which of these two still lifes (cat. no. 17 and fig. 17f), with three objects in common but in mirror image (the spiral fluting of the fruit bowl is also reversed, but not that of the oil bottle), was painted first should be seen in the context of the vexed question of Morandi's chronology as a whole in 1916. Morandi and his friends seem to have shown no especial interest in the problem: at the 1939 Quadriennale in Rome (where the sequence of the exhibited works was decided by Leo Longanesi[18]) and in the catalogue of Brandi's monograph of 1942, the July 2 painting preceded that of June 23 (by two numbers in the room at the Rome show). Lamberto Vitali corrected this in his monograph of 1964.[19] Morandi himself was involved in the choice and arrangement of the illustrations for the latter,[20] and here the two paintings with the fluted bottle and fruit bowl were placed together for the first time (though not on facing pages), with the Mattioli painting preceding Vitali 29. (In the introductory essay Vitali considered the latter "the second in order of time," for its more complex composition and greater chromatic subtlety.[21]) In 1982 Carlo Ludovico Ragghianti, who had discussed at length with Morandi the matter of sequences and series, also referred to the Mattioli *Still Life* as having been painted "a few days before."[22] Five years earlier, in 1977, the definitive *catalogue raisonné* maintained the same order for the two paintings[23] but inexplicably placed Vitali 27 (fig. 17g), which is dated on the canvas eleven days after Vitali 29, before the other two paintings.

In the present state of our knowledge and considering Morandi's own insistence on situating the Mattioli painting before Vitali 29, it is not possible to resolve the matter definitively. Morandi was working towards ever flatter forms in June–July 1916, reducing them to silhouettes against the background, with a tendency to abstraction that reached its peak in Vitali 27. (Though on one occasion Maurizio Fagiolo dell'Arco postdated Vitali 27 to 1917 there are no apparent grounds for this.[24]) The radical compression of space and of objects into a mosaic of flat shapes in Vitali 29 (fig. 17f) would argue in favor of it being the later of the two. However, information that can be found in Morandi's letters has qualified the force of this argument. One cannot exclude that Vitali 29 may have been reworked later. On July 5, 1921, Morandi wrote to Broglio that he was "adjusting" ("accomodando") a painting of 1916 in readiness for the 'Valori Plastici' exhibitions in Germany.[25] The painting in question was not Vitali 29 (this

19); Piovene 1942, pl. 19 (*Natura morta*); *Almanacco* 1942, p. 63 (*Natura morta*); Letter from Giorgio Morandi to Umbro Apollonio, dated May 21, 1948, in Bandera 2001, p. 99; Letter from Umbro Apollonio to Giorgio Morandi, dated May 22, 1948, in Bandera 2001, pp. 99–100; Mango 1949, p. 24; Zervos 1950, p. 161; Garretto 1952, p. 44; Valsecchi 1952, pl. 6; D'Ancona 1953, pl. 13, pp. 22–3; Bloch 1955, pl. 1; Castelfranco, Valsecchi 1956, pl. 36a, pp. 58, 81; Valsecchi 1957, fig. 91; Valsecchi 1958, pl. 23, p. 58; Carrieri, May 24, 1959; Ballo 1960, p. 27; Marchiori 1960, no. 43; Bellonzi 1963, pp. 101, 106; Arcangeli 1964, pp. 73, 78, fig. 11 (*Natura morta*); Ballo 1964[b], vol. I, p. 136; Valsecchi 1964, pp. 5, 12, pl. III; Vitali 1964, p. 19, pl. 22 (*Natura morta*); Siblik 1965, pl. 6; Borgese, June 18, 1966; Argan 1970, pp. 598–602, fig. p. 599; Giuffré 1970, pp. 16–17, pl. 7; Del Monte 1973, p. 39; Russoli 1976, p. 46; Vitali 1977, no. 28 (*Natura morta*); Solmi 1978, pp. 30–1, fig. 24; Ragghianti 1982, p. 226; Solmi 1985[a], pp. 34, 36–7; Castagnoli 1990, pp. 32, 34; Pasquali 1990, pp. 18, 26; Rylands 1997, p. 84; Bandera 2001, pp. 23–4, 48, 58, 65, 99–100

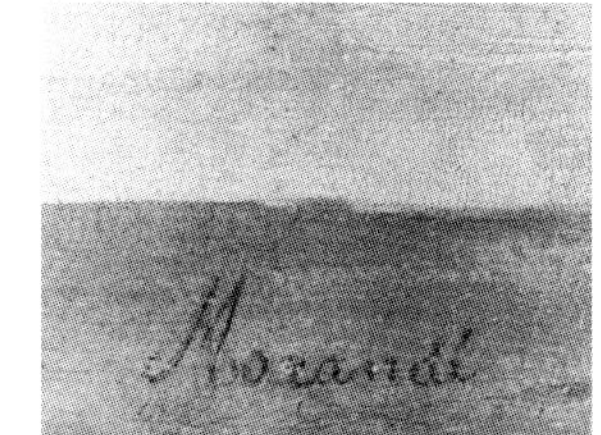

Fig. 17a. *Detail of the signature on the* recto *of cat. no. 17*

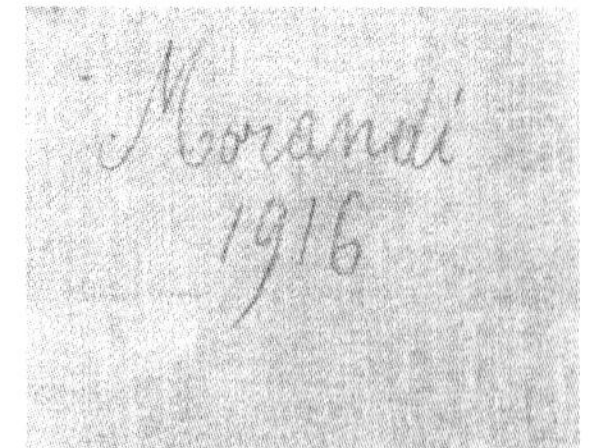

Fig. 17b. *Detail of the* verso *of cat. no. 17, with the artist's signature*

Fig. 17c. *Illustration of cat. no. 17 in A. Beccaria,* Giorgio Morandi, *1939*

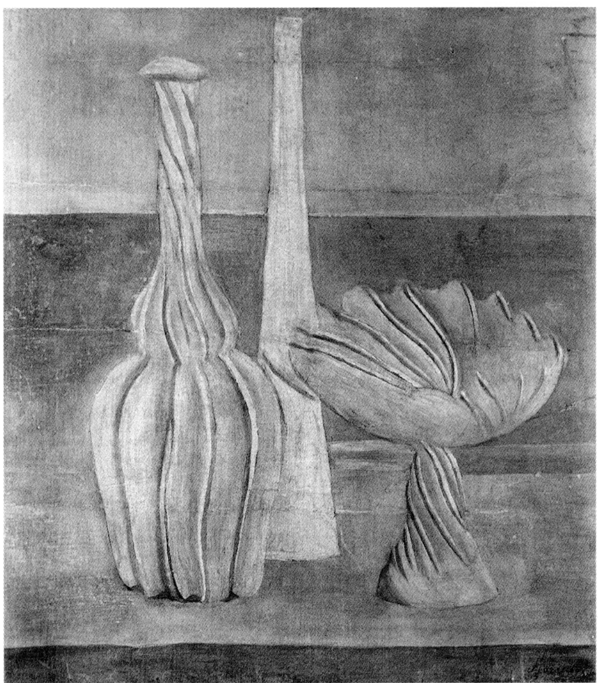

had been delivered to Broglio at least by 22 May, the date of the opening of the exhibition in Hanover where, as we have seen, it was shown). But the letter testifies to a habit of Morandi's of retouching his own works years later prior to selling or exhibiting them. If then one imagines Morandi re-painting Vitali 29 after his two year Metaphysical period (1918–19) — a period notable for the high finish and smooth, even fields of color — then the difference in texture and brushwork between this and the Mattioli painting may find its explanation. For a comparison between the two paintings in purely compositional terms, infra-red reflectography carried out on the Mattioli painting provides us with two important pieces of information (fig. 17e). The first is that Morandi had foreseen a fourth object, a bottle, placed behind the fruit bowl: this bottle was never painted but a space was reserved for it before the background was made uniform with a wash of bluish-gray. Secondly, the decision to divide the setting into four horizontal bands was made during execution of the painting: Morandi initially planned to emphasize the table top by a semi-vertical caesura to the right of the base of the fruit bowl (with an effect not dissimilar from that obtained symmetrically in Vitali 29). At the outset of the Mattioli painting, Morandi had therefore planned a more crowded painting, with more voluminous objects (fig. 17e reveals that the outline of the fruit bowl extended to the left edge of the tall central bottle and that the silhouette of the bottle was made narrower when the background was painted over). Only, then, during the execution of the painting did Morandi shift towards the more rarefied and two-dimensional image. This transition, in which Morandi, even while at work moves away from formulae already tested in a previous painting, would support the argument that the Mattioli painting came after Vitali 29; indeed, in subsequent series of still lifes of the 1930s and 1950s, we again see Morandi eliminating objects from the arrangements in front of him in mid-execution.

The Mattioli still life with *Bottles and Fruit Bowl* has completely novel formal characteristics in the panorama of contemporary Italian painting. Any notion of depth has been virtually eliminated from the spatial box (in Giulio Carlo Argan's skilful description, "there is a continuous spatial tissue, like a taut veil, on whose surface the objects, the table, the walls emerge as if by transparency"[26]). The parallel bands of the table and the 'horizons' occupy the foreground plane, intersecting the verticals of the objects at intervals of calculated and geometric

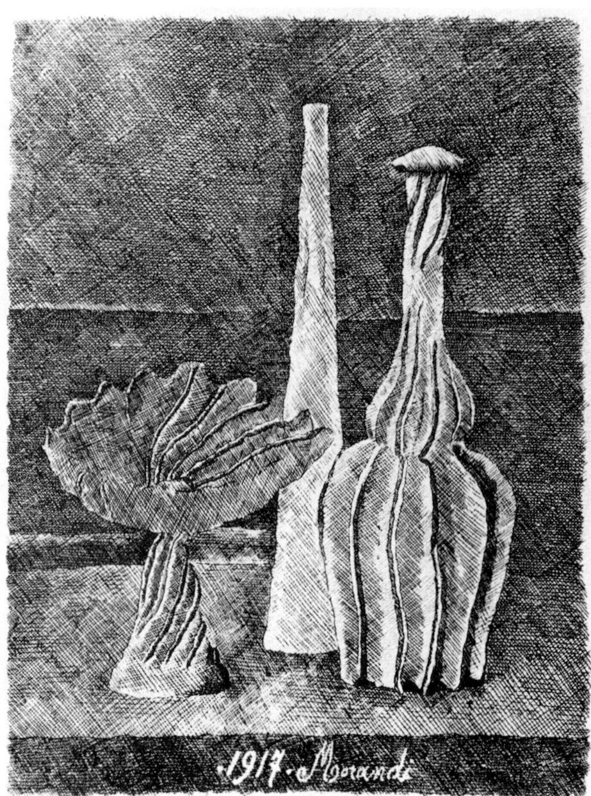

Fig. 17d. *Giorgio Morandi,* Bottiglie e fruttiera (Bottles and Fruit Bowl)*, etching, 1928*

harmony. The excess of light gives the objects a spectral look, like images on an over-exposed photograph. They cast no shadows and there is practically no chiaroscuro (Philip Rylands has observed how the dark patches on the bottom of the fluted oil bottle were painted by Morandi directly on the actual object, still today preserved in the Museo Morandi, Bologna[27]). The color scheme is composed of subtle tonal sequences ranging from the bluish color of the background to the "gray, nut brown and ivory [...] almost like a resplendent duel between variations of a tonal color and the semblance of a monochrome"[28] of the table and objects.

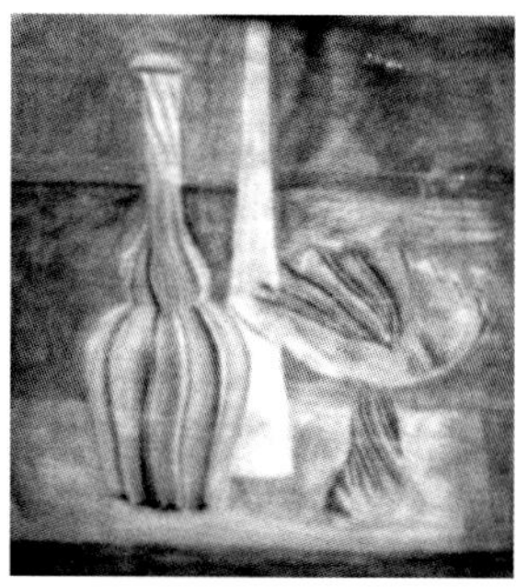

Fig. 17e. *Infra-red reflectography of cat. no. 17*

It is not easy to identify Morandi's visual sources. If indeed there were any, they were so profoundly assimilated and re-invented that any direct comparisons give meager results. Critical discussion of *Bottles and Fruit Bowl* has consisted of generic allusions to the fourteenth and fifteenth centuries (matching Carlo Carrà's essays on Giotto and Paolo Uccello published in 1916 in *La Voce*, a periodical attentively read by Morandi[29]) countered by Francesco Arcangeli's allusions to "the more silent and secret aspects of modern art in France," without specific details.[30] The only precise source to have been put forward has been Lamberto Vitali's indication of a vase of flowers by Henri Rousseau[31] (fig. 17h). The two-part neutral background and the spiral white ceramic of the vase in Rousseau's painting were certainly known to Morandi from the reproduction in 1914 in *La Voce*.[32] A similar vase, with a similar unusual chiaroscuro pattern, was the dominant formal motif in a still life by Henri Matisse, *Les tulipes*, illustrated in the May 1914 issue of *Les Soirées de Paris* (fig. 17j) and perhaps known to Morandi when painting this work.[33] Matisse may be the explanation for the division of the ground into strips that scan the composition of the foreground plane (especially evident in *La Glace sans tain*, fig. 17k, but also for example in the 1914 *La Femme assise*,[34] both illustrated in the same May 1914 issue of *Les Soirées de Paris*), or again for the reduction of the objects to ghostly apparitions, floating without shadow in a rarefied spatial container (*The Lemons*,[35] fig. 25h, another still life illustrated in Apollinaire's review, uses a method for structuring the background similar to that of Vitali 29). The solution of simple bands of color to suggest three planes — the surface on

Fig. 17f. *Giorgio Morandi,* Still Life, *oil on canvas, 1916, in C. Brandi,* Morandi, *1942*

Fig. 17g. *Giorgio Morandi,* Still Life, *oil on canvas, 1916. New York, The Museum of Modern Art, acquired through the Lillie P. Bliss Bequest*

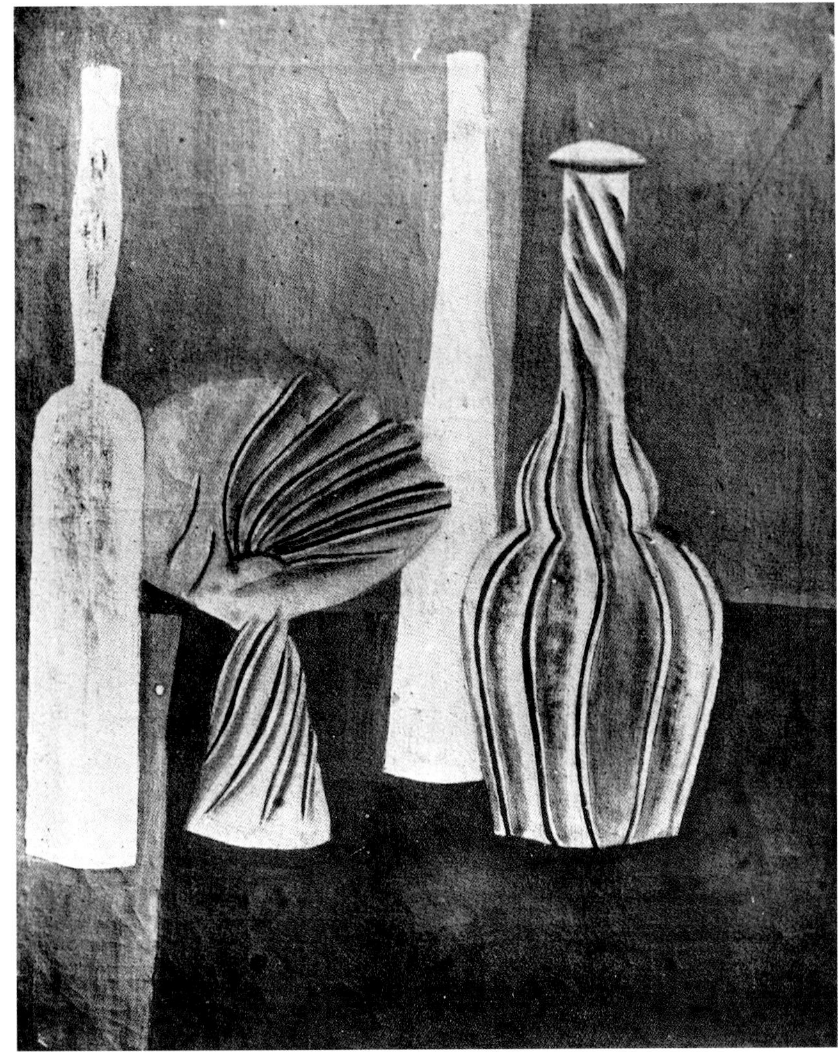

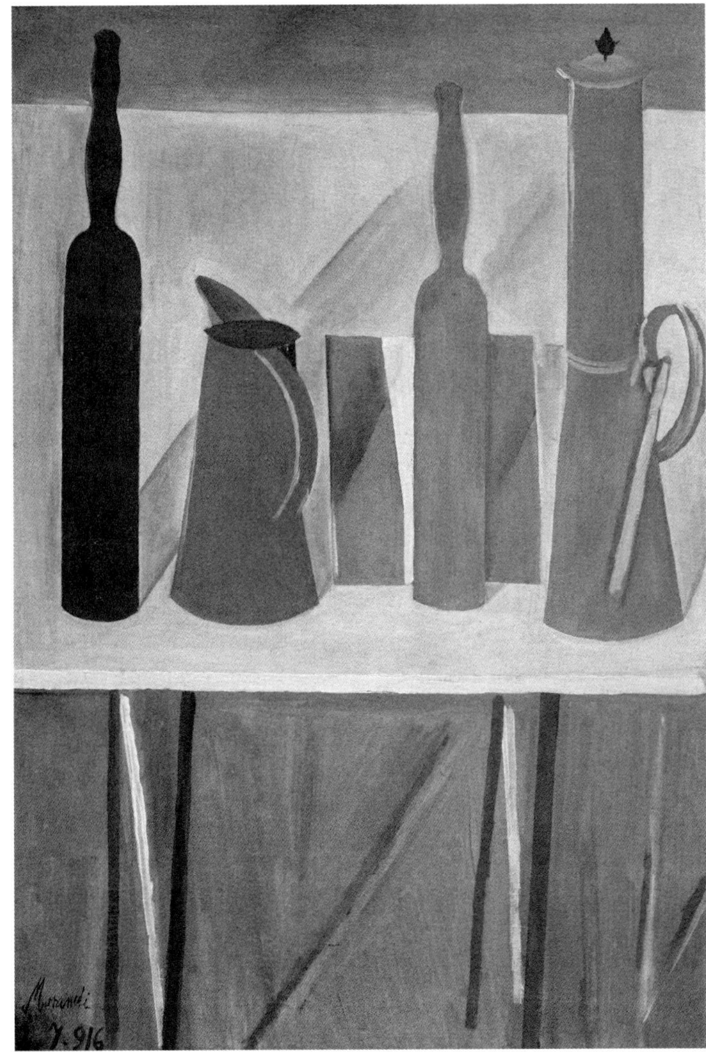

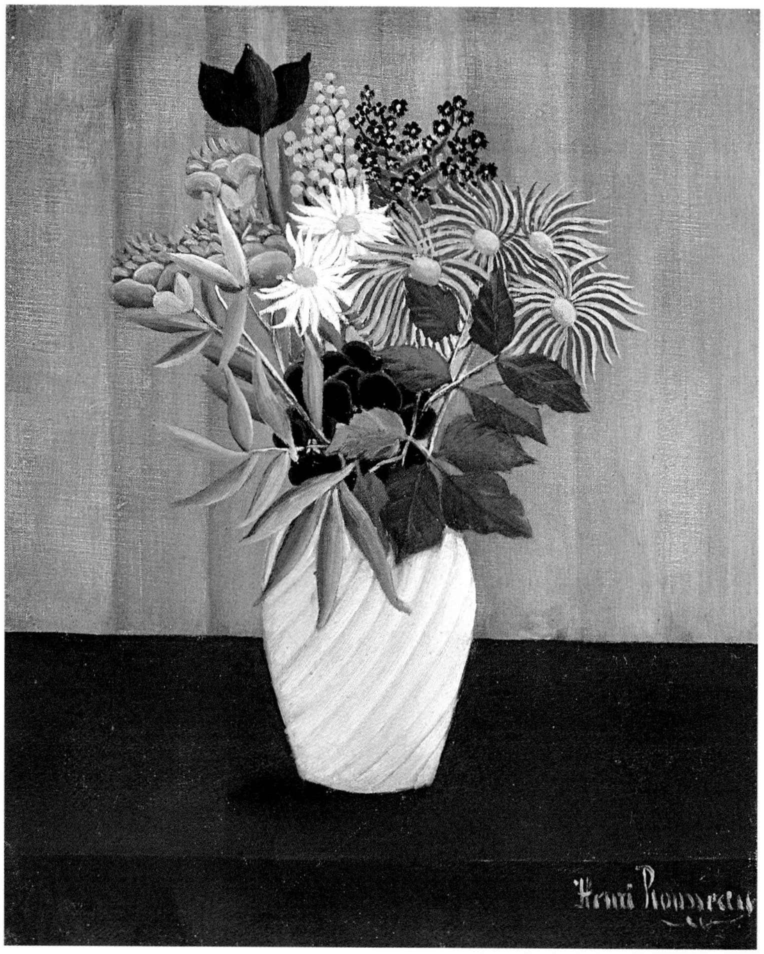

Fig. 17h. *Henri Rousseau,*
Vase of Flowers,
oil on canvas, c. 1910.
Merion (Pennsylvania),
The Barnes Foundation

which the objects are placed, and surfaces below and behind — may be derived from a painting legendary among young artists of the time, the *Still Life* with a coffee pot, lantern, pears and lemons by Henri Rousseau (fig. 17i) in the collection of Ardengo Soffici.[36] Morandi's painting shares with this the thin dark strip that opens the composition at the bottom and the concept of a still life of flattened forms seen from above and given relief by the lower of the two 'horizon' lines.

Nor is Morandi's compositional idea free of the influence of Cubism, or of Picasso in particular. For the compression of space into a flat, two-dimensional inlay, the models accessible to Morandi included the construction in parallel bands of the background of Picasso's *Violin Hanging on the Wall*[37] illustrated in *Emporium* in 1913 (fig. 17l) in the same article by Ugo Nebbia that explains his knowledge of Derain's *Bathers*.[38] The unusual corolla-shaped bowl of Morandi's compote dish echoes the shape of a bunch of bananas in a 1907 still life by Picasso,[39] illustrated in a book on Picasso published by *La Voce* in 1914[40] as well as in the *Almanacco della Voce 1915*. Finally Morandi may have remembered the almost square format and the inexorable flattening and contouring of forms in a mixed media *Still Life* by Picasso[41] (fig. 17m) published in the November 1913 issue of *Les Soirées de Paris*, whose reproductions, according to research by Paolo Fossati, influenced the compositions of Morandi's Metaphysical works in 1918.[42]

Before 1928, when Morandi exhibited the etching based on the painting now in the Mattioli Collection at the Venice Biennale, only regular visitors to Morandi's studio in Bologna wrote about the 1916 series of still lifes. In 1918, Riccardo Bacchelli was struck by compositions of "wavy porcelains [...] bottles and pitchers, which come together, rare, spaced, entire, against opaque and uniform backgrounds, with their own and shared logic. I would say that they wit-

Fig. 17i. *Henri Rousseau,* Still Life with Coffee Pot, Fruit and Lamp, *oil on canvas, 1910. Private collection*

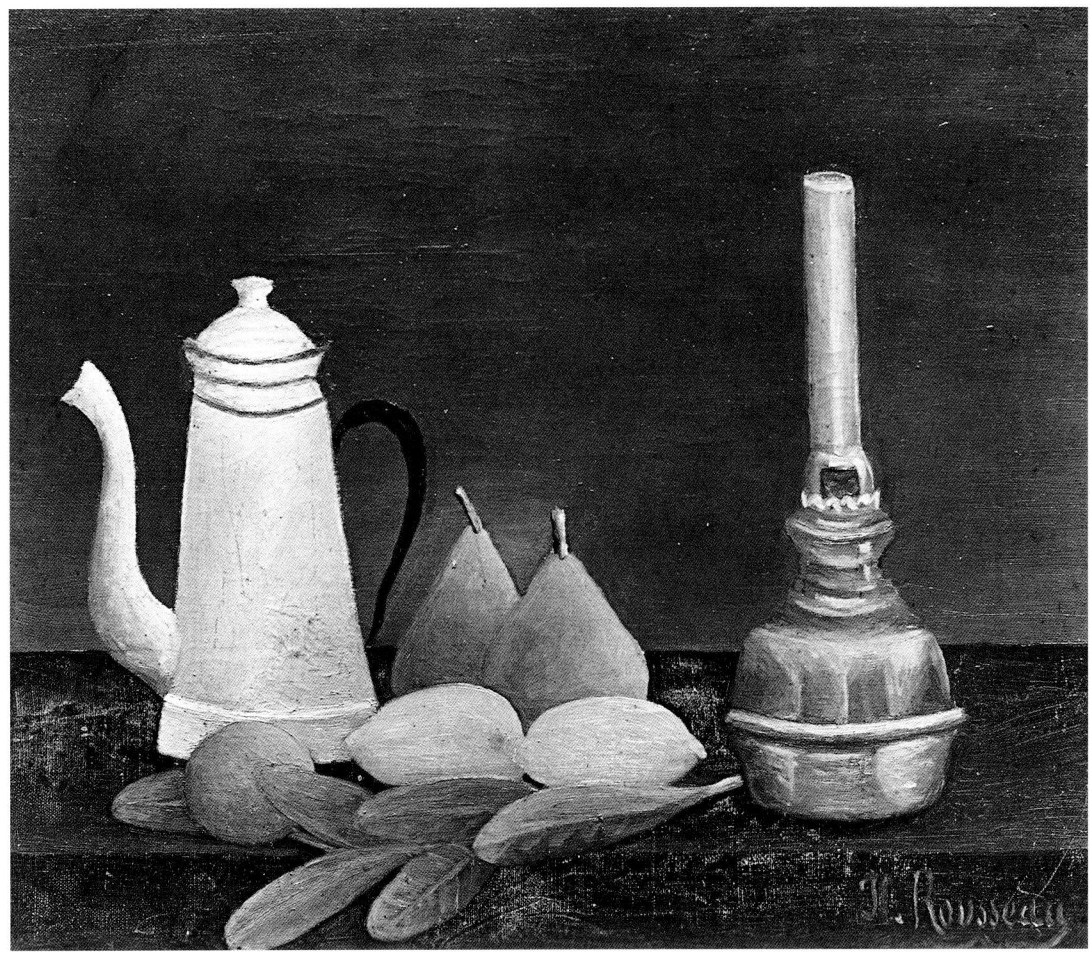

ness, so much are they necessary and alone." He considered them "the fullest and most joyous works by Morandi, and those that give the idea of having reached saturation."[43] In the same year Raffaello Franchi, in the Bolognese review *La Raccolta*,[44] writing of these still lifes, referred to the "objects arranged according to his talent" by Pablo Picasso in the reproductions of the November 1913 issue of *Les Soirées de Paris*, a further indication of how the awareness of these materials circulated in literary and artistic circles in Florence and Bologna.

Even after the execution of the *d'après* etching (1928) and through most of the 1930s, this still life was jealously guarded in the artist's studio. The canvas was detached from its stretcher and folded, as testified by losses corresponding to a fold still visible above the 'horizon' line. At a time difficult to pinpoint between 1938 and 1939 (when there was growing interest in early Morandi on the art market in Lombardy), the painting was bought by Pietro Feroldi. Neither the rather spare correspondence between Feroldi and Morandi,[45] nor the much denser correspondence between Feroldi and Carlo Belli,[46] which is full of information about the Morandis that were entering Feroldi's collection, provide us with a more definite date for the purchase of *Bottles and Fruit Bowl*. Feroldi was however enthusiastic about the work from the beginning and in 1941, when compiling the illustrations for the catalogue of his collection, he referred to the painting as the "square still life with those white elements which shines [*sic*] in all the artist's works."[47]

Bottles and Fruit Bowl was however known even before its reproduction in Beccaria's 1939 booklet: in December 1938, when compiling material for an essay to be published in *Le Arti*, Cesare Brandi wrote Morandi requesting a black and white photograph of the "*still life* with that fruit bowl and that veined bottle" which a drawing by Brandi himself identifies as the Mat-

Fig. 17j. *Henri Matisse,* Les tulipes *(*The Tulips*),* *in* Les Soirées de Paris*, 1914*

Fig. 17k. *Henri Matisse,* La Glace sans tain *(*La Fenêtre bleue*) (*The Plate-Glass *[*The Blue Window*]), oil on canvas, 1913. New York, The Museum of Modern Art, Abby Aldrich Rockefeller Fund*

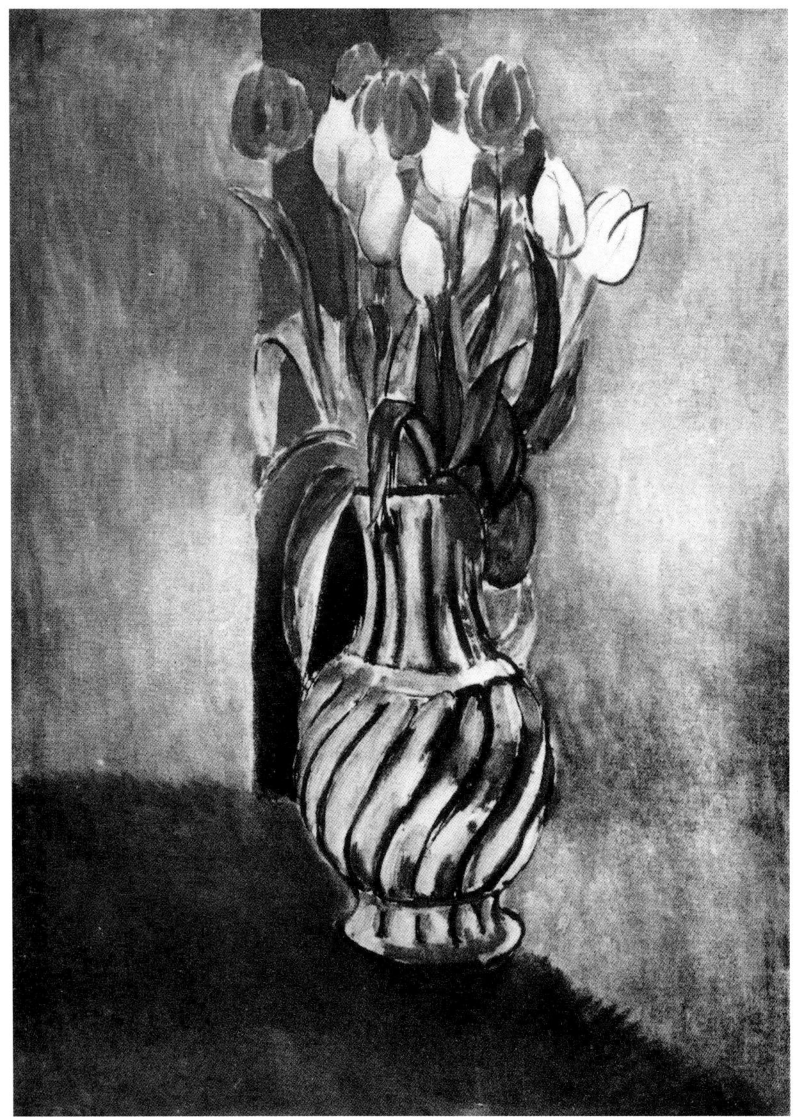

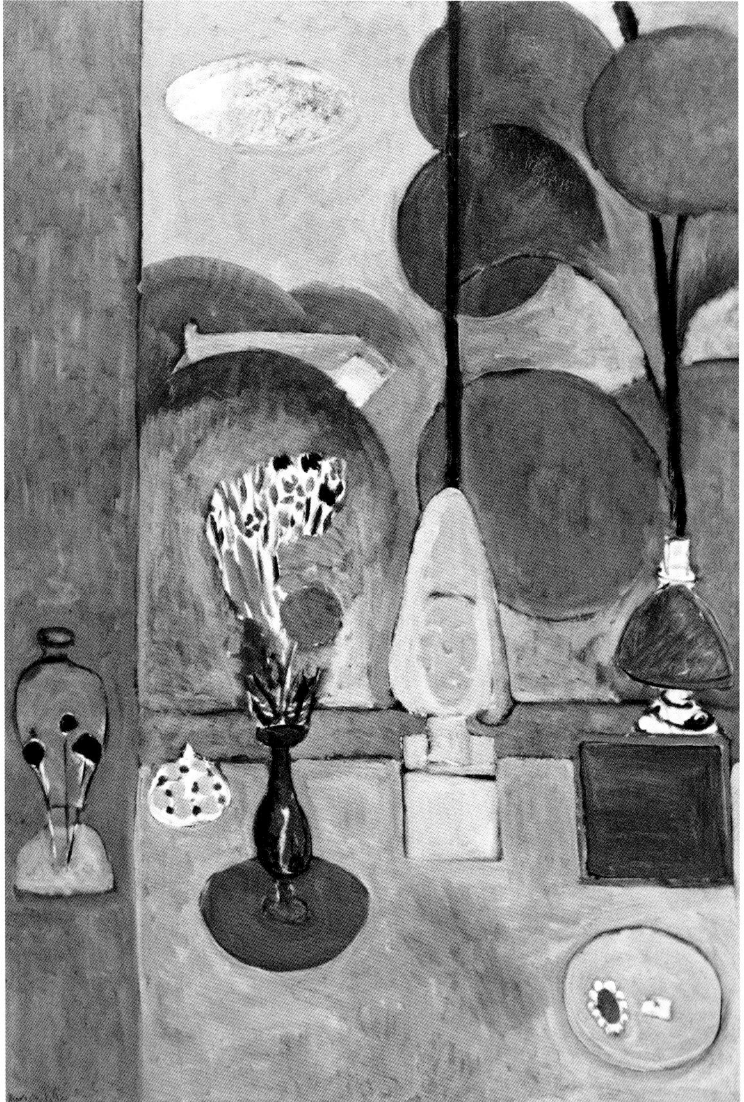

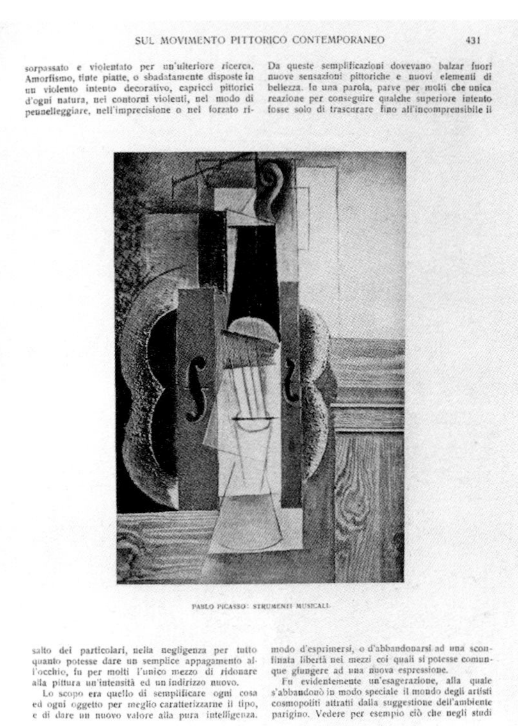

SUL MOVIMENTO PITTORICO CONTEMPORANEO 431

sorpassato e violentato per un'ulteriore ricerca. Amorfismo, tinte piatte, o sbadatamente disposte in un violento intento decorativo, capricci pittorici d'ogni natura, nei contorni violenti, nel modo di pennelleggiare, nell'imprecisione o nel forzato risalto dei particolari, nella negligenza per tutto quanto potesse dare un semplice appagamento all'occhio, fu per molti l'unico mezzo di ridonare alla pittura un'intensità ed un indirizzo nuovo.

Lo scopo era quello di semplificare ogni cosa ed ogni oggetto per meglio caratterizzarne il tipo, e di dare un nuovo valore alla pura intelligenza. Da queste semplificazioni dovevano balzar fuori nuove sensazioni pittoriche e nuovi elementi di bellezza. In una parola, parve per molti che unica reazione per conseguire qualche superiore intento fosse solo di trascurare fino all'incomprensibile il modo d'esprimersi, o d'abbandonarsi ad una sconfinata libertà nei mezzi coi quali si potesse comunque giungere ad una nuova espressione.

Fu evidentemente un'esagerazione, alla quale s'abbandonò in modo speciale il mondo degli artisti cosmopoliti attratti dalla suggestione dell'ambiente parigino. Vedere per esempio ciò che negli studi

PABLO PICASSO: STRUMENTI MUSICALI

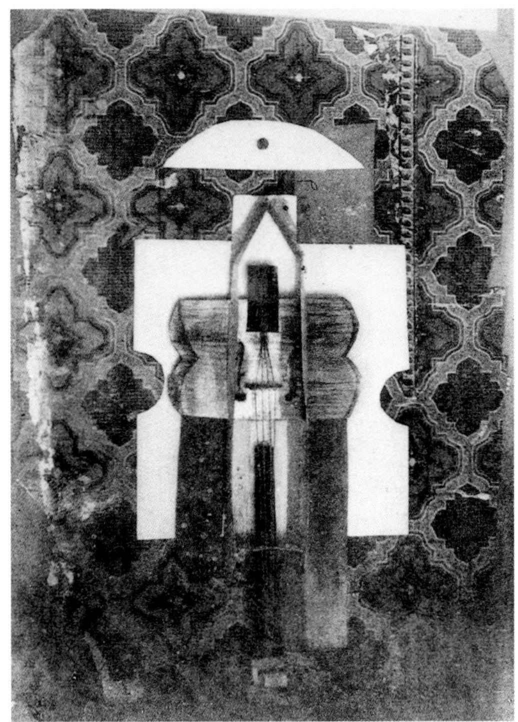

Fig. 17l. *Pablo Picasso,* Violon accroché au mur *(*Violin Hanging on the Wall*), oil on canvas, in* Emporium, *1913*

Fig. 17m. *Pablo Picasso,* Nature morte *(*Construction au violon*) (*Still Life *[*Violin Construction*]), mixed media construction, in* Les Soirées de Paris, *1913*

tioli painting.[48] Morandi sent instead a photograph of Vitali 29, which was to be exhibited at the 'III Quadriennale romana' (1939) and which was much illustrated and discussed by the press on that occasion.[49] From the early 1940s, and before the publication of the color plates in Piovene's book on the Feroldi Collection, the painting was so celebrated that it was chosen, in the popular *Almanacco Letterario Bompiani* for 1942 published late in 1941,[50] as evidence of continuity, in the finest Italian art, between the 1910s and the 1940s (it was paired with an engraving, *Dead Dragonfly*, by Luigi Bartolini). In the text which was to serve as an introduction to the Feroldi Collection catalogue (but replaced at the time of printing by Guido Piovene's introduction), Carlo Belli seems tacitly to refer to the Mattioli still life in the lines dedicated to Morandi's greatness:

> "... his chaste painting has such vitality in itself as to empty the subject of all other content [...]. See how this painting, made from highly sensitive passages, from swift and decisive strokes, from liquid and profound coloring leads the mind toward the mystery of matter, inscrutable, even if achieved by the great artist. Fluid, dense and elastic, this matter has in itself a high narrative power: every brushstroke, one could say, is a pictorial episode of sadness or joy that transports us to a higher, ultimately abstract world and which may even forego the pretext of a subject. We are at the summit of painting, in a position of extreme rarefaction compared to the weight of human emotions, in a domain only attained by angels or demons: Morandi or Picasso."[51]

Bottles and Fruit Bowl remained in the Feroldi Collection until 1949 and was shown in important exhibitions soon after the end of the war (the 1948 Venice Biennale, the 'Twentieth-Century Italian Art' show in New York in 1949) as one of the flagship Italian paintings of the first half of the century. When Gianni Mattioli bought the Feroldi Collection, it was priced at 490,000 lire (against an estimate of 750,000 lire), by far the highest price of any of the collection's numerous works by Morandi.[52] From the time of its entry to the Mattioli Collection, this still life has become the most admired and illustrated of the pre-Metaphysical Morandis. Critical per-

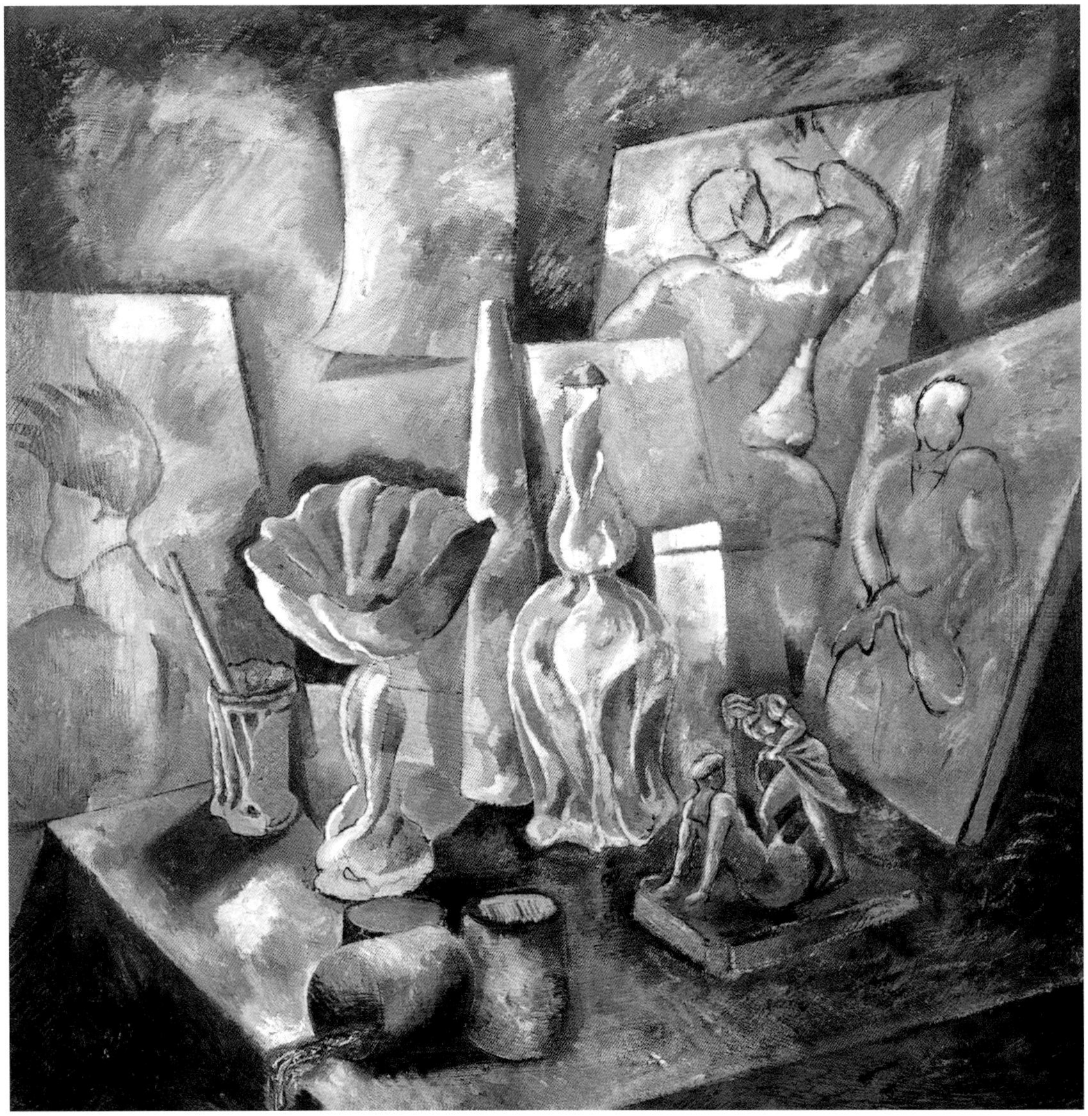

Fig. 17n. *Sandro Chia,* Dipinti, scultura e polvere (Paintings, Sculpture and Dust*), oil on canvas, 1981. Private collection*

ception of it lurched between the two extremes of an art solidly anchored to figurative values and traditional craftsmanship (in the *Corriere della Sera* in 1966, the painting was polemically illustrated as the antidote to the kinetic art exhibited at the Venice Biennale)[53] or as a work that wound up a centuries-old history of spatial research and inaugurated a new art founded on relational and existential components, as described by Giulio Carlo Argan in his memorable account of the painting in the most successful history of Italian art of the time.[54] When artists in the 1980s returned to figuration, *Bottles and Fruit Bowl* was elevated to a model of formal equilibrium, as exemplified in paintings such as Sandro Chia's *Paintings, Sculpture and Dust* (1981, fig. 17n) and Bruno Donzelli's *Morandiana, with Italian Still Life*, 1986.[55]

[1] According to Raimondi 1966, p. 53.
[2] Beccaria 1939, pl. VII.
[3] The signature is not in fact legible in the small volume itself, but instead in the original black and white print that was used for the block (today in Milan, Archivio Scheiwiller).
[4] Piovene 1942, pl. 19.
[5] Letter from Giorgio Morandi to Umbro Apollonio, dated May 21, 1948, in Bandera 2001, p. 99. The painting was sent nevertheless to the Biennale. For a full account see Bandera 2001, pp. 23–4, 54, 58, 65, 99–100.
[6] Vitali 1957, no. 50.
[7] *Venice* 1928, p. 106, no. 71; the identification of the etching is possible thanks to the notebook in which the artist listed where each impression went (Fiorani 1991, p. 57: the impression sent to the Biennale was numbered 7/50).
[8] Letter from Giorgio Morandi to Carlo Alberto Petrucci, dated December 24, 1948, in Ficacci 1991, p. 166.
[9] Trassari Filippetto 1991, p. 57.
[10] *Fiori*, Milan, Pinacoteca di Brera, Jesi Collection: Vitali 1977, no. 26; the relative etching is in Vitali 1957, no. 51.
[11] Vitali 1977, no. 29, formerly in the Frua De Angeli Collection, now in a private collection.
[12] The painting is known to have been in *Hanover* in 1921, no. 55, with the title *Fruchtschale und Flaschen*: it can be identified in an installation photograph of the 'Valori Plastici' exhibitions in Germany in 1921 published in Rivosecchi 1988, p. 142.
[13] This is the painting with the number 27 ('*Fruttiera e bottiglie*') in a contract for the definitive transfer of thirty-three paintings stipulated between Giorgio Morandi and Mario Broglio on November 22, 1928 (Milan, private archive).
[14] Letters from Giorgio Morandi to Ardengo Soffici, dated December 29, 1928 and February 27, 1929, in Cavallo 1989, pp. 78–81.
[15] *Rome* 1939, no. 5, loaned by Alberto Della Ragione.
[16] Vitali 1977, no. 27, today in New York, The Museum of Modern Art.
[17] Ragghianti 1982, p. 226.
[18] Belli, February 3, 1940.
[19] Vitali 1964, nos. 23–4.
[20] Ragghianti 1964, p. 15.
[21] Vitali 1964, p. 19.
[22] Ragghianti 1982, p. 226.
[23] Vitali 1977, nos. 28–9.
[24] Fagiolo dell'Arco 1985, p. 465.
[25] Letter from Giorgio Morandi to Mario Broglio, dated July 5, 1921 (Rome, Galleria Nazionale d'Arte Moderna, Fondo 'Valori Plastici', Inv. p. 99: *Giorgio Morandi 1921–62. Venticinque pezzi: contratti, lettere, cartoline*): an extract of the letter is quoted in Fagiolo dell'Arco 1998[b], p. 54.
[26] Argan 1970, p. 601.
[27] Rylands 1997, p. 84.
[28] Arcangeli 1964, p. 78.
[29] Brandi 1942, pp. 10–11 and Pasquali 1990, p. 26.
[30] Arcangeli 1964, p. 81.
[31] Merion (Pennsylvania), The Barnes Foundation: Vallier 1961, no. 52; Vitali 1964, p. 19.
[32] *Rousseau* 1914, no. 5.
[33] Giuseppe Raimondi (1966, p. 125) observed that in 1918 Morandi had been aware for some years of reproductions published in Apollinaire's review.
[34] *La Glace sans tain* and *La Femme assise*. Both paintings are in New York, The Museum of Modern Art, with the titles *La Fenêtre bleue* (Abby Aldrich Rockefeller Fund) and *Femme au tabouret* (Gift of Florene M. Schoenborn and Samuel A. Marx).
[35] *Les Citrons*, Providence (Rhode Island), Museum of Art, Rhode Island School of Design.
[36] Private collection: Vallier 1961, p. 93. Franco Russoli has stressed the importance of how Soffici (who was capable of making Morandi understand even the most modern painting) interpreted Rousseau: "All he needed was to see how Soffici isolated certain objects from Rousseau, to reach an understanding of Picasso and Braque's drawings of 1905–6, of the sugar coasters which opened like fans, so that he could do his wonderful white fruit bowls:" Russoli 1976, p. 46.
[37] *Violon accroché au mur* (1913), Bern, Kunstmuseum: Daix, Rosselet 1979, no. 573.
[38] Nebbia 1913, p. 431.
[39] *Nature morte aux bananes* (1907), whereabouts unknown: Daix, Rousselet 1979, no. 68.
[40] *Picasso* 1914, no. 4, called *Le banane.*
[41] *Construction au violon* (1913), lost work: Daix, Rousselet 1979, no. 629a.
[42] Fossati 1995, pp. 161–5.
[43] Bacchelli, March 29, 1918.
[44] Franchi 1918[b], p. 118.
[45] Rosazza Ferraris 1991.
[46] Feroldi's letters to Belli are preserved in the Archivio del 900 of the Museo di Arte Moderna e Contemporanea of Trento and Rovereto and will soon be published in their entirety by Giuseppe Appella: the author is grateful to Gabriella Belli and Paola Pettenella for enabling access to this material.
[47] Letter from Pietro Feroldi to Carlo Belli, dated July 1, 1941 (Archivio Mattioli, photostatic copy).
[48] Brandi 1990, p. 151.
[49] Brandi 1939, pp. 246–7; Bartolini, February 12, 1939.
[50] *Almanacco* 1942, p. 63.
[51] Unpublished typescript introduction to the Feroldi Collection catalogue by Carlo Belli, before May 1942, Rovereto, MART, Archivio del 900, Fondo Belli, p. 19.
[52] Archivio Mattioli., *Elenco raccolta Feroldi* (*Appendix I*, document no. 24).
[53] Borgese, June 18, 1966.
[54] Argan 1970, pp. 598–602.
[55] Crispolti 1998, pls. 51, 57.

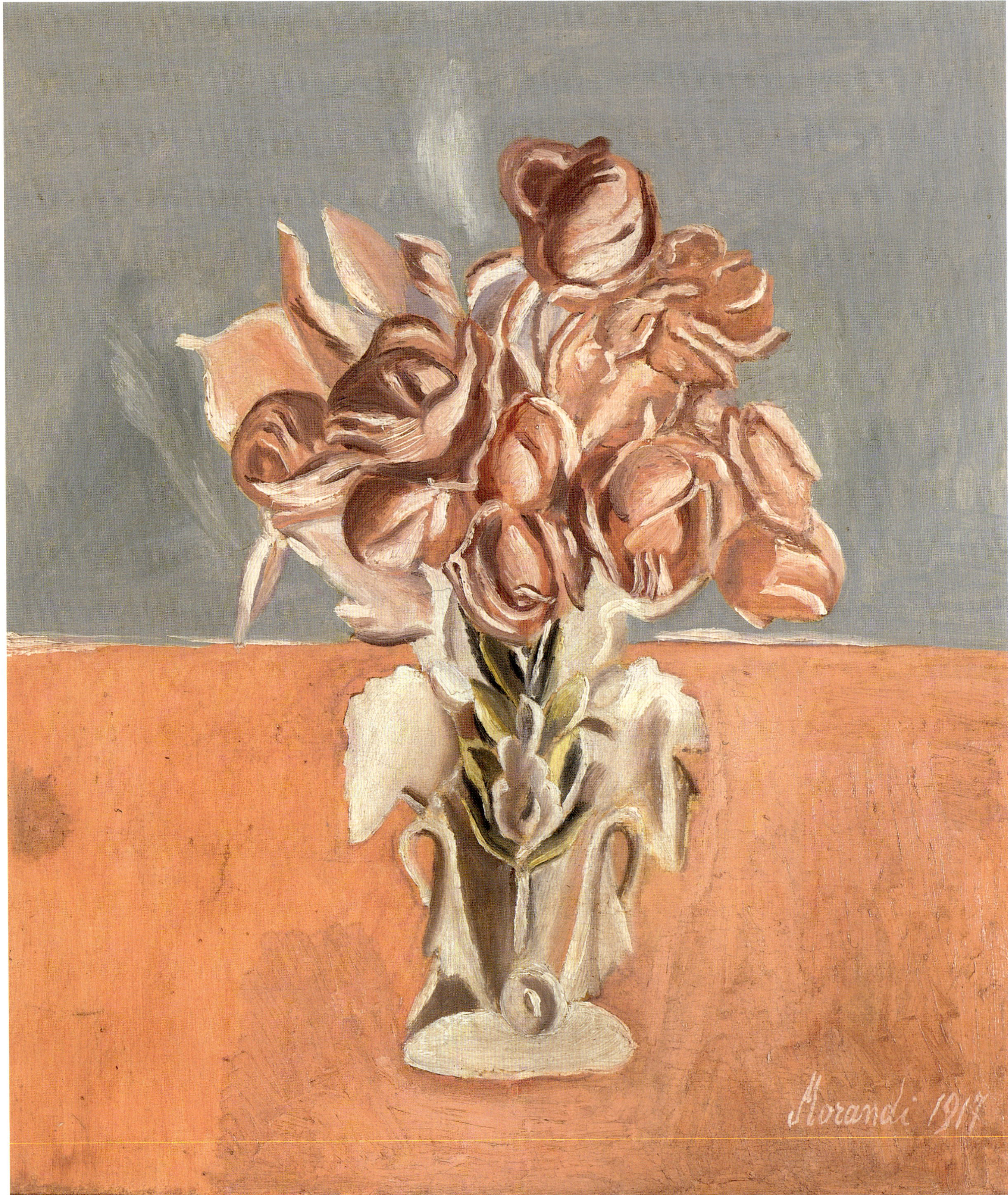
Morandi 1917

18

Giorgio Morandi

Roses (*Flowers*)

Rose (*Fiori*), 1917

Oil on canvas
58 × 50 cm

Inscription: *recto*, signed on lower right: 'Morandi 1917'

Provenance: property of the artist; between February and October 1939: Rino Valdameri, Milan; before November 1940: Carlo Frua De Angeli, Milan; May 1948: Galleria del Milione, Milan; November 1949: Adriano Pallini, Milan; October 1951: Gianni Mattioli, with the mediation of the Galleria del Milione

Exhibitions: Rome 1939, p. 177, no. 6 (*Fiori*); Zurich 1940, not in catalogue (its exhibition documented by a label on the back); Catania–Palermo 1949, no. 30 (*Fiori*); Florence 1953[a], no. 27 (*Rose*, 1918); Turin 1959, p. 43, no. 31 (*Rose*); Washington, DC 1967–Tokyo 1972, no. 79 (Washington, DC–Hamburg), no. 77 (Madrid–Seville), no. 79 (Kyoto–Tokyo); Rome 1973, no. 16; Venice 1989, pp. 366, 645; Madrid 1990–1, p. 254; Rome 1998–9, no. 78; New York 2001, catalogue not printed

Bibliography: Beccaria 1939, pl. IX (*Fiori*); Brandi 1939, pp. 245–6, fig. 3 (*Fiori*); *Domus* 1942, p. 483 (*Tela*); Letter from Marco Valsecchi to Gianni Mattioli, dated September 19, 1951 (Archivio Mattioli); Bacchelli, January 9, 1958 (*Rose*); Carrieri, May 24, 1959; Ballo 1960, p. 25; Vitali 1961, pl. IV; Arcangeli 1964, p. 84 (*Fiori*); Martini 1964, pl. IV; Vitali 1964, p. 19, pl. 26 (*Fiori*); Siblìk 1965, pl. 7; Giuffrè 1970, p. 24; Raimondi 1970, p. 98; Vitali 1977, no. 31 (*Fiori*); Solmi 1978, p. 32, fig. 26; Solmi 1985[a], pp. 35, 37; Pasini 1989, p. 39; Rylands 1997, p. 86; Arrigoni 2000, pp. 287–8

Morandi told Francesco Arcangeli that he painted only two pictures in 1917, the Mattioli *Roses* and a second which was lost at the time that Arcangeli had this conversation (1960–1).[1] The other was probably the *Landscape* of hills dated August 1917 which once belonged to Raimondi and which re-emerged on the occasion of the Morandi exhibition in Rome in 1973.[2] Lamberto Vitali, in his *catalogue raisonné*, assigned several additional works to the year 1917, by backdating known paintings such as the *Self-Portrait* (destroyed) previously published with the date 1919,[3] or *Cactus*, formerly in the Frua De Angeli Collection.[4] As a whole, Morandi's production in the two years between his masterpieces of the summer of 1916 and his first mature paintings in the spirit of *metafisica* of 1918 is still mysterious. He probably destroyed or repainted numerous pictures contemporary with *Roses*. The X-ray of the latter carried out by the Soprintendenza of Venice (fig. 18a) reveals that Morandi re-used a canvas on which he had previously painted a similar subject. In the lower right corner there is an easily recognizable rose with its coronet of leaves, turned through 90°. One of the subsequent paintings of *Flowers*, painted over a period of a few days in June 1918 (fig. 18c),[5] was also significantly repainted. Infra-red reflectography published by Luisa Arrigoni[6] (fig. 18b) has shown that Morandi first painted a bouquet of flowers stylistically similar to the Mattioli painting, in the same vase, but perpendicular with respect to the version that covered it. Thus we know at least one case of a painting plausibly datable to 1917 that was overpainted by another in 1918. The visible version testifies to a new phase of Morandi's work, following the long interruption caused by his serious illness between the winter of 1917 and the early months of 1918.

Roses is notable for its transformation of the relentless precision of draftsmanship and clarity of form of Morandi's work in 1916 into a style of luscious pigment, much worked over and richly impasted. The heavily worked vase (probably of translucent glass with a motif of open Art Nouveau-style leaves, allowing a glimpse of the rose stems inside) and the arabesques of thick paint forming the buds and leaves all seem to infect even the flat, two-part background. The lighter aura which veils the even brushwork of both the flat surface on which the vase stands and the bluish background seems mysteriously to emanate from the bouquet. In a memorable description of the painting, Francesco Arcangeli sensed a delicate thread betraying Morandi's own state of mind, the insinuation of "something heated, agitated […] a yearning for an almost animal vitality, to the limit of the expressionistic" in which "the diaphanous paler nuances are stirred as if by the hint of a repressed *scirocco*."[7] The pink tonalities that dominate Morandi's palette in 1916–19 reflect his scrupulous attention to pigment: Morandi told Carrà, whom he had just met, that he had procured some time before "the last pieces of a beautiful red earth that used to be extracted around Assisi and which has been unavailable for a long time now," and which "mixed with white makes a very beautiful pink, like that in ancient frescoes."[8]

The painting's obsessive frontality and simple two-part background are evident consequences of the 'Modernist' impact on the artist of reproductions of Henri Rousseau's still lifes (see fig. 18f; attention has also been drawn to a painting of *Flowers* by Rousseau illustrated in the monograph published by *La Voce* in 1914:[9] fig. 17f) and those by Picasso when closest to Rousseau. The now lost painting of *Flowers* by Morandi dated '5.6.1918' (fig. 18d), for its leaves spread toward the spectator and for certain details of the way the light falls on the flowers and leaves, may be indebted to Picasso's *Vase of Flowers with Glass and Spoon* from 1908[10] which seems not have been reproduced in any publication accessible to Morandi but which was owned by Kahnweiler until 1913. The richness of the handling of paint in *Roses* suggests comparison with other sources, especially a return to the cherished Impressionist models that permeated Morandi's paintings around 1913–14. In Ambroise Vollard's lavish volume on Cézanne of 1914, which Morandi could have consulted in Florence either at the Libreria della Voce or at the Biblioteca Marucelliana (the copy preserved in the Museo Morandi is, according to Marilena Pasquali, a later gift to the artist), a *Bouquet of Flowers* (fig. 18g) could have inspired the compact, inextricable tangle of flowers animated by crescent-shaped contours.[11] The same motif (this time of foliage and fruit) was repeated in a lithograph by Henri Matisse after Cézanne in a volume of Cézanne's work published the same year by Bernheim-jeune.[12] The memory of three (alas unidentifiable) paintings of *Flowers* by Auguste Renoir that Morandi saw at the 1910 Venice Biennale[13] must have provoked the choice of near monochrome and the device of outlining the flowers with heavy impasto[14] (fig. 18h).

Roses was referred to indirectly in an interesting memoir about a year after its execution: during a visit to Morandi's studio in Via Fondazza early in June 1918 together with Giuseppe Raimondi, Emilio Cecchi noted in his notebook the "reworking of the same still life, after six

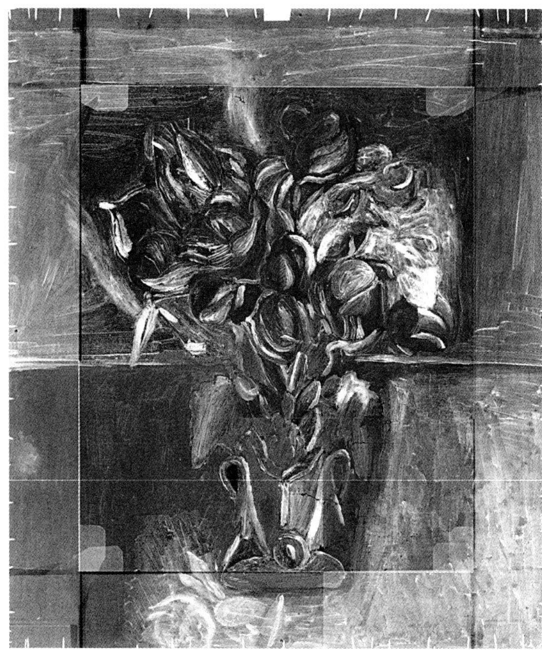

Fig. 18a. *X-ray of cat. no. 18*

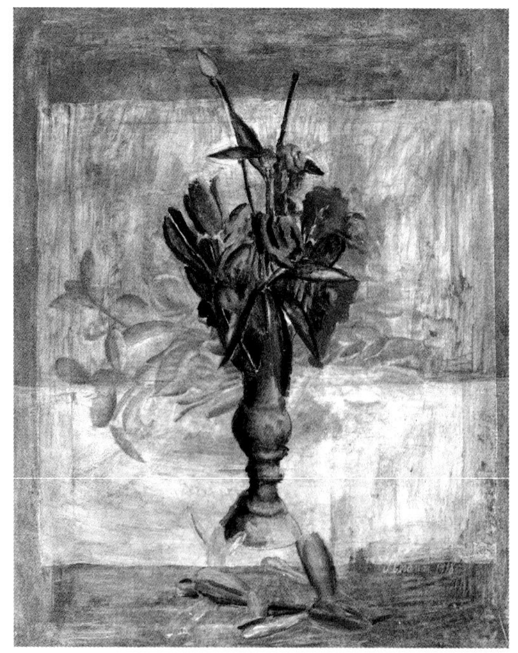

Fig. 18b. *Infra-red reflectography of fig. 18c*

Fig. 18c. *Giorgio Morandi,* Fiori (Flowers)*, oil on canvas, 1918. Milan, Pinacoteca di Brera, Bequest of Lamberto Vitali*

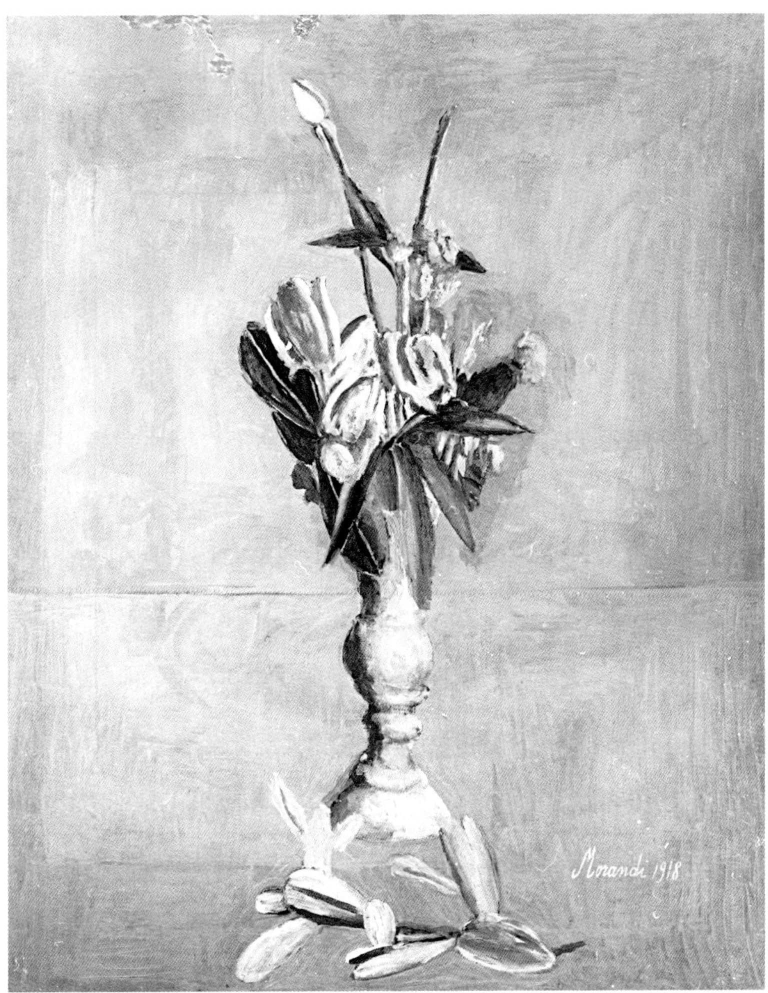

months of attacks of cerebral anemia."[15] Cecchi's visit took place before June 6 (the date of a letter from Cecchi to his wife, a painter, to whom he recounted the episode[16]), at the same time therefore as the execution of the two paintings of *Flowers* dated June 5 and 9, 1918 (figs. 18d and 18b) and soon after the execution of some watercolors with vases of flowers[17] (fig. 18e) one of which is dated May 28, 1918. The "painting [...] dubious or chalky" with bizarre tones of "gum pink, dirty green, blue and white"[18] referred to the *Flowers* of 1918, but Cecchi already perceived these as the point of arrival of a process begun with the Mattioli *Roses*, which Morandi had evidently shown to his visitors on this occasion.

In the last months of 1918 or early in 1919, *Roses* was certainly still hanging in the studio, together with Morandi's early Metaphysical works. Giuseppe Raimondi confirmed this, and related it to the magical transformation of things which the reading of Arthur Rimbaud, prompted by Ardengo Soffici's famous book of 1912, had inspired among Italian painters and poets of the time:

> "[Morandi's paintings] were hanging still on the walls of his room, and seemed to have no expectation that they would be seen by anyone other than the painter who had created them. The painting of Flowers of '17, those in the porcelain vase whose side, turned toward the observer, seems split open to show the entire structure of the flowers: the roses, down to the stems immersed in the vase, as if in a dream, a vision, an apparition of constant poetical yearning. I was haunted by a thought from Rimbaud's *Illuminations*, and around these we exercised our fantasy."[19]

If, as Raimondi claimed, these *Roses* were hanging in Morandi's studio, then they were among those which caught Carrà's enthusiastic attention during a visit in 1919, a visit described by Morandi in a letter to Raimondi in which he mentioned the "older [paintings] of flowers and bottles I had hanging on my walls."[20] However, when it came to selecting a work for exhibition, Morandi chose another painting of the same subject: the "flowers hanging on the wall next to the window"[21] was sent to Rome and exhibited in November 1919, together with a few other works, in a group show without a catalogue held in the shop of the art dealer Giosi in Via Sistina.[22] This was probably the more tightly painted *Flowers* dated June 5, 1918 (fig. 18d), now lost:[23] it passed to Mario Broglio, editor of *Valori Plastici*, as part of his December 26, 1919 contract,[24] and was exhibited in the 'Valori Plastici' show in Germany in 1921.[25] *Flowers* did not remain however, in Broglio's possession after 1928.[26]

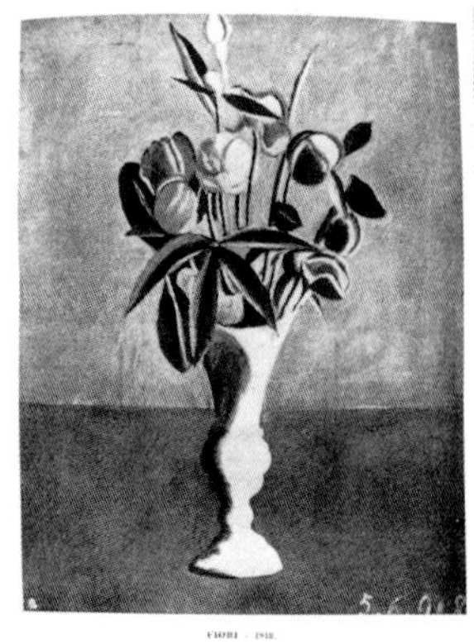

Fig. 18d. *Giorgio Morandi,* Fiori (Flowers)*, 1918, in A. Beccaria,* Giorgio Morandi*, 1939*

Instead, the Mattioli *Roses* stayed in Morandi's studio until 1939, when it was included by Leo Longanesi, together with a few other paintings owned by the artist, in a selection of forty-two works for the first solo exhibition of Morandi's work at the 'III Quadriennale romana'.[27] Descriptions of the room in the numerous reviews systematically avoided any mention of *Roses*, which was difficult to fit into the prevailing modes of interpretation of Morandi's work at the time of the Quadriennale, the one architectonic, the other tonal. However, it was illustrated in both of the two most important items in Morandi's bibliography for 1939: Cesare Brandi's article published in *Le Arti* (which emphasized its "heraldic" character, the flowers "fixed and spread, like a device," and artificial as if "coming from the blotting paper of the herbarium"[28]) and the monograph by Arnaldo Beccaria ("each note supports all the others in a reciprocal equilibrium, in an absolute order"[29]). A reproduction in *Domus* in 1942 included the simple frame in which *Roses* was mounted at the time: this reinforced both the abstract nature of the image (the title *Tela* [*Canvas*] in the caption reiterated this non-iconic aura) and its estranging frontality.

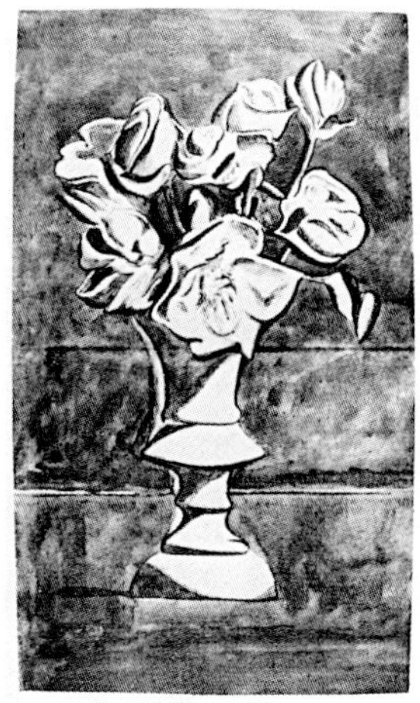

Fig. 18e. *Giorgio Morandi,* Fiori (Flowers)*, watercolor, 1918, in* Valori Plastici*, year III, no. 3, end of 1921–beginning of 1922*

The presence of *Roses* in the much-discussed and highly-praised room of the Rome Quadriennale was the beginning of a complex provenance, that we can reconstruct from archival documentation, from publications, and from labels still glued to the stretcher. In the caption to the illustration in Beccaria's book, published after the closing of the Quadriennale, *Roses* was described as belonging to the collection of Rino Valdameri, the most active buyer of early Morandis in Italy.[30] By November 1940, at the time of the 'Mostra di pittori e scultori italiani contemporanei' at the Kunsthaus Zürich, *Roses* was a part of the Frua De Angeli Collection.[31] On May 31, 1948, the Galleria del Milione took possession of the painting on deposit from Frua De Angeli.[32] The following year, the gallery sent it to a 'Mostra d'Arte Italiana Contemporanea' in Palermo and Catania[33] (organized by the Venice Biennale, which explains the otherwise inexplicable label of the 'XXIV Biennale Internazionale d'Arte di Venezia–1948' glued to the stretcher) and on November 7, 1949 the Galleria sold it to Adriano Pallini for the sum of 495,000 lire.[34] In a letter to Gianni Mattioli dated September 19, 1951, the critic Marco Valsecchi, who had recently visited the Pallini Collection, described the painting among "a group of paintings that you should not let escape you [...], paintings that I consider fundamental, both historically and aesthetically."[35] Spurred by the interest shown by the greatest collector of modern art in Italy, the Galleria del Milione bought *Roses* back from Pallini on October 5, 1951 for 400,000 lire and sold it to Mattioli four days later for 600,000 lire.[36]

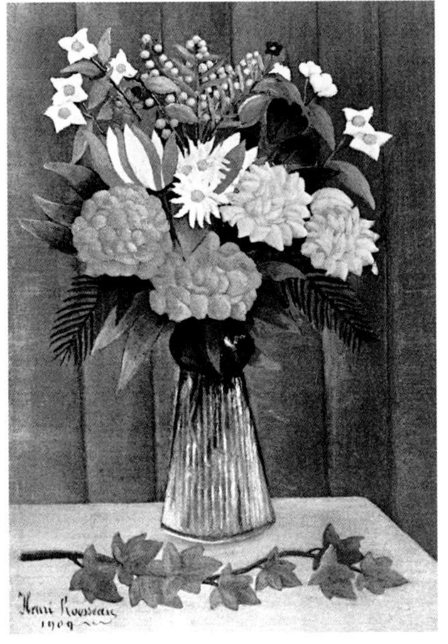

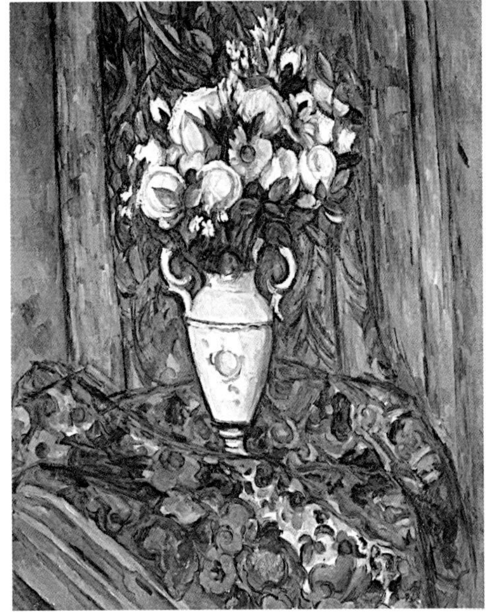

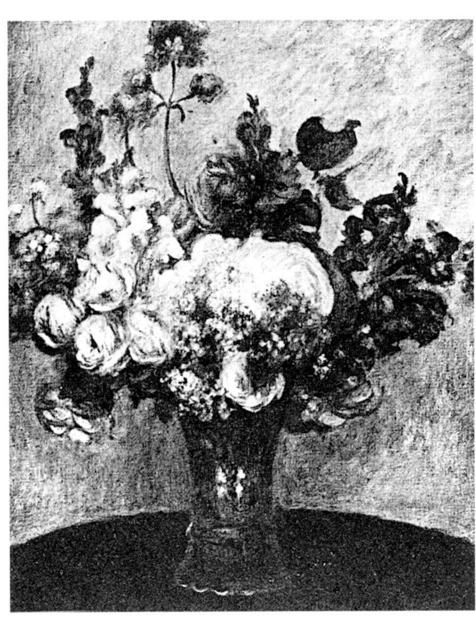

Fig. 18f. *Henri Rousseau,* Fiori (Flowers)*, oil on canvas, 1909. Private collection*

Fig. 18g. *Paul Cézanne,* Bouquet de fleurs (Bouquet of Flowers)*, oil on canvas, c. 1900, Washington, DC, National Gallery of Art, Gift of Eugene and Agnes E. Meyer*

Fig. 18h. *Auguste Renoir,* Bouquet*, oil on canvas, 1898, in* L'Atelier de Renoir*, 1931*

[1] Arcangeli 1964, p. 84.
[2] *Paesaggio*, private collection: *Rome* 1973, no. 17; Vitali 1977, no. 32.
[3] Raimondi 1951, fig. 16b; however, the 1917 date is ostensibly contradicted by a letter from Giorgio Morandi to Giuseppe Raimondi, dated October 4, 1919 (published in Raimondi 1970, p. 201) in which Morandi stated that he had only recently completed the painting.
[4] Milan, private collection: Vitali 1977, no. 34. The 1917 dating is made problematic by the date 'July 1918' on a very similar watercolor reproduced in the penultimate issue of *Valori Plastici*: Pasquali 1991, no. 1918/4.
[5] This is *Flowers*, dated 'June 9, 1918' on the back, in Vitali 1977, no. 41 (Milan, Pinacoteca di Brera, Bequest of Lamberto Vitali); a slightly earlier work is *Flowers* dated '5.6.918' on the back, illustrated in Beccaria 1939, pl. X (whereabouts unknown). See fig. 18d.
[6] Arrigoni 2000, pp. 287–8.
[7] Arcangeli 1964, p. 84.
[8] Letter from Giorgio Morandi to Carlo Carrà, dated October 14, 1919, in *Venice* 1979, p. 153.
[9] Rylands 1997, p. 86 and *Rousseau* 1914, no. 5; this painting is now in Merion (Pennsylvania), Barnes Foundation: Vallier, 1961, no. 52.
[10] *Vase de fleurs et verre avec cuiller*, St Petersburg, Hermitage: Daix, Rosselet 1979, no. 196.
[11] This is *Bouquet de fleurs* from 1900–3, Washington, DC, National Gallery of Art: Vollard 1914, pl. 52, between pp. 160 and 161; Rewald 1996, no. 893.
[12] Bernheim-jeune 1914, pl. 5.
[13] *Venice* 1910, pp. 40–1, nos. 14, 21, 22.
[14] See, for example, a *Bouquet* of 1898 in Bernheim-jeune 1931, vol. I, no. 194, pl. 63.
[15] Cecchi 1976, p. 294.
[16] Cecchi 1990, p. 28.
[17] Pasquali 1991, no. 1918/5–6.
[18] Cecchi 1976, p. 294.
[19] Raimondi 1970, p. 98.
[20] Letter from Giorgio Morandi to Giuseppe Raimondi, dated August 30, 1919, in Raimondi 1970, p. 190.
[21] Letter from Giorgio Morandi to Giuseppe Raimondi, dated September 11, 1919, *ibidem*, p. 193.
[22] Oppo (November 22, 1919) testified to the presence of Morandi's paintings in the exhibition.
[23] Beccaria 1939, pl. X.
[24] The painting could most plausibly be identified with that listed as no. 15, *Natura morta con fiori* (*Still Life with Flowers*) measuring 56 × 60 cm, in Vitali 1983, appendix of 'Contracts', unnumbered page; the installation photograph of the wall with Morandis in one of the 'Valori Plastici' shows in Germany (published in Rivosecchi 1988, p. 142) shows a painting of the same width and a slightly inferior height than the *Still Life*, Vitali 1977, no. 29, which measures 55.5 cm along its base and 65.5 cm in height.
[25] Rivosecchi 1988, p. 142.
[26] In the Broglio-Morandi contract dated November 22, 1928 (Milan, private archive), none of the thirty-three paintings definitively sold to Broglio is compatible, in title or description, with *Flowers* of June 5, 1918; it was therefore among the paintings returned to the artist ("he took back all his works excepting those described above and sold to him [Broglio], which I consigned according to the contract dated December 26, 1919").
[27] *Rome* 1939, p. 177, no. 6; a label glued to the original stretcher documents the painting's presence in the exhibition and indicates Morandi as the owner.
[28] Brandi 1939, pp. 245–6 and fig. 3.
[29] Beccaria 1939, p. 14 and pl. IX.
[30] The label on the back refers to no. 137 in his collection.
[31] The painting's presence in *Zurich* 1940 is evidenced not by the catalogue but by a label on the back of the painting specifying its ownership.
[32] Milan, Galleria del Milione, Register of incoming works, entry no. 5196.
[33] *Catania–Palermo* 1949, no. 30.
[34] Milan, Galleria del Milione, Register of incoming works, entry no. 5196.
[35] Archivio Mattioli, letter from Marco Valsecchi to Gianni Mattioli, dated September 19, 1951 (*Appendix I*, document no. 78).
[36] *Ibidem*: Milan, Galleria del Milione, statement of accounts, dated November 3, 1951; on October 29 the purchase of Morandi no. 5196 was debited to Gianni Mattioli (*Appendix I*, document no. 80).

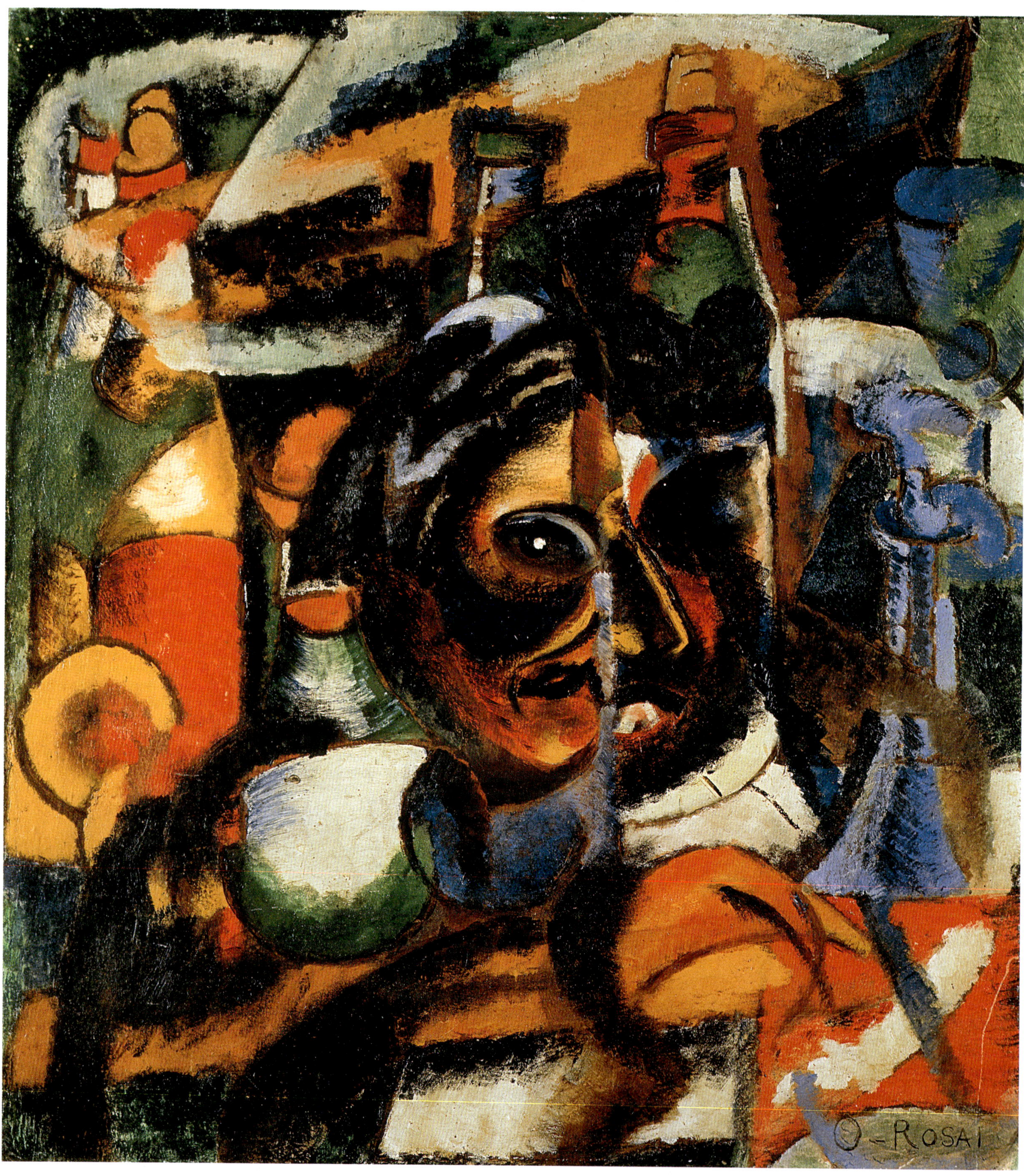
O. ROSAI

19

Ottone Rosai (Florence, 1895 – Ivrea, 1957)

Dynamism Bar San Marco (Café San Marco; Café Interior)

Dinamismo Bar San Marco (Caffè San Marco; Interno di Caffè), 1913

Oil on cardboard
laid on canvas
55 × 51 cm

Inscription: *recto*, signed on lower right: 'O. Rosai'

Provenance: before May 1916: Attilio Vallecchi, Florence; before November 1940: Galleria del Cavallino, Venice; before April 1950: Gianni Mattioli

Exhibitions: Milan–Genoa–Florence 1919, no. 258 (*Dinamismo del Bar S. Marco*); Zurich 1940, not in catalogue (its presence in the exhibition is proven by a label glued to the stretcher); Paris 1950, no. 68, (*Dynamisme dans un bar*, 1912); London 1950, no. 84 (*Dynamism in a Bar*, 1912); Florence 1953[a], no. 40 (1912); São Paulo 1953–4, p. 11, no. 24; Ivrea 1957, no. 2 (late 1913–early 1914); Rome 1959, no. 38 (*Dinamismo di Bar San Marco*); Winterthur 1959, no. 85; Munich 1959–60, no. 84; Florence 1960, no. 5 (1914); Venice 1960, p. 22, no. 108 (1913); Turin–Milan 1961, no. 46; Hamburg 1963–Frankfurt 1964, no. 51; Washington, DC 1967–Tokyo 1972, no. 53 (Washington, DC–Hamburg), no. 52 (Madrid–Seville), no. 53 (Kyoto–Tokyo); Milan 1973–4, no. 250; Venice 1986, p. 202

Bibliography: Letter from Attilio Vallecchi to Ottone Rosai, dated May 14, 1916, in Corti 1995, p. 37 (*Caffè San Marco*); *Taccuino* no. 30 (1916)?, in Rosai 1987, p. 463 (*Interno di Caffè*); Letter from Ottone Rosai to Primo Conti, dated March 25, 1919, in Rosai 1987, p. 98 (*Caffè San Marco*); *Centone* 1919, between pp. 24 and 25, illus. (*Caffè San Marco*); Zervos 1950, p. 213 (*Composition futur-*

Ottone Rosai belonged to the generation of the avant-garde after Boccioni and Soffici. When in 1909, in Florence, debate over Futurism first appeared in the pages of *La Voce*[1] he was a boy of fourteen, but five years later he was already painting in an unmistakable Futurist manner. His youthfulness, his impulsive nature, little inclined to theoretical speculation, and a genuine talent for observing working class realities in Florence, made of Rosai an atypical Futurist. In some of his earliest pictorial efforts he seems to have looked at the willful deformations and vivid colors of German Expressionism. Original paintings by the Expressionists were unknown in Florence at that time, but there is evidence that the movement was being discussed in artistic circles in Italy: reproductions of Jawlensky, Kandinsky, Macke, Marc, Münter, Campendonck and Ernst were available in, for example, the catalogue of the 'Erster Deutscher Herbstalon,' Berlin, of September–October 1913 (at which both the Italian Futurists and Ardengo Soffici also exhibited). Furthermore Theodor Daübler, an intellectual trained in Berlin and well-versed in German as well as French avant-garde art, lived in Florence at the time and frequented the *Lacerba* milieu and Rosai himself.[2] However, Rosai's Futurist period was short-lived: by 1916 his landscapes painted in war zones tended towards a realism with *naïf* accents learned from Henri Rousseau.

In an autobiographical note written in 1937,[3] Rosai described his conversion to Futurism as the immediate consequence of seeing the works exhibited in the 'Lacerba' show in Florence (November 1913–January 1914). The speed of his conversion can be judged by the difference between the emphatically Symbolist mood of pictures he showed at the 'Mostra d'arte propria' in Florence in November 1913,[4] and exercises in the style of Soffici such as the drawing (with a single pasted newspaper clipping) called *Latrina* (*Latrine*, fig. 19b) which was published in the April 1, 1914 issue of *Lacerba*. Nevertheless, evidence for a precise chronology of Rosai's early Futurist works is scarce. On February 10, 1914 he contributed to a show of drawings and sketches at the Libreria Gonnelli;[5] in a letter to Papini dated March 20, Rosai said that he was "daub[ing] on the cardboards in every direction" and was beginning to feel satisfied with the results;[6] on the same day that the April 1 issue of *Lacerba* was published with a reproduction of *Latrina*, Rosai told Aldo Palazzeschi that Filippo Tommaso Marinetti and Theodor Daübler had liked works that he was about to send to Rome (this was certainly a reference to the 'Esposizione Libera Futurista Internazionale' which was to open April 13).[7]

The date of April 1, 1914, together with the titles of his works in the catalogue of the Rome exhibition,[8] provides the first important *terminus ante quem* for Rosai's Futurist phase. By March therefore he had already executed the still life called *Zang-Tumb-Tumb + Bottle + Glass* (most likely the version in oils,[9] fig. 9b, not the now-lost collage with the same title).[10] The inclusion of the cover of Marinetti's book *Zang Tumb Tumb. Adrianopoli ottobre 1912. Parole in libertà*, which was published at the beginning of March 1914 (as stated in the March 1 issue of *Lacerba*), the execution of this painting can be narrowed to within the month. During those weeks Rosai was testing his skills combining lessons learned from Soffici (a book jacket reproduced pictorially in the foreground, as in Soffici's *Typography*;[11] the bold black outlining of the fragmentation of the glass) with the dissonant hues of Boccioni's painterly surfaces, which he was studying and admiring despite growing reservations among the Florentines.[12]

The other titles in the 'Esposizione Libera Futurista Internazionale' (*Dynamism of a Street*, two versions of *Dynamism of Objects*) indicate that *Dynamism Bar San Marco* was not among the works sent to what was Rosai's first opportunity to exhibit outside Florence. However, in a later letter, to the critic Marco Valsecchi in 1957, Rosai recalled not only that *Dynamism Bar San Marco* had been completed by this time but that it was his first Futurist painting.

> "I want to tell you the true story of the Bar San Marco. The picture was painted by me neither in 1911, nor 1912, nor 1914, as has been said and written by some, but toward the end of 1913. Between October and November of that year [actually November 1913–January 1914], the Mostra della Pittura Futurista was held in Florence in the spaces of the Gonnelli bookshop. The Gonnelli bookshop was on via Cavour, not far from the Bar San Marco. Although not among the exhibitors, I visited the show, one could say, every day. Between one visit and another I used to go to the San Marco to drink the coffee, which gave me the opportunity to represent in paint my state of mind at that time. That is how was born — at the end of 1913 — the picture which marked my official entry into the Futurist movement."[13]

Rosai's failure to send a painting so consciously Futurist (the habitués of night haunts as representatives of modern life) to the exhibition in Rome in April should not surprise us. Despite its fashionable theme ('Caffè' was the title of the most combative column in *Lacerba*; the March 15 issue of *Lacerba* published the well-known *Elogio del caffè* by Italo Tavolato, in which the bar is celebrated as the venue *par excellence* of the life of the artist; the exhibition in Rome included *Dynamism of a Café-Chantant* by Depero and *Café* by Sironi), Rosai's painting seems odd and out of place in Florence in early 1914, when avant-garde painting was dominated by Soffici's Cubist-derived formalism. From Soffici's point of view indeed, the representation of the clients' 'state of mind' was outmoded (Carrà had already disparaged this notion as *passé* in remarks which were reported in the press about Boccioni's *States of Mind* triptych at the 'Lacerba' exhibition[14]); the technique of simultaneity was clumsy (the two heads fused along their vertical axes and in the same plane as the glasses and bottles, in a busy arrangement of overlapping sheathes of light and of sensuously painted, richly varied color); the combination of a Carrà-inspired motif (compare *The Galleria in Milan* [cat. no. 6], which was exhibited at the 'Lacerba' show and acquired there by the Florentine Alessandro Magnelli) with Boccioni-style fragmentation (the two straight lines which cut through the head can be compared to those in Boccioni's *Head + Light + Ambiance*, which Rosai saw at the 'Lacerba' show and which was reproduced in a postcard; also the treatment of the blue glass to the right) was weak; the juxtaposition of the halves of the face betrays the work of a pre-1912 Futurist. Someone in Florence, perhaps Soffici himself before leaving for Paris at the end of February, may have ad-

iste, 1912); Parronchi 1952, p. 33 (*Bar San Marco*, 1912); Castelfranco, Valsecchi 1956, pp. 49–50 (*Dinamismo Bar San Marco*, 1912 but with doubts); Letter from Ottone Rosai to Marco Valsecchi, dated April 28, 1957, in Rosai 1987, p. 412; Santini 1957, pp. 50–1 (*Dinamismo Bar San Marco*, 1914); Drudi Gambillo, Fiori 1958–62, vol. I, p. 441 (*Dinamismo di un bar*), vol. II, pp. 366, 369, no. 11 (*Dinamismo del Bar San Marco*); Recupero 1959, p. 59; Valsecchi 1959, p. 27 (1913); Marchiori 1960, no. 30 (1914); Santini 1960, pp. 17, 20, 24, 26, 132, 139 (1914); Carrieri 1961, no. 144 (1913–14); Bellonzi 1963, p. 127; Calvesi 1967, p. 182 (1913–14); Cavallo 1973, pp. 38–9, 166 (1913–14); Pratesi, Uzzani 1991, pp. 98–9; Cavallo 1995[a], pp. 35–7 (1913–14); Cavallo 1995[b], p. 269; Lemaire 1995, p. 68; Rylands 1997, p. 88

Fig. 19a. *Ottone Rosai,* Bar San Marco, *collage on board, 1914. Santomato (Pistoia), Gori Collection*

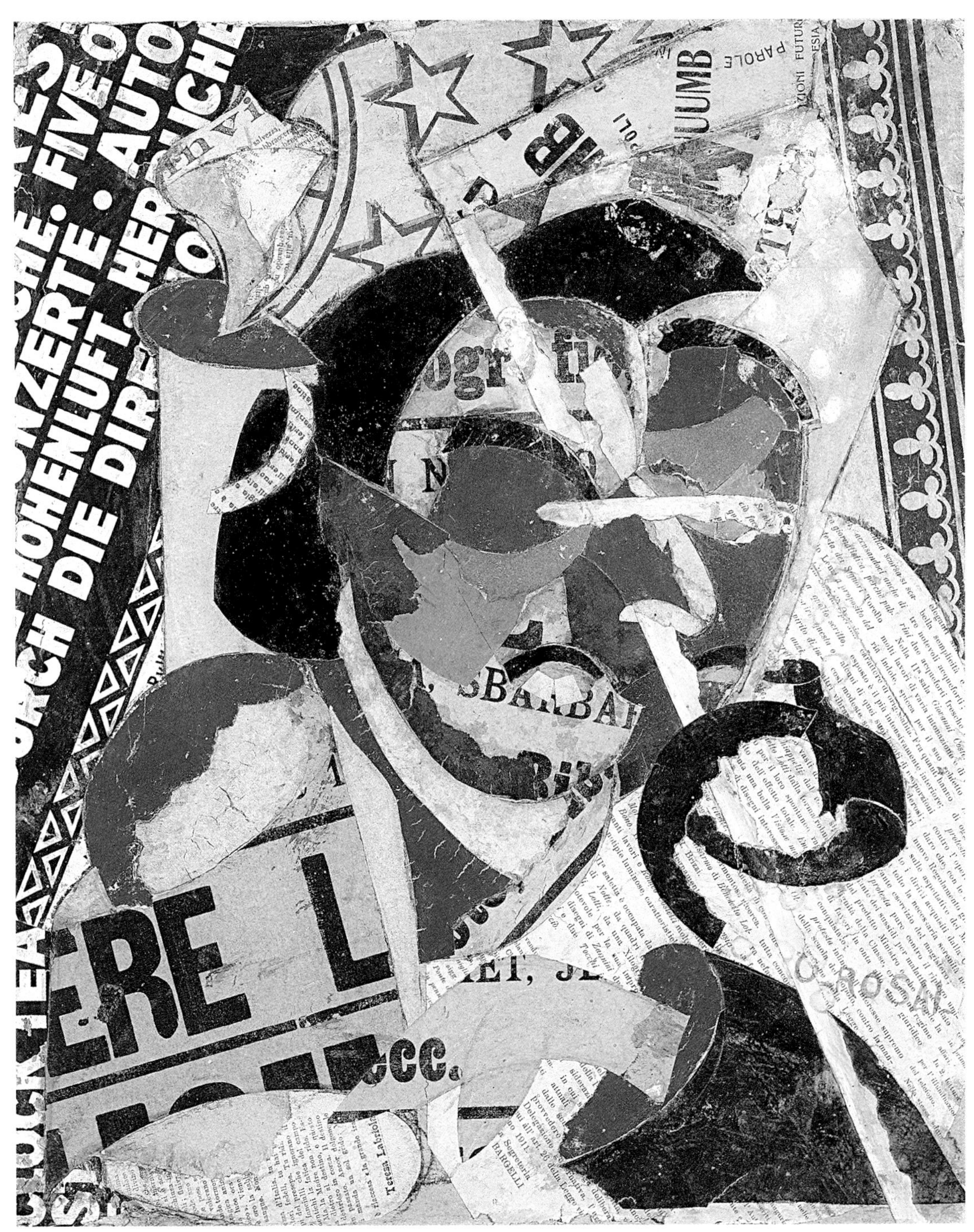

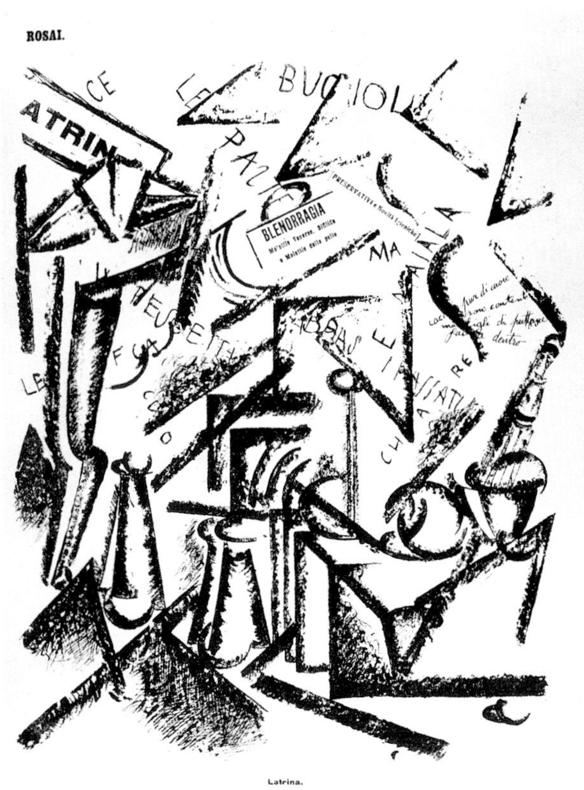

Fig. 19b. *Ottone Rosai,* Latrina (Latrine)*, drawing and collage, in* Lacerba, *April 1, 1914*

vised Rosai to focus his attention on less ambitious subjects, free of the risk of lapsing into illustration.

There are two further impediments to a confident dating of *Dynamism Bar San Marco* in the final days of 1913, in accordance with Rosai's recollection. The first stems from a comparison between it and a *Self-Portrait* in ink on paper which, though dated 1913,[15] incorporates a faithful replication of the masthead of *L'Italia Futurista*, a Florentine periodical first published in June 1916. The head of this *Self-Portrait* and the two halves of the head joined in the center of the Mattioli painting clearly have much in common stylistically: for example the pervasive crescent-shaped lines, the eye inserted in a similar almond-shaped cavity in which the precise circle of the iris is drawn (a formula used in no other surviving paintings by Rosai) and the deep shading overall. But it is also possible that Rosai, at the Front in 1916–17, isolated from his Florentine friends and eager for bold expressionist touches (to the point of coming close to Carrà's primitivism in a drawing dated 1916[16]) harked back, in the frontal portrayal of a face, to a style he had tried and proven as expressive for its raw lack of elegance.

The second problem is the sequential relationship, much discussed but not resolved,[17] between the Mattioli painting and a collage of the same subject, *Bar San Marco*[18] (fig. 19a). The collage was certainly executed after March 1, 1914, the publication date of Marinetti's *Zang Tumb Tumb*, since Rosai glued to this that part of the cover of Marinetti's book that he did not use in the above-mentioned *Zang-Tumb-Tumb + Bottle + Glass* (fig. 19c). The two collages (*Zang-Tumb-Tumb + Bottle + Glass* and *Bar San Marco*) are clearly of the same date, not only because they share the same materials (aside from the cover of *Zang Tumb Tumb*, the yellow paper printed with stars outlined in black), but also because of their stylistic similarities: the depicted objects float on a ground of clippings spatially unrelated to the foreground, and some profiles and outlines are rendered by curvilinear pieces of black paper. The date of the *Bar San Marco* collage, the only one in the series to have survived, cannot therefore be advanced by relying on the *terminus post quem* provided by the newspaper clipping. This has recently been identified as the review published in *Il Popolo Pistoiese* of an exhibition of drawings by the school of Celestino Celestini in Florence and Pistoia in June–July 1913, in which Rosai himself participated.[19] The present writer has been unable instead to identify the source of a fragment of text signed by Teresa Labriola,[20] a militant feminist active in Italy between the first and second decades of the century and a university professor of the philosophy of law.

Some observations on whether the painting or the collage came first can be made by comparing the two works. The collage is clearly more cryptic than the painting. With the painting as his point of departure, Rosai's process seems to have been that of eliminating elements (the three bottles vanish in the collage, replaced by a single blue bottle neck on the left; the glass on the right is gone; there is only one head, traversed by a single diagonal line of fragmentation). The image is tighter: the viewpoint is closer; the mood of the ambiance, which in the painting is generated by sensations of color and chiaroscuro, is transmitted by newspaper cuttings (reactionary discussions of art in the review as well as current literary debate; Marinetti's words in freedom from *Zang Tumb Tumb*; the announcement in different languages for a 5 p.m. tea-time concert; the derided feminist themes in the article by Labriola). Objects which in the painting are rendered in the Cubist analytical technique (the blue goblet) appear as flat areas of color in the collage. It would seem difficult to date the collage before Soffici's return from Paris in early April 1914, when he brought with him impressions of his visits to Picasso's studio and began to paste colored papers and newspaper clippings onto his works (as indicated by his letters to Carrà[21] and by the clippings from the Parisian press of March 14 which appear

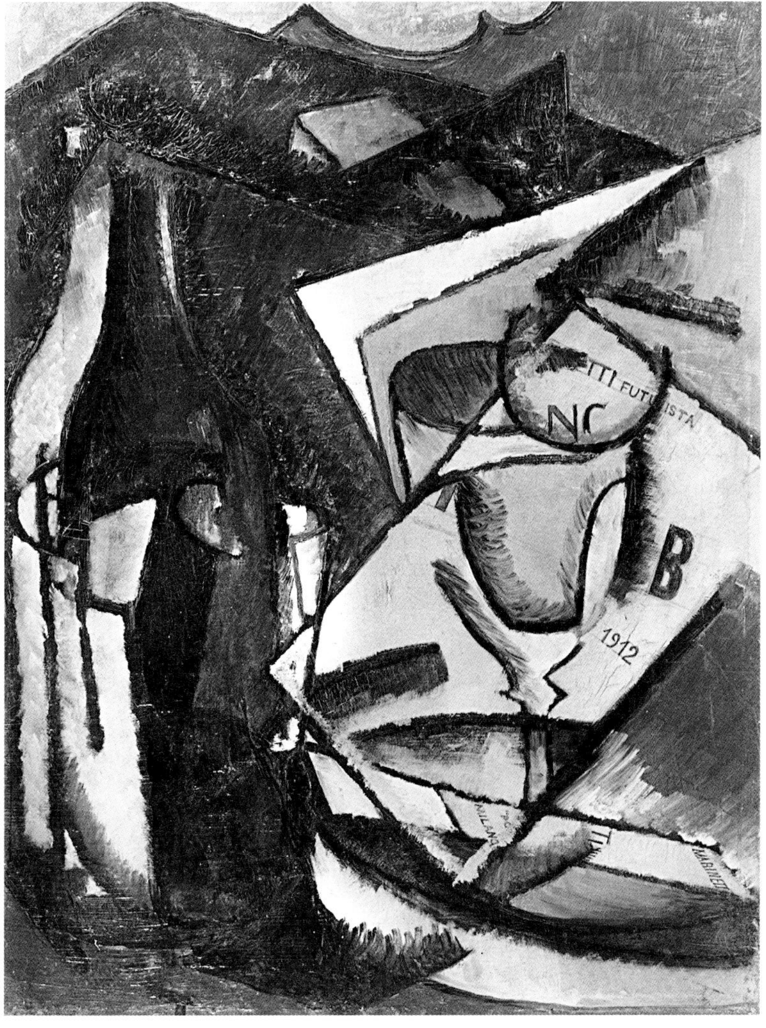

Fig. 19c. *Ottone Rosai,* Zang-Tumb-Tumb + bottiglia + bicchiere *(*Zang-Tumb-Tumb + Bottle + Glass*), oil on canvas, 1914. Milan, Civiche raccolte d'arte, Jucker Collection*

on some of Soffici's collages[22]). Only at this point, on the basis of Soffici's example and advice, would Rosai have attempted to replicate in collage earlier painted works. Together with the still life with the jacket of *Zang Tumb Tumb* that was exhibited in Rome, Rosai may then have essayed a reworking of *Dynamism Bar San Marco*, but with new and important compositional variants.

The painting was not exhibited in 1914 and did not remain long with Rosai, who was compelled by need to sell his works even at extremely modest prices (such as amazed Guillaume Apollinaire, from Paris, who was evidently told of this by Soffici).[23] A letter dated May 14, 1916 from Attilio Vallecchi to Rosai ("See if you have a few hours of time to let me too have a pictorial record of the war. I promise to pay you at least as much as that for the Café San Marco")[24] testifies that the painting had already entered the collection of the publisher of *Lacerba*, one of the most active buyers of avant-garde painting in Florence. A record of 'Quadri venduti' ('Pictures Sold') in a 1916 notebook of Rosai's, published in 1987, informs us of the selling price of the painting, then called *Interno di caffè* (*Café Interior*), the ridiculously low sum of 2 lire,[25] and removes any possible confusion with the collage of the same name (listed as *Testa + Ambiente* [*Head + Ambiance*]) which was sold instead for 10 lire to Soffici, its first owner.[26]

During the Great War years Rosai shifted towards a more narrative and popular style of painting, and for this reason *Dynamism Bar San Marco* would have grown in importance in the artist's estimation. Accordingly he had it illustrated in the second issue of the Florentine periodical *Il Centone*, already post-Futurist in content,[27] edited by Primo Conti and Corrado Pavolini and at the same time chose it to be shown in the first important postwar Futurist exhibition (the 'Grande Esposizione Nazionale Futurista') together with four paintings of war,[28] perhaps all lent from the Vallecchi Collection. Marinetti's silence about Rosai in his review of the show[29] and Rosai's simultaneous switch toward purism (Soffici advised him to remove from circulation the "ugly earlier paintings [...], mediocre or bad things that are then displeasing to see and they confuse and damage one's reputation"[30]) explain the painting's absence from early shows of Rosai's work and its omission from books on him (a still life structured in a very different way, *The Carpenter's Bench*,[31] was favored instead). The painting was only to reappear in the 'Mostra di pittori e scultori italiani contemporanei' in Zurich in November–December 1940. The exhibition label on the stretcher gives the owner as the Galleria del Cavallino, Venice, owned by Carlo Cardazzo, a dealer and collector actively buying and promoting Rosai's work from the late 1930s.[32] By April 1950, when it was illustrated in the issue of *Cahiers d'Art* dedicated to twentieth-century Italian art, *Dynamism Bar San Marco* already belonged to the Mattioli collection. It was sent at once to survey exhibitions of modern Italian art in Paris and London in 1950. Thanks to a dating of 1912 (1912 is inscribed on the back of the cardboard support, perhaps by Rosai himself, but now hidden by the relining[33]) its critical fortune peaked in the 1950s, when evidence for a Futurist tradition independent of the prevailing Cubism was particularly admired: Parronchi stressed its "turbid, whirling color"[34] and Ragghianti its characteristically Italian deformations ("the broken grimaces, torn asunder from the head, coarsely touching, share less with the young ladies of Avignon — elegant by comparison — than with certain attenuating tensions of Cimabue, in which the images are forced, without rupturing the Hellenic tradition of temporal unity, to the paroxysm of sensibility").[35]

[1] Soffici, April 1, 1909.
[2] Washton Long 1993, pp. 521–34.
[3] Rosai 1937, p. I.
[4] Three of these are reproduced in Parronchi 1959, pls. 24–5.
[5] *Florence* 1914, nos. 185–90.
[6] Letter from Ottone Rosai to Giovanni Papini, dated March 20, 1914, in Rosai 1987, p. 19.
[7] Letter from Ottone Rosai to Aldo Palazzeschi, dated April 1, 1914, *ibidem*.
[8] These were: 1. *Zang-Tumb-Tumb + bottiglia + bicchiere*; 2. *Dinamismo stradale* (*Dynamism of a Street*); 3. *Dinamismo di oggetti* (*Dynamism of Objects*); 4. another *Dinamismo di oggetti*: Rome 1914[c], p. 23.
[9] *Zang-Tumb-Tumb + bottiglia + bicchiere*, Milan, Civiche raccolte d'arte, Jucker Collection: Santini 1960, no. 212.
[10] *Ibidem*, no. 356.
[11] *Tipografia*, Switzerland, private collection: Raimondi, Cavallo 1967, no. 204.
[12] Undated letter from Ottone Rosai to Ardengo Soffici (but June 1914), in Rosai 1987, p. 20.
[13] Letter from Ottone Rosai to Marco Valsecchi, dated April 28, 1957, in Rosai 1987, p. 412.
[14] Tarchiani, December 7, 1913.
[15] Turin, Forchino Collection: Ragghianti 1956, no. 3; the 1913 date is accepted by Crispolti, Marzuoli 2000, p. 43.
[16] Franchi 1942, pl. II.
[17] The painting was placed before the collage in Santini 1957, p. 52, without explanation; it was dated after the collage and other paintings of 1914 in Recupero 1959, pp. 58–9; the sequence was considered problematic by Santini 1960, p. 139 and by Cavallo 1995[a], p. 37; the matter is not addressed by Mattarella 2000, p. 146.
[18] Santomato (Pistoia), Gori Collection: Santini 1960, no. 54.
[19] Cavallo 1995[a], pp. 31–2.
[20] The text is not included in the otherwise extensive bibliography of Teresa Labriola's work, in Taricone 1994, pp. 213–19.
[21] The first certain evidence is in a letter from Ardengo Soffici to Carlo Carrà (undated, but April 20, 1914) in Carrà, Soffici 1983, pp. 51–2.
[22] The 1913 date usually ascribed to the still life called *Piccola velocità* (*Small Speed*: Milan, Civiche raccolte d'arte, Jucker Collection: Raimondi, Cavallo 1967, no. 175), most recently in *Hanover* 2001, no. 322, should be moved to the following year, given Soffici's use of a cutting from issue number 11042 of *Le Matin* dated March 1914, reporting the imminent duel between the Finance Minister, Joseph Caillaux, and the chief editor of *Le Figaro*, Gaston Calmette.
[23] Apollinaire, May 29, 1914.
[24] Letter from Attilio Vallecchi to Ottone Rosai, dated May 14, 1916, in Corti 1995, p. 37.
[25] *Taccuino* no. 30 (1916), in Rosai 1987, p. 463.
[26] As reconstructed in Cavallo 1995[b], p. 269.
[27] Carpi 1984, p. 58.
[28] These were: 255: *Vallesina di Cadore*; 256: *Guerra + rancio*; 257: *Dinamismo di strada campestre*; 259: *Sensazione di peso + materia*, in *Milan–Genoa–Florence* 1919, p. 18.
[29] Marinetti, March 21, 1919.
[30] Letter from Ardengo Soffici to Ottone Rosai, dated April 22, 1920, in Corti 1996, p. 31.
[31] *Il banco del falegname*: Volta 1931, unnumbered plate.
[32] As evidenced by the drawings published by the gallery in Gatto, 1939.
[33] The inscription was noted by Santini 1957, p. 50.
[34] Parronchi 1952, p. 33.
[35] Ragghianti 1953, pp. 22–3.

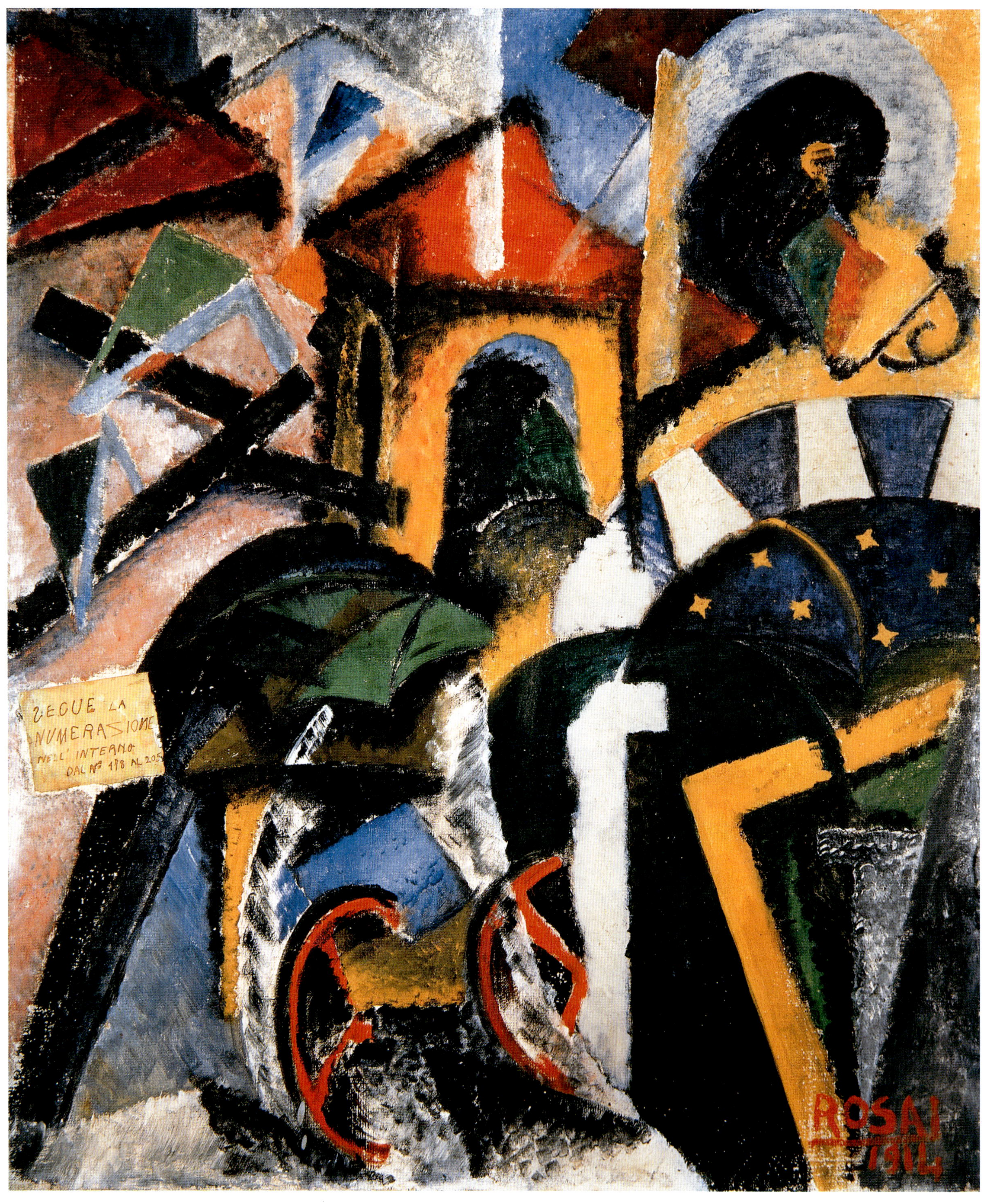
SEGUE LA
NUMERASIONE
NELL' INTERNO
DAL N° 198 AL 205
ROSAI
1914

20

Ottone Rosai

Fragmentation of a Street (*Street Dynamism*?; *Streets Simultaneity*?; *Dynamism of a Street*)

Scomposizione di una strada (*Dinamismo stradale*?; *Simultaneità stradali*?; *Dinamismo di una strada*), 1914

Oil on canvas with collage insert
63 × 53 cm

Inscriptions: *recto*, signed lower right: "ROSAI 1914"; *verso*, inscribed on the canvas: "A GIOVANNI / PAPINI offre / O. ROSAI / [PITTORE?]" (fig. 20a)

Provenance: 1914?: Giovanni Papini?; property of the artist; 1957: Francesca Rosai, Florence; April 1960: Gianni Mattioli

Exhibitions: Rome 1914[c]?, p. 23, no. 2 (*Dinamismo stradale*); Florence 1948, not in catalogue (but exhibition label on the stretcher); Florence 1953[b], no. 2 (*Scomposizione di una strada*, 1914); Rome 1955–6, p. 56, no. 29; Munich 1957, p. 59, no. 177; Rome 1959, no. 36; Winterthur 1959, no. 83; Munich 1959–60, no. 83; Florence 1960, no. 7; Venice 1960, p. 22, no. 109; Turin–Milan 1961, no. 47; Hamburg 1963–Frankfurt 1964, no. 53; Washington, DC 1967–Tokyo 1972, no. 54 (Washington, DC–Hamburg), no. 53 (Madrid–Seville), no. 54 (Kyoto–Tokyo); Milan 1973–4, no. 257; Venice 1986, p. 203

Bibliography: Letter from Fernando Agnoletti to Ottone Rosai, dated May 11, 1915, in Corti 1996, p. 37 (?) (*Simultaneità stradali*); Masciotta 1940, p. 14 and pl. I (*Scomposizione di strada*, 1914); Franchi 1946, p. 14 (*Dinamismo di una strada*); Parronchi 1952, p. 36 (*Scomposizione di strada*); Castelfranco, Valsecchi 1956, p. 55; Drudi Gambillo, Fiori 1958–62, vol. I, p. 441 (*Scomposizione di strada*), vol. II, p. 367, no. 15; Santini 1960, p. 140, no. 55; Carrieri 1961, p. 102; Ballo 1964[a], p. 210; Calvesi 1967, p. 183;

Despite Rosai's fragmentation of this townscape by means of Cubo-Futurist devices, such as the elision of volumes and the dismantling of solids (whose contours generate a dense overlapping of angled forms), several features of the street to which the title of the painting refers can easily be recognized. In the center foreground there is the back of a horse-drawn carriage with two red wheels and a cabin upholstered in dark green fabric. The white arc stippled with black on which the carriage is placed most probably indicates a curve in the street, a motif which was to dominate some of Rosai's most famous paintings after 1919. In the upper center stands a kiosk with round arches and a red tiled roof. The lower right foreground is occupied by a loggia: the two-color rusticated arch fronts a groin vault painted dark blue and speckled with stars. Above it Rosai depicted a street lamp, shaped like an upside-down pyramid, partially silhouetted against the arch of a doorway. The left side of the scene is more abstracted. The black outline of a door faces onto the street along which the carriage passes. A plaque tells us that inside the courtyard "segue la numerazione nell'interno dal n. 173 al 205" ("the numbers continue inside from no. 173 to 205"): the plaque is represented by a piece of paper pasted to the canvas with a clumsy inscription in pen, in which, to emphasize the ambiance of a poor working class neighborhood, the S and the Z are written backwards. The red triangle of a roof in the upper left corner is the only other identifiable element.

The open-sided kiosk, the striped arch, the starred vault and the mustard yellow stucco identify the location beyond any doubt as Florence. If, as this writer believes, the arch is a reference to one of the tombs along the neo-Gothic façade of the cemetery of the monks of Santa Maria Novella, Rosai has set the scene in one of the Florentine neighborhoods of which he was particularly fond, given its simultaneous presence of popular life (artisans' shops, bordellos), illustrious shrines of art and the cosmopolitan modernity of the nearby train station. Rosai, in his Futurist phase, had a strong desire always to depict the distinctive features of places, a tendency which was difficult and to some degree provocative when the subject was as blatantly *passatista* as the historic center of Florence. Even in paintings in which the impulse to distort was strongest, Rosai was reluctant to abandon a vein of realistic observation (in this case for example the gilded rib of the vault, or the calculated perspective of the kiosk in the center). Compared to *Dynamism Bar San Marco* (cat. no. 19), Rosai attained here a greater degree of fusion between these two tendencies, that of representing things and that of breaking them apart: here he isolated and emphasized curvilinear motifs (the arches, the cross-vault, the wheels and the cabin of the fiacre, the arm of the street lamp) and inserted them into a texture of angular and broken forms, extending this visual pattern across the entire canvas.

Apollonio 1970, no. 99; Cavallo 1973, pp. 39, 166, no. 14; Cavallo 1995[a], pp. 35–6; Lemaire 1995, p. 68; Rylands 1997, p. 90

In a fine passage in a long manuscript memoir of the 1930s, still-unpublished, Rosai recounted what his adherence to Futurism meant for his development as a painter, in terms of the strengthening and mastery of his innate expressive faculties:

> "Futurism for me was a direct and desperate test of all my artistic potential. In those syntheses through which each mark had to have the flavor of the most deeply ingrained personality I was able to measure the exact weight of all my most secret and inner strengths. And in the painting's outcome all of my intellectual and moral potential. I was not at all captivated by the theoretical part, but concerned instead with what I had seen and was seeing around me and I sought only to be in possession of the possibilities that my blood was able to render, and to project onto a canvas that which was the lowest or the noblest that I may have absorbed."[1]

Of the paintings Rosai executed in 1914 in the studio he rented in Viale Principe Umberto in Florence, the one most directly related to *Fragmentation of a Street* was a *Landscape* (fig. 20b) which was still in Carlo Cardazzo's collection as recently as 1973:[2] the black and white photograph[3] shows a similar deformation of the natural image by the use of diagonal lines (accented in black) and a similar insertion of arches and curves. The perspectival distortions in *Landscape* are more marked (the small house near the bottom seems to be viewed from a great height, while the houses in the central part of the painting are seen frontally and from close to) and there is a greater rigidity in the contours, especially on the left: it is as if Rosai's intentions, compared to those in the Mattioli painting, had shifted, in a way characteristic of a swiftly maturing artistic talent.

Yet the lack of fixed points in the chronology of Rosai's production in 1914 prevents us from establishing with certainty which was painted first. The Mattioli painting, by unanimous agreement among critics, seems to be the more successfully and freely resolved of the two: they have drawn attention to the gaiety of its palette (the fragmentation of form does not go beyond "the borders of things and their joyous and robust dissolution in color"[4]), to its independence from the Futurist matrix ("it is the painting in which the principles of Futurism are perhaps most compromised, most misunderstood"[5]) and to its narrative freedom (there "is an exaltation of its fairy-tale aspect and the hermetic taste of the composition, in a resolutely constructive tone"[6]).

Despite the fact that Rosai's special interest in landscapes reached a pitch in May–June 1914, when we know he produced three of them,[7] *Fragmentation of a Street* may have been painted earlier. One of the paintings by Rosai at the 'Esposizione Libera Futurista Internazionale' in Rome (which opened on April 13, 1914) was titled *Dinamismo stradale* (*Dynamism of a Street*) and it is possible that this was the Mattioli painting.[8] Certain elements are compatible with a dating prior to April 1, when Rosai's four paintings were sent to the Rome exhibition[9]: firstly, the dedication on the back to Giovanni Papini (with whom Rosai already enjoyed a relationship of mutual esteem and from whom he had received a much appreciated note in March from Paris[10]); secondly, the vivid and *naïf* palette (the lively yellows and reds and the black borders feathered at the edges are shared with those in *Zang-Tumb-Tumb + Bottle + Drinking Glass* [fig. 19c] which was almost certainly exhibited in the same 'Esposizione Libera' in Rome[11]); finally the collage insert with writing (a small advertising clipping is glued in similar fashion to the drawing *Latrine* [fig. 19b], published in the April 1 issue of *Lacerba*). Moreover, in March 1914

Fig. 20a. *The back of cat. no. 20*

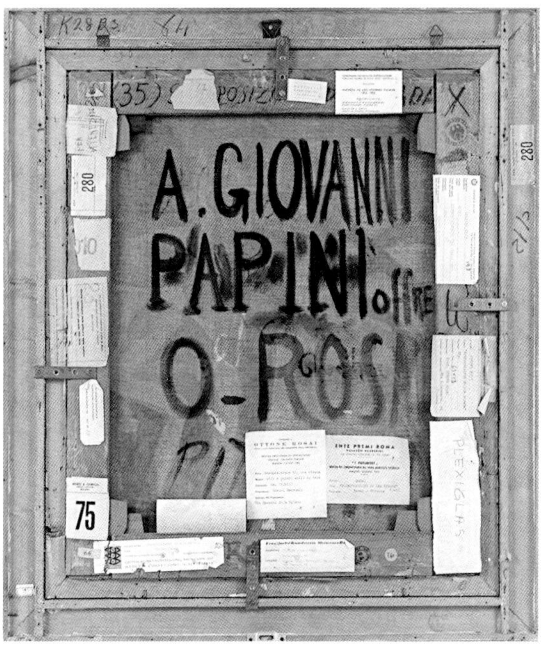

what can be considered Rosai's principal source for *Fragmentation of a Street* was already accessible. The January 15 issue of *Lacerba* published a full-page illustration of an ink drawing by Soffici, *Simultaneity Woman Carriage Street* (fig. 20d) which Rosai studied attentively and from which he appropriated several features: not just the general compositional scheme and idea (a 'simultaneous' townscape, fragmented and scanned by an oblique grid), but also some technical devices (the wide black marks, their edges blurred, with which Rosai outlined his forms) and some specific details such as the round-headed arch on the right, the carriage wheel and the street signs. Soffici added a work with the same title to the group of paintings that were sent from the November 1913–January 1914 'Lacerba' show to the February–March 1914 Futurist show at the Galleria Sprovieri in Rome.[12] It is probable that, early in 1914, Soffici wanted to try his hand at an urban subject, with people and things in motion, in a way radically different from Giacomo Balla's paintings with racing automobiles, which he had seen (and severely criticized) at the 'Lacerba' show.[13] Soffici would then have drawn the youthful and enthusiastic Rosai into doing the same thing, suggesting that he do a painting characterized by solid plastic forms and a strongly topographical quality (the working-class streets of Florence), in contrast to Balla's flat and decorative abstractions. Rosai's dependence on Soffici's moral authority was, in 1914, total: in a letter in June he declared himself "grateful for a thousand counsels, lessons and encouragements."[14] Even after the sensational breach in their relationship caused by the publication of Rosai's polemical pamphlet against Soffici in 1931,[15] he continued to acknowledge his debt and his special bond to the older artist "as a painter and a Florentine."[16]

As in the cases of *Dynamism Bar San Marco* and *Zang-Tumb-Tumb + Bottle + Glass*, *Fragmentation of a Street* had a collage pendant (whereabouts unknown) with an identical subject and title[17] (fig. 20c). It is less easy in this case however to establish the temporal priority of the painting or the collage. In the latter Rosai used a clipping from the December 13 issue of the Florentine daily *Il Nuovo Giornale* (reporting the finding of Leonardo's *Mona Lisa* in Florence after its theft two years earlier from the Louvre[18]). This precedes by some months the collage's supposed date of execution (in accordance with Soffici's practice of using papers yellowed by oxidation[19]). Rosai also included a clipping from an advertisement for the Edizioni di Lacerba, but this is not possible to date as it was never used in the regular last-page publicity in the bimonthly listings (probably a printer's proof similar to that glued to the upper left of the still life,

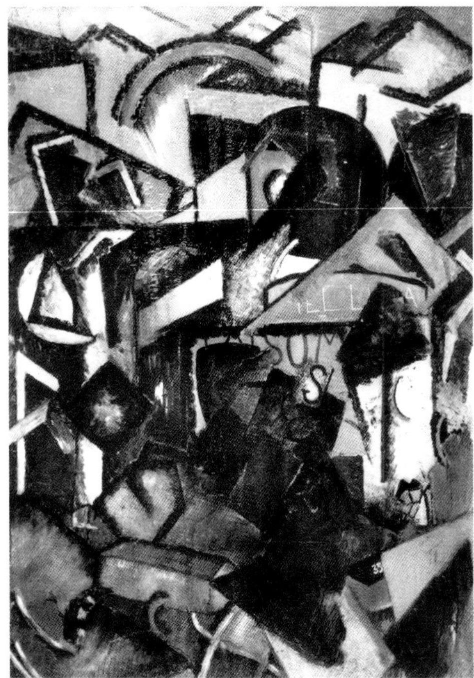

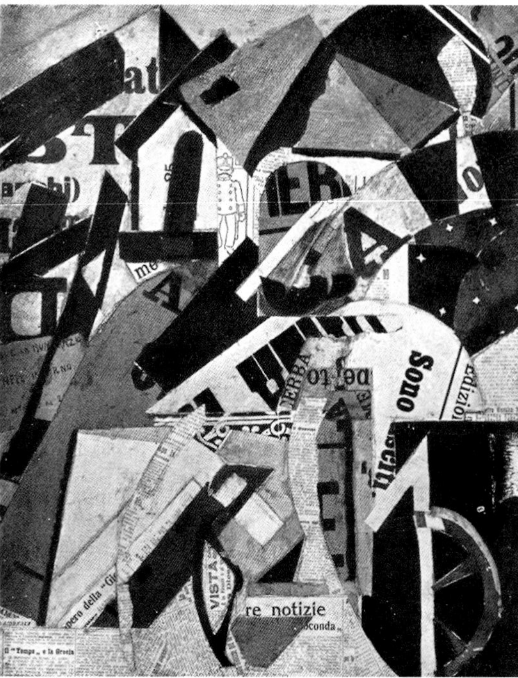

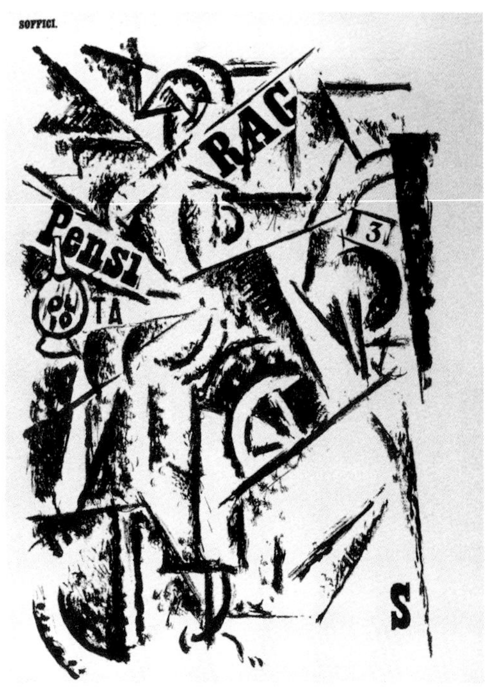

Fig. 20b. *Ottone Rosai,* Landscape, *oil on canvas, 1914. Private collection*

Fig. 20c. *Ottone Rosai,* Scomposizione di una strada *(*Fragmentation of a Street*), collage, 1914, in* Paragone, *1952*

Fig. 20d. *Ardengo Soffici,* Simultaneità donna carretto strada *(*Simultaneity Woman Carriage Street*), in* Lacerba, *January 15, 1914*

The Carpenter's Bench[20]). The daily newspaper articles cut and pasted onto the collage augment the sense of spatial complexity, but its basic design matches precisely that of the oil painting. However, to date the collage after Soffici's return from Paris (April 9, 1914), when he brought back news of Picasso's collages, is insufficient to establish that it was made after the Mattioli painting: as we have seen, the identification of the latter with the *Dinamismo stradale* (*Dynamism of a Street*) exhibited at the 'Esposizione Libera Futurista Internazionale' in April 1914 is not certain, and the painting lacks therefore a definite *terminus ante quem*.

This uncertainty is not the only impediment to reconstructing the early history of *Fragmentation of a Street*. Its entry into Giovanni Papini's collection, as implied by the dedication on the back (Rosai "offers" it to Papini: fig. 20a), is not documented: it is omitted from a 'Bilancio dei quadri venduti' ('Accounting of Paintings Sold'; this included gifts) recorded by Rosai in a 1916 notebook[21] nor does it correspond to either of the two works in Papini's collection requested by Rosai for loan to his retrospective at the Galleria del Milione in November 1930.[22] A weak hint of a putative early provenance occurs in a letter to Rosai dated April 25, 1915 from Fernando Agnoletti, a Florentine writer and collector, in which Agnoletti stated that he was keeping available a painting with the title *Simultaneità stradali* for the mooted (but never realized) second 'Lacerba' show.[23] However, it has to be remembered that Rosai's Futurist paintings were considerably more numerous than those few extant today (between forty and fifty according to the artist's later autobiographical writings[24]) and that identical or similar titles can correspond to different paintings. Given the urban and Florentine setting of *Fragmentation*, its identification with a *Dynamism of a Country Road* (as has been suggested[25]), which was sent to the 'Grande Esposizione Nazionale Futurista' in 1919,[26] is problematic. Despite the fact that the first certain evidence about the painting's history is dated twenty years later, by which time it belonged to Rosai himself,[27] an earlier passage through the Agnoletti Collection need not be ruled out: in 1940 Rosai told Emilio Jesi in a letter that he had "bought back three old things of mine from some idiots"[28] and that he was unwilling to sell them to the Milanese collector ("I have no longer any things that remind me of myself at that age and of that impassioned faith which I may never find again, and for this reason I like to have a few of them. You have some nice ones, so allow me to keep these"[29]) who, in those same years, was scouring the market for important Futurist paintings and who had acquired Rosai's still life, *The Carpenter's Bench*.[30]

Michelangelo Masciotta, author of the first critical reading of *Fragmentation of a Street* in 1940, confined it to an intermediate phase of Rosai's art ("Such a painting, even if it succeeds in conveying a flavor of the consents and contrasts, of the convergences and divergences, is still matter, all matter, outside of any spiritual emotion"[31]). But critical attitudes to Futurism changed radically in the space of a few years. *Fragmentation* became important to Rosai in the postwar era when Futurism returned to vogue and he wished to affirm his image as an avant-gardist, who was not bound only to the stereotype of illustrator of the microcosm of Florence, with its overtones of the Fascist 'Strapaese' movement. *Fragmentation of a Street* was sent to a show held at the Circolo degli Artisti at the Casa di Dante, Florence, in 1948; it was made available to the historical shows on Futurism during the 1950s and to Rosai's 1953 retrospective organized by Carlo Ludovico Ragghianti at the Strozzina, Florence. Only after Rosai's death was it sold, on April 8, 1960, by Francesca Rosai, the artist's widow, to Gianni Mattioli.[32]

[1] Florence, Gabinetto Scientifico Letterario G. Vieusseux, Archivio A. Bonsanti, *Carte Rosai*, Cas. C, insert 8, sheet 119.
[2] *Paesaggio*: Cavallo 1973, p. 166, no. 14.
[3] Marchiori 1960, fig. 31.
[4] Parronchi 1952, p. 36.
[5] Santini 1960, p. 140.
[6] Cavallo 1973, p. 39.
[7] Letter from Ottone Rosai to Ardengo Soffici, undated (but June 1914), in Rosai 1987, p. 20.
[8] *Rome* 1914[c], p. 29, no. 2.
[9] Letter from Ottone Rosai to Aldo Palazzeschi, dated April 1, 1914, in Rosai 1987, p. 19.
[10] See Rosai's reply to Giovanni Papini, dated March 20, 1914, in *ibidem*.
[11] Milan, Civiche raccolte d'arte, Jucker Collection: *Rome* 1914[c], p. 29, no. 1.
[12] *Rome* 1914[a], p. 28, no. 6.
[13] Balla's *Plasticità luci × velocità* (similar to but not identical with Lista 1982, no. 329) is reproduced in *Florence* 1913–14, unnumbered plate; Soffici's negative opinion of Balla is expressed in Soffici 1955, p. 324.
[14] Letter from Ottone Rosai to Ardengo Soffici, undated (but June 1914), in Rosai 1987, p. 20.
[15] Rosai 1931.
[16] Rosai, 1937, I.
[17] Parronchi 1952, pl. 19b.
[18] This event unleashed a widespread infatuation with Leonardo da Vinci that was ferociously derided in the circles of *La Voce* and *Lacerba*: Longhi, January 13, 1914 and 'Caffè,' January 15, 1914.
[19] As in Raimondi, Cavallo 1967, no. 206 (*Natura morta*, 1914, with a clipping from a December 1911 issue of *La Nazione*).
[20] *Il banco del falegname*, Milan, Pinacoteca di Brera, Jesi Collection: Santini 1960, no. 56.
[21] *Taccuino* no. 30 (1916), in Rosai 1987, p. 463.
[22] *Rosai* 1930, unnumbered plates.
[23] Letter from Fernando Agnoletti to Ottone Rosai, dated May 11, 1915, cited by the curator in Corti 1996, p. 37.
[24] Florence, Gabinetto Scientifico Letterario G. Vieusseux, *Carte Rosai*, Cas. C, insert 8, sheet 119: letter from Ottone Rosai to Bruno Gilardi, dated April 28, 1956, in Rosai 1987, p. 401.
[25] Santini 1960, p. 140, no. 55.
[26] *Dinamismo di strada campestre*: *Milan–Genoa–Florence* 1919, no. 257.
[27] Masciotta 1940, pl. I (the painting is among the few illustrated of which the ownership was unspecified).
[28] Letter from Ottone Rosai to Emilio Jesi, dated June 27, 1940, in Rosai 1987, p. 262.
[29] *Ibidem*.
[30] In Volta 1931, unnumbered plate, the painting was published without any indication of ownership (thus in the artist's own collection); in Parronchi 1940, pl. II, it already belonged to the della Lanterna Collection of Genoa, a pseudonym for the Jesi Collection during the years when racial laws were in effect.
[31] Masciotta 1940, p. 14.
[32] Archivio Mattioli, file for the work.

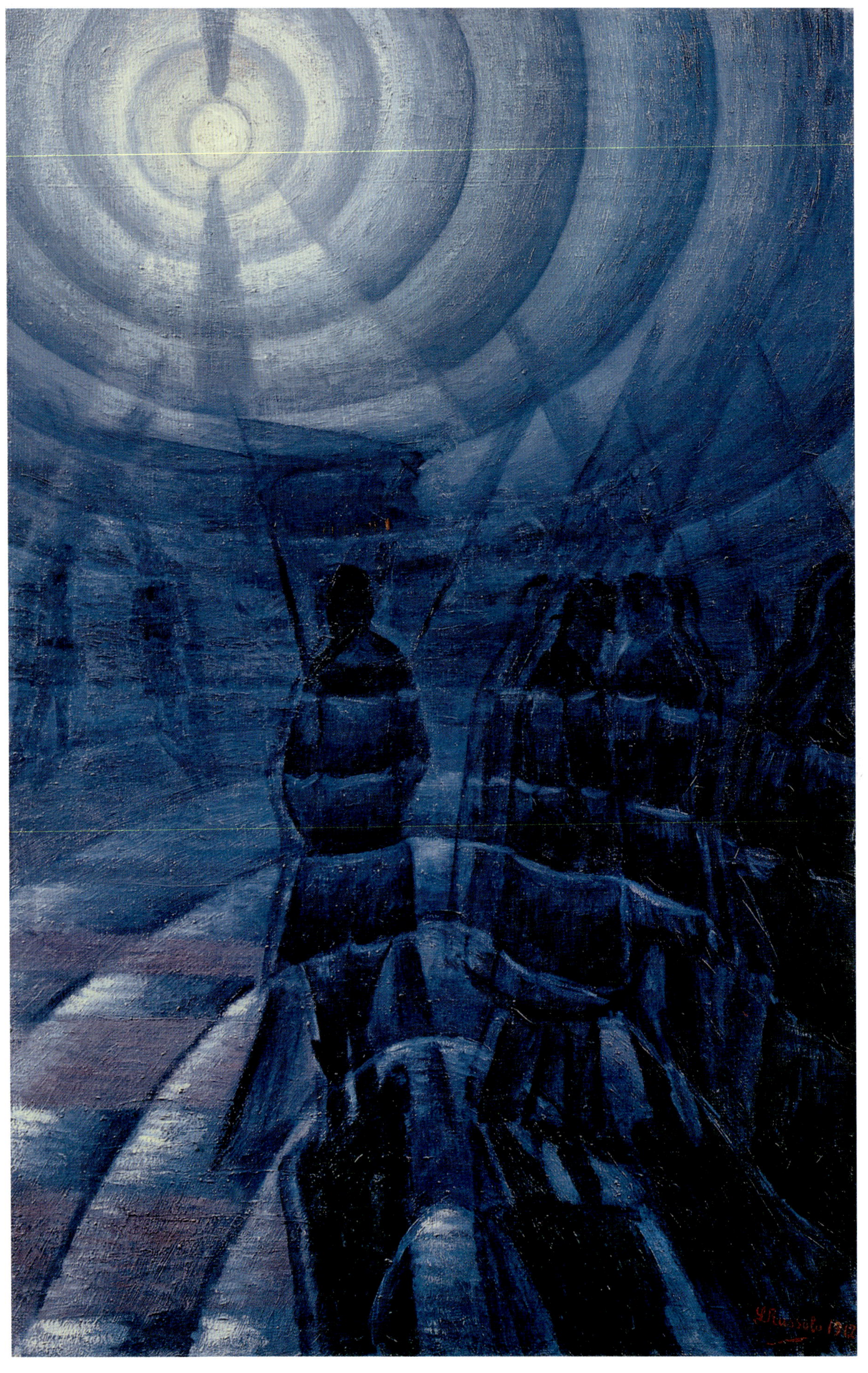

21

Luigi Russolo (Portogruaro, Veneto, 1885 – Cerro di Laveno, Varese, 1947)

Solidity of Fog (*The Fog*; *Fog over Milan*)

Solidità della nebbia (*La nebbia*; *Nebbia su Milano*), 1912

Oil on canvas
100 × 65 cm

Inscriptions: *recto*, signed lower right: 'L. Russolo 1912'; *verso*, written on the top of the stretcher: 'Russolo Solidità della nebbia', partially covered by labels

Provenance: property of the artist; ?: Margherita Sarfatti, Milan, later Rome; May 1950: Gianni Mattioli, with the mediation of Galleria del Milione

Exhibitions: Rome 1913, p. 25, no. 2 (*Solidità della nebbia*); Rotterdam 1913, no. 23; Naples 1914, p. 27, no. 1; Rome 1948, p. 32, no. 1 (*La nebbia*); New York 1949, p. 134 (*The Fog*); Venice 1950, p. 62, no. 27; Zurich 1950, no. 68; Florence 1953[a], no. 7; São Paulo 1953–4, p. 12, no. 26; New York 1954, no. 27; Barcelona–Madrid 1955, no. 12; Marseilles 1955, catalogue not traced (the presence of the work in the exhibition is documented in Archivio Mattioli, file for the work); Munich 1957, no. 56; Rome 1959, no. 20; Winterthur 1959, no. 88; Munich 1959–60, no. 86; Venice 1960, p. 22, no. 113; Paris 1960–1, no. 626; New York 1961–Los Angeles 1962, no. 92; Cologne 1962, no. g/171; Washington, DC 1967–Tokyo 1972, no. 31 (Washington, DC–Hamburg), no. 30 (Madrid–Seville), no. 31 (Kyoto–Tokyo); Milan 1970, no. 147; Newcastle upon Tyne 1972–London 1973, no. 98; Milan 1973–4, no. 243; Düsseldorf 1974, no. 131; Venice 1986, p. 207; Frankfurt 1995, no. 352; Milan 1995–6, p. 162

Bibliography: Prampolini 1913, pp. 105–6; Boccioni, January 23–30, 1916 (*La Nebbia*); Barr 1949, p. 12, pl. 17; Zervos 1950,

As a co-signer of the two Futurist painting manifestos in 1910, and as the inventor of the art of noises, Luigi Russolo has been the subject of some monographs over the past thirty years[1] and has inevitably been included in all the principle books and retrospective exhibitions on Futurism.[2] Scholars have tended to focus primarily on his experiments with music, and as a consequence his pictorial career is still poorly defined. No one yet has systematically investigated his passion for Symbolism and the (mainly French) literary influences on his training, while his paintings of 1912–13 still await definition in an international context. Little is known, for instance, about how much Russolo knew of contemporary painting in France and Germany and how it relates to his own work. This major painting of 1912 is no exception. At a 1995 exhibition in Frankfurt on the relationship of the avant-garde to the occult it was assigned special importance, as confirmed by its illustration on the catalogue cover and on the exhibition poster. But the catalogue essay offered only a generic connection to occult themes, limited to the interpretation of the concentric rings which radiate from the sky and reverberate on the earth as waves from a field of energy.[3]

When Russolo exhibited this painting for the first time in the foyer of the Teatro Costanzi in Rome, in February 1913,[4] his musical studies of noises were still unknown to the public. The music of Balilla Pratella, which in January Marinetti had hoped would be played by that "formidable pianist"[5] Russolo, was performed instead by the Teatro Costanzi orchestra conducted by Pratella himself, in two concerts on February 20 and March 9, 1913. Furthermore Russolo seems to have made no mention of the imminent turn of events in the texts that were declaimed during the two turbulent evenings.[6] Only with the publication on March 11, 1913 of the manifesto *L'arte dei rumori* (*The Art of Noises*) was Russolo linked to the new experimental music. In May his name appeared, on the official list of Futurist roles in the introduction to the catalogue of the Rotterdam exhibition, as the only representative of the *Art des Bruits*, even before his first *intonarumori* (noise intoners) performance in Modena, the evening of June 2. Russolo's reputation as a musician began only in the late spring. Twice he would defend his ideas in *Lacerba*[7] and, in November, the catalogue of the 'Lacerba' show in Florence explained that the presence of only two paintings by Russolo was owing to his overwhelming involvement with the "preparation of the imminent concerts of *intonarumori*."[8] Russolo's defection in favor of music took place therefore while *Solidity of Fog* was on display in Rome. He must initially have continued to experiment simultaneously in both arts, musical and pictorial, if it is true that for the subsequent show in Rotterdam he was the only artist able to add two paintings (*Me Movement* and *Plastic Resumé of the Movements of Woman*[9]) which were evidently not ready in time for exhibition in February at the Costanzi show in Rome. In fact Russolo's pictorial imagination had many points in common with that of his music. The pattern of concentric rings in the sky and ground of *The Solidity of Fog* resembles the emanation of sound waves in the background of *Music* (fig. 21a), a 1911 painting repainted in 1912 and exhibited as *Musical Dynamism* at the Costanzi show. Moreover, in a passage of *L'arte dei rumori*, he spoke of sounds capable of suggesting "the ample, solemn and white breathing of a city at night"[10] with visual accents (the breadth of the horizon, the white gleams) similar to those in the Mattioli painting.

The date 1912 next to the artist's signature should reasonably place the painting's execution in the months following the first Parisian Futurist exhibition at the Galerie Bernheim-jeune in February 1912. It is unlikely that a painting of such scale and ambition would not have been exhibited at the crucial show in Paris had it been ready in time.[11] Russolo was the Futurist painter who in 1912 opposed the Cubist language of fragmented form with the most determined resistance. Even after his direct contact with the Parisian scene in February he adopted independent pictorial solutions, with sinuous linear rhythms and a shrill and strident palette. His desire to represent symbolically "the universal dynamism that pervades both man and his world"[12] led him to resort to Art Nouveau-style arabesques[13] and to attempt a highly personal visual synthesis based on "spiral-shaped and concentric elements."[14] The lack of published letters that would enable us to track his progress, the relative scarcity of his Futurist paintings, and the sporadic nature of critical comment on them, all combine to make it difficult to measure the degree to which Russolo consciously pursued alternatives to the dominant Cubist style.

Of the four paintings exhibited in February 1913 at the Costanzi show in Rome, *Solidity of Fog* would seem to have been the most illustrational, with a style and subject matter characteristic still of early Futurism. More mature abstract motifs (his favorite interaction of curved or spiral lines and luminous angles) structure the now lost *Force Lines of Lightning* or *The Houses Continue into the Sky*,[15] while the Mattioli painting seems to have more in common with Futurist paintings of the winter of 1911–12.

The men wrapped in their dark overcoats who filter the color of the surrounding atmosphere are reminiscent of the figures on the left in Umberto Boccioni's *The Forces of a Street*[16] which Boccioni was working on in the months leading up to its exhibition in Paris in February 1912 (fig. 21b). The shared desire to portray a public space occupied by indeterminate human beings and the common theme of nocturnal color pierced by thickly impasted effects of stabbing light indicate how close the two painters were (and how Russolo acquiesced in 1912 to formulae essayed by Boccioni a few months earlier). Even the abstract proposition of the title itself, *Solidity*, can be compared to the titles of Boccioni's paintings in 1912 (*Elasticity*, *Materia*) which were intended to draw attention to the plastic element in the objects represented.

In 1968 Marianne Martin made an important contribution to our understanding of the painting.[17] She indicated a connection between the easily recognizable subject (men strolling at night on a street in a city immersed in fog pierced by the glow of shining electric arc lamps) and a poem by Jules Romains, *Rien ne cesse d'être intérieur* (from the 1908 anthology *La Vie unanime*). Romains's description of a foggy street, with shining lamplight and passers-by who, though strangers to one another, feel a mysterious communion, is reproduced almost literally in this painting:

p. 92 (*Brouillard sur Milan*, 1912); Apollonio 1950, p. 60; Garretto 1952, p. 43; *Russolo* 1957, unnumbered page; Zanovello Russolo 1958, p. 28, pl. 10; Drudi Gambillo, Fiori 1958–62, vol. I, p. 442, vol. II, pp. 302, 306, no. 12; Calvesi 1959, p. 32; Marchiori 1960, pp. 78–9; Carrieri 1961, pl. 70; Taylor 1961, pp. 80, 82; Bellonzi 1963, p. 70; Ballo 1964[b], pp. 67, 92; Haftmann 1965, p. 123; Pierre 1966, pp. 31, 194; Calvesi 1967, p. 93; Martin 1968, pp. 148–50; Apollonio 1970, fig. 59; Argan 1970, p. 379; Finocchi 1970, p. 147; Rye 1972, p. 60; Kozloff 1973, pp. 207–8; Lista 1975, p. 14; Maffina 1978, p. 332; Crispolti 1980[b], pp. 125, 127; Ballo 1983, p. 24; Roche-Pézard 1983, pp. 207, 483, no. 145; Crispolti 1986, p. 123; Coen 1989, p. 52; Anzani, Pirovano 1992, pp. 121, 130; Lista 1995, p. 439; Rylands 1997, p. 92; Tagliapietra 2000, pp. 52–4

Fig. 21a. *Luigi Russolo,*
La Musica *(*Music*),*
oil on canvas, 1911–12.
London, Estorick Collection

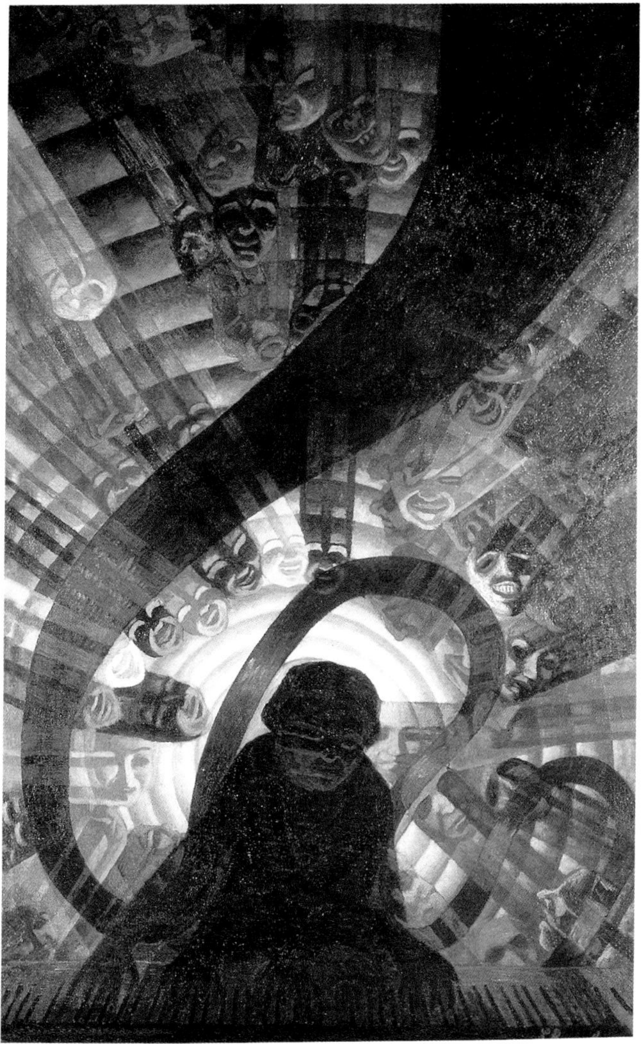

> "The street is more intimate because of the fog.
> Around the gas lamps all the air is alight;
> Each thing partakes of the rays;
> [...]
> The beings have fused their forms and their lives
> And souls have tenderly submitted.
> I have never been less free than this evening
> Nor less lonely."[18]

Romains's Unanimism has rightly been considered one of the essential sources of Marinetti's ideology,[19] and its impact on Futurist painters is evident. Apollinaire, in one of two reviews of the February 1912 Futurist show, recognized explicit references to Unanimist vocabulary in the titles of the paintings.[20] Russolo, who read French easily and felt particularly close to the recent decadent culture of Paris, seemed to find pleasure in the morose atmosphere, the surreal lights, and the spectral inhabitants of the cities described by Romains. The same themes recur in other passages of *La Vie unanime* as well as in Romains's *Premier livre des Prières* (1909): the perambulations of passers-by are less physical than they are emanations of a rhythm, their thoughts connected by invisible waves; white rays filtered through the fog are refracted at their feet; lights are often phosphorescent and movements are only half seen among the vapors.

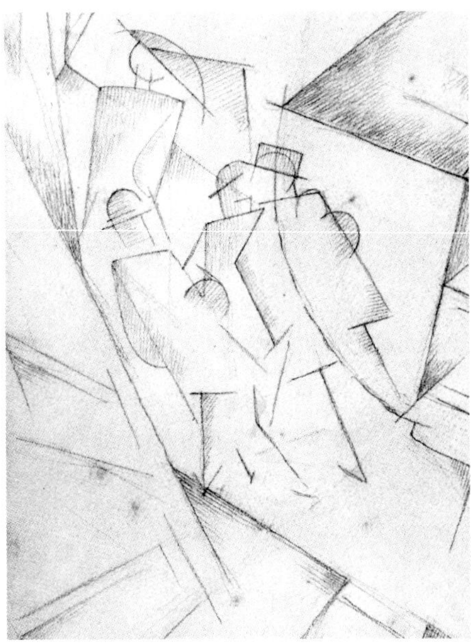

Fig. 21b. *Umberto Boccioni, Study for* Le forze di una strada, *pencil on paper, 1911, detail. Milan, Civico gabinetto dei disegni*

Other explanations than the poetry of Romains have been put forward for this difficult and mysterious painting. Philip Rylands[21] recently linked it to the imagery conjured by specific passages of the *Technical Manifesto of Futurist Painting* (itself indebted to Unanimism), and in particular to the declaration that "space no longer exists: the street pavement, soaked by rain beneath the glare of electric lamps, becomes immensely deep and gapes to the very center of the earth."[22] As already mentioned, the concentric expansion of the surfaces of the ground and the sky has suggested comparison with the propagation of electromagnetic waves, a subject central to the debate over science and the occult in the early twentieth century.[23] Moreover, a painter trained in the first decade would certainly have retained in his visual memory the plates illustrating Newton's rings and the patterns of the refraction of color that illustrated Gaetano Previati's *Principi scientifici del divisionismo*[24] (fig. 21c), one of the best known books on painting theory and among the most admired by the Milan Futurists.

The explanation of the painting as a nocturnal scene immersed in fog derives in the first place from the title Russolo gave it at its first exhibition, and later from other sporadic evidence. Enrico Prampolini, a young artist who in 1913 began to frequent the Futurists, spoke of the work in the following terms in a review of the Costanzi show published in *L'Artista Moderno* of Turin:

> "Another characteristic of Futurist painting is to impart life and solidity to the ambiance, to air, for example; thus, in Russolo's picture *Solidity of Fog*, one sees people walking through the fog who are therefore cut by it in concentric circles and solidified rays."[25]

Three years later, when beginning an art column for *Gli Avvenimenti*, Umberto Boccioni remembered the painting and hinted at a specific urban setting:

> "The thick fog which settled on Milan a few nights ago reminded me of the picture *The Fog* by Luigi Russolo and led me unintentionally to his studio."[26]

In 1950 the authors of the *Cahiers d'Art* insert on Italian art of the Novecento had no doubts about the setting, and the painting appeared with the title *Brouillard sur Milan*.[27]

However, this interpretation of the subject leaves room for a few remaining doubts. Unlike Boccioni's *The Forces of a Street*, no buildings are visible in this 'city', and the figures ap-

Fig. 21c. *Pattern of refraction of color through a thin plate of double refracting crystal, in G. Previati,* Principi scientifici del divisionismo, *1906*

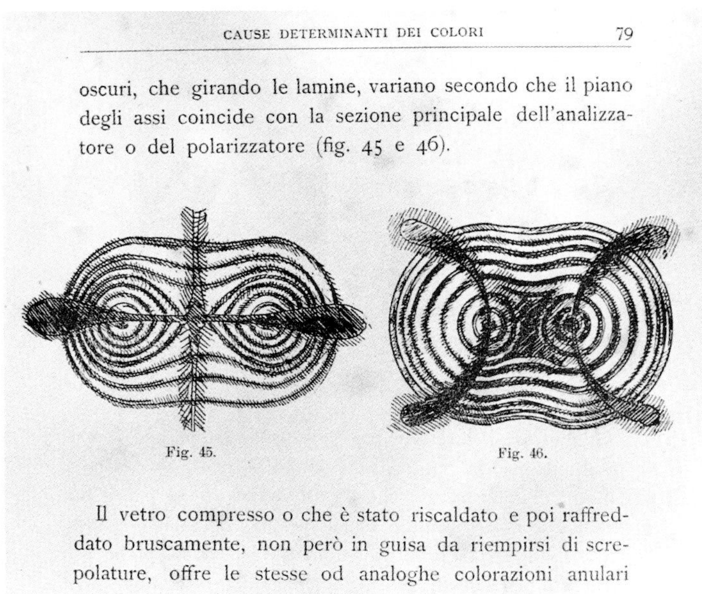

CAUSE DETERMINANTI DEI COLORI 79

oscuri, che girando le lamine, variano secondo che il piano degli assi coincide con la sezione principale dell'analizzatore o del polarizzatore (fig. 45 e 46).

Fig. 45. Fig. 46.

Il vetro compresso o che è stato riscaldato e poi raffreddato bruscamente, non però in guisa da riempirsi di screpolature, offre le stesse od analoghe colorazioni anulari

parently occupy an indefinite open space. The light source is difficult to identify either with a street lamp (incongruously, the only one in such a vast space) or with the moon, which would hardly have such intensity through a blanket of fog. Moreover, it is difficult to interpret the intersecting lines that spring from the backs of some of the figures and the flag-like cloth attached to one of these lines which unfurls over the head of the central figure. Finally, despite the provocative liberties standard with the Futurist palette, the pink reflections in the sky and the street and the series of vivid red spots in the background seem alien to a foggy night in Milan. These doubts are reinforced by one of Gianni Mattioli's recollections which his daughter, Laura, reported to the present writer. Luigi Russolo, who saw a great deal of the future collector as early as the 1920s, habitually spoke of this painting (which however entered the Mattioli Collection only in 1950, three years after Russolo's death) not as an image of nightlife in Milan with its *viveurs*, of which the Futurist group was so fond, but as a scene of war set in Africa. The date 1912 would require that it refer to the Italian campaign in Tripolitania (September 1911–October 1912) and in particular to Marinetti's interpretation of this event in six articles published between December 25 and 31, 1911 in the Paris daily *L'Intransigeant*; the articles were then collected in *La Bataille de Tripoli*, published simultaneously in French and Italian in January 1912 by Edizioni della Poesia.[28] The first three episodes of the book (sunset in the desert, the night vigil and preparations for the attack at dawn) include the kind of images that could have influenced *Solidity of Fog* and thus dispel some of the uncertainties mentioned above. Marinetti wrote of sentries who "mechanically turn their backs to one another" (p. 1), some with bayonets fixed to their rifles (p. 15); one of them, "standing straight, with his rifle slung over his shoulder," "quivered like a flag" (p. 1). The landscape in Marinetti's prose is characterized by "gray-blue tones with pink nuances" (p. 4), by the circularity of dunes "reposing in rings" (p. 2) like "liquefied curves, all painted in cosmetic pink" (p. 8). In a passage from his second letter, the floodlight of the battleship *Sicilia* inundates the trenches with light and bathes everything "in a supernatural light," creating the effect "of a big theater cut in two by a great beam of electric light" (p. 15); the floodlight "breaks into two beams of silvery dust, the second of which flows down, attenuating, [...] between the stage flats of the horizon, toward the enemy camp" (p. 16). The red dots on the horizon of the Mattioli painting would connect to the episode in which Captain Savino pointed out to Marinetti "three red fires," amongst the dunes near the enemy camp, which were bonfire beacons (p. 16).

It is not possible in the end to reinterpret *Solidity of Fog* on the basis of an aural recollection and a few similarities to a written text only. Although the Italian troops in Libya dressed for the 1911–12 winter in military greatcoats down to their knees, the appearance of the silhouetted figures refers more likely to the bourgeois dress of overcoats and bowler hats. The presence of a horse and carriage similar to a *fiacre* in the background, identified for the first time by Philip Rylands,[29] reinforces the logic of an urban setting. It is difficult to explain why Russolo would have inserted elements from Marinetti's popular wartime reports in a scene of nocturnal pedestrians on a city street: in this sense the literal significance of the painting continues to be partially elusive. On the other hand, its meaning in terms of Futurist ideology is clear. The powerful objective genitive in the title, stressing the solidity *of the* fog, invites us to consider the atmosphere that surrounds things (in particular, that of a foggy night) as a concrete, solid reality, according to a precise postulate of Futurist theory: this was formulated in the programmatic declaration which introduced the Paris show in February 1912 (one must render, in its solidity, "the invisible which stirs and lives beyond intervening obstacles, what we have on the right, on the left, and behind us"[30]); it was developed by Boccioni in the 1912 'Manifesto of Futurist Sculpture' (a need "to MODEL THE ATMOSPHERE which surrounds our objects"[31]); and it was repeated in a March 1913 text (atmosphere is "like a material substance which exists between objects"; the Futurist artist "feel[s] it, seek[s] it, seize[s] hold of it and emphasize[s] it by using all the various effects which light, shadows and streams of energy have upon it"[32]).

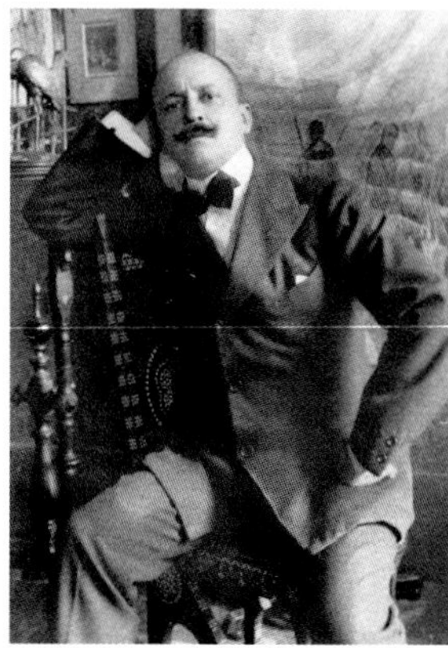

Fig. 21d. *Filippo Tommaso Marinetti in his house in Corso Venezia, Milan, 1912. Cat. no. 21 is behind him*

Whether or not *Solidity of Fog* is related to *La Bataille de Tripoli*, Marinetti admired Russolo's painting enough to have himself photographed in front of it in his apartment in Corso Venezia, Milan, in 1912 (fig. 21d).[33] It is unlikely that the work belonged to him (Futurist shows proudly declared the ownership of paintings belonging to the leader of the movement and this did not appear as such in the Costanzi catalogue); it may instead have been parked, as often happened, at Marinetti's home in-between exhibitions. At the 1913 show in Rome, Enrico Prampolini's review in *L'Artista Moderno*, quoted above, was the only critical reference to *Solidity of Fog* in the Italian press. But, according to a passage in Emilio Cecchi's review of the show, Russolo's paintings, together with those by Balla, were the most discussed and admired by the public,[34] perhaps for their quick illustrative and chromatic appeal. At the subsequent Futurist exhibition in Rotterdam (May–June 1913), *Solidity of Fog* was offered for sale for 750 florins,[35] the same price as Carrà's *Rhythms of Objects*, Boccioni's *Horizontal Construction* and Balla's *Street Lamp*. The painting's absence from the 'Lacerba' show in Florence (where Russolo sent his more recent and abstract *Automobile in corsa* (*Speeding Automobile*) and *Volumi dinamici* (*Dynamic Volumes*) and from shows in 1914 in Rome and London (where Russolo added some paintings, retrieving at least one dating from 1912, *Ombre-luci-case* [*Shadows-Lights-Houses*], and calling it *Espansioni dinamiche. Case + luci* [*Dynamic Expansions. Houses + Lights*]) perhaps meant that he had chosen to exclude works linked to the engendering phase of Futurist pictorial language, considered them too illustrative. But in May–June 1914 *Solidity of Fog* reappeared, as the only Russolo in the Futurist show at the Galleria Sprovieri in Naples.[36]

It is not known when the painting entered the collection of Margherita Sarfatti, whom Russolo had met at an early date, before 1910.[37] The passage of the review that Sarfatti wrote on Russolo for the first postwar Futurist show (in which Russolo and Balla, among the five signatories of the 1910 manifesto, were the only ones still to be exhibiting under Marinetti's aegis[38]) indicated that she was already familiar with *Solidity of Fog*, which had not been seen in public since 1914:

> "The appearances of things reveal themselves to him especially in lines of atmospheric displacement, varied in their rhythms, in orientation and in form, according to the speed and

the essential quality of the body which carves its own imprint in the air, and prolongs there in ethereal oscillations the music of its own gesture."[39]

The painting was acquired by Gianni Mattioli shortly before it was exhibited in the Futurism exhibition at the XXV Venice Biennale in 1950. Though still credited in the catalogue to the Sarfatti Collection,[40] it had in fact already been sold in May to the Milanese collector for the sum of 300,000 lire, with an additional 10% fee for the Galleria del Milione.[41]

[1] Lista 1975; Maffina 1977; Maffina 1978; Collovini 1997; Tagliapietra 2000.

[2] For instance, Calvesi 1967, pp. 92–3; Martin 1968, pp. 70–1, 83–4, 89–91, 108–9, 118–19, 148–51; Crispolti 1980b, pp. 125–8; *Venice* 1986, pp. 204–11; Coen 1996, pp. 27–8; *Hanover* 2001, nos. 287–91.

[3] Lista 1995, p. 439.

[4] *Rome* 1913, p. 25, no. 2.

[5] Letter from Filippo Tommaso Marinetti to Francesco Balilla Pratella, dated January 10, 1913, in Lugaresi 1969, p. 40.

[6] According to accounts by Civ., February 22, 1913, and f.f.m., March 11, 1913; for recollections of the musical part of the two evenings see Maffina 1978, pp. 20–1.

[7] Russolo, July 1, 1913; Russolo, November 1, 1913.

[8] *Florence* 1913–14, p. 23.

[9] *Moi mouvement* and *Resumé plastique des mouvements d'une femme*: *Rotterdam* 1913, nos. 24–5.

[10] Maffina 1978, p. 131.

[11] Crispolti 1980[b], p. 127 speculated that the painting was executed either in the first months of 1912 or even in late 1911.

[12] Taylor 1961, p. 80.

[13] Martin 1968, p. 148.

[14] Crispolti 1980[b], p. 127.

[15] *Linee forza della folgore* or *Le case continuano in cielo*. Basel, Öffentliche Kunstsammlung Basel, Kunstmuseum: Maffina 1978, p. 332.

[16] Formerly Basel, Kunstmuseum, Hängi Collection: Calvesi, Coen 1983, no. 747. The study for this is in Milan, Civico gabinetto dei disegni: *ibidem*, no. 748.

[17] Martin 1968, p. 149.

[18] "La rue est plus intime à cause de la brume. / Autour des becs à gaz l'air tout entier s'allume; / Chaque chose a sa part de rayons; [...] / Les êtres ont fondu leurs formes et leurs vies/ Et les âmes se sont doucement asservies. / Je n'ai jamais été moins libre que ce soir / Ni moins seul:" Romains 1908, pp. 30–1.

[19] Bergman 1962, pp. 216–23; Martin 1968–9, pp. 265–8.

[20] Apollinaire, February 7, 1912.

[21] Rylands 1997, p. 92.

[22] Boccioni *et al.*, April 11, 1910. The translation is that of Apollonio 1970, p. 28.

[23] Lista 1995, pp. 438–40.

[24] Previati 1906, pp. 71 and 76–7.

[25] Prampolini 1913, pp. 105–6.

[26] Boccioni, January 23–30, 1916.

[27] Zervos 1950, p. 92.

[28] Marinetti 1912[b], the text was read during the Futurist *soirées* in January 1912: Del Puppo 2000[a], p. 159.

[29] Rylands 1997, p. 92.

[30] Boccioni *et al.*, 1912, p. 6. The translation is that of Apollonio 1970, p. 47.

[31] Boccioni, April 11, 1912. The translation is from Apollonio 1970, p. 65.

[32] Boccioni, March 15, 1913. The translations are taken from Apollonio 1970, p. 88.

[33] A reproduction of the photograph dated 1912, in Marinetti, Palazzeschi 1978, between pp. 68 and 69.

[34] Cecchi, March 23, 1913.

[35] *Rotterdam* 1913 [p. 35].

[36] *Naples* 1914, p. 27, no. 1.

[37] Cannistraro, Sullivan 1993, pp. 67–8. The painter's relationship with the young art critic continued into subsequent years. In August 1916, Russolo wrote Sarfatti commenting in affectionate tones on Boccioni's tragic death.

[38] *Milan–Genoa–Florence* 1919, no. 260–4.

[39] Sarfatti, April 13, 1919.

[40] *Venice* 1950, p. 60. no. 27.

[41] Archivio Mattioli, statement of accounts between the Galleria del Milione and Gianni Mattioli, dated July 18, 1950: on May 8, 1950, a 30,000 lire debit to Mattioli was recorded as the fee for the purchase of Russolo's painting from Mar-gherita Sarfatti for the sum of 300,000 lire (*Appendix I*, document no. 50).

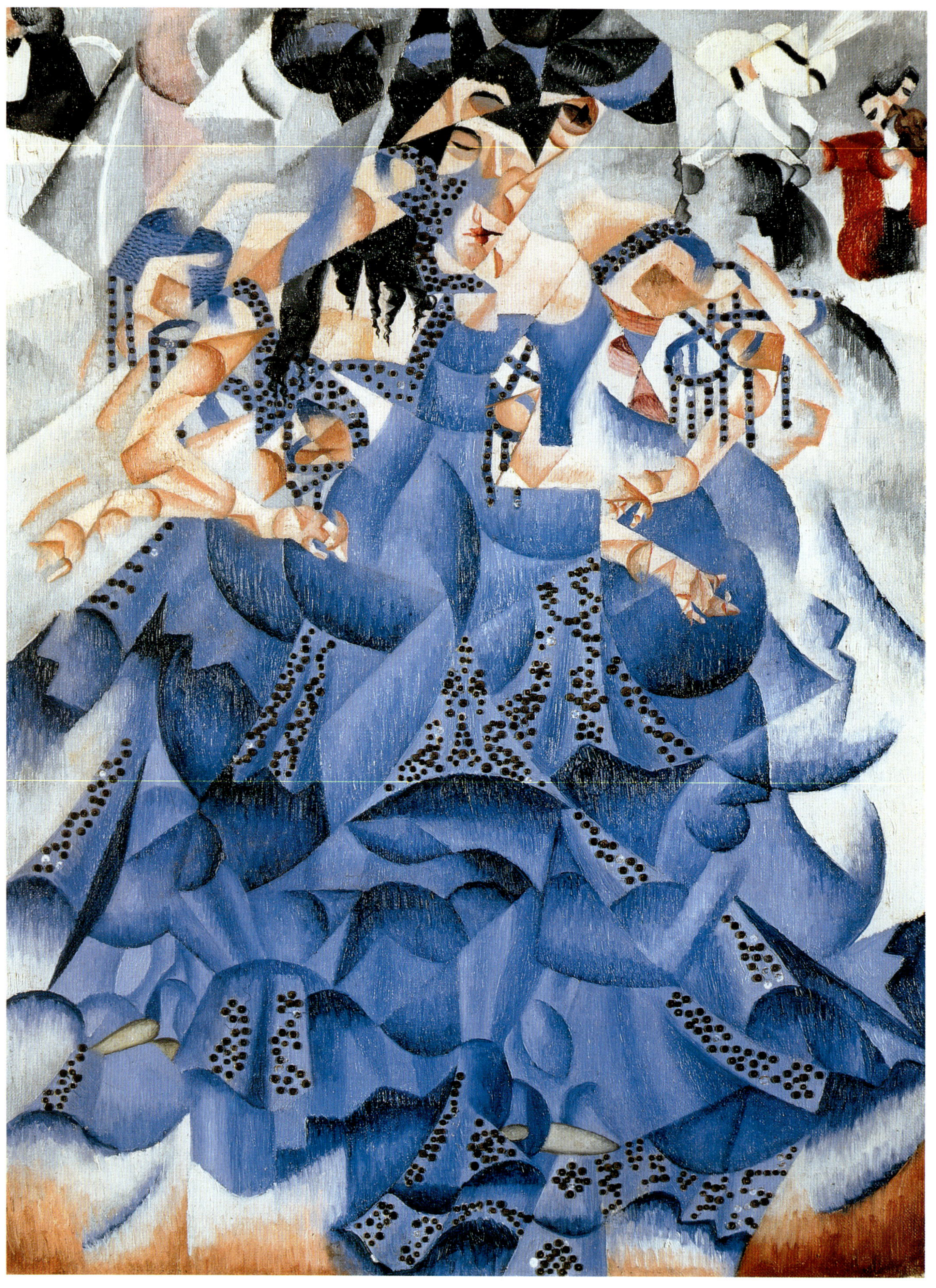

22 **Gino Severini** (Cortona, Arezzo, 1883 – Paris, 1966)

Blue Dancer (*1st Dancer* or *2nd Dancer*; *Dancer*)

Ballerina blu (*1a Danzatrice* or *2a Danzatrice*; *Danzatrice*; *Danzatrice bleu*), 1912

Oil on canvas with sequins
61 × 46 cm

Inscription: *verso*, on the canvas: 'Gino Severini "Danseuse Bleue"' (fig. 22a)

Provenance: property of the artist; January 1914: Fernando Agnoletti, Florence; 1933: Braccio Agnoletti, Florence; 1948: Romeo Toninelli, Milan; before June 1950: Gianni Mattioli

Exhibitions: Rome 1913, p. 29, no. 5 or 6 (*1a Danzatrice* or *2a Danzatrice*); Rotterdam 1913, no. 34 or 35 (*Première danseuse* or *Deuxième danseuse*); Florence 1913–14, p. 25, no. 4 or 5 (*Danzatrice*); Venice 1930, p. 146, no. 97 (*Danzatrice bleu*); Rome 1948, p. 32, no. 8 (*Danzatrice bleu*); New York 1949, p. 134 (*Blue Dancer*, 1912); Venice 1950, p. 60, no. 32; Zurich 1950, no. 83; Milan 1951, catalogue not traced (the presence of the work in the exhibition documented in Archivio Mattioli, file for the work); Milan 1952, unnumbered; Florence 1953a, no. 8 (*Danzatrice in blu*, 1912); São Paulo 1953–4, p. 13, no. 28; New York 1954, no. 29; Kassel 1955, no. 594; Rome 1955–6, p. 56, no. 30; Rome 1959, no. 5; Winterthur 1959, no. 93; Munich 1959–60, no. 89; Venice 1960, p. 23, no. 122; New York 1961–Los Angeles 1962, no. 107; Cologne 1962, no. g/180; Washington, DC 1967–Tokyo 1972, no. 33 (Washington, DC–Hamburg), no. 32 (Madrid–Seville), no. 33 (Kyoto–Tokyo); Milan 1972, no. 129; Newcastle upon Tyne 1972–London 1973, no. 88; Paris 1973, no. 50; Milan 1973–4, no. 126; Düsseldorf 1974, no. 142; Dortmund 1976, no. 4; Venice 1986, p. 228; London 1989, no. 36; Madrid

Gino Severini, native of Cortona, played a fundamental role in keeping the Italian Futurists abreast of developments in French painting. Having moved permanently to Paris in 1906 he was the first to provide them with precise information about the formal techniques of fragmentation being practiced by Cubist painters (in a letter to Boccioni, spring 1911[1]); he guided Boccioni, Carrà and Russolo around the galleries and studios of the avant-garde on their visit to Paris in October 1911; he kept them informed of the rapid evolution of the artistic avant-garde in the French capital between 1912 and 1913. Although, in his memoirs published in 1946, Severini was emphatic about his consensus with Parisian art (in particular with Pablo Picasso and Guillaume Apollinaire) and although he meticulously recorded his tensions and disagreements with the group of Italian artists led by Marinetti, he was a convinced and impassioned campaigner of the Futurist movement. His paintings from 1911 to 1915 reveal his genuine adherence to the poetics of simultaneity, his predilection for the themes of modern life dear to the Futurists, and his ambition to represent movement in its spatial and temporal dimensions. Moreover his theory of the plastic analogies of dynamism was one of the principal contributions to the theory of Futurist representation. His lively palette and the precision and elegance of his drawing were to make him the Futurist painter most esteemed outside Italy: in 1912 his paintings were unanimously admired by reviewers of the movement's first group show held in Paris, and in 1913, contrary to the Futurist practice of exhibiting only as a group, he held two successful one-man shows in London and Berlin.

Professional dancers on the stage of public dance-halls, which from the time of the Impressionists had been among the most popular representations of modern life, seem not to have formed part of the original Futurist repertoire of themes and images. In the first painting manifesto, dated February 11, 1910, the five co-signers (which originally included Aroldo Bonzagni and Romolo Romani together with Umberto Boccioni, Carlo Carrà and Luigi Russolo) expressed some interest in a particular pathological variation of night life, *nottambulismo*, and for subjects popular with the late Scapigliatura group: "the feverish figures of the *bon viveur*, the cocotte, the apache and the absinthe drinker."[2] Through 1912 dancers on stage are absent both from Marinetti's manifestos and from the anthology *I poeti futuristi*, published in 1912, which set out to exemplify the full range of images, notions and motifs in the new poetics promoted by Marinetti. Only towards the end of 1913 did Marinetti cite the rhythm of a "swift, overpowering dance," as might have been performed at the Folies-Bergères, in support of his concept of "fisicofollia" ("body-madness") in the manifesto *The Variety Theater.*[3] Severini's privileged position in Paris from 1910 to the summer of 1912 enabled him to tackle subjects quite different from those of other Futurists, in Milan. The theme of the dance was constantly before the eyes of Parisian artists, thanks to the plethora of night locales, and to posters that depicted in full-length the most famous performers[4] and accentuated their strange and provocative motions.[5]

In 1946, Severini wrote in his memoirs how he assiduously frequented the most fashionable dance halls in Paris (Le Moulin de la Galette, Moulin Rouge, Bal Tabarin, Folies-Bergères, Royal Souper, Rat Mort, Monico, Grelot), where he was admitted free of charge thanks to his reputation as an expert dancer. With his painter's eye he registered the colorful dazzle of the *can-can* dancers on stage:

> "These ballerinas were dressed like all the other women of the period, but when they raised their skirts and began to dance, caught in a band of brilliant light, all you could see was a blur of contrasting blacks and whites, and a splendor of grays, in a whole range of violets, greens and blues."[6]

Thus it was no surprise that Severini was the only artist at the first Futurist exhibition in February 1912 at the Galerie Bernheim-jeune in Paris to dedicate four paintings to the theme of the dance (the large *The Dance of the 'Pan-Pan' at Monico* [fig. 22b], *Possessed Dancer* [*Danseuse obsédante*], *The Milliner* [*La Modiste*], both illustrated in the catalogue, and *Yellow Dancers* [fig. 22c][7]). When these paintings traveled to the subsequent exhibition in London, explanatory captions under their titles in the catalogue inserted them, not without strain, into the repertoire of Futurist artistic concerns: perceptual synaesthesia in *The Dance of the 'Pan-Pan'*; simultaneity of the dancer's sensations and states of mind of the painter in *Possessed Dancer*; simultaneous interpenetrations of form in *The Milliner*; and the dismantling of form by movement and light in *Yellow Dancers*.[8]

The Mattioli *Blue Dancer* and its pendant, *White Dancer* (also known as *La Chahutteuse*) in the Jucker Collection (fig. 22d), constitute a significant development with respect to the paintings exhibited in February 1912. In the latter the artist's attention had been focused primarily on the relationship between the dancers and their surroundings and on the fragmentation

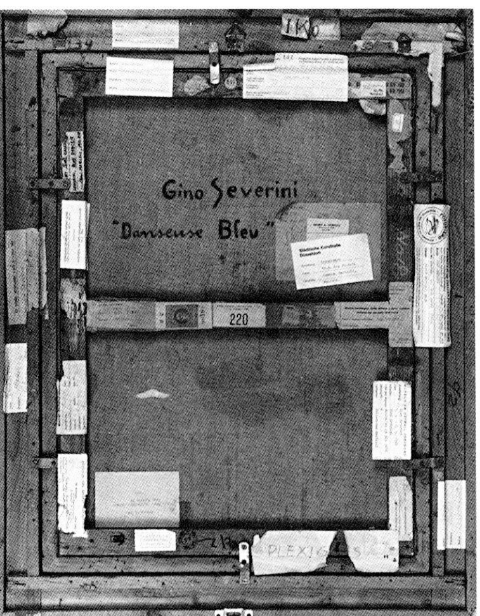

1990–1, p. 261; Saint-Paul de Vence 1992, no. 30; Barcelona 1996, no. 87; Venice 2001, no. 7

Bibliography: Letter from Gino Severini to Filippo Tommaso Marinetti, dated February 9, 1913, in Hanson 1995, pp. 144–5; Cecchi, March 23, 1913 (?); Longhi, April 10, 1913 (?); Gian de' Sordi, December 12, 1913; Tommei, December 24, 1913; Letter from Gino Severini to Giovanni Papini, dated December 30, 1913 (Fiesole, Fondazione Primo Conti, Centro di Documentazione e Ricerche sulle Avanguardie Storiche, Archivio Papini); 'Elenco', January 15, 1914; Letter from Gino Severini to Giovanni Papini, dated February 6, 1914 (Fiesole, Fondazione Primo Conti, Centro di Documentazione e Ricerche sulle Avanguardie Storiche, Archivio Papini); Courthion 1941, pl. VI (*Danzatrice bleu*, 1912); Courthion 1946, pl. VII; Severini 1946, pp. 152, 200, 204–6 and pl. facing p. 152; Carrieri 1950, p. 60; Garretto 1952, p. 43; D'Ancona 1953, pp. 11, 15; Ragghianti 1953, p. 9; Haftmann 1955, no. 72; Castelfranco, Valsecchi 1956, p. 74, pl. 10; Drudi Gambillo, Fiori 1958–62, vol. I, p. 458, vol. II, pp. 320, 339, no. 36; Haftmann 1960, vol. II, p. 160; Maltese 1960, p. 295, pl. 157; Carrieri 1961, p. 47, pl. 102; Taylor 1961, p. 66; Venturi 1961, pp. 13, 17, pl. 9; Janis, Blesh 1962, p. 40; Bellonzi 1963, pp. 69, 75; Pacini 1966, pp. 27–8, pl. 11; Calvesi 1967, pp. 110–11; Mathey 1967, p. 184; Martin 1968, pp. 139–40, pl. 91; Apollonio 1970, p. 40, fig. 50; Rye 1972, p. 72; Dorfles 1976, p. 9; Tisdall, Bozzolla 1977, p. 160; Barilli 1983, p. 16; Fagiolo dell'Arco 1983, p. 20; Roche-Pézard 1983, pp. 377, 484, no. 159, fig. 69; Bagatti, Manghetti, Porto 1984, pp. 67–8; Coen 1986, p. 42; Fonti 1988, p. 127, no. 105; Pacini 1990, pp. 48–50; Poggi 1992, pp. 21–2, 172; Hanson 1995, pp. 144–5; Lemaire 1995, p. 51; Carandini 1996, p. 17; Marziali 1996, pp. 182–4; Rylands 1997, p. 94; Del Puppo 2000[a], pp. 169–72, 177; Fonti 2001[a], pp. 20, 24–7; Fonti 2001[b], p. 80

Fig. 22a. Verso *of cat. no. 22*

Fig. 22b. *Gino Severini,* La Danse du 'Pan-Pan' à Monico *(*The Dance of the 'Pan-Pan' at Monico*), 1911, destroyed, in P. Courthion,* Gino Severini*, 1930*

Fig. 22c. *Gino Severini,* Danseuses jaunes *(*Yellow Dancers*), oil on canvas, 1911. Cambridge (Massachusetts), Fogg Art Museum, Harvard University Art Museums, Gift of Mr and Mrs Joseph H. Hazen*

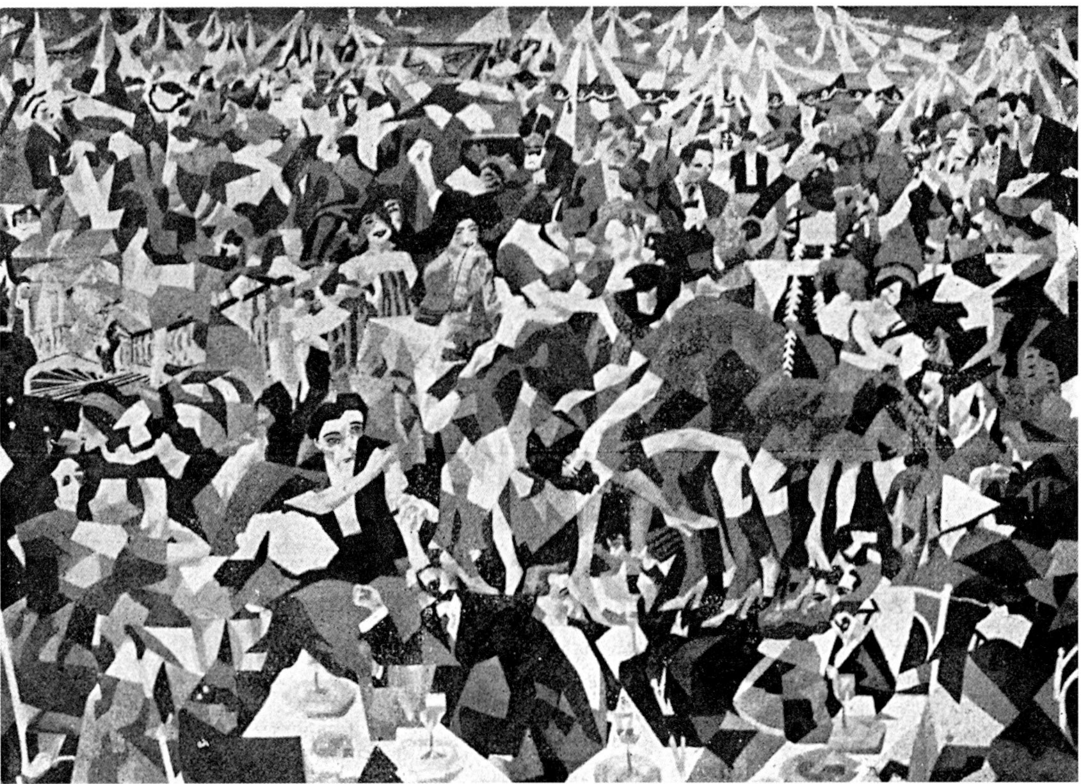

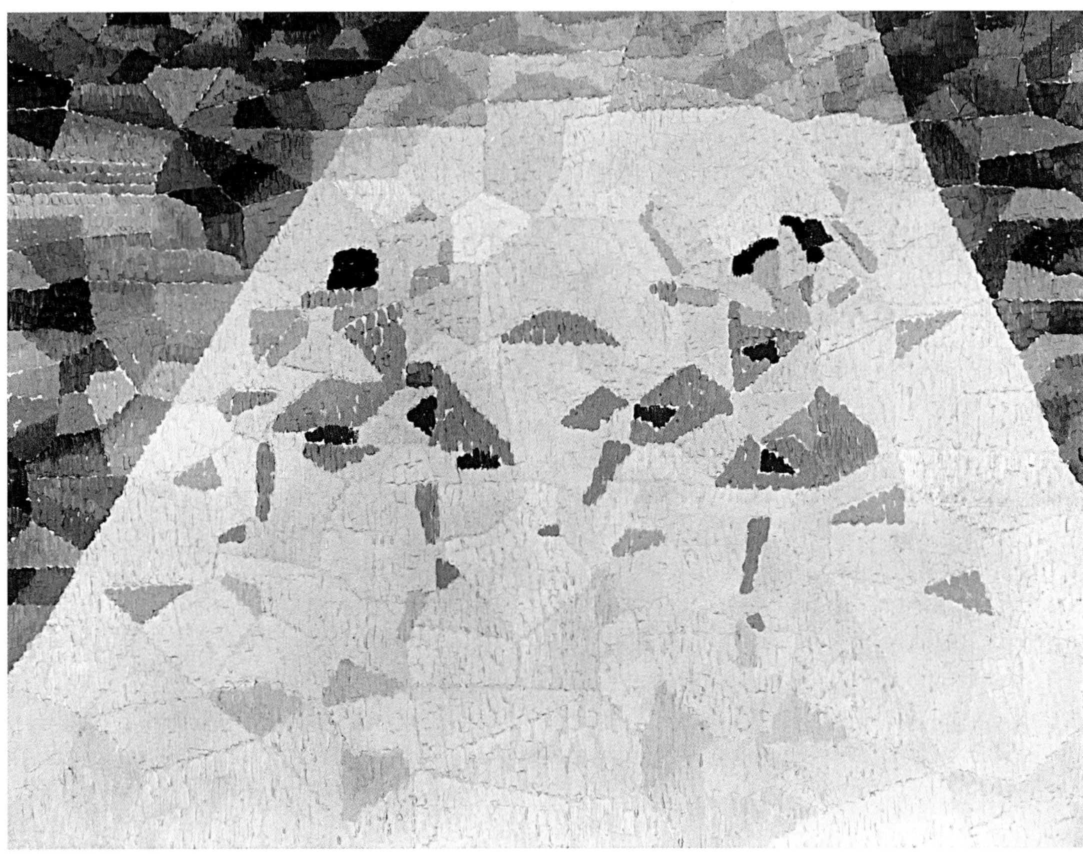

of the episode. In the two later works, Severini seems to concentrate instead on the movements of a single dancer, who fills the foreground and is placed on the vertical axis. We know from Severini himself that the Jucker dancer performs a *chahut*, a more frenzied version of the old *can-can* that had been performed in Paris for over seventy years. The dance portrayed in the Mattioli painting was most likely a flamenco (as Philip Rylands has suggested,[9] contrary to the opinions of others who interpret it as a tango[10]). The flamenco had recently become all the vogue in Parisian dance halls and was obsessively promoted in the spring of 1912 at the Monico and the Bal Tabarin. The wide flounced skirt entirely covering the legs, the fringes over the shoulders running down the bare arms, the angles of the forearms and the gestures of the fingers (that seem to suggest a snapping to the rhythm of the music, or better still the playing of castanets) are all compatible with the flamenco. Nor was Severini the only Futurist in 1912 to conjure up the image of a flamenco dancer. In a long metaphor in *Le Monoplan du pape* by Marinetti, a free verse poem published in Paris in January 1912 (and certainly known to Severini who had copies sent to him to give to his literary friends in Paris), Etna seen from an airplane spurts "Spanish flames" which dance forward; they are adorned with "shawls of smoke embroidered with sparks"; they move in time "to prolonged castanet clickings" and are dressed in "skirts / of lace of ash violet" that shape "mobile hips."[11]

The precise date of the painting was recalled in a passage of Severini's memoirs. In the spring of 1912, at the time of his growing friendship with Pablo Picasso who was then moving out of his Boulevard Raspail studio after his definitive break with Fernande Olivier, Severini continued to "work on the same line" as the paintings sent to the Bernheim-jeune show and executed, together with some portraits, "two paintings of dancers (*Danseuse bleue* and *Chahutteuse* [fig. 22d] in white and black), [taken] to Milan to show to friends, at their request."[12] Severini's departure for Milan, and then to Pienza where he spent the summer, took place, he remembered, immediately after the brawl caused by Valentine de Saint-Point's declamation of the *Manifesto of Lust* in Paris on June 27, 1912.[13] This date can reasonably be considered a *terminus ante quem* for the Mattioli painting. Aside from the two pictures of dancers and a self-portrait, Severini remembered having taken to Milan photographs and newspaper clippings with news about the most recent events in avant-garde painting circles in Paris.[14]

Three clues, however tenuous and indirect, seem to confirm Severini's account. The first is contained in a June 10, 1912 letter to Marinetti: Severini wrote that he was finishing his "current work" in view of a new exhibit to be held in Rome, and that he intended to pass through Milan as soon as possible with his new paintings.[15] The second, which reiterates Severini's role of keeping his Milanese painter friends up to date in the early summer of 1912, can be found in a letter datable to the same period: Boccioni invites Severini to bring to Milan "all possible information on the Cubists and Picasso and Braque" by going to Kahnweiler to buy "the latest photographs of works made after my departure."[16] The third occurs in a letter prior to the so-called 'peace of Florence' at the end of October 1912: Boccioni suggests to Severini, who was about to leave Pienza, that he bring his paintings to Milan "ready for packing at the first opportunity"[17] (the exhibition the following year in Rotterdam had already been decided and negotiations for a show in Rome were under way). Among these we can reasonably include the two dancers painted before the summer, which were, in fact, shown both in Rome and Rotterdam in 1913.[18]

On a strictly documentary basis, the dating of the application of sequins on the dancer's blue dress poses a difficulty. In an often-cited passage of Severini's 1946 memoirs, he recalled that towards the end of 1912 (after his return to Paris therefore, from the end of October), Apollinaire had suggested, with reference to a practice of Gothic and early Renaissance Italian artists,

Fig. 22d. *Gino Severini,* Ballerina bianca (Chahutteuse) *(*White Dancer [Chahutteuse]*), oil on canvas, 1912. Milan, Civiche raccolte d'arte, Jucker Collection*

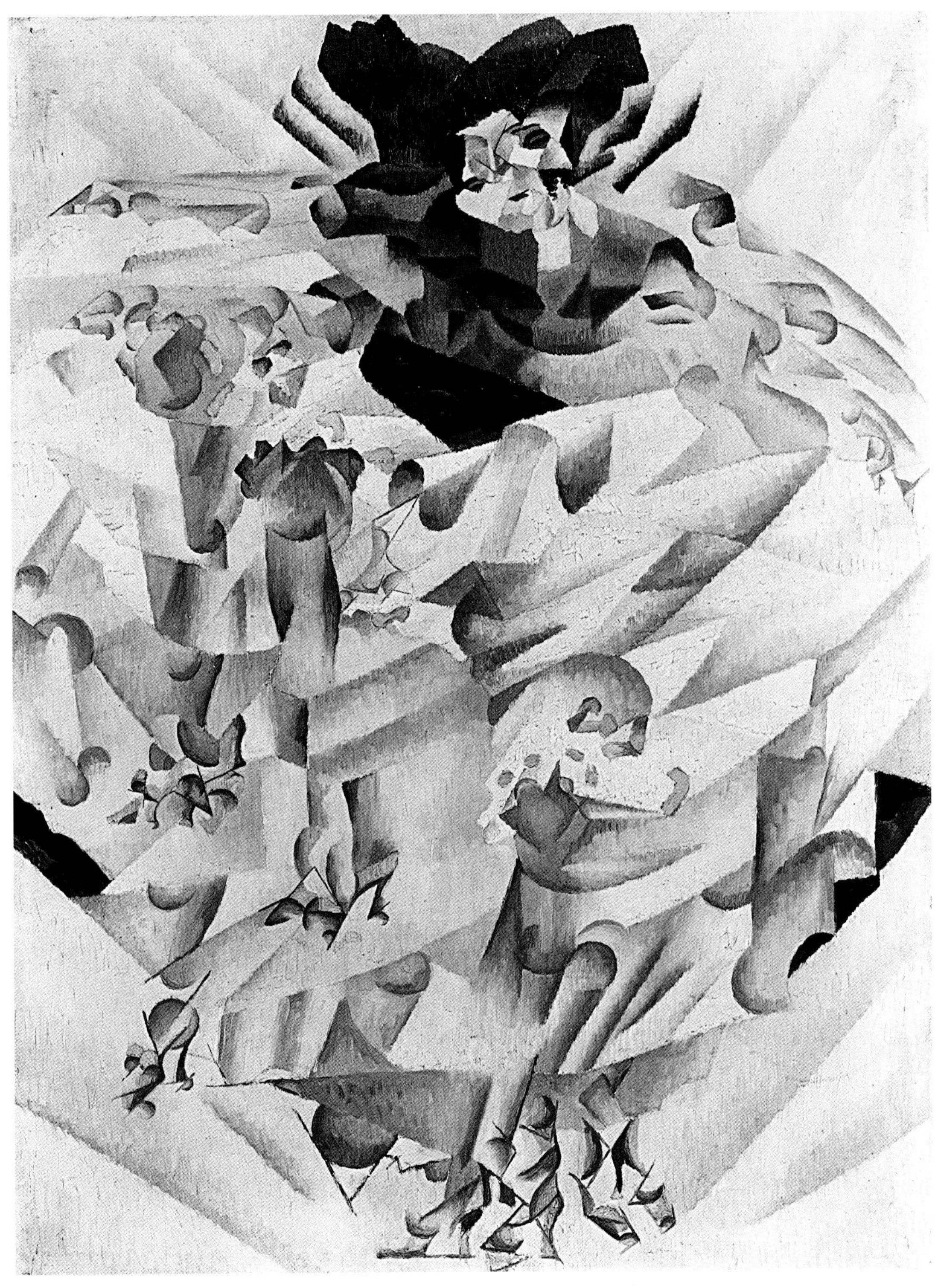

that he add to his paintings "elements of actual reality": their presence and the "contrast this provoked, increased the vitality of paintings and their whole dynamism."[19] In this context Severini mentioned specifically two works: the first a portrait of his future father-in-law, Paul Fort, made with the covers of the review *Vers et Prose*,[20] and the second a "ballerina with shapes in relief on which I glued some real dancers' sequins" (this was the *Dancer at Pigalle*,[21] which indeed has a form in relief made of plaster to indicate the swelling of a fold). However there are also sequins on the *Dynamic Hieroglyphic of the Bal Tabarin* (fig. 22e), which we know was painted during the summer in Pienza, before Apollinaire's advice (it is the "large picture" on which Severini was working when he wrote to Marinetti in August 1912[22]). Nor was Severini able to work on *Blue Dancer* again during the winter of 1912–13, in Paris, as it had been left, together with five others, in storage in Pienza.[23] In the letter that documents this, from Paris in February 1913, Severini specified that the two dancers were among the Pienza paintings but he mentioned sequins only in relation to *Dynamic Hieroglyphic of the Bal Tabarin* ("In painting number 1 I used real sequins to satisfy my need for absolute realism"[24]). The certainty that *Blue Dancer* went to Rome, together with an explicit mention of sequins in Emilio Cecchi's review of the show ("sprayed constellations of sequins, glued with gum to the hems of the dresses"[25]), leaves no room for doubt and limits the problem to the actual date that the sequins were added — whether in May–June 1912 (during the execution of the painting in Paris) or the summer (when he was painting the *Dynamic Hieroglyphic of the Bal Tabarin* in Pienza). Some thirty years on, Severini's imprecise recollection may readily be explained by the profoundly different significance of the encrusted materials he was applying to his paintings in the summer of 1912 with respect to those the following winter, 1912–13: in the *Blue Dancer* the sequins represent illusionistically themselves and were used to render with, to use Severini's own words, "absolute realism" the effect of artificial light striking a reflecting surface.

Severini's decision to pursue the subject of dancers in the months after the Bernheim-jeune show does not seem fortuitous. Critics from Paris and abroad stressed both "the vigorous, ardent movement of all those figures"[26] in the large *The Dance of the 'Pan-Pan' at Monico* and Severini's special ability to involve the spectator in the rhythm transmitted by the painting;[27] what impressed them in the *Possessed Dancer* was the confounding of foreground and background, of time and space.[28] Apollinaire defined the large painting of dancers (*The Dance of the 'Pan-Pan' at Monico*) in no uncertain terms as "the most important work that a Futurist brush has painted"[29] for its capacity to refer to "realities severely prohibited by Futurist declarations."[30] Even if a third of a century later Severini insisted that the paintings executed after the Parisian show in February (the two ballerinas, the *Self-Portrait*, the *Abstract Rhythm of Mme. M.S.*) had continued "on the same line"[31] as the works preceding them, there are clear differences. Severini seems to move closer to the sources of Picasso's Cubism with greater decision just at a time when a new, more narrative Cubism was starting to prevail, at the Salon des Indépendants which inaugurated in March. The structure of the *Blue Dancer* corresponds linguistically to Picasso's paintings of 1909, such as his *Nude Woman*[32] (fig. 22g), in which the pyramidal figure transmits the rhythms of its shattered forms to its surroundings. The chiaroscuro pattern, with clashing curved and broken lines, seems to be the outcome of Severini's pondering Picasso's still lifes and figures from the same period. It is not possible to date with precision Jean Metzinger's *Dancer at the Café*[33] (fig. 22f) the painting closest to Severini's in terms of subject and design. But it is likely that the Metzinger, usually dated 1912 yet stylistically closer to his works of the following year (*The Blue Bird* [*L'Oiseau bleu*]) than to those of the spring of 1912 (*Woman and Horse* [*La Femme au cheval*]), was influenced by the worldly *brio* and graphic elegance of Severini's dancers, rather than the other way round.

Fig. 22e. *Gino Severini,* Geroglifico dinamico del Bal Tabarin (Dynamic Hieroglyphic of the Bal Tabarin)*, oil on canvas with applied sequins, 1912. New York, The Museum of Modern Art, acquired through the Lillie P. Bliss Bequest*

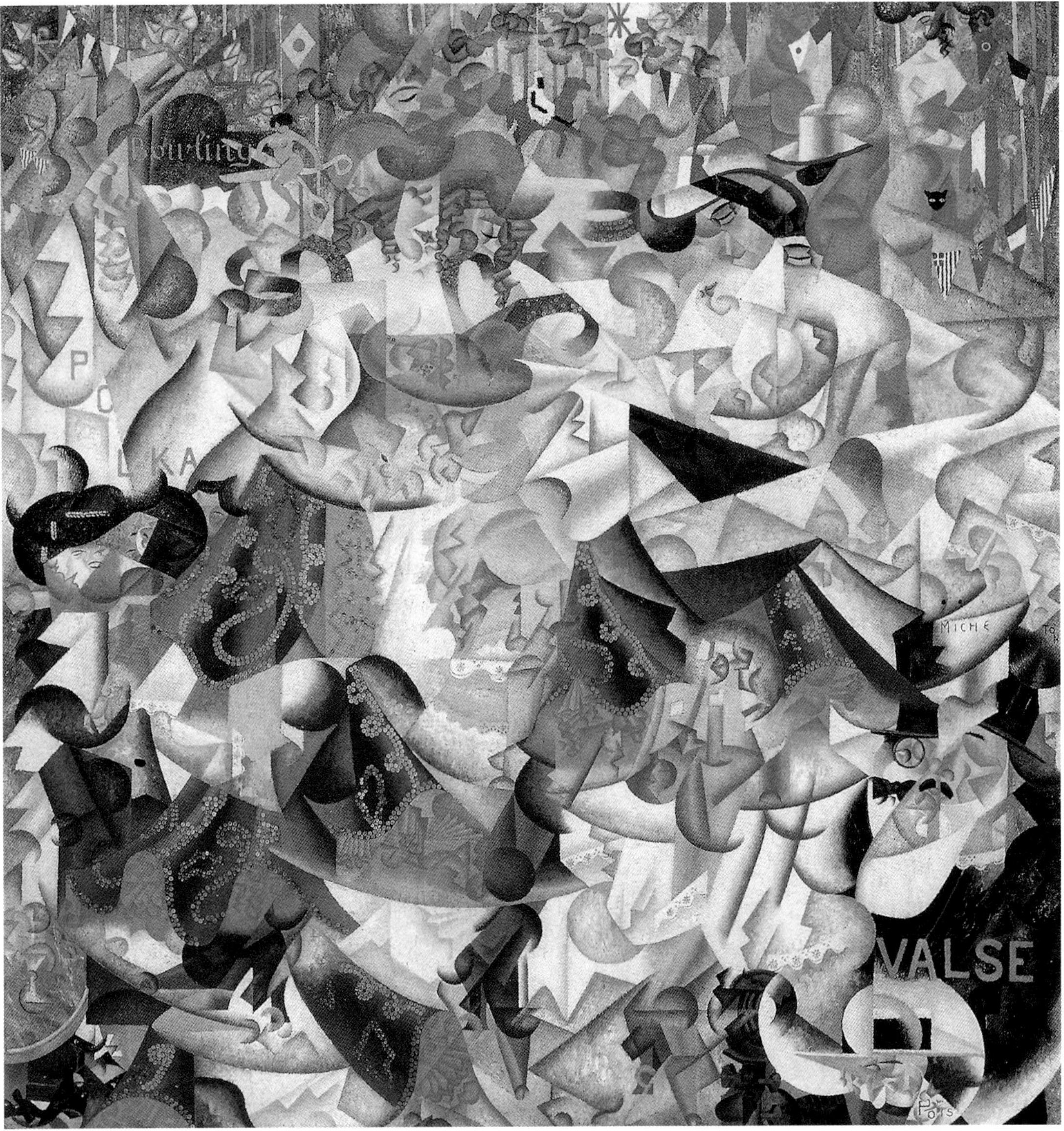

Compared to Picasso, Severini disciplined his drawing into more elegant and decorative patterns. Furthermore he emphasized those characteristics that would identify the painting as Futurist: he made the temporal element of the dance rhythm explicit (the repetition of two poses of the arms), he forced the chromatic component (the dominant blue of the dress versus the gray surroundings), and implied the modern setting by inserting a violinist and two clients in the upper corners. To meet the challenge of the more widely esteemed Cubist paintings of modern subjects (such as Jean Metzinger's *Woman and Horse* or Fernand Léger's *The Wedding*) or in the more classical vein (*The City of Paris* by Robert Delaunay or *The Bathers* by Albert Gleizes) which were exhibited at the 1912 Indépendants, he may have perceived that a reworking of Picasso's vocabulary in rhythmical and coloristic terms was his most viable option. The most astute insight into this delicate phase of Severini's work after February 1912 occurs in a letter Severini himself wrote to Soffici on September 27, 1913. The two dancers, the self-portrait, and *Mme M.S.* mark the transition from the "merely musical" ("soltanto musicale") painting of *'Pan-Pan' at Monico* and the "forms-sounds" ("forme-suoni") paintings of the winter of 1912–13:

"At the time of our exhibition chez Bernheim, the Cubists, Picasso, and my Futurist friends accused me more or less openly of objective Impressionism and of neo-Impressionism. Boccioni and Carrà liked Picasso's analytic abstraction and conceptual painting; and I thought myself almost a fool at the time since I hadn't felt even the smallest influence of this. For this reason I did a series of paintings which you know which were exhibited in Rome, in these I wish to reconcile the outside and inside of things, form conceived for itself and emotional form; luckily my intuition saves me from becoming static and from Cubist analysis almost in spite of myself."[34]

The Jucker *White Dancer* (fig. 22d) and the Mattioli *Blue Dancer*, executed when the discussion of the 1912 Futurist show was over and the Salon des Indépendants had closed, were two interpretations of the same subject intended to experiment different, perhaps consciously alternative formal solutions. The Mattioli *Dancer* was carefully set in context (on a stage, and in the background a client in a tuxedo and a lady with a hat on the left, and a violinist with a red jacket on the right); by contrast the Jucker *Dancer* is apparently placed in empty space surrounded by lines that suggest simply the irradiation of her own movements. The *Blue Dancer*'s dress is analyzed in broken lines (like those of *The Milliner*) that are linked by the more dynamic lunettes in which the blue becomes intenser and darker. Severini's technique in the Jucker *Dancer* is quite different: parallel sequences of straight lines suggest the rapid spread of movements from the two centers of irradiation, the uplifted knee rotating to the left and the hand that raises her dress on the right.[35] In place of the relatively rational chiaroscuro of *Blue Dancer*, similar in technique to the *Self-Portrait* of the same period, Severini adopted in the Jucker *Dancer* a texture based on a monochrome of white tones inserting, with emphatic dynamism, tapestry-like patches derived from *The Milliner* or *Yellow Dancers*[36] (fig. 22c). To enliven the fractured forms of the *Blue Dancer*, Severini turned to *appliqué* sequins, which give the painting a jolt of extra luminous energy: in this way the physical light reflected from the tiny disks which embellish the neckline, the shoulders and flounces of the woman's dress complements the detailed chiaroscuro pattern of the full blue dress (planned in detail in an underlying drawing visible today with infra-red reflectography: fig. 67, p. 427). Critics, especially Anglo-Saxon, have stressed the painting's novelty: "a new lightness of spirit"[37] and a desire to represent light "which does not come from a visible external source, but from the dancers themselves."[38]

As a work of art abreast with the latest accomplishments of the Parisian avant-garde, by an artist who had received the most acclaim from international critics, *Blue Dancer* was the object of keen interest when it traveled to Milan in the summer of 1912 and was shown to the Futurist painters. Its impact was considerable and it would be hard to explain the upper part of Carlo Carrà's *The Galleria in Milan* (cat. no. 6), which was most likely painted in the following months, without Carrà's knowledge of Severini's painting. If Umberto Boccioni's *Materia* was conceived during that summer and executed in the fall, then its pyramidal structure, previously unknown in Boccioni's paintings, may be indebted to the composition of *Blue Dancer*.

Blue Dancer remained in Pienza until it was dispatched, together with the self-portrait, the Jucker *White Dancer* and *Dynamic Hieroglyphic of the Bal Tabarin*, to Rome for exhibition in the foyer of the Teatro Costanzi, which opened February 21, 1913. It was exhibited adjacent to *White Dancer*, as the final pair of paintings in Severini's section, and titled *1st Dancer* and *2nd Dancer*. In a letter to Marinetti, Severini expressed his precise wish that the six works appear in the catalogue as a simple numerical sequence, from "picture number 1" to "picture number 6"[39] (a request disregarded for numbers 1-4, which were given the titles that Severini had written on the backs of the canvases). However we do not know the order in which Severini wanted the two dancers to be hung, nor even whether he intended the order to imply a for-

Fig. 22f. *Jean Metzinger,* La Danseuse au café (Dancer at the Café)*, oil on canvas, 1912. Buffalo (New York), Albright-Knox Art Gallery, General Purchase Funds, 1957*

Fig. 22g. *Pablo Picasso,* Femme nue (Nude Woman)*, oil on canvas, 1909. Private collection*

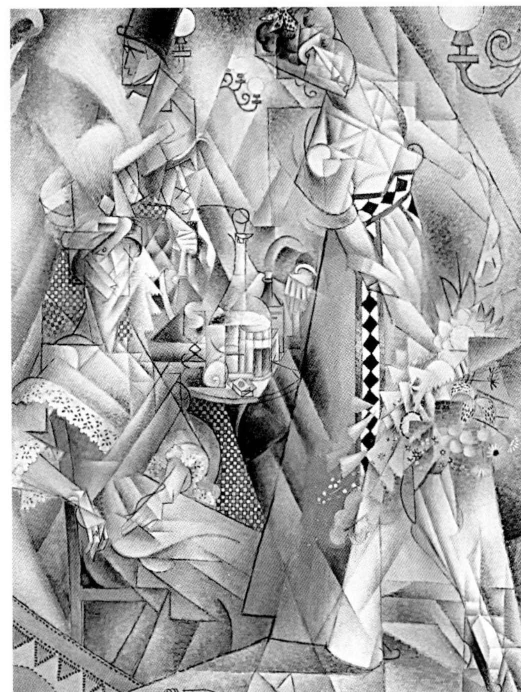

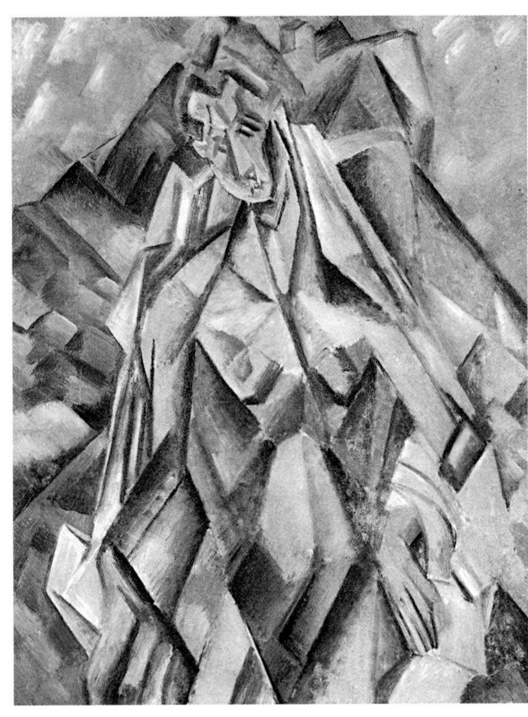

mal progression from the first to the second. Critics seemed more struck by the *White Dancer*, whose photograph was circulated in the press, but visitors tended to confuse the two paintings, to praise in them "something aesthetic which inebriates," but at the same time to reproach the overly shallow worldliness, the lack of compositional syntax, the presence of the realistic insertion of sequins ("certain stuck-on things disharmonious with the whole I do not comprehend"[40]). In Roberto Longhi's memorable reading of the paintings published in the April 10 issue of *La Voce*, details of the Jucker *Dancer* ("the sheen of a jabot, the exact archicentric curves of the dimples on the chin or the cheeks, the perspective straightening of the ring on the heel") are mixed with others more pertinent to the Mattioli *Dancer* ("the falling folds of the unwrapped robe, the concave-convex cylinder of the curls").[41] The review by Emilio Cecchi, who saw in Severini the degeneration of Boccioni's and Soffici's research into pure volumetrics, commented on the insertion of the sequins, superimposing the *Blue Dancer* on the more riotous and dazzling *Dynamic Hieroglyphic of the Bal Tabarin*:

> "Severini [...] manages to confer a dazzling semblance of 'Futurism' on his punctilious and senile sensitivity. Is he seeking a fusion of the Cubist process with the system of projections of movement? But the construction of his volumes is arbitrary, and only succeeds in segmenting the projections of planes of movement; and the segments drift down, leaving small multicolored tails like paper streamers behind them: breaths of air which are bathed in their fleeting tint. One has a kaleidoscope of scraps, held together by reflections of bright soap-bar or candy colors. Swimming inside these scraps we see [...] trifles of some embroidery, some outlines of yellow ribbons on pink thighs, sprayed constellations of sequins, glued with gum to the hems of the dresses, producing contradictions so excessive as to make one aware how much, after all, he fails to achieve his own intentions."[42]

Blue Dancer was next shown in Rotterdam,[43] where it was priced at 500 guilders, a relatively low sum compared to paintings of comparable dimensions by other artists (Carrà's *Rhythms of Objects*, 53 × 67 cm, was for sale for 750 guilders), and again at the Florentine 'Lacerba' show inaugurated in November.[44] For this Severini added other paintings executed during the summer in Paris and one from Pienza where he had returned to live,[45] to those returning from Holland at the end of the summer, all painted in 1912 and temporarily stored in Milan (the smaller paintings, including the two dancers, may have been stored at Carrà's house).[46] Instead he was not able to send to Florence the paintings in his one-man shows in London and Berlin since they had not returned yet to Italy. Inevitably comparison with the more recent works of other artists (especially those of Balla and Boccioni, which had evolved radically since the February show in Rome) worked to his disadvantage and, in a letter to Papini, his disillusionment was directed specifically toward *Blue Dancer*, which was bound too closely to the pictorial grammar of Cubism:

> "I regret that the dancer which I repudiate is hanging near the latest things by my friends. Between that and my present work there are more than 40 paintings: how can I look at it without anger. I have worked here in Anzio, and have reached important conclusions about which I will write you soon."[47]

Instead, *Blue Dancer* was much admired in Florence and was singled out and awarded a critical reading of its own for the first time, by a journalist of *La Tribuna* in Rome, who signed his articles with the pseudonym Gian de' Sordi ("There is a dancer dressed in light blue, with a numberless dress, many facial angles and several limbs as a result. That is the way for an expert eye to see a ballerina really dancing"[48]); he preferred it to the Jucker *Dancer* for its more literal adherence to Futurist theory.[49] The two dancers found a buyer from the show in Fernando Agnoletti, a Florentine writer and critic who was starting a collection of Italian avant-garde art. In Severini's autobiography, the purchase was remembered with Braccio Agnoletti, Fernando's son, being present:

> "[Braccio Agnoletti] remembers that his father took him one day to the home of an English lady named Mrs. Bee and, showing him a painting he had had the lady purchase, said to him approximately: 'Look at it carefully. It is by a great artist who is now ill.' The boy was very irritated by his father's imposition upon his own free judgment, and perhaps thought that a true and great artist would never have painted such scrawls. Today, Braccio Agnoletti possesses the two paintings *Danseuse bleue* and *Chahutteuse* which his father purchased at that time, and he is very pleased to own them."[50]

During the Florence show, according to the January 15, 1914 issue of *Lacerba*, Severini was able to sell another painting (*Abstract Rhythm of Mme M.S.*) and two pastels of his most recent series, on the theme of the *Argentine Tango*.[51] In the long and complex story of the payment for these paintings by Ferrante Gonnelli, the bookseller who had organized the Florentine show and who kept the proceeds from the tickets and the sales of paintings, we know only the price of the two tango pastels (300 lire) and of a landscape added to the list (169 lire).[52] There were no details about the sum paid by Agnoletti for the two dancers: as Severini's entire credit in September with Gonnelli had been only 210 francs[53] it is probable that Agnoletti purchased the dancers directly from Severini.

Firmly lodged in the Florentine collection, *Blue Dancer* was exhibited to the public only once over the next three decades, in the Futurist gallery curated by Marinetti at the 1930 Venice Biennale.[54] In the postwar period its fortunes changed and it was sent to the 1948 'Rassegna Nazionale di Arti Figurative' in Rome:[55] the catalogue does not specify the owner, but during those same months the painting was sold by Braccio Agnoletti to the Milanese dealer Romeo Toninelli, who made it available in 1949 for the 'Twentieth-Century Italian Art' exhibition in New York.[56] By June 1950 the painting had been added to the Gianni Mattioli Collection and was immediately loaned to the Futurist exhibition at the XXV Venice Biennale.[57]

[1] Letter from Gino Severini to Umberto Boccioni, undated (but April–May 1911) in Coen 1988, pp. XXXVIII–XLI.
[2] Boccioni *et al.*, February 11, 1910. The translation is from Apollonio 1970, p. 25.
[3] Marinetti, October 1, 1913. The translation is taken from Apollonio 1970, p.127.
[4] Carandini 1996, pp. 7–11; Carandini 2001, pp. 50–3.
[5] Martin 1985, pp. 96–7.
[6] Severini 1946, p. 73.
[7] *Paris* 1912[a], respectively nos. 28, 31, 33 and 32. *Danseuse obsédante* and *La Modiste* are now, respectively, in a private collection and formerly Slifka Collection, New York.
[8] *London* 1912, pp. 25–6; the captions, as a letter from Umberto Boccioni makes clear (Drudi Gambillo, Fiori 1958–62, vol. II, p. 41), were the responsibility of the gallery.
[9] Rylands 1997, p. 94. The suggestion was taken up by Fonti 2001[a], p. 20.
[10] Martin 1968, p. 139.
[11] Marinetti 1912.
[12] Severini 1946, p. 152; the most precise document for dating Fernande Olivier's separation from Picasso is a letter from Picasso to Georges Braque, dated May 18, 1912 (Cousins, Daix 1989, p. 390), in which Picasso mentions his definitive abandonment by Fernande on the previous day.
[13] *Manifesto della lussuria*. Lista 1988, p. 86.
[14] Severini 1946, p. 157.
[15] Letter from Gino Severini to Filippo Tommaso Marinetti, dated June 10, 1912, in Hanson 1995, p. 139.
[16] Letter from Umberto Boccioni to Gino Severini, undated (but June–July 1912) in Drudi Gambillo, Fiori 1958–62, vol. I, pp. 245–6.
[17] Letter from Umberto Boccioni to Gino Severini, undated (but October 2, 1912), *ibidem*, vol. I, p. 249.
[18] *Rome* 1913, p. 29, nos. 5–6; *Rotterdam* 1913, nos. 34–5.
[19] Severini 1946, p. 175; in Poggi 1992, pp. 171–2, Severini's recollection is used to date *Blue Dancer* at the end of 1912; Roche-Pézard 1983, p. 379 had already proposed a dating toward the end of 1912.
[20] Milan, private collection: Fonti 1988, no. 140.
[21] *Danseuse à Pigalle*, Baltimore, Baltimore Museum of Art: *ibidem,* no. 109.
[22] Letter from Gino Severini to Filippo Tommaso Marinetti, dated August 5 [1912], in Hanson 1995, p. 139.
[23] In a letter from Gino Severini to Filippo Tommaso Marinetti from Paris, dated February 9, 1913, Severini confirmed that he had given instructions for the six paintings to be sent from Montepulciano (the nearest railway station to Pienza) to Rome for the Costanzi show (Hanson 1995, pp. 144–5).
[24] *Ibidem*, pp. 144–5.
[25] Cecchi, March 23, 1913.
[26] Kahn, March 1, 1912.
[27] Salmon, February 6, 1912.
[28] Döblin 1912, p. 42.
[29] Apollinaire, February 7, 1912.
[30] Apollinaire, February 9, 1912.
[31] Severini 1946, p. 152.
[32] Chicago, private collection: Daix, Rosselet 1979, no. 301.
[33] Buffalo (New York), Albright-Knox Art Gallery; Messina, Nigro Covre 1986, p. 261 put forward the hypothesis that it was painted at the end of 1912; for a comparison of the Jucker *Dancer* with the Metzinger see Coen 1988, p. XLI.
[34] Letter from Gino Severini to Ardengo Soffici, dated September 27, 1913 in Drudi Gambillo, Fiori 1958–62, vol. I. p. 292.
[35] Marziali 1996, p. 182.
[36] Cambridge (Massachussets), Fogg Art Museum, Harvard University Art Museum, Gift of Mr and Mrs Joseph H. Hazen.
[37] Taylor 1961, p. 66.
[38] Martin 1968, p. 139.
[39] Letter from Gino Severini to Filippo Tommaso Marinetti, dated February 9, 1913, in Hanson 1995, pp. 144–5.
[40] Pascazio 1913, p. 96.
[41] Longhi, April 10, 1913.
[42] Cecchi, March 23, 1913.
[43] *Rotterdam* 1913, no. 34 or 35.
[44] *Ritmi di oggetti*: *Florence* 1913–14, p. 25, no. 4 or 5.
[45] Letter from Carlo Carrà to Gino Severini, dated November 10, 1913, in Carrà, Severini 1983, p. 284.
[46] Letter from Gino Severini to Carlo Carrà, dated November 4, 1913, *ibidem*, p. 283.
[47] Letter from Gino Severini to Giovanni Papini, dated December 30. 1913: Fiesole, Fondazione Primo Conti, Centro di Documentazione e Ricerche sulle Avanguardie Storiche, Archivio Papini.
[48] Gian de' Sordi, December 12, 1913.
[49] Tommei, December 24, 1913.
[50] Severini 1946, pp. 205–6.
[51] 'Elenco,' January 15, 1914.
[52] Letter from Gino Severini to Giovanni Papini, dated February 23, 1914: Fiesole, Fondazione Primo Conti, Centro di Documentazione e Ricerche sulle Avanguardie Storiche, Archivio Papini, letters from Gino Severini.
[53] Letter from Gino Severini to Carlo Carrà, dated September 8, 1914, in Carrà, Severini 1983, p. 298.
[54] *Venice* 1930, p. 146, no. 97.
[55] *Rome* 1948, p. 32, no. 8.
[56] *New York* 1949, p. 134.
[57] *Venice* 1950, p. 60, no. 32.

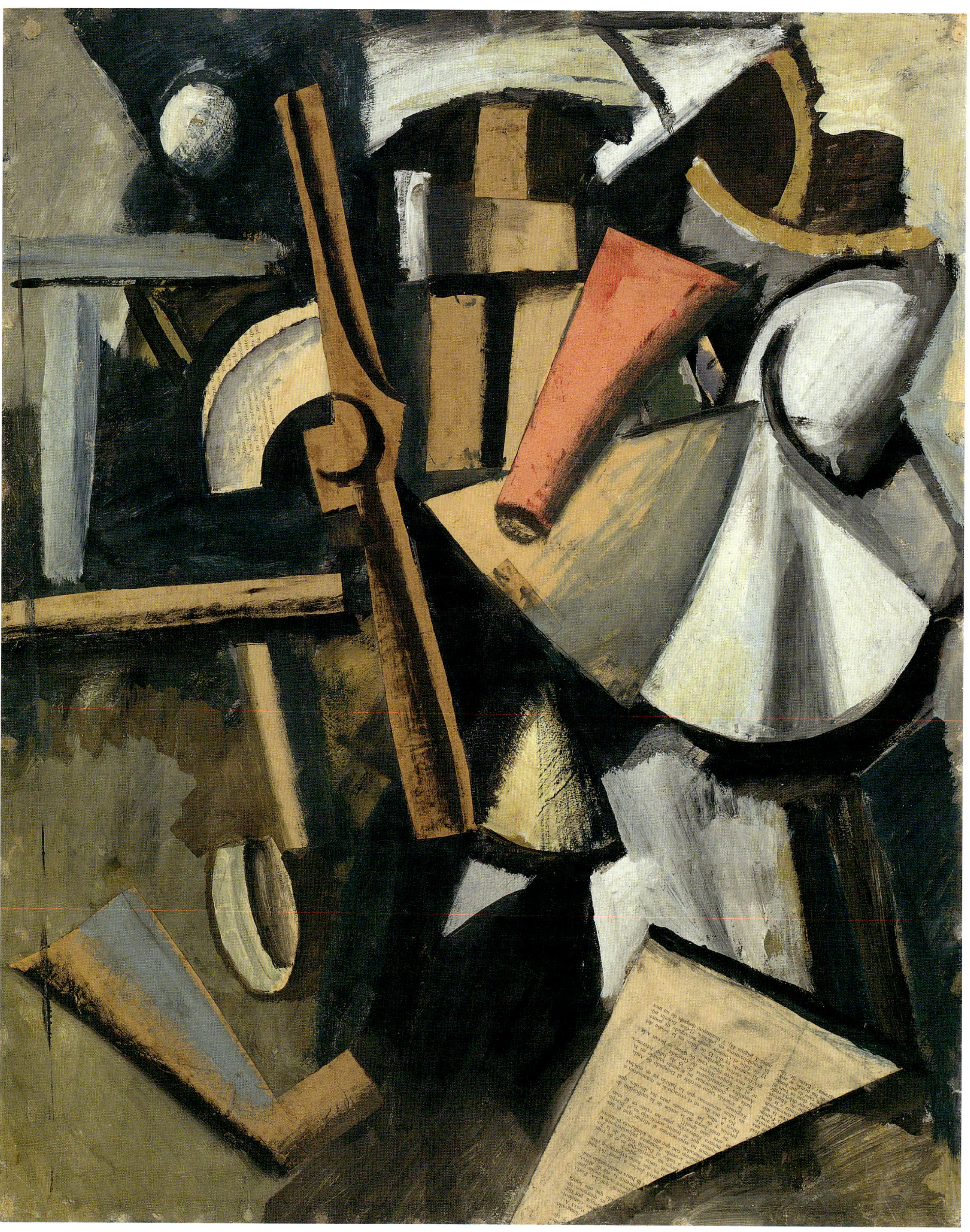

23

Mario Sironi (Sassari, 1885 – Milan, 1961)

Composition with Propeller (*Fragmentation of an Airplane*?; *The Propeller*)

Composizione con elica (*Scomposizione d'aeroplano*?; *L'elica*), 1919

Tempera and collage on board
74.5 × 61.5 cm

Provenance: property of the artist; ?: Maria Alessandra Costa?; October 1946: Galleria del Milione; after 1946: Camillo Poli, Milan; June 1950: Gianni Mattioli, with the mediation of the Galleria del Milione

Exhibitions: Rome 1919 (no. 37)? (*Scomposizione d'aeroplano*); Zurich 1950, no. 100 (*Komposition mit Propeller*); Florence 1953[a], no. 59 (*L'elica*, 1918); Rome 1959, no. 121; Winterthur 1959, no. 101 (*Composizione con elica*, 1915); Munich 1959–60, no. 93 (*Composizione con elica*, 1915); Venice 1960, p. 23, no. 131 (*Composizione con elica*, c. 1915); New York 1961–Los Angeles 1962, no. 121 (*Composition with Propeller*, 1915); Venice 1962, p. 24, no. 7 (*Composizione con elica*, 1915); Brescia 1963, no. 8 (*Composizione con elica*, 1918); Rome 1965, no. 115 (*Composizione con elica*, undated); Washington, DC 1967–Tokyo 1972, no. 47 (Washington, DC–Hamburg), no. 46 (Madrid–Seville), no. 47 (Kyoto–Tokyo); Milan 1973, p. 38, no. 13, pl. I (*Composizione con elica*, 1915); Milan 1973–4, no. 257; Düsseldorf 1974, no. 163 (1915); Venice 1986, p. 247; Düsseldorf–Baden Baden 1988, no. 19 (*Komposition mit propeller*, 1915); Madrid 1990–1, p. 358; New York 2001, without catalogue

Bibliography: Pica 1955, fig. 8 (*Elica*, 1918); Drudi Gambillo, Fiori 1958–62, vol. I, p. 464, vol. II, pp. 379, 391, no. 33 (*Composizione con elica*, 1915–16); Marchiori 1960, no. 79 (*Composizione con elica*, 1915); Taylor 1961, p. 104

Studies of Mario Sironi, which have become more numerous in recent years, have only sporadically taken into consideration this important *Composition with Propeller*: with few exceptions it has been taken to be a Futurist work executed during the Great War years. The special significance of Sironi's Futurist phase (he became an inside member of Marinetti's movement only in March 1915), his technical training which included engineering, and his impatience with the analysis of movement evidently conditioned certain aspects of this painting which are hardly compatible with Futurist poetics, such as its air of slightly disturbing fixity, or the drama of its chiaroscuro. In fact the literal meaning of the work and the date of its execution have never been the object of study.

Despite the difficulty at first of deciphering this tempera (the only interpretation offered to date has been that of a mechanistic still life with recognizable components in the form of two propellers, one aerial the other marine[1]), it is possible to identify with certainty two distinct subjects juxtaposed along the vertical axis.

On the left is the silhouette of a bi-plane seen from the front and most likely in flight, given its slight inclination with respect to the painting's vertical axis. The large wooden propeller is clearly distinguishable; the curved outline of the nose of the fuselage is indicated by a semicircular newspaper clipping; the upper portion of the wing on the left is affixed to the fuselage by a small diagonal rib and separated from the lower wing by a vertical strut; at the end of the long landing gear one of the wheels is visible. A silvery moon is painted against a dark blue sky to the left of the propeller above the wing. Sironi, a volunteer in the war in 1915, who was at the Front until the end of 1915 and from August 1917 to the end of the following year,[2] was instantly intrigued by the military use of airplanes. Beginning in 1915 he portrayed them distributing interventionist pamphlets (on the cover illustration of the May 16 issue of the Milanese periodical *Gli Avvenimenti*[3]), flying against the wartime sky,[4] silhouetted against city suburbs,[5] or crashed to the ground following an aerial accident.[6] The front part of a war plane is portrayed from a point of view similar to that of the Mattioli painting in a drawing discovered in 1968[7] (fig. 23b).

The genesis of the left part of the painting now seems clear: from the latter drawing or others like it which are now lost, sketched by Sironi at the Front and serving as annotations of the distribution of lights and darks, Sironi began a process of abstraction, simplifying forms and dispensing with the physical attachments of one part of the plane to another: some details, such as the landing gear and the propeller, become isolated elements with unbroken profiles. The make of the airplane in fig. 23b can be identified with certainty: the attachment of the propeller low down on the nose, the square-ish section of the fuselage with its slats for cooling the engine, the characteristic silhouette of the tail and undercarriage, all correspond to a small, one-man SVA,[8] a fighter and reconnaissance plane and a lightweight bomber manufactured by Ansaldo from the spring of 1918, which became famous in its two-person version thanks to Gabriele d'Annunzio's flight over Vienna on August 9, 1918.

Despite the simplified rendering of the forms, the airplane in the Mattioli painting can also be identified, with a reasonable margin of doubt. The unusual proportions of the large propeller relative to the small plane, the typical squared-off form of the propeller and the circular fuselage suggest that this is a Nieuport 11 'Bébé' with an 80 HP engine manufactured by the Società Anonima Nieuport Macchi in Varese from the second half of 1916 onwards.[9] This was the Italian Air Force's first real fighter plane (fig. 23d) and protagonist, given its light weight and maneuverability, of vivid pages dedicated to aerial warfare in the popular press of the time.

On the right Sironi seems to have arranged a composition of mechanical elements probably referring to the airplane on the left. The large metal propeller may be a component of the large front fan of some propulsion engines then in use in the aviation of the period,[10] while the object in the upper center, obtained by juxtaposing four pieces of yellowed card, which Sironi then shaded with brushstrokes of black, could be an engine axle or a transmission shaft. If, then, what we are seeing is the depiction of an airplane beside a montage of parts of its engine, *Composition with Propeller* can probably be identified with a *Fragmentation of an Airplane* exhibited at a one-man show of Sironi's work in July 1919 at the Casa d'Arte Bragaglia, documented by a leaflet with a checklist of works which has only recently been brought to the attention of scholars.[11]

However, this attempt to explain logically the relation between the two parts of the painting clashes with evidence of another nature. Certain drawings datable around 1918–19 show rather clearly how Sironi, during this phase of his career, freely inserted recurring elements in compositions very different from each other in inspiration and theme. In a drawing published with the title *Composition*[12] (fig. 23e) we see a metal propeller and the strange red cone as in the Mattioli painting combined with a woman's high-heeled shoe, thus evoking the atmosphere of the Jucker *Dancer*[13] (1918–19; fig. 23g). In a second drawing published as *Metaphysical Composition*[14] (fig. 23f), a still life with mechanical objects frames a woman walking (constructed in a way similar to a drawing by Sironi illustrated in the July 25, 1919 issue of *Cronache d'attualità*: fig. 24c): an object (perhaps a component of an airplane rudder) formed like a set square is isolated in the upper part toward the top, like the one represented in the lower left of the Mattioli painting.

As has been noted, Sironi was the first Italian Futurist to make of the airplane a pictorial subject in its own right.[15] This occurred in the war years, in the wake of a consolidated tradition of Futurist aviation literature. Since the beginning of the decade the Marinetti group of poets had been celebrating the exaltation of the senses provoked by flight (later sanctioned in a 1916 manifesto by Marinetti as "perpendicular mysticism" and the "spiral ascension of the Ego toward the Nothing-God"[16]), but also the fascination of the mechanics of an engine with "burnt cylinders"[17] and "a steel heart that rattles."[18] The propeller in particular, the instrument thanks to which man mastered the sky, had inspired pages of lively metaphorical fantasy: whether as a rotating blade scything the stars like stalks of wheat[19] or as the emanation of the pilot's feverish brain.[20] Moreover the final part of Marinetti's poem *Le Monoplan du Pape*, published in 1912, had celebrated the airplane as an instrument of war, with a detailed and prophetic description of aerial warfare on the Italo-Austrian front.[21] It is doubtful however that

(*Composition with Propeller*, 1915); Carrieri 1961, pl. 157 (*L'elica*, 1918); Valsecchi 1962[b], no. 14 (*Composizione con elica*, 1918); Bellonzi 1963, pp. 93, 98 (*Composizione con elica*, c. 1916–18); Ballo 1973[b], p. 29 (1915); Crispolti 1980[b], p. 142 (1915–17); Bellonzi 1985, p. 25, no. 6 (1915); Anzani, Pirovano 1992 , p. 131 (1916–18); Benzi 1993[a], p. 24 (1918–19); Benzi 1993[b], p. 19 (1918–19); Di Genova 1993, pp. 427–8; Rylands 1997, p. 96 (1915); Braun 2000, p. 28, pl. I (c. 1917)

Fig. 23a. *Detail of cat. no. 23*

Sironi was particularly sensitive to this genre of poetry. In the Mattioli painting the artist seems to overturn the basic ideology of such literature: the propeller is static, endowed with an almost totemic monumentality; the airplane's shapes are frozen in closed forms, with no suggestion of dynamism; the engine and the mechanical parts of the plane do not express aggressive power of the kind celebrated by Marinetti but are assembled with the impassivity of trophies.

Sironi's sources or influences must therefore be sought elsewhere. Sironi had a technical background (he had earned a diploma at a technical institute and in 1902 enrolled at the Engineering Faculty of the University of Rome, though with little success) which stirred in him a particular interest, even fascination for mechanical objects. Furthermore, the popular periodical press was full of images of innovative machinery testifying to the technological contribution of Italian industry to the war effort: an immense, stationary propeller was used to advertise the Pomilio factories (with a drawing by Guido Marussig) and the Isotta Fraschini factories (fig. 23c), while photomontages of engines and other complicated mechanical devices appeared as evidence of aggressively modern graphic design in two magazines that Sironi certainly knew, the Roman *Il Mondo* and the Milanese *Gli Avvenimenti* (for which he worked as an illustrator in 1915–16). Finally one must reckon with Sironi's response to the most important painting (and certainly the most discussed among the Italian Futurists[22]) on the subject of aviation of recent years, the large *Tribute to Blériot* by Robert Delaunay[23] (fig. 8g). This contains, on the left, a frontal view of an airplane against an abstract background of multicolored circles with its static propeller in the same position as that of Sironi's *Composition*.

Though a summary chronology of Sironi as a Futurist has been attempted,[24] a sequential ordering of his paintings of 1915–20 is still problematic. The infrequency of his participation in exhibitions, the scarcity of documents and reviews that enable the identification of works cited in catalogues, the absence of photographic reproductions in the press (as opposed to an abundance of his illustrations), Sironi's habit of not dating his paintings, and his own basic indifference to reconstructing a reliable pictorial autobiography are all factors that stand in the way of dating the extant paintings. This *Composition with Propeller* is a significant example: it was undated in the catalogue of the retrospective in which it was exhibited for the first time, in 1950,[25] and has since been dated 1915,[26] 1915–16,[27] 1915–17,[28] 1917,[29] 1918,[30] 1918–19,[31] a

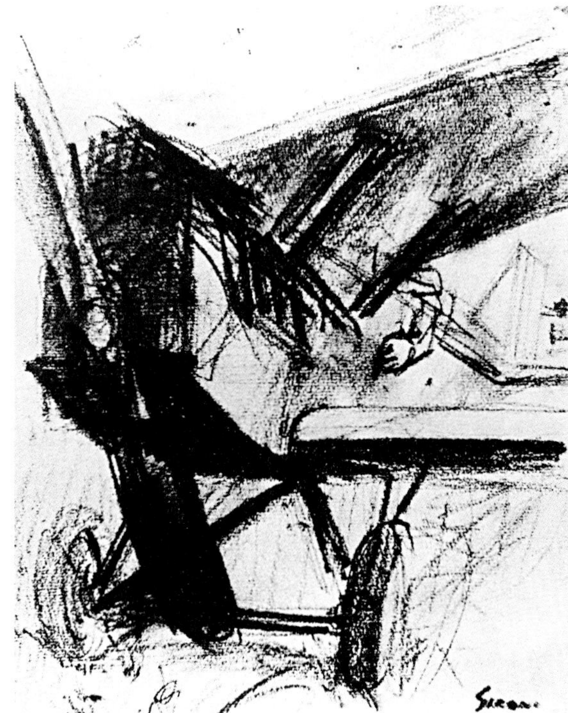

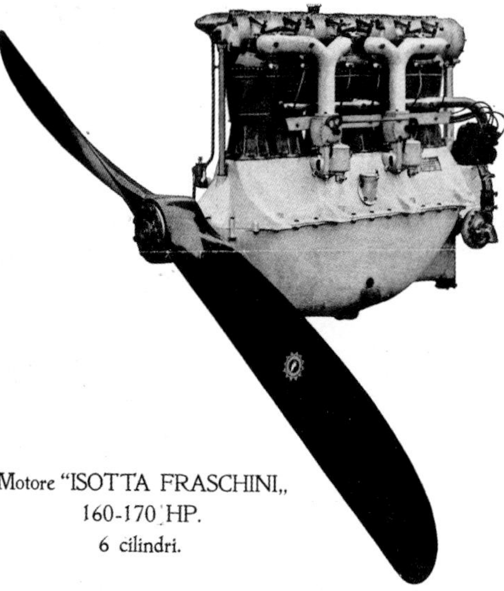

Fig. 23b. *Mario Sironi,* Aeroplano (Airplane)*, grease pencil on paper, in G. Traversi,* Mario Sironi, Disegni*, 1968*

Fig. 23c. *Advertisement for the Isotta Fraschini airplane engine, in* L'Illustrazione Italiana*, 1917*

span of time reaching from the heroic phase of Futurism to the postwar Roman era of Metaphysical painting.

The two collage inserts (both taken from a Spanish-language publication reporting administrative sanctions for certain pasta manufacturers and of illegal hoarding by a 'junta' of some kind) are not at first sight helpful in determining a significant *terminus ante quem*; they can however be usefully matched with clippings in other collages by Sironi. Fragments from a specialized Spanish bulletin called *La Pasta Alimenticia* (a title also to be found in the triangular clipping in the lower part of the Mattioli painting: fig. 23a) with characteristic two-column text (each c. 75 mm wide), with the same sort of news (the selling prices of flour, the constitution of regional manufacturers' delegations) and with advertising inserts on the same theme, are present in two works by Sironi whose dates we know: the first is *The Venus of the Ports*,[32] a tempera and collage on which Sironi was working well into 1919 (a clipping from the April 2, 1919 issue of *La Tribuna* is easily legible). Fragments of the same Spanish bulletin are pasted on the above-mentioned Jucker *Dancer*, which can be dated with certainty to after 1918 (thanks to a newspaper clipping near the top with a fragment of the triumphal report of the crossing of the Tagliamento by Italian troops, issued by the Supreme Command on the evening of November 2, 1918 and published in the press the following day). It is probable therefore that Sironi used the same issue of the Spanish publication for a series of works executed around the same time.

None of the Spanish libraries consulted by the present writer owns a complete set of *La Pasta Alimenticia: revista dedicada al fomento de las industrias de productos alimenticios*, a monthly periodical published in Saragossa. But the regularity with which it was published in the years available at the Biblioteca Nacional de España in Madrid (11 issues per year for the years XIV and XV, 1933 and 1934) and the numbers to which they refer (163–73 for 1933; 174–84 for 1934) allow us to date the inauguration of the publication to 1919 with reasonable certainty. This tends to exclude that *Composition with Propeller* was painted before 1919, or at any rate it establishes that it can only have been completed, with the two Spanish clippings, in 1919. At this point two questions remain unanswered: how did Sironi come into possession

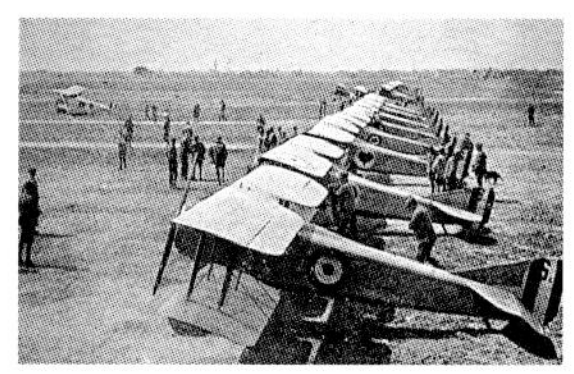

Fig. 23d. *Nieuport 'Bébe' fighter bi-planes lined up prior to military action, in* Il Mondo*, May 3, 1918*

of this esoteric Spanish publication, and why did he use it in compositions of such varying subjects? The first question may plausibly be answered by the move of Sironi's brother Edoardo to Saragossa, Spain, for reasons of work.[33] The answer to the second question is more complicated. In both *Dancer* and *The Venus of the Ports*, clippings from the foreign press evoke respectively the international cosmopolitan world of vaudeville theater and the seaport underworld (with ironic allusions such as the words 'productos alimenticios' on the prostitute's chest in *The Venus of the Ports*, as noted by Maria Grazia Messina[34]). In *Composition with Propeller* they induce an atmosphere of Metaphysical displacement, an understandable bewilderment in the viewer when coming across, in an image of mechanical technology, news reports on the commerce of pasta (in Spanish no less).

Composition with Propeller was therefore probably executed in Rome during the early months of 1919, where Sironi stayed after his January demobilization and where there was no lack of visual stimuli for a painting dominated by mechanical artifacts. In January 1919 the second issue of *Noi* contained illustrations by Prampolini characterized by the inclusion of mechanical parts (*Forma e spirito* [*Form and Spirit*] on the cover, *Costruzione* [*Construction*] on page 12). Sironi's *Dancer* in the Jucker Collection, with its marionette-like construction, has much in common with Alexander Archipenko's *Medrano*, which was illustrated in the same issue of *Noi*. Piles of incongruous geometrical objects occupied the backgrounds of metaphysical compositions by Giorgio de Chirico that were exhibited in February at the Casa d'Arte Bragaglia. The depiction of mechanical devices, with their shining, mysterious harmony, relates Sironi's work to Suprematist works of 1915 by Vladimir Tatlin,[35] Ivan Puni (*Suprematist sculpture relief*, 1915[36]), and Liubov Popova (*Caraffe on a Table*, 1915,[37] fig. 23i), though the channels for such relations are difficult to document. Printed materials reaching Italy in the wake of Marinetti's journey to Russia in January–February 1914 presented a Russian avant-garde still Cubo-Futurist in tendency (see fig. 23h), though these had been useful updates in their time for Sironi both as illustrator and as painter.[38] There is no trace of reproductions circulating in Italy of the most advanced three-dimensional experiments of Russian artists, beginning with the first exhibition of Tatlin's pictorial reliefs (May 1914) and continuing with the rich exhi-

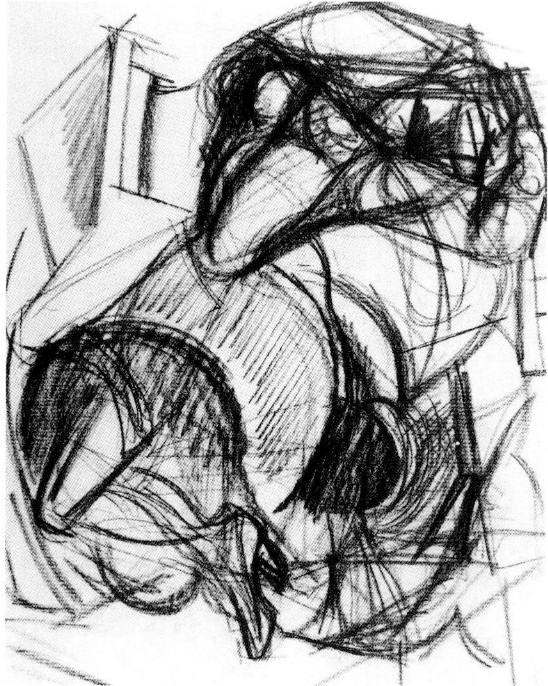

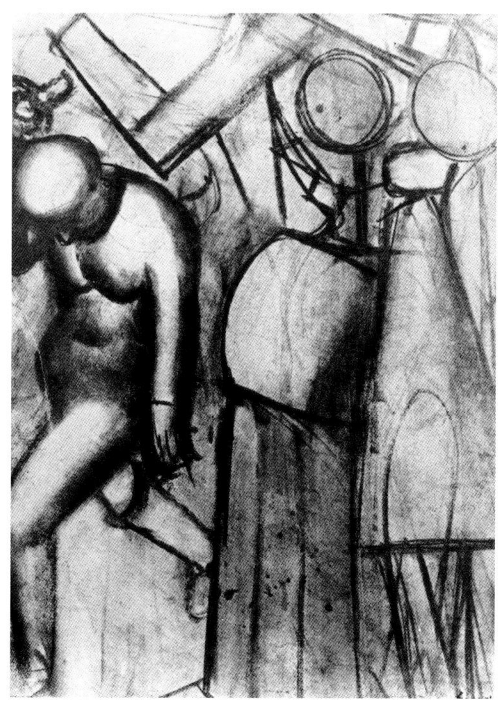

Fig. 23e. *Mario Sironi,* Composition*, pencil on paper, c. 1919. Private collection*

Fig. 23f. *Mario Sironi,* Composizione metafisica *(*Metaphysical Composition*), pencil and charcoal on paper, c. 1919. Private collection*

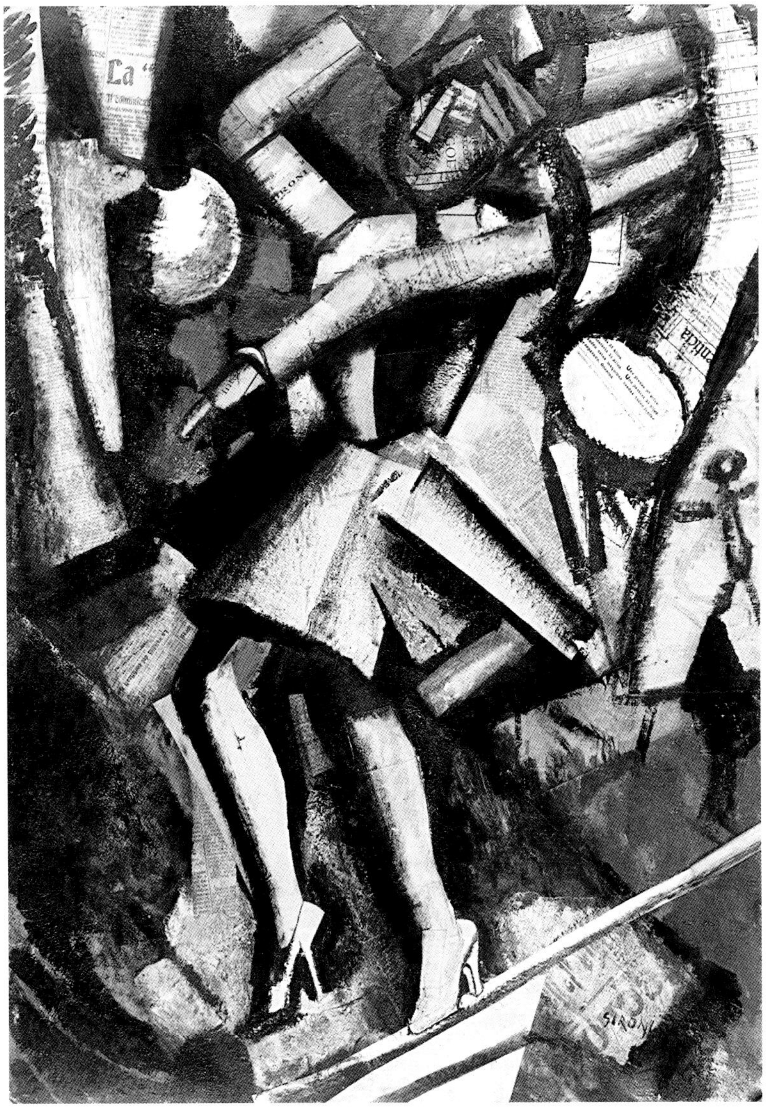

Fig. 23g. *Mario Sironi,* Ballerina (Dancer)*, tempera and collage on canvas, 1919. Milan, Civiche raccolte d'arte, Jucker Collection*

bition seasons in Moscow and St Petersburg of 1915.[39] But some news and a few photographs may have filtered through to Sironi by way of his friendship with Mikhail Larionov and Natalia Gontcharova, who were in Rome from September 1916 to April 1917 and who were in close contact with the Roman Futurists.[40]

For his one-man show at the Casa d'Arte Bragaglia in Rome in July 1919 Sironi chose paintings in varying, even discordant styles (as one review noted, "a mix [...] of various works"[41]): a dense assemblage of Metaphysical objects in *The Atelier of the Marvel*;[42] a landscape with a strong perspective framework, *The Quindici-ter*;[43] and an elementary Cubism in *Suburban Café* (exhibited in 1919 with the title *Provincial Café*[44]), to mention only those we know were in the exhibition. It should be no surprise then that he sent a work that was Futurist in structure and characterized by memories of Simultanism (if indeed one accepts its reading as an airplane flanked by parts of its engine), painted with energetic and constructive brushwork. Indeed, such vestiges of Futurism in Sironi's works at the Casa d'Arte Bragaglia are documented in the two known reviews, the only ones to be published owing to the printers' strike that paralyzed the Roman press in the summer of 1919. The critic who signed the review in the political weekly *Roma Futurista* on August 3, 1919 with the pseudonym 'A. Vibrante' insisted positively on the quality of "superior toy" of the things depicted and on the superior plastic necessity of some of the odder juxtapositions:

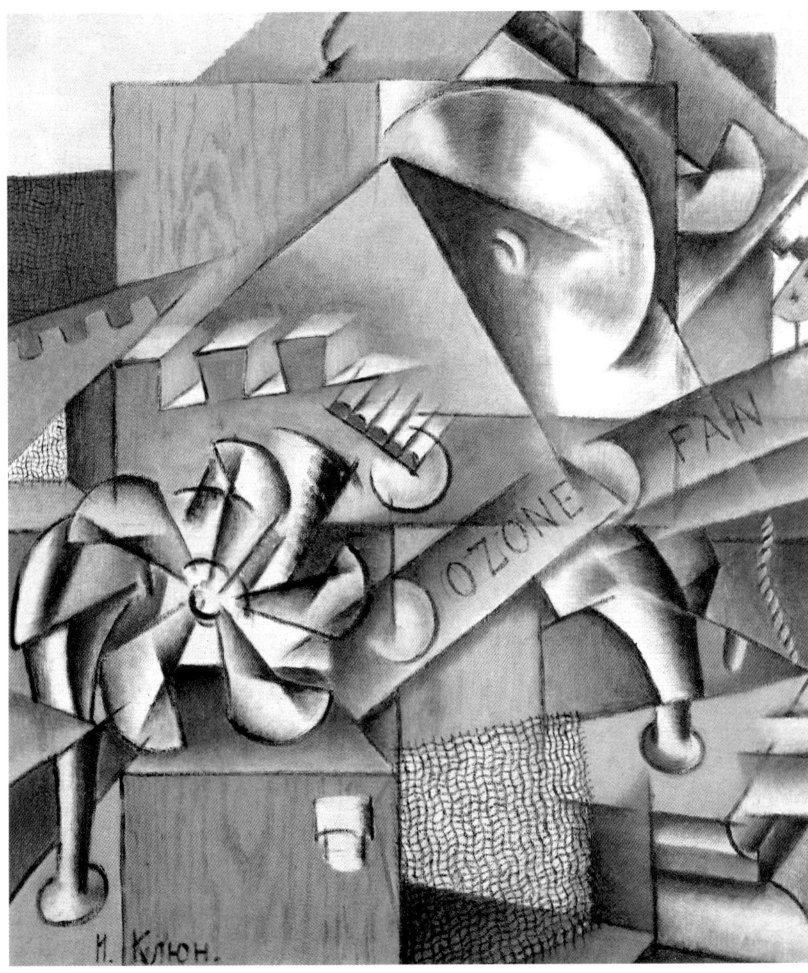

Fig. 23h. *Ivan Kliun,* Ozonizer*, 1914. St Petersburg, Russian State Museum*

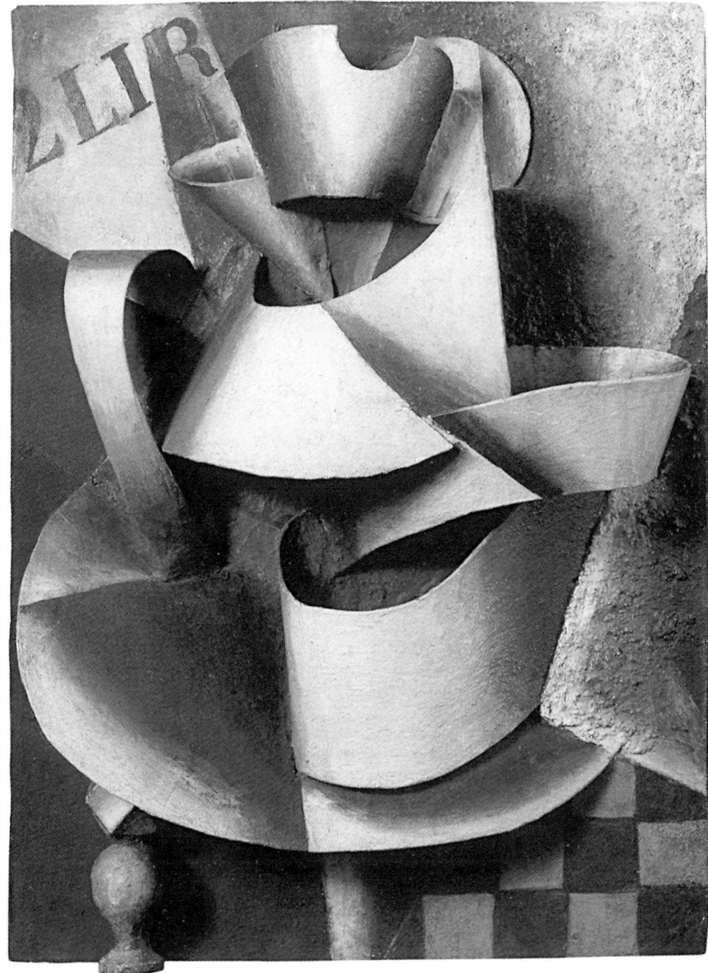

Fig. 23i. *Liubov Popova,* Caraffe on a Table (Plastic Painting)*, oil on cardboard, 1915. Moscow, Tretyakov Gallery, Gift of George Kostakis*

> "Sironi conceives the plastic life as an assemblage of toys [...] of a higher order, determining among themselves the dramas of matter and placed in relation to their settings, a panorama of forms, a complex of figures and objects which harmonize themselves in the painting, according to a personal architecture, where everything is plastically necessary."[45]

On the opposite front, Mario Broglio, editor of *Valori Plastici* and champion of an extreme detachment from the Cubo-Futurist avant-garde language, seemed to refer directly to this painting in one of the most virulent passages of his critique of Sironi's show:

> "The fragmentations, the simultanism [...] in other words, Boccioni's whole philosophy of painting, tackled with determination and without bad faith, provides him with formulae and disturbing illusions to work with."[46]

Composition with Propeller's history was interrupted in 1919 and begins again only in November 1950. It was inventoried as no. 4000 in the archives of the Galleria del Milione, with the generic title 'Futurist period tempera'[47]: it was on deposit with "signora Sironi" (almost certainly Maria Alessandra Costa, Sironi's companion in the 1920s) and was returned by the latter to the Galleria del Milione on October 1, 1946. In the immediate following years it changed hands again: in 1950 Gianni Mattioli purchased it, through the Galleria del Milione and for the sum of 75,000 lire, from the lawyer Camillo Poli.[48] Mattioli, who bought a further four paintings by Sironi on this occasion,[49] must have been in contact with Poli since at least two years: a still life by Rosai belonging to Poli was shown in April 1949 in the 'Twentieth-Century Italian Art' exhibition at the Museum of Modern Art, New York,[50] for which Mattioli was responsible for putting the American curators, Alfred Barr, Jr. and James Thrall Soby, in contact with Italian collectors. Mattioli immediately secured the public exhibition of his *Composition with Propeller*: with the title *Komposition mit Propeller* it was shown at the 'Futurismo-Pittura Metafisica' exhibition in the Kunsthaus Zürich, with an insurance value of 300,000 lire.[51]

[1] Rylands 1997, p. 96.
[2] For the most detailed chronology for Sironi in the years 1915–19 see Camesasca 1980, pp. 425–7.
[3] Benzi, Sironi 1988, p. 35, no. 76.
[4] *Aereo* (1915), Prato, Farsettiarte: *Sassari* 1985, no. 7.
[5] *Aereo e città*, Cologne, Ludwig Museum: *Rome* 1993–4, pp. 140–1; *Paesaggio urbano con aeroplano* (1918–19), Berlin, Staatliche Museen zu Berlin - Preussischer Kulturbesitz Nationalgalerie: Bellonzi 1985, no. 19.
[6] *Aeroplano con paesaggio urbano*, Milan, private collection: *Milan* 1985, no. 31.
[7] *Aeroplano*, Milan, private collection: Traversi 1968, pl. 16.
[8] Apostolo, Bignozzi 1973, pp. 185–92.
[9] Contini 1934, p. 288; Apostolo, Bignozzi 1973, pp. 9–16.
[10] Garuffa 1918, p. 582.
[11] *Scomposizione d'aeroplano*: *Rome* 1919, no. 36; Gianelli 1989, p. 638; Braun 2000, p. 233.
[12] Private collection: Baldacci, Cavallo 1993, p. 31, no. 10, dated 1919–20: the woman's shoe can be seen in the upper center, turned through 90° facing left with respect to the sheet.
[13] *Ballerina*, Milan, Civiche raccolte d'arte, Jucker Collection: *Milan* 1992–3, unnumbered plate.
[14] Private collection; *Düsseldorf–Baden Baden* 1988, no. 39; *Rome* 1993–4, p. 381.
[15] Benzi 1993[c], p. 118.
[16] Marinetti 1916[b], in Marinetti 1983, p. 137.
[17] Cavicchioli 1912, p. 217.
[18] Altomare 1912, p. 76.
[19] Cavicchioli 1912, p. 217.
[20] Marinetti 1912[a], p. 41.
[21] *Ibidem*, pp. 299–348.
[22] Breunig 1960, pp. 587–9.
[23] Basel, Öffentliche Kunstsammlung Basel, Kunstmuseum.
[24] Benzi 1993[a].
[25] *Zurich* 1950, no. 100.
[26] *New York* 1961–*Los Angeles* 1962, no. 121.
[27] Drudi Gambillo, Fiori 1958–62, vol. II, p. 391, no. 33.
[28] Crispolti 1980[b], p. 142.
[29] Braun 2000, pl. I.
[30] *Florence* 1953[a], no. 59.
[31] Benzi 1993[a], p. 24.
[32] *La Venere dei porti*, Milan, Civiche raccolte d'arte, Boschi-Di Stefano Collection: Caramel, Fiorio, Pirovano 1980, no. 1646; a brief collection of clippings can be found in Pugliese 2000, pp. 17–25.
[33] Letter to the author from Andrea Sironi, dated May 21, 2001. By 1920 the move had definitely taken place, since at least two drawings by Mario Sironi datable to that year are on sheets headed 'Edoardo Sironi-Saragozza'.
[34] Messina 1995, p. 85.
[35] The five constructions are illustrated in *Tatlin* 1915, unnumbered pages.
[36] New York, The Museum of Modern Art: *Frankfurt–New York* 1992, no. 35.
[37] Moscow, Tretyakov Gallery: Rudenstine 1981, p. 366, figs. 815–16; *New York* 1991, pp. 57 and 128, no. 41.
[38] Benzi 1993[c], p. 116; Braun 2000, pp. 28 and 228–9.
[39] Zhadova 1982, pp. 41–57; Zhadova 1988, pp. 331–8; Marcadé 1989, pp. 92–3; *Düsseldorf* 1993–*Moscow* 1994, pp. 245–59.
[40] Parton 1993, pp. 154–8.
[41] Broglio 1919, p. 29.
[42] *L'atelier della meraviglia*, Milan, Pinacoteca di Brera, Jesi Collection: Mazzocca 1993–4, vol. II, no. 894.
[43] Formerly Milan, Cesare Tosi collection: Bellonzi 1985, no. 21.
[44] *Caffè di periferia* and *Caffè di provincia*: Valsecchi 1962[b], pl. 2.
[45] Vibrante, August 3, 1919.
[46] Broglio 1919, p. 30.
[47] Milan, Archivio Galleria del Milione, register of works: the identification with *Composition with Propeller* is supported by the printed number 4000 on the stretcher and by the measurements given in the registry (61 × 73.5 cm), which are comparable to those of the Mattioli painting.
[48] Archivio Mattioli, note in the Galleria del Milione accounts dated July 18, 1950: on June 20, 1950, Gianni Mattioli was debited the sum of lire 75,000 for the purchase from Poli of the "Sironi n. 4000." On June 30 Mattioli was debited a 10% commission by the Galleria del Milione (*Appendix I*, document no. 50).
[49] These were: *Manichino*, tempera, 68 × 49 cm, register of the Galleria del Milione no. 4385, lire 45,000; *La penitente*, oil on canvas, 60 × 50 cm, register of the Galleria del Milione no. 5776, lire 65.000; *Composizione con cavaliere*, oil on panel, 28 × 20 cm, register of the Galleria del Milione no. 5782: *Alleluia*, oil on canvas, 40 × 50 cm, register of the Galleria del Milione no. 5778 (Archivio Mattioli, account of the Galleria del Milione, dated July 18, 1950).
[50] *New York* 1949, p. 133.
[51] *Zurich* 1950, no. 100 (with the generic indication 'Privatbesitz'); Archivio Mattioli, receipt signed by the Soprintendente alle Gallerie Fernanda Wittgens and dated October 27, 1950 with a list of paintings from the Gianni Mattioli Collection sent to the 'Futurismo-Pittura metafisica' show in Zurich.

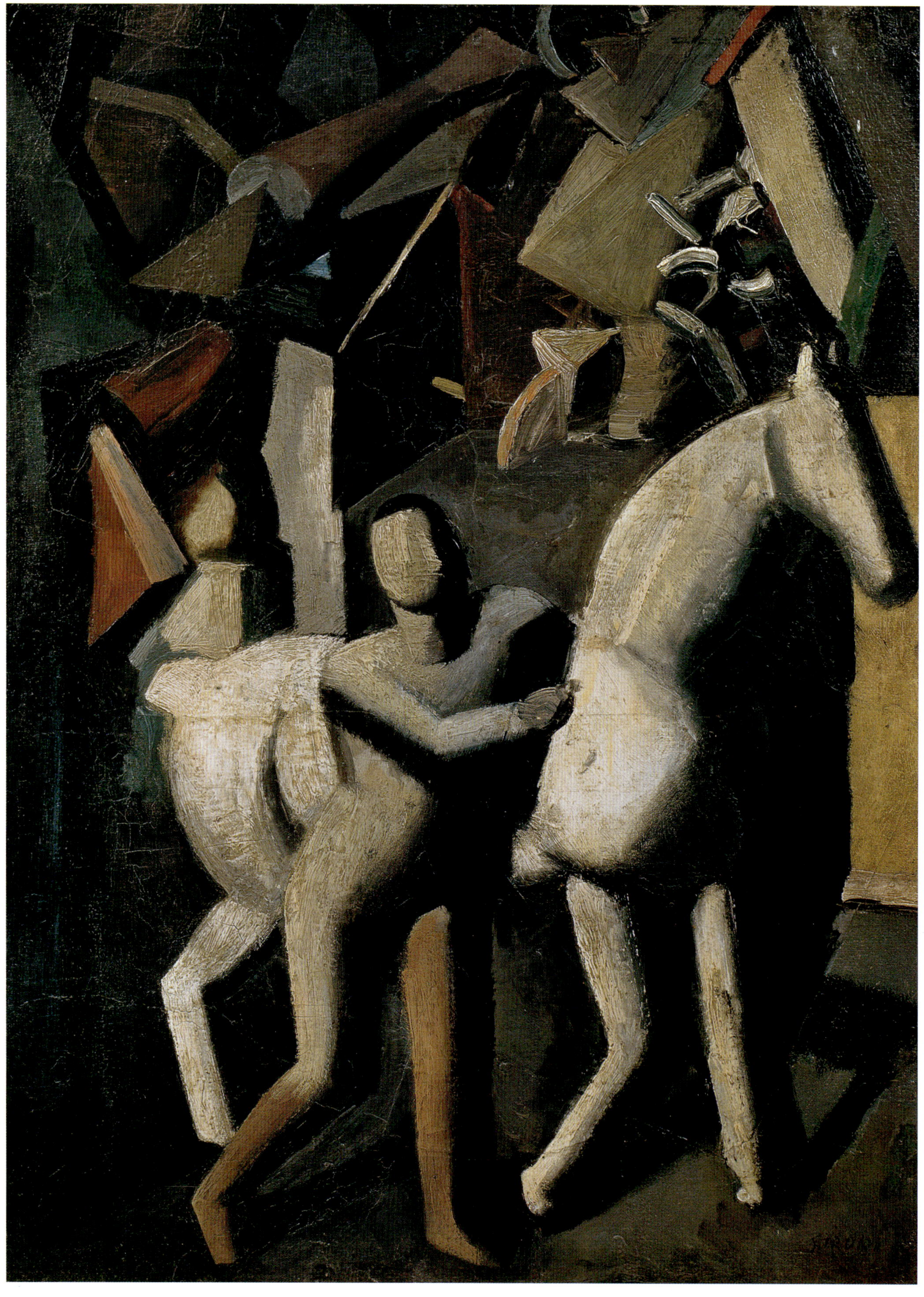

24

Mario Sironi

The White Horse (*Rider*?; *Man and Horse*)

Il cavallo bianco (*Cavaliere*?; *Uomo e cavallo*), 1919

Oil on canvas
79 × 59 cm

Inscription: *recto*, signed lower right: 'Sironi'

Provenance: property of the artist; June 1941: Pietro Feroldi, Brescia; May 1949: Gianni Mattioli

Exhibitions: Rome 1919 (no. 31)? (*Cavaliere*); Macerata 1922, no. 40 (*Uomo e cavallo*); Milan 1942[b], catalogue not printed; Zurich 1950, no. 167 (*Das weisse Pferd*, 1919); Florence 1953[a], no. 60 (*Il cavallo bianco*, 1919); Rome 1959, no. 120; Winterthur 1959, no. 106; Munich 1959–60, no. 98; Venice 1962, p. 24, no. 14; Florence 1967[a], no. 1375; Washington, DC 1967–Tokyo 1972, no. 46 (Washington, DC–Hamburg), no. 45 (Madrid–Seville), no. 46 (Kyoto –Tokyo); Milan 1973, no. 22; Düsseldorf–Baden Baden 1988, no. 40; Macerata 1995, no. 0A/4

Bibliography: Letter from Pietro Feroldi to Carlo Belli, dated June 28, 1941 (Archivio Mattioli, photostatic copy); Piovene 1942, p. XV, pl. 32 (*Il cavallo bianco*); Anceschi 1944, no. 3; Sartoris 1946, p. 11, pl. II; Carrieri 1950, pp. 156, 158; Pica 1955, pp. 25, 31, pl. III; Castelfranco, Valsecchi 1956, pp. 43–4; Drudi Gambillo, Fiori 1958–62, vol. I, p. 464, vol. II, no. 75, pp. 389, 393; Marchiori 1960, no. 80; Valsecchi 1962[b], pl. III; Valsecchi 1963, unnumbered page; Ballo 1964[b], vol. I, pp. 179–80; Camesasca 1980, pp. 426–8; Crispolti 1980[b], p. 143; Garberi 1991, p. 30, no. 9; Benzi 1993[b], p. 19; Benzi 1993[c], p. 144; Crispolti 1995, p. 150; Rylands 1997, p. 98; Braun 2000, p. 229

In 1919, like other artists connected to the Futurist movement, Sironi initiated a process of tightening up his compositions and of emphasizing the volumetric quality of his forms. The pictorial language he developed was distinct from that of his contemporaries: vestiges of mechanical dynamism, archaistic simplifications, Metaphysical sympathies and emphatic chiaroscuro are woven into a pictorial drama of somber tones, whose irrational and romantic basis was often stressed by Italian critics.[1]

The pamphlet printed for Sironi's one-man exhibition at the Casa d'Arte Bragaglia in Rome (July 3–30, 1919),[2] which has come to the attention of scholars only in recent years,[3] documents the presence of two paintings of horses and riders: *Cavaliere* (*Rider*), no. 31, and *Uomo a cavallo (costruzione plastica)* (*Man on Horseback [Plastic Construction]*), no. 33. It is not possible to identify the former as the Mattioli painting with certainty. The two known reviews of the exhibition omit details of individual works,[4] and the back of the painting, which was relined in the 1950s (the earliest visible label is that of the 1962 Venice Biennale), does not provide helpful information. Yet it is likely nevertheless that *The White Horse* was among the paintings exhibited in July 1919 at the Casa d'Arte Bragaglia. As we have seen, Sironi sent two works which testify that the equestrian theme had by this time engaged his pictorial imagination. Moreover *The Atelier of the Marvel*, a painting known to have been in the exhibition and today called *The Atelier of the Marvels*[5] (fig. 24f), depicts throughout the same mysterious array of gadgets with a Metaphysical aura that occupy the background of *The White Horse.* Finally, amidst the general difficulty of establishing a chronology of Sironi's drawings between 1919 and 1920, the illustration of a female nude on the first page of the July 25, 1919 issue of *Cronache d'attualità* (fig. 24c) constitutes a stylistic *terminus ante quem*: the volumetric construction of the woman is close to that of the horseman in the Mattioli painting, with its rounded shapes and compact shadows that wrap the anatomy in unbroken bands. The rough surface of *The White Horse* is compatible with a dating before June 1919. As X-rays reveal (fig. 24a), Sironi painted over a collage which seems to have been in the Futurist manner: densely overlapping angular planes (like those in a charcoal drawing, *Composition*, datable to 1918,[6] fig. 24b) are combined with circular elements (the portion of a circular band still visible in relief between the horseman's head and the horse's neck was a favorite motif of Sironi's in 1919, also used in *Composition with Propeller* in the Mattioli painting [cat. no. 23] and in an ink drawing with the title *Metaphysical Composition*).[7] It is likely that Sironi, given the opportunity to prepare a large show in July in an important exhibition venue associated with the Rome avant-garde (exhibitions of paintings by Giacomo Balla and Giorgio de Chirico had preceded his), worked intensely in the months prior to this event, painting over used canvases and transforming them in the spirit of the new classical mood that was beginning to pervade Rome. Thus a Futurist collage was obliterated by a painting dominated by the atavistic motif of a rider on foot leading a horse by (invisible) reins. Mario Broglio's review of the Casa d'Arte Bragaglia show in July 1919 cited, among the best works, "representations that tend to draw us outside of time and space, where an archaic spirit seems to have imbued simple and severe bodies, as if in a dream"[8]: *The White Horse* easily fits this description.

The hypothesis that *The White Horse* dates from the first half of 1919 is of particular importance for an understanding of Sironi's artistic choices in this crucial period of a few months. Following his demobilization in January 1919 he alternated between sporadic contacts with Milan (where he frequented the homes of Margherita Sarfatti and Umberto Notari, renewed his relations with Marinetti and witnessed the *volte face* of Achille Funi and Leonardo Dudreville in favor of realism[9]) and a prolonged sojourn in Rome where the direction in which art was moving had by this time become clear, between calls to reject the avant-garde in the journal *Valori Plastici* and the strong imprint of Metaphysical painting established by de Chirico's one-man show at the Casa d'Arte Bragaglia in February.[10]

The White Horse testifies to Sironi's particular awareness of de Chirico. The background is inexplicable without a knowledge of the accumulations of set squares, wooden hoops and angles with luminous outlines crowding de Chirico's paintings at the Casa d'Arte Bragaglia (*The Philosopher-Poet*, now lost but illustrated on the first page of the February 15 issue of *Cronache d'attualità*, as well as all his major paintings of 1917–19[11]) and his drawings illustrated in the spring 1919 issue of *Valori Plastici* (*Autumnal Still Life*, for example[12]). But Sironi was also attentive to the work of Carrà, whose art was stylistically more compatible with his own: the brown pyramid with a facet in shadow placed in the upper left corner seems taken whole from the first version of the *Builder's Son* (reproduced in an insert of *Valori Plastici* in April–May 1919), and was a form that evidently fascinated Sironi, since he painted it again on the green table in *The Lamp* of the same year.[13] The foreground also shows his fascination with the new Metaphysical painting. The ground tilted toward the viewer and the shadows projected diagonally across it are derived from the art of de Chirico in Ferrara in 1917; the modeling of the horseman in rounded, blank volumes compares with similarly shaped figures in de Chirico's drawings (*The Prodigal Son* from 1917; *Mannequin and Two Personages* from 1919[14]). The horse, whose color and plastic rendition resemble something sculptural, challenges the plasters illuminated by stark artificial light in Carrà's recent paintings (beginning with the head of the *Drunken Gentleman* [fig. 10h] illustrated in the catalogue of Carrà's one man exhibition at the Galleria Chini in Milan in 1917–18[15]).

Sironi, who amazed Umberto Boccioni in 1910 because he had filled "his house with plaster casts" and was copying "a Greek head from all angles, 20 or 25 times,"[16] surely welcomed the renewed attention of modern painters to antique sculpture in 1919. Despite this archaic aura, the horse and rider do not seem to derive from any specific model, whether Roman, Romanesque or Renaissance. The motif of the rider on foot leading his horse is common in antique sculptures that were accessible to Sironi in Rome at that time, such as two of the Hadrian medallions on the Arch of Constantine (though the invention of the horseman with his arm on the horse's back is absent). But in the immediate postwar period Sironi seems to have been attracted to the subject primarily because it lent itself readily to the modernist theme of the synthesis of volumes. In contemporary drawings the horse-rider duo enabled him to study,

Fig. 24a. *X-ray of cat. no. 24*

Fig. 24b. *Mario Sironi,* Composition, *charcoal on paper, c. 1918. Private collection*

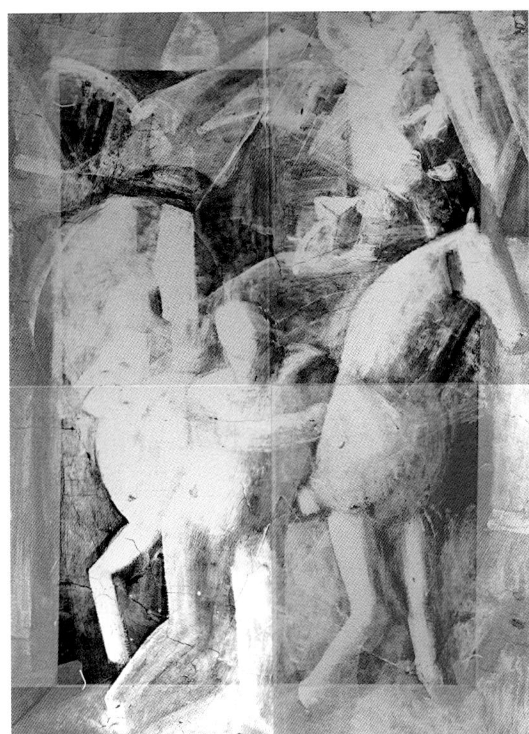

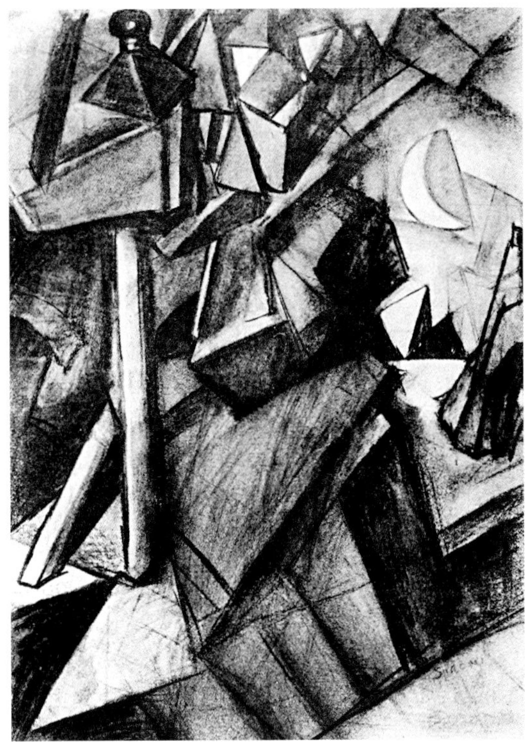

by turn, the contrived faceting of a wooden toy (*Ananke*,[17] fig. 24d), the piling-up of pure solids (*The Horse*[18]), the simplification of contours (*Horse and Rider*,[19] *Composition with Mannequin*[20]), and bold chiaroscuro (*Horse, Airplane and Guitar*,[21] fig. 24e). The Mattioli painting however seems to present us with a novelty: the man's gesture of placing his arm over the horse's back instills an unprecedented tenderness, almost a physical communion between the man and the animal, which confounds the ceremonial effect, replacing it with an anti-heroic dimension.

One of the dominant motifs of *The White Horse* is the contrast between the foreground, with its anti-heroic and archaic flavor, and the entirely different background. This is filled with forms evoking the world of mechanical technology still dear to the artist. In the upper right are forms evocative of the tail and rudder of an airplane (also present in the underlying collage, where it was depicted from a different point of view). Lower down, a stylized motorcyclist can be seen from behind (fig. 24g), a detail that was identified by its first owner Pietro Feroldi at the time he acquired the painting.[22] One can make out the rear wheel, the fork, the passenger's seat and the handlebars;[23] Sironi portrayed the cyclist's back, his leg, his arm and his head. He was evidently intrigued by the doubled-over posture of the cyclist, which occurs again in a contemporary drawing[24] and, soon after, in an illustration for the January 1920 issue of *Primato Artistico Italiano*[25] (fig. 24h).

When Sironi painted over his earlier Futurist collage in the late spring of 1919 with the oil painting of *The White Horse*, he opted for a technique in blatant opposition to the ideals promoted by the *Valori Plastici* group that had come to prevail in those months. The background is thickly painted with agitated brushstrokes whose texture is clearly visible; the horse is constructed by covering the dark ground with a dense white impasto which accentuates volume. The clear neo-Quattrocento light of which Carrà was so fond and the thin paint layers favored by de Chirico are substituted by a dramatic chiaroscuro and a material density suggestive of the uncontrollable energy of a lava flow (an early description of the painting stressed the "orgiastic and voluptuous dynamism" of its execution[26]). *The White Horse* kept the door open for

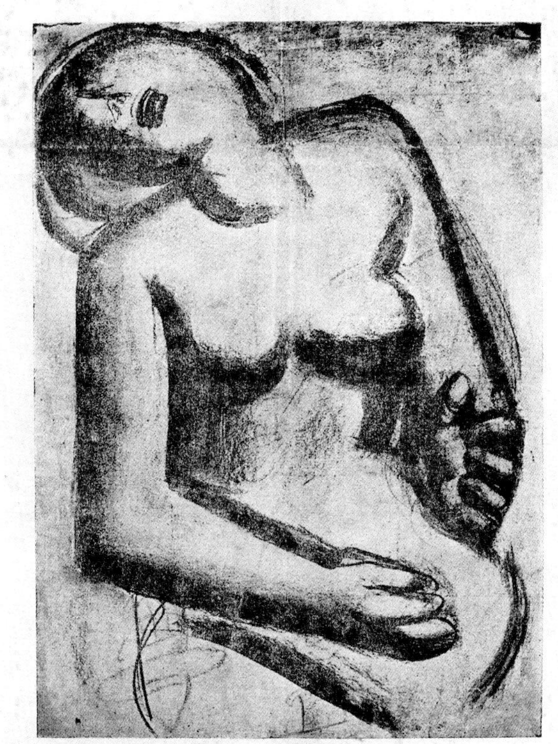

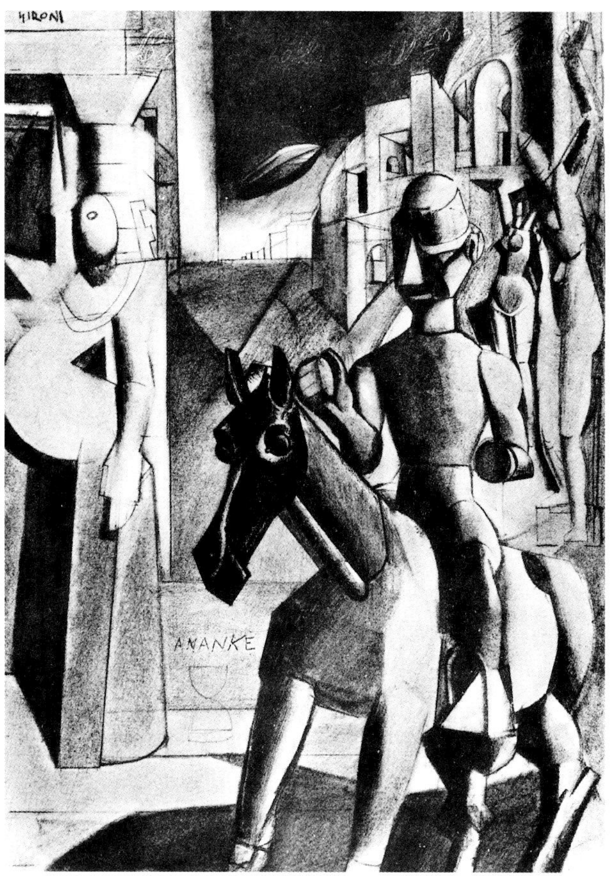

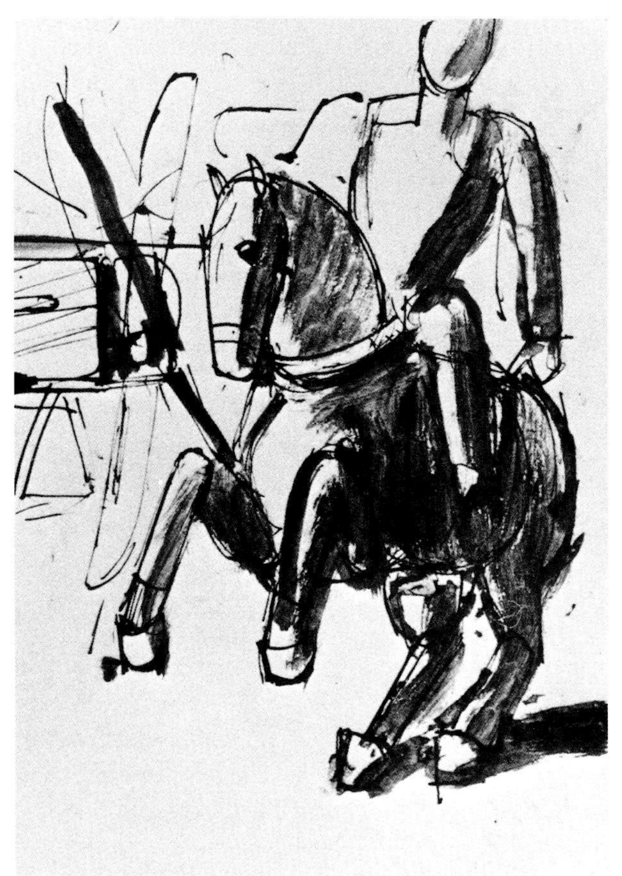

Fig. 24c. *Mario Sironi,* Drawing, *1919, in* Cronache d'attualità, *July 25, 1919*

Fig. 24d. *Mario Sironi,* Ananke, *pencil and charcoal on paper, 1919. Private collection*

Fig. 24e. *Mario Sironi,* Cavallo, aeroplano e chitarra *(*Horse, Airplane and Guitar*), pen and India ink on paper, 1919–20, detail. Rome, private collection*

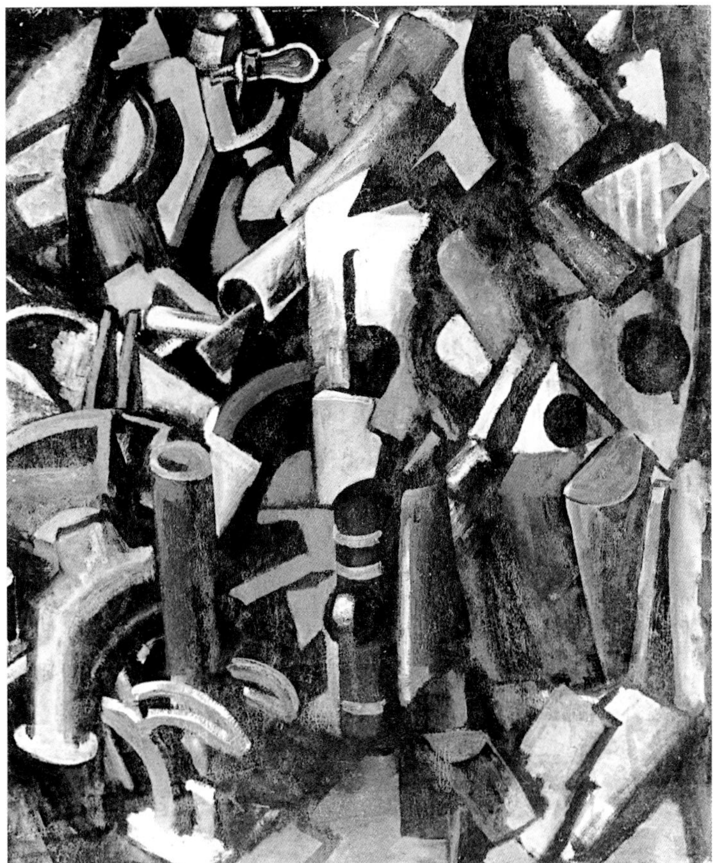

Fig. 24f. *Mario Sironi,* L'atelier delle meraviglie *(The Atelier of Marvels), oil on canvas, 1919. Milan, Pinacoteca di Brera, Jesi Collection*

a dialogue with Marinetti's circle (in February Sironi had exhibited fifteen paintings at the 'Grande Esposizione Nazionale Futurista' in Milan), by attempting a combination of the new classical vogue with the formal achievements of Futurism (as explicitly stated in the manifesto *Contro tutti i ritorni in pittura* signed by Sironi in January of the following year[27]).

Evidence of the appropriateness of interpreting the painting in a Futurist key was its presence in the 1922 'Prima Esposizione Futurista', with the title *Cavallo e cavaliere*, organized by Ivo Pannaggi in Macerata for the 'Esposizione Provinciale d'Arte'[28] (fig. 24i). The gallery, installed as a ten-year retrospective of Futurist research, opened with a tribute to Boccioni's *Scomposizione di donna a tavola* (*Fragmentation of a Woman at a Table*), continued with Balla's work of 1918 and Depero's of 1920, to conclude with the relatively mechanistic imagery of Paladini, Pannaggi and Prampolini: in this context, Sironi's *The White Horse* assumed a determining role by opening the way to a new Futurist style of plastic construction,[29] capable of rendering the "new reality" as argued by Pannaggi in an essay that explained the rationale behind the exhibition.[30]

The catalogue of the show in Macerata did not identify the owners of the works, but it is likely that *The White Horse* remained unsold in Sironi's possession for a protracted period, since it has no provenance prior to 1941 when it entered the collection of Pietro Feroldi. It was among the last paintings acquired by the Brescian collector, at a time when he had already conceived the ambition of tracing a history of modern Italian art, according to a rigorous set of aesthetic criteria. Feroldi informed Carlo Belli of his purchase in a letter dated June 28, 1941, justifying his choice as a tribute to Sironi's plastic rigor. Significantly, Feroldi compared it favorably with another masterpiece of 1919 by Sironi, *The Lamp* (*La lampada*), which had recently been bought by the collector Emilio Jesi, his fiercest rival in Lombardy in terms both of financial means and visual acumen:

"I have again purged [the collection], eliminating twelve or ten useless items, but I have added a 1922 Carrà [...] and a 70 × 60 almost Cubist Sironi: a white horse with a nude man and behind a movement of bluish-greens grayish-Sienna which compose geometrical schemes of motifs of war airplane, motorcycle, elements of houses. Plastic values pushed to the unimaginable and a stupefying pictorial matter. All told the mannequin of the lamp taken to an incomparable height."[31]

Entry into the Feroldi Collection saved the painting from the neglect it had suffered for almost two decades and made it instantly famous. It was exhibited in November 1942 with Feroldi's collection at the Brera, while the book presenting the collection that was published for the occasion included a good color illustration. It was easy for Guido Piovene, who wrote the introduction to the lavish collation of plates, to take for granted the pleasure his readers would have in a painting "with that effect of chiaroscuro which shows the tendency of the times in a 17th-century key."[32] In 1947, in a cultural climate beginning to recognize Italian *pittura metafisica* as one of the sustaining pillars of the art of the century, the plates of the monograph on Sironi by Alberto Sartoris began with the illustration of *The White Horse*, perceived by this time as a key work in the artist's *oeuvre*. In May 1949 the painting passed into the Mattioli Collection together with the rest of the Feroldi Collection, for the sum of 100,000 lire, compared to an estimated value of 180,000.[33]

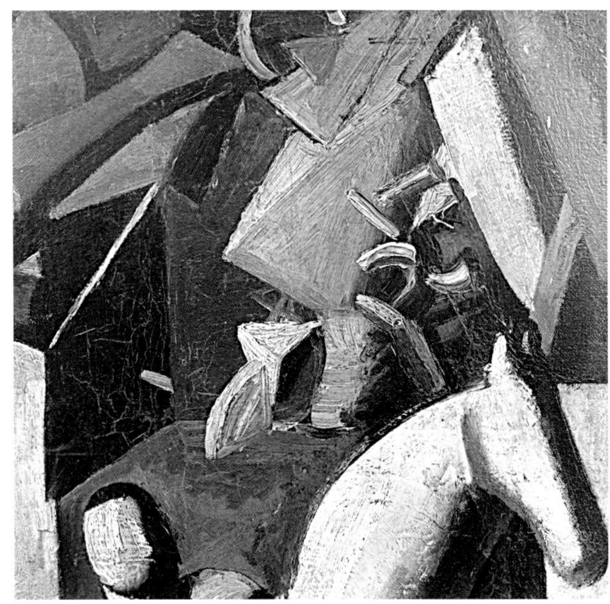

Fig. 24g. *Detail of cat. no. 24*

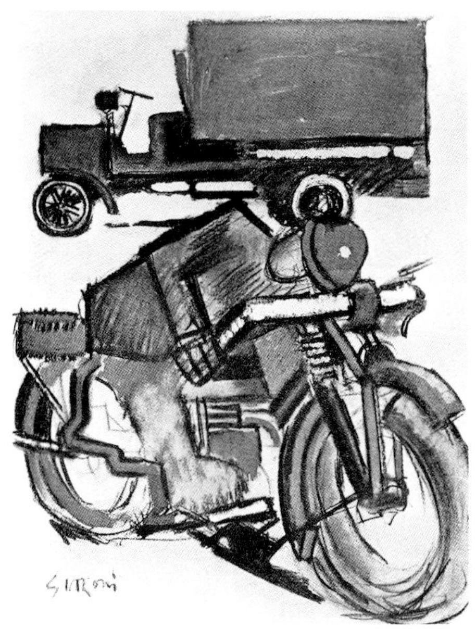

Fig. 24h. *Mario Sironi,* Motociclista *(*Motorcyclist*), in* Il Primato Artistico Italiano*, 1920*

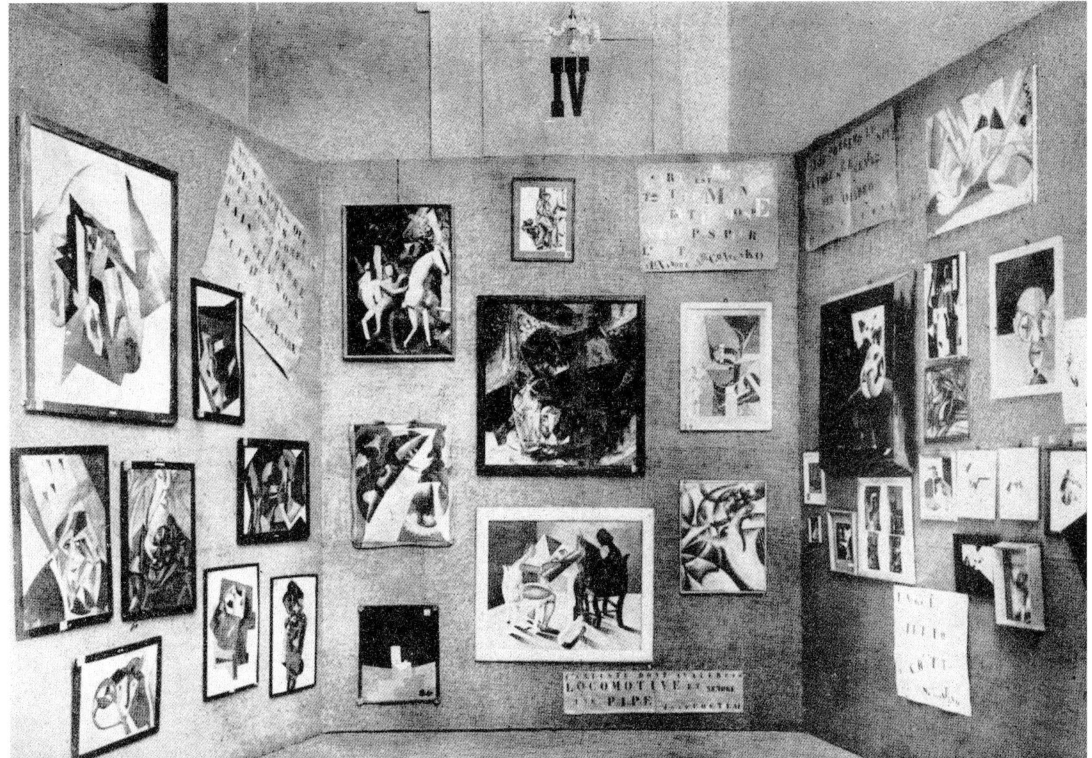

Fig. 24i. *Installation view of three walls of the 'Mostra Futurista alla Esposizione Provinciale d'Arte,' Macerata, 1922*

[1] Sartoris 1946, p. 11; Ragghianti 1953, pp. 20–1; Crispolti 1980[b], pp. 142–3.
[2] *Rome* 1919.
[3] Gianelli 1989, p. 638; Braun 2000, p. 233.
[4] Broglio 1919, pp. 29–30; Vibrante 1919.
[5] *L'atelier della meraviglia*, later *L'atelier delle meraviglie*: Milan, Pinacoteca di Brera, Jesi Collection: Benzi 1994, no. 894, pp. 800–1.
[6] New York, Barbara Mathes Gallery: *Rome* 1993–4, p. 381.
[7] *Composizione metafisica*, Rome, private collection: *ibidem*, p. 382.
[8] Broglio 1919, p. 30.
[9] Sarfatti 1919, pp. 32–3; letter from Mario Sironi to Paolo Buzzi, sent April 5, 1950, in Sironi 1980, pp. 18–19; Camesasca 1980, pp. 427–8; Braun 2000, pp. 42–3.
[10] Benzi 1933[b], p. 18.
[11] Baldacci 1997, p. 404; for identifying the paintings exhibited in the show, for which there was no catalogue, the review by Longhi is fundamental: Longhi, February 22, 1919.
[12] Baldacci 1997, D91, p. 337.
[13] *Il figlio del costruttore* and *La lampada*, the latter in Milan, Pinacoteca di Brera, Jesi Collection: Benzi 1994, no. 894, pp. 801–02.
[14] *Il figliol prodigo* and *Manichino e due personaggi*: Baldacci 1997, D 95, p. 377 and D 122, p. 409.
[15] *Gentiluomo briaco*: *Milan* 1917–18, no. 16.
[16] Letter from Umberto Boccioni to Gino Severini, dated August 1, 1910, in Boccioni 1971, p. 342.
[17] Milan, private collection: *New York* 1989[b], no. 34.
[18] Private collection, *Il cavallo*: *Milan* 1973, no. 17, dated erroneously 1914.
[19] *Cavallo e cavaliere*, private collection: Baldacci, Cavallo 1993, p. 35, no. 14.
[20] *Composizione con manichino*, formerly Milan, Grossetti Collection: *Brescia* 1963, no. 12.
[21] *Cavallo, aeroplano e chitarra*, Rome, private collection: *Düsseldorf–Baden Baden* 1988, no. 52.
[22] Letter from Pietro Feroldi to Carlo Belli, dated June 28, 1941, in Archivio Mattioli, photostatic copy.
[23] The saddle, which is set back, and the characteristic form of the forked shaft which supports make it possible that this is a two-cylinder, two-person Della Ferrera, a 500cc motorcycle manufactured from 1913 and later equipped for military purposes (*Italia motociclistica* 1950, p. 82).
[24] Dated 1919, in *Udine* 1985, no. 26.
[25] Benzi, Sironi 1988, p. 40, no. 120.
[26] Sartoris 1946, p. 11.
[27] Dudreville, Funi, Russolo, Sironi 1920.
[28] *Macerata* 1922, no. 40; the presence of the painting is certified by the photograph of the room in *Macerata* 1995, p. 153.
[29] Crispolti 1995, pp. 149–50.
[30] Pannaggi, June 22, 1922.
[31] Letter from Pietro Feroldi to Carlo Belli, dated June 28, 1941 in Archivio Mattioli, photostatic copy; the purchase of a new *Composition* of 1919 by Sironi was announced to Belli on December 1, 1941.
[32] Piovene 1942, p. XV.
[33] Archivio Mattioli, *Elenco raccolta Feroldi* (*Appendix I*, document no. 24).

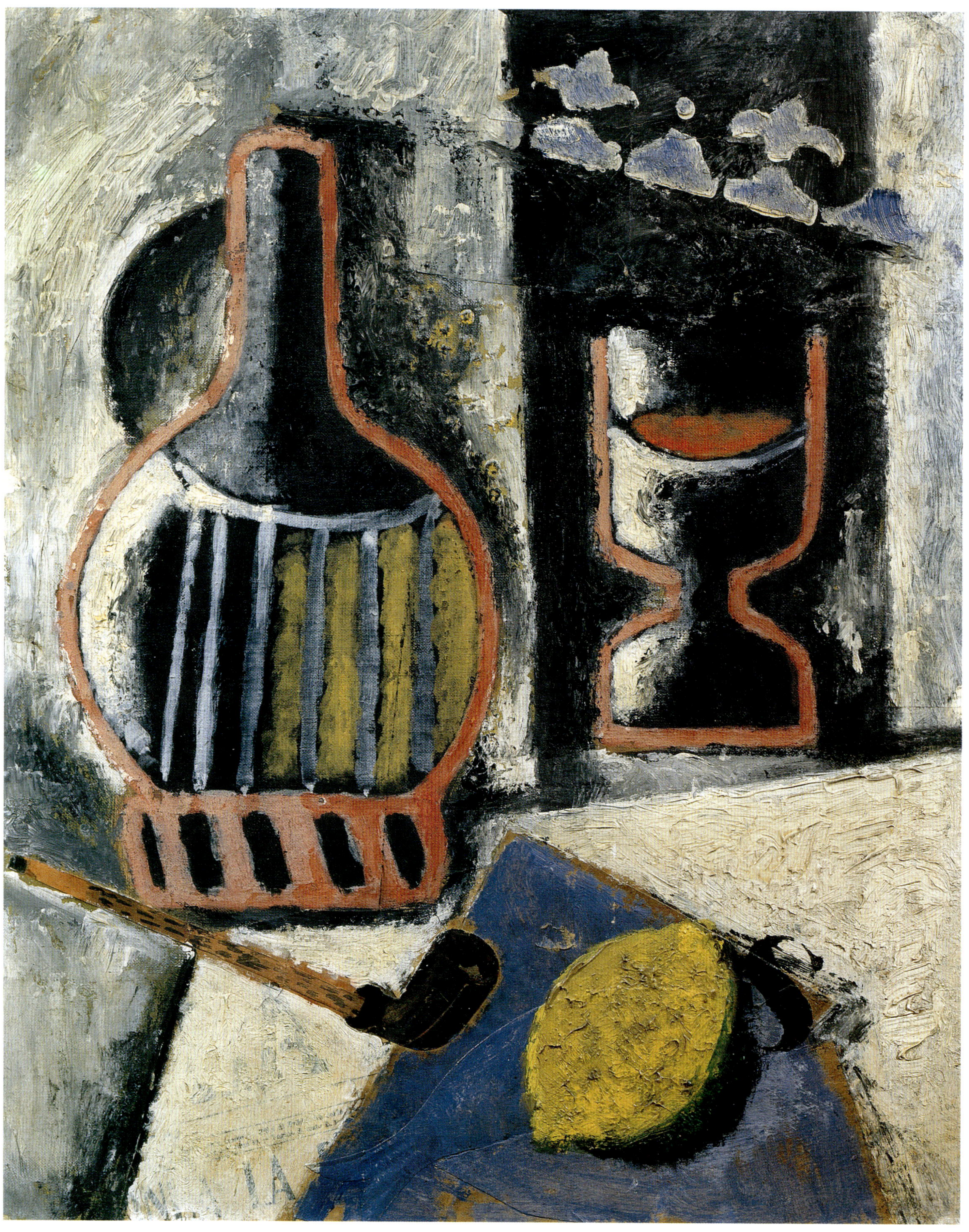

25

Ardengo Soffici (Rignano sull'Arno, Florence, 1879 – Forte dei Marmi, Lucca, 1964)

Small Trophy (*Still Life*; *Lemon, Pipe etc.*; *Still Life with Flask*; *Composition*)

Trofeino (*Natura morta*; *Limone, pipa ecc.*; *Natura morta con fiasco*; *Composizione*), 1914–15

Oil on canvas
46.5 × 38.5 cm

Inscription: *verso*, signed on the canvas: 'SOFFICI 1914' (fig. 25a)

Provenance: property of the artist; before 1920: Fernando Agnoletti, Florence; before 1933: Agnes Brown, Florence; after 1941?: Galleria del Cavallino, Venice; after 1946: Galleria del Naviglio, Milan; 1950: Gianni Mattioli

Exhibitions: Rome 1918[a], p. 8, no. 1 or 2 or 3 or 4, fig. p. 16 (*Natura morta*); Florence 1920, no. 78 (*Limone, pipa ecc.*, 1915); Milan 1950, catalogue not traced (the painting's presence in the exhibition is documented by a label on the back and its publication in Apollonio, Valsecchi 1951, pp. 69–70); Florence 1953[a], no. 25 (*Natura morta con fiasco*, 1914); Rome 1959, no. 25; Winterthur 1959, no. 114; Munich 1959–60, no. 104; Venice 1960, p. 24, no. 142 (1915); Turin–Milan 1961, p. 44; Naples 1964–Rotterdam 1965, no. 332 (Naples), no. 174 (Zurich–Rotterdam); Rome 1965–6, p. 207, no. 12 (*Trofeino*, 1915); Washington, DC 1967–Tokyo 1972, no. 39 (Washington, DC–Hamburg), no. 38 (Madrid–Seville), no. 39 (Kyoto–Tokyo); Poggio a Caiano 1975, no. 53

Bibliography: Papini 1933, pl. XIV (*Trofeino*, 1915); Giani 1942, pl. 130 (*Composizione*, 1914); Salvini 1949, pp. 186–91 (*Composizione*, 1914); Apollonio, Valsecchi 1951, pp. 69–70 (*Natura morta*, 1914); Ragghianti 1953, p. 19; Drudi, Gambillo Fiori 1958–62, vol. I, p. 466 (*Natura morta con fiasco*), vol. II, pp. 399 and 402, no. 27 (*Trofeino*); Carrieri 1961, fig. 134; Cavallo, Raimondi, Russoli 1967, p.

Ardengo Soffici was a leading protagonist of Italian cultural discourse between 1908 and 1920. Benefiting from the stimuli of sojourns in Paris (from 1900 to 1907, and again, though with long intervals, from 1910 to 1914), he revived the role of militant art critic in Italy with writings fueled by polemic and notable for their international, especially French bias. Between the end of the first decade and the middle of the second, Soffici placed Impressionism, especially Paul Cézanne, at the heart of the debate on contemporary painting in Italy; he published the first, fundamental article in Italian on Cubism in *La Voce*; he initiated discussion of the regenerative power of naive or folk art by his appreciation of Henri Rousseau; and he sustained a continual dialogue with the Milanese Futurists, proudly polemical at first and from 1913 dialectically critical. Some of his literary criticism (*Arthur Rimbaud*, 1911), fiction (*Lemmonio Boreo*, 1912) and autobiographical writings (*Giornale di bordo*, 1915) were important points of reference, thanks to their lucid visual character, for an entire generation of Italian critics and men of letters. Soffici's activity as a painter was strongly influenced by his beloved French models: when in 1914 his differences with Marinetti and Boccioni grew to the point that they could no longer be resolved, he turned to the Cubism of Braque and Picasso with an awareness and sophistication refined by the exercise of his criticism and theory over many years.

Of the forty-one paintings of 1914–15 catalogued in the fundamental monograph on Soffici, edited in 1967 by Giuseppe Raimondi and Luigi Cavallo,[1] almost all (thirty-eight) were still lifes; later additions to the catalogue have confirmed the absolute centrality of this genre over these two years.[2] Soffici's abandonment of landscape and figure painting (which had been important vehicles of experiment for him in the crucial months of 1913 when he first joined the Futurists and which were numerous among the works he sent to exhibitions in 1913–14) enabled him to focus exclusively on the components of pictorial form, with neither the distraction of content nor the need to make compromises with the modernist ideology of Marinetti's Futurism.

In *Fine di un mondo,* the memoirs of his artistic career published in 1955, Soffici attributed his conversion to the still life to two factors. The first was the impression made on him, when he visited Paris in February–April 1914, by the still lifes that he saw in Picasso's studio and by those of the Cubists that were shown at Salon des Indépendants (where "the inventions of the painters [...] covered the walls with guitars, bottles, pipes"[3]). The second factor was a conscious quest for the forms and images of popular or folk art: as early as the summer of 1913 Soffici wrote Carrà of his interest in an art which was "absolutely Italian," "plebeian, modern,"[4] but he only pursued this programmatically in the months immediately following his return from Paris. In the rural Tuscan taverns, fruit, flasks of wine and glasses, salamis and cheeses were depicted in:

63; Raimondi 1967, p. 33; Raimondi, Cavallo 1967, no. 222 (1915); Russoli 1975, p. 112 (1915); Russoli 1976, pp. 44–6; Roche-Pézard 1983, pp. 449 and 486 (1915); Cavallo 1986, p. 281; Cavallo 1992, p. 21; Rylands 1997, p. 100 (1915)

> "ingenuous images, crudely drawn and modeled, colored in unexpected combinations of tones; but as a whole they had something so spontaneous, genuine, sincere that they brought to mind our primitives and Quattrocento painters; Giotto, Paolo Uccello, for example, who were able to preserve, in their ignorant errors and roughness, the spontaneous adherence to the essential characteristics of the spirit which animated them and of the visible things of their shared native land."[5]

From this immersion in the folk world of Tuscany, Soffici recalled having derived even the title, *Trofeino*, which he supposedly gave to this and other still lifes of the same period. Historic definitions of trophy as an architectural ornament composed "of martial relics [...] and other devices pertaining to war, arranged in order" in the seventeenth-century *Vocabolario toscano delle Arti del Disegno* by Filippo Baldinucci[6] or, in eighteenth-nineteenth century usage, as "a gathering of objects of a science, an art, or similar, arranged like trophies"[7] were extended by Soffici to include that of the still life in accordance with the usage of a spokesman of the people, Guglielmo Baldinotti. Baldinotti was a maker of shop signs and was invited by Soffici to work in his studio so that Soffici could understand his untutored pictorial technique and the "strange beauty [of the] puerility of composition and execution":

> "Still life was not however the name that Baldinotti gave, as we painters do today, to that genre of paintings. He called them 'trofeini,' referring to the trophies of weapons that decorate certain rooms in palaces, but more especially to those panels representing musical instruments, pages of scores, flowers, fruits, etc., which nineteenth-century decorators painted on the ceilings of noble rooms, and which they called by the same term."[8]

However, the title of 'Trofeini' attributed to a series of still lifes in 1914–15 was certainly a matter of hindsight. In actual fact the term does not occur in any of Soffici's writings or letters of the period; furthermore none of the Cubo-Futurist paintings he exhibited during the second and third decades of the century had such a title. When the Mattioli *Small Trophy* was exhibited for the first time (in 1918, at the 'Mostra d'Arte Indipendente pro Croce Rossa' at the Galleria dell'Epoca in Rome) it was generically called *Still Life*,[9] while at the large solo exhibition of Soffici's work in 1920 at the Horne Museum, Florence, it probably corresponded to no. 78, which was given the thematically neutral title of *Lemon, Pipe etc.*[10] The first occasion of Soffici's use of the term *trofeino* was precisely in relation to the Mattioli painting, in the caption of its illustration in the monograph dedicated to Soffici with a preface by Giovanni Papini in the *Arte Moderna Italiana* series (1933).[11]

Of the forty or so still lifes datable to 1914–15, approximately half contain collage inserts. Soffici pasted to his supports (whether they were prepared canvases or cardboard) commercial or theater posters, postal stickers, or pieces of card cut into shapes and painted; in isolated instances he used a fragment of wallpaper and a matchbox with the State Monopoly band; but most often he used newspaper clippings. The ways he inserted the bits of newspaper were the most varied of all the Futurists. Sometimes they affected only a minimal part of the still life

Fig. 25a. Verso *of cat. no. 25*

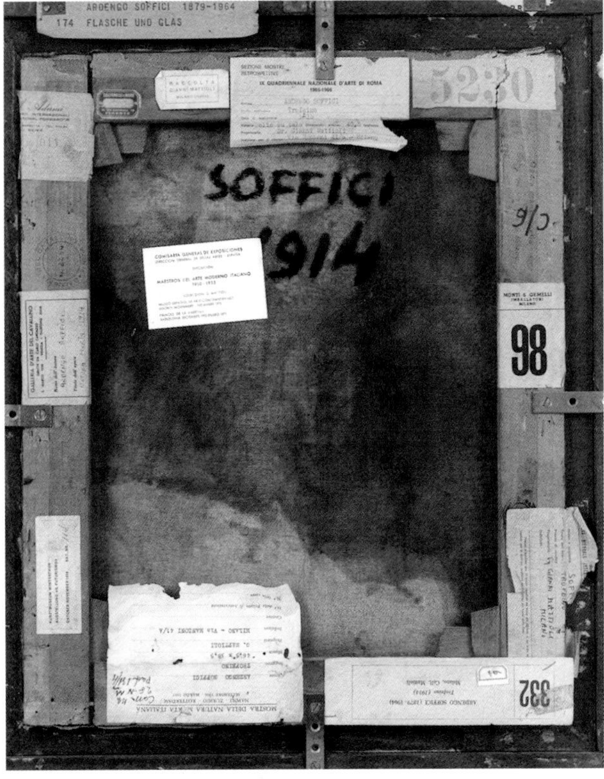

(as in the case of the *La Nazione* masthead barely visible in the lower right of *Small Trophy*); sometimes they were densely distributed to augment the spatial dislocation, as in *Watermelon, Fruit Bowl and Bottle*[12] (fig. 25b), or they formed the precise shape of an object such as the small round table in *Composition with Green Bottle*[13] (fig. 25d). Elsewhere newspaper served as the actual background of the work: either the pattern formed by the text may be perfectly legible, as in *Bottle and Glass*,[14] or the collage is veiled by a thin layer of tempera allowing only certain titles to show through, as in *Still Life with Inkwell*[15] (fig. 25f). In a text entitled *Materia*, probably written at that time but published later in the *Primi principi di estetica futurista* of 1920, Soffici claimed that the non-pictorial inserts (newspapers, posters, wallpaper) "have no 'representational' function but have only a function chromatic or tonal, or as a plastic form or, in any case, that of a harmonic element, of technical material, just like the colors."[16] It seems clear however that the purpose of the newspaper in *Small Trophy* (and in a few other works of the same period such as the *Still Life with Red Egg*,[17] fig. 25e) was to represent itself, lying on a table next to objects from daily life (in this case a lemon, a pipe, a flask of wine and a glass). The same process can be seen in Cubist still lifes by Georges Braque at the end of 1913 such as *Bottle, Newspaper, Pipe and Glass*[18] or, better yet, in many of Picasso's still lifes of 1914 (*Glass, Bottle of Wine, Packet of Tobacco, Newspaper* [fig. 25i] or *Ham, Glass, Bottle of Vieux Marc, Newspaper*[19]) which Soffici could easily have seen during either of his two stays in Paris in the first half of that year. The pasted clipping from *La Nazione*, the Florentine liberal-conservative daily to which Soffici was opposed but which he bought regularly when he was staying in Poggio a Caiano, left part of the masthead visible in accordance with the practice of the Cubists, but not with that of either Carrà or Boccioni who instead cut out inside pages or less easily identifiable text with the aim of sinking the image into the flux of often contradictory events reported in the headlines or the columns.

The few letters of the front page headline ("NIA LA C") that can be glimpsed through the light wash of white paint in the lower left are sufficient to identify the November 6, 1911 is-

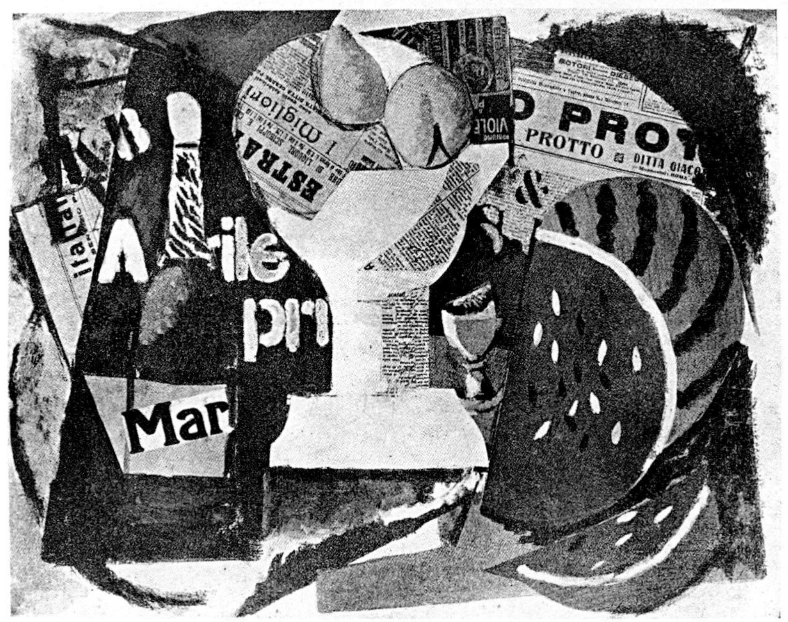
SOFFICI

Cocomero, fruttiera bottiglia.

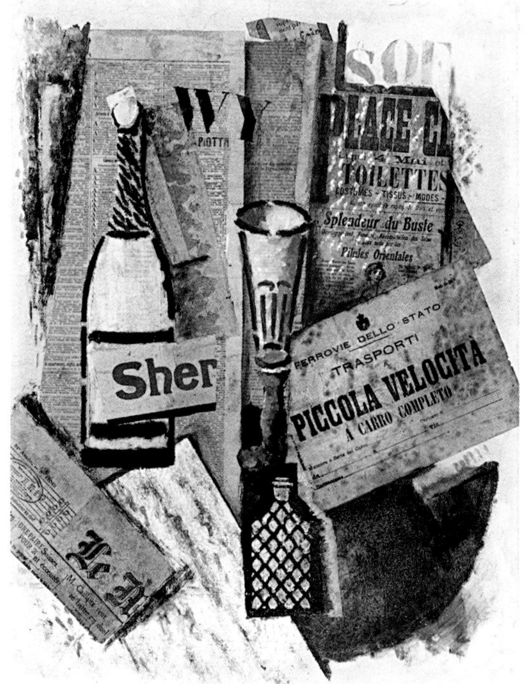

Fig. 25b. *Ardengo Soffici,* Cocomero, fruttiera e bottiglia *(*Watermelon, Fruit Bowl and Bottle*), 1914, in* Lacerba, *May 15, 1914*

Fig. 25c. *Ardengo Soffici,* Piccola velocità *(*Small Speed*), oil, tempera and collage on cardboard, 1914. Milan, Civiche raccolte d'arte, Jucker Collection*

sue of *La Nazione* (the whole phrase, in uppercase, was "La Tripolitania la Cirenaica annesse all'Italia" ["Tripolitania and Cirenaica annexed to Italy"], referring to the triumphant conclusion of the first phase of the Libyan campaign). Thus Soffici co-opted, probably for the sake of the pictorial effect of the yellowed paper, a part of a three-year-old newspaper referring to a war that was already over and at a time when, in August 1914, another war had broken out, on a worldwide scale. As Picasso did, with intentions that have been interpreted in various ways,[20] Soffici seems to have inserted a news report about war into a context of domestic peace. For Soffici, who hoped for the entry of Italy into the war on the side of France and England against the middle European empires, the presence of the newspaper may be understood not only as a reference to the way news of dramatic current affairs intrudes on the painter's daily work (such as he described in a pair of letters to Carrà[21]) but also as an implicit appeal for intervention, with a reference to an Italian victory of recent history.

Soffici studies have not yet tackled the question of the chronology of the still lifes of 1914 and 1915. Some groupings can be hazarded by matching objective data in the paintings such as the *termini post quem* provided by newspaper collages (in the strictest sense of the term: as we have seen above, Soffici kept newspapers for years[22]) with the rare reproductions of the period, with information gleaned from letters and other documents, as well as with Soffici's autobiographical recollections.

Of a group of three collages usually assigned to 1913[23] none can be convincingly dated earlier than April 1914, the date of Soffici's return from the first of two trips to Paris that year, when he was accompanied by Carrà, Papini and Palazzeschi. Discussion of Cubist collage was particularly intense at this time, and the matter of inserting real objects in paintings was the object of sharp debate between Papini and Boccioni in the pages of *Lacerba*.[24] One of the group, *Small Speed*[25] (fig. 25c), includes a legible clipping from the March 1914 issue of *Le Matin* with the announcement of a duel between the French Finance Minister Joseph Caillaux and the editor of *Le Figaro* Gaston Calmette. Raimondi-Cavallo nos. 173 and 174[26] (notwithstanding the presence of clippings from the March 15, 1913 issue of *Lacerba* and in no. 174 a bottle pictorially constructed with unusual attentiveness to its transparency) have elements of flat,

Fig. 25d. *Ardengo Soffici,* Composizione con bottiglia verde *(*Composition with Green Bottle*), tempera and collage on board, 1914. Private collection*

Fig. 25e. *Ardengo Soffici,* Natura morta con uovo rosso *(*Still Life with Red Egg*), tempera and collage on board, 1914. Private collection*

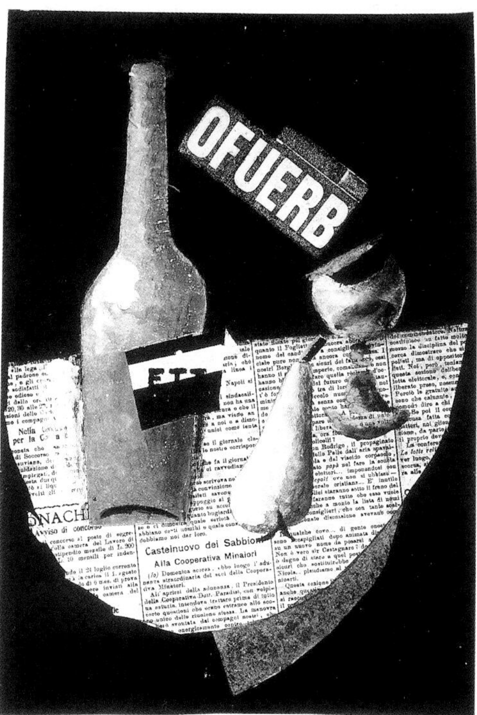

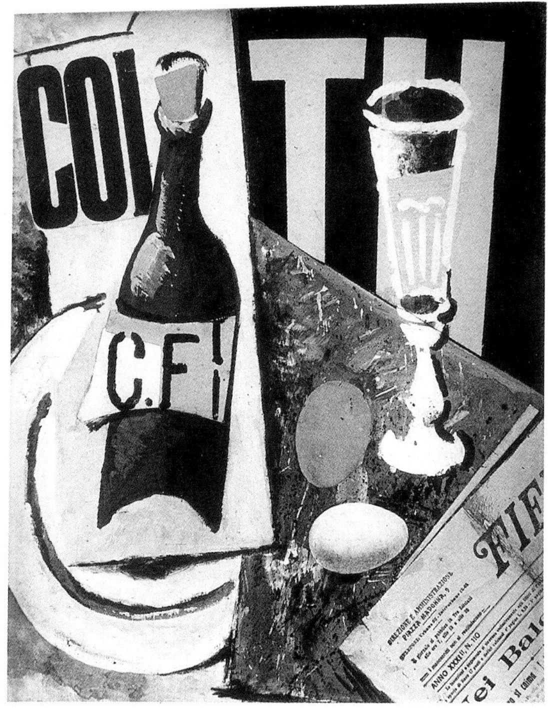

monochrome elements (the liqueur bottles in no. 173 or the slice of watermelon in no. 174) difficult to reconcile with the intense chiaroscuro pattern of Soffici's paintings of late 1913. Not until the early months of 1914 did he address the matter of depicting newsprint, though at first in the traditional way — by painting it. In *Typographical Simultaneity*,[27] painted after the Florentine 'Lacerba' show and sent to the Futurist group show at the Sprovieri Gallery in February, he simulated the new 1914 masthead of *Lacerba* and the frontispieces of two coeval publications. Upon his return from Paris in April, at the time of his keen interest in popular art, Soffici announced to Carrà that he had definitively adopted the practice of collage and that he was convinced that "the best thing in fact is to use sheets where it is necessary to obtain fresh and straightforward colors, without pausing over trifles and thousands of previous petty considerations."[28] A few weeks later he communicated that he had "achieved the industrialization of the painting" by using zinc stencils to render mechanical and impersonal forms.[29]

Watermelon, Fruit Bowl and Bottle (fig. 25b) was illustrated in the May 15, 1914 edition of *Lacerba*. Around this one can gather still lifes in which stencils have been used (as in the bottle with its scratch marks, the flûte glasses and the bottle of Cinzano) and in which newspaper clippings are more densely deployed, conforming to a practice derived from Picasso's collages: *Small Speed* (fig. 25c), *Watermelon and Liqueurs*, and the still life *Bottles and Cup* (the latter made exclusively with stencils).[30] Immediately after these come most probably the still lifes in which the newspaper pages or posters are less fragmented and inserted in a simpler, more defined space. Soffici continued to produce compositions of the latter kind, perhaps those admired by Picasso when he saw photographs of them in Paris in June,[31] until the outbreak of the war when, according to the artist's recollections, he suddenly stopped working up until the time of the French victory in the Battle of the Marne in October.[32] The only certain clues for compiling a chronology in the following months are the pages of newspaper pasted on the background of *Still Life with Inkwell*[33] (fig. 25f: the entire third page of the March 31, 1915 *Corriere della Sera*) and of *Fruit with Glass and Cup*[34] (with its fragment of an unidentified newspaper dated March 28 of the same year, reporting Bulgaria's imminent entry into the war against

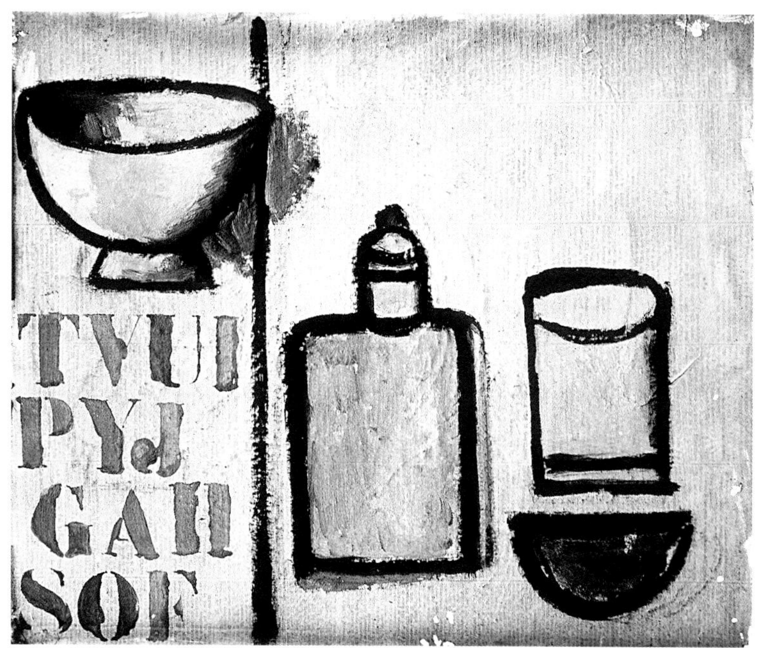

Fig. 25f. *Ardengo Soffici,* Natura morta con calamaio (Still Life with Inkwell), *tempera on newspaper, 1915. Private collection*

the middle-European empires). To these two collages (usually dated 1914 or 1914–15, but necessarily of the second quarter of 1915) one can add the still lifes catalogued in the 1967 Soffici monograph as numbers 193–6 and 198–200, given their similar, indeterminate backgrounds and thick black outlining. The two still lifes with objects reduced to flat shapes against a dark ground, blue or black (*Vase and Pear*, fig. 25g; *Fruit Bowl with Pears*[35]), can even be dated a few months later if we accept Soffici's recollection in 1955 that they were made at the time of a visit of the de Chirico brothers to Poggio a Caiano ("They found me painting, in the manner of *trofeini*, some terracotta vases and other brightly colored objects against a black background"[36]) between June 2 and 10, 1915.[37]

However, this summary chronological framework is not enough to resolve the dating of the Mattioli *Small Trophy*. Soffici dated it 1914 on the back of the canvas (fig. 25a) but exhibited it for the first time — and subsequently published it — with the date 1915. In favor of a date as late as the spring of 1915 is an identical motif of upholstery trimming made with a stencil of alternating fleur-de-lis and balls in *Vase and Pear* (fig. 25g: probably, as we have seen, datable to June 1915) and the thick rust-red contours of *Small Trophy* which, in a black variant, surround the objects of still lifes certainly executed after March 1915 (such as the *Still Life with Inkwell*, fig. 25f). In general *Small Trophy* reveals the same awareness of the work of Henri Matisse that makes itself felt in other works by Soffici plausibly dated 1915: the yellow lemon on a bright blue ground echoes a similar acid color combination in *The Lemons*[38] (fig. 25h), which was probably seen by Soffici in Matisse's studio during his February–March sojourn in Paris (there are hints of the visit in a letter to Carrà some months later[39]) and which was illustrated in the May 15, 1914 issue of *Les Soirées de Paris,* perhaps the same that Soffici sent to Carrà from Paris during the last brief (late May–late June) trip to Paris in 1914. Soffici derived from the same painting, which he evidently studied at length, the silhouette of the vase in *Vase and Pear* (fig. 25g), the vertical scansion of the painting in light, flat zones characteristic of *Still Life with Inkwell* (fig. 25f) and *Pear, Book and Cup,*[40] and the insertion of an acute-angled triangle of color that invades the picture from below in *Glass and Cup* and *Still Life.*[41]

Nevertheless, the 1914 date inscribed by Soffici on the reverse was not necessarily an attempt to predate the painting, which after all shares some of its compositional traits with still lifes of 1914: the newspaper clipping placed on a strong diagonal, the ovoid shape in the foreground, the glass on the right standing out against the black background are inventions already to be found in *Still Life with Red Egg*[42] (fig. 25e) which can plausibly be included on stylistic grounds among the collages executed after Soffici's return from Paris in April.

Thus it seems rather likely that Soffici worked on the Mattioli *Small Trophy* in two distinct moments. Certain elements which must initially have had a decisive importance, since they were made of cut-out and pasted cardboard, were later obliterated with a new layer of paint:[43] a fish lying on the newspaper was concealed by the lemon and the underlying blue surface, and is now visible only by reason of its contour in relief, as is the triangular shape above the glass which was covered by the black that forms a background for the glass and which is masked by the decorative trim running the length of its hypotenuse. As it appears today, the painting could be mistaken for a repainted collage: some elements were preserved (the pipe under the flask around which the new layer of thick paint gathers), others veiled by a semi-transparent layer of paint (the clipping from *La Nazione*), others, like the fish and the triangle, are entirely hidden. In 1915 Soffici definitively distanced himself from Futurist simultaneity and declared his revived passion for pictorial *matière*. His appropriation of Matisse's pure palette (as evinced by a poem published in *La Voce* on April 15, 1915, which comments on works already executed: in his paintings "each color / sings like a bird / an instrument / a passion / blue yellow green cobalt"[44]) did not exclude his interest in dense pigment and in the grayish incrustations of some of Picasso's and Braque's paintings of early 1914. Some specific motifs in *Small Trophy* were derived from these two artists: the glass cast as a squared-off silhouette incised against a dark background (as in a Braque still life of 1914,[45] fig. 25j) and the pipe that appears in so many of Picasso's still lifes of the spring of 1914 and in some by Braque to which *Small Trophy* can usefully be compared (for example *Pipe and Newspaper*[46]). Finally, the trim replicates almost literally the real fringe applied to Picasso's 1914 relief *Le Casse-croute* in the Tate, London.[47]

Soffici from the beginning attributed special importance to this painting and three years after it was finished included it in a small selection of works sent to the group show in Rome at the Galleria dell'Epoca in April–May 1918, choosing it for illustration in the catalogue.[48] Crit-

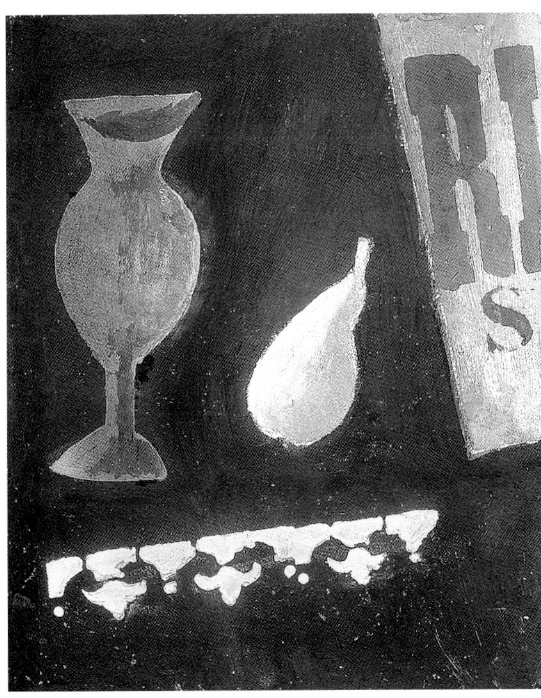

Fig. 25g. *Ardengo Soffici,* Vaso e pera (Vase and Pear)*, tempera on board, 1915. Private collection*

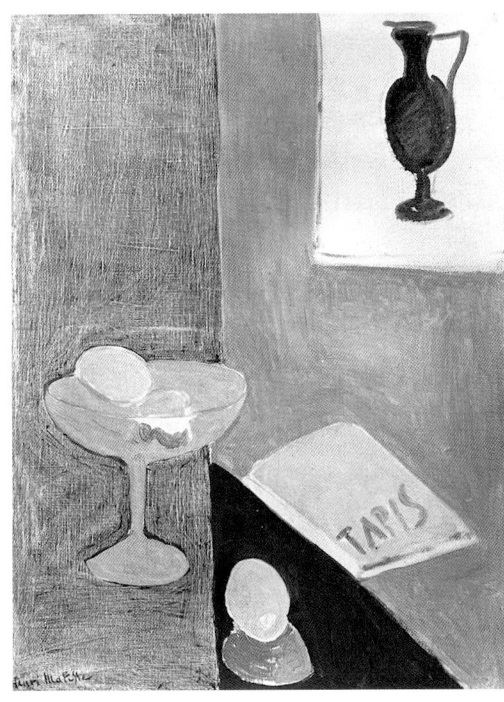

Fig. 25h. *Henri Matisse,* Nature morte aux citrons dont les formes correspondent à celles d'un vase noir dessiné sur le mur (Still Life with Lemons)*, oil on canvas, 1914. Providence (Rhode Island), Rhode Island School of Design Museum of Art, Gift of Miss Edith Wetmore*

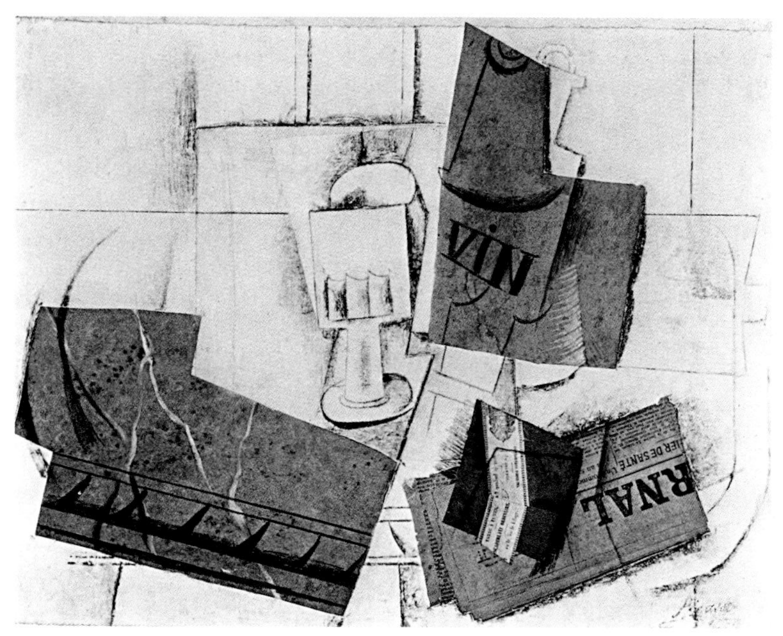

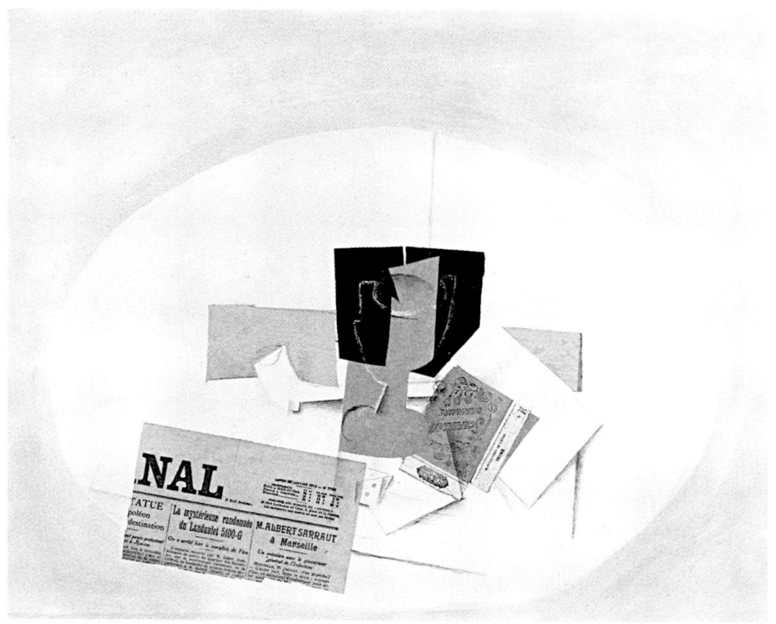

Fig. 25i. *Pablo Picasso,* Verre, bouteille de vin, paquet de tabac, journal *(*Glass, Bottle of Wine, Packet of Tobacco, Newspaper*), collage, charcoal and tempera on paper, 1914. Paris, private collection*

Fig. 25j. *Georges Braque,* Pipe, verre, dé et journal *(*Pipe, Glass, Dice and Newspaper*), charcoal and collage on paper, 1914. Hanover, Sprengel Museum Hannover*

ics praised mostly, in the four still lifes, the skilful color combinations ("certain very shrewd juxtapositions of tones, totally of the surface, matchlessly refined, of a dry and very sensible taste"[49]); but the reverential allusions to Soffici's paintings in reviews by Giorgio de Chirico (who praised "the spirit, spare and multicolor, skeletal and saturated with well-digested luminosity [...] beneath the restorative, beating sun"[50]) and by Carlo Carrà (who perceived in "that most special materialization of the Italian nature [...] the rigorous logic of the painting's lyrical architecturalness"[51]) diverted attention to themes by then typical of the return to order.

Two years later, *Small Trophy* was exhibited with a new title *Lemon, Pipe etc.* and dated 1915 at the large show of Soffici's work in Florence in May–June 1920 at the Horne Museum. It was hung in a small room of forty-two paintings and three drawings which brought together all the Cubo-Futurist works, by this time only reluctantly tolerated by critics.[52] According to the catalogue it was the property of Fernando Agnoletti, who owned, together with his companion Agnes Brown, a considerable number of paintings of the period 1913–15. As with all Soffici's paintings and collages of the period, information about the years 1920–40 is scarce. The illustration in the 1933 monograph on Soffici stated that *Small Trophy* was still in the Brown Collection.[53] There is no evidence of its exhibition in any of the one-man Soffici shows organized between 1938 and 1941 by the dealer Vittorio Barbaroux — shows which prompted the beginning of a market for Soffici's Futurist work.[54] The subsequent provenance of *Small Trophy* can be reconstructed thanks to information on the back of the canvas. It was acquired by Carlo Cardazzo at some time during the 1940s, perhaps after 1941 (it cannot be identified with any of the four paintings by Soffici exhibited with the Cardazzo Collection in 1941 at the Galleria di Roma).[55] Two rubber stamps are legible on the stretcher: the first documents its entry into the Galleria del Cavallino in Venice, owned by Cardazzo, with the number 2244, the second that it entered the Galleria del Naviglio in Milan, opened by Cardazzo in November 1946, with the number 328. A third stamp, on the canvas, certifies that the work was exhibited, in 1950, at the Galleria del Naviglio at an exhibition of Cubist paintings.[56] Gianni Mattioli instantly purchased the painting, on the recommendation of Marco Valsecchi,[57] art correspondent for several periodicals in Milan (among which the popular weekly *Oggi*) and an active militant critic in Italy in the period immediately after the end of World War II.

[1] Raimondi, Cavallo 1967, nos. 180–228 (this group of works includes Soffici's decorations for Papini's house in Bulciano, a woodcut and a drawing).
[2] Bargellini, Bellonzi 1969, pls. XVIII–XIX; *Poggio a Caiano* 1975, nos. 49–50.
[3] Soffici 1955, p. 348.
[4] Letters from Ardengo Soffici to Carlo Carrà, dated July 22 and 27, 1913, in Carrà, Soffici 1983, pp. 26 and 31.
[5] Soffici 1955, p. 416.
[6] Baldinucci 1681, p. 78.
[7] Giorgini, Broglio 1870–97, vol. IV, pp. 438–9; Petrocchi 1887–91, p. 1168.
[8] Soffici 1955, p. 421.
[9] *Natura morta*: *Rome* 1918[a], p. 16.
[10] *Limone, pipa ecc.*: *Florence* 1920, no. 78.
[11] Papini 1933, pl. XIV.
[12] Private collection: Raimondi, Cavallo 1967, no. 187; the collage, after reappearing on the market, was discussed in Cavallo 1994, p. 43.
[13] Formerly Milan, Mazzotta Collection: Raimondi, Cavallo 1967, no. 188.
[14] *Bottiglia e bicchiere*, Milan, Civiche raccolte d'arte: *ibidem*, no. 223.
[15] Prato, private collection: *ibidem*, no. 197.
[16] Soffici 1920[a], pp. 90–1.
[17] Rome, Jacovitti Collection: Raimondi, Cavallo 1967, no. 192.
[18] *Bouteille, journal, pipe et verre*, private collection: Worms de Romilly, Laude 1982, no. 224.
[19] *Verre, bouteille de vin, paquet de tabac, journal* and *Jambon, verre, bouteille de Vieux Marc, journal*, respectively, private collection: Daix, Rosselet 1979 no. 662; and Paris, Musée d'Art Moderne de la Ville de Paris: *ibidem*, no. 705.
[20] A display of black humor in search of macabre *doubles entendres* (Rosenblum 1980, pp. 33–47); political protest in an anarchical vein (Leighten 1985, pp. 659–72); the desire to overturn the late Symbolist values of the still life (Poggi 1992, pp. 141–53).
[21] Letters from Ardengo Soffici to Carlo Carrà, dated August 25 and November 20, 1914, in Carrà, Soffici 1983, pp. 61 and 67.
[22] In addition to the case of *Small Trophy*, a comparable example is the *Still Life* (private collection: Raimondi, Cavallo 1967, no. 206) which was dated 1914 by the artist and which is stylistically consistent with that date, although it incorporates pieces of newspaper dating back to December 1911.
[23] Raimondi, Cavallo 1967, nos. 173–5.
[24] Papini, February 15, 1914; Boccioni, March 1, 1914; Papini, March 15, 1914; on this subject see Del Puppo 2000[b], pp. 82–94.
[25] Milan, Civiche raccolte d'arte, Jucker Collection: Raimondi, Cavallo 1967, no. 175.
[26] *Still Life*, Florence, private collection; *Still Life*, Florence, private collection.
[27] *Simultaneità tipografica*: *ibidem*, no. 204, with the title *Tipografia* and specified as an "oil and collage on cardboard," later corrected to "oil on cardboard" in Cavallo 1986, p. 202.
[28] Letter from Ardengo Soffici to Carlo Carrà, dated April 30, 1914, in Carrà, Soffici 1983, p. 52.
[29] Letter from Ardengo Soffici to Carlo Carrà, dated May 1, 1914, *ibidem*, p. 55.
[30] Raimondi, Cavallo 1967, no. 175 (*Piccola velocità*, Milan, Civiche raccolte d'arte, Jucker Collection), no. 202 (*Watermelon and Liquors*, Milan, Pinacoteca di Brera, Jesi Collection) and no. 180 (*Glass and Cup*, Milan, private collection).
[31] As communicated by Soffici to Giuseppe Prezzolini in a letter dated May 25 [1914]: Prezzolino, Soffici 1977, p. 253.
[32] Soffici 1955, p. 427.
[33] Private collection: Raimondi, Cavallo 1967, no. 197.
[34] Private collection: *ibidem*, no. 201.
[35] *Vaso e pera* and *Fruttiera con pere*, formerly Arcangelo Distaso Collection: *Poggio a Caiano* 1975, nos. 49–50.
[36] Soffici 1955, p. 460.
[37] Letter from Ardengo Soffici to Guillaume Apollinaire, dated June 2, 1915, in Apollinaire 1992, p. 93; Baldacci 1997, p. 298.
[38] Providence (Rhode Island), Museum of Art, Rhode Island School of Design, gift of Miss Edith Wetmore: *New York* 1992, no. 181.
[39] Letter from Ardengo Soffici to Carlo Carrà, dated May 2–3, 1915, in Carrà, Soffici 1983, pp. 84–5.
[40] *Pera, libro e tazza*, private collection: Raimondi, Cavallo 1967, no. 193.
[41] *Bicchiere e tazza* and *Natura morta*: *ibidem*, nos. 194–5.
[42] Private collection: *ibidem*, no. 192.
[43] As noted by Roche-Pézard 1983, p. 449.
[44] Soffici 1915, p. 530; for Soffici's annotation in 1921 that this was a "a fleeting description of paintings by the author," see Vanden Berghe 1999, p. 79.
[45] Hanover, Sprengel Museum Hannover: Worms de Romilly, Laude 1982, no. 234.
[46] *Pipe et journal*, New York, Mr and Mrs Sidney Cohn Collection: *ibidem*, no. 213.
[47] London, Tate Modern: Daix, Rosselet 1979, no. 746.
[48] *Rome* 1918[a], p. 8, no. 1 or 2 or 3 or 4, titled *Natura morta*; fig. p. 16 (*Natura morta*).
[49] Recchi 1918, pp. 79–80.
[50] De Chirico, June 18, 1918.
[51] Carrà, June 3, 1918.
[52] Ojetti, June 16, 1920.
[53] Papini 1933, pl. XIV.
[54] In the absence of the three catalogues, there is some information on what works were shown in Tomea 1938, pp. 23–4, and in a letter from Ardengo Soffici to Giovanni Scheiwiller, dated May 22, 1942, in Cavallo 1986, p. 408.
[55] *Rome* 1941, nos. 75–8.
[56] *Milan* 1950. The exhibition of *Trofeino* is further documented by its illustration in Apollonio, Valsecchi 1951, p. 69.
[57] Archivio Mattioli, file for the work.

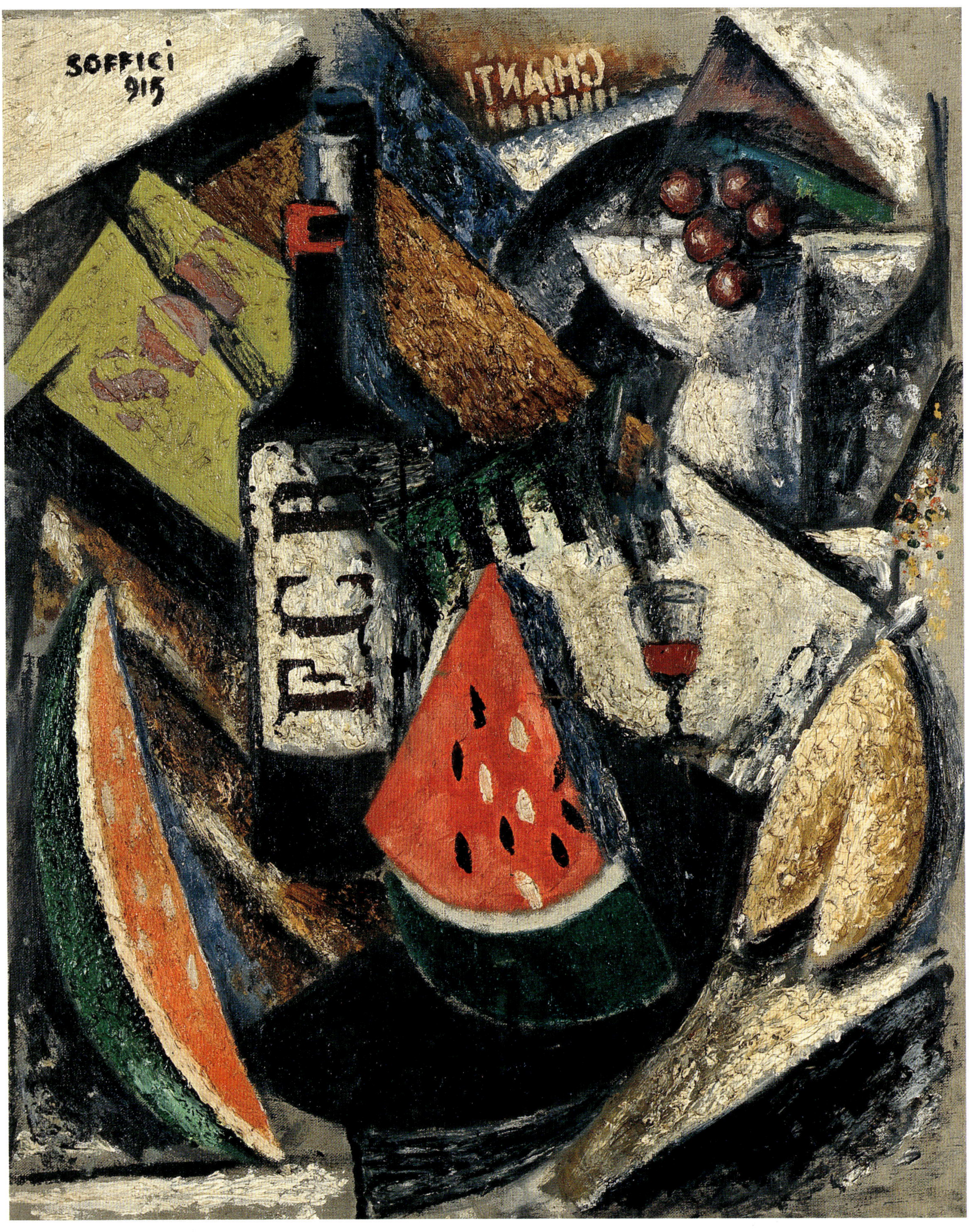
SOFFICI
915

26

Ardengo Soffici

Fruit and Liqueurs (*Fruit and Liqueur*; *Still Life*)

Frutta e liquori (*Frutta e liquore; Natura morta*), 1915

Oil on canvas
65 × 54 cm

Inscriptions: *recto*, signed upper left: 'SOFFICI / 915'; *verso*, on upper stretcher: 'SOFFICI FRUTTA [E LIQUORI]'

Provenance: property of the artist; 1942?: Galleria del Milione, Milan?; before 1945: Carlo Frua De Angeli, Milan; before November 1950: Israel Collection, Montreal; November 1950: Gianni Mattioli

Exhibitions: Florence 1920, no. 97 (*Frutta e liquore*, 1915); Milan, 1942–3, catalogue not traced (the presence of the work in the exhibition is documented by Giolli 1943, p. 84 and De Micheli 1943, pp. 76–7); Florence 1953[a], no. 46; São Paulo 1953–4, p. 15, no. 40; Rome 1955–6, p. 55, no. 20; Munich 1957, no. 219; Rome 1959, no. 30; Winterthur 1959, no. 116; Munich 1959–60, no. 106; Venice 1960, p. 141, no. 24; Turin–Milan 1961, p. 45; Hamburg 1963–Frankfurt 1964, no. 87; Rome 1965–6, p. 207, no. 7; Washington, DC 1967–Tokyo 1972, no. 40 (Washington, DC–Hamburg), no. 39 (Madrid–Seville), no. 40 (Kyoto–Tokyo); Milan 1973–4, no. 250; Poggio a Caiano 1975, no. 51; Venice 1986, p. 251; Vienna 1993–Frankfurt 1994, ex catalogue (the presence of the work in the exhibition is documented by Archivio Mattioli, file for the work)

Bibliography: Soffici 1920[b], p. 142 (*Frutta e liquori*, 1915); Bardi 1930, pl. 70 (*Frutti e liquori*, 1915); Papini 1933, pl. XV (*Frutta e liquore*, 1915); Vitali 1933, p. 407 (*Frutta e liquore*, 1915); De Micheli 1943, pp. 76–7 (*Natura morta*, 1915); Giolli 1943, p. 84

Soffici's return to painting in tempera and oil in 1915, following his experiments with collage in 1914, was not ushered in with an apparatus of theoretical writings, but can be documented instead by thoughts and observations conveyed in letters to Carlo Carrà, by this time his preferred correspondent in matters of art. In a long letter of May 21, 1915, dominated by vexation at his friend's insistence on sympathizing with Marinetti, Soffici declared his growing passion for the richness and variety of pictorial effects obtained by traditional means:

> "I speak above all about technique since technique is everything in art for me. I experience sensual pleasure from a painting; I like the strength, the distinction, the variety, the full-bodied quality or lightness of the mark, of the consistency, of the plastic texture. The only dynamism possible in painting is that deriving from the vibrations of the touch, from the tingling of the medium, from the clash of strong or delicate contrasts. It is the atmosphere of plastic creation. Boccioni's idea of the mechanical makes me smile. It's bad, horrible literature."[1]

Soffici's position was not isolated, but rather fit a pattern of ideas gaining international circulation. A month earlier Pablo Picasso had written Soffici a letter from Paris in which he reopened the question of color, perceived as central to the process he himself had begun, of a return to tradition:

> "Anyway, the time has come to concern oneself with color [,] it should not simply be a clothing, one must be acquainted with the world of color."[2]

Compared to his intentions in the still lifes of the previous year, Soffici was apparently, in *Fruit and Liqueurs*, in search of a richer, more complex arrangement of color, experimenting, even rather self-consciously, with the variety of pictorial textures listed in his letter to Carrà. Areas of uniform pigment such as the mustard-colored surface against which the letters 'SOF' are silhouetted (serving as an abbreviated signature) coexist with traces of *pointillisme* in complementary colors (in the space between the fruit bowl and the right edge of the canvas), evidently derived from Picasso's works of 1913–14 that Soffici knew from his two trips to Paris in the spring of 1914.[3] Thick and heavily-worked surfaces such as those of the yellow fruits in the lower right (probably two bananas, common fare on Italian tables after the conquest of Libya in

1912) stand out against a background in which only the grayish priming of the canvas is visible. The process of collage is not mimetically represented in paint, as has been claimed,[4] so much as superceded, and in some passages overturned. The bottle with the letters 'FCB' (most likely a reference to the initials for Ferro China Bisleri, a popular digestif and, according to the widespread advertising of the period, a tonic for fortifying the blood) was composed with the aid of the usual stencil (fig. 26a), made after his return from Paris in April[5] and serving here as a means for obtaining a new material density rather than a flat outline, as would have been the case in 1914. The slice of watermelon dominating the center (which, for Soffici, from the time he wrote his 1910 text on Rousseau, can be taken as an explicit sign of support for the aesthetics of folk art[6]) differs from the uniform triangle painted in his 1914 still lifes, and is constructed coloristically with two different tones of red. The fruit bowl is not an ambiguous void as in *Watermelon, Fruit Bowl and Bottle*[7] (fig. 25b), painted some months earlier, but is an object with a solid three-dimensionality on which rests a bunch of large grapes painted with realistic chiaroscuro.

The few documents regarding Soffici's production in 1915 do not allow us to establish if the phase to which *Fruit and Liqueurs* belongs occurs before or after that of the more rarefied '*Trofeini*' ('Small Trophies')[8] in which the image is more stylized and the paint applied in more articulated and flatter planes. If the *trofeini* executed between March and June 1915 (see cat. no. 25) are earlier, then Soffici was apparently pursuing in this *Fruit and Liqueurs* a sort of return to the more complex constructions based on diagonals that marked his works of the first half of 1914, with the clear intention of retrieving the density of their construction. Some works of 1914, which include collage, can be placed in a direct relation to this painting. The same motif of the fruit bowl with a bunch of grapes, probably deriving again from folk art, can be seen in *Melon and Flask of Wine*[9] (fig. 26c). A *Still Life* dated 1914, with newspaper clippings from late 1911[10] (fig. 26c), presents the same bottle of Ferro China Bisleri, the same glass with a red liqueur and a comparable construction of the background. In 1915 the topicality of such experiments was proven by the publication in the February 14 issue of *Lacerba* of a *Still Life* with the same objects and the same spatial structure as the Mattioli painting, but which, like others of 1914, was entirely made from newspapers and stenciled lettering and profiles (fig. 26b). The novel plastic solidity which, in the Mattioli painting, characterizes some of the objects (the slice of watermelon, the fruit bowl, the bananas, the glass) already betray the revived concern for "concrete forms located in space" discussed by Soffici and Carrà in Florence in an important meeting in November 1915.[11] There seems, then, to have been a creative period, in 1915, during which Soffici consciously returned to compositions of the previous year: compositions which occur in the contemporary paintings of Alexandra Exter (Soffici's companion during his stays in Paris), such as her *Still Life* with a piece of watermelon, bottles and cherries of 1914[12] (fig. 26d) which has the look of a variation of *Fruit and Liqueurs* in the style of Picasso. A few months later Soffici translated those same schemes into a pictorial language already reshaped to give the objects depicted a new concreteness and substance.

As in many paintings by Picasso and Braque from 1911 onwards, the written word is prominent in *Fruit and Liqueurs*. Aside from the first syllable of the artist's own name, 'SOF', in capitals, we also see the initials 'FCB' on the Ferro China Bisleri label and the word 'CHIANTI' in reverse, whose first three letters are repeated in the center of the painting, the latter evoking the convivial atmosphere of a tavern. The scripts were facilitated by stencils of the type normally used for labeling packing crates. They have an impersonal and mechanical effect but also induce, by using the stencil backwards, subtle plays on perception, "throwing into question the viewer's spatial position *vis-à-vis* the bottles."[13] After their infatuation with Cubism in

(*Natura morta*, 1915); Papini 1945, pl. 2 (*Frutta e liquori*, 1915); Carrieri 1950, p. 68; Ragghianti 1953, p. 19; Castelfranco, Valsecchi 1956, p. 77, pl. 22a; Drudi Gambillo, Fiori 1958–62, vol. I, p. 466, vol. II, pp. 400, 402, no. 33 (*Natura morta*); Marchiori 1960, pp. 90–1; Carrieri 1961, pl. 133; Bellonzi 1963, pp. 123–4; Carli, Dell'Acqua 1964, p. 450; Cavallo, Raimondi, Russoli 1967, p. 61; Raimondi 1967, p. 32; Raimondi, Cavallo 1967, no. 221; Argan 1970, p. 380; Russoli 1975, p. 110; Cavallo 1992, p. 21; Lemaire 1995, p. 66; Rylands 1997, p. 102

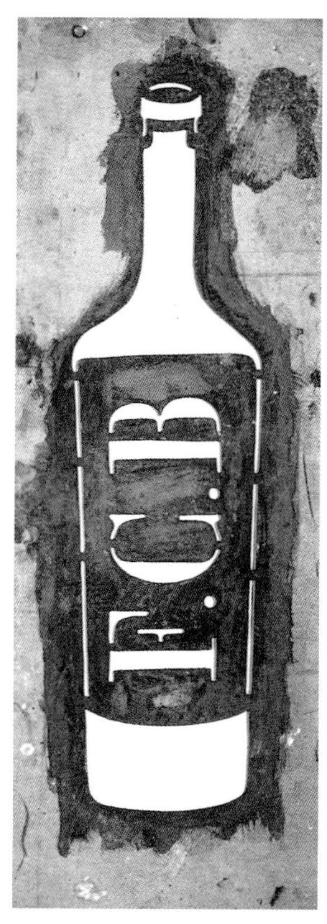

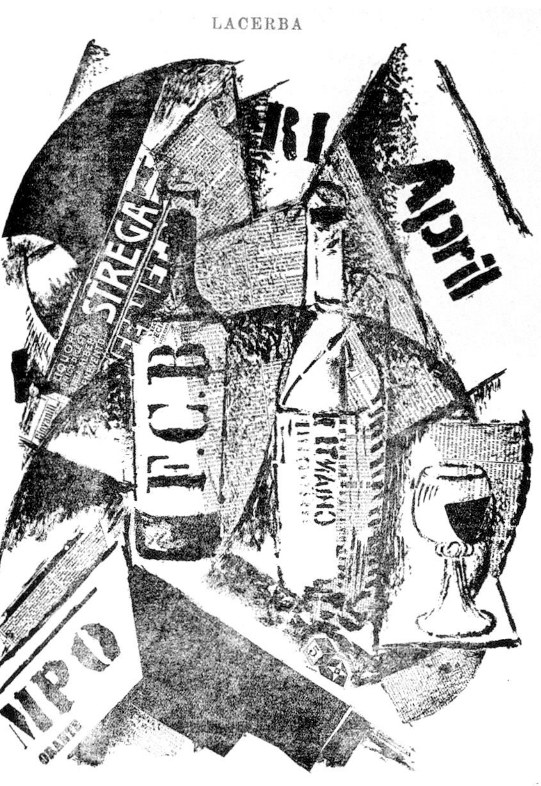

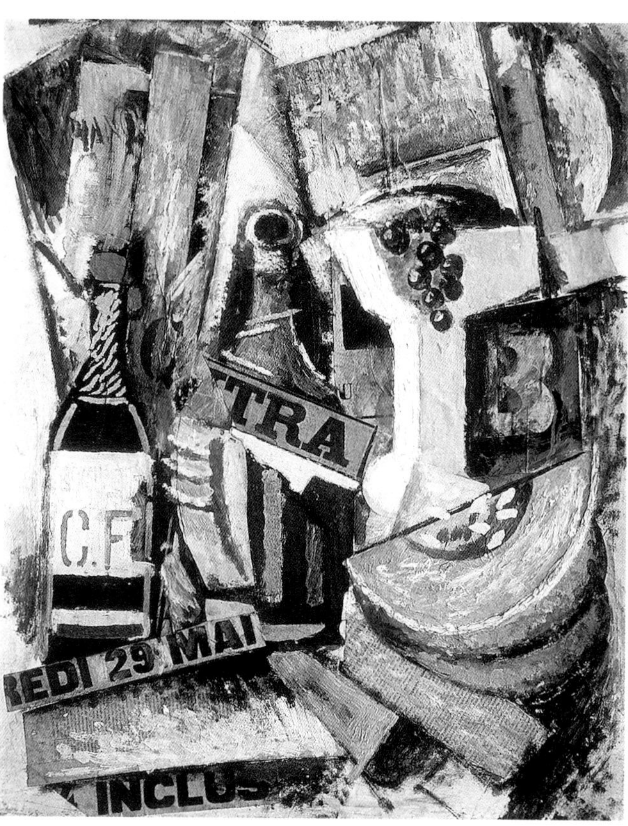

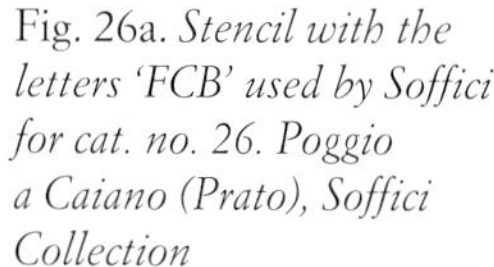

Fig. 26a. *Stencil with the letters 'FCB' used by Soffici for cat. no. 26. Poggio a Caiano (Prato), Soffici Collection*

Fig. 26b. *Ardengo Soffici,* Still Life, *in* Lacerba, *February 24, 1915*

Fig. 26c. *Ardengo Soffici,* Popone e fiasco di vino *(Melon and Flask of Wine), tempera and collage on board, 1914. Private collection*

1912, the artists and writers who gravitated around *Lacerba* rediscovered in 1914–15 a passion for the visual possibilities offered by typographically diverse words. Soffici had painted a work early in 1914 with the title *Typographical Simultaneity*,[14] in which he depicted the mastheads and front pages of the main publications of *Lacerba*, while in a text of May 1914 Giovanni Papini wrote passionately of the formal poetics of the work of the typographer.[15]

Soffici took a clear stand on the matter in a passage of the 'Typography' chapter (written sometime between 1914 and 1917, but only published in 1920) in *Primi principi di una estetica futurista*. This marked his definitive disavowal of Marinetti's words-in-freedom, already roundly censured in a letter commenting on some of Carrà's *Guerrapittura* drawings.[16] Soffici attributed a prevalently formal significance to the word inserted in a painting, confining it to the role of one of the visual components in the "matter of the image":

> "Animated by color and light, in surprising combinations, set in motion in the most vigorous outflows of our existence, its [the printed letter] efficacy becomes even more evident. Efficacy of suggestion and of figurative complement. No longer a mute conventional mark, but a living form among living forms, the letter can become part of the body of matter of the image."[17]

Fruit and Liqueurs remained in Soffici's possession for twenty years. He managed its exhibitions and publications, and certain of its formal characteristics (the balance between spatial complexity and the plastic solidity of the objects, which was admired even in the years of the return to order) meant that *Fruit and Liqueurs* was his most reproduced and best known avant-garde work in subsequent decades. When it was exhibited in the Soffici exhibition in 1920 at the Horne Museum (with the title *Fruit and Liqueur* and the date 1915),[18] it was certainly among the paintings that pleased the critics best, classing it among the "formal arabesques pleasing in color and vibrating with light and wisely balanced in its lights and darks."[19] Short-

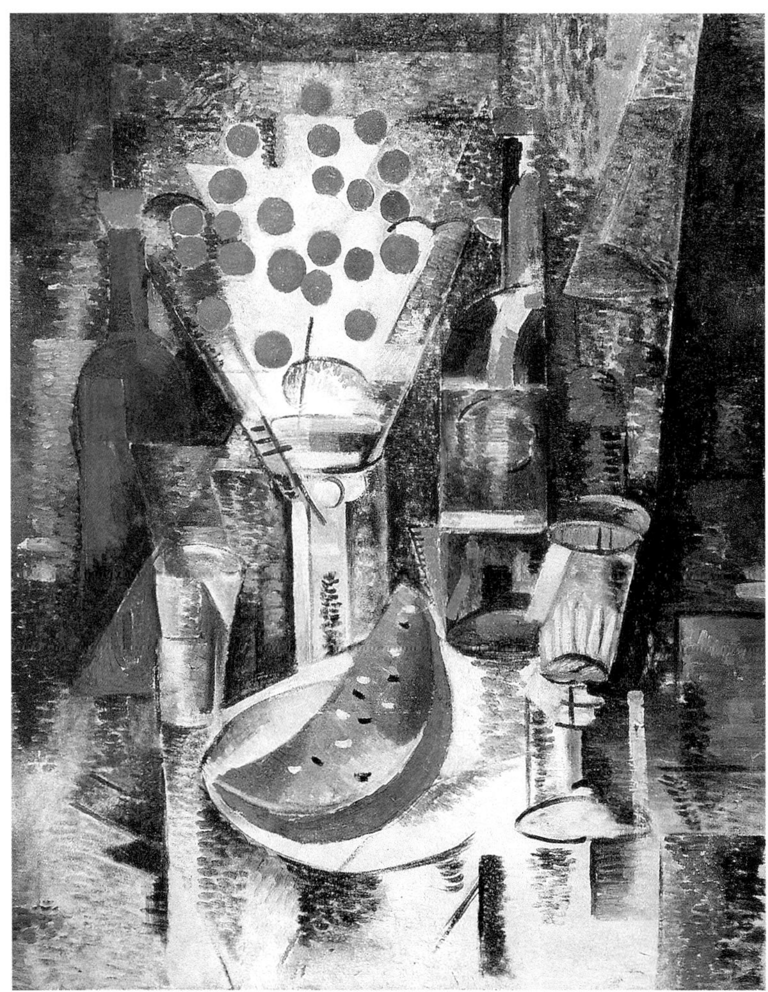

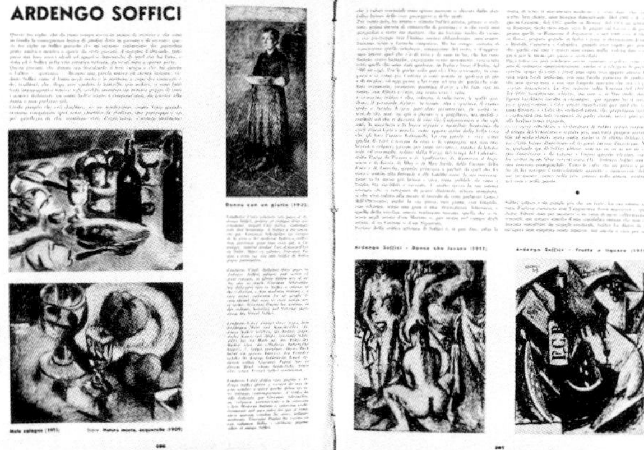

ARDENGO SOFFICI

Fig. 26d. *Alexandra Exter,* Still Life with Bowl of Cherries, *oil on canvas, 1914. Rostov (Russia), Rostov Kremlin State Museum Preserve*

Fig. 26e. *Reproduction of cat. no. 26, in* Domus, *1933*

ly after the exhibition closed, Soffici chose this still life for a key illustration in the second issue of *Rete Mediterranea*, the magazine of 1920 written entirely by the artist. By re-presenting this still life five years on, Soffici clearly intended to establish, in the altered climate of classicism, the modernity of experimental work (by that time the target of mockery) and its continuity with the formal research of the Cubo-Futurist period. An extract of the text next to the illustration emphasized the necessity for complexity of chromatic construction:

> "A strong impasto, which awakens a sense of solidity and stability in the viewer, is a notable virtue in a work of painting [...]. It is essential that its texture be rich in tones, or in variations of tones, in such a manner that any part of the painted surface appear to the eye enlivened by that combination of color ranges which generates at once both variety and unity in harmony, vibrations and compact solidity."[20]

Henceforth *Fruit and Liqueurs* was included among the few Cubo-Futurist period works appearing in the two principal publications on Soffici: Pier Maria Bardi's book *Carrà e Soffici* in 1930[21] (it was not however offered for sale at the corresponding exhibition[22]) and the volume dedicated to Soffici in the important *Arte Moderna Italiana* series, edited by Giovanni Scheiwiller, with an introduction by Giovanni Papini (1933).[23] Despite Soffici's desire to present *Fruit and Liqueurs* as a transitional work in his return to figuration (fig. 26e), it was seldom appreciated by even the most discerning critics. It seemed to exemplify a period "buried without thoughts of resurrection"[24] and at best was a witness to "pure polemic."[25] *Fruit and Liqueurs* came up for sale at the December 1942–January 1943 Soffici exhibition in the Galleria del Milione, the first attempt at a comprehensive review of his Cubo-Futurist period. It was illustrated in two reviews of the show[26] and was discussed in an article by Mario De Micheli which was one of the first critical reevaluations of Soffici's experimental work from 1913 to 1915. According to De Micheli, young militant critic for *Corrente* and a fervent admirer of Picasso, it was to be admired for its Cubist-derived compositional rigor:

> "Among these paintings [of 1913–15] the still life of 1915 is a successful piece, painted in a thick impasto in which the overlapping planes are handled with a certain confidence. In other words, there is a solidity which we do not find in the recent paintings, a solidity owed to a study of the tones and of the compositional construction, taught by Cubism."[27]

By the time of the 1945 monograph published by Il Milione, with twelve plates of Soffici's paintings and a preface by Giovanni Papini, *Fruit and Liqueurs* had entered the collection of Carlo Frua De Angeli,[28] a collector of twentieth-century Italian painting who was particularly active from the late 1930s to the early 1950s. In the years immediately following, according to information in the files of the Mattioli archive, it passed into the Israel Collection in Montreal and then, towards the end of 1950, into the Mattioli Collection.[29] In later years *Fruit and Liqueurs* continued to represent the pictorial link between two apparently irreconcilable cycles of Soffici's work. In 1953 Carlo Ludovico Ragghianti attributed to it a "quality of real density," capable of revealing concisely "the passage to his subsequent phase openly and programmatically traditionalist and realistic."[30] Giuseppe Marchiori observed how, thanks to the color enlivening the "recomposed structures [...] the objects regain an unexpected consistency."[31] To Franco Russoli in 1975 the work seemed "a point of arrival in the encounter between Cubo-Futurist syntax and a primordial sentiment for the real."[32]

[1] Letter from Ardengo Soffici to Carlo Carrà, dated May 21, 1915, in Carrà, Soffici 1983, p. 88.
[2] Letter from Pablo Picasso to Ardengo Soffici, dated April 20, 1915, in Cavallo 1986, p. 248.
[3] Numerous examples can be found in Daix, Rosselet 1979, nos. 621–760.
[4] Raimondi 1967, p. 33.
[5] The stencil is illustrated in *Rignano sull'Arno* 1994, p. 40.
[6] Soffici, September 15, 1910.
[7] Private collection: Raimondi, Cavallo 1967, no. 187, collage published in *Lacerba*, May 15, 1914.
[8] Raimondi, Cavallo 1967, nos. 193–201; *Poggio a Caiano* 1975, nos. 49–50.
[9] Private collection: Raimondi, Cavallo 1967, no. 185.
[10] Formerly Florence, Galleria Michaud; *ibidem*, no. 206.
[11] Letter from Carlo Carrà to Ardengo Soffici, dated December 27, 1915 (which refers to a meeting between the two after November 17), in Carrà, Soffici 1983, pp. 92–3.
[12] Rostov Kremlin State Museum Preserve: *Berlin* 1999, p. 146, no. 5.
[13] Rylands 1997, p. 102.
[14] *Simultaneità tipografica*, whereabouts unknown: *Rome* 1914[a], p. 28, no. 5; Raimondi, Cavallo 1967, no. 204.
[15] Papini, May 1, 1914.
[16] Letter from Ardengo Soffici to Carlo Carrà, dated April 28, 1915, in Carrà, Soffici 1983, pp. 80–1.
[17] Soffici 1920[a], pp. 87–9.
[18] *Florence* 1920, no. 97.
[19] Marangoni 1920, p. 67.
[20] Soffici 1920[b], p. 165.
[21] Bardi 1930, pl. 70.
[22] As indicated by the 'Distinta dei quadri esposti da Bardi' (Milan, Archivio Storico Civico, Biblioteca Trivulziana, Fondo Bardi, cartella 9, carta 3196).
[23] Papini 1933, pl. XV.
[24] Vitali 1933, p. 408.
[25] Giolli 1943, p. 84.
[26] De Micheli 1943, p. 76; Giolli 1943, p. 84.
[27] De Micheli 1943, p. 77.
[28] Papini 1945, pl. 2.
[29] On November 30, 1950 the Galleria del Milione debited Gianni Mattioli the sum of 3,800 lire for "travel expenses to Turin to collect painting [by] Soffici returned from America"; again, on January 12, 1951, the sum of 4,000 lire for "new stretcher and lining Soffici returned America": Archivio Mattioli, account from the Galleria del Milione dated February 7, 1951 (*Appendix I*, document no. 68).
[30] Ragghianti 1953, p. 19.
[31] Marchiori 1960, p. 91.
[32] Russoli 1975, p. 110.

List of Exhibitions Cited

Paris 1904
Societé des Artistes Français. Catalogue illustré du Salon. Paris [Grand Palais, April–June 1904]. Catalogue Paris, Librairie d'Art 1904

Milan 1910
Esposizione di duecento opere del pittore Gaetano Previati. Catalogo. Milan, Società per le Belle Arti, January–February 1910. Catalogue Milan, Capriolo e Massimino 1910

Venice 1910
IX Esposizione Internazionale d'Arte della Città di Venice. 1910. Catalogo illustrato. Venice [May–October] 1910. Catalogue Venice, Ferrari 1910

Milan 1911
Esposizione intima annuale. Milan, Famiglia Artistica, December 1911. Catalogue untraced

Paris 1912[a]
Les Peintres Futuristes Italiens. Paris, Galerie Bernheim-jeune, February 1912. Catalogue Paris, Moderne Imprimerie 1912

London 1912
Exhibition of Works by the Italian Futurist Painters. London, The Sackville Gallery, March 1912. Catalogue Southwood, Smith and Co. 1912

Paris 1912[b]
Société du Salon d'Automne. Catalogue des Ouvrages de Peinture, Sculpture, Dessin, Gravure, Architecture et Art Décoratif. Paris, Grand Palais, October–November 1912. Catalogue Paris, Kugelmann 1912

Rome 1913
Prima Esposizione [di] Pittura Futurista. Rome, ridotto del teatro Costanzi, Galleria G. Giosi [February–March] 1913. Catalogue Rome, Tipografia Carducci 1913

London 1913
The Futurist Painter Gino Severini Exhibits His Latest Works. London, Marlborough Gallery, April 1913. Catalogue London, Marlborough 1913

Rotterdam 1913
Les Peintres et les Sculpteurs Futuristes Italiens. Rotterdam, Rotterdamsche Kunstkring, May–June 1913. Catalogue Rotterdam, De Jong 1913

Paris 1913
1re Exposition de Sculpture Futuriste du Peintre et Sculpteur Futuriste Boccioni. Paris, Galerie la Boëtie, June–July 1913. Catalogue Paris, Dupont 1913

Berlin 1913
Erster Deutscher Herbstsalon, Berlin, Galerie Der Sturm [September–December] 1913. Catalogue Berlin, Verlag Der Sturm 1913

Florence 1913–14
Esposizione di Pittura Futurista di 'Lacerba'. Florence, via Cavour 48, November 1913–January 1914. Catalogue Florence, Tipografia Vallecchi, 1913

Florence 1914
318 bozzetti disegni xilografie acqueforti bronzi. Selling exhibition, Florence, Libreria Gonnelli, February 1914. Catalogue Florence 1914

Rome 1914[a]
Esposizione di Pittura Futurista. Boccioni-Carrà-Russolo-Balla-Severini-Soffici. Rome, Galleria Futurista G. Sprovieri, February–March 1914. Catalogue Rome, tipografia Patria 1914

Paris 1914
Société des Artistes Indépendants. Catalogue de la 30me Exposition 1914. Paris, Champ de Mars, March–April 1914. Catalogue Paris 1914

Rome 1914[b]
Seconda Esposizione Internazionale d'Arte 'della Secessione'. Catalogo Illustrato. Rome, Palazzo delle Esposizioni, March–April 1914. Catalogue Rome, Tipografia dell'Unione 1914

Rome 1914[c]
Esposizione Libera Futurista Internazionale. Pittori e Scultori italiani, russi, inglesi, belgi, nordamericani. Rome, Galleria Futurista G. Sprovieri, April–May 1914. Catalogue Rome, Tipografia Commerciale Moderna 1914

London 1914
Exhibition of the Works of the Italian Futurist Painters and Sculptors. London, The Doré Galleries, [April–June 1914]. Catalogue without date or place [but London 1914]

Naples 1914
Prima Esposizione di Pittura Futurista. Boccioni-Carrà-Russolo-Balla-Severini-Soffici. Naples, Galleria Futurista Sprovieri, May–June 1914. Naples, Cozzolino 1914

Rome 1915
Esposizione Fu Balla e Futurista. Rome, Sala d'Arte A. Angelelli [December 1915]. Catalogue without date or place

San Francisco 1915–16
Panama-Pacific International Exposition. Catalogue De Luxe of the Department of Fine Arts, San Francisco. San Francisco, The Palace of Fine Arts, February 1915–May 1916. Cat-

alogue San Francisco, San Francisco Art Association 1915. Curated by J. Trask and N. Laurvik

Milan 1916–17
Grande Esposizione Boccioni Pittore e Scultore Futurista. Catalogo. Milan, Galleria Centrale d'Arte, Palazzo Cova, December 1916–January 1917. Catalogue without date or place [but Milan 1916], with texts by U. Boccioni and preface by F. T. Marinetti

Capri 1917
Esposizione futurista del pittore e scultore Depero. Capri, Sala Morgano, September 1917. Catalogue Naples, Pierro 1917

Milan 1917–18
Mostra personale del pittore futurista Carlo Carrà. Milan, Galleria Paolo Chini, December 1917–January 1918. Catalogue Milan 1917, with a text by C. Carrà and poetry by P. Buzzi

Rome 1918[a]
Mostra d'Arte Indipendente pro Croce Rossa. Rome, Galleria dell'Epoca, May–June 1918. Catalogue Rome, Galleria dell'Epoca 1918

Viareggio 1918
La pittura d'avanguardia. Viareggio, Kursaal, August 1918. Catalogue untraced

Rome 1918[b]
Mostra del pittore futurista Balla. Rome, Casa d'Arte Bragaglia, October 1918. Catalogue Rome, Casa d'Arte Bragaglia 1918, with a text by G. Balla

Florence 1918
Pittori d'oggi. Florence, "Florentina Ars", Palazzo Antinori, October–November 1918. Catalogue Florence, Spinelli & C. 1918

Milan–Genoa–Florence 1919
Grande Esposizione Nazionale Futurista. Quadri, Complessi plastici, Architettura, Tavole parolibere, Teatro plastico futurista e Moda Futurista. Milan, Galleria Centrale d'Arte (Palazzo Cova) [March–April] 1919; Genoa, Galleria Centrale d'Arte [May–June] 1919; Florence, Salone della Pergola [summer] 1919. Catalogue Milan, La Presse 1919, with a text by F. T. Marinetti

Rome 1919
Mario Sironi. Rome, Casa d'Arte Bragaglia [July 1919]. Catalogue untraced

Florence 1920
Esposizione Soffici. Florence [Museo Horne], via de' Benci 6, May–June 1920. Catalogue Florence, Vallecchi 1920, with a text by M. Marangoni

Geneva 1920–1
Exposition internationale d'Art Moderne : peinture, sculpture etc. Geneva, December 1920–January 1921. Catalogue Geneva, Sadag 1920, with an introduction by E. Faure

Milan 1921
Depero e la sua Casa d'Arte. Milan, Galleria Centrale d'Arte-Palazzo Cova, January–February 1921. Catalogue Rovereto, tipografia Mercurio 1921, with a text by F. Depero

Paris 1921
Exposition des peintres futuristes italiens et conference de Marinetti. Paris, Galerie Reinhardt, May 1921. Catalogue Paris, Devambez 1921

Hanover 1921
Das junge Italien. Hanover, Kestner-Gesellschaft E. V., May–June 1921. Catalogue Hanover, Edler & Krische 1921

Alessandria 1921
Mostra Provinciale d'Arte. Alessandria, Teatro Municipale [from 7 June 1921]. Catalogue untraced

Trento 1921
XXVIa mostra del pittore futurista Depero. Trento, November 1921. Catalogue Rovereto, tipografia Mercurio 1921

Milan 1922
Pittori contemporanei italiani. Milan, Bottega di Poesia, January 1922. Catalogue untraced

Rome 1922
Umberto Boccioni. Rome, Galleria d'Arte Bragaglia, April 1922, 74th exhibition. Catalogue in *Bollettino Quindicinale della Casa d'Arte Bragaglia*, year II, no. 68, Rome, 15 April 1922

Macerata 1922
I[a] Esposizione Futurista, promoted by the Esposizione Provinciale d'Arte, organized by Ivo Pannaggi. Macerata, Palazzo del Convitto Nazionale, June–July 1922. Catalogue Macerata, Stabilimento Affeda 1922

Turin 1923
Esposizione Nazionale di Belle Arti. Turin, Palazzo al Valentino, spring 1923. Catalogue Turin, Società Promotrice di Belle Arti–La Quadriennale 1923

Milan 1924
Umberto Boccioni. Milan, Bottega di Poesia, March 1924. Catalogue Milan, Bottega di Poesia, XXI, with an introduction by F. T. Marinetti and a text by U. Boccioni

Rome 1925
Terza Biennale Romana. Esposizione Internazionale di Belle Arti. Rome, Palazzo delle Esposizioni, March–June 1925. Catalogue Rome, Pinci 1925

Milan 1926
Mostra individuale dei pittori Carlo Carrà, Giorgio de Chirico e postuma di Rubaldo Merello. Milan, Galleria Pesaro, February 1926. Catalogue Milan, Bastetti e Tumminelli 1926

Paris 1926
Salon des Artistes Indépendants. Paris, March–May 1926. Catalogue Paris, Delattre 1926

Rome 1928
XCIV Esposizione di Belle Arti. Rome, Società Amatori e Cultori di Belle Arti, February–June 1928. Catalogue Rome, Società Amatori e Cultori delle Belle Arti 1928

Venice 1928
XVI Esposizione Internazionale d'Arte della Città di Venezia. Catalogue. Venice [May–October] 1928. Catalogue Venice, Ferrari 1928

Venice 1930
XVII Esposizione Biennale Internazionale d'Arte 1930. Catalogo. Venice [May–October] 1930. Catalogue Venice, Ferrari 1930

Paris 1931
Rétrospective Modigliani, Paris, Galerie Marcel Bernheim, June 1931. Catalogue untraced

Milan 1933
Mostra retrospettiva di Umberto Boccioni. Milan, Castello Sforzesco, from June 1933. Without catalogue

Milan 1935
Mostra personale di Carrà. Milan, Galleria del Milione, November–December 1935. Catalogue Milan, *Bollettino della Galleria del Milione*, no. 43, 1935

New York 1936
Cubism and Abstract Art. New York, The Museum of Modern Art, 1936. Catalogue New York, The Museum of Modern Art 1936. Curated by A. H. Barr, Jr.

Milan 1937
20 firme in una mostra collettiva. Milan, Galleria del Milione, January–February 1937. Catalogue Milan, *Bollettino della Galleria del Milione*, no. 50, 1937

Genoa 1937
20 firme in una mostra collettiva. Genoa, Galleria Genova, April 1937. Catalogue untraced

Rome 1937
Omaggio [Tribute] a 16 artisti italiani. Rome, Galleria di Roma, June 1937. Catalogue Rome 1937, with a text by V. Guzzi

San Francisco 1939
Golden Gate International Exposition. Department of Fine Arts. Contemporary Art. San Francisco, Palace of the Legion of Honour, 1939. Catalogue San Francisco 1939

Rome 1939
III Quadriennale d'Arte Nazionale, Rome, Palazzo delle Esposizioni, February–July 1939. Catalogue Milan–Rome, Domus, 1939

Zurich 1940
Ausstellung Zeitgenössischer Italienischer Maler und Bildhauer. Zurich, Kunsthaus, November–December 1940. Catalogue Venice, Ferrari 1940, with a text by A. Maraini

Rome 1941
XLIII Mostra della Galleria di Roma con opere della raccolta di Carlo Cardazzo. Rome, Galleria di Roma, April 1941. Catalogue Rome 1941

Milan 1942[a]
Mostra di Carrà. Milan, Centro di azione per le arti, R. Pinacoteca di Brera, May–June 1942. Catalogue Milan, Esperia 1942. Curated by G. Pacchioni and G. A. Dell'Acqua

Milan 1942[b]
Mostra della collezione Feroldi. Milan, Pinacoteca di Brera [October–November] 1942. Without catalogue

Milan 1942–3
Ardengo Soffici. Milan, Galleria del Milione, December 1942–January 1943. Catalogue untraced

Milan 1948
Carlo Carrà 1903-1948. Milan, Circolo delle Arti 'Le Grazie', March–April 1948. Catalogue untraced

Rome 1948
Rassegna Nazionale di Arti Figurative promossa dall'Ente Autonomo Esposizione Quadriennale d'Arte di Roma. Rome, Galleria d'Arte Moderna, March–May 1948. Catalogue Rome, Istituto Grafico Tiberino 1948

Venice 1948
XXIV Biennale di Venezia. Catalogo, Venice, Giardini di Castello, May–September 1948. Catalogue Venice, Edizioni Serenissima 1948

Florence 1948
Dall'Otto al Novecento. Otto momenti di pittura in Toscana. Florence, Circolo degli Artisti-Casa di Dante, December 1948. Catalogue Florence-Empoli, S. T. E. T 1948, with a text by R. Franchi

Cairo 1949
Exposition de peinture Moderne Italienne depuis 1850 jusqu'à nos jours. Cairo, Ismail Pacha Palace, February–March 1949. Catalogue Venice, Alfieri 1949, with texts by N. Barbantini and U. Apollonio

Catania–Palermo 1949
Quarant'anni d'arte italiana, Catania–Palermo, January–April 1949. Catalogue untraced

New York 1949
Twentieth-Century Italian Art. New York, The Museum of Modern Art, April-September 1949. Catalogue New York, The Museum of Modern Art 1949. Curated by J. T. Soby and A. H. Barr, Jr.

Brussels 1950
Art italien contemporain. Brussels, Palais des Beaux-Arts, January–February 1950. Catalogue Brussels, Laconti 1950, with a text by G. Raimondi

Amsterdam 1950
Figuren uit de Italiaanse Kunst na 1910. Amsterdam Stedelijk Museum, March–May 1950. Catalogue untraced

Paris 1950
Exposition d'art moderne italien. Paris, Musée National d'Art Moderne, May–June 1950. Catalogue Paris, Presses Artistiques 1950, with a text by P. D'Ancona

London 1950
Exhibition of Modern Italian Art. London, The Tate Gallery, June–July 1950. Catalogue The Arts Council of Great Britain 1950, with a text by P. D'Ancona

Venice 1950
XXV Biennale di Venezia. Catalogo, Venice, Giardini di Castello, June–October 1950. Catalogue Venice, Alfieri 1950

Milan 1950
[*Mostra di pittori cubisti*], Milan, Galleria del Naviglio, November 1950. Catalogue untraced

Zurich 1950
Futurismo-Pittura Metafisica. Zurich, Kunsthaus, November–December 1950. Catalogue Zurich, Neue Zürcher Zeitung 1951, with texts by R. Wehrli and M. Bill

Milan 1951
Arte astratta italiana. I primi astrattisti italiani 1913-1940. Milan, Galleria Bompiani, March–April 1951. Catalogue untraced

Rome 1951
Omaggio a Giacomo Balla Futurista. Rome, Fondazione Origine, April 1951. Catalogue Rome, Origine 1951

Cleveland–New York 1951
Modigliani. Paintings Drawings Sculpture. Cleveland, The Museum of Art, January–March 1951; New York, The Museum of Modern Art, April–June 1951. Catalogue New York, The Museum of Modern Art 1951. Curated by J. T. Soby

Rome 1951–2
VI Quadriennale Nazionale d'Arte di Roma. Rome, Palazzo delle Esposizioni, December 1951–April 1952. Catalogue Rome, De Luca 1951

Venice 1952
XXVI Biennale di Venezia. Catalogo. Venice, Giardini di Castello, May–October 1952. Catalogue Venice, Alfieri 1952

Milan 1952
[*Mostra Antologica*]. Milan, Galleria del Milione, November 1952. Catalogue Milan, *Bollettino della Galleria del Milione*, new series, no. 1 1952

Ostend 1953
Exposition Art Fantastique. Ostend, Kursaal, July–August 1953. Catalogue untraced

Florence 1953[a]
Arte moderna in una raccolta italiana. Florence, Palazzo Strozzi, April–May 1953, with an essay by C. L. Ragghianti. Catalogue Milan, Edizioni del Milione 1953

Florence 1953[b]
Omaggio a Rosai. Florence, La Strozzina, April–May 1953. Catalogue Florence 1953. Curated by C. L. Ragghianti

São Paulo 1953–4
Futuristas e artistas italianos de hoje na segunda Bienal de São Paulo. São Paulo, Museu de Arte Moderna, December 1953–February 1954. Catalogue Venice, Ferrari 1953

New York 1954
Futurism. New York, Sidney Janis Gallery, March–May 1954. Catalogue New York, Hitchcock 1954

Barcelona–Madrid 1955
Exposición de pintura italiana contemporánea. Barcelona, Palacio de la Virreina, March–April 1955; (*Exposición de Arte Italiano Contemporáneo*) Madrid, Palacio del Retiro, May–June 1955. Catalogue Madrid, Estades 1955, with a text by P. Bucarelli

Lausanne 1955
Du futurisme à l'art abstrait. Le mouvement dans l'art contemporain. Lausanne, Musée Cantonal des Beaux-Arts, June–September 1955. Catalogue Lausanne, Musée Cantonal des Beaux-Arts 1955. Curated by E. Manganel and G. Weelen

Kassel 1955
Documenta. Kunst des XX. Jahrhunderts. Kassel, Museum Fridericianum, July–September 1955. Catalogue Munich, Prestel-Verlag 1955, with a text by W. Haftmann

Bern 1955
Modigliani Campigli Sironi. Bern, Kunsthalle, August–September 1955. Catalogue Bern, Benteli AG 1955, with a text by A. Rüdlinger

Marseille 1955
L'Art italien contemporain. Marseille, Musée Cantini, September–October 1955. Catalogue Marseille, Imprimerie Municipale 1955, edited by N. Ponente, with a text by P. Bucarelli

Ann Arbor 1955
20th Century Painting and Sculpture from The Collection of Mr. and Mrs. Harry Lewis Winston. Ann Arbor, MI, The University of Michigan Museum of Art, October–November 1955. Catalogue Ann Arbor, The University of Michigan 1955, with a text by J. P. Slusser

Rome 1955–6
VII Quadriennale Nazionale d'Arte. Rome, Palazzo delle Esposizioni, November 1955–April 1956. Catalogue Rome, De Luca 1955

Winterthur 1956
Giorgio Morandi-Giacomo Manzù. Winterthur, Kunstmuseum, June–July 1956. Catalogue Winterthur, Kunstverein Winterthur 1956, with a text by H. Keller

Ivrea 1957
Ottone Rosai. Ivrea, Centro Culturale Olivetti, May 1957. Catalogue Ivrea, Quaderni del Centro Culturale Olivetti 1957. Curated by P. C. Santini.

Munich 1957
Grosse Kunstausstellung München 1957 mit Ausstellung italienischer Kunst von 1900 bis zur Gegenwart. Munich, Haus der Kunst, June–September 1957. Catalogue Munich, Suddeutscher Verlag 1957

Turin 1957
Peintres d'aujourd'hui. France-Italie. Pittori d'oggi. Francia-Italia. Turin, Palazzo delle Arti, Parco del Valentino, October–November 1957. Catalogue Turin, TECA 1957

Amsterdam 1958
De Renaissance der XXe eeuv. Amsterdam, Stedelijk Museum, July–September 1958. Catalogue Amsterdam, Stedelijk Museum 1958

Milan 1958
Mostra di Amedeo Modigliani. Milan, Palazzo Reale, November–December 1958. Catalogue Milan, Ente Manifestazioni Milanesi 1958. Curated by F. Russoli

Rome 1959
Il Futurismo. Rome, Palazzo Barberini, June–September 1959. Catalogue Rome, De Luca 1959. Curated by J. Recupero.

Winterthur 1959
Il Futurismo. Winterthur, Kunstmuseum, October–November 1959. Catalogue Winterthur, Kunstverein Winterthur 1959, with a text by C. Giedion-Welcker

Munich 1959–60
Futuristen. Munich, Städtischen Galerie, December 1959–February 1960. Catalogue Munich, Holzinger 1959, with a text by C. Giedion-Welcker

Turin 1959
Capolavori di arte moderna nelle raccolte private. Turin, Civica Galleria d'Arte Moderna, October–December 1959. Catalogue Milan, Edizioni del Milione 1959. Curated M. Valsecchi

Milan 1960
Balla pittore futurista. Milan, Galleria Minima, May 1960. Catalogue [Milan, Galleria Minima 1960], with an unsigned text

Venice 1960
XXX Esposizione Biennale Internazionale d'Arte. Venice, June–October 1960. Catalogue Venice, Ente Autonomo la Biennale di Venezia 1960

Florence 1960
Mostra dell'opera di Ottone Rosai 1911-1957. Florence, Palazzo Strozzi May–June 1960. Catalogue Florence, Vallecchi 1960. Curated by P. C. Santini

Paris 1960–1
Les Sources du XX siècle. Les Arts en Europe de 1844 à 1914. Paris, Musée National d'Art Moderne, November 1960–January 1961. Catalogue Paris, Les Presses Artistiques 1960. Curated by J. Cassou

New York 1961–Los Angeles 1962
Futurism. New York, The Museum of Modern Art, May–September 1961; Detroit, The Detroit Institute of Arts, October–December 1961; Los Angeles, Los Angeles County Museum, January–February 1962. Catalogue New York, The Museum of Modern Art 1961, with a text by J. C. Taylor

Turin–Milan 1961
Mostra della moda, stile, costume. Da Boldini a Pollock: pittura e scultura del XX secolo. Turin [dates and venue not specified] 1961; Milan, Civico Padiglione d'Arte Contemporanea, October–November 1961. Catalogue Milan, Industrie Grafiche Moneta 1961. Curated by F. Russoli

Milan 1962[a]
Quaranta futuristi. Milan, Galleria Toninelli Arte Moderna, January–February 1962. Catalogue Milan, Toninelli Arte Moderna 1962

Milan 1962[b]
Prima retrospettiva di Fortunato Depero. Milan, Galleria Toninelli Arte Moderna, April 1962. Catalogue Milan, Toninelli Arte Moderna 1962, with a text by G. Ballo

Milan 1962[c]
Mostra di Carlo Carrà. Milan, Palazzo Reale, April–May 1962. Catalogue Milan, Bramante 1962

Venice 1962
XXXI Biennale Internazionale d'Arte di Venezia. Venice [June–October] 1962. Catalogue Venice, Ente Autonomo la Biennale di Venezia 1962

Vienna 1962
Kunst von 1900 bis heute. Vienna, Museum des 20. Jahrhunderts, September–October 1962. Catalogue Vienna, Brüder Rosenbaum 1962. Curated by W. Hofmann

Cologne 1962
Europäische Kunst 1912. Cologne, Wallraf-Richartz Museum, September–December 1962. Catalogue Cologne, Wallraf-Richartz Museum 1962. Curated by G. von den Osten

Siegen 1962–3
Giorgio Morandi. Rubenspreis 1962 der Stadt Siegen. Siegen, Haus Seel am Markt, October–November 1962. Catalogue Siegen, Vier-Quellen Verlag 1962, with a text by U. Apollonio

Brescia 1963
Mostra celebrativa di Mario Sironi. Brescia, Associazione degli Artisti Bresciani, January–February 1963. Catalogue Brescia, Apollonio 1963. Curated by M. Valsecchi

Turin 1963
Giacomo Balla. Turin, Galleria Civica d'Arte Moderna, April 1963. Catalogue Turin, Museo Civico 1963. Curated by E. Crispolti

Frankfurt 1963
Amedeo Modigliani. Frankfurt am Main, Frankfurt Kunstverein, Steinernes Haus Römerberg, June–July 1963. Catalogue Offenbach, Statz 1963. Curated by E. Rathke

Rotterdam 1963
Gino Severini. Rotterdam, Museum

Boijmans Van Beuningen, June–September 1963. Catalogue Rotterdam, Wissing 1963, with a text J. C. Ebbinge Wubben

Hamburg 1963–Frankfurt 1964

Italien 1905-1925: Futurismus und Pittura Metafisica. Hamburg, Kunstverein, September–November 1963; Frankfurt, Frankfurter Kunstverein, Steinernes Haus Römerberg, November 1963–January 1964. Catalogue Offenbach, Graphische Werkstätte 1963. Curated by E. Rathke and S. Rathke Köhl

Milan 1964

Omaggio a Gino Ghiringhelli. Milan, Galleria del Milione, November–December 1964. Catalogue Milan, *Bollettino della Galleria del Milione*, new series, no. 103

Naples 1964–Rotterdam 1965

La natura morta italiana. Naples, Palazzo Reale, October–November 1964. Catalogue, Milan, Alfieri & Lacroix 1964; Zurich, Kunsthaus, December 1964–January 1965; Rotterdam, Museum Boijmans Van Beuningen, March–April 1965

Bern 1965

Giorgio Morandi. Bern, Kunsthalle, October–December 1965. Catalogue Bern, Kunsthalle Bern 1965, with a text by W. Haftmann

Rome 1965

Rassegna di Arte Figurativa Contemporanea e Retrospettiva "Il soldato italiano". Rome, Palazzo Barberini, November–December 1965. Catalogue Rome, Ministero della Difesa 1965

Rome 1965–6

IX Quadriennale Nazionale d'Arte di Roma. Rome, Palazzo delle Esposizioni, October 1965–April 1966. Catalogue Rome, De Luca 1965

Milan 1966[a]

12 capolavori di una collezione privata. Milan, premises of *Il Giorno*, January–February 1966. Catalogue Milan, S. P. E. M. 1966, with a text by M. Valsecchi

Milan 1966[b]

Mostra di pitture, disegni, scenografie, intarsi di stoffe, grafica, manifesti pubblicitari, studi di Fortunato Depero. Milan, Galleria d'Arte Moderna, Padiglione d'Arte Contemporanea, April–May 1966. Catalogue Milan, Galleria d'Arte Moderna 1966. Curated by A. Pica

Venice 1966

XXXIII Esposizione Biennale Internazionale d'Arte. Venice, Giardini di Castello, June–October 1966. Catalogue Venice, Ente Autonomo La Biennale di Venezia 1966

Bologna 1966

L'opera di Giorgio Morandi. Bologna, Palazzo dell'Archiginnasio, 30 October–15 December 1966. Catalogue Bologna, Alfa 1966. Curated by G. A. Dell'Acqua, R. Longhi, L. Vitali

Milan 1967

Mostra dell'opera grafica di Carlo Carrà. Milan, Accademia di Brera, Sala Napoleonica. Catalogue Milan, Maestri 1967. Curated by G. Ballo

Florence 1967[a]

Arte moderna in Italia 1915-1935. Florence, Palazzo Strozzi, February–May 1967. Catalogue Florence, Marchi e Bertolli, 1967. Curated by C. L. Ragghianti.

Florence 1967[b]

Ardengo Soffici e il cubofuturismo 1911-1915. Florence, Galleria Michaud [dates not specified] 1967. Catalogue Edizioni Galleria Michaud 1967, with texts by L. Cavallo, G. Raimondi and F. Russoli

Washington, DC 1967–Tokyo 1972

Masters of Modern Italian Art from the Collection of Gianni Mattioli. Washington, DC, The Phillips Collection, November 1967–January 1968. Catalogue Washington, DC, H. K. Press 1967, curated by F. Russoli; Dallas, The Dallas Museum of Fine Arts, February–March 1968; San Francisco, The San Francisco Museum of Art, March–April 1968; Detroit, The Detroit Institute of Arts, June–July 1968; Kansas City, The William Rockhill Nelson Gallery of Art, October–November 1968; Boston, The Museum of Fine Arts, January–February 1969; New York, Olivetti store, March–April 1969; (*Maîtres de l'art moderne en Italie 1910-1935*) Brussels, Palais des Beaux-Arts, September–October 1969; (*Italiensk Kunst 1910-1935. Gianni Mattiolis Samling*) Copenhagen, Louisiana, November–December 1969; (*Italienische Kunst. Sammlung Gianni Mattioli*) Hamburg, Hamburger Kunsthalle, February–March 1970; (*Maestros del arte moderno en Italia 1910-1935*) Madrid, Museo Español de Arte Contemporáneo, November–December 1970; Barcelona, Palacio de la Virreina, December 1970–January 1971; Seville, Museo de Arte Contemporáneo, January–February 1971; (*Masters of Modern Italian Art from the Collection of Gianni Mattioli*) Kyoto, The National Museum of Modern Art, April–May 1972; Tokyo, The National Museum of Modern Art, May–July 1972

Turin 1969

Il sacro e il profano nell'arte dei simbolisti. Turin, Galleria Civica d'Arte Moderna, May–August 1969. Catalogue Turin, Galleria Civica d'Arte Moderna. Curated by L. Carluccio

Milan 1970

Mostra del Divisionismo Italiano. Milan, Palazzo della Permanente, March–April 1970. Catalogue Milan, Società per le Belle Arti ed Esposizione Permanente 1970. Curated by F. Bellonzi and others

Bassano del Grappa 1970

Fortunato Depero 1892-1960. Bassano del Grappa, Museo Civico, July–September 1970. Catalogue Bassano del Grappa, Museo di Bassano 1970. Curated by B. Passamani

Brussels–Berlin 1971

Métamorphoses de l'object. Art et Anti-art 1910-1970. Brussels, Palais des Beaux-Arts, April–June 1971; Rotterdam, Museum Boijmans Van Beuningen, June–August 1971; Berlin, Neue Nationalgalerie, September–November 1971. Catalogue Brussels, La Connaissance S. A. 1971

Prato 1971

100 opere di Carlo Carrà. Prato, Galleria d'Arte Moderna Falsetti, May–June 1971. Catalogue Prato, Falsetti 1971, with texts by M. De Micheli and M. Luzi

Milan 1971

Giorgio Morandi. Milan, Rotonda della Besana, May–June 1971. Catalogue Cinisello Balsamo, Pizzi 1971, with texts by F. Arcangeli, J. Leymarie and A. Forge

Rome 1971–2

Giacomo Balla (1871-1958). Rome, Galleria Nazionale d'Arte Moderna, December 1971–February 1972. Catalogue Rome, De Luca 1971. Curated by G. De Marchis

Milan 1972

Metamorfosi dell'oggetto. Milan, Palazzo Reale, January–February 1972. Catalogue Milan, Comune di Milano-Ripartizione iniziative culturali 1972, with a text by W. Haftmann

Rome 1972

X Quadriennale d'Arte Nazionale d'Arte. Aspetti dell'arte figurativa contemporanea. Nuove ricerche d'immagine. La linea della ricerca figurativa in Italia dal verismo dell'ultimo

Ottocento al 1935. Rome, Palazzo delle Esposizioni, November–December 1972. Catalogue Rome, De Luca 1972. Curated by E. Carli and others

Newcastle upon Tyne 1972–London 1973
Futurismo 1909-1919. Exhibition of Italian Futurism. Newcastle upon Tyne, Hatton Gallery, November–December 1972; Edinburgh, Royal Scottish Academy, December 1972–January 1973; London, Royal Academy of Arts, January–March 1973. Catalogue Edinburgh, Northern Arts and Scottish Arts Council 1972. Curated by A. Bozzolla and C. Tisdall

Bonn–Kassel 1973
Fortunato Depero. Ein Kunstler des Futurismus. Bonn, Rheinisches Landesmuseum, January–February 1973; Saarbrücken, Moderne Galerie, March–April 1973; Hanover, Kubus, April–May 1973; Kassel, Kulturhaus, June–July 1973. Catalogue Vallagarina, Calliano 1973. Curated by B. Passamani

Milan 1973
Mario Sironi. Palazzo Reale, February–March 1973. Catalogue Milan, Electa 1973. Curated by R. De Grada

Rome 1973
X Quadriennale d'Arte Nazionale d'Arte. Situazione dell'arte non figurativa. Rome, Palazzo delle Esposizioni, February–March 1973. Catalogue Rome, De Luca 1972

New York 1973
Futurism. A Modern Focus. The Lydia and Harry Lewis Winston Collection. Dr. and Mrs Barnett Malbin. New York, Solomon R. Guggenheim Museum [dates not specified] 1973. Catalogue The Solomon R. Guggenheim Foundation 1973. Curated by L. Shearer and M. W. Martin

Trento 1973
Fortunato Depero 1892-1960. Trento, Palazzo Pretorio, September–October 1973. Catalogue Vallagarina, Calliano 1973. Curated by B. Passamani

Paris 1973
Le Futurisme 1906-1916. Paris, Musée National d'Art Moderne, September–November 1973. Catalogue Paris, Editions des Musées Nationaux. Curated by G. Ballo, F. Cachin-Nora, J. Leymarie and F. Russoli

Milan 1973–4
Boccioni e il suo tempo. Milan, Palazzo Reale, December 1973–February 1974. Catalogue Milan, Arti Grafiche Fiorin 1973. Curated by G. Ballo, F. Cachin-Nora, L. De Maria, F. Russoli

Rome 1973
Giorgio Morandi (1890-1964). Rome, Galleria Nazionale d'Arte Moderna, May–July 1973. Catalogue Rome, De Luca 1973, with texts by P. Bucarelli, C. Brandi, G. De Marchis and others

Düsseldorf 1974
Futurismus 1909-1917: Wir setzen den Betrachter mitten ins Bild. Balla Boccioni Bragaglia Depero Carrà Marinetti Prampolini Romani Russolo Sant'Elia Severini Sironi Soffici. Malerei, Skulptur, Zeichnung, Musik, Architektur, Fotodynamik, Film, Bühne. Düsseldorf, Städtische Kunsthalle, March–April 1974. Catalogue Düsseldorf, Städtische Kunsthalle 1974, with texts by F. Russoli, F. W. Heckmanns and R. Langer

Turin 1974
Giacomo Balla. 30 esempi. Turin, Galleria Martano, May 1974. Catalogue Turin, Documenti Martano/due no. 47. Curated by M. Fagiolo dell'Arco

Milan 1974
50 anni di pittura italiana nella collezione Boschi-Di Stefano donata al Comune di Milano. Milan, Palazzo Reale, May–September 1974. Catalogue Milan, Electa 1974. Curated by M. Precerutti Garberi

Milan 1975
Mostra Antologica di Carlo Carrà. Milan, Galleria d'Arte Medea, October–November 1975. Catalogue Milan 1975 with a text F. Russoli

Bologna 1975
Giorgio Morandi. Antologica. Bologna, Galleria Comunale d'Arte Moderna, May–June 1975. Catalogue Bologna, Grafis 1975, with a text by L. Vitali

Poggio a Caiano 1975
Ardengo Soffici. L'artista e lo scrittore nella cultura del '900. Poggio a Caiano, Villa Medicea, June 1975. Catalogue Florence, Centro Di, with texts by G. Raimondi, M. Richter and F. Russoli

Paris 1975–6
Le Bateau-Lavoir berceau de l'art moderne. Paris, Musée Jacquemart-André, October 1975–February 1976. Catalogue Paris, Busson 1975. Curated by J. Warnod

Dortmund 1976
Gino Severini. Dortmund, Museum am Ostwall, March–April 1976. Catalogue Dortmund, Museum am Ostwall 1976, with texts by G. Dorfles and R. Langer

Berlin 1977
Tendenzen der Zwanziger Jahre. Berlin, Neue Nationalgalerie, Akademie der Kunste, Große Orangerie des Schlosses Charlottenburg, August–October 1977. Catalogue Berlin, Reimer 1977. Curated by D. Honisch and others

Frankfurt 1977–8
DaDa in Europa. Werke und Dokumente. Frankfurt am Main, Städtische Galerie im Städelschen Kunstinstitut, November 1977–January 1978. Catalogue Berlin, Reimer 1977. Curated by H. Bergius and K. Gallwitz

Venice 1979
La pittura metafisica. Venice, Palazzo Grassi, May–July 1979. Catalogue Vicenza, Neri Pozza 1979. Curated by G. Briganti and E. Coen

Milan 1979
Arte e socialità in Italia dal realismo al simbolismo 1865-1915. Milan, Palazzo della Permanente, June–September 1979. Catalogue Milan, Società per le Belle Arti ed Esposizione Permanente 1979, with texts by F. Bellonzi, R. Bossaglia and others

New York 1980
Picasso. A Retrospective. New York, The Museum of Modern Art, May–September 1980. Catalogue The Museum of Modern Art, 1980. Curated by R. Penrose and J. Golding

Turin 1980
Ricostruzione futurista dell'Universo. Turin, Mole Antonelliana, June–October 1980. Catalogue Turin, Musei Civici 1980. Curated by E. Crispolti

Philadelphia 1980–1
Futurism and the International Avant-garde. Philadelphia, Philadelphia Museum of Art, October 1980–January 1981. Catalogue Philadelphia, Philadelphia Museum of Art 1980. Curated by A. d'Harnoncourt

Paris 1981
Amedeo Modigliani 1884-1920. Paris, Musée d'Art Moderne de la Ville de Paris, March–June 1981. Catalogue Paris, Musée d'Art Moderne de la Ville de Paris 1981. Curated by B. Contensou and D. Marchesseau

New Haven 1983
The Futurist Imagination: Word + Image in Italian Futurist Painting, Drawing, Collage and Free-word Poetry. New Haven, Yale University

Art Gallery, April–June 1983. Catalogue New Haven, Yale University Art Gallery 1995. Curated by A. Coffin Hanson

London 1983
The Essential Cubism. Braque, Picasso & Their Friends 1907-1920. London, The Tate Gallery, April–July 1983. Catalogue London, The Tate Gallery 1983. Curated by D. Cooper and G. Tinterow

Anacapri 1983
Capri 1905-1940. Frammenti postumi. Anacapri, Villa Rosa, July–September 1983. Catalogue Milan, Feltrinelli 1983. Curated by L. Vergine

Cortona 1983–4
Gino Severini, prima e dopo l'opera. Cortona, Palazzo Casali, November 1983-January 1984 Catalogue Milan, Electa 1983. Curated by M. Fagiolo dell'Arco

Florence 1984
Futurismo a Firenze 1910-1920. Florence, Palazzo Medici-Riccardi, February–April 1984, Catalogue Florence, Sansoni 1984. Curated by F. Bagatti, G. Manghetti and S. Porto

Paris 1984–5
Le Douanier Rousseau. Paris, Galeries Nationales du Grand Palais, September 1984–January 1985. Catalogue Paris, Editions de la Réunion des Musés Nationaux 1984. Curated by M. Hoog, C. Lanchner and W. Rubin

Udine 1985
Sironi. 100 disegni inediti. Udine, Chiesa di San Francesco, May–July 1985. Catalogue Milan, Mazzotta 1985. Curated by C. Gian Ferrari

Sassari 1985
Mario Sironi. Opere 1902-1960. Sassari, Padiglione dell'artigianato sardo, October–November 1895. Catalogue Milan–Rome, Mondadori-De Luca 1985. Curated by M. Penelope

Milan 1985
Sironi 1885-1961. Milan, Palazzo Reale, October–December 1985. Catalogue Milan, Mazzotta 1985. Curated by C. Gian Ferrari

Bologna 1985–6
Morandi e il suo tempo. Bologna, Galleria Comunale d'Arte Moderna, 9 November 1985–10 February 1986. Catalogue Milan, Mazzotta 1985. Curated by F. Solmi

Venice 1986
Futurismo & Futurismi. Venice, Palazzo Grassi, May–September 1986. Catalogue Milan, Bompiani 1986. Curated by P. Hulten

Milan 1987
Carrà. Mostra antologica. Milan, Palazzo Reale, April–June 1987. Catalogue Milan, Mazzotta 1987. Curated by M. Carrà and G. A. Dell'Acqua.

Paris 1987
Giorgio Morandi. Paris, Hôtel de Ville, June–August 1987. Catalogue Milan, Mazzotta 1987

Düsseldorf 1987
"Die Axt hat geblüht...". Europäische Konflikte der 30er Jahre in Erinnerung an die frühe Avantgarde. Düsseldorf, Städtische Kunsthalle, October–December 1987. Catalogue Düsseldorf, Städtische Kunsthalle 1987. Curated by J. Harten

Munich 1988
Mythos Italien. Wintermärchen Deutschland. Die italienische Moderne und ihr Dialog mit Deutschland. Munich, Bayerisches Staatsgemaldesammlungen, March–May 1988. Catalogue Munich, Prestel-Verlag 1988. Curated by C. Schulz-Hoffmann

Capri 1988
Depero, Capri, il teatro. Capri, Certosa di San Giacomo, July–August 1988. Catalogue Naples, Electa Napoli. Curated by G. Belli, M. Scudiero and E. Vilas

Rovereto 1988–Milan 1989
Depero, Rovereto, Museo Fortunato Depero, November 1988–January 1989; Milan, Palazzo Reale, March–May 1989. Catalogue Milan, Electa 1988. Curated by M. Fagiolo dell'Arco

New York 1988–9
Boccioni: A Retrospective, New York, The Metropolitan Museum of Art, September 1988–January 1989. Catalogue New York, The Metropolitan Museum of Art 1988. Curated by E. Coen

Verona 1988–9
Realismo magico. Pittura e scultura in Italia 1919-1925. Verona, Galleria dello Scudo, November 1988–January 1989. Catalogue Milan, Mazzotta 1988. Curated by M. Fagiolo dell'Arco.

Düsseldorf–Baden Baden 1988
Mario Sironi (1885-1961). Düsseldorf, Städtische Kunsthalle, April–June 1988; Baden Baden, Staatliche Kunsthalle, July September 1988. Catalogue Cologne, Du Mont Buchverlag 1988. Curated by J. Harten and J. Poetter

New York 1989[a]
Twentieth-Century Modern Masters. The Jacques and Natasha Gelman Collection. New York, The Metropolitan Museum of Art, December 1989. Catalogue New York, The Metropolitan Museum of Art. Curated by W. S. Liebermann and S. Rewald

Paris 1989
Magnelli. Paris, Musée National d'Art Moderne [dates not specified] 1989. Catalogue Paris, Centre Georges Pompidou 1989. Curated by D. Abadie

Rome 1989
Casa Balla e il Futurismo a Roma. Rome, Villa Medici, September–December 1989. Catalogue Rome, Istituto Poligrafico e Zecca dello Stato 1989. Curated by E. Crispolti

New York 1989[b]
Mario Sironi. New York, Philippe Daverio Gallery, May–June 1989. Catalogue Milan–New York, Edizioni Philippe Daverio 1989. Curated by F. Benzi

London 1989
Italian Art in the 20th Century. Painting and Sculpture 1900-1988. London, Royal Academy of Arts, January–April 1989. Catalogue Munich, Prestel 1989. Curated by E. Braun

Bologna 1989
Morandi nelle raccolte private bolognesi. Bologna, San Giorgio in Poggiale, March–April 1989. Catalogue Bologna, A. G. E. 1989, with a testimonial by A. Emiliani and texts by P. G. Castagnoli and M. Pasquali

Focette, Cortina d'Ampezzo, Milan 1989
'A Prato per vedere i Corot.' Corrispondenza Morandi-Soffici per un'antologica di Morandi. Focette, Cortina d'Ampezzo, Milan, Galleria d'Arte Moderna Farsetti, July–October 1989. Catalogue Milan, Farsetti. Curated by L. Cavallo

Kamakura 1989–Kyoto 1990
Giorgio Morandi (1890-1964). Kamakura, The Museum of Modern Art, November–December 1989; Mie, Prefectural Art Museum, January–February 1990; Fukujama, Museum of Art, February-March 1990; Tokyo, Yurakucho Art Forum, March–April 1990; Kyoto, The National Museum of Modern Art, April–May 1990. Catalogue Tokyo, The Tokio Shimbum 1989, with texts by M. Garberi, M. Calvesi, R. Tardito and others

Venice 1989
Arte Italiana. Presenze 1900-1945. Venice, Palazzo Grassi, 30 April–5 November 1989. Catalogue Milan, Bompiani 1989. Curated by P. Hulten and G. Celant

Bologna 1990
Giorgio Morandi. Mostra del centenario. Bologna, Galleria Comunale d'Arte Moderna 'Giorgio Morandi', May–September 1990. Catalogue Milan, Electa 1990. Curated by M. Pasquali

Martigny 1990
Amedeo Modigliani. Martigny, Fondation Pierre Gianadda, June–October 1990. Catalogue Martigny, Fondation Pierre Gianadda 1990. Curated by D. Marchesseau

Madrid 1990–1
Memoria del Futuro. Arte Italiano desde las primeras vanguardias a la posguerra. Madrid, Centro de Arte Reina Sofia, October 1990–January 1991. Catalogue Milan, Fabbri 1990. Curated by G. Celant and I. Gianelli

Paris 1990–1
Art&Pub. Art & Publicité 1890-1990. Paris, Centre Georges Pompidou, October 1990–February 1991. Catalogue Paris, Centre Pompidou 1990. Curated by N. Ouvard

Milan 1990–1
Morandi a Milano. Milan, Palazzo Reale, November 1990–January 1991. Catalogue Milan, Electa 1990, with texts by M. Garberi, G. A. Dell'Acqua, R. Tardito and others

Rome 1990–Bologna 1991
Morandi. L'opera grafica. Rispondenze e variazioni. Rome, Istituto Nazionale per la Grafica. Calcografia Nazionale, December 1990–February 1991; Bologna, Palazzo Pepoli Campogrande, March–April 1991. Catalogue Milan, Electa 1990. Curated by M. Cordaro

New York 1991
Liubov Popova. New York, The Museum of Modern Art, February–April 1991. Catalogue New York, The Museum of Modern Art 1991. Curated by M. Dabrowoski

Gorizia 1991
Italico Brass. Gorizia, Castello di Gorizia, July–September 1991. Catalogue Milan, Electa 1991. Curated by M. Masau Dan

Rovereto 1991–2
Il mondo di Carlo Belli. Italia anni Trenta. La cultura artistica. Rovereto, Archivio del 900, November 1991–March 1992. Catalogue Milan, Electa 1991. Curated by G. Appella, G. Belli and M. Garberi

Sansepolcro 1991
Piero della Francesca e il Novecento. Prospettiva, spazio, luce, geometria, pittura murale, tonalismo 1920-1938. Sansepolcro, Museo Civico, July–October 1991. Catalogue Venice, Marsilio 1991. Curated by M. M. Lamberti and M. Fagiolo dell'Arco

Verona 1991–2
Boccioni 1912 Materia. Verona, Galleria dello Scudo, December 1991–February 1992. Catalogue Milan, Mazzotta 1991. Curated by L. Mattioli Rossi

Saint-Paul de Vence 1992
L'Art en mouvement. Saint-Paul de Vence, Fondation Maeght, July–October 1992. Catalogue Saint-Paul de Vence, Fondation Maeght 1992. Curated by J.-L. Prat

Milan 1992
Ardengo Soffici. Milan, Società per le Belle Arti ed Esposizione Permanente, September–October 1992. Catalogue Milan, Mazzotta 1992. Curated by L. Cavallo

Frankfurt–New York 1992
The Great Utopia. The Russian and Soviet Avant-garde, 1915-1932. Frankfurt, Schirn Kunsthalle, March–May 1992; Amsterdam, Stedelijk Museum, June–August 1992; New York, Solomon R. Guggenheim Museum, September–December 1992. Catalogue New York, The Guggenheim Museum 1992, with texts by P. Wood and others

New York 1992
Henri Matisse. A Retrospective. New York, The Museum of Modern Art [dates not specified] 1992. Catalogue New York, Abrams. Curated by J. Elderfield

Milan 1992–3
La collezione Jucker. Milan, Palazzo Reale, December 1992–January 1993. Catalogue Milan, Charta 1992, with texts by M. T. Fiorio, C. Bertelli and G. A. Dell'Acqua

Vienna 1993–Frankfurt 1994
Die Sprache der Kunst: die Beziehung von Bild und Text in der Kunst des 20. Jahrhunderts. Vienna, Kunsthalle, September–October 1993; Frankfurt, Frankfurter Kunstverein, December 1993–February 1994. Catalogue Stuttgart, Canz 1993. Curated by E. Louis and T. Stoss

Düsseldorf 1993–Moscow 1994
Vladimir Tatlin Retrospektive. Düsseldorf, Städtische Kunsthalle, September–November 1993; Baden Baden, Staatliche Kunsthalle, December 1993–February 1994; Moscow, Tret'jakov Gallery, March–April 1994. Catalogue Cologne, Du Mont 1993. Curated by A. Strigalev and J. Harten

Rome 1993–4
Mario Sironi 1885-1961. Rome, Galleria Nazionale d'Arte Moderna, December 1993–February 1994. Catalogue Milan, Electa 1993. Curated by F. Benzi

Marseille 1993
Poésure et Peintrie. D'un art, l'autre. Marseille, Musée Cantini, February–May 1993. Catalogue Paris, Réunion des Musées Nationaux 1993. Curated by B. Blistène and V. Legrand

Berlin 1994
Die letzten Tage der Menschheit. Bilder des Ersten Weltkrieges. Berlin, Altes Museum, June–August 1994. Catalogue Berlin, Deutsches Historisches Museum/Ars Nicolai 1994. Curated by R. Rother

Rignano sull'Arno 1994
Ardengo Soffici. Arte e storia. Rignano sull'Arno, September–November 1994. Catalogue Milan, Mazzotta. Curated by O. Casazza and L. Cavallo

London 1994
A Bitter Truth. Avant-garde Art and the Great War. London, Barbican Art Gallery, September–December 1994. Catalogue New Haven and London, Yale University Press 1994, in association with Barbican Art Gallery. Curated by R. Cork

Rome 1994–5
Carlo Carrà 1881-1966. Rome, Galleria Nazionale d'Arte Moderna, December 1994–February 1995. Catalogue Milan, Electa 1994. Curated by A. Monferini

Paris 1994–Tokyo 1996
La Ville. Art et architecture en Europe 1870-1993. Paris, Centre Georges Pompidou, February–May 1994; Barcelona, Centro de Cultura Contemporània, June–October 1994; Tokyo, Museum of Contemporary Art, July–September 1996. Catalogue Paris, Editions du Centre Pompidou 1994. Curated by J. Dethier and A. Guiheux

Paris 1994–5
André Derain. Le peintre du "trouble moderne". Paris, Musée d'Art Moderne de la Ville de Paris, November 1994–March 1995. Catalogue Paris, Paris Musées 1994. Curated by S. Pagé

Rome 1994–5
Depero. Dal Futurismo alla Casa d'Arte. Rome, Palazzo delle Esposizioni, December 1994–February 1995. Catalogue Milan, Charta 1994. Curated by G. Belli

Milan 1995
Boccioni 1912 Materia. Milan, Fondazione Antonio Mazzotta, April–

May 1995. Catalogue, Milan, Mazzotta 1995. Curated by L. Mattioli Rossi

Frankfurt 1995
Okkultismus und Avantgarde. Von Munch bis Mondrian 1900-1915. Frankfurt, Schirn-Kunsthalle, June–August 1995. Catalogue Ostfildern, Tertium 1995. Curated by V. Loers and P. Witzmann

Macerata 1995
Pannaggi e l'arte meccanica futurista. Macerata, Palazzo Ricci - Pinacoteca Comunale - Palazzo Contini, July–October 1995. Catalogue Milan, Mazzotta 1995. Curated by E. Crispolti

New Haven 1995–6
Severini futurista: 1912-1917. New Haven, Yale University Art Gallery, October 1995–January 1996. Catalogue Yale, Yale University Art Gallery 1995. Curated by A. Coffin Hanson

Prato 1995–Milan 1996
Ottone Rosai. Prato, Farsetti Arte, September–October 1995; Milan, Palazzo Reale, October 1995–January 1996. Catalogue Milan, Mazzotta 1995. Curated by L. Cavallo

Milan 1995–6
Arte a Milan 1906-1929. Milan, Fiera di Milan, November 1995–January 1996. Catalogue Milan, Electa 1995. Curated by P. Biscottini

Venice 1996
Umberto Boccioni. Dinamismo di un cavallo in corsa + case. Venice, Peggy Guggenheim Collection, February–May 1996. Catalogue New York, The Solomon R. Guggenheim Foundation 1996. Curated by F. Licht

Paris 1996
Fortunato Depero Futuriste. De Rome à Paris 1915-1925. Paris, Pavillon des Arts, March–June 1996. Catalogue Paris, Paris-Musées 1996. Curated by G. Belli

Barcelona 1996
Futurismo 1909-1916. Barcelona, Museu Picasso, May–July 1996. Catalogue Barcelona, Museu Picasso-Ambit Serveis Editorials 1996. Curated by E. Coen

Bergamo 1996
Carlo Carrà. La matita e il pennello. Bergamo, Galleria d'Arte Moderna e Contemporanea, March–June 1996. Catalogue Geneva-Milan, Skira 1996. Curated by V. Fagone

Naples 1996
Futurismo e Meridione. Napoli, Palazzo Reale, July–October 1996. Catalogue Naples, Electa Napoli 1996. Curated by E. Crispolti

Rome 1997
I capolavori Estorick. Una collezione inglese di arte italiana del XX secolo. Rome, Galleria Nazionale d'Arte Moderna, June–September 1997. Catalogue Turin, Allemandi 1997. Curated by A. Noble and L. Velani

Comacchio 1997
Casa Balla. Un pittore e le sue figlie tra futurismo e natura. Comacchio, Palazzo Bellini, June–October 1997. Catalogue Venice, Marsilio 1997. Curated by M. Fagiolo dell'Arco

Bologna 1997
Stagioni: l'autunno. Capolavori da una raccolta. Bologna, Museo Morandi, October 1997. Catalogue Bologna, Museo Morandi 1997. Curated by M. Pasquali

Verona 1997–Venice 1998
Morandi ultimo. Nature morte 1950-1964. Verona, Galleria dello Scudo, December 1997–March 1998; Venice, Peggy Guggenheim Collection, April–September 1998. Catalogue Milan, Mazzotta, 1997. Curated by L. Mattioli Rossi

Padua 1998
Giacomo Balla 1895-1911. Verso il futurismo. Padua, Palazzo Zabarella, March–June 1998. Catalogue Venice, Marsilio 1998. Curated by M. Fagiolo dell'Arco

Rome 1998
Il futuro alle spalle. Italia Francia - L'arte tra le due guerre. Rome, Palazzo delle Esposizioni, April–June 1998. Catalogue Rome, De Luca 1998. Curated by F. Pirani

Trento 1998
La Collezione Giovanardi. Capolavori della pittura italiana del '900. Trento, Museo di Arte Contemporanea of Trento and Rovereto, Palazzo delle Albere, April November 1998. Catalogue Milan, Electa 1998, Curated by M. M. Lamberti

Milan 1998
Botteghe di editoria tra Montenapoleone e Borgospesso. Libri, arte e cultura a Milan 1920-1940. Milan, Biblioteca di via Senato, September–October 1998. Catalogue Milan, Electa-Biblioteca di via Senato 1998. Curated by A. Modena

Rome 1998–9
XII Quadriennale. Valori Plastici. Rome, Palazzo delle Esposizioni, October 1998–January 1999. Catalogue Geneva-Milan, Skira 1998. Curated by P. Fossati, P. Rosazza Ferraris and L. Velani

Lugano 1999
Amedeo Modigliani. Lugano, Museo d'Arte Moderna-Villa Malpensata, March–June 1999. Catalogue Geneva-Milan, Skira 1999. Curated by R. Chiappini

Milan 1999
Gaetano Previati. Un protagonista del simbolismo europeo. Milan, Palazzo Reale, April–August 1999. Catalogue Milan, Electa 1999. Curated by F. Mazzocca

Paris 1999
Robert Delaunay 1906-1914: de l'Impressionnisme à l'Abstraction. Paris, Centre Georges Pompidou, June–August 1999. Catalogue Paris, Centre Georges Pompidou 1999. Curated by P. Rousseau

Berlin 1999
Amazons of the Avant-garde: Alexandra Exter, Natalia Goncharova, Liubov Popova, Olga Rozanova, Varvara Stepanova and Nadezhda Udaltsova. Berlin, Deutsche Guggenheim Berlin, July–October 2000. Catalogue New York, Guggenheim Museum 1999. Curated by J. E. Bowlt, M. Drutt and Z. Tregulova

Rome 1999–2000
Sul dinamismo. Opere di Umberto Boccioni dal The Metropolitan Museum of Art di New York e dalle Civiche Raccolte d'Arte del Castello Sforzesco di Milan. Rome, Galleria Comunale d'Arte Moderna e Contemporanea, December 1999–March 2000. Catalogue Rome, De Luca 1999. Curated by G. Bonasegale

Leghorn 2000
Il futurismo attraverso la Toscana. Architettura, arti visive, letteratura, musica, cinema e teatro. Leghorn, Museo Civico "G. Fattori", January–April 2000. Catalogue Milan, Silvana Editoriale 2000. Curated by E. Crispolti

Milan 2000[a]
Umberto Boccioni. Elasticità. Milan, Civiche Raccolte d'Arte - Società per le Belle Arti ed Esposizione Permanente [May] 2000. Catalogue Geneva-Milan, Skira 2000

Milan 2000[b]
Mario Sironi. Venere dei porti. Milan, Civiche Raccolte d'Arte - Società per le Belle Arti ed Esposizione Permanente [September] 2000. Catalogue Geneva-Milan, Skira 2000

Venice 2000
Cosmos. Da Goya a de Chirico, da Friedrich a Kiefer. L'arte alla scoperta dell'infinito. Venice, Palazzo Grassi [March–July] 2000. Cata-

logue Milan, Bompiani 2000. Curated by J. Clair

Barcelona 2000–1

Del Futurismo al láser. La aventura italiana de la materia. Barcelona, Palau de la Virreina, November 2000–January 2001. Catalogue Milan, Mazzotta 2000. Curated by M. Calvesi and R. Siligato

Rome 2000–1[a]

Italie 1880-1910. Arte alla prova della modernità. Rome, Galleria Nazionale d'Arte Moderna, December 2000–March 2001. Catalogue Turin-London, Allemandi 2000. Curated by G. Piantoni and A. Pingeot

Rome 2000–1[b]

Novecento. Arte e Storia in Italia. Rome, Scuderie Papali al Quirinale. Mercati di Traiano, December 2000–April 2001. Catalogue Geneva-Milan, Skira 2000. Curated by M. Calvesi, P. Ginsborg and F. Pirani

New York 2001

The Global Guggenheim. Selections from the Extended Collection. New York, Guggenheim Museum, February–April 2001. Without catalogue

Hanover 2001

Der Lärm der Strasse. Italienischer Futurismus 1909-1918. Hanover, Sprengel Museum, March–June 2001. Catalogue Hanover, Sprengel Museum, Hanover - Milan, Mazotta 2001. Curated by N. Nobis

Venice 2001

Gino Severini. La Danza 1909-1916. Venice, Collezione Peggy Guggenheim, May–October 2001. Catalogue Geneva-Milan, Skira 2001. Curated by D. Fonti

Tokyo 2001

Una storia dell'Arte in Italia nel XX secolo. Cento opere della Galleria Nazionale d'Arte Moderna e da collezioni italiane per una storia dell'arte in Italia nel XX secolo. Tokyo, Museum of Contemporary Art, September–December 2001. Curated by S. Pinto

Bibliography of Works Cited

Abadie 1989
D. Abadie, 'Chronologie de Magnelli,' in Paris 1989, pp. 171–261

Abetti 1915
A. Abetti, *Osservazioni astronomiche fatte all'Equatoriale di Arcetri nel 1914*, Florence, Galletti e Cocci 1915

Abraham 1912
M. Abraham, 'Una nuova teoria della gravitazione,' *Il nuovo cimento*, LVIII, IV, December 1912, pp. 459–81

Abramowicz 1990
J. Abramowicz, 'La tecnica dell'arte incisoria di Giorgio Morandi,' in Rome 1990–Bologna 1991, pp. XLII–XLVIII

Agnese 1996
G. Agnese, *Vita di Boccioni*, Florence, Camunia 1996

Alexandre 1993
Modigliani. Testimonianze, documenti e disegni inediti provenienti dalla collezione del dottor Paul Alexandre, collected and introduced by N. Alexandre, Turin, Allemandi 1993

Allard 1911
R. Allard, 'Sur quelques peintres,' *Les Marches du Sud-Ouest*, I, 2, June 1911, pp. 57–64

Almanacco 1914
Almanacco Italiano 1914, Florence, Bemporad e figli 1914

Almanacco 1942
'Due generazioni 1911-1941,' *Almanacco Letterario Bompiani*, XVIII, 1942

Altomare 1912
L. Altomare, 'A un aviatore,' *Poeti* 1912, pp. 75–6

Anceschi, January 1, 1939
L. Anceschi, 'Giuochi e coerenze di Carrà,' *Meridiano di Roma*, January 1, 1939

Anceschi 1944
L. Anceschi, *Mario Sironi*, Milan, Edizioni della Conchiglia 1944

Aniante, January 27, 1919
A. Aniante, 'Pittura futurista. Depero,' *Il Giornale d'Italia*, January 27, 1919

Angelucci, Rylands 1992
S. Angelucci, P. Rylands, 'Umberto Boccioni. Dinamismo di un cavallo in corsa + case: un restauro problematico,' *Bollettino d'Arte*, LXXVII, series VI, 79, 1992, pp. 133-142

Antliff 1993
M. Antliff, *Inventing Bergson. Cultural Politics and the Parisian Avant-garde*, Princeton, Princeton University Press 1993

Antliff 2000
M. Antliff, 'The Fourth Dimension and Futurism: A Politicized Space,' *The Art Bulletin*, LXXXII, 4, December 2000, pp. 720–33

Antolini 1991
A. Antolini, 'Dal Postimpressioni-smo alla Fine delle Avanguardie,' in De Vecchi, Cerchiari 1991, pp. 379–569

Anzani, Pirovano 1992
G. Anzani, C. Pirovano, 'La pittura in Lombardia nel primo Novecento (1900-1945),' in Pirovano 1992, pp. 85–241

Apollinaire, February 7, 1912
G. Apollinaire, 'La Vie Artistique. Les Peintres Futuristes Italiens,' *L'Intransigeant*, February 7, 1912

Apollinaire, February 9, 1912
G. Apollinaire, 'Chronique d'Art. Les Futuristes,' *Le Petit Bleu*, February 9, 1912

Apollinaire, March 25, 1912
G. Apollinaire, 'Vernissage aux Indépendants,' *L'Intransigeant*, March 25, 1912

Apollinaire, March 18, 1913
G. Apollinaire, 'A travers le Salon des Indépendants,' *Montjoie!*, March 18, 1913

Apollinaire, May 29, 1914
G. Apollinaire, 'Les Arts. Tableaux à bon marché,' *Paris-Journal*, May 29, 1914

Apollinaire 1960
G. Apollinaire, *Chroniques d'art 1902-1918, textes réunis avec préface et notes par L.-C. Breunig*, Paris, Gallimard 1960

Apollinaire 1992
'Guillaume Apollinaire. 202 Bd. Saint-Germain, Paris,' *Quaderni del Novecento Francese*, no. 13, ed. Lucia Bonato, Rome, Bulzoni 1992

Apollonio 1950
U. Apollonio, *Pittura moderna italiana*, Venice, Neri Pozza 1950

Apollonio 1970
U. Apollonio, *Futurismo*, Milan, Mazzotta 1970

Apollonio 1973
U. Apollonio, ed., *Futurist Manifestos* (The Documents of 20th-Century Art), New York, The Viking Press 1973

Apollonio, Valsecchi 1951
U. Apollonio, M. Valsecchi, *Panorama dell'arte italiana*, Turin, Lattes 1951

Apostolo, Bignozzi 1973
G. Apostolo, G. Bignozzi, *Storia dell'aviazione. Profili di aerei militari della Prima Guerra Mondiale*, Milan, Fabbri Editori 1973

Appella 1991
G. Appella, 'Carlo Belli e la cultura dello spirito,' in Rovereto 1991–2, pp. 13–30

Arcangeli 1942
F. Arcangeli, 'Divagazioni su Carrà,' *Architrave*, III, June 1942, pp. 9–10

Arcangeli 1948
F. Arcangeli, 'Tre pittori italiani dal 1910 al 1920,' in Venice 1948, pp. 27–8

Arcangeli 1961
F. Arcangeli, *Maestri del disegno contemporaneo in una raccolta privata di arte moderna a Milano*, Milan, Scheiwiller 1961

Arcangeli 1964
F. Arcangeli, *Giorgio Morandi*, Milan, Edizioni del Milione 1964

Argan 1970
G. C. Argan, *L'Arte Moderna 1770/1970*, Florence, Sansoni 1970

Argan 1977
G. C. Argan, *Die Kunst des 20. Jahrhunderts*, Berlin, Propylaen Verlag 1977

Argan, Calvesi 1953
G. C. Argan, *Umberto Boccioni*, selected writings, documents, bibliography and catalogue, ed. M. Calvesi, Rome, De Luca 1953

Arrigoni 2000
L. Arrigoni, 'Morandi a Brera. Due dipinti nascosti,' in Flores d'Arcais, Olivari, Tognoli Bardin 2000, pp. 285–9

'Avviso' October 1, 1913
U. Boccioni, C. Carrà, L. Russolo, G. Balla, G. Severini, A. Soffici, 'Avviso (27 settembre 1913),' *Lacerba*, October 1, 1913

Bacchelli, March 29, 1918
R. Bacchelli, 'Giorgio Morandi,' *Il Tempo*, March 29, 1918

Bacchelli, January 9, 1958
R. Bacchelli, 'Maestri della pittura contemporanea: Giorgio Morandi,' *Settimo giorno*, Milan, January 9, 1958

Bagatti, Manghetti, Porto 1984
F. Bagatti, G. Manghetti, S. Porto, *Esposizione di 'Lacerba' (1914-1914)*, Florence 1984, pp. 56–73

Baj 1942
G. Baj, 'Carrà a Brera,' *Origini*, VI, August 1942, pp. 7–8

Baldacci 1986
Ricostruzione di Casa Balla, text by P. Baldacci, Milan, Mondadori 1986

Baldacci 1997
P. Baldacci, *De Chirico 1888-1919. La metafisica*, Milan, Leonardo Arte 1997

Baldacci, Cavallo 1993
P. Baldacci, L. Cavallo, *Mario Sironi. Disegni. Opere dal 1906 al 1961. Matite, inchiostri, tempere*, Reggio Emilia, La Scaletta 1993

Baldinucci 1681
F. Baldinucci, *Vocabolario Toscano dell'Arte del Disegno*, Florence, Santi Franchi 1681

Balla 1984
E. Balla, *Con Balla*, vol. I, Milan, Multhipla Edizioni 1984

Balla 1986
[L. Balla], 'Lettere,' in Baldacci 1986, pp. 150–75

Balla, Depero, March 11, 1915
G. Balla, F. Depero, *Ricostruzione futurista dell'universo*, Milan, Direzione del Movimento Futurista, March 11, 1915

Ballo, September 10, 1952
G. Ballo, 'Le bottiglie di Morandi,' *Settimo giorno*, September 10, 1952

Ballo 1956
G. Ballo, *Pittori italiani dal futurismo a oggi*, Rome, Edizioni Mediterranee 1956

Ballo 1960
G. Ballo, 'Chiarezza di Morandi,' *Ideal-Standard Rivista*, II, 2, April–June 1960, pp. 23–31

Ballo 1962
G. Ballo, 'Fortunato Depero,' in Milan 1962[b], unnumbered pages

Ballo 1964[a]
G. Ballo, *Boccioni*, Milan, Il Saggiatore 1964

Ballo 1964[b]
G. Ballo, *La linea dell'arte italiana dal simbolismo alle opere moltiplicate*, Rome, Edizioni Mediterranee 1964

Ballo 1966
G. Ballo, 'Umberto Boccioni,' in Venice 1966, pp. 5–13

Ballo 1973[a]
G. Ballo, 'Le Futurisme,' in Paris 1973, pp. 11–20

Ballo 1973[b]
G. Ballo, 'Boccioni e il suo tempo,' in Milan 1973–4, pp. 13–31

Ballo 1982
G. Ballo, 'Boccioni a Milano,' in Milan 1982–3, pp. 11–76

Bandera 2001
M. C. Bandera, *Morandi sceglie Morandi. Corrispondenza con la Biennale 1947–1962*, Milan, Charta 2001

Barbantini, May 19, 1911
N. Barbantini, 'L'Esposizione Libera di Milano,' *L'Avvenire d'Italia*, May 19, 1911

Bardi 1930
P. M. Bardi, *Carrà e Soffici*, Milan, Belvedere 1930

Bardi 1957
P. M. Bardi, *16 dipinti di Giorgio Morandi*, Milan, Edizioni del Milione 1957

Bargellini, Bellonzi 1969
100 opere di Ardengo Soffici, texts by P. Bargellini and F. Bellonzi, Prato, Edizioni Galleria Falsetti 1969

Barilli 1983
R. Barilli, 'La sinfonia polifonica di Severini,' in Florence 1983, pp. 11–23

Barr 1936
A. H. Barr, Jr., 'Futurism,' in New York 1936, pp. 54–63

Barr 1949
A. H. Barr, Jr., 'Early Futurism,' in New York 1949, pp. 7–16

Barr 1977
A. H. Barr, Jr., *Painting and Sculpture in the Museum of Modern Art 1926-1967*, New York, The Museum of Modern Art 1977

Barricelli 1966
A. Barricelli, *Balla*, Rome, De Luca 1966

Bartolini, January 11, 1931
L. Bartolini, 'Seconda lettera dalla Quadriennale: Carlo Carrà,' *Corriere Adriatico*, January 11, 1931

Bartolini, February 12, 1939
L. Bartolini, 'Un pittore fra i pittori della Quadriennale,' *Quadrivio*, February 12, 1939

Bartolini 1940
L. Bartolini, 'Artisti contemporanei. Morandi incisore,' *Emporium*, XCI, 544, April 1940, pp. 173–80

Baumgarth 1964
C. Baumgarth, 'Die Anfänge der futuristischen Malerei,' *Mitteilungen des Kunsthistorischen Institutes in Florenz*, XI, II–III, November 1964, pp. 167–92

Beccaria 1939
A. Beccaria, *Giorgio Morandi*, Milan, Hoepli 1939

Belli 1935
C. Belli, *Kn*, Milan, Edizioni del Milione 1935

Belli, February 3, 1940
C. Belli, 'Corrispondenza indiretta sul caso Morandi,' *Corriere Padano*, February 3, 1940

Belli 1994
G. Belli, 'Depero, sensibilità futurista,' in Rome 1994–5, pp. 13–21

Belloli 1979
C. Belloli, 'A cinquant'anni dalla morte di Diaghilew,' *La Martinella*, XXXIV, XI–XII, November–December 1979, pp. 323–32

Bellonzi 1963
F. Bellonzi, *Pittura italiana. V. Il Novecento*, Milan, Martello 1963

Bellonzi 1985
F. Bellonzi, *Sironi*, bibliographical

and biographical notes by C. Gian Ferrari, Milan, Electa 1985
Beltrami 1906
Milano nel 1906, ed. L. Beltrami *et al.*, Milan 1906
Benzi 1993[a]
F. Benzi, 'Sironi Futurista. Prima che torni l'ordine,' *Art e Dossier*, no. 84, November 1993, pp. 20–4
Benzi 1993[b]
F. Benzi, 'Mario Sironi: il percorso della pittura,' in Rome 1993–4, pp. 13–37
Benzi 1993[c]
F. Benzi, 'Catalogo delle opere. Dipinti e opere monumentali,' in Rome 1993–4, pp. 87–365
Benzi 1994
F. Benzi [entries for Mario Sironi], in Mazzocca 1993–4, pp. 799–804
Benzi 2001
F. Benzi, 'Balla,' *Art e Dossier*, no. 163, Florence, Giunti 2000 [actually 2001]
Benzi, Sironi 1988
F. Benzi, A. Sironi, *Sironi illustratore. Catalogo ragionato*, Rome, De Luca 1988
Bergman 1962
P. Bergman, *"Modernolatria" et "Simultaneità". Recherches sur deux tendances dans l'avant-garde littéraire en Italie et en France à la veille de la première guerre mondiale*, Studia Litterarum Upsaliensia 2, Uppsala, Svenska Bokforlaget 1962
Bergson 1896
H. Bergson, *Matière et Mémoire. Essai sur la relation du corps à l'esprit*, Paris, Alcan 1896
Bernard 1912
E. Bernard, *Souvenirs et lettres inédites*, Paris, Société des Trente 1912
Bernheim-jeune 1914
Cézanne, texts by O. Mirbeau, Th. Duret, L. Werth, F. Jourdain, Paris, Bernheim-jeune 1914
Bernheim-jeune 1931
L'Atelier de Renoir, foreword by M. Albert André, Paris, Bernheim-jeune 1931
Berninger, Cartier 1972
H. Berninger, J. A. Cartier, *Pougny (Iwan Puni): Catalogue de l'œuvre. I. Les années d'avantgarde Russie-Berlin 1910-1923*, Tübingen, Wasmuth 1972
Bertelli, Briganti, Giuliano 1988
Storia dell'Arte Italiana, editors C. Bertelli, G. Briganti, A. Giuliano, vol. IV, Milan, Electa-Bruno Mondadori 1988
Bevilacqua, January 13, 1918
G. Bevilacqua, 'Note d'arte. La mostra Carrà,' *Il Tempo*, January 13, 1918
Bignardi 1996
M. Bignardi, *Capri e Positano futuriste: Depero e Prampolini, fra anni Dieci e Venti*, in Naples 1996, pp. 183–8
Bigongiari 1970
P. Bigongiari, 'Tra ordine cosmico e ordine storico,' in Carrà 1970, pp. 5–10
Birolli 1970
Z. Birolli, catalogue entries for 'Umberto Boccioni,' in Milan 1970, pp. 126–40
Birolli 1983
Z. Birolli, *Umberto Boccioni. Racconto critico*, Turin, Einaudi 1983
Bloch 1955
V. Bloch, *Morandi*, six color plates, Milan, Edizioni del Milione 1955
Boccioni, April 11, 1912
U. Boccioni, *Manifesto tecnico della scultura futurista* (April 11, 1912), Milan, Taveggia 1912
Boccioni 1913
U. Boccioni [Introduction], in Paris 1913, pp. 3–9
Boccioni, March 1, 1914
U. Boccioni, 'Il cerchio non si chiude,' *Lacerba*, March 1,1914
Boccioni, March 15, 1913
U. Boccioni, 'Fondamento plastico della scultura e pittura futuriste,' *Lacerba*, March 15, 1913
Boccioni, August 15, 1913
U. Boccioni, 'Per l'ignoranza italiana. Sillabario pittorico,' *Lacerba*, August 15, 1913
Boccioni 1914
U. Boccioni, *Pittura Scultura Futuriste (Dinamismo Plastico)*, Milan, Edizioni futuriste di 'Poesia' 1914
Boccioni, January 23–30, 1916
U. Boccioni, 'Arti Plastiche,' *Gli Avvenimenti*, II, 5, January 23–30, 1916
Boccioni 1971
U. Boccioni, *Gli scritti editi e inediti*, ed. Z. Birolli, Milan, Feltrinelli 1971
Boccioni 1972
U. Boccioni, *Altri inediti ed apparati critici*, ed. Z. Birolli, Milan, Feltrinelli 1972
Boccioni *et al.*, February 11, 1910
U. Boccioni, C. D. Carrà, L. Russolo, G. Balla, G. Severini, *Manifesto dei pittori futuristi*, Milan, Direzione del Movimento Futurista 1910
Boccioni *et al.* April 11, 1910
U. Boccioni, C. D. Carrà, L. Russolo, G. Balla, G. Severini, *La pittura futurista. Manifesto Tecnico* (April 11, 1910), Milan, Direzione del Movimento Futurista 1910
Boccioni *et al.* 1912
U. Boccioni, C. D. Carrà, L. Russolo, G. Balla, G. Severini, 'Les exposants au public,' in Paris 1912, pp. 1–14
Boess 1988
C. Boess [Kommentare zu den Werken. Katalog], in Munich 1988, pp. 113–279
Bohn 1979
W. Bohn, 'Circular Poem-Painting by Apollinaire and Carrà,' *Comparative Literature*, 31, 3 (summer 1979), pp. 246–71
Bohn 1982
W. Bohn, 'Carlo Carra's "Patriotic Celebration",' *Arts Magazine*, no. 56, February 1982, pp. 126–8
Bohn 1986
W. Bohn, *The Aesthetics of Visual Poetry, 1914-1928*, Cambridge–New York, Cambridge University Press, 1986
Bohn 1994
W. Bohn, 'Celebrating with Carlo Carra: Festa patriottica,' *Zeitschrift für Kunstgeschichte*, 57, 1994, pp. 670–81
Bondi 1979
F. Bondi, 'Gilbert Clavel e "Un istituto per suicidi",' in Clavel 1979, pp. 7–26
Borgese, June 18, 1966
L. Borgese, 'Boccioni e Morandi artisti di ieri salvano la Biennale tecnologica,' *Corriere della Sera*, June 18, 1966
Boschiero 1991
N. Boschiero, 'Carlo Belli: la vita,' in Rovereto 1991–2, pp. 190–235
Bowness 1972
A. Bowness, *Modern European Art*, London–New York, Thames and Hudson 1972
Bragaglia, February 29, 1912
A. G. Bragaglia, 'L'innamorato del sole,' *Patria*, February 29, 1912
Bragaglia 1913
A. G. Bragaglia, *Fotodinamismo Futurista. Sedici tavole*, Rome, Nalato undated [but 1913]
Bragaglia 1970
A. G. Bragaglia, 'Depero… ricordando,' in Bassano del Grappa 1970, pp. LV–LXII
Bragaglia 1980
A. G. Bragaglia, *Fotodinamismo Futurista*, with a list of documents and an appendix ed. by A. Vigliani Bragaglia, essays by M. Calvesi, M. Fagiolo, F. Menna, with an introduction by G. C. Argan, Turin, Einaudi 1980

Bragaglia 1988
C. L. Bragaglia, 'Carlo Ludovico Bragaglia ricorda,' in Capri 1988, pp. 26–7

Brandi 1939
C. Brandi, 'Cammino di Morandi,' *Le Arti*, Rome, I, 3, February–March 1939, pp. 245–55

Brandi 1942
C. Brandi, *Morandi*, Florence, Le Monnier 1942

Brandi 1990
C. Brandi, *Morandi*, introduction by V. Rubiu, with the Brandi–Morandi correspondence 1938–63 ed. by M. Pasquali, Rome, Editori Riuniti 1990

Braun 1992
M. Braun, *Picturing time. The Work of Etienne-Jules Marey (1830-1904)*, Chicago–London, The University of Chicago Press 1992

Braun 2000
E. Braun, *Mario Sironi and Italian Modernism. Art and Politics under Fascism*, Cambridge, Cambridge University Press 2000

Breunig 1960
L.-C. Breunig, 'Notes,' in Apollinaire 1960, pp. 559–97

Briganti, July 15, 1942
G. Briganti, 'Immagini di Carrà,' *Primato*, July 15, 1942

Brinton 1916
C. Brinton, *Impressions of the Art at the Panama-Pacific Exposition*, New York, John Lane Co. 1916

Brizio 1962
A. M. Brizio, *Ottocento-Novecento*, Turin, UTET 1962 (III ed.)

Broglio 1919
M. Broglio, 'Mostra Sironi,' *Valori Plastici*, I, VI–X, June–October 1919, pp. 29–30

Bruno 1969
G. Bruno, *L'opera completa di Boccioni*, preface by A. Palazzeschi, Milan, Rizzoli 1969

Buzzi 1933
P. Buzzi, 'Gloria a Umberto Boccioni,' *Dinamo futurista*, I, 3–5, June 1933, pp. 16–17

c.c. May 2, 1911
c.c., 'La prima Esposizione di arte libera, *Il Secolo*, May 2, 1911

'Caffè,' January 15, 1914
'Caffè. Imbecillità sicura. Si va a vedere la Gioconda,' *Lacerba*, January 15, 1914

Cajumi, December 10–11, 1913
E. Cajumi, 'Scultura futurista,' *Il Giornale di Sicilia*, December 10–11, 1913

Calvesi 1958[a]
M. Calvesi, 'Il futurismo di Boccioni: formazione e tempi,' *Arte antica e moderna*, I, 2, April–June 1958, pp. 149–69

Calvesi 1958[b]
M. Calvesi, 'Primi espositori di Ca' Pesaro. Postilla a Boccioni,' *Arte antica e moderna*, I, 4, October–December 1958, pp. 413–15

Calvesi 1959
M. Calvesi, 'Il futurismo e le avanguardie,' *La Biennale di Venezia*, IX, 36–37, July–December 1959, pp. 21–44

Calvesi, November 15, 1964
M. Calvesi, 'Marinetti e il futurismo oggi,' *La Fiera Letteraria*, November 15, 1964

Calvesi 1966
M. Calvesi, *Le due avanguardie. Dal futurismo alla pop art*, Milan, Lerici 1966

Calvesi 1967
M Calvesi, *Dinamismo e simultaneità nella poetica futurista*, Milan, Fabbri [1967]

Calvesi 1973
Umberto Boccioni. Incisioni e disegni, Florence, La Nuova Italia 1973

Calvesi 1976
M. Calvesi, 'Un Boccioni ritrovato e il tema dialettico della spirale,' *Paragone*, nos. 317–19, July–September 1976, pp. 236–65

Calvesi 1980
M. Calvesi, 'Le fotodinamiche di Anton Giulio Bragaglia,' in Bragaglia 1980, pp. 167–205

Calvesi 1981
M. Calvesi, 'Formazione, poetiche ed ideologia della metafisica,' in Calvesi, dalla Chiesa, Coen 1981, pp. 9–72

Calvesi 1982
M. Calvesi, *La metafisica schiarita. Da De Chirico a Carrà, da Morandi a Savinio*, Milan, Feltrinelli 1982

Calvesi 1983[a]
M. Calvesi, 'La corrispondenza di Boccioni: alcune date da rivedere,' in Calvesi, Coen 1983, pp. 108–9

Calvesi 1983[b]
M. Calvesi, 'Il problema di Boccioni scultore,' in Calvesi, Coen 1983, pp. 109–10

Calvesi 1992
M. Calvesi, 'Piero della Francesca, Severini, Carrà,' *Art e Dossier*, no. 72, October 1992, pp. 12–16

Calvesi 1994
M. Calvesi, 'Letture iconologiche. La città sale di Umberto Boccioni. Un cantiere galoppante,' *Art e Dossier*, no. 93, September 1994, pp. 22–5

Calvesi 2000
M. Calvesi, 'Dal Polimaterismo futurista a Burri e all'arte povera,' in Barcelona 2000–1, pp. 13–23

Calvesi, Coen 1983
M. Calvesi, E. Coen, *Boccioni. L'opera completa*, Milan, Electa 1983

Calvesi, dalla Chiesa, Coen 1981
M. Calvesi, G. dalla Chiesa, E. Coen, *La Metafisica. Museo documentario*, Bologna, Grafis 1981

Calza, July 21, 1912
A. Calza, 'Poeti futuristi... ma non tanto,' *Il Giornale d'Italia*, July 21, 1912

Camesasca 1980
E. Camesasca, *Cronologia*, in Sironi 1980, pp. 419–62

Cannistraro, Sullivan 1993
P. V. Cannistraro, B. R. Sullivan, *Margherita Sarfatti. L'altra donna del Duce*, Milan, Mondadori 1993

Cantù 1913
A. Cantù, 'Dall'impressionismo del colore all'impressionismo della linea,' *Vita d'Arte*, year VI, vol. XI (January–June 1913), pp. 133–8

Capano 1991
L. Capano, 'Catalogo delle opere,' in Verona 1991–2, pp. 138–217

Capano, Negri 1991
L. Capano, A. Negri, 'Via Adige 23,' in Verona 1991–2, pp. 255–9

Capano, Negri 1995
L. Capano, A. Negri, 'Ancora su via Adige,' in Milan 1995, pp. 258–9

Caramel, Pirovano 1973
L. Caramel, C. Pirovano, *Musei e Gallerie di Milano. Galleria d'Arte Moderna. Padiglione d'Arte Contemporanea. Raccolta Grassi*, Milan, Electa 1983

Caramel, Fiorio, Pirovano 1980
L. Caramel, M. T. Fiorio, C. Pirovano, *Musei e Gallerie di Milano. Galleria d'Arte Moderna. Collezione Boschi*, Milan, Electa 1980

Carandini 1996
S. Carandini, 'La danzatrice è una metafora. Poesia del corpo e composizione dello spazio nella danza di Loïe Fuller,' *Ricerche di Storia dell'Arte*", no. 58, 1996, pp. 5–18

Carandini 2001
S. Carandini, '"Una sera vivendo l'azione di una danzatrice": Gino Severini, Parigi e la danza,' in Venice 2001, pp. 43–55

Carli, Dell'Acqua 1964
E. Carli, G. A. Dell'Acqua, *Profilo dell'Arte Italiana. III. Dal Rinascimento ai Contemporanei*, Bergamo, Istituto Italiano di Arti Grafiche 1964

Carpi 1984
U. Carpi, 'Ideologia e politica del futurismo fiorentino,' in Manghetti 1984, pp. 45–62
Carrà, March 15, 1913
C. Carrà, 'Piani plastici come espansione sferica nello spazio,' *Lacerba*, March 15, 1913
Carrà, September 1, 1913
C. Carrà, 'La pittura dei suoni, rumori, odori. Manifesto futurista,' *Lacerba*, September 1, 1913
Carrà, June 1, 1914
C. Carrà, 'Vita moderna e arte popolare,' *Lacerba*, June 1, 1914
Carrà 1915
C. Carrà, *Guerrapittura. Futurismo politico. Dinamismo plastico. 12 disegni guerreschi. Parole in libertà*, Milan, Edizioni futuriste di 'Poesia' 1915
Carrà 1916[a]
C. Carrà, *Boccioni*, Milan [anonymous publisher] 1916
Carrà 1916[b]
C. Carrà, 'Orientalismo. Soliloquio critico. Monologo cantato. Analisi e sintesi sul mio recente quadro Il gentiluomo briaco,' *La Voce*, year VIII, June 30, 1916, pp. 269–71
Carrà, June 3, 1918
C. Carrà, 'La pittura metafisica a Roma,' *Il Popolo d'Italia*, June 3, 1918
Carrà 1920[a]
C. Carrà, 'Noterelle polemiche,' *Valori Plastici*, II, V–VI, May–June 1920, pp. 67–8
Carrà 1920[b]
C. Carrà, 'Misticità e ironia nella pittura contemporanea,' *Valori Plastici*, II, VII–VIII (1920), pp. 69–73
Carrà, June 22, 1933
C. Carrà, 'Ricordo di Umberto Boccioni,' *L'Ambrosiano*, June 22, 1933
Carrà 1943
C. Carrà, *La mia vita*, Rome, Longanesi 1943
Carrà 1967–8
M. Carrà, *Carrà. Tutta l'opera pittorica*, with an essay by A. Gatto, 3 vols., Milan, Edizioni dell'Annunciata co-published with Edizioni della Conchiglia 1967–8
Carrà 1970
L'opera completa di Carrà dal futurismo alla metafisica e al realismo mitico 1910-1930, introduction by P. Bigongiari, philological and critical apparati by M. Carrà, Milan, Rizzoli 1970
Carrà 1978
C. Carrà, *Tutti gli scritti*, ed. M. Carrà, with an essay by V. Fagone, Milan, Feltrinelli 1978
Carrà 1996
M. Carrà, 'Le matite di Carrà,' in Bergamo 1996, pp. 45–54
Carrà, Waldberg, Rathke 1968
C. Carrà, P. Waldberg, E. Rathke, *Metafisica*, Milan, Mazzotta 1968
Carrà, Russoli 1977
Carrà. Disegni, ed. M. Carrà and F. Russoli, Bologna, Grafis 1977
Carrà, Severini 1983
C. Carrà, G. Severini, 'Carteggio (1912-1941),' ed. M. Carrà, *Paradigma*, no. 5, 1983, pp. 275–310
Carrà, Soffici 1983
C. Carrà, A. Soffici, *Lettere 1913-1929*, Milan, Feltrinelli 1983
Carrà, Papini 2001
Documenti. Il carteggio Carrà-Papini. Da "Lacerba" al tempo di "Valori Plastici", ed. M. Carrà, Geneva–Milan, Skira 2001
Carrieri 1947
R. Carrieri, *12 opere di Amedeo Modigliani*, Milan, Edizioni del Milione 1947
Carrieri 1950
R. Carrieri, *Pittura Scultura d'Avanguardia (1890-1950) in Italia*, Milan, Edizioni della Conchiglia 1950
Carrieri, May 24, 1959
R. Carrieri,'I maestri della pittura contemporanea in Italia: Giorgio Morandi,' *Epoca*, Milan, May 24, 1959
Carrieri 1961
R. Carrieri, *Il futurismo*, Milan, Edizioni del Milione 1961
Caruso, Martini 1974
Tavole parolibere futuriste (1912-1944), anthology edited by L. Caruso and S. M. Martini, Naples, Liguori 1974
Castagnoli 1990
P. G. Castagnoli, 'Inizi di Morandi,' in Bologna 1990, pp. 29–36
Castelfranco, Valsecchi 1956
G. Castelfranco, M. Valsecchi, *Pittura e scultura italiana dal 1910 al 1930*, Rome, De Luca 1956
Castieau-Barrielle 1987
T. Castieau-Barrielle, *La Vie et l'œuvre de Amedeo Modigliani*, Courbevoie, ACR 1987
Cavallo 1973
L. Cavallo, *Ottone Rosai*, Milan, Edizioni Galleria Il Castello 1973
Cavallo 1986
L. Cavallo, *Soffici. Immagini e documenti (1879-1964)*, in collaboration with V. Soffici, Florence, Vallecchi 1986
Cavallo 1989
L. Cavallo, 'Corrispondenza Morandi-Soffici per un'antologica del maestro bolognese' in Focette–Cortina d'Ampezzo–Milan 1989, pp. 5–34
Cavallo 1992
L. Cavallo, 'Ardengo Soffici. La pittura di una vita,' in Milan 1992, pp. 9–24
Cavallo 1994
L. Cavallo, 'Aggiornamenti sul lavoro cubofuturista di Soffici (1912-15),' in Corsetti, Moretti 1994, pp. 69–84
Cavallo 1995[a]
L. Cavallo, 'Ottone Rosai, una traccia di lettura,' in Prato 1995–Milan 1996, pp. 23–62
Cavallo 1995[b]
L. Cavallo, 'Catalogo delle opere,' in Prato 1995–Milan 1996, pp. 265–336
Cavallo 1999
L. Cavallo, 'Nota su due disegni di Picasso,' in Richter, Rodriguez 1999, pp. 11–18
Cavallo, Raimondi, Russoli 1967
L. Cavallo, G. Raimondi, F. Russoli, *Ardengo Soffici e il Cubo Futurismo 1911-1915*, Florence, Edizioni Galleria Michaud 1967
Cavicchioli 1912
E. Cavicchioli, 'Fuga in aeroplano,' *Poeti* 1912, pp. 217–19
Cecchi, March 23, 1913
E. Cecchi, 'Esposizioni romane. La mostra futurista,' *Il Marzocco*, March 23, 1913
Cecchi, May 21, 1925
E. Cecchi, 'Pitture di Carlo Carrà, *L'Ambrosiano*, May 21, 1925
Cecchi 1976
E. Cecchi, *Taccuini*, ed. N. Gallo and P. Citati, Milan, Mondadori 1976
Cecchi 1990
E. Cecchi, *Lettere da un matrimonio*, ed. M. Ghilardi, Florence, Sansoni 1990
Celoria 1914
G. Celoria, 'Sulla eclissi totale di sole del 21 agosto 1914 e sul passaggio di Mercurio sul disco solare avvenuto il 7 novembre 1914. Osservazioni fatte al R. Osservatorio Astronomico di Brera,' *Rendiconti del Regio Osservatorio Astronomico di Brera*, XLVI-II, 14–15, 1915, pp. 797–810
Centone 1919
[O. Rosai, reproduction of *Caffè San Marco*], *Il Centone*, I, 2, March 1919, between pp. 24 and 25
Ceroni 1958
A. Ceroni, *Amedeo Modigliani peintre*, Milan, Edizioni del Milione 1958
Cézanne 1914
Sedici opere di Cézanne, Maestri moderni, 1, Florence, Libreria della Voce 1914

Chiappelli, May 7, 1911
A. Chiappelli, 'Il filosofo di moda,' *Il Marzocco*, May 7, 1911
Cinelli 1991
B. Cinelli, 'Derivazioni pierfrancescane nel Novecento: modelli e varianti,' in Sansepolcro 1991, pp. 211–27
Civ., February 22, 1913
Civ. [G. Civinini], 'L'esibizione del futurismo al Costanzi. Uno spettacolo burrascoso,' *Corriere della Sera*, February 22, 1913
Clavel 1918
G. Clavel, 'Picasso e il Cubismo,' *Valori Plastici*, I, I, November 15, 1918, pp. 11–13
Clavel 1919
G. Clavel, 'Teatro plastico,' *Valori Plastici*, I, XI–XII, November–December 1919, pp. 10–14
Clavel 1920
G. Clavel, 'Espressioni d'Egitto,' *Valori Plastici*, II, IV–V, March–April 1920, pp. 25–32
Clavel 1979
G. Clavel, *Un istituto per suicidi* (1920), trans. I. Tavolato, illus. by F. Depero, Venice, Edizioni del Cavallino 1979
Coen 1986
E. Coen, *Futurismo*, Florence, Giunti Barbera 1986
Coen 1988[a]
E. Coen, 'The Futurists and Their Contemporaries,' in New York 1988–9, pp. XXXVII–LVI
Coen 1988[b]
E. Coen, 'Umberto Boccioni. Paintings and drawings,' in New York 1988–9, pp. 3–199
Coen 1989
E. Coen, 'The Violent Urge Towards Modernity. Futurism and the International Avant-garde,' in London 1989, pp. 50–6
Coen 1996[a]
E. Coen, 'Dinamismo di un cavallo in corsa+case: dalla teoria alla forma,' in Venice 1996, pp. 61–7
Coen 1996[b]
E. Coen, 'Marinetti y los Futurista: un desafío a las estrellas,' in Barcelona 1996, pp. 13–32
Collovini 1997
D. Collovini, *Luigi Russolo, un'appendice al futurismo*, Venice, Supernova 1997
Comanducci 1934
A. M. Comanducci, *I pittori italiani dell'Ottocento*, Milan, Artisti d'Italia 1934
Conti 1919
P. Conti [review of], C. Carrà, *Guerrapittura*, *Il Centone*, I, 2 (March) 1919
Contini 1934
L. Contini, *L'aviazione italiana in guerra*, Milan, Marangoni 1934
Cooper, Tinterow 1983
D. Cooper, G. Tinterow, catalogue, in London 1983, pp. 36–440
Coquiot 1914
G. Coquiot, *Cubistes, futuristes, passéistes. Essai sur la jeune peinture et la jeune sculpture*, Paris, Librairie Ollendorff 1914
Cordaro 1991
Morandi. Incisioni. Catalogo generale, ed. M. Cordaro, Milan, Electa 1991
Cork 1994
R. Cork, *A Bitter Truth. Avant-garde Art and the Great War*, New Haven–London, Yale University Press 1994
Corsetti, Moretti 1994
'Nuovi contributi critici su Ardengo Soffici,' ed. L. Corsetti and M. Moretti, *Quaderni Sofficiani*, no. 1, Poggio a Caiano, Associazione Culturale 'A. Soffici' 1994
Corti 1994
V. Corti, *Lettere a Rosai*, Rome, Lo Faro 1994
Corti 1995
Nel mondo di Rosai, ed. V. Corti, Florence, Giorgi e Gambi 1995
Corti 1996
V. Corti, *Rosai e Soffici. Carteggio 1914-1951*, Florence, Giorgi e Gambi 1996
Costantini 1933
V. Costantini, 'Cronache milanesi. Umberto Boccioni,' *Emporium*, XXXIX, 464, August 1933, pp. 127–31
Costantini 1934
V. Costantini, *Pittura italiana contemporanea dalla fine dell'800 a oggi*, Milan, Hoepli 1934
Costantini 1936
V. Costantini, 'Cronache. Milano. Carlo Carrà,' *Emporium*, XLII, 493 (January 1936), pp. 42–4
Costantini 1937
V. Costantini, 'Cronache milanesi. "Venti firme",' *Emporium*, LXXXV, 507, March 1937, p. 164
Costantini 1940
V. Costantini, *Scultura e pittura italiana contemporanea (1880-1926)*, Milan, Hoepli 1940
Courthion 1941
P. Courthion, *Gino Severini*, Milan, Hoepli 1941
Courthion 1946
P. Courthion, *Gino Severini*, Milan, Hoepli 1946
Cousins, Daix 1989
J. Cousins (with the collaboration of Pierre Daix), 'Documentary Chronology,' in Rubin 1989, pp. 335–452
Cremona, June 15, 1932
I. Cremona, 'Visite: Carlo Carrà,' *Il Selvaggio*, IX, 4, June 15, 1932
Crispolti 1960
E. Crispolti, 'Cubismo e futurismo,' *Enciclopedia* 1958–67, vol. IV (1960) pp. 163–75
Crispolti 1963
E. Crispolti, 'Situazione e percorso di Balla. Alcune considerazioni generali,' in Turin 1963, pp. 1–40
Crispolti 1967
E. Crispolti, 'Improvvisazioni e imprecisioni (con qualche inedito),' *Palatino*, XI, no. 3, July–September 1967, pp. 319–28
Crispolti 1968
E. Crispolti, 'Vicende dell'immagine fra naturalismo, divisionismo e fauvismo,' in Crispolti, Russoli, De Micheli 1968, pp. 1–32
Crispolti 1980[a]
E. Crispolti, 'La metropoli futurista,' in Turin 1980, pp. 52–97
Crispolti 1980[b]
E. Crispolti, 'Dinamismo, immaginazione meccanica, simultaneità urbana,' in Turin 1980, pp. 100–81
Crispolti 1986
E. Crispolti, *Storia e critica del Futurismo*, Bari, Laterza 1986
Crispolti 1988
E. Crispolti, 'Appunti su Depero "astrattista futurista" romano,' in Rovereto 1988–Milan 1989, pp. 183–203
Crispolti 1992
E. Crispolti, 'La pittura del primo Novecento a Roma (1900-1945),' in Pirovano 1992, pp. 457–566
Crispolti 1995
[E. Crispolti], 'La "Ia Esposizione Futurista" a Macerata,' in Macerata 1995, pp. 149–69
Crispolti 1998
E. Crispolti, *L'oggetto Morandi*, Fiesole, Cadmo 1998
Crispolti, Drudi Gambillo 1963
E. Crispolti, M. Drudi Gambillo, 'Catalogo,' in Turin 1963, pp. 41–136
Crispolti, Russoli, De Micheli 1968
E. Crispolti, F. Russoli, M. De Micheli, *La continuità dell'immagine: realtà naturale, realtà lirica e realtà sociale*, Milan, Fabbri 1968
Crispolti, Marzuoli 2000
E. Crispolti (with A. Marzuoli), 'Pittura e scultura. Itinerario espositivo

e schede,' in Leghorn 2000, pp. 26–146

d.b. May 1–2, 1911
d.b., 'Esposizione libera,' *La Perseveranza*, May 1–2, 1911
Daix, Rosselet 1979
Le cubisme de Picasso. Texte de Pierre Daix. Catalogue raisonné de l'œuvre peint 1907-1916 par Pierre Daix et Joan Rosselet, Neuchâtel, Ides et Calendes 1979
Dalai 1991
M. Dalai, 'Dalla trasparenza della mimesis all'opacità della poiesis,' in Verona 1991–2, pp. 65–80
Dalrymple Henderson 1995
L. Dalrymple Henderson, 'Die moderne Kunst und das Unsichtbare: Die verborgenen Wellen und Dimensionen des Okkultismus und der Wissenschaften,' in Frankfurt 1995, pp. 13–31
D'Ancona 1953
P. D'Ancona, *I classici della pittura italiana del Novecento*, Milan, Edizioni del Milione 1953
De Chirico, June 18, 1918
G. de Chirico, 'L'arte metafisica della mostra di Roma,' *La Gazzetta Ferrarese*, June 18, 1918
De Chirico 1919
Giorgio de Chirico. 12 tavole in fototipia precedute da giudizi critici, Rome, Valori Plastici 1919
De Chirico 1920
G. de Chirico, 'Classicismo pittorico,' *La Ronda*, I, 7, July 1920, pp. 506–11
De Grada 1962
R. De Grada, *Boccioni: Il mito del moderno*, Milan, Club del Libro 1962
De Marchis 1977
G. De Marchis, *Giacomo Balla. L'aura futurista*, Turin, Einaudi 1977
De Maria 1983
L. De Maria, 'Marinetti poeta e ideologo,' in Marinetti 1983, pp. XXIX–C
De Micheli 1943
M. De Micheli, 'Cronache. Milano. Personale di Soffici alla Galleria del Milione,' *Emporium*, XLIX, 578, February 1943, pp. 76–7
De Micheli 1959
M. De Micheli, *Le avanguardie artistiche del '900*, Milan, Schwartz 1959
De Micheli 1971
M. De Micheli, 'Il realismo mitico e quotidiano di Carlo Carrà,' in Prato 1971, pp. 7–22
de Pisis, February 12, 1918
F. de Pisis, 'Carlo Carrà, Giorgio de Chirico,' *Gazzetta Ferrarese*, February 12, 1918
De Vecchi, Cerchiari 1991
P. De Vecchi, E. Cerchiari, *Arte nel tempo*, vol. III, *Dall'Illuminismo al Postmoderno*, Milan, Bompiani 1991
Decroocq 1999
M.-C. Decroocq, 'Catalogo dei dipinti,' in Lugano 1999, pp. 181–203
Del Monte 1973
A. Del Monte, 'Dipinti e disegni,' in Rome 1973, pp. 23–154
Del Puppo 2000[a]
A. Del Puppo, *'Lacerba' 1913-1915: arte e critica d'arte*, Bergamo, Lubrina 2000
Del Puppo 2000[b]
A. Del Puppo, 'Realtà brutta. Una polemica tra Papini e Boccioni,' *Prospettiva*, no. 97, January 2000, pp. 82–94
Del Puppo 2001
A. Del Puppo, *ad vocem* 'Balla, Giacomo,' in Godoli 2001, pp. 103–7
Del Re 1913
A. del Re, 'Cronaca d'arte inglese. La seconda mostra dei post-impressionisti alle "Grafton Galleries",' *Rassegna contemporanea*, year VI, series II, no. 1, January 10, 1913, pp. 132–8
Della Porta, October 1, 1938
A. F. Della Porta, 'Esaltazione e denigrazione della razza,' *Perseo*, October 1, 1938
Dell'Acqua 1950
G. A. Dell'Acqua, 'La Peinture métaphisique,' in Zervos 1950, pp. 121–65
Dell'Acqua 1990
G. A. Dell'Acqua, 'Morandi e i collezionisti lombardi,' in Milan 1990–1, pp. 34–8
Depero 1919
F. Depero, 'Il teatro plastico. Principi e applicazioni,' *Il Mondo*, V, 17, April 27, 1919
Depero 1933
F. Depero, 'Umberto Boccioni,' *La Rivista Illustrata del Popolo d'Italia*, XI, 7, July 1933, pp. 35–42
Depero 1940
Fortunato Depero nelle opere e nella vita, Trento, Legione trentina, Tipografia Editrice Mutilati e Invalidi 1940
Des Prureaux, June 11, 1911
H. des Prureaux, 'Della natura morta,' *La Voce*, June 11, 1911
Des Prureaux, December 7, 1911
H. des Prureaux, 'Intorno al cubismo,' *La Voce*, December 7, 1911
Des Prureaux, October 31, 1912
H. des Prureaux, 'Il soggetto nella pittura,' *La Voce*, October 31, 1912
Descargues 1954
P. Descargues, *Amedeo Modigliani 1884-1920*, Paris, Braun & Cie 1954
D'Harnoncourt 1980
A. d'Harnoncourt, 'Futurism and the International Avant-garde,' in Philadelphia 1980–1, pp. 11–34
Di Genova 1993
G. Di Genova, *Storia dell'Arte Italiana del '900. Generazione maestri storici*, vol. I, Bologna, Bora 1993
Di Milia 1998
G. Di Milia, 'Boccioni,' *Art e Dossier*, no. 131, Florence, Giunti 1998
Döblin 1912
A. Döblin, 'Die Bilder der Futuristen,' *Der Sturm*, no. 110, May 1912, pp. 41–2
Domus 1942
'Giorgio Morandi,' *Domus*, no. 179, November 1942, pp. 483–5
Doran 1995
M. Doran, *Cézanne. Documenti e interpretazioni*, Rome, Donzelli 1995
Dorfles 1976
G. Dorfles, 'Severini,' in Dortmund 1976, pp. 7–13
Dortch Dorazio 1970
V. Dortch Dorazio, *Giacomo Balla. An album of his life and work*, New York, Wittenborn & Co and Venice, Alfieri undated [but 1970]
Drudi Gambillo, Fiori 1958–62
Archivi del Futurismo, collected and edited by M. Drudi Gambillo and T. Fiori, Rome, De Luca, vol. I, 1958, vol. II, 1962
Dudreville, Funi, Russolo, Sironi 1920
L. Dudreville, A. Funi, L. Russolo, M. Sironi, 'Contro tutti i ritorni in pittura-Manifesto futurista (11 gennaio 1920),' *Roma Futurista*, April, 25–May 2, 1920
Durieu 1995
P. Durieu, *Modigliani*, Paris, Hazan 1995

Einstein 1915
A. Einstein, 'Erklärung der Perihelbewegung des Merkur aus der allgemeinen Relativitätstheorie,' *Königlich Preussische Akademie der Wissenschaften zu Berlin. Sitzungsberichte*, 1915, pp. 831–9
Einstein 1995
The Collected Papers of Albert Einstein. Volume 4. The Swiss Years: Writings 1912-1914, ed. M. J. Klein, A. J. Kox, J. Renn, R. Sculmann, Princeton, Princeton University Press 1995
Einstein, Grossmann 1913
Entwurf einer verallgemeinerten Re-

lativitätstheorie und einer Theorie der Gravitation. I Physikalischer Teil by A. Einstein, *II. Mathematischer Teil* by M. Grossmann, Leipzig–Berlin, Teubner 1913

'Elenco', January 15, 1914
['Elenco delle opere vendute all'Esposizione Futurista di "Lacerba"'], *Lacerba*, January 15, 1914

Enciclopedia 1929–37
Enciclopedia Italiana, Milan–Rome, Istituto Giovanni Treccani 1929–37

Enciclopedia 1958–67
Enciclopedia Universale dell'Arte, Venice–Rome, Istituto per la Collaborazione Culturale 1958–67

f.m.m., March 11, 1913
f.m.m., 'Can-can futuristico al Costanzi. Fracasso, tiro a segno e boxe,' *La Tribuna*, March 11, 1913

Fagiolo dell'Arco 1967
M. Fagiolo dell'Arco, *Omaggio a Balla*, Rome, Bulzoni 1967

Fagiolo dell'Arco 1968
M. Fagiolo dell'Arco, *Balla: le 'compenetrazioni iridescenti,'* Rome, Bulzoni 1968

Fagiolo dell'Arco 1974
M. Fagiolo dell'Arco, 'Analisi e sintesi. Un taccuino di Balla,' in Turin 1974, pp. 5–35

Fagiolo dell'Arco 1983
M. Fagiolo dell'Arco, 'Tutta la vita di un pittore,' in Cortona 1983–4, pp. 11–78

Fagiolo dell'Arco 1985
G. de Chirico, *Il meccanismo del pensiero. Critica, polemica, autobiografia 1911-1943*, ed. M. Fagiolo dell'Arco, Turin, Einaudi 1985

Fagiolo dell'Arco 1988
Depero, ed. M. Fagiolo dell'Arco, with N. Boschiero, Milan, Electa 1988

Fagiolo dell'Arco 1997
M. Fagiolo dell'Arco, '"Esistere per dare". Giacomo, Luce, Elica Balla,' in Comacchio 1997, pp. 13–25

Fagiolo dell'Arco 1998[a]
M. Fagiolo dell'Arco, 'Giacomo Balla verso il futurismo,' in Padova 1998, pp. 13–39

Fagiolo dell'Arco 1998[b]
M. Fagiolo dell'Arco, '"Modernità e tradizione". Schizzi per un ritratto di Mario Broglio,' in Rome 1998–9, pp. 45–68

Fagone 1978
V. Fagone, 'Le tre stagioni di Carlo Carrà,' in Carrà 1978, pp. V–XLIV

Fallacara 1913
L. Fallacara, 'La Vita. Firenze,' *Humanitas*, III, 50, December 14, 1913, pp. 369–70

Fanciulli, January 10, 1918
G. Fanciulli, 'Mostra Carrà,' *La Perseveranza*, January 10, 1918

Faure 1911
E. Faure, 'Paul Cézanne,' *L'Art Décoratif*, XXVI, II semester 1911, pp. 113–28

Fechheimer 1914
H. Fechheimer, *Die Plastik der Ägypter*, Berlin, Cassirer 1914

Fergonzi 1993
F. Fergonzi, 'Firenze 1910-Venezia 1920: Emilio Cecchi, i quadri francesi e le difficoltà dell' impressionismo,' *Bollettino d'Arte del Ministero per i Beni Culturali e Ambientali*, LXXVIII, series VI, 79, May–June 1993, pp. 1–26

Fergonzi 1998
F. Fergonzi, 'Catalogo delle opere. Giorgio Morandi,' in Trento 1998, pp. 48–89

Fermani, Lambiase 1983
E. Fermani, S. Lambiase, 'Clavel e Depero,' in Anacapri 1983, pp. 149–71

Ficacci 1991
L. Ficacci (ed.), 'Il carteggio Morandi-Petrucci,' in Cordaro 1991, pp. 138–79

Finocchi 1970
A. Finocchi [catalogue entries for] 'Luigi Russolo,' in Milan 1970, pp. 148–50

Fiorani 1991
F. Fiorani, 'Catalogo delle opere [1927-1929],' in Cordaro 1991, pp. 34–78

Fiori 1968
Archivi del Divisionismo, ed. T. Fiori, with an introduction by F. Bellonzi, 2 vols., Rome, Officina Edizioni 1968

Flammarion 1904
C. Flammarion, *Le stelle e le curiosità del cielo*, Milan, Sonzogno 1904

Flammarion 1913
C. Flammarion, *L'Astronomia popolare. Descrizione generale del cielo*, Milan, Sonzogno 1913

Flores d'Arcais, Olivari, Tognoli Bardin 2000
Arte lombarda del secondo millennio. Saggi in onore di Gian Alberto dell'Acqua, ed. F. Flores d'Arcais, M. Olivari, L. Tognoli Bardin, Milan, Federico Motta 2000

Fonti 1988
D. Fonti, *Gino Severini. Catalogo Ragionato*, Milan, Mondadori-Daverio 1988

Fonti 2001[a]
D. Fonti, 'Gino Severini. "La danza",' in Venice 2001, pp. 11–31

Fonti 2001[b]
D. Fonti, 'Severini. La danza' [catalogue of the works], in Venice 2001, pp. 69–167

Forti, March 22, 1914
Ask. [A. Forti], 'La mostra dei "secessionisti" al Baglioni,' *Il Resto del Carlino*, March 22, 1914

Fossati 1988
P. Fossati, *La pittura metafisica*, Turin, Einaudi 1988

Fossati 1995
P. Fossati, *Storie di figure e di immagini. Da Boccioni a Licini*, Turin, Einaudi 1995

Francastel 1959
P. Francastel, 'Il futurismo e il suo tempo,' *La Biennale di Venezia*, IX, 36–7, July–December 1959, pp. 2–10

Franchi 1918[a]
R. Franchi, 'Carlo Carrà,' *La Raccolta*, I, 3, May 15, 1918, p. 47

Franchi 1918[b]
R. Franchi, 'Giorgio Morandi,' *La Raccolta*, I, 9–10, November, 15 – December 15, 1918, pp. 117–18

Franchi 1942
R. Franchi, *Disegni di Ottone Rosai*, Milan, Hoepli 1942

Franchi 1946
R. Franchi, 'Ottone Rosai,' *Lettere ed Arti*, II, 11–12, November–December 1946, pp. 10-15

Fratelli 2000
M. Fratelli, 'Un cavaliere in un paesaggio moderno,' in Milan 2000[a], pp. 5–25

Frontisi 1994
C. Frontisi, 'La Création et son double,' in Majastre, Peuchlestrade 1994, pp. 9–22

Fugazza 1988
S. Fugazza, 'L'Italia fascista tra reazione classicista, modernismo e società di massa,' in Bertelli, Briganti, Giuliano 1988, IV, pp. 375–427

Funcken 1970
L. and F. Funcken, *L'uniforme et les armes des soldats de la guerre 1914-1918*, vols. I–II, Tournai, Casterman 1970

Gaehtgens 1993
Kunstlerischer Austausch Artistic Exchanges, ed. Th. W. Gaehtgens, Berlin, Akademie 1993

Gambi, Gozzoli 1982
L. Gambi, M. C. Gozzoli, *Milano*, Bari, Laterza 1982

Garberi 1990
M. Garberi, 'Morandi e Milano,' in Milan 1990–1, pp. 20–33

Garretto 1952
P. Garretto, 'Garçonnière per so-

gni,' *Arbiter*, XVIII, January–February 1952, pp. 42–7
Garuffa 1918
E. Garuffa, *Motori a scoppio e loro applicazioni pratiche all'automobile, all'autoscafo, all'aeroplano*, Milan, Hoepli 1918
Gatto 1939
A. Gatto, *Disegni di Ottone Rosai*, Venice, Edizioni del Cavallino 1939
Gian de' Sordi, December 12, 1913
Gian de' Sordi, 'Fra l'arte e la vita. La mostra futurista di Firenze,' *La Tribuna*, December 12, 1913
Giani 1942
Pittori Italiani Contemporanei, ed. G. Giani, Milan, Edizioni della Conchiglia 1942
Giani 1951
G. Giani, *Fortunato Depero Pittore*, Milan, Edizioni della Conchiglia 1951
Giani 1958
Pittori del Novecento, presented by G. Giani, Milan, Edizioni della Conchiglia 1958
Gianelli 1989
I. Gianelli, 'Cronologia 1900-1945,' in Venice 1989, pp. 589–729
Giedion Welcker 1959
C. Giedion Welcker, 'Vergängliches und Zukünftiges in Futurismus,' in Winterthur 1959, unnumbered pages
Ginex 1999
G. Ginex, '"Un sogno che svanisce nella luce della modernità": Gaetano Previati nella lettura della critica, dalle suggestioni antipositiviste all'influsso su Umberto Boccioni,' in Milan 1999, pp. 69–75
Giolli 1942
R. G. [Giolli], 'Quarant'anni di pittura di Carrà,' *Domus*, no. 174, June 1942, pp. 260–1
Giolli 1943
R. G. [Giolli], 'Quadri, sculture: quel che avviene,' *Domus*, no. 182, February 1943, pp. 83–5
Giorgini, Broglio 1870–97
Nòvo vocabolario della lingua italiana secondo l'uso di Firenze, Ministero della Pubblica Istruzione, compiled, under the presidency of Comm. E. Broglio by S. Bianciardi, P. Dazzi, G. B. Giorgini, A. Gotti, G. Meini, M. Ricci, Florence, Cellini 1870–97
Giuffré 1970
G. Giuffré, *Giorgio Morandi*, Florence, Sansoni 1977
Gleizes, Metzinger 1912
S. Gleizes, J. Metzinger, *Du "cubisme"*, Paris, Figuière 1912
Gnudi 1946
C. Gnudi, *Morandi*, Florence, Edizioni U 1946
Gobetti, July 11, 1923
P. Gobetti, 'La Quadriennale al Valentino,' *Il Popolo di Roma*, July 11, 1923
Gombrich 1990
E. H. Gombrich, *Styles of Art and Styles of Life*, London, Royal Academy of Art 1990
Godoli 2001
Il Dizionario del Futurismo, ed. E. Godoli, Florence, Vallecchi 2001
Govoni, March 15, 1913
C. Govoni, 'La città morta,' *Lacerba*, March 15, 1913
Green 1976
C. Green, *Léger and the Avant-garde*, New Haven–London, Yale University Press 1976
Guzzi 1994[a]
D. Guzzi, 'I tempi lunghi della pittura carraiana, ovvero, analisi delle cronologie,' in Rome 1994–5, pp. 125–66
Guzzi 1994[b]
D. Guzzi, 'Dipinti,' in Rome 1994–5, pp. 167–413

Haftmann 1955
W. Haftmann, *Malerei im 20. Jahrhundert*, Munich, Prestel 1955
Haftmann 1960
W. Haftmann, *Enciclopedia della pittura moderna*, Milan, Il Saggiatore 1960
Hamilton 1970
G. H. Hamilton, *19th and 20th Century Art. Painting, Sculpture, Architecture*, New York, Abrams 1970
Hanson 1995
A. H. Hanson, 'Marinetti Papers. Letters and Postcards from Gino Severini to F. T. Marinetti 1910-1915,' in New Haven 1995–6, pp. 135–77
Hergott 1994
F. Hergott, 'Il "punto di semplicità" di Carlo Carrà,' in Rome 1994–5, pp. 105–9
Hess 1961
H. Hess, *Lyonel Feininger*, London, Thames and Hudson 1961
Hofmann 1971
W. Hofmann, *Turning Points in Twentieth-Century Art: 1890-1917*, New York, Braziller 1971
Holtzmann 1899
H. Holtzmann, *Mailand. Ein Gang durch die Stadt und ihre Geschichte*, Leipzig, Neumann 1899
Hoog 1984
M. Hoog, 'Catalogue,' in Paris 1984–5, pp. 107–258
Italia motociclistica 1950
1901-1950. Italia motociclistica. Storia, tecnica, industria, sport, organizzazione, Milan, Edisport 1950
Ivanoff 1941
N. Ivanoff, 'La scuola vecchia dell'Abbazia della Misericordia e i suoi tesori,' *Emporium*, XCII, 554, February 1941, pp. 71–80

Janis, Blesh 1962
H. Janis, R. Blesh, *Collage. Personalities, Concepts, Techniques*, Philadelphia–New York, Chilton 1962

Kachur 1992
L. Kachur, *The Word-image in Contemporary Art: (pour un art de l'écriture)*, Union (New Jersey), James Howe Gallery 1992
Kahn, March 1, 1912
G. Kahn, 'Les Futuristes Italiens,' *Mercure de France*, March 1, 1912, pp. 184–6
Kandinsky 1912
W. Kandinsky, *Über das Geistige in der Kunst. Insbesondere in der Malerei*, Munich, Piper 1912
Kandinsky 1913
Kandinsky 1901-1913. Berlin, Der Sturm 1913
Kellermann 1992
M. Kellermann, *André Derain. Catalogue raisonné de l'œuvre peint*, vol. I (1895-1914), Paris, Galerie Schmit 1992
Koenigliche 1895
Koenigliche Museen zu Berlin. Aegyptische und Vorderasiatische Alterthümer aus den Koeniglichen Museen zu Berlin, Berlin, Mertens & Cie 1895
Kozloff 1973
M. Kozloff, *Cubism/Futurism*, New York, Charterhouse 1973
Kruszynsky 1996
A. Kruszynsky, *Amedeo Modigliani, Akte und Porträts*, Munich–New York, Prestel-Verlag 1996

Lacerba, August 1, 1914
[Reproduction of C. Carrà, *Festa patriottica-dipinto parolibero*], in *Lacerba*, August 1, 1914
Lamberti 1995
M. M. Lamberti, 'Milano nell'arte contemporanea: la città dei futuristi,' in *Milano e la Lombardia nella civiltà nazionale*, Milan, Istituto Lombardo di Scienze e Lettere, 1995, pp. 260-95
Lamberti 1997
M. M. Lamberti, 'Convenzioni e convinzione di un genere pittorico,'

in Verona 1997–Venice 1998, pp. 27–40
Lamberti 2000
M. M. Lamberti (ed.), *Lionello Venturi e la pittura a Torino 1919-1931*, Turin, Fondazione Cassa di Risparmio di Torino 2000
Lancellotti 1926
A. Lancellotti, *La Terza Biennale Romana d'Arte*, Rome, Pinci 1926
Lanthemann 1970
J. Lanthemann, *Modigliani. Catalogue raisonné*, Barcelona, Condal 1970
Larousse 1866–76
Grand Dictionnaire Universel du XIXe siècle Français, by P. Larousse, Paris, Administration du Grand Dictionnaire Universel 1866–76
Lassaigne 1981
J. Lassaigne, *Amedeo Modigliani. Werkwerzeichnis*, Berlin, Ullstein Kunstbuch 1981
La Stampa, June 18, 1921
[unsigned article], 'La mostra d'Arte di Alessandria,' *La Stampa*, June 18, 1921
Lavagnino 1956
M. Lavagnino, *L'Arte Moderna*, vol. II, Turin, UTET 1956
Lebel 1959
R. Lebel, *Marcel Duchamp*, New York, Grove Press 1959
Lega, January 15, 1927
A. Lega, 'Carlo Carrà,' *Il Selvaggio*, January 15, 1927
Leighten 1985
P. Leighten, 'Picasso's Collages and the Threat of War, 1912-13,' *The Art Bulletin*, 67, no. 4, December 1985, pp. 653–72
Lemaire 1995
G.-G. Lemaire, *Futurisme*, Paris, Editions du Regard 1995
Licht 1996
F. Licht, 'Catalogue,' in Venice 1996, pp. 167–86
Lindsay, Vergo 1982
K. C. Lindsay, P. Vergo, *Kandinsky. Complete Writings on Art*, Boston 1982
Lipchitz 1954
J. Lipchitz, *Amedeo Modigliani*, New York, Abrams 1954
Lista 1973
G. Lista, *Futurisme*, Lausanne, L'Âge d'Homme 1973
Lista 1975
G. Lista, *Luigi Russolo. L'Art des Bruits*, Lausanne, L'Âge d'Homme 1975
Lista 1979
G. Lista, *Futurismo e fotografia*, Milan, Multhipla 1979
Lista 1980
G. Lista, *Arte e politica. Il futurismo di sinistra in Italia*, Milan, Multhipla 1980
Lista 1982
G. Lista, *Balla*, Modena, Edizioni Galleria Fonte d'Abisso 1982
Lista 1984
G. Lista, *Giacomo Balla Futuriste*, Lausanne, L'Âge de l'Homme 1984
Lista 1988
G. Lista, *Les Futuristes*, Paris, Veyrer 1988
Lista 1993
G. Lista, *Entre dynamis et physis ou les mots en liberté du futurisme*, in Marseille 1993, pp. 46–67
Lista 1994
G. Lista, 'Le Culte de la frénesie urbaine. Les futuristes et leur influence en Europe,' in Paris 1994, pp. 76–84
Lista 1995
G. Lista, 'Futurismus und Okkultismus,' in Frankfurt 1995, pp. 431–44
Lista 2000
G. Lista, 'Il cosmo come finitudine. Dalla cromogonia di Boccioni all'arte spaziale di Fontana,' in Venice 2000, pp. 93–7
Lista 2001
G. Lista, *Le Futurisme. Création et Avant-garde*, Paris, Les Editions de l'Amateur 2001
Loize 1966
J. Loize, 'Frank Burty,' *Reflets du Roussilion*, 13, Spring 1966, pp. 27–32
Longhi, April 10, 1913
R. Longhi, 'I pittori futuristi,' *La Voce*, April 10, 1913
Longhi, January 13, 1914
R. Longhi, 'Le due Lise,' *La Voce*, January 13, 1914
Longhi 1914
R. Longhi, *Scultura futurista Boccioni*, Florence, Libreria della Voce 1914
Longhi, February 22, 1919
R. Longhi, 'Al Dio ortopedico,' *Il Tempo*, February 22, 1919
Longhi 1937
R. Longhi, *Carlo Carrà*, Milan, Hoepli 1937
Longoni, May 23, 1913
E. Longoni, 'La nuova vittoria,' *La Gazzetta dello Sport*, May 23, 1913
Lorenzoni 1995
[L. Lorenzoni], 'Il contesto. Lettere,' in Milan 1995, pp. 261–71
Lugaresi 1969
Lettere ruggenti a F. Balilla Pratella Marinetti Papini Balbo Boccioni de Pisis Severini Folgore Mascagni Russolo, ed. G. Lugaresi with a 'clarification' by G. Prezzolini, Milan, Quaderni dell'Osservatore 1969

Maffina 1977
G. F Maffina, *L'opera grafica di Luigi Russolo*, Varese, CEAL 1977
Maffina 1978
G. F. Maffina, *Luigi Russolo e l'arte dei rumori. Con tutti gli scritti musicali*, Turin, Martano 1978
Maiocchi 1985
R. Maiocchi, *Einstein in Italia. La scienza e la filosofia italiane di fronte alla teoria della relatività*, Milan, Franco Angeli 1985
Majastre, Peuchlestrade 1994
Le Texte, l'œuvre, l'émotion, ed. J.-O. Majastre, G. Peuchlestrade, Brussels, La lettre volée 1994
Malni Pascoletti 1991
M. Malni Pascoletti, '"Una delle gallerie private più interessanti del mondo intero." Note su Italico Brass collezionista d'arte,' in Gorizia 1991, pp. 43–52
Maltese 1960
C. Maltese, *Storia dell'arte in Italia 1785-1943*, Turin, Einaudi 1960
Manghetti 1984
Futurismo a Firenze 1910-1920, ed. G. Manghetti, Verona, Bi & Gi Editori 1984
Mango 1949
R. Mango, 'Il Museum of Modern Art di New York,' *Domus*, 241, December 1949, pp. 22–5
Mann 1980
C. Mann, *Modigliani*, London, Thames and Hudson 1980
Manzoni 1900
A. Manzoni, *I Promessi Sposi. Storia milanese del secolo XVII scoperta e rifatta da Alessandro Manzoni*, illus. edition with 278 drawings and 13 heliotype plates by Gaetano Previati, Milan, Hoepli 1900
Marangoni 1920
M. Marangoni, 'Mostra Ardengo Soffici,' *Valori Plastici*, II, 5–6, May–June 1920, pp. 64–7
Marc 1912
F. Marc, 'Zwei Bilder,' in W. Kandinsky, F. Marc, *Der Blaue Reiter*, Munich, Piper 1912, pp. 8–12
Marcadé 1989
J. C. Marcadé, *Le Futurisme russe*, Paris, Dessain et Tolra 1989
Marchesseau 1990
[D. Marchesseau], 'Notices des œuvres exposées,' in Martigny 1990, pp. 205–40
Marchiori 1960
G. Marchiori, *Arte e artisti d'avan-*

guardia in Italia (1910-1950), Milan, Edizioni di Comunità 1960

Marey 1878
E.-J. Marey, *La Méthode graphique dans les sciences expérimentales et particulièrement en physiologie et en médecine*, Paris, Masson undated (1878)

Marey 1890
E.-J. Marey, *Physiologie du Mouvement. Le Vol des oiseaux*, Paris, Masson 1890

Margheri 1982
C. Margheri, *Trilogia*, Milan, Rusconi 1982

Marinelli 1991
S. Marinelli [entry for] Francesco Bonsignori, 'Pala Dal Bovo,' in Verona 1991–2, pp. 142–4

Marinetti, February 20, 1909
F. T. Marinetti, 'Le Futurisme,' *Le Figaro*, February 20, 1909

Marinetti 1909
F. T. Marinetti, *Poupées Electriques. Drame en trois acts. Avec une préface sur le futurisme*, Paris, Sansot & Cie 1909

Marinetti 1912[a]
F. T. Marinetti, *Le Monoplan du Pape. Roman politique en vers libres*, Paris, Sansot et Cie 1912

Marinetti 1912[b]
F. T. Marinetti, *La Bataille de Tripoli (26 octobre 1911) vécue et chantée par F. T. Marinetti*, Milan, Edizioni futuriste di 'Poesia' 1912 (Italian trans., *La battaglia di Tripoli*, Milan, Edizioni futuriste di 'Poesia' 1912)

Marinetti, June 15, 1913
F. T. Marinetti, 'L'immaginazione senza fili e le parole in libertà (Milano, 11 maggio 1913),' *Lacerba*, June 15, 1913, pp. 121–4

Marinetti, October 1, 1913
F. T. Marinetti, 'Il teatro di varietà. Manifesto futurista,' *Lacerba*, October 1, 1913

Marinetti, November 15, 1913
F. T. Marinetti, *Dopo il verso libero le parole in libertà*, *Lacerba*, November 15, 1913

Marinetti 1916[a]
F. T. Marinetti [Introduction], in Milan 1916–17, pp. 7–11

Marinetti 1916[b]
F. T. Marinetti, 'La nuova religione della velocità. Manifesto futurista di Marinetti (11 maggio 1916),' *L'Italia Futurista*, I, 1, June 1, 1916

Marinetti, March 21, 1919
F. T. Marinetti, 'L'esposizione nazionale futurista,' *Il Popolo d'Italia*, March 21, 1919

Marinetti 1919
F. T. Marinetti, 'Il pittore e scultore futurista Boccioni,' *Il Primato Artistico Italiano*, I, 1, October 1919, pp. 28–9

Marinetti 1920
F. T. Marinetti, *Elettricità sessuale. Sintesi futurista*, Milan, Facchi 1920

Marinetti 1969
F. T. Marinetti, *La grande Milano tradizionale e futurista. Una sensibilità italiana nata in Egitto*, ed. L. De Maria, Milan, Mondadori 1969

Marinetti 1983
F. T. Marinetti, *Teoria e invenzione futurista*, ed. L. De Maria, Milan, Mondadori 1983

Marinetti 1987
F. T. Marinetti, *Taccuini 1915-1921*, ed. A. Bertoni, Bologna, Il Mulino 1987

Marinetti *et al.* April 27, 1910
F. T. Marinetti, U. Boccioni, C. D. Carrà, L. Russolo, 'Contro Venezia passatista,' in Marinetti 1983, pp. 33–8

Marinetti *et al.* October 15, 1913
F. T. Marinetti, U. Boccioni, C. Carrà, L. Russolo, 'Programma poliico futurista,' *Lacerba*, October 15, 1913

Marinetti, Palazzeschi 1978
F. T. Marinetti, A. Palazzeschi, *Carteggio, con un'appendice di altre lettere a Palazzeschi*, ed. P. Prestigiacomo, Milan, Mondadori 1978

Martin 1968
M. Martin, *Futurist Art and Theory 1909-1915*, Oxford, Clarendon Press 1968

Martin 1968–69
M. Martin, 'Futurism, Unanimism and Apollinaire,' *Art Journal*, XXVIII, Winter 1968–9, pp. 265–8

Martin 1973
M. Martin, 'Works in the Exhibition,'in New York 1973, pp. 29–205

Martin 1985
M. Martin, 'The Futurist Gesture: Futurism and the Dance,' in *Akten des XXV Internationalen Kongresses für Kunstgeschichte (Vienna September 4-10, 1983),* vol. II, *Kunst, Musik Schauspiel*, Graz–Vienna, Böhlaus 1985, pp. 95–113

Martini 1964
A. Martini, *Giorgio Morandi*, Milan, Fabbri 1964

Marziali 1996
L. Marziali [Comentario a las obras], in Barcelona 1996, pp. 137–92

Mascherpa 1967
I cento anni della Galleria, ed. G. Mascherpa, Milan, Arti Grafiche Ricordi 1967

Masciotta 1940
M. Masciotta, *Ottone Rosai*, Florence, Parenti 1940

Mastrigli, February 23–4, 1913
F. Mastrigli, 'La mostra futurista al "Costanzi". Dinamismo, stati d'animo, ritmi e linee-forza,' *La Vita*, February 23–4, 1913

Mathey 1967
F. Mathey, *Le strutture del reale nella visione cubista*, Milan, Fabbri 1967

Matitti 1998
F. Matitti, 'Balla e la teosofia,' in Padova 1998, pp. 40–45

Mattarella 2000
L. Mattarella [entry for] Ottone Rosai, 'Bar San Marco,' in Rome 2000–1[b], p. 146

Mattioli 1951
G. Mattioli, 'Come ho formato la mia raccolta,' *La Biennale di Venezia*, I, 3, January 1951, pp. 25–6

Mattioli Rossi 1991[a]
L. Mattioli Rossi, 'C'era una volta,' in Verona 1991–2, pp. 17–26

Mattioli Rossi 1991[b]
'Appendice 1. Documenti' [ed. L. Mattioli Rossi], in Verona 1991–2, pp. 231–52

Mattioli Rossi 1997
L. Mattioli Rossi, 'Gianni Mattioli,' in Venice 1997, pp. 9–20

Mattioli Rossi 1999
L. Mattioli Rossi, 'I restauri: interventi e interpretazioni,' in *Vincenzo Foppa: la Cappella Portinari*, ed. L. Mattioli Rossi, Milan, Motta 1999, pp. 81–113

Mattioli Rossi, Braun 1997
Masterpieces from the Gianni Mattioli Collection, essays by L. Mattioli Rossi and E. Braun, New York, The Solomon R. Guggenheim Foundation - Milan, Electa 1997

Mazzocca 1993–94
Pinacoteca di Brera. Dipinti dell'Ottocento e del Novecento. Collezioni dell'Accademia e della Pinacoteca, ed. F. Mazzocca, Milan 1993 (vol. I) and 1994 (vol. II)

Mazzuccato, March 22, 1914
Mazz. [P. Mazzuccato], 'La mostra di pittura e scultura al Baglioni. Artisti d'avanguardia,' *Giornale del Mattino*, March 22, 1914

Meier-Graefe 1912
J. Meier-Graefe, 'Greco peintre baroque,' *L'Art Décoratif*, XXVIII, October 1912, pp. 213–48

Messina 1995
M. G. Messina, 'Per una nuova lettura del primitivismo di Sironi,' *Ricerche di Storia dell'Arte*, no. 57, 1995, pp. 84–94

Messina 1998
M. G. Messina, '"Valori Plastici", il confronto con la Francia e la questione dell'arcaismo nel primo dopoguerra,' in Rome 1998, pp. 19–35
Messina, Nigro Covre 1986
M. G. Messina, J. Nigro Covre, *Il cubismo dei cubisti. Ortodossi/eretici a Parigi intorno al 1912*, Rome, Officina 1986
Meyer 1900
G. Meyer, *L'Universo stellato. Trattato di astronomia popolare*, Turin, Unione Tipografico-Editrice 1900
Milione 1933, no. 20
'Mostra protesta del collezionista,' *Il Milione*, no. 20, December 23, 1933
Milione 1936, no. 45
'Commenti,' *Il Milione*, no. 45, March 2, 1936
Milione 1937, no. 50
'20 firme in una mostra collettiva,' *Il Milione*, no. 50, January 20, 1937
Milione 1937, no. 51
'Commenti,' *Il Milione*, no. 51, February 18, 1937
Milione 1952, no. 1
Il Milione, new series, no. 1, Milan, Edizioni del Milione, 1952
Möbius 1906
A. F. Möbius, *Astronomie. Grösse, Bewegung und Entfernung der Himmelskörper*, Leipzig, Göschen 1906
Modigliani 1958
J. Modigliani, *Modigliani senza leggenda*, Florence, Vallecchi 1958
Monferini 1994
A. Monferini, 'Il platonismo di Carrà e le opere metafisiche tra il 1916 e il 1919,' in Rome 1994–5, pp. 81–8
Monferini 1996
A. Monferini, 'Carrà: dall'arte popolare alla "realtà metafisica",' in Bergamo 1996, pp. 61–71
Monti 1967
R. Monti, 'Arte in Italia 1915-1935,' *Critica d'Arte*, XV, 91–2, December 1967
Morelli 1988
F. R. Morelli (ed.), 'Corrispondenza. Carrà e l'Europa,' in Verona 1988–9, pp. 333–6
Moretti, January 28, 1937
B. Moretti, 'La mostra delle "Venti firme" al Milione,' *L'Italia*, January 28, 1937
Muller, Elgar 1967
J. E. Muller, F. Elgar, *Un secolo di pittura moderna*, Milan, Il Saggiatore 1967
Museum of Modern Art 1991
The Museum of Modern Art, New York. The History and the Collection, New York, Abrams in association with The Museum of Modern Art, New York 1991

Naccari 1911
G. Naccari, *Atlante astronomico*, Milan, Vallardi 1911
Naubert-Riser 2000
C. Naubert-Riser, 'L'immaginario cosmico. Dal Simbolismo all'arte astratta,' in Venice 2000, pp. 119–27
Nebbia 1913
U. Nebbia, 'Sul movimento pittorico contemporaneo,' *Emporium*, XXXVIII, no. 228, December 1913, pp. 421–38
Negri 1991
A. Negri, 'Uno sguardo circolare,' in Verona 1991–2, pp. 27–42
Negri undated
Il sistema dell'arte a Milano 1945-1956. Gallerie ed esposizioni, ed. Antonello Negri. Research by M. Fratelli and P. Rusconi, Milan, Hestia undated
Nicodemi, July 16, 1933
G. Nicodemi, 'Umberto Boccioni,' *L'Illustrazione Italiana*, LX, 29, July 16, 1933, pp. 102–3
Nicodemi 1935
G. Nicodemi, 'Carlo Carrà,' *Emporium*, LXXXI, April 1935, pp. 206–16
Noble 1997
A. Noble, 'Eric Estorick: una vita nei quadri,' in Rome 1997, pp. 11–34

Ojetti, November 8, 1912
U. Ojetti, 'Cubismo,' *Corriere della Sera*, November 8, 1912
Ojetti, June 16, 1920
U. Ojetti, 'Soffici pittore,' *Corriere della Sera,* June 16, 1920
Olivier 1933
F. Olivier, *Picasso et ses amis*, Paris, Stock 1933
Oppo, November 22, 1919
C. E. Oppo, 'Note d'Arte. Dal mercante Giosi in via Sistina,' *L'Idea Nazionale*, November 22, 1919
Orban 1997
C. Orban, *The Culture of Fragments: Word and Image in Futurism and Surrealism*, Amsterdam–Atlanta, Rodopi 1997
Ostwald 1912
W. Ostwald, *L'Evolution de l'électrochimie*, Paris, Alcan 1912

Pacchioni 1945
G. Pacchioni, *Carlo Carrà*, Milan, Edizioni del Milione 1945
Pacchioni 1959
G. Pacchioni, *Carlo Carrà pittore*, Milan, Edizioni del Milione 1959
Pacini 1966
P. Pacini, *Severini*, Florence, Sansoni 1966
Pacini 1970
P. Pacini, 'Futurismo ed oltre. Contributo agli "Archivi del Futurismo",' *Critica d'Arte*, XVII, new series, no. 111, May–June 1970
Pacini 1990
P. Pacini, 'Gino Severini, l'unanimismo di Jules Romains e le danze cromatiche di Loïe Fuller. 1,' *Antichità viva*, XXIX, 6, 1990, pp. 44–53
Padovan 1914
A. Padovan, *Il libro del cielo*, Milan, Istituto Editoriale Italiano 1914
Pallucchini 1958
R. Pallucchini, 'L'Art contemporain en Italie,' in W. George, R. Cogniat, M. Fourny, Paris, Prisme des Art-Editions d'Art et d'Industrie 1958
Pampaloni, Verdone 1977
G. Pampaloni, M. Verdone, *I futuristi italiani*, Florence, Le Lettere 1977
Pannaggi, June 22, 1922
I. Pannaggi, 'Futurismo,' *La Provincia Maceratese*, June 22, 1922
Papini, February 15, 1914
G. Papini, 'Il cerchio si chiude,' *Lacerba*, February 15, 1914
Papini, March 15, 1914
G. Papini, 'Cerchi aperti,' *Lacerba*, March 15, 1914
Papini, May 1, 1914
G. Papini, 'Dichiarazione al tipografo,' *Lacerba*, May 1, 1914
Papini 1933
G. Papini, *Ardengo Soffici*, Milan, Hoepli 1933
Papini 1945
12 opere di Ardengo Soffici, presentate da Giovanni Papini, Milan, Edizioni del Milione 1945
Papini, Carrà 1986
'Ai tempi di "Lacerba". Trentadue lettere di Giovanni Papini a Carlo Carrà (marzo 1913–maggio 1916),' ed. M. Carrà, *Paradigma*, 7, 1986, pp. 339–62
Parisot 1991
C. Parisot, *Modigliani. Catalogue raisonné. II. Peintures, dessins, acquarelles*, Leghorn, Grafis 1991
Parronchi 1941
A. Parronchi, *Ottone Rosai*, Milan, Hoepli 1941
Parronchi 1952
A. Parronchi, 'Preistoria di Rosai (1911-1919),' *Paragone*, 25, January 1952, pp. 31–40
Parronchi 1959
A. Parronchi, 'Rosai 1913,' *Paragone*, 113, May 1959, pp. 66–70

Parton 1993
A. Parton, *Mikhail Larionov and the Russian Avant-garde*, London, Thames and Hudson 1993
Pascazio 1913
N. Pascazio, 'La pittura futurista,' *Humanitas*, II, no. 16, April 20, 1913, pp. 95–7
Pasini 1989
R. Pasini, *Morandi*, Bologna, Clueb 1989
Pasquali 1985
'Quaderni morandiani n. 1. Morandi e il suo tempo,' in *Primo Incontro Internazionale di Studi su Giorgio Morandi*, November 16–17, 1984, ed. M. Pasquali, Milan, Mazzotta 1985
Pasquali 1989
M. Pasquali, 'Morandi e il collezionismo a Bologna,' in Bologna 1989, pp. 21–8
Pasquali 1990
M. Pasquali, *Morandi*, Florence, Giunti 1990
Pasquali 1991
M. Pasquali, *Morandi. Acquerelli. Catalogo generale*, Milan, Electa 1991
Pasquali 1996
Museo Morandi. Catalogo generale, ed. M. Pasquali, II ed. revised and enlarged, Bologna, Grafis 1996
Pasquali 1997
'Morandi e il mondo dell'arte. Lettere 1950-1964,' in Verona 1997–Venice 1998, pp. 213–28
Pasquali, Tavoni 1994
M. Pasquali, E. Tavoni, *Morandi. Disegni. Catalogo generale*, ed. M. Pasquali with L. Selleri, Milan, Electa 1994
Passamani 1970[a]
B. Passamani [Introduction], in Bassano del Grappa 1970, pp. XII–XXXVII
Passamani 1970[b]
B. Passamani, 'Catalogo,' in Bassano del Grappa 1970, pp. 3–101
Passamani 1981
B. Passamani, *Fortunato Depero*, Rovereto, Comune di Rovereto-Musei Civici 1981
Patani 1991
O. Patani, *Amedeo Modigliani. Catalogo generale. Dipinti*, Milan, Leonardo 1991
Patani 1992
O. Patani, *Amedeo Modigliani. Catalogo generale. Sculture e disegni 1909-1914*, Milan, Leonardo 1992
Patani 1994
O. Patani, *Amedeo Modigliani. Catalogo generale. Disegni 1906-1920, con i disegni provenienti dalla collezione Paul Alexandre (1906-1914)*, Milan, Leonardo 1994
Perloff 1986
M. Perloff, *The Futurist Moment: Avant-garde, Avant-guerre, and the Language of Rupture*, Chicago, University of Chicago Press 1986
Perocco 1965
G. Perocco, *Artisti del Primo Novecento Italiano*, Turin, Bolaffi 1965
Petrella 1991
F. Petrella, 'La "materia" inquieta e le sue trasformazioni. Appunti per una ricerca,' in Verona 1991–2, pp. 83–114
Petrie 1974
B. Petrie, 'Boccioni and Bergson,' *The Burlington Magazine*, vol. CXVI, no. 852, March 1974, pp. 140–7
Petrocchi 1887–91
P. Petrocchi, *Nòvo dizionàrio universale della lingua italiana*, Milan, Treves 1887–91
Peyrefitte 1959
R. Peyrefitte, *L'esule di Capri*, Milan, Longanesi 1959
Pfannstiel 1929
A. Pfannstiel, *L'Art et la vie. Modigliani*, Paris, Seheur 1929
Pfannstiel 1956
A. Pfannstiel, *Modigliani et son œuvre. Étude critique et catalogue raisonné*, Paris, La Bibliothèque des Arts 1956
Pianigiani 1937–8
O. Pianigiani, *Vocabolario etimologico della lingua italiana*, Milan, Sonzogno 1937–8
Pica 1908
V. Pica, *Gl'Impressionisti Francesi*, Bergamo, Istituto Italiano di Arti Grafiche 1908
Pica 1955
A. Pica, *Mario Sironi pittore*, Milan, Edizioni del Milione 1955
Picasso 1914
Dodici opere di Picasso, Maestri moderni, 3, Florence, Libreria della Voce 1914
Pierre 1966
J. Pierre, *Le Futurisme et le dadaïsme*, Lausanne, Rencontre 1966
Piovene 1942
Le grandi raccolte d'arte contemporanea. La Raccolta Feroldi, presented by G. Piovene, Milan, Edizioni del Milione 1942
Pirani 1989
F. Pirani, 'Anni cruciali per Dorazio,' *La Tartaruga. Quaderni d'arte e di letteratura*, nos. 5–6, 1989, pp. 49–57
Pirovano 1992
La pittura in Italia. Il Novecento/1. 1900-1945, ed. C. Pirovano, Milan, Electa 1992
Pittori 1938
Pittori italiani contemporanei, vol. III: 11 color plates (De Pisis, Garbari, Modigliani, Morandi, Sironi), Milan, Edizioni del Milione 1938
Pittori 1946
Pittori italiani contemporanei, color plates, Milan, Edizioni del Milione 1946
Poeti 1912
I poeti futuristi, Milan, Edizioni futuriste di 'Poesia' 1912
Poggi 1992
C. Poggi, *In Defiance of Painting: Cubism, Futurism, and the Invention of Collage*, New Haven–London, Yale University Press 1992
Poggi 1997
C. Poggi, 'Dreams of Metallized Flesh: Futurism and the Masculine Body,' *Modernism/Modernity*, IV, 3, September 1997, pp. 19–43
Poggi 2002
C. Poggi, 'Folla/Follia: Futurism and the Crowd,' *Critical Inquiry*, vol. 28, no. 3, Spring 2002, pp. 709–48
Poggialini Tominetti 1979
M. Poggialini Tominetti [entry for] 'La città che monta o Giganti e pigmei,' in Milan 1979, pp. 79–80
Poggianella 1995
S. Poggianella, 'Okkulte Elemente und das Licht im Werk Ballas,' in Frankfurt 1995, pp. 459–63
Ponente 1969
N. Ponente, *Modigliani*, Paris, Flammarion 1969
Prampolini 1913
E. Prampolini, 'Pittura futurista. Prima Esposizione Italiana,' *L'Artista Moderno*, XII, 6, March 25, 1913, pp. 103–6
Pratesi, Uzzani 1991
M. Pratesi, G. Uzzani, *L'arte italiana del Novecento. La Toscana*, Venice, Marsilio 1991
Previati 1906
G. Previati, *Principi scientifici del divisionismo. (La tecnica della pittura)*, Turin, Bocca 1906
Prezzolini, February 15, 1912
G. Prezzolini, 'Io devo...,' *La Voce*, February 15, 1912
Prezzolini, Soffici 1977
G. Prezzolini, A. Soffici, *Carteggio, I. 1907-1918*, ed. M. Richter, Rome, Edizioni di Storia e Letteratura 1977
Primato 1922
Anonymous, 'Le mostre e le sale di "Bottega di Poesia". Milano, via Monte Napoleone 14,' *Il Primato*

Artistico Italiano, IV, 2, February 15, 1922, pp. 43–6
Pugliese 2000
M. Pugliese, 'Dentro la Venere,' in Milan 2000[b], pp. 17–25
Quadrone, April 14, 1923
E. Quadrone, 'Il "vernissage" alla Quadriennale di Belle Arti che si inaugura oggi a Torino,' *La Gazzetta del Popolo*, April 14, 1923

Ragghianti 1936
C. L. Ragghianti, 'Studi sull'arte italiana contemporanea: Carrà,' *La Critica d'Arte*, I, V, June 1936, pp. 251–8
Ragghianti 1953
C. L. Ragghianti [Introduction], in Florence 1953, pp. 5–40
Ragghianti 1956
C. L. Ragghianti, 'Ottone Rosai. Cinquant'anni di disegno,' *Critica d'Arte*", III, no. 15, April 1956, pp. 199–210
Ragghianti 1964
C. L. Ragghianti, 'Un'antologia di Morandi,' *Critica d'Arte*, XI, no. 62, May 1964, pp. 11–21
Ragghianti 1965
C. L. Ragghianti, 'Boccioni prefuturista,' *Critica d'Arte*, XII, no. 69, March 1965, pp. 14–25
Ragghianti 1969
C. L. Ragghianti, 'Bologna cruciale 1914,' *Critica d'Arte*, XVI, nos. 106–7, October–November 1969, pp. 1–140
Ragghianti 1982
C. L. Ragghianti, 'Morandi o l'architettura della visione,' in *Opere di Carlo L. Ragghianti. VIII. Bologna cruciale 1914 e saggi su Morandi, Gorni, Saetti*, Bologna, Calderini 1982
Raimondi 1941
G. Raimondi, 'Cartella di disegni. Giorgio Morandi,' *Le Arti*, III, 3, February–March 1941, pp. 164–7
Raimondi 1942
G. Raimondi, *Disegni di Carlo Carrà*, Milan, Hoepli 1942
Raimondi 1948
G. Raimondi, 'Le stampe di Giorgio Morandi,' *Prospettive*, II, 1948, pp. 147–58
Raimondi 1951
G. Raimondi, 'La congiuntura metafisica Morandi-Carrà,' *Paragone*, 19, July 1951, pp. 18–27
Raimondi, November 24, 1966
G. Raimondi, 'Morandi e i cubisti,' *Il Resto del Carlino*, November 24, 1966
Raimondi 1966
G. Raimondi, *I divertimenti letterari (1915-25)*, Milan, Mondadori 1966
Raimondi 1967
G. Raimondi, 'Ardengo Soffici 1907-1920,' in Raimondi, Cavallo 1967, pp. 11–37
Raimondi 1970
G. Raimondi, *Anni con Giorgio Morandi*, Milan, Mondadori 1970
Raimondi, Cavallo 1967
G. Raimondi, L. Cavallo, *Ardengo Soffici*, with the Galleria Michaud, Florence, Nuovedizioni Enrico Vallecchi 1967
Rambosson 1904
Y. Rambosson, 'La sculpture au Salon (Société des Artistes Français),' *L'Art Décoratif*, VI, II semester 1904, pp. 28–34
Recchi 1918
M. Recchi, 'Mostra d'arte Indipendenti in Roma,' *La Raccolta*, I, 5, July 15, 1918, pp. 79–80
Recupero 1959
J. Recupero [catalogue], in Rome 1959, pp. 53–91
Répaci 1942
L. Répaci, 'Carrà a Brera,' *L'Illustrazione Italiana*, LXIX, 21, June 14, 1942, p. 575
Rewald 1983
J. Rewald, *Paul Cézanne. The Watercolors. A Catalogue Raisonné*, Boston, Little-Brown 1983
Rewald 1989
S. Rewald, 'Catalogue,' in New York 1989
Riccòmini 1985
E. Riccòmini, 'Morandi: memoria e presenza,' in Bologna 1985, pp. 11–43
Richter, Rodriguez 1999
'Omaggio a Soffici nel 35 anniversario della scomparsa,' ed. M. Richter, J. F. Rodriguez, *Quaderni Sofficiani*, 5, Prato, Pentalinea 1999
Rigutini, Fanfani 1875
Vocabolario italiano della lingua parlata compiled by G. Rigutini and P. Fanfani, Florence, Tipografia Cenniniana 1875
Riva, April 20, 1937
A. Riva, 'Le Venti Firme alla "Genova",' *Il Giornale di Genova*, April 20, 1937
Rivosecchi 1988
V. Rivosecchi, 'Catalogo delle opere,' in Verona 1988–9, pp. 121–269
Roche-Pézard 1983
F. Roche-Pézard, *L'Aventure Futuriste 1909-1916*, Rome, Collection de l'École Française de Rome 1983
Roches 1910
F. Roches, 'La Section française des Beaux-Arts à l'Exposition Internationale de Buenos-Air,' *L'Art Décoratif*, XII, II semester 1910, pp. 1–27
Rodriguez 1994
J. F. Rodriguez, *La Réception de l'impressionisme à Florence en 1910*, Venice, Istituto Veneto di Scienze, Lettere ed Art (Memorie. Classe di Scienze Morali, Lettere ed Arti) 1994
Roethel, Benjamin 1982
H. K. Roethel, J. K. Benjamin, *Kandinsky. Catalogue Raisonné of the Oil Paintings. Volume one: 1900-1915*, London, Sotheby's 1982
Romains 1908
J. Romains, *La Vie unanime. Poème*, Paris, Editions de l'Abbaye 1908
Rosai 1930
Ottone Rosai, with texts by F. Agnoletti, B. Ricci, D. Giuliotti, D. Garrone, C. O. Cochetti, V. Montebugnoli, G. Contri, A. Palazzeschi, Milan, Galleria del Milione 1930
Rosai 1931
O. Rosai, *Alla ditta Soffici-Papini & Compagni*, Florence, Edizioni Fiorentine 1931
Rosai 1937
[O. Rosai], 'Artisti italiani. Ottone Rosai,' *Il Frontespizio*, IX, April 4, 1937, pp. I–VIII
Rosai 1987
O. Rosai, *Niente altro che un artista. Lettere e scritti vari*, ed. V. Corti, Piombino, TraccEdizioni 1987
Rosazza Ferraris 1991
[ed. P. Rosazza Ferraris], 'Cronaca di un'ossessione. Sei lettere inedite da Feroldi a Morandi 1938-1939,' *Bresciaoggi*, April 14, 1991
Rosazza Ferraris 1998
P. Rosazza Ferraris, 'Mercato, collezionismo, committenza e pubbliche acquisizioni: appunti per una storia economica dei Valori Plastici,' in Rome 1998–9, pp. 165–70
Rosci 1991
M. Rosci, 'La materia e lo stato d'animo plastico,' in Verona 1991–2, pp. 43–64
Rose 1990
J. Rose, *Modigliani. The Pure Bohemian*, London, Constable 1990
Rosenblum 1962
R. Rosenblum, *La storia del cubismo e l'arte del XX secolo*, Milan, Il Saggiatore 1962
Rosenblum 1980
R. Rosenblum, 'Picasso and the Typography of Cubism,' in New York 1980, pp. 49–75
Roseveare 1982
N. T. Roseveare, *Mercury's Perihelion from Leverrier to Einstein*, Oxford, Clarendon Press 1982

Rossi 1995
G. Rossi, 'Osservazioni tecniche sull'esecuzione di Materia,' in Milan 1995, p. 222
Rousseau 1914
Dodici opere di Rousseau, Maestri moderni, 2, Florence, Libreria della Voce 1914
Rousseau 1999
P. Rousseau, 'Anthologie,' in Paris 1999, pp. 238–68
Rovati 2000
F. Rovati, '"A Torino dormono tutti". Mostre di pittura e scultura dal 1919 al 1931,' in Lamberti 2000, pp. 277–311
Rovati 2001
F. Rovati, 'La mostra su Boccioni del 1933,' *ACME. Annali della Facoltà di Lettere e Filosofia dell'Università degli Studi di Milan*, LVI, III, September–December 2001, pp. 303–24
Rubin 1989
W. Rubin, *Picasso and Braque. Pioneering Cubism*, New York, The Museum of Modern Art 1989
Rudenstine 1981
A. Rudenstine, *The George Kostakis Collection: Russian Avant-garde Art*, New York, Abrams 1981
Rudenstine 1985
A. Rudenstine, *Peggy Guggenheim Collection, Venice*, New York, The Solomon R. Guggenheim Foundation and Abrams 1985
Rusconi 1998
P. Rusconi, 'Cataloghi e monografie d'arte,' in Milan 1998, pp. 87–93
Russoli 1958
F. Russoli, *Modigliani*, Milan, Silvana 1958
Russoli 1975
F. Russoli, 'Dipinti,' in Poggio a Caiano 1975, pp. 54–148
Russoli 1976
F. Russoli, 'Soffici pittore,' in *Atti del Convegno di Studi Ardengo Soffici. L'artista e lo scrittore nella cultura del '900*. Poggio a Caiano, June 7–8, 1975. Florence, Centro Di 1976, pp. 44–9
Russoli 1977
F. Russoli, 'Il disegno di Carrà,' in Carrà, Russoli 1977, pp. 11–14
Russolo, July 1, 1913
L. Russolo, 'Gl'intonarumori futuristi,' *Lacerba*, July 1, 1913
Russolo, November 1, 1913
L. Russolo,'Conquista totale dell'enarmonismo mediante gl'intonarumori futuristi,' *Lacerba*, November 1, 1913
Russolo 1938
L. Russolo, *Al di là della materia*, Milan, Bocca 1938
Russolo 1957
Luigi Russolo. Omaggio all'artista e allo scienziato in occasione del decennale della morte, Milan, Fenarete-Letture d'Italia 1957
Rye 1972
J. Rye, *Futurism*, London, Studio Vista/Dutton Pictureback 1972
Rylands 1997
P. Rylands [Catalogue], in Venice 1997, pp. 49–103

Sabachnikoff, Piumati 1893
I manoscritti di Leonardo da Vinci. Codice sul volo degli uccelli e varie altre materie published by T. Sabachnikoff, transcriptions and notes by G. Piumati, Paris, Rouveyre 1893
Salaris 1985
C. Salaris, *Storia del Futurismo*, Rome, Editori Riuniti 1985
Salmon, February 6, 1912
A. Salmon, 'Les Futuristes,' *Paris-Journal*, February 6, 1912
Salmon 1913
A. Salmon, 'Odilon Redon,' *L'Art Décoratif*, XV, I semester 1913, pp. 5–20
Salmon, March 18, 1914
A. Salmon, 'Le Salon,' *Montjoie!*, March 18, 1914
Salvagnini 2000
S. Salvagnini, *Il sistema delle arti in Italia 1919-1943*, Bologna, Minerva 2000
Salvini 1949
R. Salvini, *Guida all'Arte Moderna,* Florence, L'Arco 1949
Sanders, Bernstein 2001
Poetry plastique, eds. J. Sanders, C. Bernstein, New York, Marianne Boesky Gallery 2001
Sandroni 1991
'Schede tecniche delle opere esposte,' ed. F. Sandroni, in Verona 1991–2, pp. 218–24
Sani, March 23, 1914
S. Sani, 'Pittori d'avanguardia,' *L'Avvenire d'Italia*, March 23, 1914
Sani 1971
B. Sani [Catalogue entries], in Rome 1971–2, pp. 141–97
Santamaria, August 15, 1920
E. Santamaria, 'Conversando con Giacomo Balla,' *Griffa*, I, 6, August 15, 1920
Santini 1957
P. C. Santini [Catalogue], in Ivrea 1957, pp. 48–60
Santini 1960
P. C. Santini, *Rosai*, Florence, Vallecchi 1960
Sarfatti, December 12, 1911
M. G. Sarfatti, 'L'esposizione "Intima" alla Famiglia Artistica,' *Avanti!*, December 12, 1911
Sarfatti, September 24, 1916
M. G. Sarfatti, 'L'opera di Umberto Boccioni,' *Gli Avvenimenti*, September 24, 1916
Sarfatti 1917
M. G. Sarfatti, 'Umberto Boccioni,' *Rassegna d'Arte Antica e Moderna*, IV, 1917, vol. II ('Vita d'Arte Moderna'), pp. 41–50
Sarfatti, April 13, 1919
M. G. Sarfatti, 'L'Esposizione futurista a Milano. Terzo e ultimo articolo,' *Il Popolo d'Italia*, April 13, 1919
Sarfatti 1919
M. G. Sarfatti, *La fiaccola accesa*, Milan, Istituto Editoriale Italiano 1919
Sarfatti, March 27, 1925
M. G. Sarfatti, 'La seconda Biennale di Roma,' *Il Popolo d'Italia*, March 27, 1925
Sarfatti 1925[a]
M. G. Sarfatti, 'Pittori d'oggi. Carlo Dalmazzo Carrà,' *La Rivista Illustrata del Popolo d'Italia*, III, 5, May 15, 1925, pp. 39–43
Sarfatti 1925[b]
M. G. Sarfatti, *Segni colori e luci. Note d'arte*, Bologna, Zanichelli 1925
Sarfatti 1930
M. G. Sarfatti, *Storia delle pittura moderna*, Rome, Cremonese 1930
Sartoris 1946
A. Sartoris, *Mario Sironi*, Milan, Hoepli 1946
Scheiwiller 1930
Art italien moderne, preface by G. Scheiwiller, Paris, Bonaparte 1930
Scheiwiller 1950
G. Scheiwiller, *Amedeo Modigliani*, V ed., Milan, Hoepli 1950
Schmalenbach 1991
W. Schmalenbach, *Modigliani*, Prestel 1991
Schmid, Weddingen 1998
S. Schmid, E. Weddingen, 'Jean Metzinger und die "Königin der Klassiker". Eine Cyclopädie des Kubismus,' *Wallraf-Richartz Jahrbuch*, LIX, 1998, pp. 229–58
Schmidt 1987
H.-W. Schmidt [Entry for Giacomo Balla, *Mercurio transita davanti al sole*], in Düsseldorf 1987, pp. 36–7
Schneede 1994
U. Schneede, *Umberto Boccioni*, Stuttgart, Hatje 1994
Schulz-Hoffmann 1988
C. Schulz-Hoffmann, *Futurismus*, in Munich 1988, pp. 114–43

Scudiero 1987
M. Scudiero, *Fortunato Depero. Opere*, with essays by G. Belli and E. Crispolti, Trento, Reverdito 1987
Seitz 1961
W. C. Seitz, *The Art of Assemblage*, New York, The Museum of Modern Art and Doubleday and Co. 1961
Severini 1913
G. Severini, 'Introduction,' in London 1913, pp. 3–7
Severini 1933
G. Severini, 'Ricordi su Boccioni,' *L'Esame Artistico e Letterario*, V, 6, July 1933, pp. 345–52
Severini 1946
G. Severini, *Tutta la vita di un pittore. Volume primo: Roma-Parigi*, Milan, Garzanti 1946
Severini 1959
M. Severini, *La collezione Sebastiano Timpanaro nel Gabinetto disegni e stampe dell'Istituto di Storia dell'Arte dell'Università di Pisa*, Venice, Neri Pozza 1959
Shell 2000
O. Shell, *Cleansing the Nation: Italian Art, Consumerism, and World War I*, Ann Arbor UMI, 2000
Siblik 1965
G. Siblik, *Giorgio Morandi*, Prague, Soucasné Svetové Umeni 1965
Siligato 2000
R. Siligato, 'Dal polimaterismo futurista alla comunicazione interattiva,' in Barcelona 2000–1, pp. 25–37
Simoni 1916
R. Simoni, 'Tragica morte del futurista Boccioni,' *Corriere della Sera*, August 19, 1916
Sironi 1980
M. Sironi, *Scritti editi e inediti*, ed. E. Camesasca with C. Gian Ferrari, Milan, Feltrinelli 1980
Sironi, Zervos 1950
M. Sironi, C. Zervos, 'Omaggio a Boccioni,' *Spazio*, I, 1, July 1950, pp. 12–14
Sketch, April 29, 1914
'Dynamism or Dynamite? More Futuristic Puzzles,' *The Sketch*, April 29, 1914
Smith 1997
In Visible Touch. Modernism and Masculinity, ed. T. Smith, Chicago, The University of Chicago Press 1997
Soby 1949
J. T. Soby, 'The Scuola Metafisica,' in New York 1949, pp. 17–23
Soffici 1908
A. Soffici, 'Paul Cézanne,' *Vita d'Arte*, I, I (1908), pp. 320–31
Soffici, April 1, 1909
A. Soffici, 'La Ricetta di Ribi buffone,' *La Voce*, April 1, 1909
Soffici, September 15, 1910
A. Soffici, 'Henry [*sic*] Rousseau,' *La Voce*, September 15, 1910
Soffici, September 22, 1910
A. Soffici, 'Divagazioni sull'arte,' *La Voce*, September 22, 1910
Soffici, August 24, 1911
A. Soffici, 'Picasso e Braque,' *La Voce*, August 24, 1911
Soffici, July 11, 1912
A. Soffici, 'Commentari del Louvre. Giornata seconda,' *La Voce*, July 11, 1912
Soffici, November 21, 1912
A. Soffici, 'Ojetti e il cubismo,' *La Voce*, November 21, 1912
Soffici, July 1, 1914
A. Soffici, 'Raggio,' *Lacerba*, July 1, 1914
Soffici, April 15, 1913
A. Soffici, 'Chicchi del grappolo. Teoria del movimento nella plastica futurista,' *Lacerba*, April 15, 1913
Soffici 1913
A. Soffici, *Cubismo e oltre*, Florence, Libreria della Voce 1913
Soffici 1914
A. Soffici, *Cubismo e futurismo*, with 32 illustrations of Balla, Boccioni, Braque, Carrà, Cézanne, Picasso, Russolo, Severini, Soffici, Florence, Libreria della Voce 1914
Soffici 1915
A. Soffici, 'Simultaneità liriche. Atelier,' *La Voce*, VII, April 15, 1915, pp. 530–2
Soffici 1920[a]
A. Soffici, *Primi principi di una estetica futurista*, Florence, Vallecchi 1920
Soffici 1920[b]
A. Soffici, 'Arte,' *Rete Mediterranea*, no. 2, June 1920, pp. 163–7
Soffici 1926
A. Soffici, 'Carlo Carrà,' in Milan 1926, pp. 7–17
Soffici 1928
A. Soffici, *Carlo Carrà*, Milan, Hoepli 1928
Soffici 1932
A. Soffici, 'Giorgio Morandi,' *L'Italiano*, VII, 10, March 1932, pp. I–VIII
Soffici 1955
A. Soffici, *Fine di un mondo. Autoritratto d'artista italiano nel quadro del suo tempo. IV. Virilità*, Florence, Vallecchi 1955
Solmi, December 6, 1935
S. Solmi, 'Carrà alla Galleria del Milione,' *L'Ambrosiano*, December 6, 1935
Solmi 1978
F. Solmi, *Morandi: storia e leggenda*, Bologna, Grafis 1978
Solmi 1985[a]
F. Solmi, 'Dagli esordi alla metafisica,' in Bologna 1985, pp. 20–43
Solmi 1985[b]
F. Solmi, 'Giorgio Morandi, gli anni della formazione,' in Pasquali 1985, pp. 19–34
Solmi 1987
F. Solmi, 'La peinture de Morandi: un lieu de l'infini,' in Paris 1987, pp. 9–23
Somaré 1920
E. Somaré, 'Notizie d'arte. Pittura e scultura. Milano. Galleria delle Mostre temporanee, via Dante 10,' *Il Primato Artistico Italiano*, II, 3, March–April 1920, p. 33
Spate 1979
V. Spate, *Orphism. The Evolution of Non-figurative Painting in Paris 1900-1914*. Oxford, Clarendon Press 1979
Spate 1997
V. Spate, 'Mother and Son: Boccioni's Painting and Sculpture 1906-1915,' in Smith 1997, pp. 107–38
Spinazzè 2000
S. Spinazzè [Entry nos. 94–100], in Rome 2000–1[a], pp. 252–64
'Sprovieri' 1983
'Intervista a Giuseppe Sprovieri,' in Anacapri 1983, pp. 144–6
Stoss 1993
T. Stoss, 'Am Anfag,' in Wien 1993–Frankfurt 1994, pp. 1–48

Tagliapietra 2000
F. Tagliapietra, *Luigi Russolo pittore musicista filosofo*, Quinto di Treviso, Europrint 2000
Tarchiani, December 7, 1913
N. T. [Tarchiani], 'I pittori futuristi a Firenze,' *Il Marzocco*, December 7, 1913
Taricone 1994
F. Taricone, *Teresa Labriola. Biografia politica di un'intellettuale tra Ottocento e Novecento*, Milan, Franco Angeli 1994
Tatlin 1915
Anonymous, *Vladimir Evgrafovich Tatlin*, Petrograd 1915
Tavolato, Kheiri undated
Miniature indiane dell'epoca islamica, with a foreword by I. Tavolato and a critical essay by S. Kheiri, Rome, Edizioni di Valori Plastici undated
Taylor 1961
J. C. Taylor, 'The Futurist Achievement,' in New York 1961–Los Angeles 1962, pp. 17–120
Taylor, Martin 1973
J. C. Taylor, revised by M. W. Mar-

tin, 'Umberto Boccioni. Drawings and Prints,' in New York 1973, pp. 207–28
Testori 1942
G. Testori, 'Considerazioni sulla mostra di Carrà a Brera,' *Stile*, July–August 1942, pp. 6–7
Thovez, May 20, 1923
E. Thovez, 'La sala degli analfabeti,' *La Gazzetta del Popolo*, May 20, 1923
Tisdall, Bozzolla 1977
C. Tisdall, A. Bozzolla, *Futurism*, London, Thames and Hudson 1977
Titta Rosa 1970
G. Titta Rosa, *Milano di ieri*, Florence, Sansoni 1970
Tomea 1938
F. Tomea, 'Mostre d'Arte,' *Broletto*, III, 36, December 1938, pp. 23–6
Tommaseo, Bellini 1861–79
N. Tommaseo, B. Bellini, *Dizionario della lingua italiana*, 6 vols., Turin, Pomba 1861–99
Tommei, December 24, 1913
U. Tommei, 'L'esposizione di pittura futurista di Firenze,' *Quartiere latino*, I, 4, December 24, 1913
Torriano 1942
P. Torriano, *Carlo Carrà*, Milan, Garzanti 1942
Trassari Filippetto 1991
G. Trassari Filippetto, 'Catalogo delle opere [analysis and description of the matrices],' in Cordaro 1991, pp. 3–136
Traversi 1968
G. Traversi, *Mario Sironi. Disegni, illustrazioni, scenografie e opera grafica*, Milan, Ceschina 1968

Uhde 1911
W. Uhde, *Henri Rousseau*, Paris, Figuière 1911
Uomo di pietra, May 6, 1911
Anonymous, 'Esposizione d'Arte Libera,' *L'Uomo di Pietra*, May 6, 1911

Vallier 1963
D. Vallier, *Geschichte der Malerei im 20. Jahrhundert 1870-1940*, Cologne, Du Mont Schauberg 1963
Vallier 1969
L'opera completa di Rousseau il Doganiere, critical and philological apparati by D. Vallier, Milan, Rizzoli 1969
Valsecchi 1950
M. Valsecchi, *Umberto Boccioni*, Venice, Edizioni del Cavallino 1950
Valsecchi 1952
M. Valsecchi, *24 dipinti in una raccolta d'arte moderna*, Milan, Edizioni del Milione 1952
Valsecchi, May 23, 1953
M. Valsecchi, 'Mezzo secolo a Firenze,' *Tempo*, May 23, 1953
Valsecchi 1956
M. Valsecchi, *Maestri moderni*, Milan, Garzanti 1956
Valsecchi 1958
M. Valsecchi, *La pittura metafisica: G. de Chirico, C. Carrà, G. Morandi*, Milan, Garzanti 1958
Valsecchi 1959
M. Valsecchi, 'Biografie degli artisti,' in Turin 1959, pp. 15–35
Valsecchi 1962[a]
M. Valsecchi, *Carrà*, Milan, Garzanti 1962
Valsecchi 1962[b]
M. Valsecchi, *Mario Sironi*, Rome, Editalia 1962
Valsecchi 1963
M. Valsecchi [Presentation], in Brescia 1963, unnumbered pages
Valsecchi 1964
M. Valsecchi, *Morandi*, Milan, Garzanti 1964
Van Lennep undated
J. Van Lennep, *Musées Royaux des Beaux-Arts de Belgique. Catalogue de la Sculpture. Artistes nés entre 1750 et 1882*, Brussels, Musées Royaux des Beaux-Arts de Belgique, undated
Vanden Berghe 1999
D. Vanden Berghe, 'L'autocommento inedito di Soffici a Simultaneità e chimismi lirici,' in Richter, Rodriguez 1999, pp. 95–112
Velani 1971
L. Velani, 'Regesti biografici e bibliografici,' in Rome 1971–2, pp. 23–140
Velani 1999
L. Velani, 'Catalogo,' in Rome 1999–2000, pp. 53–81
Venedig, Mailand 1899
Venedig, Mailand, über St Gothard, Brenner, Semmering, Griebens Reisebücher, vol. 72, Berlin, Goldschmidt 1899
Venna, January 15, 1918
L. Venna, 'Una visita a Giacomo Balla,' *L'Italia Futurista*, II, 37, January 15, 1918
Venturi 1936
L. Venturi, *Cézanne. Son art, son œuvre*, Paris, Rosenberg 1936
Venturi 1961
L. Venturi, *Gino Severini*, Rome, De Luca 1961
Verdone, Pagnotta Guidetti, Bidetti 1992
M. Verdone, F. Pagnotta Guidetti, M. Bidetti, *La Casa d'Arte Bragaglia 1918-1930*, Rome, Bulzoni 1992
Verzotti 1989
G. Verzotti, *Boccioni. Catalogo completo*, Florence, Cantini 1989
Vibrante, August 3, 1919
A. Vibrante, 'La mostra di Mario Sironi,' *Rome Futurista*, August 3, 1919
Vigliani Bragaglia 1980
'Fotodinamismo e cinema d'avanguardia,' compiled by A. Vigliani Bragaglia, in Bragaglia 1980, pp. 133–48
Vitali 1933
L. Vitali, 'Ardengo Soffici,' *Domus*, no. 68, August 1933, pp. 406–8
Vitali, April 21, 1934
L. Vitali, 'Le incisioni di Carlo Carrà,' *L'Italia Letteraria*, April 21, 1934
Vitali 1950
L. Vitali, *Preferenze*, Milan, Editoriale Domus 1950
Vitali 1957
L. Vitali, *Giorgio Morandi. Opera grafica*, Turin, Einaudi 1957
Vitali 1961
L. Vitali, *Giorgio Morandi*, Ivrea, Olivetti 1961
Vitali 1964
L. Vitali, *Giorgio Morandi pittore*, Milan, Edizioni del Milione 1964
Vitali 1977
L. Vitali, *Morandi. Catalogo generale*, Milan, Electa 1977
Vitali 1983
L. Vitali, *Morandi. Catalogo generale* (II ed.), Milan, Electa 1983
Vollard 1914
A. Vollard, *Paul Cézanne*, Paris, Galerie A. Vollard 1914
Volta 1931
S. Volta, *Ottone Rosai*, Milan, Hoepli 1931
Von Bissing 1914
Denkmäler Ägyptischer Sculptur herausgegeben und mit erlänternden Texten versehen von Fr. W. Freiherrn von Bissing, Munich, Bruckmann 1914

Warnod, March 18, 1913
A. Warnod, 'Le Salon des Indépendants. Fauves et cubistes,' *Comœdia*, March 18, 1913
Warnod 1975
J. Warnod, *'Le Bateau lavoir' 1882-1914*, Paris, Les Presses de la Connaissance 1975
Warnod, June 21, 1913
A. Warnod, 'Les Sculptures futuristes de Boccioni, les Tableaux de Thomas Couture,' *Comœdia*, June 21, 1913
Washton Long 1993
R.-C. Washton Long, 'National or international? Berlin critics and the

question of Expressionism,' in Gaehtgens 1993, pp. 521–34

Werner 1967
A. Werner, *Amedeo Modigliani*, Milan, Garzanti 1967

Windsor 1977
A. Windsor, 'Apollinaire, Marinetti and Carra's "Dipinto Parolibero",' *Gazette des Beaux-Arts*, no. 89, April 1977, pp. 144–52

Worms de Romilly, Laude 1982
N. Worms de Romilly, J. Laude, *Braque. Le Cubisme (fin 1907-1914)*, Paris, Maeght 1982

Zanchi, Bottelli undated
P. Zanchi, F. Bottelli, *Un secolo di Galleria*, Cernusco sul Naviglio, Severgnini undated

Zanotto 1996
S. Zanotto, *Filippo de Pisis ogni giorno*, Vicenza, Neri Pozza 1996

Zanovello Russolo 1958
Russolo. L'uomo e l'artista, memoir by M. Zanovello Russolo, foreword by U. Nebbia, preface by P. Buzzi, Milan, Corticelli 1958

Zanzi, May 10, 1923
E. Zanzi, 'Alla Quadriennale. Ancora la sala degli scandali. Da Carlo Carrà a Gigi Chessa,' *Il Momento*, May 10, 1923

Zervos 1938
C. Zervos, *Histoire de l'art contemporain*, Paris, Cahiers d'Art 1938

Zervos 1950
'Un demi-siècle d'art italien,' ed. C. Zervos, *Cahiers d'Art*, XXV, 1, 1950, pp. 3–276

Zhadova 1982
L. A. Zhadova, *Malevich. Suprematism and Revolution in Russian Art 1910-1930*, London–New York, Thames and Hudson 1982

Zhadova 1988
Tatlin, ed. L. A. Zhadova, London–New York, Thames and Hudson 1988

Zuccoli, May 11 1913
L. Zuccoli, 'Il futurismo a casa sua,' *Il Marzocco*, May 11, 1913

Nicola Ludwig

Importance, Physical Fundamentals and Technological Evolution of Infrared Reflectography

The technique for the reflectographic examination[1] of paintings exploits the transparency of many pigments and binders in the near infrared region of the spectrum, i.e. the region characterized by longer wavelengths than those of visible light. Its first applications date from the early 1930s.

At the outset the examination of works of art under infrared light was of interest chiefly to restorers and conservators, as it allowed them to discriminate between those pigments which, although different, display identical optical properties in the visible region of the spectrum. This made it possible to identify earlier restorations.

It was with the progressive improvement of the technology used for the acquisition and recording of infrared images that this type of analysis entered the field of study of the work in the proper sense, providing important information on its genesis (with particular regard to the possibility of identifying possible earlier versions, painted over later) and on the underdrawing (the underdrawing made directly on the light-colored priming of the surface of the canvas or panel).

Examination of the underdrawing in a large number of works by the same artists has made it possible to acquire more and more information on their personal techniques of execution, on the evolution of an artist's method of working over time and on the mode of operation within workshops and studios. In some cases it has also led to the discovery of different versions on a single support, to the finding of important clues for dating or attribution — such as signatures, inscriptions or dates on which there was no reliable information — and to the identification of works that were thought to have been lost.

While the contribution made by the technique to settling controversial problems of attribution appears to have been only partially effective, where some artists are concerned the understanding of their stylistic development that can be gained from examination of the underdrawings appears to have become increasingly indispensable to anyone compiling a *catalogue raisonné* or writing a monograph.

The use of photographic films sensitive to infrared light, very widespread partly as a consequence of their low cost, has attracted a great deal of attention to infrared reflectography. It has been utilized not just to identify drawings underneath layers of paint, but also for the interpretation of inscriptions on papyri, bandages, tablets and all sorts of fragments that have survived from ancient times. In the specific case of the reading of underlying marks, however, photographic films have one drastic limitation: a threshold of sensibility that does not exceed 0.9 micrometers (millionths of a meter) in the near infrared.

It was not until the 1960s, with the studies carried out by the Dutch physicist Van Asperen de Boer, that the second great revolution in the field of reflectography came about, through the use of apparatus capable of detecting infrared radiation in the specific bands where pictorial materials (pigments and binders) are most transparent.

According to the theory of the propagation of light, if an ideally transparent and homogeneous medium contains dispersed particles of material (which can be considered non-absorbent for illuminating radiation and which are of a small size compared with the wavelength of the radiation itself), the phenomenon of attenuation of the incident radiation is due to scattering, which diminishes as the wavelength increases. Since the layer of paint is made up of particles of pigment dispersed in a homogeneous medium that is to a first approximation transparent, increasing the wavelength diminishes the layer's opacity to infrared, while augmenting the optical contrast between the underdrawing and the background to which it is applied, as it is detected on the outside through the layer itself following reflection off the background.

In elementary terms, this explains the experimental observation that the use of instruments to detect radiation of increasing wavelength in the infrared greatly increases the possibility of visualizing the underdrawing in a clearly legible manner.

Through a series of experimental trials, and drawing on the theories of the Russians Kubelka and Munk on the transparency of thin films of paint,[2] Van Asperen settled on the band of wavelengths between 1.5 and 2 micrometers as the optimal one for infrared reflectography (i.e. in the near infrared — NIR — region of the electromagnetic spectrum, in which the interaction of the radiation with the pictorial material produces the effect of maximum transparency).[3]

The basic mechanisms characteristic of NIR radiation, responsible for the phenomenon, are essentially its low interaction (by absorption or by diffusion) with the majority of pigments, which are in the form of a suspension in the binder (oil or tempera), and the high optical absorption of the underlying drawings with respect to a sufficiently reflective surface.

A background that reflects infrared well is a light-colored priming. In particular, owing to the fact that the transparency of the pigments and the absorption of the materials of the underdrawing are both dependent on wavelength, it is difficult to identify a precise working range for infrared reflectography, but realistically it can be located — as has been pointed out — between 1 and 2 micrometers. Over such broad bands of the spectrum the effect of chromatic aberration due to the focusing of the different wavelengths by the optics used can produce images that are not always sharp. This is also due to the fact that the optical systems utilized have not generally been constructed specifically for infrared radiation, but for the wavelengths characteristic of the visible spectrum.

This phenomenological theory makes it possible to calculate the value of the thickness of obscuration, i.e. the minimum thickness at which a drawing traced on the ground of the painting can no longer be detected. The consideration that we can expect an increase in the thickness of obscuration with the wavelength of the radiation is not a general indication sufficient to obtain the optimal conditions for reflectography. In fact these depend on the specific material of the paint as well as the thickness of the layers, and in the case of a real painting these data have to be averaged out to some extent. It is possible to experiment with suitable optical filters for this purpose. So the insurmountable limits in finding optimal working conditions are in any case provided by the characteristics of the instrument used for detection. And for wavelengths within the limits of the instrument's sensitivity, the value of the thickness of obscuration of different pigments has to be assessed.

A further consideration on the wavelengths utilizable in reflectography regards the presence of the characteristic absorption bands of the O-H group (around 2.9 micrometers) and of the C-H group (around 3.3 micrometers) due to the oils and proteins contained in the binding medium, which produce a marked absorption of the radiation at these wavelengths. From this we can derive the maximum value of the wavelength utilizable. Employing radiation of an even greater wavelength will generally result in interference between the radiation emitted by molecular compounds and reflected radiation.

In the region of the near infrared, which extends as far as 2 micrometers, the use of Vidicon tubes (which exploit the variation in electrical resistance induced by the radiation on a thin deposit of lead sulfide) has proved so effective that it is still the technology most widely used by museums and conservators for reflectographic analysis, in spite of the low quality of the images. The emergence of solid-state devices for the detection of radiation at the end of the 1980s has led to an exponential increase in the sensitivity of instruments: in fact these detectors are based on the principle that each photon (the minimum packet of electromagnetic energy into which radiation can be broken down) that comes into contact with the detector produces a separation of charges that can in principle be registered and counted, and therefore a signal that is closely correlated with the incident radiation. These detectors, reduced to tiny dimensions (a few tens of micrometers) and combined in arrays (known as charge-coupled devices or CCDs), permit a high definition of the image and good legibility, as each micro-detector picks up the radiation coming from a single point of the actual object. Thus the image is formed by conversion of the signal recorded simultaneously by all the detectors.

This type of camera, developed for applications in the visible spectrum, uses a material (silicon) that is also sensitive in the near infrared range (0.7-1.1 micrometers). So by making suitable modifications to a normal video camera and replacing the optical filter that cuts down the infrared radiation with one that eliminates visible wavelengths, it is possible to create a device for use in reflectography that, while not operating in the optimal range defined above, produces images of high quality. Comparative studies[4] have demonstrated the clear superiority of solid-state systems (CCDs) with regard to the reduction in the geometric distortion of the image, the stability of the signal of the different elements of the detector and the linearity of the response to different light stimuli. Images obtained with this technology have particularly high contrast and a good resolution of detail. Yet it seems beyond question that the reduced spectral bandwidth of CCDs based on silicon detectors makes these devices essentially blind to certain pigments in reflectographic analysis, so that the use of this technology is in fact of little advantage in some situations.

The dilemma created by the need to choose between systems based on CCDs, which produce images of high quality but in regions where not all the pigments are transparent, and those based on Vidicon tubes, which produce images that are not always sharp, but in bands of the spectrum that are of high transparency for the majority of pigments, has only very recently been overcome by the use of solid-state detectors operating in bands of the infrared that are optimal for reflectographic analyses, made out of materials like platinum silicide and gallium antimonide of indium and germanium.[5]

A further improvement that has taken place in the last few years consists in the possibility of transferring the data that make up the image in digital format directly from the source — the detector — to the memory of a personal computer. This permits elimination of both the 'noise' (i.e. that part of the signal due to disturbances generated in the transmission of the data in analogic form) and errors introduced during digitalization by the frame grabber of the PC.

In all modern techniques of reflectography, whether using cameras equipped with Vidicon tubes or solid-state cameras, digital processing of the images assumes great importance. For example, it permits improvement of contrast or the re-creation of the entire work by combining individual images of details, useful when you want to examine the underdrawing as a whole. It is often necessary to take close-up images as they provide greater information (spatial discrimination of the details) and create less distortion than overall images, which are taken from a greater distance.

To meet these needs and in particular to permit automatic high-quality recomposition of the image of the whole work of art, a prototype infrared scanner for use in reflectography has been developed at the laboratories of the Istituto Nazionale di Ottica Applicata in Florence. In schematic terms, it consists of a mechanical drive that through the high-precision movement of a solid-state optical sensor for infrared radiation (an InGaAs photodiode), allows the point-by-point examination (at a resolution of four pixels per mm) of the surface of the painting without introducing geometric distortions. A PC controls the movement of the sensor and the digitalization of the signal coming from the mobile measuring head. This includes the sensor, which operates in the band of wavelengths comprised between 1 and 1.7 micrometers, an extremely simplified optical system and the electronics for the detector. The system of illumination is an integral part of the head and moves with it. This has made it possible to limit the illuminated zone to a small area around the point under examination, with the further advantage that each point of the painting is examined under the same lighting conditions, maintained at a very low level thanks to the high sensitivity of the sensor and the high signal-to-noise ration of the associated electronics. Thus the analysis is carried out in conditions of low and precise illumination, reducing to a minimum the threat to the conservation of the painting.

In brief, the scanning system provides art historians and restorers with images characterized by a notable resolution of detail and of shades of gray. In this way they can also obtain information on the pigments used in the shading carried out by the artist in the initial phase of the work, for instance with thin glazes laid on with the brush or light hatching, whose density can vary greatly from case to case.

Although still a prototype, the infrared scanner has already made it possible to carry out important campaigns of measurement. The ones conducted at the Pinacoteca di Brera[6] and the Museo Poldi Pezzoli in Milan, at the Accademia Carrara in Bergamo and the Uffizi in Florence are of particular significance, with the examination of dozens of works.[7]

Unfortunately the instrument, in its current configuration, is extremely unwieldy and cannot be used when museum structures do not have premises set aside for measurement or where it is necessary to operate in particularly difficult conditions, as in the case of works that cannot be removed from their usual location and which are in positions where access is not easy, for instance on altars in churches. Experiments are currently being carried out at the INOA laboratory in Milan on a prototype that operates directly on the flat image instead of on the real object, considerably reducing the size of the equipment and the time required to take measurements.

Finally, it is important to stress that techniques of scientific analysis applied to works of art are only capable of developing their full potential within the ambit of coordinated and multidisciplinary programs of research, in which different types of information and techniques are integrated and used to build up a body of knowledge that is at once coherent and wide-ranging.

[1] R. A. Lyon, 'Infrared Radiations and Examinations of Paintings', in *Technical Studies in the Field of Fine Arts*, vol. 2, 1934.
[2] P. Kubelka, F. Munk, 'Ein Beitrag zur Optik der Farbanstriche,' *Zeitschr. f.techn. Physik*, vol. 12, 1931.
[3] J. R. J. van Asperen de Boer, *Infrared Reflectography. A contribution to the examination of earlier European painters*, PhD thesis, Central Research Laboratory for Objects of Art and Science, Amsterdam, 1970.
[4] E. Wamlsley, C. Fletcher, J. K. Delaney, 'Evaluation of system performance of near-infrared imaging devices', *Studies in Conservation*, vol. 37, pp. 120–30, London 1992.
[5] E. Walmsley, C. Metzger, J. K. Delaney, C. Fletcher, 'Improved visualization of underdrawings with solid state detectors operating in the infrared', *Studies in Conservation*, vol. 39, pp. 217–31, London 1994.
[6] *Oltre il visibile, indagini riflettografiche*, ed. by D. Bertani, Università degli Studi di Milano, Milan, 2001.
[7] Further information on the application of reflectographic techniques to the study of paintings can be found at the websites: http: //www.ino.it / %7eluca/rifle/rifle_it.html; http://albinoni.brera.unimi.it/istituto/ARCHEO/rifletto.htm.

Gianluca Poldi

Reflectographic Analysis of Some Paintings in the Mattioli Collection

It is not common practice to examine twentieth-century art by techniques like infrared reflectography, especially if unconnected with the requirements of restoration or conservation. The mass of documents in our possession, including first-hand accounts and sometimes even photographs of different stages in the execution of modern paintings, makes such studies unnecessary in many cases. In addition, experience has taught us that it is usually difficult to obtain good results from this technique with paintings apart from those of the Middle Ages and Renaissance, which normally have colors with excellent characteristics of transparency and a high degree of reflection from the chalk priming underneath.

Yet some art historians have now realized that information obtainable by the technique of reflectography can also be of considerable interest for twentieth-century works as it is able sometimes to provide data on the genesis of the painting (underlying versions and drawings) and on the artist's technique (such as the use of preparatory drawings, the succession of layers of paint, certain characteristics of the brushwork).

In the specific case of the Mattioli Collection, it was felt that the study of reflectograms might solve a number of problems in the interpretation of certain works.

The choice of the works to be examined was the outcome of a balance between the specific interests of the art historians, emerging out of conversations with Laura Mattioli Rossi and Flavio Fergonzi, and the results of a direct examination of the works on our part, and in particular of the thickness of the layers of paint, the type of preparation of the canvas and the technique used by the artist, in order to assess the usefulness of taking infrared reflectograms, considering the limitations of the technique.

In fact the transparency to infrared of a picture's paint layers is determined by several factors. These include: the transparency of the binders used and the pigments suspended in them in the infrared spectrum, the concentrations of the pigments in the binders — i.e. the transparency and concentration of the individual colors in the case of prepared colors in tubes or the like — and the transparency of their mixtures or overlays, as well as the thickness of each layer of paint. In addition, there has to be a sufficiently reflective support (the priming of the canvas or panel, or the canvas itself) to permit reflection of the infrared component of the radiation striking the painting into the video camera.

Over the course of the reflectographic studies conducted at the Peggy Guggenheim Collection in Venice in October 2000 and June 2002, we carried out not only an examination of the ten paintings covered in the following reflectographic reports, but also a rapid inspection of other works, including Sironi's *The White Horse*, Boccioni's *The City Rises* and Balla's *Mercury Passing Before the Sun*, without obtaining significant results to add to what was already visible to the naked eye.

Equipment Used

During the two programs of measurement, two different sets of equipment were used, operating in different bands of the spectrum. This was done in order to permit crosschecking of the results obtained and to make a comparison between the two kinds of apparatus that would help to define their limitations and the respective qualities of the images produced.

The equipment we used consisted of a video camera sensitive to infrared light, connected to a laptop computer fitted with a frame grabber. The video camera used to capture the infrared images had a solid-state detector with an indium-gallium arsenide focal plane array, sensitive to the near infrared over a bandwidth ranging from 0.9 and 1.7 micrometers, which did not require a cooling system. The detector was an array of 320 × 240 elements, each 40 micrometers on a side, and the frequency of image capture was 60 Hz. The device (model SU320-1, 7RT), manufactured and kindly made available to us by Sensors Unlimited, had a quantum efficiency of over 75% (more than three quarters of the radiation reaching the detector was converted into an electronic signal) in the bandwidth between 1 and 1.6 micrometers, and a peak of maximum response around 1.5 micrometers. The dimensions of the image provided were 560 × 620 pixels.

The device used to take measurements in June 2002 was a prototype developed in the laboratory of Archeometry at the Istituto di Fisica Generale Applicata (Institute of General Applied Physics) in Milan. It consisted of a digital camera fitted with a CCD (charged couple device) detector and a high band-pass filter that made it possible to operate in the infrared band of 0.8-1.1 micrometers. The dimensions of the image produced were 2560 × 1900 pixels. So this second instrument had the advantage of a distinctly higher definition, but operated in a smaller range of wavelengths, a band over which a small number of colors are transparent, especially where the layers of paint are thick (in the order of half a millimeter).

Method of Exposure and Treatment of the Images

In the case of the first device, the lens chosen for the exposures, as well as the distance from which the pictures were taken, depended on whether it was necessary to identify significant details or produce an overall image. In the second case, i.e. for reflectograms of the whole work, or for works of large format, a lens with a focal length of 25 mm and video optics was used. For the details, except where otherwise stated, a suitable 70-mm telephoto lens was used. In general, images of details were only taken where an inspection of the whole picture had revealed noteworthy characteristics of transparency on the part of the pigment, such as to make the drawing or the version underneath more clearly visible than in an overall reflectogram. The use of a telephoto lens requires a greater intensity of radiation in infrared, just as it does with visible light.

The ideal conditions for reflectography require a uniform distribution of light — or rather of infrared radiation — which is normally provided by diffuse lighting, in our case natural as well as artificial. The lighting conditions are specified for each reflectographic study. By artificial light we mean here the conditions of normal illumination of the rooms in which the works are exhibited in Venice, where the light sources — which have a spectrum of emission extending into the near infrared — are sufficient, thanks to the high sensitivity of the detector, to provide an adequate amount of light. In a few cases, during the first program of measurement, the glass protecting some of the works was removed to avoid reflections.

In the case of the CCD camera, which was fitted with a built-in zoom lens (5×), it was necessary to illuminate the works with a 350-watt lamp for photography.

For pictures of larger size two or more images were taken and then combined by means of suitable graphics programs.

Care was taken, during the exposure, to set the axis of the video camera as perpendicular as possible to the plane of the picture, so as to avoid distortions of perspective. The images, recorded in shades of gray directly onto a digital support, were brought back to their correct proportions with graphic software (Adobe Photoshop), compensating for the slight deformation caused by the system of capture, and then the number of shades of gray was optimized and the luminosity and contrast improved to make the image clearer.

Several standards of reflectance (white, gray and black, omitted in subsequent reflectograms for the sake of convenience) were included in each image. This was done in order to permit reproduction of the studies under conditions as close as possible to the original ones, as well as to allow measurement of a quantitative type (and not just a qualitative one, as usually happens in reflectography), i.e. numerical data on the response of each color to infrared, normalized by means of the standard, in the bandwidth in which the video camera operated.[2]

The Reflectographic Reports

In addition to a comment on the results of the infrared studies and the problems raised, the reports that follow provide information on the conditions under which the images were taken, so that the principal parameters are known which, along with the characteristics of the reflectographic video camera used, allow experts to understand its operating limits and to make comparisons between these studies and any subsequent analyses.[3] The indications on exposure conditions refer solely to the indium-gallium arsenide camera, while for the CCD camera the conditions were always the following: distance about 2 m, direct light from suitably positioned 350-watt lamp. When reflectograms were taken with the latter device this is specified in the captions. Where this is not specified the first telecamera was used.

Where appropriate, the reflectographic images are compared with black and white images of the painting, so as to permit an optimal interpretation of the information obtained, emphasizing lines and tones rather than colors, for which readers are generally referred to the images in the historical sections. As a result of damage to some elements of the array of detectors a short series of blank pixels appears in the upper right-hand part of some images taken with the indium-gallium arsenide camera, but this does not compromise interpretation of the reflectograms.

Umberto Boccioni, Dynamism of a Cyclist

The picture is painted with generally short and detached brushstrokes on yellowish-white priming visible chiefly in the interstices of the canvas, as in the zones (fig. 1) not covered with paint present around the cyclist's head, while the latter is painted with thicker and more closely spaced brushstrokes. The points where warp and weft intersect, in relief, are devoid of priming and dark tints.

In this case almost the only thing the reflectograms (figs. 2–3) reveal, thanks to the good contrast with several areas less absorbent of infrared, is the dark lines that delimit the forms and that are painted on top of the areas of color — evidently not preparatory. But it shows almost nothing that is concealed from view except, owing to the partial transparency of the violet in the left-hand part, the presence of a pair of dark lines perhaps belonging to a not yet definitive version of the painting. This is not necessarily part of a preparatory drawing, as the lines may have been made on top of another layer of paint. It is more likely a variation in the course of the work, i.e. lines erased in a method of working that proceeded by successive approximations to the final result. Owing to the thickness of the layers and the use of colors that are little or not at all transparent, nothing is visible of the sketch relating to the version of the painting at its first stage of elaboration such as can be seen behind the picture *Materia* in photographs from the summer of 1913, except perhaps the arc of the left shoulder. Thus we are bound to ask whether the simple, clearly visible and dark drawing of that time has been scraped off (as in front of the cyclist, where it would otherwise be visible), which would explain the state of the priming, with the raw canvas exposed, and perhaps in other zones simply covered with thicker layers, as at bottom left and under the violet arc.

Some ocher and green tints and a few shades of blue are transparent, letting us see how in the lower half of the figure in particular Boccioni traced the outlines with the color blue, since they are invisible or barely visible in the reflectograms, just like the areas of color themselves. The same situation is to be found in the broad arc that runs from left to right under the number 15.

The dark tracing shows that particular care was taken over the clear definition of the diagonal lines that frame the shape of the cyclist, especially on the right, as if to convey a thrust or a limit exceeded, and over some details such as the profile of the tibia and the parts of the foot in movement, which remain visible even to the naked eye, as do the lines around the hub of the rear wheel and the ones that cross in a triangle above it.

A few interesting comments can be made about certain colors and their infrared properties that can provide us with further information about the painting technique. The pinkish-red curved line at top left, for example, disappears in the reflectograms taken with the gallium arsenide camera, showing that this color is very transparent to infrared. The red next to the number 15 behaves differently: it only partially disappears in the reflectogram, where the zone of separation between the areas of red and green remains distinct. This can be explained in two ways: either Boccioni used two different kinds of red, one of them more transparent to infrared, the other more reflective, or — and this is a more plausible hypothesis — just one kind of red paint, relatively transparent to infrared, was laid on top of a fairly reflective color (perhaps to accentuate its brilliance), for example a white or a pink, from which the radiation not absorbed by the red is reflected back to the video camera. In general the blues are not very transparent to infrared where they are mixed with white or with a dark tint.

Conditions of exposure: distance about 1.5 m, natural light from above, the picture was protected by glass

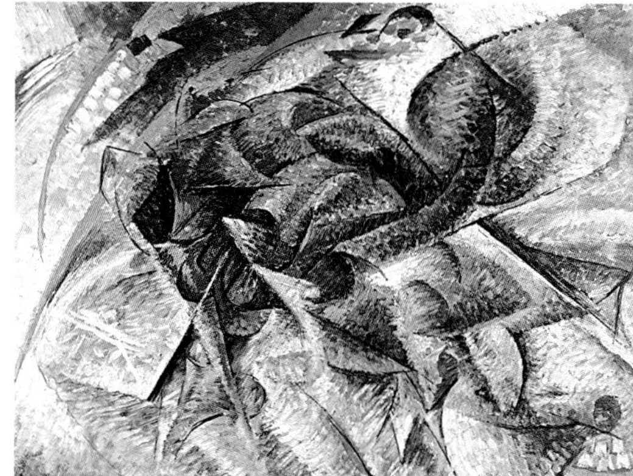

Fig. 1. *Total in visible light, in black and white*

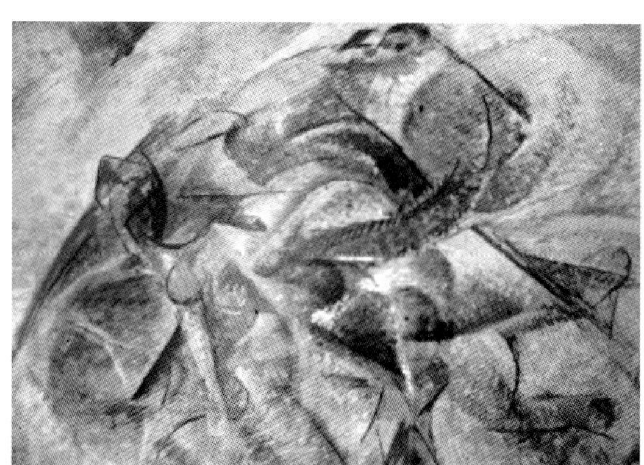

Fig. 2. *Total in infrared*

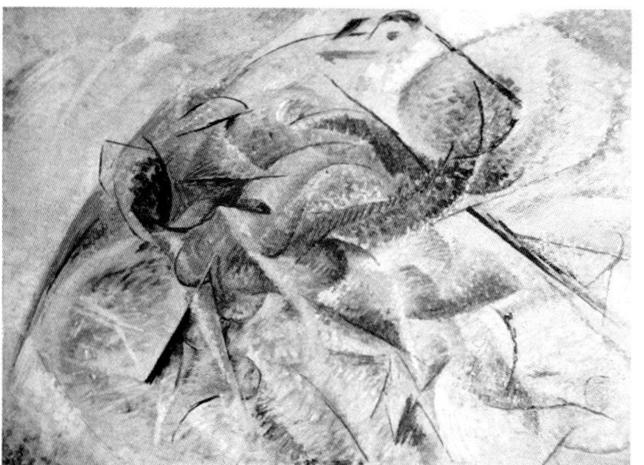

Fig. 3. *Total in infrared by* CCD *camera*

Fig. 4. *Visible light: detail of the canvas near the cyclist's head*

Fig. 5. *Visible light: detail of the head*

Fig. 6. *Visible light in color: detail of the head*

Fig. 7. *Infrared by* CCD *camera: detail of the head*

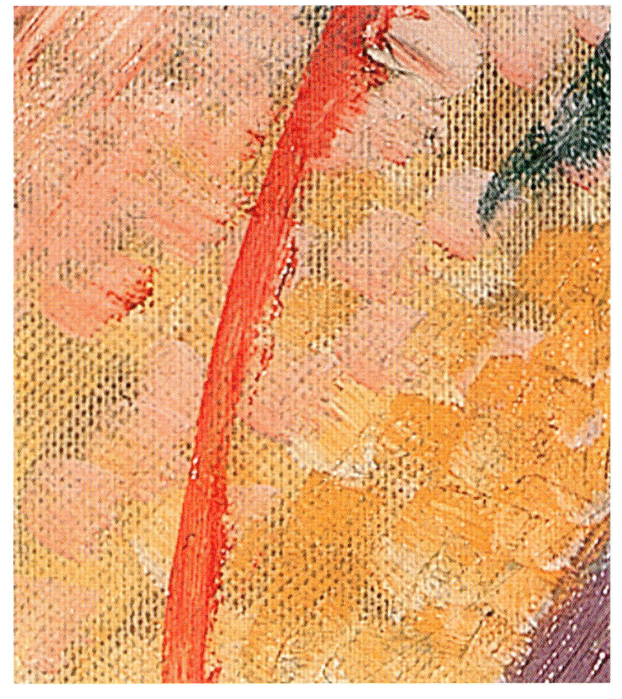

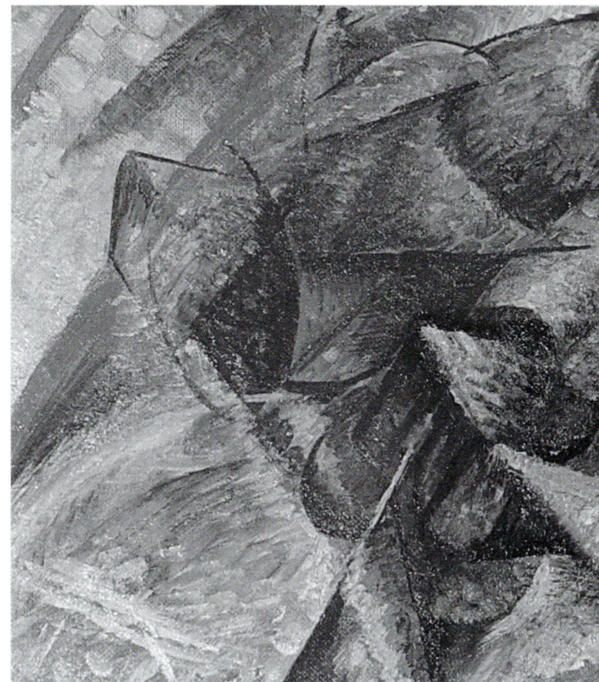

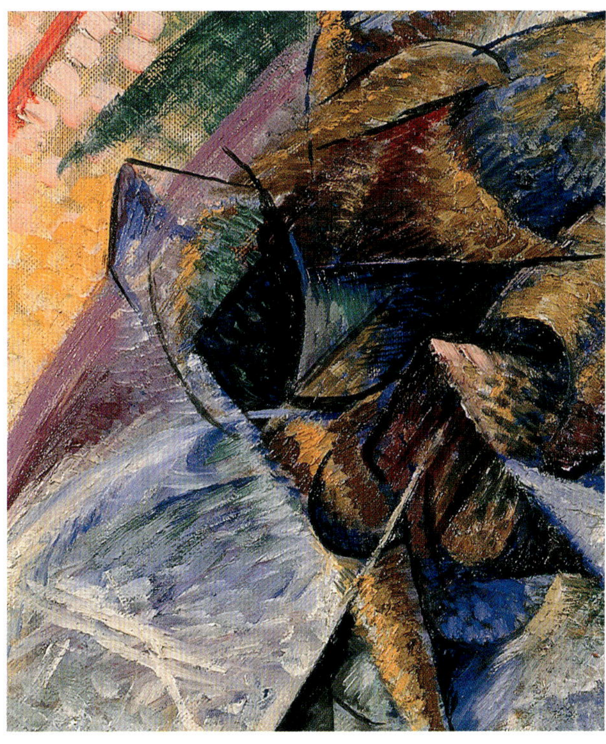

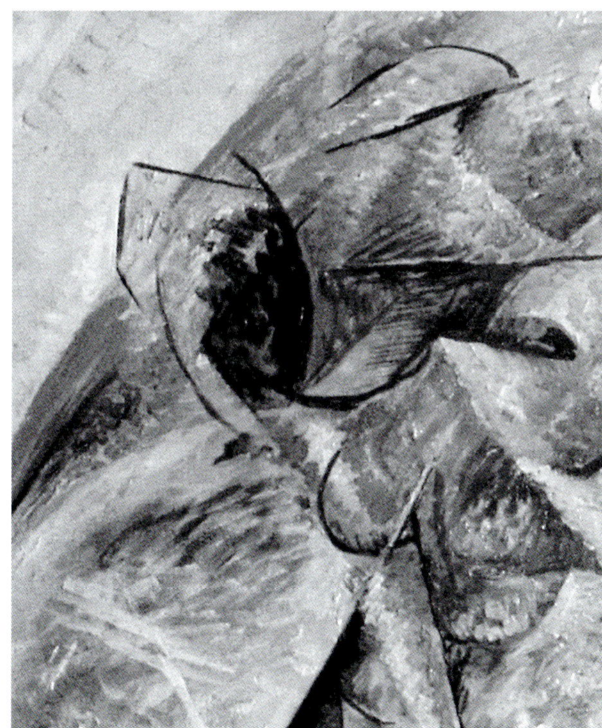

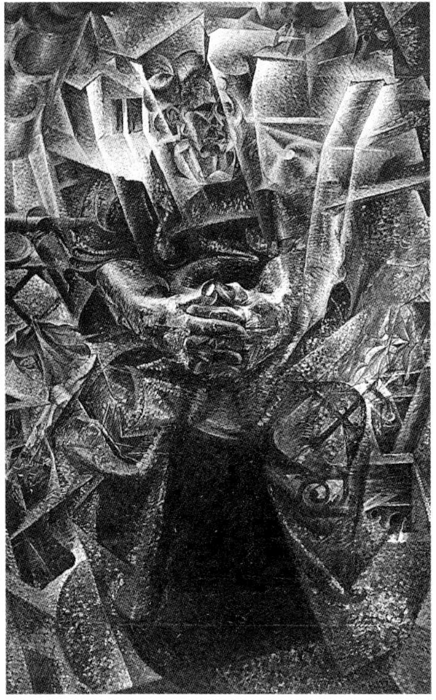

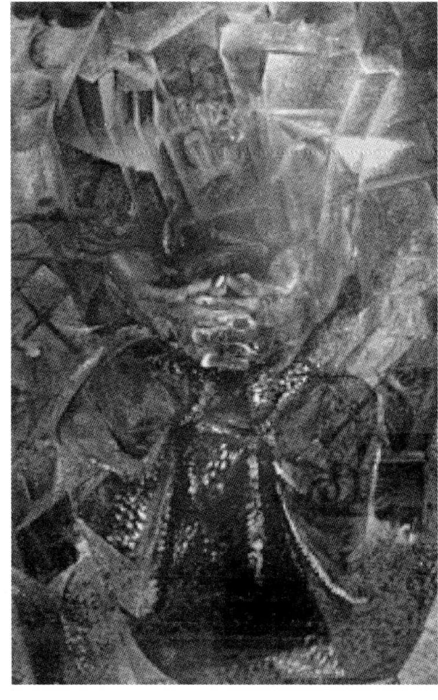

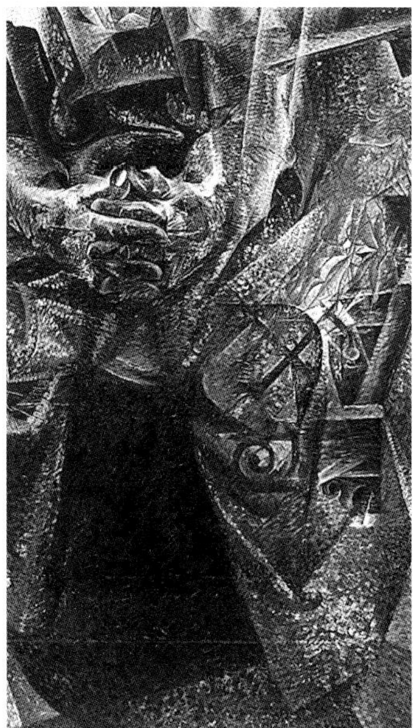

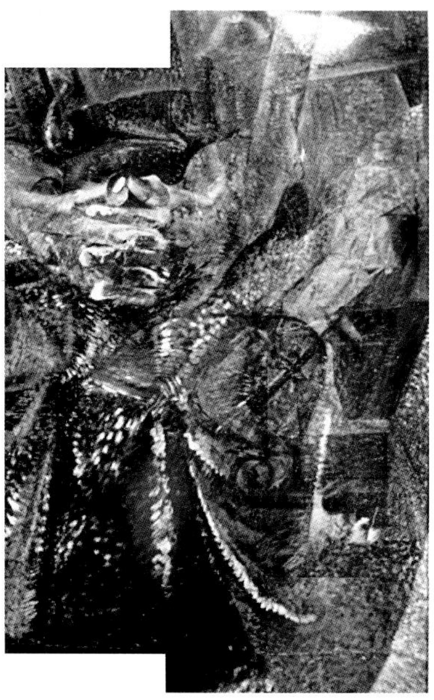

Fig. 8. *Total in visible light, in black and white*

Fig. 9. *Total in infrared*

Fig. 10. *Visible light: detail of right-hand part*

Fig. 11. *Infrared: detail of right-hand part*

Umberto Boccioni, Materia

The great complexity of this painting in terms of the layers and variety of colors used makes interpretation of the reflectographic images difficult. This is exacerbated by the difficulty of taking reflectograms under uniform conditions of diffuse light, avoiding specular reflections and over- and underexposed zones, owing to the large dimensions of the work and the variety of color.
The first thing we note is that in infrared (figs. 9, 11–13, 15–18), where the tracing of lines and planes visible to the naked eye is substantially present, characteristic details of brilliance of several colors are brought out, such as the red, the dark ochers and in general all the blues of the lower half (as is clearly evident in the skirt), while the greens are decidedly adsorbent, even when the shades are paler in visible light.
I do not believe that the question of whether the brilliance of red, ocher and blue under infrared depends on the high reflectivity of the pigments in question or on their high degree of transparency, allowing radiation to be reflected from the layer underneath, which could be white, can be resolved with this analysis alone, at least with regard to the blues, of which more will be said later. As far as the ochers and reds are concerned, I think we could be dealing with an intermediate situation.
Some valuable information about the technique of execution can be derived from a careful examination of the X-radiograph of the work, published in the catalogue of the exhibition 'Boccioni 1912 Materia'.[4] As is well-known, in X-radiographs colors with a higher density than the others show up lighter (they are radio-opaque). Pigments containing heavy elements, such as white lead, are typically opaque, while pigments of organic origin and earths are much less so. The effect of opacity can also be determined or accentuated by the thickness of the layer of paint. In the case of *Materia* it is precisely the radio-opaque zones that indicate the likely presence of areas painted in white before being covered by colors, or areas where the paint contains an abundance of white pigment (which is considered to be white lead or perhaps white zinc, and certainly not titanium dioxide, not available until around 1920).
The trapezoidal shape (a roof), highly reflective under infrared (figs. 11, 18), next to the left shoulder of the woman is painted with very thick strokes of red (in fact it is the only place that red appears in this work) and orange, perhaps with the addition of white. It appears, at least in the upper part, to be as opaque to X-rays as the zones in which white is present in abundance to the naked eye, such as the illuminated walls of the houses. This suggests that Boccioni had painted a glaze of white as preparation for the red. Where the man walking under the balconies, on the left of the mother, there is the same effect but only to a lesser degree. Hence we can assume that the brown ocher paint used was partially laid on a colored base — as can be seen — and partially on a thin white base, at least where it is more reflective in infrared. A similar consideration applies to the horse on the left of the picture (fig. 17). The white base can be made out in the oblique band that runs across the figure of the man as far as the mother's knee, a band that is opaque in the X-radiograph and wider than it appears in the final version. The reflectogram reveals, under the forms that mark the man's head, a clearer oval outline, invisible to the naked eye.
The horse, painted in the same colors as the man walking, is not reflective in infrared, and is therefore much less visible in the reflectogram.
Even though this does not appear to be the case on close examination of the picture, it is not impossible that some of the short green and blue brushstrokes were laid on top of light tints: in fact the X-radiograph suggests that some of the blue areas in the lower part of the canvas (fig. 12) are painted on a white base, with touches of the brush, to accentuate their luminosity and in some cases may actually be a light-colored priming of the canvas. At the same time we can exclude the significant presence of white under the blue areas of the upper part of the canvas, which are not radio-opaque.

Fig. 12. *Infrared by CCD camera: lower half*

Fig. 13. *Infrared by CCD camera: detail of lower left corner*

Fig. 14. *Visible light: detail of hands and man to left of the mother*

Fig. 15. *Infrared by CCD camera: detail of hands and man to left of the mother*

Fig. 16. *Infrared by CCD camera: detail of upper left part, chimneys and buildings*

Fig. 17. *Infrared by CCD camera: detail or the racing horse*

Fig. 18. *Infrared by CCD camera: detail of mother's bust and red roof*

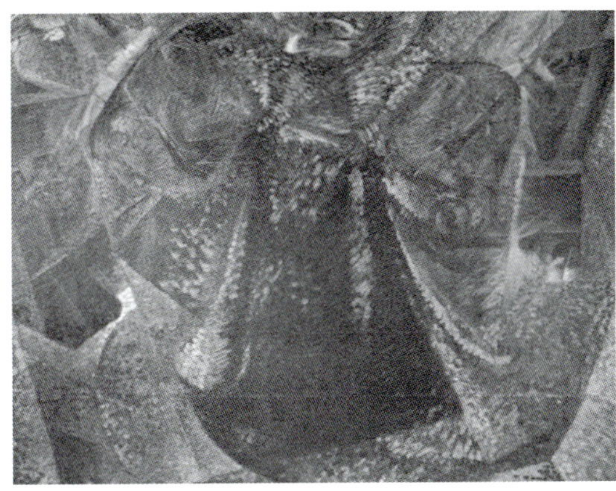

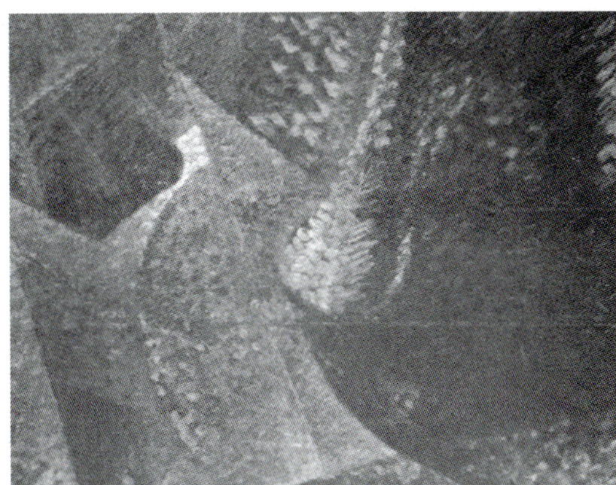

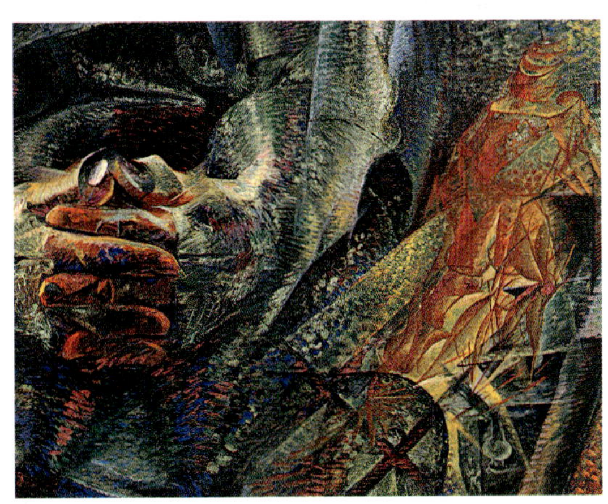

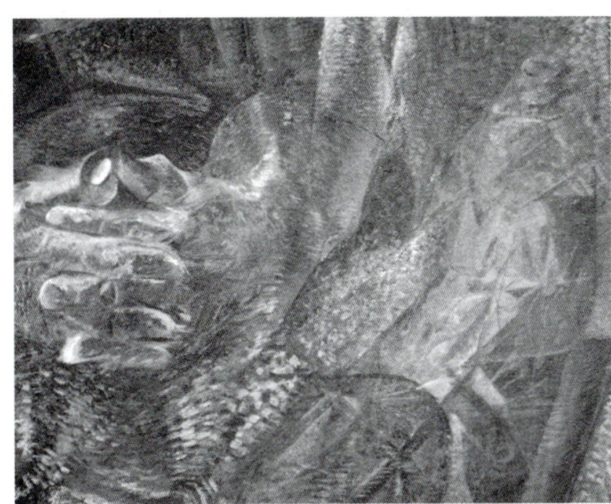

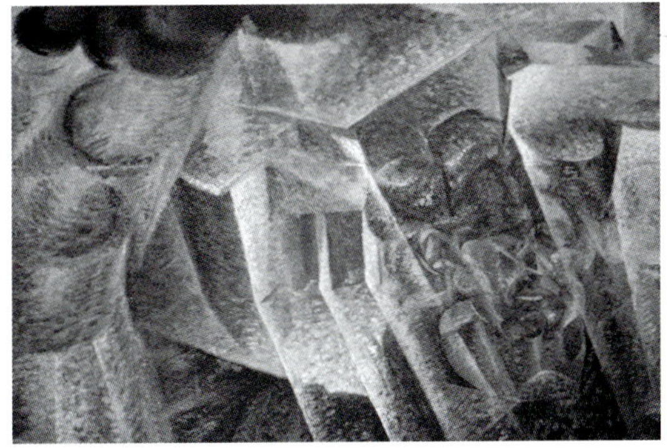

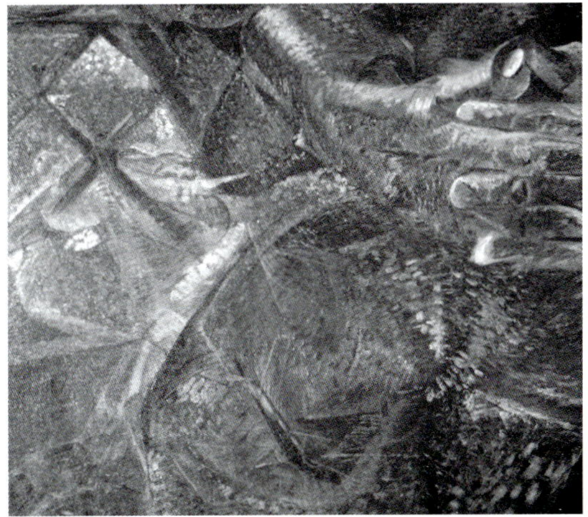

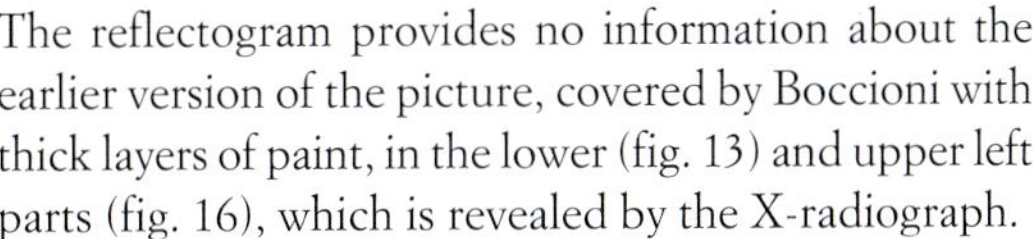

The reflectogram provides no information about the earlier version of the picture, covered by Boccioni with thick layers of paint, in the lower (fig. 13) and upper left parts (fig. 16), which is revealed by the X-radiograph.

Conditions of exposure: distance about 4 m for the overall view and 2 m for the details, both with a 25-mm lens artificial light from above and two lateral light sources from below

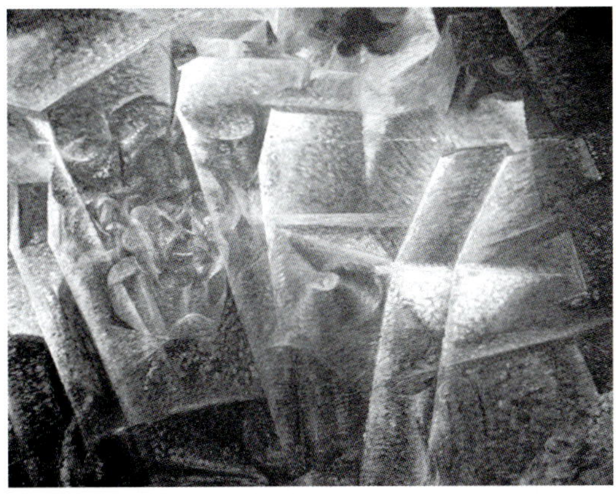

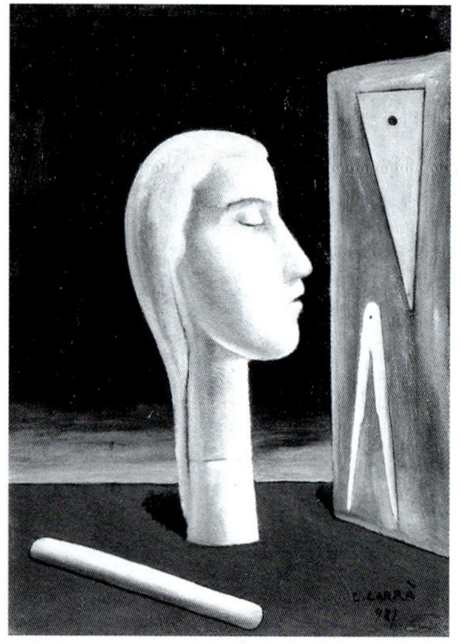

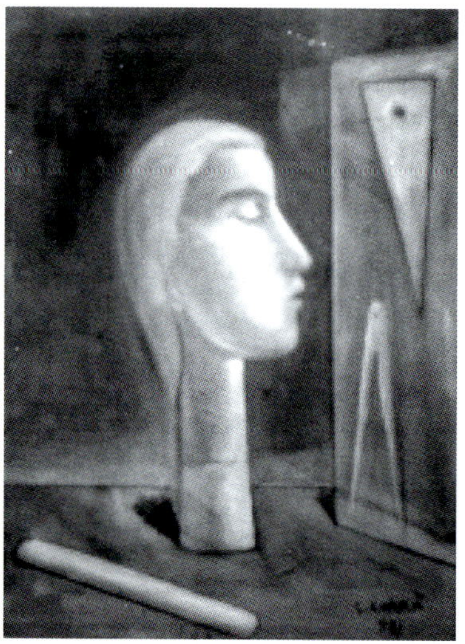

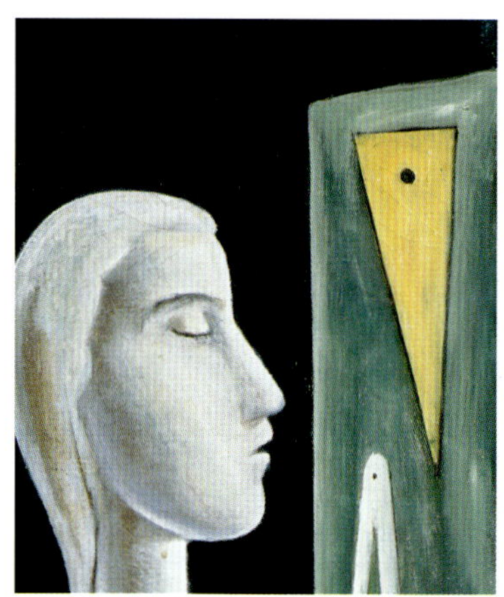

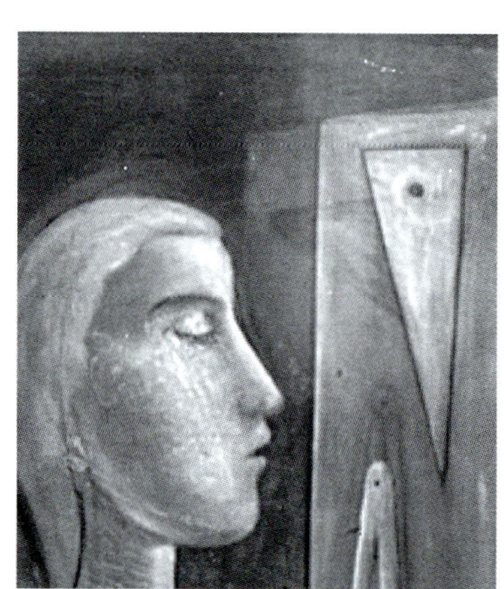

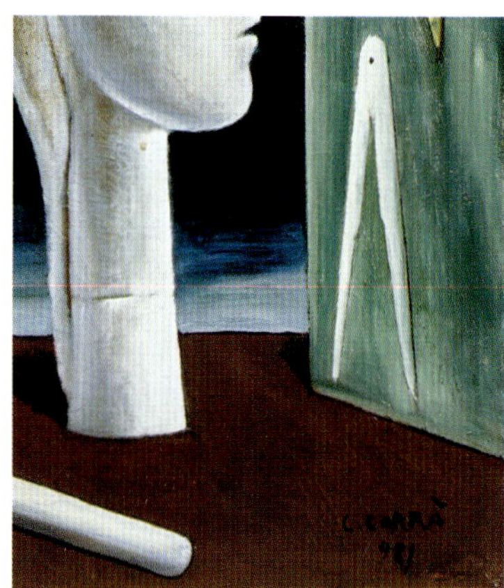

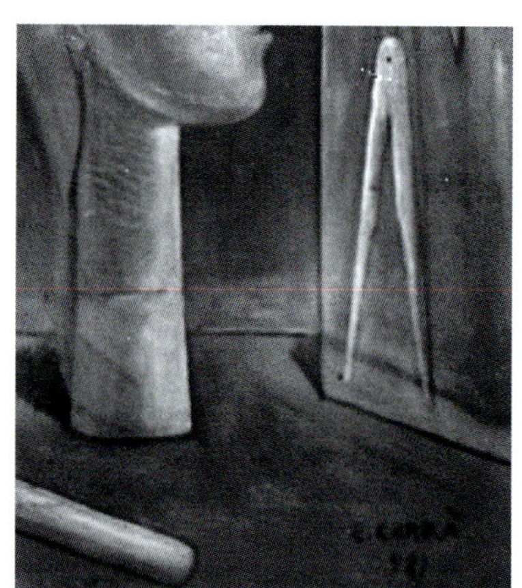

Fig. 19. *Total in visible light, in black and white*

Fig. 20. *Total in infrared*

Fig. 21. *Visible: detail of upper part*

Fig. 22. *Infrared: detail of upper part*

Fig. 23. *Visible: detail of lower part*

Fig. 24. *Infrared: detail of lower part*

Carlo Carrà, The Engineer's Mistress

Examination of the reflectograms made with the indium-gallium arsenide camera (no information could be obtained in infrared with the CCD camera) permits us to make some interesting discoveries about this work, which shows — thanks to the moderate transparency of some of the pigments used in the infrared band in which the apparatus operates — several fairly marked signs of a concealed drawing (figs. 20, 22, 24, 26). In particular, what we see here must be a *pentimento*, or a variant in the course of execution, to judge by the considerable differences between the tracing underneath and the finished work. The forms revealed are defined by an outline that is not only drawn but — at least in some cases — already painted (as with the vertical table and the set square hanging from it), inasmuch as the areas enclosed by contours present different characteristics of reflection of infrared than the surrounding zones, even though they are covered with the same color in visible light.

In particular, we note that in the first version underneath the definitive one, Carrà painted the vertical wall broader toward the back, so that it extends beyond what now appears as the line of the horizon, and that its lower edge had a different inclination, so that it appeared to be shifted further back and located in part under the present pro-

Fig. 25. *Visible: detail of eye and nose*

Fig. 26. *Infrared: detail of eye and nose*

Fig. 27. *Infrared: total with reconstructive hypothesis following the tracing of the lines underneath*

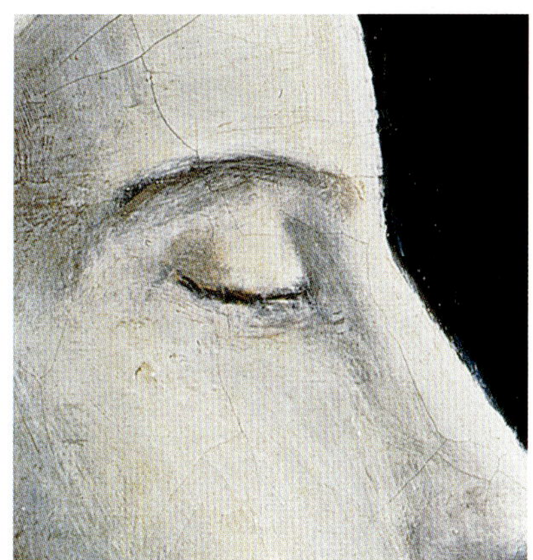

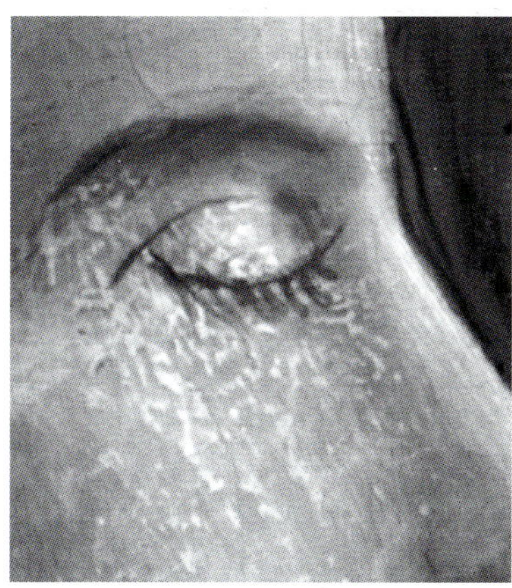

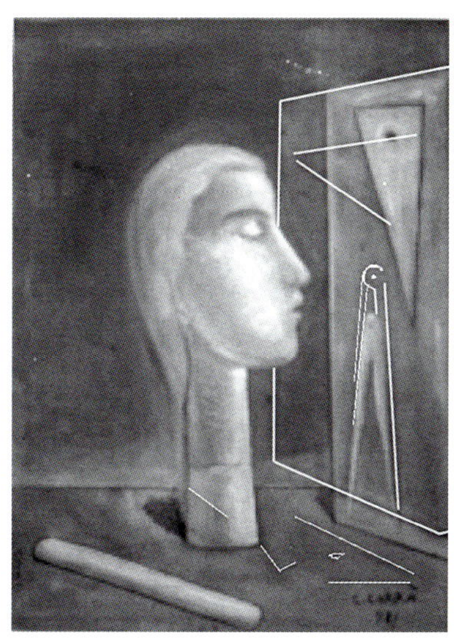

file of the head. In that version the drawing instruments were different in shape from the ones we see now: thus the set square was not of the 30-60-90 type, but with 45-degree angles, and covered at the rear the greatest extension of the support; the compasses were located in a slightly higher position, level with the tip of the nose of the head, and had a slightly different shape, with more care taken over the definition of the articulation, drawn in a dark color, and the upper part of the legs (fig. 22).

As for the line of the horizon, no variation can be seen in the tracing (fig. 24). The underlying surface, although its ocher color does not appear transparent to infrared, exhibits some discontinuities in its application, which suggest the presence of marks that are no longer visible, perhaps another set square laid flat, painted or sketched between the base of the neck and the vertical table.

A few diagonal lines on the neck, in the left-hand part in shadow (in fact the surrounding white pigment is more reflective), do not provide any significant additional information.

Examination of the reflectographic details of the face reveals a number of features, such as the correction of the line of the nose (fig. 26), perhaps outlined in black with a brush, giving it a more snub profile, the eyebrow, which appears better defined in infrared than in visible light, and above all the greater richness of the drawing of the eye, with the painted eyelashes and the line of the upper fold of the eyelid. The sort of pale halo that surrounds the head in the reflectogram may be a finishing touch executed with brushstrokes that follow its contours, whose optical properties in visible light differ little or not at all from the dark ground on which it is painted. Or else, owing to the considerable thickness of the paint evident in grazing light both above the head, on the left, and in front of the nose, it might be a mark of a difficult elaboration, for a head that was perhaps planned and originally painted about a centimeter larger than it is now, a hypothesis that could only be confirmed by an X-radiograph.

It can be deduced that Carrà decided to eliminate the details in the final version, as if they had turned out to be unsuited to the elementary simplicity of the forms he was representing.

Conditions of exposure: distance about 1.5 m details with telephoto lens artificial light from above

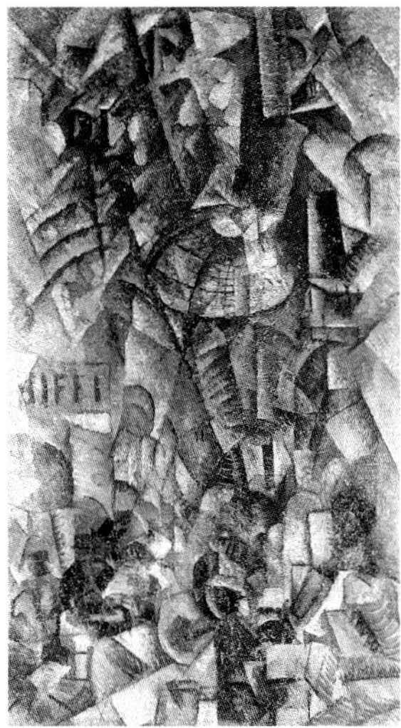

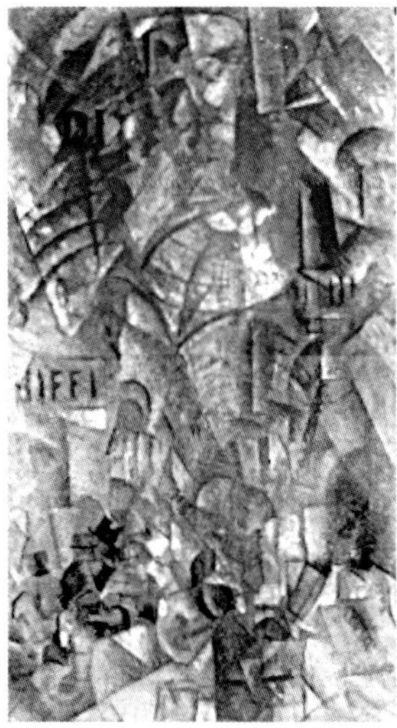

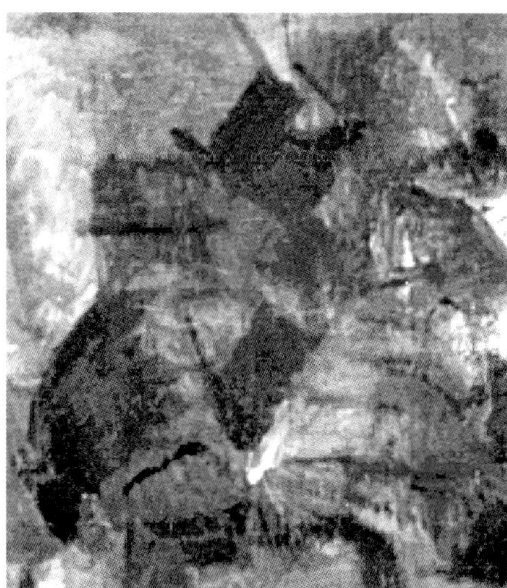

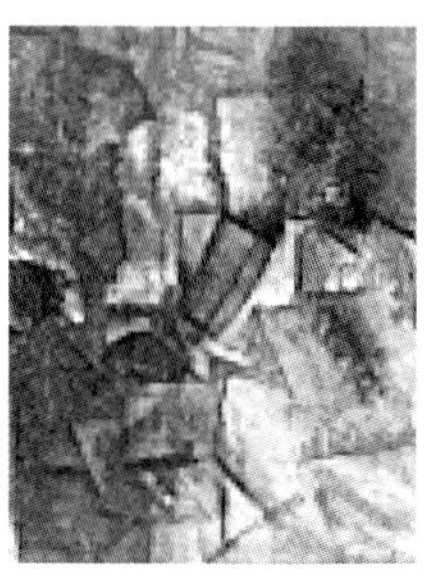

Fig. 28. *Total in visible light, in black and white*

Fig. 29. *Total in infrared*

Fig. 30. *Infrared: detail at bottom right (man reading newspaper)*

Fig. 31. *Infrared: detail at bottom right*

Carlo Carrà, The Galleria in Milan

The prevalence of grays, blacks and dark shades of color, as well as the thickness of the brushwork, make it difficult for infrared to penetrate beyond the surface. On the other hand, the light areas are in general highly reflective, perhaps because they are mixed with white or laid on top of zones of white. Rarely do the light areas turn out to be absorbent, i.e. dark in reflectography, and this is probably only when they are partially transparent but painted over dark zones. A few tints prove to be completely transparent to infrared radiation: in particular we note that the figure at the bottom right from the viewpoint of the observer, perhaps that of a waiter entering the scene, loses many of the pinkish-brown brushstrokes that suggest the rotation of the volumes (in the vicinity of the left sleeve of the jacket and the pants) in reflectography (fig. 31), bearing witness to the essential transparency of this color, made evident here by the fact that it is laid on top of the light-colored base of the grayish-white jacket.
As far as it is possible to tell amidst the dense tangle of lines and different colored planes, the reflectographic images show, for the reason just pointed out, a considerable degree of agreement with the visible image, so that it is impossible to detect either underdrawings or *pentimenti*, except perhaps for the accentuation of certain details, such as the silhouette-head of the aforementioned waiter, which is merely a black mark in visible light, and for a slightly finer view of the black figures at bottom left, in the background, but in any case insufficient for a better characterization (fig. 30).

Conditions of exposure: distance about 1.5 m, detail with telephoto lens, artificial light from above

Amedeo Modigliani, Portrait of the Painter Frank Haviland

The picture, painted on light paperboard with no priming, presents detached brushstrokes in the Impressionist manner that leave large portions of the support uncovered and expose a number of pencil lines used in the construction of the image, as well as areas of more homogeneous color, mostly in the central vertical band of the work and in the clothing worn by the man portrayed. It is precisely in the jacket of brown color, probably a lake, that we can see (fig. 37) a significant variation. This consists in the different location of the hand with the pipe, initially the left hand, set in the foreground right in front of the observer, and not the right one shown in profile as in the final version. In my view the cuts above the stem of the hidden pipe (fig. 35) should not be interpreted as corrective scrapings, but as an indication of the edge of the jacket lapel.
An examination of the rest of the painting permits a better appreciation of the outlines of the face, with the double profile of the forehead and nose (fig. 33), and the variation in the profile of Haviland's left shoulder.
Overall, the reflectography reveals traces of a rapidly sketched preparatory drawing consisting essentially of an outline, with parts that are often detached, but which also marks a few details like folds or the knot of the red necktie. If a necktie is what it is, and not a shirt, as is suggested by the fact that traces of red can be detected with the naked eye under the brown of the jacket as well (fig. 34), which may have been added only later, perhaps to cover up the left hand. The outline of the fingers and pipe that were later concealed was traced in fairly fluid brushstrokes, perhaps following indications in pencil.

Fig. 32. *Visible light: detail of the face*

Fig. 33. *Infrared by* CCD *camera: detail of the face*

Fig. 34. *Visible light: detail lower right*

Fig. 35. *Infrared by* CCD *camera: detail lower right, revealing the presence of the hand with the pipe, later covered up*

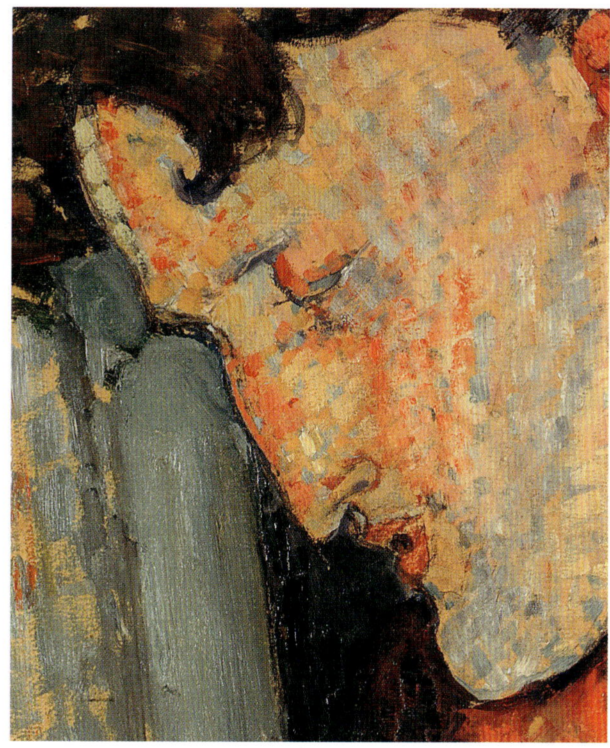

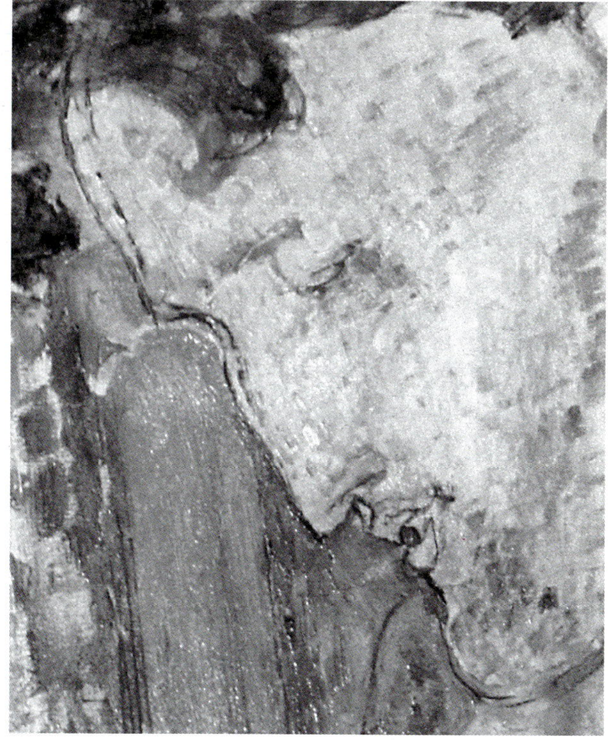

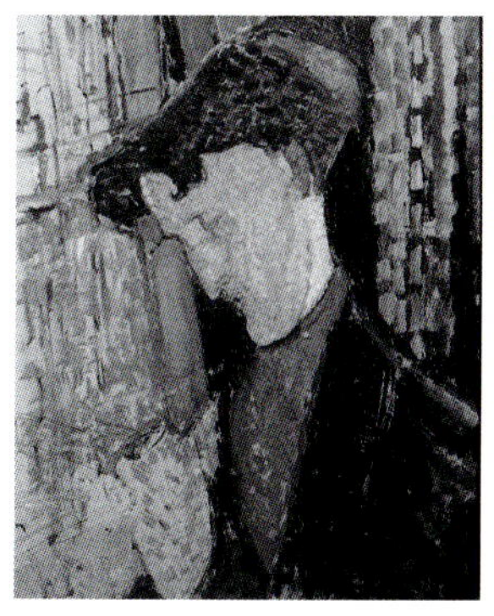

Fig. 36. *Total in visible light, in black and white*

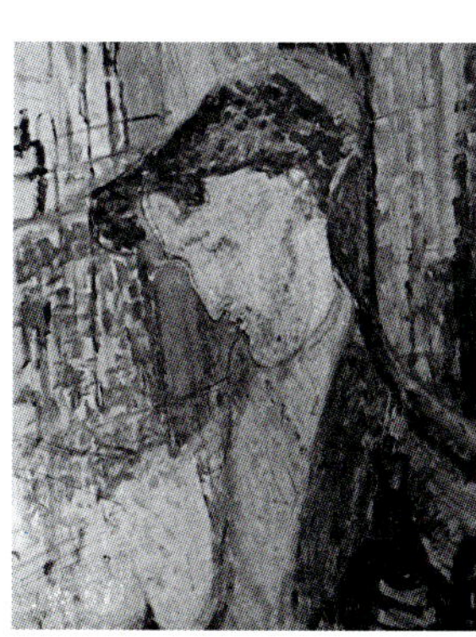

Fig. 37. *Total in infrared by* CCD *camera*

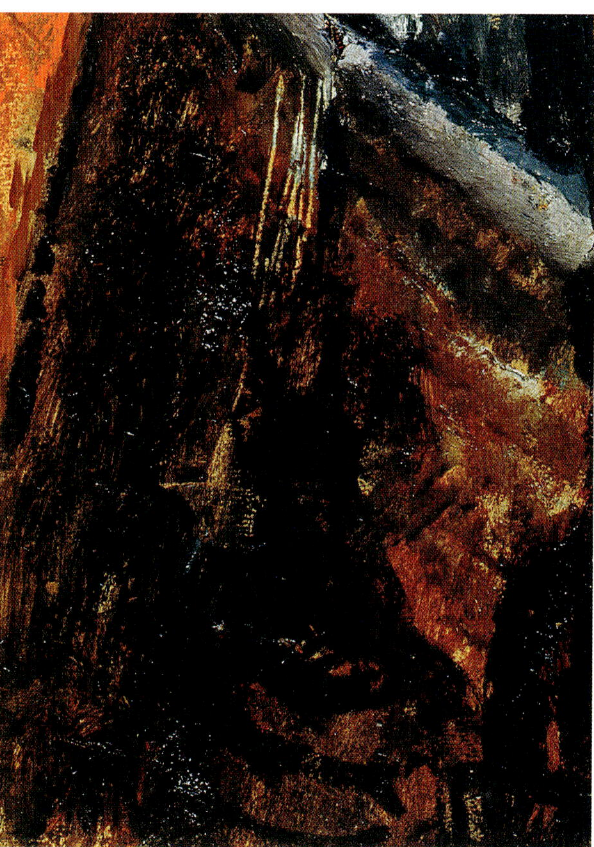

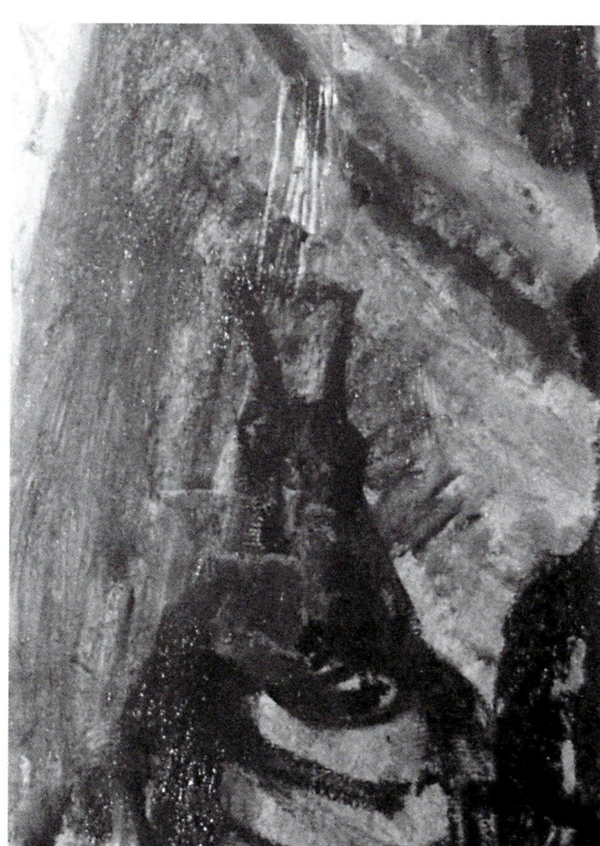

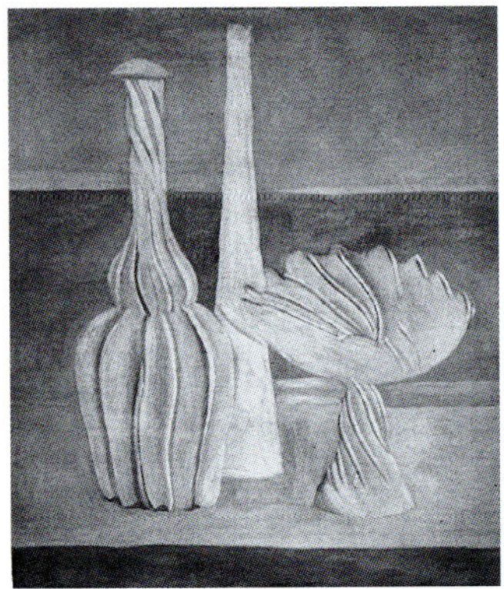

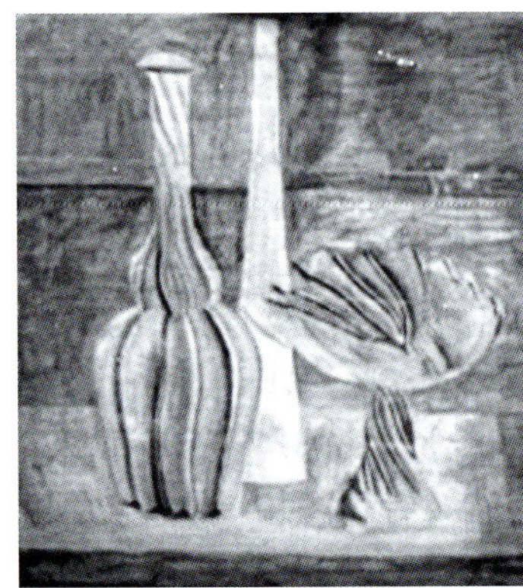

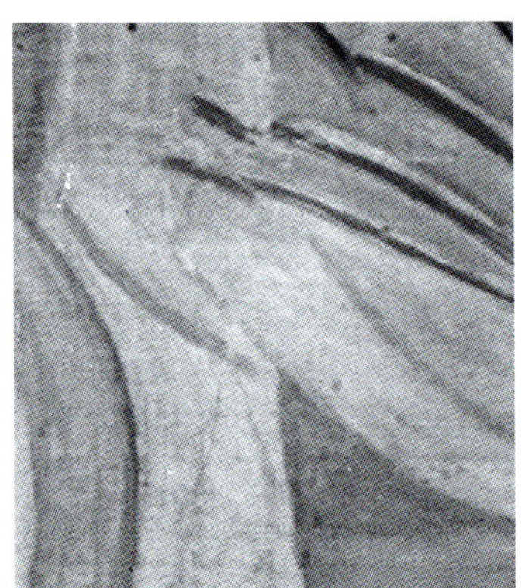

Fig. 38. *Total in visible light, in black and white*

Fig. 39. *Total in infrared*

Fig. 40. *Infrared: detail of the central zone*

Giorgio Morandi, Bottles and Fruit Bowl

Partly as a consequence of the light-colored and uniform, although thin, priming, and the thinness of the layer of paint, we are able to see the unevenness of the painted surface, including abrasions, in infrared, and to obtain information that is invisible to the naked eye, as well as appreciate the quality of the broad and light brushwork, growing denser only where the objects are represented.

The shape of a bottle above the fruit bowl, barely visible to the eye, can be clearly distinguished in infrared: probably not painted, the painter must have originally intended it to occupy the space in the background.

The white bottle at the center of the composition was originally slightly wider, to judge by the brushwork that runs along its right-hand side.

The reflectogram (fig. 44) also reveals a different handling of the white band on which the objects stand: it is bounded on the right by a border, perhaps double, similar to the one below and made up, as far as can be made out from a close examination, of two thin pencil lines almost entirely covered by the paint. Pencil lines can also be seen along the base of the taller bottle.

Still in the right half of the canvas, the infrared image reveals a few uncertainties in the construction of the fruit bowl, probably initially conceived with a wider bowl. All that remains in visible light is the oblique beige and white line on the central bottle, while in infrared we can see two more similar arcs under the whorls of the left-hand part (fig. 40).

Taking the observations as a whole, we get the impression of a certain lack of homogeneity (in the thickness of the paint and in the brushwork) between the left-hand side of the work (including the central bottle) and the right side, as if the picture had been painted in two stages.

An intervention of restoration to fill a loss can be identified above the fruit bowl in the vicinity of the right edge of the picture (fig. 43): the paint has also lifted off slightly above the horizon, forming a thin and continuous line, certainly the result of a folding of the painted canvas.

Conditions of exposure: distance about 1.5 m, details with telephoto lens, natural light behind the picture and, for the details only, artificial light from above

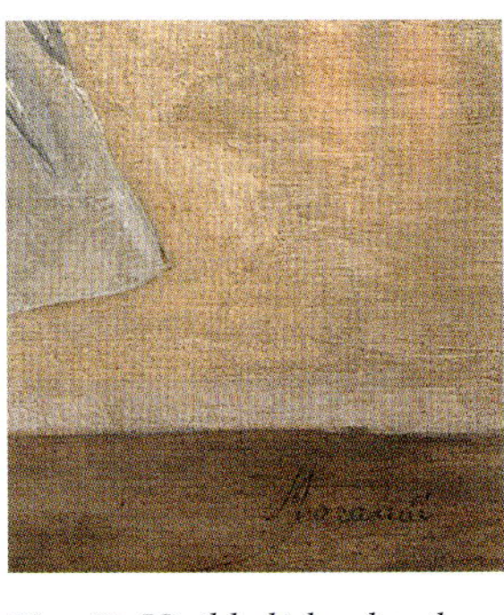

Fig. 42. *Visible light: detail of the lower right-hand corner*

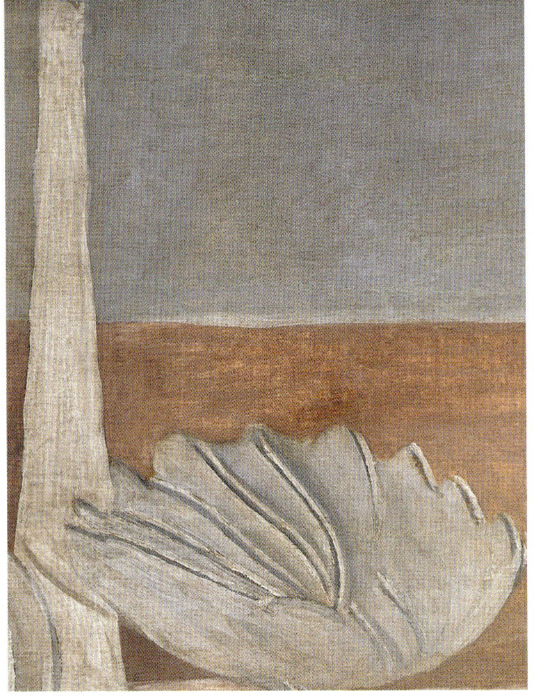

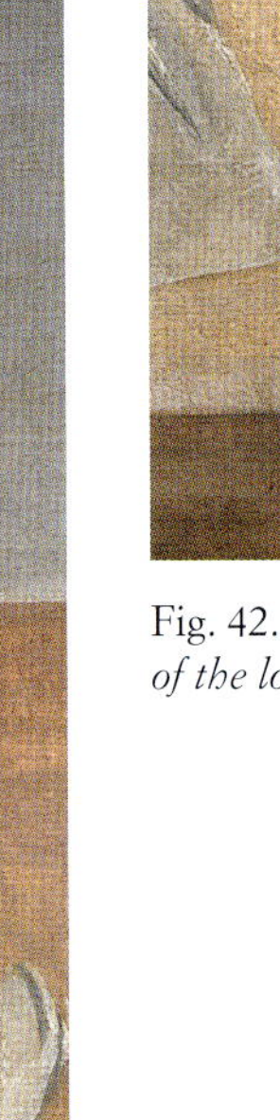

Fig. 41. *Visible light: detail of the zone above the fruit bowl*

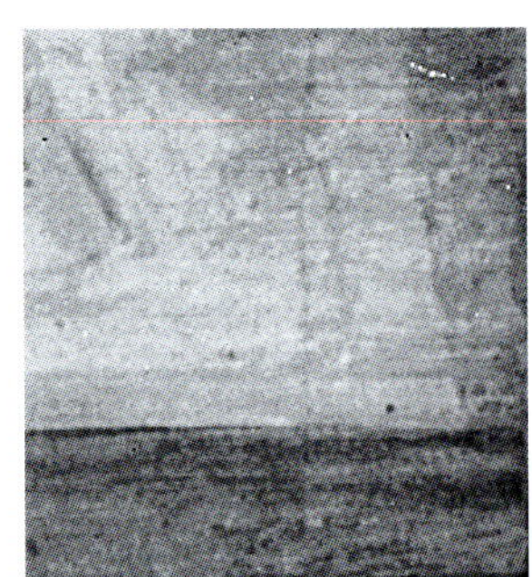

Fig. 44. *Infrared: detail of the lower right-hand corner*

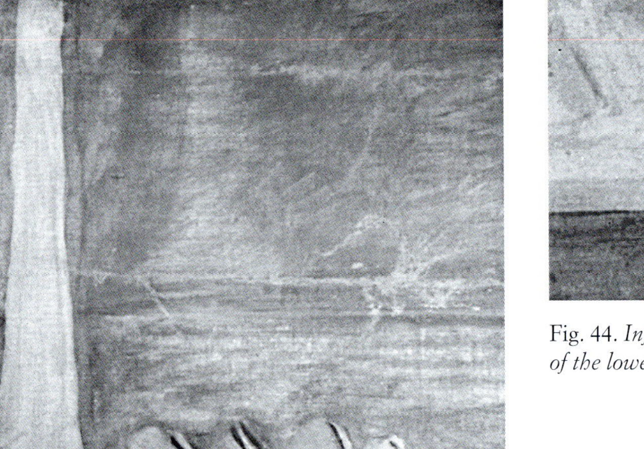

Fig. 43. *Infrared by* CCD *camera: detail of the zone above the fruit bowl*

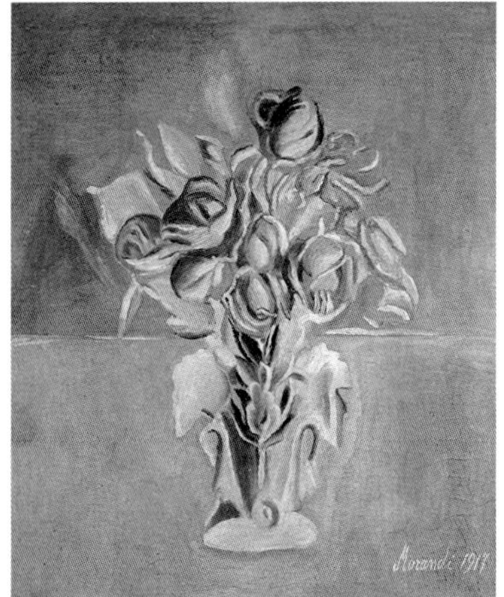

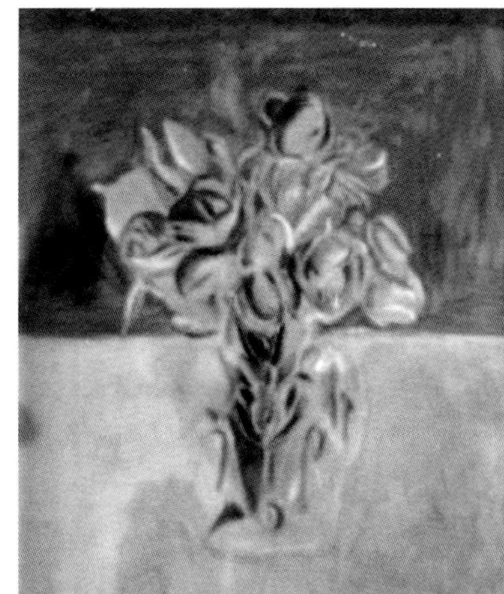

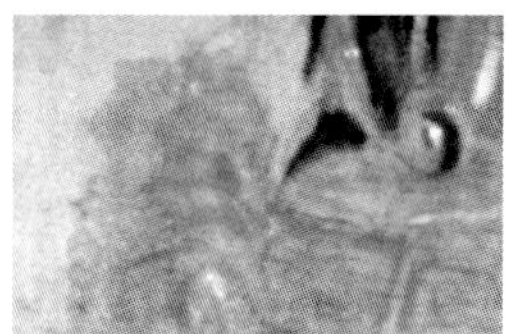

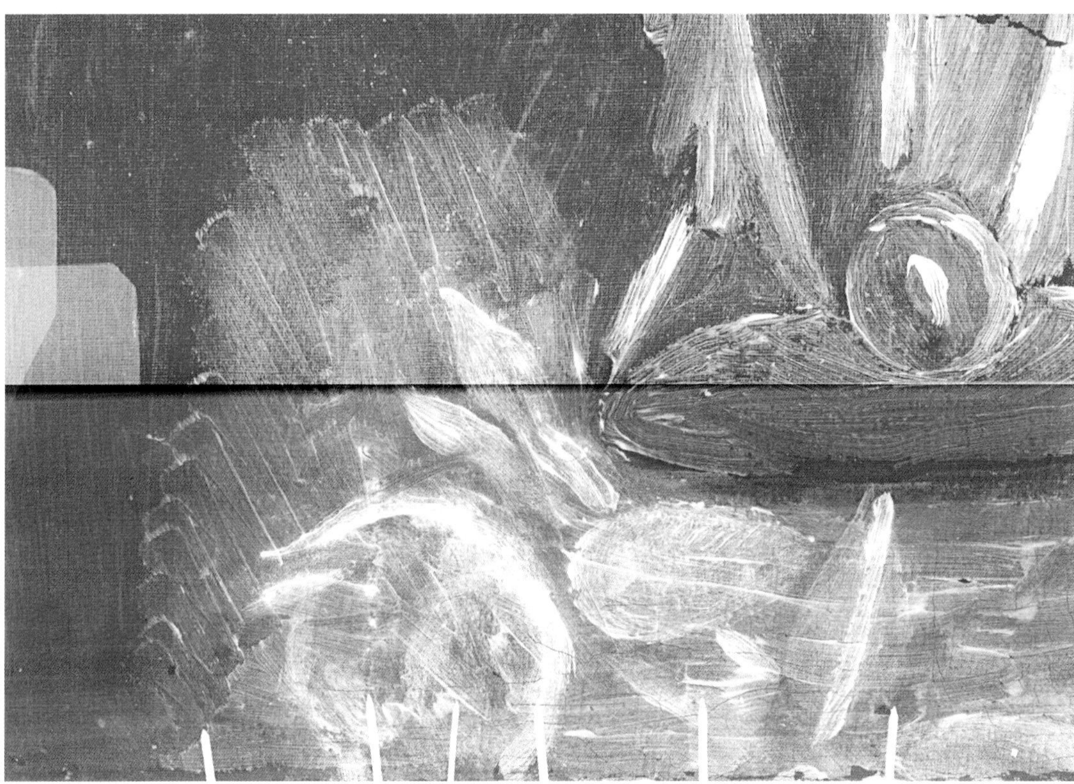

Fig. 45. *Total in visible light, in black and white*

Fig. 46. *Total in infrared*

Fig. 47. *Infrared by platinum silicide telecamera: detail at the base of the vase*

Fig. 48. *X-radiograph: detail of the repainting in the lower left-hand part of the picture, which conceals a rose*

Giorgio Morandi, Roses

During the campaign of measurement, the decision was taken to examine Morandi's painting of *Roses*, which, like *Bottles and Fruit Bowl*, has a light-colored and uniform priming of the canvas and not very thick layers of paint, in order to find out whether the pale halos along the edge of the vase and the floral composition covered up *pentimenti* present in the painting underneath. The reflectograms, made both with our apparatus (fig. 46) and, for comparison, with the one used at the Soprintendenza of Venice (a Mitsubishi IR M700 video camera with a platinum silicide detector that operates between 1.2 and 3 micrometers), showed no significant difference with respect to what is visible to the naked eye, essentially because the pigments used are for the most part opaque to infrared. What is evident, however, is Morandi's broad brushwork, with thick and covering strokes, as in the zone to the left at the foot of the vase, where the reflectogram just hints at the presence of an earlier variant (fig. 47). The hypothesis of a *pentimento* in that zone is confirmed by the X-radiograph, made by the technicians of the Soprintendenza of Venice (using a Gilardoni ART machine — 29 kV, 4 mA — with one minute of exposure at a distance of one meter and with the image captured on Imation 3M film, then digitalized). In fact the X-radiographic image (fig. 48) reveals the presence of a rose flower, with leaves, at the foot of the vase, covered with a thick layer of paint. To judge by its opacity to X-rays, the flower must have been painted with a fairly dense color, perhaps containing a higher proportion of white (lead?) than the other flowers. A further variation over the course of the work, or after it was finished, can be found in the flowers in the vase, on the right-hand side, above the rose suspended on the line of the horizon, where there may have been another flower, or leaves, rather

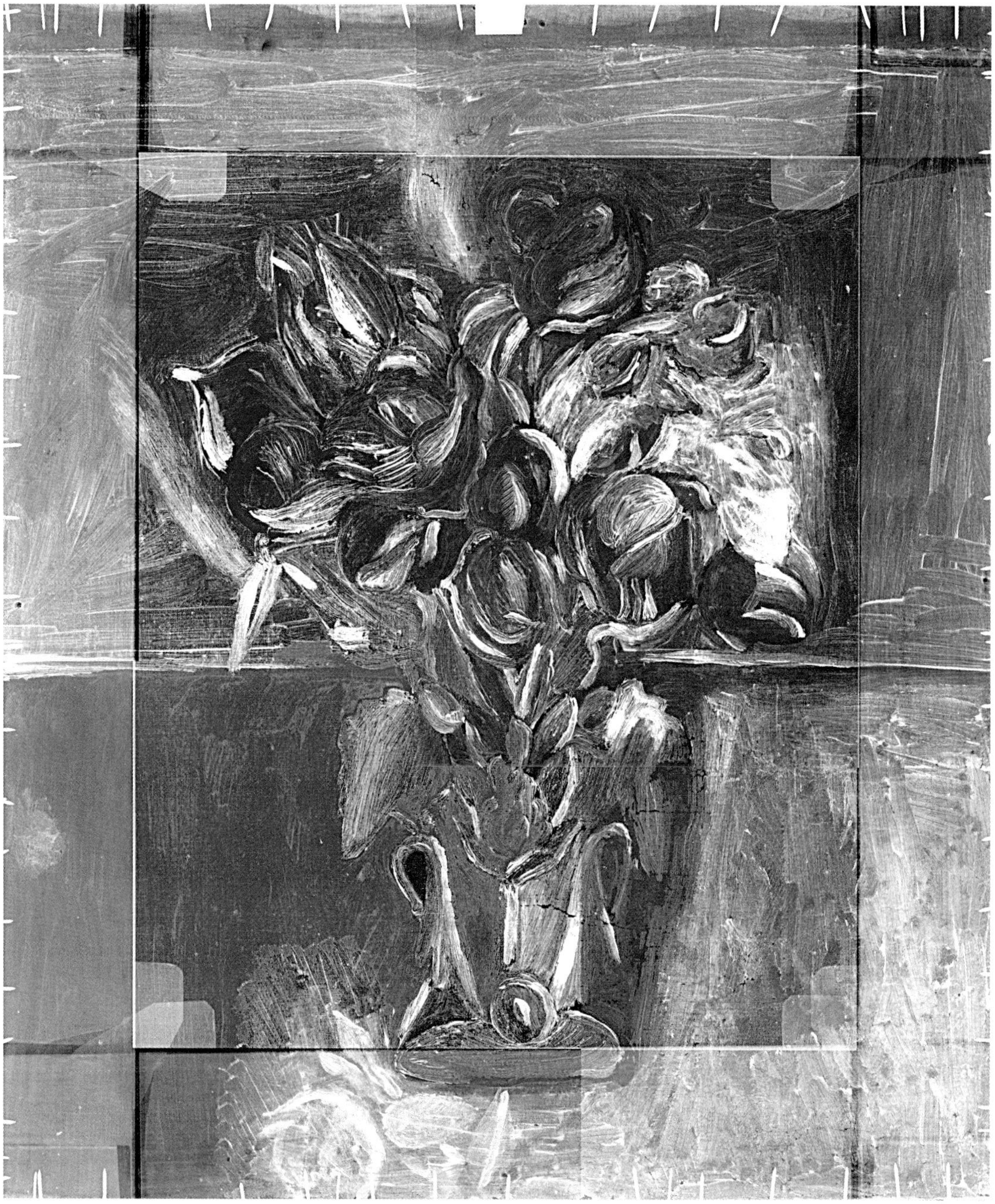

Fig. 49. *Total in X-radiography*

Fig. 50. *Infrared by* CCD *camera: detail of Morandi's brushwork*

than the single bud now present. The X-radiograph (fig. 49) also makes it possible to exclude the possibility that the white haloes above and to the left of the flowers and the lighter zone to the right of the vase cover *pentimenti*, while it allows, together with the reflectogram (fig. 50), the complexity of Morandi's brushwork to be studied in detail.

On visual examination, the other works by the artist present in the collection appear to have been executed with a technique for which the infrared reflectogram does not normally produce any significant results (owing to the thickness of brushstrokes, the stratification and the type of pigments used). For this reason it was decided to carry out no further analyses of them.

Conditions of exposure: distance about 1.5 m, natural light behind the picture

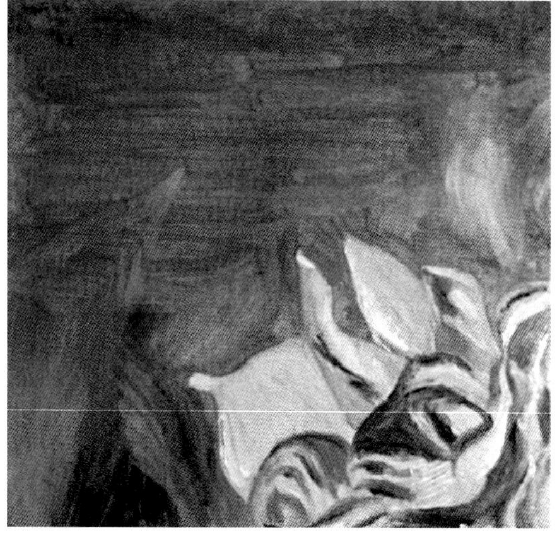

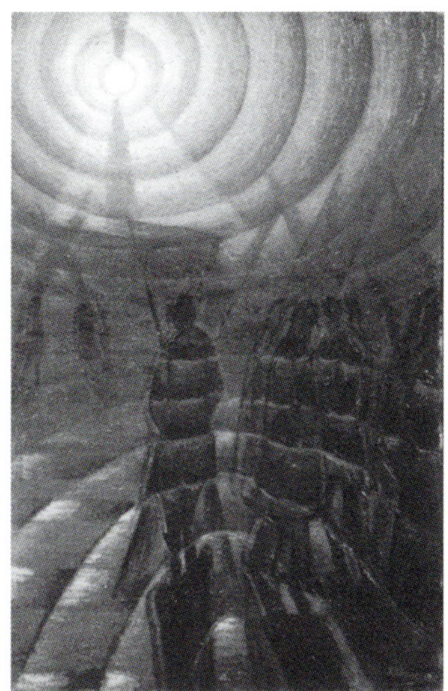

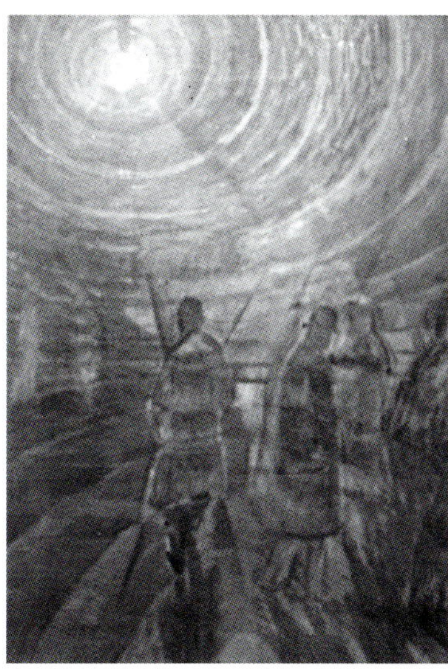

Fig. 51. *Total in visible light, in black and white*

Fig. 52. *Total in infrared*

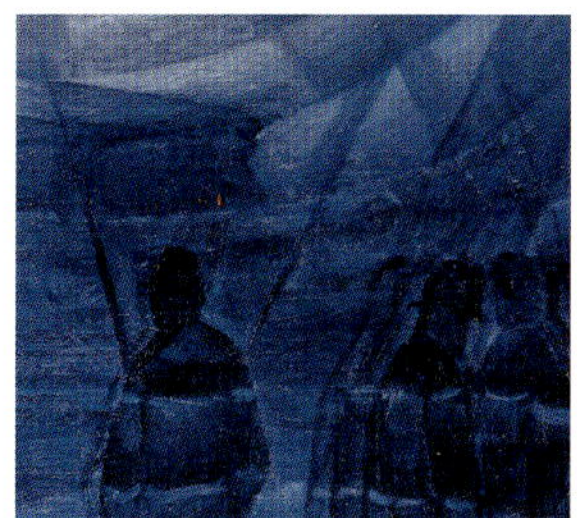

Fig. 53. *Visible: detail of central band*

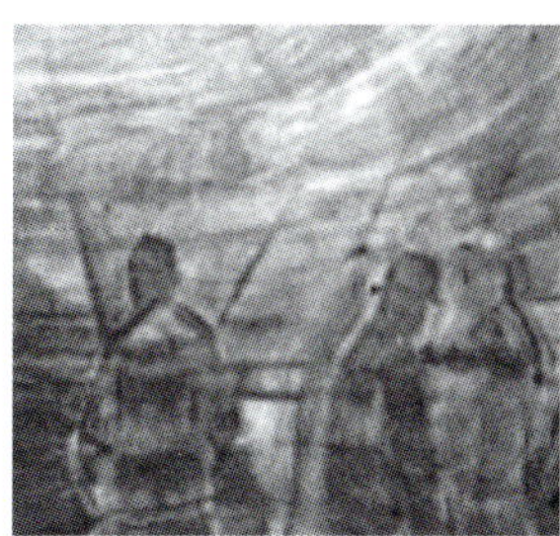

Fig. 54. *Infrared: detail of central band*

Luigi Russolo, Solidity of Fog

The interpretation of the reflectographic image is fairly complicated owing to the consistent and stratified way the paint has been laid on.
In the upper part of the work the blues show a certain amount of transparency, especially in the areas where they are most intense, such as the edge of the concentric circles, the large vertical band of blue — which vanishes under infrared — or the diagonals. The whites are more reflective, as in the source of light and the two pale irradiations toward the bottom.
The lower part of the painting has absorbent colors. This is true of the white tones, perhaps because they are painted in a thin layer over a darker color, and of the blues, perhaps because of a non-reflective priming of the canvas or the superimposition of layers of different colors, and black in particular, extensively used to mark the profiles of the figures in the foreground and to trace their shadows. Black lines made clearly visible in reflectography allow us to appreciate the technique of execution.
The central part of the canvas presents a greater number of problems of interpretation. From left to right, the reflectogram permits clear identification of the figures in the background, whose blue turns out to be relatively transparent to infrared. No preparatory drawing is discernible, but it can be deduced that the figures were painted before the surrounding space, which is more opaque. The same characteristics of transparency are found in the zone around the head of the man viewed from behind in the center of the foreground, and in the band behind the man in a bowler hat, seen in profile, on his right, which is shifted further to the left of the visible blue border (fig. 56). Perhaps Russolo originally intended to place that figure further to the left, or to place the man seen from behind in that position, or to put another one with a similar posture alongside them, given that the edge of this pale band has a similar profile to the left-hand side (i.e. to the left sleeve) of the man viewed from behind. As for the colors, it can be noted that in the infrared, as we have already seen, the blues are generally fairly transparent. Even the darker colors — such as black — do not appear completely opaque in some cases, where the brushwork is thin and blurred over a blue base or mixed with blue, as in the coats of the figures in the foreground.
Between the two figures referred to above, the reflectogram taken with the indium-gallium arsenide telecamera (fig. 54) reveals a dark structure, opaque to infrared, made up of two parallel segments and one vertical near the man viewed from behind. This structure, invisible to the naked eye, appears to be a fence or stockade.
The blue shape above the figure seen from behind, which can be interpreted as a flag, is transparent to infrared, as are the blue brushstrokes above the heads of the figures just to the right, which together with the presumed flag convey the impression, as Rylands has pointed out,[5] of a horse (head, neck, mane, bridle) drawing a carriage with a driver (wearing a top hat). An attempt has been made to bring out this form in the fig. 55, by means of the chromatic subtraction of black from cyan and magenta from blue. Thanks to the greater transparency of the blue with which this form was painted (similar to the blue of the figures in the background on the left) with respect to the surrounding, more opaque, blue tint, it is possible to make out the form of the presumed coach in the reflectogram as well, in particular the position of the rear wheel, to the left of the oblique shaft that partly overlaps it (figs. 53-54). It is not possible to detect any sign of an underdrawing.
As far as the two groups of figures on the right are concerned, all that reflectography reveals is the presence between them of two dark horizontal segments, covered in visible light by blue paint — too parallel to be a continuation of the concentric arcs and perhaps too high up to be lines of the horizon — and a dark jagged structure that runs between the shoulder of the man in a bowler hat and the one on his right. It is hard to tell what it is, although it might be the profile of some construction on the horizon.

Conditions of exposure: distance about 2 m, artificial light from above

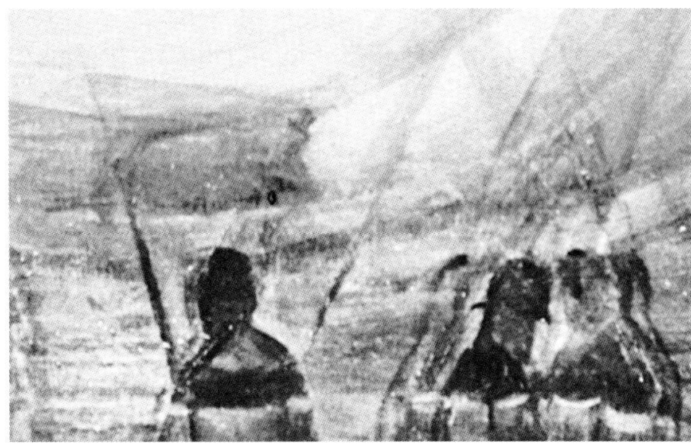

Fig. 55. *Visible: detail of central band with chromatic adjustments to bring out as far as possible the figures in the background (carriage, driver and horse?)*

Fig. 56. *Infrared by* CCD *camera: detail of figure at center*

Fig. 57. *Total in visible light, in black and white*

Fig. 58. *Total in infrared by* CCD *camera*

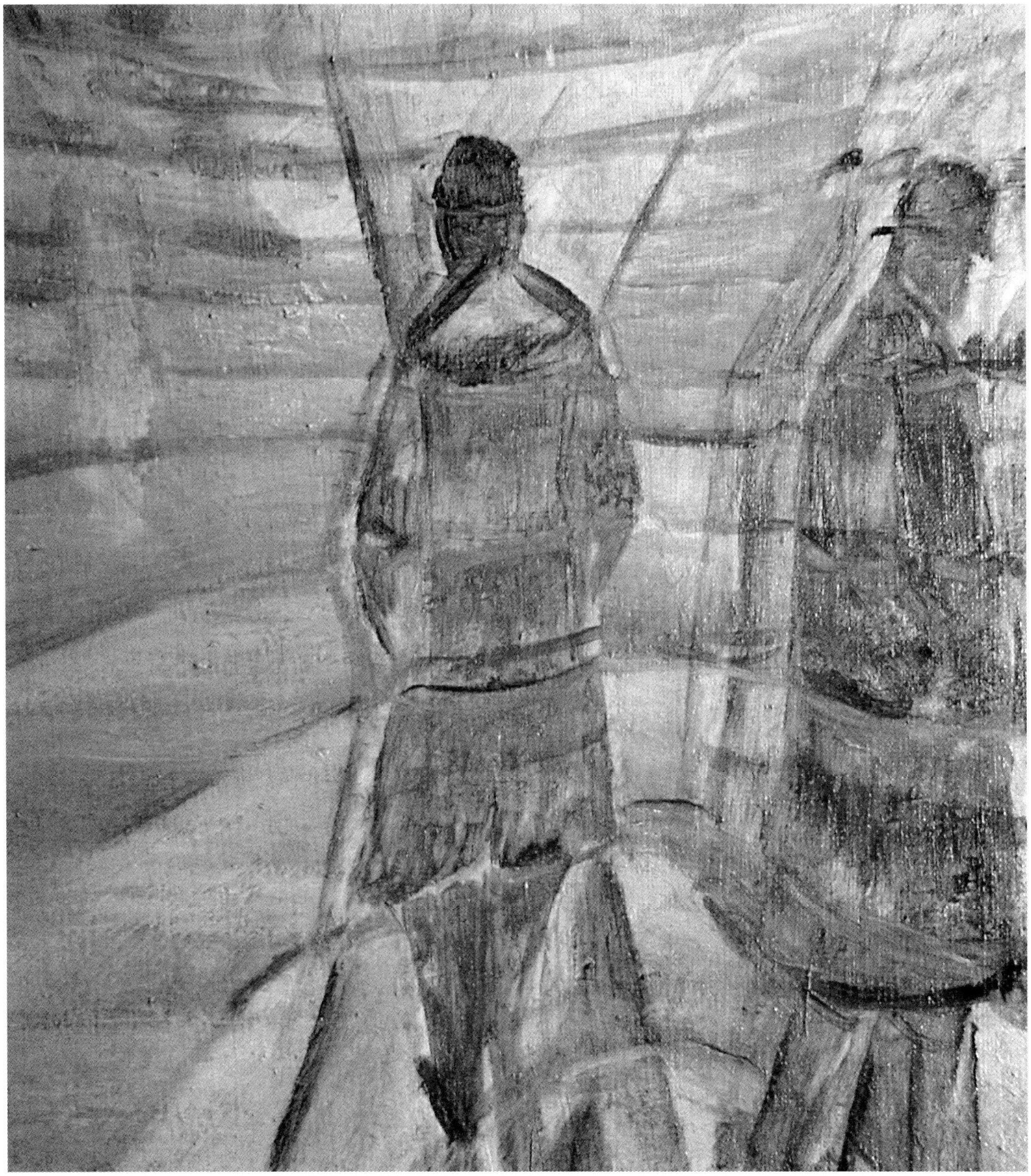

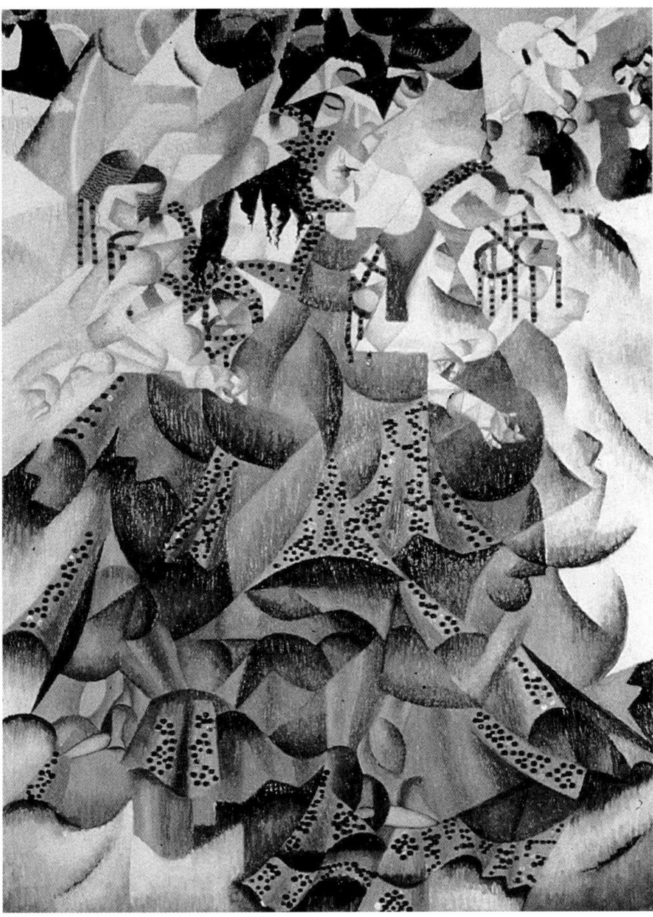

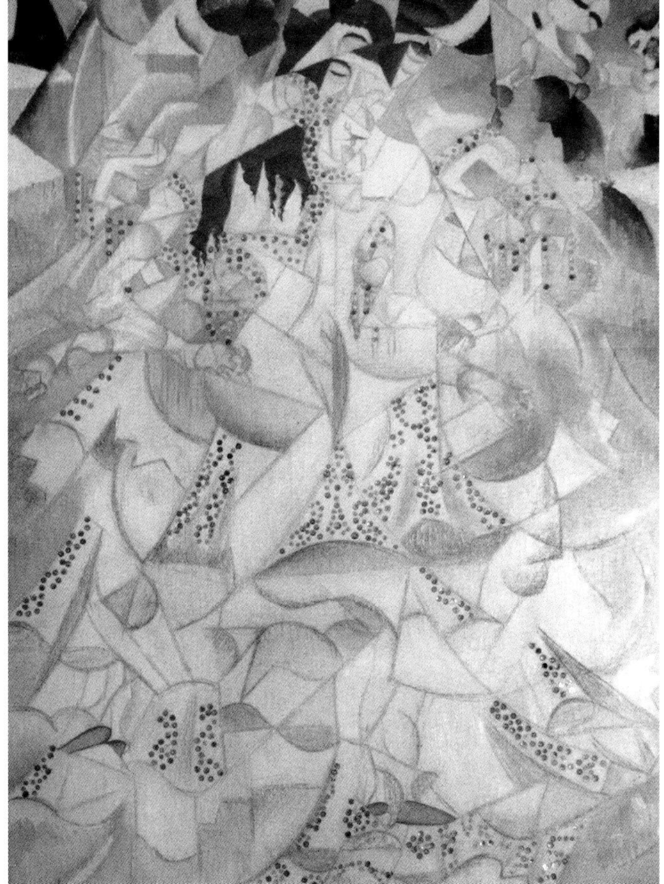

Gino Severini, Blue Dancer

A careful examination of the reflectographic images, and of the details in particular, permits the identification of a precise drawing under the painting, in this case clearly a preparatory drawing with outlines of the forms and shading inside them, darker in the zones to be painted with more intense color (fig. 67). The drawing is clearly evident in infrared at the edges of the homogeneous areas of color, showing that Severini almost always followed faithfully a highly detailed preparatory tracing, except inside a few patches of light blue and pink, where he has marked passages of tone with less distinct lines and softer contours. In general one gets the impression that the use of straight lines in the drawing, clearly evident in the reflectograms, was softened by the brushwork. An example of this can be seen above the left shoulder, where the painted line is given a slight curve and appears blurred, while in infrared the tracing is more distinct and some of the excessively accentuated triangular shapes (in gray, in the background) to the left of the head are eliminated, limiting the geometric decomposition to the structure of the face alone. It is in the face that the drawing is richest in detail, executed with precision as in the case of the lines of the nose and the mouth, and partly softened by the blue color in the middle of the face and by the more intense tones of pink, as in the chin. The drawing generally appears richer than in visible light, and this applies to the arms and hands as well. The drawing of the arms and the hands appears a little richer than in visible light, as in all the flesh tones.
The reflectogram of the dancer's right hand (fig. 64), in movement, reveals the complexity of the underdrawing, and a number of variations with respect to the definitive work can also be discerned. In fact the infrared image shows the lower left hand of the dancer with a more tapering wrist and devoid of the triangular shapes painted in pink, while in the painted version the forearm is a little wider (it is possible that the impression of a more slender wrist in infrared is due to the partial covering up of the original line of the wrist with blue, later restored with the laying on of the pink). In addition, we can make out under the blue color a *pentimento* in the position of the upper left hand, well masked even in infrared, which was originally inclined more sharply downward. A careful examination of the surface of the picture with the naked eye does not allow any certain conclusions to be drawn with regard to all the details and the possible variations, but does show clearly that the pink parts are painted on top of the blue ones. A comparison with the drawings made by Severini in those years throws light on the construction of the preparatory drawing, most of which seems to have been executed directly in charcoal, at least in the shaded parts and perhaps many of the outlines as well, which appear to be thicker than typical lines drawn in pencil. Charcoal was used, for example, in a similar way in the drawing *Argentine Tango* of 1913 (private collection), which is a study for the painting of the same name now in the Morton G. Neumann Family Collection.[6]

Conditions of exposure: distance about 1.5 m, details with telephoto lens, artificial light from above

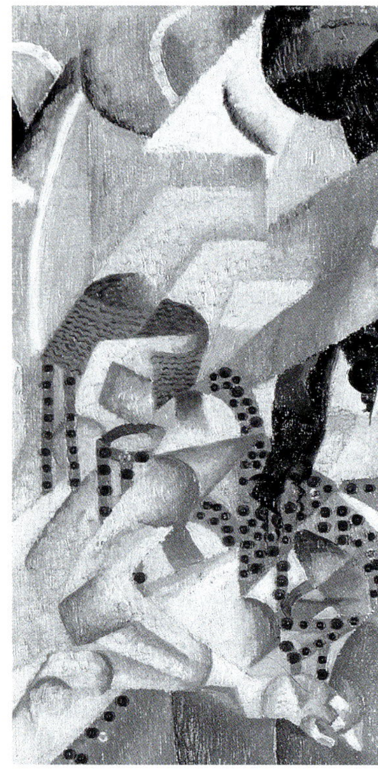

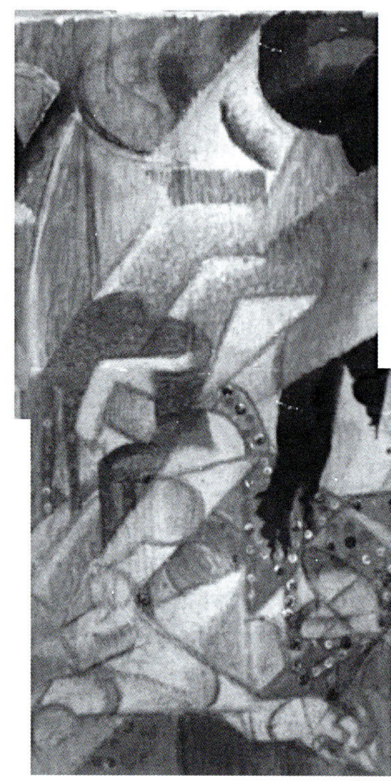

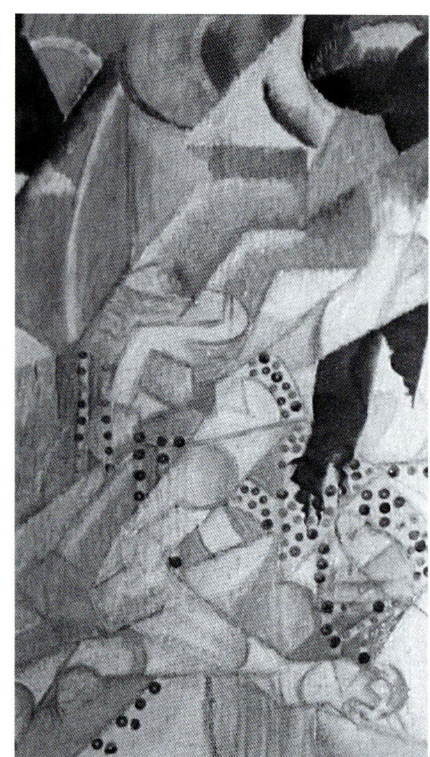

Fig. 59. *Visible light: detail of the right arm*

Fig. 60. *Infrared: detail of the right arm*

Fig. 61. *Infrared by* CCD *camera: detail of the right arm*

Fig. 62. *Visible light: detail of the face and left arm*

Fig. 63. *Visible light in color: detail of the face and left arm*

Fig. 64. *Infrared by* CCD *camera: detail of the face and left arm*

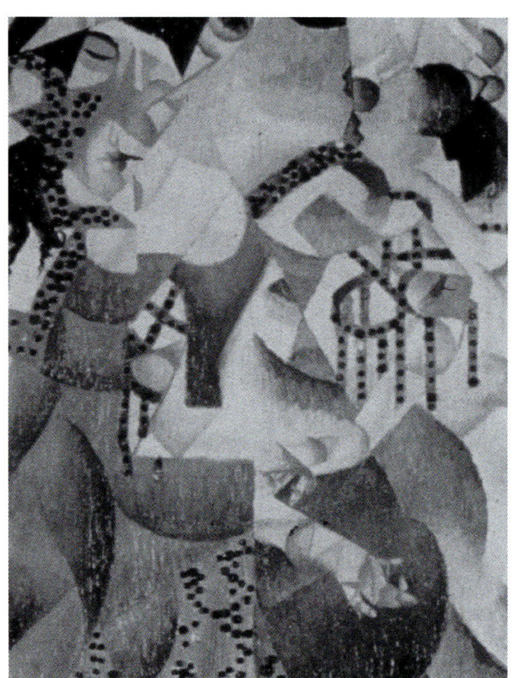

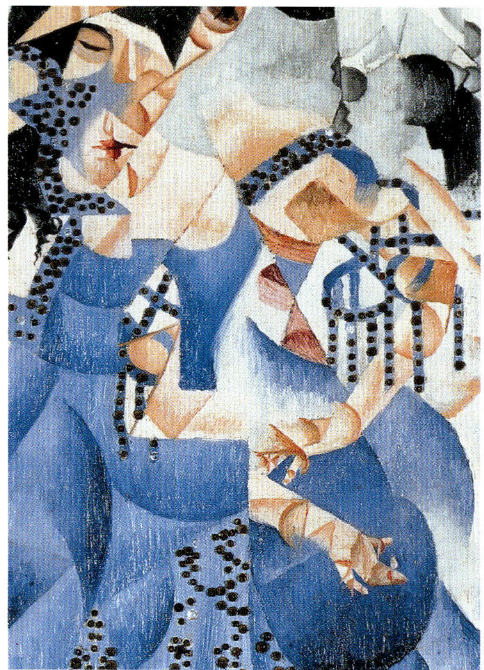

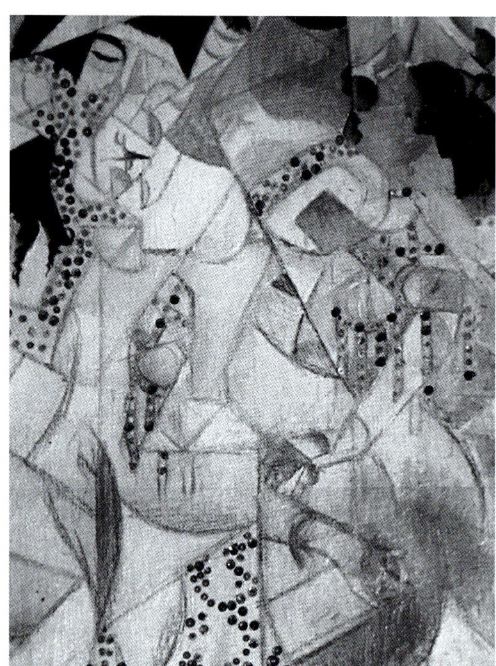

Fig. 65. *Visible light: detail of the lower portion of the dress on the right*

Fig. 66. *Visible light in color: detail of the lower right-hand portion of the dress*

Fig. 67. *Infrared: detail of the lower right-hand portion of the dress*

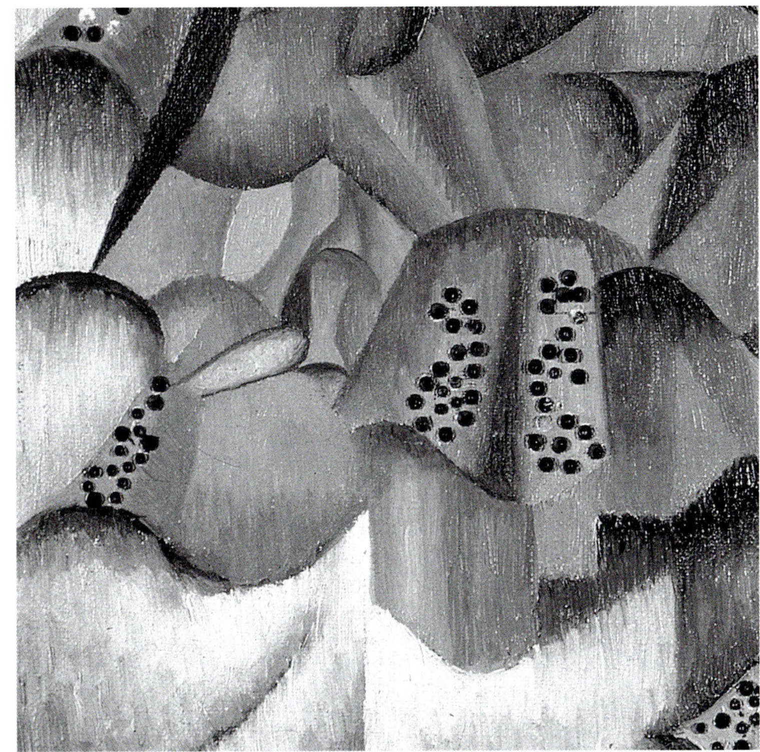

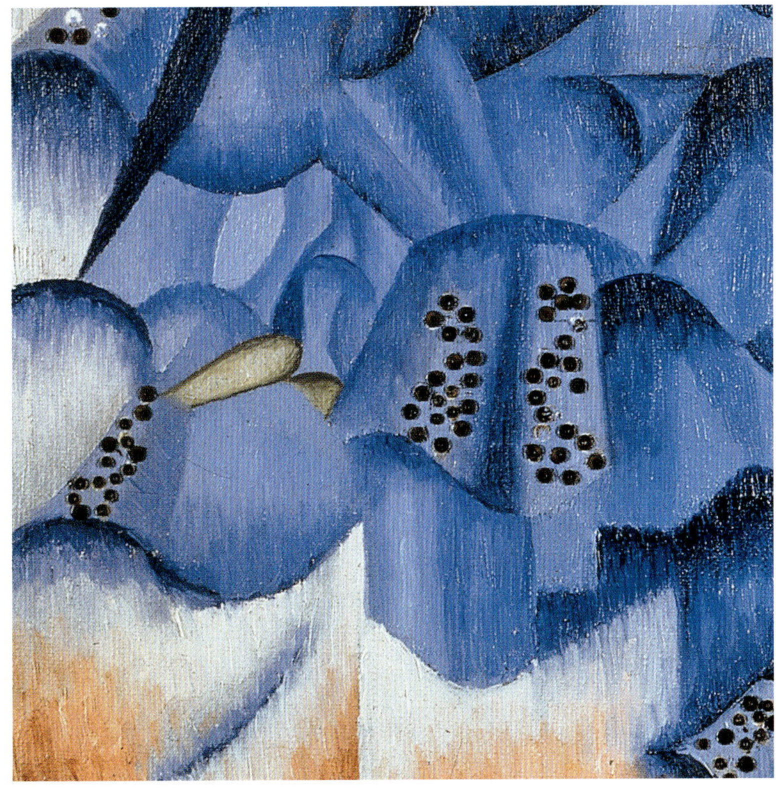

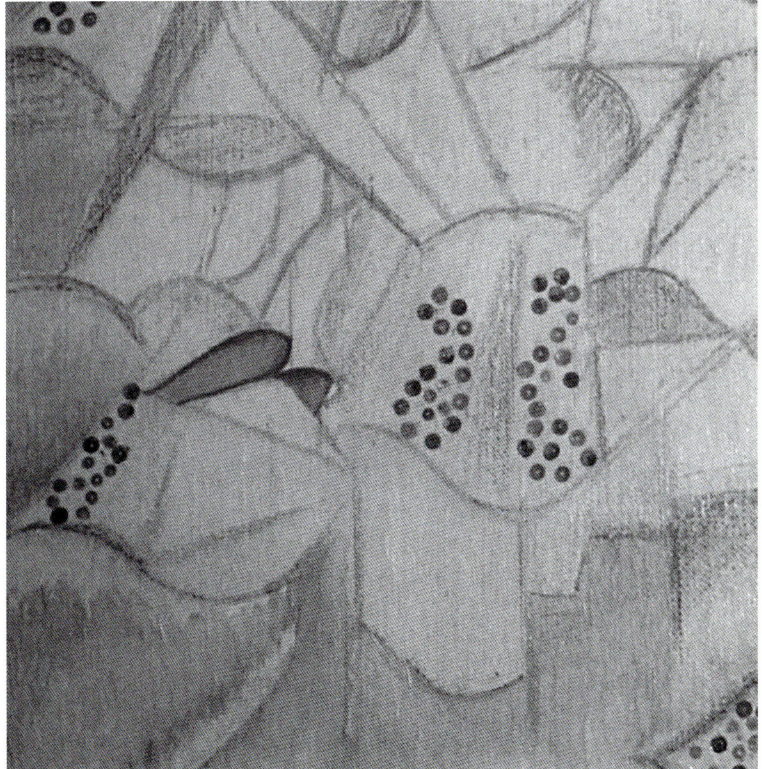

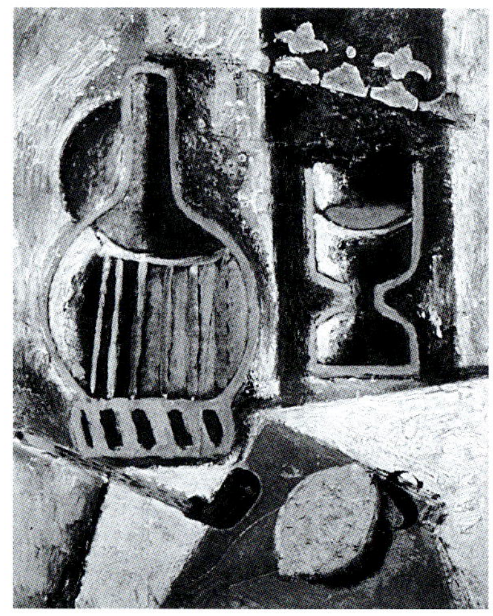

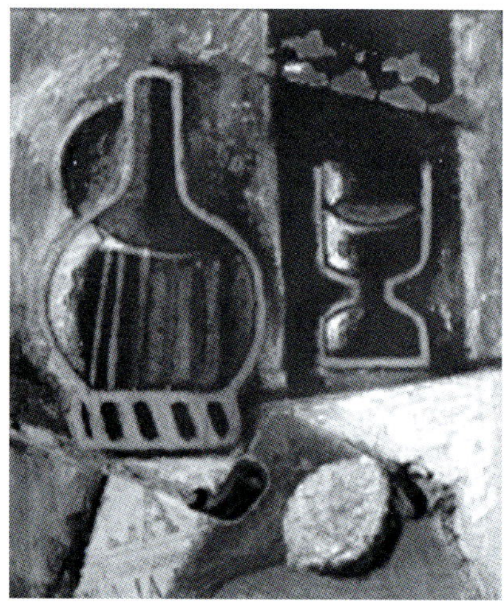

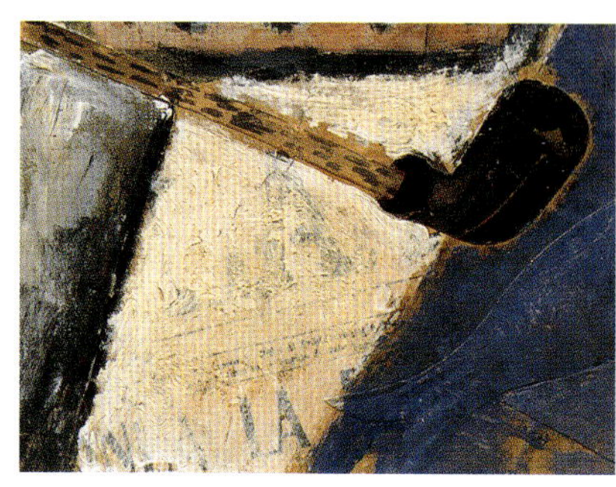

Ardengo Soffici, Small Trophy

The thickness of the paint and above all the use of a mixed technique of collage and painting, with dark (brownish-ocher) paper glued onto the canvas and painted over without any priming, as well as some of the pigments employed, including the black or dark bases, make it impossible to find any transparent parts of the painted surface (fig. 68), with the exception of the square in the foreground made up of a cutting from a newspaper covered with a not very dense layer of white paint, whose letters are printed on white paper. In fact, as has already been pointed out, the absence of a light-colored priming means that the amount of infrared light reflected through the layer of paint is so small that it is only barely detectable by the instruments. On the other hand, it is possible that no preparatory drawing was made under the painting in a collage of this kind.
Part of the masthead of the newspaper becomes visible, and it is possible to recognize clearly the letters 'LA' (fig. 71) and, partially hidden by the pipe bowl and separated by a space, an 'N'. All that can be deciphered under the masthead is a portion of the first headline (or half title?) of the page with the letters 'N[letter that could be a U]A LA' followed, after a spacc, by thc first strokc of a letter that might be a D, an E, an R, a B or a P. Clearly recognizable, just as it is to the naked eye, is the cutout shape of the paper fish, whose front part is covered by the lemon.

Conditions of exposure: distance about 1.5 m, artificial light from above

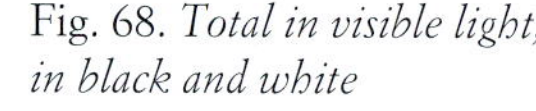

Fig. 68. *Total in visible light, in black and white*

Fig. 69. *Total in infrared*

Fig. 70. *Visible: detail of the newspaper in the foreground*

Fig. 71. *Infrared: detail of the newspaper with adjustment of the contrast so as to bring out the letters*

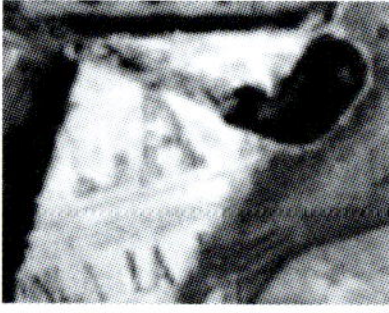

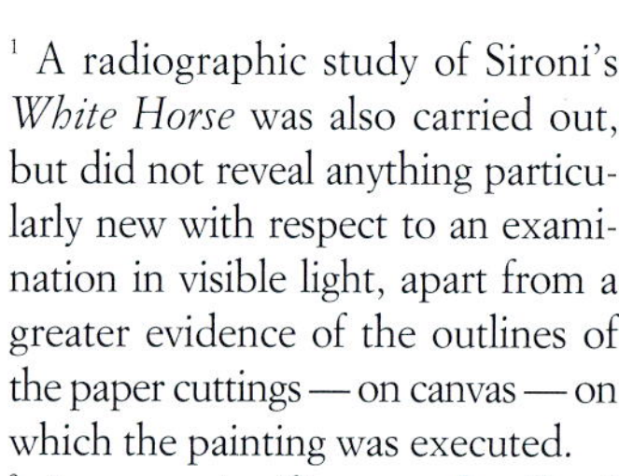

These studies owe a great deal to the generous cooperation of Sensors Unlimited Inc. of Princeton, and in particular of Dr. Kimberly Olsen, who gave permission for the loan of the apparatus and supervised the taking of the images, carried out in the Archeometry section of the Istituto di Fisica Generale Applicata (Institute of General Applied Physics) at the State University of Milan, by Dr. Nicola Ludwig, the author and Silvia Romagnoli. The studies of June 2002 were carried out by Nicola Ludwig and the author. Naturally, we would like to thank the staff of the Peggy Guggenheim Collection in Venice, and in particular the director Philip Rylands, Chiara Barbieri and Siro de Boni, for their kind collaboration.

[1] A radiographic study of Sironi's *White Horse* was also carried out, but did not reveal anything particularly new with respect to an examination in visible light, apart from a greater evidence of the outlines of the paper cuttings — on canvas — on which the painting was executed.

[2] A more significant and refined method, which goes by the name of multispectral analysis, allows each image to be taken in contiguous narrow bands of infrared radiation, obtained by means of suitable band-pass filters, so as to obtain more detailed information on the response of the pigment to infrared. This allows a so-called curve of reflectance (ratio of incident radiation to reflection) to be traced point by point for the individual tint, and its identification under certain conditions without the need to take a physical sample.

[3] Unfortunately, there are no international standards for the presentation of reflectographic analyses, and so it has been necessary to introduce a number of parameters that, while perhaps not sufficient, are in our view scientifically necessary.

[4] *Boccioni 1912 Materia*, ed. L. Mattioli Rossi, exhibition catalogue, Milan, Mazzotta 1995, p. 223.

[5] *Masterpieces from the Gianni Mattioli Collection*, Milan, Electa 1997, p. 92.

[6] See, for example, in the catalogue of the exhibition in Venice *Gino Severini. The Dance 1909-1916* (Milan, Skira 2001), the reproductions on pages 23 and 111, as well, for comparison, as those on pages 125, 131 and 163.

Index of Proper Names and Works of Art

This index lists proper names (excluding bibliographical references and the names of collectors in the captions to the illustrations) and works of art by title, including 'words-in-freedom'. The works of art are listed under the names of their authors, in chronological order. They are indexed in the language in which they appear in the text — hence, generally in their English translation but not always. For example, many of the titles of works of art appearing in 'Appendix I – Documents' have not been translated and are therefore listed here in Italian. The numbers refer to pages. When the reference is to an illustration (or its caption) the page number is given in italics.

Photographic Credits

Color reproductions are by Studio Gherardo Mari, and Sergio Martucci. Illustrations in Laura Mattioli Rossi's text are courtesy of Archivio Mattioli. Infrared reproductions in Gianluca Poldi's text are by Gianluca Poldi. Unless otherwise indicated in the respective captions, illustrations in the entries of the individual works are by:

1a, 14c, 16e, Rome, Galleria Nazionale d'Arte Moderna, Courtesy of the Ministero per i Beni e le Attività Culturali; 1b, Courtesy of Galleria Fonte d'Abisso, Milan; 1d, 1e, 3a, 3b, 17g, 17k, 22e, Digital Image © 2002 The Museum of Modern Art, New York; 1f, 2a, 4a, 4p, 5a, 6f, 6g, 8i, 8j, 9a, 11h, 13d, 17a, 17b, 20a, 22a, 23a, 24g, 25a, Photo Sergio Martucci, Venice; 1h, © Collège de France; 1m, Centro Studi Anton Giulio Bragaglia, Rome; 1n, 2c, 4g, 4i, 5f, 5g, 5j, 6a, 9d, 9k, 9l, 11e, 19c, 21b, 22d, 23g, 25c, Civiche Raccolte d'Arte, Castello Sforzesco, Milan. Foto Saporetti, Milan; 2f, © MUMOK, Museum of Modern Art Ludwig Foundation Vienna; 2j, Munson-Williams-Proctor Institute Museum of Art; 3f, GAM, Galleria Civica d'Arte Moderna e Contemporanea di Torino, Courtesy of the Musei Civici di Torino; 3h, 8c, 14g, Collezione Calmarini, Milan; 3i, 5c, 21a, Estorick Collection, London, UK / Bridgeman Art Library; 3j, 6d, 10f, 10g, 18b, 24f, Courtesy of the Ministero per i Beni e le Attività Culturali; 3l, © A.C.L. Bruxelles; 3m, Courtesy of Associazione Mutilati e Invalidi di Guerra, Rome. Photo Flavio del Monte, Rome; 4b, Courtesy of Galleria dello Scudo, Verona. Photo Jacopo Cima; 4c, 5h, Archivio Pollini, Verona; 4f, Courtesy of Galleria dello Scudo, Verona; 4h, Bayerische Staatsgemäldesammlungen, Pinakothek der Moderne, Munich; 4k, 25j, Sprengel Museum Hannover. Photo Michael Herling; 4m, The Philadelphia Museum of Art, The Louise and Walter Arensberg Collection. Photo Graydon Wood 1994; 4n, 16b, Centre Pompidou-MNAM-CCI, Paris © Photo CNAC/MNAM Dist. RMN; 4o, Kunstsammlung Nordrhein-Westfalen, Düsseldorf. Photo Walter Klein, Düsseldorf; 4q, © Tate, London 2002; 4s, 12g, © 2002 The Art Institute of Chicago; 4t, Staatliche Museen zu Berlin – Preussischer Kulturbesitz Nationalgalerie. Photo Jörg P. Anders; 4u, 8g, 14e, Öffentliche Kunstsammlung Basel, Martin Bühler; 5e, Yale University Art Gallery; 5k, 6e, 6h, © 2002 The Solomon R. Guggenheim Foundation, New York. Photo David Heald; 5l, 18g, © Board of Trustees, National Gallery of Art, Washington; 5m, Centre Pompidou-MNAM-CCI, Paris © Photo CNAC/MNAM Dist. RMN Bertrand Prévost; 8d, 17j, 17m, Courtesy of Bibliothèque d'Art et d'Archéologie "Jacques Doucet", Paris; 8h, 9e, 9g, Archivio Carrà; 9o, Foto Gian Sinigaglia, Milan; 9p, © Photo RMN; 9q, Museum Boijmans Van Beuningen, Rotterdam; 10i, 12d, © Photothèque des Musées de la Ville de Paris / Photo Delepelaire; 11a, 11b, 11d, 11f, 2 p. 14, Museo di Arte Moderna e Contemporanea of Trento and Rovereto; 12c, © All rights reserved. The Metropolitan Museum of Art; 12e, © 2002 Museum Associates / LACMA. All Rights Reserved; 12h, Collection of Museu de arte de São Paulo Assis Chateaubriand, São Paulo, Brazil. Photo Luiz Hossaka; 15a, © Photo RMN – Hervé Lewandowski; 15b, Università degli Studi di Pisa, Dipartimento di Storia delle Arti; 16a, Fondo Giovanardi; 16h, © State Hermitage Museum, St. Petersburg; 17h, BF#580 © reproduced with the Permission of the Barnes Foundation™, All Rights Reserved; 18c, Courtesy of the Ministero per i Beni e le Attività Culturali. Foto Patrizia Mancinelli; 20b, Archivio Galleria del Cavallino; 22c, © President and Fellows of Harvard College. Photographic services; 22f, Albright-Knox Art Gallery, Buffalo, New York; 23h, © State Russian Museum, St. Petersburg; 23i, © State Tretiakov Gallery, Moscow; 25d, 25e, 25f, 25g, 26a, 26c, Archivio Luigi Cavallo; 25h, Museum of Art, Rhode Island School of Design, Gift of Miss Edith Wetmore